ENCYCLOPEDIA OF

HUMAN

BEHAVIOR

VOLUME 1   A-CON

ENCYCLOPEDIA OF

HUMAN

BEHAVIOR

EDITOR-IN-CHIEF

V. S. Ramachandran

University of California, San Diego
La Jolla, California

VOLUME 1   A- CON

ACADEMIC PRESS

San Diego   New York   Boston   London   Sydney   Tokyo   Toronto

This book is printed on acid-free paper. ∞

Copyright © 1994 by ACADEMIC PRESS, INC.

All Rights Reserved.
No part of this publication may be reproduced or transmitted in any form or by any
means, electronic or mechanical, including photocopy, recording, or any information
storage and retrieval system, without permission in writing from the publisher.

Academic Press, Inc.
A Division of Harcourt Brace & Company
525 B Street, Suite 1900, San Diego, California 92101-4495

United Kingdom Edition published by
Academic Press Limited
24–28 Oval Road, London NW1 7DX

Library of Congress Cataloging-in-Publication Data

Encyclopedia of human behavior / edited by V. S. Ramachandran.
    p.   cm.
   Includes index.
    ISBN 0-12-226920-9 (set). -- ISBN 0-12-226921-7 (v. 1)
    ISBN 0-12-226922-5 (v. 2) -- ISBN 0-12-226923-3 (v. 3)
    ISBN 0-12-226924-1 (v. 4).
    1. Psychology--Encyclopedias. I. Ramachandran, V. S.
   BF31.E5 1994
   150'.3--dc20   93-34371
                                                        CIP

PRINTED IN THE UNITED STATES OF AMERICA
   95 96 97 QW 9 8 7 6 5 4 3 2

CONTENTS

B

C

VOLUME 2

C

D

E

F

G

H

I

Volume 3

J

L

M

VOLUME 4

R

S

T

U

V

W

PREFACE

The social scientists have a long way to go to catch up, but they may be up to the most important scientific business of all, if and when they finally get to the right questions. Our behavior toward each other is the strangest, most unpredictable, and almost entirely unaccountable of all the phenomena with which we are obliged to live.

Lewis Thomas

Psychology, the study of the human mind, has made many rapid strides during the past three decades. There is now, more than ever before, a real need for a standard reference work covering all aspects of human behavior. The *Encyclopedia of Human Behavior* is the most up-to-date and comprehensive collection of reviews currently available. The essays will be of interest not only to clinical and experimental psychologists but also to students in fields such as psychiatry, neuroscience, philosophy, cognitive science, and medicine. Indeed, given the enormous range of topics covered, no one interested in human nature can fail to find something of interest in each volume. The format of the volumes lends itself just as readily to casual perusal as it does to serious inquiry.

My colleagues and I are often asked questions such as What is the superego? What is repression? How reliable is eyewitness testimony? How much sleep do we need? What do we know of the psychology of laughter, language, cruelty, or politics? Or of love, cunning, and deceit? We have all had the frustrating experience of not being able to answer the question or even to find the answer quickly without recourse to extensive library research. This encyclopedia should prove to be an invaluable resource in such situations. Also, students of psychology and related health professions will find this collection of articles useful as a starting point when they embark on new research projects dealing with specific aspects of human behavior.

The study of human behavior is an enterprise that covers an enormous variety of subjects, ranging from the minutiae of neurophysiology to such familiar but poorly understood topics as Freudian psychology. Psychology is a science that is still very much in infancy even though it has had a very long history, almost as long as that of physics and biology. Anyone interested in the history of ideas should

be puzzled by the differences between advances in biology and advances in psychology. The progress of biology has been characterized by a number of landmark discoveries, each of which resulted in a breakthrough in understanding, for example, the discoveries of cells, Mendel's laws of heredity, chromosomes, mutations, and most recently DNA and the genetic code. Psychology, however, has until recently been characterized by an embarrassingly long sequence of "theories," each of which was really nothing more than a passing fad that rarely outlived the person who proposed it. I have always found this contrast to be quite remarkable and can think of no simple explanation for it other than the fact that human behavior is inherently more complex, quixotic, and difficult to fathom. Fortunately, the picture has changed radically over the past three decades, particularly in psychiatry and cognitive neuroscience. There are two reasons for this change: First, there has been a growing dissatisfaction with metaphorical explanations (Peter Medawar calls explanations of this kind "analgesics," for "they dull the ache of incomprehension without removing the cause") and a healthy trend toward replacing them with more mechanistic explanations. Second, progress has been aided by the advent of several new technical innovations for studying the structure and function of the human brain. This encyclopedia covers as many of these recent advances as possible within a four-volume set.

My own experience is mainly in neuropsychology, medicine, and visual science, and I am therefore especially indebted to Nikki Fine of Academic Press who, in conjunction with the editorial advisory board, selected the authors in other areas and who saw each essay through the long process of peer review, revisions, and copy-editing. Most of the entries are by acknowledged experts in the field. Given the nature and scope of this enterprise, some degree of overlap among the essays was not only inevitable but also desirable since our goal was to ensure that each article was a self-contained summary of one specific aspect of human behavior. Given the space limitations, each author was encouraged to provide an overview and convey the general flavor of an area of research rather than attempt an exhaustive review. The result is a very stimulating and informative collection of essays.

I have no doubt that this work will prove useful to specialists. If it also succeeds in kindling a spark of interest in some aspect of human behavior among undergraduate and graduate students, then our efforts will have been amply rewarded, for no enterprise is more important to the future of our species than an understanding of human nature in all its diverse manifestations.

V. S. RAMACHANDRAN

ABOUT THE EDITOR-IN-CHIEF

V. S. RAMACHANDRAN is a professor with the Neurosciences Program and the Department of Psychology at the University of California, San Diego. He also has appointments at the Institute of Computational Neurosciences and the Cognitive Sciences Program.

Dr. Ramachandran originally trained as a physician and obtained an M.D. from Stanley Medical College, where he was awarded Gold Medals in pathology and clinical medicine. He then went on to obtain a Ph.D. in neurophysiology from Trinity College, Cambridge University, in 1978. Before moving to La Jolla, he held visiting appointments at several institutions, including Oxford University and Caltech (Pasadena), where he studied the development of binocular neural mechanisms in sheep and cats. His experiments revealed that the neurons which mediate stereoscopic depth perception are present at birth and are probably specified largely by genetic mechanisms.

Dr. Ramachandran's research is concerned mainly with human visual perception and human neuropsychology (the study of patients with focal brain damage). He is on the editorial board of several international journals and has published over 70 scientific papers in professional journals, including three review articles that appeared in *Scientific American*. In 1989 he was invited to give the presidential lecture at the annual meeting of the Society of Neurosciences and also received a Certificate of Appreciation for "Outstanding Contributions to Visual Science" from the Optometric Vision Development Society of America. In addition to his contributions to the professional literature, he has been actively involved in helping the public to understand science and medicine. He has appeared in several television programs and his work has been featured in publications such as *Discover, National Geographic,* and *The New York Times*.

Since moving to La Jolla, Dr. Ramachandran's work has been concerned mainly with human vision; more recently he has also begun investigating the behavioral correlates of neural plasticity in adult human subjects, including phenomena such as "phantom limbs." His current research goal is to link perceptual experience with neurophysiology by studying both normal individuals and patients with focal brain damage.

ABOUT THE EDITORIAL ADVISORY BOARD

AARON T. BECK is a professor of psychiatry at the University of Pennsylvania School of Medicine and director of its Center for Cognitive Therapy. A fellow of the Royal College of Psychiatrists, he has been honored with many awards, including the American Psychiatric Association's Fund Prize for Research in Psychiatry, the Paul Hoch Award of the American Psychopathological Association, the Distinguished Scientific Award for the Applications of Psychology from the American Psychological Association, and the Louis Dublin Award of the American Association of Suicidology. Dr. Beck's most recent awards include the Albert Einstein Award from the Albert Einstein School of Medicine and the Westwood Lodge Award. He has also been listed as among the top two or three most influential psychotherapists by *American Psychologist* and *Canadian Psychologist*. Author of nine books and over 300 articles and creator of the Beck Depression Inventory, he is best known for his research efforts on the understanding and treatment of depression, anxiety, and suicidal behavior.

DAVID M. BUSS is a professor of psychology at the University of Michigan, Ann Arbor, and director of the International Consortium of Personality and Social Psychologists. He has been a guest editor of the *Journal of Personality* and currently sits on the editorial board for six journals of personality and social psychology. Winner of the American Psychological Association's G. Stanley Hall Award and Distinguished Scientific Award for Early Career Contribution to Psychology, he has also received a fellowship at the Center for Advanced Studies in the Behavioral Sciences at Stanford, a Distinguished Faculty Recognition Award at the University of Michigan, and the Hoopes Prize for supervising an award-winning thesis at Harvard University. Author of over 75 scientific papers and editor of two books on personality, he is currently at work on three additional books.

ANTONIO R. DAMASIO is Van Allen Distinguished Professor and head of the Department of Neurology at the University of Iowa. In 1989 he was appointed adjunct professor at The Salk Institute for Biological Studies, La Jolla, and in 1990 he received the American Medical Association's William Beaumont Prize, which recognizes landmark contributions to medical science through neuropsychological research. Over the past decade, Damasio's research team has made important contributions to the understanding of vision, memory, language, and decision making. The laboratories that he and his wife, Hanna Damasio, created at the University of Iowa are a leading center for investigating the neural substrates of mental functions based on neurological lesions. In 1992 they shared the Pessoa Prize, the highest distinction for intellectual achievement from their native Portugal. Damasio is a member of the American Neurological Association, a fellow of the American Academy of Neurology, and a board member of leading neuroscience journals and research foundations. He is a past president of the Academy of Aphasia and of the Behavioral Neurology Society.

WILLIAM G. IACONO is a professor of psychology and neuroscience at the University of Minnesota in Minneapolis. Winner of two Distinguished Scientific Awards for Early Career Contributions to Psychophysiology and Psychology, he is also a fellow in the American Association for the Advancement of Science, the American Psychological Association, and the American Psychological Society. He is a consulting editor for the *Journal of Abnormal Psychology* and has long served as a consultant to a host of other journals, societies, granting agencies, and government and private organizations. He is currently conducting research projects for the National Institute of Drug Abuse, the National Institute of Alcohol Abuse and Alcoholism, and the National Institute of Mental Health. Author of over 100 scientific papers, his recent areas of study include the behavioral genetics of cognitive ability, psychopathology, schizophrenia, depression, psychophysiological correlates of psychopathology, and polygraph use.

EDWARD E. JONES (1926–1993) was a professor of psychology at Princeton University. Known as one of the founding fathers of the field of "person perception" in social psychology, he published over 80 scientific papers and five books investigating how people understand one another's motives and dispositions. Awarded the American Psychological Association's Distinguished Scientific Contribution Award and the Society of Experimental Social Psychology's Distinguished Scientist Award, he was also a past president of the Society for Personality and Social Psychology, a fellow of both the American Academy of Arts and Sciences and the American Psychological Society, and a two-time fellow at the Center for Advanced Study in the Behavioral Sciences.

JEROME KAGAN is a professor of psychology at Harvard University. Best known for his research on human development, he has published widely in this area and has authored eight books. A fellow in the American Association for the Advancement of Science and the American Academy of Arts and Sciences, he has been the recipient of many awards, including the American Psychological Association's Hofheimer Prize for Research, William James Award, and Distinguished Scientist Award; Yale University's Wilbur Cross Medal; Cambridge University's Kenneth Craik Award; the Distinguished Scientist Award from the Society for Research in Child Development; and the Aldrich Award from the American Academy of Pediatrics. He is also a member of the National Advisory Council of the NICHD and the National Academy of Sciences Institute of Medicine.

How to Use the Encyclopedia

The *Encyclopedia of Human Behavior* is intended for use by both students and research professionals. Articles have been chosen to reflect major disciplines in the study of human behavior, common topics of research by professionals in this realm, and areas of public interest and concern. Each article thus serves as a comprehensive overview of a given area, providing both breadth of coverage for students and depth of coverage for research professionals. We have designed the encyclopedia with the following features for maximum accessibility for all readers.

Articles in the encyclopedia are arranged alphabetically by subject. A complete table of contents appears in Volume 1. Here, one will find broad discipline-related titles such as "Educational Psychology" and "Psychopathology," research topics such as "Memory" and "Motor Control," and areas of public interest and concern such as "Divorce" and "Pornography, Effects on Attitudes and Behavior." Volumes 2–4 contain contents specific to those volumes only.

The Index is located in Volume 4. Because the reader's topic of interest may be listed under a broader article title, we encourage use of the Index for access to a subject area. For instance, the Index will lead the reader to the articles "Anger," "Defense Mechanisms," and "Oedipus Complex" for coverage of the topic "Repression." Because a topic of study in human behavior is often applicable to more than one article, the Index provides a complete listing of where a subject is covered and in what context.

Each article contains an outline, a glossary, cross references, and a bibliography. The outline allows a quick scan of the major areas discussed within each article. The glossary contains terms that may be unfamiliar to the reader, with each term defined *in the context of its use in that article*. Thus, a term may appear in the glossary for another article defined in a slightly different manner or with a subtle nuance specific to that article. For clarity, we have allowed these differences in definition to remain so that the terms are defined relative to the context of each article.

Each article has been cross referenced to other articles in the encyclopedia. Cross references are found at the end of the paragraph containing the first mention of a subject area covered elsewhere in the encyclopedia. We encourage readers to use the cross references to locate other encyclopedia articles that will provide more detailed information about a subject.

The bibliography lists recent secondary sources to aid the reader in locating more detailed or technical information. Review articles and research articles that are considered of primary importance to the understanding of a given subject area are also listed. Bibliographies are not intended to provide a full reference listing of all material covered in the context of a given article, but are provided as guides to further reading.

ACCOUNTABILITY AND SOCIAL COGNITION

Jennifer S. Lerner and Philip E. Tetlock
University of California at Berkeley

Social cognition The mental processes through which people come to understand and interpret social events and information. Social factors influence both what people think about and how they think.

Glossary

Accountability A universal feature of social interaction through which people hold other people implicitly or explicitly responsible for their actions. Although accountability is a universal feature of social systems, the specific norms to which people are held accountable vary from one culture and historical period to another.

Cognition Thinking processes through which persons achieve awareness or knowledge of the world.

Heuristic A problem-solving strategy or "rule of thumb" which has worked in the past and is thought likely to work again. A heuristic strategy is a cognitive short-cut (in contrast to more systematic, logically defensible but less time-consuming strategies).

Integrative complexity A measure of the multidimensionality of cognition. Complexity is defined in terms of two cognitive structural properties: evaluative differentiation and conceptual integration. Differentiation refers to the number of evaluatively distinct or contradictory dimensions of a problem an individual takes into account. Integration refers to the development of complex connections among differentiated characteristics.

ACCOUNTABILITY refers to the implicit or explicit expectation of decision makers that they may be called upon to justify their beliefs, feelings, and actions to others. Under Section I, we introduce accountability as a universal feature of social life that inevitably arises from the norm-enforcement needs of groups and organizations. How people cope with accountability is, however, a relatively new and growing area of study. Under Section II, we discuss the motivational and cognitive assumptions underlying this emerging literature. Under Section III, we draw on experimental research to explicate four major coping strategies activated by accountability demands. Under Section IV, we discuss when scholarly observers applaud these strategies as adaptive or criticize them as maladaptive, and comment on the complexities of making such determinations. Section V summarizes what we currently know about accountability and decision making, and what remains unanswered.

I. THE FOUNDATION OF ACCOUNTABILITY

A. Introduction to Accountability

Semin and Manstead propose that people inevitably create accountability systems to cope with common problems of group life. Further, they assert that social order could not be maintained without accountability practices. Accountability, in this view, serves as a critical rule and norm enforcement mechanism—the social psychological link between individual decision makers on the one hand and social systems on the other.

Accountability rules and conventions vary dramatically from one culture and historical period to another. The underlying functions served by accountability arrangements are, however, remarkably similar. Specifically, accountability systems arise whenever two conditions are satisfied:

1. One group member acts in a manner that harms others.
2. Those harmed are sufficiently alarmed to incur the costs of monitoring and censuring the responsible party. In short, accountability is a universal feature of all known systems of social control, from economic markets to government bureaucracies to informal peer and community networks.

B. Accountability and Decision Making

Expectations of accountability constrain virtually every decision people make. Whether one is an architect designing a building, a politician contemplating next year's budget priorities, or a research scientist preparing a manuscript for a peer-refereed journal, there is strong pressure to anticipate the objections of potential critics (what will I say if they advance this or that argument?). [*See* DECISION MAKING, INDIVIDUALS.]

Field studies underscore the ubiquity of accountability in decision making. Experimental studies shed light on the mechanisms underlying the effects of accountability on judgment and choice.

II. ASSUMPTIONS UNDERLYING ACCOUNTABILITY RESEARCH

A. Motivational Assumptions Underlying Accountability Research

Why do people generally seek the approval and avoid the disapproval of those to whom they feel accountable? Theorists offer three categories of answers:

1. Economic self-interest
2. Self-esteem needs
3. Impression management needs

The economic and self-esteem approaches view approval motivation as a means to ends, the ends being either material-enhancement or self-enhancement.[1] By contrast, impression management theories hold that people seek approval as an end in itself.

Although logically distinct, these three categories of motives are empirically intertwined. On the one hand, these motives are sometimes related in positive feedback loops: as one's material wealth increases, so too might one's status or esteem in which one is held by others. Similarly, purchasing particular possessions can be seen as the symbolic action of self-affirmation. On the other hand, these motives are sometimes in direct tension with each other. Conspicuous consumption can also lead to negative feedback from others.

B. Cognitive Assumptions Underlying Decision-Making Research

Most researchers start from the premise that people are limited-capacity information processors who rely on simplifying heuristics to cope with an otherwise intolerably complex world. Perhaps the most influential framework to date has been the cognitive miser which depicts people as prone to a variety of judgmental failings. The miser attempts to minimize mental strain by employing simple heuristics, but

---

[1] Traditionally, theories explaining approval motivation have focused on the private self, explaining motives as a means to an end. Theories ranging from Freud's view of the unconscious all the way to current theories of self-schemata are examples of this "private self" approach. Typically, such theories explain approval motivation in terms of inner cognitions, traits, and emotions.

In economic theories of human behavior, assessing the costs and benefits of social action is an individual's main objective. In this view, the decision maker is an intuitive economist whose aim is to increase power while maximizing rewards and minimizing costs. A range of theories exist in terms of economic effectiveness. At one end, economic theories posit near perfect rationality on the part of the decision maker. At the other end, theories argue that decision makers are wired up in fundamentally wrong ways to be perfectly rational.

By contrast, symbolic interactionists have focused on the "public self." Symbolic theories assert that the trait attributions made by others are essential to the definition of the self. The "looking glass self," for example, represents the idea that a person's self-concept is actually a reflection of that person's perceptions of how he or she appears to others.

the price of cognitive economy is susceptibility to a host of errors, including being too quick to draw strong conclusions about others' personalities from fragmentary and unrepresentative evidence, too slow to revise hypotheses in response to new evidence, overconfident, and too quick to lose faith in genuinely diagnostic evidence when that evidence is embedded among irrelevant or distracter variables.

Recently, the cognitive miser framework has been challenged by a new generation of contingency theories of judgment and choice which rely instead on the "cognitive manager" metaphor. Central to these contingency theories is the assumption that people think in different ways in different situations. There is, moreover, considerable evidence that people can indeed shift from simpler to more complex cognitive strategies in response to situational demands.

In this article, we use the cognitive miser metaphor as a starting point; bounded rationality is a useful first approximation for predicting how people cope with accountability predicaments. All other things being equal, people do prefer least-effort solutions. But, all other things are not always equal. Under certain conditions, accountability can motivate substantial effort, sometimes with beneficial consequences, sometimes without.

III. HOW PEOPLE COPE WITH ACCOUNTABILITY: STRATEGIES AND HEURISTICS

To recap, accountability is a universal feature of the natural decision environment; people are motivated to seek the approval and respect of those to whom they are accountable; and, people are capable of thinking critically or heuristically depending on situational factors. These assumptions lay the framework for introducing a social contingency model of judgment and choice.

A. Social Contingency Model of Judgment and Choice

Proposed by Tetlock, this model posits how motivational and cognitive dispositions of decision makers interact with the social context (especially accountability) to shape individual judgment and choice. Just as there are middle-range theories that depict people as more or less effective intuitive psychologists and economists, so one can imagine theories

that depict people as more or less effective politicians. This model of judgment and choice falls near the midpoint of the effectiveness continuum.[2]

1. The Acceptability Heuristic

This low-effort solution to accountability predicaments is activated when the socially acceptable option is obvious, likely to come to mind quickly, and likely to be bolstered by supportive arguments readily available in the environment.[3] Under these conditions, people simply adopt positions likely to gain the favor of those to whom they feel accountable, thereby allowing them to avoid much "unnecessary" cognitive work (analyzing the pros and cons of alternative courses of action, interpreting complex patterns of information, making difficult trade-offs).

An example is strategic attitude shifting. Studies show that when subjects know the views of the audience and do not feel locked into any prior attitudinal commitment, they shift their views toward those of the prospective audience. Field studies tell a similar story of decision makers in business and politics often tailoring the message to the audience.

2. Pre-Emptive Self-Criticism

The social contingency model posits, however, that the solutions to accountability predicaments are not always so straightforward. In some situations, the most acceptable option is not obvious. The model predicts that under conditions of normative ambiguity and pressure to justify future action, people abandon their cognitive-miserly ways and become relatively flexible, multidimensional thinkers.

To test these predictions, Tetlock *et al.* asked subjects to report their positions on controversial issues (capital punishment, affirmative action) under one of four conditions: expecting their positions to be confidential or expecting to justify their positions to an individual with liberal, conservative, or unknown views. In addition, subjects were asked to

---

[2] On one end of the continuum would be theories that posit Machiavellian levels of political cunning. People, in this view, are incessant schemers who actively seek out information about the expectations and preferences of others, carefully calculate the impact of possible decisions on others, anticipate potential objections, and craft accounts to preempt these objections. At the other end of the effectiveness continuum would be theories that portray people as hopelessly inept politicians who may try to maintain good working relations with important constituents, but who instead frequently wind up antagonizing them.

[3] This is especially true in group polarization and concurrence-seeking group situations.

TABLE I

Integrative Complexity of Thought Varies in a Predictable Pattern According to Perceived Audience Characteristics

		Mean integrative complexity scores	
Strategy	Condition	Tetlock (1983)	Tetlock *et al.* (1989)
—	No accountability	1.83	1.56
Acceptability heuristic	Accountable to liberal audience	2.00	1.66
Acceptability heuristic	Accountable to conservative audience	2.06	1.76
Pre-emptive self-criticism	Accountable to unknown audience	2.61	2.05

Note: Higher scores indicate more complex responses. Ratings ranged from 1 to 7.

report their thoughts on each issue *prior* to committing themselves to a position. These thought protocols were then subjected to detailed content analysis to assess the integrative complexity of subjects' thinking on the issues.

Subjects who were accountable to an unknown audience employed a pre-emptively self-critical strategy; in their thought protocols, they displayed much more tolerance for evaluative inconsistency (recognizing both good and bad features of particular policies) and much more recognition of value trade-offs. This cognitive reaction can be viewed as an adaptive strategy to protect one's self- and social-image. Expecting to justify one's views to an unknown audience raised the prospect of failure: The other person might find serious flaws in the positions taken. To reduce the likelihood of such an esteem-threatening and embarrassing event, subjects demonstrated their awareness of alternative perspectives on the issues. The implicit goal was to justify the position taken by showing an understanding of the counter-arguments.

Recall that integrative complexity is a measure of the multidimensionality of cognition. Table I summarizes mean values of integrative complexity ratings that correspond to use of the acceptability heuristic and pre-emptive self-criticism. Presumably, accountability to an unknown audience induces more complexity because people try to anticipate arguments that potential critics might raise.

3. Defensive Bolstering

The model also identifies a third major coping strategy. When people have irrevocably committed themselves to a course of action,[4] accountability will

---

[4] Here we refer specifically to cases of postdecisional accountability

again motivate cognitive effort. The result will not, though, be self-critical, flexible, and complex thought. Rather, the result will be rigid, defensive, and evaluatively consistent thought. Accountability will prompt people to engage in *defensive bolstering,* that is, to generate as many reasons as they can why they are right and potential critics wrong.

Note the difference between predecisional versus postdecisional accountability. Tetlock *et al.* showed how a minor variation in the timing of an accountability manipulation can dramatically influence coping strategies. Subjects who felt accountable and reported their thoughts after making attitudinal commitments became much less integratively complex than accountable subjects who reported their thoughts prior to taking a stand.

Once accountable subjects had publicly committed themselves, the major function of thought became the generation of justifications for those stands. As a result, the integrative complexity of the thoughts reported plunged (subjects were less likely to see the other point of view), and the number of pro-attitudinal thoughts increased (subjects generated thoughts that were evaluatively consistent with their public attitudinal stands). Table II shows the systematic variation in integrative complexity according to the timing of accountability.

4. Decision Avoidance

Finally, the model predicts a fourth coping pattern. When people are accountable to conflicting audiences, when it is necessary to impose losses on a well-defined constituency in order to promote the general good, and when the risks posed by a decision are moderate to high, people are likely to engage in decision avoidance tactics. Under these conditions, people cope by buckpassing and procrastinating.

TABLE II
Integrative Complexity Varies Systematically According to the Timing of Accountability

Condition	Mean integrative complexity scores
Accountable to unknown audience	
Predecisional accountability	2.01
Postdecisional accountability	1.4
Accountable to liberal audience	
Predecisional accountability	1.7
Postdecisional accountability	1.3
Accountable to conservative audience	
Predecisional accountability	1.8
Postdecisional accountability	1.5

Note: Higher scores indicate more complex responses. Ratings ranged from 1 to 7. Data drawn from Tetlock *et al.* (1989).

TABLE III
Primary Strategies Used to Cope with Accountability Demands and the Activating Situational Conditions

| Coping strategy | Situational conditions | |
	Perceived audience motives	Temporal factors
Acceptability heuristic	Known	Predecisional accountability
Pre-emptive self-criticism	Unknown	Predecisional accountability
Defensive bolstering	Unknown or known	Postdecisional accountability
Decision avoidance[a]	Conflicting[b]	Predecisional accountability

[a] Tactics such as procrastination and buckpassing are activated when subjects want to avoid decision making responsibility.
[b] Evidence also indicates that the necessity of imposing losses on a well-defined constituency in order to promote the general good activates decision avoidance.

To test these predictions, Tetlock and Boettger conducted a laboratory simulation of Food and Drug Administration decisions to admit new drugs onto, or keep old drugs on, the United States pharmaceuticals market. Specifically, the study assessed: (a) the degree of risk the drug subjects were willing to tolerate; (b) the tendency to blame by buckpassing or procrastinating; and (c) the degree of conflict or ambivalence experienced in decision making.

After subjects received information about the likely risks and benefits of the drug, they made decisions under either total anonymity or public accountability conditions. Results indicate that accountable subjects focused on the relative ease of justifying choices in setting levels of acceptable risk. All subjects were more accepting of a drug the lower the anticipated risks and the greater the anticipated benefits. Accountable subjects were especially unwilling to accept risk when the drug was not yet on the market and posed moderate or high risk. Under these conditions accountable subjects procrastinated (sought to delay decision making until further evidence was available) and buckpassed (passed responsibility for decision making onto another governmental agency).

In summary, the model posits that the social context of decision making can activate qualitatively distinct strategies of coping with accountability demands: the acceptability heuristic; pre-emptive self-criticism; defensive bolstering; and decision avoidance tactics (Table III).

B. Cognitive Implications of Coping Strategies

One possible objection to the foregoing research is that accountability merely affects response thresh-olds, not how people actually reason their way through problems of judgment and choice. If so, then accountability manipulations should be equally effective whether they are introduced before or after people are exposed to the evidence on which they must base their judgments and decisions.

Contrary to this prediction, accountability is much more effective in preventing than in reversing judgmental biases. Once subjects have assimilated or integrated information into their impressions of a person or event, they have a hard time reinterpreting that information. Accountability has a marked impact on the initial impression-formation process (it places subjects in a vigilant mental set that confers some protection from inferential biases), but it has little impact after the initial processing has occurred. Accountability cannot undo biased thinking at earlier processing stages. [*See* IMPRESSION FORMATION.]

C. Individual Differences in Coping with Accountability

Although most work has focused on situational determinants of thinking strategies, some studies have looked at individual differences in relation to accountability. Though individual differences have not appeared as a locus for explaining variance, there are significant cognitive style and social motivational correlates of coping responses. Key findings include the following.

1. Dogmatism

Dogmatic subjects tend to be less complex in their thinking. This suggests that high scorers on the dogmatism scale are less likely than low scorers to adopt a pre-emptively self-critical strategy, but are equally likely to adopt the acceptability heuristic.

2. Social Anxiety

Anxiety plays a limited but significant role by moderating the activation of pre-emptive self-criticism; subjects high in social anxiety report more integratively complex thoughts in response to predecisional accountability. High social anxiety subjects are also more likely to engage in defensive bolstering than low social anxiety subjects. Overall, social anxiety and need for approval help predict how motivated people are to gain the approval of prospective audiences as well as the strategies they use to achieve that goal.

D. Boundary Conditions on Accountability Effects

There are noteworthy cases in which accountability fails to motivate changes in cognitive effort, suggesting boundary condition on its effects. As expected, when accountable to someone believed to be a legitimate judge, people are more likely to engage in analytic thought and to be able to describe their judgment policies after a judgment task. On the other hand, when accountable to someone without a perceived legitimate right to judge, people are less accurate at describing their policies, and they engage in more intuitive, rapid thinking.

Furthermore, accountability is not effective in reducing decision errors when the correct response is unknown and is not likely to be revealed with more thorough processing of information. In contrast to recency bias (which accountability does eliminate), accountability is ineffective with the curse of knowledge. The curse of knowledge exists when individuals are influenced by outcome knowledge that is irrelevant to the decision at hand. Kennedy suggests that this is due to the fact that curse of knowledge is due to the way data are used by the decision maker rather than insufficient attention or effort.

IV. EVALUATION OF COPING RESPONSES

Conventional wisdom tells us that increasing accountability promotes effective decision making.

Experimental inquiry and political case studies, on the other hand, suggest that increasing accountability can trigger a variety of both welcome and not-so-welcome responses. We have seen, for example, that accountability can motivate cognitive effort which can take the form of either pre-emptive self-criticism, on the positive side, or increased buck-passing and procrastination and susceptibility to judgmental biases, such as dilution,[5] on the negative side. These findings suggest that accountability is no social panacea; there is often a trade-off between costs and benefits involved.

We now probe beyond these generalizations and develop a more nuanced understanding of accountability's benefits. The key questions are: When do these coping strategies lead to behavioral outcomes that scholarly observers applaud as adaptive or deplore as maladaptive? And, what standards should we use to make such determinations? In the next section, we proceed strategy by strategy (with reviews and comments on the existing literature) to answer these questions. [See COPING.]

A. Acceptability Heuristic

Motivating adherence to social norms is the primary effect of this strategy. Results from considerable research allow us to explore both its micro- and macro-implications.

1. Advantages

The acceptability heuristic is a stabilizer; it turns social interaction into social order. Because people are concerned with what others will deem acceptable behavior, people are less likely to transgress important social and cultural norms. Indeed, accountability is a vital component of the social matrix; no social order can survive for long if its members do not recognize the legitimacy of its rules and accountability procedures.

The acceptability heuristic is a cognitive shortcut that sometimes serves us well. For example, when subjects believe that ignoring sunk costs[6] would appear more rational to an audience, the acceptability heuristic improves decision making.

Another advantage is promoting creativity. All creative acts depend on risk taking and some evi-

---

[5] Tetlock and Boettger (1989) documented increased susceptibility to the dilution effect, but also questioned whether this same effect is profitably considered a bias or a normative response.

[6] Sunk cost bias is the tendency to consume an object after sinking money in it because people anticipate feeling regret later for having wasted resources on something they left unconsumed.

dence suggests that collective accountability increases risk seeking in groups. On the other hand, there is evidence that accountability reduces the amount of risk groups are willing to take. One possibility is that accountability will magnify risk taking only if individual group members sense that riskiness is valued by the group.[7]

2. Disadvantages

By motivating decision makers to adopt the least objectionable course of action, the acceptability heuristic can lead individuals into decision traps. Research on bargaining has documented entrapment in groups. Several studies have found that accountability to constituents leads to tough, contentious bargaining, with a relatively high probability of deadlocks. Similarly, Adelberg and Batson found that accountability impaired rather than enhanced the effective use of resources by decision makers. When resources were insufficient, accountability made subjects award all applicants equally small and insufficient grants. The desire for social approval/acceptability shifts the decision-maker's focus away from the potential effectiveness of outcomes to the justifiability of actions.

B. Defensive Bolstering

This strategy directs decision makers to devote the majority of their mental effort to justifying whatever position they feel committed to.

1. Disadvantages

Defensive bolstering can lead to a host of problems, including overconfidence in the correctness of decisions, discounting contradictory evidence, denying difficult value trade-offs, and susceptibility to entrapment. As already discussed, when decision makers are accountable for past commitments, they are more likely to up the ante. For example, research reveals that people who are personally responsible for an investment decision that produces bad results are more likely than people not personally responsible to pursue a failing policy instead of choosing a new course of action that would prevent further

losses. Personal responsibility also causes groups to perceive successive decisions as more strongly related and to feel more confident about those decisions. Moreover, individual accountability fails to stimulate entrapment *only* when decision makers can shift to alternative options that are not associated with a loss of prestige.

2. Advantages

Of course, it is not always a good idea to abandon a policy at the first sign of trouble. Decision makers who practice defensive bolstering as opposed to preemptive self-criticism are more likely to stick with a fundamentally good policy that has recently run into serious short-term difficulties. There is a fine, normative line between principled determination to "stay the course" and stubborn refusal to "acknowledge the facts."

C. Pre-Emptive Self-Criticism

Predecisional accountability to unknown audiences directs people to anticipate objections that others might raise and to incorporate those objections into their own position.

1. Advantages

a. Improves Social Judgment

Many psychologists believe that there is a systematic bias in the person perception process: a pervasive tendency among observers to overestimate personality or dispositional causes of behavior and to underestimate the influence of situational constraints on behavior. Indeed, this behavior is referred to in the literature as the fundamental attribution error.

To examine this "error" in the context of accountability, Tetlock conducted an essay attribution experiment that explicitly manipulated whether subjects felt accountable for their attributional judgments and when they learned of being accountable. The classic overattribution effect was replicated when subjects did not feel accountable for their attributional judgments or when subjects learned of being accountable only after exposure to all the evidence. However, subjects who learned of being accountable prior to exposure to the evidence successfully resisted the overattribution effect. The effects suggest that the accountability manipulation encouraged people to consider the empirical facts presented rather than to rely on top-down interpretations.

---

[7] To qualify this finding, we note that Weigold and Schlenker (1991) found that accountability only reduced risk avoidance for individuals who had characterized themselves as low risk takers. Subjects who rated themselves as high risk takers were not affected by accountability in their preference for risk. According to Weigold and Schlenker, accountability made subjects rely on their own ideas about what kind of behavior would be socially appropriate.

The perseverance of first impressions, otherwise known as the primacy effect, is another bias that can be reduced by accountability. Using evidence from a criminal case, Tetlock found that having to justify one's impressions to others leads people to process information more vigilantly, and, as a result, reduces the undue influence of early formed impressions on final judgments. Accountability *prior to the evidence* also improved free recall of the case material, presumably because accountability affects how people initially encode and process stimulus information.

Similarly, Kennedy found that recency bias, the tendency to overweight evidence received later in a sequence, was reduced by accountability. Also in this study, however, Kennedy found that the curse of knowledge is not mitigated by accountability.

b. Induces Appropriate Confidence

A substantial literature indicates that people are often excessively confident in the correctness of their factual judgments and predictions. Yet, accountability can attenuate or eliminate overconfidence. Tetlock and Kim demonstrated that accountability reduces overconfidence in a personality prediction task. When people learn of the need to justify their responses *before* seeing the personality test responses of others, they form more integratively complex first impressions of people's personalities, make more accurate behavioral predictions, and report more appropriate confidence in those predictions. Observers who learn of the need to justify their responses *after* seeing the test takers' responses show no improvement in performance.

This debiasing effect has many potential applications. For example, evidence that accountability elicits confidence estimates from eyewitnesses that are more predictive of accuracy may be used to improve legal proceedings. Contrary to conventional wisdom, an individual's confidence about an identification is often only weakly related to the accuracy of an identification. But, if accountability is introduced in the proper way, this correlation should improve.

c. Stimulates Bottom-Up Rather Than Top-Down Information Processing

Several studies indicate that accountability stimulates data-driven as opposed to theory-driven information processing. We know, for example, that accountability leads decision makers to employ more consistent patterns of cue utilization. Similarly, a combination of accountability and forewarning in a

memory based interpersonal judgment task induces people to store and review all relevant information prior to making a judgment. By contrast, when not otherwise prompted, people tend to base interpersonal judgments on previous decisions and stored beliefs or inferences about someone.

There is also evidence that accountability can encourage data-driven and discourage theory-driven information processing. Previous work on person perception has shown that characteristics of the *perceiver* are frequently more important determinants of person perception than are characteristics of the person being judged. Perceivers tend to offer undifferentiated descriptions of stimulus persons (a given perceiver tends to see different stimulus persons as similar to each other) as well as idiosyncratic descriptions of stimulus persons (little overlap exists in the descriptions that different perceivers offer of the same stimulus person). This pattern is exactly what one would expect if people were theory-driven (top-down) thinkers who rely on their own implicit theories of personality and give little weight to actual properties of the persons being judged.

Under high importance and high accountability conditions, however, experimenters found a reversal of the typical finding: (1) differentiated perceiver descriptions of stimulus persons and (2) substantial agreement among judges in the descriptions offered of the same stimulus persons. In short, accountability appeared to sensitize perceivers to "what was actually out there."

d. Improves Human Performance

Accountability leads to more analytic choice strategies and greater investments of time and effort in decision making. This increase in investment helps explain why accountability reduces social loafing in groups. To test the effect of accountability, researchers manipulated whether subjects were accountable for their individual performance in a group task by telling subjects that the experimenter either would or would not be contacting them later to ask further questions. Mathematical models of subjects' judgments indicated that subjects who were not held accountable for their group work used less complex judgment strategies than those working alone. But, they also found that this kind of social loafing could be significantly reduced by holding members responsible for their individual performance. [*See* SOCIAL LOAFING.]

2. Disadvantages

a. Induces Excessive Searches for Meaning

Increased integrative complexity increases the tendency to make inappropriately regressive predictions when diagnostic evidence is accompanied by diverse bits of nondiagnostic information (what has been called the dilution effect). In one scenario, Tetlock and Boettger asked subjects to predict the grade point averages of target students. Subjects received either only diagnostic evidence (number of hours studied per week) or diagnostic evidence plus a host of irrelevant information (tennis playing habits, dating patterns). Accountable subjects tried to be "good," complex information processors and to integrate both the diagnostic and nondiagnostic evidence in making predictions about grade point average. In short, pre-exposure accountability to an unknown audience motivated subjects to be more integratively complex thinkers, but it did not make them wiser—it did not make them more discriminating consumers of the information at their disposal.

b. Increases Susceptibility to Status Quo Bias and Sensitivity to Risk

Another example of the arguably maladaptive effects of integrative complexity comes from a Tetlock and Boettger study that examined judgments of the acceptability of a drug on the United States pharmaceutical market. As noted earlier, accountable subjects were much more responsive to the level of risk posed by the drug, and especially so when they believed the drug had not yet been admitted into the market. Analysis of covariance indicated that subjects who thought about the issues in more integratively complex ways were largely responsible for the three-way interaction between the status quo manipulation, the accountability manipulation, and the level of risk manipulation. Examination of the thoughts reported by these subjects revealed a preoccupation with worst-case scenario thinking and explicit concern for what they would say to those who would be injured by their decisions. There is, of course, nothing immoral or irrational about such concerns. It is noteworthy, however, that these subjects were much more tolerant of risk created by a drug that was already on the market (the status quo effect). Removing a drug with a high benefit–cost ratio from the market would antagonize those constituencies who currently benefit from it. Introducing a drug with an equally positive benefit–cost ratio focuses attention on those constituencies who would be hurt. In short, accountability pressures that motivate integrative complexity make people reluctant to put themselves out on a limb and take stands that require painful trade-offs.

D. Determining the Value of Strategies

Having considered numerous cases in which the literature presents each coping strategy as either adaptive or maladaptive, we return to an earlier question: What standards are appropriate to determine the appropriateness of each strategy? Here we urge caution. There are many possible standards and a lack of clear guidelines. For example, when does the desire of good team players to do what is most acceptable stimulate mindless conformity and groupthink as opposed to much needed enthusiasm and unity of purpose? Is the dilution effect better thought of as a cognitive bias or a prudent response to the conversational norm "assume the information people give you is relevant to the task at hand?" Response tendencies that look like judgmental flaws from one perspective frequently look quite reasonable from other perspectives (see Tetlock, 1992, for several examples).

Before labeling a response tendency a cognitive flaw, we should consider the interpersonal, institutional, and political goals that people are trying to achieve by making judgments of a particular type: Do people seek to achieve causal understanding or to express their moral approval/disapproval? Do people attempt to maximize expected utility or to minimize risk of serious criticism?

V. SUMMARY AND CONCLUSIONS

Accountability is an inevitable feature of decision environments—it is the social psychological link between individual decision makers on the one hand and social systems on the other. Nevertheless, its effects have been largely overlooked by psychologists. Only recently are some psychologists beginning to systematically study the strategies people develop for coping with this ubiquitous problem of social life.

Research to date identifies four major coping strategies for dealing with accountability: the acceptability heuristic, defensive bolstering, pre-emptive self-criticism, and decision avoidance tactics. Our analysis of the pros and cons of each strategy lead us to conclude that each of the coping responses is appropriate under some circumstances and inappropriate under others. We argue that the criteria for assessing utility of a strategy must factor in the social context in which that strategy operates. For example, labeling the dilution effect a cognitive error fails to take into account the conversational norms operating in the social context. Such a label downplays the adaptive value of sensitivity to conversational norms.

Although the number and diversity of field and laboratory studies on this topic are growing, numerous gaps exist in the literature. There is little work on accountability to self, to conflicting audiences, and to challenging (rather than threatening) audiences. We also need comparative ethnographic studies of organizational culture to document the diverse forms that accountability relationships take and the style of decision making associated with these relationships. People do not make decisions in a social vacuum. It is crucial, therefore, that we expand our investigation of accountability and social cognition through complementary research programs of experimentation and field study.

Bibliography

Adelberg, S., and Batson, C. D. (1978). Accountability and helping: When needs exceed resources. *J. Pers. Soc. Psychol.* **36,** 343–350.

Cvetkovich, G. (1978). Cognitive accommodation, language and social responsibility. *Soc. Psychol.* **41,** 149–155.

Fiske, S. T., and Taylor, S. (1984). "Social Cognition." Addision-Wesley, Reading, MA.

Ford, J. K., and Weldon, E. (1981). Forewarning and accountability: Effects on memory-based interpersonal judgments. *Pers. Soc. Psychol. Bull.* **7**(2), 264–268.

Hagafors, R., and Brehmer, B. (1983). Does having to justify one's judgments change the nature of the judgment process? *Organizational Behav. Hum. Performance* **31,** 223–232.

Kennedy, J. (1992). "Debiasing Audit Judgment with Accountability: A Framework and Experimental Results." Unpublished dissertation, Duke University.

Kroon, M. B. R. (1992). "Effects of Accountability on Groupthink and Intergroup Relations." Thesis, University of Utrecht, The Netherlands.

McAllister, D. W., Mitchell, T. R., and Beach, L. R. (1979). The contingency model for the selection of decision strategies: An empirical test of the effects of significance, accountability, and reversibility. *Organizational Behav. Hum. Performance* **24,** 228–244.

Ross, J., and Staw, B. M. (1993). Organizational escalation and exit: Lessons from the Shoreham Nuclear Power Plant. *Acad. Manag. J.* **36,** 701–732.

Schlenker, B. R. (1980). "Impression Management: The Self Concept, Social Identity, and Interpersonal Relations." Brooks-Cole, Monterey, CA.

Semin, G. R., and Manstead, A. S. R. (1983). "The Accountability of Conduct: A Social Psychological Analysis" Academic Press, London.

Simonson, I., and Nye, P. (1992). The effect of accountability on susceptibility to decision errors. *Organizational Behav. Hum. Decision Processes* **51,** 416–446.

Tetlock, P. E. (1992). The impact of accountability on judgment and choice: Toward a social contingency model. *Adv. Exp. Soc. Psychol.* **25,** 331–376.

Weigold, M. F., and Schlenker, B. R. (1991). Accountability and risk taking. *Pers. Soc. Psychol. Bull.* **17,** 25–29.

ACTOR–OBSERVER DIFFERENCES IN ATTRIBUTION

George R. Goethals
Williams College

Glossary

Actor–observer bias The tendency for actors to attribute their behavior to external and situational causes while observers attribute actors' behavior to the actors' personal dispositions and traits.

Behavior engulfing the field The phenomenon first noted by Fritz Heider whereby perceivers pay so much attention to behavior that they do not notice situational factors that might be responsible for that behavior.

Correspondence bias People's tendency toward attributing other people's behavior to traits directly corresponding to their behavior, such as attributing friendly behavior to a friendly disposition.

Ego-centricity People's tendency to perceive themselves as central and causal actors in a wide range of situations.

Salient Attention getting, easily noticeable; in social perception behavior is often attributed to salient plausible causes.

Self-serving bias People's tendency to take credit for success but deny responsibility for failure.

ACTORS explain their behavior very differently from observers who are perceiving their behavior. Specifically, actors themselves attribute their behavior to external or situational factors, that is, to forces in the environment that led them to perform particular actions. In contrast, observers of the actor are much more likely to attribute the actor's behavior to internal or personal causes, that is, to traits of the actor that led him or her to perform a particular action. That is, people attribute their own behavior to external causes and other people's behavior to internal causes.

One reason that actors and observers differ is that they have different information about possible causes. Actors know about all the times they have behaved differently in different situations, while observers do not. This makes it easier for observers to conclude that the behavior is consistent and reflects a personal trait. Also, people are likely to attribute behavior to noticeable and salient potential causes, and actors are more likely to notice the situation in which they have to act while observers are more likely to notice the actors themselves. Actor's egocentric and self-serving biases can also contribute to actor–observer differences in attribution.

The actor–observer can lead to misunderstandings between people and between groups, including nations. For years the Soviet Union and the United States struggled to overcome hostility and conflict that in part reflected actor vs observer differences in attribution. Each country armed itself and viewed its own behavior as a necessary response to the armaments of the other. At the same time they each perceived the other country as arming itself in order to try to dominate world politics and to intimidate other peaceful countries.

I. THE THEORY OF ACTOR–OBSERVER DIFFERENCES IN ATTRIBUTION

During the 1970s social psychologists Edward E. Jones and Richard E. Nisbett developed a theory concerning the differences between the ways actors themselves and observers of actors explain actors' behavior. In effect, they proposed that the way people explain their own behavior is different from the way they explain other people's behavior. In explaining their own behavior they have the perspective of the actor. In explaining other people's behavior they have the perspective of an observer.

The basic difference between actors and observers is that actors explain behavior in terms of external or situational factors that caused or elicited their behavior while observers explain other people's behavior in terms of personal traits or dispositions that produced the behavior. Actors view their behavior as caused by the environment and as an appropriate response to that environment while observers view behavior as a reflection of their individual abilities, motives, attitudes, temperaments, moods, or tastes. These differences in attribution can cause important misunderstandings and create interpersonal conflict.

As an example of actor–observer differences, consider a woman who decides to take a trip to the southwest United States to see the Grand Canyon. The woman herself is the actor in this example. She might explain her decision by noting that the price of airline tickets is extremely low this time of year or that the Grand Canyon is one of America's most spectacular natural wonders, and that it would be fascinating for anyone to see. That is, she sees her behavior as caused by the situation, and as an appropriate and entirely reasonable response to the situation. Observers in this example, for instance, people who know the woman at work, might explain her trip by noting that she is a nature lover with a lot of energy who is clever enough to recognize a good deal when she sees it. That is, other people explain the woman's behavior in terms of one or more personal qualities that led her to take the trip. They see the behavior as corresponding to or reflecting these personal qualities. Clearly, the woman herself does not agree with the acquaintances who are observing her behavior. In this case the differences in explanation may have no serious or adverse consequence. In other cases they might.

II. EVIDENCE FOR THE ACTOR–OBSERVER BIAS

A great deal of research has demonstrated that actors and observers make different attributions for behavior. For example, when male college students were asked to explain why they liked their girlfriend or chose their major they made attributions that were quite different from the attributions made by their friends. The students themselves, as actors explaining their own behavior, spoke of the particularly positive and attractive qualities of their girlfriends and the utility and desirability of their majors. That is, they saw their choices as reflecting the qualities of what they chose, not their own personal qualities. Observers, in this case friends and acquaintances of the students, were much more likely to explain a specific student's choices in terms of his or her personal interests and needs. They might explain that their friend was highly attracted to athletic women or that he wanted to make a lot of money and to prepare himself for a career that would satisfy the value he put on financial security. A second study considered actors working on a set of difficult intellectual problems and solving only a few at the beginning of the set and nearly all of them at the end. Actors explain their increasing success as due to the problems getting easier, an external cause. Observers explain the increasing success as reflecting the actors' extra effort, an internal cause. As a result of these attributions, actors predict that they will do well on another set of problems, while observers tend not to. Misunderstanding is clearly possible. Another study showed that people writing to advice columnists such as Dear Abby or Ann Landers are much more likely to explain their own problems in terms of external forces that create those problems and other people's problems in terms of the personal shortcomings of those people that land them in difficulty. Again, we see our own behavior as a natural, appropriate, and common response to situations, and therefore caused by those situations, and other people's behavior as caused by their unique personal dispositions and abilities.

III. COGNITIVE EXPLANATIONS FOR THE ACTOR–OBSERVER BIAS

There are several factors that have been proposed as explanations for the differences between actors' and observers' causal explanations. Some of these point to cognitive or informational variables. One such explanation emphasizes the fact that actors and observers have different information about the actor. Actors know that their behavior varies and is not always like the way they just behaved in one specific instance. Therefore, they see any particular behavior as caused by the unique circumstances in which it was performed. The observer often does not know how the actor has behaved in the past, in similar or different circumstances, and can easily assume that the actor's specific behavior is common and representative, and reflective of the actor's personal inclinations or abilities. This makes it easy for the observer to attribute the actor's behavior to his or her personal qualities.

Another cognitive explanation emphasizes differences in what information is salient to actors and observers, and therefore what each one views as causal. This explanation builds on research showing that perceivers attribute behavior to salient or noticeable causes. For example, people watching a conversation between two other people are likely to think that the person whom they can see the best is exerting the most control in directing the flow of the conversation. Similarly, we are more likely to attribute interpersonal behavior to people who are more noticeable because they are wearing bright-colored clothes or sitting in a rocking chair. That is, we attribute behavior to plausible causes that are noticeable and therefore perceptually salient.

How do plausible causes vary in noticeability or salience to actors and observers? For the actor the salient factors are the force and the constraints of the situation. The actor must be alive to these pushes and pulls and perform within them. Because of their salience, these pushes and pulls will probably seem like very plausible causes to the actor, and will be used to explain their behavior. For the observer watching the actor, the salient factors are likely to be the actor's specific behaviors and reactions. The forces that the actor sees and responds to are not likely to be noticed by the observer. The actor's responses will attract the observers attention. The great psychologist Fritz Heider stated that "behavior has such salient properties it tends to engulf the field." By that Heider meant that observers find actors' behavior highly noticeable, indeed so noticeable that it tends to block out other factors that ordinarily might be noticed, such as the subtle pressures in the situation that caused the behavior. Consider for example a man in an argument with two

other people who is subtly needled or put down by the others, and subsequently loses his temper and yells at them. While the man himself will find the other people's needling very salient and view it as causal, an outside observer is more likely to notice the man's dramatic yelling, and overlook the other people's subtle needling. The observer would attribute the actor's behavior to the actor's bad temper and excitability.

There is some research that supports the salience interpretation for the actor–observer effect. When actors are shown videotapes of their own behavior, so that they themselves become the focus of attention and the salient plausible cause, they tend to attribute their behavior to themselves, to their personal characteristics.

IV. MOTIVATIONAL EXPLANATIONS FOR THE ACTOR–OBSERVER BIAS

The two explanations above focus on cognitive factors that produce differences in the attributions of actor and observers. They both assume that actors and observers make judgments rationally and sensibly but because they have different information or pay attention to different information they make different and potentially erroneous attributions. Other research has focused on motivational factors that may lead people to make biased inferences about the causes of behavior.

One motivational factor is that people are often motivated to perceive themselves in certain ways. In most cases, however, they are not motivated to perceive other people in the same way. Thus, these motivations would come into play when we are actors explaining our own behavior but not when we are observers explaining someone else's behavior. One motivational factor is called psychological reactance. People react against any threat to their free behaviors. If people attribute a particular behavior, say friendliness, to a corresponding internal disposition or trait of friendliness, they may feel that the trait of friendliness will limit their freedom to act unfriendly in a later situation. Since they want to maintain the view that they are free to act in either manner, friendly or unfriendly, they may be reluctant to attribute their friendly behavior to the friendly disposition. That is, they may not want to perceive the friendly disposition as causal. Thus, they would see their friendly behavior as caused by the specific circumstances of the situation in which they acted friendly. They would see subsequent unfriendly behavior in the same way, as reflecting the special circumstances of the situation in which they were unfriendly. In this way they can see themselves as free to behave as either friendly or unfriendly, and not as one whose friendly disposition would normally cause them to act friendly, and to restrict their freedom to be unfriendly when necessary. This motive to see oneself as free does not apply to other people. We have no such wish to see them as free. In fact, we gain some sense of having control ourselves if we can see other people as predictable. To the extent that we can infer that they possess personal traits and dispositions, and that these traits and dispositions guide their behavior, we gain a sense that we can predict and even control their behavior. For this reason we may be especially biased toward inferring traits and toward seeing them as the cause of other people's behavior. [*See* MOTIVATION, EMOTIONAL BASIS.]

Another motivational factor is people's desire to see themselves as having behaved appropriately in the situation they are in. They want to see themselves as responsive to the situation that they are in, and able to act the right way in it. One way that people gain a sense that their actions are appropriate is to perceive that most other people would respond in the same way and that their actions are caused by the situation. In contrast, people have no similar need to see the behavior of others as appropriate.

Another closely related self-perception bias is the tendency to see our selves as adaptive and flexible. We like to perceive not only that we behaved appropriately in any specific instance, but also that we have the richness, versatility, and depth of personality to behave appropriately in the future. As a result we perceive ourselves as generally well-adapted, rich in personal resources, flexible, and multifaceted.

There has been a great deal of research on the question of whether the fact that we do not attribute our behavior to traits means that we do not think we have traits. Early research supported the notion that people believe that traits are things that other people—but not themselves—have. For example, when people were asked to indicate whether they are "serious" or "carefree," or that it "depends on the situation," or whether they are "subjective" or "analytic," or that it "depends on the situation," and so forth, they are distinctly more likely to say that it depends on the situation in thinking about themselves than in thinking about an acquaintance.

In other words, in this study people do not report having traits as often as they assign traits to others. This suggests that we think of other people, but not ourselves, as having traits. [*See* TRAITS.]

Later research presents a more complex picture. If people are presented with two traits, such as serious and carefree, and also presented with the alternative of marking "both" or "neither," the results quite clearly show that people report "both" more often and "neither" less often for themselves. That is, people think that they have not less but more traits than other people. It is simply that they do not think their behavior in any particular situation is caused by these traits. They think that their behavior is less predictable than that of others. That seems to be because they perceive themselves as having pairs of contradictory traits, such as introverted and extraverted, but they believe their friendly or unfriendly behavior is not likely to be attributable to either one of these traits but to the specific constraints and forces characterizing a particular situation. In short, we think of ourselves as complex, multi-faceted, responsive to situations, adaptive, and flexible. We have no such biases about other people. They are predictable and understandable, and have traits in one direction or the other; for example, they are either introverted or extraverted, not both, and those traits are likely to determine their behavior in specific situations.

Although the various cognitive and motivational explanations that have been proposed to explain actor vs observer differences in attribution can be seen as conflicting, they are not mutually exclusive. It is probable that a range of factors contribute to the differences.

V. IS THE ACTOR OR THE OBSERVER CORRECT?

One important question that is related to these differences pertains to who is correct, the actor or observer. Of course it is important to remember that each of us is both actor and observer at different times, or on occasion both at once. Are we correct when we are making attributions about ourselves as actors or about others as observers? Actors feel that their behavior is caused by external forces. Observers feel that it is caused by internal forces. Who is right?

In answering the question of above, it is useful to know that the actor vs observer differences in attribution are closely tied to, and probably reflect, another important bias in person perception. This bias is known by several names, including the "fundamental attribution error" and the "correspondence bias." It is the tendency that people have to let "behavior engulf the field," to ignore or underweight the force of external constraints on behavior, and to assume that behavior is a direct reflection of corresponding personality trait or disposition. In this way, friendly behavior is seen as being caused by a friendly personality, and not the norms of the situation, the way we have been taught to treat other people, or the desire to win someone's admiration, respect, or financial support. We are much more aware of the external forces shaping our own behavior, and it is tempting to conclude that actors are more accurate than observers. However, current research does not definitively support that conclusion. It seems to be correct, but we need more evidence. [See ATTRIBUTION.]

VI. THE ACTOR–OBSERVER BIAS IN EVERYDAY LIFE

Actor vs observer differences in attribution come into play in many spheres of interpersonal, intergroup, and international relations. A few instances are important. One comes from the area of family dynamics and family therapy. Often relationships, for example, between a husband and wife, are characterized by stable, repeating, and interdependent patterns. One well-known example concerns a bickering husband and wife, where one nags and the other withdraws. This pattern is repeated over and over. Both husband and wife perceive it, but each interprets it differently. The husband perceives the situation as one in which he nags because his wife withdraws frequently, and leaves him alone and frustrated. He perceives that she withdraws because she has lost interest in their relationship and is unloving. The wife perceives that she withdraws because her husband is always nagging at her and criticizes her. She perceives that he nags and criticizes because he is insecure and hostile. In short, both the husband and wife are showing the actor–observer bias. They see their own behavior in the relationship as responsive to the other one's behavior, and they perceive the spouse's behavior as reflecting his or her own personal qualities and dispositions. Again, we can ask which one is correct, the husband or wife. Many family systems analysts would say

that the question is irrelevant, that both husband and wife contribute to the pattern of behavior in the family system equally and that the important thing is to change their perceptions and change their behavior.

A similar kind of misunderstanding can be seen when two people play interpersonal bargaining games in the laboratory. In many such games, such as the Prisoner's Dilemma, individuals can choose to cooperate or compete. If both people cooperate they will both obtain moderately positive outcomes, if both compete they will obtain moderately negative outcomes, and if one competes while the other cooperates, the competing person, by exploiting the cooperating person, will get very positive outcomes while the cooperating person will get very negative outcomes. Sometimes both players in such a laboratory game will begin by competing. When this happens each one often explains his or her own behavior as self-protective and the other person's as competitive, hostile, and exploitative. They report that because they are not sure they can trust the other, they have to begin by being competitive. If the other shows he or she wants to be cooperative, then later they will arrange to be cooperative together. But the other person's initial competitive response, the same as their own, is seen as hostile. Thus, their own initial competitive response is seen as cautious and self-protective, and caused by the likely possibility that the other will compete, while the other's response is seen as hostile. Very quickly, any chance for mutual cooperative action becomes difficult. Misunderstandings that are very difficult to overcome grow out of actor vs observer differences in attribution.

A very similar pattern of behavior and misunderstanding characterized relations between the United States and the Soviet Union for nearly five decades following World War II. Both countries armed themselves and built expensive weapons systems. In the case of the Soviet Union, the expense of these armaments overwhelmed its financial and political system and led to the breakdown of a 70-year-old empire. Like the two individuals deciding whether to cooperate or compete, both nations behaved in the same way. They viewed their own behavior as self-protective, as an appropriate response to the aggressive designs and dispositions of the other. The other nation's behavior was seen as reflecting imperialistic dispositions and hostile intentions. Both sides manifested the actor–observer bias in their analyses of their own behavior and the other's, even though their own behavior and the other's were identical.

VII. LIMITS ON THE ACTOR–OBSERVER BIAS

The actor–observer bias is very common, and frequently causes misunderstanding and friction between individuals and groups. However, like most social psychological phenomena, it does not operate in every situation. Sometimes actors attribute their own behavior to personal dispositions or other internal causes, and sometimes observers recognize the external constraints that cause other people's behavior.

What are some of the factors that qualify the general tendency for actors to attribute their behavior to situations and observers to attribute actors' behavior to personal dispositions? First, there are two other biases that compete with the actor–observer bias, or, more specifically, with actors' general tendency to attribute their behavior to external causes. First, some research has suggested an egocentricity bias, a tendency for people to see themselves as a central locus of causality. For example, people often recall their own contributions to a group decision more than those of other people, and attribute that decision to their own contributions. People see themselves as important, and sometimes this view of themselves leads them to perceive that their personal qualities, or at least their behaviors, produced certain outcomes. It is possible for the actor–observer bias and the egocentricity bias to exist side by side. People can believe that their behaviors caused certain outcomes, but still perceive the situation as causing their behavior. The intersection between the two biases is complex, but at times the egocentricity bias will lead actors to attribute their behavior to internal causes.

Another bias affecting self-perception is the self-serving bias, the tendency to take credit for success but deny responsibility for failure. Thus, a person might attribute a successful behavior to high ability but a failure to the difficulty of the task he or she is facing, or simply to bad luck. The self-serving bias is a strong one, and when personal success is involved it can reverse the usual tendency to attribute one's own behavior to external factors.

There are also factors that can alter the strength of the general tendency for observers to attribute other people's behavior to internal characteristics. For example, when people are "active observers" themselves, that is, when they are interacting with the people whose behavior they are judging, their tendency to make internal attributions actually increases. Actively interacting with others makes attribution less thoughtful and more likely to fall back on established habits, like underweighing external forces and letting behavior engulf the field. On the other hand, when observers are encouraged to be empathetic to the actors they are observing, they tend to be slightly more aware of the situational factors that impinge on the actors, and more likely to make actor-like external attributions for behavior.

In conclusion, the actor–observer bias is a common phenomenon in social perception. It is produced by a number of cognitive and motivational factors. While it can be lessened on occasion, it is frequently a factor in generating misunderstanding between people and conflict between nations. Edward E. Jones and Richard E. Nisbett's discovery of the divergent perspectives of actors and observers is a major contribution to social psychology.

Bibliography

Fiedler, K., Semin, G., and Koppetsch, C. (1991). Language use and attributional biases in close personal relationships. *Pers. Soc. Psychol. Bull.* **17,** 147–155.

Fischer, K., Schoenenman, T. J., and Rubanowitz, D. E. (1987). Attributions in the advice columns. II. The dimensionality of actors' and observers' explanations for interpersonal problems. *Pers. Soc. Psychol. Bull.* **13,** 458–466.

Greenwald, A. G. (1980). The totalitarian ego: Fabrication and revision of personal history. *Am. Psychol.* **35,** 603–613.

Heider, F. (1958). "The Psychology of Interpersonal Relations." Wiley, New York.

Jones, E. E., and Nisbett, R. E. (1971). "The Actor and the Observer: Divergent Perceptions of the Causes of Behavior." General Learning Press, Morristown, NJ.

Jones, E. E., Rock, L., Shaver, K. G., Goethals, G. R., and Ward, L. M. (1968). Pattern of performance and ability attribution: An unexpected primacy effect. *J. Pers. Soc. Psychol.* **10,** 317–340.

Nisbett, R. E., Caputo, C., Legant, P., and Marecek, J. (1973). Behavior as seen by the actor and as seen by the observer. *J. Pers. Soc. Psychol.* **27,** 154–164.

Sande, G. N., Goethals, G. R., and Radloff, C. E. (1988). Perceiving one's own traits and other's: The multifaceted self. *J. Pers. Soc. Psychol.* **54,** 13–20.

Storms, M. (1973). Videotape and the attribution process: Reversing actor's and observer's points of view. *J. Pers. Soc. Psychol.* **27,** 165–175.

Taylor, E. E., and Fiske, S. T. (1978). Salience, attention and attribution: Top-of-the-head phenomena. In "Advances in Experimental Social Psychology" (L. Berkowitz, Ed.), Vol. 11. Academic Press, New York.

ADOLESCENCE

Grayson N. Holmbeck
Loyola University Chicago

Glossary

Adolescence A transitional developmental period between childhood and adulthood which is characterized by a host of biological, psychological, and social role changes. Although the period is typically viewed as spanning the age range of 10–20, the actual onset and endpoint of adolescence vary depending on individual differences and the manner in which one assesses the onset and endpoint.

Adolescent psychopathology Includes problem behaviors that develop during adolescence due to difficulties in managing the important developmental tasks of this period. They can include internalizing (e.g., depression, suicide, anxiety, eating disorders) or externalizing forms of psychopathology (e.g., conduct disorders, aggression).

Contexts of adolescence Include contexts which shape the impact of the primary changes of adolescence. For example, how parents and peers respond to the physical and cognitive changes of adolescence will have an effect on how these primary changes are experienced. Contexts include family, peer, school, and work settings.

Primary changes of adolescence Include changes in the biological, cognitive, and social role domains. Although the timing and nature of these changes vary across culture, they are viewed as universal and as occurring temporally prior to the other changes that typically characterize the adolescent period (e.g., changes in identity development, autonomy, etc.).

Secondary changes of adolescence Include the following psychosocial issues of adolescence: iden-

tity, achievement, sexuality, intimacy, autonomy, and attachment. Most of these issues are of concern at all periods in a person's life, but they have special significance during the adolescent developmental period. The manner in which the individual manages each of these issues is impacted upon by the primary changes and contexts of adolescence.

ADOLESCENCE is a transitional period between childhood and adulthood which is characterized by a host of biological, psychological, and social role changes. Scholars who have written about adolescence from a psychoanalytic perspective have viewed this developmental period as a time of storm and stress when extreme levels of conflict with parents result in a reorientation toward peers. Despite disconfirming empirical evidence, it appears that public policy and the public's beliefs are still in line with this perspective. The main purpose of this article is to describe an empirically based framework for understanding adolescent development. This framework is based on the notion that there are primary changes that occur during adolescence (i.e., pubertal, cognitive, and social role changes), all of which impact on a set of secondary changes (i.e., changes in identity, achievement, sexuality, intimacy, autonomy, and attachment). The primary changes have an impact on the secondary changes *via* the contexts in which adolescents develop (i.e., family, peer, school, and work settings). An additional purpose of this article is to discuss the implications that developmental psychology has for clinical interventions with adolescents.

I. A FRAMEWORK FOR UNDERSTANDING ADOLESCENT DEVELOPMENT

Scholars who have written about adolescence from a psychoanalytic perspective have viewed this developmental period as a time of storm and stress when extreme levels of conflict with parents result in a reorientation toward peers. Given that such views have been based on clinicians' observations of adolescents with adjustment difficulties, it is not surprising that recent research involving large representative samples of adolescents has not supported these early storm and stress notions. Despite such disconfirming empirical evidence, it appears that public policy and the public's beliefs are still in line with the psychoanalytic perspective. Moreover, those who write for mass media publications will often invoke concepts such as rebelliousness, parent–adolescent conflict, early onset of sexual behaviors, and identity crises to make points about the negative nature of adolescence.

The main purpose of this article is to describe an empirically based framework for understanding adolescent development. This framework is based on the notion that there are primary changes that occur during adolescence, all of which impact on a set of secondary changes. The primary changes have an impact on the secondary changes *via* the contexts in which adolescents develop, namely, family, peer, school, and work settings. This framework is presented in Figure 1. In this framework, concepts such as sexuality and identity are not afforded primary status, but instead are viewed as "secondary changes." The biological, cognitive, and social role changes of adolescence are viewed as "primary changes." Although the timing and nature of these primary changes vary across culture, they are viewed as primary because they are universal and because they occur temporally prior to the secondary changes that characterize the adolescent period. The goal of this first section is to provide a brief overview of the research findings which relate to each of the concepts included in the framework. At the end of this section, several examples which make use of the framework are provided.

It is critical to note at the outset that there are a host of factors which will impact on the connections that occur between the different components of the framework for understanding adolescent development. For example, mesosystemic factors include bidirectional effects between contexts, such as between family relationships and child functioning in the school setting. Exosystemic factors include effects on adolescent development which arise from environments where parents spend their time, such as the parents' work setting. Finally, the meaning of the primary changes, contexts, and secondary changes of adolescence will vary across different cultures (i.e., a macrosystemic factor), thus influencing the interconnections between the components of the framework.

A. Primary Changes of Adolescence

From infancy until late adolescence, children experience dramatic intraindividual changes across a number of domains, namely, biological, psychological,

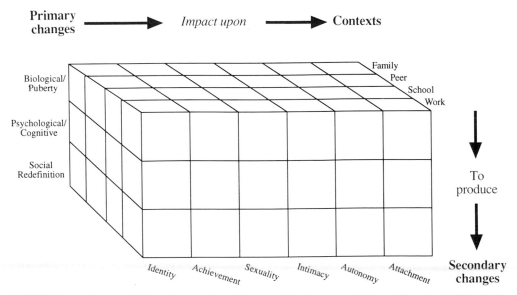

FIGURE 1 A framework for understanding adolescent development. [Adapted from J. P. Hill (1980). "Understanding Early Adolescence: A Framework." Center for Early Adolescence, Carrboro, NC.]

and social (see Fig. 1). It is important to note that changes within and across these domains are asynchronous and vary between individuals in terms of both rate and pattern.

1. Biological/Pubertal Changes

More than any other stage of life except the fetal/neonatal period, adolescence is a time of substantial physical growth and change. Changes in body proportions, voice, body hair, strength, and coordination are found in males and changes in body proportions, body hair, and menarcheal status are found in girls. Crucial to the understanding of this process is the knowledge that the peak of pubertal development occurs 2 years earlier in the modal female than in the modal male and that there are substantial variations between individuals in the time of onset, the duration, and the termination of the pubertal cycle. Thus, not only is there intraindividual variation in terms of the onset of the different pubertal changes but there is interindividual variation in the many parameters of these changes as well. Both pubertal status (an individual's placement in the sequence of predictable pubertal changes) and pubertal timing (timing of changes relative to one's age peers) should be taken into account.

Unlike the newborn, adolescents are aware of these changes and this awareness may be pleasing or horrifying; lack of information about puberty/sexuality can contribute to emotional upset. On the other hand, pubertal changes are not traumatic for the majority of adolescents. Most of the psychological effects of pubertal changes are probably not direct, but rather are mediated by the responses of the adolescent or the responses of significant others to such changes. Significant others may assume, for example, that physical changes indicate development in psychological areas. At present, however, there are no known direct links between physical and psychological development.

2. Psychological/Cognitive Changes

Jean Piaget has provided us with a comprehensive theory of cognitive development that has general applicability to infants, children, and adolescents. Piaget has enumerated a series of four stages of cognitive development, each of which is assumed to be: (1) qualitatively different than the stage before or after, (2) a structured whole in a state of equilibrium, (3) universal across cultures, and (4) part of an invariant set of stages. It is worth noting that there is some controversy regarding the usefulness

and accuracy of Piagetian theory and there exist alternative theories of adolescent thinking. One of these theories, which highlights the role of social interactions in cognitive development, is discussed below. [*See* COGNITIVE DEVELOPMENT.]

According to Piaget, the sensorimotor period (birth to 2 years of age) involves a series of substages whereby the infant develops from "a bundle of reflexes" to one who can physically manipulate his/her world with a set of organized and progressively more advanced set of behaviors. Preoperational children (2 to 7 years of age) can use mental images to represent events but are limited (in comparison to their older peers) in that they tend to be highly "egocentric." These children do not view others as having perspectives different from theirs and their speech is not tailored to the listener. The thinking of children in the concrete operational period (ages 7 to 11) is more dynamic and involves what Piaget refers to as cognitive operations. Thought is more in tune with the environment and is increasingly logical and flexible.

Though less overtly observable, the cognitive changes of adolescence are probably as dramatic as the physical changes. Piaget is credited with the identification of adolescence as the period of formal operational thinking. Adolescents who have achieved such thinking abilities are able to think more complexly, abstractly, and hypothetically. They are more able to think in terms of possibilities and they are increasingly able to think about the future. Some adolescents can think about their own thinking (meta-cognition). Interestingly, however, this latter skill is not without potential difficulties. Some have suggested that the adolescent may become obsessed with this new ability. Even if not obsessed, adolescents are not fully developed in a social cognitive sense and may misperceive others as equally interested in their own thoughts and actions but as unable to understand their emotional experiences (i.e., adolescent egocentrism). [*See* METACOGNITION.]

According to Piaget, development does not occur in a vacuum, but rather is fostered or hindered via interactions with the social world. This viewpoint has led several researchers to explore the interface between cognitive development and social relations (i.e., social cognitive development). The development of role-taking and empathy skills, the role of affect in understanding people versus things, attributional processes in social situations, and prosocial behavior are a few of the research areas that have interested developmental and social psychologists working in this area.

Although too numerous to discuss in detail, many other theories of psychological development have also been suggested. Kohlberg describes six stages of moral reasoning with two stages comprising each of the following three levels: preconventional, conventional, and principled (or postconventional). People at lower stages tend to be rule- and obedience-bound whereas people at higher stages recognize the arbitrary nature of rules and laws and that such laws can be changed if they are unjust. These postconventional individuals base their decisions on a universal set of ethical principles as well as on their own conscience. Kohlberg's notions are social cognitive in nature in that experiences with the social world shape development. Loevinger's theory of ego development is also a stage theory which involves increasing levels of maturity. Stages differ along dimensions of impulse control, maturity of interpersonal relations, and cognitive style. Research with Loevinger's Sentence Completion Test has revealed, for example, that adolescents at higher levels of ego development evidence less psychopathology. [*See* MORAL DEVELOPMENT; PERSONALITY DEVELOPMENT.]

3. Changes in Social Role

A variety of changes in the social status of children occurs during adolescence. Although such social redefinition is universal, the specific changes vary greatly across different cultures. In some nonindustrial societies, public rituals (i.e., rites of passage) take place soon after the onset of pubertal change. Norms for appropriate social behaviors are altered at this time and the adolescent is now viewed as an adult. In Western industrialized societies, the transition is less clear, but analagous changes in social status do take place. Changes can occur across four domains: interpersonal (e.g., changes in familial power status), political (e.g., late adolescents are eligible to vote), economic (e.g., adolescents are allowed to work), and legal (e.g., late adolescents can be tried in adult court systems). In addition, adolescents are able to obtain a driver's permit and can get married. Homeleaving in late adolescence also serves to redefine one's social role.

Given that the primary changes of adolescence have now been discussed, the next section concerns the contexts of adolescence.

B. Normative Contextual and Environmental Changes

Contextual changes during childhood and adolescence can occur in the following domains: family, peers, school, and work (see Fig. 1). Changes in each domain will be reviewed, in turn.

1. Changes in Family Relationships

Not only does the family play a principal role in the socialization of an adolescent, but there are developmental changes in this role as well. Recent research suggests that *both* parents and siblings appear to play significant and unique roles in this process. The role of fathers in adolescent development is beginning to receive attention as are the effects of divorce and maternal employment on adolescent adjustment. [*See* FAMILY SYSTEMS.]

Although those from the family therapy tradition have shown an interest in dimensions of parenting and family functioning, an extensive developmentally oriented literature exists that concerns parenting behaviors and their corresponding adolescent adjustment outcomes. Based on factor-analytic studies of parental warmth and control, a two-dimensional classification scheme of parenting has been developed which includes the following parenting patterns: authoritarian–autocratic, indulgent–permissive, authoritative–reciprocal, and indifferent–uninvolved.

Authoritative parents are similar to authoritarian parents in their emphasis upon explicit standards and guidelines, the difference being that the former are likely to be more affectionate and to permit more say in the construction and application of rules. Permissive parents are those that do not clearly state or explain their rules and are more likely to submit to their children's demands. Regarding socialization outcomes, authoritarian and authoritative parenting have been found to have a negative and a positive impact, respectively, on children's (and especially boys') social competence, initiative, spontaneity, moral development, motivation for intellectual performance, self-esteem, and locus of control. Permissive parents tend to have children who are more aggressive and impulsive. [*See* AUTHORITARIANISM.]

Adolescence is a time of transformation in family relations. Changes in adolescent attachment and autonomy as well as changes in the life circumstances of the parents themselves have an impact on the adolescent and the family system. Families with young adolescents are more likely to engage in conflict over mundane issues (rather than basic values) than are families with older or younger children; parents and adolescents tend to have roughly one conflict every 3 days. On the other hand, *most* adolescents negotiate this period without severing ties with parents *or* developing serious disorders. Despite the lack of serious relationship trauma during adolescence, there does appear to be a period of increased emotional distance in parent–adolescent relationships during early adolescence, particularly during the peak of pubertal change. A therapist who works with an adolescent should be aware that transformations in attachments to parents are to be expected during adolescence and that some normative familial problems may arise because of difficulties in negotiating this transition.

2. Changes in Peer Relationships

Most now agree that an adolescent's peer relationships are necessities rather than luxuries and that these relationships have a positive impact on cognitive, social–cognitive, linguistic, sex role, and moral development. Indeed, there is considerable support for the hypothesis that children and adolescents with poor peer relations are at risk for later personal and social difficulties (e.g., dropping out of school and criminality). One might argue that quality relationships with parents can take the place of peer relationships or at least buffer any negative effects of problematic relationships with other adolescents. On the other hand, research findings suggest that it is often through interactions with age-mates that an individual is able to learn skills such as cooperation and empathy. In short, peer relationships appear to provide a *unique* contribution to adolescent adjustment.

Peer relationships during childhood and adolescence appear to evolve through a series of developmental stages. Stage theories of interpersonal understanding and social perspective-taking have been proposed. Some have argued that an individual's personality is best understood by an examination of his/her interpersonal interactions. Harry Stack Sullivan, for example, describes his notion of "chumship" and maintains that this (typically) same-sex friendship is a critical developmental accomplishment. It is with this relationship that the young adolescent presumably learns about intimacy, and this friendship serves as a basis for later close relationships.

Although we have stressed, as have others, that families and peers provide unique contributions to

development and adjustment, it is also true that the family can provide a secure base for a child's exploration into the world of peers. Healthy family relations are a necessary basis for the development of healthy peer relations, especially in light of the following findings: (a) children and adolescents usually adhere to their parents' values even during increases in peer involvement, (b) parent and peer values are typically quite similar, especially with regard to important issues, and (c) differences between parent and peer values are more likely when adolescents have distant relationships with their parents *and* when they associate with peers who endorse and exhibit antisocial behaviors. Thus, we must be careful not to treat the world of peers and the world of the family as separate. Each affects the other, with both contributing uniquely to adolescent development and adjustment. [*See* PEER RELATIONSHIPS AND INFLUENCES IN CHILDHOOD.]

3. Effects of the School Context

Another context of adolescent development is the school environment. Scholars have argued not only that we should be interested in the school's effect on cognition and achievement, but that we should also look at the school as an important environment for the development of one's personality, values, and social relationships.

With increasing age, children are exposed to more complex school environments. Movement between schools (such as between elementary and junior high school) can be viewed as a stressor, with multiple school transitions producing more deleterious effects. Past research suggests that children (and particularly girls) who switch from an elementary school into a junior high school (as opposed to staying in a K–8 school) will show significant self-esteem decrements and that recovery in self-esteem is not likely for a sizeable number of these girls. Boys and girls who make such a transition also evidence decrements in grade point average and extracurricular activities. Presumably, these adjustment difficulties are due, at least in part, to movement from a protected environment (elementary school) to an impersonal environment (junior and senior high school).

The school environment also impacts on adolescent development. The physical setting of the school, limitations in resources, philosophies of education, teacher expectations, curriculum characteristics, and interactions between teacher and student have been found to be related to a host of adolescent outcomes, and these findings are maintained even after social background is held constant. For example, high school students appear to profit from non-authoritarian teaching approaches. We know that smaller schools and less authoritarian school environments promote commitment on the part of the student (i.e., fewer students drop out) and that the high rate of drop outs in some school districts indicates that the environment has not been well matched to student needs.

4. Effects of Working

The last context that will be considered is the work environment. Although more than 80% of all high school students in this country work before they graduate, little research has been done on how work impacts on adolescent development or the adolescents' relationships with significant others.

The research that has been done suggests that the work environment has important positive *and* negative effects on adolescent development. Although adolescents who work tend to develop an increased sense of self-reliance, they also tend to (a) develop cynical attitudes about work, (b) spend less time with their families and peers, (c) be less involved in school, (d) be more likely to abuse drugs or commit delinquent acts, and (e) have less time for self-exploration and identity development. The primary problem seems to be the monotonous *and* stressful nature of adolescent jobs.

C. Secondary Changes of Adolescence

As discussed earlier, there are a number of psychosocial issues that are impacted upon by the primary changes of adolescence as well as the nature of the adolescent's contextual environment. The secondary changes that will be discussed in this section are as follows: identity, achievement, sexuality, intimacy, autonomy, and attachment (see Fig. 1).

1. Identity

A major psychological task of adolescence is the development of an identity. Adolescents develop an identity through periods of role exploration and role commitment. One's identity is multidimensional and includes self-perceptions and commitments across a number of domains, including occupational, religious, sexual, and political commitments. Development occurs at different rates across each domain. Although the notion that all adolescents experience identity crises appears to be a myth, identity development is recognized as an important adolescent issue.

Research in the area of identity development has isolated at least four identity statuses which are defined with respect to two dimensions: commitment and exploration. These identity statuses are as follows: identity moratorium (exploration with no commitment), identity foreclosure (commitment with no exploration), identity diffusion (no commitment and no systematic exploration), and identity achievement (commitment after extensive exploration). A given adolescent's status can change over time, reflecting increased maturation and development or, alternatively, regression to some less adaptive identity status.

When an adolescent systematically explores various roles prior to making a serious commitment to any one role, the adolescent is in a state of identity moratorium. This can often involve a painful and deliberate decision to take time off from current stressors to create breathing space for exploration. This person is not drifting aimlessly—instead, the adolescent searches systematically as a preparation for commitment. The adolescent who is identity foreclosed has not made an autonomous choice. A commitment to a role has taken place, but the adolescent has made the commitment with little or no exploration. Such individuals typically adopt an identity that has been prescribed by important people in their life (i.e., parents, friends). It could be said that such people miss out on their full range of potential. The adolescent who is identity diffused has an incomplete sense of self, with no commitments to an identity. Such a person lacks beliefs and principles and tends to "live for the moment." Roles are tried on quickly but are abandoned just as quickly. Finally, the identity achieved individual has made a firm commitment after a period of exploration.

Regarding gender and cultural differences, it appears that the process of identity formation differs for males and females. Identity development in males appears to involve struggles with autonomy and themes of separation whereas identity development in females is more likely to be intertwined with the development and maintenance of intimate relationships. Researchers have also explored the possibility that identity development may proceed in different ways for different socioeconomic and ethnic groups. Adolescents low in socioeconomic status, for example, are usually unable to explore options (given their financial constraints), thus making them less likely to experience a period of identity moratorium.

2. Achievement

Decisions made during one's adolescence can have serious consequences for one's future education and career. Some adolescents decide to drop out of school whereas others complete their education and graduate from high school. Some decide to continue on to college or graduate school. For those who remain in school, it is during high school that most adolescents are, for the first time, given the opportunity to decide which classes they want to take. Such decisions present the adolescent with new opportunities but also limit the range of possible employment and educational options available to the adolescent. After graduation from high school, adolescents typically decide whether they want to pursue more education or whether they wish to seek full-time employment—a decision which is certainly affected by one's socioeconomic status. Finally, adolescence is a time of preparation for adult work roles, a time when vocational training begins. Given the complexity of achievement decisions, adolescents benefit from the cognitive changes that characterize this developmental period. Those who have developed these abilities are at an advantage when they begin to make education- and career-related decisions.

It has been suggested that adolescents will exert more or less effort in school depending on their level of achievement motivation (which is considered to be a relatively stable personality trait) and their fear of failure (which produces anxiety in achievement-related situations). These two drives come into conflict (i.e., an approach–avoidance conflict) with the former making it more likely that the adolescent will engage in achievement-related behaviors and the latter making it less likely that the adolescent will engage in such behaviors. Others have stressed the importance of one's attributions concerning successes and failures in predicting whether an adolescent will exhibit achievement-related behaviors. Past research suggests that some adolescents attribute their successes and failures to internal factors (e.g., one's innate intelligence), whereas other adolescents tend to attribute their successes and failures to external factors (e.g., the difficulty or fairness of a test).

In terms of gender differences, boys are more likely than girls to enroll in higher level math and science classes—despite similar ability levels in these areas. Scholars studying such differences have argued that parents are differentially supportive of boys and girls in these academic areas, with most parents being more supportive of boys' efforts. Moreover, it appears that girls are socialized to expect that they will not do well in mathematics classes. In general, girls are more likely than are boys to make internal attributions in failure situations.

3. Sexuality

Most children have mixed reactions to becoming a sexually mature adolescent. Parents also have conflicting reactions to such increasing maturity. Despite the importance of this topic, we know very little about normal adolescent sexuality, primarily due to the difficulty in conducting studies on this topic.

There are a host of factors which are associated with the onset and maintenance of sexual behaviors. Pubertal changes of adolescence have both direct and indirect effects on sexual behaviors. Direct activational effects of hormones exert an influence on sexual interest and behaviors (particularly for boys). Regarding indirect effects, visible secondary sex characteristics are social stimuli that signal the physical maturity of the adolescent to potential dating partners. Ethnic and religious differences in the onset of sexuality also exist. Finally, personality characteristics (e.g., the development of a sexual identity) and social factors (e.g., parent and peer influences) also serve as antecedents to adolescent sexual behaviors. [See SEXUAL BEHAVIOR.]

Unfortunately, sex education programs in this country have not been entirely successful at impacting on adolescent contraceptive knowledge or behaviors. Many of these programs are too brief to have any lasting impact on students. Partnerships between schools and family planning clinics, increased access to contraceptive services at appropriate ages, a reduction in the media's mixed messages regarding teenage sexuality, and a more secure legislative position regarding consent for contraception would all be helpful in reducing the fertility rate, delaying the onset of sexual activity, and preventing high-risk sexual behaviors. Sensitivity to cultural issues and the targeting of particularly at-risk groups would also be important additions to available programs. The increasing rates of sexually transmitted diseases among adolescents and the fact that many young adults with AIDS (acquired immune deficiency syndrome) probably became infected as adolescents would suggest that adolescent sexuality is deserving of considerable national attention (from researchers, school administrators, public policy advocates, and public health officials).

4. Intimacy

It is not until adolescence that one's friendships have the potential to become intimate. An intimate relationship is characterized by trust, mutual self-disclosure, a sense of loyalty, and helpfulness. Intimate sharing with friends increases during adolescence as does adolescents' intimate knowledge of their friends. All relationships become more emotionally charged during the adolescent period and adolescents are more likely to engage in friendships with opposite-sex peers than are children. Girls' same-sex relationships are described as more intimate than are boys' same-sex relationships. Having intimate friendships is adaptive; adolescents with such friendships are more likely to have high self-esteem. Some scholars have proposed that friendships change during the adolescent period because of accompanying social–cognitive changes. The capacity to exhibit empathy and take multiple perspectives in social encounters makes it more likely that friendships will become similarly more mature and complex. [*See* LOVE AND INTIMACY.]

5. Autonomy

Autonomy is a multidimensional construct in the sense that there is *not* just one type of adolescent autonomy (i.e., there are at least three types: emotional autonomy, behavioral autonomy, and value autonomy). Emotional autonomy is the capacity to relinquish childlike dependencies on parents. Adolescents increasingly come to de-idealize their parents, see them as people rather than simply as parenting figures, and be less dependent on them for immediate emotional support. Despite such increases in emotional distance between parent and child during the adolescent period, research with healthy adolescents suggests that autonomy from mothers and fathers does not develop at the expense of their relationships with their parents.

When adolescents are behaviorally autonomous, they have the capacity to make their own decisions, to be less influenced by others, and to be more self-governing and self-reliant. Being autonomous in this way does not mean that adolescents never rely on the help of others. Instead, they are able to recognize those situations where they have the ability to make their own decisions versus those situations where they will probably need to consult with a peer or parent for advice. Susceptibility to peer pressure increases to a peak in early adolescence, due in part to an increase in peer pressure prior to early

adolescence and an accompanying decrease in susceptibility to parental pressure.

Finally, the development of value autonomy also occurs during the adolescent period. Adolescents' views of moral, religious, and political issues become more complex and abstract. Adolescents are also increasingly likely to have values of their own rather than simply internalizing their parents' or peers' values. As noted earlier, however, value sharing is common between parents and adolescents, with adolescents tending to select as friends peers that have the same values as their parents.

6. Attachment

The last secondary change that will be considered is attachment. As suggested earlier, past research suggests that one task of adolescence is to gain increasing levels of behavioral autonomy without sacrificing the attachment that one has to his/her primary caregivers (an attachment that developed between infant and parent many years earlier). Interestingly, parental disapproval is anticipated to be more upsetting than peer disapproval by most adolescents. Discontinuities in the parent–child relationship during the transition to adolescence tend to occur against a backdrop of relational continuity (with respect to level of connectedness, warmth, and cohesiveness between parents and adolescents). Over the course of adolescence, the attachment relationship between parent and adolescent tends to be transformed from one of unilateral authority to one of mutuality and cooperation.

D. Use of the Framework for Understanding Adolescent Development

Having reviewed the different components of the Framework for Understanding Adolescent Development, a few examples of how this framework can be used to understand the behavior of adolescents are provided. Recall, that the primary changes of adolescents impact on the contexts of adolescence which, in turn, influence the secondary changes of adolescence.

Example 1 Suppose that a young preadolescent girl begins to physically mature much earlier than her age-mates. Such early maturity will impact on her peer relationships. For example, early maturing girls are more likely to date and intiate sexual behaviors at an earlier age than are girls who mature on time. Such impacts on male peers will influence her own self-perceptions in the areas of identity and sexuality.

Example 2 Suppose that a young adolescent boy has recently begun to develop cognitively and is now able to take multiple perspectives in social interactions, think hypothetically, and conceive of numerous possibilities for his own behaviors. Such increased cognitive skills will impact on his familial relationships insofar as he is now able to imagine how his relationships with his parents could be different. He begins to challenge the reasoning of his parents and requests more decision-making power in his family. The accompanying changes in his relationships with his parents will also impact on his level of behavioral autonomy, the nature of his attachments to his parents, and his identity.

Example 3 A 16-year-old girl has just obtained a driver's license and has decided that she will look for her first job to earn some spending money. Because she is now 16 years old, she has recently gained a number of privileges that she did not have before (i.e., her social role has changed). She takes a job in a fast food restaurant several miles from home and, because she now has a driver's license, she can get to work on her own. Her experiences at her job produce increases in feelings of autonomy and achievement as she begins to develop an occupational identity.

As can be seen by these examples, this framework is very useful in describing and understanding the behaviors of individual adolescents as well as promoting a more general understanding of adolescent development. Now that several examples of the framework have been provided, the discussion now turns to the next section of this article, which concerns the implications of developmental psychology for clinical interventions with adolescents.

II. IMPLICATIONS OF ADOLESCENT DEVELOPMENT FOR CLINICAL INTERVENTIONS WITH ADOLESCENTS

After providing a rationale for examining the interface between developmental psychology and treatment, two types of knowledge that appear to have implications for the treatment of adolescents and for treatment-based research are examined: (a) knowledge of developmental norms, level, and transitions,

and (b) knowledge of developmental psychopathology.

A. Rationale

Clinical child psychologists often mistakenly endorse what has been termed the *developmental uniformity myth*—the assumption that children and adolescents of different ages and developmental level are more alike than they are different and that all can be handled similarly in the treatment setting. Many scholars writing in this area have maintained that most existing treatments for adolescents are not sensitive to the developmental level of the client. Given that many are concerned with the lack of interface between developmental psychology and treatment, it is surprising that so few developmentally gauged treatments have been designed. Although developmental psychology and psychopathology have been brought together in the new field of *developmental psychopathology,* there is room for greater consideration of treatment issues.

B. Using Knowledge of Developmental Norms, Level, and Transitions

In the first portion of this article, a variety of normative intraindividual and contextual changes that occur during adolescence were discussed. Given the primacy of change during the second decade of life, it appears that researchers and therapists who are knowledgeable about normal and maladaptive development are at a great advantage when attempting to design a treatment, determine the conditions under which a treatment is efficacious, and/or apply a given treatment. In short, the quality of adolescent treatment is likely to "move up a notch or two" when knowledge of developmental psychology is taken into account.

Although the existing clinical literature has not been attentive to normal development, this does not mean that efforts which do take developmental factors into account do not exist. In this section, research efforts and discussions of clinical practice that have attempted to take developmental norms, level, and transitions into account in the design, assessment, or implementation of treatment approaches are discussed.

1. Developmental Norms and Treatment

Knowledge of developmental norms serves as a basis for making sound diagnostic judgments, assessing the need for treatment, and selecting the appropriate treatment. In terms of diagnosis, both overdiagnosis and underdiagnosis can result from a lack of knowledge of developmental norms. A clinician who lacks the knowledge that a behavior is typical of the adolescent age period (e.g., interest in sexuality) is much more likely to overdiagnosis and to inappropriately refer such an adolescent for treatment. With regards to underdiagnosis, it is a common belief (as discussed earlier) that adolescents have stormy and stressful relations with their parents and that "detachment" from parents is the norm. On the other hand, research has not supported this notion—it appears that approximately 20% (rather than 100%) of adolescents have such relationships with their parents. It is interesting to speculate about the clinical implications of such erroneous "storm and stress" beliefs. Some have warned that adolescents who are experiencing severe identity crises or extreme levels of conflict with their parents are not experiencing normative adolescent "growing pains." A clinician who overlooks this possibility will underdiagnose the psychopathology owing to storm and stress beliefs.

Some changes during adolescence are normal and these have implications for the selection of treatments. Given the adolescent's normal developmental trend toward greater autonomous functioning, certain treatments are more appropriate for this age group. Self-control strategies are probably more useful with older adolescents than are behavioral programs where parents are employed as behavior change agents. Also, different cognitive problem-solving strategies are relevant at different ages.

2. Cognitive Developmental Level and Treatment

The importance of cognitive development as a moderator of treatment effectiveness has been stressed by many but has rarely received empirical attention. Given that most efforts thus far have been in the form of theoretical discourse, rather than empirical study, it appears that this is a new research area that shows great promise for the future. Some have argued that treatment effectiveness will be moderated by the developmental level of the adolescent. For example, children at different cognitive developmental levels will have different understandings of traumas such as sexual abuse and divorce.

Although the developmental differences in adolescents' understandings of major life events have been discussed in this literature, we need more informa-

tion concerning the actual type of intervention strategy to employ. What is needed are developmentally gauged, step-by-step strategies that could be employed after assessing a child's cognitive developmental level. It would be helpful if clinicians could develop alternate forms of their treatments that could be appropriately applied to those of varying developmental level.

In the area of adolescent pregnancy, for example, few intervention programs have considered the cognitive developmental level of the adolescent. Given the availability of contraception and sex education classes, many are puzzled by the "irrationality" of adolescent contraception nonuse. The reasoning behind the link between adolescent cognitive development and contraceptive use involves the notion that adolescents who are less cognitively mature may not appreciate the seriousness of contraceptive nonuse, anticipate the difficulties that will be encountered in the future if pregnancy results, or properly evaluate the probability of pregnancy. The less cognitively mature male may also not "take the role" of his partner and, as a consequence, may not take seriously the risk of pregnancy or the consequences for the female if she should become pregnant. It is important to note that, as yet, there is little empirical evidence for connections between level of adolescent cognitive development and sexual decision-making.

3. Developmental Transitions and Treatment: The Importance of Prevention Efforts

Past research suggests that an adolescent who must confront multiple life changes and transitions simultaneously (e.g., school change, pubertal change, early dating, geographical mobility, and major family disruption) is at risk for adjustment difficulties. For example, an adolescent who has just moved to a new school may be unable to seek emotional support at home if his/her parents are also going through a divorce (two life changes which are frequently linked).

What implications do these findings have for treatment? This line of research suggests that prevention efforts are needed for adolescents who are about to experience multiple transitions. The focus of such prevention should be on the development of appropriate adolescent coping strategies. Here the focus would be on coping *with future events* rather than focusing on coping with *current* stressors. Indeed, how often are sixth graders prepared (in any way) for their upcoming move to junior high school? More to the point, could we not easily target children who are about to experience multiple life changes? Finally, are different coping strategies going to be helpful with children and adolescents at different developmental levels? Prevention could be applied in conjunction with changes in developmental level as well. The obvious application of this notion is to sex education. If they are cognitively ready, should we not educate preadolescents about sexuality and contraception *before* they are reproductively mature?

In sum, although there has been much more discussion of the interrelatedness of developmental level and child psychotherapy than actual research, it appears plausible that our treatment strategies could be improved by incorporating findings from developmental research into our clinical work.

C. Using Knowledge of Developmental Psychopathology

Developmental psychopathology is a field concerned with the continuity and discontinuity of certain psychological maladies (i.e., the developmental transformations in the types and nature of psychopathology—all of which have important implications for treatment). The nature and frequency of most disorders appear to vary across age level. For example, the findings of current research suggest that the nature of attention-deficit hyperactivity disorder (ADHD) varies with age, with the various components of the disorder (i.e., impulsivity, inattention, and hyperactivity) being exhibited in varying degrees at different ages. That is, inattention and impulsivity appear to continue into adolescence and adulthood, whereas gross motor disturbance is most likely to peak in early to middle childhood. Regarding depression, adolescent girls tend to exhibit symptoms of withdrawal, whereas younger depressed girls are less likely to exhibit this symptom. Age differences have also been noted for other disorders falling within both the externalizing and internalizing categories (e.g., conduct disorders and anxiety, respectively). [*See* ATTENTION-DEFICIT HYPERACTIVITY DISORDER.]

Just as there is discontinuity across age in the manifestation of certain disorders, there is considerable continuity as well. Most depressed adults, adolescents, *and* children evidence distortions in their perceptions of their own abilities and they tend to make attributions for negative events that are both internal and global. Thus, at least for depression, it may be that there is cognitive continuity. [*See* DEPRESSION.]

Roughly half of all adolescent disorders are continuations of those seen in childhood. Those that are new during adolescence (e.g., anorexia) tend to be quite different than those that began during childhood. There are increases in the rates of the following disturbances during adolescence, relative to rates during childhood: depression, bipolar affective disorders, attempted suicide, completed suicide, and schizophrenia. There are increases in the frequency of antisocial activities but not in the number of individuals involved. Animal phobias become less common during adolescence and agoraphobia and social phobias become more common. The incidence of enuresis and encopresis is also less during adolescence. It is critical to note, however, that most adolescents do *not* develop mental disorders and that the actual percentage of adolescents who do show symptoms (most estimates are between 10 and 20%) is only slightly higher (perhaps less than 5% higher) than the rates for children or adults. Antisocial behavior tends toward continuity insofar as antisocial adults have almost always been antisocial children. Depressed adults tend not to have been depressed children—with the onset of depression being less common in childhood. Finally, schizophrenia disorders are often not preceded by psychotic disorders during childhood. [*See* AGORAPHOBIA; ANTISOCIAL PERSONALITY DISORDER; SCHIZOPHRENIA; SUICIDE.]

In short, there is not a simple continuous relationship between childhood and adolescent disorders. Clinicians would want to have this knowledge of developmental psychopathology to enable them to develop hypotheses about the course of a given child's disturbance. Is it likely that the disturbance will change or abate or stay the same over time? Is the disturbance typical of the problems that are usually seen for a child of that age? Without answers to these questions, the therapist may be prone to apply inappropriate treatments or to be overly concerned about the presence of certain symptoms.

III. CONCLUDING COMMENTS

In this article, a framework for understanding adolescent development was discussed and examples of interconnections between the different parts of the framework were provided. Implications of developmental psychology for the treatment of adolescents were also discussed. The importance of knowledge in the following areas, for both researcher and therapist alike, was stressed: knowledge of developmental norms, level, and transitions, and knowledge of developmental psychopathology. Unfortunately, it appears that there is still an appreciable lack of interface between developmental psychology and clinical treatment—and this applies to those who do research as well as to those who do clinical work with adolescents. Therefore, we must teach clinicians (and parents and teachers) to "think developmentally" so that the integration of these two areas may proceed.

Bibliography

Feldman, S. S., and Elliott, G. R. (Eds.) (1990). "At the Threshold: The Developing Adolescent." Harvard University Press, Cambridge, MA.

Hende, W. R. (Ed.) (1991). "The Health of Adolescents." Jossey-Bass, San Francisco, CA.

Hill, J. P. (1980). "Understanding Early Adolescence: A Framework." Center for Early Adolescence, Carrboro, NC.

Lerner, R. M., Petersen, A. C., and Brooks-Gunn, J. (Eds.) (1991). "Encyclopedia of Adolescence." Garland, New York.

Steinberg, L. (1989). "Adolescence," 2nd ed. McGraw-Hill, New York.

Van Hasselt, V. B., and Hersen, M. (Eds.) (1987). "Handbook of Adolescent Psychology." Pergamon, New York.

◆

ADRENAL GLANDS

Lawrence N. Parker

University of California at Irvine

Glossary

Androgens Steroid hormones which cause the development of a male phenotype during embryonic life, and male secondary sex characteristics during and after puberty.

Catecholamines Hormones such as epinephrine (adrenaline), secreted by the adrenal medulla, and norepinephrine (noradrenaline), secreted by sympathetic nerve fibers, as well as the adrenal medulla, which have cardiovascular and metabolic actions.

Glucocorticoids Steroid hormones which have multiple actions, including stimulation of glucose production (gluconeogenesis) and glycogen synthesis by the liver; and metabolism of triglycerides to free fatty acids and glycerol (lipolysis) in adipose tissue.

Mineralocorticoids Steroid hormones which regulate mineral metabolism, such as that of sodium and potassium.

Sympathetic nervous system Part of the autonomic nervous system, which mediates reactions to stressful stimuli and includes the adrenal medulla.

ADRENAL GLANDS play an integral part in the human response to stress, by way of secretion of steroids, such as cortisol, and catecholamines, such as epinephrine. In addition, other adrenal steroids of the androgen class affect female reproduction and, possibly, sexual behavior. The structure and function of the adrenal glands are covered here, with a discussion of the involvement of the adrenal glands in behavior relating to stress and reproduction.

The human adrenal glands are paired structures located at the superior pole of each kidney. They are compound glands, composed of an outer cortex and an inner medulla. The cortex secretes three classes of steroid hormones: glucocorticoids, androgens, and mineralocorticoids. In humans, examples of these hormones are cortisol (glucocorticoid), dehydroepiandrosterone (DHA; androgen), and aldosterone (mineralocorticoid). [*See* HORMONES AND BEHAVIOR.]

The medulla secretes nonsteroidal hormones with a catechol nucleus, such as epinephrine and norepinephrine (catecholamines), which are primarily involved in the biological alarm mechanism of the sympathoadrenal system. The embryological development of the cortex and medulla is different, as are their control mechanisms and functions, and in some nonhuman vertebrates, including fish, they are located separately. [*See* CATECHOLAMINES AND BEHAVIOR.]

I. STRUCTURE OF THE ADRENAL GLANDS, AND HORMONES SECRETED

A. Adrenal Cortex

The location and surrounding structures of the human adrenal glands are shown in Figure 1. The weight range of each adrenal gland is approximately 3.5 to 5 g, and the cortex comprises approximately 90% of the gland volume. Chronically increased ACTH secretion causes adrenal weight to increase. Occasionally, accessory adrenal tissue is found in the connective tissue near the main glands. Embryologically, the adrenal cortex is derived from the mesoderm. A unique fetal zone, which secretes DHA sulfate (DHAS), involutes shortly after birth, leaving the structure described above.

By light microscopy, three zones can be identified in the cortex, as shown in Figure 2. The outer zone,

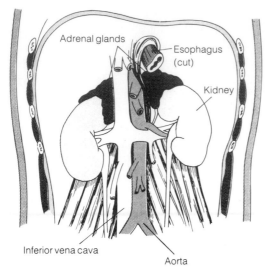

FIGURE 1   Location and surrounding structures of the human adrenal glands. [Reproduced with permission from Gaudin, A., and Jones, K. (1989). "Human Anatomy and Physiology," p. 423. Harcourt Brace Jovanovich, San Diego.]

the zona glomerulosa, is relatively thin, and contains cells which secrete aldosterone. The middle zone, the zona fasiculata, is usually the thickest layer of the adrenal cortex, and has a columnar structure. Its cells are relatively clear, since they are large and have a high lipid content. The inner zone, the zona reticularis, surrounds the medulla. Its cells are relatively dark staining and compact in appearance, and often contain lipofuscin pigment granules. Both the zona fasiculata and the zona reticularis produce cortisol and androgens, but in the human, the zona reticularis has sulfotransferase activity, and is the probable source of DHAS. Chronically increased ACTH concentrations result in lipid depletion from the zona fasiculata, and an increase in the width of the zona reticularis.

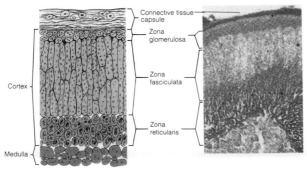

FIGURE 2   Histology of the human adrenal gland. [Reproduced with permission from Gaudin, A., and Jones, K. (1989). "Human Anatomy and Physiology," p. 423. Harcourt Brace Jovanovich, San Diego.]

B. Adrenal Medulla

The adrenal medulla is part of the sympathetic nervous system, which arises from cells of the neural crest. Storage granules which stain brown with chromic acid, due to oxidation of catecholamines to melanin, give the cells which contain them the name chromaffin or pheochrome cells. These cells are also found on both sides of the aorta, and comprise the paraganglia. The largest collection of these cells is found near the inferior mesenteric artery, where they fuse to form a fetal structure termed the Organ of Zuckerkandl, which undergoes involution within the first year of life.

The remainder of the chromaffin cells in the paraganglia and adrenal medulla persist during adult life, and secrete epinephrine (adrenaline), norepinephrine (noradrenaline), and dopamine. In the adrenal medulla, the cells are arranged in an irregular network with a rich blood supply, and are in contact with sympathetic ganglia. The cells of the adrenal medulla are innervated by preganglionic fibers of the sympathetic nervous system. Most of the blood supply of the adrenal glands enters through the cortex and drains into the medulla, except for some vessels which supply the medulla directly.

II. PHYSIOLOGICAL EFFECTS OF ADRENAL GLAND HORMONES

A. Adrenal Cortex

Cortisol exerts major effects on glucose metabolism in several different ways. Cortisol combines with cytosolic glucocorticoid receptor proteins, and after interaction with nuclear acceptor sites, increases hepatic gluconeogenesis markedly, partly by stimulation of transcription and translation to synthesize enzymes which convert amino acids to glucose, and also by increasing amino acid mobilization from muscle and other tissues. Cortisol also causes an increase in glycogen synthesis by the liver, and decreases the rate of peripheral glucose utilization.

With respect to protein and fat metabolism, cortisol stimulates catabolism of nonhepatic proteins, and increases the rate of amino acid uptake into liver. In adipose tissue, cortisol stimulates lipolysis and subsequent release of glycerol and free fatty acids, while enhancing the rate of fatty acid oxidation.

Cortisol is a major stress hormone, and is secreted in so many different forms of stress that an increase in cortisol secretion is often considered the result of what may be defined as a stressful stimulus. It has been speculated that cortisol functions to aid survival in stress by improving the metabolic milieu by means of the energy-producing and biosynthetic pathways noted above. The inflammatory process is common in stress due to illness or injury. Cortisol may also help to minimize damage to the body due to excessive inflammation by stimulating mechanisms such as lysosomal membrane stabilization, which prevents release of proteolytic enzymes, and reduction in capillary permeability to avoid leakage of plasma and blood cells into an inflamed area. Cortisol also has numerous other effects, such as maintenance of normal cardiac output and renal blood flow, and modification of immunological responses. [*See* STRESS.]

DHAS and other adrenal androgens circulate in young adults at concentrations much higher than those of cortisol. However, their functions have not been as clearly elucidated as have those of cortisol. Evidence has been presented that these steroids have a nonglucocorticoid receptor, and that they may prevent osteoporosis, facilitate the birth process by causing cervical softening, modify immune responses, mediate female libido, and serve as precursors for more potent sex steroids. In animal studies, these steroids have been shown to protect against obesity, diabetes, and certain types of infections and tumors. DHAS is present in the human brain, and has been shown to be synthesized in rat brain, but its function in the nervous sytem of either species is not known.

Aldosterone and other mineralocorticoids maintain normal sodium and potassium concentrations and intravascular volume. Aldosterone combines with an intracellular cytosol mineralocorticoid receptor and exerts actions at the nuclear level of the target cell by induction of protein synthesis and subsequent activation of a sodium pump, whose effect is to transport sodium across cell membranes. In the kidney, sodium is absorbed, and hydrogen ion and potassium are secreted. Therefore, under the influence of aldosterone, sodium is conserved, and potassium and hydrogen ion are excreted into the urine. Aldosterone has similar effects in sweat glands, salivary glands, and the intestinal lumen.

B. Adrenal Medulla

Catecholamines exert their actions through two types of receptors, alpha and beta. Norepinephrine stimulates alpha receptors. This results in a variety of actions, such as vasoconstriction, blood pressure elevation, iris dilatation, and bladder sphincter contraction. Epinephrine also stimulates alpha receptors. However, in addition, it stimulates beta receptors, which results in actions such as vasodilatation, acceleration of the heart rate, bronchodilatation, glycogenolysis, and lipolysis. These actions are part of the physiological response to stressful stimuli, and complement those of cortisol, secreted by the cortex.

III. REGULATION OF SECRETION OF ADRENAL GLAND HORMONES

A. Adrenal Cortex

Cortisol is produced by the adrenal cortex in response to adrenocorticotropin (ACTH) secreted by the human pituitary gland. ACTH secretion occurs in response to decreased circulating concentrations of cortisol, as part of a negative feedback system, and in response to stressors of many types, including surgery, hemorrhage, thermal injury, and hypoglycemia. In addition, there is a circadian rhythm of pulsatile ACTH and cortisol secretion which results in increased secretion toward the end of the sleep period, and therefore higher levels of circulating cortisol in the morning than at night.

ACTH is a 39 amino acid peptide derived from the larger molecule pro-opiomelanocortin (POMC), whose secretion is under the control of neurotransmitters and hypothalamic corticotropin-releasing hormone (CRH), as shown in Figure 3. CRH is a 41 amino acid peptide which is secreted into the hypophysial portal system. The relationship of ACTH to POMC is shown in Figure 4. While there is considerable interspecies variability of POMC structure in many parts of the molecule, the first (N-terminal) 24 amino acids of ACTH are highly conserved among species, and are biologically active. There is evidence from animal experiments that non-ACTH POMC peptides may synergize with ACTH in control of glucocorticoid secretion.

ACTH binds to specific adrenal cell membrane receptors, activates adenyl cyclase, and thereby causes an increase in intracellular concentration of cyclic 3',5'-monophosphate (cAMP). This in turn causes an increase in cellular protein kinase activity, and an increase in activity of cholesterol ester hydrolase, which produces free cholesterol for the rate-limiting conversion of cholesterol to pregnenolone. This is mediated by the mitochondrial side-chain cleavage enzyme. Plasma lipoproteins also provide cholesterol for steroidogenesis.

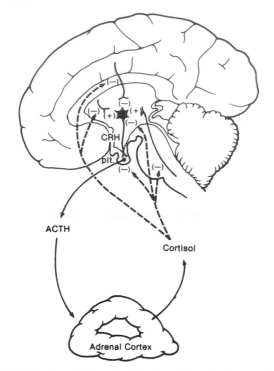

FIGURE 3 Simplified cortisol feedback loop in the hypothalamic–pituitary–adrenocortical system. CRH, corticotropin-releasing hormone. Cortisol feedback shown by dotted lines. [Re-
produced with permission from Darlington, D., and Dallman, M.
(1990). Feedback control in endocrine systems. In "Principles
and Practice of Endocrinology and Metabolism," p. 40. L. B.
Lippincott, Philadelphia.]

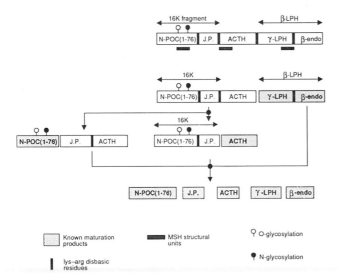

FIGURE 4 Structure and processing of pro-opiomelanocortin
(POMC; POC). LPH, lipotropin; endo, endorphin; JP, joining
peptide. [Reproduced with permission from Seidah, N., Rochem-
ont, J., Hamelin, J., Benjannet, S., and Chretien, M. (1981).
Biochem. Biophys. Res. Commun. **102,** 710.]

As shown in Figure 5, pregnenolone can be converted to mineralocorticoids, glucocorticoids, or androgens. Many of the microsomal enzymatic steps
are controlled by ACTH by means of regulation of
the rate of steroidogenic enzyme synthesis. In contrast to the situation in the human, in rodents there
is little activity of the enzyme 17-hydroxylase (Fig.
5), and therefore the main glucocorticoid is cortico-
sterone.

Adrenal androgens are also secreted in response
to acute ACTH stimulation, but their control is more
complex since in some situations they are not secreted in conjunction with cortisol. These situations
include adrenarche, puberty, aging, polycystic ovarian syndrome, stress, and starvation. Adrenarche
is the process of adrenal gland maturation, which
occurs before puberty at approximately age 7, and
which involves increased secretion of DHA and
DHAS with constant secretion of cortisol. During
aging, while the circadian rhythm of cortisol secretion remains unchanged, that of DHA is absent or
minimal, and while basal levels of cortisol are unchanged, as shown in Figure 6, basal concentrations
of DHAS undergo marked variation, with a peak in
the third decade of life. Evidence indicates that at
least part of the explanation for the dissociation in
cortisol and adrenal androgen concentrations may
be due to the influence of non-ACTH POMC-related
peptide secretion.

Aldosterone is produced only by the zona glomerulosa, because it is the only zone with 18-hydroxy-
lase and 18-dehydrogenase activity. The zona glomerulosa does not contain 17-hydroxylase activity,
and does not produce cortisol. ACTH causes acute
stimulation of aldosterone secretion. However,
there are other important control mechanisms in addition to ACTH. Angiotensin II is the major regulator of aldosterone secretion. Secretion of angiotensin II is controlled by renin, as shown in Figure 7.
Renin release is controlled primarily by the sodium
concentration of fluid in contact with the renal juxtaglomerular cells, and the renal blood pressure, as
sensed by renal baroceptors. Increased renin release
is caused by decreased sodium concentration or
blood pressure. Renin mediates the conversion of
hepatic renin substrate (angiotensinogen) to the 10
amino acid peptide angiotensin I, which in turn is
converted to the 8 amino acid peptide angiotensin
II by the converting enzyme in lung and other tissues. The 7 amino acid peptide angiotensin III is
also bioactive.

Angiotensins II and III bind to receptors in zona
glomerulosa cells and stimulate aldosterone secre-

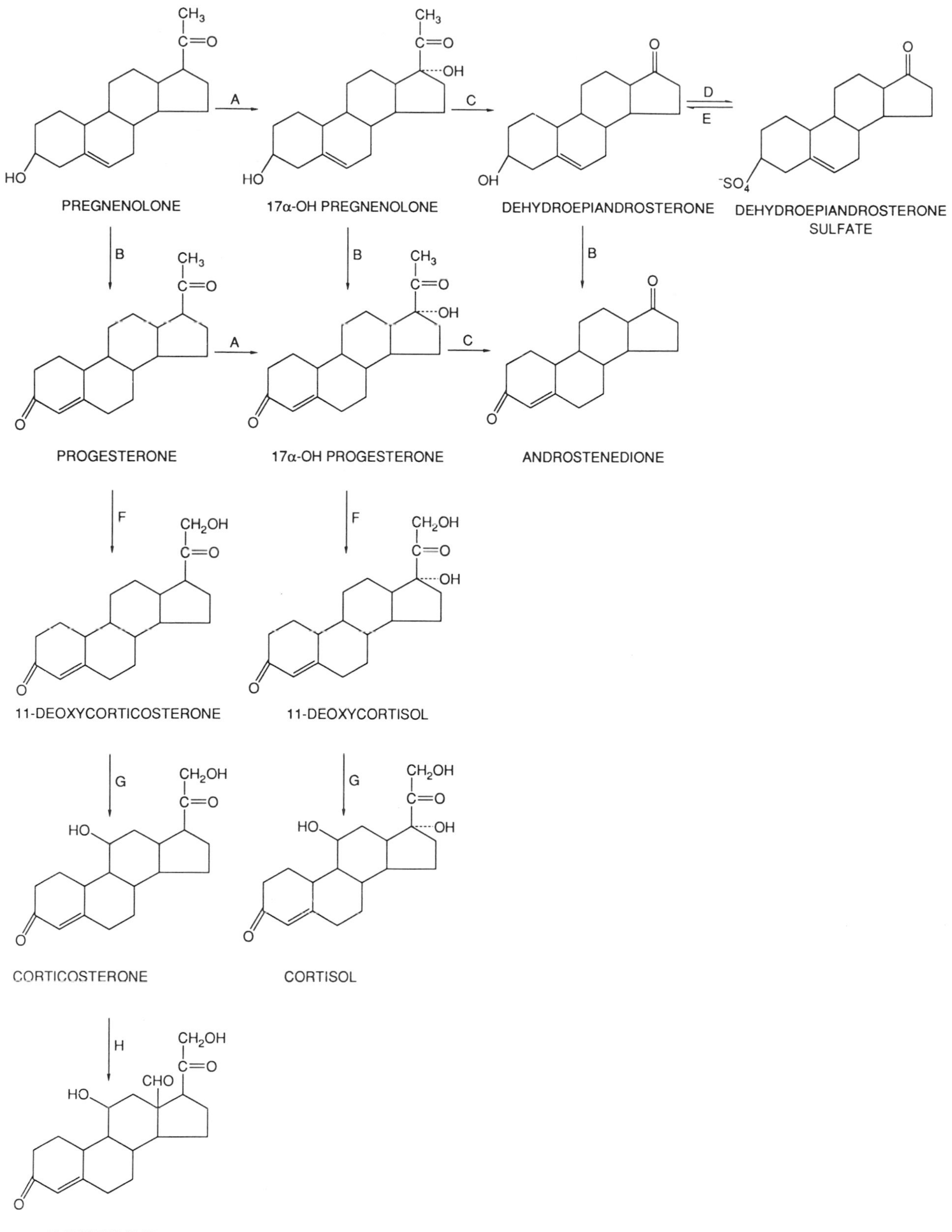

FIGURE 5 Human adrenocortical steroidogenic pathways. Enzyme activities. (A) 17-Hydroxylase; (B) 3-β-hydroxysteroid dehydrogenase-isomerase; (C) C17-20-desmolase; (D) steroid sulfotransferase; (E) steroid sulfatase; (F) 21-hydroxylase; (G) 11-hydrodylase; (H) 18-hydroxylase, 18-dehydrogenase. [Reproduced with permission from Parker, L. (1989). In "Adrenal Androgens in Clinical Medicine," p. 4. Academic Press, San Diego.]

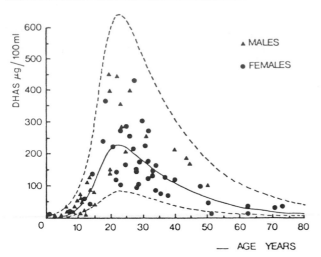

FIGURE 6   Serum concentrations of DHAS in normal subjects 1–73 years of age. [Reproduced with permission from Smith, M., *et al.* (1975). *Clin. Chim. Acta* **65**, 5.]

tion by a calcium-dependent mechanism involving activation of C kinase, independent of cAMP. The action of angiotensins may be mediated by prostaglandins, especially of the E series, and inhibitors of prostaglandin synthesis inhibit the effects of angiotensin II on aldosterone secretion.

Potassium ion also influences aldosterone secretion. An increase in serum potassium ion concentration of 1 meq/l may triple the rate of aldosterone secretion. This effect is a direct one on zona glomerulosa cells, and forms the basis for a feedback mechanism to regulate the concentration of extracellular potassium ions. Concentrations of potassium ion have the opposite effect on renin concentrations, but the direct effect on aldosterone secretion is pre-

dominant. In addition, as in the case of cortisol and adrenal androgen secretion, there is evidence that additional control of aldosterone secretion may be exerted by non-ACTH POMC-related peptides.

B. Adrenal Medulla

Control of secretion of the adrenal medulla is best understood in context of the mechanism of function of the sympathetic nervous system. Whereas preganglionic fibers of the parasympathetic branch of the autonomic nervous system emerge from cranial and sacral spinal nerves, those of the sympathetic nervous system emerge from thoracic and lumbar spinal nerves and innervate many organs, including the adrenal medulla. These fibers then terminate in ganglia of the paraspinal sympathetic trunk, nearby plexuses, or in the adrenal medulla.

Preganglionic nerve impulses are transmitted to postganglionic fibers by liberation of acetylcholine at nerve terminals. This results in secretion of catecholamines by the peripheral sympathetic nervous

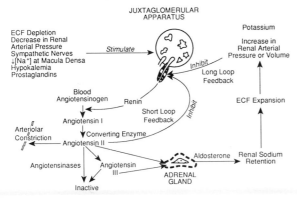

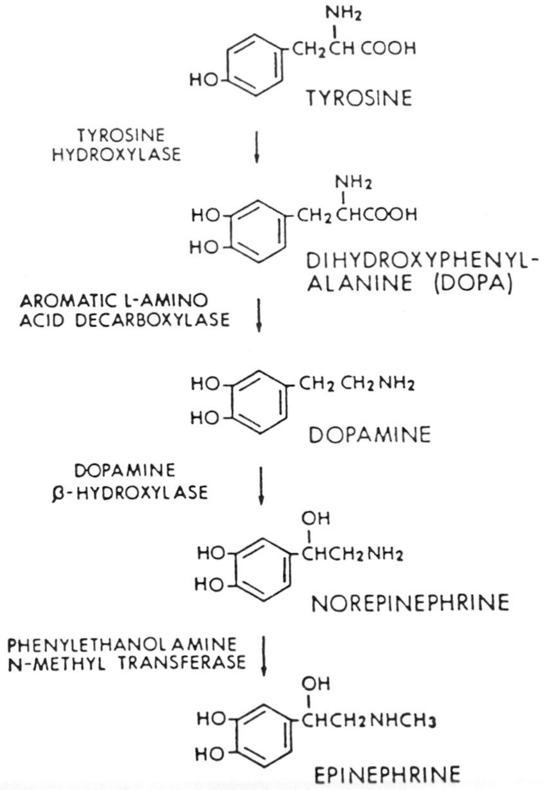

FIGURE 7   Control of aldosterone secretion by the renin–angiotensin system. ECF, extracellular fluid. [Reproduced with permission from Bondy, P., and Rosenberg, L. (1980). "Metabolic Control and Disease," 8th ed. W. B. Saunders, Philadelphia.]

FIGURE 8   Catecholamine biosynthetic pathway of the sympathetic nervous system. [Reproduced with permission from Cryer, P. (1987). In "Endocrinology and Metabolism," 2nd ed. (Felig, P., Ed.). McGraw-Hill, New York.]

system and by the adrenal medulla. Norepinephrine is the major secretory product of the peripheral nervous system. In the human adrenal medulla, the ratio of epinephrine to norepinephrine secretion is approximately 4:1.

Catecholamine biosynthetic pathways are shown in Figure 8. The rate-limiting step in catecholamine biosynthesis is the initial conversion of tyrosine to DOPA by tyrosine hydroxylase. Tyrosine itself is derived from the diet, or converted in the liver from phenylalanine by phenylalanine hydroxylase. Dopamine is also found in sympathetic neurons and the adrenal medulla. The major difference between the pathways of the adrenal medulla and the peripheral sympathetic nervous system is the presence of the enzyme phenylethanolamine-N-methyl transferase (PNMT) in the former. This enzyme is induced by high concentrations of cortisol which are present in the capillary sinusoidal circulation from the adrenal cortex to the medulla.

A large percentage of synaptically released catecholamines are inactivated by reuptake into storage granules. Metabolism of circulating catecholamines occurs via two main pathways, mediated by the enzymes catechol-O-methyl transferase (COMT) and monoamine oxidase (MAO), as shown in Figure 9. The end product of norepinephrine and epinephrine metabolism, after conversion by both enzymes is 3-methoxy-4-hydroxy-mandelic acid (vanillylmandelic acid; VMA).

The hypothalamus is the main regulator of sympathetic nervous system function. Impulses from the posterior and lateral hypothalamus result in generalized discharge of the sympathetic nervous system, including the adrenal medulla. As discussed above, this occurs in response to a variety of noxious, threatening, or stressful stimuli. In addition, the sympathetic nervous system is instrumental in maintaining an appropriate circulating volume and cardiac output during changes of posture from supine

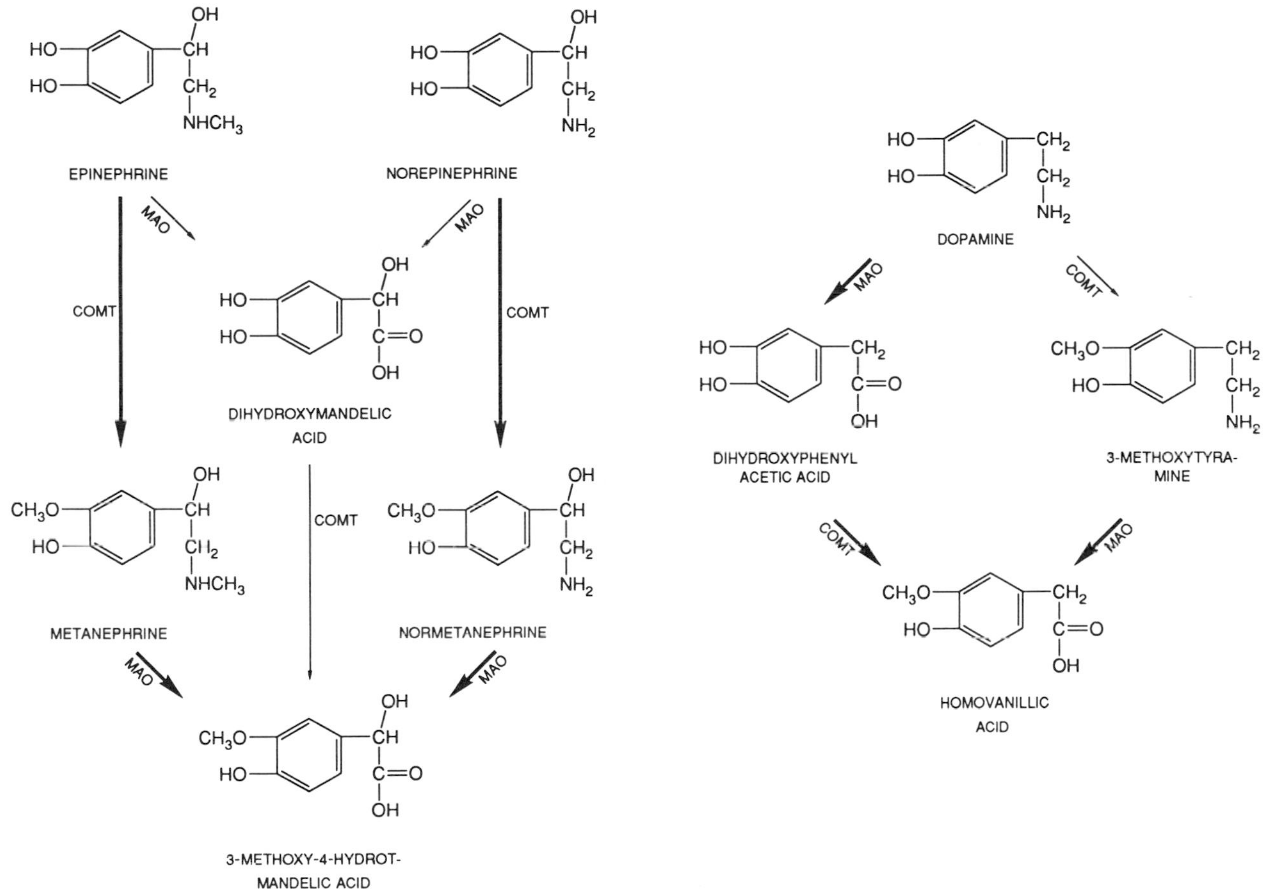

FIGURE 9 Metabolism of catecholamines by catechol-O-methyltransferase (COMT) and monoamine oxidase (MAO). [Reproduced with permission from Goldfien, A. (1986). In "Basic and Clinical Endocrinology," 2nd ed. (Greenspan, F., and Forsham, P., Eds.), p. 326. Lange, Los Altos, CA.]

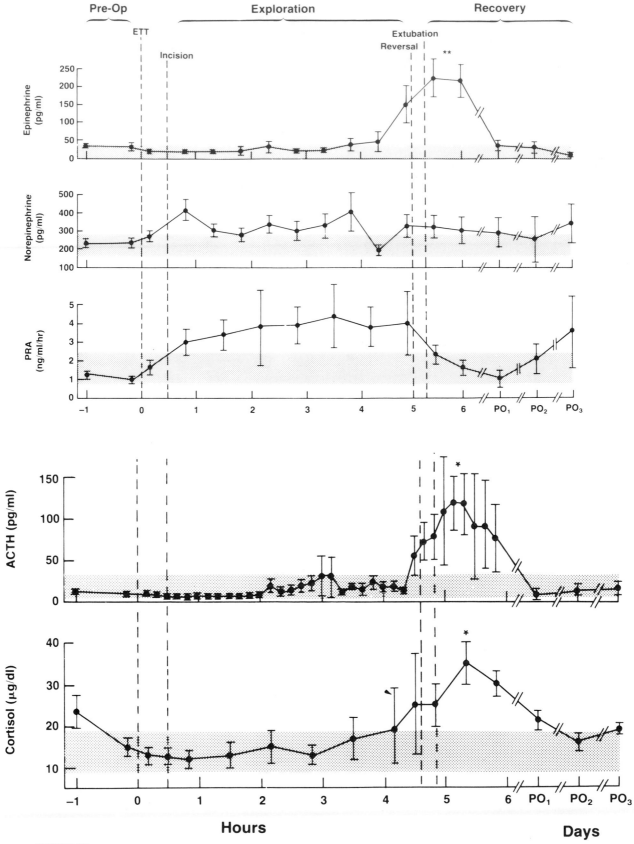

FIGURE 10   Mean plasma epinephrine, norepinephrine, PRA (plasma renin activity), ACTH, and cortisol concentrations in 11 patients before, during, and after neck exploratory surgery under general anesthesia. PO, postoperative. The shaded areas represent the normal morning ranges. [Reproduced with permission from Udelsman, R., *et al.* (1987). *J. Clin. Endocrinol. Metab.* **64,** 986. © The Endocrin Society.]

to upright. These feedback systems are mediated by sensors in the carotid sinuses, aorta, and medulla, which detect changes in circulatory volume and blood pressure. [See HYPOTHALAMUS.]

IV. THE ADRENAL GLANDS AND BEHAVIOR

As described above, the adrenal cortex and medulla, although of different embryological origins, and operating via different regulatory mechanisms, complement each other in the maintenance of homeostasis in the fact of stress. A difference between the adrenal cortex and medulla exists, however, in that generally less stress is necessary to stimulate an increase in catecholamine secretion than to stimulate an increase in cortisol secretion. Also, some situations characterized by arousal, without anxiety, may cause an increase in catecholamine, but usually not cortisol secretion. More severe stresses cause increases in both catecholamine and glucocorticoid secretion. Examples of this include prolonged exercise, sharp or blunt physical trauma, and thermal burns. For reasons which are not clear, these stressors are often accompanied by decreased gonadal and adrenal androgen secretion. An example of the adrenal medullary and cortical changes in major stress is shown in Figure 10, which demonstrates hormonal changes during the stress of the preoperative, operative, and postoperative phases of neck surgery. It is interesting that the anesthetic techniques used in this study minimized stress hormone increases often seen during surgery, and therefore demonstrate most of the increase in ACTH, cortisol, and epinephrine secretion to occur in the postoperative, rather than the operative, period.

A psychiatric stress, anorexia nervosa, has been studied with respect to adrenocortical secretion. This condition, which occurs mainly in young women, is characterized by an inappropriate fear of gaining weight, depressive symptoms, and ritualized eating habits. Reflecting the degree of stressfulness of this condition, cortisol concentrations are often increased, and those of adrenal androgens, such as DHA, are decreased, as shown in Figure 11. This hormonal secretory pattern, reminiscent of that seen in physical injury or illness, is reversible upon resolution of the anorexia nervosa. Other changes in adrenal hormone metabolism in psychiatric disorders include decreased dexamethasone suppressibility of cortisol secretion in depression, possibly re-

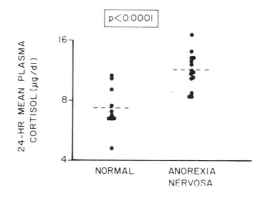

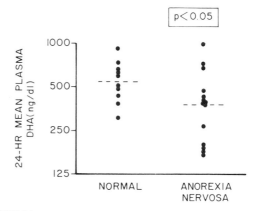

FIGURE 11   Averaged 24-hour mean plasma cortisol and DHA concentrations in women with anorexia nervosa and age-matched control women. [Reproduced with permission from Zumoff, B. *et al.* (1983). *J. Clin. Endocrinol. Metab.* **56,** 668. © The Endocrin Society.]

lated to stress, and a desynchronization of cortisol and DHA circadian rhythms in schizophrenia.

It is also worthwhile to consider the opposite relationship, that of excess catecholamine or adrenal steroid secretory states and behavior. A pheochromocytoma, which is a tumor of the adrenal medulla, secretes an excess of catecholamines, and patients with this condition often suffer from extreme anxiety, as well as physical manifestations, such as headaches, sweating, and high blood pressure. There is evidence that female libido is at least partly dependent on the secretion of adrenal androgens, and states of adrenal androgen excess are often accompanied by disturbances in menstruation, ovulation, and libido, as well as in physical signs, such as hirsutism and acne. Finally, hypercortisolism from medication excess or adrenal production, known as Cushing's syndrome, is often associated with depression, menstrual disturbances, mania, or psychosis. Much research is necessary to explore the interrelationships between behavior and the hormonal families of catecholamines and steroids.

Bibliography

Baxter, J., and Tyrrell, J. (1987). The adrenal cortex. In "Endocrinology and Metabolism" (P. Felig, Ed.). McGraw-Hill, New York.

DeQuattro, V., Myers, M., and Campese, V. (1989). Anatomy and biochemistry of the sympathetic nervous system. In "Endocrinology" (L. DeGroot, Ed.). W. B. Saunders, Philadelphia.

Esler, M., and Meredith, I. (1992). Responses of the human sympathetic nervous system to stressors. In "Stress and Reproduction" (K. Sheppard, J. Boublik, and J. Funder, Eds.). Raven Press, New York.

Grebb, J., Reus, V., and Freimer, N. (1992). Neurobehavioral chemistry and physiology. In "A Review of General Psychiatry" (H. Goldman, Ed.). Appleton and Lange, Norwalk, CT.

Guyton, A. (1986). The adrenocortical hormones. In "Textbook of Medical Physiology." 7th ed. W. B. Saunders, Philadelphia.

Hale, A., and Rees, L. (1989). ACTH and related peptides. In "Endocrinology" (L. DeGroot, Ed.). W. B. Saunders, Philadelphia.

Loriaux, D. L. (1990). The adrenal glands. In "Principles and Practice of Endocrinology and Metabolism" (K. Becker, Ed.). J. B. Lippincott, Philadelphia.

Parker, L. (1989). What is the biological role of adrenal androgens? In "Adrenal Androgens in Clinical Medicine." Academic Press, San Diego.

Rose, R. (1984). Overview of the endocrinology of stress. In "Neuroendocrinology and Psychiatric Disorders" (G. Brown, S. Koslow, and S. Reichlin, Eds.). Raven Press, New York.

AGGRESSION

Ronald Baenninger
Temple University

Glossary

Amygdala A small subcortical brain structure which is part of the limbic system; important in regulating aggressiveness and emotionality, as well as memory processes.

Androgen Any maleness-promoting substance, usually a hormone.

Castration Removal of the testes of males; the corresponding operation in females is called ovariectomy.

Cognitive Mental processes such as thinking and problem-solving.

Conspecific A member of the same species.

Dizygotic The type of twinning in which two different eggs are both fertilized to form fraternal (non-identical) embryos.

Endocrine The system of ductless glands which secrete hormones important in reproduction and many other bodily functions.

Hypothalamus A small subcortical brain structure important in regulating many basic motives, e.g., hunger and thirst.

In-group solidarity The feeling of closeness and support experienced by those who belong to a cohesive group.

Monozygotic The type of twinning in which a single fertilized egg divides to form genetically identical embryos.

Neural Having to do with nerve cells or the nervous system.

Operant conditioning A learning process in which the likelihood of a particular behavioral act is increased or decreased by rewards or punishments that occur whenever that act occurs.

Personality trait A way of behaving or thinking that is so consistent that it is characteristic of an individual.

Primates The taxonomic order of mammals to which humans belong, along with monkeys and apes.

Progesterone A steroid hormone secreted by the ovaries during parts of the female reproductive cycle.

Septal region A subcortical brain region concerned with the regulation of emotions.

Social facilitation A process in which the presence of others makes an activity more likely to occur.

AGGRESSION is a physical or verbal behavior that is intended to injure or destroy. The question of whether aggression is always a response to environmental events that produce pain, fear, or frustration is discussed. The extent to which learning is involved in aggressive behavior is examined, as well as the role of instinct. The relevant neural and endocrine mechanisms are described, as is the probable role of evolution in aggressive behavior.

I. WHAT DOES AGGRESSION MEAN?

Like many words that we use all the time, aggression turns out to be difficult to define precisely. The behavior of living organisms is fluid, fleeting, and rarely repeats itself exactly. In order to study aggression or any kind of behavior we must know or define what we are looking for so that we can examine which events precede it, and what kinds of consequences the behavior is likely to have.

Over 30 years ago A. H. Buss, a leading research psychologist who has devoted much of his career to studying aggression, defined it as ". . . a response that delivers noxious stimuli to another organism." While this appears straightforward and objective it is not very helpful outside the scientific laboratory. In examining why it is not helpful, and what it leaves out, we may understand just how complex aggression is.

First of all, the definition above refers only to behavior. Feelings that most people would consider part of aggression, feelings like hostility, anger, or rage, are not considered to be aggressive according to this objective, scientific definition. Feelings are subjective. Suppose you have been waiting in a long line and someone slips in front of you just as your turn comes up. You are likely to feel rage, or anger, or at least hostility toward the cheater, but unless you make an overt response that "delivers noxious stimuli" (by telling him off, or shoving or hitting) you would not be aggressive, according to a scientific definition of aggression.

Notice also that the scientific definition includes nothing about the intent that lies behind the noxious stimuli. We cannot know what another person's intention was, in any objective sense, so we attribute an intention to the person who harms another. Suppose that in your eagerness to reach that ticket window you step on the heel of someone in line ahead of you. According to the objective definition, that *would* be considered aggressive, even if you had no intention of hurting the person in front of you. Sometimes we hurt people or animals by accident, without intending to: driving a car over an animal on the road is not considered aggression, even though the poor creature is dead. Soldiers who are killed by "friendly fire" are not considered as victims of aggression by their own artillery. People are often injured or put in agony by people intending to do something important or helpful for them. A dentist or a surgeon who injures you would be considered aggressive toward you if their intentions are not taken into account. One may "deliver noxious stimuli" without intending to.

It is also possible to intend harm or injury without actually doing it. Suppose a terrorist rigs an explosive device to rid the world of a political opponent. The intended victim gets in his car, turns the key, but the bomb fails to go off. Surely, most people would consider the terrorist's attempt to be an aggressive act, even though there was no harm done. In this case, the deliberate act of rigging the explosive

device tell us that there was an intention. Intention is a central aspect of defining an act as aggressive, but in most cases it is not possible to determine the intentions of another person objectively.

People may, of course, state their intentions. In many species of animals there are threatening postures or signals that signal an intention by one individual to attack another. Male Siamese fighting fish extend a gill cover and flare their large fins as part of what is called a "threat display" toward other males, and even toward their own mirror images. Dogs bare their teeth, and in some bird species threatening individuals may posture or strut in a particular way, wave an enlarged claw (as in certain crabs), or give a particular call (as in howler monkeys of Central America). The male songs of many common bird species serve to attract females and to threaten other males. People may shake their fists or verbally threaten others. None of these signals actually harm anyone so they could not be considered aggressive by a strict objective definition.

A final difficulty with trying to define aggression objectively concerns a concept from the field of psychiatry, the idea of "passive aggression." Here the aggressor does nothing, but the effect is to harm the victim. For example, a prison guard who ignores a fight that is brewing between two prisoners may be behaving in a passive aggressive manner—by not intervening he ensures that someone will be harmed. Someone who pretends not to hear or understand your request for assistance may be behaving in a passive aggressive manner, by forcing you to repeat your request, speak louder, or do without their help. While the harm done to you may be minimal, and not physical, the effect can be unpleasant, particularly if it is a repeated pattern of behavior.

How can we define aggression? Not very easily, but a basic definition that most specialists would accept is ". . . physical or verbal behavior with the intent to injure or destroy." In what follows the emphasis will be on explaining and understanding aggression by individuals rather than by groups, societies, or cultures. The major causes and theories will be described from the perspective of scientific psychology.

II. JUSTIFYING AGGRESSION

If violence or aggression can be justified as self-defense it may be overlooked, or go unpunished. When Hitler invaded Poland in 1939 he tried to make it appear like self-defense by first staging a phony attack against Germany, complete with Nazi soldiers dressed up in Polish army uniforms. If anyone had believed this ploy to be genuine they would presumably have believed that Hitler's sudden, violent invasion of Poland was justified. A home owner who kills an intruder in self-defense will not usually be convicted of murder.

Aggressive acts are often excused if there is a clear provocation, or a pattern of harassment. For example, in their legal defense, spouse abusers or child batterers may attempt to prove that their violent behavior was provoked by the behavior of the spouse or child. The idea is that the abuse or battering would not have occurred if the victim had not provoked the person accused. Such a defense assumes that violence or aggression is a response to external circumstances or events, a view shared by many social scientists.

III. IS AGGRESSION INEVITABLE?

This question has concerned social and biological scientists for much of this century. It is an important matter, having to do with the basic nature of living creatures. Is it always external circumstances like pain, suffering, threats, provocations, or harassment that elicit aggression or violence? In a world without such instigators of violence would people and other animals live in peace and serenity with each other? Sigmund Freud denied this optimistic view. Instead, he asserted that aggression was one of the two most basic internal drives that we have. By this he meant that aggression, like sex, is a motive that wells up in us all even when there are no external circumstances or events that might justify it.

In opposition to Freud's pessimism is the idea, espoused by many social scientists, that aggression and violent behavior are a way of responding to unpleasant circumstances in one's environment. One early example of such a theory was the frustration–aggression hypothesis of Dollard *et al.,* which sought to explain all aggression as a reaction to frustration. While it is certainly true that aggression is a common reaction to frustration in both humans and other animals, it is clearly not the only reaction. Because of their past learning and personality development some people react to serious frustrations by turning their aggression inward against themselves (intropunitive) and become depressed, withdrawn, or guilt-ridden.

An alternative theory came from the animal laboratory, where it was found that painful stimulation in the presence of another individual was sufficient to produce immediate, vicious attacks. The basic result was replicated in a remarkable variety of different species from nearly every vertebrate class. Even laboratory pigeons sought out the chance to attack other pigeons when they received electric shocks.

Several theorists have suggested that fear or terror is the most important instigator of aggression. It is clear that fear may provoke aggressive attacks, as when a frightened wild animal is backed into a corner, or a fugitive is cornered. Some have argued that fear is important in aggression on the international scale, as when armed nations each believe that they are in danger of being attacked. So-called "pre-emptive strikes" become likely under these circumstances. [*See* ANXIETY AND FEAR.]

Irritable or impulsive violence may be increased by certain environmental events. High temperatures increase the aggressive interactions of laboratory mice, and similar effects have been found in people. The rate of homicides in the United States is higher in the hotter regions of the country; rape and other violent assaults rise with the temperature during the summer months in all parts of the country. [*See* HOMICIDE.]

Aggressive behavior is often interpreted as a learned reaction to life's difficulties, a way of coping with pain, fear, or frustration. The learning process may include simple operant conditioning, in which aggressive acts become characteristic of an individual because they are frequently rewarded. It is a common observation that *assertive* behavior is often rewarded financially, or with other signs of material, political, or social success, but assertiveness is not the same as aggressiveness. An assertive person is one who is firm about achieving goals, and unwilling to give up easily. Their behavior is aggressive only to the extent that they hurt or injure others in their zeal.

IV. LEARNING AND AGGRESSION

When an individual resorts to aggression as a way of achieving his or her goals in life it is a serious matter for the rest of the population; such people are a danger to the rest of us. A child who gets his way by hitting, punching, and screaming is learning to behave aggressively and is likely to carry the results of such learning into adulthood. In one study, male children who were aggressive at age 5 were still high at age 12, and it would be a fairly safe bet that these individuals would still be aggressive as young adults.

The psychologist Albert Bandura worked out a "social learning" theory of aggression. He described violence as including a wide range of behavior based on past experience, that is meaningfully related to the context in which it occurs, and which is maintained because it makes sense to the person who is behaving violently. Other people are part of our environmental context. If Person A is nasty and punitive toward Person B then B has an unpleasant environment partly created by A.

One way in which violence is learned is by observing it, especially in situations in which the model is respected, or in which violence leads to success. The process is more complex than simple operant conditioning by reward and punishment, and involves both imitation learning and social facilitation. In one experiment concerned with how social learning might occur, nursery school children observed an adult who was solving a problem. The adult's behavior included punching of an inflated Bobo doll, as well as other acts that were irrelevant to the solution of the problem. When the children later found themselves in the same problem-solving situation they did many of the same things the adult had done, including hitting the Bobo doll.

Observing and imitating the aggressive acts of a model whom one admires can be an important cause of aggression. One reason that many psychologists and educators avoid the use of physical punishment with school children is that parents and teachers are important and respected by children; if admired authority figures hit children then it must be alright to use such methods.

Through the influence of punishment people and other animals can learn what *not* to do, rather than learning what to do. The effects of punishment on aggressive behavior are of great interest because they are rather contradictory. When an animal or a person is punished for behaving aggressively it means that a noxious, painful stimulus is presented to them whenever they are aggressive. Their aggressive acts may temporarily cease. But as we have already seen, painful stimuli are one of the causes of aggression. The training procedure that is intended to decrease aggression may eventually increase it. This result has been found in a variety of experiments with different species (including people). Thus, spanking a child for hitting another child

may result in even more hitting. [*See* OPERANT LEARNING.]

V. AGGRESSION AS AN INSTINCT

Among the Hopi of the American Southwest the ideal of living at peace with others has long been practiced, but it is unusual to find a culture or nation which has never resorted to overt aggression; most individuals and groups show violence and aggression on occasion. Does all this mean that aggression is a human instinct? Sigmund Freud argued that it is an instinct, the destructive counterpart of the life-promoting force (libido) that each of us has from the moment of birth. He believed that this aggressive, destructive energy accumulated, and that if it is not released in socially acceptable ways (such as sports) it will spill over in socially unacceptable ways. Konrad Lorenz argued that this destructive energy evolved because it was required for every creature's survival. Aggression is ubiquitous and nearly universal among vertebrate species. One kind of evidence that led respected scientists to portray aggression as an instinctive behavior pattern is that it has genetic, neural, endocrine, and biochemical aspects. The existence of these biological influences may imply a kind of "hard-wired" system that is independent of environmental influences like learning. This system may be responsible for an aggressive drive or motive state that is internal; the implication is that even when no frustration, fear, pain, or irritating stimulus is present that aggressive behavior may surface like oil from an oil well.

VI. INTERNAL STIMULI
FOR AGGRESSION

There are clear differences between species: wolverines are more aggressive than rabbits. And there are strain differences: Dobermans or pit bull terriers are more likely to attack people than are spaniels or Irish setters. Such mundane observations imply hereditary aspects to aggressiveness, because different species and strains have different gene pools. Experiments with selective breeding and cross-breeding of laboratory rats, mice, and other species have confirmed that aggressiveness has hereditary aspects. Such experiments cannot be done with humans, of course, so we have no direct evidence of the heritability of aggressiveness in our own species. The fact that violent behavior may characterize individuals who are genetically related proves little. Family members usually share their environments as well as genes, and the influences cannot easily be separated. In one questionnaire survey that measured aggressiveness the scores of 179 fraternal (dizygotic) twin pairs were virtually uncorrelated, but the correlation between the aggressiveness of 286 identical (monozygotic) twin pairs was +.40, a highly significant relationship. Explicitly genetic theories of aggression and criminally violent behavior (such as those of Lombroso, or the Y–Y male chromosome) have had limited explanatory success.

In most species of vertebrates there are differences between the sexes in aggressiveness. Males usually are the more aggressive sex (in the sense of fighting more) and male hormones (androgens) appear to be involved. In species where females are more aggressive, such as an Arctic bird called the phalarope, it is the female whose androgen output is higher than in males. In our species levels of testosterone, an androgen, rise dramatically during adolescence; it is not coincidental that every human society has difficulty with male adolescents who get in trouble with the law and with each other as they adjust to their adult levels of testosterone. A similar developmental pattern exists among non-human primates. Androgens appear to promote aggressiveness. [See HORMONES AND BEHAVIOR.]

During the 1930s several European nations made castration legal as a way of dealing with aggressive criminals. The results of such Draconian treatment were mixed. In some cases the reduction of androgen was accompanied by decreased aggressiveness while in others there was little apparent effect. Laboratory experiments with other species are fairly clear: in species such as mice and rats, where learning is not a very important component of aggressive or sexual behavior, there is a clear decrease in these behaviors following castration. But in species where cognitive aspects appear important, such as non-human primates and carnivores, such decreases are less reliably found. Gender identity, social or cultural learning, and personality factors that result from childhood learning and adjustment appear to be more critical than hormone levels in the determination of aggressive or sexual motivation. In human adults the injection of testosterone does not have marked effects on aggressiveness.

K. Dalton studied the irritable aggression which is sometimes a part of the so-called premenstrual syndrome. Low levels of the ovarian hormone progesterone appeared to cause aggressive and even violent behavior of some adult women during the week prior to menstruation. Supplemental progesterone in many cases alleviated such symptoms, although social and personality factors were clearly critical. Relatively few women experience uncontrollable aggressive urges, and those who do are not reliably helped by progesterone administration. [See PREMENSTRUAL SYNDROME.]

Dietary factors may be important. Low blood sugar levels (hypoglycemia) have been found to be determinants of human aggressiveness in some studies. Although alcohol depresses central nervous system activity it appears to facilitate aggression in a variety of species. A genetically determined disorder of purine metabolism, Lesch-Nyhan syndrome, increases aggressiveness of those who suffer from it. Such factors as these may increase irritability and impulsiveness rather than exerting specific effects on the central nervous system.

A wide variety of neural structures have been shown to increase or decrease the likelihood of different kinds of aggression in different kinds of animals. Karli has reviewed these animal studies. In laboratory rats, for example, damage to several subcortical brain areas increases aggression. Removal of olfactory (receptor) bulbs increases irritability, while septal area lesions produce hyperreactivity. Damage to the ventromedial hypothalamus similarly affects reactivity to external stimuli (including prey and conspecifics) in rats and cats. Damage to the periaqueductal grey area of the brain has the specific effect of increasing defensive aggression.

In humans, deliberate damage to neural tissue for research would be ethically abhorrent, but naturally occurring cases have implicated a variety of brain tumors (i.e., in subcortical areas and the temporal and frontal lobes of the cerebral cortex). One famous case occurred in 1966 when Charles Whitman deliberately climbed a tall tower from which he shot 38 people, killing 14. Whitman's autopsy disclosed a probable tumor in the temporal lobe near the amygdala, although his brain was severely damaged by the police marksmen who had to shoot him. The uncontrollable nature of Whitman's impulses was clear from his history of seeking psychiatric help for his aggressiveness. Epilepsy and closed head injuries have resulted in uncontrollable aggression in some cases. [See EPILEPSY.]

VII. THE SOCIAL CONTEXT

Aggressiveness appears to be a consistent personality trait. But we all live in a social context, and social factors may enhance or reduce personality traits. If violence is portrayed in a group or subculture as acceptable or even praiseworthy, then its members will be affected by that view. Otherwise nonviolent individuals may change temporarily by imitating the violence around them. In the United States, for example, homicides have been found to increase following particularly violent events such as prize fights. [*See* TRAITS.]

For nearly a quarter century there has been a debate among social scientists about whether violence on TV engenders violent acts by viewers, and a great many experiments have found this to be true. But another result is possible, and has been found in some other experiments, namely that observing violence may induce a catharsis in viewers, an experience that will reduce their personal emotions of anger and hostility. Just as physical exercise can leave one feeling drained and relaxed, an experience of catharsis, in which one's emotions are exercised, can leave one feeling drained. The concept of catharsis was used by Aristotle to explain the manner in which public drama builds and then purges or cleanses the intense emotions of an audience. On balance, modern research suggests that while aggressive *feelings* may be reduced by observing violence, the performance of aggressive *acts* is likely to be increased. [*See* VIOLENCE, OBSERVATIONAL EFFECTS ON BEHAVIOR.]

People who are already prone to violent acts may respond differently to violent TV, films, or theater as compared to nonviolent individuals. This is a complex issue that has not yet been clearly worked out. Even the presence of weapons can enhance aggression in perfectly normal people. In a series of laboratory experiments Leonard Berkowitz and his colleagues found that weapons, or even pictures of weapons, significantly increased the expression of anger and hostility. [*See* ANGER.]

One of the earliest psychological experiments involving real aggression was carried out at an American boys' camp by Sherif and Sherif. Two groups of normal boys were assigned to different bunkhouses, and kept separate for daily activities. Next, a spirit of rivalry between the two groups was engendered in competitive events. As predicted, in-group solidarity was increased, and produced unfavorable stereotypes of the out-group and its members. After losing a tug-of-war one group burned the other's flag. Retaliation then occurred back and forth for several days, with bunkhouse raids, name-calling, fist fights, and much hostility between the groups.

The groups resisted attempts to bring them into contact with each other in pleasant circumstances, and the warfare only ended when the groups needed to cooperate in solving big problems (as when the camp water supply stopped, or a truck had to be pulled from a muddy ditch). [*See* PREJUDICE AND STEREOTYPES.]

VIII. THE VIOLENCE-PRONE PERSONALITY

Many heroes of history and mythology are portrayed in literature as using violence to solve their problems and overcoming the difficulties in their paths. News reports in the media make it clear that some people still resort to violence as a way of achieving their aims in life. Why? Are they somehow innately aggressive (as Freud and Lorenz would perhaps suggest)? Or do they live their lives in environments where their violence and aggression are perceived as solutions?

In his book *Violent Men,* the research criminologist Hans Toch formulated a typology of violence, based on his extensive work with violent criminals in prisons and on parole. These characterizations of the motives of violent men help us (and the law enforcement agencies for whom Toch was a consultant) to understand the interplay of personality factors with social environments in motivating violent behavior.

1. Reputation defending. Many people expect a champion prize fighter, football hero, or hockey player to defend his reputation for violence outside the ring, as well as inside it. A man who believes that he has such a reputation to uphold, whether such a belief is realistic or not, may use violence in doing so.

2. Norm enforcing. These people assign to themselves the mission of enforcing rules of conduct that they believe are universal. In some of the cowboy heroes of the early American West we can find examples of this motive.

3. Self-image compensating. We all have an image of ourselves that we strive to maintain. Men in this category, Toch suggested, feel it necessary to defend or promote their self-image more vigorously than most of us. A man whose self-image is securely masculine would have less need to show violent aggression in his daily life.

4. Self-defending. Someone whose early life was spent in an environment where other people were often physically dangerous to him or to those he loved may believe, not unreasonably, that other people are likely to be dangerous. Attacking or intimidating others before they can be harmful is understandable.

5. Pressure removing. The fears, demands, pressures, and frustrations of social life or economic circumstances may build up to the point where a violent explosion seems to be the only option available.

6. Bullying. For these people it is simply a pleasure to terrorize or intimidate others through violent means.

7. Exploitation. This category is like the previous one, with the additional gratification of forcing others to comply with one's wishes, and using them to do one's bidding. Gangsters and members of organized crime syndicates provide examples of this category.

8. Self-indulging. For a sadistic individual, delivering noxious stimuli to others may itself be gratifying. For these people, their own gratification is assumed to be the most important matter in social interactions.

9. Catharting. If performing violent, aggressive acts is followed by the experience of catharsis such acts will be repeated. The audiences of ancient Greece were swept up in the emotions engendered by performances of classic tragedies, as audiences have been ever since.

These motives that Toch identified are not simple ones. And like other human motives, they are not mutually exclusive. Their existence does not rule out the possibility of brain tumors like that found in Charles Whitman.

IX. THE EVOLUTION OF AGGRESSION

Like other aspects of our behavior, human aggression and violence have a history in the evolution of our species. Since behavior is fleeting, and leaves no fossil remains, we must resort to indirect methods for discovering how the behavior patterns that now exist in our species might have evolved from our evolutionary ancestors. One approach is to study the behavior of other species that now exist, species whose evolutionary relationship to our own is known to some extent. If several species that share

a common ancestor all have a particular trait in common, and the trait does no exist in unrelated species, then it is likely that the trait existed in the early ancestor.

A major difference between humans and other species in their aggression is that we have developed weapons which allow us to injure others at a distance, so that human aggressors are often spared the potentially dangerous consequences of their attacks on others. But what do other species fight about? Much of the violence and aggression that occur in other animal species are related to competition and predation. According to the data from the classic field studies of Jane Goodall, threat and attack among chimpanzees (our closest living relatives) occur in the following situations:

1. Competition over food.
2. Defense of an infant by its mother.
3. Dominance ranking and/or the prerogatives associated with it. Changes in dominance status over time are also associated with fights.
4. Redirected aggression, in which an individual who has lost an encounter with a higher ranking individual will in turn attack another of lower rank.
5. Failure of an individual to comply with a signal given by the aggressor.
6. Strange appearance, including physical deformity.
7. Fighting among males for access to receptive females.

These situations occur among humans is well, but overt aggression or violence about these matters is unusual in people who have learned the normal social rules that human cultures have established. In circumstances of hardship or scarcity these rules may break down, and we humans then fight like our fellow primates over food, mates, or dominance ranking. The motives for violence identified by Toch are clearly more complex, having to do with self-image, reputation, and perceptions of "psychological" harm.

It seems likely that human aggressiveness evolved early, in circumstances similar to those of our primate relatives, but it is clear that we have evolved beyond them, so that more cognitive, abstract reasons now underlie most of our aggression. We have psychological and cultural reasons for fighting that are different, and the weapons that we can use are devastatingly effective compared to the teeth and hands used by other primates. New ways to settle our inevitable human differences are urgently needed.

Bibliography

Bandura, A. (1973). "Aggression: A Social Learning Analysis." Prentice Hall, Englewood Cliffs, NJ.

Buss, A. H. (1961). "The Psychology of Aggression." Wiley, New York.

Dalton, K. (1964). "The Premenstrual Syndrome." Charles C. Thomas, Springfield.

Dollard, J., Doob, L. W., Miller, N., Mowrer, O. H., and Sears, R. R. (1939). "Frustration and Aggression." Yale University Press, New Haven.

Freud, S. (1920). "A General Introduction to Psychoanalysis." Boni & Liveright, New York.

Karli, P. (1991). "Animal and Human Aggression." Oxford: Oxford University Press.

Lorenz, K. (1966). "On Aggression." Harcourt, Brace and World, New York.

Moyer, K. E. (1987). "Violence and Aggression: A Physiological Perspective." Paragon House, New York.

Phillips, D. P. (1983). The impact of mass media violence on U.S. homicides. *Am. Soc. Rev.* **48**, 560–568.

Sherif, M., and Sherif, C. W. (1953). "Groups in Harmony and Tension." Harper and Row, New York.

Toch, H. (1984). "Violent Men." Schenkman, Cambridge, MA.

AGING, PERSONALITY, AND ADAPTATION

Michael R. Levenson and Carolyn M. Aldwin
University of California at Davis

Glossary

Cohort A group of people sharing a common characteristic, usually year or decade of birth.

Cross-sectional A study design which compares different age groups at the same time.

Dementia Impairments in cognitive performance, usually produced by neurological damage.

Life expectancy The average number of years an individual in a cohort is expected to live.

Lifespan The maximum number of years an individual member of a species can live.

Longitudinal A study design which follows one or more cohorts over a period of time.

Senescence Declines in function thought to be associated with age.

Wisdom The ability to understand problems and life situations comprehensively in the face of uncertainty.

THE BIGGEST DEVELOPMENT in gerontology, or aging research, has been the recognition that the aging process is not simply senescence—most people over the age of 65 are not senile, bedridden, isolated, or suicidal. Indeed, the current cohorts of people in their 60s and 70s are probably the healthiest in history, and researchers distinguish between the "young-old" (ages 65–79), most of whom are still relatively healthy and active, and the "old-old"

(80+), who are more likely to show impaired health and cognition.

Gerontologists also differentiate among impaired, normal, and optimal aging. Impaired aging is related to disease states; normal aging tends to show slight decrements in functioning; and optimal aging shows either few changes or increases in some capacities. Further, when decrements do occur, most older adults adapt by compensating for difficulties and optimizing their capabilities, and thus maintain a fairly high level of functioning. Much of the most exciting research is focusing on identifying factors which are associated with optimal aging, such as health behavior habits, personality traits, social integration, and attitudes toward aging. This article concentrates most heavily on these topics, but also addresses current trends in cognition, creativity, and wisdom.

I. PERSONALITY AND AGING

Early theorists such as Erik Erikson posited the existence of developmental stages in adulthood—that is, qualitative shifts in personality which are universal, sequential, and irreversible. Erikson's identification of three adult stages (intimacy vs isolation, generativity vs stagnation, and ego integrity vs despair) represents the best known schema for adult development. However, sociologists were quick to criticize these theories, arguing that they ignored the contribution of social roles, class, gender, and culture to change in adulthood, and averred that there was no evidence for systematic shifts in adult personality and values which were not due to changes in social roles.

In response, some theorists posited less rigid models in which development is based either on interactional processes between the individual and the sociocultural environment or on volitional, conscious effort. In other words, developmental change is something which might occur in adulthood, but it is not necessarily teleological, universal, sequential, or irreversible. What that development might consist of, however, is a matter of debate. Development has been characterized variously in terms of individuation, ego development, mastery, wisdom, and mindfulness, to name only a few examples. Whatever it may consist of, development is something which adults *do,* not something which happens to them, and it is not driven primarily by biological maturation.

Most of the adult developmental theorists relied heavily on clinical interviews of rather small numbers of individuals (usually men). More recent research has taken a more quantitative approach, utilizing standardized measures of personality traits given to larger samples of men and women. In cross-sectional designs, respondents of different ages are sampled at one time point, and either correlations with age or mean differences across age groups are computed. Longitudinal designs follow respondents across time, and utilize stability coefficients (cross-time correlations) or repeated measures analysis of variance to examine rank order or mean level change.

Most studies utilizing these designs find relatively little change in personality with age, with the possible exception of interiority, suggesting that older individuals may withdraw from the world in later life. On the basis of numerous studies in which moderate to high stability coefficients (.6 to .8) were found, some believe that personality is stable—at least from age 30 onward, and there is little, if any, personality change in adulthood. Further, studies comparing mean scores generally find very small, if any, differences in personality with age.

However, there are several limitations to this line of research. To the extent that personality inventories assess temperament, researchers utilizing these measures may be focusing on the most stable component of personality, in part because temperament is probably the most heritable aspect of personality. Other components, such as conceptions of the ideal self, may show more systematic changes with age. Further, researchers who utilize archival data to examine personality over several decades have demonstrated impressive evidence of change, although there are substantial differences in individual trajectories. Even the personalities of monozygotic twins tend to diverge with age.

In part, whether personality is viewed as stable or changeable depends upon both the type of measure and the statistical design. Aggregate statistics (e.g., correlations or mean change over time) usually suggest that personality is stable, while examining individual trajectories (ipsative statistics or idiographic studies) often yields substantial evidence of change. The two methods are actually assessing two different kinds of stability. Longitudinal statistics which assess change or stability by means of correlations of aggregated scores cannot yield evidence about individual change or stability. Instead, observed coefficients of this kind largely reflect the stability of an assessment instrument in a population. In other words, a group as a whole may be stable even though individuals within the group may have changed.

While most people appear to have fairly stable temperaments in adulthood, Caspi, Bem, and Elder have asked the stability question in a different way: Given the incentive many people might have to change traits that are self-defeating, why is personality as stable as it is? They found that interactional styles established in childhood affect the range of choices available to a person across the life course. For example, people who have limited (and aversive) interactional styles, such as being hot-tempered, may elicit anger from others. This type of feedback tends to encourage the maintenance of that interactional style which led to the restriction of choices in the first place. [*See* TRAITS.]

Caspi and his colleagues identified two types of continuity: "cumulative continuity," behavior maintained by the effects of its own accumulating consequences, and "interactional continuity," the interdependence of one's behavior and the response of his or her environment. Together, these combine to increase the likelihood of the expression of traits which, in the case of maladaptive behavior, ultimately benefit no one. For example, an ill-tempered youth may incur repeated frustrations which increase the bad temper and elicit further frustrating responses. The ill-tempered youth thus becomes the abusive and economically downwardly mobile adult and, finally the irascible old man or woman.

Questions of personality change in adulthood overlap questions of adult development but are by no means equivalent to them. An introvert may become wise, but still be an introvert; conversely, an introvert may become relatively extraverted without becoming any wiser. Rather than asking whether personality can change with age, it is better to ask how or under what circumstances personality does change. Further, can people direct their own changes in ways which can reasonably be interpreted as developmental, for example, in ways which maximize their psychological and physical health?

II. PSYCHOSOCIAL EFFECTS ON THE AGING PROCESS

Species, and individuals within species, have different lifespans, the maximum length of life possible for individuals within a species. In general, smaller creatures such as insects and small mammals have very short lives, while larger animals have longer lifespans. Currently, humans, tortoises, and parrots have the longest lifespans. At present, the longest a human can live is about 120 years, while parrots can live to be 130 or older. The lifespan for humans has not changed in recorded history, but the average life expectancy, the average length of time a person in a given cohort can expect to live, has increased dramatically in the past century. Most of the increase in life expectancy is due to the striking decrease in infant mortality, improved sanitation, and better nutritional and medical practices. Indeed, the over 80 cohort is the fastest growing segment of the population.

A truism in gerontology is that individual differences increase with age. That is, as we grow older, our life histories result in unique constellations of experiences which emphasize our individuality. A corollary of this observation is that we appear to age at different rates. At age 55, some people are crippled with chronic illness; others are running the Boston Marathon. Some 70 year olds suffer from cognitive dementia which impairs recognition of even their own children; others are writing books, giving concerts, or starting new careers. Some of this variation is undoubtedly genetic; however, much of it may be due to psychosocial factors such as health behavior habits, personality, social ties, and education.

A. Health Behavior Habits

Choices of lifestyles has a large impact on health. Smoking, alcohol consumption, nutrition, and exercise all affect the rate at which our bodies age by promoting or retarding disease processes. Utilizing tobacco products greatly increases levels of carcinogens and free radicals, both in the body of the user and in his or her immediate environment. This exposure increases risk of cardiovascular diseases and cancer. Smoking also promotes cosmetic changes such as wrinkles and deep furrows in the skin, as does excessive exposure to the sun. Further, cardiovascular disease may impair cognitive functioning by decreasing blood flow to the brain.

Maintaining good nutrition is another obvious way to promote health, and poor nutrition, especially in the elderly, may increase risk of disease and cognitive impairment. Presumably, excessive intake of fats and meat may also damage health, while many studies have shown that diets high in complex carbohydrates, fruit, and vegetables may provide protection against the development of some diseases.

Lifelong aerobic exercise may also protect against the development of disease, and may even prolong life. Indeed, much of the decline in pulmonary function typically seen with age actually occurs among smokers and the sedentary. The Baltimore Longitudinal Study on Aging found little or no decline in cardiac output in healthy subjects up to age 79. While over-exercising can suppress both neuroendocrine and immune function, moderate exercise may both delay the onset of chronic illnesses and help in their regulation once they occur. Further, cross-sectional studies show that active older men tend to have higher performance scores on cognitive tasks than do sedentary older men, although longitudinal studies suggest that the causal directionality between exercise and better cognitive function is not always clear. Interestingly, aerobic fitness appears to decline in introverts at a more rapid rate than in extraverts, perhaps mediated through the greater likelihood of extraverts to exercise.

B. Personality and Health

One of the most interesting but controversial areas of current research is whether certain personality types are at higher risk for disease. Friedman and Rosenman identified a link between Type A personality and heart disease. Type A's are characterized by hostility, explosive speech and behavior patterns, and extreme time pressure, often performing two or more tasks at once. However, subsequent research suggested that hostility is probably the most important component in the development of heart disease and in premature mortality. [See TYPE A–TYPE B PERSONALITIES.]

Further, there is some suggestion that emotional repression and/or depression may increase the risk of cancer. Temoshok and her colleagues have found that "Type C" women, who were characterized by suppression of negative emotions and a compliant, appeasing facade were more likely to have melanoma, and perhaps breast cancer as well. Other studies have shown that individuals high in depression are at greater risk for developing cancer, especially among those who also smoke.

Some of the most interesting research in healthy psychology suggests that a sense of control or mastery may also affect longevity. Ellen Langer and Judith Rodin conducted an interesting experiment on elderly residents in a nursing home. In many of these institutions, especially those which follow a biomedical model, the residents have little control over anything that happens to them. Langer and Rodin's intervention was to induce a sense of control in the experimental group by giving them the ability to make small choices in their everyday life, such as being able to select among entrees at dinner or when to see a movie. Further, both the experimental and the control group were given a plant. However, the experimental group was told that they should take care of the plant, while the control group was told that the nursing staff would have that duty. Over the next few months, the residents in the experimental group expressed more satisfaction, were less depressed, more alert, less cognitively impaired, and more social. Eighteen months later, a larger percentage of the control group had died. [See CONTROL.]

Physiological functioning in the elderly may be surprisingly malleable. Many anecdotal reports exist of instances of nearly deaf older persons who can suddenly "hear perfectly well" if they are the subject of conversations, or how playing an instrument alleviates arthritis in the hands of a venerable musician. Langer and her colleagues attempted to experimentally demonstrate this phenomenon in two groups of 70 to 75-year-old men. Both groups went on a retreat for 5 days. The control group was instructed to concentrate on reminiscing about life 20 years before. The experimental group was instructed to allow themselves to *be* exactly who they were 20 years before. They were assisted in this task by activities such as seeing and discussing movies from 20 years before, debating the merits of sports figures and politicians, and reading magazines from that era. By the end of a week, the experimental group, relative to the controls, had improved on a number of physiological parameters, including joint flexibility, manual dexterity, and near-point vision, and cognitively on a measure of digit symbol substitution. Langer *et al.* appear to be showing that if one does

not "act one's age," one may, in important ways, not *be* one's age.

Much of the research on psychosocial effects on health remains controversial in part because the physiological pathways have as yet to be worked out. However, we know that psychosocial factors affect neuroendocrine function, which in turn can affect immune function. Currently, a new field of research, psychoneuroimmunology, is investigating the mechanisms through which psychosocial factors affect this aspect of health, but to date only a relative handful of studies have been done on the elderly. [See STRESS AND ILLNESS.]

It is also true that the relationship between personality and health outcomes is often weak. Scores on personality inventories often fail to predict behavior very well, and it would be naive to expect them to do much better for physiology. Further, inference from a relationship between attributes in a population to a relationship between these attributes in an individual necessarily entails a logical fallacy. Although personality is associated with disease in population studies, not everyone who is hostile develops heart disease, and most people who are depressed do not develop cancer (and vice versa). But we will all die of something, and chances are quite likely that it will be either CHD or cancer. Rather, psychosocial factors may be best thought of as factors which affect the risk of the premature development of illness and disability.

C. Social Integration and Health

Social integration may be an important influence on health in older adults. Relatively simple measures of social integration (marital status, number of organizations, number of friends, and going to church) predict mortality, even controlling for standard biomedical risk factors and existing health problems. The mechanisms through which social integration influences health are unclear. Spouses, friends, and relatives may promote better nutrition and health behavior habits, and encourage the older adult to get adequate health care. Work in younger adults, however, suggests that social ties may have direct effects on health outcomes. Whatever the mechanism, the relationship between social integration and health will continue to be an important area of research in gerontology. [See SOCIAL SUPPORT.]

III. AGING AND MENTAL HEALTH

A common assumption is that older adults are particularly vulnerable to mental health problems, especially loneliness and depression. It is true that white males over the age of 65 have the highest suicide rates of any demographic group. Some clinical estimates have put the depression rate as high as 65% among elderly adults. However, many depression inventories include somatic symptoms such as fatigue, aches and pains, and sleep disturbances, which may reflect common health problems in the elderly, rather than depression per se. When somatic symptoms are removed, there is often little or no relationship between age and depression. Indeed, the Epidemiological Catchment Area Studies have shown that older adults have lower rates of mental illness than younger adults. [*See* DEPRESSION.]

Some of the contradictions in the literature may be due to the existence of a nonlinear relationship between aging and depression. Studies which compare young adults with middle-aged ones often find a negative correlation between age and depression, while studies comparing middle-aged to older adults sometimes find a positive correlation, suggesting a J-shaped curve between overall psychological symptoms and age (see Fig. 1). Symptom levels appear

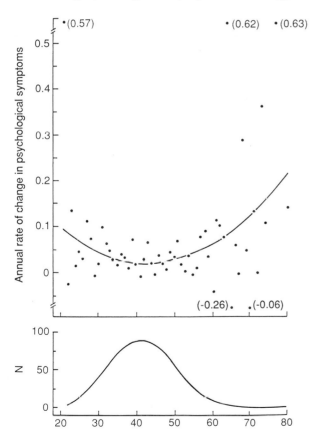

FIGURE 1   J-shaped curve of the relationship between age and psychological symptoms. [From Aldwin, C. M., Spiro, A., III, Levenson, M. R., and Bossé, R. (1989). *Psychol. Aging* **4**, 295–306.]

to decrease from young adulthood to middle age, remain stable in mid-life, and then increase again after age 65. Further, some of the change in mental health may be in part be predicted by personality. For example, neuroticism may predict both the future occurrence of and increase in psychological symptoms with age. However, it should be emphasized that getting older per se does not necessarily lead to poorer mental health, but psychological symptoms may accompany health problems. While new cases of nonorganic psychosis are very rare in later adulthood, other problems, such as adverse reactions to medications, surgery, or poor nutrition, may lead to confusional or psychotic states, which are reversible if properly diagnosed and treated. Organic brain disorders, such as strokes, transitory ischemic attacks (TIAs), and Parkinson's and Alzheimer's diseases may also lead to mental health problems which are more intractable. Indeed, rapid personality change accompanied by aggression or mood swings may be an early indicator of neurological dysfunction in the elderly. Further, as physical health declines, it is not surprising that depression may accompany chronic pain, extreme disability, or a terminal illness.

A particularly important problem in geriatric psychiatry involves the overuse of psychotropic medications. The elderly, especially those in skilled nursing facilities (SNFs), are probably the most overmedicated segment of society. While only constituting 12% of the population, the elderly account for 60% of all psychotropic medication prescriptions. Further, medications clear much more slowly in the elderly, taking two to three times as long to dissipate as in younger people. Overmedication may lead to confusional states or pseudo-dementias, which then are sometimes misdiagnosed as true dementia. The current federal regulations for SNFs are attempting to limit the use of psychotropic drugs by nursing staff, but overmedication in the elderly remains a major public health problem.

Another drug problem among the elderly is alcohol abuse. The prevalence of alcohol problems in the elderly is not well established. Estimates range from 7 to 70%, but the more generally accepted figure is 10 to 15%. Cross-sectional studies generally find that older people consume less alcohol, but it is not clear whether this is an age or a cohort effect. Some researchers think that the older cohorts, having lived through Prohibition, have always consumed less alcohol. Other researchers, however, believe that older people actually do drink less alcohol, perhaps because they drink less at each occasion, although the occasions may be just as frequent. Alcohol is processed more slowly in older people, and so older people cannot tolerate as much alcohol as when they were younger. Further, alcohol can adversely interact with many medications, so that alcohol problems tend to be associated with health problems in older populations. [*See* SUBSTANCE ABUSE.]

Given the potential seriousness of alcohol abuse in the elderly, some researchers have tried to identify predictors of alcohol problems in later life. However, there appears to be only a weak relationship between personality and alcohol abuse, and some suggest that alcohol consumption is more a source of personality problems than it is the result of them. Further, older adults with chronic alcohol problems tend to report more stress and have fewer social resources.

Nonetheless, in the absence of major dementing illness, alcoholism, serious physical health problems, or major stressors such as spousal bereavement, an older individual's mental health is likely to be just as good as that of a younger individual. Further, there is little direct relationship between aging and depression; rather, how older people cope with stress may be more important.

IV. AGING, STRESS, AND COPING

The elderly are more vulnerable to physical stressors. They are less able to regulate their body temperature, and are thus susceptible to both extreme heat and extreme cold. In natural disasters, famines, and population dislocations, the very young and the very old are at highest risk for death. However, there is very little evidence that the elderly are necessarily more vulnerable to psychosocial stressors, unless, of course, they are in very frail health.

While some have found that the elderly report fewer major life events, others have pointed out that stressful life event inventories typically oversample events that younger adults are more likely to experience, such as starting or losing a job, going to jail, or becoming a parent. However, when events are sampled that older adults are likely to experience, such as retirement, bereavement, health declines, and child's divorce, there is little relationship between age and the occurrence of major life events. Nonetheless, older adults may report fewer hassles or daily stressors, perhaps because they have fewer social obligations, and they consistently rate problems as less stressful than do younger adults. In

part, experiencing many difficulties over the lifespan may increase one's perspective on the true seriousness of problems. For example, losing a spouse or a child to cancer may make hassles such as a delayed bus or long lines in a grocery store pale by comparison. [*See* STRESS.]

Other life events which typically occur to older adults are simply not as stressful as previously thought, such as the departure of adult children from the home (the "empty nest" syndrome) or retirement, which is problematic primarily for individuals with health or financial problems. Further, unless it is accompanied by a precipitous decrease in estrogen levels, menopause is not associated with major depression. Nor do most people appear to experience a mid-life crisis.

As a group, the elderly tend to be well-off financially, with only about 12% below the poverty line (as opposed to 25% for children). However, the elderly cannot be treated as a homogenous group. While married couples in their 60s and 70s tend to be fairly well off, the old-old, widows, and minority elderly often experience high rates of poverty—reaching as much as 80% among African-American elderly widows. Indeed, poverty tends to be intractable among the elderly, but transient for children. In other words, most children are only poor for relatively short periods of time, but once an elderly person is impoverished, that situation will last for the rest of his or her life. Further, many elderly are "tweeners"—they have incomes just above the poverty line, and are ineligible for various forms of public assistance, but do not have enough funds to cope with medical or other emergencies.

There are major sources of stress for older adults. Middle-aged adults are sometimes called the "sandwich generation," as they often take care of both their children and their parents. Given the rapid demographic growth of those over 80, many people in their 60s and 70s are providing care to their parents, other elderly relatives, and sometimes their spouses as well. Further, it is a myth that Americans abandon their elderly. Only 5% reside in nursing homes, and families provide most of the care for the older generation. Indeed, a major predictor of institutionalization is a breakdown in the social support system, often due to the development of health problems in the caretakers.

Declines in health status and functional abilities are also stressful. Many elderly people live with chronic pain and face increasing limitations in activities of daily living (ADLs), such as shopping, bathing, or toileting. Although women typically live longer than men, the quality of that life tends to be poor, especially among the old-old. Further, older adults are very familiar with death, losing both friends and family members on an increasingly frequent basis. Losing one's spouse may be especially traumatic and is associated with increased risk of CHD in the following year, although a third of adults surprisingly do not appear to grieve very much at the death of their spouse. Sometimes death may be welcome when a loved one has undergone much suffering. [*See* GRIEF AND BEREAVEMENT.]

A major controversy is whether older adults are better or poorer copers than younger ones. Gutmann proposed that there is a shift from active mastery in early adulthood, to "passive" mastery in middle adulthood, to "magical" mastery in late life, based upon TAT responses in several cultures. However, studies which examine the actual coping strategies used by older adults in real life situations have found a somewhat more complicated picture. Most studies find that older people are just as likely to use problem-solving strategies as younger people, but are less likely to use maladaptive strategies such as escapism, wishful thinking, and drugs and alcohol to cope with problems. Where there are age differences in coping, this can often be attributed to the fact that older individuals are usually dealing with very different types of problems than younger ones. Even if elderly people do use fewer strategies, this does not necessarily mean that they are passive copers. Rather, they maybe more effective, in that they have, through long experience, determined which strategies work and which are ineffective in different situations, and thus expend less energy by using fewer but more effective techniques. [*See* COPING.]

In support of Gutmann's hypothesis, Aldwin did find that older people said that they feel less control or responsibility for problems than did younger people, which may lead to the assumption that they are more passive. However, even though they said they had little or no control, they used just as much problem-focused coping, and appraised their efforts just as efficacious as younger adults. Thus, older adults may have a more complex view of the world, in which they recognize the limitation of personal agency, but nonetheless do what they can. Labouvie-Vief has also suggested that mature adults have more complex understanding of both their emotions and those of others, which also guides their choice of coping strategies. Again, an elderly person whose health is very frail or who is experiencing cognitive impairment may have a diminished capacity to cope with stress. Often such individuals adopt a general strategy of selecting and simplifying—that is, narrowing the scope of their world and developing routines to reduce complication. For example, older people with diminished capacity may go to only one grocery store with which they are familiar and insist upon the same person driving them, preferably at the same time of day. But under optimal or even normal conditions, the older person may be a coping resource for other people—a wise person to whom younger individuals turn to for advice in coping with stress.

V. AGING, COGNITION, AND CREATIVITY

One of the most widely accepted findings in the gerontological literature is decrements in cognitive performance with advancing age, especially on memory and learning tasks. The more complex and/or novel the task, the more age differences are likely to emerge. However, controlling for educational differences attenuates the relationship between age and performance on most cognitive tasks. Recent evidence suggests that decrements in memory performance up to age 80 were primarily a function of cohort differences in education, and there is a wide range of differences in age of onset of deficits, with some elders showing no deficits even in late life. Note, however, that all studies find that reaction time slows with age, regardless of health or educational status.

It is also true that older people are at significant risk of developing dementing illnesses. These produce neurological damage which results in cognitive deficits such as memory loss or confusion as to time or place. Some studies estimate that nearly 50% of people over the age of 85 have some dementia. Further, cognitive function can also be impaired by such common chronic illnesses as diabetes and hypertension, as well as common medications such as those for hypertension. [*See* DEMENTIA.]

In part, whether aging deficits in cognition are to be expected in late life depends on how the question is posed. Laboratory studies of memory and learning in the elderly often show performance decrements, even in the apparently healthy and well-functioning. However, the same elder may be entirely competent in performing tasks outside the laboratory, leading some researchers to question the ecological validity of laboratory cognitive tests (although certainly neuropsychological testing for effects due to disease and injury is well-established).

Indeed, Cornelius and Caspi found that the problem-solving ability in everyday life increased with age, even though scores on more conventional cognitive tests decreased. Thus, age-related decline in some types of cognitive functions may occur in the "average" case, especially after age 70. However, these will not *necessarily* occur, and even if they do, there may be ways of minimizing these effects. Further, some types of functions may actually increase, including cognitive complexity.

Some of the most interesting research focuses on ways of improving cognitive performance with age. Several researchers have shown that elderly people can be taught to improve their cognitive performance, although these interventions do not work very well in Alzheimers' patients. Nonetheless, in the absence of disease, the plasticity of neuropsychological (and presumably neurological) functioning in late life is quite remarkable. As Marion Diamond has remarked, "Use it or lose it."

A similar picture emerges for creativity in later life. Researchers who analyze aggregated data find declines in creativity in late life, with peak quality of work appearing in young adulthood in some fields such as poetry, mathematics, physics, and painting. However, declines in creativity may also be confounded with illness or injury which are not necessarily age-related, or with increased responsibility for teaching or administration. Further, some persons remain highly creative in later life. [*See* CREATIVE AND IMAGINATIVE THINKING.]

In general, the quantity of production tends to decline but the quality of work may increase in late life. The term *altersstil* has been used by German students of artistic style to refer to a deepening or "essentialization" of the artistic vision in late life. This distinct late life pattern of creativity is exemplified, among painters, by Michelangelo, Titian, Donatello, Rembrandt, El Greco, Goya, Monet, and Matisse, to mention some of the more illustrious.

Ellen Langer has argued that older people may be interested in different cognitive tasks than younger people. This shift can be interpreted as "decline" when it is actually a change in orientation. In the course of adult development, the search for wisdom or holistic understanding may supersede acquisition of the knowledge of particulars as the dominant cognitive task in late life. Nevertheless, we must also face the reality of declines associated with less than optimal aging.

VI. SUMMARY

The study of aging, personality, and adaptation provides a fascinating window onto the human condition. By examining impaired, usual, and optimal aging, it shows us the depths of human suffering, what is probably going to happen to us in late life, and what achievements are possible. Paul Baltes has remarked that development in late life is a balance between gains and losses. We will certainly lose energy, relatives, and friends, and some social roles. On the other hand, we will gain experience, knowledge, other relatives such as grandchildren and great-grandchildren, and perhaps wisdom.

Given the plasticity of the aging process, Langer's model of development and aging is also promising. She argues that development across the lifespan entails mindful involvement, creating new categories rather than being enslaved to old ones, including the category of the "inevitable declines associated with aging." Diamond's admonition to "use it or lose it" applies to nearly every psychological and physiological process affected by aging, including physical activity, sexual performance, and cognitive abilities. It is important to remember that, barring accidental death, chronic illness, disability, and eventually death will occur to everyone. Nonetheless, the quality of life and to a certain extent longevity are affected by psychosocial factors and therefore by choice.

Acknowledgments

Preparation of this article was supported by grants from the National Institute on Alcohol Abuse and Alcoholism (AA08941) and the National Institute on Aging (R29 AG07465) to the first and second authors, respectively. Correspondence concerning this article should be addressed to Michael R. Levenson, Ph.D., Department of Applied Behavioral Sciences, University of California, Davis, CA 95616.

Bibliography

Aldwin, C. (1991). Does age affect the stress and coping process? The implications of age differences in perceived locus of control. *J. Gerontol: Psycholog. Sci.* **46**, P174–180.

Alexander, C., and Langer, E. (Eds.). "Higher Stages of Human Development: Perspectives on Adult Growth." Oxford University Press, New York.

Baltes, P. B., and Baltes, M. M. (1990). "Successful Aging: Perspectives from the Behavioral Sciences." Cambridge University, New York.

Binstock, R. H., and George, L. K. (Eds.) (1990). "Handbook of Aging and the Social Sciences," 3rd ed. Academic Press, San Diego.

Birren, J. E., and Schaie, K. W. (Eds.) "Handbook of the Psychology of Aging," 3rd ed. Academic Press, San Diego.

Friedman, H. S. (Ed.) (1990). "Personality and Disease." Wiley, New York.

Langer, E. J. (1990). "Mindfulness." Addison-Wesley, New York.

McCrae, R. R., and Costa, P. T. (1990). "Personality in Adulthood." Guilford, New York.

Pervin, L. A. (Ed.) "Handbook of Personality: Theory and Research." Guilford, New York.

Salthouse, T. A. (1991). "Theoretical Perspectives on Cognitive Aging." Erlbaum, Hillsdale, NJ.

Sternberg, J. (Ed.) (1990). "Wisdom: Its Nature, Origins, and Development." Cambridge University Press, New York.

AGORAPHOBIA

Geoffrey L. Thorpe
University of Maine

Glossary

Cognitive therapy A system of psychotherapy focused upon identifying and restructuring dysfunctional thoughts and schemas linked to psychopathology.

DSM-III (and DSM-III-R) Abbreviations for the 1980 third edition (and its revision in 1987) of the *Diagnostic and Statistical Manual of Mental Disorders* published by the American Psychiatric Association.

Exposure *in vivo* The structured treatment of anxiety disorders by systematic confrontation of feared external situations to reduce avoidance behavior and anxiety.

Exposure to somatic cues Extends the methods of exposure *in vivo* to those internal cues and bodily sensations associated with panic attacks.

Limited symptom attack An anxiety episode with a few subjective anxiety symptoms, insufficient in number to qualify as a panic attack.

Panic attack A discrete period of intense fear, not explained by a continuing organic factor, that arises rapidly with at least 4 anxiety symptoms from a 13-item list specified in the DSM-III-R.

Pharmacological dissection The identification of qualitatively separate anxiety patterns by examining the differential effects of certain medications.

AGORAPHOBIA is an anxiety disorder characterized by marked fear of entering crowded, public places; of traveling away from home, especially by public transportation; of feeling trapped or confined; and of being separated from a place or person associated with safety. Sudden, brief episodes of extreme anxiety—panic attacks—are commonly associated with agoraphobia, and may lead to avoidance of situations in which they occur. Often there is a "fear of fear" pattern, in which the bodily sensations of mounting panic are themselves a source of anxiety. Generally more debilitating than simple (specific) or social phobias, agoraphobia causes some people to remain entirely housebound. As a syndrome of anxiety elements in physiological, behavioral, and subjective domains, agoraphobia represents a distinct disorder with a typical clinical presentation and course. It usually arises in early adult life, with a prevalence in the Western world of approximately 4%; there is a significant preponderance of females in surveys of agoraphobia in clinical and community settings. Since about 1970, clinical researchers have developed effective pharmacological and psychological treatments to reduce or eliminate agoraphobic avoidance behavior and panic attacks.

I. AGORAPHOBIA: PAST AND PRESENT

The term "agoraphobia" was introduced by the German psychiatrist C. F. O. Westphal (1822–1890) in a classic monograph of 1871, *Die Agoraphobie*. He chose the term to describe the abnormal fears of a series of three men who experienced anxiety episodes when walking alone in public places. Feared situations included city squares, concert halls, churches, open streets and fields, crowded rooms, and traveling by carriage, bus, or train; typical anxiety symptoms were trembling, heart palpitations, and "an immediate breakout of intense anxiety," or feeling "strange all at once, almost like a 'hangover.'" Westphal gave prominence to the patients' fear of walking alone in streets or across squares, and therefore used agoraphobia to denote "fear of spaces"; however, he acknowledged that the term was not exhaustive because it did not embrace all features of the disorder. Contemporary commentators have noted that the Greek ''agora'' refers to a marketplace or place of assembly, and find Westphal's choice of term felicitous in aptly describing the chief situational fears associated with agoraphobia today.

Despite the enthusiasm of some American psychiatrists, interest in agoraphobia waned in the years following the publication of *Die Agoraphobie*. The taxonomist Emil Kraepelin later described a patient similar to those of Westphal, but referred neither to him nor to agoraphobia. The field of psychiatry rapidly became dominated by the psychoanalytic paradigm at the turn of the century, and, while agoraphobia received some attention from psychoanalysts, it was viewed as but one of many psychogenic disorders, not meriting particular notice. Sigmund Freud was more interested in all-encompassing theories of psychosexual development and neurotic symptom formation than in the classification of specific syndromes.

The development of behavior therapy in the 1950s by Joseph Wolpe and others was closely connected with the study of phobias and other anxiety disorders; interest in agoraphobia revived with American and British research on systematic desensitization and related methods in the 1960s, and with the publication of Isaac Marks' *Fears and Phobias* in 1969. Systematic desensitization produced disappointing outcomes with agoraphobia, but treatment based on graduated or full-flooded real-life exposure to relevant situations was successful in reducing avoidance behavior and anticipatory anxiety. [*See* ANXIETY DISORDERS; ANXIETY AND FEAR; PHOBIAS.]

The work of Donald Klein on ''pharmacological dissection'' suggested that benzodiazepines are helpful in relieving anticipatory anxiety, whereas monoamine oxidase inhibitors and tricyclic compounds attenuate panic attacks. Such findings raise the question of different, co-existing anxiety patterns in agoraphobia.

This progress in psychological and pharmacological treatment of agoraphobia in the 1970s influenced the diagnostic classification itself in the United States, so that in 1980 agoraphobia appeared for the first time as a distinct category. Further developments in the 1980s gave prominence to the panic attack as the central feature of agoraphobia and, indeed, of panic disorder, a parallel syndrome not marked by phobic avoidance of situations. Psychological treatment of both syndromes focused on ther-apeutic exposure to panic sensations, and on encouraging patients to make more realistic and benign ascriptions as to the source of their anxiety; exposure to somatic cues and cognitive therapy have become the leading psychological interventions.

II. DESCRIPTIVE PSYCHOPATHOLOGY AND EPIDEMIOLOGY

A. Description of Agoraphobia

People with agoraphobia usually fear, and often avoid, situations in which it would be difficult or embarrassing to obtain help if overwhelmed by anxiety. Such situations include (a) traveling away from home, especially by bus, train, or car; (b) crowded, public places, such as government buildings, supermarkets, concert halls, shopping malls, and places of worship; and (c) confined places, such as elevators, the dentist's or beautician's chair, and—when driving—passing through tunnels, over bridges, or along a limited-access highway. Agoraphobia is commonly associated with highly distressing attacks of panic that appear to arise spontaneously and unpredictably, often—but not always—in the situations typically feared and avoided. When confronted by such typical agoraphobic situations as a large auditorium or a crowded shopping mall, a person with the disorder may experience rapid heartbeat, a compelling urge to escape from the situation, apprehensions about dying or losing control, and a sense of depersonalization or unreality. A ''fear of fear'' pattern often develops in which the appearance of any bodily sensation associated with anxiety engenders fear of an impending panic attack, thus arousing further anxiety. Some people with agoraphobia restrict their lives substantially, sometimes to the point of remaining housebound, in order to avoid the anxiety or panic aroused by entering public places.

For many patients, dysphoric mood, somatoform disorders, interpersonal conflict, or substance abuse accompany agoraphobia. Untreated, agoraphobia tends to follow a chronic, fluctuating course. It is common for people with agoraphobia to experience daily variations in anxiety severity; most describe having ''good days'' and ''bad days.'' For some patients, there may be weeks or months of near-normal functioning followed by a resurgence of the original symptoms. For others, gradual improvement leading to complete recovery may occur without professional intervention, but this is not typical. In one study, patients interviewed 8 years following successful treatment reported general maintenance of improvement but with some interim exacerbations. When agoraphobic problems had reappeared temporarily, the most common context was acute objective stress such as the loss of employment or a bereavement.

B. Diagnostic Classification

The psychiatric taxonomy accepted in the United States is the *Diagnostic and Statistical Manual of Mental Disorders* (DSM), published since 1952 by the American Psychiatric Association and revised in 1968, 1980, and 1987. Before 1980, agoraphobia was not listed as a distinct disorder in the DSM classification, but could be found among lists of the Greek names for specific phobias in textbooks on psychiatry and abnormal psychology. By the time the third edition of the DSM was published in 1980 it had become clear that agoraphobia was in no sense a simple phobia—its prevalence, its resistance to treatment, its distressing and disabling consequences, and the broad range of its symptoms all clearly set it apart from such specific fears as phobias of heights, snakes, blood, or the number 13.

Agoraphobia does include fear of situations (shopping malls, crowded buses, public meetings, etc.), but patients show varied patterns of specific fears, and there is no standard list of situations that must be feared for the diagnostic criteria to be met. Given that it is quite typical in agoraphobia for the patient to fear having a definite appointment, or even the ringing of the doorbell, it is difficult indeed to specify exactly what external situation constitutes the phobic stimulus. Some commentators note that what is chiefly feared in agoraphobia is the absence of safety signals, not the presence of disturbing objects. Most recently, "fear of the panic attack" (or, in patients who do not panic, fear of limited symptom attacks or circumscribed anxiety episodes) has been cited as a central feature of agoraphobia. The significance of the panic attack in many cases of agoraphobia further sets it apart from the simple phobias.

In the 1980s, with such considerations in mind, the compilers of the DSM considered listing agoraphobia as a distinct diagnostic category. Renewed interest in agoraphobia in turn sparked interest in the panic phenomenon, and it was soon recognized that the overlapping of agoraphobia and panic attacks allowed several possible patterns: Agoraphobia with or without panic attacks, and panic attacks with or without agoraphobia. Accordingly, in the DSM-III of 1980 agoraphobia appeared in two forms, with and without panic attacks, and panic disorder was allotted a distinct category. The most recent change was seen in the DSM-III-R of 1987, which gave precedence to panic in the syndrome that includes panic attacks and agoraphobia.

C. The DSM-III-R Classification

Agoraphobia appears twice in the DSM-III-R, as *panic disorder with agoraphobia* and as *agoraphobia without history of panic disorder;* both are found among the anxiety disorders. The former category is listed as one of the two types of panic disorder.

1. Panic Disorder with Agoraphobia

This diagnosis is used when the patient's pattern of problems meets criteria (a) for panic disorder, and (b) for the "with agoraphobia" subtype. The chief characteristic of panic disorder is the recurrence of panic attacks as distinct episodes of extreme anxiety or distress, not explained by the presence of a continuing organic factor. Panic attacks include at least 4 of a 13-item list of typical anxiety symptoms, which by definition are initially unexpected and are not produced in response to stimuli associated with simple or social phobias. The list of typical symptoms in a panic attack includes shortness of breath, dizziness, heart palpitations or rapid heart rate, trembling or shaking, sweating, the sensation of choking, depersonalization or derealization, and fear of dying, losing control, or developing an acute mental illness. By definition, the anxiety symptoms in a panic attack arise suddenly and rapidly increase in intensity. The diagnostic criteria require a pattern of at least four panic attacks in as many weeks, or, failing that, one or more initial attacks followed by continued fear of further attacks. An organic factor may have been influential in early panic attacks (for example, the patient may have experienced dizziness as a result of a viral infection of the vestibular system, or depersonalization following ingestion of an illicit drug) but, by definition, the attacks will have continued despite successful treatment or removal of the initiating organic factor. [*See* PANIC DISORDER.]

To meet criteria for panic disorder with agoraphobia, the patient has panic disorder and also fears situations in which it could be difficult to obtain help if a panic attack arose. The diagnosis applies even if the person's fear and avoidance of situations are not attributed to fear of having a panic attack.

2. Agoraphobia without History of Panic Disorder

A person with this disorder has never had problems that meet criteria for panic disorder. Instead, he or she fears, and may avoid, situations in which it would be difficult or embarrassing to leave in the event of the sudden onset of anxiety, which may represent a "limited symptom attack" that would not include the range of symptoms associated with a panic attack. Agoraphobia entails difficulties with travel: either avoidance of travel altogether, or being able to travel only with the aid of a trusted companion, or despite significant discomfort.

Finally, it should be noted that patterns meeting criteria for panic disorder but not agoraphobia are classified as *panic disorder without agoraphobia;* patterns consistent with panic disorder but in which an organic factor initiates and maintains the problems are classified as *organic anxiety syndrome,* provided that *delirium* has been ruled out.

D. Epidemiology

Appropriate methodology requires assessing the prevalence and correlates of agoraphobia in the general community as well as in clinic samples (which tend to be unrepresentative). Because of recent changes in the taxonomy, allowance has to be made for the different terms and criteria in studies conducted in different decades. Accordingly, the most informative studies have separated the agoraphobic syndromes from panic disorder without history of agoraphobia and have used accurate community survey techniques. In the studies cited, about half of the respondents with agoraphobia would be classified as having panic disorder with agoraphobia, and half as having agoraphobia without history of panic disorder. However, in clinical samples of agoraphobia panic disorder with agoraphobia predominates, justifying extensive coverage of panic in discussions of treatment.

The largest and most authoritative epidemiological investigation to include assessment of anxiety disorders was the Epidemiological Catchment Area study, reported in the 1980s. The fully structured Diagnostic Interview Schedule was used in a survey of 18,572 appropriately sampled adults in five communities in the United States (New Haven, Baltimore, St. Louis, Durham, and Los Angeles). The

life-time prevalence of agoraphobia was estimated as 4.8%. A smaller study with similar methodology conducted in the former West Germany showed a life-time prevalence of 5.7% for agoraphobia; a similar Canadian study gave 2.9%. A rate of 6.9% was found for a Hispanic population in Puerto Rico with a Spanish form of the interview schedule. Generally, the estimates of the 6-month prevalence of agoraphobia in these studies were one or two percentage points lower than the life-time estimates.

Overall, the findings on the prevalence of agoraphobia are consistent across countries and cultures in studies using the same instrument and careful sampling procedures. Across studies, the life-time prevalence of agoraphobia, with or without panic attacks, is about 5%; the 6-month prevalence is about 4%. These rates are markedly higher in women than in men; for the five sites in the Epidemiological Catchment Area study the ratio of women to men with agoraphobia was 2.7 : 1.

Agoraphobia is associated with more severe impairment than other phobias and has a markedly higher comorbidity rate for depression. Substance abuse, hypochondriasis, somatization disorder, and personality disorders are often associated with agoraphobia. The usual course is chronic. The age of onset in agoraphobia varies but is usually in the 20s or 30s with a mean of about 28 years. There is no general agreement on an association between agoraphobia and specific childhood experiences. Maternal overprotection has been studied, but findings are mixed. [*See* PERSONALITY DISORDERS; SUBSTANCE ABUSE.]

The estimated morbidity risk of anxiety disorders in the first-degree relatives of patients with agoraphobia is 32%; there is also a greater risk of an alcohol disorder. Concordance rates for panic disorder with and without agoraphobia are significantly higher in monozygotic than in dizygotic twins; a Norwegian study showed 31% concordance in 32 monozygotic twins but 0% in 53 dizygotic twins. Such results have been taken to indicate some genetic predisposition for agoraphobia and panic disorder.

III. ETIOLOGICAL THEORIES

A. Biological Theories

The observations that anxiety syndromes seem to run in families and that pharmacological treatment

AGORAPHOBIA 61

can be helpful have understandably led to considerable interest in biological mechanisms underlying agoraphobia and related disorders. Attention has been paid to the heritability of agoraphobia, to possible biological variables increasing vulnerability to agoraphobia, and to potential specific mechanisms that may explain agoraphobia.

There is general agreement that a predisposition toward agoraphobia (and panic) may be inherited, but it is not possible to predict who will develop agoraphobia even among people with a number of close relatives with the disorder. (It is also widely accepted that mental disorders in general defy attempts to fit a classical model of single-gene heredity.) Agoraphobia probably conforms to a diathesis-stress model in which an inherited vulnerability is necessary, but not sufficient, for the eventual appearance of the syndrome. That would require the additional operation of certain environmental factors in interaction with the predisposing conditions.

Physiological variables distinguishing agoraphobia from normal functioning, and from less pervasive anxiety disorders like simple phobia, include resting heart rate and forearm blood flow (both higher in agoraphobia) and skin conductance (higher and more variable in agoraphobia). However, such findings have not produced clear conclusions with implications for etiology or treatment.

The most promising candidates for the inherited vulnerability factor (if there is but one) in people with agoraphobia can be described as personality traits such as neuroticism, emotionality, trait anxiety, or "nervousness." Studies of animals and humans have consistently indicated a genetic component in emotionality; it is well known that rats can be bred for emotional reactivity, for example, and in the human studies, there is even stronger evidence for the heritability of trait anxiety or neuroticism than there is for the heritability of anxiety disorders.

Neuroticism is thought to result from lability of the limbic system, of the autonomic nervous system, or of specific neurotransmitter processes. For example, one animal study showed that rats bred for emotionality had more brain benzodiazepine receptors than rats bred normally. Malcolm Lader has noted that many of the data on panic may be explained by positing an instability or hypersensitivity of central noradrenergic mechanisms centering on locus coeruleus function. Despite these observations, few definite conclusions may be drawn from the many physiological and endocrinological studies. The best-supported generalization is that patients with agoraphobia and related anxiety disorders have chronically overaroused central nervous systems and are slow to habituate to noxious stimuli.

Several physiological processes and physical disorders produce symptoms like those of panic, arousing interest in possible mechanisms for agoraphobia. These include hyperventilation, asthma, limbic seizures, abnormalities of thyroid function, hypoglycemia, and mitral valve prolapse. Of particular interest has been the phenomenon of provocation of panic by sodium lactate infusions; people with a history of panic disorder, but not those with no prior experience of panic, tend to react to the infusion with panic. Furthermore, pharmacological treatment by means of imipramine can abolish the lactate provocation of panic. Although such observations may appear to confirm a biological basis for panic disorder (and, therefore, of at least one of the agoraphobic syndromes), the mechanism is a subtle one that interacts with environmental and cognitive factors. The lactate provocation of panic can also be blocked by psychological treatment; hence, it would be misleading to focus exclusively on biological processes in interpreting panic phenomena.

There is as yet no clear evidence of a particular biological variant that explains all of the features of agoraphobia. There is likely to be an inherited predisposition toward a labile limbic or autonomic nervous system, associated with chronic overarousal and slow habituation. This diathesis may in turn interact with certain behavioral and cognitive mechanisms to produce agoraphobic syndromes. David Barlow has pointed out that "The fact that language and meaning structures are the most common stimuli for anxiety in humans requires a complex neurobiological system."

B. Psychodynamic and Interpersonal Theories

Psychoanalytic theory proposes that mental experience and behavior are influenced profoundly by the dynamic interaction of largely unconscious intrapsychic forces. All disorders are viewed as having important unconscious determinants, but this is particularly poignant in such disorders as agoraphobia because of the pivotal importance of anxiety to psychoanalytic theory. Early childhood experiences, particularly interactions with parents and other significant people, are given prominence not only because they form the prototypes for adult social interactions, but also because they influence the development of the mental apparatus itself. Particularly relevant to agoraphobia are the person's inner representations of other people. It is vital to one's sense of safety and security to develop stable "object relations," or internal representations of others. If object relations are disturbed, due, for example, to a poor quality or consistency of early actual relationships, then the person may be vulnerable to insecurity and anxiety later in life. Studies have shown that in humans and animals early separation from parents can be linked to agoraphobia-like behavior. [See OBJECT RELATIONS THEORY.]

Freud's initial theory of anxiety dealt with its somatic aspects. He described "anxiety neurosis" as an *actual* neurosis ("condition of the nerves"), not a psychoneurosis, because it results from undischarged neural excitation (caused by emotional trauma, for example). To Freud, such actual neuroses involve disturbed bodily processes, particularly difficulties in breathing. He later described psychoneuroses in which undischarged tension results from unacceptable ideas rather than from external stimulation.

Eventually Freud turned his attention away from physical explanations of anxiety and emphasized its role as an ego function that is aroused in response to danger, a sense of helplessness when confronted by internal or external threat. Relevant to agoraphobia, Freud's ideas are consistent with the views that the ego responds with anxiety to (1) real danger, (2) physiological processes involving the autonomic nervous system, and (3) the arousal of emotions like anger or frustration. [See ID, EGO, AND SUPEREGO.]

An important issue for clinicians taking a psychodynamic approach is to separate manifestations of anxiety that stem from biological disturbances from those that stem from intrapsychic problems, such as an underlying conflict or a disorder of object relations. Psychodynamicists argue that, because environmental stimuli influence neurophysiological reactivity, and because the *meaning* of those stimuli mediates their impact, there is an important role for psychodynamic hypotheses and therapy in application to agoraphobia.

An integrative theory put forward by Alan Goldstein and Dianne Chambless in 1978 uses behavioral and psychodynamic concepts to explain the various phenomena of agoraphobia, including typical personality factors and interpersonal styles. It is argued that the person with agoraphobia (a) fears panic attacks rather than particular places; (b) has difficulties with self-sufficiency, independence, and assertiveness; (c) is unable to trace the antecedents of emotional feelings when they arise; and (d) develops the initial symptoms of agoraphobia in a climate of interpersonal conflict. The interaction of these factors produces agoraphobia. The typical patient in this model is a woman who feels trapped in a troubled marriage. Although she wishes to leave, she lacks the necessary autonomy, independence, and self-sufficiency to make leaving a realistic option. Dealing directly with her feelings and asserting her opinions toward her husband are unfamiliar and difficult for her, so she attempts to tolerate this unsatisfactory situation. An argument with her husband early in the day elicits dysphoric mood but not a specific, identifiable emotion. Out in public later in the day, she still feels ill at ease, but is unsure of the origin of this feeling. Waiting in line somewhere (or using an elevator, traveling through an underpass, etc.), she feels trapped, and at some level this is reminiscent of being trapped in the unsatisfactory marriage. A panic attack suddenly arises. She later begins to avoid places similar to the site of the panic attack. Eventually becoming housebound, she is no longer able to contemplate leaving her husband, and this has the advantage of settling the matter so that she is no longer troubled by her mixed feelings about leaving.

This view of agoraphobia draws attention to the potential role of adjunctive treatments like assertiveness training, marital therapy, or therapeutic work on recognizing and identifying feeling states. The work of some behavior therapists attests to the value of assertiveness training in programs for agoraphobia, and marital therapy has brought benefit to at least some patients with agoraphobia, as judged by anecdotal reports. However, marital distress has not been shown to have general etiological significance in agoraphobia. [See MARITAL DYSFUNCTION.]

C. Behavioral and Cognitive Theories

1. Conditioning Theories

The most familiar behavioral theory of the etiology of agoraphobia calls attention to classical conditioning as a possible mechanism. According to this view, previously innocuous stimuli such as streets, shops, and crowds acquire fear-eliciting properties through systematic pairing with noxious events. Although these noxious events are usually not specified, there are various plausible possibilities, such as witnessing an accident while in town, or being taken ill while shopping. Suddenly becoming ill, for example, creates reflex responses of distress and discomfort. By their pairing with the stimuli that elicit distress, certain stimuli in the immediate environment could become conditioned stimuli that on later occasions call forth anxiety as a conditioned response. [*See* CLASSICAL CONDITIONING.]

An immediate objection to classical conditioning as an explanation of agoraphobia is that extinction of the acquired anxiety would be expected when the person encounters the newly feared situations without the original noxious stimuli. However, Mowrer's two-factor theory posits the operation of a second process, instrumental or operant learning, to explain the persistence of conditioned fear. Once fear is acquired by means of classical conditioning, avoiding the feared situations will be reinforced because avoiding these situations means removing anxiety. At the same time, avoidance of conditioned stimuli prevents the exposure to them that would be necessary to allow extinction to occur. [*See* OPERANT LEARNING.]

So many objections have been raised to two-factor theory in this context that it can no longer be supported as a general explanation of agoraphobia. In agoraphobia, levels of fear and avoidance behavior are not closely correlated, yet two-factor theory explains avoidance behavior as motivated by conditioned fear. Conditioning does not explain the common phenomenon of daily fluctuations in anxiety severity, or the fact that general stress is often associated with an exacerbation of agoraphobia. It is not clear from two-factor theory why agoraphobia so often represents a syndrome of fears of travel, crowds, confinement, and so forth, if indeed conditioning takes place haphazardly and involves whichever stimuli happen to be prepotent at the time. Conditioning theories do not obviously explain the comorbidity of agoraphobia with depression or hypochondriasis. Even the survivors of serious accidents or natural disasters do not necessarily develop an anxiety disorder, despite having been subjected to highly anxiety-provoking experiences. By contrast, most people with agoraphobia cannot recall having had an aversive experience with the situation or object they fear. Conditioned fear is very difficult to produce in humans in laboratory experiments, and there are many contradictory findings. Several attempts to replicate landmark studies of classical fear conditioning in humans were notorious failures.

There is the paradox that, although unadorned conditioning accounts of agoraphobia have been discredited, treatments that seem based on extinction procedures have been quite successful. Exposure *in vivo*, in which the patient learns to confront agoraphobic situations without leaving at the onset of anxiety, can be helpful in overcoming a pattern of avoidance of situations *and* can attenuate panic attacks. However, the success of such treatment does not confirm a two-factor theory account of the etiology of agoraphobia.

When the panic attack itself is considered to be the noxious event that allows classical conditioning of fear to external situations, the conditioning explanation becomes more credible. That leads to the proposition that it will be most helpful to explain the origin and maintenance of panic attacks. A panic attack may be viewed as the result of a vicious circle or upward spiral in which, at each point, stimuli associated with anxiety elicit conditioned anxiety responses, which in turn produce further anxiety-eliciting stimuli. This is an interoceptive conditioning view in which it is assumed that the conditioned stimuli are the bodily sensations that result from initial anxiety arousal, and that each conditioned response has a greater amplitude than its immediate predecessor. It follows from this view of panic attacks that it will be helpful therapeutically for the patient to confront anxiety sensations themselves rather than simply the external situations in which they commonly arise. If the patient fears the bodily sensations of anxiety (heart pounding, dizziness, shortness of breath, and so forth), then the exposure principle would predict that systematic confrontation of these sensations will ultimately diminish their power to evoke anxiety.

Problems with this view of panic attacks include the following. If any arousal of anxiety leads inexorably to a vicious circle that culminates in a panic attack, then people with panic disorder would never experience limited episodes of mild or moderate anxiety. However, it is usual for panic disorder patients to display moderate levels of generalized anxiety between their panic attacks. The theory also fails to explain who will be vulnerable to the escalation of mild anxiety into panic attacks. The cognitive therapy approach to which we turn next attempts to address this problem.

2. Cognitive Theories

Aaron Beck's cognitive therapy rests upon several theoretical assumptions that center upon the individual's appraisal of events. Such appraisals range from fleeting "automatic thoughts" in the form of accessible, though covert, verbalizations (e.g., "Oh, no. I knew I'd get anxious if I came to the mall, and I feel slightly dizzy already!") to deeper and more enduring "cognitive schemas," not necessarily verbalized, reflecting a more fundamental attitude (e.g., strange feelings could indicate a serious medical catastrophe).

Central to the application of cognitive therapy assumptions to panic attacks is the patient's appraisal of the bodily sensations or somatic cues connected with mounting anxiety. David Clark has argued that people with panic disorder have developed cognitive schemas concerning vulnerability to medical catastrophes, and he and others have demonstrated that people with panic disorder show cognitive biases in that direction. (The notion of fear of medical catastrophes as one variant of agoraphobia was introduced by Joseph Wolpe in 1970.) This model complements the conditioning of somatic cues model by indicating who is vulnerable to panic and why not all anxiety episodes culminate in panic. Variations in cognitive appraisals between and within individuals may account for the unpredictability of panic attacks. In Clark's model, the sequence begins when the client experiences sensations from a flushed face or pounding heart. It is immaterial to the model whether these sensations result from pathological (developing a fever in response to an infection) or normal (having run up the stairs) processes. Next, the patient makes a "catastrophic misinterpretation" of the bodily sensations, viewing them as signals of a medical disaster such as a heart attack. The misinterpretation itself arouses increased anxiety, and the vicious circle continues when further alarming appraisals are made.

3. A Comprehensive Model

Perhaps the most comprehensive contemporary theory is that of David Barlow, who suggests that panic results from activation of an ancient alarm system, and is the basic emotion of fear, while anxiety is a more general cognitive–affective structure. Panic occurs in response to three types of alarm. *True alarms* are panic attacks elicited by genuine danger. *False alarms* are panic attacks in the absence of objective danger, and result from a genetically determined predisposition in interaction with an accumulation of general stress. (Anyone may experience a false alarm, not only people with anxiety disorders.) *Learned alarms* are panic attacks that are triggered by cues, which may be specific objects, as in simple phobia, or internal physiological changes, as in panic disorder. Anxious apprehension also plays a part in

explaining the development of anxiety disorders; a cognitive schema containing propositions concerning anxiety elicits negative affect when triggered, and the sequence of events that follows includes directing attention to internal self-evaluations, increased arousal, narrowing of attention, and hypervigilance concerning sources of apprehension.

In summary, Barlow's model of agoraphobia is his model of panic disorder with the addition of the development of agoraphobic avoidance. Biological vulnerability interacts with objective stress to produce an initial uncued panic attack, or false alarm. The connection of the panic attack with interoceptive cues leads to the development of cued learned alarms. As a result, there is a psychological vulnerability characterized by anxious apprehension about future panic attacks. Next, panic attacks are triggered unpredictably by a combination of autonomic and cognitive symptoms of anxiety with additional somatic cues. Depending on the presence or absence of safety signals and various cultural and environmental factors, avoidance behavior may develop, giving rise to the panic disorder with agoraphobia syndrome.

IV. ASSESSMENT AND DIAGNOSIS

The assessment of agoraphobia in clinical practice proceeds through several stages. First, the diagnosis is established. Second, identification of the specifics of a patient's level of distress and disability allows development of an individualized treatment plan. Third, evaluating concomitant problems or issues, ranging from diagnosable disorders to matters of life circumstances, permits deployment of adjunct treatments or influences the sequence in which treatments for agoraphobia are provided. Fourth, monitoring the patient's progress throughout the course of therapy is essential in determining response to treatment and alerting the clinician to needed procedural changes.

A. Diagnosis

People with agoraphobia may be self-referred, referred by friends or relatives, or referred by other professionals. It is not uncommon for a patient to seek treatment having made a self-diagnosis of agoraphobia after reading a magazine article or viewing a television presentation about agoraphobia. It is also quite common for a patient to be referred to a mental health professional by emergency room staff after one or more visits for urgent treatment during panic attacks. Because many people with agoraphobia are either entirely housebound or have a limited range of travel, clinicians working with this disorder become accustomed to making home visits, at least in the early stages of assessment and treatment.

Because there are several physical conditions that give rise to symptoms like those of agoraphobia, it is important that the patient receive a physical examination before mental health interventions begin. If anxiety persists despite successful treatment of a precipitating or complicating physical condition, then treatment of agoraphobia proceeds. It should be noted that having certain physical conditions is not incompatible with having agoraphobia, but accompanying physical disorders demand attention first.

Assessment is needed to identify other psychiatric disorders that may co-exist with agoraphobia, including mood, somatoform, substance use, and personality disorders. Also relevant for assessment are issues like marital conflict, social skills deficits, and difficulty with personal autonomy that may not require a formal diagnosis but may yet be important foci for intervention. By no means do all people who experience anxiety when in public places or who have had panic attacks have problems that meet diagnostic criteria for agoraphobia syndromes. Social and simple phobias may center upon some of the situations commonly avoided in agoraphobia, and panic attacks may occur in mood disorders, psychosis, and in people without psychiatric disorders. Treatments usually deployed with agoraphobia may be misdirected in these other diagnostic contexts.

B. Assessing the Range and Extent of Agoraphobia

Simply applying the appropriate diagnostic label is insufficient to guide treatment. The clinician seeks to know the patient as a unique individual and accordingly conducts the usual psychosocial history and mental status examination. Beyond that, the nature and extent of the agoraphobic problems will need to be charted in sufficient detail to allow formulation of an appropriate individual treatment plan and continued evaluation of progress toward treatment goals.

The Anxiety Disorders Interview Schedule—Revised (ADIS-R) is the most widely used structured interview protocol in the assessment of agoraphobia

and other anxiety disorders. Developed by Barlow and his colleagues, the ADIS-R allows detailed and accurate characterization of the person's anxiety problems and permits authoritative diagnosis in DSM-III-R terms. The instrument is primarily employed in research trials to ensure uniformity of diagnostic practices. Although the complete protocol is too lengthy for routine clinical use, subsets of the ADIS-R may be used appropriately and conveniently in most clinical settings.

Self-report questionnaires like the Fear Questionnaire, the Anxiety Sensitivity Index, and the Mobility Inventory are all useful for treatment planning and charting progress in respect of the specific agoraphobic symptoms. Questionnaires on other related issues, such as assertiveness, depression, or marital harmony, are generally helpful in initial evaluations and may be germane to the issues of particular clients throughout the course of treatment.

It is highly desirable to have the patient self-monitor general anxiety, panic attacks, and agoraphobic avoidance daily. Individualized forms may be used so that details of the specifics of the patient's situation may be accommodated therein. For example, daily ratings may be made of a patient's degree of avoidance of, fear in, and self-confidence about each item in a customized graded hierarchy of feared situations. Daily ratings of the frequency and intensity of panic attacks allow records to be made by the client of the circumstances surrounding each episode, situational, cognitive, and interpersonal.

The nature of agoraphobia allows the use of a hierarchically ordered behavioral test for most patients. This takes the form of an unaccompanied journey—walking, driving, or using public transportation—to take in as many situations relevant to the patient's fear and avoidance as possible. The clinician asks the patient to proceed as far as possible, and takes the distance actually traveled as a helpful datum in sampling current levels of agoraphobic avoidance.

Physiological monitoring has been a customary component of research trials designed to provide generalizable information on treatment effectiveness, but is far less common in routine clinical practice. The typical finding that measures of anxiety in the different domains—self-report, behavioral observation, and psychophysiological—do not covary as might be predicted should not daunt the clinician unduly. When all such measures are available, it is recommended that treatment proceed until clear reductions have been seen in each measurement modality.

V. TREATMENT

A. Pharmacological Treatment

Pharmacological treatment has several advantages for the patient and significant progress has been made in this area since 1970, improving the general outlook for agoraphobia. Many people with agoraphobia have their first clinical contacts with physicians, either in emergency rooms following an initial panic attack or in family practice settings, and medication is readily available and convenient to use. (Despite this, surveys show that the general public and people with agoraphobia tend to disfavor drug therapy.)

Agoraphobia subsumes anxiety and avoidance behavior, and is often associated with dysphoric mood if not clinical depression. The medications most commonly used, and extensively studied, in the treatment of agoraphobia are those that are generally prescribed for anxiety and depressive symptoms.

1. Tricyclic Compounds

Together with the monoamine oxidase inhibitors, the tricyclic compounds are chiefly used in treating depression, but the term "antidepressants" commonly applied to them may be misleading in this context because there is controversy about their role in agoraphobia treatment (do they attenuate dysphoric mood, facilitating other treatments, or do they act specifically to block panic attacks?).

Imipramine has been the most extensively studied, but the related tricyclics desipramine and clomipramine may be similar in effectiveness. Early studies appeared to show that imipramine reduced panic attacks, but patients continued to avoid agoraphobic situations.

Later studies demonstrated imipramine's superiority to placebo medication and indicated that it brought additional benefit when added to behavioral treatment. However, this additional benefit was not attributable to the blockade of panic. When imipramine is used in conjunction with the anti-therapeutic recommendation to avoid confronting feared situations, improvement in mood, but not in agoraphobia, is the result. Empirically, imipramine plus exposure therapy seems more effective than either treatment alone. It has been argued that inconsistencies in research findings with imipramine may result from marked differences in doseage across studies.

2. Monoamine Oxidase Inhibitors (MAOIs)

The MAOIs phenelzine and iproniazid have received most attention. Whereas some studies have shown little if any difference between phenelzine and placebo in application to agoraphobia, another has shown that phenelzine reduces general disability and avoidance behavior. In that study phenelzine was more effective than imipramine. For reasons that are unclear, phenelzine appears to potentiate self-initiated exposure.

3. Benzodiazepines and Triazolobenzodiazepines

The benzodiazepines are minor tranquilizers that have been extensively prescribed for various forms of anxiety and stress reactions, clinical and subclinical, for decades. Donald Klein's initial work on imipramine had suggested that it is specific for blocking panic, whereas the benzodiazepines are effective only with generalized or anticipatory anxiety. Later work suggests that high doses of benzodiazepines may be effective in treating panic attacks. The recent development of high-potency benzodiazepines like alprazolam and clonazepam has brought substantial benefit in the treatment of agoraphobia and panic. Alprazolam, a triazolobenzodiazepine, has been the subject of a multi-center world-wide double-blind study of people with panic disorder (with and without agoraphobia). Fifty percent of the alprazolam patients and 30% of placebo patients were panic-free 3 weeks after the start of the trial.

Strong withdrawal reactions after discontinuance of alprazolam pose a significant problem, as does the phenomenon of "rebound panic" in which a minority of patients may experience even worse panic attacks after withdrawal from medication than before treatment.

4. Summary

Imipramine, phenelzine, and alprazolam are helpful in the treatment of agoraphobia. The related medications desipramine, clomipramine, tranylcypromine (an MAOI), and clonazepam have received less attention but may be as helpful. Some medications not noted above, like the beta-blocker propranolol, have been shown ineffective for agoraphobia. The mechanisms underlying successful pharmacological treatment are unclear.

B. Psychological Treatment

Psychodynamic approaches to agoraphobia have received far less attention than biological, behavioral, and cognitive approaches in recent decades, and there is no corpus of empirical research on psychodynamic formulations of etiology or on the results of psychodynamic treatment. However, its proponents suggest that psychodynamic approaches are particularly germane to some of the common clinical issues in agoraphobia, and applying psychodynamic reasoning could be especially fruitful in this context. It is argued that these approaches may be particularly helpful with treatment-resistant patients, in guiding the strategy of supportive psychotherapy, and in using the therapeutic relationship in a supportive context and as a potential therapeutic tool.

Behavior therapists treating agoraphobia in the late 1950s and early 1960s emphasized its commonalities with the phobias, and sought to reduce situational fear and avoidance behavior by means of techniques effective for simple phobia. In the 1970s the differences between agoraphobia and other phobias began to be recognized, and treatment by systematic desensitization was replaced by imaginal flooding and exposure *in vivo*. Attention was paid to panic attacks as well as to avoidance behavior. Since the 1980s the focus has been on direct psychological treatment of panic attacks.

1. Treatment of Agoraphobic Avoidance Behavior

Despite initial enthusiasm for Joseph Wolpe's technique of systematic desensitization as a therapeutic breakthrough for phobias, its application to agoraphobia in controlled clinical trials in the 1960s brought disappointing results. The technique was largely abandoned as treatment for agoraphobia when developments in the 1970s established flooding in fantasy and graded practice in real life as effective treatments. Researchers in Vermont led by Stuart Agras showed that graded practice—with or without praise for specific accomplishments—could quickly reduce agoraphobics' avoidance of unaccompanied journeys away from the clinic. This work converged with that of Isaac Marks in the United Kingdom to identify exposure *in vivo* as the central ingredient of psychological treatment for agoraphobic avoidance.

Procedural variations such as brief or prolonged exposure duration, massing or spacing of treatment sessions, and terminating exposure at the point of increasing or decreasing anxiety were examined assiduously by clinical researchers, but the consensus is that these technical details are less important than the general recommendation to confront, rather than avoid, feared situations. This exposure principle is as well-founded as any in the entire field of mental health work.

Improved functioning after exposure treatment for agoraphobia has been shown to persist for several years post-treatment. Not all patients accept or remain in exposure treatment; the attrition rate during therapy has been estimated at 12%. Of those who complete a course of treatment, approximately 70% have successful outcomes.

Exposure treatment may proceed intensively and rapidly. In some studies, an entire course of treatment was completed in 2 weeks of prolonged, daily sessions. While the data on adverse complications from rapid treatment are equivocal, particularly those concerning the possibility of social and marital disruptions, gradual treatment is recommended in order to facilitate patients' thorough consolidation of therapeutic gains at each step. Treatment of avoidance through exposure preferably includes weaning patients from "safety signals," items like written instructions from the therapist, bottles of minor tranquilizers (even empty ones), or canes or umbrellas that are carried more for their associations with a sense of security than for any more obviously practical benefit.

2. Treatment of Panic

The current diagnostic classification assigns central importance to panic attacks in most cases of agoraphobia seen in clinical settings. If panic is primary, and avoidance behavior a secondary complication thereof, then treatment could logically be directed at panic phenomena. This is not incompatible with treatment of avoidance by exposure, which can itself reduce panic attacks. But, as David Barlow has put it, "treating avoidance behavior will always be necessary. Nevertheless, the primary goal should be the treatment of panic."

The essential technique in the psychological treatment of panic is *exposure to somatic cues*, or reproduction of and confrontation by the bodily symptoms that the patient associates with panic attacks. The patient is asked to create sensations of panic deliberately in treatment sessions. Running in place, voluntary hyperventilation, and spinning around in a swivel chair are examples of procedures for creating such sensations. Clinicians match particular procedures to patient's most troublesome symptoms; someone who is most troubled by dizziness will practice spinning around, while someone disturbed by the sensations of a rapid heart-rate will run up and down the stairs.

In early trials, this approach has brought the most impressive results yet seen in the treatment of panic and agoraphobia, the success rates approaching 100% in some studies. Advances in methodology that have allowed the daily monitoring of panic attacks have permitted accurate tracking of panic attack frequency. "Percentage of patients panic free" has become a standard datum to report in contemporary treatment trials.

The success of exposure to somatic cues as treatment for panic has prompted a reinterpretation of some early studies that lacked a theoretical context at the time. Inhalation of carbon dioxide as treatment for generalized anxiety, the "running treatment" for agoraphobia, the utility of imaginal flooding to phobia-irrelevant themes in reducing phobic sensitivity, and the lactate provocation of panic as treatment for anxiety episodes—all found in the literature of the last few decades—may be readily understood today as consistent with the exposure principle in its most recent application to panic sensations.

The efficacy of exposure to somatic cues has been attributed to various theoretical processes. These include the exposure principle, possibly resting upon the extinction or habituation of conditioned anxiety responses to panic sensations, or upon the development of coping skills by the patient. The success of the method is consistent with the specific hypothesis that chronic hyperventilation underlies panic disorder. It is also consistent with the cognitive therapy view that the patient makes catastrophic misinterpretations of the bodily sensations of panic, ascribing to them morbid significance as harbingers of a medical emergency.

Parallel to exposure to somatic cues is *cognitive therapy* in the contemporary treatment approach to panic. Consistent with David Clark's model of an interaction of sensitivity to somatic cues and catastrophic misinterpretation thereof, patients are engaged in a cognitive treatment process of collaborative empiricism in which implicit schemas construing panic sensations as signals of dire illness are carefully assessed, gently challenged, and empirically tested. Cognitive therapy involves exploring, in a sympathetic and accepting way, the specific idiosyncratic cognitions that are assumed to underlie emotional distress. Wherever possible, real-life "experiments" are undertaken in attempting to challenge unrealistic assumptions. There is no standard, structured format that must be applied systematically to all patients; rather, the principles of cognitive therapy guide a creative treatment approach with each individual. The results of preliminary trials of cognitive therapy have been as encouraging as those of exposure to somatic cues, and the combination of these treatments has brought the best outcomes.

3. Comprehensive Treatment of Agoraphobia

In addition to the central psychological treatment approaches of exposure *in vivo*, exposure to somatic cues, and cognitive therapy, relaxation training and breathing retraining have been found helpful in the treatment of agoraphobia and are recommended as optional components of a treatment plan. There is a consensus that in the typical case of panic disorder with agoraphobia treatment should proceed deploying all of these techniques in sequence, beginning with self-paced exposure *in vivo*. Some authorities argue that, because it is not associated with deleterious side-effects or complications from withdrawal, psychological treatment should be used first, and pharmacological treatment brought in as necessary subsequently. [*See* RELAXATION.]

VI. CONCLUSIONS AND PROSPECTS

Although it is fragmented by the current nomenclature into two distinct disorders, agoraphobia is a coherent syndrome with a range of symptomatology extending far beyond the limited compass of specific phobias. Recognized since 1871 as an unusually debilitating anxiety disorder, agoraphobia has only recently yielded to effective pharmacological, behavioral, and cognitive treatments.

The conclusions of a recent Consensus Development Conference on the Treatment of Panic Disorder, sponsored by the National Institutes of Health and the National Institute of Mental Health in the United States, are pertinent and may be summarized as follows. Although perhaps most patients receiving psychological treatment are also taking medication, little is known about the effectiveness of combined pharmacological and psychological treatment. Not enough is known about the mechanisms of action of contemporary treatments, patient factors predicting success or permitting matching to the most appropriate treatment, the long-term effectiveness of the new treatments for panic, and the value of treatment for associated mental health problems and issues.

Also in need of further attention by clinicians and researchers are the following. Whereas pharmacological treatment is readily available, it is difficult for many patients to gain access to psychological treatment, especially in rural areas. Innovations in service delivery are needed, and studies should address the viability of psychological treatment of agoraphobia from remote sites by means of the latest communications technology. Many communities are underserved by mental health professionals, and not only individuals housebound by agoraphobia have difficulties in obtaining psychological services.

Bibliography

Barlow, D. H. (1988). ''Anxiety and Its Disorders.'' Guilford Press, New York.

Chambless, D. L., and Goldstein, A. J. (Eds.) (1982). ''Agoraphobia: Multiple Perspectives on Theory and Treatment.'' Wiley, New York.

Gournay, K. (Ed.) (1989). ''Agoraphobia: Current Perspectives on Theory and Treatment.'' Routledge, London.

Hecker, J. E., and Thorpe, G. L. (1992). ''Agoraphobia and Panic: A Guide to Psychological Treatment.'' Allyn and Bacon, Boston.

Knapp, T. J. (Ed.) and Schumacher, M. T. (Trans.) (1988). ''Westphal's 'Die Agoraphobie'.'' University Press of America, Lanham, MD.

Marks, I. M. (1987). ''Fears, Phobias, and Rituals: Panic, Anxiety, and Their Disorders.'' Oxford University Press, New York.

Mathews, A. M., Gelder, M. G., and Johnston, D. W. (1981). ''Agoraphobia: Nature and Treatment.'' Guilford, New York.

Thorpe, G. L., and Burns, L. E. (1983). ''The Agoraphobic Syndrome: Behavioural Approaches to Evaluation and Treatment.'' Wiley, Chichester, UK.

Walker, J. R., Norton, G. R., and Ross, C. A. (Eds.) (1991). ''Panic Disorder and Agoraphobia: A Comprehensive Guide for the Practitioner.'' Brooks/Cole, Pacific Grove, CA.

AGRAPHIA

Daniel N. Bub and Martin Arguin
Montreal Neurological Institute

Glossary

Allographic code To write, we must know how to generate the spatial form of each upper- or lower-case letter in the correct order. These output codes are termed *allographs* and are relatively abstract in nature; allographic code must specify the shape of each letter independent of its size or the actual muscle system (hand, foot, etc.) executing the response.

Deep agraphia An unusual acquired disorder with the following characteristics: Writing and spelling of concrete words (referring to objects) is much better than performance to words denoting abstract concepts. Verbs, adjectives, and grammatical function words (e.g., words like *if, but, from,* etc.) are also written very poorly, and pronounceable nonsense words cannot be written at all. In addition, some errors are semantically related to the target words (e.g., "table" may be written as "chair," "boat" as "ship," and so on). Deep agraphia need not co-occur with the analogous reading disorder termed *deep dyslexia*.

Graphemic buffer Writing or oral spelling inherently demands that letter codes be retrieved individually from left to right; for this procedure to occur smoothly, a specialized working memory component—a graphemic output buffer—is needed to temporarily maintain the linear form of the orthographic representation generated from higher levels of processing.

Orthographic form The internal representation of the spelling of words (and pronounceable nonwords) that is acted on by more peripheral output mechanisms. Whole word orthographic units exist independently of their corresponding spoken form.

Phonological agraphia A disorder in which spelling relies on access to the orthography of the entire word. The patient writes words correctly, but cannot assemble the orthography of an unfamiliar word or nonsense word.

Surface agraphia A disorder in which spelling and writing performance is mediated by subword orthographic units rather than word-specific orthography. In languages like English, there are often several ways of spelling a word on the basis of its pronunciation, and correct performance for such items requires knowledge of entire word forms as orthographic representations. Patients with surface agraphia make numerous errors when asked to spell words that are not predictable from their pronunciations (e.g., the word "comb" may be rendered as "coam," "beef" as "beaf").

AGRAPHIA is the general clinical term referring to an acquired disorder of writing and/or oral spelling. The impairment can be highly specific in particular cases, reflecting damage to any one of a number of discrete functional components that, working together, allow us to produce the orthographic description of words as an organized sequence of letters on the page.

I. INTRODUCTION

There is now a very substantial body of evidence indicating that language is mediated by a large number of separate functional components that together enable the complex communicative acts that are such a unique aspect of human cognition. Written language is a fairly recent occurrence in the development of human culture, and from a neuropsychological standpoint, must be thought of as a latent or potential capability of preexisting linguistic mechanisms that has now been realized or discovered by us. Since we are using old "machinery" to carry out a new trick, we should not be surprised to learn that much of our writing skills depends on the same language processes that we need for spoken comprehension and production. But there is also a sense in which the ability to translate words and sentences into an orthography that is ultimately expressed by fine-grained hand movements to form print or script must depend on a number of functional systems that exist independently of the major components of language. We must acquire procedures that map speech sounds into their equivalent orthographic units. We must also learn how to spell a large number of words with an orthography that is essentially quite arbitrary with respect to their pronunciation, like *yacht* or *soup*. These words (which should on the basis of regular correspondences be spelled *yot* and *soop*) and a huge number of other equally unpredictable patterns must be learned and maintained as permanently available orthographic code that cannot be equated with the representation of the words' spoken form. And we must acquire the skilled, highly articulated movements that are necessary to construct the spatial form of letters on the page, or to translate the pattern into a sequence of letter names that we can retrieve for oral spelling.

The study of neurological cases has yielded important insights into the question of the relationship between spoken and written language. We now have begun to arrive at an understanding of the specialized mechanisms on which the acquisition of orthographic skills must depend. In this article, we will review the evidence and arguments that cognitive neuropsychologists have marshalled to reach our current interpretation of the processes that underly writing and spelling. Our discussion will be chiefly focussed on the performance of brain damaged patients—in certain cases, it is possible to observe impairment of discrete subcomponents of the functional mechanisms responsible for written language. This in itself is a remarkable fact, because it implies that even linguistic procedures that are derivative, in the sense that they have been developed as by-products of the natural, innate components of language, can exhibit a modular organization. By analyzing the varieties of agraphia (acquired disorders of writing and/or spelling), we hope to construct a detailed picture of the *normal* mechanisms developed by the brain to enable the production of ortho-graphic code transformed by brain damage to yield the specific pattern of results observed in different cases.

II. HISTORICAL BACKGROUND

We began by noting that there is likely to be considerable specialization of the functional components mediating written language. It is worth pointing out that a long time was needed for this point to be understood. The earliest theorists on the neuropsychology of language were largely of the opinion that the difference between spoken and written forms only depended on the fact that written language required a knowledge of the spatial representation of letters to generate a spelling pattern. In all other respects, the most influential thinkers believed that the two methods of language production must be considered equivalent.

The erroneous assumption that writing or spelling disorders were primarily contingent on more general language or cognitive impairments effectively blinded neurologists to a range of observations that have only quite recently emerged on the specificity of writing mechanisms. Thus, some neurologists argued, for example, that isolated disorders of writing in brain-damaged cases were often due to intellectual impairment and confusion, which they believed affected written performance more severely than less demanding, automatic aspects of language.

Of course, there were dissenting voices, even at the beginning. Charcot described a patient who appeared to rely on the internal orthographic code of a word to recover its pronunciation. Dejerine also invoked the concept of a visual word form center to account for a selective disorder of reading (with intact writing and spelling) in cases of *pure alexia*, but rejected the possibility that writing took place from this center without first activating the spoken form of the word. Wernicke, in one of his last publications, took care to explicitly distinguish his view from Dejerine's:

> Certainly, on the basis of Dejerine's ideas regarding the extent of the speech center, it is obvious that he feels that the optic word center, so named by him, exerts the same influence on oral language as does the acoustic word center. This view . . . we cannot accept, since in normal individuals visual images exist only for letters and not words.

III. COMPONENTS OF WRITING

A. The Subword Routine

If we pause to consider Wernicke's argument that writing does not entail a knowledge of the orthographic (or visual) form of words, we will soon discover that on logical grounds alone the notion is hard to accept, given the nature of a spelling system like English (and many other orthographies). Take for example sets of words like "meet," "meat," and "mete," or "rain," "reign," and "rein." How can their correct spelling be determined without explicitly representing each of the different patterns that must then be separately matched to their corresponding meaning? There are a huge number of such ambiguities in many orthographic systems, and yet they present no difficulty to the average individual with a high school education.

One of the first to emphasize that a disorder of spelling may be confined to the retrieval of word-specific orthographic patterns was Pick, who attempted to marshall evidence in favor of a distinction between "phonetic and orthographic writing." Unfortunately, the relevant observations available from different sources were rather weak and anecdotal in nature; Pick discussed such modest phenomena as a patient who wrote "tonge" instead of "tongue," another who wrote "here" instead of "hear," "to" instead of "too," and "toothack" for "toothache." The possibility that these errors were merely slips due to inattention or even lack of education was discussed but never convincingly refuted.

In more recent years, however, abundant evidence has been obtained supporting the notion advocated by Pick. Thus, if one component of normal spelling is based on retrieving whole-word orthography, and if this component can be selectively damaged, then there must be a form of acquired agraphia in which the patient will have particular difficulty spelling words with orthographic forms that bear an arbitrary relationship to their pronunciation (i.e., any word that can be plausibly spelled in more than one way). There have been a number of published cases that provide clear examples of this disorder, now termed *surface agraphia* or *lexical agraphia*. In one such case, a patient, R. G., experienced spelling difficulty after surgery for a left parieto-occipital angioma. He could accurately write nonsense words to dictation, showing adequate knowledge of the correspondences between sound and print, but he made numerous errors when asked to write orthographically ambiguous or irregular words. The degree of ambiguity was indicated by the number of silent letters in the words or by the relative frequency of the orthographic value for a given speech segment (e.g., the vowel in "care" can be denoted by "ea" as in "pear" and "wear," but this particular correspondence is quite infrequent). The patient's accuracy deteriorated systematically as the orthographic ambiguity of the word increased, though the effect was less pronounced for familiar words. The influence of word frequency on spelling accuracy is typical of surface agraphia, and implies that the availability of whole-word orthographic units is a function of their previous history of activation.

We can describe surface agraphia as writing via the mechanisms that transcode subword units from their phonemic to their graphemic correspondence in the *absence* of word-specific retrieval of orthography. Can we learn more about the nature of this procedure by looking at the kind of errors made by surface agraphic patients? The answer obtained so far has turned out to be rather complex: Patients may use different size units for translating the sound of a word into print. In some cases, responses are based on a procedure that simply assigns one letter to a phoneme. Thus, errors in one reported case include "motor" as "mota" (the patient spoke and therefore "wrote" with a Cockney accent), "tone" as "ton," and "goes" as "goz." The very reduced size of these units is not typical of all cases, however, nor would we expect to see normal spellers relying on such a primitive set of correspondences when asked to write unfamiliar words. Indeed, other patients have demonstrated considerable flexibility in the assignment of a spelling pattern to items with a similar pronunciation. The most we can conclude at present is that in some cases, damage has affected not only the retrieval of whole-word orthography, but the subword routine as well, so that multi-letter graphemes are no longer assigned to an auditory sequence. If the units available to the patient extend to multiple letters for a given speech segment, a greater variety of mapping options become available, which may be selected on a probabilistic basis according to their frequency of occurrence in written language. Finally, still larger units (e.g., an entire word ending) may re-introduce constraints on the possible values that could mediate a response: for example, the word "priest" could never be written "preest" if the terminal segment "eest" is taken as the relevant unit, because that particular orthographic sequence does not occur in English.

We do not yet have a complete theory of the mechanisms that surface dysgraphics rely on to translate speech segments into orthographic code. Such a theory would require that we understand both the full range of subword units that are *normally* available and the effect of brain damage on the mechanisms and representations that underly this spelling procedure.

B. The Whole-Word Routine

Our interpretation of surface agraphia is that the patient is unable to retrieve word-specific orthography and must instead rely on subword units to produce a response. If the word-specific routine exists as an alternative spelling mechanism to subword translation, then it should follow that patients can be observed who demonstrate the *reverse* of the impairment that is characteristic of surface agraphia. These cases should *only* be able to derive the spelled form of whole words and not the spelling of a pattern that must be assembled *de novo*.

There have been a number of reports on this unusual dissociation, now termed *phonological agraphia,* which together with the opposing category surface agraphia, provides very clear support for the functional separability of word and subword orthographic routines.

In 1981, Shallice documented a patient who could only transcribe 26% of single-syllable pronounceable nonsense words to dictation, but averaged 90% on a large sample of words varying in concreteness, frequency of occurrence, and spelling regularity. This patient's difficulty was not merely the outcome of impaired auditory discrimination or of an inability to hold the dictated nonsense items in memory, because he could easily repeat them back to the examiner *after* he had failed to derive their spelling pattern.

The existence of phonological agraphia, now confirmed in many reports, offers clear proof that there is indeed a functional component of the writing mechanism holding word-specific orthographic forms, contrary to Wernicke's supposition. But we still need to know the role of the word's pronunciation in retrieving its spelling pattern—is it the case that the sound of the word must be activated to derive whole-word orthography, or can we directly address an orthographic representation from the meaning of a word without contacting its sound. We should note that the former viewpoint was based on the strong impression, shared by all normal language users, of automatic access to the sound pattern of words when we read or write. But we must be careful about reaching any conclusion about a *causal* relationship between the activation of the sound pattern of a word (i.e., the stored phonological representation) and its orthography. While there is no doubt that the two representations are activated conjointly during the act of writing or spelling, we cannot infer that the retrieval of an orthographic code is necessarily dependent on a prior access to phonology.

In fact, we now have dramatic evidence from an unusual subclass of phonological agraphia indicating that this intuition is wrong. Certain aphasic patients can write down the name of an object that they are unable to produce in spoken form. It is not the case that the naming disorder is simply the outcome of impairment to lower-level mechanisms responsible for articulation. Consider for example the patient M. H., whose spontaneous speech, though fluent, was almost totally devoid of content words. Her naming of line drawings, three-dimensional objects, and reading aloud was very poor, and the difficulty appeared to reflect a complete failure to access the underlying pronunciation of the word. M. H.'s performance on a variety of tasks requiring the internal manipulation and comparison of speech codes (for example, picture–word rhyme matching) demonstrated that her ability to derive the sound of most words was very seriously limited. In spite of this profound inability to generate the spoken form of words, M. H. showed no such constraint on written labeling. She correctly wrote the names of 19/20 objects and 15/20 line drawings even though she could only produce the spoken names of 3/40 of these items. Further aspects of M. H.'s writing were typical of phonological agraphia: she could not write pronounceable nonsense words (1/20 correct) or even nonsense syllables to dictation, yet her transcription of dictated words (even relatively infrequent words with unusual spelling) was very accurate. Like the patient described by Shallice, M. H.'s ability to repeat an auditory nonsense word after a failed spelling attempt was found to be excellent.

The evidence from this patient and other similar cases indicates that the orthography of a word can be available for production in the complete absence of its spoken form. As a point of interest, M. H. eventually learned to use the spelling of a word to evoke its pronunciation. For example, presented with the picture of a mountain, her response was "M-O-U-N-T-A-I-N, mountain." This adaptive strategy, which we observed when her oral reading of single words began to improve, apparently took place by generating the visual form of a word and then translating it into sound.

There is one further remarkable and complex variant of phonological agraphia that has been documented. We have pointed out that certain patients must generate the orthography of a word directly from meaning, without the mediation of speech codes. In some cases, this procedure is itself partially deficient, and selective difficulty occurs when the patient is asked to write or spell words belonging to a particular semantic category.

There is documentation of patients who write concrete words to dictation much more accurately than abstract words, while verbs and grammatical functional words (e.g., "the," "and," "before") were written very poorly. Errors may be semantically related to the target. For example, one patient wrote "funny" instead of "happy," "boat" for "yacht," "smile" for "laugh," etc. In addition, and not surprisingly, this patient's ability to write nonsense words to dictation was completely abolished.

We termed this unusual class of writing disorder *deep agraphia* to emphasize the link between it and the analogous reading disorder observed in patients with deep dyslexia. Unlike deep dyslexic patients, however, cases of deep agraphia may have no trouble reading and comprehending written words from a full range of semantic and syntactic categories, so that the difficulty is specific to the *production* of an orthographic code. Indeed, under these circumstances the patient will become aware of the writing errors on completion of a response because there is no difficulty reading single words. We can see, then, that there is considerable functional independence between the mechanisms for encoding and producing whole-word orthography. This issue will be returned to at a later point. [*See* DYSLEXIA.]

The nature of deep agraphia suggests a disturbance in the process that recovers the spelling of a word *after* the meaning has been correctly determined. Clear evidence that the patient has understood the word even when the response is a semantic paragraphia (e.g., "table" written for "chair") has been obtained—in the relevant cases, adequate comprehension can be demonstrated for all words (regardless of their semantic or syntactic class) prior to transcription. If the disturbance responsible for the category effects on spelling was more central, of course, we would expect impaired understanding of low imagery words, verbs, and function words.

IV. PERIPHERAL OUTPUT MECHANISMS

Thus far we have discussed the components of the writing mechanism that derive the spelled form of words—either directly from the meaning or indirectly by using speech codes to assemble an orthographic pattern made up of subword units. We can refer to these procedures as collectively functioning at a *pre-graphemic* stage of processing, in that the representations constructed do not deal with the spatial characteristics or physical realization of the letters making up the word. The theoretical division between pre- and postgraphemic systems immediately raises a fundamental question on the nature of the operations that must ultimately deliver graphemic units in their correct order. Writing or oral spelling inherently demands that letter codes be retrieved individually from left to right; there is general agreement that for this procedure to occur smoothly, a specialized working memory component—a graphemic output buffer—is needed to temporarily maintain the linear form of the orthographic representation generated from higher levels of processing.

A. The Graphemic Buffer

A number of criteria may be specified for identifying selective damage to this component of the writing mechanism. Since the graphemic buffer is the point at which both word-specific and subword orthographic units are maintained for output, we should expect damage at this level to yield the same pattern of errors in all writing tasks (written naming, writing to dictation, spontaneous writing, and delayed copying). There should also be no effect of variables like word class, imageability, spelling regularity, or word familiarity on performance, because the function of the graphemic buffer is to act as a temporary register for *any* orthographic string, regardless of the procedures that generated it. Finally, performance should be strongly affected by the *length* of the graphemic string that is organized for production, as more elements will place a greater burden on the damaged buffer during retrieval if the mechanism is acting as temporary storage device.

The performance of an Italian patient, L. B., documented by Caramazza and colleagues, is illustrative: He made spelling errors on all tasks, regardless of modality of input or output. Mistakes were almost exclusively letter substitutions (svolta → svonta), additions (taglio → tatglio), deletions (nostro → nosro), and transpositions (stadio → sdatio)—i.e., obvious deformation of the graphemic string for both words and pronounceable nonwords. L. B. also showed a dramatic length effect on spelling accuracy; he could spell correctly all two-letter stimuli but only 30% of 8- and 9-letter items. This pattern stands in marked contrast to the kind of the spelling errors made by agraphic patients with damage to more central components of the writing mechanism (compare, for example, the performance of a deep agraphic patient, who would be unable to write short function words like "to," "be," "on," etc., but who would be much more successful producing the spelled form of longer, high imagery words).

More recent analyses have further clarified the nature of the impairment to the mechanisms that organize and maintain graphemic strings for output. It is not the case that we can simply think of this level in the architecture as responsible for maintaining the identity and order of letters that comprise a word. If the operation of the buffer were so straightforward, then damage to graphemic representations should result in errors (e.g., omissions or transpositions) that are unrelated to the actual orthographic structure in which the letters occur. But results in fact demonstrate important constraints on the distribution of spelling mistakes. Thus, L. B.'s substitutions and transpositions invariably preserve the status of the target letter as a consonant or vowel—the patient almost never replaces one with the other. Second, there appeared to be disproportionately fewer errors on double consonant (geminate) clusters (e.g., canna) than words of the same length but without double letters (e.g., canta). Finally, L. B. is reliably better at spelling regularly alternating consonant–vowel (CV) sequences than other orthographic patterns.

To explain these results, Caramazza and Miceli argue that graphemic representations should be thought of as minimally having a three-layered organization: one tier for establishing abstract letter identities, another for the CV structure, and a third (an ortho-syllabic representation adapted from linguistic theories of phonological structure) that specifies the syllabic organization of the graphemes that comprise a word. Using this framework, the authors interpret the complexities underlying L. B.'s orthographic errors as follows:

1. *Substitution and transposition errors:* The patient must have access to information about CV structure even when the details of the specific abstract letter identities are lacking. The error is the outcome of a "repair" operation that the system uses, directed by preserved knowledge of the array's CV configuration, to complete an underspecified element. A substitution, on this

interpretation, may be due to the *random* selection of a vowel or consonant when the actual identity of the target letter has been lost; transposition errors may be the outcome of a *misselection* from the set of letter elements that comprise the word.

2. *Enhanced performance for double-letter clusters:* The identity of double letters might be specified only once. Letter doubling would then be marked by associating a single-letter identity with *two* positions at the CV level. STELLA, for example, might be represented $C_{(S)} C_{(T)} V_{(E)} CC_{(L)} V_{(A)}$. This type of format implies that fewer elements would actually be registered for double-letter words than comparable words with no letter doubling. The patient's accuracy is strongly determined by array length, and so a double-letter configuration (in fact, a smaller number of buffered identities) would enhance performance.

3. *Alternating CV sequences are better than less regular ones:* Caramazza and Miceli assume that graphemic representations determine syllabic boundaries in addition to CV structure and letter identities. Damage to the buffer means that the orthographic array is underspecified, and there may be default mechanisms that attempt to reconstruct or "repair" it. An irregularly alternating CV sequence might permit repair solutions that violate the original structure (for example, a sequence like CCVCCV—say, the word "stanco"—might be reconstituted by placing a vowel in the third *or* fourth position, or by completely deleting a nonvowel position, yielding a gross distortion of the original structure of the target). For a recurring CVCVCV sequence, the same reconstructive procedure will either maintain the original format or would require the deletion of an entire CV segment if no vowel is inserted in the appropriate location. Consistent with this analysis, deletions by L. B. were much more frequent in nonsystematically alternating CV patterns than regularly alternating ones, and the converse was true for substitution errors.

The detailed work on the disruption of mechanisms responsible for graphemic output has revealed a complex but principled organization. Spelling patterns are not merely passively registered as an ordered array of letters; rather, the nature of impairment following damage to this peripheral stage points to a number of hierarchical levels of representation in which the graphemes are embedded. Just as the psycholinguistic analysis of normal speech errors ("slips of the tongue") has allowed us to clarify the multi-layered, interactive nature of the phonemic structures that determine the production of a spoken utterance, so has research on one class of agraphic patients begun to show the complexity of the orthographic representations that are needed for accurate retrieval of a spelling pattern.

B. The Allographic Procedure

We must distinguish between the procedures that derive the graphemic structure of a word and the actual mechanisms that produce the sequence as letters on the page. To write, we must know how to generate the spatial form of each upper- or lowercase letter in the correct order. These output codes are termed *allographs* and are relatively abstract in nature; allographic code must specify the shape of each letter independent of its size or the actual muscle system (hand, foot, etc.) executing the response. It is reasonable to infer that certain writing errors inadvertently made by normal individuals could reflect a momentary disturbance of the allographic component. Thus, occasional "slips of the pen" include letter substitutions and reversal of allographically similar forms (*n* for *m*, *p* for *b*, etc.), indicating the possibility that they arise through misselection of a graphic motor pattern with a spatially close alternative.

It is difficult to study the writing mistakes made by normal spellers because they occur infrequently, and we cannot always be clear on their origin. But there are agraphic cases that have been documented where the disturbance is plainly confined to the retrieval of allographic code. In these cases, preserved knowledge of the word's orthography can be demonstrated, because *oral spelling* is carried out correctly. When tested, other methods of producing the form of a written word (typing or use of block letters) may also yield a high degree of accuracy. Writing, however, is marred by numerous errors of omission, substitution, reversals, and insertions. This form of agraphia is not merely the result of a disturbance in the production of a motor pattern for individual letters, because the patients have no trouble writing single letters to dictation; their impairment shows only when they are asked to form an array of letters. In a recent report of one case, performance was influenced by the frequency of occurrence of a grapheme; the patient made fewer substitution errors if the target letter was relatively common and many more errors if the frequency of the letter in English orthography was moderate or low. While the highly selective nature of the writing disorder provides clear support for the dissociability of this level from previous graphemic stages, we have yet to achieve a detailed understanding of the mechanisms that govern the planning and execution of an allographic sequence.

C. Graphic Motor Output

The motor schema for a letter differentiates between the shape of a letter and more general parameters that govern factors like size and orientation. Cases of apractic agraphia reveal a loss of the motoric representations necessary for producing letters. Written characters are poorly formed and may in fact be illegible, though even very impaired patients maintain the distinction between cursive and printed letters and between upper- and lowercase. The disturbance may dissociate from limb apraxia, suggesting that the motor codes for graphemes are separately represented from motoric schemas for other complex acts. Finally, there are patients who exceed the number of strokes when forming letters, particularly those that demand iteration of the same movement (e.g., *w*, *m*, *b*). These errors reflect a disruption of sensory and proprioceptive feedback on the finely articulated movements of writing.

V. RELATIONSHIP BETWEEN WRITING AND OTHER COGNITIVE FUNCTIONS

We have described the major functional components responsible for producing the orthography of single words. The architecture may be summarized as follows: Word-specific orthographic representations may be activated directly from the meaning or the auditory form, or a sequence may be built up from subword units corresponding to a particular pronunciation. There are thus mechanisms for deriving orthography that require contact with phonemic codes and additional systems that operate independently of speech. The output of both systems converges on a graphemic buffer, where the spelling pattern is organized and maintained for a written response. The spatial composition of the letters is then developed in allographic form and the graphic motor patterns are executed as an overt response.

A number of points should be made about the formulation of the system. First, the components are not to be taken as literal statements about neuro-anatomical regions; the hypothesized mechanisms are first-order abstractions based on dissociations in the performance of brain-damaged patients that must be further elaborated to the point where they can be validly thought of in neurological terms. Indeed, though there does appear to be some consistency in the location of focal damage associated with different agraphic subtypes, there is little of immediate theoretical interest that follows from these observations. While we are still a long way from understanding how individual components of the functional architecture emerge from the neural activity of particular brain regions, the recent success in connectionist modeling of higher-level functions offers an interesting direction to pursue.

A more tractable question for now concerns the general issue of the relationship between the components mediating the production of orthography and the rest of the language system. Recall that we began by noting that there is a sense in which writing is completely dependent on the systems that mediate spoken language. Certainly, this would be true for grammar; it is hard to imagine a fundamental distinction between the syntactic knowledge responsible for our ability to produce a well-formed sentence in the spoken and written modalities. The statement is also obviously true for conceptual (semantic) representations; if the meaning of a word has been totally lost, neither the spoken nor written form could be retrieved by semantic mediation, given the reasonable assumption, of course, that concepts are represented in a format that does not depend on the kind of response that must be generated. [See SEMANTICS; SYNTAX.]

But unfortunately, the true situation is rather more complex. The grammar of a language and the meaning of a word must be accessed by specialized procedures, and *their* operating characteristics may well differ according to the particular language output system. Thus, it is quite possible to observe an agraphia for certain categories of words (e.g., low imagery words) that the patient has no difficulty understanding or producing in spoken form (e.g., documented cases of "deep" agraphia). Our conclusion here is that there are modality-specific retrieval procedures affected by the semantic neighborhood of a word. If these routines sustain only partial damage, certain classes of words may be more adequately retrieved in one particular response mod-

ality. Of course, if the damage to the stored meaning of words is more central, then production errors will occur in all tasks that require the mediation of semantic representations.

In the domain of sentence construction, the same arguments apply. Many theorists have argued that smooth written production of text demands the temporary storage of words and phrases in a memory buffer that preserves information while the sentence is organized and executed. The most suitable code for this kind of storage is thought by many investigators to be phonemic in origin.

It is true that errors made by normal writers (slips of the pen) reveal a significant proportion of mistakes that are connected to the underlying sound of the target words. Thus, we find homophone substitutions ("weight" instead of "wait," "write" instead of "right"), phonological confusions ("28" for "20A," "3" for "C"), and even occasional errors that suggest a reliance on subword correspondences ("ques" for "cues"). Since there is good reason to assume that the writers actually knew the correct spelling of these words, the mistakes indicate that the spoken form of the word is exerting an overriding influence on the orthographic mechanism.

Unfortunately, the evidence from the appropriate cases of agraphia does not offer clear-cut support for the idea that written sentence production necessarily demands the concurrent influence of speech-based representations. M. H., a patient who accurately wrote single words without access to their pronunciation, did in fact show a dramatic impairment of her ability to write sentences. Of interest, the nature of her errors indicated poor control of grammatical morphemes (e.g., function words like "the," "but," etc., and word affixes like "ing," "ment," and "er"), as well as complete omission of verbs. For example, M. H.'s written description of a picture showing a boy closing a window was "At boy is close the window." By contrast, her spoken response, tested approximately one hour later, revealed correct use of grammar along with the anticipated failure to produce content words ("It looks as if he is putting down the . . . ."). Another very similar case (E. B.), however, was found to be quite different in this respect: his syntax was sophisticated, and his writing included frequent compound sentences, complex sentences, and participal phrases. Unless we are willing to accept the suggestion that E. B.'s performance was based on highly atypical skills, the preservation of syntax indicates that while speech codes may influence written sentence production, they are not an essential requirement.

There is one writing procedure that clearly does depend on the activation of phonemic codes, however. To transcribe a pronounceable nonsense word, the acoustic pattern has to be converted to abstract phonological segments which are then given a corresponding orthographic value. Damage to auditory-phonological conversion would result in impaired repetition as well as transcription of nonwords. This is not to imply that phonological agraphia is always associated with a failure to repeat nonsense words, and indeed the pure cases described in the literature show very good oral repetition. The mechanism responsible for deriving orthography from speech segments can be selectively affected if the damage occurs beyond the point in the architecture where the phonology of the target utterance has been determined, at a level that determines the actual mapping between phonemic and graphemic units.

Thus far we have discussed the relationship between writing and other components of language. But the issue of the dependence of orthography on other kinds of representation also extends to the visual system: just how much reliance does writing, and perhaps more crucially spelling aloud, place on mechanisms dealing with spatial or visual structure? Some patients with phonological agraphia have commented that they feel they are writing by looking at the word as if it were registered on an "inner screen." One documented case involved a patient who often wrote the letters comprising the word in a nonlinear order, sometimes beginning with the last or intermediate letters before attempting to reconstruct the rest of the word. The inference has been that nonlinear retrieval of graphemes can take place over a visual representation.

But we should be careful before reaching any strong conclusions from these incidental findings. The orthographic description of whole words is more abstract than a stored configuration of letter patterns. If spelling literally depended, under certain circumstances, on "reading off" letters from a mental image, we would be faced with the absurd question of whether the patient is "viewing" upper- or lowercase letters on the inner screen, and what determines the nature of the display format. Is the word seen in script, print, and with what spacing between letters? Clearly, these are not sensible questions, and their very absurdity gives pause to any simplistic notion of spelling as directly based on the visualization of an orthographic sequence.

Finally, we take up the question of writing in relationship to reading. Both systems require access to the orthographic form of words and a knowledge of the correspondence between subword units and pronunciation. To what extent is there functional overlap between the components of the system that map letter strings onto orthographic and phonological representations for reading and the system that accomplishes the reverse operation of deriving the orthography to produce a written word?

There is no doubt that the reading performance of many patients can be startlingly different from their spelling. It is possible to observe cases that cannot spell nonsense words (phonological agraphia) but read them aloud with no difficulty. One instance of surface agraphia has been documented as displaying the opposite dissociation in reading performance; i.e., the patient (R. G.) was *unable* to read nonsense words that he could easily write to dictation, and he had no trouble reading the orthographically unusual words that he could not spell! This extreme dissociation led some authors to infer that the orthographic knowledge necessary for word recognition in reading is different from the orthographic knowledge necessary for correct spelling in writing.

The assumption of separate orthographic representations for reading and writing, though frequently made, has been the subject of much controversy. It has been argued that reported *dissociations* between reading and writing/spelling are in fact theoretically neutral with respect to the question of separate orthographic components for input and output. It may be that a given case of surface agraphia with preserved reading of irregular words is the result of central damage to representations that are specific to an output orthographic system. Alternatively, the results are equally compatible with the hypothesis that written language is mediated by a single orthographic component, with functionally distinct procedures that gain access to this information for reading and retrieve the same representation for spelling.

There have been a number of attempts to distinguish these possibilities by analyzing cases in which the disturbance to reading and writing is qualitatively the same. Thus, we make use of *associated* deficits rather than dissociations in performance to test the hypothesis of dual orthographic components. In 1987, Coltheart and Funnell documented a case of surface dyslexia and surface agraphia (H. G.) that showed similar performance in reading and spelling. The authors obtained a set of homophone words (e.g., "read" and "reed"), yielding consistent accuracy in a test of visual word identification (Set A) and a further set (Set B) that produced errors on at least one out of two occasions. H. G.'s spelling of Set B words was much less accurate than his spelling of words in Set A, even when frequency effects of the words were partialled out. The idea is that written homophones by definition require word-specific orthographic knowledge if they are to be understood and produced correctly, because the pronunciation offers no way of disambiguating them. The fact that H. G.'s ability to spell a homophone can be predicted from his reading comprehension (the patient, who had no language disorder, was asked to define the meaning of each visual word) is taken as evidence that there is a single orthographic lexicon, used for both reading and spelling, and the entry for each of these words in this lexicon has been impaired. A similar argument has been put forward by a number of other investigators.

The research on agraphia indicates that we have made some progress in understanding the basic functional components of the writing mechanism. It can be seen that the production of written words and sentences demands specialized systems that bear a complex relationship to their counterparts in the auditory domain. While spoken and written language are close partners from a neuropsychological perspective, the performance of brain damaged cases has begun to clarify the nature of their interaction as well as their divergence.

Bibliography

Baxter, D. M., and Warrington, E. K. (1987). Ideational agraphia: A single case study. *J. Neurol. Neurosurg. Psych.* **49,** 369–374.

Beauvois, M. F., and Derouesné, J. (1981). Lexical or orthographic agraphia. *Brain* **104,** 21–49.

Behrmann, M., and Bub, D. (1992). Surface dyslexia and dysgraphia: Dual routes, single lexicon. *Cog. Neuropsychol.* **9,** 209–251.

Bub, D., and Kertesz, A. (1982). Evidence for lexicographic processing in a patient with preserved written over oral single word naming. *Brain* **105,** 697–717.

Caramazza, A., and Miceli, G. (1992). The structure of orthographic representations in spelling. "Reports of the Cognitive Neuropsychology Laboratory," No. 50. The Johns Hopkins University.

Caramazza, A., Miceli, G., Villa, G., and Romani, C. (1986). The role of the graphemic buffer in spelling: Evidence from a case of acquired dysgraphia. *Cognition* **26,** 59–85.

Coltheart, M., and Funnell, E. (1987). Reading writing: One lexicon or two? In "Language Perception and Production: Shared Mechanisms in Listening, Speaking, Reading and Writing." (D. A. Allport, D. G. MacKay, W. Prinz, and E. Scheerer, Eds.), Academic Press, London.

Friedman, R. B., and Alexander, M. P. (1984). Pictures, images and pure alexia: A case study. *Cog. Neuropsychol.* **1,** 9–23.

Friedman, R. B., and Hadley, J. A. (1992). Letter-by-letter surface alexia. *Cog. Neuropsychol.* **9,** 185–208.

Hotopf, W. H. N. (1980). Slips of the pen. In "Cognitive Processes in Spelling" (U. Frith, Ed.), pp. 288–307. Academic Press, London.

Hotopf, W. H. N. (1983). Lexical slips of the pen and tongue: What they tell us about language production. In "Language Production" (B. Butterworth, Ed.), pp. 147–199. Academic Press, London.

Levine, D., Calvanio, R., and Popovics, A. (1982). Language in the absence of inner speech. *Neuropsychologia* **20,** 391–409.

Margolin, D. I. (1984). The neuropsychology of writing and spelling: Semantic, phonological, motor and perceptual processes. *Quart. J. Exp. Psychol.* **36A,** 459–489.

McCarthy, R. A., and Warrington, E. K. (1990). "Cognitive Neuropsychology." Academic Press, San Diego.

Newcombe, F., and Marshall, J. C. (1985). Reading and writing by letter sounds. In "Surface Dyslexia" (K. E. Patterson, J. C. Marshall, and M. Coltheart, Eds.), pp. 35–51. Erlbaum, Hillsdale, NJ.

Pick, A. (1925). On the pathology of orthography. (Translated from German by R. De Bleser, 1989). *Cog. Neuropsychol.* **6** (5), 71–586.

Shallice, T. (1981). Phonological agraphia and the lexical route in writing. *Brain* **104,** 413–429.

Wernicke, C. (1908). The aphasia symptom complex. In "Diseases of the Nervous System" (A. Church, Ed.), pp. 265–324. Appleton, New York.

◆ AIDS AND SEXUAL BEHAVIOR

Michael P. Wilbur
The University of Connecticut

Glossary

Adolescent Persons between the ages of 15 and 24, as defined by the World Health Organization (WHO).

AIDS Acquired immune deficiency disorder. A serious condition characterized by a defect in natural immunity against disease and caused by a virus called HIV. HIV is not highly contagious. It is specifically transmitted through unprotected sexual intercourse, sharing needles, direct infusion of tainted blood products, or the birth process (from an infected mother to her child).

Antibody A blood protein produced in response to exposure to a specific antigen: a critical component of the body's immune system.

Asymptomatic Having an infectious organism within the body but showing no outward symptoms (i.e., swollen lymph glands, fever, cough).

Attitude A relatively constant feeling, predisposition, or set of beliefs directed toward an object, person, or situation.

Behavior An action that has a specific frequency, duration, and purpose, whether conscious or unconscious.

Belief A statement or proposition, declared or implied, that is emotionally and/or intellectually accepted as true by a person or group.

Bisexual A person who is sexually attracted to persons of either sex.

CDC Centers for Disease Control; located in Atlanta, Georgia.

Chronic Of long duration; prolonged; describes disease that persists for a long period of time.

Condom A latex sheath used to cover the penis during intercourse to prevent pregnancy and sexually transmitted diseases, including HIV-infection.

Cunnilingus A sexual activity involving oral contact with the female genitals.

Diagnosis Health or behavioral information that designates the problem or need; its status, distribution, or frequency in the person or population; and the probable causes or risk associated with the problem or need.

ELISA Enzyme-linked immunosorbant assay antibody test. The initial screening test used to detect antibody to HIV-infection. More sensitive than the Western blot antibody test.

Epidemic Any unusual outbreak of the number of disease cases present at one time in a defined geographic region.

Epidemiology The study of the causes and means of controlling disease.

Fellatio A sexual activity involving oral contact with the male genitals.

HIV Human immunodeficiency virus. The name that scientists have given to the virus that causes HIV-disease and AIDS.

HIV-disease The continuum between HIV-infection and possible death resulting from AIDS.

Homophobia The fears, myths, and prejudices people have about homosexuals or attraction to people of the same sex.

Homosexual A person who is sexually attracted to people of the same sex (gay or lesbian).

Intravenous Inside the veins; HIV transmission occurs when a person who has HIV uses a needle and then shares that needle with someone else without first cleaning the needle, thereby infecting that person.

Kaposi's sarcoma (KS) A tumor of the walls of blood vessels. Usually KS appears as pink to purple, painless spots on the skin but may also occur internally in addition to or independent of the skin lesions. KS is one example of an opportunistic infection.

Mucous membrane The soft, moist skin that lines the body cavities such as the mouth, vagina, urethra, eyelids, rectum, and so on.

Neurologic Pertaining to the nervous system or brain. Persons infected with HIV often develop neurologic infection.

Nonoxynol-9 A chemical included in spermicides that kills sperm, which also helps prevent some transmission of the HIV.

Opportunistic infections Those diseases that are caused by agents that are frequently present in our bodies or environment but which cause disease only when there is an alteration from normal healthy conditions such as when the immune system becomes depressed. Kaposi's sarcoma (KS) and pneumocystis carinii pneumonia (PCP) are examples of opportunistic infections.

Pandemic Prevalent over a whole area, country, universal, general, etc.; an epidemic over a large region; said of a disease—a pandemic disease.

PWA Person with AIDS, also known as PLWA, person living with AIDS. Many people with AIDS prefer this term over AIDS patient because they see themselves as active participants in their treatment and not as helpless victims.

Retrovirus A particular family of viruses, including HIV, that have a method of reproduction different from that of other viruses. Retroviruses are difficult to treat or cure, and to date, there are no vaccines successful against human retroviruses.

Risk Characteristics of individuals (genetic, behavioral, environmental, and sociocultural conditions) that increase the probability that they will experience a disease or specific cause of death as measured by population relative risk factors.

Safer sex Those practices which reduce the risk of transmission of sexually transmitted diseases.

Seroconversion The point at which a recently infected person begins to produce antibodies against an invading antigen.

Seropositive In the context of HIV, this indicates that an individual has been exposed to HIV by the presence of antibodies in the blood. Seropositivity usually develops 3 to 6 months after being infected.

Syndrome A pattern of symptoms and signs, appearing one by one or simultaneously, that together characterize a particular disease or disorder.

T-cells A type of lymphocyte which protects against viruses, parasites, and fungi. T-cells regulate the various cellular (i.e., cell-mediated defense) and humoral (i.e., antibody-mediated defense) components of the immune system.

Vaccine A preparation introduced into the body to produce immunity to a disease. While some vaccines are undergoing trials, no effective vaccine exists for HIV-infection.

Virus Minute, parasitic organism which depends on nutrients inside cells for its metabolic and reproductive needs. Some viruses, like HIV, are very fragile and cannot survive outside the host cell for more than a few minutes. Antibiotics do not affect viruses.

Youth Persons between the ages of 10 and 24 years, as defined by the Centers for Disease Control.

THE HUMAN IMMUNODEFICIENCY VIRUS (HIV) results in a chronic immunodeficiency disorder called HIV-disease. The symptoms of HIV-disease occur in a sequence of phases, with the most advanced phase of HIV-disease called acquired immune deficiency disorder (AIDS). Through December 1992, the Centers for Disease Control and Prevention (CDC) has received reports of over 250,000 cases of AIDS in the United States.

The topic of HIV/AIDS is a multifaceted issue which cannot, and should not, be reduced to medical terminology and factual information alone. HIV/AIDS is very much a human and social problem that cannot be addressed merely as a public health and medical issue. However, a basic understanding and knowledge base of factual information is a necessary prerequisite to our grasp of the scope and complexity of this human, social, medical, and public health problem. In addition to possessing a factual knowledge base, a more thorough understanding of HIV/AIDS also requires that we focus upon our attitudes and beliefs, as well as the emotional components concerning the virus and syndrome, and the behaviors that place others and ourselves at-risk of contracting the virus.

As with most human conditions and behavior, there is often a gap between what we know and what we do. That is, regardless of how much knowledge we possess, people still make poor decisions, people still engage in risk-taking behaviors that disregard possible outcomes or known consequences, and people still make mistakes.

Beginning with the premise that it is much more difficult to "live with AIDS" than to live without AIDS, the following discussion will emphasize four facets of the HIV/AIDS epidemic: (1) a basic knowledge base of factual information; (2) attitudes and belief systems concerning the virus and syndrome; (3) the decisions and behaviors that place individuals at-risk of contracting HIV; and (4) the emotional issues surrounding HIV/AIDS. It also should be noted that discussions of this topic remain sensitive and controversial due to its sexually graphic material and prevailing stereotypes surrounding its cause, transmission, and lack of cure.

I. KNOWLEDGE BASE: HISTORY, STATISTICS, AND TRANSMISSION

There is inevitably some uncertainty about what does and does not transmit HIV. However, in the first decade since HIV was officially identified in France and the United States in 1983, there is little doubt within the medical community that the presence of HIV is necessary to cause AIDS.

A. History

Originally called human T-cell lymphotropic virus, Type III (HTLV-III) in the United States and lymphadenopathy-associated virus (LAV) in France, HIV was given its current name in 1985.

The World Health Organization (WHO) has estimated that 9 to 11 million people are infected worldwide. As of January 1993, the Centers for Disease Control has received reports of 250,000 cases of AIDS in the United States, estimating that 1 to 1.4 million people are currently infected with the HIV-disease and will be in need of physical health care and mental health care. Estimates are that approximately 1 in 250 people in the United States are HIV-infected: 1 in 100 men and 1 in 800 women. It also has been predicted that 1 in 10 people in the United States will be infected with HIV in the next decade, with about 40,000 new infections occurring each year. For the past 10 years, in North America, Europe, and Australia, HIV has been predominantly transmitted as a result of unprotected intercourse between two men and by needle sharing. Worldwide, the major mode of transmission is heterosexual contact (71%), and 40% of HIV-infected people are women.

In 1990 HIV-infection was among the top 10 causes of death in the United States. Among persons 24 to 44 years old AIDS was the third leading cause of death and accounted for 13% of all deaths. In the next decade, however, it is predicted that AIDS will have a dramatic impact among young and middle-aged adults. Of the 47,106 cases of AIDS reported to the CDC in 1992, over one-half were men who have sex with men, 25% were injecting drug users (IDUs), and 14% were women. Nationally, the fastest increasing population of people with AIDS is the result of the sexual transmission of the human immunodeficiency virus (HIV). The epidemiology of AIDS in some states, however, differs significantly from national patterns. In Connecticut, for example, one-half of all AIDS cases reported in 1992 were among persons who were intravenous drug users, with 60% of all cases related to the transmission of HIV through the infected blood of shared needles. It has been estimated that every 13 minutes in the United States someone is injected intravenously, with 40,000 new injections each year. This traditional occurrence of HIV through sexual transmission and IDUs has been called "Pattern I."

In other countries, such as Africa, South and Central America, parts of Asia, and the Caribbean, the majority of cases have resulted from another pattern (Pattern II): heterosexual transmission. In these countries it is unusual for HIV to result from male to male sexual contact or from needle sharing. There is also another blended pattern that includes elements of Patterns I and II, called "Pattern III," that is the result of mixing the two major patterns from various countries.

Additionally, there are at least two variants of HIV, and probably more than two: HIV-1 and HIV-2. HIV-1 is the cause of almost all HIV-disease in the United States and other Pattern I countries. HIV-2 occurs primarily in West Africa and rarely in the United States. And although HIV-2 is not as well understood as HIV-1, the HIV-2 disease appears to be transmitted in the same ways as HIV-1, but it progresses at a slower rate than does HIV-1 disease. The present discussion is concerned with only HIV-1.

One-third of the people living in the United States currently know or have known someone with HIV-disease. Based on available data there is evidence that the yearly incidence of HIV/AIDS will plateau by 1995, to around 60,000 to 75,000 new cases per year, and demographic data indicate that some populations within the United States are more at-risk of contracting HIV/AIDS than others: gay men, Hispanic Americans, African Americans, IDUs, women, and adolescents and individuals in their 20s.

B. Multicultural Considerations

These specific populations within the United States are statistically more at-risk due to social contexts related to race, class, socioeconomic status, poverty, etc. However, it should be carefully noted that the reported disproportion of HIV/AIDS among some U.S. populations does not occur due to racial or biological differences.

This notwithstanding, of the 1 to 1.4 million reported cases of HIV-infection in United States, 54% are white and 29% are African Americans. Cumulative AIDS mortality rates from 1981 to 1987 were higher for Puerto Rican born males (362 per 100,000), other Latinos (217 per 100,000), and African Americans (267 per 100,000) than for white males (182 per 100,000). African and Hispanic Americans combined account for 70% of all AIDS cases among heterosexual males, 70% of all cases among women, and 75% of all pediatric cases.

1. Men

Homosexual and bisexual sexual behaviors are considered to be the major means of HIV/AIDS transmission. It is estimated that 46% of HIV-infected Hispanic men and 44% of HIV-infected African American men became infected through homosexual and bisexual sexual behaviors; while 60% of white males with AIDS were IDUs or had sex partners who were IDUs. Of men who fall into this category of becoming HIV-infected (i.e., IDUs or had sex partners who were IDUs), 35% are African American and 39% are Hispanic.

2. Latinos

Latinos represent approximately 8% of the U.S. population and account for 16% of cumulative AIDS cases. Hispanic Americans also account for 14% of all adult cases of AIDS and 22% of all pediatric AIDS cases. On a national level, there has been a 53% increase in cumulative cases of AIDS among Latino women, with Latino women comprising 20% of the women diagnosed with AIDS. Puerto Ricans represent the racial/ethnic group most affected by the HIV/AIDS epidemic.

3. African Americans

African Americans represent 26% of all cases of AIDS and 58% of all pediatric AIDS cases. African Americans are contracting AIDS in numbers far greater than their relative percentage in the U.S. population. Fifty-two percent of all children with AIDS are African Americans, and 52% of all women with AIDS are African American.

4. Women and Youth

Other identifiable groups who appear at-risk include women in general, adolescents and college-age youth, and Asian Americans and Pacific Islanders. Between 1985 and 1988, HIV/AIDS became one of the 10 leading causes of death among women of reproductive age. As of 1992, women and their infants represent the two fastest growing groups of individuals in the United States diagnosed with AIDS.

HIV has become one of the critical causes of premature mortality among adolescents and young adults in the United States. Latino adolescents account for around 18% of AIDS cases among 13 to 19 year olds, with 21% of Latino adolescents in this age group with AIDS being female. In general, however, youth are at an increasing risk of becoming HIV-infected. It is estimated that around 2 to 8 per 1000 college and university students in the United States are HIV-infected. This number increases to 10 per 1000 HIV-infected college and university students on campuses located in geographic and urban areas with high incidence of HIV/AIDS. There is evidence of the increasing occurrence of heterosexual HIV transmission among U.S. adolescents and college-age youth, as well as among the heterosexual U.S. population in general.

Between 1983 and 1987 statistics were not kept for the 43 different Asian and Pacific Islander groups. In 1990, however, there were 757 AIDS cases reported to the Centers for Disease Control for Asian and Pacific Island groups. Of the reported cases for these groups, 75% were due to male homosexual/bisexual sexual contact, 4% due to IDUs, and 10% due to blood-related transmission. As of June 1990, 159 Native Americans were diagnosed with AIDS. It is estimated that HIV-infected Native Americans include 4.4 per 1000, with more members of this group infected through intravenous drug use than homosexual/bisexual sexual behaviors.

C. Transmission

Based on our current knowledge, the transmission of HIV has been associated only with the following sources: blood and direct derivatives of blood, semen, vaginal and cervical secretions in the female genital tract, and possibly breast milk. That is, HIV is transmitted only by direct exposure to blood or blood derivatives, sexual intercourse of certain types, from women to fetus during gestation and birth, or possibly from mother to infant during breast feeding.

1. Blood Transmission

In general, there are three ways HIV can be transmitted via blood or blood derivatives: needle sharing (IDUs), accidental injuries resulting in direct exposure to HIV-infected blood (the intact skin provides an effective barrier to HIV), and transfusion of blood or blood derivatives, or the transplantation of tissues or organs from an infected donor.

The majority of blood transmitted cases of HIV in the United States are due to the transfer of infected blood in shared needles, most frequently in the use of illicitly injected drugs. Accidental exposures to HIV-infected blood are about 3 chances out of 1000 for a health care worker to be infected by an HIV patient (e.g., a needle stick injury) and the transmission of HIV from an infected surgeon to a patient occurs about once in every 42,000 to 420,000 medical procedures. Before 1985, HIV infection through transfusion was a significant form of transmitting HIV/AIDS, especially for hemophiliacs. And currently, the risk of transmitting HIV cannot be entirely eradicated, since some individuals may have donated blood, tissue, or organs after being HIV-infected but prior to being assessed as HIV positive through HIV antibody testing.

2. Sexual Transmission

The transmission of HIV sexually is solely associated with intercourse, with insertive and receptive anal intercourse, and insertive and receptive vaginal intercourse resulting in HIV. The probability of transmitting HIV during unprotected anal intercourse is greater for the receptive partner than the insertive partner among men, and the risk of transmitting HIV from man to woman is greater during anal intercourse than vaginal intercourse. The chance of transmitting HIV from male to female during vaginal intercourse also is higher than of female to male transmission; however, the probability of transmitting HIV from female to male is increased if menstrual blood is present during intercourse. Although it may require several acts of sexual intercourse to become infected by an HIV-infected sexual partner, an individual may become infected with HIV with a single event of intercourse.

The probability of transmitting HIV through fellatio appears to be much lower than through anal and vaginal intercourse; however, some HIV cases have been reported to have been transmitted from an infected man to this sexual partner via the semen or pre-ejaculatory fluid during oral sex. There is also some evidence that seroconversion to HIV may be associated with cunnilingus, but the chance of transmitting HIV from a infected woman to her sexual partner through vaginal or cervical secretions during oral sex is uncertain.

No evidence exists for the transmission of HIV via oral–anal contact (rimming) or by manual–anal contact (fisting). It is possible, however, that rimming (oral–anal contact) may transmit an agent (different from HIV) that is responsible for Kaposi's sarcoma (KS).

3. Mother to Fetus/Infant Transmission

The virus is transmitted from mothers to their fetus or infant during pregnancy, during the birth process, and during breast feeding. In the United States over 4000 cases of AIDS have been reported in children less than 13 years old, comprising 1.7% of the entire cases of AIDS. Virtually all current transmission of HIV infection to children in the United States occurs perinatally. About 10 to 40% of infants born to women who have HIV are infected. In many cases, however, the maternal HIV antibody disappears during the infant's first year of life and the seropositive infants may not be truly infected. Over two-thirds of infants born to seropositive mothers will not be HIV-infected. It still remains a difficult clinical task to determine whether an infant is truly infected, although 80 to 100% of infected infants can be identified at 3 months of age.

Other than by the means of transmission just discussed, there is no evidence that HIV is transmitted by kissing, or kissing with blood or lesions in the mouth that have resulted from braces on the teeth or from brushing and flossing the teeth. In addition, the transmission of HIV has not been associated with the rare presence of HIV in saliva; with respiratory droplets released during coughing/sneezing; with any kind of insects or animals; with ordinary social contact in residential, occupational/career, academic, or recreation contexts; with sharing toothbrushes, razors, dishes, drinking glasses, eating utensils, chairs, toilet seats, or tables; or with air and water.

D. Diagnosis of HIV

Sixty-five percent of all patients with AIDS receive their diagnosis as a result of pneumocystic carinii pneumonia (PCP) and 78% of HIV-infected people develop immune related disorders within 7 years after infection. About 35% of the 78% of HIV-infected people develop full-blown AIDS within 7 years. Although various testing procedures exist for detecting HIV disease (e.g., antigen testing, the polymerase chain reaction (PCR), etc.), in most instances HIV is inferred from detecting antibodies to the virus in an individual's blood. These antibodies in the blood are identified by an enzyme-linked immunosorbant assay (ELISA) technique. If the antibodies are detected in the blood, the results are then confirmed by immunoblotting or immunofluorescent antibody tests, such as the Western blot. Around 20 to 70% of positive ELISA tests are confirmed by Western blot.

1. The Window Period

The interval between an individual's exposure to HIV and when he or she seroconverts to HIV is typically called the "window period." In most cases, the period of time between an individual's exposure to HIV and his or her seroconversion to HIV is 6 to 8 weeks. However, the time between exposure to seroconversion to HIV (i.e., the "window period") can be from 6 weeks to 6 months. The interval between infection and development of AIDS is much shorter, however, in young children than adults, and so is their lifespan. For an HIV-infected infant the average age of diagnosis of AIDS is 9 months, and the average age of death is 18 months.

E. The Progression of the HIV Disease

The progression of the HIV disease consists for four phases: primary HIV disease, chronic asymptomatic disease, chronic symptomatic disease, and advanced disease, or AIDS. The first phase is a short one (10 to 21 days) and occurs after infection and before positive antibody tests (seroconversion). Individuals in the first phase usually experience acute fever, enlargement of lymph nodes, fatigue, and minor loss of appetite. The chronic asymptomatic phase is variable in length, depending upon individual differences, and is marked by a period of latent symptoms but progressive reduction of the immune system. Within 6 weeks to 6 months from HIV exposure and infection, antibody tests become positive during the chronic asymptomatic phase. This phase may last from less than 1 year to more than 12 years, with most people progressing to the next phase, chronic symptomatic disease, between 6 and 11

years after HIV infection. Symptoms of the chronic symptomatic disease consist of fever, night sweats, fatigue and loss of appetite and weight. In addition, there is enlargement of the lymph nodes as well as problems with the skin and mucous membranes, such as dermatitis, shingles, canker sores, thrush, and lesions on the tongue. The transition from the chronic symptomatic disease to "full-blown" AIDS is characterized by four categories of illnesses: opportunistic infections, neoplasms, neurologic disease, and wasting.

Opportunistic infections are the most dangerous to people living with AIDS and include pneumocystic carinii pneumonia (PCP), meningoencephalitis, retinitis, cytomegalovirus (CMV) infection, esophagitis or enteritis, and tuberculosis. Neoplasms are less frequent than opportunistic illnesses, and it is usually the opportunistic illnesses that cause death for PWAs. The two primary neoplasms, however, are Kaposi's sarcoma (KS) and lymphomas. KS is a pink to purplish, bruise-like lesion that involves the skin, mucous membranes, and lungs. It typically occurs on the face, neck, lower extremities, and the oral cavity. Although it is believed that KS is transmitted by an agent other than HIV, there is evidence to suggest its transmission via oral–anal intercourse (rimming). Tumors of the lymph nodes and lymphoid tissue (lymphomas) are very frequent among people living with AIDS. Most people living with AIDS also have some type of neurologic disorder: deficits in memory, lack of concentration and attentiveness, emotional instability and apathy, and pyschomotor retardation. Extreme loss of body mass and weight (wasting) and malnutrition are also characteristic manifestations of AIDS.

F. Treatment

In the first 10 years of the HIV/AIDS epidemic, 63% of the people diagnosed with AIDS have died. Of the people diagnosed with HIV-disease between 1978 and 1983, 92 to 96% had died by 1987. We do know more about the onset and progression of HIV-disease than we did in 1987. But, no cure for HIV/AIDS exists.

There are currently about 70 treatment procedures, and people with HIV-disease are living longer. Antiretroviral drug therapy, vaccines such as Zidovudine (ZDV or AZT), dideoxyinosine (ddI), and dideoxycytidene (ddC), limits the replication of HIV and has improved the chances of survival for people living with AIDS. Another significant treatment procedure is to prevent complications from infection by vaccination against hepatitis B, measles, flu virus, and prophylaxis against pneumocystis carinii pneumonia (PCP).

II. ATTITUDES AND BELIEF SYSTEMS

Any discussion of the HIV/AIDS epidemic in regard only to its related statistics, its treatment, its diagnosis, means of transmission, and history would be insufficient. Such a discussion must be unrestricted by the consideration of the attitudes and beliefs associated with HIV/AIDS; social or economic status; class and poverty; intravenous drug use; and sexual, ethnic, and racial attitudes and beliefs. The nature and duration of the HIV-disease involves attitudes and beliefs in all of these areas.

Because HIV-infected people [frequently referred to as people with AIDS (PWAs) and/or people living with AIDS (PLWAs)] are too often considered to be outside the mainstream of our society (e.g., homosexuals, bisexuals, intravenous drug users, and other groups discriminated against and ostracized), they are often characterized according to stereotypic attitudes and beliefs based on limited knowledge about and experiences with such individuals. Coupled with these stereotypic attitudes and beliefs is the absence of any cure for the HIV-disease.

Research on attitudes toward people with AIDS indicates homophobic attitudes to be common (i.e., fear of homosexuals or of one's own homosexual feelings). Because AIDS is typically associated with homosexual/bisexual sexual behaviors and intravenous drug use, many people rationalize their feelings that most people who get ADIS are getting what they deserve, or only have themselves to blame. These types of beliefs and attitudes cause people to avoid those with AIDS, or to reject people with AIDS based on their lifestyle or their HIV-disease. Although such attitudes and beliefs may be congruent with avoiding and rejecting behaviors, such attitudes, beliefs, and behaviors are not consistent with what we know about HIV/AIDS or the people who are living with AIDS. HIV-disease is pandemic. That is, everyone who engages in risk-behavior is vulnerable to contracting HIV, regardless of their class, socioeconomic level, ethnic or racial group, or sexual orientation. And, risk-behavior includes unprotected heterosexual sexual behavior.

Other studies of peoples' attitudes toward and willingness to work with PWAs indicate a values-

conflict between empathizing with the AIDS patient and the larger social attitudes of avoidance, rejection, and ostracization of people with AIDS.

Our knowledge that there is no cure for the fatal HIV-disease and AIDS, our stereotypic beliefs associated with who transmits and acquires AIDS, and our avoiding and rejecting behaviors toward people with AIDS make if difficult to establish caring attitudes toward and relationships with those who are HIV-infected or who have AIDS. Successful educational efforts must be directed at developing caring attitudes toward people with AIDS.

III. SOCIAL CONTEXT AND PUBLIC POLICY

The first decade of the HIV/AIDS epidemic has seen social attitudes and public health policy decisions reflective of those manifested by many individuals. That is, HIV/AIDS is a disease of intravenous drug users and homosexuals, and they have only themselves to blame. Since HIV/AIDS has become a pandemic disease transmitted through heterosexual sexual intercourse with "mainstream" society, social attitudes and public health policy are slowly beginning to change.

Although there remain many pockets of resistance to providing health and sex education about HIV/AIDS, condom availability and distribution, needle exchange programs, and the elimination of discrimination and ostracization of HIV/AIDS patients, public health officials are beginning to provide increased funding for HIV/AIDS research, treatment, and educational/prevention efforts. In July 1991, for example, the National Commission on AIDS recommended removing legal barriers to the purchase and possession of needles and syringes as part of a strategy for reducing the spread of HIV among IDUs. As a further example, the state of Connecticut enacted laws in July 1992 that allowed the purchase, in pharmacies and without prescription, of up to 10 needles and syringes at one time and the possession of up to 10 clean needles and syringes. Connecticut legislators further approved and funded additional needle-exchange programs in the cities of Hartford and Bridgeport.

These changes in social attitudes and public health policy, however, have come slowly and not without the continued protests and demands that the HIV-disease be responded to and recognized for the pandemic disease it is, rather than being treated as a disease of homosexuals and intravenous drug users.

And, much of the change in attitude, policy, and increased funding have been due to the efforts and persistence of the homosexual community. Despite all this, educational and prevention measures remain inadequate and additional funding is needed for health care, social services, research, and treatment.

The difficulty, of couse, is that attitudes and belief systems (caring or otherwise) are composed of one's knowledge, one's personal life experiences, and one's awareness of and sensitivity to emotions, all of which develop in a social and cultural context. Beliefs and attitudes are also typically expressed within the framework of the historical, familial, and developmental contexts in which they are formed.

Thus, to adequately address AIDS, and the attitudes and beliefs associated with AIDS and sexual behavior, we must also address our personal and life experiences with HIV/AIDS and people living with AIDS; our emotional awareness and sensitivity to others; and the development of caring attitudes, behaviors, relationships, and social policy toward PWAs and AIDS.

IV. AIDS AND SEXUAL BEHAVIOR

Because one significant means of transmitting HIV/AIDS is through the physical intimacy and privacy of sexual intercourse and behaviors, and often in the context of insufficient sexual knowledge, experience, and/or a meaningful and caring relationship, people will continue to engage in risk-behavior.

A. Experience

However, we know that HIV is largely preventable by behaviors that reduce risks. Abstinence from vaginal, anal, and oral sex eliminates the sexual transmission of AIDS. Also, sexual intercourse in monogamous relationships between sexual partners who have not had intercourse with another sexual partner prior to the beginning of the present monogamous sexual relationship presents no risk of becoming HIV-infected. Additionally, the routine, systematic use of latex condoms, in addition to the spermicide nonoxynyl-9, for vaginal and anal (and perhaps oral) sex reduced the risk of transmitting HIV sexually. The use of latex condoms versus animal skin/membrane condoms is extremely important, because HIV can permeate animal membrane condoms whereas it cannot permeate latex membranes.

Unfortunately, there are no guarantees or absolutes when it comes to human behavior, or human sexual behavior. Although one may believe he or she has made a commitment to sexual abstinence and/or *safer sex*, not all situations are controllable and not all commitments and decisions are final. People do get themselves into difficult situations where they lose control of what is happening to them sexually (e.g., acquaintance rape). And, given the necessary mix of people, relationships, and events (including alcohol and/or other "recreational" drugs), people do change, or are persuaded to change, their priorities and previous commitments. For example, most condom failures are due to the user's lack of motivation and commitment to use condoms, or they are due to the user's inexperience and lack of skill in condom use, not defective condoms.

By definition, life is ambiguous and involves certain elements of uncertainty and risk. At times life is uncomfortable, painful, insecure, difficult, controversial, and unsafe. And, despite our attempts to quantify, measure, and isolate the critical variables that predict and control human behavior, it remains elusive, unpredictable and in many cases uncontrollable. Accidents happen, mistakes occur, poor decisions are made, and people do what they want to do rather than what they are told to do or warned against.

Some people do seem to learn, however, that even though life is not totally safe, certain, secure, risk-free, or free from pain and controversy, life can be safer, more certain, less risky, more secure, and less painful. Somewhere within this process, most people also learn they are not immortal and that earlier life-risks are no longer worth taking, or that risks can be taken in a *safer* manner. This process, however, appears to involve the integration of our personal life experiences with what we know (our knowledge base), and with what we do (our behavior).

In the absence of such experience, young people will experiment to acquire their own life experiences. Not everyone has the same opportunities, however, and the kinds of experiences individual's have may be limited or enhanced by class, ethnicity/race, social level, etc. And the decisions one makes are related to one's personal experiences.

B. Decision-Making and Sexual Behavior

Most decision-making theorists believe that the use of statistics, based on the probability of predicting the specific outcomes of specific decisions, are more effective and reliable in making "good" decisions, while others believe that one's judgment, based on personal experience and sometimes intuition, is more effective in making decisions and predicting the outcomes of those decisions. Experience also provides the opportunity of retrospectively analyzing one's prior decisions. Much of the initial knowledge about HIV/AIDS was based on anecdotal information provided by gay men and retrospectively analyzed in terms of their sexual behaviors and patterns, the numbers of sexual partners, and other personal experiences. But, experience provides us with insight and information only in terms of the decisions that were made, and no information about the other possible options that could have been chosen or the outcomes associated with decisions involving other available alternatives.

There is also the danger of overgeneralizing from one's own experience, denying the experiences one has had, or deleting and distorting selective information from one's experiences. People often assume that what is true in their experience is also true in others' experience. Not everyone, however, has the same experiences, experiments with life's options in the same way, engages in the same level of risks, or experiences the same outcomes as a result of similar decisions. Not everyone experiments with smoking tobacco, using alcohol, taking illicit drugs, having intercourse with same-sex partners, permarital intercourse, or bungee jumping. Similarly, not everyone experiments with or has experiences that involve the same combination of events, people, or situations in the same temporal context.

For example, some people may experiment with alcohol and/or drug use at the same time that they have sexual intercourse; while others may experiment with alcohol and/or drug use independent of sexual intercourse. And, any of these behaviors may occur with different people in different contexts that involve different antecedent events and consequences. Everyone does not have the same number of sexual partners, everyone does not drink the same number of drinks, and not everyone drives an automobile while drunk or impaired. There are varying degrees of risk associated with various combinations of experimental behaviors and life experiences. Consequently, the outcomes vary. Some people drink and drive with no negative consequences, while the outcomes for others who drink and drive may be tragic automobile accidents and death.

No amount of statistical evidence or life-experience can ever accurately predict the outcome of

such behaviors. There will always be some degree of uncertainty and chance involved in living life. However, the probability or chance of certain outcomes occurring, or the risk involved, can be estimated on the basis of statistical evidence and the experiences of ourselves and others.

In regard to AIDS and sexual behavior, statistical evidence and the experience of others do indicate that the probability and risk of becoming HIV-infected as a result of unprotected sexual intercourse is dramatically high. In reality there is no such thing as safe sex today, outside a monogamous sexual relationship between sexual partners who have not had previous sexual intercourse with others prior to the current monogamous sexual relationship. Popular advice suggests that people discuss with potential sexual partners their prior sexual histories and behaviors, and the probability of their exposure to HIV-infection. Even then, there is no guarantee that the sexual partner who says he or she has never had sexual intercourse prior to the present monogamous sexual relationship is telling the truth. But, sexual intercourse may be made *safer* through the use of protected sex: using latex condoms during vaginal, oral, and anal intercourse.

C. Emotional Awareness and Sensitivity

In addition to the information attained from statistical evidence and personal experience, there is another variable that requires consideration in the discussion of AIDS and sexual behavior: emotional awareness and sensitivity to others. As in other human behavior, emotions and emotional awareness are significant aspects of sexual behavior. To increase the consistency between what people know and what people do, an undersatnding of emotions is a necessary addition to the factual knowledge people possess and the personal experiences of ourselves and others.

Because emotions are often difficult to understand and, like personal experiences, are subjective in nature, many people attempt to "get-rid-of" their feelings rather than attempting to understand them. Because emotions are such a significant part of life-decisions, relationships, and behaviors, a lack of awareness about emotions may be as significant an omission as not possessing the required knowledge or having insufficient experience in making important decisions.

It also appears that the emotions most people attempt to avoid, "get-rid-of," or keep from their awareness are negative ones. Pleasant, uplifting feelings typically do not create difficulties in peoples' lives. Unless, of course, we consider people who engage in unprotected sexual intercourse merely for its physical pleasure and satisfaction, in the absence of emotional intimacy and understanding. In the present consideration, pursuing the attainment of positive feelings associated with physical, unprotected sexual satisfaction alone may result in the aftermath of dramatically negative emotions.

The personal accounts and experiences of HIV-infected and AIDS patients reflect common emotional responses to the HIV-disease: fear, hurt, anger, and loneliness. It is extremely frightening to think that we, or someone we love, might become HIV-infected and die of AIDS because of the high-risk behaviors we, or they, may have engaged in prior to becoming aware of, or in spite of, the dangers and risks associated with HIV-disease.

The opportunistic infections involved in AIDS-related death also are dramatically fearful and painful: pneumocystic carinii pneumonia (PCP), meningoencephalitis, retinitis, cytomegalovirus (CMV) infection, esophagitis or enteritis, and tuberculosis; neoplasms that involve the skin, mucous membranes, oral cavity, and lungs (e.g., Kaposi's sarcoma); tumors of the lymph nodes and lymphoid tissue (lymphomas); neurologic and psychomotor disorders and deficits in memory, concentration, and attentiveness; emotional instability and apathy; and the extreme loss of body mass and weight through chronic diarrhea and malnutrition. These are not easy infections with which to cope, emotionally or physically, whether we are the patient who is dying or the person who is watching someone we love die of such dreadful and painful illnesses.

Because such opportunistic infections can be lingering in their progression, it also is not uncommon for much of the physical and emotional suffering to occur alone. Initially, friends, partners, and family members often do not realize the emotional commitment or time investment involved in the process of AIDS-related death. As the opportunistic illnesses progress, there is typically the realization that a cure will not be found in time. And prior to the acceptance of death's inevitability and the completion of the loss and grieving process, anger becomes a dominant theme for the AIDS patient and those close to him or her. In short, the process of losing someone to AIDS can be chronically hurtful because of the hideousness of the opportunistic diseases and the slow

wasting of the patient. Not only is the loss significant but the hurt and pain are prolonged.

Ironically, the negative emotional consequences of becoming HIV-infected also may be the very same emotions, if avoided and blocked from awareness, that put people at-risk of becoming HIV-infected: fear, hurt, and anger. Earlier discussions of such negative feelings have evolved in an emotional paradigm that, if understood and applied rather than avoided and ignored, may be an important antecedent to engaging in sexual behaviors that place people at-risk of contracting HIV/AIDS.

The paradigm involves a sequence of emotions that describes fear, hurt and anger as the common-core of feelings that are typically ignored, blocked from awareness, or discouraged from expression in our present society. If the three common-core emotions are not expressed and/or blocked from awareness, an individual's emotional responses usually progress through the sequence of boredom, guilt, frustration and confusion, depression, symptomatic self-defeating behaviors (such as sexual promiscuity, "acting-out" behavior, alcohol and substance abuse, and combinations of these), and in the most severe-case scenario, suicide or homicide.

Popular observations and perceptions among the lay-population are that many people in the United States today are mistrusting of others, disclose very little about themselves, keep to themselves ("cocoon"), are lonely and alienated from others, are somewhat narcissistic, and are fearful of people outside their immediate family, especially strangers and people with whom they are not acquainted. Another popular lay-perception is that many people today do not have a good sense of their self-identity and self-worth.

Although this may be a fairly pessimistic description and view of individuals and relationships in our current society, it also may be worthy of further consideration in regard to AIDS and sexual behavior. If such popular observations are even remotely accurate, in combination with individual's avoidance or lack of awareness of their negative feelings, the importance of becoming aware of, understanding, and expressing such emotions may be a significantly neglected aspect of AIDS and sexual behavior. That is, if people are aware of the danger and risk involved in having unprotected sexual intercourse, their emotional awareness and response, if consistent with their existing knowledge and experience, should be one of fear and healthy skepticism. And, if fear is understood as the feeling of anticipated and potential loss, most people should realize that emotional pain and hurt are in response to a real and actual loss in one's life. Emotional awareness tells us that fear and pain are inevitable aspects of living life.

We do anticipate losses in our lives (fear) and we do experience real as well as anticipated losses in our lives (emotional pain and hurt). Relationships do end, people do get fired and laid-off from their jobs, significant people in our lives do move away from us to new geographic locations, accidents and physical impairments do occur, and ultimately people do die. At some point, and in addition to fear and hurt, most people usually feel angry in response to an anticipated or real loss. Anger is typically part of the emotional process of grieving a significant loss. [See ANGER.]

If unexpressed, these feelings of fear, hurt, and anger underlie the feelings of boredom, guilt, frustration and confusion, depression, and symptomatic "acting-out" and self-defeating behaviors. Boredom is often used synonymously with apathy. But regardless of the term used, a bored or apathetic person is also an angry, hurt, and fearful person. Boredom usually leads to feelings of guilt, or an expression of anger directed at oneself. And self-directed anger (or guilt) typically progresses to frustration and/or confusion about what one is feeling. The next steps in the progression of avoided and unexpressed fear, hurt, and anger are depression and "acting-out," self-defeating behavior. [See GUILT.]

In this case, the "acting-out," self-defeating behavior may be that of a fearful, hurt, angry, and depressed person, unsure of her or his self-identity and with low self-worth, engaging in unprotected sexual intercouse. The high-risk consequences of such emotional avoidance and self-defeating behavior being that of HIV-infection. Avoided and unexpressed fear, hurt and anger beget further fear, hurt, and anger and the cycle is complete and perpetuated. [See SELF-DEFEATING BEHAVIORS.]

If one doubts the legitimacy of the described emotional paradigm, or its significance in becoming HIV-infected as a result of engaging in high-risk sexual behaviors, all one needs do is listen to HIV/AIDS patients recount their personal sexual histories and experiences and describe their current emotional responses of fear, hurt, anger, and loneliness. In fact, opening oneself to listening to the "life-stories" of HIV-infected people and people living with AIDS provides an excellent, and safe, means of increasing one's own emotional awareness and sensitivity to those with HIV-disease.

D. Caring Relationships

Most HIV/AIDS patients are willing to speak candidly and honestly to others about the sexual histories, experiences, and behaviors that resulted in their becoming HIV-infected, as well as to express the feelings associated with their being HIV-infected or living with AIDS. For many HIV/AIDS patients this is a way for them to give to others, to educate others about HIV-disease, to provide some sense of meaning and significance to their lives, to help others learn from their experiences, and to demonstrate their caring for others.

The honesty and caring demonstrated by many HIV/AIDS patients, perhaps motivated by the daily awareness of their own mortality and the feelings associated with that awareness, are the honest and caring qualities that could benefit most of us if emulated in our own personal and sexual relationships. Rarely in our society today is honesty the best policy in terms of financial gain and freedom from suffering and pain. But, in terms of AIDS and sexual behavior honesty is the only policy in terms of freedom from unnecessary suffering and pain.

Unfortunately, many people react to HIV/AIDS patients with responses of fear, anger, disgust, blame, discrimination, and ostracization—missing the important emotional information and relationship messages being conveyed by HIV/AIDS patients. Rather than using such information to increase their own emotional awareness and sensitivity toward others, too many people respond to HIV-infected people and people living with AIDS by choosing to avoid or to "get-rid-of" their own negative feelings by displacing and projecting them onto the HIV/AIDS patient. Such dishonesty with self and lack of awareness are the antithesis of developing caring attitudes and relationships with HIV/AIDS patients, let alone developing emotionally intimate, honest, and caring relationships with others.

V. CONCLUSIONS

The World Health Organization (WHO) has estimated that 9 to 11 million people are HIV-infected world wide. As of January 1993, the Centers for

Disease Control has received reports of 250,000 cases of AIDS in the United States, estimating that 1 to 1.4 million people are currently infected with the HIV-disease and will be in need of physical health care and mental health care. Estimates are that approximately 1 in 250 people in the United States are HIV-infected: 1 in 100 men and 1 in 800 women. In some states the estimates are even more severe. In Connecticut, for example, it is estimated that 1 in 125 people are currently HIV-infected or have AIDS: 1 in 80 men and 1 in 330 women. What is dramatic about these data is that Connecticut is a state known for its health care, high standard of living, and internationally renowned educational institutions. It also has been predicted that 1 in 10 people in the United States will be infected with HIV in the next decade, with about 40,000 new infections occurring each year.

Of the 47,106 cases of AIDS reported to the CDC in 1992, over one-half were men who have sex with men, 25% were injecting drug users (IDUs), and 14% were women. Based on available data there is evidence that the yearly incidence of HIV/AIDS will plateau by 1995, to around 60,000 to 75,000 new cases per year. To place the pandemic HIV-disease in clearer perspective, over 39,000 lives were lost in the Vietnam War between 1967 and 1973. AIDS has claimed over 150,000 lives in its first decade.

There is still much we do not know about the virus and the treatment of HIV-infection and AIDS. There is still much we need to do to educate people about what we do know about HIV/AIDS, its consequences, and prevention. And, there is still much we need to do to help people integrate their current knowledge with caring attitudes and emotional awareness and sensitivity in their behaviors toward and relationships with HIV/AIDS patients and others. To know and care about others, however, we must first know and care about ourselves.

To truly understand AIDS and sexual behavior, we must possess the necessary knowledge and factual information acquired through formal education and teaching, self-learning and reading, and the personal experiences of ourselves and others. This content knowledge must then be incorporated with the information obtained from the self-exploration of our own attitudes and belief systems concerning HIV/AIDS, sexual orientation, sexual relationships, intravenous drug use, ethnic and racial groups, differences in class and socioeconomic level, poverty, public health policies, and health-care issues. In addition to the aquired knowledge and the development of caring attitudes and belief systems, we must also integrate an awareness of our own emotions and sensitivity with the emotions of others.

Armed with the appropriate knowledge, attitudes, and emotional awareness and sensitivity, we may then begin to engage in sexual relationships and behaviors that are caring toward ourselves and others. Without such knowledge, attitudes, and emotional awareness and sensitivity, HIV/AIDS will continue to be a pandemic disease transmitted by what we do to ourselves and others through one of the most intimate of human behaviors: sexual intercourse.

Bibliography

Callen, M. (1990). "Surviving AIDS." Harper Collins, New York.

Centers for Disease Control. (1992). "HIV/AIDS Surveillance—United States. AIDS Cases Reported through December 1991." United States Department of Health and Human Services, Washington, DC.

Douce, L. A. (Ed.). (1993). AIDS and HIV [Special feature]. *J. Counsel. Dev.* **71,** 259–309.

Friedland, G. H. (1990). Early treatment of HIV: The time has come. *N. Engl. J. Med.* **332,** 1000–1002.

Goedert, J. J. (1987). What is safe sex? Suggested standards linked to testing for human immunodeficiency virus. *N. Engl. J. Med.* **316,** 1339–1342.

Holmes, K. K., Karon, J. M., and Kreiss, J. (1990). The increasing frequency of heterosexual acquired AIDS in the United States. *Am. J. Public Health* **80,** 858–863.

Keeling, R. P. (1991). HIV disease: Current concepts (Special feature: AIDS and HIV). *J. Counsel. Dev.* **71,** 261–274.

Lifson, A. R., Rutherford, G. W., and Jaffe, H. W. (1988). The natural history of HIV infection. *J. Infect. Dis.* **158,** 1360–1368.

Lorin, R. P., and Newbrough, J. R. (Eds.). (1990). AIDS and the community [Special issue] *J. Comm. Pyschol.* **18** (4).

Perlman, J. A., Kelaghan, J., and Wolf, P. H. (1990). HIV risk difference between condom users and non-condom users among U.S. heterosexual women. *J. AIDS* **3,** 155–165.

Shilts, R. (1988). "And the Band Played On." St. Martin's Press, New York.

Sloand, E. M., Pitt, E., Chairello, R. J., and Nemo, G. J. (1991). HIV testing: State of the art. *J. Am. M. Assoc.* **266,** 2861–2868.

ALTRUISM AND HELPING BEHAVIOR

E. Gil Clary
College of St. Catherine

Glossary

Altruistic helping Helping behavior motivated by concern for the person in distress; selfless helping.

Egoistic helping Helping behavior motivated by concern for the benefits and costs to the helper for helping; selfish helping.

Helping behavior Action that attempts to relieve another person's distress.

Prosocial behavior Positive forms of behavior, including helpfulness; the concept stands in contrast to antisocial behavior.

HELPING BEHAVIORS are activities where people provide assistance in solving the problems of other people. Altruism designates the case where the assistance is motivated by concern for the other person, whereas helping motivated by concern for the self is regarded as egoistic. Motivational processes, other intrapersonal factors, and situational forces influence whether people will help in a situation where help is needed. In addition to addressing this question of "will a person help?," the questions "how will a helper help?" and "will the help be helpful?" are explored.

I. RANGE AND FREQUENCY OF HELPING BEHAVIOR

While human beings are clearly capable of extreme cruelty and violence toward their fellow human beings, people also display extraordinary acts of kindness, generosity, and sacrifice on behalf of others. Amidst the horrors of Nazi-dominated Europe were cases of Gentiles rescuing and hiding Jewish victims of the Final Solution. In the southern United States during the 1950s and 1960s were white participants in the civil rights movement, working actively with black participants in political organizing and voter registration. And in 1992, in the riots sparked by the verdicts of the four Los Angeles policemen involved in the Rodney King beating, we saw four black men and women rescue a white truck driver being beaten by a group of black youths.

These dramatic acts of helpfulness may well be infrequent occurrences, yet smaller and more ordinary acts occur with great regularity. During the course of our everyday social lives, we have opportunities to give directions to people who are lost, assist stranded motorists, provide small change to worthy causes, and engage in countless other acts of assistance. In addition to these brief help-giving encounters, many people are involved in helpfulness on a sustained basis, oftentimes in the form of volunteer work. We find, for example, people providing companionship to young people or the elderly, counseling those who are psychologically distressed, tutoring illiterate adults or disadvantaged children, and delivering meals to the homebound. Moreover, national surveys conducted in recent years have found that approximately half of all American adults reported performing some kind of volunteer work in the 12 months prior to the survey.

Clearly, prosocial activities are widespread and include a broad range of actions. In one attempt at discovering the underlying differences among this wide assortment of helpful acts, multidimensional scaling procedures were applied to many of the helping behaviors utilized as dependent measures in research. According to the analysis of these researchers, helping situations vary along three dimensions. To illustrate these dimensions, Table I presents helpful actions representative of the combination of the three dimensions.

TABLE I

Dimensions of Helpful Actions and Representative Acts

	Planned help		Unplanned help	
	Serious situation	Not serious situation	Serious situation	Not serious situation
Indirect help (giving)	Donate blood	Save cartons for art students	Telephone for medical emergency	Give money for bus fare
Direct help (doing)	Crisis counseling	Volunteer for experiment	Perform CPR for a heart attack victim	Look for lost contact lens

The first dimension concerns whether the helper performs an action that *directly* helps the person in need or *indirectly* helps by providing a resource that can be used to alleviate the need. Essentially, is the action something the helper does that in itself provides relief or some resource the helper gives that can then be used by another helper or the recipient to provide relief? The second dimension is whether the helping situation arises *unexpectedly*, with the helper surprised by the need for help, or is *planned*, with the helper deliberating before acting and perhaps even seeking out the opportunity. In other words, is the helpful response unplanned (e.g., emergencies) or anticipated (e.g., the decision to help, and the help itself perhaps, unfolds over time)? Finally, the situation in which the need for help arises may be *serious* or *not serious*. That is, how badly does the recipient of help need help and what are the potential consequences if help does not occur?

Helpful actions, then, differ in terms of the context in which they arise (whether the need occurs unexpectedly or not), nature of the recipient's need (serious or not serious), and type of action required (direct or indirect). Furthermore, these differences serve as important qualifications as we attempt to understand helping behavior. As an illustration, national surveys of charitable and voluntary actions consistently find a larger number of American adults reporting that they give money to charities (indirect help) than engage in volunteer work (direct help). With these categories and actions as a backdrop, the following examination of prosocial behavior will focus on three questions related to helping. First, will a person help in a situation where another is in need of help? Second, given that a person has decided to help, in what way will the helper help?

And third, will the help be effective in reducing the recipient's need?

II. CONDITIONS AFFECTING THE OCCURRENCE OF HELPING

A. Situational Factors

The vast majority of studies conducted by behavioral scientists on the subject of human helpfulness has been devoted to the question of whether a potential helper will help when faced with another person's need for help. The interest has been in identifying factors operating within the situation and within the potential helper that increase or decrease the likelihood that help will occur. A major impetus for behavioral scientists' attention to helping behaviors was a dramatic episode of a failure to help. In 1964, Kitty Genovese was murdered by a knife-wielding attacker as she returned to her New York City apartment building in the early hours of the morning. The attack actually consisted of three separate attacks over an approximately 45-minute time period and was witnessed by at least 38 people who were watching from their apartments. None of the observers assisted her.

Out of this tragic episode has emerged a body of literature devoted to the phenomenon of *bystanders' intervention into emergencies*, with the investigations attempting to duplicate the emergency nature of the Kitty Genovese case under controlled conditions. College students participating in an experiment, for example, have been exposed to an unexpected fall and injury to a workman in an adjoining room. Or customers in stores have witnessed staged thefts, with the key behavior being whether the theft was reported. From these studies, one consistent finding has emerged: the presence of other people, and particularly strangers, inhibits intervening in emergencies.

From the attempts to explain the inhibitory effect of others have come a framework for the intervention process in emergencies (Fig. 1 presents the sequence of events). The first condition that must be met before a potential helper can intervene is attention to the event. While it seems implausible that a dramatic emergency would be unnoticed, several factors can actually lead to a failure to notice an emergency. These include being overwhelmed by stimuli as might be the case when one lives in a large urban area, distracted from external events because one is focusing attention on one's own problems, or under time pressures. If, however, a potential helper notices the event, then the next step concerns whether the person interprets the episode as a situation that requires help. An interpretation that the episode is an emergency is hindered by any set of conditions that make it ambiguous—is an altercation between a man and woman, for example, an attack or a lover's quarrel?

The conditions mentioned up to this point could occur regardless of whether one is facing a possible emergency alone or with others. More directly related to the inhibiting effect of other people is the social process of *evaluation apprehension*. This involves people's desire to present themselves as "calm, cool, and collected," and avoid actions that might embarrass them. In this case, people are fearful of acting as if the situation is serious when, in fact, it is not, and thereby being embarrassed by overreacting. The unfortunate upshot of this process is that when a group is faced with a potential emer-

gency, individuals present a calm mask while looking around at others' faces to determine if the situation is serious but other people in the situation are also presenting a calm mask as they look around at others. The end result is often an interpretation that the event is not an emergency and no one intervenes. When alone, the absence of others removes an audience for embarrassment and gives the individual more latitude in making an interpretation that an emergency has occurred.

Having made an interpretation that the event is an emergency, a person must still decide whether he or she will intervene. Again, several factors affect this final step, including an estimation of one's own competence to help: i.e., that one possesses the skills necessary to assist the person in need. In terms of the inhibiting presence of others, an important aspect of this final decision is *diffusion of responsibility*. When alone, the responsibility for helping a victim rests solely with the individual. When others are present, however, the several individuals psychologically distribute responsibility for action and each individual's own sense of responsibility is lessened. Thus, the tendency for evaluation apprehension and diffusion of responsibility to occur when one is exposed to a potential emergency with other people results in a decreased probability that anyone will help.

Several other factors in helping situations inhibit help-giving, functioning primarily as costs to the helper. One such cost comes from the process of evaluation apprehension when witnessing emergencies with others, with its concern for possible embarrassment arising from intervening when one should have "minded one's own business." Helpful actions can also cost the helper time, energy, or money. Moreover, some situations are clearly dangerous for the intervener; rescuers of Jewish victims of the Holocaust, for example, were often executed if caught. Finally, even in the absence of physical harm, some situations involve victims who are severely injured and suffering and people can find exposure to these situations psychologically distressing. This is well illustrated by the discomfort of passersby who are exposed to bloodied victims of severe automobile accidents.

While helping can certainly be costly, there are also costs for failing to help (e.g., the disapproval of others). Yet helpful actions are not simply a matter of calculating potential losses. People who help can benefit through helping and the availability of these rewards increases the likelihood that help will

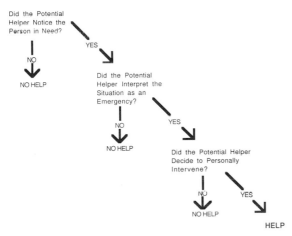

FIGURE 1   The bystander intervention process.

occur. Many of the benefits available to helpers seem to center on approval, whether the approval of others for helping, the gratitude of the recipient of help, or self-approval. With respect to self-approval, helpers can reinforce themselves for acting in accordance with their values and/or for having "made a difference." Moreover, through helping, a helper can experience an increase in self-confidence and more generally self-esteem. Thus, although a considerable amount of research has been devoted to the social processes that inhibit intervention, behavioral scientists have also investigated social processes that promote helpful actions.

One important promotive influence involves *modeling*—learning by observing the behavior of others. Modeling influences can have long-term effects, as in the case of parents acting as prosocial models (discussed more fully in the next section), as well as short-term effects. For example, when presented with unexpected opportunities to help, witnessing another's help increases the incidence of behaving helpfully. Charitable donations to sidewalk Salvation Army solicitors have increased when the potential helper first observes a model providing a donation. Similarly, a motorist with a flat tire received more offers of assistance when travelers had earlier observed another motorist with a flat tire receiving assistance. In part, witnessing the helpfulness of another increases the observer's helpfulness by teaching new behaviors and demonstrating that certain behaviors are appropriate in a situation.

In addition, exposure to helpful models reminds observers of norms about helping others, especially the *norm of social responsibility*. According to this norm, we should help those who are dependent on us, such as young children, the sick, and people in need. While research is consistent with the prediction that helping increases as dependency increases, explanations which focus on norms like social responsibility are often criticized on the grounds that they are vague, general, and appear to be present in situations where there is a failure to help (e.g., Kitty Genovese). Furthermore, there are social norms that discourage helping, as exemplified by such admonishments as "don't get involved" and "mind your own business." Nonetheless, many societies have norms like social responsibility that serve as a backdrop to events where others are in need and exert an influence when combined with other factors. For example, exposure to a helpful model reminds people of the social responsibility norm.

A clearer case of a help-related norm influencing helping behavior concerns the *norm of reciprocity*—we should help those who have helped us. This guideline is not just limited to the realm of helping, but applies more broadly to our relations with others. Reciprocity also appears to represent a universal norm and some societies have very clear-cut guidelines about how and when one returns a gift (e.g., the Kula ring among the Massim peoples found in several small islands near New Guinea). Yet, receiving help is no guarantee that the recipient will later return the help. Recipients of help seem to feel less obligation to reciprocate when the gift represents a small portion of the helper's overall resources or if the original help was given accidentally rather than deliberately. Reciprocal help also seems to be less likely if the helper is judged to have ulterior motives for acting helpfully. In this case, recipients may experience "psychological reactance"—a negative motivational state where people wish to reassert their freedom to act, which may result in a refusal to reciprocate.

The conditions under which prior help is more versus less likely to be returned raise a larger question about the potential recipient of help as a situational determinant of helping—when are people in need more likely to receive help? As discussed earlier, there is an increased tendency to help when the need of the victim increases. This tendency, however, is moderated by potential helpers' judgments about whether the victim deserves help. People help more when the victim is viewed as needing help because of circumstances beyond his or her control versus having created one's own predicament. Subway riders, for example, were more likely to help a fallen rider when his fall appeared to be due to sickness rather than drunkenness. In a related vein, more help is forthcoming when the need seems legitimate and necessary, as in requesting money for purchasing milk, rather than a more unnecessary and trivial need (e.g., requesting money for beer). Finally, there is a tendency to help others more when the person in need appears to be similar to us, as signaled by the person's dress.

B. Personal Factors

The vast majority of psychological studies conducted on the topic of helping behavior has focused on identifying situational variables that inhibit or promote help-giving rather than internal factors. When studies did include helper-related factors, however, the findings tended to not support the person-based approach and instead pointed to the power of situational forces in determining individuals' helpfulness (e.g., bystander intervention studies that included trait measures have typically found weak associations, at best, between the traits and helping). There were exceptions, as in a study of people who had intervened in naturally occurring crimes (e.g., assaults, burglaries, and hold-ups). Relative to a matched group of noninterveners, people who had intervened were physically larger, reported more first-aid, life-saving, and police training, had been exposed to more crimes, and described themselves as more aggressive, emotional, and principled.

That *intrapersonal* processes exert important influences on helping behavior comes from research on the effects of mood states. It should be pointed out that although most of the research has utilized situational manipulations to induce mood states, the focus is clearly on this internal condition. Whether induced by finding a coin in a phone booth, receiving a free cookie, or having an experience of success, people are more likely to help when they are in a *positive mood*. Several psychological mechanisms appear to contribute to this relationship, including the tendency for people in a good mood to view things in a more positive light, be reminded of one's own good fortune, and desire to maintain the positive mood state. All in all, these several mechanisms appear to result in an increased salience of obtaining positive reinforcement.

The relationship of negative moods and helping is a more complex one, with the association heavily dependent on the specific negative mood. Guilt is generally associated with increased helping, and especially when one feels responsible for the potential recipient's state of need, as helping provides a mechanism for reducing that guilt. The relationship of sadness and helping, however, is more variable. Helping becomes more likely if the sadness is directed at the distress of another person, but less likely if the sadness is directed at oneself. As an illustration, one study asked some subjects to imagine a terminally ill friend's reaction to the illness, while other subjects' attention was directed to their own reactions to their friend's illness; only the former group revealed an increased tendency to help. Thus, a potential helper's internal mood state, positive or negative, can clearly influence helpfulness.

More broadly, recent research has shown that personal factors are more likely to affect helping behav-

ior in some kinds of situations versus others. Specifically, situational factors seem to operate as more powerful influences in situations where the opportunity to help arises unexpectedly and the resulting help is unplanned (e.g., emergencies). On the other hand, in situations where the help is planned and may even involve the helper seeking out the opportunity to help (e.g., volunteer activities), there is a tendency for important differences between helpers and nonhelpers to emerge. In fact, this variation in the strength of situational and personal factors as a function of the type of situation seems to be a more general relationship: situations possessing highly salient external cues for behavior reveal situational determinants, whereas situations possessing less salient external cues reveal personal dispositions and desires guiding behavior.

Given that personal factors affect helpfulness under some conditions, the question then arises as to the specific intrapersonal characteristics that are involved in this social behavior. Before considering specific characteristics, let us turn to an issue central to personal factors associated with help-giving, and indeed underlying much of the discussion of helping behavior generally—is help ever given for the ultimate benefit of the recipient of help or is all helpfulness reducible to benefitting the helper? This issue, known as the *altruism–egoism debate,* centers on the question of people's motivations for helping. The debate has a very long tradition in philosophy and goes to the heart of questions about human nature. As applied to helping behavior, is the help given to others always selfish and instrumental in that its object is maximizing gains and minimizing costs to the self, the helper? Or is help sometimes given selflessly, with the benefits to the other the primary or only end?

In psychological research, much of the contemporary debate over altruism and egoism centers on the potential helper's emotional responses to seeing another in distress and the resulting motivational states. The emotion of primary interest is *empathy*, and research has uncovered two empathic responses aroused by the plight of another person. *Personal distress* involves the potential helper's own distress at the sight of another in need, and is characterized by such feelings as being "troubled," "alarmed," and "upset" in a situation requiring help. *Empathic concern* is an emotional state marked by feeling "sympathetic," "compassionate," and "tender" in response to another's need and represents an orientation toward the other person's distress. According to research, personal distress tends to arouse egoistic motivation, with the potential helper's primary aim being the termination of one's own distress. This can be achieved by either escaping from the situation or helping the person in need if escape is too difficult. On the other hand, empathic concern leads to altruistic motivation, where the goal is reducing the distress of the other person, and this can be achieved only by the other receiving help. [See EMPATHY.]

In addition to this connection between altruistic motivation and empathic concern, known in the literature as the *empathy–altruism hypothesis,* altruism has been associated with specific values. Values related to helpfulness include humanitarian concerns, contributing to the community, and social responsibility. Moreover, it appears that helpful people adopt these values more strongly, with the motivation including the desire to express these values in action. Research on people involved in volunteer work serves as an example. Studies have found that helping-related values are characteristic of volunteers, distinguish volunteers from nonvolunteers, and even distinguish more committed volunteers from less committed volunteers. This is also seen with volunteer blood donors, where these values have been found to gain in strength with repeated donations; for some donors, in fact, the result is that the blood donor role becomes a significant part of the individual's self-conception. [See SOCIAL VALUES.]

The question has also been asked whether specific personality traits are associated with helping behavior and perhaps even altruistic helping. Relative to nonvolunteers, volunteers have been observed to possess greater degrees of self-efficacy, emotional stability, empathy, internal locus of control, and intrinsic religiosity. Under conditions of unplanned (unexpected) opportunities to help, traits observed to be related to helpfulness have included self-esteem, ascription of responsibility, dispositional empathic concern, and high need for nurturance combined with low need for succorance. Two important qualifications have been noted regarding the relationship of personality traits and helping behavior, especially helping that occurs in unexpected/unplanned situations. First, stronger relationships between traits and helping are obtained when one combines several traits into a composite measure, as this composite more adequately captures the more general predisposition to help others. Second, it appears that whether a particular trait correlates with helping depends on the fit between the trait and the specific situation. Nurturance, for example, was

found to be correlated with willingness to counsel high school students but unrelated to willingness to collate and assemble class materials; this latter activity, however, was related to autonomy.

Given that intrapersonal factors affect helping behavior, it is important to consider the origin of these factors. One important mechanism by which help-related emotions, motivations, and traits are acquired is through the process of *socialization* during childhood and adolescence. Parents, teachers, and other influential adults can encourage and reinforce children's helpful behaviors so that these behaviors become habitual. Parents and others can also model helpfulness, demonstrating to children the appropriateness of acting prosocially. For example, a group of committed civil rights activists reported that their parents had been activists of an earlier era (i.e., modeled helpfulness), as well as having established warm, positive relationships with their children. This combination appears to be especially important for internalization (of help-related characteristics, in this case) to occur: children are more likely to adopt as their own those standards that are modeled by a nurturant model. Research has also shown that preaching helpfulness in the absence of action is ineffective. Not surprisingly, children exposed to a model who preaches but does not practice helpfulness tend to imitate the model's (nonhelpful) behavior.

In concluding this section on the relationship of personal factors and helping behavior, we return to the central issue of altruistic versus egoistic motives. Specifically, is help ever altruistic? If by altruism one means a "pure" version where a person helps out of concern for the other and without concern for the self, then altruism is probably rare, if it exists at all. Research on the empathy–altruism hypothesis, for example, obtains positive correlations between empathic concern and personal distress. There would appear to be altruistic helping, however, if altruism is viewed as a motive that can coexist with other motives; i.e., a person can care about others at the same time as caring about the self. Research on volunteerism provides a case in point, as investigations consistently find volunteers attempting to satisfy several motives. Some volunteers combine altruistic values with the desire for new learning opportunities, others appear motivated by values and career-related concerns, and still other volunteers couple a desire to increase self-esteem with expressing one's altruistic values. Thus, research with people engaged in volunteer work especially points to the multimotivational nature of helping behavior.

III. WAYS OF HELPING

In the preceding section, the primary emphasis was on the question of whether a potential helper will help. Having decided to help, the helper is then faced with the decision of how he or she will help. In other words, given the need of the other and the capabilities of the helper, what kind of help will be given? Two variations on this question are considered: first, what type of action will the helper perform; and second, what style, approach, or orientation will the helper take toward the recipient of help?

A. Types of Helping Activities

One important distinction noted earlier was that help might be given directly or indirectly. That is, the helper might *do* something to assist in solving the person's problem or *give* something that can then be used to solve the problem. When faced with a victim of a heart attack, for example, one might help by performing CPR or by finding someone who can perform CPR or some other medical procedure. Similarly, in the civil rights movement, some activists engaged in direct activities like voter registration, while others helped through such indirect means as providing financial support. Furthermore, large organizations whose mission is to help others such as the Red Cross are likely to provide the opportunity to help both directly (e.g., providing disaster relief or teaching swimming) and indirectly (e.g., giving money or blood, or working on tasks which support the organization, as in clerical tasks). In cases like these latter examples, where people are engaged in planned helping, helpers are particularly likely to rely on their internal states to guide how they will help. Thus, whether one helps directly or indirectly depends on a number of factors, including the time, energy, and resources available to a helper, and the helper's skills, talents, and psychological dispositions.

B. Models of Helping

While the distinction between direct and indirect help centers on the actions themselves, another concerns the *model of helping* adopted by the helper as he or she approaches the task of helping others.

This distinction is not about the type of action one performs but rather the underlying assumptions a helper makes about the helping situations with which he or she is faced. In other words, people holding different models of helping may engage in similar direct helping activities, but differ in the way that help is given and the objective that one hopes to accomplish. Models of helping may be seen most clearly in situations where help occurs with regularity; for example, in sustained helping situations represented by the work of members of the "helping professions."

According to conceptual analyses of helping, helpers (and recipients) faced with a situation where help is needed make attributions about the degree of responsibility the person with the problem has for (1) causing that problem and (2) solving the problem. The two attributional dimensions combine to result in four models of helping: the moral model (the person with the problem is viewed as having a high degree of responsibility for both the problem and solution); the medical model (the target person is seen as having little responsibility for either the problem or solution); the enlightenment model (the target person is seen as having a high degree of responsibility for the problem but a low degree of responsibility for the solution); and the compensatory model (the person with the problem is viewed as not responsible for the problem but is responsible for the solution). People endorsing different models of helping are believed to differ in their perceptions of people with problems, the role of helpers, and the appropriate kind of interaction between helper and recipient. Table II summarizes the models and the consequences of each.

While each model might be applied most appropriately to specific problems and helping situations, for purposes of illustration consider one situation where each model has been applied at one time or another—approaches to the problem of alcohol abuse. The moral model, with its ideas about people creating their own problems and the necessity for people to change themselves, appears to be represented by Prohibition-era conceptions of alcoholism. The medical model is represented by the disease model of alcohol abuse, with the assumption that alcoholism has biological roots and therefore requires medical treatment. The enlightenment model is illustrated by Alcoholics Anonymous, where a person takes responsibility for his or her problems but must turn to the support group and a higher power for change to occur. Finally, the compensatory model, with its

TABLE II

Consequences of Attribution of Responsibility in Four Models of Helping

Attribution to recipient of responsibility for problem	Attribution to recipient of responsibility for solution to the problem	
	High	Low
High	Moral model	Enlightenment model
Perception of recipient	Lazy	Guilty
Actions expected of recipient	Striving	Submission
Others besides recipient who must act (helpers)	Peers	Authorities
Actions expected of helpers	Exhortation	Discipline
Implicit view of human nature	Strong	Bad
Low	Compensatory model	Medical model
Perception of recipient	Deprived	Ill
Actions expected of recipient	Assertion	Acceptance
Others besides recipient who must act (helpers)	Subordinates	Experts
Actions expected of helpers	Mobilization	Treatment
Implicit view of human nature	Good	Weak

Source: Adapted with permission from "Models of Helping and Coping," by P. Brickman, V. C. Rabinowitz, J. Karuza, D. Coates, E. Cohn, and L. Kidder (1982), *American Psychologist,* 37, p. 370. Copyright 1982 by the American Psychological Association.

emphasis on other factors causing one's problems but viewing the person as the source of the solution, is found in approaches that view addiction as stress-related and treatment as adapting and adjusting to those stresses.

Psychological research on the models of helping has included conceptual applications of the models to specific helping situations (e.g., the work of nurses and psychotherapeutic practice) as well as empirical examination. Empirical investigations have provided support for the underlying structure of the four models. Research has also uncovered some interesting differences among people in terms of their preferences for how they wished to be helped by others. Older people, for example, appear to prefer models of helping that attribute less responsibility for the solution to the person with the problem (i.e., the medical and enlightenment models). Another study found sex and social class differences in preferences for receiving help: males, regardless of social class, appeared to prefer styles in which the recipient was not responsible for solutions to problems; females of the working and lower classes were comparable to males, while middle class fe-

males preferred a style where they, as recipients, retained responsibility for the solutions. Thus, there appear to be very real differences in how helpers approach the task of helping others, that the approaches differ in some fundamental ways, and that recipients of help have some distinct preferences for how others help them. Whether these preferences are actually in recipients' best interests is one of the questions addressed in the next section.

IV. EFFECTIVE HELPING

Thus far we have considered two questions related to situations where help is needed—will a potential helper help, and if so, in what way will the helper help? The final question to be examined concerns whether the help given is effective. This question can be phrased in several ways: was the help helpful; did the assistance actually solve the problem or reduce the distress experienced by the recipient; and did the helper possess the competence to successfully help another? Helpful actions do not necessarily carry guarantees of success, as attested to by the proverb that "the road to hell is paved with good intentions."

It seems unlikely that there is some basic skill that leads to effective helping in a wide range of situations. Rather, successful help is more likely related to specific skills being applied to the specific demands of a situation. This has been implicit in several examples previously discussed. Recall the finding that people who had intervened in criminal activity reported relevant training experiences, saw themselves as more aggressive, and were physically large (interveners also reported being larger than the criminal offender). While these qualities are important in this kind of situation, it is unlikely that the same features would necessarily make one a better psychological counselor. An additional illustration comes from blood donations: blood donors, despite intentions, must meet certain health requirements before donating blood, and the blood collected is not used until undergoing a screening process. It bears pointing out that research has shown that possessing relevant skills also affects the decision to help in the first place. In a staged emergency involving a victim of electrical shock, subjects having experience with electrical equipment were more likely to intervene than those lacking this experience.

At the same time, a relevant skill is not just another variable influencing the decision to help. This was demonstrated in a recent experiment where subjects, either before or after receiving Red Cross training, were exposed to a mock arterial bleeding emergency. *Whether* subjects intervened or not was influenced by some of the usual bystander intervention variables (e.g., the presence or absence of other people), but *how* people helped was affected by training—those with training were more likely to provide direct help (the application of direct pressure to the wound) whereas those without training were more likely to engage in indirect help (finding other assistance). This suggests that whether a person will help is not the same as how one will help. Moreover, in the context of the medical emergency used here, it is clear that acts of helpfulness are not equally effective. In actual severe arterial bleeding cases, failure to apply direct pressure within 4 to 10 minutes usually results in death, so that indirect help may be of no help.

The models of helping discussed earlier are also relevant to the issue of the effectiveness of help. The investigation that observed that the elderly preferred the medical and enlightenment models (i.e., approaches to helping that attributed less responsibility for the solution to the person with the problem) also found that psychological well-being was *positively* associated with taking responsibility for solutions to problems. Investigations from several areas are generally consistent on this point, with improvement being more likely when recipients of help become active participants in solving their own problems. Research on psychotherapy provides one example in which successful outcomes are associated with clients' attributing change to their own efforts. This is not to argue that models that do not assume recipient responsibility for solutions have no place in helping relationships; after all, virtually everyone would prefer the immediate application of the medical model over the moral model following a head injury in a motorcycle accident. Later on, however, the moral model might well be appropriate, particularly if the victim of the motorcycle accident was not wearing a helmet. Thus, it is unlikely that some models are always more effective than other models, but rather that each model will be effective in certain situations and/or at certain points in the helping process.

In concluding this section on effective help, we should also consider the literature on recipients' reactions to help. While receiving help can certainly be beneficial for the recipient, there are also psychological costs attached to being a recipient. Studies on recipients' reactions have tended to focus on the *threat to self-esteem* that can accompany help. That is, helping often involves a relationship that is unequal in power and carries with it the suggestion that the recipient is incompetent. Needing help, in other words, can be embarrassing and humiliating. And helpers vary in the ways in which they give assistance, with some being caring and supportive, whereas others assist in more negative and threatening ways. Certainly, help that is given in a more negative and threatening manner is experienced as more unpleasant for recipients. However, this approach may actually be more effective in the long-run, at least for some recipients: recipients may become motivated to eliminate this loss of self-esteem and thereby engage in greater efforts at self-help in the future. [*See* SELF-ESTEEM.]

V. HELPERS AND HELPING OPPORTUNITIES

As with human behavior generally, prosocial action is a complex phenomenon affected by a variety of factors and considerations. Whether one helps in a situation where another person is in need depends on social forces operating in the situation, characteristics of the particular needs present in the situation, and the motivations and abilities of the potential helper. Having decided to help, the helper must decide how and in what way to help, with the specific type of help and approach to helping influenced by some of these same factors as well as others (e.g., the helper's fundamental assumptions about the helping process). Yet, having provided help of a specific sort and in a specific way does not necessarily result in the termination of the recipient's distress. Furthermore, help that is immediately successful may not be effective in the long-run.

An act of helping, then, can be broadly constructed as an interactive function of characteristics of the helper and characteristics of the helping situation. Within this context, we might revisit an issue central to many questions about human helpfulness—the debate over altruistic versus egoistic motivation. One aspect of this debate has concerned the question of the "altruistic personality": a type of person who is consistently helpful, more helpful than others, and whose helpfulness arises out of altruistic motives. Given the earlier concerns about the existence of "pure altruism," an altruistic personality seems doubtful. And within an interactive framework, one can probably expect only so much consistent helpfulness if by consistency one means acting helpfully across a wide variety of helping situations. Even with a *willingness* to help, a helpful person may not possess the *ability* to help. To expect a helpful person to act helpfully in a large number of very different situations seems as unreasonable as expecting an intelligent person to make important contributions in many different intellectual domains. But consistency can also refer to a sustained commitment to performing one kind of helping activity (e.g., performing volunteer work on a regular basis). Moreover, it appears that some people are consistently more helpful than others. Some researchers

describe such people as possessing a "prosocial orientation," which consists of several psychological characteristics (e.g., valuing helpfulness, feeling a greater responsibility for others, and operating at a higher level of moral development).

In several respects helping behavior is not the simple issue that it may appear to be at first glance. As we have seen, there are times when helping may not be the most appropriate response. Despite good intentions, for example, a helper may not be competent to help. Or some acts of intervention may not be capable of reducing a victim's needs (e.g., indirect help when time is critical). Furthermore, being caring and supportive sometimes lead to a recipient becoming dependent on the assistance of others. Lastly, there may be times when the best response is to allow a person in need to act as the helper. After all, as research on peer tutoring has shown, the person who benefits the most from a tutoring situation is the tutor.

Bibliography

Batson, C. D. (1987). Prosocial motivation: Is it ever truly altruistic? In "Advances in Experimental Social Psychology" (L. Berkowitz, Ed.), Vol. 20. Academic Press, New York.

Carlson, M., Charlin, V., and Miller, N. (1988). Positive mood and helping behavior: A test of six hypotheses. *J. Personality and Soc. Psychol.* **55**, 211–229.

Clary, E. G., and Snyder, M. (1991). A functional analysis of altruism and prosocial behavior: The case for volunteerism. In "Review of Personality and Social Psychology" (M. S. Clark, Ed.), Vol. 12. Sage, Newbury Park, CA.

Eisenberg, N., and Mussen, P. (1989). "The Roots of Prosocial Behavior in Children." Cambridge University Press, Cambridge.

Kohn, A. (1990). "The Brighter Side of Human Nature: Altruism and Egoism in Everyday Life." Basic Books, New York.

Krebs, D., and Miller, D. T. (1985). Altruism and aggression. In "The Handbook of Social Psychology" (G. Lindzey and E. Aronson, Eds.), Vol. 2, 3rd ed. Random House, New York.

Oliner, S. P., and Oliner, P. M. (1988). "The Altruistic Personality: Rescuers of Jews in Nazi Europe." Free Press, New York.

Smithson, M., Amato, P., and Pearce, P. (1983). "Dimensions of Helping Behavior." Pergamon Press, Oxford.

ALZHEIMER'S DISEASE

George G. Glenner
University of California at San Diego

Glossary

Microglial cell Scavenger or phagocytic cell capable of protein digestion by packets of enzymes (lysosomes) in its cytoplasm.

Neuroreceptor Membrane segment of a nerve cell to which neurotransmitter chemicals (see below) bind prior to activating the cell.

Neurotransmitter Chemical compound responsible for transmitting a signal from one nerve cell to another.

Normal pressure hydrocephalus A condition of unknown cause producing dilatation of the ventricles (cisterns) of the brain in the absence of an increase in pressure of the cerebrospinal fluid.

Tomography Recording of internal body images by X ray at a predetermined plane.

ALZHEIMER'S DISEASE is the most common cause of dementia, affecting over 4 million individuals, and it is the fourth most frequent cause of death in the elderly in the United States. It has, as its major pathologic manifestations, destruction of large nerve cells and neural pathways in the cortex throughout the brain as the result of the deposition of silk-like fibers (amyloid fibers) in the walls of blood vessels (cerebrovascular amyloidosis), in aggregates and clumps outside of nerve cells ("senile" plaques, and within nerve cells (neurofibrillary tangles). This leads initially to loss of recent memory, anxiety, depression, deterioration of reasoning and perceiving abilities (cognitive functions), and disorientation, and ultimately to pneumonia and death. It results in 50% of nursing home admissions and 120,000 deaths per year. The direct costs to care for the ravages of the disease in 1992 were over $90 billion—a figure greater than that for heart disease, cancer, and stroke combined. Although Alzheimer's disease is age related, it is not caused by aging. Its etiology is unknown at present.

I. DEMENTIA AND ITS FORMS

"Senility" is a lay term referring to the slow deterioration of bodily functions during the aging process. Dementia, signifying "loss of mental acuity," was considered an inevitable concomitant of this process and it was suggested that all individuals—if they grew old enough—would become demented. This concept is of course unprovable and in fact discounted by the fact that there are many examples of nonagenarians and centenarians who have led productive lives until the time of death. Age, however, is a risk factor for dementia, as it is for numerous other disease processes such as diabetes and osteoarthritis, being 400 times more prevalent at age 80 than at 60. [*See* DEMENTIA.]

There are two main categories of dementia. Secondary dementia represents 20% of the total cases and refers to treatable and often reversible conditions (Table I). The use of multiple medications, often prescribed by different physicians without the other's knowledge, may lead to toxic cocktails and subsequent symptoms of dementia that are easily reversible by withdrawal of medication if irreversible damage has not intervened. This is also true of primary vitamin B_{12} deficiency, most often manifested as pernicious anemia, where vitamin B_{12} injections given in the early stages of the disease can reverse the symptoms of dementia and prevent pro-

TABLE I

Factors Responsible for Secondary Dementia

Nutritional factors
Vitamin B_{12} deficiency (pernicious anemia)
Malnutrition
Chronic malabsorption
Heavy metal intoxication

Toxic factors
Multiple drug administration
Alcoholism
Barbiturate overdosage
Electrolyte disturbances
Metabolic disorders

Endocrine dysfunction
Hypothyroidism
Adrenal insufficiency
Hypopituitarism
Insulin secreting tumor

Infectious factors
Pulmonary tuberculosis
Subacute bacterial endocarditis
Chronic respiratory disease (with cardiac failure)

Brain lesions
Tumors
Normal pressure hydrocephalus
Cerebral emboli
Subdural hematoma

gression. It is this category of dementias that the physician must eliminate first by thorough history, physical examination, and laboratory tests. "Benign senescent forgetfulness of Kral" is a condition in some older people with none of the symptoms of dementia other than moderate memory loss. Psychiatric depression often mimics dementia and has been designated by some as a "pseudodementia."

The primary dementias represent 80% of the remaining causes of dementia (Table II) and are usu-

TABLE II

The Primary Dementias

Dementia	Incidence at autopsy
Alzheimer's disease	62.6%
Multi-infarct dementia	21.4%
Mixed Alzheimer's disease and multi-infarct	6.3%
Parkinson's disease	5.7%
Pick's disease	3.0%
Creutzfeldt-Jacob (including Gerstmann-Sträussler)	0.5%
Adult leukodystrophy	0.1%

ally untreatable and of unknown etiology (with the exception of dementia caused by multiple small strokes, or multi-infarct dementia, which may be caused by a treatable hypertensive condition). Although Alzheimer's disease was initially described as a disease of younger individuals (i.e., those less than 65 years of age) and designated "presenile dementia," subsequent pathologic examination of the brains of demented people over age 65 revealed over 60% of them to have the pathologic lesions characteristic of Alzheimer's disease. Thus, the terms "presenile" and "senile dementia" were unified under the term Alzheimer's disease, and this represents the most frequent cause of dementia. Multi-infarct dementia caused by hardening of the arteries (atherosclerosis and/or arteriosclerosis) with or without hypertension is the next most prevalent cause. Numerous much rarer and obscure diseases make up the remainder of the primary dementias. Of note is Creutzfeldt-Jakob disease, which is caused by a slow-acting transmissible agent. The process is not contagious, but can be passed from individual to individual by corneal grafts, ingestion of human pituitary extracts, and implantation of contaminated cerebral electrodes.

One of the most common behavioral abnormalities seen in the Alzheimer's patient is depression. Indeed it is a rare patient that does not present with such symptoms and this is perhaps the cause that the initial physician encountered is a psychiatrist. Not infrequently an Alzheimer's patient may demonstrate episodes of violence that must be distinguished from the manic state. On occasion paranoia is a prominent symptom as it was with Alzheimer's first patient. In these patients these abnormalities must be distinguished in the differential diagnosis from a psychiatric illness. [*See* DEPRESSION.]

II. THE LESIONS OF ALZHEIMER'S DISEASE

The silk-like fibrils (neurofibrillary tangles) found inside cerebral nerve cells (neurons), first described by Alois Alzheimer in 1907, the clumps and aggregates of silk-like fibers (senile plaques) located outside cells in the grey matter of the cerebral cortex, and similar fibers involving the walls of cerebral vessels represent the characteristic lesions of Alzheimer's disease (Fig. 1). Amyloidosis is defined as the deposition of a fibrillar proteinaceous material having the characteristics of silk fibers and, thus,

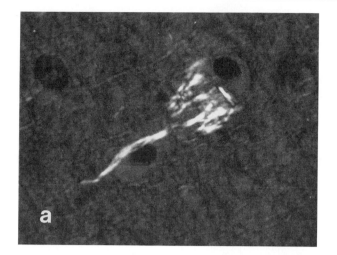

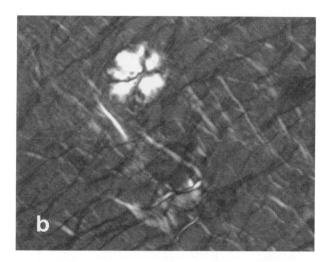

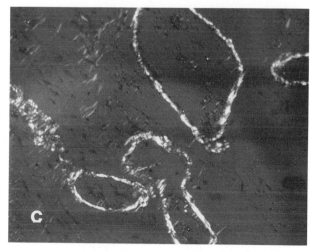

FIGURE 1 (a) Neurofibrillary tangle; (b) senile plaque; (c) cerebral vessels with amyloid deposits in walls. All photographs made with a polarizing microscope after Congo red staining.

insoluble in body fluids and resistant to enzymatic digestion. X-ray crystallographic examination reveals these fibers to have a β-pleated sheet configuration, a structure first described by Pauling and Corey in 1951 having the conformation of a corrugated, elongated fiber that is composed of protein subunits arranged perpendicularly and at periodic intervals to the long axis of the fiber. On electron microscopic examination these amyloid fibers have a twisted-ribbon appearance. This β-pleated sheet configuration and twisted-ribbon appearance have been found in the paired helical filaments that make up the neurofibrillary tangles and in the fibrillar deposits of the senile plaques and cerebral vessels in the cortex (Fig. 2). Thus, the major defining lesion of Alzheimer's disease is composed primarily of amyloid fibers. Amyloid fibers have been created in the test tube by enzyme digestion from a variety of proteins. It appears that the tangles are formed in certain large (pyramidal) neurons in the brain and accumulate and destroy them. The senile plaques, at least in their early stages, probably compress and destroy nerve fibers in their path, while the vascular deposits of amyloid fibers weaken the vessel walls to cause leakage of blood serum into the brain substance and at times rupture to produce intracerebral hemorrhage and strokes.

The loss of specific neurons and the destruction of cerebral tissue by plaques lead to the reduction in the volume of grey matter, causing shrinkage of the brain, otherwise known as cerebral atrophy (Fig. 3). Thus, the separation of the brain from the skull increases, the cervices of the brain (sulci) widen, and the ventricles (cisterns for cerebrospinal fluid) dilate. The number of plaques present in the grey matter has been correlated with the degree of dementia. The only other pathologic condition known to have the three characteristic lesions of Alzheimer's disease is Down's syndrome, in individuals over the age of 40. Thus far in all such individuals the tangles, plaques, and vessel abnormalities have been found. In aged normal (undemented) individuals infrequent plaques and tangles may be seen.

III. GENETICS AND EPIDEMIOLOGY

Alzheimer's disease has been proven at autopsy in an individual as young as 38 and, though infrequent, it is not rare in individuals in their 40s and 50s. The vast majority of patients with Alzheimer's disease are over age 65, with the average being about 71.

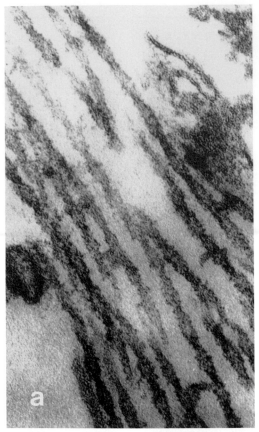

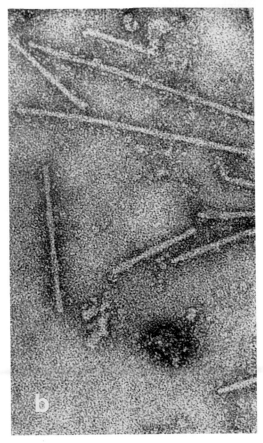

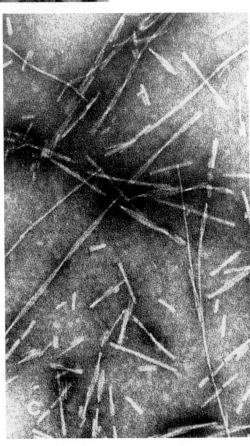

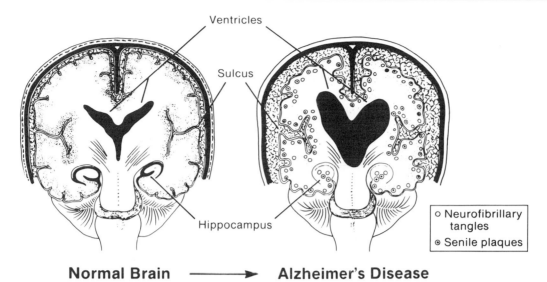

FIGURE 3 (Left) Normal brain with ventricles and hippocampus (site of recent memory) labeled. Grey matter (cortex) stippled. (Right) Cerebral atrophy of Alzheimer's disease with destruction of grey matter and hippocampus by plaques and tangles, dilation of ventricles, shrinkage of brain from skull, and widening of crevices (sulci) between convolutions.

There is no significant sex predilection. The length of time from diagnosis to death ranges from 5 to 15 years. Familial cases of Alzheimer's disease are known and the majority, but not all, are those with a younger age of onset. These are thought to be genetically transmitted in an autosomal dominant manner. However, identical twins are not invariably affected by the disease. It is estimated that about 10–15% of Alzheimer's cases are genetically predisposed. The only known risk factor for sporadic (nongenetic) Alzheimer's disease is age. This increases dramatically from age 60 and tends to level off at age 85. There does not appear to be a geographical, ethnic, or racial predilection for this disease. There is no animal model known for Alzheimer's disease.

IV. CLINICAL DIAGNOSIS

Alzheimer's disease can usually be diagnosed with a fair degree of accuracy with a good medical history, clinical examination, and laboratory tests—even though there is no specific diagnostic test for the disease. The patient almost invariably presents with a history of loss of recent memory such that they cannot remember major events occurring only days previously. This is believed to be due to damage by tangles in cells of the hippocampus (Fig. 3). Often such patients become lost driving in familiar surroundings. Concomitant anxiety, depression, agitation, and confusion are prominent. Cognitive defects slowly become apparent, with progressive difficulty in calculations, writing, recognizing time, verbalizing, and reasoning. Combativeness may occur. In the early stages neurologic defects are usually absent unless another process coexists. These symptoms progress until the patient becomes almost mute, loses voluntary reflexes (e.g., swallowing), becomes incontinent, and cannot walk, sit, or dress without assistance. Hemorrhages induced by amyloid angiopathy can cause strokes (most frequently nonparalytic). Death usually results from pneumonia due to failure to swallow properly so that food is inhaled into the lungs (aspiration pneumonia). Many patients become comatose and must be fed by a nasogastric tube.

In the initial stages computerized axial tomography (CAT) scans and other radioimaging studies may inconstantly reveal cerebral atrophy. Use of positron emission tomography (PET) scans and a radio-

FIGURE 2 (a) Paired helical filaments composing neurofibrillary tangles; (b) amyloid fibers from a case of systemic amyloidosis; (c) "amyloid" fibers formed artificially from insulin. Note twisted ribbon appearance. All photographs taken through an electron microscope and magnified about 150,000×.

labeled glucose analogue can demonstrate failure to metabolize nutrients in cortical areas of the brain. Laboratory tests are used primarily to rule out other dementing processes, such as brain tumors or vitamin B_{12} deficiency. Despite the fact that no specific diagnostic text exists, a correct diagnosis of Alzheimer's disease in a specialized dementia clinic is usually over 90% while throughout the United States it averages about 80%.

V. COMMON REACTIVE STATES

The catastrophic reaction is a response of the Alzheimer's patient to a variety of conflicting stimuli which can induce a hostile response. Several of these include: the request to make a decision between more than two alternatives; conflicting requests or orders; excessive caregiver attention. Simple decision-making, distraction of the patient, and a replacement of one caregiver with another can frequently avoid or abort a violent response. Excess disability occurs when the caregiver responds vocally or physically for the patient with the subsequent diminution of the patient's speaking or activity skills. "Sundowner's syndrome" is a phase of confusion and irritation seen at the close of day. It is probably due to general tiredness of the patient and an inability to process any more information after a long day of struggling to interpret their environment correctly. A reduced level of activity consisting of familiar undemanding tasks is best at this time of the day. Some type of meaningful activity is necessary to keep patients from escalating into a catastrophic reaction because of their anxiety and confusion.

VI. TREATMENT AND MANAGEMENT

There is no curative, arrestive, or prophylactic treatment for Alzheimer's disease. However, supportive or symptomatic treatments to alleviate the anxiety, agitation, and depression are available. The greatest difficulty usually arises with the caregiver, who is frequently elderly, has medical problems, and lives on a fixed income. Long-term care is at present not subsidized to a significant degree by Medicare or third-party (insurance) reimbursement. In-home care and adult day-care can provide relief (respite) for many of these caregivers and an optimal quality of life and dignity for the patient.

VII. THE NATURE OF ALZHEIMER'S DISEASE

Specific theories as to the pathogenesis of Alzheimer's disease have been presented that lend themselves to experimentation. It is these theories that hold the potential of an insightful approach to our understanding of Alzheimer's disease.

A. Infectious Agent Theory

Since the demonstration that the dementing processes (Creutzfeldt-Jakob disease, kuru, and Gerstmann-Sträussler syndrome) are caused by a slow-acting, viral-like, transmissible agent, numerous investigations to demonstrate such an infectious process in Alzheimer's disease have been attempted without success. The finding that a fibrillar protein (termed "prion") intimately associated with the infectious process in Creutzfeldt-Jakob disease has many of the characteristics of amyloid fibrils and is found in the form of plaques in varying frequency in these diseases also suggested a relationship with Alzheimer's disease. However, the chemical structure (amino acid sequence) of the amyloid fibrils of Alzheimer's disease deposits was found to be distinctly different from that of the prion, thereby invalidating a chemical identity between these two types of dementia. Although the prion has been suggested as the infectious agent per se, unequivocal proof of this is lacking and any association with the pathogenesis of Alzheimer's disease is strictly conjectural.

B. Cerebrotoxic Agents

Aluminum toxicity as a causative factor in the pathogenesis of Alzheimer's disease has been the most frequently mentioned potential agent of this type as a result of evidence of increased aluminum levels in the brain correlated with aging, chemical evidence of aluminum silicates in plaques, and chemical evidence of aluminum concentration in tangles. The pathogenesis has been variously proposed as via ingestion (aluminum utensils, and aluminum containing antacids), inhalation with olfactory nerve involvement, and by absorption (deodorants). Against the significance of these findings is the lack of Alzheimer's-type lesions in patients suffering from aluminum intoxication during renal dialysis ("dialysis dementia"), the absence of an increased incidence of Alzheimer's disease in aluminum factory workers, and in the invariable presence of Alzheimer's disease lesions in Down's syndrome. Silicon is another agent proposed as a potential causative agent.

C. Vascular and Blood–Brain Barrier Changes

Physical alterations of capillary walls, presumably other than by amyloid fibrils, have been noted in ultrastructural studies of Alzheimer's disease brains. It has been suggested, but not proven, that these changes may lead to a compromise of the blood–brain barrier. This barrier regulates macromolecular transport across the walls of blood vessels in the brain tissue. Evidence that amyloid deposition in the walls of blood vessels in the cerebral grey matter is an almost invariable concomitant of Alzheimer's disease has been demonstrated within recent years and has led to the suggestion that these vascular lesions result in blood–brain barrier incompetence. Evidence that a protein, present solely in the serum, can be identified and isolated from the amyloid core of plaques provides some evidence that altered blood–brain barrier permeability exists in Alzheimer's disease, but sufficient proof of this has not as yet been provided.

D. Neurotransmitter and Neuroreceptor Deficiencies

The consistent finding of a depletion of choline acetyltransferase (an enzyme involved in the synthesis of the neurotransmitter acetylcholine) activity in brains of Alzheimer's disease patients led to many studies based on several hypothetical premises: Alzheimer's disease was the result of an enzyme (neurotransmitter synthesizing) deficiency; Alzheimer's disease was the result of depletion or absence of a neurotransmitter; and cortical neuronal destruction in Alzheimer's disease was caused by destruction of a group of cells at the base of the brain, the nucleus basalis of Meynert, cells which are believed to innervate the cortical cells. Loss of this innervation by the basal cells was thought to result in cortical cell death. Upon this "cholinergic hypothesis" were based therapeutic attempts to increase the level of acetylcholine by use of its precursors, lecithin and choline, and by direct infusion in the brain of acetylcholine and the introduction of enzyme inhibitors such as physostigmine and tetrahydroaminoacridine (THA) to prevent the enzymatic destruction (by cholinesterases) of acetylcholine. Thus far these ap-

proaches have led to only minimal success. Neurotransmitter deficiencies in Alzheimer's disease are not limited to the cholinergic system, however, but also involve levels of other neurotransmitters, for example, norepinephrine and serotonin. In Alzheimer's disease dysfunction in a variety of neuronal systems is associated with neurotransmitter receptors. These are proteins incorporated in nerve cell membranes that bind specific neurotransmitter molecules. Reduction in many types of receptors (e.g., of serotonin and acetylcholine) occurs in the cortex in Alzheimer's disease, but a consistent receptor abnormality occurring in Alzheimer's disease has yet to be revealed. [*See* BRAIN CHEMICALS; SYNAPTIC TRANSMITTERS AND NEUROMODULATORS.]

E. Abnormal Proteins and Protein Products

The consistent evidence of fibrillar deposits in tangles as paired helical filaments, plaques, and cerebral vessels and X-ray diffraction demonstration that these are twisted β-pleated sheet fibrils has led to the conclusion that Alzheimer's disease is a form of cerebral amyloidosis. This signifies that the above lesions are directly or indirectly responsible for neuronal cell death and are the final stage of the pathogenetic process leading to Alzheimer's disease.

The recent discovery of the β protein (the major protein comprising the amyloid fibril deposits of the plaques, tangles, and cerebral vessels in both Alzheimer's disease and Down's syndrome) has initiated a flurry of biochemical and molecular biological studies. This protein was first isolated, purified, and its amino acid sequence determined from amyloid-laden vascular tissues of Alzheimer's disease and Down's syndrome. It was found to be a unique polypeptide composed of a minimum of 28 amino acids having a molecular weight of approximately 4.2 kDa with an essentially identical amino acid sequence in both Alzheimer's disease and Down's syndrome. Subsequently, the same protein was found comprising the amyloid fibrils of the plaques and the paired helical filaments of the neurofibrillary tangles. Based on its presence as amyloid fibrils in 100% of Down's syndrome individuals it was suggested that it was a chemical characteristic (phenotype) for Down's syndrome and that the gene encoding for its precursor would be found on chromosome 21, the abnormally tripled chromosome found in Down's individuals.

Four research groups working independently subsequently isolated complementary DNA clones coding for the amyloid β protein precursor (βPP) by the use of recombinant DNA techniques and found that the gene coding for the βPP was localized to chromosome 21. An analysis further revealed that the gene coded for a 695 amino acid βPP. A small portion of this βPP had an amino acid sequence identical with that of the β protein. It was suggested that βPP is a cell-surface receptor. An insert of a group of amino acids has also been found in two species of βPP that is similar to an inhibitor of enzymes cleaving certain proteins. The synthesis of the β protein can potentially occur in several cell types in the brain and many other tissues including the heart, kidney, and spleen.

Considerable evidence has accumulated that many amyloid fibril proteins are formed from larger precursor proteins by enzyme cleavage (proteolysis) to produce a β-pleated sheet fibril. These precursor proteins have been found to be chemically abnormal. It would, therefore, appear logical that the β protein of cerebrovascular amyloid fibrils, having about 28 amino acids, and that of plaques, having about 43 amino acids, would be formed by enzyme cleavage from an abnormal 695 amino acid βPP. The above-noted precedent that amyloid fibers are usually formed from abnormal precursor proteins has recently been demonstrated in a small number of familial cases where a mutation in the βPP occurs. This finding definitively relates the β protein in these cases to Alzheimer's disease.

It is still not known whether the source of the βPP originates from the brain or blood. The diverse cellular sites of potential synthesis strongly suggest, but do not prove, that βPP is disseminated via the bloodstream to eventuate in intracerebral amyloid deposits.

Our lack of knowledge of the exact chemical composition of βPP prevents any statement as to whether abnormalities during the cascade of events (e.g., addition of sugars and enzyme cleavage) affecting βPP after it is coded for by the gene distinguishes the βPP of Alzheimer's disease and Down's syndrome individuals from that of normal.

VIII. HYPOTHESIS FOR THE PATHOGENESIS OF ALZHEIMER'S DISEASE

From the present state of our knowledge a pathogenic sequence of events leading to cerebrovascular amyloidosis, plaques, and tangles can be devised

(Fig. 4). The amyloid β protein gene codes for a normal βPP that is subsequently abnormally modified as the result of a defective enzyme (by aberrant addition of sugars or by anomalous enzyme cleavage—as during proteolytic enzyme saturation, e.g., in Down's syndrome). Assuming the primary source of cerebral amyloid deposits is in peripheral body sites, the abnormal βPP is disseminated via the bloodstream where it is acted upon preferentially by the proteolytic enzyme complement of cerebrovascular endothelial cells (cells lining the inner walls of blood vessels) that cleave the β protein from the βPP and release it to form the amyloid fibers. Accumulation of these fibers may disrupt the blood–brain barrier and permits seepage of βPP into the brain substance where it is acted upon by the proteolytic complement of cerebral digestive cells (microglia) to form plaques. βPP (or another serum protein) acts to block vital chemical receptors on the surface of large neurons in the cortex to perturb their metabolism, inducing the formation of the abnormal paired helical filaments. The plaques compress and destroy nerve fibrils and filaments. The paired helical filaments of the tangles prevent transport of neuronal components, which are essential to cell survival, and destroy those cells in which they are deposited.

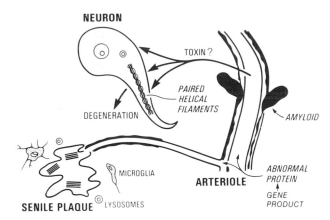

FIGURE 4   Diagrammatic representation of a postulated pathogenesis of Alzheimer's disease. An abnormal or normal serum β protein precursor (βPP), coded for by a gene on chromosome 21, is taken up specifically by cerebrovascular endothelial cells to be proteolytically cleaved by their enzyme complement (lysosomes) to form amyloid fibrils. The amyloid fibril deposition breaks the blood–brain barrier and the (abnormal?) serum protein(s) binds to neuronal cell membranes perturbing their environment. These neurons form abnormal neurofibrils (paired helical filaments), which cause the cell's death. Proteolytic cleavage by microglial enzymes of the βPP, which has seeped through amyloid-laden capillary walls, produces the amyloid cores of senile plaques. [From G. G. Glenner and E. F. Osserman (Eds.) (1984) "Amyloidosis," Plenum Press, New York. Reprinted with permission.]

The possible relationship of proteolytic enzyme defect to Alzheimer's disease is intriguing since cellular enzyme differences have been implicated in the preferential localization of amyloid fibrils in Alzheimer's disease solely to the cerebral vessels (and not to those in the rest of the body). This signifies quantitative or qualitative differences in the enzyme complement, possibly of endothelial cells, between the cerebral and peripheral vasculature. Identification of an abnormal enzyme could lead to specific approaches to therapy by its selective inhibition. Such a finding could also lead to a specific diagnostic test for the abnormal enzyme and, thus, for Alzheimer's disease.

Acknowledgment

Reproduced in part, with permission, from the *Annual Review of Medicine*, Vol. 40. Copyright 1989 by Annual Reviews, Inc.

Bibliography

Davies, P., and Finch, C. E. (Eds.) (1987). "Banbury Report 27: Molecular Neuropathology of Aging. Cold Spring Harbor Symposium." Cold Spring Harbor Laboratory, Cold Spring Harbor, New York.

Glenner, G. G. (1980). Amyloid deposits and amyloidosis: The β-fibrilloses. *N. Engl. J. Med.* **302**, 1283 and 1333.

Glenner, G. G. (1983). Alzheimer's disease: Multiple cerebral amyloidosis. In "Banbury Report 15: Biological Aspects of Alzheimer's Disease. Cold Spring Harbor Symposium" (R. Katzman, Ed.). Cold Spring Harbor Laboratory, Cold Spring Harbor, New York.

Glenner, G. G. (1988). Alzheimer's disease: Its proteins and genes. *Cell* **52**, 307.

Stehman, Z., Strachan, G., Neubauer, J., Glenner, J., and Glenner, G. G. (Eds.) (1991). "Training Manual for Alzheimer's Care Specialists." Alzheimer's Family Center, Inc., San Diego, CA.

Tomlinson, B. E., and Corsellis, J. A. N. (1984). Aging and the dementias. In "Greenfield's Neuropathology" (J. H. Adams, J. A. N. Corsellis, and L. W. Duchen, Eds.), 4th ed. Wiley, New York.

AMNESIA

John F. Kihlstrom and Elizabeth L. Glisky
University of Arizona

Glossary

Alcoholic blackout Amnesia without loss of consciousness, in which the intoxicated person retains the ability to perform certain "automatized" behaviors without any subsequent memory for the episode.

Amnesia A special case of forgetting in which the memory loss is greater than would be expected under ordinary circumstances. Anterograde amnesia affects memory for events occurring after the instigating event; retrograde amnesia affects memory for events occurring before the instigating event.

Amnesic syndrome A profound deficit in learning and memory usually associated with bilateral damage to the diencephalon or to the medial portions of the temporal lobe. It always involves an anterograde amnesia and may involve a retrograde amnesia as well.

Functional amnesia A significant loss of memory attributable to an instigating event, usually stressful, that does not result in insult, injury, or disease affecting brain tissue. Its most common forms are psychogenic amnesia, psychogenic fugue, and multiple personality disorder.

Infantile and childhood amnesia An amnesia observed in adults, affecting memory for personal experiences occurring in the first 5–7 years of life. Infantile amnesia commonly covers the period before language and speech develop.

Posthypnotic amnesia A retrograde amnesia induced by means of hypnotic suggestion; it may be canceled by a prearranged reversibility cue.

Transient global amnesia A benign and temporary amnesia characterized by sudden onset, apparently caused by momentary vascular insufficiencies affecting brain tissue.

Traumatic retrograde amnesia A retrograde amnesia resulting from a concussive blow to the head; most of the affected memories are eventually recovered, except for a "final RA" affecting the accident itself.

AMNESIA may be defined as a special case of forgetting, in which the loss of memory is greater than would be expected under ordinary circumstances. A head-injured patient is no longer able to learn things that he was once able to master easily; a patient with psychogenic fugue loses her identity as well as her fund of autobiographical memories. Amnesia includes frank pathologies encountered in neurological and psychiatric clinics, such as Korsakoff's syndrome, Alzheimer's disease, traumatic retrograde amnesia, and multiple personality disorder. But it also includes abnormalities of memory observed ubiquitously, such as infantile and childhood amnesia, the exaggerated forgetfulness associated with healthy aging, and the memory failures associated with sleep and general anesthesia. These naturally occurring pathologies of memory have their counterparts in amnestic states induced in otherwise normal, intact individuals by means of experimental techniques, such as electroconvulsive shock in laboratory rats and posthypnotic amnesia in college sophomores.

Experimental research on memory began with the publication of Ebbinghaus' *Uber das Gedachtniss* in 1885, but the clinical description of amnesia dates from even earlier. Korsakoff described the amnesic syndrome that bears his name in 1854. And in 1882 Ribot published *Les Maladies de la memoire*, with a detailed description of the consequences for memory of brain insult, injury, and disease, as well as a theory of memory and amnesia. On the basis of his observations, and Hughlings Jackson's principle that ontogeny recapitulates phylogeny, he concluded that brain disorder produces a progressive loss of memory that affects memories in the reverse order of their development. Thus, in traumatic retrograde amnesia, memories for events occurring immediately before the accident are most likely to be lost. This principle, now known as Ribot's Law, does not always hold, but it was an important first step in the journey from clinical description to scientific theory.

For reasons that are not completely clear, clinical and experimental study of amnesia languished for the first half of the 20th century, but was revived by Talland's 1965 monograph *Deranged Memory*, which reported an extensive psychometric and experimental study of patients with Korsakoff syndrome. Talland's work ushered in a new age of research in which clinicians and experimentalists joined forces under the banner of *cognitive neuropsychology*—a discipline that attempts to integrate evidence obtained from the intensive study of brain-damaged patients with theories of normal cognitive function. In this article, we provide a summary of this research, as it pertains to the major disorders of memory—pathological and normal, natural and artificial—and discuss the role of this research in the contemporary psychology of memory. [*See* MEMORY.]

I. THE AMNESIC SYNDROME

The amnesic syndrome represents a profound deficit in learning and memory; it is by far the most commonly studied pathology of memory. Its characteristic feature is a gross anterograde amnesia (AA), meaning that the person cannot remember events that have occurred since the time of the brain damage. Short-term memory (as measured by digit span, for example) is unimpaired; but after even a few moments' distraction, these patients cannot remember what they have said or done, or what has been said or done to them, just recently. In the classic cases, the patient's cognitive deficits are specific to long-term memory: general intelligence, perception, reasoning, and language functions are spread. But this anterograde amnesia is associated with several different etiologies, and careful examination indicates that these disparate origins are associated with

somewhat different patterns of memory and cognitive deficit.

One form of the amnesic syndrome, now known as *diencephalic amnesia*, was first described by Korsakoff in association with alcoholism. At the time, chronic alcoholics frequently suffered from a deficiency of vitamin B_1 (thiamine) which results in bilateral damage to structures of the diencephalon, including the upper portion of the brainstem, the mammillary bodies, the dorsomedial nucleus of the thalamus, and the mammillothalamic tract (unilateral lesions produce "material-specific" amnesias for verbal or nonverbal memories, depending on which hemisphere is damaged). Although this disease is now effectively prevented by the introduction of vitamin-enriched commercial foods, other etiologies, including vascular insufficiencies, tumors, and fronto-temporal brain damage can have similar effects. These patients typically show a retrograde amnesia (RA) as well as AA, meaning that they also have difficulties in remembering events from their premorbid life, especially those from the years immediately preceding their disease. Remote memory, such as for childhood events, is apparently preserved. Note that such a pattern conforms to Ribot's Law.

Another form of amnesic syndrome, known as *temporal lobe amnesia*, stems from bilateral lesions in the medial portion of the temporal lobe, and especially the hippocampus, entorhinal cortex, and surrounding structures (again, there are also material-specific amnesias resulting from unilateral damage to these structures). The most famous case is Patient H. M., who displayed a profound AA after surgical resection of his medial temporal lobes, including the hippocampus, in a desperate attempt to relieve intractable epileptic seizures. Other cases have been caused by brain tumors, ischemic episodes, head trauma, and herpes encephalitis. Temporal-lobe patients always show AA; when they show RA, it is not always as extensive as in diencephalic patients.

There is also a *frontal-lobe amnesia*, which is qualitatively different from the amnesic syndrome. Frontal-lobe patients are not globally amnesic, but they frequently show deficits on tasks requiring memory for temporal order, as well as memory for the source of newly acquired knowledge. They also lack *metamemory* capabilities—they have little appreciation of the contents stored in their own memories, or in the availability of appropriate memory strategies. Patients who have frontal damage in addition to diencephalic or medial-temporal lobe damage experience their greatest difficulties on memory tasks requiring strategic planning and organization.

Finally, *transient global amnesia* is a temporary (typically lasting several hours) condition characterized by sudden onset. It closely resembles the permanent diencephalic and medial-temporal lobe amnesias, in that it involves both AA and RA, but, as its name implies, it is brief. The condition, while frightening, is benign: after remission, there are no signs of permanent brain damage (and little risk of another episode in the future). Transient global amnesia appears to be caused by temporary vascular insufficiency affecting brain tissue; interestingly, many cases appear in association with physical exertion or mental stress.

In the absence of permanent brain damage, something akin to the amnesic syndrome may be observed in cases of *alcoholic blackout*. Blackout involves amnesia without loss of consciousness. The intoxicated individual may engage in conversation or perform other actions normally, but after regaining sobriety, he or she will have no memory for the episode. Blackouts are most commonly observed in chronic alcoholics, though they do occur to nonalcoholics who are severely intoxicated. In any case, blackout is most likely to occur when the person ingests large quantities of alcohol rapidly, especially when fatigued or hungry. Alcohol folklore suggests that the amnesia is an instance of state-dependent retrieval—that the memories return when the person resumes drinking. However, laboratory research clearly indicates that the memories covered by blackout are unrecoverable, and thus that the amnesia reflects an encoding deficit. Sedative drugs, such as the barbiturates and benzodiazepines, also produce irreversible AA.

The different patterns of task performance offer clues about the nature of the memory deficit in the amnesic syndrome. In principle, any instance of forgetting may be attributed to a failure at one or more of three stages of memory processing: encoding (the creation of a memory trace of a new experience), storage (the retention of trace information over time), and retrieval (the recovery of trace information for use in ongoing experience, thought, and action). Logically, a syndrome that affects memory for postmorbid but not premorbid events is most likely due to encoding failure. And, in fact, it has been suggested on the basis of laboratory experiments with lesioned rats and monkeys that the hippocampus and other structures in the medial-temporal lobe mediate that consolidation and stor-

age of new memories. An alternative formulation assumes that representations of the various elements of an event are distributed widely in the cortex, and that the hippocampus creates a "cognitive map" to index and bind them together. In either case, the occurrence of AA means that the hippocampus is crucial for memory formation, even though the memories themselves are not stored there.

What about the RA? Some degree of RA is usually, but not always, observed in the amnesic syndrome. Logically, damage to a structure that consolidates and organizes new memories should have no effect on old memories. In some cases, RA may reflect the disruption of premorbid memories that were incompletely consolidated at the time of disease onset; this would produce a temporal gradient, but the extent of RA observed would seem to imply that proper consolidation requires weeks, months, or years instead of seconds, minutes, or hours. On the other hand, if the hippocampus serves a binding and indexing function, its destruction will create an RA by effectively preventing the retrieval of memories that remain available in storage; this would produce an amnesia for remote as well as recent memories and would not necessarily produce a temporal gradient. Finally, in some cases what appears as RA may in fact be AA, reflecting the slow onset of an insidious disease process and producing the appearance of a temporal gradient; this suggestion is particularly plausible in the case of diencephalic amnesia associated with chronic alcohol abuse, but cannot account for amnesias of sudden onset.

The nature of RA in the amnesic syndrome remains unresolved. In the final analysis, it is important to remember that in real life outside the laboratory, pure cases of amnesic syndrome are exceedingly rare. Patients may suffer primary damage to one area, but collateral damage to another, and the precise combination of lesions may determine the presence and extent of RA.

Even conclusions about encoding deficits must be qualified to some extent. At first glance, the AA observed in the amnesic syndrome appears to be a complete inability to acquire new information. However, closer examination indicates that certain aspects of learning and memory are spared even in the densest cases of amnesia. Thus, Patient H. M. has learned to solve the Tower of Hanoi puzzle, but he does not recognize the puzzle as familiar. Amnesic patients who study the word *ELATED* do not remember it just minutes later; but when presented the stem *ELA-* and asked to complete it with the first word that comes to mind, they are more likely to produce *ELATED* (as opposed to *ELASTIC* or *ELABORATE*) than would be expected by chance. The ability of amnesic patients to acquire cognitive and motor skills, and to show priming effects in word-stem completion, shows that they are able to acquire new information through experience, although, somewhat paradoxically, they are not aware that they possess this knowledge.

The limits of such learning are still being studied, but already they have motivated a distinction between two expressions of episodic memory, *explicit* and *implicit*. Explicit memory (EM) refers to the conscious recollection of a previous episode, as in recall or recognition. By contrast, implicit memory (IM) refers to any change in experience, thought, or action that is attributable to such an episode, such as skill learning or priming. The dissociation between EM and IM in amnesic patients indicates that some forms of learning and memory are preserved. According to one view, amnesics suffer from a specific inability to encode declarative knowledge about specific events, but retain an ability to acquire procedural (or other non-declarative) knowledge. This would account for their ability to acquire new cognitive and motor skills. Preserved priming has been attributed to the automatic activation of declarative knowledge structures that were stored prior to the brain damage, or to the encoding of new episodic representations in a primitive perceptual memory system that lacks the kinds of information (e.g., about the meaning of an event, or its spatiotemporal context) that would support EM. [*See* EPISODIC MEMORY; IMPLICIT MEMORY.]

II. TRAUMATIC RETROGRADE AMNESIA

Another form of amnesia occurs as a consequence of head trauma. A very severe blow to the head can bruise gray matter and shear white matter, producing both cortical and subcortical damage that may result in AA and RA similar to that observed in the amnesic syndrome. Even in the absence of such damage, some blows to the head can result in a concussion or temporary cessation of electrical activity in the cortex and loss of consciousness. The recovery of consciousness begins with the return of simple reflexes, then the gradual return of purposeful movement, and then speech (this pattern would be predicted by Ribot's Law). After the victim appears fully oriented, he or she will display an AA for some

time, as well as an RA for the accident itself and the events leading up to the accident. Typically, the AA is immediate, i.e., it will start at the time of the trauma. But if the loss of consciousness is delayed, the onset of the AA will be delayed as well. Such *lucid intervals* suggest that the AA is a result of vascular complications that may take some time to develop.

The RA is characterized by a temporal gradient, meaning that it is densest for events nearest the time of the accident—another example of Ribot's Law at work. However, the gradient is broken by *islands of memory* consisting of isolated events, not necessarily personally important, that are remembered relatively well. The extent of the RA is correlated with the extent of the AA. Although the memories covered by the AA are permanently lost, apparently reflecting an encoding deficit, the RA gradually remits. It was once thought that this recovery began with the earliest memories and proceeded forward, which again would be predicted by Ribot's Law. Although the most recent events are generally recovered last, more careful studies show that the shrinkage of amnesia is accomplished by filling in the gaps that surround the islands of memory, leaving a *final RA* covering the accident itself and the moments or minutes leading up to it, and perhaps a few *islands of amnesia*. The shrinkage of amnesia clearly indicates that traumatic RA is a disorder of retrieval, and that the islands of memory act as anchors to support the recovery process. However, the final RA may reflect either a loss of memory from storage or more likely a disruption of consolidation.

A nontraumatic form of retrograde amnesia is observed in psychiatric patients who are administered *electroconvulsive therapy* (ECT) for acute affective disorder. In ECT, electrical stimulation (e.g., 100 V, 500 mA for 500 msec), delivered from surface electrodes applied over the temporal lobe, induces a convulsive, tonic–clonic seizure not unlike those of grand mal epilepsy; after a short series of such treatments (e.g., 6–10 sessions over 2–3 weeks), patients often experience a rapid return to their normal mood state (ECT is not a cure, as episodes of depression or mania may recur).

Because they are anesthetized when the treatment is delivered, patients experience no pain or distress from the convulsions themselves; because they receive muscle relaxants, the convulsions do not result in bone trauma. However, the seizure does produce both AA and RA as adventitious consequences (i.e., unrelated to treatment success). The RA shows the same sort of temporal gradient observed following concussive blows to the head. Because there is less memory impairment (though no difference in treatment outcome) with unilateral than with bilateral electrode placement, ECT is usually delivered to the nondominant hemisphere. The RA gradually clears up (except for the moments before ECT is actually delivered), but memories affected by the AA cannot be recovered.

The amnesia induced by ECT shows a dissociation between EM and IM similar to that observed in the amnesic syndrome. In one experiment, patients who studied a list of words within 90 minutes following administration of ECT showed a deficit in recognition, but no deficit in priming on a word-stem completion test. In another study, patients who read word strings presented in mirror-reversed fashion before delivery of ECT later showed an advantage in reading those words, even though they failed to recognize these words as familiar.

What about the memories covered by the final RA? Although electroconvulsive shock may disrupt encoding processes, it does not appear to remove the memory traces from storage. The relevant evidence comes from studies of the effects on memory of *electroconvulsive shock* (ECS) administered to animals. A common research paradigm is called one-trial, step-down, passive avoidance learning. A rat is placed on a shelf above an electrified floor. If the animal steps down, it receives a footshock and jumps back up on the shelf. Under ordinary circumstances, the animal will not return to the floor: it learns in one trial to avoid the shock by doing nothing. But in the experiment, the animal received a dose of ECS similar to that delivered to patients in ECT. After the animal recovers, it steps down onto the floor after being placed on the shelf—as if it has forgotten all about the shock.

ECS-induced amnesia shows a temporal gradient similar to that observed in other forms of traumatic retrograde amnesia. If the ECS is delayed from the time of the original learning experience, there is less amnesia than if it is administered immediately afterward. But the extent of amnesia also depends on how memory is measured. The amnesic animal steps down immediately, as if the footshock never happened. At the same time, it shows a marked increase in heart rate. Moreover, if the animal receives *reminder treatments,* such as tail shock in another environment or immersion in circulating ice water, it will remain on the shelf and avoid the floor. The *desynchrony* between behavioral and psychophysio-

logical indices of fear is analogous to the dissociation between EM and IM observed in human amnesic patients; and the effectiveness of reminder treatments shows that at least some aspects of the forgotten event have been preserved. Memories covered by the final RA may never be accessible to conscious recollection, but they may nonetheless be expressed as implicit memories.

III. FUNCTIONAL AMNESIAS

Clinically significant amnesias are not confined to cases of organic brain syndrome. Psychiatrists and clinical psychologists also encounter forms of *functional amnesia* in a group of mental illnesses known as the *dissociative disorders*. Functional amnesia may be defined as a loss of memory that is attributable to an instigating event (often, mental stress) that does not result in insult, injury, or disease to the brain. For example, victims of violent crimes such as rape, or other sorts of traumatic stress, often display an amnesia for the event itself. Although this might be an AA reflecting encoding deficits caused by high levels of arousal, there is often an RA covering the events leading up to the trauma as well—sometimes extending to a large portion of the person's life. Because there is no evidence of head injury, such memory failures are labeled as *psychogenic amnesia*. Compared to traumatic retrograde amnesia, psychogenic amnesia appears to be more extensive and longer lasting. Clinical lore holds that psychogenic amnesia can be reversed by hypnosis or barbiturate sedation, but evidence for the reliability of recollections produced by these techniques is largely lacking. [*See* DISSOCIATIVE DISORDERS.]

Another dissociative disorder, *psychogenic fugue,* entails a more extensive loss of autobiographical memory, covering the whole of the person's life, a loss and/or change in identity, and sometimes physical relocation (from which symptom the syndrome derives its name). Such cases often come to the attention of police and health providers when a person cannot identify himself; or when she comes to herself in a strange place and does not know how she got there. Interestingly, fugue patients lose self-knowledge and autobiographical memory, but they do not seem to lose their fund of semantic memory, or their repertoire of procedural knowledge.

Upon recovery the patient is left with an amnesia covering the events of the fugue state itself, and retains no knowledge of whatever identity he or she may have adopted in that state. Examination of such cases after they are resolved often reveals an instigating episode of psychological stress. [*See* AUTOBIOGRAPHICAL REMEMBERING AND SELF-KNOWLEDGE; SEMANTIC MEMORY.]

Multiple personality disorder (MPD), in which two or more personalities appear to inhabit a single body, alternating control over experience and action, also involves a disruption of memory and identity. One of these personalities is often "primary," in that it is the one that has been manifest the longest and known by most other people. Most important in the present context, the various personalities appear to be separated by an amnesic barrier that prevents one alter ego from gaining access to the memories of another. In many cases, the amnesia is asymmetrical, in that Personality A may be aware of Personality B, but not the reverse. The amnesia largely affects identity and autobiographical memory; as a rule, the various personalities share semantic memory and procedural knowledge in common. The most widely accepted theory of MPD holds that it develops in defense against abuse, trauma, or deprivation in early childhood. [*See* CHILD ABUSE; PERSONALITY DISORDERS.]

Reports of MPD were relatively common in the clinical literature before 1920, and then virtually disappeared. There has been a resurgence of MPD, bordering on epidemic, in recent years. However, it is not clear how many of these are iatrogenic in nature or simply misdiagnosed. Where the alternate personalities are initially elicited through hypnosis or other special techniques, or when an amnesic barrier is absent, the case is suspect. MPD is sometimes offered as an insanity defense, claiming that a second personality is actually responsible for crimes of which the first personality is accused. MPD raises interesting issues of criminal law: in principle, the actions of one personality may be outside another personality's ability to control; interpersonality amnesia may prevent the accused from assisting in the defense; and techniques intended to elicit testimony from a personality may violate constitutional safeguards against self-incrimination. However, MPD has rarely proved successful as a defense against criminal charges.

There are several experimental studies that confirm the existence of interpersonality amnesia in MPD. Thus, for example, one alter ego is often unable to recall or recognize a list of items studied by another. Interestingly, there is some evidence that IM may be spared in these cases. Thus, one alter ego may show savings in relearning, interference, transfer of training, or priming effects involving a list studied exclusively by another one. Although the available research is somewhat ambiguous, in general it seems that the amnesic barrier is permeable in the case of implicit memories.

Just as the amnesic syndrome finds its experimental analog in drug-induced amnesia, and traumatic retrograde amnesia in ECT and ECS, the functional amnesias seen clinically have their laboratory parallel in posthypnotic amnesia. Following appropriate suggestions and the termination of hypnosis, many subjects cannot remember the events that transpired while they were hypnotized. After the hypnotist administers a prearranged cue, the critical memories become accessible again; the fact of reversibility marks posthypnotic amnesia as a disruption of memory retrieval. The amnesia does not occur unless it has been suggested (explicitly or implicitly), and memory is not reinstated merely by the reinduction of hypnosis; thus, posthypnotic amnesia is not an instance of state-dependent memory. Response to the amnesia suggestion is highly correlated with individual differences in hypnotizability: while hypnotic "virtuosos" typically show a very dense amnesia, their insusceptible counterparts show little or no forgetting. [*See* HYPNOSIS.]

Like the organic amnesias, posthypnotic amnesia is selective. The subject may forget which words appeared on a study list, but retains the ability to use these words in speech and writing. Skills acquired in hypnosis transfer to the posthypnotic state, and suggestions for amnesia have no impact on practice effects. Subjects who learn new factual information while hypnotized may retain it despite suggestions for amnesia, but these same subjects may well forget the circumstances in which this knowledge was acquired—a phenomenon of *source amnesia* that has also been observed in the amnesic syndrome. Finally, there is good evidence that priming effects are preserved in posthypnotic amnesia. That is, subjects who cannot remember words from a study list are more likely to use those words as free associations or category instances than would be expected by chance. Thus, posthypnotic amnesia shows the familiar dissociation between EM and IM.

Because functional amnesia occurs in the absence of brain damage, and because posthypnotic amnesia occurs in response to suggestion, questions inevitably arise about malingering, simulation, and behavioral compliance. Unfortunately, it is difficult to distinguish between genuine and simulated amnesia in either clinical or experimental situations. Claims of amnesia are readily accepted when there is palpable evidence of brain damage. It should be understood, however, that evidence of a significant interpersonal or sociocultural component does not necessarily mean that functional amnesia is faked. Rather, it means that functional amnesia is complex. Hypnosis may be a state of altered consciousness, but it is also a social interaction; thus, it should not be surprising to discover that the subject's response to amnesia suggestions will be influenced by the precise wording of the suggestion, the discourse context in which it is embedded, the subject's interpretation of the hypnotist's words, and perceived social demands. The social context is probably important in the organic amnesias, but its role is magnified in their functional counterparts.

IV. AMNESIA THROUGH THE LIFESPAN

Some forms of amnesia occur naturally in the course of psychological development. For example, adults rarely remember much from their early childhoods; the earliest memory is typically dated between the third and fourth birthdays, and is limited to a relatively small number of isolated fragments until about 5 or 7 years of age. The appearance of childhood amnesia is not merely an artifact of the long retention interval between childhood encoding and adult retrieval; something special seems to happen to memories for childhood events. Infantile amnesia, covering the first year or two of life, may be attributed at least in part to the lack of language and to the immaturity of the neocortex and other critical brain structures. However, the exact mechanism for childhood amnesia, covering the years after the second birthday, remains uncertain.

The classic explanation for childhood amnesia was proposed by Freud. In his view, during the phallic stage of psychosexual development the child resolves the Oedipus complex by repressing infantile sexual and aggressive impulses, as well as any thoughts, images, and memories that might be related to them. Since (according to the theory) all the young child's mental life is concerned with these topics, all of early childhood is repressed—except a couple of banal *screen memories* that aid repression by giving the person something to remember. Recall that the major goal of psychoanalysis is to lift the repressive barrier so that patients can acknowledge and cope realistically with their primitive instinctual urges. Other theories emphasize the relationship between cognitive processes employed at encoding and retrieval. For example, Schachtel proposed that memories encoded by pre-oedipal, primary-process modes of thought cannot be retrieved by post-oedipal, secondary-process schemata. A similar account can be offered from Piaget's perspective, emphasizing the incompatibility between sensory-motor and preoperational encodings and the retrieval processes characteristic of concrete and formal operations. Note that all these theories predict that memories of childhood experience should be accessible to young children, who have not undergone the "five-to-seven shift." In contrast, some theorists have argued that young children simply do not possess the information-processing capacity—specifically, the ability to pay attention to two things at once, like an event and its episodic context—required to encode retrievable memories. In this case, the prediction is that children will know little more about their childhood histories than adults do. [*See* COGNITIVE DEVELOPMENT.]

It should be noted that infantile and childhood amnesias affect only memories for personal experiences. Children acquire a vast fund of information, and a considerable repertoire of cognitive and motor skills, which they carry into adulthood. Whether this selectivity reflects merely the effects of constant rehearsal, or reveals a dissociation between EM and IM similar to that observed in the clinical amnesias, is not clear.

At the other end of the life cycle, it appears that even the healthy aged have difficulty learning new information and remembering recent events. Aging has little effect on primary or short-term memory, as reflected in digit span or the recency component of the serial-position curve; but it has substantial effects on secondary or long-term memory, especially after moderately long retention intervals. Again, the deficit primarily affects episodic memory: the elderly do not lose their fund of semantic information (although they may be slower on such tasks as word-finding) and their repertoire of procedural knowledge remains intact, provided that they have been able to maintain these skills through practice.

At the same time, it should be noted that episodic–semantic comparisons almost inevitably confound type of memory with retention interval. Memories for recent experiences have, by definition, been encoded recently; most semantic knowledge was acquired while the individual was relatively young. Surprisingly, little is known about the ability of older individuals to learn new vocabulary or acquire new world knowledge. The aged do show an impairment in episodic memory for remote events, but it is not clear whether this reflects age differences in retrieval processes or simply the effects of the retention interval and opportunities for proactive and retroactive interference.

A relatively recent topic in research on aging memory compares EM and IM. Compared to the young, the aged show definite impairments on EM (especially free recall, less so on recognition); but they show less deficit, or none at all, on IM tasks such as stem-completion. Part of the reason for their problems with EM may lie in the difficulty that the elderly have in processing contextual information. Spatial context, temporal context, and source are necessary for distinguishing one event from another, and thus crucial to conscious recollection. Whether this difficulty is specific to contextual features of events, or merely a reflection of a more general limitation on cognitive resources, is unclear.

Memory problems are confounded in the dementing illnesses often associated with aging, e.g., Alzheimer's disease (AD). The severe memory problems associated with AD are likely related to the increase of neuritic plaques and neurofibrillary tangles, particularly in medial temporal regions of the brain. These changes, as well as neuronal loss and depletion of neurotransmitters in other cortical and subcortical areas, contribute to the extensiveness of the disease process. Both AA and RA emerge early in the course of these diseases and progressively worsen. In contrast to the amnesic syndrome, however, the memory deficit in dementia affects primary as well as secondary memory and forms part of a larger cluster of deficits affecting a broad swath of cognitive and emotional life, including the loss of premorbid semantic and procedural knowledge as well as episodic memory. In the latter stages of their illness, demented patients may show *anosognosia* or a lack of awareness of their deficits. [*See* ALZHEIMER'S DISEASE.]

Does the abnormal forgetting observed in aging and dementia extend to implicit as well as explicit memory? Research on this question is still at a very early stage, but already it seems fairly clear that implicit memory is relatively spared in normal aging. Thus, elderly subjects will fail to recognize studied words, but show priming effects on word-fragment completion. With respect to AD and other forms of dementia, however, some controversy remains. There is some evidence of intact motor-skill learning in AD patients, but there is also evidence of impaired performance on priming tasks. The issue is complicated by the fact that AD is a progressive illness. Although impairments in explicit memory may be observed quite early in the course of the disease, deterioration of implicit memory may wait until later stages.

V. AMNESIAS OF EVERYDAY EXPERIENCE

Amnesia is a symptom of neurological or psychiatric disorder, but it is also something that occurs in the ordinary course of everyday living. The most familiar example is sleep. A great deal transpires while we are asleep, including events in the external environment and endogenous activity such as dreams, nightmares, and (in some cases) episodes of somnambulism (sleepwalking) and somniloquy (sleeptalking), but virtually none of this is remembered in the morning. In fact, our inability to remember what has been happening is often the phenomenological basis for inferring that we have been asleep. Similarly, attempts at sleep learning have been almost uniformly unsuccessful, leading investigators to conclude that we are able to learn during sleep only to the extent that we stay awake. [*See* SLEEP: BIOLOGICAL RHYTHMS AND HUMAN PERFORMANCE.]

Most investigators explain sleep-induced amnesia in terms of an encoding deficit or consolidation failure. According to this view, the low levels of cortical arousal characteristic of sleep effectively impair complex information-processing functions. Thus, events in the environment are not noticed, relevant information in memory is not retrieved, and traces of new experiences are not encoded in retrievable form. Some evidence favoring this view comes from studies of memory for dreams. Sleepers who are awakened during REM sleep almost invariably report a dream, apparently by virtue of retrieval from primary memory; but dreams are rarely reported upon awakening in the morning, a task that requires access to trace information in secondary memory. However, subjects will remember a dream in the morning if they awaken directly out of REM sleep. And dreams reported during REM awakenings will be accessible in the morning, provided that the dreamer has remained awake long enough to rehearse the dream before returning to sleep. [*See* DREAMING.]

Most evidence of sleep-induced amnesia comes from studies of EM, leading to speculation that evidence of memory for sleep events, including successful sleep learning, might be obtained with measures of IM. Research on this topic has only just begun, but the available evidence is negative. When care is taken to ensure that there is no evidence of cortical arousal indicative of awakening, subjects show neither EM nor IM for events that occurred while they were sleeping. Even if positive evidence for sleep learning were obtained, it would almost certainly not be as efficient as learning in the normal waking state.

Amnesia is also an important component of general anesthesia induced in surgical patients. Clinically, the success of general anesthesia is indicated by the patient's lack of response to instructions, suppression of autonomic and skeletal responses to incisions and other surgical stimuli, and absence of retrospective awareness of pain and other events occurring during surgery. Thus, by definition, amnesia is a consequence of adequate general anesthesia. But, as with sleep, the amnesia is always assessed in terms of EM, leaving open the possibility that even adequately anesthetized patients might show IM for surgical events. Some anecdotal evidence favoring this proposition is provided by occasional cases in which patients awaken from surgery with an inexplicable dislike of their surgeon—an attitudinal change which is plausibly traced to unkind remarks made about the patient by members of the surgical team.

In recent years, this question has been the object of considerable investigation, and in fact research employing paradigms derived from studies of the amnesic syndrome has sometimes, but not always, provided evidence of spared IM. Thus, patients who are presented a list of words during surgery sometimes show significant priming effects. Such effects are not always obtained, however; and even when they are obtained, they are relatively small. Certainly the scope of information processing during general anesthesia cannot compare to what is possible when the patient is awake and properly oriented; for example, IM after anesthesia may well be limited to the processing of the physical properties of stimuli, but not their meaning. What accounts for the different outcomes across the available research is not clear. Perhaps some anesthetic agents impair EM but spare IM, while others impair both. Such a result might yield interesting insights about the biological foundations of memory.

VI. THEORETICAL AND PRACTICAL IMPLICATIONS

Research on amnesia is intrinsically interesting, but it also has theoretical and pragmatic implications. At the theoretical level, amnesia engages our attention because it seems to carve nature at its joints. Amnesia is selective, and the difference between those aspects of memory that are impaired in amnesia and those that are spared promises to provide information about the processes underlying memory functioning and the organization of memory into different systems. Such conclusions are based on the *logic of dissociation*. In *single dissociations*, variable *A* affects performance on task *Y* but not task *Z*; in *double dissociations*, variable *A* affects *Y* but not *Z*, while variable *B* affects *Z* but not *Y*; in *reversed associations*, changes in *A* increase *Y* and decrease *Z*, while changes in *B* decrease *Y* and increase *Z*; in *stochastic independence*, performance on task *Y* is uncorrelated with performance on task *Z*. All other things being equal, differences such as these suggest that the tasks in question differ in qualitative terms. If they were only quantitatively different, they would be correlated with each other and influenced by the same variables.

Such dissociations are commonly observed in amnesia. For example, the fact that the amnesic syndrome affects the recency portion of the serial-position curve, but not the primacy component, has been cited as evidence that primary (short-term) and secondary (long-term) memory are qualitatively different memory systems, perhaps with different biological substrates (one affected by the brain lesion, the other not). Evidence from amnesia also has been used to support other structural distinctions: between declarative and procedural knowledge and, within the domain of declarative knowledge, between episodic and semantic memory. Thus, amnesic patients have difficulty learning new factual information, but retain an ability to acquire new cognitive and motor skills; and if they do retain new factual knowledge, they display an amnesia for the circumstances in which this information was acquired. Logic and experience tell us that when something breaks, it tends to do so along natural boundaries, which form lines of least resistance. When a disorder of memory separates past memory from new learning, procedural and declarative knowledge, or episodic and semantic memory, it tells us that these distinctions, conjured in the minds of theorists, actually mean something in the real world. The fact that these kinds of dissociations are observed in all sorts of amnesia—not just the amnesic syndrome, but in traumatic retrograde amnesia, psychogenic amnesia, and posthypnotic amnesia as well—strengthens the conclusion that the theoretical distinctions are psychologically and biologically valid.

Of particular interest in recent theory are the various dissociations between explicit and implicit expressions of episodic memory. To date, three broad classes of theories have been proposed to explain these dissociations; each has several exemplars. According to the *activation* view, the activation, by a current event, of pre-existing knowledge representations is sufficient for IM; but EM requires elaborative activity, in which individually activated structures are related to each other. According to the *processing* view, IM is an automatic consequence of environmental stimulation, while EM occurs by virtue of controlled processes that are limited by attentional resources. According to the *memory systems* view, IM reflects the activity of a perceptual representation system, which holds information about the form and structure of the objects of perception, and EM reflects the activity of an episodic memory system that represents knowledge about the meaning of events and the context in which they occur.

Research on the amnesic syndrome, including studies of both human patients and animal models, indicates that the medial-temporal lobe, including the hippocampus, entorhinal cortex, and perirhinal and parahippocampal cortex, forms the biological substrate of explicit memory. But the diencephalic form of amnesic syndrome seems to indicate that the mammillary bodies and the dorsomedial nucleus of the thalamus are also critical for memory. As research continues, investigation of amnesia will make a unique and valuable contribution to understanding the relation between explicit and implicit memory, and the biological foundations of each. [*See* MEMORY, NEURAL SUBSTRATES.]

At the same time, evidence of preserved memory functioning offers new insights concerning amelioration and rehabilitation in cases of amnesia. Loss of explicit memory has debilitating consequences for afflicted individuals in everyday life. They are often unable to keep track of events, remember appointments or schedules, engage in educational or vocational pursuits, or manage home activities. Attempts at rehabilitation have frequently focused on restoration of damaged explicit memory processes either through the use of repetitive drills or by teaching patients mnemonic strategies such as visual imagery or verbal elaboration. These retraining attempts have met with limited success. There is no evidence that exercising damaged neural or cognitive mechanisms leads to positive outcomes; and although patients have sometimes been able to acquire a few pieces of information by using mnemonic techniques, they do not use the strategies spontaneously in everyday life.

On the other hand, rehabilitation strategies that have focused on providing compensatory devices designed to bypass problems in daily life have been somewhat more promising. External aids such as notebooks, diaries, alarm watches, and environmental labels have enabled some amnesic patients to function somewhat more independently, although use of such devices often requires considerable amounts of training and practice. The microcomputer, potentially a powerful prosthetic for people with memory impairments, has yet to be extensively used for this purpose.

The finding that implicit and procedural memory often remain intact even in cases of severe amnesia has recently prompted researchers to begin to explore ways in which these preserved processes might be exploited beneficially for rehabilitation purposes. Cuing techniques, which take advantage of amnesic patients' ability to respond normally to word-stem or fragment cues, have been used successfully to teach individuals new factual information such as vocabulary as well as procedural tasks such as data-entry and word-processing. Continued research in this direction, paralleling more theoretically based research concerning preserved memory functions in amnesia, should enable further progress toward improving the ability of amnesic individuals to function effectively in their everyday lives.

Acknowledgments

Preparation of this article, and the research that supports the point of view represented herein, was supported by Grants MH35856 from the National Institute of Mental Health and AG09195 from the National Institute of Aging, the McDonnell-Pew Program in Cognitive Neuroscience, and the Flinn Foundation. We thank Terrence Barnhardt, Jeffrey Bowers, Jennifer Dorfman, Martha Glisky, Michael Polster, Barbara Routhieaux, Victor Shames, Michael Valdesseri, and Susan Valdisseri for their comments.

Bibliography

Eich, E. (1990). Learning during sleep. In "Sleep and Cognition" (R. R. Bootzin, J. F. Kihlstrom, and D. L. Schacter, Eds.).

pp. 88–108. American Psychological Association, Washington, DC.

Glisky, E. L., and Schacter, D. L. (1989). Models and methods of memory rehabilitation. In "Handbook of Neuropsychology" (F. Boller and J. Grafman, Eds.), Vol. 3, Part 5, pp. 233–346. Elsevier, Amsterdam.

Kihlstrom, J. F., and Schacter, D. L. (1990). Anaesthesia, amnesia, and the cognitive unconscious. In "Memory and Awareness in Anaesthesia" (B. Bonke, W. Fitch, and K. Millar, Eds.), pp. 21–44. Swets & Zeitlinger, Amsterdam.

Schacter, D. L., and Kihlstrom, J. F. (1989). Functional amnesia. In "Handbook of Neuropsychology" (F. Boller and J. Grafman, Eds.), Vol. 3, pp. 209–231. Elsevier, Amsterdam.

Shimamura, A. P. (1989). Disorders of memory: The cognitive science perspective. In "Handbook of Neuropsychology" (F. Boller and J. Grafman, Eds.), Vol. 3, Part 5, pp. 35–74. Elsevier, Amsterdam.

Squire, L. R., Knowlton, B. J., and Musen, G. (1993). The structure and organization of memory. *Annu. Rev. Neurosci.* **44,** 453–495.

Tulving, E., and Schacter, D. L. (1990). Priming and human memory systems. *Science* **247,** 301–306.

ANALOGICAL REASONING

Denise Dellarosa Cummins
University of Arizona

I. Philosophical Foundations
II. Psychological Investigations
III. Theoretical Models

Glossary

Analog An object or event that is similar to another object or event by virtue of isomorphic structures.
Base The primary object to which subsequent objects are compared.
Encoding Constructing a mental representation of a stimulus.
Mapping Putting structural features common to two analogs in correspondence with each other.
Target The problem or analogy that a reasoner endeavors to solve or understand by comparing it to the base.

AN ANALOGY is a relational similarity. Analogical reasoning involves identifying and working out correspondences between two sets of relations, usually referred to as the *target* and the *base* sets. Consider the statement "The structure of the atom is analogous to the structure of the solar system." Understanding this statement requires that the reasoner work out a meaningful set of correspondences between the atom (target) and the solar system (base), such as mapping the sun onto the nucleus of the atom and the planets onto electrons.

I. PHILOSOPHICAL FOUNDATIONS

A. Ancient and Medieval Uses of the Term

The term "analogy" was originally developed by the ancient Greeks to refer to mathematical proportionalities, but came to be used by them to refer more generally to similarity relations. Two types of similarity relations were distinguished, "analogy of proportionality" and "analogy of attribution." In the first, a relational likeness is said to hold between two sets of entities, as in "A is to B as C is to D." In the second, two terms are compared with respect to a property that is attributed to them in some non-univocal way. For example, the term "healthy" can be attributed to a human being and to medicine, but the meaning of the term is not identical in the two cases. "Healthy" as an attribute refers intrinsically and properly to the biological state of a human being, but because medicine contributes causally to health, the term can also be predicated of it. These distinctions were adopted by medieval theologians (notably Thomas Acquinas) to explain how beings with finite resources could come to understand an infinite being. Using analogy of proportionality, God's qualities were said to stand to God's nature as human qualities stand to human nature. Using analogy of attribution, God was assigned the role of the primary analog (e.g., base) to whom qualities such as "goodness" and "wisdom" are intrinsic and complete. When predicated of finite beings, these terms were considered merely analogous.

B. Models and Analogy in Science

Formally speaking, a model is an interpretation of a set of axioms, that is, a set of entities that satisfy the axioms. For example, certain characteristics of space satisfy the axioms of Euclidian geometry and hence constitute a model of that formal system. In addition to formal models, physical models (e.g., wind tunnels) and analogies (e.g., hydraulic models of economic supply and demand) also play an important role in scientific explanation. The similarity relation between a model and the system modeled is called an isomorphism. For example, a swinging pendulum satisfies the formal relations described in a wave equation, hence the two are isomorphic in that respect.

Models and analogy play two crucial roles in science. First, physical models and analogies are useful when the mathematical specification of the system is unknown or too complex to be used to make predictions about the system. Second, models of any kind often provide an explanatory content for a theory. For example, point particles moving about at random in a vessel constitute a model of the elementary theory of gases. The model allows theoretical concepts such as molecule, position, and velocity to receive an interpretation in particle mechanics. Combining this model with the gas laws (e.g., Boyle's law), also provides a more satisfying and coherent explanation of the lawlike behavior of gases than do the gas laws alone.

C. The Logic of Reasoning by Analogy

Analogical reasoning is a form of inductive inference. Analogical arguments have the following form:

> Entity A has attributes a, b, c, and z.
> Entity B has attributes a, b, c, and z.
> Entity C has attributes a, b, c.
> Therefore, entity C has attribute z.

This is an inductive argument because the conclusion is not entailed by the premises—it goes beyond the information given. One vitally important function of analogical reasoning is its use in generating hypotheses. Notice that the conclusion to the argument above can serve as a hypothesis—one could now attempt to test whether entity C in fact has attribute z. The analogical similarity between entities A, B, and C suggests the hypothesis that C also has z.

There are no formal methods for determining the validity of analogical arguments. Instead, they are evaluated in terms of their strength using the following six criteria:

1. The greater the number of entities having the attributes in question (a, b, c, and z), the stronger the conclusion that C also has z.
2. The greater the number of elements shared by A, B, and C the stronger the conclusion that C also has z.
3. The argument is strengthened in direct proportion to the weakness of the conclusion. For example, concluding "C probably has z" is weaker than concluding "C has z." The premises above constitute a stronger argument for concluding "C probably has z" than they do for concluding "C has z." So the strength of the

argument is inversely related to the weakness of the conclusion.
4. As the number of dissimilar elements among A, B, and C increases, the conclusion is weakened.
5. If a, b, and c are believed to cause or lead to z, then as the number of entities in the premises that have other dissimilar attributes increases, the argument is strengthened. For example, adding these premises strengthens the belief that z is caused or determined by a, b, and c; hence, they strengthen the argument that C has z as well:

> Entity R has q, t, $\underline{a}$, $\underline{b}$, $\underline{c}$, and $\underline{z}$.
> Entity G has m, n, $\underline{a}$, $\underline{b}$, $\underline{c}$, and $\underline{z}$.
> Entity Q has w, u, $\underline{a}$, $\underline{b}$, $\underline{c}$, and $\underline{z}$.

6. The conclusion is strengthened when a, b, and c are known in fact to have a causal or other determining influence on z.

In summary, normative accounts of analogy classify it as a species of induction. It is a means of drawing conclusions about an entity's unseen or unmeasured attributes on the basis of similarities which it shares with another better known or better understood entity. There are no formal means of assessing an analogical argument's validity. Rather, guidelines have been established for evaluating the strength of such arguments.

II. PSYCHOLOGICAL INVESTIGATIONS

Investigations into analogical reasoning divide into two literatures, research on reasoning with four-term analogy problems and research on analogical transfer during problem solving and knowledge acquisition.

A. Investigations of Reasoning with Four-Term Analogy Problems

The atom–solar system analogy discussed above can be reframed as a four-term analogy problem, such as "Sun : Planet :: Nucleus : ?"; the required answer is "Electron." Analogies of this type are typically used on standardized intelligence tests, and performance on them correlates positively with other measures of intelligence. Restating analogies in this format also provides a means of isolating each component of the reasoning process for study. To do this, reasoners are required to solve the analogy after viewing the entire four-term problem, or after being given a "preview" of each successive component, i.e., "*A*" followed by "*A : B :: C : D*," or "*A : B*" followed by "*A : B :: C : D*," or "*A : B :: C*" followed by "*A : B :: C : D*." The number of differences between the first two terms and between the first and third terms is varied as well. As the number of differences increases, so does the number of transformations the reasoner must undertake in order to complete the analogy. Examples using geometric analogies are illustrated in Figure 1.

One explanation of how reasoners solve four-term analogies is that they compare the first and second terms to see what they have in common, and then apply that common relation to the third and fourth terms. In fact, there is considerable evidence that a comparison of the first and third terms is involved as well. For example, in one set of studies using the "preview" methodology, reasoners spent approximately the same amount of time (13% of overall solution time) comparing the first two terms as they did comparing the first and third terms. The time required to process the analogy components and the number of errors made increased systematically as the number of transformations increased. Moreover, the amount of time spent encoding the terms was substantial, varying from 36% for geometric analo-

gies to 54% for verbal analogies. Importantly, encoding time and comparison time correlated with overall intelligence, but in opposite directions. Reasoners with high overall intelligence scores took *longer* to encode items but were quicker when carrying out comparisons. [*See* REASONING.]

These and other results suggest that solving four-term analogy problems involves (1) encoding the four terms, (2) inferring a relation between the first and second terms, (3) mapping the relation between the first and third term, and (4) applying the relation to the final term.

B. Analogical Transfer

In its most general sense, analogical transfer involves using knowledge from past experiences to solve novel problems. The basic empirical paradigm involves showing reasoners how to solve one or more types of problem (base problem or problems), and then requiring them to solve another problem (target) that is analogous—but not identical—to one of the base problems. If the newly learned procedure is used to solve the target problem, then analogical transfer of the learned skill is said to have occurred. Cross-domain transfer refers to instances in which the reasoner uses a procedure learned in one domain to solve a problem in another domain (e.g., physics to chemistry). Intra-domain transfer refers to instances in which the reasoner uses a procedure associated with a certain type of problem in one domain to solve another type of problem in the same domain. [*See* PROBLEM SOLVING.]

A major difference between analogical transfer and reasoning with four-term analogy problems is that in analogical transfer, the target is presented to the reasoner, but the base somehow must be retrieved from memory before the mapping process can take place. The processes involved can be summarized as follows:

1. Constructing representation of the target
2. Selecting an appropriate base from memory
3. Mapping the correspondences between the base and target
4. Extending the mapping to generate a solution

The summary results reported below are based on the use of numerous types of problems, including "insight" problems, algebra word problems, elementary probability problems, and physics prob-

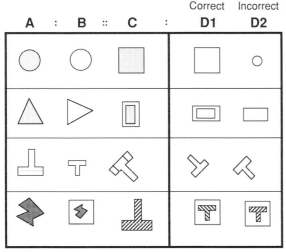

FIGURE 1 Examples of four-term geometric analogies, showing correct and incorrect solutions to the problems. The problems increase in difficulty as one proceeds down the list due to the number of transformations the reasoner must undertake to complete the analogy. For example, to complete the first analogy, the reasoner must simply remove the shading. To complete the last analogy, the reasoner must reduce the object, invert it, change the orientation of its stripes, and enclose it within another shape.

lems. The major results of work on analogical transfer can be summarized as follows.

1. Similarity in both structural and surface features influences whether a base analog will be retrieved. Once the base is retrieved from memory, however, only the degree of structural similarity between it and the target influences transfer performance.

For example, consider the following insight problem: A patient has an inoperable tumor in the center of his body. The tumor can be destroyed using X-rays, but the intensity needed to destroy it would also destroy all living tissue in its path, killing the patient. At lower intensities, the X-rays are harmless to the healthy tissue, but are insufficient to destroy the tumor. How can the rays be used to destroy the tumor without damaging healthy tissue?

One solution to this problem is to surround the patient with X-ray machines each delivering rays at intensities low enough to avoid harming healthy tissue, yet all converging on the tumor so that their intensities sum to a level high enough to destroy the tumor at its center. Left to their own devices, reasoners produce the convergence solution for this problem less than 10% of the time. If reasoners are taught the solution using a base analog that differs from this target in terms of surface features, the spontaneous transfer rate increases, but only to about 30%. For example, the base story might use converging ultrasound waves to fix light bulbs or converging armies to destroy fortresses instead of converging X-rays to kill tumors. These superficial differences hinder the reasoner from retrieving the appropriate base from memory. This is consistent with the results of other research showing that problem-solvers are often spontaneously "reminded" of previous problem-solving episodes only if those episodes are superficially similar to the problem they are currently working on.

Reasoners are not entirely insensitive to deeper similarities, however; if the target differs from the base in terms of structural features only, the same increase to about 30% obtains. For example, the target might refer to X-rays and tumors just as the base did, but now the major structural constraint is that the X-ray machine is incapable of delivering a dose high enough to kill the tumor. This differs from the constraint that the X-ray machine can deliver a high enough dose, but a dose of that intensity would kill the patient. The convergence solution still applies, but the structural constraints differ in the two problems, and this difference is enough to hinder the reasoner's retrieval of the base from memory.

Finally, if the target differs in terms of both surface and structural features, the rate of transfer is not appreciably different than baseline (i.e., about 13%). There must be some overlap (surface or structural) between the base and target problems in order for spontaneous retrieval to occur.

2. If reasoners are explicitly told to use the solution procedure encountered in an earlier problem, only structural similarity influences transfer. Continuing with the X-ray problem, after receiving a hint to use the base problem, transfer levels increase to about 80% regardless of surface feature overlap if the structural similarity is high, but only to about 50% if structural similarity is low. For example, if told to use the base story to solve the X-ray target problem, it doesn't matter whether the base refers to armies and fortresses, ultrasound waves and light bulbs, or X-rays and tumors. As long as the structural constraints are the same (e.g., a force of too great intensity must be divided into smaller units), reasoners can readily understand how to apply the base solution to the target. If the structural constraint differs, however (e.g., the force is too weak to be used alone), they fail to see the usefulness of the convergence solution.

3. Content embedding hinders analogical transfer. For example, transfer occurs more readily if an arithmetic progression solution procedure is taught as a content-free algebraic procedure using acceleration problems as examples than if it is taught specifically as a procedure for solving problems involving acceleration (i.e., all quantitative expressions explained in terms of motion). The more abstract the learning, the more likely that learning is to transfer to other problems within the domain and to problems in other domains.

4. Requiring reasoners to compare two or more analogs with differing surface features prior to attempting to solve the target produces the most robust transfer results. This can be done using four-term analogy problems, or by simply requiring them to write out descriptions of the problems structural similarities. This is typically explained in terms of generalization or schema

formation. Comparing two or more analogs produces an abstract problem category representation, or schema, that specifies content-neutral conditions for applying a given solution procedure. Using the X-ray problem as an example, this means that the reasoner forms an abstract category, or schema, for *problems that require the converging of weak forces into a single powerful force*. Notice that the description is quite general, and can be applied regardless of whether the objects in the problem are X-rays and tumors, armies and fortresses, etc.

5. Expert problem-solvers are less strongly influenced by surface similarity than novice problem-solvers, and the degree to which they are influenced varies with the level of expertise. For example, college students who score below 550 on the quantitative section of the Scholastic Aptitude Test (SAT) tend to be more influenced by surface feature similarity than are students who score 700 and above. This latter group, however, is more influenced by surface feature similarity than mathematics and physics graduate students. Requiring students to compare numerous base problems (as described in 4 above) significantly reduces the differences between expert and novice performance on target problems.

III. THEORETICAL MODELS

Current models of analogical transfer can be divided into two classes, content-driven models and content-free models. Content-driven models define analogy and transfer in terms of the reasoner's goals, the context in which the analogy occurs, and the meaning of the analogs' contents. Content-free models define analogies and analogical transfer in terms of formal relationships between the target and base analogs. Two summary examples of these classes are given below:

A. A Content-Driven Model

Analogs are represented in memory as mental models, that is, as states and transition functions that relate each state to its successor. For example, the X-ray problem would be represented as follows: An initial state in which the goal is to destroy the tumor, the resources available are powerful X-rays, the operators (legal moves) include reduc-

ing ray intensity, moving the rays, and administering the rays, and the constraint that the high-intensity rays cannot be safely administered from one direction only; a transition function in which application of the operators yield destruction of the tumor (satisfaction of goal state). Analogical transfer involves establishing a tentative mapping between goal descriptions (e.g., "destroy tumor" is mapped tentatively onto "destroy fortress"), and then systematically establishing mappings between the remaining elements in the X-ray and the "fortress" analogs. Only those features that are causally relevant to achieving the goal are mapped. Mapping continues until the problem is solved (i.e., the transition function is used to satisfy the goal), or until analogy breaks down. A breakdown occurs when too many structure-violating differences are detected between the base and target analog. A structure-violating difference is one which prevents the application of corresponding operators (e.g., multiple X-ray machines are not available). These are distinguished from structure-preserving differences which do not prevent application of the operators, although the operators may need to be modified in order to be applied (e.g., "divide army into smaller units" is physically different from "reduce X-ray intensity," but the X-ray operator can be modified to "divide into several low intensity rays" to provide a match.)

B. A Content-Free Model

In this model, the goals of the reasoner are irrelevant, as are the particular contents of the analogs. The analogs are represented as collected structures of predicates. Analogical transfer consists of putting objects into one-to-one correspondence so as to maximize depth of predicate structure. The mapping principle that accomplishes this is called the systematicity principle. This principle, simply stated, is that predicates that participate in higher-order, coherent structures are preferred over isolated, simple predicates during mapping.

Consider our example of the solar system and the atom. The solar system contains the sun and planets, the atom a nucleus and electrons. Assume the reasoner's understanding of the solar system is that the sun is a yellow star that is hotter than and more massive than the planets, and that the planets revolve around the sun because the sun acts as an attractive force. This knowledge can be represented as a set of predicates, such as

HOTTER-THAN (Sun, Planet)
IS-YELLOW (Sun)

CAUSES $\begin{cases}$ MORE-MASSIVE-THAN (Sun, Planet)
ATTRACTS (Sun, Planet)
REVOLVES-AROUND (Sun, Planet). $\end{cases}$

Assume the only knowledge the reasoner has about atoms is that they contain a nucleus and electrons, and that the nucleus is more massive than the electrons. This knowledge can be represented by the following predicates:

MORE-MASSIVE-THAN (Nucleus, Electron).

The reasoner's task is to complete the analogy by mapping relations from the base analog (solar system) to the target analog (atom).

The reasoner begins by looking for identical predicates. There is only one relation that matches, MORE-MASSIVE-THAN, so a tentative mapping between nucleus and sun and between planet and electron is constructed. Attributes are ignored in this model, so the predicate IS-YELLOW would not be mapped even if it did match a predicate in the target analog. But what about the remaining predicates? According to the systematicity principle, predicates that are part of a higher-order, coherent predication structure should be preferred over isolated predicates during mapping. The predicates AT-TRACTS and REVOLVES-AROUND are joined by MORE-MASSIVE-THAN as subpredicates in the larger structure CAUSES. For this reason, they are selected for inclusion in extending and completing the analogy. HOTTER-THAN, since it participates in no higher-order predicate system, is not selected for inclusion. The resulting atom analog can be represented as

CAUSES $\begin{cases}$ MORE-MASSIVE-THAN (Nucleus, Electron)
ATTRACTS (Nucleus, Electron)
REVOLVES-AROUND (Nucleus, Electron). $\end{cases}$

The major distinction between this model and the preceding one is that analogical mapping and transfer proceed without reference to the meaning of the predicates under consideration or the goals of the reasoner. Mapping is done solely on the basis of matches between identical elements, and selection of predicates for transfer is guided solely by structural (syntactical) properties of the representations.

Bibliography

Cummins, D. D. (1992). Role of analogical reasoning in the induction of problem categories. *J. Exp. Psychol. Learning, Memory, Cog.* **18,** 1103–1124.

Ferre, F. (1967). Analogy in theology. In "The Encyclopedia of Philosophy" Vols. 1 and 2, pp. 94–97. Macmillan, New York.

Gentner, D. (1989). The mechanisms of analogical reasoning. In "Similarity and Analogical Reasoning" (S. Vosniadou and A. Ortony, Eds.), pp. 199–241. Cambridge University Press, Cambridge.

Hesse, M. (1967). Models and analogy in science. "The Encyclopedia of Philosophy," Vols. 1 and 2, pp. 94–97. Macmillan, New York.

Holyoak, K. J. (1985). The pragmatics of analogical transfer. In "The Psychology of Learning and Motivation" (G. Bower, Ed.), Vol. 19, pp. 59–87. Academic Press, New York.

Holyoak, K. J., and Thagard, P. (1989). Analogical mapping by constraint satisfaction. *Cog. Sci.* **13,** 295–355.

Hurley, P. J. (1991). "A Concise Introduction to Logic, 4th ed. Wadsworth, Belmont, CA.

Sternberg, R. J. (1977). Component processes in analogical reasoning. *Psychol. Rev.* **84,** 353–378.

ANGER

James R. Averill
University of Massachusetts at Amherst

Glossary

Aggression The intentional infliction of harm on others, against their wishes and not for their own good.

Anger An emotional state that involves both an attribution of blame for some perceived wrong and an impulse to correct the wrong or prevent its recurrence.

Category mistake The logical fallacy of assuming that what is true of one category (e.g., aggression) is also true of a related category (e.g., anger); category mistakes are particularly common when the relation between the categories is one of class inclusion, part–whole, or cause–effect.

Catharsis A purgation ("cleansing") or clarification of emotion; used to explain the benefits sometimes associated with vicarious emotional experiences, for example, during theatrical performances (Aristotle) and psychotherapy (Freud).

Crime of passion Legal terminology for homicide committed while in an emotional state, typically anger; also termed *voluntary manslaughter*.

Emotional state A short-term disposition to respond based on an evaluative judgment (e.g., that something is good or bad, challenging or threatening, just or unjust); as traditionally conceived, emotional states differ from other short-term dispositions in that the relevant evaluation is nondeliberate and the ensuing response is beyond personal control (a passion rather than an action).

Social constructionism The view that emotions are not an intrinsic part of human nature (i.e., genetically determined) but, rather, are constructed from elementary processes in conformance with social norms and rules.

ANGER and aggression are often discussed under one heading, a fact that has distorted discussions of both. Anger need not be, and typically is not, manifested in aggression; conversely, aggression is frequently manifested for reasons that have little to do with anger. This article focuses on anger as an emotion; the orientation is social–psychological. Psychologically, anger is an accusation of wrongdoing—an attribution of blame—and a determination to correct the perceived wrong; socially, anger functions as a kind of informal judiciary that helps regulate interpersonal relationships.

I. TWO CONCEPTS OF ANGER

The concept of anger is often used in two distinct ways: first, as a generic term to cover a wide range of related emotional responses, such as envy, jealousy, fury, frustration, annoyance, contempt, and the like; and second, as a specific emotion on a par with other emotions in the same general category (e.g., anger versus envy). Linguistically, when a single term is used to refer to phenomena at two different levels of generality, the term so used is known as a synecdoche. "Anger" is often used as a synecdoche, in both everyday speech and psychological theory.

It is important to distinguish the generic and specific uses of the concept of anger, for what is true of a category at one level of generality need not be true at another (higher or lower) level. To conflate levels of generality is to commit a "category mistake." Category mistakes are particularly common when synecdoches are involved, for the use of the same term makes it easy to transverse between levels of generality without realizing the shift in meaning.

Consider, first, the meaning of anger as a generic category. What do members of the category (e.g., envy, jealousy, and fury, as well as anger as a specific emotion) have in common? On some occasions, at least, all are associated with aggressive behavior. In its generic sense, then, anger may be used to refer to almost any aggressive emotional response. Angry aggression in this sense is typically contrasted with instrumental aggression, that is, aggression deliberately used as a means for achieving some extrinsic reward (as in a robbery). [*See* AGGRESSION.]

Now consider anger as a specific emotion. How does anger in a narrow sense differ from other members of the general category of angerlike emotions, such as envy, jealousy, and fury? As will be explained more fully below, anger as a specific emotion involves an attribution of blame for wrongdoing and a desire for reparation. Only rarely is anger in this sense accompanied by aggression, at least by physical aggression. The main objective of anger is not to harm the instigator, but to correct the perceived wrong and prevent recurrence.

Category mistakes can proceed from the top down (generic to specific categories) or from the bottom up (specific to generic categories). An example of a top–down mistake is the common assumption that because anger (in the generic sense) connotes aggression, then anger (in the specific sense) must also involve a tendency toward aggression, even if that tendency is repressed, bottled-up, disguised, or otherwise made unobservable. An example of a bottom–up mistake is the inclination on the part of perpetrators to excuse aggression of all sorts, from child abuse to urban riots, with the plea: "It wasn't my fault; he/she/they made me angry."

The following discussion focuses on anger *as a specific emotion*. No attempt is made to review the vast amount of research related to aggression in general. Considerable advances have been made in our understanding of the biological (evolutionary) and physiological bases of aggressive behavior; as important as that understanding may be, it is only tangentially related to anger as a social–psychological phenomenon. On the other hand, data relevant to anger come from a wide range of sources, including historical (ethical) teachings, legal proceedings, surveys of everyday experience, experimental studies, cross-cultural research, and clinical practice.

II. ANGER IN HISTORICAL PERSPECTIVE

Historically and today, anger appears on nearly every list of "basic" emotions. Often this is taken to mean that anger is somehow prior to society, for example, that anger is a relic of biological evolution. Anger, however, does not arise from the depths of some presocial self. It embodies a history of social meanings. From early infancy, we are emotional apprentices, first to our parents, and then to teachers, ministers, artists, entertainers, and other formal agents of cultural transmission. The apprenticeship continues on a less formal basis throughout life as we interact with family, friends, and acquaintances in everyday, face-to-face encounters. In the process, we learn the rules and norms that constitute our emotions and the skills to enact them properly. Subsequently, we may refine and transform what we have acquired, but we can never completely escape the vestiges of our cultural heritage.

Western culture has been greatly influenced by the confluence of two main streams of thought, Greco-Roman philosophy and Judeo-Christian theology. Each stream has contributed its share to current conceptions of anger. Shortly, we will consider briefly the views of three early representatives of these traditions, namely, Aristotle, Seneca, and Lactantius. But first, a bit of etymology may be helpful.

Anger is an emotion. On that, everyone would agree. But what is an emotion? On that, few psychologists agree. For most of Western history, from the time of the ancient Greeks until about the middle of the 18th century, what we now call emotions were commonly referred to as passions. As traditionally conceived, a passion is anything a person (or physical object) "suffers"; this would include, in the case of humans, both emotions and diseases. Hence, from the same root (the Greek *pathe* and the Latin *pati, passiones*) we get such emotion-related terms as "passion," "pathos," and "sympathy" and such disease-related terms as "patient," "pathogen," and "pathology."

Aristotle considered that the passions formed 1 of 10 fundamental categories of being. Actions—things a person does deliberately and with forethought—formed another distinct category. This distinction between passions and actions is embedded in our ordinary language, as when we say of a person that he was "gripped," "seized," and "overcome" by emotion. Anger in particular is often depicted as a "wild beast" that must be "tamed," or as an "inner force" that will "explode" if not adequately "released." Such conventional ways of speaking help constitute the way we think and feel. But linguistic conventions can mislead as well as inform.

When addressing the practical concerns of rhetoricians, as opposed to the theoretical concerns of metaphysicians, Aristotle defined anger "as an impulse, accompanied by pain, to a conspicuous revenge for a conspicuous slight directed without justification towards what concerns oneself or towards what concerns one's friends" (*Rhetoric*, 1378a30). Two aspects of this definition are specially noteworthy. First, the "slight" (by which Aristotle meant any show of contempt, spite, or insolence, especially by a friend or inferior) had to be "without justification." A reprove that is deserved is not an adequate provocation to anger. Second, the revenge must be "conspicuous"; otherwise the offender will not realize that he or she is being punished for the slight. To these two points, we should add a third important feature of Aristotle's analysis, namely, the response must be appropriate to the provocation and the situation, being neither too weak nor too strong.

Aristotle's analysis contains a paradox. If anger is a passion, how can it be so finely tuned to the social context, in both initiation and expression? One way to resolve this paradox is to deny that anger, at least under ordinary circumstances, is beyond personal control; to assert, in effect, that the classification of anger as a passion is based more on metaphor than on fact. More will be said about this possibility below. Another possible resolution is to regard anger as a primitive reaction to painful stimuli, an impulse that is regulated but not constituted by social rules. This is the position of many current psychological theories of anger and aggression. It was also the position taken by Aristotle, who believed that the physiological changes that accompany anger (e.g., a "boiling of blood" about the heart) can impel a person to act in a nondeliberate and irrational manner.

Aristotle's answer, however, hardly seems adequate. The physiological changes that accompany a brisk walk, say, exceed those that accompany most episodes of anger, and yet a brisk walk does not lead a person to act irrationally. Conversely, some of the worst deeds committed in the name of anger are done in a cold and calculated manner, with no more than usual physiological involvement.

The Roman philosopher and statesman Seneca (4 B.C.–A.D. 65) wrote the first full work devoted entirely to the topic of anger. As a follower of Stoicism, Seneca defined passion as a form of false judgment, the mental analogue of a physical disease. (After all, who would deliberately, "in his right mind," make a false judgment?) This definition of passion led Seneca to reject the notion that anger is necessarily tied to one's bodily condition or that it could be anything but a human emotion. A false judgment, no less than a true judgment, is born of reason, no matter how ill-begotten the false judgment might be. Seneca also rejected the Aristotelian notion that anger, properly directed and in moderation, can be considered good. If on occasion a false judgment produces a beneficial outcome, that is a fortunate happenstance. Whatever good is done in anger, according to Seneca, can be done even better and with greater surety following rational deliberation. In a manner prescient of current cognitive therapies, Seneca offered advice on how to reinterpret events so that they are no longer judged offensive; or when that is not possible because the offense is too egregious, then to correct the wrong in a rational and deliberate manner.

Stoicism was the dominant philosophy of the Roman Empire, and views such as those expressed by Seneca were very influential—in theory if not in practice. And although it might at first seem like a relatively minor footnote to the history of thought, Seneca's treatment of anger also posed a major challenge to the ascendancy of Christianity. Jehovah of the Old Testament is often depicted as wrathful, vengeful, and punishing. The biblical Christ, too, was not without anger, as when he drove the moneychangers from the temple. How could an all-knowing, all-powerful, and all-loving god be susceptible to anger, if anger is indeed a passion (whether conceived as a form of false judgment or a physiologically based impulse)?

This question was addressed by Lactantius, a Roman convert to Christianity and confidant to the Emperor Constantine (4th century A.D.). Lactantius criticized the notion that anger involves a desire for revenge. Rather, anger in the strict sense (that is, righteous or just anger) is a mental act motivated to restrain offenses. Such anger is proper to God and necessary to humankind, according to Lactantius, for no one who is good and just can fail to be moved at the sight of evil. We therefore rise to punishment, not for the sake of revenge, but in order that morals be preserved and license suppressed. Of course, Lactantius recognized that angry people sometimes do more harm than good. That, however, is a feature of "unjust" anger, a debasement of true anger that (in a manner similar to Aristotle) he attributed to interference from bodily reactions.

The views of Aristotle, Seneca, and Lactantius, although presented here in the most cursory manner, highlight some of the issues and controversies that still divide contemporary theories of anger.

Is anger a passion or an action? In terms of the language we use to describe anger in everyday discourse, it is clearly a passion. On this point, Aristotle, Seneca, and Lactantius would agree; however, the reasons they give for this classification are very different, a fact which might call into question the nature of the classification itself. Indeed, Lactantius comes close to denying that anger is a passion, at least when he speaks of divine or (in humans) righteous anger. Perhaps the closest modern analogue of Lactantius's divine anger (a fully rational, disembodied anger) can be found in the area of Artificial Intelligence. Computers can be programmed to simulate righteous anger, that is, to evaluate "offenses," interrupt ongoing activity, and take corrective measures. We need not postulate special circuitry, no less some primitive anger "instinct" or "drive" on the part of the computer. All that is required is the programming of appropriate rules.

What is the role of physiological arousal in anger? To the extent that anger leads to vigorous action, it may be accompanied by noticeable bodily changes. There is also evidence that the physiological changes associated with anger are somewhat different than those typically associated, say, with fear. (Anger shows a norepinephrine-like pattern; fear, an epinephrine-like pattern.) Moreover, research suggests that when a person is physiologically aroused, for whatever reason and regardless of the patterning of the arousal, he or she may be more prone to anger—or to any other emotion appropriate to the situation—than would otherwise be the case. Thus, the potential importance of physiological arousal during anger should not be underestimated, but neither should it be overestimated. Physiological arousal is neither a necessary nor a sufficient condition for anger. Fundamentally, anger is to be understood primarily in cognitive rather than physiological terms. This fact was recognized by Aristotle and even more unequivocally by Seneca and Lactantius.

What is the function of anger? When appropriately experienced and expressed, anger serves an important social function, namely, the restraint of offense (Aristotle, Lactantius); indeed, when faced with adequate provocation, anger is not only appro-

priate, it is a god-given duty (Lactantius). Needless to say, anger can be, and too often is, used for selfish and even anti-social ends (Seneca). But a phenomenon must be understood in terms of its normative application, not its misapplication, although the latter may be more dramatic and in need of attention.

To conclude this section, we might ask with regard to historical teachings in general: Does anger exist outside of a particular socio-historical context, or is it a product of that context? Theorists who adopt the first alternative are sometimes referred to as "naturalists," for they believe that anger is an inherent part of human nature. Those who favor the second alternative are known as "social constructionists," for they believe that anger is constituted, not just regulated, by social norms and rules. For social constructionists, views such as those presented by Aristotle, Seneca, and Lactantius are of more than historical interest; they help form the cultural matrix within which anger is constituted.

III. ANGER IN COURTS OF LAW

In contemporary society, the law of homicide both embodies and promotes social norms and rules with respect to anger. In Anglo-American common law, two grades of criminal homicide are generally recognized, murder and manslaughter, and each of these is divided into two subcategories, first- and second-degree murder and voluntary and involuntary manslaughter. Murder is homicide committed with "malice aforethought," that is, deliberately and with the intent of gain (cf. instrumental aggression). Second-degree murder differs from first-degree murder in that there are mitigating circumstances. Manslaughter is a lesser crime than murder. Voluntary manslaughter is the technical name for a "crime of passion," that is, homicide committed during emotion, typically anger. It is "voluntary" because the angry person *wants* to attack the victim. Involuntary manslaughter is accidental but nevertheless culpable homicide, for example, due to negligence. [*See* HO-MICIDE.]

As just noted, anger serves to mitigate a charge of homicide from murder to voluntary manslaughter. This is no trivial matter. A conviction for murder can mean a life sentence or even the death penalty. By contrast, voluntary manslaughter carries a much lighter sentence—typically little more than a few years in prison, and often probation. Why should this disparity exist? And how does a jury decide whether a defendant was truly angry at the time of the crime?

The law stipulates four major criteria for deciding whether a person was truly angry at the time of a killing: adequacy of provocation, heat of passion, insufficient cooling time, and a causal connection between the provocation and the crime. "Heat of passion" is a vague reference to the behavior of the individual at the time of the homicide; and "causal connection" refers to the fact that the aggression must be a direct response to the provocation. The other two criteria—the adequacy of provocation and insufficient cooling time—are the most interesting from an analytical point of view, for they are judged by the so-called "reasonable-man test." This test stipulates that the provocation be sufficient to arouse an ordinary member of the community to anger so intense that it might lead to homicide; and, again according to community standards, that there be insufficient time for the anger to dissipate before the homicide is committed.

The reasonable-man test provides ostensibly objective criteria (the norms and standards of the community) against which the feelings and reactions of the defendant can be compared. If there is a match, the defendant may be considered to have been in an angry state; if there is no match, the defendant is not judged to have been angry, regardless of his or her feelings at the time. Put differently, the reasonable-man test objectifies anger; no longer does anger refer simply to a state of mind of the defendant, but to an objectively existing state of affairs to which the individual may or may not have attained. The so-called "reasonable man" is, after all, no actually existing person, but is, rather, an idealized embodiment of the norms and standards of the community.

The above considerations suggest that the attribution of anger in courts of law is a kind of social subterfuge. The crime of passion is still a crime, but one that is to some degree excusable. The angry person was, after all, doing his "duty" by correcting some wrong as defined by community standards. He is therefore given a two-way out. First, the victim is, in a sense, put on trial along with the defendant; and if the victim (instigator) was sufficiently guilty (committed a provocation egregious enough to be judged "adequate") then he or she must share the blame for having provoked the incident. Second, since anger is classified as a passion, the defendant cannot be held fully responsible for behavior that was presumably beyond personal control.

IV. ANGER IN EVERYDAY AFFAIRS

Crimes of passion present a misleading picture of anger in one very important respect—they are crimes. The presumed "reasonable man" has proven himself to be unreasonable in his resort to excessive violence. To what extent can we generalize from crimes of passion to anger in everyday affairs?

Anger is a very common emotion. When asked to keep diary records, most people report becoming mildly angry once or twice a day, and seriously angry once or twice a week. The most frequent targets of anger are loved ones and friends; the most common instigations involve some perceived misconduct, for example, an intentional wrongdoing or avoidable accident; and the motivation of the angry person is to correct or prevent recurrence of the "wrong," not to hurt the instigator.

Anger may be expressed in a great variety of ways depending on the person and situation. Common responses include talking the incident over with the instigator, verbal reprimands, withdrawal of privileges, brooding, and so on. At higher levels of intensity, an angry episode may include such behaviors as shouting, slamming doors, and stomping out. Only rarely does anger result in direct physical aggression against the instigator, at least among adults. In fact, being unusually kind to or solicitous of the instigator—a "contrary reaction"—is more common than direct physical aggression.

Needless to say, it is easy to think of episodes of anger that do not conform to the above pattern. For example, on occasion we all have become angry at an inanimate object, as when our car stalls in the middle of an intersection; in such instances, however, we typically imbue the object with human qualities (the car had no "right" to stall). Overwhelmingly, anger is an interpersonal emotion; it is directed at persons or other entities (the self, human institutions) that in some way can be held accountable for their actions.

Few people find pleasure in their own anger; to be the target of another person's anger is even more unpleasant. Nevertheless, surveys indicate that the consequences of most everyday episodes of anger are evaluated positively. Even instigators (the "wrongdoers") report that, in the majority of cases, they gain from being the target of anger, for example, by coming to realize their own faults or by gaining a better understanding of the angry person's point of view.

An important caveat must be added to this last observation: The more aggressive the response, the less likely it is that anger will have a positive outcome. Rather than being a typical manifestation of anger, aggression reflects a failure of anger to achieve its purpose, which is to correct the wrong, not to hurt the target.

V. RULES OF ANGER

On the basis of historical teachings, legal procedures, and everyday experience, it is possible to infer the rules that help determine the way anger is experienced and expressed. Some of the more general rules are presented in Table I.

All theorists recognize the importance of rules for the experience and expression of emotion. There is a crucial difference among theorists, however, in the way the rules are presumed to work. Naturalists assume that anger is an inherent part of human nature and that rules function only to regulate how the emotion is experienced. Social constructionists, by contrast, believe that the rules not only regulate but also help constitute anger as a distinct emotion. There are other differences among these two positions as well. For example, naturalists search for the origins of anger in biological evolution, whereas social constructionists look toward history; naturalists see an essential link between anger and aggression, whereas social constructionists believe that aggression is only one of many ways that anger may

be expressed; and naturalists regard anger as universal, whereas social constructionists consider anger to be culturally specific.

The Utku Eskimos supposedly do not have a name for, nor do they express, an emotion equivalent to anger. Social constructionists take such data as support for their contention that anger is not a biologically based, universal phenomenon; naturalists, on the other hand, argue that the Utku simply suppress their anger, or express it in subtle and indirect ways, in order to preserve harmonious social relationships. There is no easy way to resolve these divergent interpretations, for the issue depends partly on how anger is defined, for example, as a general category or as a specific emotion (cf. the earlier discussion of anger as a synecdoche). However, this much can be said: As cross-cultural research continues to reveal the great diversity of ways that human societies have developed to deal with potential frustrations and interpersonal conflicts, the case for the universality of anger as a *specific* emotion becomes increasingly problematic.

Consider *liget*, a fundamental emotion among the Ilongot, a headhunting people indigenous to the Philippines. Like anger, *liget* can be occasioned by insults, slights, and other affronts to the self, and the violation of social norms. The most important occasion for *liget*, however, is cutting off the head of another person. The taking of a head helps establish one's place as an equal and honored member of society. The identity of the victim is largely irrelevant—a man, woman, child, anyone will do, prefera-

TABLE I

Some Rules of Anger as Inferred from Historical Teachings, Legal Procedures, and Self-reports of Everyday Experiences

1. A person has the right (duty) to become angry at intentional wrongdoing or at unintentional misdeeds if those misdeeds are correctable (e.g., due to negligence, carelessness, or oversight).

2. Anger should be directed only at persons and, by extension, other entities (one's self, human institutions) that can be held responsible for their actions.

3. Anger should not be displaced on an innocent third party, nor should it be directed at the target for reasons other than the instigation.

4. The aim of anger should be to correct the situation, restore equity, and/or prevent recurrence, not to inflict injury or pain on the target nor to achieve selfish ends through intimidation.

5. The angry response should be proportional to the instigation; that is, it should not exceed what is necessary to correct the situation, restore equity, or prevent the instigation from happening again.

6. Anger should follow closely upon the provocation and not endure longer than is needed to correct the situation (typically a few hours or days, at most).

7. Anger should involve commitment and resolve; that is, a person should not become angry unless appropriate follow-through is intended, circumstances permitting.

Source: Averill, J. R. (1993). Illusions of anger. In "Aggression and Violence: A Social Interactionist Perspective" (R. B. Felson and J. T. Tedeschi, Eds.). American Psychological Association, Washington, DC.

bly a stranger. *Liget* also finds expression in a variety of ways other than headhunting. For example, male *liget* is implicated in both courtship and childbirth; "concentrated" in the sperm, it helps make babies. *Liget* also stimulates work and provides the strength and courage to overcome obstacles. From these few remarks, it is evident that *liget* is constituted by different rules than is anger. A crazed American might cut off the head of another, but only a well-socialized Ilongot could experience *liget*. Moreover, if a crazed American did cut off the head of another, we would not attribute the response to anger—not in a court of law (cf. previous discussion of crimes of passion) nor in everyday affairs.

In short, the rules presented in Table I may seem self-evident, but that is not because they are universally or necessarily true. Rather, they are culturally based norms that, when internalized, become part of our "second nature." Other cultures have different rules, different emotions, different "second natures."

VI. ANGER AND THE SOCIAL ORDER

We question the sincerity and even the character (or mental health) of a person who claims to be angry but who declines to take action, circumstances permitting (see Rule 7, Table I). This link between anger and action is not due simply to the fact that anger is a reaction to unpleasant events. Of greater importance is the fact that anger involves a commitment to the shared values that make social life possible. The demand for action is thus a social as well as a psychological imperative. In traditional moral teachings, the failure to become angry under appropriate circumstances was regarded as sinful as excessive or unjustified anger. In the words of the 17th century divine Thomas Fuller, "anger is one of the sinews of the soul; he that wants it hath a maimed mind." A modern extension of this traditional teaching can be found in the current popularity of "assertiveness training."

In most everyday episodes, the transgressions that provoke anger are relatively minor—breaking a promise, ignoring a responsibility, being inconsiderate. This fact tends to obscure the role that anger plays in maintaining the social order. No matter how trifling our everyday promises, responsibilities, and considerations may seem to be, they are the threads from which the fabric of society is woven. If they are too frequently broken without mend, society

unravels. In a very real sense, then, the many small mendings that are the everyday experiences of anger, each minor in its own right, help sustain a way of life.

Anger can be a tool for social change as well as maintenance. There may come a time when we commit ourselves to values other than those embraced by the larger society. In a fight for civil rights and equality, for example, we may turn our anger on people and institutions to whom we previously held fealty. But the new values we now seek to establish are, typically, old values applied to new circumstances or extended to new groups (e.g., women, minorities). Even as a tool for radical social change, anger tends to be conservative of the values it embodies.

VII. ANGER IN HEALTH AND DISEASE

Anger has implications for the health of the individual as well as society. For example, patients suffering from serious diseases such as cancer have a better prognosis if they become angry at their condition than if they become merely frightened or depressed. Although the underlying mechanisms are not clear, a possible explanation is that the angry person is more likely to "fight" the illness, for example, by taking an active role in his or her treatment.

More frequently, anger has been postulated to have a negative impact on a person's health. Specifically, pent up or suppressed anger has been implicated in a wide variety of psychosomatic disorders, including coronary disease, ulcerative colitis, and depression. Evidence for an etiological role of anger in such conditions is often contradictory. Nevertheless, there are two ways in which unexpressed anger can have a deleterious effect on health. First, if a person is caught in a frustrating or threatening position and takes no action, for whatever reason, the sustained stress that is experienced can lead to tissue damage in susceptible organs, and even to inhibition of the immune system, thus increasing vulnerability to a wide variety of disorders.

A second way that anger has been postulated to have a deleterious effect on health is through the mechanism of repression. The concept of repression owes much to Freud and psychoanalysis, although it is no longer tied to any one theoretical position. The notion of repressed anger has even passed into the legal system (thus extending the "insufficient cooling time" criterion for crimes of passion). The basic idea is that, due to situational or personal constraints, anger is too threatening for the individual even to admit experiencing. Banned from consciousness, the anger nevertheless finds outlet in a disguised and maladaptive fashion. [See DEFENSE MECHANISMS.]

Of all the conditions commonly attributed to repressed anger, the most frequently mentioned is depression. Depression can have many causes, both physiological and psychological. It need not, and typically does not, have anything to do with repressed anger. There are occasions, however, when depressive-like symptoms can take on some of the qualities of an angry response. Consider the case of a woman who is so fatigued that she finds it difficult to get out of bed in the morning, feels despondent through most of the day, and is haunted by frequent thoughts of suicide. Life becomes a burden both to herself and to those around her. Now add the following considerations: The woman's husband treats her with neglect; nevertheless, she sincerely believes that she has no right to be angry with her husband, for his neglect of her is somehow deserved. Still, in subtle ways her behavior causes considerable inconvenience to her husband; and, moreover, she derives barely concealed satisfaction from her husband's discomfort. In such a case, we might well speak of the woman's depression as being a manifestation of "repressed" anger. That, however, is a metaphorical way of speaking, for the woman's behavior follows only some, but not all, of the standard rules for anger. A more parsimonious explanation might be that the woman has acquired, in this situation, at least, a set of personal rules that helps constitute an emotion that resembles both anger (retaliation for a perceived wrong) and depression (fatigue, despondency, self-reproach). [See DEPRESSION.]

Recall the emotion of *liget* described earlier. It bears some semblance to anger within our own culture, but it is constituted by different rules and hence represents a different emotion. Rules of emotion can vary *within* as well as between cultures. There exist subcultures of increasingly smaller scope, down to the level of the family and ultimately the individual. An emotion that is the product of personal (idiosyncratic) rules, is particularly subject to misinterpretation since usual forms of consensual validation are lacking. But nothing is gained by way of clarity, and much may be lost, if we label the nonconforming emotion by some common name ("anger," say, or "depression") and attribute its idiosyncrasy to repression.

A. Catharsis

The idea of repression is closely tied to that of catharsis. During psychoanalytic therapy (what Freud originally called the "cathartic method") presumably repressed impulses are brought to consciousness and expressed in an adaptive fashion. Using a rather graphic metaphor, Freud compared catharsis to the draining of pus from an infected wound. Continuing with the example of depression, suppose the woman described earlier turns to psychotherapy for help. During treatment, she may come to recognize on a conscious level the unfairness of her treatment, and, blaming her husband rather than herself, she may resolve to do something to change the situation. From a psychoanalytic perspective, it might be said that her depression "lifts" as her repressed anger is "released." An alternative explanation is that one kind of emotional response (an ill-defined anger/depression combination) has been replaced by a more adaptive response (normative anger).

A good deal of experimental research has also been devoted to the possible cathartic effects of emotional expression, especially with respect to anger and aggression. On the whole, the results have not been kind to the catharsis hypothesis. More often than not, the expression of anger on one occasion facilitates and encourages its expression on subsequent occasions. This is opposite to the mitigating effect predicted by the catharsis hypothesis. In the case of anger and aggression, as in so many other areas, practice makes perfect—or at least easier.

VIII. GENDER DIFFERENCES

A common stereotype is that women are less capable of anger than are men. This stereotype is also sometimes used to explain the greater frequency of depression diagnosed among women than men (cf. previous discussion of repressed anger). However, surveys of the everyday experience of anger suggest that women become angry as often as men, as intensely, and as effectively. Gender differences in anger, to the extent that they exist, must be sought on a more subtle plane than the stereotype suggests.

In the conduct of interpersonal relations, men tend to place greater emphasis on competition and individual rights, whereas women tend to place greater emphasis on cooperation and affiliation. Men also tend to be physically more aggressive than women. Such differences in orientation and response style cannot help but have reverberations on the way anger is experienced and expressed. Some of the things that a man finds offensive may not offend a woman, and vice versa; and when angry, a man may do and say things that a woman typically would not (for example, men are more likely than women to engage in physical violence when angry, and women are more likely than men to cry). But as important as such differences may be, they should not be interpreted to mean that anger is less appropriate to women than to men, or that women are less capable of anger than are men. "Different" does not necessarily imply "more" or "less." Women are as sensitive as men to unfair treatment; and in response to provocations they deem adequate, women are as likely as men to make their feelings known clearly and effectively.

IX. WRONGFUL ANGER

The rules presented in Table I suggest that anger, properly constituted, serves to correct socially recognized wrongs, and that the anger should not exceed what is necessary to achieve that end. And, as described earlier, the majority of episodes fit that description. However, the rules of anger are easily broken, either unintentionally or willfully, with consequences that are harmful to the self and interpersonal relationships.

When the rules are violated, we may speak of wrongful anger (provided the violation is not so egregious as to preclude the response from being classified as anger altogether). Three types of wrongfull anger have already been discussed in passing, namely, anger that goes unexpressed, resulting in continued provocation and unrelieved tension; anger that is expressed indirectly or in accordance with idiosyncratic rules; and anger that is expressed intemperately, resulting in violence against the target. To these we could add anger that is unduly prolonged, is displaced on innocent third parties, is oft-repeated without adequate follow-through, and so forth.

The rules of anger may be violated for many reasons, some of which are beyond the immediate control of the individual—for example, inadequate socialization, neurological dysfunction, inordinate stress, or fatigue. However, with a better understanding of what constitutes an adequate provocation and with the acquisition of more effective coping skills, violations typically can be curbed. That, at least, is the rationale behind most assertiveness training and anger treatment programs. But the outcome of anger—whether beneficial or harmful—does not depend exclusively on the behavior of the angry person. Anger is more like a dialogue than a soliloquy; or, put differently, there are "rules of engagement" for the target as well as for the angry person. The most beneficial response for a target (assuming the anger is justified) is an explanation to correct any misunderstanding, an apology if no misunderstanding exists, and a resolve to prevent recurrence. Too often, unfortunately, anger provokes anger, and conflict escalates.

Constructive (as opposed to wrongful) anger presumes good will on the part of the angry person. When good will is absent, the rules of anger may be violated "wantonly," so to speak. That is, anger may be used deliberately, if not consciously, to achieve ends that are only tangentially related to the instigation. The concept of anger, it will be recalled, has exculpatory implications, and this in two ways: First, since anger is commonly interpreted as a passion rather than an action, the angry person presumably cannot control his or her own behavior; second, if the anger is accepted as justified, the blame for initiating the incident is shifted from the angry person to the instigator. Not surprisingly, therefore, perpetrators and their apologists often seek to excuse vicious behavior—child abuse, spouse battering, mugging and robbery, gang warfare, urban riots, etc.—by attributing it to anger. And in a multitude of more minor ways, we all sometimes resort to anger to intimidate and coerce others in the pursuit of selfish goals.

Wrongful anger is unwittingly fostered by the misguided advice, often found in popular psychology books, that it is healthy to "let your anger out." If a response is inappropriate to begin with, letting it out in the name of anger is doubly inappropriate, for a response cannot be labeled as anger without endorsing, no matter how unwittingly, its exculpatory implications. Far better it would be to heed the warning of Aristotle: "Anyone can get angry—that is easy; . . . but to do this to the right person, to the right extent, at the right time, with the right motive, and in the right way, that is not for everyone nor is it easy; wherefore goodness is both rare and laudable and noble" (*Nichomachean Ethics,* 1109a25).

Bibliography

Averill, J. R. (1982). "Anger and Aggression: An Essay on Emotion." Springer-Verlag, New York.

Averill, J. R. (1993). Illusions of anger. In "Aggression and Violence: A Social Interactionist Perspective" (R. B. Felson and J. T. Tedeschi, Eds.), American Psychological Association, Washington, DC.

Friedman, H. S. (Ed.) (1991). "Hostility, Coping, and Health." American Psychological Association, Washington, DC.

Geen, R. G. (1990). "Human Aggression." Brooks/Cole, Pacific Grove, CA.

Tavris, C. (1989). "Anger: The Misunderstood Emotion," (revised ed.). Simon and Schuster, New York.

Thomas, S. P. (Ed.) (1993). "Women and Anger." Springer, New York.

Wyre, R. S., and Srull, T. K. (Eds.) (1993). "Advances in Social Cognition" Vol. 6. "Perspectives on Anger and Emotion." LEA, Hillsdale, NJ.

ANTISOCIAL PERSONALITY DISORDER

Robert G. Meyer
University of Louisville

Daniel Wolverton
University of Louisville

Sarah E. Deitsch
University of Kentucky

Glossary

Burnout The notion that the passage of time, repetition, or aging generates a behavior change.

Criminal personality A concept that overlaps with that of antisocial personality disorder. It is more inclusive as it refers to more criminal behavior patterns.

Primary–secondary psychopathy A further delineation of the concept of psychopathy. Primary psychopaths show even lower levels of anxiety, avoidance learning, and remorse, and higher levels of violence and sensation-seeking.

Psychopath A term that also overlaps but is more narrow in focus than the antisocial personality disorder. Psychopaths show even less remorse and ability to profit from experience, and more violence, glibness, callousness, and sensation-seeking.

Psychopathy checklist—revised (PCL-R) The premier instrument for the assessment of psychopathy.

Recidivism The return to a prior criminal-antisocial behavior pattern.

Sensation-seeking A need for increased stimulation of various sorts, as well as an increased need for thrills and danger.

ANTISOCIAL PERSONALITY is arguably the most important personality disorder, in terms of both impact on society and complexity of psychological and legal issues. The concept of the antisocial personality disorder is confused by the common usage of three overlapping terms: the criminal personality, the antisocial personality, and the psychopath (sociopath). The criminal personality is a sociological term, not a DSM category. As we will see, it includes a variety of different personalities who are involved in some way in criminal activity. Many different personality types function as criminals in our society; of these, the antisocial personality, or the related term "psychopath," is only one specific psychological syndrome. Antisocial personalities apparently account for no more than about 30% of the overall prison population.

I. CHARACTERISTICS OF THE CRIMINAL

Several overall patterns characterize the criminal. Four principal characteristics of the criminal lifestyle are (1) irresponsibility, (2) self-indulgence, (3) interpersonal intrusiveness, and (4) social rule breaking. The young or "apprentice" criminal is typically motivated by peer influence, combined with stimulation-seeking, which gradually give way to more antisocial components as the criminal career develops. More specifically, the majority of offenses are caused by individuals aged 21 and younger, and approximately 80% of adult chronic offenders were chronic offenders before age 18. Criminals tend to be male, at about a 5:1 ratio, up to as high as 50:1 in some specific categories of aggressive crime. With the rise in feminism, we are increasingly closer to gender parity in "white-collar crime," but the high ratio of males has persisted in aggressive crimes. As to the general causes of crime, both poor sociocultural conditions and heredity are major factors, while more specific factors are cold, rejecting, harsh, inadequate, and/or inconsistent parenting; a high level of stimulation-seeking; psychopathy; impulsivity; low intelligence, especially low verbal intelligence; mesomorphic body type; and a history of hyperactivity, handicap, and/or being abused as a child. [See CRIMINAL BEHAVIOR.]

Psychodiagnostician Edwin Megargee and several colleagues have developed an ongoing research program that has generated an excellent typology of the criminal personality. Using data primarily from the MMPI, they differentiated 10 criminal types in one prison population. On the basis of behavioral observations, social history data, and other psychological tests, they obtained validation for this classification and subsequently extended its use to other prison populations. Most importantly from the perspective of good research design, researchers working independently of Megargee established the validity of the system in other prisons, and others have independently validated similar patterns. It is clear from this and other data that there is no single criminal type. Their empirically derived and applicable system is likely to remain the standard one for many years. Another helpful way of conceptualizing different criminal "paths" is provided in Table I.

II. ANTISOCIAL PERSONALITY DISORDER—PSYCHOPATH TERMINOLOGY

The term *antisocial personality* reflects an evolution through a number of terms, the most widely known of which has undoubtedly been "psychopath." In about 1800, Philippe Pinel coined the term *Manie sans délire* to reflect the fact that these individuals manifest extremely deviant behavior but show no evidence of delusions, hallucinations, or other cognitive disorders. While Pinel was certainly including several personality disorder categories other than the antisocial personality in his descriptions, James Prichard's label of "moral insanity," denoted in 1835, is a clear forerunner of the antisocial personality grouping. This general conceptualization grew in acceptance, and late in the 19th century the label *psychopathic inferiority*, introduced by Johann Koch, became the accepted term. Later variations included "psychopathic character," "psychopathic personality," and "psychopath." Expositions by a

TABLE I

Tracks to Various Antisocial Patterns

The aggressive/versatile track leading to "cafeteria style" offending, including violent, property, and/or drug offenses/abuse	The nonaggressive antisocial track leading to more specialized offending including property and drug offenses/abuse
Characteristics	*Characteristics*
Higher rate of genetic, prenatal and/or birth disorders	Lower rate of genetic, prenatal and/or birth disorders
Onset of conduct problems in preschool years	Onset in late childhood or early to middle adolescence
Aggressive and concealing problem behaviors	Mostly nonaggressive conduct problems
More hyperactive/impulsive/attention problems	No appreciable hyperactive/impulsive/attention problems
Poor social skills	Capable of social skills
Poor peer relationships	Association with deviant peers
Academic problems	Sporadic or minimal academic problems
High rate of instigation of offenses	Low rate of instigation of offenses
Low remission rate	Higher remission rate, at least for delinquency
More males than females	Higher proportion of females than in aggressive/versatile path
Higher rate of drug abuse	Lower rate of drug abuse
Higher rate of stimulation-seeking	Lower rate of stimulation-seeking

Source: Adapted in part from R. Loeber (1990), *Clin. Psychol. Rev.* **10**, 1–42.

number of individuals, particularly by Hervey Cleckley, brought the term into common usage.

Despite the foundation for the condition, the first (1952) edition of the American Psychiatric Association's *Diagnostic and Statistical Manual of Mental Disorders* (DSM-I), the generally accepted "bible" of mental disorder classifications, muddied the issue by substituting the term "sociopathic personality" to cover the patterns that had traditionally been subsumed under the psychopath label. "Sociopathic" was used to emphasize the environmental factors allegedly generating the disorder and to de-emphasize the moralistic connotations that had become encrusted on the old terminology. Nevertheless, both concepts remained in lay and professional usages. The confusion was further heightened with the 1968 revision of the *Diagnostic and Statistical Manual* (DSM-II), which included neither term; instead, the DSM-II substituted the label "antisocial personality disorder." Although this new term carries an inherent implication of specifically criminal behavior, many professionals believed that it was a clear improvement in that it emphasized observable behavioral criteia: that is, to patterns of observable, definable behavior that conflict chronically with agreed-upon societal norms.

The trend toward objective criteria for the application of the term continues in the latest revisions of the *Diagnostic and Statistical Manual,* and the term "antisocial personality" disorder is also retained. It would be helpful if a specific psychopathic disorder diagnosis was included in the DSM, especially if references to overt criminality were minimized. Incidentally, if the individual is younger than 18, the appropriate diagnosis is conduct disorder.

From early on, studies have found that the term "psychopathic personality" is meaningful and useful in diagnosis. Also, in an early, landmark study, Spitzer and his associates (1967) checked for the diagnostic reliability of all of the standard mental health diagnostic categories, and found the highest level of agreement ($r = .88$) in the respondents' ability to label persons in the category of antisocial personality.

As we see, there is considerable overlap between the terms "antisocial personality disorder" (the present official DSM term), the "psychopath," and the "sociopath." Throughout this article, we will use the overall term "antisocial personality," recognizing that the psychopath (or sociopath) is typically seen as a subgroup of this category. [*See* PERSONALITY DISORDERS.]

III. CHARACTERISTICS OF THE ANTISOCIAL PERSONALITY (AP)

The essential characteristic of the antisocial personality disorder (AP) is the chronic manifestation of antisocial behavior patterns in amoral and impulsive persons. They are usually unable to delay gratification or to deal effectively with authority, and they show narcissism in interpersonal relationships. The pattern is apparent by the age of 15 (usually earlier) and continues into adult life with consistency across a wide performance spectrum, including school, vocational, and interpersonal behaviors.

A consensus of the research on the specific characteristics of the antisocial personality (and this research typically focuses on that narrower range of individuals seen as psychopathic) presents the following, i.e., relative to normals, they are (a) less physiologically responsive (e.g., by EKG, GSR, and EMG measures) to fearful imagery: (b) less psychologically responsive to social disapproval: (c) less responsive psychologically to affect-laden words, i.e., they respond cognitively but not affectively: (d) perseverate in behaviors with negative consequences even when they are intellectually aware of these consequences; (e) show more evidence of "cortical immaturity" but not significantly greater indices of brain dysfunction; and (f) show higher levels of sensation- and thrill-seeking behaviors.

Although the DSM-III-R discusses only the overall category of AP, there is good evidence that it can be further subdivided into categories of primary psychopath and secondary psychopath. Primary psychopaths are distinguished by the following characteristics: (1) they have very low levels of anxiety, avoidance learning, or remorse; (2) they are even more refractory to standard social control procedures; (3) they are higher in sensation- and thrill-seeking behaviors, particularly the "disinhibition" factor that refers to extroverted, hedonistic pleasure seeking.

Both the secondary and the primary psychopath are quite different from those individuals who are antisocial because they grew up in and adapted to a delinquent subculture. These delinquent individuals are normal in relation to the subculture they were reared in; they follow (often almost obsessively) the rules and mores of this group. They can be as conformist as the good middle class, middle management person. As we have already noted, not all criminals are psychopaths, and not all psychopaths are criminals.

Cleckley (1955), a particularly influential early theorist, asserted that psychopaths are often intellectually superior, and this concept has unduly influenced attitudes toward the AP. However, Cleckley was clearly in error here; such a characterization best fits the unique subsample that he usually encountered with in his clinical practice. It is not surprising that those rare psychopaths who (a) were willing to participate and stay in therapy and, especially, and who (b) could pay a private therapist's fees would be brighter than the average psychopath. As a whole, all subgroups of antisocial personalities actually show lower than average scores on intelligence tests. This is logical considering their inability to adjust to school, and is especially so if genetic dysfunction and/or brain immaturity are involved.

Violent crimes of nonpsychopaths are often characterized by extreme emotional arousal and frequently occur in situations of domestic dispute. They are more often perpetrated against women who are known to the aggressor and can be loosely characterized as "crimes of passion." On the other hand, the violent crimes of psychopaths are less affectively laden, being perpetrated most commonly against men unknown to the aggressor. Violence of psychopaths is often callous and cold-blooded, frequently stemming from a dispassionate search for revenge or retribution and displays of machismo.

IV. HERITABILITY OF PSYCHOPATHY

Cesare Lombroso's very early theory that one can tell a criminal by certain physical features, such as a low forehead, has been discarded. However, though some still believe the genetic effect is not very strong, most modern researchers have shown that criminal behavior is affected by heredity, thus providing strong, though indirect, support for the belief that the AP also is affected by heredity.

V. DIFFICULTIES IN STUDYING THE PSYCHOPATH

There is a reasonable concern that some of the research data available on AP's are not based on adequate sampling techniques. Two populations are a favorite target of researchers: (1) persons (often college students) who score high on the Psychopathic Deviate (Pd (4)) scale of the Minnesota Multiphasic Personality Inventory (MMPI) and (2) incarcerated criminals. There are problems with both groups. Individuals high on the Pd scale (as is true for a significant number of psychology graduate students and medical students) may be creative, productive individuals who are contributing positively to society even though they do not accept some of the standard social mores.

The use of an incarcerated criminal population is also a questionable practice. First, it assumes that the great majority of AP's are unsuccessful and, second, that they are lodged in prisons. There are data (some cited earlier) that refute both of these assumptions, and logic would argue otherwise. The most critical error lies in the assumption that the criminal population is largely composed of AP's. Anyone familiar with prisons is all too aware of the polyglot of individuals in residence.

VI. ASSESSMENT MEASURES WITH AP

Numerous tests, e.g., MMPI-2, provide a narrow or indirect evaluation of psychopathy. However, empirical evidence gathered over the course of the past 10 years indicates that Hare's Psychopathy Checklist (PCL) and its revised form (PCL-R) offer one of the most promising methods of assessing psychopathy directly and comprehensively, yet reliably. The PCL-R is a 20-item revision of the original 22-item scale (Hare, 1980) designed to measure not only behaviors, but also inferred personality traits central to the traditional clinical conceptualization of psychopathy. Assessment is based on a semistructured interview (about 90–120 minutes) and a review of file information. The interview serves not only as a source of information about the subject, but also allows the examiner an opportunity to observe the person's interpersonal style. [*See* CLINICAL ASSESSMENT.]

Scoring is based on a three-point scale (0, 1, or 2). Scoring criteria are well delineated and allow satisfactory interrater reliability of .83 for a single rating and .92 for the average of two ratings. The total score can range from 0 to 40 with higher scores indicating a closer match to the psychopathic prototype. Although scores fall along a continuum, a cutting score of 30 is recommended as the best diagnostic indicator and this cutoff is currently being used in most studies of forensic populations. In such populations the mean score is usually between 20 and 25 with a standard deviation of approximately 7.

The psychometric properties of the PCL-R have been well documented and there is extensive evidence to support the measure's reliability and validity. Also, the base rate of psychopathy and the psychometric properties of the PCL for adolescents are similar to those obtained with adult male offenders.

In addition, it does not appear that shortening the test severely compromises the positive psychometric properties, especially in civil populations. The PCL:SV (Hare *et al.*, 1989), a 12-item screening version of the PCL-R, has been tested on both criminal and civil populations and has shown good psychometric properties. It has slightly lower reliability than the full-length version, with which it correlates at about .80. Testing is based on a 30- to 45-minute interview and less extensive file information. Scores range from 0 to 24 with a score of 18 or higher being a good indicator of psychopathy. While this measure is easier to administer and flexible enough to be used in a variety of populations, the full-length version is still the best measure in forensic populations and should be used whenever this is feasible.

VII. PCL(R)-GENERATED CONCEPTS

There is substantial evidence that psychopathy, as measured by the PCL-R, consists of two stable, main factors, and both factors show good interrater reliability and internal consistency. The more behaviorally oriented Factor 2 demonstrates slightly higher reliability than Factor 1 which is not surprising since there is less subjectivity involved in the scoring of Factor 2 items. However, greater internal consistency is shown by items loading on Factor 1 which is consistent with the idea of a core set of psychopathic personality traits. The factor components are as follows:

Factor 1:
(1) Glibness/superficial charm,
(2) egocentricity/grandiose sense of self-worth,
(3) pathological lying,
(4) conning/lack of sincerity,
(5) lack of remorse,
(6) shallow affect,
(7) callousness/lack of empathy,
(8) failure to accept responsibility.
Factor 2:
(1) Need for stimulation/proneness to boredom,

(2) parasitic lifestyle,
(3) poor behavioral controls,
(4) early behavior problems,
(5) lack of realistic long-term plans,
(6) impulsivity,
(7) irresponsibility,
(8) juvenile delinquency,
(9) revocation of conditional release.

Factor 1 is positively related to clinical ratings of psychopathy and with personality measures of narcissism, dominance, and machiavellianism. It is negatively correlated with nurturance, agreeableness, empathy, anxiety, and DSM diagnoses of avoidant and dependent personality disorders. Factor 2 is related to disruptive prison behavior, drug and alcohol problems, and DSM-III-R APD. It is negatively correlated with conscientiousness, socialization, SES, employment, education, and IQ.

There is evidence that the diagnosis of psychopathy via the PCL-R predicts recidivism even after such variables as criminal history, previous conditional release violations, and relevant demographic characteristics have been controlled for. The behavioral and lifestyle variables of Factor 2 are important in the prediction of general recidivism, while the personality characteristics that compose the first factor are more important in predicting violent recidivism. This finding is consistent with the view that violent psychopaths are more persistent and instrumental in their use of violence than nonpsychopaths.

Yet, while the PCL-R demonstrates impressive incremental validity in predicting violence, especially considering the severe restriction of range under which it functions, the usefulness of the PCL-R should not be overgeneralized. One should not infer from extant supporting research that the PCL-R is able to consistently predict violent behavior in the general population. So far, it appears that the usefulness of the psychopathy construct in predicting violence presupposes some history of violent behavior.

VIII. THE PSYCHOPATH AND THE MAJOR THEORETICAL ORIENTATIONS

This section presents conceptualizations of the psychopath within the framework of the dominant theoretical orientations in psychology, e.g., psychodynamic, learning/behavioral, cognitive, existential, and finally biological, followed by a proposed etiological model.

A. Psychodynamic Concepts

Blending psychodynamic and ethological perspectives, psychodynamic theorists such as John Bowlby have argued for the selective advantage of strong emotional attachments on the part of young animals toward their primary caregivers. Studying children in orphanages who had been reunited with their parents after long separations, Bowlby extended these ethological theories to humans and elaborated on a number of pathological attachment styles, e.g., clinging–dependent, anxious–ambivalent, and avoidant.

Clearly the attachment style of the psychopath would be "avoidant," since an inability to form meaningful attachments with others is a cardinal symptom of psychopathy. Given the frequency of lax, inconsistent, and often violent parenting in the families of psychopaths, it is not surprising that a budding antisocial would learn that social independence, self-sufficiency, and even interpersonal manipulation are the best defenses in a hostile, unsupportive, unnurturing world. To remain unattached is the best prevention against frustrated attachment.

This viewpoint may account for the psychopath's peculiar blend of affective blandness interspersed with occasional fits of angry, gratuitous violence. The great majority of the time, the psychopath is the ultimate "well-defended" person—cold, unfathomable, and unflappable. The angry, frustrated inner child is usually buried so deeply that it is seldom available to the others, or to the psychopath himself.

His developmental needs for nurturance, trust, and acceptance gone sorely unmet in childhood, the psychopath rises above his blocked needs by developing a "moving against" interpersonal style. Feeling profoundly inferior at one psychological level, the psychopath "rises above" others by dragging them down—manipulating, exploiting, humiliating, and perhaps even physically tormenting them to this end. Generally lacking education and socially accepted skills, the psychopath may even come to take special pride in his talent for antisocial and criminal pursuits.

B. Learning/Behavioral Concepts

The issue of conditionability is noted earlier in this chapter. To amplify, the learning viewpoint also emphasizes early experience with primary caregivers, but frames these interactions more in terms of reinforcement and punishment. The basic notions here are that the parents of psychopaths are inconsistent and punitive in their parenting behavior. The apparently random quality of the caregivers' behavior teaches the young psychopath that others' treatment of him is not contingent upon his behavior. Moreover, because he is so frequently punished, and most often on a noncontingent basis, he eventually becomes enured to punishing consequences in general. Child-rearing patterns such as these may contribute to the fact that adult psychopaths do not learn from the punishing consequences of life mistakes, as well as the finding that, in learning experiments, psychopaths ignore negative consequences and focus only on potential rewards.

C. Cognitive Concepts

At first glance, the cognitive model seems to have little to add to the discussion of the origins of psychopathy. Especially as articulated in the early writings of Aaron Beck and Albert Ellis, this model has focused less on etiology and more on here-and-now intervention. However, the following existential model certainly provides a cognitive perspective. Also, consider the underlying cognitive schemas that Beck finds to be facilitative of psychopathic behavior, as discussed in the upcoming treatment section.

D. Existential Concepts

It is interesting to view the psychopath from this perspective because of its heavy emphasis on such notions as guilt, anxiety, and freedom. From a point of view influenced by Friedrich Nietzsche's writings, the psychopath is the most free person in the world (this may sound odd given the frequency with which psychopaths are incarcerated). Because he has suppressed it, or is not capable of experiencing it, he is not encumbered by the guilt and anxiety which would interfere with free, self-determined action in the world—he is not a "lamb." He has transcended the conflict and discontent befalling most who struggle to have their needs met in the context of a prohibiting society. He is willing to live with "dirty hands."

Existentialists often focus not only on freedom, but also on death, isolation, and meaninglessness. We might even admire the psychopath in terms of his ability to confront, accept, and embrace death in the form of reckless and dangerous behavior; we might admire his ability to embrace his ultimate isolation and "go it alone"; and we might even grudgingly come to respect his having grasped the purposelessness of existence and then choicefully imposed his own meaning on it, however cruel and perverse its manifestations might be.

But upon closer examination, we see that the psychopath does not really comfortably fit within the existentialist model. He has not really grappled and struggled with the conflicts inherent in choicefulness, e.g., the anxiety which follows from passing up opportunities which will never come again, the guilt which comes with inadvertently hurting others by one's decisions (the psychopath is willing to live with dirty hands because he does not experience them as dirty). And, not having struggled, the psychopath can never experience the wholeness which comes from growth through pain.

We see that he is reacting against others rather than for himself. We see that he is a slave to his impulses, not master of his fate. From a gestalt point of view, we see that he is so hardened and defended that he does not really experience the world. He is not in touch with, or "aware" of the environment in a way that would allow him to act freely in accord with it, rather than haphazardly against it. We see that he is not only alienated from others, but almost completely alienated from his deeper self.

E. Biological Concepts

This article already notes that heritability has a strong role in the development of psychopathy, and some authors have hypothesized a biological link with such childhood disorders as attention-deficit hyperactivity disorder (ADHD). Additionally research has noted several biologically based correlates, including reduced arousal to fear-inducing stimuli, minimized startle responses, restricted affective range, inability to respond affectively to emotion-laden words, reduced conditionability, and a tendency to perseverate in terms of attention allocation. But there is more to be said. [See ATTENTION-DEFICIT HYPERACTIVITY DISORDER.]

Whereas learning and psychodynamic models emphasize the effects of parents' temperaments on children's behavior, biologically based models emphasize the effects of children's temperaments on parents' behavior. For example, consistent with this thinking, research has shown that because of failure

to obey, antisocial children were able to elicit punitive behavior from mothers of children who had never even met them before. Psychopaths apparently elicit relatively rejecting responses from parents by being underemotional and unresponsive, by being overly active and thereby annoying, and/or by having little natural tendency to engage their parents socially.

Also, research supports the notion that some individuals (especially psychopaths) have lower baseline levels of arousal than others. In order to achieve optimal levels of arousal, these individuals require more frequent and intense environmental stimulation. It follows that in their attempts to seek out sensational experiences they would be more likely to engage in antisocial acts, i.e., low levels of conditionability and high needs for sensation-seeking combine to create high levels of antisociality and impulsivity.

IX. PROPOSED "COMMON PATH" FOR THE DEVELOPMENT OF PSYCHOPATHY

A. Pre-existing Risk Factors

1. Biological (prenatal, birth) disruption
2. Low SES
3. Family history of vocational–social–interpersonal dysfunction
4. Family history of psychopathy

B. From Birth to School Age

1. Child temperament factors
   (a) Child's lack of emotional responsiveness and lack of social interest fosters rejecting responses from parents
   (b) Child's high activity levels may cause parental annoyance and elicit punitive responses
2. Parental factors
   (a) Inconsistent parenting results in child's failing to learn behavioral contingencies
   (b) Aggressive, punitive parenting results in child's modeling aggression, experiencing hostility, becoming enured to punishing consequences, and developing a repressive defensive style (emotional "hardness")
3. Parent–child interaction
   (a) Unreliable parenting results in insecure attachment (i.e., interpersonally

"avoidant" attachment style); child "goes it alone" rather than risk rejection and disappointment associated with unreliable and/or abusive parents

C. School Age to Adolescence

1. Predisposing personality factors
   (a) Low baseline level of arousal (i.e., Eysenck's biological extraversion) contributes to impulsive, undercontrolled, and sensation-seeking behavior
   (b) A synergy of physiological underarousal, repressive psychodynamics, and habitual "numbness" to social contingencies results in child being insensitive to, and unable to, "condition" to environmental events; therefore, does not learn or "profit" from experience
   (c) ADHA/"soft" neurological disorder overlay may exacerbate behavior problems
2. Personality development
   (a) Peer/teacher labeling may result in self-fulfilling prophecy effects
   (b) School and social failure result in sense of inferiority and increased interpersonal hostility; child develops "moving against" interpersonal style
   (c) Initial forays into antisociality (e.g., theft, fire setting, interpersonal violence) occur; evidence for diagnosis of conduct disorder mounts

D. Adolescence

1. The young psychopath hones exploitative style in order to express hostility and "rise above" feelings of inferiority; "proves superiority" by hoodwinking and humiliating teachers, parents, peers
2. Continued antisocial behavior results in initial scrapes with the law
3. Physiological impulsivity, inability to profit from experience (exacerbated by a perseverative attentional style), and interpersonal hostility and antagonism combine to make repeated legal offenses highly probable
4. Contact with other antisocials in the context of juvenile-criminal camps or prison results in "criminal education"; increased criminality results; criminal and antisocial behavior

become a lifestyle at which the psychopath can "excel"

E. Adulthood

1. Antisocial behavior escalates through the psychopath's late 20s; increasingly frequent incarceration results in increased hostility and hardened feelings
2. Unable to profit from experience, lacking in insight, and unable to form therapeutic bonds, the psychopath becomes a poor therapy-rehab risk and bad news for society
3. Antisocial behavior decreases or "burns out" in an uneven fashion beginning in the early 30s (less so with violent offenses); this may be due to lengthier incarcerations, to changes in age-related metabolic factors which formerly contributed to sensation-seeking and impulsive behavior, or perhaps to decrements in the strength and stamina required to engage in violent or felony-property crimes

X. INTERVENTION ISSUES

Nearly all significant theorists and researchers suggest that psychopaths are poor therapy candidates, and there is some evidence that the more severe, or primary, psychopaths may get worse with psychotherapy, i.e., psychotherapy may provide a "finishing school" experience for them. The treatment problem with all the personality disorders—getting the client into therapy and meaningfully involved—is acute in the antisocial personality disorder. And, to the degree the person shows primary psychopathy, the poorer are the chances for any meaningful change, no matter what treatment is used. [See PSYCHOTHERAPY.]

Most effective are (1) highly controlled settings, (2) with personnel who are firm and caring yet sophisticated in controlling manipulations, (3) and in which the antisocial client resides for a significant period of time (and these appear to be effective only while the psychopath is in residence). Any inpatient treatment program should include four major components: (1) supervision, manipulation of the environment, and provision of education by the staff to facilitate change; (2) a token economy system that requires successful participation for one to receive anything beyond the basic necessities; (3) medical-psychiatric treatments to deal with ancillary psychopathology, e.g., neurological disorders, depression; and (4) a system of necessary social cooperation to maximize conformity and encourage development of the group ethic. This last component is seldom a consideration. In such a program every task that can be found that can reasonably be performed by another and which is not essential to health should be required to be performed only by one inmate for another. This is truly an area where the psychopath is a neophyte.

Attention should also be paid to the AP's high level of stimulation-seeking. This need can be interpreted to the person with an antisocial personality disorder as similar to that of the alcoholic, in that the person will be driven to fulfill this appetite in one way or another. Therapists should attempt to work with psychopaths to develop methods, e.g., developing a consistent pattern of engagement in sports and other strenuous and/or exciting activities and jobs that provide for a high level of activity and stimulation. [*See* SENSATION SEEKING.]

Overall, a therapist would generally need to

1. As noted, expect resistance to entering therapy, and then to staying in therapy.

2. As noted, consider their proneness to boredom and their high level of stimulation-seeking.

3. Expect such clients to be deceptive about their history and present status. To the degree feasible, independently corroborate any critical questions about history or present behaviors. Contract ahead of time that if you feel it necessary, you will obtain such data from significant others, etc.

4. In line with the above, clearly confront the individual's psychopathy and any record of deviant behavior. The presentation of "objective" profiles from tests like the MMPI-2 or 16 PF can be effective here. Confront the psychopathology as a lifestyle disorder that will require treatment of a significant duration (and cost); thus, one might contract for some financial penalty for early withdrawal. At the same time, avoid the role of judge, and stay as much as possible in the role of collaborator. Maintaining a degree of adequate rapport is critical. Any exercises that help to develop empathy or social sensitivity are useful.

5. Challenge the following underlying beliefs as adapted from Beck *et al.* (1990): (a) rationalization—"My desiring something justifies whatever actions I need to take"; (b) the devaluing of others—"The attitudes and needs of others don't effect me, unless responding to them will provide me an advantage, and if they are hurt by me, I need not feel responsible for what happens to them"; (c) low-impact consequences—"My choices are inherently good. As such, I won't experience undesirable consequences or if they occur, they won't really matter to me"; (d) "I have to think of myself first; I'm entitled to what I want or feel I need, and if necessary, can use force or deception to obtain those goals"; (e) "rules constrict me from fulfilling my needs."

A. The Issue of Antisocial Burnout

Some solace may be achieved in the notion that psychopathic-antisocial behavior may diminish with age, independent of intervention. Fortunately, there is some empirical validation of this notion. Usually the downward trend begins after age 40, but unfortunately there appears to be no significant dropoff in violent crime for the true (high on Factor 1) psychopaths. And, though often at a diminished rate in nonviolent crime, more recent research suggests that more than a third of psychopath offenders remain criminally active throughout their adulthood.

XI. SUMMARY

The antisocial personality presents a murky conflux of five axioms: (1) an apparent rationality and social appropriateness; (2) an apparent inability to process experience effectively under standard social controls and punishments; (3) some evidence of behavior-determining variables, such as genetic defect and/or brain dysfunction; (4) an absence of evidence of mediating variables between these possible causes and eventual antisocial behavior; and (5) a disinterest in changing oneself, and a lack of positive response to imposed treatment methods.

However pessimistic the picture regarding treatment potential, more psychopathic treatment and outcome studies are warranted, even if they focus on only the small improvements which are made by that small percentage of psychopaths who would stay in treatment. Since psychopaths, as a relatively small percentage of the population, commit such a large percentage of violent and property crimes, even a 5–10% success rate may pay dividends in terms of overall reduction of the most severe offenses.

Bibliography

Beck, A., and Freeman, A., *et al.* (1990). "Cognitive Therapy of the Personality Disorders." Guilford, New York.

Cleckley, H. (1955). "The Mask of Sanity." Mosby, St. Louis.

Eysenck, H., and Gudjonsson, G. (1989). "The Causes and Cures of Criminality." Plenum, New York.

Hare, R. (1991). "The Hare Psychopathy Checklist-Revised." Multi-Health Systems, Toronto.

Hare, R., Harpur, T., Hakstian, A., Forth, A., Hart, S., and Newman, J. (1990). The Revised Psychopathy Checklist: Reliability and factor structure. *Psychol. Assess.* **2,** 338–341.

Megargee, E., and Bohn, M. (1979) "Classifying Criminal Offenders." Sage, Beverly Hills.

Meyer, R. (1992). "Abnormal Behavior and the Criminal Justice System." Lexington Books, Lexington, MA.

Serin, R. (1991). Psychopathy and violence in criminals. *J. Interpersonal Violence* **6,** 423–431.

Spitzer, R., *et al.* (1967). Quantification of agreement in psychiatric diagnosis: A new approach. *Arch. Gen. Psychiatry* **17,** 83–87.

ANXIETY AND FEAR

Daniel W. McNeil, Cynthia L. Turk, and Barry J. Ries
Oklahoma State University

Glossary

Anxiety An emotional state characterized by verbal reports of distress (e.g., apprehension, worry), physiological arousal (e.g., increased heart rate), behavioral activation (e.g., avoidance), and/or disruption of cognitive processing (e.g., hyperawareness about possible threat cues in the environment). Anxiety is associated with more cognitive symptoms and less visceral activation, and cues for its manifestation are more diffuse and changeable, relative to fear.

Fear An emotional state involving verbal reports, physiological arousal, overt behavior, and/or cognitive disruption similar to that of anxiety. Fear, however, involves greater mobilization for physical action. Typically, it is triggered by specific objects or situations.

Panic Sudden onset of a discrete period of intense anxiety and/or fear, typically involving feelings of terror, and often accompanied by a sense of imminent doom. Physiological (e.g., hyperventilation) and/or cognitive (e.g., feelings of unreality) symptoms are involved. Panic attacks can either be associated with specific situations or are manifested with no known situational trigger; they can be either expected or unexpected. Anticipatory anxiety/fear about having a panic attack often develops after the first occurrence(s). When panic is of psychopathological proportions, it is sometimes associated with agoraphobia, distress about being in places from which escape would be difficult or assistance would be unavailable if panic were to occur.

Phobia Extreme and persistent anxiety and/or fear of an object(s) or a situation(s) that is out of proportion to any actual danger involved, typically provokes an immediate response, is recognized by the person affected as excessive, involves avoidance or enduring exposure to the object(s) or situation(s) with considerable discomfort, and, according to diagnostic criteria, results in interference with life activities or involves great distress in the person afflicted.

ANXIETY AND FEAR are emotional states with multidimensional structures. There is considerable similarity between these constructs, but current scientific thinking suggests they are not identical, even though these terms are used interchangeably in everyday language. Fear is often described as a fundamental emotion which is present across ages, cultures, ethnic groups, and species, and functions as an alarm system which physiologically activates an organism to respond to a threat. Anxiety is typically considered to be more diffuse, primarily cognitive relative to fear, and is less likely to be associated with overt behavior such as avoidance. Anxiety is characterized by feelings of distress and worry, maladaptive shifts in attention due to off-target thinking, and the perception that aversive events are occurring in an unpredictable and uncontrollable manner.

I. WHAT IS ANXIETY AND WHAT IS FEAR?

A. Usage and Origins of the Words *Fear* and *Anxiety*

The importance of anxiety and fear in the human experience is reflected by the rich vocabulary that describes these emotions. Just a few of the many words used in everyday language to describe fear and anxiety include agitation, alarm, apprehension, aversion, concern, consternation, disquiet, distress, dread, edginess, fretfulness, fright, horror, hysteria, jitters, nervousness, qualm, restlessness, scare, tension, terror, trepidation, torment, uneasiness, vigilance, wariness, woe, and worry. Historically, the word *fear* evolved from the Old English word *faer,* which originally meant peril or calamity but later came to mean a feeling of uneasiness caused by possible danger. The word *anxiety* originated from the Latin word *anxius* which means troubled in mind, solicitous, or uneasy.

B. Fear and Anxiety as Described in Models of Emotion

Multifactor models of emotion propose the existence of a finite number of basic, fundamentally different emotions. Izard, for example, proposes 10 fundamental emotions including anger, fear, sadness/distress, contempt, disgust, guilt, shame/shyness, joy, interest/excitement, and surprise. These individual emotions may combine or blend with one another to produce a large variety of affective states. In models such as these, fear is typically regarded as a basic emotion while anxiety is viewed as a variable blend of emotions in which fear combines with one or more other basic emotions such as guilt, sadness, shame, or anger.

Dimensional models generally assert that all emotions can be classified in terms of their relationship to two or three major orthogonal, bipolar dimensions of affect. Two dimensions proposed by Watson and Tellegen are positive affect (feeling active, elated, excited versus drowsy, dull, sleepy) and negative affect (feeling distressed, fearful, hostile, nervous versus calm, placid, relaxed). These dimensions are usually depicted visually as two axes intersecting at a 90° angle within a circumplex; different emotions are placed within the circumplex in order to reflect their relationship to the two axes as well as to each other. In Watson and Tellegen's model, anxiety is associated with heightened negative affect. The bioinformational theory of emotion by Lang and colleagues suggests there are three rather than two orthogonal, bipolar dimensions that can be identified in self-reports. These dimensions are: (a) a valence dimension, pleasantness–unpleasantness (feeling happy, enthusiastic, content versus afraid, upset, sad), (b) an activity dimension, arousal–calm (feel-

ing excited, astonished, tense versus relaxed, sleepy), and (c) a control dimension, dominance–submissiveness (feeling influential, in control, dominant versus submissive, awed, guided). These dimensions are visualized as three axes intersecting at 90° angles in three-dimensional space. Various emotional states are defined as being located in the different regions created by these three axes. According to this model, fear and anxiety involve the experience of unpleasantness, arousal, and relative lack of control.

C. Components of Anxiety and Fear

It is common to view fear and anxiety as emotion states that exist *inside* people (and perhaps other organisms). Traditional psychological perspectives, such as psychodynamic theories, have embraced this idea, and regard overt motoric behaviors (e.g., avoidance of a feared situation) and physiological activation (e.g., heavy perspiring) as *manifestations* of anxiety and/or fear. Critics have labeled these as *lump* theories, in that fear and/or anxiety are regarded as some amorphous entity *inside* an individual. The lump perspectives have been criticized as being unscientific and nonconducive to empirical verification in the study of anxiety and fear.

Over the past 25 years, fear and anxiety have been regarded as comprising three dimensions: verbal reports, physiological response, and overt behaviors. This conceptualization has been particularly applied to the assessment of anxiety and fear and is often known as the "three systems approach." Viewed in this manner, fear and anxiety are *not* seen as lumps of emotion within people causing thoughts, physical reactions, and avoidance behavior. Rather, these three systems are fear and anxiety themselves, and compose their structure. Interestingly, these systems appear to operate somewhat independently of one another. This phenomenon is known as *desynchrony* or *discordance;* anxiety or fear is present in one or more systems, but to a lesser or greater degree in others. For example, some people appear outwardly calm while making a speech and do not avoid or escape, but their hearts pound and they later report having been terrified.

Anxiety specifically has been viewed by Spielberger as being either state or trait in nature. State anxiety is a transitory emotional condition characterized by feelings of tension and apprehension which fluctuate over time as a function of environmental stressors and the individual's coping response to them. Trait anxiety is a relatively stable personality attribute that is an individual difference in proneness to appraise stressors as distressing. [See TRAITS.]

Barlow's work suggests anxiety, fear, and panic may be described as cued or uncued, expected or unexpected. Panic is considered cued when the individual is able to identify an external or internal event that precipitates it; panic is considered uncued when the individual is not able to identify a trigger. If a panic attack is anticipated, then it is expected; otherwise, it is unexpected. Thus, panic attacks fall into one of four categories: cued and expected, cued and unexpected, uncued and expected, uncued and unexpected. For example, a panic attack is both cued and expected when a person with a snake phobia encounters a snake. Spontaneous panic that comes "out of the blue" is uncued and unexpected. In this conceptualization, fear is largely cued, while anxiety is uncued. [See PANIC DISORDER.]

D. Relationship of Anxiety and Fear to Anger, Depression, and Courage

Fear, anxiety, and anger are common emotional responses to stressful situations and are often difficult to distinguish because all involve unpleasant feelings and psychophysiological arousal. Some evidence suggests that anxiety and fear can be differentiated from anger according to feelings along the dominance–submissiveness continuum. People who are angry may feel in control of events while people who are anxious or fearful may feel out of control or vulnerable. Studies have also differentiated anxiety and fear from anger physiologically. For example, fear and anxiety have been associated with increases in skin conductance and respiration rate, while anger has been involved in increased diastolic blood pressure. [See ANGER.]

Depression is another unpleasant affective state that can be difficult to differentiate from anxiety and fear. A great deal of evidence suggests that anxiety and depression are strongly related emotional states which frequently occur at the same time; there is conceptual overlap in these constructs as well. Some studies have suggested a common genetic vulnerability for psychopathological disorders involving anxiety, fear, and depression. Anxiety is more strongly related to apprehension, worry, and somatic symptoms, while depression is more often associated with feelings of hopelessness and helplessness, motor retardation, and negativistic

thinking, sometimes including suicidal thoughts. (Certain kinds of depression, however, involve agitation, which makes differentiation from anxiety all the more difficult.) [See DEPRESSION.]

Courage is persistence in the face of fear and anxiety. To carry on with behavior despite both responding physiologically and acknowledging fear or anxiety verbally is to act courageously. For example, most people would agree that rescuing a child from a burning building would constitute courageous behavior for a fire fighter. However, it is also courageous for someone with an intense fear of public speaking to give a speech to an audience. In both cases, the individual is continuing to perform despite physiological arousal and self-reports of fear and anxiety. In this way, courage provides an example of discordance in the three response systems mentioned earlier. Repeated and successful practice of courageous behavior leads to a decrease in verbal reports of fear and psychophysiological responsivity, which can lead to a state of fearlessness.

II. WHAT MAKES HUMAN BEINGS ANXIOUS AND/OR FEARFUL?

A. Anxiety and Fear as Normal, Adaptive Emotional States

Fear and anxiety are normal responses in everyday life. To some extent, they are experienced by virtually all people. These emotions are an important part of being human. Fear and anxiety can be adaptive reactions to realistic threats or to the possibility of some negative event(s). In dangerous situations, these emotional states can mobilize people to respond rapidly and efficiently. Without this capacity, human beings would not have been able to survive for very long in ancient times when faced by the dangers present in the natural environment.

According to recent theories, individuals develop anxiety and/or fear when exposed to events, particularly stressful ones, that are either unpredictable, uncontrollable, or both. Lack of predictability regarding when aversive events occur leads to chronic anxiety because the individual remains constantly vigilant and does not relax. Uncontrollability results in feelings of helplessness and subsequent emotional states of anxiety and depression. A vast animal research literature focusing on the effects of exposure to unpredictable and uncontrollable stimuli has had a great impact upon current theorizing; Seligman is one of the pioneers in this area.

In their simplest forms, anxiety and fear prepare the organism psychophysiologically to meet the demands of life. Cannon's emergency action tendencies of "fight or flight" are involved. These responses represent the organism's alarm reaction to life-threatening emergencies. The most primitive of these responses, and ones that have been selected in an evolutionary sense, are the urges to escape ("flight") or to stand and face the threat ("fight").

Fear and anxiety continue to have adaptive value in everyday life today. Without some minimal amount of fear and anxiety, people might become careless and lack the motivation to accomplish things that need to be done. People might drive recklessly on the highway, approach dangerous animals, neglect work, or not plan for the future. According to the Yerkes-Dodson law, both human and animal performance generally improves with increases in arousal until some optimal level is reached, at which point further increases in arousal will hinder performance. With too little arousal, a pilot may become inattentive and make a critical mistake; with too much activation, the pilot may become paralyzed with fear and unable to respond effectively to danger.

People do not always avoid situations which provoke fear and anxiety and at times may actively seek out dangerous activities. Bomb disposal operators report that they find going on missions to disarm bombs preferable to the boredom of sitting around their quarters between tasks. Many sky divers, mountain climbers, and race car drivers enjoy the challenge of mastering danger. Most people enjoy some sort of danger vicariously, by watching hazardous sports, viewing horror or thriller movies, or reading suspense novels. Some individuals also enjoy the anxiety/fear in riding roller coasters and going to Halloween "haunted houses."

B. Dimensions of Anxiety and Fear

A considerable amount of research has been directed at identifying the objects and situations that evoke fear in human beings. Given the myriad of human concerns in various age groups, societies, and cultures, as well as throughout the course of history, a complete list would be virtually impossible to construct. New fears and anxieties emerge or are lessened periodically. Only in the last several decades have there been concerns about nuclear weapons

and AIDS; concern about contracting certain diseases which were common early in this century is considerably less now due to the availability of certain medications. Nevertheless, work by Arrindell and others has made it possible to categorize anxieties and fears of adults into the following five basic dimensions:

1. Social situations
2. Environmental and/or agoraphobic
3. Blood, bodily injury, illness, and death
4. Sexual and aggressive scenes
5. Small animals

Viewing fears and anxieties in categories prompts questions about whether these states necessarily have an external trigger. Is it possible to be afraid, or to feel anxious, without such a feeling being in response to some stimulus cue? Can people be anxious or fearful about some object or situation without conscious awareness? Various theoretical formulations disagree on answers to these questions. There has been some attention paid to "free floating anxiety" that is not tied to any particular environmental cues. Nevertheless, behavioral theories emphasize the importance of "situation specificity" in fear/anxiety responding (i.e., reacting to particular objects or situations in the environment as cues for fear/anxiety).

C. Pathological Fears and Anxieties

While a bit of fear and anxiety keeps people alert and ready for action, excessive amounts are disruptive and even paralyzing. It is important to clarify the relationship of normal fears and anxieties to pathological states, diagnostically known as anxiety disorders. As illustrated in Figure 1, fears and anxieties exist along a continuum of severity, ranging from fearlessness on one end, to typical levels of anxiety and fear, to their pathological manifestations in anxiety disorders, including phobia, on the other side. Inherent in this model is the idea that normal anxieties and fears are continuous with psychopathological states. The anxiety disorders are not disease states completely unlike that found in "normal" individuals. They are, however, quite extreme and persistent versions of emotional states experienced by almost all people, to different degrees in various circumstances. [See ANXIETY DISORDERS; PHOBIAS.]

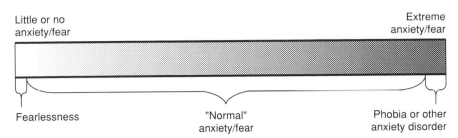

FIGURE 1   Continuum of severity for anxiety/fear.

Anxiety and fear are considered pathological when they are out of proportion to the actual threat present, interfere with one's daily activities, involve maladaptive behavior such as avoidance or escape, and are recognized by the individual as excessive or unreasonable. The prevalence of anxiety disorders surpasses that of any other mental health problem in the general population. Chronic fear and anxiety can contribute to physiological problems such as ulcers or cardiovascular disease. Additionally, substance abuse, especially alcohol abuse, is common among individuals suffering from anxiety disorders and sometimes reflects an attempt at self-medication. [*See* SUBSTANCE ABUSE.]

D. The Origins of *Angst*

Both philosophers and clinicians have pondered the cause(s) of diffuse and objectless anxiety. Kierkegaard, one of the philosophical founders of existentialism, used the German word *angst* to describe this experience. For Kierkegaard, *angst* results from the distinctively human, self-conscious capacity to discern the ''possibility of freedom'' and the ultimate threat of nonbeing. Kierkegaard believed that *angst* is rooted in fear generated by self-awareness of one's own possibilities in both individual development and in relationship to others, as well as in fear generated by the threat of nonexistence. Kierkegaard thought that the achievement of selfhood was possible only if one was able to recognize and confront anxiety and to move ahead and actualize one's possibilities despite it.

Freud used the word *angst* (anxiety) to refer to vague, objectless anxiety and the word *furcht* (fear) to label such distress when it was focused on an object. Freud viewed anxiety as the reaction to and signal of unconscious memories of real or imagined threats to the child, which are elicited in the adult through learned associations. Anxiety is related to fantasized situations that were perceived as real and

dangerous to the child, who felt helpless in the face of them. Infantile fears of separation, loss of love, or castration may be activated by a wish or symbolically linked situation for the adult. The generation of anxiety acts as a signal to elicit the psychological defense mechanisms, which, if adequate, reduce anxiety and allow for a high level of functioning. If the defenses are not adequate, phobic or compulsive symptoms symbolically related to the unconscious source of anxiety may arise.

E. Fear and Anxiety across the Lifespan

While fears and anxieties can develop at any time of life, certain ones have a greater incidence in particular age ranges or developmental stages. Fears identified as being common in infancy typically include fear of heights, loss of physical support, loud noises, and other sudden, intense, unexpected stimuli from the environment. A fear of strangers typically develops between 6 and 12 months; this distress is interesting in that it is present across societies and cultures, and in lower animals, including mammals and birds. Stranger fear appears to be different from distress associated with separation from parents, which can emerge as early as 4 months and peaks between 13 and 18 months. A program of research by Kagan and colleagues on temperament evident in infancy suggests that some human beings are constitutionally predisposed to being anxious and/or fearful, inhibited, and physiologically reactive, which may have long-lasting implications.

Common fears of children 1, 2, and 3 years old include fear of toilet training activities, injury, loud noises, animals, dark rooms, masks, and novel stimuli. During preschool, kindergarten, and first grade, prominent fears include fear of separation from parents, animals, darkness, bodily harm, thunder, lightning, sleeping or staying alone, and supernatural beings such as ghosts, witches, and monsters. Older elementary school children frequently experience fears and anxieties related to test taking, grades, physical appearance, injury, illness, death, and natural phenomena such as tornados, earthquakes, thunder, and lightning. Most of the fears and anxieties of adolescents are focused on personal adequacy, school events, physical health, sexual matters, and political and economic concerns. In general, over the course of childhood, fears and anxieties change from having a formless and imaginary quality to being specific and reality-based.

Many fears and anxieties are common in the general population. The five most common fears among adults, in order of prevalence, are:

1. Snakes (most common)
2. Heights
3. Storms
4. Flying in an airplane
5. Dental treatment

Fear and anxiety in the elderly have received relatively little attention. The study of fear and anxiety in older persons is often complicated by frequent coexistence with other disorders such as depression, dementia, or medical illness. Surveys suggest that most anxiety disorders actually decrease in prevalence with age.

What human beings fear and find anxiety-provoking changes across the lifespan. Research has consistently shown that during the course of development, virtually all children display a large number of fears (e.g., of injections, doctors, darkness, and strangers), most of which are transitory or short-lived. Fears of snakes, animals, heights, storms, enclosures, and social situations are frequently acquired during childhood and adolescence, but appear to be more long lasting, as their prevalence remains relatively high throughout adulthood and into old age. Fears which are acquired throughout the first six decades of life and reach their peak of prevalence at the upper end of the lifespan include fears of crowds, death, injury, illness, and separation.

F. Sex and Gender Differences

Studies have consistently shown that men generally report less fear and anxiety, while women report more such distress. This sex difference is also seen during childhood: girls tend to report a greater number of fears and anxieties than boys, regardless of age. What males and females fear and find anxiety-provoking seem to differ as well. Women express more environmental and agoraphobic fears, distress about small animals, and concern about sexual and aggressive scenes than men. Fears of social situations, as well as fears about bodily injury, death, and illness appear to be more equivalent. During childhood, girls report more fears and anxieties related to animals and physical injury and illness, while boys report more fears and anxieties related to economic and academic failure.

Variables other than biological sex may account for many of the differences observed between females and males regarding the prevalence of fears, anxieties, and anxiety disorders. Nathanson proposed that women may report more physical and mental illness (including fears and anxieties) for a variety of reasons: (a) more cultural acceptability for women to report illness than for men; (b) female roles in Western societies being more compatible with sick role behaviors relative to male roles; and (c) greater prevalence of actual illness in women due to stressful social roles.

Gender role orientation may be another variable which contributes to the sex differences observed for fear and anxiety. Using the Bem Sex-Role Inventory, individuals (regardless of biological sex) can be conceptualized as having one of four orientations: masculine (high masculinity, low femininity), feminine (high femininity, low masculinity), androgynous (high masculinity, high femininity), or undifferentiated (low masculinity, low femininity). The literature suggests that low masculinity, rather than high femininity, is associated with psychopathology in general, including fear and anxiety. [See SEX ROLES.]

G. Cross-Cultural and Subcultural Comparisons

Fear and anxiety are emotional states that are experienced by people across the world. However, while similar overall levels of anxiety and fear have been found across societies, cultures, and between majority and minority ethnic groups within societies, their environmental content and context are very different. Traditional Aboriginals in Australia, for example, prefer open areas that are not closed in, and some may react quite negatively to being shut in a room. This reaction may be related to thousands of years of nomadic existence, in which closed in shelters were uncommon. As another example, Chinese males in Southeast Asia may suffer from koro, the fear of the penis retracting into the abdomen and death occurring as a result. This phenomenon results in acute panic and various devices may be employed to prevent retraction of the penis. Occasionally this disorder is seen among women as well; they fear retraction of the nipples, the breasts, or the labia. In this culture, male genitals are considered to be vital for life and excessive sexual activity is believed to be unhealthy. Therefore, it is not surprising to find that patients who experience *koro* may relate the cause to a past sexual transgression.

Fright-related disorders are interesting phenomena that have been observed in many different cultures. In Iranian society, a variety of problems ranging from physical illness to psychotic episodes may be explained as being caused by a prior startle or fright experienced by the individual. Similarly, in some Hispanic cultures, *susto* is a condition that is caused by a sudden fright, the "evil eye," or the casting of a spell and is characterized by a state of anxiety, fearfulness, or illness.

H. Comparisons across Species

Fear and anxiety responses have been instrumental in the survival of both human beings and other species throughout the course of evolution. Humans and other species often experienced similar hazards to their existence and, through natural selection, have come to share many similar, adaptive fears. For example, human infants, like the young of other land-dwelling species such as cats, goats, and monkeys, display an adaptive fear of heights and withdraw from a visual cliff. Aquatic species such as ducks show no such fear. Similarly, novel objects, foods, and situations elicit adaptive approach–avoidance behaviors in humans and other species such as birds and primates; such behaviors are beneficial to organisms in that the unfamiliar carries with it the possibility of both danger and opportunity. Other fears common to both humans and many other species include fear of too much or little light or space, fear of sudden touch, seizure, proximity, or movement, and fear elicited by visual and auditory alarm cues from members of the same species.

III. DEVELOPMENT AND MAINTENANCE OF ANXIETY AND FEAR

A. Role of Learning

Most fears and anxieties are learned. They can be acquired through direct contact with the feared stim-

uli, or through indirect means, such as absorbing fear/anxiety-evoking information about the stimuli or observing others who interact with the stimuli in a fearful or anxious manner.

A fundamental law of learning that describes how fear and anxiety develop is classical conditioning. In this type of learning, an unconditioned stimulus (UCS), such as pain, is the original source of fear. After pairing of the UCS with a new, previously neutral stimulus, this second stimulus becomes the conditioned stimulus (CS). The CS then can elicit a fear response without the UCS being present. Generalization occurs when stimuli that are similar to the CS also elicit a fear response. [*See* CLASSICAL CONDITIONING.]

In a historic study, Watson and Raynor demonstrated the role of classical fear conditioning in human behavior. In this study, a child, Albert, was exposed to a very loud noise (UCS) while viewing a rat (CS). Little Albert soon developed a conditioned fear to rats. This fear generalized to other objects that resembled rats, such as rabbits and other soft, furry animals. Another example of a conditioned response involves the acquisition of conditioned nausea in oncology patients who are undergoing chemotherapy. Patients may develop moderate to severe nausea reactions to previously neutral stimuli paired with chemotherapy administration, such as the sights, sounds, and smells associated with the staff dispensing the therapy and the setting in which it is conducted.

Conditioning alone, however, does not account for the development and maintenance of all anxiety and fear. Difficulties for the theory include: not accounting for the selectivity of phobias, learning to fear some objects or situations more than others, and failure of the fear that is associated with certain objects to decrease despite repeated exposure to the stimulus without negative consequences. An early adaptation to classical fear conditioning theory was the avoidance learning model, which hypothesized that fears fail to decrease or remit completely if the individual learns to avoid the stimulus. Mowrer stated that the learned fear of the conditioned stimulus was acquired according to classical conditioning principles, and that the motor response of avoidance was learned by instrumental conditioning. As it involves both classical conditioning and instrumental conditioning, it is known as "two-factor theory." It purported to explain why phobias do not resolve even with repeated exposure. Mowrer reasoned that the motor response was first made to escape a negative situation, but on subsequent trials, the behavior was an avoidance response motivated by fear, and maintained by fear reduction. Despite the fact that the two-factor theory has not fared well when subjected to rigorous empirical investigation, it has made a significant contribution toward the understanding of the maintenance of fear and anxiety. The basic principles of conditioning have not been abandoned; rather, it appears that cognitive and emotional processes are used in determining fear and anxiety responsivity.

Another mechanism by which fear and anxiety may be learned is observational or vicarious learning. Vicarious learning occurs by observing or participating in the experience of others. A study which introduced laboratory-reared adolescent rhesus monkeys (who had demonstrated no prior snake fear) to their wild-reared parents illustrated this sort of learning in the social transmission of snake fear. By the end of the sixth encounter in which the adolescents observed their parents behaving fearfully in the presence of snake stimuli, the adolescent monkeys' avoidance and behavioral disturbance was indistinguishable from that of their parents.

Given that much of fear and anxiety is learned, it can be unlearned. This premise is the basis for much behavioral and cognitive–behavioral treatment of extreme forms of fear and anxiety in anxiety disorders. As already noted, anxieties and fears change over the lifespan, partly in concert with developmental changes. Learning through life experiences has perhaps an even greater impact in the waxing and waning of distressing emotional states. It is unlikely that anxiety or fear about an object or situation would emerge and then remain unchanged throughout an individual's lifetime. Rather, it is probable that the fear or anxiety would change in terms of its intensity and triggering features, dependent upon various life events. For example, a person who is phobic of flying in an airplane might initially be very distressed while flying, becoming less fearful after some successful trips on an airliner, later feeling discomfort only in certain parts of the journey, such as take-offs. This would be an example of exposure, in which confronting the feared situation first intensifies anxiety and then allows the individual to habituate. It is also possible, however, for sensitization to take place, for the distress to worsen, as a result of escaping after fearful confrontation with a feared stimulus. Desensitization, however, is another method for reducing fear and anxiety. It can happen in a programmatic way in psychotherapeutic treat-

ment, or can be naturally occurring, such as when an individual gradually becomes more and more comfortable dealing with members of the opposite sex, never having become so fearful during encounters that escape was prompted.

B. Trauma

Exposure to traumatic events, including natural disasters such as destructive tornados, almost invariably produces fear and anxiety on an immediate basis, preparing threatened people physically and cognitively for action. Traumas such as war and rape not only trigger immediate anxiety and/or fear, but, for some people, may result in longer term symptoms after the danger has passed. Sometimes these difficulties are extreme and persistent in which individuals reexperience the event through distressing thoughts, dreams, or dissociative flashbacks, avoid stimuli associated with the event, display a general numbing of responsiveness, and experience symptoms of elevated arousal such as difficulty sleeping, irritability, difficulty concentrating, hypervigilance, and an exaggerated startle response. In this pronounced form, an anxiety disorder, specifically posttraumatic stress disorder, can be present. [See POST-TRAUMATIC STRESS DISORDER.]

Research suggests that the onset and exacerbation of fears and anxieties can be prompted by contextually unrelated aversive events, such as trauma. In some instances, trauma and development or exacerbation of fear/anxiety are quite distant from one another in time. An example would be a person who develops fear of flying sometime after treatment for cancer.

C. Genetic and Familial Transmission

A variety of studies have asked, "Are fear and anxiety inherited?" and "Are fear and anxiety acquired through learning in the family and other environments?" These questions are an example of the "nature versus nurture" debate that permeates much of psychology. Researchers have looked at family histories, parenting characteristics, and prevalence rates of anxiety disorders within families to answer these questions. Comparative psychologists have demonstrated that it is possible to breed anxiety/fear in rats and dogs and have observed severe social anxiety to be naturally occurring in a subset of certain non-human primates. When exploring the heritability of the global category of "anxiety neurosis," one study noted that as many as 50% of the children with parents with an anxiety neurosis also carried that diagnosis. Studies with twins suggest a genetic component in transmission of anxiety disorders. Most studies with humans support the idea that in some individuals, tendencies to develop problem fear and anxiety are inherited, but learning through familial transmission has been demonstrated to be extremely influential as well.

This heritability has ignited another question: "What is it that is inherited?" The most widely accepted answer is that one inherits a vulnerability to fear and anxiety, which may or may not develop in pathological proportions based on an individual's environment. Chronic stress is an example of an environmental influence that may induce problem fear and/or anxiety in a vulnerable person. Without that stress, the individual might never have developed an anxiety disorder. [See STRESS.]

D. Evolutionary Significance and Biologically Prepared Stimuli

Encounters with environmental stressors that cause fear and anxiety have been present throughout the history of humankind. Early encounters included contact with feared beasts that have shaped humans' reactionary responses. It has been proposed that animal fear originates in a predatory defense system that allows animals, including humans, to avoid or escape potentially dangerous animals such as poisonous snakes.

The evolutionary significance of fear and anxiety is directly linked to the biological idea of survival of the species. Fear and anxiety serve a protective function for all members of the animal kingdom that are capable of experiencing this biological warning. Some theorists believe that the ability to plan for the future is also dependent on anxiety and fear.

Humans, and some lower animals, are "prepared" or predisposed to fear certain animals and other stimuli. Human beings more frequently fear or are anxious about stimuli that can potentially cause harm (e.g., rodents). This theory of evolutionary "preparedness" implies that some aspects of what humans learn to fear, along with the fear response, may be innate. For example, investigators have suggested that humans may have an innate fear of small stimuli that move rapidly and/or abruptly (e.g., snakes, spiders). It is somewhat less frequent for people to fear things that have little or no apparent danger, although quite unusual fears are observed

clinically (e.g., distress about opening large dictionaries, fear of stimuli that have pointed characteristics).

IV. ANXIETY AND FEAR AS RESPONSES

As previously noted, anxiety and fear have been regarded as having a three systems structure, including verbal reports, overt behaviors, and responses in physiological systems. A recent theoretical formulation by Eifert and Wilson, however, suggests that the three systems approach involves a confounding of content and method of assessment. They propose that current conceptualizations of emotions involve four content areas: affective, cognitive, motoric, and physiological. It is further suggested that these content areas can be assessed via three methods: self-report (both verbal and nonverbal), observation, and use of instrumentation. Given this conceptualization, and because of the current emphasis on cognition in the scientific literature, cognitive factors will be considered as a separate category.

A. Verbal Reports

In many cases, verbal report is the most salient of anxiety/fear responses: People acknowledge fear and sometimes complain about it. The verbal report component of fear and anxiety is quite complicated in that people can describe private, internal states, such as feelings and thoughts, but can also report on their overt behaviors and physiological responses. Accuracy and reliability of reporting are an issue, due to the effects of social desirability and acquiescence, reactive effects of measurement, bias, and faking. Readiness to complain is another factor that determines whether and how vociferously an individual will communicate about fear and/or anxiety.

B. Cognitive Processes

Research suggests there are three particular categories of anxiety/fear-linked cognitive bias. Specifically, individuals experiencing anxiety (a) attend selectively to threat-related information, (b) show facilitated memory for threat-related information, and (c) demonstrate an interpretive bias favoring more threatening meanings of ambiguous information. In terms of content of thinking, anxiety has been found to include negative self-talk, obsessive worrying, low self-efficacy, and self-abnegation, based on verbal reports of cognitive activity. These same qualities of thought are present in fear, albeit to a lesser degree.

C. Overt Behaviors

Behaviors associated with fear and anxiety are often motoric and observable (e.g., a person running away after spotting a snake). In fact, actual avoidance of an object or situation has long been a hallmark of phobia, which is a severe instantiation of fear and/or anxiety. Escape is a related behavior, but instead of avoiding the object or situation altogether, the individual confronts it, but leaves prematurely (e.g., an individual appears for a dental appointment, sits in the waiting room, but leaves after a few minutes, prior to being seen in the examination room).

Human beings not only share some specific fears with other species, they also have in common defensive strategies that have obvious survival value and are designed to ward off danger. Avoidance and escape are examples of flight, in reference to the previously mentioned fight or flight responses. While avoidance and escape behaviors are the most classic signs, Marks has identified other types of overt behaviors associated with fear and anxiety as well, as listed here:

1. Withdrawal (avoidance, escape)
2. Immobility (freezing, unresponsiveness)
3. Submission (vulnerable posturing, appeasement)
4. Aggression (verbal attack, threats)

Immobility is often seen in the animal kingdom as an adaptive response to threatening situations, such as when predators are nearby and neither escape nor aggression would be prudent. As identified by Marks, immobility can either be attentive, in which an animal freezes but has heightened awareness of possible danger, or tonic, in which an organism is unresponsive, perhaps appearing dead. A rabbit freezing at the sight of a fox is an example of immobility. This sort of fear/anxiety response may be less common in human beings, but can be seen in extreme reactions to major stressors. Victims of brutal attacks and rapes have reported reacting by being paralyzed and unable to respond during the event, consistent with the idea of immobilization for survival. Muted forms of immobility are seen in some social situations, such as when a person delivering a speech freezes and cannot continue to talk.

In submission, organisms attempt to deflect attacks on themselves (or their young) or try to appease a threatening organism. In human beings, appeasement can be observed in a variety of social encounters, such as in situations in which individuals with less status attempt to placate higher status persons by avoiding eye contact, acknowledging weaknesses, or making self-deprecating remarks.

Aggression is not typically regarded as being associated with fear or anxiety. Nevertheless, "fight" is one option in the fight or flight reaction described earlier. Sometimes, colorful aggressive displays, like threatening rustling of plumage in some peacocks, and other complex ritualistic behaviors, are involved in such reactions. Responding to threat with fear- or anxiety-associated aggression can be adaptive, discouraging attack by others. [See AGGRESSION.]

D. Physiological Responses

Anxiety and fear are associated with changes in various bodily organs and systems. Of greatest interest in this area has been the nervous system, particularly the autonomic nervous system, although others, such as the endocrine system, have garnered considerable attention as well. The parasympathetic and sympathetic nervous systems (divisions of the autonomic nervous system) are associated with changes in physiological function related to anxiety and fear.

In fear/anxiety responses, cardiovascular and other systems are activated. Heart rate is increased. Blood flow to the extremities is decreased because of the constriction of peripheral blood vessels. In order to aid in defense, blood pressure increases as excess blood is directed to the large skeletal muscles. Blood is stored in the torso so that it is readily available for vital organs. Skeletal muscles prepare to contract and so generate electrical activity. Muscles of the face change, which may be evident in facial expression. Sweat gland activity increases to prepare the organism to cool itself after exertion. The skin surface becomes cooler because of decreased blood flow to the skin. Breathing becomes more rapid to supply the blood with increased oxygen. An increase in the release of glucose into the bloodstream prepares the muscles and organs for response. Pupils dilate and hearing becomes more acute. These responses are engaged as part of the "fight or flight" reaction already noted.

This mobilization of the organism for action is not the only route for fear. A unique and very different type of diphasic response, specific to blood, injury, and/or illness stimuli, ultimately deactivates the cardiovascular system by decreasing heart rate and blood pressure, sometimes causing the organism to faint. This response is usually triggered by sight of injections, blood, or injury. Blood flow is reduced, presumably to lessen the danger of shock if an injury were actually to occur, thereby rendering an organism more likely to survive.

V. MEASUREMENT OF ANXIETY AND FEAR

In assessment, the question arises as to which of the three (or four) systems is the standard, determining whether anxiety and/or fear is in fact present, and to what degree. Not surprisingly, there is no simple answer. No one system has precedence over the others, nor is any one considered the most important. In nonclinical research investigations, as well as in clinical work with pathological manifestations of anxiety and fear, the use of multiple measures of fear and anxiety is almost universally recommended. No one system (i.e., self-reports, cognitive processes, overt behavior, or physiology) has emerged as the standard for assessment. Rather, use of various measures from each system, and use of methods from each of the categories of self-report, observation, and instrumentation are the ideal.

A. Self-Report

The method most relied upon in terms of determining whether and how much a person is fearful or anxious is that of self-reports, what people indicate through spoken or written communication. For example, it is relatively simple to ask people if, and how much, they are afraid. Nevertheless, this area of response becomes very complicated because people can also make reports not only about their thoughts and feelings, but also concerning overt behaviors and physiological responses (e.g., "I've been avoiding dental treatment for years. When I even think about it, my heart races").

Interviews are one of the most effective methods for gathering information about a person's experience with anxiety and fear. They can be used with both nonclinical and clinical populations. The format can be unstructured and general, such as open-ended interviews conducted by most mental health professionals in purely clinical settings. Structured interview protocols can be utilized to assess broadly (e.g., Anxiety Disorders Interview Schedule–Re-

vised) or in highly specific areas (e.g., Dental Fear Interview).

Questionnaires that directly prompt the individual to indicate the presence and intensity of anxiety/fear, typically using numerical ratings, are another self-report assessment strategy. These can be omnibus questionnaires, such as the Fear Survey Schedule–III or the Marks and Mathews Fear Questionnaire. These instruments assess discomfort associated with a variety of objects and situations and have subscales, in such areas as those detailed previously in this chapter as dimensions of anxiety and fear. Other questionnaires are shorter and more specific to a particular stimulus or class of stimuli. Examples include social situations (e.g., Social Phobia and Anxiety Inventory), snakes (e.g., Snake Fear Questionnaire), and pain (e.g., Fear of Pain Questionnaire–III).

Subscales of general personality assessment instruments (e.g., Minnesota Multiphasic Personality Inventory–2) are also used to evaluate anxiety and fear, sometimes with indirect questions. Symptom checklists (e.g., Symptom Check List–90–Revised) can also be used, particularly to evaluate self-report of physiological responses. This method is self-report if completed by the individual being assessed, but may best be considered observation if rated by a researcher or clinician. Finally, self-report is frequently used to assess cognitive processes. Thought listing is a method in which the person assessed lists all conscious and remembered thoughts after confronting a distressing object or situation. Thought endorsement questionnaires (e.g., Social Interaction Self-Statement Test) involve numerical ratings of frequency of thoughts commonly reported in response to feared and/or anxiety-provoking stimuli. [See PERSONALITY ASSESSMENT.]

Some nonverbal assessment methods involve presentation of symbolic stimuli and require an individual to select stimuli that match internal feeling states. For example, the Self-Assessment Mannikin prompts individuals to rate dimensions using an abstract stick figure, changing characteristics of the mouth (for smiling or frowning), body activity (to indicate arousal), and body size (to report on feelings of dominance).

B. Observation

In work with fear and anxiety, overt motoric behaviors are the most common measures evaluated with observation. Observation of behavior can take place in the clinic, laboratory, or natural environment.

As a measurement modality, observation is perhaps properly considered to be conducted by researchers, clinicians, or collateral sources (e.g., spouse, relatives) other than the person who is being assessed. It is possible to utilize trained personnel to do standardized observations, such as monitoring of facial expressions or assessment of social skills.

The most common standardized strategy for observing behavior in clinical and research settings is the behavioral assessment test (BAT). With this method, the individual being assessed is asked to confront a fear/anxiety-eliciting stimulus in a standardized format. Typically, measures involve approach (e.g., how close a person can get to a snake in a snake fear BAT) or endurance (e.g., how long an individual can stay in a closet in a BAT for closed-in spaces fear). It should be noted that BAT's can also involve self-reports (e.g., ratings of anxious feelings) and use of instrumentation (e.g., to assess physiological responses).

Other behaviors that may be assessed with BAT's include, but are not limited to, approaching a dog, giving a speech to an audience, riding alone in an elevator, or walking alone along a predetermined course. It is also possible for there to be observation of more subtle behaviors. For example, there are sometimes interference effects in ongoing social performance (e.g., stammering, blocking of speech) which can be quantified.

C. Instrumentation

Specialized instruments allow evaluation of anxious and/or fearful actions that would ordinarily be impossible to measure accurately or at all. Instruments are commonly used to measure psychophysiological responses, as well as to record speed and accuracy of cognitive processing. Moreover, brain imaging techniques are available that allow measurement of very basic physiological processes.

Novel assessment methods have been introduced to accurately record cognitive processes. These techniques can be used to assess responses to stimuli that are either within consciousness (supraliminal) or outside of awareness (subliminal). Assessing cognitive processes in fear/anxiety research has focused on attention and memory, assessing reaction time, processing time for complex tasks, accuracy of recall and recognition, comprehension of ambiguous stimuli, and effects of interfering probe stimuli, among others.

An example is the Stroop color-naming test, which is one methodology that has been modified for fear/anxiety work and used to measure selective attending of supraliminal cognitive processes. In one of the original Stroop color-naming tasks, response time in color-naming stimuli was recorded. Subjects performed slower on a task involving incongruent stimuli (i.e., color words in antagonistic ink colors) than on naming solid-color squares. This phenomenon is the Stroop interference effect; it has been found not only with words that involve interference from color, but also with words that presumably cause interference due to their specificity to a person's fears and/or anxieties. For example, Stroop interference effects have been found for social-relevant words (e.g., *interview, party*) for persons with social phobia.

Psychophysiological data are most frequently collected in the laboratory or clinic, but can be acquired in the natural environment using ambulatory monitoring equipment. Typically, psychophysiological levels are measured at resting baselines, and then compared to precisely timed events that are fear and/or anxiety provoking. The psychophysiological methods most often used in fear/anxiety work are cardiovascular, electromyographic, and electrodermal ones. Typically, electrodes are attached to the epidermis in specific areas or configurations, allowing for measurement of electrical activity produced by internal organs or systems.

The most frequently utilized measures of physiological arousal in fear and anxiety research are cardiovascular. Of these, heart rate has been the most often selected index, although others such as blood pressure are quite important as well. Another commonly used physiological measure is electromyography (EMG), the assessment of skeletal muscle activity. EMG levels are recorded from particular muscle sites. By measuring electrical activity from a muscle, it is possible to infer muscular tension. The most common area is the frontalis muscle, which is across the forehead, because it is believed to be highly sensitive to general tension and arousal. Assessment of electrodermal activity is yet another type of psychophysiological measurement; it focuses on sweat gland activity in the skin, using measures of skin conductance and resistance. An increase in perspiration will be reflected in a decrease in resistance and an increase in conductance. Because of the concentration of sweat glands, the hands and feet are common areas for such measurement. Other ways of measuring psychophysiological fear and anxiety reactions include endocrinological measures. Research has examined changes in catecholamine levels before, during, and after stress in both normal and anxious subjects. Endocrinological studies have also investigated changes in epinephrine, norepinephrine, and adrenocortical functioning.

VI. CONCLUSIONS

The knowledge base about anxiety and fear is continually growing. There are now scientific journals devoted to anxiety and anxiety disorders as their exclusive subject matter. In the last decade, national organizations (e.g., Anxiety Disorders Association of America) have come into being, with memberships including lay people afflicted with problem fear and/or anxiety, and professionals who provide treatment and/or research in the area. Anxiety and fear are important emotional states, but are in truth like the proverbial double-edged sword. They are motivating emotional states, prompting people to behave in healthy and safe ways. Conversely, in extreme forms, they are associated with misery and distress, causing lifelong problems that can disrupt an individual's life entirely and indefinitely. Anxiety and fear are scientifically fascinating. Undoubtedly, intensive research and clinical work on fear and anxiety, as well as their pathological manifestations, will continue for some time to come.

Bibliography

American Psychiatric Association (1987). "Diagnostic and Statistical Manual of Mental Disorders," 3rd ed., revised. American Psychiatric Association Press, Washington, DC.

Arrindell, W. A., Kolk, A. M., Pickersgill, M. J., and Hageman, W. J. J. M. (1993). Biological sex, sex-role orientation, masculine sex-role stress, dissimulation and self-reported fears in a non-clinical sample from Britain. *Adv. Behav. Res. Ther.* **15**, 103–146.

Barlow, D. G. (1988). "Anxiety and Its Disorders: The Nature and Treatment of Anxiety and Panic." Guilford, New York.

Barrios, B. A., and O'Dell, S. L. (1989). Fears and anxieties. In "Treatment of Childhood Disorders" (E. J. Mash and R. A. Barkley, Eds.), pp. 167–221. Guilford, New York.

Beck, A. T., and Emery, G. (1985). "Anxiety Disorders and Phobias: A Cognitive Perspective." Basic Books, New York.

Marks, I. M. (1987). "Fears, Phobias, and Rituals: Panic, Anxiety, and Their Disorders." Oxford University Press, New York.

McNeil, D. W., Vrana, S. R., Melamed, B. F., Cuthbert, B. N., and Lang, P. J. (1993). Emotional imagery in simple and social phobia: Fear versus anxiety. *J. Abnormal Psychol.* **102**, 212–225.

Rachman, S. J. (1990). "Fear and Courage," 2nd ed. Freeman, New York.

Tuma, A. H., and Maser, J. D. (Eds.) (1985). "Anxiety and the Anxiety Disorders." Erlbaum, Hillsdale, NJ.

Zinbarg, R. E., Barlow, D. H., Brown, T. A., and Hertz, R. M. (1992). Cognitive-behavioral approaches to the nature and treatment of anxiety disorders. *Annu. Rev. Psychol.* **43**, 235–267.

ANXIETY DISORDERS

Elizabeth A. Meadows and David H. Barlow
University at Albany, State University of New York

Glossary

Agoraphobia Avoidance of a cluster of situations from which escape may be difficult or embarrassing in the event of a panic attack or related event, or endurance of these situations with dread.

Diagnosis The process of identifying specific disorders.

***Diagnostic and Statistical Manual of Mental Disorders* (DSM)** The reference manual used by mental health professionals, including descriptions and diagnostic criteria for psychiatric disorders. The edition in use since 1987, DSM-III-R (third edition, revised), will be replaced by DSM-IV in spring 1994.

Exposure A treatment technique in which feared stimuli, including thoughts, sensations, or situations, are confronted until anxiety diminishes.

Panic attack A sudden rush of fear, accompanied by strong physical sensations.

Phobia An excessive fear of some event, object, or situation.

ANXIETY is a normal emotion experienced by everyone. Excessive anxiety is also among the most common problems for which people seek psychological treatment. Both adaptive and maladaptive anxiety will be discussed here, with emphasis on the varieties of anxiety disorders, their assessment, and treatment.

I. WHAT IS ANXIETY?

Almost everyone knows the feeling of anxiety, although a universal definition is difficult to come by. Anxiety is our body's natural response to perceived danger or threat; without anxiety, we would have no motivation to protect ourselves or others from harm. Thus, anxiety can be very adaptive, such as when it prompts us to be vigilant while walking alone on a dark street, alert to any signs of danger. Anxiety can be helpful in less dangerous situations as well. For example, people tend to perform better with mild levels of anxiety than they do with none at all; being *too* relaxed can impede performance as greatly as being overly anxious.

When it is excessive for a given situation, however, or occurs too frequently, anxiety can be maladaptive, and quite disruptive. Examples of maladaptive anxiety include the hypervigilance described above, but in an objectively safe situation such as walking down the hallway at work, or worrying a great deal about the possibility of some misfortune. The revised third edition of the *Diagnostic and Statistical Manual of Mental Disorders* (DSM-III-R) lists eight different categories of anxiety disorders, each describing a different form of maladaptive anxiety; two new disorders are listed in DSM-IV.

Because anxiety is a normal part of life that can also become problematic, it is important to recognize that features of each of the anxiety disorders are considered normal and healthy, within limits. For example, everyone worries about things from time to time, but when the worry become excessive or the person feels it is uncontrollable, it might fall into the diagnostic category of generalized anxiety disorder. Similarly, one of the characteristics of obsessive–compulsive disorder is a need to perform certain rituals. The typical bedtime rituals of children, such as having a parent read a story, kiss a teddy bear, and tuck the child in, would not be considered abnormal behavior. If, on the other hand, the child developed a more elaborate series of rituals that involved tremendous amounts of time and energy, or that greatly disrupted household functioning, this would be considered clinically significant.

Generally speaking, features of anxiety disorders may be seen frequently. These features are not considered clinically significant disorders unless they involve marked distress or interference with functioning. Thus, a fear of large dogs that prompts one to cross the street occasionally to avoid a dog may not be seen as particularly bothersome to the individual. If this same person were to begin avoiding going outside at all, just in case a dog was nearby, this would obviously cause more interference. Alternatively, if this person were to begin a relationship with the owner of a large dog, the fear might prompt greater amounts of distress. Thus, distress or interference with functioning may be prompted by a more intense or more frequent symptom, or by the same symptom in a new setting. Without distress or interference, symptoms constitute nonclinical features of a disorder, rather than a clinical disorder itself.

II. THE ANXIETY DISORDERS

A. Panic Disorder and Agoraphobia

Panic disorder is characterized by panic attacks, or sudden rushes of intense fear or feelings of impending doom. These attacks include physical sensations such as shortness of breath, palpitations or accelerated heart rate, and dizziness, and fears of dying, going crazy, or losing control. A panic attack is defined as an unexpected rush of intense fear or discomfort accompanied by at least four of 13 symptoms, such as those listed above, and peaking in intensity within 10 minutes. Attacks consisting of fewer than four symptoms are called limited symptom attacks. [See PANIC DISORDER.]

The occurrence of panic attacks alone does not constitute panic disorder. In addition to the attacks themselves, in panic disorder there is also persistent fear of future attacks or of the consequences of the attacks; this fear of panic can be the most debilitating aspect of panic disorder, consuming enormous amounts of energy and attention. Frequently, panic disorder is accompanied by agoraphobia, or avoidance of situations from which escape may be difficult or embarrassing or in which help may not be available in the case of a panic attack. The person with agoraphobia may also fear or avoid situations in which panic attacks have occurred in the past. Agoraphobia varies widely in degree. Mild agoraphobia, manifested by fear or dread of situations, and occasional avoidance or escape, need not impact largely on a person's daily life. Agoraphobia can also become so severe that the person is literally housebound. [See AGORAPHOBIA.]

About 8–10% of the population experience an unexpected panic attack in a given year, but only 3–6% go on to develop agoraphobia. An additional 1% develop panic disorder without agoraphobia. Agoraphobia is much more commonly seen in women than in men. One possible explanation for this is that it is easier or more acceptable for women to avoid than for men; men might instead cope with their panic attacks by self-medicating with alcohol. While it is also possible that women actually do experience more panic attacks than do men, this seems less likely given that the gender differences in panic prevalence are substantially less than those of agoraphobia prevalence.

More infrequently, agoraphobia may be experienced in the absence of panic disorder. Thus, various situations are avoided or feared, yet the person has never had panic disorder. The most common reason reported by these people for their avoidance is fear of limited symptom attacks, which are like panic attacks with only one or two specific symptoms. For example, someone who experiences diarrhea may begin to avoid any situations without ready access to a bathroom. Some people have never experienced the symptoms they fear, but avoid situations because "it could still happen." Finally, a smaller number of people report avoiding similar situations, but are unable to specify their fears.

B. Social Phobia

Social phobia is characterized by a fear of negative evaluation by others, or the fear that one might do or say something that might be embarrassing or humiliating. Social phobia can be very specific, limited to just certain situations such as public speaking or using public restrooms, or it can be quite pervasive, generalized to almost all social situations. When faced with the feared social situations, people with social phobia became anxious, in many cases experiencing panic attacks in these situations.

Almost everyone has experienced some social anxiety, such as being nervous on a first date, or when making a formal presentation. While this may be uncomfortable or unpleasant, it does not necessarily constitute a clinical problem. In approximately 1–2% of people, however, these fears become so strong that their lives are greatly affected. For example, a person who is overly concerned with the possibility of sounding silly or stupid may avoid social interactions such as conversation or parties, thus affecting social life. This person might also feel unable to speak out in class or at meetings, thus leading to poorer grades or work performance. In extremely severe forms, *any* situation in which one might be observed would be avoided, leading one to drive only at night, for example, so as not to encounter other drivers while at a stop light.

C. Specific Phobia

Specific phobias are irrational or excessive fears of a specific object or situation. Some common targets of these fears include heights, animals (especially snakes or spiders), small enclosed places, flying, and blood or injury. DSM-IV lists four subtypes of specific phobias: animal; natural environment (e.g., heights, storms); blood, injection, injury; and situational (e.g., airplanes, enclosed places). Phobias not fitting these categories, such as a fear of situations that may lead to vomiting, are classified as "other."

Because of the discrete nature of these fears, it is possible to have an extremely strong fear of a particular target, yet not have a clinically significant phobia. A common example is fear of harmless snakes. A person who is quite frightened of snakes and would be terrified to encounter one may never actually be confronted with this situation if he or she lived in a city and rarely ventured into more rural areas. On the other hand, this same person would have a big problem upon moving to the country, where suddenly snakes might be encountered any time the front door was opened. Alternatively, if this city-dweller's circle of friends became interested in hiking, this fear might then interfere in his or her social life, thus also causing difficulties.

The prevalance rate of specific phobias in the general population is between 5 and 15%. However, specific phobias are among the least frequent disorders prompting treatment-seeking, because they rarely cause marked interference in everyday functioning. In addition, specific phobias vary in content across age groups. For example, fears of monsters and the dark are quite common in young children, but rarely seen in adults, while fears of air travel begin most frequently in adulthood.

D. Obsessive–Compulsive Disorder

Of all the anxiety disorders, obsessive–compulsive disorder (OCD) has the greatest potential to require hospitalization or otherwise totally disrupt daily functioning. Its features can be the most bizarre-looking, and can easily be mistaken for psychotic features if the full clinical picture is not known. [*See* OBSESSIVE–COMPULSIVE BEHAVIOR.]

Obsessions are defined in DSM-IV as "recurrent and persistent thoughts, impulses, or images that are experienced, at some time during the disturbance, as intrusive and inappropriate, and cause marked anxiety or distress." Compulsions are defined as "repetitive behaviors or mental acts that the person feels driven to perform in response to an obsession, or according to rules that must be applied rigidly." A crucial feature of both obsessions and compulsions is that they are ego-dystonic; that is, the person considers the thoughts or behaviors as intrusive or foreign, and not purposeful or rational. Behaviors such as eating or gambling considered "compulsive" by some would not be included in the category of OCD, as both are enjoyable, albeit perhaps regretted after the fact.

People with obsessive–compulsive disorder may experience both obsessions and compulsions, or just one of these. In the most straightforward examples of OCD, people experience very disturbing obsessions, which they then try to ignore or suppress. When this fails to eliminate the horrific thought, anxiety about the thought grows to intolerable levels, and some behavior is then used to counteract or neutralize the thought. For example, the common obsession of contamination would be neutralized by compulsive washing, to restore a sense of cleanliness and safety. In other cases, the neutralizing compulsions are covert, so that the obsession is counteracted by some other thought or image, rather than by an overt behavior. Finally, some people with OCD do not identify any specific obsessions, but feel compelled to engage in rigid or stereotyped rituals; resisting these rituals leads to intense anxiety, although no specific negative consequence is named.

As with other disorders, OCD can range greatly in severity. In milder forms, a person might have to count silently to four, for example, whenever she has the thought that something bad might happen to her children, as a way of preventing that from coming true. Another example would be a person who is certain he locked all the doors and windows, but just doesn't feel quite right about it unless he checks them in a certain pattern two or three times each night. In many cases, milder forms of OCD, while somewhat distressing, can be dismissed by others as quirks or idiosyncrasies. In more severe forms, however, OCD can take on disturbing and bizarre qualities. For example, people with contamination fears might wash their hands until raw, to ensure that no dirt or other contaminant could remain. Any activity that could pose a threat of contamination is intensely feared, and avoided if possible. Thus, any contact with others might require wearing gloves, to forestall such contamination. Even situations that objectively pose no threat, such as *seeing* dirt, might trigger the need to wash. Generally, people with OCD recognize that the obsessions and compulsions are senseless, and that the neutralizing behavior is either unrealistic (as in the case of counting silently to prevent harm) or excessive (as in washing to the point of raw, bleeding skin). In some cases, obsessions become "overvalued," and it is much harder for the person to recognize the irrational nature of these beliefs.

In the past, OCD was believed to be very uncommon. Recent studies, however, indicate that between 1 and 2% of the general population meets criteria for OCD. The disorder typically begins in adolescence or early adulthood, although children may also have OCD.

E. Post-Traumatic Stress Disorder

Post-traumatic stress disorder (PTSD) is the only anxiety disorder to include an identifiable onset. Encompassing such disturbances as "shell shock" or "rape survivor trauma," PTSD is defined by a constellation of symptoms developed in response to some extraordinary trauma. These symptoms are grouped into three categories: re-experiencing, numbness/avoidance, and increased arousal. Of these, the re-experiencing symptoms most clearly delineate PTSD from other disorders, as both avoidance and arousal are common components of most anxiety disorders as well. Re-experiencing can take several forms. Both dreams and recollections may occur recurrently and intrusively. People with PTSD may suddenly feel as if they are reliving the event, or have flashbacks. They may also become intensely distressed or physiologically reactive upon exposure to events or situations that remind them of the event, such as the anniversary of the event, or colors, sounds, or smells associated with it. [*See* Post-Traumatic Stress Disorder.]

Numbness/avoidance symptoms include deliberate avoidance of thoughts or activities associated with the traumatic event, inability to remember aspects of the event, and general decreased responsiveness. Symptoms of increased arousal include sleep difficulties, hypervigilance, anger outbursts, and exaggerated startle response. An important aspect of these latter two categories is that these symptoms must represent a change from the person's status prior to the traumatic event. Therefore, insomnia that was present prior to the trauma would not be included in PTSD symptomatology unless it increased markedly following the event.

There is not much consistent information on the prevalence of PTSD in the general population. Studies examining rates of PTSD in groups of people who have undergone specific traumas report wide ranges of such incidence. In part, this is complicated by the range of stressors. PTSD can develop in response to a single event such as rape, or a more long-term event such as war. PTSD can also develop in response to witnessing a traumatic event, in addition to experiencing it oneself. Thus, a very low rate of PTSD may be expected for some stressors, and a higher rate from others. However, merely experiencing or witnessing a traumatic event is not sufficient to induce PTSD, as there are others who undergo the same traumas without developing PTSD; therefore, simply grouping by type of trauma does not explain the discrepancies in PTSD incidence. In other words, while trauma must be present for PTSD to develop, such trauma is not sufficient to explain the development of the disorder. Other factors, such as biological vulnerability, social support, and coping responses, interact with the experience of trauma, leading to a range of psychological sequelae.

In 1984, the U.S. Congress mandated the development of the National Center for Post-Traumatic Stress Disorder. The National Center is a consortium of divisions located at four different Veterans Administration hospitals, and is designed to carry out research, education, and training programs on war-related PTSD in veterans. Therefore, war-related PTSD is probably the most widely studied currently. Crime-related PTSD, including rape and domestic violence, seems to be increasingly targeted as an important area of study as well.

F. Generalized Anxiety Disorder

In the past, generalized anxiety disorder (GAD) was considered a residual category for people who experienced anxiety symptoms that did not meet any of the above diagnoses. Currently, however, GAD has become more specifically defined, and refers to chronic high levels of anxiety and pervasive worry regarding a variety of topics. This anxiety or apprehension leads to impaired concentration or ability to focus, and is difficult to control. People with GAD frequently say they worry about "everything," and tend to see themselves as worriers. The anxiety must be problematic more days than not for a period of at least 6 months. In this way, people who are responding to a specific stressor (i.e., a student severely worried about final exams during the study period prior to the exams) would be excluded from this category. GAD also includes concomitant physical symptoms of anxiety, such as muscle tension, restlessness, irritability, and sleep disturbances.

Generalized anxiety disorder is seen in approximately 4% of the general population. In addition, generalized anxiety is a common component of most other anxiety disorders; when combined with other such disorders, generalized anxiety is experienced by about 10–12% of the population, clearly a sizeable number. The onset of GAD is commonly in the 20s and 30s, and GAD tends to follow a fairly chronic course. In fact, while many people with GAD may report that their worrying or anxiety became problematic in early adulthood, they also note that they had a tendency to worry excessively since childhood.

G. Secondary Anxiety Disorder due to a General Medical Condition

This is a new DSM-IV disorder, in which anxiety symptoms such as panic attacks, obsessions, or phobic responses are judged as caused by some general medical condition.

H. Substance-Induced Anxiety Disorder

The second new DSM-IV anxiety disorder, substance-induced anxiety disorder, is similar to the previous category; anxiety symptoms are clearly present, but can be attributed, in this case, to substance use. Anxiety that precedes the substance use, that persists following cessation of substance use, or that is in excess of what would be expected for that substance use would not be classified in this category, as it would be better accounted for by another anxiety disorder.

III. TREATMENT

A. Cognitive–Behavioral Treatments

One of the most widely used methods in the behavioral treatment of anxiety disorders is exposure, or forcing oneself to face feared situations, thoughts, or sensations. Exposure can be done gradually, beginning with the easiest situations and progressing to more difficult ones. An alternative to gradual exposure is flooding, in which the person is confronted with the most anxiety-provoking situations. Exposure in which the person actually confronts feared situation is called *in vivo*, or real life, exposure; exposure can also be done imaginally. Imaginal exposure is helpful both in preparing for *in vivo* exposure and in those cases where *in vivo* exposure is unrealistic.

One form of exposure, called interoceptive exposure, has proven useful in targeting panic attacks. In interoceptive exposure, it is the physical symptoms of panic, such as racing heart or shortness of breath, that are confronted, via exercises that induce these symptoms.

Because of the circumscribed nature of specific phobias, they lend themselves readily to exposure-based treatments. Modeling has sometimes been added to exposure, so that the person first observes the therapist approach the feared stimulus. In general, exposure treatments for the various specific phobias vary only in terms of the target, with one exception. Whereas the most common response to a phobic stimulus is increased arousal, blood phobics tend to respond to phobic cues by fainting, an opposite physiological reaction. For this reason, muscle tension, in which muscles are deliberately clenched to inhibit the fainting response, is a useful adjunct to exposure treatment for blood phobics.

In treating obsessive–complusive disorder, exposure to the feared thoughts or objects is accompanied by response prevention, in which the person is instructed not to engage in the neutralizing thoughts or actions (i.e., washing or checking) that serve to reduce anxiety.

A number of techniques from cognitive therapy have also been used in treating anxiety. In cognitive therapy, people are taught to evaluate their thoughts, such as, "If I don't get out of this mall right away I'm going to collapse," and to challenge inaccurate, negative thoughts. Another component of cognitive therapy is to completely draw out all of one's fears, and to exaggerate them to the fullest extent possible. For example, a person who fears embarrassing himself at a party by saying something foolish might imagine the entire room of people turning to stare at him, running out and telling all of their friends, having his faux pas printed in the newspaper, and never being able to face any of these people ever again. In this way, the irrationality of some of the original fears is seen more clearly. [See COGNITIVE BEHAVIOR THERAPY.]

B. Medication Treatments

A number of medications have also been used to treat anxiety. The three major classes of medications that have been used are benzodiazepines, antidepressants, and beta-blockers. One of the most widely used anxiolytic drugs is alprazolam, or Xanax, a high-potency benzodiazepine. While alprazolam has been shown to block panic, it also is associated with high relapse rates once people are withdrawn from the drug. In some cases, "rebound" panics that are more severe or frequent than predrug panics occur.

Some antidepressant drugs have also been used in the treatment of anxiety. Imipramine, a tricyclic antidepressant, has had the most proven efficacy in controlled studies in the treatment of panic and agoraphobia. Phenelzine, a monoamine oxidase inhibitor (MAOI) antidepressant, has also been effective. With regard to blocking panic specifically, alprazolam, imipramine, and phenelzine all have success rates of between 50 and 90%; they vary greatly, however, in side effects, effects on panic-related symptomatology such as anticipatory anxiety and avoidance, and effects on additional anxiety symptomatology such as social phobia. In addition, other factors may make the drugs more or less acceptable to the patient. For example, phenelzine generally leads to fewer side effects than the tricyclic imipramine, and is not associated with the rebound panics of alprazolam. However, patients on MAOIs must adhere to a very strict diet in which foods containing amines such as tyramine and related compounds are prohibited; these foods, including beer, red wines, and aged cheeses can cause a severe hypertensive crisis or rise in blood pressure that can lead to death.

Another class of drugs that has been used to treat anxiety is beta-blockers, most commonly prescribed for high blood pressure. Because of the effects of beta-blockers on cardiovascular symptoms, they seemed to have potential for treating these symptoms of anxiety. However, the research has not been as promising. Beta-blockers seem to have little effect on panic, agoraphobia, or generalized anxiety, although there is some indication they might be more useful in social phobia, in which alleviating the cardiovascular symptoms such as flushing and palpitations is enough to allow the person to perform successfully.

While drug treatment of obsessive–compulsive disorder has also focused primarily on the same groups of drugs discussed above, there is one that seems to stand out in this category. The tricyclic antidepressant clomipramine (Anafranil) has shown greater effectiveness than other medications in treating OCD. More recently, a third type of antidepressant, fluoxetine (Prozac), has also shown promise in this area. Both of these drugs specifically affect the serotonergic neurotransmitter system.

Post-traumatic stress disorder has received scant attention compared with other disorders. There have been indications that benzodiazepines, antidepressants, and beta-blockers all have some effect, but this has yet to be tested in large, controlled studies. Finally, specific phobias tend to be unresponsive to medication treatment, probably due to the circumscribed nature of the feared stimulus and response.

C. Psychodynamic Treatment

Psychodynamic treatment of anxiety disorders has none of the proven success that cognitive–behavioral and medication treatments enjoy. Within this approach, the anxiety symptoms themselves are not targeted for treatment; rather, they are seen as symptoms of an underlying disturbance that is to be understood and resolved. Thus, instead of focusing upon symptoms, the meaning of these symptoms to the patient and associated issues that may trigger or exacerbate these symptoms are targeted. Psychodynamic approaches also place more emphasis on the therapeutic relationship as a tool than do cognitive–behavioral or medication approaches.

Because there is no good evidence that psychodynamic approaches are successful in treating anxiety, this is rarely the first treatment of choice. Psychodynamic treatment may, however, prove useful to patients who want to gain more insight regarding the origins of their difficulties. There is some evidence that this is best conducted following symptom relief. For example, patients who have controlled their anxiety via behavioral or drug treatment may then choose to explore related issues using a psychodynamic approach.

IV. ISSUES IN CLASSIFICATION

A. Classification Systems

While the focus of classification within this article has been the DSM-IV, this is not the only classification system in use. The categories of disorders listed in the DSM-IV are roughly matched by those listed in the mental disorders section of the 10th edition of the International Classification of Diseases (ICD-10), a diagnostic system for all medical conditions. Other classification systems incorporate a variety of components to assist in sorting psychological difficulties into useful categories.

B. Differential Diagnosis

1. Treatment Implications

As can be seen from the descriptions of the various anxiety disorders, there is a great deal of symptom overlap. For example, a panic attack that occurs out-of-the-blue may be part of panic disorder, whereas the same attack may more accurately reflect specific phobia, if in response to seeing a dog, or social phobia, if in response to an evaluative situation. Avoidance of a shopping mall is likely to reflect agoraphobia, as it would be difficult to get to an exit quickly from the middle of the mall. However, this same avoidance can be seen in PTSD, because the open space of the mall makes it difficult to "watch your back" and remain vigilant.

Because these same symptoms may reflect different disorders, it is important to make accurate diagnoses with which to guide treatment decisions. Treating all panic attacks in a similar fashion ignores the reality that some people fear the attack itself, whereas others fear only the external trigger of the attack. Both fears may be unrealistic, yet the content of the fear is very different. Thus, the treatment for a dog phobic might involve exposure to dogs so that it can be learned that one can encounter a dog and remain safe. Once the fear of dogs decreases, it is unlikely that panic attacks will continue, as the trigger (in this case, dogs) no longer evokes fear. In panic disorder, in contrast, the attack itself might be targeted for treatment.

2. Boundary Issues

Correct classification of the anxiety disorders is very important, especially given the varying treatment implications just discussed. However, in situations where the symptoms fall on the boundary between two disorders, it can be difficult to get a clear picture of one or the other disorder. For example, the primary concern in social phobia is the fear of evaluation by others, whereas the primary concern in panic disorder is of the physical symptoms experienced and their potential consequences. But many people who fear panic attacks report one of their main concerns is that others will notice their anxiety, thus causing them embarrassment. In this way, the boundary between panic disorder and social phobia is somewhat blurred; if there were no symptoms of anxiety, there would be no social concerns, yet the fear of the anxiety is primarily social.

In this particular example, there are several ways in which one might determine whether this picture fits panic disorder or social phobia. Additional support for the diagnosis of panic disorder might be provided if the person reports that there is still some fear of panic while alone, even though the main fear is of others noticing. Alternatively, further support for social phobia might come from a report that panics never occur outside of social evaluative situations, or that anxiety symptoms outside of these situations are not troublesome.

Similar boundary concerns exist among the other anxiety disorders, as well as between anxiety and other disorders, such as depression. Sometimes, a more extended assessment can reveal the additional information needed to clarify the clinical picture to the point that an appropriate treatment program can be begun. In other cases, an inaccurate diagnosis might not become apparent until treatment is already in progress, at which point a revision might be made. The difficulty in sorting through anxiety symptoms to develop the most accurate conceptualization underscores the importance of the necessity of training in assessment; by simply trying to match symptoms to a checklist of DSM-IV criteria, for example, it is likely that the nuances involved in discriminating between the disorders would be missed.

V. SPECIAL POPULATIONS

A. Children

Children can develop any of the anxiety disorders discussed previously. In many cases, children with these anxiety disorders complain of symptoms that are slightly different than those of adults with the same disorder. Sometimes, this is because many children are not yet at a stage where they would be able to describe their situation with the specificity that adults do. For example, an adult experiencing a panic attack might say, "My heart started racing, and then my whole body tensed up and I got short of breath, and I was sure I would die of a heart attack right there." A child, on the other hand, might only be able to say, "I started to feel really funny, and my stomach got all upset, and I thought I'd be sick." Similarly, adults typically report the re-experiencing symptoms of PTSD as flashback episodes, or as recurrent thoughts or dreams. Children might not describe these at all, but rather continually act out the trauma in their play. It is therefore important to consider the child's developmental level in determining his or her capacity to either experience or report the symptoms of the various anxiety disorders.

In addition to the disorders previously discussed, there is another disorder specific to children (although technically, adults are not precluded from receiving this diagnosis). In separation anxiety disorder, the child is excessively anxious when separated from caretakers or others to whom the child has become attached. In many cases, this leads to refusal to leave home for school or camp, or social activities such as sleepovers. These children may become quite afraid that some misfortune might befall significant others, or they may fail to return for the child for some other reason. They may also fear that separation will occur for other reasons, such as the child's getting lost or kidnapped. The fear can be expressed via nightmares, as well as by distress or physical complaints when faced with separation.

B. Geriatric Patients

Until recently, elderly patients were treated primarily with medication; psychological treatments were believed to be ineffective because these patients were too old to begin changing long-standing habits. Current research, however, belies these claims, and there is increasing evidence that geriatric patients can respond well to cognitive–behavioral treatments. In fact, these treatments may be preferable, as geriatric patients are more likely than others to be on additional medications, thus increasing the risk of overmedication and harmful interaction effects of medications.

In general, the same approaches to assessment used in any other patient should be used in a geriatric population. There are, however, some areas that become especially important in this population. First, neurological difficulties increase with age, and can complicate the clinical picture. For example, impaired concentration is a common anxiety symptom, yet this can also be due to a host of neurological disorders. Conversely, such symptoms of anxiety might be more easily missed in the elderly patient if they are just attributed to aging. In these cases, a complete neuropsychological assessment might be especially useful in determining the presence of a treatable anxiety disorder.

Other realities of aging must be kept in mind as well. Because the elderly *are* disproportionately likely to become crime victims, or to fall ill or become injured, some increased anxiety in these areas is to be expected. Rather than treating this as excessive anxiety, targeting the source of concern by, for example, teaching self-defense and other ways of avoiding victimization might be more appropriate. Anxiety can also prove more debilitating in elderly patients due to decreased levels of social support, and thus this may need to be more specifically addressed in their treatment.

C. Mentally Ill/Dually Diagnosed Patients

As was noted earlier, many people self-medicate with alcohol or drugs to mask their anxiety symptoms. Therefore, it is important to assess for the presence of such symptoms in substance abusers. If an alcoholic patient was drinking primarily due to anxiety, tracking these symptoms during the course of alcohol treatment will allow patient and therapist to prepare for the re-emergence of anxiety, which can suddenly become prominent. If such symptoms are not prepared for, the patient might be at greater risk for relapse because of inability to tolerate these new symptoms. On a similar note, a person who is abusing drugs or alcohol to mask anxiety might benefit from specific anxiolytic treatment.

Anxiety disorders can be seen in people with other types of disorders as well. In some cases, treating symptoms of anxiety may alleviate some distress in these patients, even if this treatment is unlikely to effect change in other areas. For example, a person with schizophrenia who also presents with a strong fear of elevators could benefit greatly from behavioral treatment targeting this specific fear. If this particular patient must regularly enter a multistoried hospital or halfway house, this fear could cause enough additional distress for the patient that treatment is warranted. Even anxiety symptoms that are more attributable to a nonanxiety disorder, such as the compulsive rituals sometimes seen in schizophrenia, might be decreased or eliminated by targeting them as a specific focus of treatment.

D. Non-Western Cultures

If anxiety is our natural and normal survival mechanism, designed to protect us from danger, it stands to reason that anxiety should be experienced in every culture. And, in fact, anxiety symptoms similar to those described above have been found in many cultures. In addition, however, anxiety can present very differently across cultures, reflecting culturally specific fears. In some Chinese cultures, a particular fear called *koro* creates intense anxiety and panic. Men with *koro* fear that their sexual organs are retracting into their bodies, and that death might occur upon total retraction. More infrequently, women might fear retraction of nipples, breasts, or external genitalia as well. Another fear specific to Chinese cultures is *pa-leng,* or fear of the cold. This fear stems from the Asian concept of balance between *yin* and *yang; pa-leng* symptoms represent an excess of *yin* that may then be life-threatening.

In Iran, "heart distress" refers to a focus on somatic symptoms related to the heart, such as palpitations. In some cases, these patients resemble Western patients suffering from depression, whereas others are more similar to panic disorder. This again reflects the symbolic meaning of these symptoms within the culture. "Fright disorders," also seen in Iran, as well as in Latin America, refer to observable fear responses attributed to some external event. Anxiety symptoms associated with black magic, voodoo, or the "evil eye" fall into this category.

Shinkeishitsu, a disorder seen in Japan, seems to resemble social phobia in its symptoms: shyness, preoccupation with how one appears to others, and extreme fear that one might offend others in some way. In some cases, the presentation is more similar to panic, with the focus of attention more on somatic symptoms. These patients tend to be perfectionistic and quite self-conscious.

E. Medically Ill Patients

Many anxiety symptoms can also reflect medical problems, thus underscoring the importance of a complete medical and psychological assessment. For example, thyroid disorders can be almost indistinguishable from panic disorder; a simple thyroid test can reveal whether to proceed with medical treatment or panic treatment. Recent advances in assessment make these distinctions easier, and thus it is more likely that appropriate treatment programs will be instituted.

For people who have anxiety as well as other medical problems, treatment can be tailored, if necessary, to accommodate the specific medical problems. In some cases, the two problems have a synergistic effect, especially when their symptoms are similar. A common example is the asthmatic who also has panic disorder. One of the fears reported by these patients during panic is that an asthma attack will be triggered. In these cases, treatment might take several approaches. If the person suffers from severe asthma attacks that frequently require hospitalization, it is unlikely that he or she will be able to undergo the interoceptive exposure to induce respiratory symptoms. Therefore, a more cognitive approach to these symptoms, combined with exposure to other panic symptoms, might be better received. In another patient, whose asthma is not quite as severe, this interoceptive exposure might be a perfect way to learn that it is possible to experience respiratory symptoms and not suffer some devastating consequence.

Bibliography

American Psychiatric Association (1994). "Diagnostic and Statistical Manual of Mental Disorders," 4th ed. American Psychiatric Association, Washington, DC.

Barlow, D. H. (1988). "Anxiety and Its Disorders: The Nature and Treatment of Anxiety and Panic." Guilford, New York.

Gittelman, R. (Ed.) (1986). "Anxiety Disorders of Childhood." Guilford, New York.

Orsillo, S. M., and McCaffrey, R. J. (1992). Anxiety disorders. In "Handbook of Neuropsychological Assessment: A Biopsychosocial Perspective" (A. E. Puente and R. J. McCaffrey, Eds.), Plenum Press, New York.

Rapee, R. M., and Barlow, D. H. (1991). "Chronic Anxiety: Generalized Anxiety Disorder and Mixed Anxiety-Depression." Guilford, New York.

Walker, J. R., Norton, G. R., and Ross, C. A. (Eds.) (1992). "Panic Disorder and Agoraphobia." Brooks/Cole, Pacific Grove, CA.

APHASIA

Howard S. Kirshner
Vanderbilt University School of Medicine

Glossary

Agraphia (also called dysgraphia) An acquired inability to write.

Alexia (also called dyslexia) An acquired disorder of reading.

Language A system of symbols used to convey thoughts, or internal, nonverbal images and representations, from one individual to another.

Lexical Of or pertaining to a word.

Literal (phonemic) paraphasic error An incorrect utterance based on substitution of an erroneous sound.

Morpheme A word ending which may vary depending on the use of a word, e.g., in singular or pleural, masculine or feminine, present or past tense.

Phoneme The smallest unit of speech which can alter the meaning of a word.

Semantics The meaning of words.

Syntax A system of grammatical rules used in language.

Verbal (semantic) paraphasic error An incorrect utterance based on substitution of an erroneous word.

APHASIAS are disorders of language, or symbolic communication, acquired as a result of brain disease. Aphasia strikes at that most human of capabilities, symbolic language, and deprives the subject of communication with others.

By this definition, aphasia can be distinguished from several related conditions. First, aphasia is a disorder of language, and not a motor speech disorder. Motor speech disorders are abnormalities of speech articulation brought about by weakness or incoordination of the muscles of the speech apparatus. Motor speech disorders include dysarthrias, abnormalities of speech articulation; dysphonias, disorders of voice; and speech apraxias, impairments of the ability to sequence a series of phonemes. In motor speech disorders, language comprehension and production are normal; language output can be ascertained by examining the patient's writing or by transcribing speech output into type. Second, aphasia is an acquired language disorder, not a congenital or developmental disorder. In North America, developmental language disorders are often called "dysphasias," just as developmental reading disorders are termed "dyslexias." Finally, the language disorder of aphasia must relate to brain disease, and not to psychiatric disorders which frequently derange thought, or the content of language. This last distinction is the most problematic, in that language is difficult to separate from thought. Even severely aphasic patients seem capable of nonverbal thought, and patients with psychoses such as schizophrenia usually express their disturbed thoughts in normal articulation and syntax.

I. INTRODUCTION

A. History of Aphasia

Historically, language was the first of the higher cortical functions to be correlated with focal lesions of the brain. Broca, in 1861, provided a clear description of nonfluent speech associated with lesions of the dominant hemisphere, and especially the left frontal lobe. The principal syndrome of nonfluent aphasia is still called "Broca's aphasia." Other 19th century physicians similarly correlated areas of brain damage, usually resulting from stroke, with specific syndromes of abnormal language. Wernicke described the fluent aphasia syndrome which now bears his name, as well as conduction aphasia; Lichtheim outlined the "transcortical" aphasias; and Dejerine designated the syndromes of pure alexia with and without agraphia. The late 19th and early 20th century saw slow progress in the understanding of aphasia, largely because physicians had to outlive their patients to correlate an aphasic syndrome with a brain lesion at autopsy. In addition, the early 20th century witnessed a decline in interest in behavioral syndromes, in favor of the "hard" neurological deficits of paralysis, sensory loss, and incoordination. The higher cognitive functions were either accorded little interest or assumed to have a diffuse distribution throughout the brain.

B. Modern Techniques in Aphasia Research

In the later years of the 20th century, aphasia has undergone a revolutionary expansion of knowledge. First, new brain imaging techniques such as computed tomographic (CT) and magnetic resonance imaging (MRI) scans have permitted the study of brain lesions in living patients, simultaneously with behavioral studies. Functional brain imaging modalities such as positron emission tomography (PET) and single photon emission computed tomography (SPECT) allow the mapping of brain regions which are metabolically active or show increased blood flow during specific behavioral tasks in normal subjects or patients with aphasia. Finally, the language tasks themselves have been refined. Speech/language pathologists administer standardized test batteries to compare performance across subjects or in the same subject over time. Neuropsychologists and linguists have constructed language tasks to test specific steps in language processing at which deficits occur, thereby creating models of the language process. Finally, the study of epilepsy has brought the techniques of electrical stimulation of the brain into routine use in the mapping of functional cortical anatomy, used in planning surgical excision of epileptic foci. Stimulation of the language cortex in patients with normal language function has added to knowledge acquired by study of patients with aphasia. While confirming the general concepts of the localization of language functions derived from stroke patients, electrical stimulation has identified new language areas and has suggested that the tradi-

tional areas may be smaller and more variable than previously thought.

C. Handedness and Cerebral Dominance

As Broca observed, the vast majority of right-handed patients with aphasia have left hemisphere lesions, suggesting that the left hemisphere is dominant for language function. In general, at least 95% of right-handed patients and a majority of left-handed patients have relative left hemisphere dominance for language. Cerebral dominance can be determined definitely by Wada testing, in which sodium pentobarbital is injected into the internal carotid artery, thus temporarily "putting to sleep" the frontal, temporal, and parietal cortical areas of one hemisphere. Wada testing is carried out to determine whether an area of the brain can be surgically removed without producing aphasia. The dominance of language in the left hemisphere appears genetically programmed, since it is present even in illiterate people. Geschwind and Levitsky pointed out that most human brains have a larger superior temporal plane ("planum temporale") in the left hemisphere as compared to the right. Subsequent measurements using CT and MRI scans have shown similar asymmetries in living patients. The most reliable measurement is the occipital length, which is longer in the left hemisphere in most right-handed people. This asymmetry is present at birth, again indicating that the enlargement of the left language cortex is genetically programmed, rather than acquired through use in language function. Some as yet controversial studies have suggested that patients with atypical cortical asymmetries on CT scan may have abnormal language dominance and atypical recovery patterns after injury to the language cortex.

Occasional right-handed patients with acquired right hemisphere lesions develop aphasia, a phenomenon termed "crossed aphasia in dextrals." These patients presumably have atypical cerebral dominance, and some have atypical hemispheral asymmetries on CT scan. The specific "crossed aphasia" syndromes are frequently atypical, milder than would be expected with a lesion of similar size in the left hemisphere.

Aphasia in left-handed patients also differs from the typical syndromes of right-handed patients with aphasia secondary to left hemisphere lesions. More left-handed patients than right-handed patients develop aphasia after a stroke, regardless of the side of the stroke, suggesting that left-handed patients have some language representation in both cerebral hemispheres. Though aphasia is more common in left-handers, recovery may be better. Taken together, these findings imply that the language dominance of left-handed patients is less rigid than that of right-handers, and either hemisphere can subserve recovery of language function. Most left-handed aphasic patients in a recent series had typical aphasia syndromes, but two patients had large right hemisphere infarctions, with nonfluent aphasia but preserved comprehension. These patients appeared to have language expression arising from the right hemisphere, but language comprehension from the left. Most left-handers, like right-handers, have left hemisphere dominance for speech and language, but there may be separate loci of dominance for handedness, motor speech, and auditory comprehension. [*See* HANDEDNESS.]

D. Epidemiology and Etiologies of Aphasia

Aphasia has classically been described in association with focal brain lesions. The most common such lesion is stroke, long the leading etiology of aphasia in research studies. Stroke can be thought of as an "experiment of nature," in which one area of the brain is damaged, while the rest remains intact. Both cerebral infarctions, in which the brain is damaged by reduced blood flow, and hemorrhages, or bleeds into the brain, cause aphasia. Approximately 500,000 strokes occur annually in the United States. About 20% of stroke patients, or 100,000 persons each year, are rendered aphasic by stroke. The total prevalence of aphasic stroke victims in the United States approaches 1 million.

Head injury frequently disrupts discourse and produces other language impairments, which are admixed with general cognitive dysfunction. Penetrating brain injuries cause focal areas of damage which resemble strokes, except that the lesion locations are different, and the "remote effects" of swelling, increased intracranial pressure, and contrecoup injuries are greater with head injuries than with stroke.

Brain tumors, abscesses, and other mass lesions may also disrupt language. These syndromes typically develop gradually, unlike the abrupt onset of aphasia secondary to stroke or head injury. As in head injuries, there are remote effects related to mass effect and edema, in addition to the focal damage. For this reason, these disorders have been less useful than stroke in aphasia research. Focal brain damage from encephalitis and other infections also causes aphasia. The Herpes simplex virus produces an encephalitis with a predilection for the orbital frontal lobes and temporal lobes. Patients may present with fluent aphasia, as well as confusion, memory loss, seizures, and fever. Patients undergoing epilepsy surgery have also provided new knowledge of the language areas of the brain, as discussed earlier.

In addition to the language disorders associated with focal brain lesions, generalized brain diseases produce language disorders. Aphasia accompanies such diffuse syndromes as encephalopathies, or acute confusional states, and dementias, chronic syndromes of memory and cognitive loss. These syndromes will be discussed after the focal aphasias.

II. EVALUATION OF APHASIA

A. Bedside Evaluation

Language functions are tested informally at the bedside to arrive at a preliminary syndrome diagnosis of aphasia. Deliberate testing is carried out for spontaneous and automatic speech, naming, repetition, comprehension, reading, and writing. Physicians correlate these language tests with other findings of the neurological examination such as motor paralysis, visual field defects, and sensory loss to arrive at a localization of the responsible brain lesion. Brain imaging studies are then performed to confirm the diagnosis.

B. Standard Aphasia Batteries

In addition to the bedside language evaluations carried out by neurologists and other physicians, a number of standardized aphasia tests are available. Most are used by speech/language pathologists or neuropsychologists for documentation of the type and severity of aphasic deficits and of progress during recovery. Among the widely used batteries are the Boston Diagnostic Aphasia Examination (BDAE), its Canadian adaptation the Western Aphasia Battery (WAB), and the Porch Index of Communicative Ability (PICA). More specific language tests have also been developed by cognitive psychologists, linguists, and speech pathologists for research studies.

III. CLASSIFICATION OF APHASIAS

Aphasia experts have used a variety of terminologies and classification systems. This article utilizes the

TABLE I
Characteristics of Aphasic Syndromes

Syndrome	Fluency	Naming	Repetition	Comprehension	Reading	Writing
Broca	−	−	−	+	±	−
Wernicke	+	−	−	−	−	−
Global	−	−	−	−	−	−
Conduction	+	±	−	+	±	+
Anomic	+	−	+	+	+	+
TCM	−	+	+	+	+	±
TCS	+	−	+	−	−	−
Isolation	−	−	+	−	−	−

"Boston" aphasia classification, developed from classical neurology, as reflected both in the bedside examination and in the BDAE and WAB. Table I summarizes the language characteristics of the major aphasia syndromes.

A. Broca's Aphasia

Broca's aphasia was the first syndrome described, and the first correlated with a specific brain region. The syndrome involves reduced speech output, sometimes with complete mutism or hesitant, struggling efforts to produce single words or short phrases. Subjects utter the most important, meaningful words of a sentence, leaving out the small grammatical words. This speech pattern is called "telegraphic speech" or "agrammatism." Patients struggle to recall names, often stuttering on the initial phoneme ("tip-of-the-tongue" phenomenon). Repetition is hesitant, like spontaneous speech. Auditory comprehension is intact for simple conversations, but detailed testing reveals deficits, especially for complex grammatical relationships, which also cause difficulty in expressive speech. Reading is often less preserved than auditory comprehension. Writing is influenced by the usual association with right-sided paralysis, or hemiparesis, but Broca's aphasics cannot write well even with the nonparalyzed left hand, indicating the presence of an expressive language disorder. Interestingly, recent studies have found that patients write better with the paralyzed right arm, aided by a mechanical device resembling a skate. This technique removes the necessity of transmission of language information to right hemisphere motor centers.

The lesions of Broca's aphasia traditionally involve the inferior frontal gyrus, just anterior to the face area of the motor cortex (Fig. 1). Small lesions in this area are associated with excellent recovery of language function. Larger lesions, involving the frontoparietal cortices, produce an early global aphasia, or loss of all language function, followed by gradual evolution toward Broca's aphasia. Recent studies by the Boston VA group of CT scans in patients with nonfluent aphasia have established three lesion patterns: (1) lesions restricted to the lower motor cortex of the precentral gyrus produce only dysarthria and mild expressive disturbance; (2) those involving the more anterior frontal operculum (Brodmann areas 44 and 45) result in difficulty initiating speech without true language difficulty (see discussion of "transcortical motor aphasia," be-

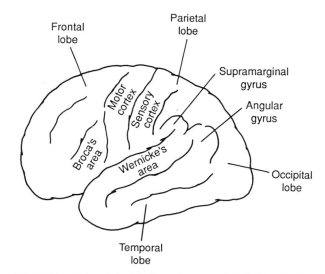

FIGURE 1   A drawing of the lateral surface of the left hemisphere of the brain. The approximate locations are given for Broca's area in the left inferior frontal convolution, Wernicke's area in the left superior temporal convolution, and the angular and supramarginal gyri of the inferior parietal lobule.

low); and (3) lesions combining these two lesion sites, plus the subcortical white matter and periventricular white matter cause deficits of Broca's aphasia. These additional aphasic disturbances may result from interruption of pathways from the posterior language areas. Damage to two subcortical areas, the rostral subcallosal fasciculus deep to Broca's area and the periventricular white matter adjacent to the body of the left lateral ventricle, appears necessary for the permanent loss of functional expressive speech.

1. Aphemia

The term "aphemia," which Broca originally chose for the syndrome now called Broca's aphasia, now refers to a transitory syndrome of muteness or nonfluent speech with initiation difficulty, dysarthria, and phoneme substitutions. Repetition is impaired in a similar way to spontaneous speech. Both auditory and reading comprehension are preserved, and writing is superior to speech. Most patients have right facial weakness, and some have right hemiparesis. Aphemia is more closely related to motor speech disorders than to aphasia, especially to the syndrome of apraxia of speech. Aphemia is associated with lesions of the lower motor cortex for the face in the precentral gyrus, with extension in some cases into the inferior frontal gyrus and underlying white matter.

B. Wernicke's Aphasia

In contrast to the nonfluent speech of the Broca's aphasic, the Wernicke's aphasic speaks fluently, with abnormal language content. Speech contains empty phrases, circumlocutions, neologisms (new words), and errors reflecting sound substitutions (literal or phonemic paraphasic errors) and word substitutions (verbal or semantic paraphasic errors). Sometimes no meaning at all is conveyed, despite fluent verbiage which sounds normal to a non-English-speaking listener. Naming often produces paraphasic utterances which have no obvious relationship to the target word, and repetition is also disturbed. Comprehension of spoken language is severely impaired. Reading is typically affected much as comprehension, but occasional cases show interesting dissociations between comprehension of auditory versus printed language. Spared reading comprehension may be important in allowing communication with the patient. Writing is often well formed, since patients with Wernicke's aphasia usu-

ally have no hemiparesis, but the written productions share the same lack of meaningful nouns and words as the speech output. Written language productions also contain misspellings; patients with mild Wernicke's aphasia may be detected most easily by analysis of writing.

Patients with Wernicke's aphasia typically have no motor or sensory deficits; some have a partial or complete loss of vision in the right visual field. As Wernicke originally demonstrated in 1874, the lesions of patients with Wernicke's aphasia typically involve the posterior portion of the left superior temporal gyrus. Recent studies have suggested that damage to the superior temporal gyrus is necessary for lasting loss of comprehension, while more temporary loss of comprehension can be seen with lesions elsewhere in the left temporal lobe or inferior parietal lobule. Reading may be more affected than auditory comprehension in Wernicke's aphasia secondary to left inferior parietal lesions.

1. Pure Word Deafness

Pure word deafness is a rare syndrome involving an inability to understand or repeat spoken language, in the absence of other language difficulty. The patient is not deaf to pure tones or to meaningful nonverbal noises such as animal sounds. Classically, the deficit occurs secondary to bilateral temporal lesions which disconnect the left hemisphere Wernicke's area from both auditory cortices. Destruction of the auditory cortices themselves causes cortical deafness or complex auditory disorders referred to as "auditory agnosia." A single left hemisphere lesion can also produce pure word deafness by disrupting bilateral auditory connections to Wernicke's area. Some patients with Wernicke's aphasia have more severe loss of auditory comprehension than of reading, resembling pure word deafness.

C. Global Aphasia

Global aphasia may be thought of as the sum of Broca's and Wernicke's aphasia. It is a loss of all six of the commonly tested language functions: spontaneous speech is mute or severely nonfluent, naming is reduced, repetition and comprehension are severely impaired, and the patient cannot read or write. Most such patients have large areas of damage in the left hemisphere and profound neurological deficits such as right hemiplegia, right-sided sensory loss, and right hemianopsia. When lesser degrees of deficit are seen across all language functions, the syndrome is called "mixed aphasia."

D. Conduction Aphasia

Conduction aphasia is an unusual but interesting language syndrome in which repetition is affected out of proportion to all other aphasic deficits. Patients speak relatively fluently, though some make frequent literal paraphasic errors and pause frequently for self-correction, giving the speech output a hesitant, choppy pattern. Naming is often impaired, but auditory comprehension is intact. Reading aloud and copying may be affected in a similar way to repetition.

Wernicke originally postulated that conduction aphasia might be caused by a lesion which did not damage either Wernicke's or Broca's area but disrupted the connections between the two areas. Geschwind rediscovered this explanation of conduction aphasia as a "disconnection syndrome." Brain lesions in conduction aphasia generally occur either in the left temporal lobe, without complete destruction of Wernicke's area, or in the left inferior parietal lobule. While the disconnection theory of conduction aphasia has remained popular, some investigators have favored a memory deficit for immediate storage of words.

E. Anomic Aphasia

As its name implies, anomic aphasia involves the selective loss of naming ability, out of proportion to other language deficits. Patients speak fluently, though with word-finding pauses and circumlocutions; repetition, auditory comprehension, reading, and writing are intact. This syndrome is less well correlated with focal pathology than the other classical aphasia syndromes, though anomic aphasia is seen with a focal lesion of the left temporal or inferior parietal region. Anomic aphasia is also common in the early stages of dementing conditions such as Alzheimer's disease.

F. Transcortical Aphasias

The transcortical aphasias were named to describe the sparing of the perisylvian language circuit, and thereby of repetition. The word "transcortical," as used by Lichtheim, implies that the damage is not to the language cortex itself, but to other areas of the brain which project onto the language cortex, referred to as the "area of concepts." The three transcortical aphasia syndromes share the sparing of repetition, despite marked aphasic deficits.

Transcortical motor aphasia is similar to Broca's aphasia, in that the patients speak nonfluently, often with long pauses before utterances and single word or whispered replies to questions. Auditory comprehension is usually quite good. These patients, unlike Broca's aphasics, can repeat long sentences, even with complex grammatical constructions. The lesions of transcortical motor aphasia spare Broca's area itself but involve adjacent portions of the left frontal cortex or subcortical white matter.

Transcortical sensory aphasia resembles Wernicke's aphasia in fluent, paraphasic speech and poor auditory comprehension, but these patients can repeat normally. The lesions are located posteriorly, in the left temporo-occipital confluence. This syndrome is also seen in patients with Alzheimer's disease, in later stages of the disease than anomic aphasia.

Mixed transcortical aphasia, also called the "syndrome of the isolation of the speech area," is a syndrome resembling global aphasia except for the sparing of repetition, which may even be excessive or palilalic. These patients cannot speak spontaneously or comprehend spoken or written language, but they can repeat fluently. Some patients tend to complete utterances left incomplete, as in poetry lines or common idioms. Geschwind and colleagues reported the case of a young woman who had extensive, bihemispheral damage from carbon monoxide poisoning, sparing the perisylvian language circuit. This patient could even memorize new lyrics to songs which had not been popular before her illness, implying that the medial temporal lobe memory circuit was also spared. Mixed transcortical aphasia has also been reported in patients with severe dementia.

G. Subcortical Aphasias

Unlike all of the aphasia syndromes described to this point, subcortical aphasias are defined more by the location of the responsible brain lesion than by the language characteristics of the aphasia. While aphasia is usually thought of as a cortical phenomenon, several patterns of aphasia with subcortical lesions have been described, all within the past few years. First, lesions of the left thalamus have been shown to cause a fluent aphasia, usually with better comprehension and repetition as compared to Wernicke's aphasia. A "dichotomous state" has been described, in which the patient may speak clearly while awake, but drift into incomprehensible, paraphasic speech when sleepy. The thalamus has a role in activating the language cortex; Luria has referred to thalamic aphasia as a "quasi-aphasic disturbance of vigilance."

Ischemic lesions of the basal ganglia and subcortical white matter also cause aphasia. Lesions of the head of the caudate, anterior limb of internal capsule, and anterior putamen produce a nonfluent aphasia with dysarthria. In comparison to Broca's aphasics, these patients often have longer phrase length and better comprehension and repetition. Lesions which extend posteriorly in the basal ganglia and laterally into the deep temporal lobe white matter can cause syndromes resembling global and Wernicke's aphasia. Similar aphasias are seen with hemorrhages into the basal ganglia, but deficits tend to be more severe because of pressure effects on surrounding structures and on the overlying language cortex.

H. Alexias

Alexia with agraphia is an acquired illiteracy in which patients cannot read or write, but spoken language, repetition, naming, and auditory comprehension remain intact. In fact, most patients with this syndrome have a mild fluent aphasia, and the syndrome overlaps with Wernicke's aphasia. The lesion involves the inferior parietal region, particularly the angular gyrus.

Pure alexia without agraphia is a linguistic blindfolding. Patients cannot read but speak normally and understand spoken language, even when words are dictated in spelled form. These patients can write, but they cannot read their own written productions, a striking feature of the disorder. Naming for objects is usually preserved, but patients may be unable to name colors. They have not lost the concept of color names, as shown by their ability to name the usual colors of common objects such as bananas or apples, but they cannot name a perceived color. In addition, they usually have short-term memory loss and a right visual field defect. Pure alexia is associated with a lesion of the left occipital cortex, usually also involving the splenium of the corpus callosum. This is a classical disconnection syndrome, as originally postulated by the French physician Dejerine in 1891. The nondamaged right occipital cortex can subserve vision in the left visual field, but visual language and

color information cannot be accessed by the left hemisphere language cortex. Some recent investigators have pointed to a disturbance of visual short-term memory as a factor in pure alexia. As the patient improves, reading of single letters may return, and printed words can then be read letter by letter; an alternate name for the syndrome is "letter-by-letter" alexia.

Many patients with aphasia have associated reading disturbance, termed "aphasic alexia." The "third alexia" syndrome of Broca's aphasia, named by Benson to follow the syndromes of alexia with and without agraphia, can vary from a mild alexia related to difficult syntactic material to a severe alexia, in which patients can read only by recognition of a few familiar words. Wernicke's aphasics often have deficits in reading and writing similar to the syndrome of alexia with agraphia, though patients have been described with more partial, selective deficits.

In recent years, neurolinguists and cognitive psychologists such as Marshall, Newcombe, and Coltheart have divided alexias according to the specific stages in the reading process which go awry (Fig. 2). Four patterns of alexia (or "dyslexia," as these investigators often call it) have been recognized: letter-by-letter, deep, phonological, and surface dys-

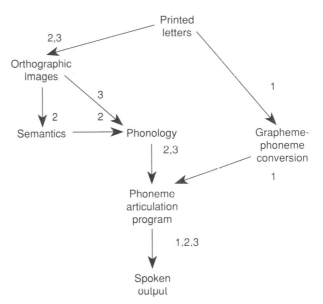

FIGURE 2 Three separate routes to reading. (1) The grapheme–phoneme conversion system used in learning reading. This is the only route available in surface dyslexia. (2) Reading only from recognizing the meaning of familiar words, the only route available in deep dyslexia. (3) A direct conversion of words to sounds, available in phonological dyslexia.

lexia (Table II). Letter-by-letter dyslexia is equivalent to pure alexia without agraphia, while the other three patterns are usually seen with aphasia.

Deep dyslexia involves several distinctive features: intact reading of familiar words, inability to read nonsense syllables or nonwords, semantic and visual errors in reading aloud, and pronounced effects of word frequency, word imageability, and word class. Imageable words are read more accurately than abstract words, while nouns and verbs are read better than adjectives, adverbs, and prepositions. Word reading is not much affected by word length or by regularity of spelling; for example, a patient might be able to read "be" but not "B," and "ambulance" but not "am." Examples of semantic errors are "jail" for "prison" and "soccer" for "football"; examples of visual errors are "perform" for "perfume" and "banish" for "blush." Deep dyslexia involves the loss of reading by the "phonological" or grapheme-to-phoneme conversion route, with residual reading involving only recognition of familiar words (route 2 in Fig. 2). Most cases have severe aphasia, with extensive left frontal and parietal damage. The residual reading of patients with deep dyslexia may involve the right hemisphere.

Phonological dyslexia is similar to deep dyslexia, except that single content words are read in a nearly normal fashion, and semantic errors are rare. As in deep dyslexia, reading of nonwords is poor. Patients sometimes read words without access to meaning. The syndrome of phonological dyslexia, like deep dyslexia, involves the loss of grapheme-to-phoneme conversion. In deep dyslexia, only words whose meaning is recognized can be read aloud; only a semantics-to-phonology reading route can operate.

In phonological dyslexia, words can also be read via a lexical–phonological route (route 3 in Fig. 2). Only the nonlexical–phonological route, by which nonwords must be read, is inoperative. Most patients with phonological alexia have severe, nonfluent aphasia.

In surface dyslexia, subjects can read laboriously by grapheme–phoneme conversion, but they cannot recognize words at a glance. They can read nonsense syllables but not words of irregular spelling, such as "yacht" or "colonel." Their errors tend to be phonological rather than semantic or visual; an example would be to pronounce "pint" as if it rhymed with "lint." Reading in these patients is accomplished without access to semantics until the word is pronounced. Individual graphemes are sounded out by the most common way they are pronounced in the language, producing errors for both irregularly spelled words and regular words which have atypical pronunciations. For example, a surface dyslexic might pronounce "rough" and "though" alike. Surface dyslexia represents a syndrome in which only one route of reading, the grapheme–phoneme route, is operative (route 1 in Fig. 2). Patients cannot read words without pronouncing their component graphemes.

I. Agraphias

Like reading, writing may be affected either in isolation ("pure agraphia") or in association with aphasia ("aphasic agraphia"). In addition, writing can be deranged by motor disorders, by visuospatial or constructional impairments, and by apraxia. Isolated agraphia has been described with left frontal and occasionally left parietal lesions. In the past, a cortical writing center called "Exner's area" was postulated, just above Broca's area. The existence of a specific writing area has not been supported, however, either by stroke cases or by electrical stimulation studies; stimulation of Broca's area interferes with writing, while excitation of other frontal regions does not produce agraphia without disturbing speech.

Agraphias have also been analyzed in similar ways to the alexias. A syndrome of "phonological agraphia" has been described in which patients cannot convert speech sounds (phonemes) into letters (graphemes). These patients cannot write pronounceable nonsense words but can write familiar words, even when irregular in spelling. Reported cases have been relatively few, with limited neuro-

TABLE II

Characteristics of Alexic Syndromes

Characteristic	Deep dyslexia	Phonological dyslexia	Letter-by-letter dyslexia	Surface dyslexia
Nonwords	−	−	−	+
Word class effect	+	+	−	−
Imageability	+	−	−	−
Word length	−	−	+	+
Regular spelling	−	−	−	+

After Patterson (1981). Neuropsychological approaches to the study of reading. *Br. J. Psychiatry* **72**, 151–174.

anatomic data, but some cases have had lesions of the supramarginal gyrus. Most patients have had associated aphasia, but of varied types. "Deep" dysgraphia is similar to phonological agraphia, but with a marked word class effect.

A "lexical agraphia" syndrome, also called "surface agraphia," has also been described. Patients can write regularly spelled words and pronounceable nonsense words, but not irregularly spelled words. These patients have intact phoneme–grapheme conversion but cannot write by a whole word, or "lexical" strategy. Lesions have been reported in the posterior angular gyrus and occipitotemporal gyrus, with one case of a left precentral gyrus lesion. [*See* AGRAPHIA.]

IV. RECOVERY OF APHASIA

Patients with aphasia from acute disorders such as stroke generally show spontaneous improvement over the first several months. The prevailing opinion has been that this improvement is maximal during the first 3 months, but global aphasics may actually improve more in the second 6 months than the first. The aphasia type often changes during this improvement; global aphasia often evolves into Broca's aphasia, and Wernicke's aphasia may evolve into conduction or anomic aphasia. The neuroanatomical correlates of language recovery appear to involve the taking over of language functions by adjacent cortical areas of the left hemisphere, and the right hemisphere may also participate. Studies of activation of language areas by PET and SPECT scanning techniques promise to advance our understanding of the neuroanatomy of language recovery.

Speech therapy, carried out by trained speech/ language pathologists, seeks to facilitate improvement in language function by a variety of techniques. Repetitive exercises are carried out to promote better articulation, and matching and vocabulary tasks are designed to improve receptive language. New techniques in speech therapy include melodic intonation therapy, which attempts to involve the right hemisphere in speech production through the use of melody, and computer techniques originally developed for primate communication. Patients who cannot speak can learn to produce major nouns and verbs and associate them into simple phrases or sentences. A variety of augmentative devices are also available to help make language outputs available to others via printers or voice simulators. Therapy techniques are now chosen based on the patient's aphasia test results, and some investigators are using brain imaging studies to predict which techniques are likely to succeed. While many speech therapy techniques have been developed empirically, large, randomized trials have clearly indicated that patients who undergo formal speech therapy function better than untreated patients.

A new area of development in language rehabilitation is the use of pharmacologic agents to improve speech. Albert and colleagues have shown that the dopaminergic drug bromocriptine is useful in increasing spontaneous speech output in transcortical motor aphasia. Use of stimulant drugs may also have a place in rehabilitation.

V. MISCELLANEOUS TOPICS IN APHASIA

A. Aphasia in Polyglots

Aphasia in patients who speak more than one language ("polyglots") has been the subject of considerable interest. In 1895, Pitres postulated that the language used most before the onset of aphasia would be the first to recover. In contemporary terms, the language in which the patient works every day, and in which hospital personnel and therapists speak, is likely to recover faster and better. Ribot, in 1906, predicted that the first-learned or native language would be the most resistant to later brain injury. These two rules are now known as Pitres' and Ribot's laws. Other investigators have considered both the time of acquisition and the relative skill level in each language. Thus, Canadians who acquired French and English simultaneously in growing up ("compound bilinguals") have more congruent language involvement than those who learned one language later than the other ("coordinate bilinguals"). In recent studies, coordinate bilinguals have even developed different aphasia syndromes in two languages; for example an Israeli patient was globally aphasic in Hebrew but had only a mild anomic aphasia in Russian. In general, the language used more extensively before the brain injury, as Pitres originally postulated, appears to be less disturbed than the less used language, regardless of which was learned first.

B. Aphasia in Acute Confusional States and Dementias

Patients who develop acute delirium or confusion frequently utter meaningless or nonsensical phrases.

In most cases this involves abnormal thought, or language content, rather than abnormal language, but some patients produce fluent, paraphasic speech and even neologisms. Naming is frequently disturbed in acute confusional states. Comprehension is at least partially preserved, if the patient's attention and memory can be entrained to the task. Many delirious patients have abnormal writing.

Patients with dementing diseases such as Alzheimer's disease frequently demonstrate abnormal language functions. The dementia of Alzheimer's disease usually begins with memory loss, and among the earliest symptoms is a loss of memory for names. Recollection of proper names and rapid generation of series of names are very sensitive to aging and dementia. For example, patients with early dementia have marked difficulty with the "animal naming" subtest of the BDAE, which requires the subject to name as many animals as possible in one minute. Articulation, repetition, and auditory comprehension tend to remain intact into later stages of dementia. At an early stage, an Alzheimer's disease patient often shows the profile of anomic aphasia. As the disease advances, reading and writing deteriorate, and auditory comprehension begins to decline. Repetition and articulatory fluency remain preserved, and the patient may then show the language profile of transcortical sensory aphasia. The content of expressive speech is also severely impoverished, devoid of abstract content. Ultimately, language expression becomes limited almost to statements of biological need. Some patients become mute in late stages, resembling global aphasia, while others repeat fluently. [See ALZHEIMER'S DISEASE; DEMENTIA.]

Alzheimer's disease is a "diffuse" degeneration of the cerebral cortex, but pathological studies indicate early involvement of the association cortex, particularly of the parietal and later the frontal lobes. Medial temporal structures such as the hippocampus, which are important to memory function, and medial forebrain structures such as the nucleus basalis, also show neuronal loss and senile plaques.

Other dementing diseases also produce language disorders. Pick's disease is a lobar atrophy involving predominantly the frontal and temporal cortices. Some cases begin with "frontal" syndromes of behavioral abnormality, others have isolated aphasia at onset. Creutzfeldt-Jakob disease is a more rapidly progressive dementia, often with myoclonus and seizures, secondary to a transmissible agent or "prion." Aphasia can precede or accompany other symptoms of this disease. After Alzheimer's disease, the most common cause of dementia is multi-infarct or vascular dementia. The specific features depend on the size and location of the cerebral infarcts, but many patients manifest aphasia.

Primary progressive aphasia is a rare syndrome in which middle aged or elderly patients show progressive loss of language functions suggestive of a focal aphasia. Some cases have been followed for several years, with steadily worsening language function, but no significant memory loss or generalized dementia. Brain imaging studies show only a lobar atrophy. Recent PET studies have consistently shown left temporal hypometabolism, with more advanced cases showing more widespread metabolic changes. While a specific degenerative disease of the frontotemporal language cortex has been suspected, postmortem studies have included a variety of pathologies including Alzheimer's and Pick's diseases, nonspecific neuronal loss with microvacuolation of the cortex, Creutzfeldt-Jakob disease, and neuronal achromasia.

C. Language and the Right Hemisphere

While the right hemisphere has traditionally been called the "minor" hemisphere because of its lack of language dominance, recent studies have shown that patients with right hemisphere disease have significant problems with verbal communication. While they can produce and understand appropriate words and sentences, patients with right hemisphere lesions speak monotonously, lacking the emotional tone or "prosody" which makes normal language colorful. These patients lose the ability to understand emotional tone, connotation, irony, sarcasm, satire, and humor, responding only to the literal meaning of the words; they understand what is said, but not how it is said. The right hemisphere may have a similar organization to the left in terms of speech prosody; frontal lesions disturb production of prosodic speech, while temporal lesions disturb comprehension of emotional tone. Right hemisphere stroke patients have difficulty even with nonemotional aspects of prosody, such as placement of emphasis within sentences or inflections, as in the difference between a statement and a question. Despite their intact language skills, these patients are at a great disadvantage in normal human communication.

Aside from these effects of right hemisphere disease, the right hemisphere appears to have considerable linguistic ability. Patients with surgical commissurotomy, or section of the corpus callosum, are able to recognize words flashed in the left visual field, or presented in tactile fashion to the left hand. They can perform simple matching tests between words or short phrases which are semantically related. The mystery about these abilities is the failure of patients with left hemisphere lesions and global aphasia to perform similar tasks, despite the presence of an intact right hemisphere. It is possible that the corpus callosum contains fiber tracts which inhibit the right hemisphere from expressing its full language capability. If such systems could be therapeutically disrupted, the recovery of aphasia might be significantly enhanced.

VI. CONCLUSION

The subject of aphasia is a rich field. Language was the first higher function to be analyzed in terms of specific localization of brain lesions, and it remains the best studied and understood of all of the cognitive functions. Increased understanding of both normal language and aphasia is likely to emerge from new studies combining specific language testing measures with precise neuroanatomic techniques such as magnetic resonance imaging and functional activation methodologies such as positron emission tomography. The result should be not only a better

knowledge of language and the brain, but also improved therapies for patients afflicted with aphasia.

Bibliography

Albert, M. L., Bachman, D. L., Morgan, A., and Helm-Estabrooks, N. (1988). Pharmacotherapy for aphasia. *Neurology* **38**, 877.

Alexander, M. P., and Benson, D. F. (1993). The aphasias and related disturbances. In "Clinical Neurology" (Joynt, R. J., Ed.), Vol. 1. J. B. Lippincott, Philadelphia.

Faber-Langendoen, K., Morris, J. C., Knesevich, J. W., LaBarge, E., Miller, J. P., and Berg, L. (1988). Aphasia in senile dementia of the Alzheimer type. *Ann. Neurol.* **23**, 365.

Kirshner, H. S. (1986). "Behavioral Neurology: A Practical Approach." Churchill Livingstone, New York.

Kirshner, H. S. (in press). "Handbook of Neurological Speech and Language Disorders." Marcel Dekker, New York.

Naeser, M. A., Palumbo, C. L., Helm-Estabrooks, N., Stiassny-Eder, D., and Albert, M. L. (1989). Severe nonfluency in aphasia. Role of the medial subcallosal fasciculus and other white matter pathways in recovery of spontaneous speech. *Brain* **112**, 1.

Posner, M. I., Petersen, S. E., Fox, P. T., and Raichle, M. E. (1988). Localization of cognitive operations in the human brain. *Science* **240**, 1627–1631.

Sarno, M. T. (1991). "Acquired Aphasia," 2nd ed. Academic Press, San Diego.

Weintraub, S., Rubin, N. P., and Mesulam, M. (1990). Primary progressive aphasia: Longitudinal course, neuropsychological profile, and language features. *Arch. Neurol.* **47**, 1329.

Wertz, R. T., Weiss, D. G., Aten, L. J., Brookshire, R. H., Garcia-Bunuel, L., Holland, A. L., Kurtzke, J. F., Greenbaum, H., Marshall, R., Vogel, D., Carter, J., Barnes, N., and Goodman, R. (1986). Comparison of clinic, home and deferred language treatment for aphasia: A VA cooperative study. *Arch. Neurol.* **43**, 653.

APPETITE

Nori Geary

Cornell University Medical College

Glossary

Anorexia Reductions in appetite and food intake due to abnormal interference with physiological hunger or satiety processes.

Appetite Subjective experiences and behaviors associated with the urge to eat; appetite is sometimes limited to the desire to eat aroused by anticipation of sensory pleasure (cf., hunger). Appetite and hunger are referred to in psychological theory as intervening variables because they are not directly observable quantities, but must be inferred indirectly.

Flavor Olfactory, gustatory, and tactile responses to food during ingestion, including both a discriminative dimension (i.e., sensory intensity and quality) and a hedonic dimension; the sensory dimension appears essentially innate and invariable, whereas the hedonic dimension is mainly learned and is affected by physiological, contextual, and experiential variables.

Food Object of appetite, whether macronutrient, micronutrient, or nonnutritive material, in pure or combined forms.

Food reward Capacity of food to elicit positive hedonic experiences, stimulate continued ingestion, and reinforce learning.

Hedonics Psychology of pleasant and unpleasant subjective states and the behaviors associated with them.

Hunger Synonym for appetite; sometimes limited to urges to eat elicited by the physiological consequences of nutrient depletion or of body weight loss (homeostatic or regulatory motivation).

Palatability The hedonic aspect of flavor that affects liking, choice, or ingestion of food.

Postprandial satiety Subjective state and associated behaviors that replace appetite as a consequence of eating; in common, but not scientific, usage, satiety often includes the feeling of surfeit caused by gluttony.

Specific appetite An urge to eat a particular nutrient or foods whose flavors mark the nutrient's presence; specific appetites result from nutritional shortcomings.

APPETITE, in particular the appetite for food, is the focus of intensive study in experimental and clinical psychology, physiology, neuroscience, and medicine. Because no single theoretical or operational definition adequately fits the variety of ways in which the concept of appetite is used in these disciplines, its common English definition remains the most appropriate. Appetite is the desire to eat. Appetite, or aspects of it, are reflected both in subjective experience and in food-related behaviors. This article outlines current understanding of the physiological psychology of normal appetite, based on empirical studies of humans and animals. Sources covering clinical issues in human appetite are included in the Bibliography.

I. SUBJECTIVE AND BEHAVIORAL ASPECTS

A. Perception of Appetite

Although humans are used to describing subjective experiences verbally, beyond merely indicating the presence of a certain state (i.e., "I'm hungry"), such reports are usually too imprecise to be of scientific value. Fortunately, a number of psychophysical techniques have been developed that permit quantification and measurement of subjective states. The visual analogue scale is one common psychophysical technique. Subjects are asked to judge their appetite by placing a mark on a standard length line, often about 10 cm, which is usually appropriately anchored (e.g., by labeling one end "most possible" and the other end "not at all"). Responses are then measured and analyzed quantitatively. This kind of technique can be used to rate the intensity of hunger, the appetite for particular foods (which may be simply named or actually tasted), and many other subjective aspects of appetite. Psychophysical techniques minimize, but cannot eliminate, the role of language in the analysis of human subjective experience. Therefore, because people use words in different ways, appetite research usually employs several different psychophysical tests.

The subjective experience of appetite includes sensations, moods, and dispositions. For example, the sensations usually labeled gastric emptiness and fullness are associated with appetite (the actual origins of these sensations, however, are unknown). The moods or emotions of restlessness and irritability often accompany hunger, whereas satiety may be associated with relaxation and a general sense of satisfaction. Finally, dispositions refer to a person's perceived urge or willingness to eat. This is the aspect of subjective experience which seems closest to the psychological construct of motivation. It is important to note that the urge to eat may vary depending on the specific food in question. One may be simultaneously sated for some foods and hungry for others. For example, if unexpectedly offered a favorite dessert after having finished a meal to satisfaction, most people can begin again with enthusiasm. [*See* MOTIVATION.]

B. Eating Behavior

The disposition to eat can be inferred from observations of behavior as well as from reports of perceptions. Indeed, because eating behaviors do not appear to mirror the subjective experience of appetite in a straightforward way, observations of eating behavior are the most important data for the study of human appetite. Behavioral observations are also, of course, the only possibility for study of appetite in animals.

In humans and most animal species, eating is organized into well-defined bouts that we call meals. Thus, the central problems in the science of appetite are understanding what controls the initiation of

meals, the choice of foods to be consumed, and the amount consumed during meals. For this reason, appetite is reviewed here in relation to the physiological control of meals in humans and animals.

The psychological constructs of hunger and satiety provide useful heuristics for the analysis of meals. As shown in Figure 1, hunger increases during the interval between meals and leads to food seeking, food selection, and meal initiation. Food-seeking behavior is often referred to as the *appetitive phase* of the motivation to eat and the actual ingestion of food as the *consummatory phase*. When eating begins, ingestion elicits negative feedback, or satiating, stimuli that contribute to the end of the meal and the inhibition of eating during the subsequent intermeal interval. Satiety signals appear to arise from a variety of food stimuli that occur between the acceptance of food in the mouth and the metabolic utilization of absorbed nutrients.

Food ingestion also elicits positive feedback, or rewarding, stimuli. Food stimuli are rewarding in three ways. First, they elicit pleasure. Second, they elicit positive feedback signals that help maintain ingestive behavior and increase meal size. Preferred flavors are the most obvious example of these aspects of food reward. According to drive reduction theories of motivation, hunger is an aversive state that is escaped by eating. Given that eating is a pleasure, however, meals may be equally well initiated solely by the urge to enjoy the rewards of eating. The third way in which food is rewarding is that eating reinforces the learning of responses associated with obtaining food.

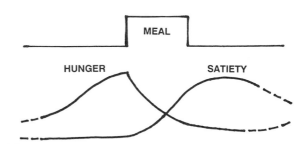

FIGURE 1   Schematic diagram of the intensity of hypothetical hunger and satiety processes in relation to a meal. Hunger increases during the intermeal interval until a meal is initiated, and then decreases. Satiety is at a low level at meal onset and increases during the meal. The combination of decreased hunger and increased satiety ends the meal and inhibits feeding through the subsequent intermeal interval. These processes represent hypothetical integrated values rather than the strengths of particular hunger and satiety signals or the subjective experiences of hunger and satiety. Food reward processes, not shown, also contribute to the control of feeding.

The differentiation of particular controls of appetite as hunger, reward, or satiety signals is a theoretical convenience which awaits empirical verification. For example, it is often supposed that hunger signals cause meal initiation, whereas satiety signals decrease meal size. But alternative conceptions have not been tested. So, for example, it is possible that signals that terminate meals decay in strength during the intermeal interval and that this release from inhibition, rather than a separate hunger signal, causes initiation of the next meal. That the subjective experiences of hunger and satiety seem to differ qualitatively is sometimes taken as evidence that the two processes are fundamentally different. This argument is faulty because qualitatively different subjective states can arise from a single neural process. The hues blue and yellow, for example, are psychological primaries that differ qualitatively and cannot be perceived simultaneously; nevertheless, they apparently originate from a single neural mechanism.

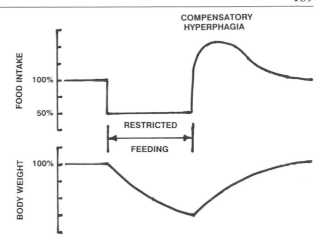

FIGURE 2 Compensatory hypophagia reveals that control of food intake contributes to the regulation of energy balance and body weight. Rats normally maintain stable body weights (100%). If they are restricted to a fraction of their normal daily food intake, body weight drops. When they are then again allowed free access to food, daily food intake increases above the usual level until body weight returns to its normal level.

C. The Meal and the Scale

Food is the organism's source of metabolic energy (i.e., calories). Thus, because ingested energy must be either expended or stored, appetite is inescapably linked to growth, adiposity, and body weight. The nearly constant level of body weight maintained by most adults suggests that energy balance is regulated as a homeostatic variable, as, for example, is body temperature. Several types of experiments in animals and humans prove that energy balance is indeed regulated and that appetite is actively controlled to help achieve this regulation. Figure 2 diagrams one such demonstration, the compensatory hyperphagia that follows forced weight loss. Other examples include compensatory hypophagia after weight gain and compensatory adjustments in food intake in response to alterations of the caloric density of the diet. Because feeding occurs as meals, the feedback signals related to energy balance and body weight must have access to the mechanisms controlling individual meals. At least in rats, these compensatory effects appear to be achieved primarily through changes in the number of meals rather than in meal size. Some possible mechanisms of this control are discussed below. Unfortunately, not all controls of appetite are regulatory, and nonregulatory controls sometimes overwhelm the regulatory controls. For example, the continuous availability of very palatable foods can disrupt regulation. Laboratory animals eat more and gain weight when a variety of palatable foods is available. Easy access to palatable foods may well contribute to the increasing incidence of overweight in developed societies in this century. [*See* HOMEOSTASIS.]

II. FOOD SELECTION

A. The Nature of Flavor

Flavor is an exceedingly complex perception. Gustatory (taste), olfactory, tactile, and thermal sensory signals elicited by food all typically contribute to flavor. Nociceptive (pain) signals, for example, during ingestion of chili pepper, and proprioceptive (movement) signals elicited by chewing or swallowing may also contribute. Further, flavor, especially its gustatory and olfactory components, elicits a prominent hedonic response. The hedonic dimension of flavor includes a dispositional component, i.e., a more or less strong urge to ingest or reject the stimulus. This hedonic–motivational dimension is weak or absent in other sensory modalities, with the exception of nociception.

For most foods, olfaction provides the dominant component of flavor. Its importance is illustrated by the consequences of anosmia (loss of the sense of smell). In complete anosmia, which is a relatively common neurological trauma, flavor perception is impoverished. Food may become so aversively monotonous that appetite is reduced, and patients have difficulty maintaining proper nutrition. The transient partial anosmia accompanying head colds is a familiar, if less severe, example. [*See* SENSE OF SMELL.]

Although some flavor stimuli have innately determined hedonic values, most likes and dislikes are learned. Thus, food preferences and food reward are shaped in large part by individual experience. Further, some forms of this learning apparently involve unique biological adaptations that are accessible only to flavor stimuli and ingestive behavior. Flavor stimuli, especially olfactory stimuli, appear to have unusual access to the brain's limbic memory systems. Presumably as a result, odor memories are more resistant to interference and evoke more immediate and powerful emotional responses than other types of memory. Because of importance of learning in food preference and reward, subsequent sections consider innate and learned mechanisms separately. [*See* LIMBIC SYSTEM.]

B. Innate Mechanisms

Like of sweet tastes and dislike of bitter and sour tastes are probably the strongest innate flavor preferences. Neonates respond to sweet foods with positive facial expressions and consume them enthusiastically, as do animals with no prior experience with sweetness. Conversely, bitter and sour tastes elicit rejection and negative facial expressions. The evolution of these preferences may have resulted from the association of sweet tastes with safe, nutritious foods such as ripe fruits and of bitter tastes with foods containing alkaloids or other toxins. In contrast to these innate preferences, preferences for olfactory stimuli, even the odors of feces or putrefication, appear learned. [*See* TASTE.]

More is known about the responses to purified simple food stimuli than to the complex flavors of foods that humans typically eat. This is unfortunate because, for example, the hedonics of pure sugar solutions do not accurately predict the hedonics of the same sugar concentrations in real foods.

C. Learned Mechanisms

1. Culture

Culture is an extremely important influence on human food preferences and food selection. People tend to eat the foods that they are raised on, perhaps due in part to social learning and in part because mere exposure to food stimuli may increase preference for them. As a result, culture determines what is considered an acceptable food (e.g., insects), how frequently foods are eaten (e.g., how often meat is eaten), how foods are processed (e.g., whether foods are eaten raw), and the particular flavor combinations characteristic of various cuisines (e.g., Hungarian paprika, Italian garlic, French herbs).

Cultural determinants of eating can be of sufficient potency to override strong biological biases (e.g., the innate dislikes of bitter or spicy food). This again emphasizes the importance of learning in food selection and reward. Dining rituals, for example, may classically condition food preferences. If some nutrient-rich foods are flavored in characteristic ways, the pleasantness of satiety may be associated with those flavors and, thus, increase liking and preference for any similarly flavored food. Conditioned flavor preferences of this kind have been demonstrated in animals by pairing flavors with intragastric or intravenous administration of nutrients. A similar mechanism may contribute to the perpetuation of food processing practices that result in improved nutrition, such as the frequent combination of beans and rice in Hispanic cuisine, which results in an amino acid pattern that is more biologically useful than that of either food alone.

2. Dietary Restraint

Although animals whose body weight has been experimentally increased voluntarily restrain their food intake until body weight is renormalized, only humans appear to deny hunger in the absence of physiological reasons. Social and cultural pressures have made preoccupation with body image prevalent. This in turn may affect food attitudes and habits. "Cognitive restraint" is indicated by positive responses in personality inventories to statements such as "I count calories," or "I consciously hold back at meals." Many overweight people and normal-weight people are restrained eaters. The characteristic attitudes of these people correlate with unusual eating patterns. For example, restrained eaters may actually eat *more* than unrestrained eaters in situations that temporarily dissolve restraint. Thus, although unrestrained eaters reduce intake after consuming experimental food preloads, restrained eaters may eat more than they usually do without preloads. Perhaps the restrained eater, feeling his or her self-imposed limit is exceeded by the preload, temporarily gives up any further attempt at dieting. The restrained eating phenomenon suggests that chronic dieting is a psychological stressor that reduces people's capacity to deal with the normal demands of self-regulation. Severe restraint may facilitate the development of serious eating disorders or influence psychological functioning in noneating contexts. According to some measures, dieters are more emotionally reactive, anxious, and depressed than nondieters, although whether this is an effect of dieting remains unclear.

3. Conditioned Taste Preferences and Aversions

If food ingestion, especially of novel foods, is followed by illness, a strong aversion to the flavor of the food often develops. This associative process appears to be a unique form of classical conditioning in which an arbitrary flavor is a conditional stimulus that is paired with the unconditional stimulus of illness. The evidence that animals have a special preparedness for conditioned taste aversion learning is that learning occurs with only a limited range of conditional stimuli (taste and odor are most effective in mammals, food color may be more effective in some birds), that the conditioning occurs exceptionally rapidly (one pairing usually suffices, in comparison to scores of trials in typical classical conditioning paradigms), that conditioning occurs despite the unusually long interval between exposure to the flavor and occurrence of illness (hours rather than seconds), and that conditioning extinguishes very slowly. The rapidity of acquisition and the intensity of the avoidance differentiate conditioned taste aversions from learned preferences. [See CLASSICAL CONDITIONING.]

Food dislikes based on conditioned taste aversions may be distinguished from foods rejected because they are known to be dangerous. Only taste aversions render flavors unpleasant and disliked. People often continue to like foods that they know to be dangerous because they previously elicited headaches, allergic reactions, or even some types of lower intestinal cramps (including those suffered by lactose-intolerant people).

Postingestive consequences of eating can also produce conditioned taste preferences. For example, rats learn to prefer flavors that have been associated with intragastric delivery of fat or carbohydrate.

Social influences can markedly affect taste aversion learning in rats. Rats may develop conditioned taste aversions more readily if they are allowed to interact with other rats that have previously acquired the aversion and may fail to develop the aversion entirely if exposed to other rats that have safely eaten the conditional stimulus. This interesting form of social learning appears to depend on communication mediated by olfactory signals in the animals' breaths. Whether analogous mechanisms exist in humans is not yet clear. Taste aversions presumably do help humans avoid toxins. They probably also decrease the preference for perfectly nutritious foods whose consumption is linked by chance to illness, as happens, for example, in cancer patients undergoing chemotherapy.

4. Specific Appetites

Depletion of certain nutrients that are required for the maintenance of homeostasis, for example, calcium loss during lactation, can elicit nutrient-specific appetites that facilitate increased consumption of the nutrient. The specific appetite for sodium is dramatic. Animals and humans normally find dilute concentrations of salt (sodium chloride) palatable, but dislike extremely salty foods. Sodium-deficient animals or people, however, avidly ingest salty foods or even pure salt. Sodium appetite is innate. It occurs during the first episode of sodium depletion, even in animals that have never had the opportunity to ingest sodium. During salt appetite, the normal preference for dilute rather than strong salt solutions is reversed. This palatability shift appears to result from changes in the way the brain processes salt gustatory stimuli rather than from a change in the response of salt taste receptors. This change in the brain's response is apparently caused by the increases in blood levels of the hormones aldosterone and angiotensin II which follow sodium depletion. Increases in one hormone in the absence of increases in the other fail to elicit salt appetite, but their simultaneous action elicits the complete response. In endocrinological terms, salt appetite is both an *activational effect* of the hormones, because it occurs transiently as a result of acute changes in hormone levels, and an *organizational effect*, because the hormones elicit a lasting change in the brain's responsiveness to subsequent episodes of salt depletions.

Specific appetites exist for several, but not all, micronutrients. Most specific appetites, however, differ from salt appetite in that the flavor of the needed nutrient is not innately recognized. Rather, animals learn to identify and select dietary sources of the nutrient based on association of the flavor of the nutrient-containing food with its physiologically beneficial effects. For example, vitamin B deficient animals learn within a few days to increase their intake of vitamin B containing foods only if those foods are distinctively flavored. If the flavor marker of the vitamin B containing food is then shifted to a vitamin B poor food, the animals select that food rather than the still available, but unmarked, vitamin B rich food. Thus, the appetite is learned only if the nutrient consistently occurs in a recognizable food source. This kind of specific appetite, like the conditioned taste aversions discussed above, is an example of biological preparedness for learning special types of ingestive responses.

There may be similar specific appetites for macronutrients. When animals are offered foods that differ in protein quantity or quality (i.e., amino acid pattern), they learn, within limits, to select a diet that contains adequate amounts and qualities of protein. Formation of this type of specific appetite is markedly facilitated by social interactions of experienced and inexperienced rats. Appetites for protein and carbohydrate may be activated on a meal to meal basis. Carbohydrate ingestion increases and protein ingestion decreases brain levels of the neurotransmitter serotonin (5-hydroxytryptophan), and drug studies suggest that serotonergic neural function may control the relative intakes of carbohydrate and protein when a choice of foods of differing macronutrient content is available. It also has been suggested that excessive "carbohydrate craving" is associated with obesity in some humans and can be treated by drugs that influence the function of serotonergic neurons. Most obese people, however, name predominately high fat foods as their favorites, with men preferring high fat/high protein foods and women preferring high fat/high carbohydrate and sweet foods.

III. HUNGER AND MEAL INITIATION

A. Peripheral Physiological Controls

Normal hunger was once thought to result simply from "hunger contractions" in the empty stomach or from decreases in blood glucose when the body's ready energy stores are depleted. It does not. Although hunger sensations are often referred to the epigastric area, modern techniques (i.e., psychophysical measures that are free of bias and motility measures that do not themselves affect motility) demonstrate that no relationship exists between gastric motility and the intensity of hunger. In fact, even trained humans usually fail to detect their own gastric motor activity. Further, the hunger sensation of people whose stomachs have been removed is not impoverished. The source of epigastric hunger sensations remains mysterious. Similarly, although hunger may be stimulated by extreme decreases in glucose utilization, such as occur during the biochemical hypoglycemia that can be elicited by large insulin injections, this is an emergency mechanism rather than a normal control of appetite.

Two peripheral physiological hunger signals have been identified in rats. The first is related to the *pattern* of blood glucose levels. A transient (about 15 min), small (about 10%) decline in systemic blood glucose precedes spontaneous meal initiation in rats. If the decline is blocked by glucose infusion, rats do not begin meals, whereas if a similar decline is pharmacologically induced, they do. This signal may also be sensed in the liver. If the branch of the vagus nerve that projects mainly to the liver is cut (hepatic vagotomy), transient blood glucose declines still occur, but no longer predict meal onset. Hunger is apparently signaled by the pattern of blood glucose rather than by metabolism per se, because pharmacologically induced blood glucose declines that are larger than normal do not stimulate feeding. Preliminary evidence suggests that transient declines in blood glucose may also signal hunger in humans.

A second peripheral signal appears directly related to the rate of oxidative metabolism in the liver. The key evidence is that pharmacological antagonism of oxidation of either carbohydrates or fat in the liver stimulates feeding in rats. When this is done in free-feeding rats, the primary effect is to increase meal frequency, suggesting that meal initiation is stimulated by decreases in energy metabolism. As discussed above, whether this is labeled the stimulation of hunger or the decay of satiety appears arbitrary. This signal appears to arise in the liver because hepatic portal vein infusions of metabolic fuels inhibit feeding more effectively than do infusions via other routes and because hepatic vagotomy blocks the effects of antagonism of hepatic metabolism. Because overweight increases the concentration of metabolic fuels in the blood, this mechanism provides an attractive candidate for the link between regulation of energy balance and the control of meals.

B. Endogenous Rhythms

Internal physiological clocks produce rhythmic changes in appetite. The daily, or circadian, rhythm is the most prominent of these. Rats caged with constant access to food do not space their meals regularly, as might be expected if the gut's capacity to store food or metabolic utilization of food were the only determinants of hunger. Rather, rats eat about four times as many meals during the dark as during the light. Humans consume about two to four meals and snacks each day, and fast much longer overnight than during the day. Although cultural and social factors probably influence this pattern, so do internal clocks. For example, humans living in laboratory environments in the complete absence of temporal cues increase the duration of their "free-running" sleep–wake cycles by several hours. These subjects often also increase their intermeal intervals so that they eat about the same number of meals per sleep–wake cycle. This suggests that the physiological mechanisms regulating sleeping and waking rhythms also contribute to the timing of meals.

Another endogenous rhythm of appetite is related to the ovarian cycle. In many animal species, females markedly reduce food intake prior to ovulation. A preovulatory decrease in appetite has also been observed in women. This change in appetite may be caused by the cyclic variation in secretion of the ovarian hormone estradiol. This is because in rats ovariectomy increases food intake and eliminates this feeding rhythm, whereas estradiol administration decreases food intake.

C. Learned Controls

External cues regularly associated with eating become potent conditioned controls of feeding in animals. If a stimulus such as a tone is paired with each presentation of food to food-deprived rats, subsequent presentations of the stimulus when the rats have free access to food causes initiation of large meals. The unconditional stimulus in this paradigm is presumably the normal hunger that stimulates feeding after food deprivation. This associative process also affects food choice. If more than one food is available when the conditioned hunger stimulus is presented, the food paired with the stimulus during the conditioning will be chosen. Conditioned hunger undoubtedly also plays an important role in human appetite.

Conditioned taste aversions influence the amount of food eaten as well as food selection. Rats offered only a food to which a taste aversion has been previously formed eat less and lose weight. Thus, conditioned taste aversions may cause or potentiate the anorexia that is frequently associated with cancer, gastrointestinal surgery, and anorexia nervosa, each of which is associated with some physical signs, such as nausea or gastrointestinal cramps, that might serve as such unconditional stimuli for taste aversion learning.

IV. SATIETY AND MEAL SIZE

A. Physiological Controls

1. Gastrointestinal Signals

Both the volume and the nutrient content of the gastric contents may contribute satiety signals. In rats, gastric distension appears to be effective only when relatively large volumes are ingested. This signal appears to be relayed to the brain via the vagus nerve. Other evidence points to a satiety signal related to intragastric nutrient concentration. Gastric emptying probably also plays an important, if indirect, role in appetite. Gastric emptying obviously affects gastric distension. Gastric emptying, rather than intestinal digestion or absorption, is usually the rate-limiting step in the delivery of ingested nutrients to the postabsorptive compartment. Thus, changes in gastric emptying will affect any intestinal or postabsorptive control of appetite. Unfortunately, attempts to manage food intake by controlling gastric function surgically or pharmacologically have to date met with little success.

The presence of nutrients in the small intestine, especially fats, also elicits potent satiety signals. The satiating mechanism of fat is clearly preabsorptive, as it occurs before absorbed fats appear in the circulation. Both fat-sensitive vagal sensory fibers and cholecystokin appear to contribute to this mechanism.

2. Peptide Satiety Signals

A great deal of recent research indicates that satiety may be signaled by peptides (that is, chains of up to about 100 amino acids) that are synthesized by specialized cells in various gut organs and are secreted during and after meals. Many peptides may function as peripheral satiety signals; present evidence for a normal physiological role is most compelling, however, for three: cholecystokinin (CCK), secreted by the upper small intestine, glucagon, secreted by pancreatic α cells, and bombesin-family peptides (BFP), localized in the stomach wall. The main lines of evidence supporting a role in satiety are similar for each of these (Fig. 3). First, extensive research has established their potency to specifically reduce meal size in animals. Second, double-blind tests of human volunteers reveal that they reduce meal size without physical or subjective side effects. Thus, in rats and humans they appear to produce satiety, not anorexia. Third, localized infusion studies reveal that they exert their initial action peripherally, in the abdomen. Fourth, this action is relayed to the brain via afferent nerves, especially the abdominal vagus. Fourth, the initial brain processing of these signals occurs in the dorsal hindbrain. This area is especially interesting because, in addition to abdominal vagal sensory inputs, it receives gustatory and other visceral inputs that seem to make it an ideal integratory site for the control of appetite. Fifth, availability of potent and selective antagonists has made possible demonstrations that endogenous CCK and glucagon are required for the control of meal size in rats.

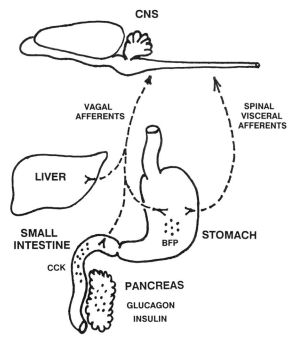

FIGURE 3   Peripheral mechanisms involved in signaling satiety from the gut to the central nervous system (CNS). Peptides thought to be involved in satiety include bombesin-family peptides (BFP), released from nerve cells in the stomach; cholecystokinin (CCK), released from the upper small intestine; and the pancreatic hormones glucagon and insulin. Peripheral nerves relay these and other feeding control signals from several sites in the abdomen. Vagal afferents connect the gut to the brain directly; spinal visceral afferents connect the gut to the brain via the spinal cord.

There are also interesting differences in the actions of these peptides. They may be related to ingestion of different nutrients (CCK, for example, probably accounts for much of the preabsorptive satiating effect of fat, whereas BFP may contribute to gastric satiety), and may contribute to different aspects of satiety (glucagon may only affect meal size; BFP may act more during the intermeal interval). These peptides may also have different modes of action. Glucagon appears to act in the classic hormonal pattern. It is released from glandular cells (pancreatic α cells) into the blood and acts on another organ (the liver). CCK is also secreted into the blood by upper small intestinal glandular cells but its satiating action may depend on local, or paracrine, rather than blood-born actions. At present it does not appear that BFP are secreted into the blood, and their mode of action remains unclear.

Insulin is another peptide with a hormonal action that may participate in the control of appetite. Insulin, secreted from the pancreatic β cells, is necessary for the utilization of glucose and other metabolic fuels by muscle and other tissues. The brain appears to extract insulin from the blood in proportion to basal insulin concentration, which in turn increases with increasing body weight. Increased brain insulin tends to reduce food intake, thus closing an apparent negative feedback loop between body weight and appetite. Insulin may affect appetite by amplifying the brain's response to other, peripheral satiety signals. This is suggested by observations that the satiating effects of CCK and some other possible peripheral peptide satiety signals are increased synergistically in the presence of elevated insulin.

Whether disturbances in peptide satiety mechanisms play a role in the etiology of human eating disorders, or whether they can be used in their treatment are questions of growing interest.

B. Variety

Humans and animals eat more when a choice of several foods of differing flavors is available than when only a single food is offered, even if nutrient composition and palatability are controlled. This is labeled sensory specific satiety. The effect is largest when more varied foods are offered, as in the more elaborate meals of all cuisines. It is not related to gustatory or olfactory adaption, and may reflect an urge to maximize food reward. In rats, caloric intake and body weight increase markedly when a variety of palatable foods are offered instead of just the stock diet. This suggests that minimizing the variety of food available might be an effective dieting strategy.

Alliesthesia is a closely related phenomenon. Alliesthesia is a decrease in pleasantness (but not in perceived intensity) of the flavors of foods that occurs as they are ingested. This change can be quite dramatic in some people, especially for sweet foods. Alliesthesia suggests that rapidly acting internal signals related to nutrient repletion can influence appetite.

V. BRAIN MECHANISMS OF APPETITE

A. Hunger and Satiety

It has been known for a half century that small lesions in particular parts of the hypothalamus, an area at the base of the brain, can dramatically disrupt normal food intake. After lateral hypothalamic damage rats stop eating voluntarily and may starve themselves to death if not carefully nursed. Subsequently, it was observed that healthy rats eat immediately if the lateral hypothalamus is electrically stimulated. Lesion and stimulation of the ventromedial hypothalamus produced the opposite results. These findings gave rise to the idea that these areas are the brain's "hunger center" and "satiety center," respectively. This idea now seems inappropriate. These areas do not appear directly involved in the processing of normal physiological controls of appetite. Rather, their feeding effects may be indirect consequences of disturbances in digestion and metabolism caused by ventromedial or lateral hypothalamic manipulations. Further, the concept of motivational centers also appears grossly oversimplified in light of current knowledge. Rather, motivational functions, like other brain functions, appear to be mediated by a diffuse, complex neural network. [See HYPOTHALAMUS.]

Neuropharmacological techniques have provided many advances in knowledge of brain mechanisms of appetite. Subpopulations of neurons in discrete areas can be manipulated by local application of neurotransmitter substances, their analogues, or their antagonists in order to identify and analyze neural pathways underlying particular behaviors. The picture that emerges from this work is of a neural network involving scores of areas and particular neurotransmitters distributed widely through both the hindbrain and the forebrain. Figure 4 shows a few of the areas that are discussed here. Progress in understanding these systems suggests that it may be possible to develop specific, pharmacological therapies for the control of appetite. A great deal of effort in the drug development industry is now focused on brain serotonin, opiate, and benzodiazepine modulators. In contrast, amphetamines are of decreasing interest because they appear to be nonspecific anorectics with dangerous side effects.

Numerous hypothalamic areas participate in brain appetite mechanisms. For example, NPY neurons (i.e., neurons that secrete neuropeptide Y as their transmitter substance) that project from the arcuate nuclei to the paraventricular nuclei of the hypothalamus appear to be involved in meal initiation. Microinfusion of small amounts of NPY into the paraventricular nuclei in sated rats immediately elicits voracious eating. When rats are offered a choice of macronutrients and are tested early in the dark phase, NPY-injected rats specifically increase their intake of high carbohydrate foods, which they normally prefer at this time. This mechanism may also involve the steroid hormone cortisol, because there are cortisol receptors in the arcuate NPY neurons and because cortisol administration has feeding effects similar to those of NPY. The nature of the rest of the networks of which these NPY neurons are part remains unclear.

Despite the extensive contributions of hypothalamic and other forebrain mechanisms to appetite, neural circuitry in the hindbrain alone may be suffi-

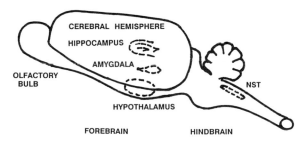

FIGURE 4   Some brain areas implicated in the control of appetite, shown in a schematic side view of the rat brain. The same structures are also found in the human brain, although their relative sizes are very different. Dotted lines indicate structures hidden deep in the brain. The hippocampus and amygdala are deep in the cerebral hemispheres; the hypothalamus is in the brain stem under the hemispheres; and the nucleus of the nucleus of the solitary tract (NST), which is the target of vagal afferent projections, is in the hindbrain. The disconnections of the forebrain discussed in the text were done by cutting through the brain just posterior to the cerebral hemisphere.

cient to mediate many aspects of appetite. When the forebrain, including the hypothalamus, is surgically disconnected, rats no longer display any of the spontaneous behaviors associated with the appetitive phase of hunger. However, when food is delivered into their mouths, they demonstrate a highly organized consummatory phase of appetite. They consume sweet solutions energetically, but reject bitter fluids. Further, they terminate ingestive bouts in ways that indicate many normal hunger and satiety controls are operating as they do in intact rats. That is, they eat more after food deprivation, after metabolic antagonists are injected, or when sweeter fluids are offered, and they eat less after gastric preloads or when CCK is injected. These impressive behavioral capacities of the lower brain suggest that appetitive functions are hierarchically and redundantly represented in several areas or levels of the brain, with each contributing additional facets to the repertoire of the intact system. Note, for example, that in these animals the mouth and gut are disconnected from the cerebral hemispheres, the presumed seat of consciousness. Thus, whatever the contribution of the subjective response to sweet taste to appetite, it is apparently unnecessary for relatively normal ingestion of sucrose solutions in the rat.

Much less is known about the contribution of more rostral brain areas to appetite. Studies of forebrain lesions suggest that the hippocampus and amygdala, two structures deep in the temporal lobe of the cerebral hemispheres, contribute to the perception of internal signals related to appetite. Patients (or rats) with damage to these areas do not seem know whether they are hungry or satiated, in that their verbal or behavioral measures of hunger state are not influenced by eating. Although patients with this type of brain damage also suffer from amnesia, this deficit does not appear to result from their memory loss. The result of their insensitivity to satiety cues combined with their failure to remember previous meals is that if offered a second meal shortly after clearing away the remains of an identical meal just finished, they eat almost as much again. [*See* HIPPOCAMPAL FORMATION.]

B. Food Reward

Neuropharmacological studies implicate several brain neurotransmitters in food reward. Of these, the role of dopamine (DA) is most firmly established. DA antagonists reduce both appetitive and consummatory responses maintained by food reward. Although central DA also contributes to brain control of movement, the effect of DA antagonism on food reward can be obtained without any signs of a motor deficit. Nor does DA antagonism produce an aversive effect. DA antagonists also have been demonstrated to specifically reduce the hedonic intensity of sucrose solutions without affecting their discriminative or sensory intensity. Neurochemical measurements also indicate that DA is released in several brain areas thought to be part of the neural reward networks, including various hypothalamic areas and the amygdala. Finally, DA may contribute both to mediation of aspects of reward specific to food as well as to more general reward functions produced by rewarding stimuli other than food.

VI. CONCLUSION

This overview introduces the broad range of subjective and behavioral phenomena of human appetite and the complex interplay of peripheral physiological, experiencial, and brain mechanisms that mediate them. Although much has been learned, it is clear that the greatest challenges for appetite research remain ahead. For example, little is yet understood about the interactions and connections among the very different levels of analysis discussed. Perhaps the greatest challenges, however, are to determine how disturbances in the basic mechanisms of appetite contribute to the etiology of eating disorders such as anorexia nervosa, bulimia, and obesity and whether manipulation of basic controls of appetite might provide effective therapies for these disorders.

Bibliography

Anderson, G. H., and Kennedy, S. H. (Eds.) (1992). "The Biology of Feast and Famine: Relevance to Eating Disorders." Academic Press, San Diego.

Barker, L. M. (Ed.) (1982). "The Psychobiology of Human Food Selection." AVI Publishing, Westport, CT.

Bernstein, I. L., and Borson, S. (1986). Learned food aversion: A component of anorexia syndromes. *Psychol. Rev.* **93**, 462.

Björntorp, P., and Brodoff, B. N. (Eds.) (1992). "Obesity." Lippincott, Philadelphia.

Blundell, J. (1991). Pharmacological approaches to appetite suppression. *Trends Pharmacol. Sci.* **12**, 147.

Geary, N. (1990). Pancreatic glucagon signals postprandial satiety. *Neurosci. Biobehav. Rev.* **13**, 323.

Hoebel, B. (1988). Neuroscience and motivation: Pathways and peptides that define motivational systems. In "Stevens' Handbook of Experimental Psychology," 2nd Ed. (R. C. Atkinson, R. J. Herrnstein, G. Lindzey, and R. D. Luce, Eds.), p. 547. Wiley, New York.

Langhans, W., and Scharrer, E. (1992). Metabolic control of eating. In "World Review of Nutrition and Dietetics," Volume 70 (A. P. Simopoulos, Ed.), p. 1. Karger, Basel, Switzerland.

Rolls, B. J. (1986). Sensory-specific satiety. *Nutr. Rev.* **44,** 93.

Scharrer, E., and Langhans, W. (1990). Mechanisms for the effect of body fat on food intake. In "The Control of Body Fat Content" (J. M. Forbes and G. R. Hervey, Eds.). Smith-Gordon, London.

Smith, G. P. (1994). Dopamine and food reward. In "Progress in Psychobiology and Physiological Psychology," Vol. 15 (A. R. Morrison and S. J. Fluharty, Eds.), in press. Academic Press, New York.

Smith, G. P., and Gibbs, J. (1992). The development and proof of the cholecystokinin hypothesis of satiety. In "Multiple Cholecystokinin Receptors in the CNS" (C. T. Dourish, S. J. Cooper, S. D. Iversen, and L. L. Iversen, Eds.), p. 166. Oxford, Oxford, UK.

Stellar, J. R., and Stellar, E. (1985). "The Neurobiology of Motivation and Reward" Springer-Verlag, New York.

Stricker, E. M. (Ed.) (1990). "Handbook of Behavioral Neurobiology," Vol. 10. "Neurobiology of Food and Fluid Intake." Plenum, New York.

Stunkard, A. J., and Stellar, E. (Eds.) (1984). "Eating and Its Disorders." Raven Press, New York.

Weingarten, H. (1985). Stimulus control of eating: Implications for a two-factor theory of hunger. *Appetite* **6,** 387.

APRAXIA

Robert E. Hanlon
Baylor Institute for Rehabilitation

Jason W. Brown
New York University Medical Center

Parapraxic errors Errors produced by individuals with apraxia when attempting to execute learned and purposeful movements to command or to imitation. Parapraxic errors are commonly manifested following a left hemisphere stroke.

Glossary

Apraxia A disorder of learned and purposeful movement, which is not due to weakness, sensory loss, dyscoordination, abnormal tone, comprehension impairment, inattention, or intellectual disturbance. The primary types of apraxia include ideomotor apraxia, ideational apraxia, and oral apraxia. Apraxia is commonly manifested following a left hemisphere stroke.

Buccofacial apraxia *See* Oral Apraxia.

Ideational apraxia A disturbance in the performance of sequential tasks, requiring the successive demonstration and integration of multiple objects necessary to achieve a functional goal. Ideational apraxia is uncommon, but may be manifested following a left hemisphere stroke involving the posterior parietal lobe.

Ideomotor apraxia Defective execution of gestures and movements, including transitive, intransitive, symbolic, and expressive gestures, as well as nonrepresentational movements, to command and to imitation. Ideomotor apraxia is commonly manifested following a left hemisphere stroke.

Limb-kinetic apraxia A form of limb ataxia characterized by the loss of fine motor dexterity; manifested as clumsiness and lack of fine manipulative control.

Oral apraxia Inability to perform orofacial movements, involving the tongue, lips, and face, to command and to imitation. (*See* Ideomotor Apraxia.)

APRAXIA is a disorder of learned and purposeful movement, which is diagnosed when the effects of weakness, sensory loss, dyscoordination, abnormal tone, comprehension impairment, inattention, and intellectual decline have been ruled out. As stated, apraxia is diagnosed by exclusion. Apraxia is manifested as a disturbance in the execution of skilled movements, which may be observed in any or all of the following conditions: inability to accurately produce a movement, whether it be a gesture, pantomime, or nonrepresentational movement, in response to a verbal command; inability to accurately produce a movement on imitation; inability to accurately demonstrate the functional use of common objects; inability to sequentially organize and integrate a series of movements involving more than one object intended to achieve a functional goal.

I. INTRODUCTION

The term *apraxia*, historically, has been used overinclusively to describe a number of disorders and functional impairments that are not due to a disturbance of learned and purposeful movement. Examples include visuoconstructional impairments (i.e., constructional apraxia), difficulties in motor learning and planning (e.g., maze learning), ataxia, akinesia, dyscoordination, and clumsiness. However, in this article, apraxia will be exclusively used to refer to disorders of learned and purposeful movement. Apraxia of eyelid opening, oculomotor apraxia, and gait apraxia will not be discussed.

The three classic subtypes of apraxia include the following: ideomotor apraxia, ideational apraxia, and limb-kinetic apraxia. Although these three subtypes were originally differentiated as distinct forms of apraxia, only the ideomotor and ideational subtypes constitute true apraxia, as defined above. Limb-kinetic apraxia is actually a form of limb ataxia, characterized by fine motor dyscontrol. Oral or buccofacial apraxia is generally recognized as a subcomponent of ideomotor apraxia and will be briefly discussed. Although typically less obvious and restrictive, with regard to functional performance, than many other disorders of higher cortical function (e.g., aphasia, agnosia, alexia), the study of apraxia, phenomenologically and experimentally, has enhanced our understanding of brain–behavior relationships.

II. DIFFERENTIAL DIAGNOSIS

In the examination of apraxia, it is imperative to rule out other forms of movement disorders, sensory dysfunction, verbal comprehension impairment, and other cognitive dysfunctions, which may singularly or collectively result in failure to produce skilled, purposeful movements. Apraxic patients are commonly aphasic with hemiparesis and/or hemianesthesia, or the apraxia is often a manifestation of dementia. The presence of aphasia, sensorimotor impairment, or dementia does not negate the diagnosis of apraxia, but merely requires systematic assessment of a disturbance of praxis. [See APHASIA; DEMENTIA.]

Patients with unilateral sensory or motor loss, secondary to a focal lesion of the contralateral hemisphere, may undergo practic assessment of the intact limb. Apraxia commonly co-occurs with aphasia, due to the proximity of neural mechanisms of the dominant hemisphere which mediate language and skilled movement sequences, and it is often difficult to determine if failure to properly execute a movement is the result of apraxia or defective comprehension. However, detailed examination of the limits of auditory comprehension (i.e., yes/no questions, pointing responses, and single-to-multiple step commands) should discern the degree to which failure to accurately produce a movement is due to poor comprehension. Movements should be assessed to imitation in addition to command, which may help to rule out the effects of a comprehension deficit. While some movements may improve on imitation,

relative to command, execution of a given movement generally remains defective. Apraxia is commonly manifested in the middle-to-late stages of dementia, but again, as with aphasia, the examiner must be careful to rule out the influence of other cognitive deficits on praxis.

III. HISTORICAL REVIEW

Although Hughlings Jackson first discussed a disorder of voluntary action in his description of aphasic patients' loss of oral–motor control, Steinthal is credited with coining the term "apraxia" in 1871. More importantly, Liepmann provided the first single case report of apraxia in 1900 in his detailed analysis of the patient, the Regierungsrat M.T., who was unable to perform gestures or pantomine object use to command and was unable to imitate hand positions with his right hand, despite the ability to perform such movements to command and imitation with the left hand. The patient's capacity to perform such movements with the left hand, as well as whole body movements to command, effectively ruled out the confounding problems of an auditory comprehension impairment and agnosia. As a result, this case represented the first conclusive description of a pure disorder of the execution of voluntary action. Postmortem analysis revealed subcortical lesions of the frontorolandic region and the left parietal region, including the supramarginal gyrus, superior parietal lobule, and the angular gyrus in addition to nearly complete destruction of the corpus callosum.

The fundamental premise of apraxia, in Liepmann's view, held that the manifestation of such disorders was the resultant effect of a dissociation between the formulation and the execution of a movement. In opposition to Liepmann's view was the model that apraxia, like aphasia, was a disturbance in the expression of symbols, or "asymbolia." This view, as originally presented by Finkelnburg, held that apraxia was a manifestation of a central communication disorder involving a defect in both the expression and comprehension of symbols, regardless of the modality through which they are conveyed.

Based on the premise that apraxia involved the separation of the idea of the movement from the execution of the movement, Liepmann, through his own work, and through the influence of others, including Pick, Kleist, and Von Monakow, proposed a unitary theory of apraxia. This theoretical model, as presented in 1920, provided a detailed and systematic analysis of apraxia, including the clinical features, anatomic structures involved, and physiological mechanisms disrupted. While he delineated three distinct forms of motor apraxia, based on different clinical manifestations and lesion site, he believed that the three forms of apraxia represented disturbances at different stages in the singular process of voluntary purposeful movement. The following is a precis of Liepmann's model of apraxia.

1. *Limb-kinetic apraxia:* A disruption of the kinetic engrams established during the acquisition of simple overlearned movements occurs following frontoparietal lesions, particularly those involving the precentral cortex.

2. *Ideomotor apraxia:* A disruption of the process at the stage between the formulation and the execution of the movement occurs with left parietal lesions located between the posterior parietal region implicated in the ideational stage and the precentral region responsible for execution.

3. *Ideational apraxia:* Complex sequential movements require a tacit understanding of the purpose or intent of the movement, as well as the body parts involved, the speed, and the sequential order of the individual movements necessary to realize the objective. A disturbance in the ideational stage of the process is manifested following left posterior parietal lesions. Figure 1 is a schematic representation of Liepmann's neuroanatomical model of apraxia.

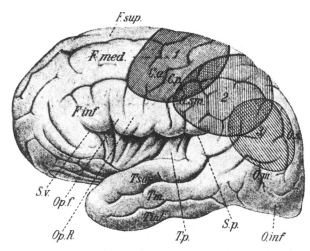

FIGURE 1 Schematic of Liepmann's neuroanatomical model of apraxia. (1) Limb-kinetic apraxia; (2) ideomotor apraxia; (3) ideational apraxia.

The association between apraxia and aphasia remained a controversial issue among neurologists and particularly, aphasiologists. While concluding that the left hemisphere controls skilled and purposeful movements and that apraxia is invariably associated with left hemisphere damage, Liepmann noted that all aphasic individuals are not apraxic, and of those who do manifest apraxia, there is no consistent relationship based on severity. Furthermore, he observed that not only were apraxic individuals impaired on motoric responses to command, they were typically unable to accurately imitate movements demonstrated by the examiner. For Liepmann, this final point was evidence that gestural disturbance was due to defective motor control and organization, rather than a general representational or symbolic deficit.

Despite the efforts of Liepmann, the view that apraxia is inextricably related to aphasia, both of which are manifestations of a generalized symbolic disturbance, became increasingly popular through the 1940s as a result of support from Head, Jackson, Critchley, and others. However, Goodglass and Kaplan's seminal investigation of the gestural disturbance in aphasia in 1963 attempted to clarify the issue of apraxia vs a central communication disorder, by means of a controlled group study of the gestural ability of aphasics and nonaphasic brain-injured controls. They hypothesized that if the gestural disorder is an exclusive manifestation of apraxia, then both imitative and spontaneous gestural actions should be defective, in addition to gestural responses to commands.

While demonstrating that aphasics were more impaired on both gestures and pantomimes than nonaphasic brain-injured controls, there was no direct correlation between severity of aphasia and level of gestural disorder. Furthermore, the aphasics as a group did not significantly improve their gestural performance on attempts at imitation, suggesting that the gestural disturbance marks a deficiency in executing purposeful movements—an apraxic disorder. Their findings lent strong support to Liepmann's view that the gestural disturbance should be categorized as ideomotor apraxia, refuting the concept of a central communication disorder.

The last 30 years has seen increasing interest and a proliferation of research on apraxia. This has been, to a large degree, due to the emphasis and attention directed toward apraxia by behavioral neurologists, such as Geschwind, Hecaen, Brown, and Heilman. Equally important to the reawakening of interest in apraxia has been the experimental work of neuro-psychologists like Goodglass, Kaplan, Kimura, and Roy. Contemporary theoretical views will be reviewed below.

IV. EXAMINATION

The assessment of apraxia should consist of a thorough examination of the patient's capacity to perform limb, buccofacial, and axial movements to verbal command and on imitation of demonstrated movements. With regard to limb movements, both sides should be tested independently, followed by movements requiring bilateral involvement. On all movements patients should first be assessed to verbal command, once the preservation of auditory comprehension has been ascertained. If the patient inaccurately performs the movement to verbal command, the command should be repeated and the movement reassessed. If performance remains inaccurate to command on the second trial, the examiner should model the correct movement and instruct the patient to imitate the modeled movement. Naturally, during the assessment of movements to verbal command, it is important that the examiner does not provide any additional verbal or visual cues.

After movements have been assessed both to verbal command and on imitation, movements involving the use of an object should be assessed in the presence of the object. First, the patient should be asked to demonstrate object use following visual presentation of the object, but without manipulation of the object. Finally, actual object manipulation and functional demonstration of use should be completed. An important component of the assessment is the inclusion of sequential tasks with multiple steps and more than one object (e.g., fold a letter for mailing, insert in an envelope, seal the envelope, and place the stamp on the envelope).

Assessment of buccofacial, axial, and whole body movements should proceed in the same manner. Buccofacial movements, involving the oral and lingual musculature, should be assessed to verbal command, on imitation, and with the object. Axial movements, involving the trunk (e.g., bend forward, lean to the left), neck (e.g., bend your head down, turn your head to the right), eyes (e.g., look up, turn your eyes to the left), eyelids (open your eyes, close your eyes), and whole body movements (e.g., stand up, step forward, sit down) are intransitive move-

ments that should be assessed to verbal command and on imitation.

A systematic assessment of apraxia should incorporate the predominant components of gestural behavior. Although inclusion of all aspects of gestural communication is well beyond the limits of an apraxia screening assessment or even a comprehensive examination, the major elements of gestural behavior should comprise the structural organization of the apraxia examination.

The elements of gestural behavior that should be taken into consideration include the following: transitive gestures (i.e., involving the depiction of object use or pantomime); intransitive gestures (i.e., movements that do not involve the depiction of object use); conventional symbolic gestures (e.g., salute, O.K. sign); conventional expressive gestures (e.g., threatening with a fist, command to stop); relational gestures (e.g., pointing); and nonrepresentational movements (e.g., place your hand on top of your head). [See GESTURES.]

It is important to consider the motor system and musculature responsible for the execution of the movements assessed. The examination should include distal, proximal, axial, and oral movements. Distal limb movements involve those in which the crucial component of the gesture or movement is performed by the fingers, hand, and/or wrist. Proximal limb movements include those upper limb gestures and movements in which the movement is primarily driven by the proximal (i.e., shoulder) musculature. Axial movements include eye, neck, trunk, and whole body movements. Oral movements involve the buccofacial musculature. Limb movements should be assessed unilaterally and bilaterally, if possible. Table I presents items which comprise a comprehensive apraxia examination.

Although the determination of the presence and severity of apraxia is the primary objective of the clinical examination, it is often important and certainly informative to note the types of errors revealed during the assessment. While the diagnosis of apraxia is an important element of a patient's neurobehavioral status and is crucial to thoroughly understanding a neuropsychological profile, the types of errors made during attempts to perform purposeful movements help to clarify the underlying basis of the disorder. Innovative research involving three-dimensional computergraphic analysis and multimodal assessment, which enables comparisons, based on the sensory modality through which a response is elicited, has enhanced our understanding of apraxia.

TABLE I
Apraxia Examination

I. Axial and whole body movements
  1. Turn your eyes upward (look up)
  2. Bend your head back (bend neck backward)
  3. Turn your head to the right
  4. Lean to the left
  5. Turn your eyes to the right (look right)
  6. Bend your head down (bend neck forward)
  7. Lean to the right
  8. Turn your eyes to the left (look left)
  9. Close your eyes
 10. Turn your head to the left
 11. Stand up
 12. Step forward
 13. Step backward
 14. Sit down

II. Oral (buccofacial)
  1. Stick out your tongue
  2. Lick your lips
  3. Show your teeth
  4. Open your mouth
  5. Cough
  6. Puff up your cheeks
  7. Blow out a match
  8. Whistle
  9. Sip on a straw
 10. Hiss

III. Proximal upper limb
  A. Unilateral (transitive movements on the body)
    1. Comb your hair
    2. Brush your teeth
    3. Shave your face
    4. Drink from a glass
    5. Eat with a spoon
  B. Unilateral (transitive movements away from the body)
    1. Throw a baseball
    2. Hammer a nail
    3. Use a saw
    4. Open a door
    5. Shake hands
  C. Unilateral (intransitive movements)
    1. Salute like a soldier
    2. Hold your hand over your heart
    3. Throw a kiss
    4. Command someone to stop
    5. Threaten someone with your fist
  D. Unilateral (nonrepresentational movements)
    1. Place your hand on top of your head
    2. Hold your arm straight up
    3. Place your hand on your opposite shoulder
    4. Hold your arm straight out to the side
    5. Make a circle in the air with your arm
  E. Bilateral (transitive movements)
    1. Drive a car
    2. Swing a bat
    3. Climb a rope
    4. Jump rope
    5. Hang a painting

  F. Bilateral (intransitive movements)
    1. Fold your arms
    2. Move your arms when you run
    3. Put your hands up, as in a robbery
    4. Move your arms when you swim
    5. Shrug your shoulders
  G. Bilateral (nonrepresentational movements)
    1. Put each hand on the opposite shoulder
    2. Place both hands on top of your head
    3. Put both hands behind your back
    4. Make a circle in the air with each arm
    5. Hold each arm straight out to the side

IV. Distal upper limb
  A. Unimanual (transitive movements)
    1. Use scissors (to cut paper)
    2. Flip a coin
    3. Use a key (to unlock a lock)
    4. Dial a telephone
    5. Write with a pencil
  B. Unimanual (intransitive movements)
    1. Snap your fingers
    2. Give the O.K. sign
    3. Wave goodbye
    4. Beckon someone to come to you
    5. Point to me
  C. Unimanual (nonrepresentational movements)
    1. Touch your thumb to your middle finger
    2. Hold up your little finger
    3. Make a circle in the air with your index finger
    4. Put your thumb between your index and middle fingers
    5. Hold up your three middle fingers
  D. Bimanual (transitive movements)
    1. Thread a needle
    2. Wind a watch
    3. Play the piano
    4. Put a ring on your finger
    5. Sharpen a pencil
  E. Bimanual (intransitive movements)
    1. Fold your hands
    2. Clap your hands
    3. Hold your hands to pray
    4. Wring your hands
    5. Twiddle your thumbs
  F. Bimanual (nonpresentational movements)
    1. Put the finger tips of both hands together
    2. Place the palm of one hand on the back of the other hand
    3. Place the back of one hand on the back of the other hand
    4. Make a circle in the air with each index finger
    5. Pull on your thumb

V. Lower Limb
  A. Lower limb (representational movements)
    1. Kick a ball
    2. Tap your foot
    3. Stamp out a cigarette

(continued)

TABLE I (*Continued*)

4. Press down on a gas pedal	7. Fork
5. Clean your feet on a door mat	8. Telephone
B. Lower limb (nonrepresentational movements)	9. Scissors
1. Put one foot in front of the other foot	10. Comb
2. Put one foot on top of the other foot	VII. Object use (multiple objects—sequential tasks)
3. Stretch out your right leg	1. Fold a letter, insert in an envelope, seal envelope, and place stamp
4. Touch your heels together	2. Pour coffee into a cup, add sugar, stir with a spoon, and drink
5. Touch your toes together	3. Open a can of soup, heat, stir with a spoon, and eat
VI. Object use (single object)	4. Open a pack of cigarettes, remove one cigarette, light it, and smoke
1. Hammer	5. Call Directory Assistance on the telephone, request a number, write the number, make the call
2. Gun	
3. Screwdriver	
4. Pencil	
5. Water Pitcher	
6. Key	

Note: The verbal command to produce all limb movements should be initiated with "Show me how you. . . ."

Apraxia researchers have developed quantitative and qualitative systems of error analysis, but no uniform scoring system of parapraxic errors has been developed. This is due, in part, to the fact that the errors produced by apraxic patients (i.e., parapraxic errors) often do not fall within one error category, but rather, are characterized by elements of two or more errors. Errors of limb apraxia may range from no response to both verbal command and imitation to subtle errors in spatial orientation and slightly augmented responses.

Parapraxic errors commonly arise from disruption of one or more variables involved in the formulation and execution of purposeful movement, including the following: initiation of movement; limb positioning in relation to either self or object; movement organization; direction of movement; movement sequencing; isolation of a movement from other movements; and termination of response. Limb gestures, in particular, require postural adjustments, joint stabilization, and limb positioning prior to and during execution of the movement which, if improperly controlled, may result in failure to complete an otherwise accurate response. Furthermore, errors may occur as a result of failure to properly stabilize the axial musculature, the improper alignment of proximal musculature, or maladroit fine manipulation. The stage at which the breakdown occurs and the specific motor systems involved (i.e., axial, proximal, or distal) help to elucidate the neuromotor mechanisms which are disrupted.

One type of parapraxic error of particular interest is the body-part-as-object error, which was first described by Goodglass and Kaplan in 1963 in their study on the disturbances of gesture and pantomime in aphasic patients. This error form consists of the tendency of many apraxic patients to conform and use part of their body, mainly the hand, to represent an object when attempting to demonstrate object use in transitive gestures or pantomime. Examples include the following: use of the index finger to represent a toothbrush and moving it across the teeth during attempts to pantomime brushing the teeth; alternating abduction and adduction of the index and middle fingers in a vertical plane to represent the action of scissors; pounding the fist on a table to represent a hammer. The significance of body-part-as-object errors has generated some controversy among aphasiologists and apraxia researchers, due to the fact that normal children often perform transitive gestures in this manner and the tendency has also been reported among normal adults. However, it is generally accepted that the frequency of body-part-as-object errors among apraxic patients exceeds that of normals and nonapraxic brain-damaged patients.

Another type of error, which differs from the positioning, spatial orientation, and movement errors described above, is referred to as "vocal overflow." This involves the spontaneous emission, among aphasics, of the word which is being gesturally represented at a given moment. Examples of vocal overflow include the following: saying "okay" during attempts to gesturally produce the O.K. sign; saying "blow" instead of a directed oral exhalation in response to the command to show me how you blow out a match.

The increased emphasis on the systematic and detailed assessment of apraxia has resulted in the development of various systems for classifying and scoring parapraxic errors. While it is not possible, within the limits of this brief overview, to discuss all of these systems, a representative list of parapraxic errors is presented in Table II.

TABLE II
Limb Parapraxic Errors

Error type	Description
Correct	Spatially and temporally accurate movement with no omitted or augmented movements
Approximation	Nearly accurate movement, but with the omission of a movement component or the inclusion of an additional movement component
Fragmentation	Disconnected or dysfluent movement within the correct plane of action
Delay	Excessive latency of the initiation of the movement
Spatial configuration error	Correct or approximation of the correct movement executed with incorrect spatial orientation, regarding either the hand-to-object relationship (internal configuration) or the relationship between the pantomimed or manipulated object and the object receiving its action (external configuration)
Plane of action error	Correct or approximation of the correct movement executed within the wrong plane of action
Semantic substitution	Replacement of the directed movement with a complete or partial alternative movement from the same semantic class
Nonsemantic substitution	Replacement of the directed movement with a complete or partial alternative movement from a different semantic class
Body-part-as-object	A body part is used to represent an object in transitive gestures
Vocal overflow	Verbalization of the word which represents the directed movement
Onomatopoetic responses	Vocalized imitation of the sound made by a given object during attempt to pantomime its use
Perseveration	Production of a movement that includes all or components of a previously produced movement
No response	Failure to produce any movement in response to either verbal command or imitation

V. TYPES OF APRAXIA

The types of apraxia which will be discussed will be limited to the three classic subtypes of limb apraxia (i.e., ideomotor, ideational, and limb-kinetic) and oral or buccofacial apraxia. As mentioned, the term apraxia has been used inclusively and ambiguously, if not inappropriately, to describe various disorders which are not primarily due to a disruption of learned and purposeful movement. As a result, constructional apraxia and dressing apraxia will not be discussed. Additionally, due to the spatial and conceptual limitations herein, gait apraxia, oculomotor apraxia, and eyelid apraxia will not be addressed.

Ideomotor apraxia is a relatively common manifestation of left hemisphere lesions, particularly lesions occurring within the distribution of the left middle cerebral artery (MCA). It has been estimated that approximately 75% of patients who have suffered a cerebrovascular accident within the left MCA distribution reveal varying degrees of ideomotor apraxia. Ideomotor apraxia is characterized by the defective execution of single gestures and movements of either a simple (e.g., "give me the O.K. sign") or relatively complex (e.g., show me how you thread a needle) nature and may involve transitive, intransitive, symbolic, and expressive gestures, as well as nonrepresentational (i.e., meaningless) movements. Performance to verbal command is typically the most defective, with some improvement generally demonstrated on imitation. However, despite improved performance on imitation, the performance of a patient with ideomotor apraxia on the whole remains defective. As previously described, it is imperative for the diagnosis of ideomotor apraxia to determine that impaired performance is not due to poor comprehension, primary motor dysfunction, sensory loss, or general intellectual decline.

The execution of axial movements is an important component of neuromotor integrity and may be disrupted in patients with ideomotor apraxia. Geschwind believed that patients with ideomotor apraxia are generally able to accurately perform axial movements (i.e., eye, neck, trunk, and whole body movements) to command, due to the fact that such movements are controlled by the nonpyramidal motor system, whereas limb movements are mediated by the pyramidal motor system. Although evidence has been presented challenging this view, it is clear that while axial movements may not be intact, the execution of such movements in patients with ideomotor apraxia is generally preserved, relative to limb movements.

The defective nature of the movements of patients with ideomotor apraxia is typically characterized by one or more parapraxic errors (see Table II), rather than clumsiness or fine motor dyscontrol, which characterizes limb-kinetic apraxia. It is uncommon and only in severe cases that a patient will demonstrate aspects of ideomotor apraxia in spontaneous activity. It is not unusual for patients who perform very poorly to verbal command and on imitation during an apraxia examination to accurately produce communicative gestures in social situations and demonstrate no difficulty in the functional use of common objects.

Ideational apraxia is a disturbance in the performance of sequential tasks, typically requiring the successive demonstration and integration of multiple objects, in order to achieve a goal. Although the individual movements representing each step in the sequence are intact, unlike those of ideomotor apraxia, the sequential organization necessary to successfully complete the task is disrupted. For example, when asked to demonstrate the procedure for preparing a letter for mailing, a patient with ideational apraxia may fold the letter, place the stamp in the upper right hand corner of the letter rather than the envelope, and then seal the envelope without inserting the letter.

Ideational apraxia is comparatively uncommon and unlike ideomotor apraxia, is often evident during spontaneous behavior, particularly when attempting to perform activities of daily living, such as self-care, preparing meals, conducting household chores, and managing personal affairs. These two forms of apraxia may be seen together, but more commonly occur independent of each other, with ideomotor apraxia being much more common than ideational apraxia. However, it is important to note that ideational apraxia is not merely a severe form of ideomotor apraxia, but rather, they are autonomous conditions. They differ qualitatively, representing distinct stages, or the disruption thereof, in the production of purposeful movement: conceptual organization (i.e., ideational apraxia) and execution (i.e., ideomotor apraxia).

Limb-kinetic apraxia, despite its name, is not a true form of apraxia, but rather is a form of limb ataxia. However, since this disturbance was included in the original conceptualization of apraxia as a distinct subtype, it will be briefly discussed. It is characterized by a loss of fine motor dexterity in the execution of adroit movements, particularly involving object manipulation using the distal musculature. This form of motor disorder is manifested as clumsiness and lack of speed and fine manipulative control. As a result, Luria characterized limb-kinetic apraxia as a loss of the "kinetic melody" involved in the execution of fine, fluent dextrous movements. Examples include difficulty with the following: operating closures, such as buttons and zippers, picking up a coin from a flat surface, typing, writing, and playing musical instruments such as the piano or guitar.

The disorder is unilateral occurring in the limb contralateral to a lesion in the sensorimotor cortex or premotor cortex, although the site of lesions which result in limb-kinetic apraxia has remained a controversial issue. There is evidence that pyramidal lesions may cause clumsiness and loss of fine manipulative control, in the absence of strength or tone changes. In light of this controversy, Hecaen has proposed that limb-kinetic apraxia is an intermediary disorder of purposeful movement, between paresis and apraxia.

Oral or buccofacial apraxia has traditionally been considered a subcomponent of ideomotor apraxia, but it will be discussed separately here. This form of apraxia is due to the disruption of the execution of learned and purposeful buccofacial movements, involving the tongue, lips, face, and thorax. Consistent with ideomotor apraxia, oral apraxia is manifested as an inability to perform orofacial movements to command or on imitation, despite the capacity to perform such movements spontaneously and automatically during functional oral motor engagement. Patients with oral apraxia are typically unable to perform the following movements to command or on imitation: blow, protrude the tongue, lick their lips, show teeth, smile, swallow, cough, etc. (see Table I). However, the same movements are performed without difficulty during engagement in functional tasks, such as eating, drinking, casual conversation, and when confronted with a lit match.

Verbal apraxia or apraxia of speech, which is commonly associated with nonfluent aphasia, is considered by some theorists to represent a distinct class of oral apraxia. While sharing fundamental elements of the diagnostic criteria for apraxia (i.e., defective selection, sequencing, and execution of learned movements), the fact that verbal apraxia is characterized by a disruption of the phonological process in speech production suggests that this disturbance is not merely a subclass of oral apraxia, despite their interrelatedness.

VI. NEUROPATHOLOGY

Apraxia typically occurs following left hemisphere lesions in right-handed patients and is most commonly manifested following infarctions in the distribution of the left middle cerebral artery. Ideomotor apraxia is generally associated with posterior parietal and temporoparietal lesions, particularly involving the supramarginal and angular gyri. Lesions located in the posterior parietal region will often result in bilateral ideomotor apraxia. Unilateral ideomotor apraxia occurs following anterior lesions of the corpus callosum which disrupt the neural communication between the motor control centers of the left hemisphere and the primary motor cortex of the right hemisphere. Another common form of ideomotor apraxia, which is manifested unilaterally, is the so called "sympathetic apraxia." Sympathetic apraxia is frequently seen in the left limb of patients with Broca's aphasia and right hemiparesis. The left-sided apraxia results from a frontal lesion that extends subcortically from Broca's area disrupting the projection fibers from the left motor region that pass through the corpus callosum to the right primary motor area. Subcortical lesions, involving the left basal ganglia and thalamus, have been implicated in selective cases of ideomotor apraxia. There is also evidence that lesions of the supplementary motor area may result in bilateral ideomotor apraxia.

Ideational apraxia, which is exclusively bilateral, and, as mentioned, is a comparatively uncommon phenomenon, may occur following large left posterior parietal lesions. Limb-kinetic apraxia, which is a unilateral disorder, and not a pure disorder of learned and purposeful movement in the same sense as ideomotor and ideational apraxia, may result from lesions of the sensorimotor or premotor cortex of the contralateral hemisphere.

Oral or buccofacial apraxia is associated with ideomotor apraxia (e.g., sympathetic apraxia) and is commonly seen in patients with Broca's aphasia. This form of apraxic disorder is often seen following lesions of the left frontal operculum, the inferior precentral gyrus, and the anterior insula. However, there are reports of oral apraxia, secondary to left posterior parietal lesions.

VII. RECOVERY FROM APRAXIA

Unlike aphasia, with which it commonly co-occurs, apraxia is not an obvious impairment and generally goes unnoticed to casual observation, unless it is quite severe. Additionally, unlike aphasia or amnesia, patients typically do not complain about disorders of praxis, primarily because they are not aware and/or do not experience notable functional limitations secondary to apraxia, unless it involves defective object manipulation.

Apraxia is most severe during the acute stage following the causative lesion, which is typically a stroke. There is generally ongoing resolution of the disorder during the postacute stage and the greatest degree of recovery occurs during the first 6 months postonset. Recovery does not appear to be related to age, education, sex, initial severity, type of aphasia, or lesion size.

However, there is evidence that recovery may follow an orderly progression, based on the motor systems involved. Axial movements, which are generally preserved, relative to limb and oral movements, resolve rapidly during the acute stage. Proximally driven upper limb movements recover at a slower rate and the resolution of distal movements is comparatively delayed and often characterized by incomplete recovery. There is also some evidence suggesting that recovery of the capacity to produce intransitive gestures surpasses that of transitive gestures (i.e., pantomimed object use).

VIII. THEORETICAL MODELS OF APRAXIA

The modern interpretation of the apraxias is still deeply rooted in the disconnection concepts of Liepmann. According to this model, an interruption of the flow from the idea or plan of the act to its motor implementation produces ideomotor apraxia, while ideational and limb-kinetic apraxia represent a disruption of the plan and motoric phase, respectively. Left-sided or sympathetic apraxia is due to a callosal or deep frontal lesion interrupting left to right hemisphere control of the left side.

The disconnection model of apraxia, as originally proposed by Liepmann, was elaborated and popularized by Geschwind. An important component of this model holds that the left hemisphere not only mediates language, but is also specialized for the control of purposeful movement (a view shared by many neuromotor and apraxia theorists). However, this remains a controversial matter, particularly in light of evidence from split-brain research demonstrating the role of the right hemisphere in the motoric expression of selective nonverbal processes. Although the disconnection model has had great influence in neuropsychology, there are some drawbacks to the fundamental concept of disconnection theory, as it applies to learned and purposeful movement, which holds that the idea of the action is disconnected from the motor cortex responsible for the movement of the muscle groups involved in the action.

Among the problems with the disconnection model are the impairment to imitative movements, which should be preserved through right hemisphere mediation, the lack of anatomical cases with a pure intrahemispheric pathway lesion, and the failure to find sympathetic apraxia in patients with a right subcortical lesion, as predicted by Liepmann. The theory does not relate apraxia to limb and bodily action generally, nor does it convincingly explain the proximal–distal or whole body dissociations. Finally, it does not account for *motoric* deficits with damage to posterior (perceptual) zones.

Less well known is the fact that Liepmann proposed a posterior to anterior unfolding model of action development (see Fig. 1), the apraxias representing disruptions at successive stages in action generation. This "genetic" aspect of Liepmann's theory could be viewed as the inception of a microgenetic account of action and apraxic disorders.

On this view, an act consists of a rapid depth-to-surface traversal of action and perception systems. The action component consists of a sequence of oscillators or kinetic rhythms that discharge into motor systems at successive evolutionary stages in the brain. The discharge gives the physical movements, while the internal action process gives the feeling of an active (self-initiated) movement. The perceptual component develops in parallel with the action component, but is based on secondary central (reafferent) and peripheral (feedback) sensory input from the action structure and the moving limb. This component provides the awareness of the action content and the conscious plan or goal.

Disruption of the *action* component in the deep stages of limbic-derived neocortex leads to a disturbance of the initiation of upper limb movement (supplementary motor area syndrome, alien hand), lower limb movement ("gait apraxia"), or vocalization (mutism). Damage to the ensuing phase mediated by systems in premotor cortex leads to derailment (idemomotor apraxia) of the limb en route to the target. The initiation of the act and the distal motility are adequate.

Damage to concurrent levels in the perceptual component gives a disturbance of the conceptual aspect or plan (ideational apraxia) of the action and disorders of the body image. The occurrence of ideo-motor apraxia with a parietal lesion is due to a disruption of the *perceptual* component. The action is incorrectly "read off" a perceptual representation, created by feedback from the limb and the internal motor structure.

While purely theoretical, this hierarchically organized, parallel process model explains the dissociations that occur between axial or proximal actions, and actions involving the distal musculature. An explanation is also provided for the role of reafference and perceptual systems, and the effects on action of posterior brain lesions.

Another hierarchically organized model of apraxia was presented by Luria as part of a unitary model of neuropsychological processing. Like all other cognitive functions, praxis is a complex functional system mediated by the dynamic interaction of cortical and subcortical zones. The integrity of the afferent field is crucial to the effective operation of a functional system. Voluntary movement is dependent on several afferent fields, including kinesthesia, proprioception, touch, and vision.

Departing from Liepmann's classification of the apraxias, Luria differentiated subtypes of apraxia, based on the functional systems disrupted by lesions to specific cortical analyzers. Afferent apraxia typically occurs following lesions of the postcentral motor cortex of the left hemisphere, due to a disruption of kinesthetic processing and is similar to limb-kinetic apraxia. Lesions of the premotor region result in the disintegration of the dynamic structure of complex skilled movements, similar to the difficulties seen in ideomotor and ideational apraxia.

Roy proposed a functionally oriented typology of apraxia, incorporating elements from disconnection theory and the hierarchically organized models of neurocognitive processing, described above. In this classification, the apraxias are differentiated according to the functional processes considered to be disturbed as a result of localized lesions.

Planning apraxia involves a disturbance in the sequential and spatial organization of voluntary movement, similar to ideational and ideomotor apraxia, and results from parieto-occipital or prefrontal lesions. In executive apraxia, the sequential planning and spatial organization of the movement are preserved, but execution of the motor act is defective, following premotor lesions. Finally, unit apraxia involves the disordered execution of individual movements, despite the preservation of planning, spatial organization, and execution of the movement sequence. Unit apraxia is manifested following either precentral or postcentral lesions of the motor cortex and is similar to Liepmann's limb-kinetic apraxia and Luria's afferent apraxia, respectively.

More recently, Heilman and his colleagues have extended interpretations based on the disconnection model to include two additional subtypes of apraxia: disassociation apraxia and conceptual apraxia. Theoretically, disassociation apraxia may occur following callosal lesions which disconnect language mediation areas from movement formulation areas. Such patients will be unable to formulate or perform movements to command with the left hand, producing no recognizable movement. However, they may be able to imitate and use objects correctly with the left hand or may show classic ideomotor apraxia errors on imitation and demonstration of object use. Conceptual apraxia, on the other hand, is a disorder of conceptual knowledge associated with lesions of the left posterior parietal lobe and temporoparietal region. Whereas ideomotor apraxia is characterized by production errors involving the temporospatial elements of the execution of a movement, conceptual apraxia is defined by content errors in which a tool is used as if it were another tool (e.g., using a saw as if it were a hammer). Tool selection errors in response to situations requiring specific tool use and/or description of a given tool's function also characterize conceptual apraxia.

The disconnection theory originally proposed by Liepmann and extended by Geschwind remains the predominant model of apraxia. Although largely unproven, theoretical models, such as the microgenetic process model described above, represent alternative approaches which may help to explain previously unexplained aspects of disorders of learned and purposeful movement. Other unitary models of praxis and apraxic disorders, including Luria's theory of complex functional systems, and other typologies of apraxia, such as those of Hecaen and Roy, should be seriously considered by students and incorporated by researchers.

Bibliography

Alexander, M. P., Baker, E., Naeser, M. A., Kaplan, E., and Palumbo, C. (1992). Neuropsychological and neuroanatomical dimensions of ideomotor apraxia. *Brain* **115,** 87–107.

Basso, A., Capitani, E., Della-Sala, S., Laicona, M., and Spinnler, H. (1987). Recovery from ideomotor apraxia: A study on acute stroke patients. *Brain* **110,** 747–760.

Brown, J. W. (Ed.) (1988). "Agnosia and Apraxia: Selected Papers of Liepmann, Lange, and Potzl." Erlbaum, Hillsdale, NJ.

DeRenzi, E., and Lucchelli, F. (1988). Ideational apraxia. *Brain* **111,** 1173–1185.

Geschwind, N. (1975). The apraxias: Neural mechanisms of disorders of learned movement. *Am. Sci.* **63,** 188–195.

Goodglass, H., and Kaplan, E. (1963). Disturbances of gesture and pantomime in aphasia. *Brain* **86,** 703–720.

Hanlon, R. E. (Ed.) (1991). "Cognitive Microgenesis: A Neuropsychological Perspective." Springer-Verlag, New York.

Hecaen, H. (1981). Apraxias. In "Handbook of Clinical Neuropsychology." (S. Filskov and T. Boll, Eds.), Wiley, New York.

Heilman, K. M., and Rothi, L. J. G. (1985). Apraxia. In "Clinical Neuropsychology" (K. M. Heilman and E. Valenstein, Eds.). Oxford University Press, New York.

Poizner, H., Mack, L., Verfaellie, M., Rothi, L. J. G., and Heilman, K. M. (1990). Three-dimensional computergraphic analysis of apraxia. *Brain* **113,** 85–101.

Roy, E. A. (1978). Apraxia: A new look at an old syndrome. *J. Hum. Movement Stud.* **4,** 191–210.

Roy, E. A. (Ed.) (1985). "Advances in Psychology," Vol. 23. Elsevier, Amsterdam.

APTITUDE TESTING

Anne Anastasi
Fordham University

Glossary

Aptitude Skill or knowledge required to perform a specified kind of activity (e.g., school work, music, carpentry).

Battery A set of interrelated tests (sometimes called subtests) that can be combined to yield one or more scores for specific purposes.

Psychometrics Psychological specialty concerned with the construction, use, interpretation, and evaluation of tests through the application of statistical methodology and psychological research on individual differences.

Test Objective and standardized measure of a sample of an individual's behavior, used for diagnosis or prediction, or to assess effect of a given condition on behavior.

Trait Psychological construct for describing individual differences in behavior, derived from statistical analysis of measured behavioral consistencies.

MODERN APTITUDE TESTING, which arose out of 19th century efforts to measure human intelligence, permits the assessment of cognitive functioning at various levels of specificity or generality. Aptitude and achievement tests represent the two ends of a continuum of developed abilities. Guided by the individual's motivation, interests, and other affective traits, these abilities develop throughout the learning history of a lifetime.

I. HISTORICAL ANTECEDENTS AND EVOLUTION

Some of the clearest antecedents of the modern aptitude-testing movement can be traced to an awakening interest in the humane treatment of mentally abnormal persons during the 19th century. With the growing concern for proper care came the need for uniform criteria for identifying and classifying such cases. First it was necessary to distinguish between persons then described as "insane" and those considered "feebleminded." The former manifested emotional disorders that might or might not be accompanied by intellectual deterioration from an initially normal level; the latter were characterized essentially by intellectual defect that had been manifested from birth or early infancy. What is probably the first explicit statement of this distinction is found in a two-volume work published in 1838 by the French physician Esquirol, in which he also noted that there are many degrees of what is now termed mental retardation, varying along a continuum from normality to "low-grade idiocy." In his attempt to develop some system for classifying the different degrees and varieties of mental retardation, Esquirol tried several procedures but concluded that the person's use of language provides the most dependable criterion of intellectual level. It is noteworthy that current criteria of mental retardation are also largely linguistic and that present-day intelligence tests are heavily loaded with verbal content. [*See* MENTAL RETARDATION.]

Of special significance are the contributions of another French physician, Seguin, who pioneered in the training of the mentally retarded. Having rejected the prevalent notion of the incurability of mental retardation, Seguin experimented for many years with what he termed the physiological method of training. Accordingly, in 1837 he established the first school for the special education of mentally retarded children. In 1848 he emigrated to the United

States, where his ideas gained wide recognition. Some of the procedures developed by Seguin for sense training and muscle training of the mentally retarded were eventually incorporated in what became known as performance or nonverbal tests of intelligence. An example is the Seguin Form Board, which requires the insertion of variously shaped blocks into the corresponding recesses as quickly as possible.

A. Intelligence Tests

The English biologist Francis Galton was largely responsible for launching the modern aptitude testing movement. In his research on human heredity, Galton soon recognized the need for exact measures to assess the degree of resemblance between related persons, such as parents and offspring, siblings, twins, or cousins. With this end in view, Galton devised a series of simple aptitude tests with which he gathered extensive data on children in several schools and on adults who visited the anthropometric laboratory he had established in London in 1884. The tests included measures of visual, auditory, tactual, and kinesthetic discrimination, muscular strength and coordination, reaction time, and other simple sensorimotor functions. Galton argued that sensory discrimination tests could provide an index of intelligence, insofar as all information concerning external events reaches us through our senses. This view was further strengthened by his observation that severely retarded persons are often unable to perceive heat, cold, and pain.

A major contributor to the development of aptitude testing was the American psychologist James McKeen Cattell. After obtaining the Ph.D. with Wilhelm Wundt at Leipzig, Cattell spent some time in London with Galton. Upon his return to the United States, he was active both in the establishment of psychological laboratories and in the development of a series of tests administered to college students. This series was modeled partly on Galton's sensorimotor instruments but was also expanded to cover memory and other simple mental processes. Cattell's tests were typical of those developed in several countries in the 1890s. Attempts to evaluate these early tests proved disappointing. Performance showed little correspondence from one test to another and exhibited little or no relation to estimates of intelligence from school achievement or other real-life criteria.

Among the late 19th century psychologists who were exploring ways of measuring intelligence was Alfred Binet. Eventually Binet became convinced that the most promising approach was through the direct—albeit crude—measurement of complex intellectual functions. An opportunity to put this idea into practice arose in 1904, when Binet was appointed to a commission for the study of educationally retarded school children. The immediate result was the development of the first Binet–Simon scale in 1905. This was followed by two subsequent revisions and by many translations and adaptations in several countries, including two in the United States. The first was by H. H. Goddard, then research psychologist at the Vineland Training School (for mentally retarded children). The Goddard revision was influential in the acceptance of intelligence testing by the medical profession. It arrived at a propitious moment to meet the urgent need for a standardized measure to diagnose and classify mentally retarded persons. As a testing instrument, however, this revision was soon outdistanced by the more extensive and psychometrically refined Stanford–Binet, developed by L. M. Terman and his associates at Stanford University. First published in 1916, the Stanford–Binet has undergone several major revisions, the latest appearing in 1986.

The aptitude tests developed thus far, whether through precise measures of simple functions or through judicious sampling of more complex intellectual tasks, were basically designed to assess individual differences in general intelligence. Their results typically yielded a single, comprehensive estimate of an individual's intellectual level. Procedurally, they required the testing of one person at a time by an experienced examiner. The Binet type of test eventually led to what is now known as clinical assessment, which means essentially the intensive study of each individual through the use of tests in conjunction with other available data sources. Then World War I gave us group testing. Derived from a psychometrically crude instrument that was developed under urgent time pressure, group intelligence tests spread rapidly after the war, for use with both adults and children. The popularization of these tests far outran their technical quality. The testing boom of the 1920s probably did more to retard than to advance the progress of testing. [See INTELLIGENCE.]

B. Tests of Special Aptitudes

As the early intelligence tests were applied in various practical contexts, it soon became apparent that such tests were limited in their coverage. Efforts were then made to fill the major gaps by means of what were originally termed "special aptitude tests." There tests were designed chiefly to supplement the global score yielded by traditional tests of intelligence.

Among the first and the most numerous special aptitude tests were those for mechanical and for clerical aptitudes. The development of these tests was stimulated predominantly by the demands of personnel selection and classification for jobs in business and industry. Mechanical aptitude tests cover a variety of functions, ranging from simple psychomotor dexterity, through perceptual and spatial aptitudes, to mechanical reasoning. Clerical aptitude tests focus most commonly on perceptual speed and accuracy in dealing with words and numbers. Eventually special aptitude tests were constructed for other areas of vocational (or avocational) interest, such as art and music. Not surprisingly, the most recent development is a growing number of aptitude tests for several computer-related skills, relevant to the work of computer operators as well as programmers.

C. Multiple Aptitude Batteries

Concurrently with the development of special aptitude tests came a growing realization that general intelligence tests themselves covered two or more distinctly identifiable aptitudes, such as verbal, quantitative, and spatial. Counselors and clinical psychologists who administered individual intelligence tests soon began to look for areas or item clusters within each test that revealed special strengths and weaknesses within the individual's performance. Newly developed instruments for group administration, from kindergarten to graduate school, typically yielded two or more subscores, either in addition to or in lieu of the traditional total score. Familiar examples are the College Board's Scholastic Aptitude Test (SAT) and the Graduate Record Examination (GRE).

Finally, full-fledged multiple aptitude batteries were constructed and began to replace the former combination of general intelligence and special aptitude tests for many testing purposes. This type of battery proved most effective in the testing of normal adults, for whom identifiable aptitudes had become most clearly differentiated. Two examples of widely used multiple aptitude batteries are the Armed Services Vocational Aptitude Battery (ASVAB), developed for admission and placement in military services, and the General Aptitude Test Battery (GATB), developed by the United States Employment Service as an aid in personnel selection within industrial and business settings.

D. Emerging Resolution: Hierarchical Models and Multilevel Scoring

The transitions from the testing of general intelligence to the acceptance of special aptitude tests as necessary supplements, and hence to the decomposition and reorganization of aptitudes into comprehensive aptitude batteries, did not occur smoothly or with complete unanimity. On the contrary, it was accompanied by lively and lingering controversies between the exponents of different approaches. It was not until the 1980s and 1990s that what looks like a resolution of the various conflicts began to emerge. The key to this resolution is the growing acceptance of a hierarchical model of human aptitudes, first proposed by Cyril Burt and P. E. Vernon in England and promoted by Lloyd Humphreys among others in the United States. According to this hierarchical model, human aptitudes can be described and assessed by constructs of varying levels of breadth. At the bottom level are narrowly defined aptitudes corresponding to specific sensorimotor, perceptual, or other simple intellectual functions needed to perform particular tasks. These simple aptitudes can be grouped into constructs of increasing breadth at successively higher levels, such as verbal comprehension, mathematical aptitude, or spatial reasoning. These broad constructs can in turn be combined to yield a single, comprehensive intellectual measure.

For each testing purpose, the most appropriate constructs may be those at any one level of breadth in this hierarchy. For example, for college admission, such fairly broad constructs as verbal and quantitative aptitudes are probably most suitable. A somewhat larger number of more narrowly defined constructs are more useful for choice of a college major or for career counseling. To identify persons qualified for highly specific jobs, such as electronic troubleshooting, a set of much narrower performance constructs would be most effective. Recently developed test batteries have used the hierarchical approach both in the construction of the battery and in the scoring alternatives offered to its users. These batteries combine comprehensive content coverage with maximum flexibility of scoring patterns for multipurpose usage. Two outstanding examples of this approach to aptitude testing are provided by the fourth edition of the Stanford–Binet, published in 1986, and the Differential Ability Scales, published in 1990. Both are individually administered tests. The same approach to test construction and use, however, is also having an impact on group administered batteries, such as the Cognitive Abilities Test and the Otis–Lennon School Ability Test.

II. APTITUDE PATTERNS AND TRAIT FORMATION

A. Statistical Research on the Composition of Intelligence

The major aptitude-testing developments that occurred in response to immediate practical demands were also supported by concurrent findings of basic research on the nature and composition of human intelligence. The first theory of intelligence based on a statistical analysis of aptitude-test scores was formulated in the 1920s by the British psychologist Charles E. Spearman. Through a study of correlations found within sets of test scores, Spearman concluded that all intellectual activities share a single common factor, which he called the general factor (g). In addition, his theory postulated numerous specific (s) factors, each strictly specific to a single activity. Positive correlation between any two functions was attributed to the g factor. The more highly the two functions were saturated, or loaded, with g, the higher was the correlation between them. The presence of specifies, on the other hand, tended to lower the correlation between them.

The development of mathematical techniques of factor analysis by subsequent researchers, largely in England and the United States, led to the identification of group factors of intermediate breadth, falling between the general and specific factors. From the 1930s to the 1950s, simplified and computationally feasible procedures of factor analysis were commonly used. With the increasing availability of high-speed computers since midcentury, more sophisticated and mathematically precise procedures replaced the earlier, crude approximations. The more refined procedures had already been developed but were heretofore impracticable.

During the same period, there were also parallel conceptual developments regarding the factors, or traits, identified by factor analysis. These traits are no longer regarded as *the* primary units of human intelligence, as originally proposed; nor are they considered to be underlying causal entities. They are essentially constructs derived from empirically measured behavioral consistencies (i.e., correlation coefficients) that facilitate the description of behavior at different levels of generality. By the substitution of a small number of common factors for the multitude of variables or tests included in a factor analysis, the description of the assessed behavior can be simplified and adapted to particular purposes. The hierarchical model of traits, with its multiple levels of factorial breadth, can reconcile the findings of different factor-analytic investigations and provide the flexibility needed for the diversity of testing purposes. [*See* TRAITS.]

B. Trait Formation

What determines the behavioral consistencies from which traits are derived? How are identifiable aptitudes, or cognitive traits, formed? In contrast to trait development, which refers to the individual's relative standing in different aptitudes, trait or aptitude formation refers to the organization of behavior into the very traits in terms of which a person's performance is reported. It has been repeatedly demonstrated that one's performance in, for example, verbal or quantitative aptitude can be improved by appropriate learning procedures. But the question under consideration is more fundamental: What brings about the correlational pattern that leads to the identification of a verbal trait or quantitative trait in the first place?

Several mechanisms have been proposed to explain trait formation. One type of explanation focuses on the continuity or co-occurrence of learning experiences. For example, children are likely to develop a broad verbal-educational factor running through all activities taught in school. A narrower factor of numerical aptitude may result from the fact that all mathematical processes tend to be taught together, by the same teacher or in the same class period. Hence, the student who is bored, discouraged, or antagonized during the math instruction will tend to lag behind in learning *all* mathematical processes; the one who is stimulated and gratified in the math class will tend to learn thoroughly all that is taught during that class period, and to develop attitudes that will enhance her or his subsequent mathematical learning.

A second type of explanation, which has received considerable attention in research on trait formation, is that of differential transfer of training. Such transfer may occur within different categories of acquired knowledge as in concept formation; through the establishment of learning sets; through the development of cognitive skills; or through the acquisition of information-processing strategies. For example, if a learning set is established, the individual is able to learn more quickly and efficiently when presented with a new problem of the same kind. Certain efficient problem-solving techniques can be utilized in solving many different problems. Some of the skills developed through formal schooling, as in reading or arithmetic computation, are applicable to a wide variety of subsequent learning situations. Individual differences in the extent to which any of these skills has been acquired will thus be reflected in the performance of a large number of different tasks; and in a factor analysis of these tasks these widely applicable skills will emerge as broad group factors. The breadth of the transfer effect, or the variety of tasks to which the skill is applicable, determines the breadth of the group factor. The resulting factor could be as broad as verbal comprehension or as narrow as a specialized perceptual discrimination.

There is a growing body of evidence demonstrating the influence of experiential variables in the formation of the traits identified by factor analysis. Differences in factor patterns have been found to be associated with different cultural contexts, socioeconomic levels, and types of school curriculums. Changes in factor patterns also occur over time. These include long-term changes, which may reflect the cumulative effects of everyday life experiences, as well as short-term changes resulting from practice and other experimentally controlled learning experiences. The traits or aptitudes identified through factor analysis are descriptive constructs that reflect the changing interrelationships of performance in a variety of situations. These aptitudes are not static entities but are the products of a person's cumulative experiential history. Insofar as the interrelationships of experiences vary among individuals and groups, different factor patterns may be expected among them. As the individual's experiences change through formal education, occupational functions, or other continuing activities, new aptitudes may become differentiated or previously existing aptitudes may merge into broader composites.

III. VIEW FROM ANOTHER ANGLE: APTITUDE AND ACHIEVEMENT TESTS

A. Some Persistent Myths

Since the 1970s, psychometricians have become increasingly aware of the hazards of retaining test labels that carry misleading surplus meanings. For example, test authors and publishers have largely replaced the term "intelligence" with more neutral terms. This change was introduced earlier and more widely in group tests than in individual tests for at least two reasons. First, individual tests are usually administered by examiners with specialized training that should provide some safeguards against unwarranted conclusions. Second, in individual testing, the examiner has an opportunity to obtain background information about the examinee—information that is of the utmost importance for the proper interpretation of test scores.

A particularly deplorable distortion of reality is found in the popular use of the term "IQ test." The IQ is neither a type of test nor an identifiable quality of a person that could be assessed by a test. It is a type of score, originally found by dividing the individual's mental age, as obtained from a Binet type of test, by her or his chronological age (actual age from birth). Because of insurmountable technical deficiencies, this type of score was generally abandoned by midcentury. It was readily shown that IQs obtained at different ages were far from comparable. Consequently, children retested at different ages would appear to be conspicuously gaining or losing ability simply because of an intrinsic fallacy in the score system. Unfortunately, the discarded IQ appears to have survived in the so-called deviation IQ. This is a different sort of score altogether—itself statistically sound but made to look superficially like the traditional IQ. The term was probably adopted in response to popular demand for the familiar IQ, which seemed to provide a convenient numerical label for a person's alleged, overall intellectual level.

Aptitudes are typically defined more precisely than intelligence, to designate more narrowly limited cognitive domains. Like intelligence, however, aptitudes have traditionally been contrasted with achievement in testing terminology. This contrast dates from the early days of testing, when it was widely assumed that achievement tests measured the effects of learning, while intelligence and aptitude tests measured so-called innate capacity independently of learning. This approach to testing in turn reflected a simplistic conception of the operation of heredity and environment which prevailed in the 1920s and 1930s.

The common misconception about the relation between aptitude and achievement tests was highlighted by an index introduced in the 1920s for use with school children. Designated as an achievement quotient (AQ), this index was found by dividing the child's educational age, obtained from an educational achievement test, by her or his mental age, obtained from an intelligence test. In addition to its various statistical deficiencies, this quotient was based on a misconception of the nature of the two types of tests. That intelligence (or aptitude) tests are not essentially different from achievement tests was demonstrated as early as 1927 by Truman L. Kelley. In this connection, Kelley coined the expression "jangle fallacy," to represent the opposite of the jingle fallacy, whereby things called by the same name are assumed to be the same. The jangle fallacy results from the use of two different names to designate what is basically a single thing; but sounding different, these names foster the assumption of two different things. Through an extensive analysis of correlational data, Kelley showed that widely used intelligence tests and achievement batteries overlapped by about 90%. Subsequent investigators repeatedly found extensive overlap between the two types of tests. In some instances, the correlation between intelligence tests and achievement batteries was about as high as the reliability coefficients of each.

By midcentury, the AQ itself had in fact disappeared, at least from the major textbooks on educational testing. Nevertheless, its ghost lingered on, as exemplified in the general concept of underachievement and overachievement. These terms had first appeared in attempts to interpret deviant AQs. If children were performing up to capacity, it was expected that their AQs would be close to 100. Those with AQs under 100 were designated underachievers; those with AQs above 100 were the overachievers.

Actually, the question of underachievement or overachievement can be more properly formulated as overprediction or underprediction from the first

to the second test. It was effectively demonstrated in a 1963 monograph by Robert L. Thorndike that such intraindividual differences from one test to another simply reflect the well-known fact that no two tests are perfectly correlated. Underprediction or overprediction occurs regardless of the type of test used. It occurs, not only when an intelligence (or aptitude) test is used to predict subsequent achievement-test performance, but also if an achievement test is used to predict subsequent intelligence-test performance. Moreover, the same prediction errors are likely to occur in either direction, whether we estimate scores on the later test from scores on the earlier test, or vice versa. From a practical standpoint, the administration of alternate forms or different levels of an appropriate achievement test, before and after a course of instruction, permits a more accurate analysis of a student's accomplishment than does the use of two different kinds of tests. To take an extreme sample, if achievement in reading comprehension is predicted from a nonverbal intelligence test that is heavily loaded with spatial aptitude, the students with higher spatial than verbal aptitude will look like underachievers, whereas those with higher verbal than spatial aptitude will look like overachievers.

A current re-emergence of the AQ ghost can be seen in the monumental muddle surrounding the definition of learning disabilities (LD) among school children. Practical interest in this definition was stimulated by the enaction of a federal law providing funds for the special education of LD children. These are children who, while otherwise normal, manifest specific learning disabilities in one or more psychological processes required in understanding or using language. The most common example is a reading disability; other disabilities may affect writing, spelling, or arithmetic skills. For diagnostic purposes, the legal definition requires the establishment of a "severe discrepancy" between expected and achieved performance in one or more of these functions.

The official definition of LD has been widely recognized as too vague and subjective for proper implementation. As a result, it has been interpreted and applied in a wide variety of ways. Local implementation differs conspicuously in both assessment procedures and statistical formulas for data analysis. Specially appointed committees of experts have clearly shown that the common use of erroneous formulas to demonstrate "severe discrepancy" has produced large spurious differences in the proportion of children qualified for special education among different states—and even among districts within a state. Although serious efforts have been made to derive a proper formula for this purpose, the conceptual confusion persists. The need to predict the child's "expected" performance level has opened the way for traditional misconceptions and misapplications pertaining to IQs, tests of g, and other misuses of the aptitude construct.

A heartening note can be found in the resurgence of interest in the specific disabilities manifested in each case. Concurrently, there is a growing accumulation of research data indicating a probable neurological basis for particular disabilities. The use of intensive clinical assessment of individual children is also coming to be widely recommended both for diagnosis of disabilities and for planning of individualized educational programs. This represents a more defensible approach, which avoids involvement with predictions from dubiously labeled general aptitude tests.

B. The Continuum of Developed Abilities

To avoid the excess meanings that have become associated with aptitude and achievement tests, the more neutral term "ability" is being substituted more and more in psychometric usage. Calling an instrument an ability test simply classifies it as a measure of cognitive behavior, as distinguished, for example, from a measure of sensory acuity, muscular coordination, or emotional response. Any cognitive test, regardless of what it has traditionally been called, provides a sample of what the individual knows and has learned to do at the time he or she is tested; it measures the level of development attained in one or more abilities. No test reveals how or why the individual reached that level. To answer the latter questions, one must delve into other concomitant variables, and especially into the person's experiential background. In this sense, every test score has a past, which needs to be explored for a proper understanding of the individual who produced it. The same test score also has a future, insofar as it permits some prediction of what that individual will do in other, nontest situations, as well as at some future time.

Further clarification was introduced in the 1980s through the increasing adoption of the more explicit term "developed abilities" to cover both aptitude and achievement tests. For example, in publications distributed by the College Entrance Examination Board to test takers and to counselors and others who utilize test results, the Scholastic Aptitude Test (SAT) is described as a measure of developed verbal and mathematical reasoning abilities that are related to successful performance in college. It is further explained that SAT scores are subject to improvement through educational experience, both in and out of school. The College Board achievement tests are differentiated as measures of the student's knowledge—and his or her ability to apply such knowledge—in specific subject areas. The distinction that emerges is primarily one of breadth versus specificity of antecedent learning experience. More visible evidence of this changing orientation is provided by the new names for the College Board tests, which became effective in 1994. The widely known SAT acronym now stands for Scholastic Assessment Tests (rather than Scholastic Aptitude Test). At the same time, the College Board tests were regrouped under two headings, namely, SAT-I: Reasoning Tests (replacing former Scholastic Aptitude Test) and SAT-II: Subject Tests (replacing former achievement tests). These name changes were accompanied by significant innovations in the nature and coverage of the various tests.

Concurrent actions by the Graduate Record Examinations Board point in the same direction. In 1982 the GRE Board officially changed the name of its Aptitude Test to General Test. Its former Advanced Tests were renamed Subject Tests. These name changes were explained as an effort to avoid potential misunderstanding about the purpose of the tests. From a broader perspective, a 1982 report by a committee of the National Academy of Sciences on ability testing concluded that both aptitude and achievement tests measure developed abilities, and that both serve as indicators of the ability to learn.

Available tests of developed abilities may be ordered along a continuum in terms of the specificity of experiential background that they presuppose. This continuum is illustrated in Figure 1. At one extreme are the course-oriented achievement tests covering narrowly defined factual information or technical skills. A test on Chinese vocabulary or television maintenance would fall at this end. Many of the specialized achievement tests employed for personnel selection or classification in industry or the armed services are of this type. Teacher-made classroom examinations also belong in this category. Next in the continuum come the broadly oriented achievement batteries, commonly used to assess the attainment of major, long-term educational goals.

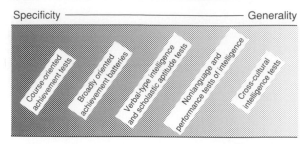

Specificity ——————————————— Generality

FIGURE 1   Tests of developed abilities: continuum of experiential specificity. [Adapted from Anastasi, A. (1988). "Psychological Testing," 6th ed. Macmillan, New York, p. 413. Reproduced by permission.]

Here are found tests focusing on the understanding and application of scientific principles, the interpretation of literature, or the appreciation of art. Still broader in orientation are tests of basic cognitive skills that affect performance in a wide variety of activities, as illustrated by reading comprehension and arithmetic computation. At the broadest level are found achievement tests designed to measure the effects of education on logical thinking, critical evaluation of conclusions, and problem-solving techniques. It is apparent that at this point achievement tests fuse imperceptibly with traditional intelligence and aptitude tests.

Further reference to Figure 1 shows a wide disparity in the experiential specificity underlying instruments designed to assess intelligence and aptitudes. The predominantly verbal, cognitive batteries, traditionally designated as intelligence tests, are close to the broadest achievement tests. Next come nonlanguage and performance tests, usually requiring no reading or writing. At the extreme generality end are the cross-cultural tests designed for use with persons of widely varied experiential backgrounds.

When instruments traditionally labeled aptitude and achievement tests are arranged in the continuum of developed abilities, we can nevertheless discern some meaningful and useful distinctions between the two test categories. Although aptitude and achievement tests near the center are virtually indistinguishable, close observation of tests at the opposite ends of the continuum reveals two principal differences. The first pertains to the degree of precision versus vagueness with which the relevant domain of antecedent experience is defined. Achievement tests measure the effects of relatively standardized sets of experiences, such as a course in elementary French, trigonometry, or computer programming. In contrast, aptitude test performance reflects the cumulative influence of a multiplicity of experiences in daily life. In other words, aptitude tests assess the effects of learning under largely unknown and uncontrolled conditions, whereas achievement tests assess the effects of learning under known and systematically controlled conditions, as in formal schooling or a specialized course of instruction.

The second difference pertains to the use of the test scores. Aptitude tests typically serve to predict subsequent performances. They are utilized to estimate the extent to which the individual will profit from a specified course of instruction or to forecast the quality of his or her performance in a job situation. Does this person have the prerequisites to take the next step in the direction he or she wants to move? Achievement tests, on the other hand, generally represent a terminal evaluation of the individual's status at the completion of training, as in passing a course, graduating from college, or obtaining a license to practice a designated specialty.

It is noteworthy, however, that under certain conditions achievement tests may also serve as predictors. For example, the progress a student has made in arithmetic, as shown by an achievement test score, can predict subsequent success in algebra. Achievement tests on premedical courses can serve as predictors of medical school performance. If aptitude is regarded as a descriptive behavioral construct, rather than a test title, it would include all the characteristics that predispose an individual to success or failure in subsequent learning or in the performance of some future activity. According to this view, an aptitude test is only one indicator of aptitude; other indicators include achievement tests, records of prior performance, and information regarding relevant physical and personality qualities.

IV. APTITUDE TESTS AND AFFECTIVE TRAITS

Since midcentury, psychologists have shown an increasing interest in reintegrating those aspects of behavior traditionally classified as cognitive and affective—or in looser and more popular terms, ability and personality. The interrelations have been investigated from many angles, and the research findings have implications for several fields of psychology. Within psychometrics, the separation between cognition and affect has tended to persist longer. Moreover, available testing instruments typically deal with the assessment of *either* cognitive or affective characteristics.

In the interpretation and use of test scores, however, a consideration of the relations between cognitive and affective variables is essential for a proper understanding of individual differences. These relations include both the effects of transient states on current behavior and the cumulative effects of more durable dispositions or traits on the development of the individual. It should also be recognized that the effects of cognitive and affective characteristics may be mutual and reciprocal rather than unidirectional. Either can influence the manifestation and development of the other. Affect is here used as a broad term to cover all noncognitive characteristics, including feelings, moods, emotions, attitudes, and motives. States refer to temporary conditions; traits denote more lasting behavioral variables or dispositions.

A. Affective Variables and Task Performance

An individual's performance on an aptitude test, as well as her or his performance in school, on the job, or in any other situation, is influenced by affective variables. A considerable body of available data indicates significant effects of temporary affective states on a person's current performance. An example is provided by studies of so-called test anxiety, which can be more broadly regarded as covering any evaluative situation perceived as personally threatening. Standardized self-report questionnaires have been developed for assessing such feelings. Anxiety states can impair performance by arousing negative feelings and such associated physiological reactions as muscular tension and increased heart rate. In addition, a cognitive component, commonly perceived as "worry," includes negative self-oriented thoughts, such as expectations of doing poorly and concern about the consequences of failure. Both the negative feelings and the disturbing thoughts tend to draw attention away from task performance and thereby lead to inferior achievement. Research with school children and college students indicates that both academic achievement and test performance are negatively correlated with measures of test anxiety.

Although test anxiety has been extensively investigated because of its immediate practical implications, the effects of many other feeling states have also been widely studied. There is evidence that even the mild pleasant or unpleasant feelings that are likely to be aroused by minor events of daily living can lead to significant differences in problem-solving strategies, in learning, and in recall. What the findings show is that temporary affective states, however mild, can influence task performance among both adults and children. [*See* TEST BEHAVIOR.]

Even more important is the cumulative effect of more enduring dispositions, or personality constructs, on the individual's performance. An affective state that is experienced repeatedly and in a diversity of contexts is well on the way to becoming an affective trait or construct for that individual. Such a personality construct will influence that person's behavior consistently across time and situations. Principal among the constructs investigated in relation to test performance are achievement motivation and self-concept. Research on what was first identified by H. A. Murray in the 1930s as the need to achieve has continued over the decades. The broad construct of achievement motivation gradually proved to be multidimensional and describable at different levels of the hierarchical model. Research through factor analysis and other statistical procedures yielded several constructs such as competitive striving, desire to meet some standard of excellence, competitive acquisitiveness, and attainment of status with peers.

A second major personality construct is the self-concept, which is also multifaceted. Studies using global self-concepts may fail to show significant correlations with performance in certain fields, whereas a more narrowly defined self-concept (e.g., academic, social, athletic) would reveal a significant relation. A person's global self-concept may be slanted to reflect his or her own value system. For instance, within a cultural group in whose value system academic achievement does not rank high, a high global self-concept would not necessarily be associated with superior academic achievement or intellectual functioning.

B. Affective Traits and the Development of Aptitudes

Affective traits influence not only immediate task performance, but also the development of aptitudes throughout the lifespan. Suggestive findings of this effect are provided by large-scale longitudinal studies of children and adults with periodic follow-ups at different ages. But such findings represent only a first step. They do not explain *how* affective variables influence aptitudes. Through what mechanisms do the individual's attitudes, interests, and motives affect the relative development of his or her aptitudes? Promising leads to an answer can be found in research on a diversity of problems pertaining to motivation, learning, and human performance. The contributions include both provocative theoretical analyses and some well-designed empirical studies.

One way that motivation and other affective variables may contribute to aptitude development is through the cumulative amount of time the individual spends on a particular kind of activity relative to other, competing activities. This effect of sheer time-on-task is enhanced by attention control. What one attends to, how deeply attention is focused, and how long attention is sustained contribute to aptitude growth. The selectivity of attention leads to selective learning—and this selection differs among persons exposed to the same objective situation. Such selective learning, in turn, may influence the relative development of different aptitudes and thereby contribute to the formation of different trait patterns. Essentially, the several aspects of attention-control serve to intensify the effect of time devoted to different activities and hence increase its influence on aptitude development.

The relation between personality and aptitudes is reciprocal. Not only do personality characteristics affect aptitude development, but aptitude level also affects personality development. The success an individual attains in the development and use of her or his aptitudes is bound to influence that person's emotional adjustment, interpersonal relations, and self-concept. In the self-concept, we can see most clearly the mutual influence of aptitudes and personality traits. The child's achievement in school, on the playground, and in other situations helps to shape her or his self-concept; and this concept at any given stage influences her or his subsequent performance. In this respect, the self-concept operates as a sort of private self-fulfilling prophecy. [*See* SELF-FULFILLING PROPHECIES.]

C. Affective Traits and Aptitude Prediction

Some long-term longitudinal studies have provided incidental evidence suggesting that the prediction of adult intellectual performance can be improved by combining affective data with aptitude test scores. Beginning in the 1970s, a more direct approach has been explored in a number of research projects on infant behavior, with follow-ups at ages ranging from

1 to 6 years. Several investigators found substantial correlations between ratings of infant behavior on affective variables and subsequent cognitive performance on such instruments as the Stanford–Binet, the Wechsler Preschool and Primary Scale of Intelligence, and the Bayley Scales of Infant Development. Affective ratings were obtained from such sources as videotaped laboratory observations, standardized ratings of infant behavior samples, and parental reports on infant temperament scales.

In general, infants who exhibited positive affect, active interest in their surroundings, and responsiveness in a testing situation tended to learn more and to advance faster than did their age peers. As a result of their early experiences, such children are also likely to respond favorably to later academic activities that involve interaction with adults in goal-oriented tasks. A further advantage stems from the influence that such infant behavior exerts on the perceptions and responses of adult caretakers, which will in turn advance the child's opportunities for further learning.

Among the affective variables investigated, special interest has centered on environmental-mastery motivation. Although applicable throughout the lifespan, this motivation has been studied most thoroughly at the infant level. Known by a diversity of names (e.g., sensation-seeking, exploration, environmental manipulation, experience-producing motivation, information-processing motivation), environmental-mastery behavior includes essentially the observation, exploration, manipulation, and control of one's immediate environment. It begins with the infant's earliest efforts to gain information from her or his world through visual fixation of objects. Visual exploration is soon combined with auditory and tactual exploration. There is evidence that such exploratory behavior is more than just a random response to stimulation. Rather, it is a specific way of processing relevant information, as demonstrated by the appropriateness of the behavior to particular changes in object properties. For example, in one experiment, changes in object texture evoked an increase in time spent in looking and fingering, together with a decrease in pushing and throwing; changes in object shape had the same effects, while also eliciting an increase in rotating the object and in transferring it from one hand to the other. Through manipulation, the child also discovers that he or she can affect the environment, as in dropping a block to see it fall and hear it hit the floor, or waving a bell to make it ring. Environmental mastery is later manifested in more complex problem-solving and goal-directed activities; it also expands to include efforts to influence the behavior of caretakers and other associates.

Because of its very nature, the environmental-mastery motive should be a prime contributor to aptitude development. And there is increasing evidence from experimental research that it does so contribute. Available findings suggest that a child's motivation for environmental mastery may be a better predictor of later intellectual competence than are earlier measures of competence.

A final implication of the relation between affect and cognitive development is the possible role of motivation and other affective variables in mediating the influence of heredity on aptitudes. That genes could directly determine individual differences in, for example, verbal or mathematical aptitude seems unlikely in the light of current knowledge about both the operation of heredity and the development of human behavior. What is needed is more information about the many intervening steps in the etiological chain of events from genes to behavior. The role of motivation may represent one such step. Supporting data are provided by research on early childhood development, as well as studies of strain differences in behavior within several animal species, including both natural and selectively bred strains. The available findings suggest that cognitive aptitudes are acquired by learning, and that inherited motivational makeup influences what one learns and how much is learned.

Bibliography

Anastasi, A. (1984). Aptitude and achievement tests: The curious case of the indestructible strawperson. In "Social and Technical Issues in Testing: Implications for Test Construction and Usage" (B. S. Plake, Ed.). Erlbaum, Hillsdale, NJ.

Anastasi, A. (1985). Reciprocal relations between cognitive and affective development—With implications for sex differences. In "Psychology and Gender" (T. B. Sonderegger, Ed.). University of Nebraska Press, Lincoln.

Anastasi, A. (1986). Experiential structuring of psychological traits. *Dev. Rev.* **6**, 181–202.

Anastasi, A. (1988). "Psychological Testing," 6th ed. Macmillan, New York.

Anastasi, A. (1993). A century of psychological testing: Origins, problems, and progress. In "A Centennial Celebration—From Then to Now: Psychology Applied" (G. R. VandenBos and T. K. Fagan, Eds.). American Psychological Association, Washington, DC.

Delaney, E., and Hopkins, T. (1987). "Stanford–Binet Intelligence Scale—Examiner's Handbook: An Expanded Guide for Fourth Edition Users" (Chapts. 6 and 7). Riverside, Chicago.

Elliott, C. D. (1990). "Differential Ability Scales: Introductory and Technical Handbook" (Chapt. 2). The Psychological Corporation, San Antonio, TX.

Yarrow, L. J., and Messer, P. J. (1983). Motivation and cognition in infancy. In "Origins of Intelligence: Infancy and Early Childhood" (M. Lewis, Ed.). Plenum, New York.

ARBITRATION

Steven L. Thomas
Southwest Missouri State University

Robert D. Bretz, Jr.
Cornell University

Glossary

Chilling effect The tendency to hold back or fail to make concessions during bargaining in anticipation that an arbitrator will "split the difference" between the final positions.

Final-offer arbitration A form of arbitration in which the arbitrator is constrained to choose either the award suggested by one party or that suggested by the other, and may not impose any compromise solution.

Lemon laws Laws that exist in several states requiring arbitration between manufacturers and dissatisfied consumers when a product has not been repaired after a reasonable number of attempts.

Mediation A process in which a neutral third-party encourages the disputing parties to informally explore settlement alternatives, offer concessions, and reach agreement in a mutually acceptable settlement, but does not have the authority to impose a solution.

Narcotic effect The tendency to continue using arbitration as a dispute resolution mechanism rather than reaching mutually agreeable settlements in the normal bargaining forum.

Past practice doctrine When, by their consistent and frequent actions over a period of time, the parties involved have given meaning to ambiguous contract language.

ARBITRATION is a formal third-party intervention into the dispute resolution process. Traditionally, arbitration has been used to resolve disputes arising over the interpretation of various provisions of collectively bargained agreements. Recently, however, arbitration has become increasingly important as an alternative dispute resolution mechanism in a variety of conflict resolution situations including business, financial, and consumer-related issues. The arbitration process begins when disagreeing parties agree to submit a dispute to a mutually acceptable third-party neutral and abide by the decision rendered. The parties to the dispute present evidence and testimony to the neutral third-party (the arbitrator), who then renders a legally binding decision.

I. ARBITRATION AND COLLECTIVE BARGAINING

A. Arbitration versus Mediation

Third-party dispute resolution procedures including both mediation and arbitration have been mainstays of the American industrial relations system. Mediation, an informal intervention into the collective bargaining process, is a widely used process where a neutral third-party (the mediator) assists union and management representatives reach a mutually acceptable settlement. The mediator has no formal authority and cannot force the parties to settle. The role of the mediator is to encourage the parties to informally explore settlement alternatives, offer concessions, and reach agreement.

Arbitration is separate and distinct from mediation, and the role of the arbitrator is much different from that of the mediator. Arbitration is a formal third-party intervention into the collective bargaining process in which the parties agree to bring a dispute to a mutually agreeable neutral third-party for adjudication. It is a quasi-judicial function. Arbitration is judicial in character in the sense that the arbitrator's decision is binding and legally enforceable. Arbitration is not truly judicial, however, for it is essentially private, contractual, and subject to relaxed rules regarding procedure, testimony, and evidence.

B. A Taxonomy of the Forms of Arbitration

A definition of arbitration must include an explanation of the different forms that the process can assume. Arbitration can be either voluntary or compulsory. In voluntary arbitration the parties mutually agree to submit their differences to a third-party. In compulsory arbitration, however, at the insistence of either party (as required either by contract language or by law), disputes must be submitted to arbitration.

Arbitration can be further classified by the nature of the conflict and the nature of the award. The conflict can involve either interest or rights issues. Interest arbitration involves disputes over the final contractual language. These might include wage levels, benefit provisions, seniority rights, management rights, and related issues. Rights disputes, by contrast, arise over interpreting the language of the contract already in force. Common rights disputes involve individual grievances arising over disciplinary infractions, overtime pay, or promotions. Although arbitration over rights issues is very common in both private and public sectors, interest arbitration is rarely used in private sector American labor relations.

The scope and finality of the award serve to further define the arbitration process. Arbitration can be advisory, conventional, or final-offer. Advisory arbitration, or fact-finding, occurs most commonly in interest cases when the third-party neutral hears testimony from both parties and makes an award that one or both of the parties may reject. Advisory arbitration is common in the public sector where the award is often (but not always) binding on the union but not the public entity.

Under conventional arbitration, the arbitrator has considerable discretion in the determination of award. He or she can select the benefit or relief suggested by either party, select an award that represents a compromise between the two positions, or select any outcome he or she deems reasonable. In final-offer arbitration, however, the arbitrator is constrained to choose either the award suggested by one party or that suggested by the other, and may not impose any compromise solution. While conventional arbitration may involve either interest or rights issues, final-offer arbitration is normally reserved for interest issues, and the case may be decided issue-by-issue or as a total package. The most visible system of final-offer arbitration is in major league baseball where players with more than 2 years in the major leagues can insist on resolving salary disputes through this procedure.

C. Evaluating Arbitration

Evaluating the success of arbitration requires separate consideration for interest and rights cases. The criteria for evaluating interest arbitration include (1) how successful arbitration has been in preventing strikes or bargaining impasses, and (2) the extent to which arbitration interferes with the parties' ability to resolve disputes without outside assistance.

The research on the success of arbitration is somewhat mixed. Advisory arbitration or fact-finding, despite its relatively common use, has not been demonstrated to be a very effective tool for dispute resolution in the public sector. Clearly, conventional arbitration tends to perform better than fact-finding in preventing strikes. The overutilization of conventional interest arbitration, however, has been criticized for having a "chilling effect" and a "narcotic effect" on negotiations. The chilling effect occurs when the parties fail to make concessions during bargaining because they anticipate that an arbitrator will "split the difference" between their positions. In essence, arbitration "chills" the willingness of the parties to compromise. Similarly, the narcotic effect occurs over time when the parties' excessive reliance on arbitration discourages bargained settlements.

Relative to conventional arbitration, final-offer arbitration reduces chilling effects. While most disputes are resolved without resort to arbitration, some research has indicated that overreliance on arbitration may occur in certain situations. In any event, the general antipathy toward interest arbitration by the private sector makes any conclusions about interest arbitration somewhat suspect.

By contrast, rights arbitration is well accepted in both public and private sectors as the final step in resolving disputes arising over the terms of a labor agreement. Although rights arbitration has been criticized for delays and costs, as a mechanism to promote industrial peace it has worked relatively well and participants are generally satisfied with the process.

II. THE LEGAL STATUS OF ARBITRATION

Arbitration was seldom used prior to World War II. Its status and wide utilization in the private sector today are largely the result of the influence of the War Labor Board, the language of the Taft-Hartley Act, and a series of court cases dating from the mid-1950s. The use of arbitration for federal public sector employees has grown relatively recently as a result of changing federal law.

A. The Influence of the War Labor Board

Prior to World War II, disputes arising over the terms and conditions of a labor contract were typically resolved through strikes, boycotts, or other forms of concerted activity. The War Labor Board, in an effort to maintain the productive capacity of American industry during the war effort, encouraged arbitration as a peaceful alternative for resolving disputes.

B. Taft-Hartley and Arbitration

The original 1935 Wagner Act governed many aspects of union organizing and collective bargaining, and created the National Labor Relations Board (NLRB) to prosecute unfair labor practices (activities that violated the Act). Breach of contract, however, was not an unfair labor practice. Under common law, the parties had little legal recourse to enforce the terms of a collective bargaining agreement. The Taft-Hartley amendments of 1947, however, included language favoring mediation and arbitration as preferred mechanisms for resolving disputes. In addition, Section 301 of Taft-Hartley provided for suits in federal court to enforce contract terms. Thus, Taft-Hartley spurred the growth of arbitration since it was far less expensive and much faster for the parties to take contract disputes to arbitration than to litigate in court.

C. Arbitration and the Courts

A number of legal decisions beginning in the mid-1950s served to both expand the scope of arbitration and define its finality. In the 1957 *Lincoln Mills* case, the Supreme Court ruled in favor of the Textile Workers union in deciding that the company could be compelled to use a contractual arbitration clause. Essentially, the Court stated that a firm's agreement to arbitrate labor disputes is the *quid pro quo* for the union's agreement not to strike. Arbitration reflected the national interests for it insured industrial peace. As a result, arbitration provisions in labor contracts could be enforced in federal courts.

Three court cases in 1960, widely known as the Steelworkers' Trilogy because all three involved the United Steelworkers Union, further defined the legal status of arbitration. The Court concluded that:

1. Doubts about whether an issue is subject to arbitration will be resolved in favor of arbitration.
2. The courts will determine whether an issue is arbitrable, not the merits of a grievance.
3. Courts should not review the merits of an arbitrator's award so long as it is based on the collective bargaining agreement.

The decisions in these cases served to enhance the authority of the arbitrator, to limit the role of the courts in reviewing an arbitrator's decision, and to preserve the final and binding nature of the arbitration process. Additional cases, such as *John Wiley and Sons v. Livingston* in 1964, continued to define the arbitrator's authority by concluding that, in general, the arbitrator, not the courts, decides whether a case is arbitrable under the collective bargaining agreement.

D. Arbitration and the NLRB

Historically, the NLRB has given great deference to the arbitrator's decision in arbitration cases involving unfair labor practices (ULP). In *Spielberg Manufacturing Co.* (1955), the NLRB said that it would not hear ULP cases where an arbitrator had previously made a ruling on the issue as part of a grievance hearing, so long as the proceedings were "fair and regular" and in keeping with the spirit of the labor laws. In *Collyer Insulated Wire* (1971) and subsequent cases, the NLRB has ruled that they will defer to arbitration those ULP complaints that can be heard through the arbitration process, limiting their review to situations in which grievances were not submitted in a timely fashion or to those in which the grievance and arbitration procedures were not fair and regular. This deference to arbitration reflects the widespread acceptance of the arbitrator's expertise and the use of arbitration as the preferred means to maintain industrial peace.

E. Legal Review of the Arbitration Process

While the courts and the NLRB have shown considerable deference to arbitration, the arbitration process is subject to limited review. The courts have modified arbitrators' decisions and awards on the basis of fraud, partiality, or corruption on the part of the arbitrator, arbitrator misconduct, or where arbitrators have exceeded their authority. In addition, though the union decides which grievances have merit and which should go to arbitration, it has the duty to fairly represent every employee. In situations where the union fails to fairly represent a member during the grievance process, the arbitrator's decision is not binding and can be vacated.

F. Arbitration for Federal Employees

The use of arbitration for disputes involving federal government employees and their unions has grown largely as a result of federal legislation. The Civil Service Reform Act (CSRA) of 1978 codified earlier executive orders from the Nixon administration creating a labor relations system for federal employees. The CSRA created a federal counterpart to the NLRB called the Federal Labor Relations Authority (FLRA) to hear disputes, and the Federal Services Impasse Panel (FSIP) to help resolve bargaining impasses. The CSRA stimulated the use of arbitration in both interest and rights cases. Regarding the former, the FSIP may approve binding arbitration over the terms of labor agreements. Concerning rights cases, the CSRA requires that all collective bargaining agreements contain grievance and arbitration procedures. The arbitrator's decision is reviewable by the FLRA in either situation upon the filing of an "exception" by either the agency or union involved.

III. THE ARBITRATION PROCESS IN INDUSTRIAL RELATIONS

Labor arbitration is a unique and important part of the American industrial relations system. This section details the mechanics and the procedures of labor arbitration: how disputes progress to arbitration, how the arbitrator is chosen, and how cases proceed. Also in this section, the criteria arbitrators use to make decisions (the "Common Law of Arbitration") are explored.

A. From Disputes to Arbitration: Grievance Procedures and the Arbitration Clause

The labor contract normally specifies how disputes between labor and management may be resolved, and under what circumstances disputes may be sub-

mitted to arbitration. Most labor agreements require that disputes be adjudicated through a set of steps called a grievance procedure. A typical procedure (as outlined below) introduces higher levels of both union and management involvement at each step:

1. The employee, the union steward, and the immediate supervisor discuss the grievance and attempt to resolve the problem.
2. If the employee and the steward feel that the problem has not been resolved, the grievance is put in writing and submitted to a designated manager. Line management (frequently with assistance from industrial relations staff) and the union business agent discuss the grievance, and management's response is submitted in writing.
3. The grievance may be appealed to upper management and industrial relations staff. Additional union officials become involved at this point.
4. The grievance is submitted to arbitration for a binding decision.

Individual employees may initiate and process grievances through the initial steps of the process, but the ultimate decision to arbitrate the grievance is made by the union. In addition, the union can file grievances based on the perceived violation of union rights, or on behalf of a large number of employees.

If the parties cannot resolve their dispute, the issue may proceed to arbitration, consistent with the terms of the bargained agreement. Typically, either party can initiate arbitration by serving the other with a written *Demand for Arbitration* containing the issue to be decided. Alternatively, the parties may jointly file a *Submission Agreement* that outlines the question for the arbitrator to decide and the contract language relevant to the question. The arbitrator may decide the wording of the issue if the parties cannot agree. Regardless, the language of the submission agreement is important because it defines the issue to be decided, and thereby places limits on the arbitrator's authority.

B. The Arbitration Hearing

There are different forums for arbitration. The most common is an *ad hoc* arbitrator, or one who is selected by the parties for a specific dispute. Other arrangements include permanent umpire systems where a single permanent arbitrator serves the parties, generally for the duration of the labor agreement. One other system is a *tripartite* format where a neutral serves as the chairperson of a board composed of one representative from labor and one from management.

Direct selection of the arbitrator by mutual consent is probably the most common method of selecting an arbitrator. Neutral agencies such as the American Arbitration Association (AAA) or the Federal Mediation and Conciliation Service (FMCS) provide lists of experienced arbitrators from which the parties can select. If the contract specifies that the AAA should assist with arbitrator selection, they will typically respond with a list of five arbitrators. Management and labor alternatively reject names until one arbitrator is chosen.

When an arbitrator is selected, he or she has the duty to arrange and conduct the arbitration proceeding. This process is designed to give the parties a "full and fair" hearing in which each party has the opportunity to present their arguments, witnesses, and evidence. The arbitrator rules on matters of evidence and testimony, and it is his or her obligation to reach a decision based on the record in the case.

Commonly, the labor contract will specify that the arbitration costs will be borne equally by the parties. Some contracts specify that the loser will bear the costs of the proceeding. The contract may also specify restrictions regarding compensation for witnesses and employee advocates such as union officials.

The arbitration hearing typically is private, open only to the persons directly involved in the case. The location of the hearing frequently is a conference room at the work site, or a similarly convenient location. Off-site locations may offer more privacy and a neutral setting; however, they increase hearing costs and may cause delays and inconvenience.

Once the submission agreement has been framed, the presentation of the case begins with an opening statement by each party. The union usually goes first in contract interpretation cases, while management usually begins in cases involving employee discipline. Witnesses are sworn in, then advocates for each party examine witnesses to determine the facts in the case. Just as in a court of law, direct examination of a party's own witnesses is followed by cross-examination by the other party. Advocates may be attorneys, or they may be union and management officials.

After the hearing, the arbitrator will issue an oral or written decision (sometimes the contract will specify the time limits and the form of the decision). Arbitrators are not required to issue an opinion explaining the decision, although many choose to do so. With permission of the parties, these opinions may be published in reporting services. The arbitrator's decision is final, binding, and enforceable on the parties involved.

C. Arbitrability

The issue of *arbitrability*—a question about whether an issue is subject to arbitration—is central to the arbitration process. If either party can show that a matter is not arbitrable, then the arbitrator has no jurisdiction and there can be no hearing.

Issues of arbitrability can be either substantive or procedural. Substantive issues involve questions about the arbitrator's jurisdiction and can be raised at any time during the process: before, during, or even after the arbitration hearing. A party challenging the arbitrator's authority on jurisdictional grounds would claim that the labor agreement forbids taking certain types of disputes to arbitration. Issues of substantive arbitrability are ultimately decided by the courts. However, the parties may empower the arbitrator to resolve jurisdictional issues.

Procedural arbitrability problems arise, not over the merits of an issue, but over matters of procedure. One party, while acknowledging the arbitrator's jurisdiction under the agreement, challenges the arbitration hearing on the basis of procedural problems such as failure to meet time restrictions in filing a grievance or appeal, or absence of signatures from required forms. The parties are normally required to file procedural complaints at the earliest possible step in the grievance process. The arbitrator is empowered to resolve procedural disputes.

D. Contract Language, Management's Rights and Implied Obligations

There are two basic types of arbitration cases that involve quite different kinds of issues: (1) contract interpretation cases, and (2) cases involving employee discipline. Contract interpretation cases involve disputes arising over the interpretation of contract language, and may address a wide variety of issues including wages, job classifications, pay for time not worked, layoff and recall rights, seniority, promotions, and management rights. Discipline and discharge cases deal with the reasonable and consistent application of company rules and negotiated agreements to problems of employee performance and behavior. Although contract interpretation cases require the arbitrator to explore the meaning of the labor agreement as it applies to the issue, the focus of discipline and discharge cases tends to be on reasonable and even-handed treatment of employees with respect, not only to the contract, but to established practices of progressive discipline.

The arbitrator's decision is based on the submission agreement and the record of the hearing (evidence and testimony), but it must find agreement in the language of the labor contract. No decision can be contrary to the intent of the labor agreement. While this seems clear in theory, contract language is seldom unambiguous, and the meaning of the contract frequently must be gleaned from principles of contract interpretation.

Clear and unambiguous language in the labor agreement is usually the controlling factor in the arbitrator's decision. The arbitrator will usually not look beyond clear language for evidence of intent. The parties cannot, of course, anticipate every aspect of the employment relationship and reduce it to written language. Thus, where contract language is ambiguous, the arbitrator may infer meaning through principles of contract construction such as management's rights, past practice, or other devices.

Management's rights, or the reserved rights doctrine, is basic to interpreting the collective bargaining agreement. The doctrine of management's rights suggests that management has the right to run the business. Management's authority is, therefore, foremost in all matters except those that it has explicitly conceded in the labor contract. Most arbitrators would probably agree that the employer retains all rights not restricted or not mentioned in the agreement. In contract interpretation cases, the burden is on the union to show that these rights were conceded. Along with management's rights, however, is a "doctrine of implied obligations." This doctrine states that although management may alter or abolish employee benefits during contract negotiations, once negotiations conclude management has an "implied obligation" to maintain them for the duration of the contract.

Past practice is invoked when it is shown that the parties, by their consistent and frequent actions over a period of time, have given meaning to ambiguous contract language. The party invoking this interpretation must demonstrate that the practice was uniform, consistent, and mutually accepted as the customary practice. When this is established, past practice provides a useful guide for interpreting vague language.

In addition to management's rights and past practice, the arbitrator may use principles from the laws of contract interpretation as guidelines to interpret the contract. First of all, contract language is only interpreted in the context of the entire agreement. Therefore, any specific provision of a labor contract will tend to be interpreted so that it is compatible with the rest of the contract. When two conflicting provisions are present within one agreement, the arbitrator will assume that the more specific provision prevails over the general language that it contradicts.

In general, common usage and the ordinary dictionary meaning of terms prevail. Where there is technical language in the contract, words are given their meaning common to the industrial practice. Contract language is always interpreted in context so that language is not incongruent with the remainder of the contract. If the parties include long "laundry lists" of items in a contract, arbitrators will conclude that those items omitted from the list were not meant to be included or covered by that provision of the agreement.

The parties and the arbitrator may also look to the history of negotiations to resolve disputes. The most recent labor contract represents an evolutionary process in that it is based on prior agreements that serve to define the parties' intent. A failed attempt by the union to include a particular provision, for example, could be used by management as evidence of the employer's intent to abolish a longstanding past practice.

E. Evidence and Proof

A labor arbitration hearing is not a court of law. The proceedings are private and designed to preserve a working relationship that must prevail long after the hearing concludes. Since the focus, however, is on maintaining industrial peace by giving the parties full opportunity to be heard, strict rules of evidence generally do not apply. The arbitrator has considerable discretion over issues of evidence and testimony.

Arbitrators, unlike juries in a court of law, are considered to be experts who know how to appropriately weigh all evidence and testimony, and do not need to be protected from hearsay and irrelevant information. The inclination in most arbitration cases is to give the parties considerable latitude in the presentation of evidence, under the theory that a full hearing is of cathartic value to the parties. The arbitrator is able to weigh the evidence and testimony appropriately, rejecting the irrelevant and immaterial.

Evidence in an arbitration case can be real and tangible, it may be circumstantial, or it may come in the form of oral testimony. Often, the arbitrator must judge the truthfulness of testimony, particularly when two witnesses contradict each other. In these instances, the arbitrator will consider the testimony on the basis of (a) the witness's demeanor and character for honesty, (b) the extent of his or her ability to recall and communicate the matter, (c) the existence of any bias or self-interest in the matter, (d) inconsistencies with evidence or previous testimony, or (e) any admissions of deceit on the part of the witness.

The burden of proof in arbitration cases is different from that in the courts. In contract interpretation cases, the burden of proof is normally on the union to demonstrate how the company violated the agreement. Conversely, in cases of discipline and discharge, the burden of proof is on the company. However, the burden of proof is a function of the evidence and testimony presented during the course of the hearing. Thus, either party may find that it has the burden to rebut evidence or testimony presented by the other party as the hearing proceeds.

There is no clear criterion for the extent of proof necessary for either party to win. Most arbitrators take the position that a stricter standard of proof is required in cases involving employee discipline. Clearly, legal standards such as "proof beyond a reasonable doubt," or even less stringent standards such as "clear and convincing proof" do not apply in arbitration cases. All that is necessary is for a party to provide enough evidence to persuade the arbitrator that the party's position is supported.

F. Discipline and Discharge

In their examination of discipline and discharge cases, arbitrators give great deference to the "just cause" standard for assessing the reasonableness of actions taken by the employer. The just cause standard creates an obligation on the part of the employer to first conform to procedural due process, then to convince the arbitrator that an employee was disciplined for cause, and, finally, that the disciplinary action fits the offense.

Management clearly has the right to formulate reasonable work rules in order to maintain an efficient, orderly, and productive establishment. While work rules can be negotiated, they frequently are not part of the labor agreement. Most often, company rules are developed outside the contract and are communicated to employees through employment manuals and written notices.

Thus, the first step in procedural just cause is to make the rules known to employees. Procedural due process also requires that an employer complies with procedures specified in the collective bargaining agreement regarding "just cause." The arbitrator will require the employer to specify the infraction in writing, provide information to the employee and union, and provide opportunities for investigation and appeals.

If the procedural aspects of a case are adequate, the arbitrator will determine whether the penalty meets the just cause standard. The arbitrator will look for uniform and consistent application of plant rules. Employees must know that certain behavior is prohibited and that a disciplinary action will be the result of an infraction. If the employer fails to enforce plant rules or discriminates against some employees in the application of those rules, the arbitrator will rarely uphold the disciplinary penalty. Lack of uniformity and consistency in enforcing rules can create a false sense of security because employees come to believe that violations will be tolerated. An experienced arbitrator will rarely tolerate this kind of uneven application of discipline.

The concept of progressive corrective discipline is at the heart of the just cause doctrine. Most arbitrators regard discipline not as punishment, but as a means to correct behavior. Even when the steps of a system of progressive discipline are not spelled out in the agreement, arbitrators will look to evidence of escalating penalties (increasingly severe penalties for repeated infractions) as in indication of just cause in the administration of discipline because it provides the employee with an opportunity to correct inappropriate behavior. Although progressive discipline provides for escalating penalties (oral warnings, written warnings, suspension, and discharge), the arbitrator is aware that for certain serious infractions (fighting, employee theft, reporting to work under the influence, for example), discharge may be appropriate on the first offense.

If the arbitrator finds for the employer, the disciplinary penalty will stand. Alternatively, the arbitrator may decide, based on the evidence presented at the hearing, that although the employee committed an infraction, the disciplinary action was too harsh. Whether the employee was found to have committed a lesser infraction than that suggested by management, or because extenuating circumstances exist (e.g., seniority or a good work record), the arbitrator may modify the disciplinary action (such as reducing a discharge to a suspension). If, however, the arbitrator rules that for either procedural or substantive reasons the employee was disciplined without cause, the arbitrator must fashion a remedy. Remedies typically are of the "make whole" variety, and may include reinstatement or backpay awards.

IV. ARBITRATION IN ALTERNATIVE DISPUTE RESOLUTION

This final section is devoted to the increasing tendency to use arbitration in a variety of nonlabor disputes. These include business disputes, securities-related disputes, and a variety of consumer-related issues such as "lemon-laws" (laws in several states that require arbitration between manufacturers and dissatisfied consumers).

A. Alternative Dispute Resolution in the Business Community

Many businesses, frustrated with the high costs of litigation and the delays in the courts system, have recently begun to rely on *alternative dispute resolution* (ADR) procedures such as arbitration to resolve disputes with other parties. Statistics reported by the AAA indicate that the number of annual commercial case filings has increased from less than 5000 in the late 1970s, to more than 12,000 by 1990.

ADR may involve a number of techniques other than arbitration and mediation to resolve business disputes involving issues ranging from complex environmental disputes to creditor–debtor relationships. Because of crowded court dockets and prolonged and expensive litigation, the value of ADR techniques has become more apparent to many organizations.

ADR techniques, however, may not work well in all circumstances. Mediation will work best (a) where both parties desire a continuation of the business relationship, (b) where they have relatively equal financial resources and experience, and (c) where the parties have relatively high levels of mutual trust. Regardless, either mediation or arbi-

tration is likely to be less destructive to the business relationship than a protracted court battle since it is not nearly so adversarial. In addition, the process is more predictable, and the dispute resolution process can be contractually prearranged.

ADR techniques have a number of characteristics that make their use advantageous (these attributes, however, may not be desirable in all circumstances). Specifically, when disputes are litigated managers have less direct control over their resolution than when disputes are arbitrated. Arbitration reduces the role of the attorney and requires more involvement by operating management.

In many cases, arbitration is less expensive and less time consuming than litigation. Trial preparation expenses, which occasionally approach settlement costs, can be substantially reduced through the arbitration process. However, whereas the public bears the cost of the forum in the court system, the parties must pay for the third-party services provided by the arbitrator. These direct expenses, however, are, typically more than offset by the savings produced by the limited prehearing expenses of arbitration.

Nonmonetary issues also make arbitration attractive. Because arbitration, unlike most litigation, is a private process, it insures some degree of confidentiality and little publicity. Unlike decisions in a court of law, the process does not create a legal precedent that binds the parties in the future. Thus, while arbitration and other ADR techniques clearly are not appropriate for all business-related disputes, they are being increasingly and successfully used where the interests of both parties are served by resolving disagreements in an expedient and relatively inexpensive forum.

B. Small Claims, Consumer Arbitration, and Lemon Laws

The small claims court system was established during the early part of this century to hear minor civil claims including the collection of debts and consumer complaints. Small claims courts were initiated as a reaction to the expense and complexity of a regular court system that had become an inadequate mechanism for resolving minor disputes. In recent years, however, small claims courts also have become the object of criticism due to delays, burdensome procedures, expense, and inaccessibility. A good deal of the criticism has resulted from the inability of the courts to deal effectively with cases involving consumer complaints spawned by the consumer protection movement.

In recent years, one important and innovative technique used to address these problems has been the development of mediation/arbitration programs. Most of the current mediation/arbitration programs were developed during the 1970s to handle minor civil disputes. The parties to the dispute could initially be offered mediation as an aid in reaching a mutually acceptable solution to their problem. Alternatively, the parties could agree in court to binding arbitration by a third-party neutral to resolve the complaint. Arbitration also has benefitted the court system by reducing caseloads. Additionally, the parties benefit because the hearing process is normally more convenient and expedient than a court decision.

One of the best examples of consumer arbitration in recent years has been the development of arbitration programs aimed at resolving complaints regarding automobile purchases under a variety of state-enacted "lemon laws." Consumer dissatisfaction with automobile purchases and warranties is well documented. Since the court system has been of limited value in addressing consumer complaints regarding automobile purchases, the states began passing legislation in the early 1980s aimed at getting automobile manufacturers to provide refunds or replacement vehicles to consumers whose vehicles were "lemons," or not repaired after a certain number of attempts. In 1982, Connecticut became the first state to pass such a bill. Since then, 45 states have followed with "lemon laws" of some variety.

State lemon laws vary considerably in terms of coverage, filing and time limit requirements, and costs. One commonality, however, is that arbitration plays a predominant rule in the adjudication of disputes. Some state laws have been the subject of criticism because consumers are required to go through dispute resolution programs run by the automobile industry. Observers have noted that these programs offer inadequate relief to consumers because the panels of volunteer arbitrators generally are not adequately trained, and frequently have close ties to the industry resulting in biases against the consumer.

As a result of problems with early lemon laws, a number of states (e.g., Florida) have amended their laws to be more responsive to consumer needs. The Florida attorney general screens applicants, and the state trains and appoints them for a 1-year term to the Florida New Motor Vehicle Arbitration Board.

The board is the final step for consumers with complaints regarding defective new automobiles. The Florida law covers new automobile purchases for 1 year, and requires consumers to give the manufacturer four opportunities to repair the automobile. At that point, the consumer can demand a refund or replacement. The consumer must first attempt to resolve the dispute through the manufacturer's dispute resolution process. If that process fails, the consumer may pay a $50 filing fee and take the dispute to the state's arbitration program where the consumer must demonstrate that the vehicle is not in conformity with the warranty and that nonconformity has had an adverse impact on the value or safety of the vehicle.

Florida, like other states with similar laws, has experienced an increasing volume of cases. As these arbitration programs mature, it appears that more cases tend to be resolved prior to arbitration. In Florida, for example, during 1990 about 40% of all cases were settled in the prehearing stage. Since consumers prevail in over two-thirds of arbitration cases heard, it appears that manufacturers are becoming increasingly inclined to settle prior to arbitration.

The Better Business Bureaus in most states operate voluntary arbitration programs to resolve consumer disputes. A number of automobile manufacturers and other businesses voluntarily participte in the arbitration programs. Although participation is currently limited, the program appears to be growing as both the public and the business community have come to place greater trust and acceptance in the arbitration process.

C. Arbitration in the Securities Industry

Securities industry arbitration involves disputes between investors and brokerage houses that arise over improper or unauthorized trading, or over misrepresented investments. Arbitration in the securities industry has a long and checkered history. Some of the earliest arbitration cases date from the late 1800s. The courts, however, had a generally hostile attitude toward compulsory arbitration in the securities industry, perceiving the mechanism to be an infringement of investors' rights. It was not until the 1980s when a series of cases inolving securities firms (*Dean Witter Reynolds Inc. v. Byrd, Mitsubishi Motors Corp. v. Soler Chrysler-Plymouth Inc.*, and *Shearson/American Express Inc. v. McMahon*) produced decisions that established the scope and finality of compulsory arbitration in the securities industry. This group of cases firmly established that when investors sign a predispute agreement to arbitrate, said agreement is enforceable, and the investors are precluded from turning to the courts for relief.

While arbitration has generally been hailed as an expedient, inexpensive, and satisfactory means to resolve disputes, arbitration in the securities industry has not enjoyed the same success. The public perception of securities arbitration is that the process is biased and unfair to the general public.

Securities arbitration is perceived to be unfair primarily because it is clearly not voluntary. To open a brokerage account the customer must generally sign a form with a provision agreeing to mandatory arbitration. Critics suggest that the unsophisticated investor frequently has little understanding of the provision or its importance. This practice has made the mandatory arbitration provision the subject of recent (albeit unsuccessful) legal challenges. In response, many brokerage firms have adopted procedures that offer more complete disclosure of the arbitration provision.

The actual arbitration procedure also has been the target of much public criticism. Because the securities industry is responsible for regulating itself, securities arbitration is accomplished through the industry arbitration system. The industry requires that a securities expert be part of the arbitration panel. While the industry argument that complex cases require securities experts is logical, the public's perception is that participation by industry insiders on the arbitration panel introduces favoritism into the process. Although the securities industry has historically been opposed to arbitration outside the industry arrangement, the recent trend appears to be toward allowing more disputes to go to external forums such as the AAA.

V. ARBITRATION: AN OVERVIEW

Arbitration, as an alternative dispute resolution mechanism, remains an integral component of the United States' industrial relations, business, consumer, and financial institutions.

Within the American system of labor relations, arbitration remains a highly institutionalized and well-accepted system of industrial jurisprudence, and it continues to promote industrial peace by resolving disputes between labor and management.

Although arbitration is less integral to business dispute resolution, as litigation becomes more expensive and time consuming the business community appears to be submitting disputes to arbitration and other ADR techniques with increasing frequency. Court decisions in the recent past, the consumer movement, and general legislative developments have served to reinforce the trend toward arbitration by encouraging its use and by increasing its legitimacy.

The future for arbitration is bright. In general, companies are less resistant to arbitration than in the past, and both consumers and business people appear less likely to view arbitration with suspicion and mistrust. As court calendars fill and litigation costs rise, arbitration is increasingly likely to be viewed as the formal means of choice for resolving an increasing variety of disputes.

Bibliography

American Arbitration Association. ''Arbitration and the Law'' (various editions). New York.

American Arbitration Association. ''The Arbitration Journal'' (various issues). New York.

Cane, M. B., and Shub, P. A. (1991). ''Securities Arbitration Law and Procedure.'' BNA Books, Washington, D.C.

Elkouri, F., and Elkouri, E. A. (1973). ''How Arbitration Works,'' 3rd ed. Bureau of National Affairs, Washington, D.C.

Fossum, J. A. (1992). ''Labor Relations,'' 5th ed. Richard D. Irwin, Homewood, IL.

Kochan, T. A., and Katz, H. C. (1988). ''Collective Bargaining and Industrial Relations,'' 2nd ed. Richard D. Irwin, Homewood, IL.

LaCugna, C. S. (1988). ''An Introduction to Labor Arbitration.'' Praeger, New York.

Zack, A. M. (1992). ''A Handbook for Grievance Arbitration.'' Lexington Books, New York.

Zack, A. M. (1989). ''Grievance Arbitration.'' Lexington Books, New York.

ASSOCIATIVE LEARNING

Ken-ichi Hara
Ishinomaki Sensyu University, Japan

Tatsuo Kitajima
Yamagata University, Japan

Glossary

Autoassociative recall Recall of the memory stored as connection weights between units in the network by evoking the most selective response to a key stimulus.

Competitive learning Learning rule that only the most strongly activated neuron can modify its synaptic efficacy, but other neurons cannot change the efficacy of synaptic transmission.

Hebbian synapse Synapse that increases its efficacy of synaptic transmission when the pre- and post-synaptic cells are conjunctively active.

Long-term depression A long-lasting decrease in the efficacy of synaptic transmission following brief and high-frequency stimulus.

Long-term potentiation A long-lasting increase in the efficacy of synaptic transmission following brief and high-frequency stimulus.

LEARNING is the process for acquisition of new knowledge, and memory is the process for maintaining the acquired knowledge. Associative memory can be divided into two types: autoassociative and pattern associative memory. In autoassociative memory, even if a part of the original pattern is presented, the perfect pattern (the stored pattern) is recalled. This process is termed completion. Pattern association produces an output pattern in response to the input pattern. The paired associates can be selected freely, independently of each other. If a pattern similar to one stored in the memory is pre-sented, the previously stored pattern is recalled. This property is termed generalization.

I. ANALYTICAL MODEL

In this section, a model proposed by Kohonen will be briefly described (Kohonen *et al.*, 1981). We consider physical system models as an associative memory model, in which the basic functions of associative memory are realized using a collection of simple elements connected to one another. Among the various physical system models which realize the basic memory functions, we are interested only in the biological memory mechanisms.

The network shown in Figure 1 illustrates a model for associative memory. The vertical units represent the dendritic membranes of a set of neurons. The horizontal lines correspond to a set of axons or axon collaterals having synaptic connections on the dendrites. They send the stimulus patterns, $s_j (j = 1, \ldots, k)$, to the network. The vertical units send out the response, $r_i (i = 1, \ldots, n)$, respectively. In the idealized model, the synaptic connection m_{ij} exists between vertical unit i and horizontal line j. The array of m_{ij} values is called the synaptic matrix.

The basic function of associative memory is definable as any process by which an input to the network is able to generate selectively a specific response associated with the input. Thus associative memory implies a selective stimulus–response (S-R) type of mapping in the network and the S-R mapping must be encoded into the set of synaptic connections. The encoding is adaptively formed when pre- and postsynaptic signals are mutually conditioned at the synaptic connections. In the network of Figure 1, the stimulus pattern and the forcing stimulus pattern, $f_i (i = 1, \ldots, n)$, must be conditioned at the synapses for associative learning to take place. During associative learning, each forcing stimulus pattern is equal to the corresponding desired response,

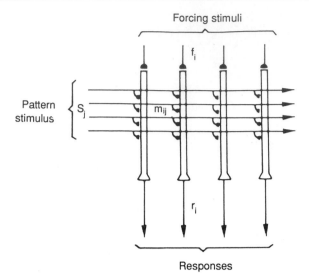

Forcing stimuli

Pattern stimulus

Responses

FIGURE 1   Associative network with a set of connected neurons. S_j = elements of the stimulus pattern; r_i = elements of the response pattern; f_i = elements of the forcing stimulus pattern; m_{ij} = synaptic connections. [From Kohonen, Oja, and Lehtiö, 1981. Reprinted with permission.]

which thus becomes associated with the conditioning stimulus pattern. During associative recall, there is no input at the forcing stimulus lines.

It will be described how associative recall is achievable in the network of Figure 1. The ith response component, r_i, is assumed to be expressed as follows:

$$r_i = \sum_{j=1}^{k} m_{ij} s_j + f_i, \qquad (1)$$

where m_{ij} represents the strength of the synaptic connection.

Let us assume that the strengths of the synaptic connections in Figure 1 are changed during a learning stage only when both the input stimulus and the forcing stimulus converging on a cell are active simultaneously. In a mathematical form, the conjunction is expressed by the product of both stimuli. The following correlation-type learning equation is obtained:

$$\frac{dm_{ij}}{dt} = \lambda f_i s_j, \qquad (2)$$

where λ is a scaler which represents the plasticity of the synaptic connections and is assumed to be constant for simplicity.

A stimulus pattern, $\mathbf{s} = (s_1, \ldots, s_k)$, at a group of input lines is defined as an ordered set. Similarly, a forcing stimulus pattern, $\mathbf{f} = (f_1, \ldots, f_n)$, at another group of input lines and a response pattern, $\mathbf{r} = (r_1, \ldots, r_n)$, at the output lines are defined. We construct a matrix M of $n \times k$ dimensions from the synaptic strengths m_{ij}. Let the pattern $\mathbf{s}$ be a column vector of k dimensions and the patterns $\mathbf{f}$ and $\mathbf{r}$ be column vectors of n dimensions, respectively.

In the description of associative recall, matrix algebra will be used. Eqs. (1) and (2) are rewritten by using the pattern vectors $\mathbf{s}$, $\mathbf{f}$, and $\mathbf{r}$ and the matrix M are follows:

$$\mathbf{r} = M\mathbf{s} + \mathbf{f}, \qquad (3)$$

$$\frac{dM}{dt} = \lambda \mathbf{f}\mathbf{s}^{\mathrm{T}}, \qquad (4)$$

where $\mathbf{s}^{\mathrm{T}}$ denotes the transpose of vector $\mathbf{s}$.

Let us assume that there are p different stimulus pattern vectors, $\mathbf{s}^{(1)}, \ldots, \mathbf{s}^{(p)}$, and p different forcing stimulus pattern vectors, $\mathbf{f}^{(1)}, \ldots, \mathbf{f}^{(p)}$. Furthermore, let us assume that all the synaptic strengths m_{ij} are initially 0. From the time $t = 0$, the first pair of stimulus and forcing stimulus pattern vectors, $(\mathbf{s}^{(1)}, \mathbf{f}^{(1)})$, appears at the input lines in the network of Figure 1 and stays constant for a short period. From Eq. (4), $M(t)$ is approximately given by the following equation:

$$M(t) = \lambda t \mathbf{f}^{(1)} \mathbf{s}^{(1)\mathrm{T}}. \qquad (5)$$

Subsequently, the second and the third pair, $(\mathbf{s}^{(2)}, \mathbf{f}^{(2)})$, $(\mathbf{s}^{(3)}, \mathbf{f}^{(3)})$, appear and so on. For convenience, it is assumed that each stimulus pair is provided to the network for a short time period whose length is $1/\lambda$. Then, $M(t)$ becomes the matrix given by the following equation:

$$M = \sum_{i=1}^{p} \mathbf{f}^{(i)} \mathbf{s}^{(i)\mathrm{T}}. \qquad (6)$$

Matrix M takes the form of a cross-correlation matrix.

On the basis of this matrix, it is possible to recall associatively the forcing stimulus patterns using the patterned stimuli as keys. The associative operation is defined by Eq. (3) without the forcing stimulus patterns $\mathbf{f}$, which was only necessary during the learning phase. Once the conjunctive learning has been completed, the values of the elements in the matrix are determined by Eq. (6) and are stored at the synaptic connections in the network. If one of the earlier stimulus pattern vectors, such as $\mathbf{s}^{(j)}$, is used as the key stimulus, the response is expressed by using Eq. (6) as follows:

$$\begin{aligned} \mathbf{r}^{(j)} &= M\mathbf{s}^{(j)} \\ &= (\mathbf{s}^{(j)\mathrm{T}}\mathbf{s}^{(j)})\,\mathbf{f}^{(j)} + \sum_{i \neq j}(\mathbf{s}^{(i)\mathrm{T}}\mathbf{s}^{(j)})\mathbf{f}^{(i)}. \quad (7) \end{aligned}$$

In some cases, different stimulus patterns have representations in the network that may be assumed to be statistically independent. This independence can be expressed as a mathematical property called orthogonality; if $\mathbf{s}^{(i)\mathrm{T}}\mathbf{s}^{(j)} = 0$ $(i \neq j)$, then vectors $\mathbf{s}^{(i)}$ and $\mathbf{s}^{(j)}$ are orthogonal. Further, if the stimulus values are standardized, it can be assumed that $\mathbf{s}^{(j)\mathrm{T}}\mathbf{s}^{(j)} = 1$. Then, the response $\mathbf{r}^{(j)}$ becomes equal to $\mathbf{f}^{(j)}$. If the key stimuli are not orthogonal, the second term in Eq. (7) will not be zero. Accordingly, this implies that there exists crosstalk between the different stored patterns. The less orthogonal the key stimuli are, the higher the level of crosstalk is.

An interesting problem has been led by the occurrence of crosstalk: Is it possible to construct a network which realizes associative recall with ideal selectivity? Mathematically, is it possible to realize the desired S-R mapping for arbitrary pairs of patterns $(\mathbf{s}^{(j)},\mathbf{f}^{(j)})$ using a hypothetical synaptic matrix M expressed by the following relation?

$$\mathbf{f}^{(j)} = M\mathbf{s}^{(j)} \qquad \text{for all } j. \quad (8)$$

It has a simple solution which is expressed as follows: If all the stimulus pattern vectors $\mathbf{s}^{(j)}$ are linearly independent, then a solution of Eq. (8) exists and is given by

$$M = F(S^{\mathrm{T}}S)^{-1}S^{\mathrm{T}}, \quad (9)$$

where $F = (\mathbf{f}^{(1)}, \ldots, \mathbf{f}^{(p)})$ and $S = (\mathbf{s}^{(1)}, \ldots, \mathbf{s}^{(p)})$. When the stimulus pattern vectors $\mathbf{s}^{(j)}$ are not linearly independent, an approximate solution is obtained in the sense of least squares, i.e.,

$$M = FS^{+}, \quad (10)$$

where S^{+} is the pseudoinverse of S. If the stimulus vectors $\mathbf{s}^{(j)}$ are linearly independent, then $S^{+} = (S^{\mathrm{T}}S)^{-1}S^{\mathrm{T}}$.

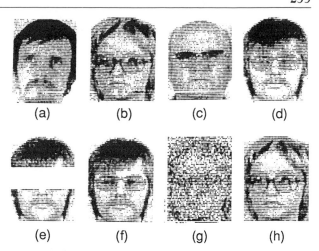

(a)   (b)   (c)   (d)

(e)   (f)   (g)   (h)

FIGURE 2   Example of autoassociative recall. Parts (a) through (d): 4 of the 100 original images. Parts (e) and (g): an incomplete version of (d) and a noisy version of (b). Parts (f) and (h): the original appearance. Parts (d) and (b) are reconstructed from (e) and (g), respectively. [From Kohonen, Oja, and Lehtiö, 1981. Reproduced with permission.]

One example of autoassociative recall is shown in Figure 2. The patterns $\mathbf{f}^{(j)}$ stored in memory are facial images of different persons: 100 pattern vectors are stored. Four of the images are shown in Figures 2a–2d. An incomplete or noisy version of one of the stored images, Figure 2e or 2g, respectively, is taken as the key $\mathbf{f}$. The optimal projection $\hat{\mathbf{f}}$ is shown to reconstruct the original appearance in Figures 2f and 2h, respectively.

II. ASSOCIATIVE LEARNING IN OLFACTORY CORTEX

In this section, a model proposed by Bower *et al.* will be briefly described. A broad range of behaviors in mammals requires the discrimination of odors. The recognition of some basic odors may be innate. However, animals can learn new odors specific to individuals or objects. It is interesting to understand how the olfactory system of mammals is able to learn and discriminate complex odor stimuli. [*See* SENSE OF SMELL.]

Mathematical models of autoassociative memory are able to generate stable outputs to complex input patterns. Furthermore, they can also generate a previously learned output pattern to the associated input pattern even if that input pattern is degraded or appears in a different circumstance. On the other hand, mammals have the ability to discriminate odors at very low concentrations or under very different conditions.

In addition to the similar functional capabilities of autoassociative memories and the olfactory system, according to the physiology and anatomy of the olfactory system odor identification may be based on the function of autoassociative memory. In particular, by some characteristics of the piriform cortex it is suggested that this region might be the site of an autoassociative memory. In the piriform cortex, both the afferent projection from the olfactory bulb and the intrinsic connections within the cortex are extensive and diffuse in their distribution. As shown in Figure 3, such distributed connectivity reminds us of mathematical autoassociative memory models.

Before constructing a complex model for the structurally complex piriform cortex, we first make use of a simplified cortical model. The model consists of a set of units and their activity levels are described by the following equation:

$$a_i(t + 1) = \sum_{j=1}^{n} (f(B_{ij}) - H_{ij}) g(a_j(t)) + A_i, \quad (11)$$

where the level of activity $a_i(t)$ $(i = 1, \ldots, n)$ represents the membrane potential of a neuron at time t. An input pattern A_i $(i = 1, \ldots, n)$ represents the effect of afferent synaptic input from the olfactory bulb. The output of all units is determined by a sigmoid response function $g(a_j(t))$ $(j = 1, \ldots, n)$.

The output directly excites other pyramidal cells in proportion to an intrinsic connectivity matrix B_{ij} $(i,j = 1, \ldots, n)$, where $f(\cdot)$ is a saturating function. It in turn stimulates interneurons which mediate local feedback inhibition on other pyramidal cells, which is represented by the inhibitory connectivity matrix H_{ij} $(i,j = 1, \ldots, n)$.

During the learning phase, a Hebb-type learning rule, which is given by the following equation, is used at the connections of intrinsic fibers.

$$\Delta B_{ij} = Cg(a_i(t))(a_j(t) - \theta), \quad (12)$$

where the increment ΔB_{ij} $(i,j = 1, \ldots, n)$ denotes the change in synaptic strength, the constant C determines the sensitivity of the synapse to synaptic modification, and the postsynaptic activity $a_j(t)$ must exceed a threshold θ for learning to take place.

In order to study the function of autoassociative memory, input intended to represent loosely the activity of single neurons in the olfactory bulb was given to the model. Synaptic connections between bulbar neurons and neurons in the olfactory cortex were determined randomly. These connections are shown in Figure 3. To examine learning capacity in the network, the strengths of the synaptic connections were altered based on their activity through the application of a Hebb-type correlation learning rule.

Although quite complex network properties are required for the learning of natural olfactory stimuli,

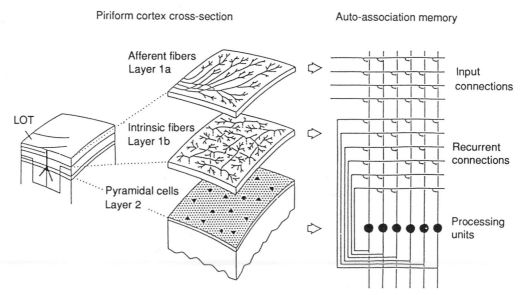

FIGURE 3   An autoassociative matrix memory model for the piriform cortex. [From Hasselmo, Wilson, Anderson, and Bower, 1990. Reproduced with permission.]

we look into two simple properties of associative learning. The first one is the function of the model whose outputs converge on consistent patterns of neuronal activity in response to particular input patterns. The second one is the capacity of the model, which generates a stable output pattern of neural activity to an incomplete version of the input pattern. As shown in Figure 4, in the case of no synaptic modification, even if the identical input pattern was presented repeatedly, a continually changing output pattern was obtained. However, when the same input pattern was presented repeatedly and synaptic modification was allowed, the output of the model converges to a stable pattern of neural activity after several stimulus presentations. In the small network of 100 units shown in Figure 4, the convergence was obtained only after a small number of presentations.

The second interesting question is as follows: Once an input pattern has been learned, what extent of changes in the input pattern will be allowed for the model to provide a stable output. The response under the condition of reducing the number of active bulbar inputs by half was compared to that with the original full input pattern. Figure 5a shows the cortical responses of two different patterns of afferent input after learning. The diagram at the far right demonstrates a relatively stable pattern of response to pattern 1 even after training with pattern 2. In Figure 5b, before training, the response to the input pattern in which 5 of the original 10 bulbar neurons are active shows only 56% similarity to the one to the original full input pattern. After training, the response to the degraded stimulus shows 80% overlaps with that evoked by the original input pattern.

Next, the locus of synaptic modification was examined in the network. To examine whether the function of the model is dependent on the particular locus of synaptic modification, the network performance was compared through the application of a Hebb-type learning rule to the afferent or intrinsic fiber synapses. The results of simulations showed that the associative memory function of the piriform cortex model was dependent on the Hebb-type synaptic modification in the intrinsic fiber synapses. If synaptic modification was limited to the afferent fiber synapses, the model did not converge to a stable output pattern in response to a consistent input. Furthermore, when synaptic modification was limited only to the afferent fibers, the function of the model for the completion of incomplete input patterns was reduced considerably in comparison to the case of modifying the intrinsic fiber synapses. From these results it is suggested that the intrinsic fiber synapses represent the principal site of synaptic learning in the olfactory cortex.

III. ASSOCIATIVE LEARNING IN THE HIPPOCAMPUS

In this section, the model proposed by Rolls will be briefly described. Figure 6 shows a schematic diagram of the connections of the hippocampus. The major inputs to the hippocampus come from the association areas of the cerebral cortex. There are three processing stages, that is, the dentate granule cells, the CA3 pyramidal cells, and the CA1 pyramidal cells. Outputs of the hippocampus return to the cerebral cortex through the subiculum, entorhinal cortex, and parahippocampal gyrus. [*See* HIPPOCAMPAL FORMATION.]

One of the major characteristics of the hippocampus is that the CA3 cells have recurrent collaterals. The axons of the CA3 cells have collaterals which make synaptic connections with the dendrites of the

Before training
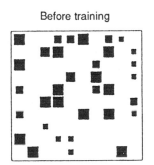

After training
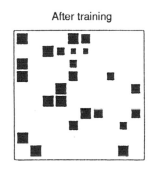

Learning curve
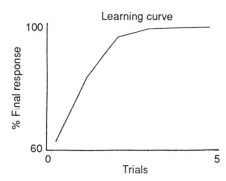

FIGURE 4 Simulations of the piriform cortex autoassociative memory properties. [From Bower, 1990. Reproduced with permission.]

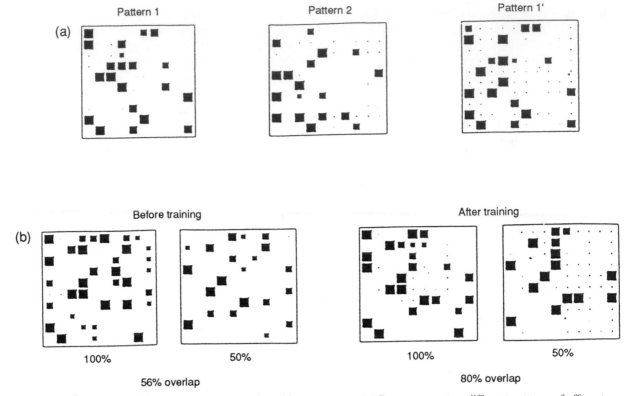

FIGURE 5   Properties of autoassociative learning of input patterns. (a) Responses to two different patterns of afferent input after learning. (b) Similarity of the response to the degraded stimulus before and after training. [From Bower, 1990. Reproduced with permission.]

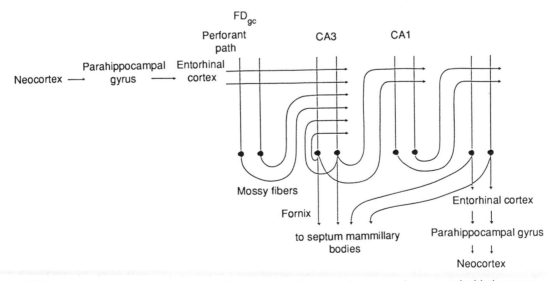

FIGURE 6   Schematic representation in the hippocampus. The cerebral neocortex is connected with the respective area via the parahippocampal gyrus and entorhinal cortex. Also, the hippocampus projects onto the neocortex via the subiculum, parahippocampal gyrus, FD_{gc}, and granule cells in the dentate gyrus. [From Rolls, 1990. Reproduced with permission.]

other CA3 cells. The probability of an axon collateral being connected with one of the dendrites is relatively high. Also, the axon collaterals of the CA3 cells are broadly distributed so that they can approach almost all other CA3 cells. Studies of long-term potentiation in the hippocampus have revealed that the synapses of the recurrent collaterals are Hebbian synapses. In other words, when strong postsynaptic and presynaptic activities occur conjunctively, they are potentiated.

From the functional anatomy of the CA3 cells, it is suggested that the CA3 cell stage functions as an autoassociation matrix memory. The outputs of the CA3 cells are fed back by the recurrent axon collaterals which make Hebb synaptic connections with the dendrites of the other CA3 cells and the autoassociation occurs.

During learning, the synaptic weights store information regarding the correlations between activities of the CA3 cells. Consequently, this type of memory is called an autocorrelation or autoassociation matrix memory. In recall, a part of the original pattern of activity of the CA3 cells occurs; it causes the firing of all the cells that were originally conjunctively activated. This property of memory is termed "completion." Further, during recall, if a pattern which is similar to one previously learned is presented, the previously stored pattern is recalled as long as some of the cells activated by a key stimulus are also part of a pattern of the active cells stored previously in the memory. This property is called "generalization." Another property of this type of memory is that even if it is partially destroyed, it continues to function moderately well. This property is called "graceful degradation" or "fault tolerance."

The function of this autoassociative matrix memory at the systems level is the association of events which occur conjunctively in different parts of the association areas to form an episodic memory. The spatial memory of a snapshot, whole-scene may be formed by associating together all parts of a whole scene. The importance of the hippocampus in episodic memory and whole scene memory may be derived from the fact that the CA3 cell stage has one autoassociation matrix memory which receives information on events occurring conjunctively in many different areas of the cerebral cortex. [*See* EPISODIC MEMORY.]

In order to understand the function of autoassociation matrix memory located at the CA3 cell stage, the roles of the dentate granule cell stage that precedes the CA3 cell stage and the CA1 cell stage that

follows the CA3 cell stage should be examined. The matrix memory in the CA3 cell stage can store a large number of different memories and has emergent properties, such as completion, generalization, and graceful degradation, due to sparse encoding and a sufficiently interconnected matrix. Then, a sparse yet efficient representation in the CA3 neurons may be produced in two ways in the dentate granule cell stage: (1) The perforant path–dentate granule cell system performs as a competitive learning matrix. (2) A very low contact probability in the mossy fiber–CA3 neurons connections accomplishes relatively orthogonal representations.

One major set of the perforant path fibers makes synaptic connections with the dentate granule cells. These synapses are modified by the rules of long-term potentiation in the hippocampus. Furthermore, strongly activated cells can inhibit other cells via inhibitory interneurons. In the network model shown in Figure 7, the synaptic connections between the horizontal axons and the vertical dendrites are initially determined randomly. Owing to these random synaptic connections, different input patterns on the horizontal axons will tend to activate different output cells. This kind of tendency can be enhanced further by providing mutual inhibition via inhibitory interneurons between the output neurons.

The modification of synaptic connections occurs on the basis of the rules of long-term potentiation. The effect of the synaptic modification is as follows: When the same stimulus is presented repeatedly, the neuron with strengthened synapses is more activated and inhibits other neurons more strongly. Consequently, this in turn produces greater selectivity

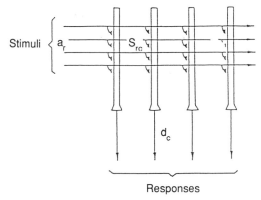

FIGURE 7 Matrix for competitive learning. Input stimuli are provided along input axons. The input axons make modifiable synaptic connections with dendrites of output cells. The dendrites construct the columns of the matrix. [From Rolls, 1990. Reproduced with permission.]

between output cells. According to computer simulations, a few neurons obtain strong synaptic connections and are highly activated in response to almost any stimulus which has any input to the neurons. To solve such a problem, it is necessary to limit the total synaptic weight of each output neuron. In computer simulations, this is performed by normalizing the sum of the synaptic weights to a constant. According to experimental evidences in some parts of the brain, synapses from inactive axons onto strongly activated neurons become weaker.

In order for the autocorrelation matrix in the CA3 cell stage to possess large memory capacity and operate with minimal interference, relatively orthogonal representations are required. Since the neurons have positive continuous firing rates, relatively orthogonal representations can be obtained by making the number of active neurons relatively low for any input stimulus. Since the probability of synaptic connection in the mossy fibers–CA3 neurons connections is very low, the sparse representation is achieved by the low contact probability.

Next, the function of the CA1 cell stage seems to be related to the CA3 autoassociation effect. At the CA3 cell stage, several sparse patterns of firing occur together and are associated to form an episodic or whole-scene memory. The CA1 cells receive these groups of simultaneously active ensembles and may detect the conjunctions of the activities of the different ensembles. Each episodic memory is assigned a relatively few neurons by competitive learning performed among the CA1 cells. Thus, in the CA1 cell stage, new economical representations of the conjunctions are built and the hippocampus provides an output appropriate to directing information storage in the cerebral cortex.

IV. CELLULAR AND MOLECULAR MECHANISMS UNDERLYING ASSOCIATIVE LEARNING AND MEMORY

A. Properties of LTP

Brief and high-frequency stimulation (tetanic stimulation) to afferent pathways causes a long-lasting increase in the efficacy of synaptic transmission. This effect, first reported by Bliss and Lømo in 1973, is called long-term potentiation (LTP). LTP has been found in all excitatory pathways in the hippocampus. In addition to a long-lasting increase in the efficacy of synaptic transmission, LTP is characterized by three essential properties: (1) input specificity, (2) cooperativity, and (3) associativity. The first property is that the induction of LTP requires a combination of presynaptic activity and strong postsynaptic depolarization. The second one is that an intensity threshold exists for the induction of LTP. Weak tetanic stimulation does not trigger LTP. The third one is that a weak input can be potentiated if a strong input is active at the same time as a weak input.

The mechanisms responsible for LTP can be divided into three phases: induction, expression, and maintenance. The induction phase refers to the initial stage that triggers the process of synaptic enhancement. The expression phase refers to the physiological changes that constitute the cause of the synaptic enhancement. The maintenance phase refers to the stage that causes the permanence of the synaptic potentiation.

B. Types of Synaptic Modification

There are five types of long-term synaptic modification. For explanation, a neuron is assumed to receive two sets of synaptic inputs, one weak (W) and the other strong (S).

1. Tetanic stimulation of the S-input produces *homosynaptic LTP* in the stimulated pathway.
2. Concurrent tetanic stimulation of the S-input following the W-input produces *associative LTP* in the W-input pathway.
3. High-frequency stimulation of the W-input alone produces *homosynaptic LTD* in the stimulated pathway.
4. Tetanic stimulation of the S-input and the spontaneous activity of the W-input pathway produce *associative LTD* in the W-input pathway.
5. Stimulation of the S-input alone produces *heterosynaptic LTD* in the W-input pathway which is not stimulated.

C. Induction of LTP

The neurotransmitter at most excitatory synapses in the hippocampus is an excitatory amino acid, probably glutamate. Glutamate can bind to at least three subtypes of receptor protein, two of which are coupled to transmembrane ion channels, and the other one is called a metabotropic receptor. The three types of excitatory amino acid receptors are as follows: *N*-methyl-D-aspartate (NMDA) receptors, α-amino-3-hydroxy-5-methy-4-isoxazolepropionate (AMPA) receptors, and *trans*-1-aminocyclopentate-1,3-dicarboxylate (ACPD) receptors.

The NMDA receptor channel exhibits a strong voltage-dependence. When the postsynaptic membrane is hyperpolarized, the NMDA receptor channel is normally blocked by Mg^{2+}. When the postsynaptic cell is depolarized, this channel block is removed and other ions can flow into the cell. Consequently, two factors are necessary for the induction of LTP: (1) In response to glutamate, the NMDA channel must open. (2) The postsynaptic cell must be depolarized to remove the Mg^{2+} block. [*See* SYNAPTIC TRANSMITTERS AND NEUROMODULATORS.]

According to experimental results, injection of calcium chelators such as EGTA into postsynaptic cells prevents the induction of LTP in those cells. It is strongly supported that an elevation of postsynaptic Ca^{2+} plays an important role in LTP. If an increase of postsynaptic Ca^{2+} is necessary for the induction of LTP, what are the biochemical processes activated by Ca^{2+} that are responsible for LTP?

There exist different Ca^{2+}-sensitive enzymes. LTP has been shown to be associated with a translocation of Ca^{2+}-phospholipid-dependent protein kinase (protein kinase C, PKC) from cytosol to the membrane and increased phosphorylation of a substrate protein of PKC. Furthermore, injection into postsynaptic cells of a specific inhibitor of PKC blocks LTP. Another kinase that has been proposed as an important role in LTP is the Ca^{2+}/calmodulin-dependent kinase II (CaMKII). Direct evidence for a role of postsynaptic CaMKII in LTP indicates that LTP is blocked by injection into postsynaptic cells of peptide that inhibits calmodulin.

D. Pre- versus Postsynaptic Mechanisms in LTP

It is known that the mechanisms for LTP induction exist, at least in part, within the postsynaptic cells. If the expression of LTP is due to an increase in transmitter release, then the postsynaptic cell must communicate with the presynaptic terminal, perhaps by releasing some substance that acts on recently activated presynaptic terminals. A possible candidate for such a messenger is arachidonic acid. Direct evidence for the role of arachidonic acid in LTP comes from the fact that an increase in extracellular arachidonic acid can be found from the dentate gyrus during LTP and application of arachidonic acid can

enhance synaptic transmission. Recently, an electrophysiological approach has been used to examine possible presynaptic mechanisms in LTP. The approach is based on the quantal nature of transmitter release and uses a statistical analysis of excitatory postsynaptic currents. The results of this analysis show that a presynaptic mechanisms is responsible for the expression of LTP.

Although there is strong evidence for presynaptic mechanisms in LTP, there exist other experimental facts explained by postsynaptic modification. During LTP, the postsynaptic potential mediated by non-NMDA receptors is increased, whereas the one mediated by NMDA receptors is little affected.

The data concerning the pre- or postsynaptic locus of LTP show that significant progress has been made toward solving this problem. It is also clear that data supporting either a pre- or postsynaptic mechanism will need to be reconciled.

E. Induction of LTD

Long-term depression (LTD), which is conversely a long-lasting decrease in the efficacy of synaptic transmission, has also been reported. In 1982, Ito *et al.* found that upon conjunctive stimulation of both climbing fibers and parallel fibers, an associative LTD can be induced at parallel fiber-Purkinje cell synapses. Although LTD has been mainly studied in the mammalian cerebellum, it has recently found in the hipppocampus and cerebral cortex.

When glutamate or quisqualate is exposed to Purkinje cells and the climbing fibers are stimulated simultaneously, the sensitivity of the Purkinje cells to glutamate decreases. However, the stimulation of climbing fibers alone or exposure of glutamate or quisqualate alone does not induce LTD. This result suggests that LTD may involve long-term desensitization of the quisqualate receptors. It has also been confirmed that an increase in the Ca^{2+} concentration of Purkinje cells plays a role for the induction of LTD. The rise in the Ca^{2+} concentration in Purkinje cell dendrites is considered to be generated by voltage-dependent Ca^{2+} channels and not through the NMDA receptor channels. Recent evidence suggests that the rise in intracellular Ca^{2+} activates the Ca^{2+}/calmodulin-dependent enzyme, nitric oxide (NO) synthetase, and NO then activates guanylate cyclase leading to production of cyclic guanosine $3',5'$-monophosphate (cGMP). LTD is blocked by a blocker of cGMP-dependent protein kinase.

F. Switching between LTP and LTD

Recently, it was reported that in slices of the rat visual cortex, tetanic stimulation can induce either LTP or LTD, depending on the level of depolarization of the postsynaptic cell. Furthermore, it was suggested that LTD is induced if postsynaptic depolarization exceeds a certain critical level but remains below some second threshold. On the other hand, LTP is induced if this second threshold is reached.

Next, it was also found that tetanic stimulation which should have induced LTP induces LTD if the postsynaptic Ca^{2+} is chelated sufficiently by intracellular injection of a Ca^{2+}-chelator. This finding suggests that whether LTP or LTD is induced is dependent on the concentration of postsynaptic Ca^{2+} during tetanic stimulation. The level of the concentration of postsynaptic Ca^{2+} may play a role in switching between LTP and LTD.

V. A MODEL FOR THE INDUCTION MECHANISM OF LTP

A. The Construction of a Model

A model is constructed for the mechanisms of the induction of LTP, having the cooperative and associative properties of LTP.

A schematic model of a nerve cell consists of two spines, A and B, located on a dendrite as shown in Figure 8. NMDA receptor channels and AMPA receptor channels in each spine head are activated by transmitters released from the presynaptic terminal. The time course of synaptic current through an ionic channel can be approximately expressed by an α function. Let $g_{Ax}(t)$ and $g_{Nx}(t)$, $(x = a,b)$, describe the conductance changes of AMPA receptors and NMDA receptors, respectively, and be expressed by corresponding sequences of α functions

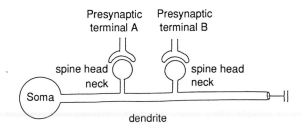

FIGURE 8 A schematic model of a nerve cell consisting of two spines located on the dendrite. [From Kitajima and Hara, 1991. Reproduced with permission.]

for a sequence of impulses which have reached the presynaptic terminal.

From the equivalent circuit of the model shown in Figure 8, the following differential equations are derived with respect to the postsynaptic membrane potentials in the heads of spines A and B, v_a and v_b, the somatic potential v_s, and the potentials at three sites of the dendrite, v_1, v_2, and v_3:

$$C_x \frac{dv_x}{dt} = -\frac{1}{R_x}(v_x - E_h) - M(v_x)g_{Nx}(t)(v_x - E_N)$$
$$- g_{nx}(t)(v_x - E_n) - \frac{v_x - v_x^*}{R_{sx}} \quad (x = a,b), \tag{13}$$

$$C_s \frac{dv_s}{dt} = -\frac{1}{R_s}(v_s - E_s) - \frac{v_s - v_1}{r_1}, \tag{14}$$

$$C_1 \frac{dv_1}{dt} = -(v_1 - E_r) - \frac{(v_a^* - v_1) - (v_1 - v_s)}{r_1}, \tag{15}$$

$$C_2 \frac{dv_2}{dt} = -\frac{1}{R_2}(v_2 - E_r) - \frac{(v_b^* - v_2) - (v_2 - v_a^*)}{r_2}, \tag{16}$$

$$C_3 \frac{dv_3}{dt} = -\frac{1}{R_3}(v_3 - E_r) - \frac{v_b^* - v_3}{r_3}, \tag{17}$$

where

$$v_a^* = \left(\frac{v_1}{r_1} + \frac{v_2}{r_2} + \frac{v_a}{R_{sa}}\right)\Big/\left(\frac{1}{r_1} + \frac{1}{r_2} + \frac{1}{R_{sa}}\right)$$
$$v_b^* = \left(\frac{v_2}{r_2} + \frac{v_3}{r_3} + \frac{v_b}{R_{sb}}\right)\Big/\left(\frac{1}{r_2} + \frac{1}{r_3} + \frac{1}{R_{sb}}\right). \tag{18}$$

In Eq. (13), $M(v)$ represents the voltage-dependent inhibition of the NMDA receptor channel by extracellular Mg^{2+} ions. It is assumed to be expressed by the following sigmoid function:

$$M(v_x) = \frac{1}{1 + \exp(-\delta_m(v_x - \varepsilon_t))}, \tag{19}$$

where δ_m is the parameter representing the inhibitory effect and ε_t is the membrane potential at which 50% inhibition occurs in the NMDA receptor channel. When the postsynaptic potential is sufficiently depolarized, Ca^{2+} flows into the spine head via the NMDA receptor channels. Then, the calcium current is given by

$$I_c(t) = M(v_x)g_{Nx}(t)(v_x - E_N). \tag{20}$$

The postsynaptic entry of Ca^{2+} ions raises the Ca^{2+} concentration in the spine head. We assume that it increases in proportion to the difference between the increased Ca^{2+} concentration and its resting level. Consequently, the Ca^{2+} concentration is subject to the following differential equation:

$$\frac{dCa^{2+}}{dt} = -k_a(Ca^{2+} - Ca_0) + \frac{k_b I_c(t)}{V_h}, \quad (21)$$

where Ca_0 is the resting Ca^{2+} concentration in the spine head, k_a is the decreasing velocity of Ca^{2+} concentration, k_b is the increase in the Ca^{2+} concentration due to unit calcium current per unit time, and V_h is the volume of the spine head.

Here we assume that the CaMKII (Ca^{2+}/calmodulin-dependent kinase II) contributes to the induction of LTP. In the spine head, each calmodulin is activated by the binding of four calcium ions and can phosphorylate the CaMKII. A single CaMKII molecule has 12 subunits and each subunit has a few sites, which are practically phosphorylated by calmodulin molecules. It is known that such phosphorylation was caused by autophosphorylation between subunits in a kinase molecule and that at least two to four sites should be phosphorylated to cause such autophosphorylation. Let a single kinase molecule have N_0 sites and N_c be the number of phosphorylated sites necessary to activate a single CaMKII molecule by autophosphorylation. Then the probability of a kinase II molecule being activated at time t is

$$P_{on}(t) = 1 - \sum_{m=N_0-N_c+1}^{N_0} \binom{N_0}{m} (1-e^{-rzt})^{N_0-m} e^{-mrzt}, \quad (22)$$

where r is the proportional constant and z is the average increase in Ca^{2+} concentration from the resting level over a certain period.

If N_k is the total number of CaMKII molecules in the spine head, $N_k P_{on}$ kinase molecules have been activated on average when the Ca^{2+} concentration returns to the resting level. The activated kinase molecules are responsible for phosphorylating the substrate protein of AMPA receptors or the proteins closely associated with them. Here, an increase in synaptic efficacy in the AMPA receptor channel is assumed to be proportional to $N_k P_{on}$. Consequently, the non-NMDA conductance, $g_{na}(t)$, in Eq. (13) is changed as follows:

$$g_{na}(t) \Rightarrow g_{na}(t)(1 + k_{eff}N_k P_{on}). \quad (23)$$

B. Computer Simulations

We used tetanic stimulus patterns similar to those in physiological experiments. A weak input (W-input) is a stimulus of 60 impulses at 100 Hz and a strong input (S-input) is that of 40 impulses at 100 Hz.

To simulate the associative properties of LTP with the model, we took the distance between A and B as 100 μm. The probability of a single CaMKII molecule in each spine head being activated was evaluated under vaious stimulus conditions, and by varying the number of phosphorylated sites required for autophosphorylation from two to four. These conditions were (1) spine B receives the S-input alone, (2) spine A receives the W-input alone, and (3) spine A receives the W-input and spine B receives the S-input. Table 1 shows the probability of each spine being activated evaluated under the above conditions.

The temporal specificity of associative LTP has been examined by physiological experiments. Figure 9a shows one of such experimental results in the CA1 region of the hippocampus. On the other hand, Figure 9b shows the probability of a single

TABLE I

The Probability That a Single Kinase II Molecule in the Head of Each Spine Is Activated (P_{on}) under Three Stimulus Conditions

Stimulation		Spine A			Spine B		
		Number of phosphorylated sites (N_c)					
A	B	2	3	4	2	3	4
No	S-input	0	0	0	1.000	1.000	1.000
W-input	No	0.266	0.078	0.017	0	0	0
W-input	S-input	0.938	0.816	0.628	1.000	1.000	1.000

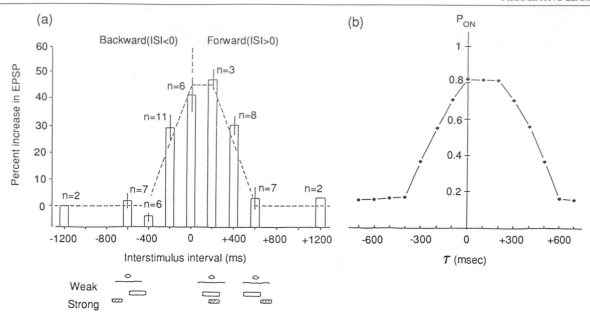

FIGURE 9 (a) The experimental result in the CA1 region of the hippocampus. (b) The probability that a single kinase molecule in the head of spine A is activated by varying the interval between two tetanic stimuli. Positive values of τ indicate that the delivery of the W-input to spine A precedes that of the S-input to spine B. [From Kitajima and Hara, 1991. Reproduced with permission.]

CaMKII molecule in the head of spine A being activated, while varying the interval between two stimulations to spines A and B from −700 to +700 msec.

From these simulation results, the cellular mechanisms of cooperativity and associativity has been interpreted as follows: a strong input which is capable of producing LTP can depolarize the postsynaptic cell above a certain threshold. Though a weak input cannot sufficiently deporalize the postsynaptic cell, a sufficient depolarization is provided by the strong input. A postsynaptic mechanism for such an interaction could be considered to be due to the transmission of intracellular potential. According to our simulation results, the cooperative and associative properties of LTP can be produced by the spread of synaptic potentials. Furthermore, not only postsynaptic potentials above a certain threshold but also their average postsynaptic potentials over a certain period are crucial in producing LTP. It is considered that this model has a fundamental mechanism of associative memory and learning.

Bibliography

Baudry, M., and Davis, J. L. (Eds.) (1991). "Long-Term Potentiation: A Debate of Current Issues." MIT Press, New York.

Bower, J. M. (1990). Reverse engineering the nervous system: An anatomical, physiological, and computer-based approach. In "An Introduction to Neural and Electronic Networks" (Zornetzer, S. F., Davis, J. L., and Lau, C., Eds.). Academic Press, San Diego.

Byrne, J. H., and Berry, W. O. (Eds.) (1989). "Neural Models of Plasticity." Academic Press, San Diego.

Churchland, P. S., and Sejnowski, T. J. (Eds.) (1992). "The Computational Brain." MIT Press, New York.

Hasselmo, M. E., Wilson, M. A., Anderson, B. P., and Bower, J. M. (1990). Associative memory function in piriform olfactory cortex. In "Cold Spring Harbor Symposia on Quantitative Biology," Vol. LV (Kandel, E., Sejnowski, T. J., Stevens, C. S., and Watson, J., Eds.). Cold Spring Harbor Laboratory Press, New York.

Kitajima, T., and Hara, K. (1991). A model of the mechanism of cooperativity and associativity of long-term potentiation in the hippocampus: A fundamental mechanism of associative memory and learning. *Biol. Cybern.* **64,** 365.

Kohonen, T., Oja, E., and Lehtiö, P. (1981). Storage and processing of information in distributed associative memory systems. In "Parallel Models of Associative Memory" revised. (Hinton, G. E., and Anderson, J. A., Eds.), Erlbaum, Hillsdale, NJ.

McGaugh, J. L., Weinberger, N. M., and Lynch, G. (Eds.) (1990). "Brain Organization and Memory: Cells, Systems and Circuits." Oxford University Press, Oxford.

Rolls, E. T. (1990). Principles underlying the representation and storage of information in neural networks in the primate hippocampus and cerebral cortex. In "An Introduction to Neural and Electronic Networks" (Zornetzer, S. F., Davis, J. L., and Lau, C., Eds.). Academic Press, San Diego.

ATTENTION-DEFICIT HYPERACTIVITY DISORDER

V. L. Schwean and D. H. Saklofske
University of Saskatchewan, Canada

Glossary

Attention-deficit hyperactivity disorder Neurobehavioral disorder characterized by developmentally inappropriate levels of inattention, impulsivity, and hyperactivity.
Neurobehavioral Behavior having neurological substrates.
Self-regulation Cognitive activity of fine tuning and adjusting behavior in response to internal and external feedback.

ATTENTION-DEFICIT HYPERACTIVITY DISORDER, one of the most studied childhood disorders, is a relatively common neurobehavioral disability characterized by inappropriate degrees of inattention, impulsivity, and hyperactivity. While much remains unknown about the disorder, burgeoning research has enriched our knowledge with respect to issues such as prevalence, primary symptoms, underlying mechanisms, co-existing disorders, onset, course, outcome, family patterns, assessment, and intervention. These findings will be elaborated upon here.

I. DIAGNOSTIC LABELS

Over the years, numerous diagnostic terms have been used to label the neurobehavioral disorder we now refer to as attention-deficit hyperactivity disorder (ADHD). Descriptions of the disorder first appeared in the clinical literature with Still's 1902 reference to children exhibiting "defects in moral control." As research advanced understanding of the disorder, changes in nosology followed and included, among others, "minimal brain dysfunction," "hyperkinetic reaction of childhood," "hyperactive child syndrome," and "attention deficit disorder (with or without hyperactivity)." The most recent diagnostic label, ADHD, adopted by the American Psychiatric Association's *Diagnostic and Statistical Manual of Mental Disorders: Third Edition—Revised* (DSM-III-R), reflects the contemporary clinical understanding of this disorder.

II. DIAGNOSTIC CRITERIA

The most widely accepted psychiatric system of classification is the DSM-III-R. According to the DSM-III-R criteria for ADHD, developmentally inappropriate degrees of inattention, impulsivity, and hyperactivity are of primary significance. Operationalized, "developmentally inappropriate" means that the child's behavior on the prescribed domains deviates significantly from that of his or her normative group. Standardized assessments are used to make this determination.

The DSM-III-R criteria list 14 behavioral symptoms characteristic of inattention, impulsivity, and hyperactivity in ADHD children. A sample of these behaviors is presented in Table I. "Inattention," the inability to sustain attention to tasks, may be evidenced by frequent shifts in activity or distracti-

TABLE I

Behavioral Characteristics of ADHD According to DSM-III-R

Inattention
  Is easily distracted by extraneous stimuli
  Has difficulty sustaining attention in tasks or play activities
  Often does not seem to listen to what is being said to him
    or her

Impulsivity
  Has difficulty awaiting turn in games or group situations
  Often blurts out answers to questions before they have been
    completed
  Often interrupts or intrudes on others

Hyperactivity
  Often fidgets with hands or feet or squirms in seat
  Has difficulty remaining seated when required to do so
  Has difficulty playing quietly

bility and disorganization. "Impulsivity" refers to the propensity to respond prematurely, before sufficient information has been gathered. An impulsive cognitive style leads to behaviors such as inappropriate turn-taking, failure to listen fully to instructions, and extreme risk-taking, among others. Fidgeting, difficulty remaining seated, and excessive talking are evidence of hyperactivity or excessive bodily movement.

Chronicity is also an important diagnostic issue: since evidence suggests that ADHD has a strong organic component, the diagnostician seeks evidence for longevity of the disorder, as well as to rule out environmental mismatches (e.g., a temperamentally active, intellectually curious youngster placed with a rigid, inflexible teacher) or psychosocial stressors (e.g., anxiety associated with physical or sexual abuse) as causal. Further, children presenting with qualitative impairments in the development of social interaction, communication, and imaginative activity are excluded from receiving the diagnosis of ADHD. Last, the DSM-III-R criteria recognize that symptom severity may fall along a continuum from mild to moderate to severe and find expression only in specific situations (e.g., school) or across many situations.

III. COGNITIVE CONCEPTUALIZATION

In addition to the core features of inattentiveness, impulsivity, and hyperactivity referenced in DSM-III-R, considerable research has documented the abnormal response of ADHD children to reinforcement. For example, studies have shown that relative to normals, ADHD children exhibit a differential response to partial and delayed reinforcement schedules. Other studies have shown that ADHD children are unable to modulate physiological arousal levels to meet situational demands. While the non-ADHD child is able to estimate and even change the amount of attentional energy directed into a particular activity, the ADHD child is less able to regulate arousal levels and, consequently, exhibits considerable variability in performance.

In recent years, attention has been directed toward identifying underlying mechanisms that would account for ADHD symptomatology. Investigators appear to be converging on the view that faulty self-regulatory processes are causal. Self-regulation is a cognitive activity that involves continuously fine tuning and modulating behavior in accordance with internal and external feedback. While the nature of the defective self-regulatory processes involved remains controversial, there appears to be evidence that inhibitory, attention, reinforcement, and arousal abnormalities are exacerbated by situational variables that exact heavy demands on self-regulatory processes (e.g., highly structured settings).

IV. ASSOCIATED FEATURES

While current accounts characterize ADHD as consisting of several essential features, it is often the case that other disorders and/or features co-exist with the ADHD. For example, research has shown that anywhere from 30 to 50% of children with ADHD exhibit significant problems with aggression, 15 to 75% present with mood disorders (e.g., depression), while about 25% manifest anxiety disorders. Deficits in social skills and emotional immaturity are also noted in approximately 50% of children with ADHD. Moreover, considerable comorbidity between ADHD and learning disabilities has been reported. Other features that may occur together with ADHD include immature motor coordination, functional encopresis and/or enuresis, minor physical anomalies, and sleep disturbances, among others. [*See* AGGRESSION; ANXIETY DISORDERS; DEPRESSION.]

A subgroup of attentional disorders that has received treatment in the clinical and research literature has been referred to as *attention deficit disorder without hyperactivity*. Children manifesting this disorder present as inattentive and cognitively sluggish and passive and may exhibit memory retrieval and perceptual processing speed problems. It is thought that anxiety frequently co-exists with the disorder.

Unlike the child with ADHD, behaviors characteristic of hyperactivity and impulsivity are not evident.

V. DEVELOPMENTAL FEATURES AND OUTCOME

Like so many other behavioral disorders of childhood, ADHD symptomatology varies to some degree as a function of the developmental stage of the child and consequent environmental demands. During the preschool years, behaviors associated with gross motor overactivity (e.g., frequent running and climbing) are most prominent. Parents may also reference the ADHD child's inattentiveness (e.g., frequent activity change) and impulsiveness (e.g., extreme "risk-taking" behaviors). Secondary problems such as noncompliance, temper tantrums, toilet training and sleep difficulties, and motor and speech problems may also be noted.

School entrance may presage a myriad of problems for the ADHD child. It is likely that no other environment places as great a demand on self-regulatory processes as the school. Inability to attend to task, erratic performance, difficulties in self-management and organization, and an impulsive cognitive style can be reflected in secondary academic and social difficulties. While the primary symptoms of ADHD may decline measurably in adolescence, secondary problems assume even more prominence. Follow-up studies of ADHD children into adolescence clearly show that well over half of these youngsters display significant impairments in academic achievement, social relationships, and psychological well-being. Lower levels of educational and occupational achievement and higher rates of psychiatric disorder continue to plague these same ADHD adolescents into adulthood.

Why outcomes are more negative for some ADHD children than for others has recently been addressed in several studies. Substantive evidence points to aggression in ADHD children as a marker variable for a wide range of adaptive (e.g., academic and occupational attainment) and psychological (e.g., antisocial behavior) disorders. In turn, family dysfunction (e.g., parental psychopathology, marital discord, ineffective child management techniques) is highly predictive of aggression in ADHD children.

VI. FAMILY PATTERNS

There is little question that the myriad of problems exhibited by ADHD children, particularly those children exhibiting co-existing oppositional problems, significantly interferes with positive family functioning. Studies examining the psychological well-being of parents of ADHD children show them to experience higher rates of stress, marital discord, and psychological and psychiatric disorders. Relative to normal children, parental interactions with ADHD children are characterized by more controlling and negative interchanges, particularly as tasks become more demanding of the child's self-regulatory abilities. Peer and teacher exchanges would appear to follow similar patterns. Support for the hypothesis that the ADHD child's behavior is causal in these negative interactions comes from research showing that parental behavior changes positively when the child is placed on stimulant medications such as Ritalin.

The direction of influence is, however, not unidirectional; indeed a reciprocal effect is present such that not only does the ADHD child alter family functioning but family functioning alters the ADHD child. For example, there is evidence indicating that maternal depression may lead to critical evaluations of the ADHD child which in turn, increases the likelihood of noncompliant behavior in the child. Moreover, a cyclical effect is often observed where parental aggression predicts oppositional problems in the ADHD child which leads to escalation of parental aggression and family conflict.

VII. PROPOSED ETIOLOGIES

Over the years, numerous etiologies have been proposed for ADHD. Postulated mechanisms have included brain damage resulting from infections or trauma or from pre- or postnatal complications. Research has shown that this theory would account for only a small number of ADHD children. Various food additives (e.g., salicylates, food dyes), as well as refined sugar, have also been popular targets. Scientific evidence for the latter explanatory hypotheses, however, is negligible, although some studies have reported a correlational, but not causal, relationship between environmental toxins such as body lead and maternal alcohol consumption and cigarette smoking during pregnancy. Psychosocial and environmental factors (e.g., poverty, poor parenting, family discord) have been discounted as causal.

At the present time, data seem to converge on a hypothesis that references a biological predisposition expressed through organic dysfunction (e.g., orbital-frontal and orbital-limbic impairments). Support for a hereditary mechanism in ADHD derives from research showing a high concordance rate for ADHD among identical twins, as well as studies affirming a higher prevalence rate of ADHD among relatives of ADHD children. Evidence for neurological underpinnings stems from neurotransmitter and cerebral blood flow studies.

The endorsement of ADHD as having neurological substrates carries with it the implication that children experiencing this disorder do not have the same degree of volitional control over certain actions as do normal youngsters. Not unlike the diabetic who can do little to exact insulin from a nonproductive pancreas, the ADHD child cannot willfully determine an impaired neurological system to enact intact self-regulatory abilities.

VIII. PREVALENCE

Because of inadequacies in defining and measuring ADHD, prevalence estimates of the disorder have varied widely. There is agreement, however, that ADHD is one of the most common developmental disorders. Contemporary accounts indicate that approximately 3 to 5% of school-age children present with clinical symptoms of ADHD. Proportionally, males are three to six times more likely to present with the disorder. Prevalence rates also vary as a function of geographical locale and socioeconomic status: rates seem to be slightly higher in urban regions and in lower socioeconomic areas.

IX. ASSESSMENT

Because environmental/task demands play a determinative role in the expression of ADHD symptoms, it is imperative that multisource, multimodal assessment techniques be employed. Multisource, multimodal assessment ensures that information about the child's behavior in a variety of contexts is gathered from a number of sources using a wide spectrum of techniques. The parent(s) and teacher(s) together with the child supply data through completion of various rating scales, interviews, observational formats, and standardized tests. Psychologists, social workers, and physicians play important roles in ruling out physical, emotional, or social problems that may account for behavioral abberations. For example, medical diagnosis is necessary to identify potential chronic and acute medical conditions

associated with ADHD and to make decisions regarding the appropriateness of specific medical interventions (e.g., treatment with psychostimulants).

A variety of interview formats, rating scales, and standardized instruments developed specifically to assist in the identification and diagnosis of ADHD are available. For example, the Childhood History Form for Attention Deficit Disorder is designed to compile relevant developmental, medical, social, behavioral, and educational information through a structured interview. The ADHD Rating Scale provides teachers and parents with the opportunity to rate the child on the 14 criteria for ADHD of the DSM-III-R. Rating scales of this sort permit a determination of whether a particular behavior is developmentally inappropriate by allowing for a comparison with a normative group. Table II presents examples of items typically included on rating scales assessing ADHD symptomatology.

More direct assessment of the child's regulatory skills may be undertaken using measures like the Stroop-Word Color Association Test, designed to assess distractibility, the Matching Familiar Figures Test, a measure of impulse control, continuous performance tests like the Gordon Diagnostic System, developed to measure vigilance or attention span,

TABLE II
Sample Items from ADHD Rating Scales

Has difficulty following instructions

Often loses things necessary for tasks

Excitable, impulsive

Wants to run things

Cries easily or often

Restless in the "squirmy" sense

Destructive

Mood changes quickly and drastically

Easily frustrated in efforts

Disturbs other children

Acts too young for his or her age

Confused or seems to be in a fog

Poorly coordinated or clumsy

Inattentive, easily distracted

Talks too much

Fails to finish things he or she starts

Can't concentrate, can't pay attention for long

Daydreams or gets lost in his or her thoughts

and various subtests from the Wechsler Intelligence Scale for Children (3rd ed.), which purport to assess distractibility and concentration.

A number of other rating scales and tests designed to assess features that frequently co-exist with ADHD (e.g., academic deficits) are also readily available and should be included in a comprehensive assessment. Direct observations of the child's behavior are also necessary; observations not only provide a check on the accuracy of other assessment data but also give insight into the role environmental variables play in the expression of problematic behaviors. Informal observational techniques and/or structured observational formats may be used to glean information about the environmental stimuli that may be directly or indirectly influencing the child's behavior. [See CLINICAL ASSESSMENT.]

X. INTERVENTIONS

A. Pharmacological Treatment

The myriad of problems exhibited by ADHD children calls for a multifaceted intervention program. For some ADHD children, pharmacologic approaches may be an integral component. Psychostimulant medications most notably methylphenidate (Ritalin), dextroamphetamine (Dexedrine), and pemolin (Cylert) are the most frequently used pharmacological interventions. While the mode of action of these medications is not well understood, it would appear they achieve their effect by temporarily correcting deficiencies in the self-regulatory system. Psychostimulant medications are described as "fast-acting drugs." Effects are produced approximately 45 minutes after oral ingestion, with a peak effect observed in 2 to 3 hours. Positive effects of the medication dissipate within 4 to 5 hours which may necessitate the administration of a second dose if benefits are to be maintained throughout the day.

The use of psychostimulant medications with ADHD children, particularly Ritalin as it is the most commonly prescribed psychostimulant, has come under criticism. Primary among those criticisms is that the medications enact minimal short-term improvements. Considerable research has documented, however, the positive effects of psychostimulant medications for about 75% of ADHD children on the primary behavioral symptomatology of ADHD and on secondary social and behavioral problems. Concerns that the medications failed to produce improvements in learning have also been dispelled by recent research showing direct short-term beneficial effects on various aspects of learning and memory. Other studies have addressed criticisms that long-term effects are negligible by documenting lower rates of delinquency and motor vehicle accidents and more positive interpersonal relationships and psychological well-being in ADHD adolescents treated for several years with Ritalin.

Concern has also been expressed about potentially unacceptable side-effects of Ritalin including diminished appetite, insomnia, abdominal fullness, overemotionality, increased heart rate and blood pressure, oversedation, and growth suppression. Investigation has shown that such effects are dose related and can be controlled with careful monitoring. There is some evidence that Ritalin may induce tics and possibly precipitate Tourette's syndrome in a very small number of ADHD children. A family or personal history of multiple tics or Tourette's syndrome, therefore, contraindicates the use of Ritalin. Support for a causal link between Ritalin use and substance abuse is negligible.

B. Family and Educational Interventions

The provision of training and counselling to families is another integral component of a comprehensive treatment plan for ADHD children. Demonstrated utility has been found for behavioral, cognitive–behavioral, and systems approaches to intervention for families of ADHD children. Regardless of the theoretical underpinnings, most intervention formats attempt to improve family functioning through educating families as to the nature of ADHD and by teaching them behavioral (e.g., contingency management techniques) and cognitive strategies (e.g., communication and problem-solving training) known to improve the psychosocial functioning of ADHD children. Several also place a strong emphasis on cognitive restructuring (i.e., altering distorted belief structures).

Finally, a comprehensive treatment plan would not be complete without the inclusion of interventions situated within the context of the school. Because this environment places heavy demands on self-regulatory processes, it is likely to be the recipient of many of the ADHD child's behavioral problems. Interventions that facilitate immediate change together with those that alter cognitive processes thereby effecting long-term change are both important.

Case Study: "Michael"

Michael, age 8 years, was referred by the school to the psychologist for assessment because of behavioral concerns. A developmental history, obtained from the parents, revealed that Michael exhibited infancy feeding problems, colic, and sleep pattern difficulties. Gross and fine motor problems as well as difficulties with speech articulation were evident. Interview data and observation suggested that the parents were experiencing considerable difficulty coping with Michael's volatile and disorganized behavior.

School reports revealed that Michael presented with significant behavioral concerns. Within the classroom, he was noted to disrupt class discipline, to manifest explosive and unpredictable behavior, and to exhibit considerable aggression. Teachers also reported that Michael was cognitively impulsive, exhibited concentration and attentional difficulties, and was unusually fidgety and restless. Academically, he was reported to be underachieving.

Assessment was undertaken using a variety of parent and teaching behavioral ratings scales, as well as direct assessment and observational techniques. Results from parent and teacher rating scales suggested the presence of ADHD, as Michael scored within the clinical range on all subtests tapping characteristics of ADHD. Secondary characteristics of ADHD were also evident (e.g., interpersonal problems, emotional immaturity). Scales assessing aggression problems showed an escalation of scores into the clinical range. Direct assessment confirmed the existence of the essential features of ADHD and observational assessment in the classroom provided verification for problems with aggression. Measures evaluating family dynamics revealed considerable stress.

A multicomponent intervention plan was developed for Michael. To facilitate an evaluation of the appropriateness of pharmacological intervention, Michael was referred to a child psychiatrist. As the family was currently "in stress," immediate parenting assistance was provided by a social service agency. The parents were also encouraged to enroll in a cognitive–behavioral parenting group sponsored by the local ADHD parent group. Additional supports (e.g., marital and individual therapy) were made available. At the school level, a systematic behavioral modification program was developed and a mechanism to ensure daily parent/teacher liaison was established. Cognitive and anger management training, as well as academic remediation, were offered through consultation with the special education teacher and school social worker.

Interventions of the first kind are primarily behavioral in nature and seek to alter behavior through manipulation of the environment (i.e., control is externally applied). Included among these modifications are adaptations to the physical environment (e.g., situating ADHD children away from distractors), to the classroom climate (e.g., increasing teachers' awareness of ADHD), to time management and scheduling (e.g., providing clear and paced transitions), to the instructional structure (e.g., decrease work load and/or shorten work periods), to verbal structure (e.g., making rules and directions clear, specific, and external), and to reinforcement practices (e.g., enhancement of traditional behavior modification techniques).

A second type of intervention is designed to enhance the development of internal control through changing thinking patterns. Generally referred to as cognitive training, these approaches seek to teach the ADHD child generic cognitive problem-solving techniques that enhance social, academic, and cognitive functioning. A self-directive component which assists the child in bringing behavior under the control of internal language is often an integral component of cognitive interventions. Finally, preventative (e.g., training in school survival skills) and remedial (e.g., content and process-based) instruction are indicated for ADHD children experiencing academically related deficits.

XI. SUMMARY

The case of "Michael" is an example of an ADHD child referred for psychological assessment and intervention planning. While this case is given only cursory treatment, it illustrates the complexities involved in defining, assessing, and treating ADHD.

Descriptions of children like Michael have long appeared in children's literature (e.g., "Fidgety Phil," mid 1800s) and as early as 1902, in the clinical literature. Over the years, frequent changes in diagnostic terminology reflected a growing empirical understanding of the disorder. The most recent diagnostic classification system adopted the term attention-deficit hyperactivity disorder to capture those characteristics at present seen as essential to the disorder; namely, developmentally inappropriate levels of inattention, impulsivity, and hyperactivity. Contemporary theoretical formulations have argued that underlying the behavioral symptomatology of ADHD is a fundamental neurological defect in self-regulation (i.e., the ability to fine tune and modulate one's behavior).

Research studies have shown that considerable heterogeneity exists among ADHD children. Core deficits co-exist in varying degrees and may be situationally specific or pervasive in their expression. A variety of other associated features may also be present, including disorders of conduct and mood, social skills deficits, and learning and academic disabilities. Manifestations of the primary symptoms of ADHD occur initially in early childhood. During the later developmental and adult years, co-existing secondary problems often assume prominence. The family system appears to be more vulnerable to the stresses resulting from ADHD behaviors when aggression is present in the child.

Diagnosis of ADHD in children must follow from a comprehensive assessment wherein data are gathered from a number of individuals familiar with the child utilizing a variety of techniques. A multidisciplinary complement of professionals should participate in such an assessment plan. Treatment, too, must be multifaceted and should include an evaluation of the appropriateness of medical interventions such as treatment with psychostimulant medications, family-based counseling and training, and school-based behavioral and cognitive training.

Bibliography

American Psychiatric Association (1987). "Diagnostic and Statistical Manual of Mental Disorders," 3rd ed.—Revised. American Psychiatric Association, Washington, DC.

Barkley, R. A. (1990). "Attention-Deficit Hyperactivity Disorder: A Handbook for Diagnosis and Treatment." Guilford, New York.

Douglas, V. I. (1983). Attention and cognitive problems. In "Developmental Neuropsychiatry" (M. Rutter, Ed.). Guilford, New York.

Goldstein, S., and Goldstein, M. (1990). "Managing Attention Disorder in Children: A Guide for Practitioners." Wiley, New York.

ATTENTION-DEFICIT HYPERACTIVITY DISORDER, ASSESSMENT

George J. DuPaul
Lehigh University

Glossary

Attention-deficit hyperactivity disorder (ADHD) A disruptive behavior disorder wherein an individual exhibits significant problems with inattention, impulsivity, and hyperactivity.

Behavior modification Intervention procedures that involve the manipulation of environmental events (e.g., rewards) to change specific, target behaviors.

Behavior rating scales Questionnaires completed by teachers, parents, or children to determine the frequency and/or severity of target behaviors over a specified time interval.

Continuous performance test A test of vigilance that involves the presentation of visual or auditory in a random sequence wherein an individual must make a response (e.g., push a button) following each occurrence of a specific target stimulus or stimuli (e.g., every "A" followed by an "X").

Functional analysis of behavior The collection of assessment data to determine the environmental events or stimuli that are causing and/or maintaining problematic behavior.

Methylphenidate (Ritalin) A psychostimulant medication that is one of the most popular and effective treatments for ADHD.

On-task behavior Visual attention that is directed to a task or activity that is considered appropriate for that time and place.

Oppositional defiant disorder A psychopathological disorder that comprises a pattern of negativistic, hostile, and defiant behaviors beginning in childhood.

ASSESSMENT OF ATTENTION-DEFICIT HYPERACTIVITY DISORDER (ADHD) involves the use of multiple evaluation techniques to determine whether an individual displays developmentally inappropriate frequencies of inattention, impulsivity, and overactivity. An individual's behavior is assessed across various situations (e.g., home, school, community) using multiple sources of data. The assessment is conducted in several stages including: (a) screening, (b) multimethod assessment, (c) interpretation of results, (d) development of treatment plan, and (e) ongoing measurement of treatment response.

ADHD has been defined and conceptualized in a variety of ways over the past several decades, thus leading to confusion among professionals regarding proper diagnosis and evaluation procedures. More recently, there is an emerging consensus that ADHD is characterized by the display of developmentally inappropriate frequencies of inattention, impulsivity, and overactivity. The behaviors or "symptoms" comprising ADHD according to the revised third edition of the *Diagnostic and Statistical Manual of Mental Disorders* (DSM-III-R) published by the American Psychiatric Association are listed in Table I. To be considered symptoms of ADHD, the behaviors must have been initially exhibited in early childhood (i.e., prior to the age of 7 years old) and must be displayed across a variety of settings on a chronic basis. The ADHD diagnosis is usually arrived at by establishing the developmental deviance and pervasiveness of symptoms. At the same time, it is im-

TABLE I

Symptoms of Attention-Deficit Hyperactivity Disorder

1. Often fidgets with hands or feet or squirms in seat.
2. Has difficulty remaining seated when required to do so.
3. Is easily distracted by extraneous stimuli.
4. Has difficulty awaiting turn in games or group situations.
5. Often blurts out answers to questions before they have been completed.
6. Has difficulty following through on instructions from others.
7. Has difficulty sustaining attention in tasks or play activities.
8. Often shifts from one uncompleted activity to another.
9. Has difficulty playing quietly.
10. Often talks excessively.
11. Often interrupts or intrudes on others.
12. Often does not seem to listen to what is being said to him or her.
13. Often loses things necessary for tasks or activities at school or at home.
14. Often engages in physically dangerous activities without considering possible consequences.

Source: Adapted from the American Psychiatric Association (1987). "Diagnostic and Statistical Manual for Mental Disorders," 3rd ed., revised, pp. 52–53. Washington, DC.

portant to "rule out" alternative causes for the child's inattention, impulsivity, and motor restlessness including poor academic instruction and management practices as well as gross neurological, sensory, motor, or language impairment, mental retardation, or severe emotional disturbance. [*See* ATTENTION-DEFICIT HYPERACTIVITY DISORDER.]

I. STAGE MODEL FOR THE IDENTIFICATION AND ASSESSMENT OF ADHD

Following a parent or teacher referral for attention and behavior control difficulties, the evaluation of ADHD is conducted in five stages (see Fig. 1). First, teacher ratings are obtained and a brief interview is conducted with the teacher to screen for the severity and frequency of possible ADHD symptoms. Next, if the findings of this screening are significant, then multiple assessment methods are used across sources and settings to document the child's functioning across a number of areas. Third, the evaluation results are interpreted such that classification and diagnostic decisions can be made. Fourth, a

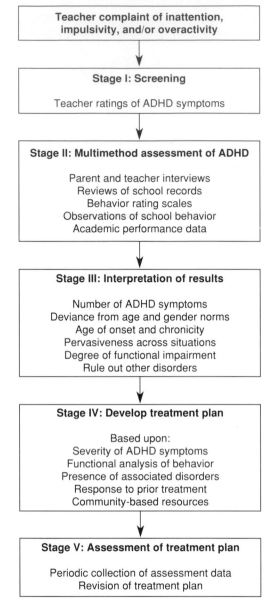

FIGURE 1   A stage model for the assessment of ADHD in childhood and adolescence. [Adapted from DuPaul, G. J., and Stoner, G. (1994). "ADHD in the Schools: Assessment and Intervention Strategies." Guilford, New York.]

treatment plan is developed based on the obtained assessment data. Finally, the child's school behavior and academic performance are assessed on an ongoing basis to determine the success of and the need for changes in the intervention program.

II. SCREENING FOR ADHD

Screening for possible ADHD should be conducted whenever a teacher seeks assistance due to a student's difficulties paying attention during instruction, inconsistent completion of independent tasks, inability to remain seated at appropriate times, or display of impulsive, disruptive behavior. In similar fashion, screening would be conducted based on a parent referral for child problems related to non-completion of chores, a high activity level, or impulsive behavior (e.g., frequent interruptions of adult or sibling activities). A brief interview with the teacher or parent is conducted to specify the behavioral concerns and to identify environmental factors which may be eliciting and/or maintaining the child's problem behaviors. Teacher or parent ratings of the frequency of ADHD symptoms are then obtained to determine whether further evaluation is necessary. If a more than a few of the symptoms of ADHD are reported (see Table 1), then the assessment would move to stage 2, as discussed below.

III. MULTIMETHOD ASSESSMENT OF ADHD

A. Measures with Diagnostic Utility

Multiple assessment techniques typically are employed across home and school settings in the comprehensive evaluation of children who may have ADHD. In particular, emphasis is placed upon obtaining reliable information regarding a child's symptoms from parents and teachers as well as from first-hand observations of the child's behavior. Therefore, the major components of the evaluation of ADHD include interviews with the child's parent(s) and teacher(s), questionnaires completed by parents and teachers, and observations of child behavior across multiple settings and under variant task conditions. Although many of these same procedures are used when evaluating adolescents, some modifications (e.g., inclusion of self-report data) are necessary to maintain the reliability and validity of the assessment data.

Interviews with the parent(s), teacher(s), and child are conducted to determine the presence or absence of various DSM-III-R symptoms as well as to enumerate possible historical and/or current factors which may be serving to maintain identified problem behaviors. Behavior rating scales completed by the student's parent(s) and teacher(s) provide data which establish the severity of ADHD-related behaviors relative to a normative sample. To supplement parent and teacher report, several direct measures of child behavior are used. The child's

behavior is observed across settings (e.g., classroom, playground, clinic playroom) on several occasions to establish the frequency and/or duration of various target behaviors. If possible, behavioral frequencies are compared to those displayed by several of the child's classmates to determine the deviance of the referred individual's behavior. Finally, the products of the child's behavior (e.g., completion and accuracy of academic work, quality of desk organization) can be collected and/or examined.

Standardized measures of sustained attention and impulse control have been incorporated routinely into the diagnostic evaluation of ADHD. Purportedly, such tests provide objective data that are less influenced by factors (e.g., parental psychopathology) which may bias parent and teacher report. Although scores on clinic-based measures such as the Continuous Performance Test discriminate between children with ADHD and their normal counterparts at a *group* level, the utility of these measures in assessing *individual* children may be limited by several factors. First, several investigations have failed to obtain significant correlations between criterion measures (e.g., teacher ratings) and scores on various tests of vigilance and impulse control. Second, when the effects of age, sex, and receptive vocabulary skills are partialled out, scores on these measures have failed to discriminate among children with ADHD, children with other behavior disorders, and their normal peers. Even when significant correlations are obtained between clinic-based tests and criterion measures, these typically are of low magnitude (i.e., between absolute values of .21 to .50) suggesting that the results of clinic-based tasks account for minimal variance of criterion indices. Thus, according to Barkley, the use of such instruments in the evaluation of ADHD is limited by rather suspect ecological validity.

B. Measures with Limited Diagnostic Utility

Several assessment techniques typically employed by psychologists have limited utility in the diagnostic evaluation of ADHD. The results of cognitive, neuropsychological, projective, and educational tests typically are not helpful in determining whether a child has ADHD or not. To date, no individually administered test or group of tests has demonstrated an acceptable degree of ecological validity to be helpful in the diagnostic process. For example, the test most frequently employed by clinical child and school psychologists (i.e., Wechsler Intelligence Scale for Children-Revised and now the WISC-III) has not been found to reliably discriminate ADHD from normal children or students with learning disabilities. More importantly, below average scores on the freedom from distractibility factor (i.e., arithmetic, digit span, and coding subtests) of the WISC-R are not necessarily a diagnostic indicator of ADHD. Further, children with ADHD often display appropriate levels of attention and behavioral control under task conditions which are highly structured and involve one-to-one interaction with a novel adult as is found in most testing situations. Thus, while individually administered tests may be helpful in determining the child's intellectual and educational status, they are not necessary components of the diagnostic evaluation of ADHD.

Self-report questionnaires completed by the child have become increasingly popular in recent years. Although a number of psychometrically sound self-report checklists are available, at least two factors limit their use in the assessment of ADHD. First, children with disruptive behavior disorders are typically poor reporters of their own behavior. The reliability and validity of self-report data provided by children with ADHD have not been established. Second, many of the self-report measures available do not have separate factors or subscales specific to ADHD, thus limiting their diagnostic utility.

IV. INTERPRETATION OF RESULTS

Although each of the assessment techniques, listed above, have limitations, the advantage of using a multimethod approach is that each of their strengths and weaknesses are balanced as part of the larger evaluation package. The overriding goals are to derive consistent information regarding the frequency and severity of ADHD-related behaviors across caregivers and settings, as well as to determine possible causes for these difficulties. To the extent that these goals are achieved, relative confidence can be placed in conclusions drawn as a result of the assessment. The results of multimethod assessment data are used to determine the diagnostic status of the referred individual by reviewing the following questions:

1. Does the child exhibit a significant number of behavioral symptoms of ADHD according to parent and teacher report?
2. Does the child exhibit ADHD symptoms at a frequency that is significantly greater than that

demonstrated by children of the same gender and chronological age?
3. At what age did the child begin demonstrating significant ADHD-related behaviors and are these behaviors chronic and evident across many situations?
4. Is the child's functioning at school, at home, and with peers significantly impaired?
5. Are there other possible problems (e.g., academic skills deficits) or factors (e.g., teacher intolerance for active behavior) that could account for the reported display of ADHD symptoms?

A. Number of ADHD Symptoms

Parent and teacher interview data are used to determine the number of ADHD-related behaviors that the individual exhibits. Their reports are evaluated vis a vis the criteria listed in Table I.

B. Frequency of ADHD-Related Behaviors

The parent and teacher questionnaires discussed above all contain at least one factor related to ADHD (e.g., labeled "hyperactivity," "attention problems," "overactive–restless"). If a child's score on this factor is greater than 2 standard deviations above the mean for his or her gender and chronological age, this is considered significant for ADHD. Scores on these same factors that are between 1.5 and 2 standard deviations above the mean are considered to be in the borderline significant (i.e., mild) range for ADHD. Thus, children receiving scores in the upper 2 to 7% of ADHD symptoms for their age and gender may be identified as having ADHD (depending upon other assessment findings).

C. Age of Onset and Chronicity of Problem Behaviors

Parent report of the onset of ADHD symptoms is obtained during the interview. Typically, the age of onset is reported to be when the child begins formal schooling (i.e., kindergarten or first grade) or earlier. The consistency of ADHD-related behaviors across grades or time can be confirmed through inspection of the child's previous report cards in the school record. According to the American Psychiatric Association, the onset of ADHD symptoms should be reported to be prior to the age of 7 and must be occurring on a daily basis for at least 6 months.

D. Problem Behaviors Occurring across Situations

At a general level, if both the parent(s) and teacher(s) are reporting significant display of ADHD-related behaviors across home and school environments, then this criterion is met. The pervasiveness of inattentive behaviors and/or conduct problems across situations *within* home and school environments can be determined using behavior rating scales. To the degree that significant ADHD-related behaviors are reported to occur across home and school settings, relative confidence can be placed in the conclusion that within-child variables (i.e., presence of ADHD) account for the behavioral control difficulties to a large degree. When inconsistencies between parent and teacher report are obtained, confidence in the diagnosis of ADHD is reduced. In general, teacher ratings are given more credence as the school is the more problematic setting for children with ADHD and teachers have greater exposure to children within a specific age range.

E. Functional Impairment

The degree to which the child's academic, social, and emotional functioning is impaired is determined through examination of all of the measures discussed above. The most frequently encountered signs of impairment associated with ADHD are academic achievement below expectations for the child and poor acceptance by peers. Thus, the child would be expected to produce less complete and accurate work than classmates based on observational data and teacher ratings. Further, ratings for the child on scales of social competence and peer relationships would be below average for his or her age and gender. Observational data may confirm the latter, as the child may exhibit high rates of aggressive behavior on the playground or may be ignored by classmates during free-play periods.

F. Other Factors Accounting for ADHD-like Behavior

The ADHD diagnosis usually is made by establishing the developmental deviance and pervasiveness of symptoms, as discussed above. At the same time, it is crucial to consider alternative causes for the child's inattention, impulsivity, and motor restlessness. For example, poor or inconsistent academic instruction and/or behavior management practices are possible "causes" of apparent ADHD symptoms. Alternatively, the individual may appear to be "inattentive" due to willful misbehavior associated with a conduct disorder.

Once a diagnostic decision is reached, the findings and resultant treatment recommendations must be communicated to the individual's teachers and parents, as well as any community-based professionals (e.g., pediatrician) who may be working with the child. Typically, a written report is generated and results and recommendations are orally reviewed with pertinent school personnel and parents.

V. TREATMENT PLANNING

The assessment does not conclude with a diagnosis, as the latter is one part of a process to determine which intervention strategies are most likely to be successful. Thus, the assessment data are used to generate an appropriate treatment plan. The intervention strategies which have the greatest research support in the treatment of ADHD are the prescription of psychostimulant medication (e.g., Ritalin) and behavior modification procedures.

Interventions for ADHD typically are designed to impact target behaviors across academic and social domains. Because ADHD symptoms are, by definition, exhibited across settings, then treatment strategies must be outlined for multiple caretakers (e.g., parents and teachers) to be used across a number of situations. Although an explicit goal of the intervention program is to decrease the frequency of various ADHD-related behaviors (e.g., inattention to task materials), the primary emphasis is on enhancing competencies in a number of areas. Thus, treatment targets are behaviors which should increase in frequency as a function of treatment, such as completion of independent work, compliance with teacher directives, accuracy of academic responding, and positive interactions with peers. Behavioral objectives must be designed on an individual basis using data from direct observations of classroom behavior, as well as the results of parent and teacher ratings. Assessment results also will identify behavioral competencies (e.g., adequate peer relations) which possibly could aid in the amelioration of the child's deficits. Those behaviors occurring at the lowest frequencies and/or deemed most crucial to classroom functioning by the teacher usually serve as initial intervention targets.

A number of factors are considered in the process of choosing appropriate interventions for an individual child with ADHD. First, the severity of ADHD symptoms helps to determine the need for medication treatment in addition to behavior modification. Second, a functional analysis of behavior is used to determine what environmental factors can be altered to enhance the child's performance. Third, the presence of additional disorders (e.g., oppositional defiant disorder) will necessitate designing interventions to address behavior control difficulties beyond ADHD (e.g., parent training in behavior modification strategies). Finally, an individual's response to prior interventions can be used to gauge what additional treatments will be necessary.

VI. ONGOING MEASUREMENT OF TREATMENT RESPONSE

The assessment of the child with ADHD does not conclude with the diagnosis, but continues on an ongoing basis as intervention procedures are implemented. In this context, the initial evaluation data not only contribute to diagnostic decisions but also serve as baseline or pre-intervention measures. Once the intervention program is designed and implemented, ongoing assessment is conducted to determine whether: (a) target and collateral behaviors are changing; (b) treatment-related improvements are socially valid and clinically significant; and (c) target behaviors are "normalized." If assessment data are not collected once treatment begins, one can never be sure that the intervention is successful or requires adjustments. Single-subject design methodology typically is employed to evaluate treatment-related changes in target behaviors.

Throughout the treatment process, the student serves as his or her own "control" and behavioral change is evaluated in comparison to baseline or nonintervention conditions. This process requires the repeated acquisition of assessment data across settings and caretakers at various points in the intervention program. In addition, treatment integrity is evaluated to ensure the accurate application (e.g., treatment compliance) of the prescribed intervention. If the intervention is implemented as designed and reliable behavior change occurs, then one can assume that the treatment is working as planned. If not, then changes to the intervention or the way that it is implemented by teachers or parents must be

made. Thus, ongoing assessment is crucial to the treatment process and the two are inexorably linked.

Although it is important to demonstrate that an intervention has led to reliable changes in the student's behavior and performance, it is crucial to determine whether such changes are socially valid and clinically meaningful. For example, a mean increase in the percentage of on-task behavior from 50 to 65% during independent work may be statistically significant, but the end result is that the student still spends too much time off-task and is not any more productive academically. The clinical significance and social validity of behavioral change can be assessed in a variety of ways. For instance, consumer satisfaction ratings could be completed by the student, teacher, and/or parents at the conclusion of treatment or at various points during the intervention. Each participant's views on specific components of the intervention could be obtained in this manner.

Another method of determining the clinical significance of an intervention is to assess whether it has led to the "normalization" of behavior. Stated differently, does the intervention enhance the student's attention span, academic productivity, and social behaviors to the point where his or her performance is indistinguishable from that of his or her peers? This can be evaluated by collecting assessment data on one or more classmates during various points in the intervention. In this way, the treated child's performance can be compared directly to that of his or her normal counterparts.

VII. ASSESSMENT OF ADHD IN ADULTS

Over the past decade, the results of longitudinal investigations have indicated the chronic nature of ADHD symptoms. Approximately 50% of children with ADHD will continue to exhibit significant symptoms of the disorder through adulthood. Thus, there is an increasing need to identify and treat adults with ADHD. Unfortunately, there is a dearth of empirical data regarding the accurate diagnosis of this disorder among adults.

Clinical assessment of ADHD in adulthood is hampered by several factors. First, the diagnostic criteria for this disorder were written to reflect the expression of symptoms in childhood and adolescence (see Table I). Thus, clinicians must surmise how specific childhood symptoms (e.g., difficulty sustaining attention to schoolwork) would be expressed in adulthood (e.g., difficulty sustaining attention to job-related activities). Second, the diagnosis of ADHD in childhood is strongly related to the reports of significant others (e.g., teachers, parents) rather than self-report. In the assessment of adults, the reports of significant others may not be available. Finally, inattention and disorganization are symptoms of many disorders (e.g., bipolar disorder) including ADHD. This complicates the differential diagnosis of this disorder in adulthood.

Currently, the evaluation of ADHD in adults comprises several assessment procedures. First, a clinical interview is conducted with the identified patient. It is important that retrospective report of ADHD symptoms are attained in addition to data regarding current problems. The probability of attaining an adequate history of symptoms is enhanced when a patient's family member, preferably a parent, is interviewed. An interview with the patient's spouse also can aid in obtaining reliable information about current symptoms. A second assessment technique is to have the patient complete a variety of self-report measures. These may be completed regarding both current and past symptomatology. If one of the patient's parents is available, then retrospective parent ratings regarding the patient's ADHD symptoms in childhood are obtained. Finally, a variety of laboratory-based tests of vigilance, impulse control, and organizational skills can be administered. It is important to note that the validity of clinic-based tests in making the diagnosis of ADHD in adults has yet to be investigated.

In summary, ADHD is a chronic disruptive behavior disorder that affects functioning in a number of domains throughout the lifespan. It is relatively common in the general population, especially among males. Assessment usually involves obtaining structured information from parents and teachers as well as directly observing individual behavior in home, school, or clinic settings. The evaluation of ADHD is conducted in five stages including screening, multimethod assessment, interpretation of results, treatment planning, and ongoing measurement of treatment response. It is important not only to make reliable and valid diagnostic decisions, but to collect assessment data that lead to effective treatment outcomes.

Bibliography

Barkley, R. A. (1990). "Attention Deficit Hyperactivity Disorder: A Handbook for Diagnosis and Treatment." Guilford, New York.

Barkley, R. A. (1988). Attention deficit-hyperactivity disorder. In "Behavioral Assessment of Childhood Disorders" (E. J. Mash and L. Terdal, Eds.). Guilford, New York.

DuPaul, G. J., and Stoner, G. (1994). "Attention Deficit Hyperactivity Disorder in the Schools: Assessment and Intervention Strategies." Guilford, New York.

Matson, J. L. (Ed.) (1993). "Handbook of Hyperactivity in Children." Allyn & Bacon, Boston.

Shaywitz, S. E., and Shaywitz, B. A. (Eds.) (1992). "Attention Deficit Disorder Comes of Age: Toward the Twenty-First Century." Pro-Ed, Austin, TX.

Whalen, C. K. (1989). Attention deficit and hyperactivity disorders. In "Handbook of Child Psychopathology" (T. H. Ollendick and M. Hersen, Eds.), 2nd ed. Plenum, New York.

◆

ATTITUDE CHANGE

John T. Cacioppo, Richard E. Petty, and Stephen L. Crites, Jr.
The Ohio State University

Glossary

Affection Emotional responses which can be expressed verbally or nonverbally.

Attitude The general and enduring evaluative perception of some person, object, or issue.

Attitude change Modification of an individual's general evaluative perception of a stimulus or set of stimuli.

Belief Information, factual and nonfactual, that a person has about other people, objects, or issues.

Cognition Mental processes involved in achieving awareness or knowledge of an object.

Compliance Acting in accordance with the demands or sanctions by others.

Conation Behavioral tendency or actual behavior.

Education The teaching of certain factual information and the teaching of how to think logically so that a person will be capable of making up his or her own mind.

Influence The effect of events and others on behavior.

Persuasion An active attempt to change a person's attitude through information.

ATTITUDE CHANGE refers to a modification of an individual's general evaluative perception of a stimulus or set of stimuli. Thus, changes for any reason in a person's general and enduring favorable or unfavorable regard for some person, object, or issue fall under the rubric of attitude change. Not included under the rubric of attitude change are changes in knowledge or skill (i.e., education), and changes in behavior that require another's surveillance or sanctions (i.e., compliance). Innate predilections to approach or withdraw—such as reflexes or fixed action patterns—and irreversible changes in parameters of approach or withdrawal—such as diminished response vigor due to aging—may be related to attitude change but are not themselves considered instances of attitude change. Attitude change, therefore, represents a specific form of self-control and social control that does not rely on coercion.

I. HISTORY

A. The Scientific Study of Attitudes and Attitude Change

The term attitude comes from the Latin words *apto* (aptitude or fitness) and *acto* (postures of the body), both of which have their origin in the Sanskrit root *ag*, meaning to do or to act. The connection between attitude and action carried into the 18th century, when attitude referred to a physical orientation or position in relation to a frame of reference. Herbert Spencer and Alexander Bain introduced the term attitude into psychology in the 1860s, when they used it to refer to an internal state of preparation for action. Sir Francis Galton subsequently suggested that the interpersonal attitudes (sentiments) of guests at a dinner party could be measured by gauging their bodily orientation toward one another, but it was Louis Thurstone's seminal 1928 paper, "Attitudes Can Be Measured," that precipitated empirical research on the determinants of attitudes. Drawing upon his background in psychophysics, Thurstone conceived of an attitude as the net affective perception of (i.e., feeling toward) a stimulus rather than as a bodily orientation. He demonstrated in pioneering research that these feelings could be scaled by constructing a set of relevant belief statements that were ordered along a unidimensional continuum ranging from maximal positivity to maximal negativity. Since that time, research on attitudes and attitude change has relied largely on self-report measures, and the dual questions of the determinants of attitude change and of attitude–behavior correspondence have been a focus of research for the past half century.

Dissection and identification of the processes underlying attitude change have occasionally been assailed as fostering the manipulation of the meek. Historical evidence indicates, however, that appeals to people's attitudes as a means of achieving social control have played a central role in only four historical periods: Athens in 427 B.C. to 338 B.C. (during which time Plato and Aristotle considered the processes underlying persuasion), Rome from approximately 150 B.C. to 43 B.C. (during which time Cicero wrote about oration and persuasion), in Europe from approximately 1470 to 1572 (during the Italian Renaissance), and the present period of the mass media which began to take form in the 18th century. The key modes of achieving political, social, and economic control during the remaining periods of human history have been physical force and intimidation rather than attitude change.

B. The Ubiquity of Attitude Changes

This historical context is easy to overlook in light of the emphasis placed in contemporary society on attitude change to motivate consumer selections, resolve conflicts, and modify maladaptive behavior. Based on the billions of dollars spent annually each year on advertising, it has been estimated that the average person in the United States has the potential to be exposed to several thousand persuasive appeals per day. Even if only a small fraction of these appeals are effective, this deluge of appeals suggests that an individual's attitudes are under nearly constant challenge.

Indeed, one of the more surprising findings in the area of attitude change is that repeated, unreinforced exposures to a novel or unfamiliar stimulus result in a positive attitude toward the stimulus. That is, repeated exposure to a novel stimulus that results in neither reward nor punishment breeds preference for this stimulus over a similar stimulus to which an individual has not been exposed. This *mere exposure*

effect has been demonstrated using stimuli as diverse as nonsense words, ideographs, polygons, and faces, and the mere exposure effect is enhanced by factors such as a heterogeneous exposure sequence, a moderate number of presentations of the target stimulus (e.g., less than 100), brief exposure durations (e.g., less than 5 sec), and a delay between the stimulus presentations and attitude measurement. Attitude change due to information emanating from the environment has also been documented *in utero* and appears to be a variation on the mere exposure effect.

II. CLASSIC AND CONTEMPORARY APPROACHES TO ATTITUDE CHANGE

A. Conditioning and Modeling Approach

Although repeated unreinforced presentations of a novel stimulus can influence attitudes, early research drew upon the basic principles of learning from studies of classical and operant conditioning to explain attitude formation and change. The focus of the theories falling under this approach has been on the effects of the direct administration of rewards and punishments to the subject. Thus, attitudes toward stimuli were posited to become more favorable/unfavorable if they were associated with pleasant/unpleasant contexts (classical conditioning) or led to positive/negative outcomes (operant conditioning). Although the roles of contingency awareness and demand characteristics have spawned controversies over the interpretation of the observed attitude changes, evaluative conditioning now appears to be well established and to be more powerful in attitude formation than in attitude change. Studies of modeling further indicated that the classical and operant conditioning of attitudes could occur vicariously. [*See* CLASSICAL CONDITIONING; OPERANT LEARNING.]

B. Verbal Learning Approach

The study of attitude change gained momentum during World War II, when the mass media played an important role in recruiting and indoctrinating troops, maintaining the morale of the Allied forces and residents, and assaulting the morale of the Axis troops. This early research, headed by Carl Hovland, was organized by the question "who said what to whom, how and with what effect." Thus, research on the determinants of message learning and persuasion was organized in terms of the effects of source factors (e.g., expertise, trustworthiness), message factors (e.g., one-sided, two-sided), recipient factors (e.g., sex, intelligence), and modality or channel factors (e.g., print, auditory). Moreover, the attention to, comprehension of, and retention of the arguments contained in a persuasive message were thought to be the information processing stages underlying attitude change. Experiments were designed initially to assess the simple (e.g., main) effects of source, message, recipient, and channel factors on recall and attitude change, but a disarray of results across experiments led to the use of more complex designs and the discovery of interactive effects on attitude change. The effects of source, message, recipient, and channel factors on attention, comprehension, retention, and attitudes were also often quite discrepant, further calling into question the heuristic value of the processing stages outlined by Hovland and his colleagues. Nevertheless, Hovland and his colleagues' classification of independent variables as source, message, recipient, and channel factors and dependent variables as measures of attention, comprehension, and retention, and their rigorous experimental approach to the study of attitude change, moved the study of attitude change from rhetorical to scientific analyses.

C. Judgmental Approach

A third approach encompasses perceptual–judgmental theories of attitude change. These theories have in common their focus on how attitude judgments are made in the context of a person's past experiences and in the stimulus context in which the attitude question or object is embedded. The judgmental distortions of assimilation and contrast, and their antecedents, have been especially important in perceptual theories of attitude change because these distortions can produce both changes in a person's attitude rating and changes in the attitude. Assimilation refers to a shift in judgments toward an anchor, whereas contrast refers to a shift in judgments away from the anchor. What constitutes an anchor varies across various perceptual theories, but have included the mean affective value of salient contextual stimuli (adaptation level theory), an individual's initial attitude (social judgment theory), and the endpoints of the scales (accentuation theory).

One important contribution stemming from this work is that a host of variables ranging from cultural background to the order, content, and scale-anchors in attitude surveys can alter attitude ratings even though the underlying attitude may be unaffected or can alter attitudes while leaving attitude ratings unaffected. In an illustrative study, college students read a case about a Mr. R. K. who had been found guilty of threatening to bomb a hospital. Students were then asked to rate themselves in terms of their sentencing disposition on a stern–leniency scale, and they wrote a paragraph justifying this rating. The stern–leniency rating was taken as an indicant of the students' attitude rating, and the justifying paragraph was used to commit the student to this rating. Next, students received the perspective manipulation. Half of them learned that the maximally lenient punishment allowable for this crime was 1 year and the maximally stern punishment was 5 years (narrow perspective); the other half of the subjects were told that the maximally lenient punishment was 1 year but that the maximally stern punishment was 30 years (wide perspective). Afterward, the students were asked how many years they felt Mr. R. K. should be imprisoned for his crime. As expected, the students exposed to the narrow perspective advocated fewer years of imprisonment than subjects exposed to the wide perspective even though both groups would still describe their attitude positions the same.

D. Motivational Approach

A fourth approach focuses on the different human motives as they relate to attitudes and persuasion. The most researched motive is the need to maintain cognitive consistency. Balance theory, cognitive dissonance theory, and congruity theory are among the most influential cognitive consistency theories. There are several characteristics that cognitive consistency theories of attitudes have in common. First, each describes the conditions for equilibrium and disequilibrium among cognitive elements (units of information). Second, each asserts that disequilibrium motivates the person to restore consistency among the elements, usually in order to remove the feeling of unpleasant tension. Third, each describes the means by which equilibrium might be accomplished. Balance theory, for instance, emphasizes the person's point of view about elements of information and their interconnections. Balance, Fritz Heider posited a half century ago, was a harmonious, quiescent motivational state in which all of the elements appeared to the individual to be internally consistent. Balance was described by Heider as occurring when recipients agree with sources they like or disagree with sources they dislike. These situations were said to be the most pleasant, desirable, stable, and expected state of relationships among any set of elements to which a person heeded. When imbalance exists, as when recipients disagree with sources they like, a motivation to maintain cognitive consistency is aroused and creates a pressure to change one or more relations among cognitive elements to reinstitute cognitive balance.

One of the major criticisms of balance theory is that there are no provisions for degrees of liking or belongingness between elements. Congruity theory overcomes this objection by quantifying gradations of sentiment and belongingness between elements. Nonetheless, congruity theory can be considered a special case of balance theory, in which there are two elements, the source and a concept, and on the assertion made by the source about the concept.

Leon Festinger's theory of cognitive dissonance is perhaps the most widely researched theory in social psychology and is unique among consistency theories in two important regards. First, most consistency theories can consider the interrelationships among a number of elements simultaneously to determine whether the structure of elements is balanced. Dissonance theory considers only pairs of elements at a time. The magnitude of cognitive dissonance within a set of many elements is determined by the proportion of relevant elements that are dissonant and the importance of the elements to the person. Research has also emphasized the importance of perceived choice and foreseeable negative consequences as factors influencing the arousal of cognitive dissonance. Second, cognitive dissonance theory has led to a number of nonobvious predictions regarding attitude change. For instance, dissonance theory specifies conditions in which a low credible source, a low incentive, high effort, or mild threat each leads to greater attitude change than a high credible source, a high incentive, low effort, or severe threat, respectively. The nonintuitiveness of these predictions, coupled with the creative and provocative methods used to confirm these predictions, did much to stimulate research in attitude change.

E. Attributional Approach

The fifth general approach to attitude change involves attitude-inference, or attributional processes. The notion common to the theories that fall under this heading is that a person's inferences about the cause of a behavior is the proximal mediator of the resulting attitude. These attitude-inferences might concern the communicator's behavior ("why is he or she saying that?") or they might concern the person's own behavior ("why did I do that?"). When a behavior is attributed to something about the person, the person's attitude can be a convenient candidate for the cause of the behavior. When a behavior is attributed to the situation, in contrast, the notion of an attitude is unnecessary to account for the behavior.

There are two general attributional principles that have guided much of the attribution research in the area of attitude change. The first is the discounting principle, which states that to the extent that a response (or effect) has a number of plausible causes, the viability of any single cause is discounted or weakened. The second is the augmentation principle, which states that a response or behavior that is unexpected (i.e., unique) given the contextual cues is especially likely to be attributed to something about the person, such as his or her personal attitude. Thus, sources who argue against their vested interests are more persuasive than are sources who argue for their vested interests. [See ATTRIBUTION.]

F. Combinatory Approach

The sixth, combinatory approach to attitudes and attitude change includes mathematical models that have been developed to account for how the attributes of or beliefs about an attitude target are evaluated and integrated to form an overall attitude about the stimulus. In Bill McGuire's probabilogical model of attitude change, for instance, attitude-relevant beliefs are represented in terms of syllogisms, and attitude change is predicted to occur as a mathematical function of changes in these beliefs. Consider the following attitude syllogism:

First premise: Reading *Time* magazine keeps one
   informed.
Second premise: A magazine that keeps one
   informed is valuable.
Conclusion: *Time* magazine is valuable.

Research on this model indicates that attitude change varies as a function of both logical consistency and hedonic consistency (wishful thinking). Logical consistency is demonstrated, for instance, as when the conclusion is more likely to be accepted the more likely is the first or second premise to be true. Hedonic consistency, on the other hand, refers to the tendency for individuals to see things as consistent with their personal desires or wishes. They might therefore tend to see conclusions and premises as more likely the more desirable they are, even if this goes against pure logic. Thus, changes in the probability that an underlying belief is true also produce changes in a person's attitude, but these changes are biased by wishful thinking, a distortion that is especially pronounced in uneducated persons.

Martin Fishbein and Izek Ajzen's theory of reasoned action also focuses on the beliefs underlying an attitude and the rational basis of attitudes, but also emphasizes the correspondence between attitudes and behaviors. According to this theory, the single best predictor of behavior is a person's intention to perform a behavior (i.e., the behavioral intention), which is posited to be a function of two factors: the person's attitude toward the behavior, and the person's subjective norms. Attitudes, in turn, are viewed as determined by the beliefs that a person holds about the consequences of a behavior, including the likelihood that the behavior would lead to certain outcomes, and the person's evaluation of those consequences. Specifically, the attitude is derived by summing the product of the strength of each belief with the evaluative component of the belief. The subjective norm, on the other hand, is posited to be a function of what the person perceives the opinion of significant others regarding the performance of the behavior to be (e.g., the expectations of parents or the opinion of friends), and the person's motivation to comply with their judgments. The subjective norm is derivable by summing the product of the strength of the belief that significant others think one should engage in the behavior with the motivation to comply component. The theory of reasoned action, therefore, suggests that to achieve behavior change, the attitudes and subjective norms for that behavior should be targeted. This theory has proven useful in predicting voluntary or deliberative behaviors, such as voter behavior, but it has done less well in predicting motivated or consistent but "unintentional" behaviors such as smoking cessation or dieting behavior. Although recent theory and research suggest that attitudes may influence behaviors directly as well as indirectly through their influence on behavioral intentions, this theory has contributed to a specification of the factors that moderate attitude–behavior correspondence. A re-

cent variation on this theory, the theory of planned behavior, posits that behavioral intentions are determined by the degree of the subject's perceived control over the action in addition to a person's attitude and subjective norm. Other recent theories of attitude–behavior correspondence have emphasized factors such as the extent to which attitudes are based on issue-relevant thinking, the attitude itself is accessible in memory, the individual's level of self-monitoring and need for cognition, and the behavior being deliberative rather than habitual in nature.

G. Self-Persuasion Approach

The final general approach discussed here is termed self-persuasion because attitude change is not viewed as the consequence of the externally provided information per se, but rather as the consequence of thoughts, ideas, and arguments that the recipients themselves generate. This approach is similar to that of Hovland and his colleagues in recognizing the importance of attention to and comprehension of a persuasive message. However, advocates of this approach make the assumption that when a person anticipates or receives a persuasive communication, an attempt is made to relate issue-relevant information (e.g., message arguments) to the preexisting knowledge that the person has about the attitude stimulus. In doing this, a person considers a substantial amount of information that is not found in, for instance, a persuasive communication or attitude stimulus. These self-generated thoughts may be positive, neutral, or negative toward the stimulus or they may be completely irrelevant to the stimulus. The notion underlying theories that fall under the self-persuasion approach is that the hedonic balance of the issue-relevant thoughts determines the nature and amount of attitude change. If a stimulus evokes primarily favorable thoughts, a positive attitude is fostered; but if a stimulus evokes primarily unfavorable thoughts, a negative attitude is nourished. The goal of theory and research falling under this rubric, therefore, has been to determine how various features of attitude stimuli and persuasive communications influence the hedonic tone of issue-relevant thinking.

III. TWO ROUTES TO ATTITUDE CHANGE

Although these various theoretical approaches postulate different mechanisms as underlying attitude change, they generally focus on one of two processes: (a) one in which individuals respond to various superficial cues or heuristics in the situation (e.g., celebrity status of the source), and (b) one in which attitude-relevant information is generated and processed (e.g., cogency or speciousness of the message arguments). Thus, these various approaches to attitude change can be conceptualized within a general framework for organizing, categorizing, and understanding the basic processes underlying attitude change. Richard Petty and John Cacioppo have proposed that the many different empirical findings and theories in the field have been viewed as emphasizing one of two relatively distinct *routes to persuasion*. The first is attitude change that occurs as a result of a person's careful and thoughtful consideration of the merits of the information presented in support of an advocacy (*central route*). The second is that occurring as a result of some simple cue in the persuasion context (e.g., an attractive source) that induces change without necessitating scrutiny of the merits of issue-relevant information (*peripheral route*). This model of the psychological operations underlying persuasion highlights that attitudes are multiply determined and that attitudes whose verbal expression is similar may have different antecedents and consequences. For instance, the issue-relevant thinking that characterizes the central route to persuasion can result in the integration of new arguments, or one's personal translations of them, into one's underlying belief structure for the attitude object. In addition, by scrutinizing the strengths and weaknesses of a recommendation, the information and the consequent attitude are rendered more coherent, accessible, and generalizable. Attitudes formed through the central route, therefore, are relatively persistent, resistant to counterpersuasion, and predictive of behavior.

Even though individuals might be motivated generally to hold correct attitudes, the numerous stimuli that individuals must evaluate daily, coupled with their limited time and cognitive resources, make it imperative that they sometimes use cognitively less demanding short-cuts (e.g., simple cues, habits, rules-of-thumbs) to guide attitudinal reactions. That is, people do not have the luxury of adopting only those attitude positions about which they have had the time and opportunity to research if they are going to be able to venture into novel situations or respond to the myriad stimuli to which they are exposed each day. Although the use of superficial persuasion cues or heuristics for attitude change (peripheral route)

can guide responses to a wide variety of stimuli while minimizing the demands on individuals' limited cognitive resources, the resultant attitudes and behavior are based on information that is only superficially or peripherally related to the actual merits of the position. Hence, some responses potentiated by this generally adaptive mechanism may be unreasonable and maladaptive. These maladaptive features of attitudes derived through the peripheral route are diminished somewhat by their relatively short persistence, susceptibility to change, and weak influence on behavior.

IV. THE ELABORATION LIKELIHOOD CONTINUUM

The model outlined in Figure 1 has provided a general framework for understanding how a variety of factors, such as unconditioned stimuli, speed of speech, and source credibility, can increase, decrease, or have no effect on attitude change. If the central route is followed, the perceived cogency of the message arguments and factors that may bias argument processing (e.g., prior knowledge, initial opinion) are predicted to be important determinants of the individual's acceptance or rejection of the recommendation, whereas factors that might serve as persuasion cues are relatively unimportant determinants of attitudes. If, on the other hand, the peripheral route is followed, then the strength of the message arguments and factors that bias argument processing become less important and persuasion cues become more important determinants of attitudes. That is, there is a trade-off between the central and the peripheral route to persuasion.

Importantly, the conditions that lead to influence through the central versus the peripheral route have also been specified. Many attitudes and decisions either are perceived to be personally inconsequential or involve matters about which people are uninformed. In these situations, people may still want to be correct in their attitudes and actions, but they are not willing or able to think a great deal about the arguments for or against a particular position. Peripheral cues provide a means of maximizing the likelihood that one's position is correct while minimizing the cognitive requirements for achieving this position. Processes such as mere exposure and classical or operant conditioning also appear to have stronger effects on attitudes when pre-exposure to

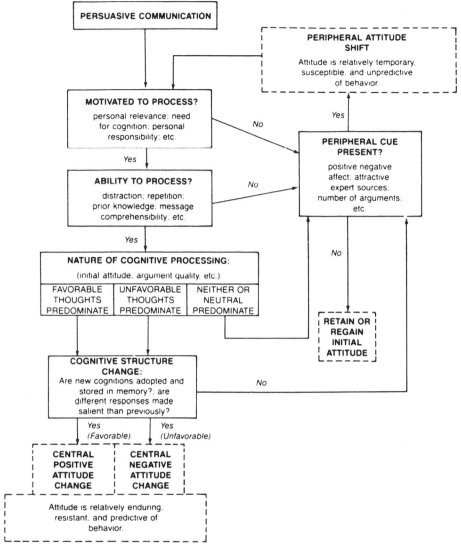

FIGURE 1   The elaboration likelihood model of persuasion. This figure depicts the two anchoring endpoints on the elaboration likelihood continuum: the central and peripheral routes to persuasion. [From R. E. Petty and J. T. Cacioppo (1986), "Communication and Persuasion: Central and Peripheral Routes to Attitude Change." Springer-Verlag, New York.]

and prior knowledge about the attitude stimulus are low rather than high.

Implicit in the central route, on the other hand, is the notion that people must relate the incoming message arguments to their prior knowledge in such a way as to evaluate the cogency and scope of the arguments; that is, they expend cognitive effort to examine the information they perceive to be relevant to the central merits of the advocacy. When conditions foster people's motivation and ability to engage in this issue-relevant thinking, the *elaboration likelihood* is said to be high. This means that people

are likely to attend to the appeal, attempt to access relevant information from both external and internal sources, and scrutinize or make inferences about the message arguments in light of any other pertinent information available. Consequently, they draw conclusions about the merits of the arguments for the recommendation based upon their analyses and derive an overall evaluation of, or attitude toward, the recommendation. Thus, the central and the peripheral routes to persuasion can be viewed as anchors on a continuum ranging from minimal to extensive message elaboration or issue-relevant thinking.

Factors governing an individual's motivation and ability to scrutinize the truthfulness of various attitude positions determine whether the central or the peripheral route operates.

Motivational variables are those that propel and guide people's issue-relevant thinking and give it purposive character. There are a number of variables that have been found to affect a person's *motivation* to elaborate upon the content of a message. These include task or stimulus variables such as the personal relevance of the recommendation, individual difference variables such as need for cognition (i.e., people's chronic tendency to engage in and enjoy effortful thinking), and contextual variables such as the number of sources advocating a position. These kinds of variables act upon a directive, goal-oriented component, which might be termed intention, and a nondirective, energizing component, which might be termed effort or exertion. [*See* MOTIVATION.]

Intention is not sufficient for high elaboration likelihood. One can want to think about an attitude stimulus or issue but not exert the necessary effort to move from intention to thought and action. If both intention and effort are present, then motivation to think about the advocacy may exist, but issue-relevant thinking may still be low because, for instance, the individual does not have the ability to scrutinize the message arguments. There are a number of variables that can affect an individual's *ability* to engage in message elaboration, including task or stimulus variables such as message comprehensibility, individual difference variables such as intelligence, and contextual variables such as distraction and message repetition. Contextual variables that affect a person's ability to elaborate cognitively on issue-relevant argumentation can also be characterized as factors affecting a person's opportunity to process the message arguments. [*See* INTENTION.]

Experiments have demonstrated that if task, individual, and contextual variables in the influence setting combine to promote motivation and ability to process, then the arguments presented in support of a change in attitudes or behavior are thought about carefully. If the person generates predominantly favorable thoughts toward the message, then the likelihood of acceptance is enhanced; if the person generates predominantly unfavorable thoughts (e.g., counterarguments), then the likelihood of resistance or boomerang (attitude change opposite to the direction advocated) is enhanced. The nature of this elaboration (i.e., whether favorable or unfavorable issue-relevant thinking) is determined by whether the motivational and ability factors combine to yield relatively objective or relatively biased information processing and by the nature of the message arguments. If elaboration likelihood is low, however, then the nature of the issue-relevant thinking is less important, and peripheral cues become more important determinants of attitude change (see Fig. 1).

A number of recent experiments have explored ways to stimulate or impair thinking about the message arguments in a persuasive appeal. Distraction, for instance, can interfere with a person's scrutiny of the arguments in a message and thereby alter persuasive impact. In an illustrative experiment on distraction and persuasion, students listened to a persuasive message over headphones while monitoring in which of the four quadrants of a screen a visual image was projected (a distractor task). In the low distraction condition, images were presented once every 15 seconds, whereas in the high distraction condition images were presented once every 5 seconds. Importantly, neither rate of presentation was so fast as to interfere with the students' comprehension of the simultaneously presented persuasive message, but the students' argument elaboration was much more disrupted in the high than low distraction condition. The results revealed that the students were less persuaded with distraction when the arguments were strong, but more persuaded with distraction when the arguments were weak.

Numerous task, contextual, and individual difference variables have been identified that enhance or impair argument elaboration by affecting a person's motivation or ability. Moderate levels of repetition of a complicated message can provide individuals with additional opportunities to think about the arguments and, thereby, enhance argument processing. Messages worded to underscore the self-relevance of the arguments enhance individuals' motivation to think about the arguments. Being singly responsible rather than one of many assigned to evaluate the recommendation can induce more issue-relevant thinking, as individuals are unable to diffuse their responsibility for determining the veracity of the recommendation.

V. ARGUMENT ELABORATION VERSUS PERIPHERAL CUES AS DETERMINANTS OF ATTITUDE CHANGE

The hypothesis that there is a tradeoff between argument scrutiny and peripheral cues as determinants of a person's susceptibility or resistance to persuasion has also been supported by recent research. In an illustrative study, two kinds of persuasion contexts were established: one in which the likelihood of relatively objective argument elaboration was high, and one in which the elaboration likelihood was low. This was accomplished by varying the personal relevance of the recommendation: students were exposed to an editorial favoring the institution of senior comprehensive exams at their university, but some students were led to believe these comprehensive exams would be instituted next year (high elaboration likelihood) whereas others were led to believe the exams would be instituted in 10 years (low elaboration likelihood).

To investigate the extent to which students' argument scrutiny determined attitudes, half of the students heard eight cogent message arguments favoring comprehensive exams, and the remaining students heard eight specious message arguments favoring the exams. Finally, to examine the extent to which peripheral cues were important determinants of attitudes, half of the students were told the recommendation they would hear was based on a report prepared by a local high school class (low expertise), whereas half were told the tape was based on a report prepared by the Carnegie Commission on Higher Education (high expertise). Following the presentation of the message, students rated their attitudes concerning comprehensive exams and completed ancillary measures. Results indicated that argument quality was the most important determinant of the students' attitudes toward comprehensive exams when they believed that the recommendation was consequential for them personally, but that the status or expertise of the source was the most important determinant of the students' attitudes when they believed that the recommendation would not affect them personally. These results held even though comprehension of the message arguments and judgments of the expertise of the source were equal across the experimental groups.

VI. OBJECTIVE VERSUS BIASED INFORMATION PROCESSING

Message processing in persuasion research was traditionally thought to imply objective processing. This, too, was an oversimplification. When an individual is motivated to scrutinize arguments for a position, there are no assurances that the information processing will be objective or rational. *Objective argument processing* means that a person is trying to seek the truth wherever that may lead. When a variable enhances argument scrutiny in a relatively objective manner, the strengths of cogent arguments and the flaws in specious arguments become more apparent. Conversely, when a variable reduces argument scrutiny in a relatively objective fashion, the strengths of cogent arguments and the flaws of specious arguments become less apparent. Objective processing, therefore, has much in common with the concept of "bottom–up" processing in cognitive psychology because elaboration is postulated to be relatively impartial and guided by data (in this case, message arguments).

In contrast, *biased argument processing* means that there is an asymmetry in the activation thresholds for eliciting favorable or unfavorable thoughts about the advocacy. Consequently, the encoding, interpretation, and recall of the message arguments are distorted to make it more likely that one side will be supported over another. Biased processing has more in common with "top–down" than "bottom–up" information processing, because the interpretation and elaboration of the arguments are governed by existing cognitive structures, such as relevant knowledge or attitude schema, which guide processing in a manner favoring the maintenance or strengthening of the original schema. Research on factors such as the role of initial attitudes has demonstrated that people are sometimes motivated and able to augment even specious arguments to arrive at a more cogent line of reasoning for their desired position.

VII. MULTIPLE AND INTERACTIVE EFFECTS

Another reason the processes underlying persuasion have appeared enigmatic is that some variables may increase argument processing at one level of the factor, but may actually bias or decrease argument processing at a different level of that factor. For instance, repeating a long or complicated persuasive message can provide individuals with additional opportunities to think about the message arguments and, therefore, enhance relatively objective argument scrutiny. Excessive exposures to a persuasive message can become tedious, however, and can actually motivate a person to reject the recommendation. Hence, the same stimulus factor—message repetition—had quite different effects on issue-relevant thinking as the amount of this factor increased.

Factors previously thought to have simple effects on information processing and persuasion have also been found to have quite different effects depending on the presence or absence of other factors. For instance, presenting a persuasive message on a non-involving issue in rhetorical rather than declarative form can increase an individual's propensity to think about the message arguments. When the recommendation is already personally involving, however, the insertion of rhetorical questions in the message arguments can actually interfere with the individual's ongoing idiosyncratic argument scrutiny. Thus, the introduction of new factors (e.g., arguments presented in rhetorical rather than declarative form) can have striking but explicable effects on people's cognitive processes and attitudes.

In sum, two assumptions underlying early work were that each of source, message, channel, and recipient factors had general and independent effects on persuasion; and a close correspondence existed between attitude change and behavior change across situations. Both assumptions proved to be oversimplifications. Indeed, after accumulating a vast quantity of data and a large number of theories, there was surprisingly little agreement concerning if, when, and how the traditional source, message, recipient, and modality variables affected persuasion. The existing literature by the mid-1970s supported the view that nearly every independent variable studied increased persuasion in some situations, had no effect in others, and decreased persuasion in still other contexts. This diversity of results was even apparent for variables that on the surface, at least, appeared to be quite simple. For example, although it might seem reasonable to propose that by associating a message with an expert source, agreement could be increased (e.g., see Aristotle's *Rhetoric*), experimental research suggested that expertise effects were considerably more complicated. Sometimes expert sources had the expected effects, sometimes no effects were obtained, and sometimes reverse effects were noted. Research since the early to mid-1970s has resulted in theoretical advances that better account for these and other complicated patterns of data by specifying the cognitive processes that are activated by the presentation of an attitude stimulus or persuasive appeal.

Bibliography

Bornstein, R. F. (1989). Exposure and affect: Overview and meta-analysis of research, 1968–1987. *Psychol. Bulletin* **106,** 265–289.

Fazio, R. H. (1990). Multiple processes by which attitudes guide behavior. The MODE model as an integrative framework. *Adv. Exp. Soc. Psychol.* **23,** 1–74.

McGuire, W. (1985). Attitudes and attitude change. In "Handbook of Social Psychology" (G. Lindzey and E. Aronson, Eds.), 3rd ed., pp. 233–346. Random House, New York.

Petty, R. E., and Cacioppo, J. T. (1986). "Communication and Persuasion: Central and Peripheral Routes to Attitude Change." Springer-Verlag, New York.

Pratkanis, A. R., Breckler, S. J., and Greenwald, A. G. (1989). "Attitude Structure and Function." Erlbaum, Hillsdale, NJ.

Robertson, T. S., and Kassarjian, H. H. (1991). "Handbook of Consumer Behavior." Prentice–Hall, Englewood Cliffs, NJ.

Schwartz, N., Bless, H., and Bohner, G. (1991). Mood and persuasion: Affective states influence the processing of persuasive communications. *Adv. Exp. Soc. Psychol.* **24,** 161–201.

Tesser, A., and Shaffer, D. R. (1990). Attitudes and attitude changes. *Annu. Rev. Psychol.* **41,** 479–523.

ATTITUDE FORMATION

David S. Douglass and Anthony R. Pratkanis
University of California at Santa Cruz

Glossary

Attitude An evaluation of an object stored in memory.

Attitude accessibility The ease (or difficulty) with which an attitude is retrieved from memory.

Attitudinal knowledge Information stored with an attitude; it may include arguments for or against a proposition, technical information, social implications for adopting a certain position, and guidelines for how to behave toward the object.

Knowing function Attitudes can be used to simplify and make sense of the complex world in which we live.

Object label How an attitude object is defined and interpreted; the evaluation of an object can be influenced by this object definition.

Self function Attitudes can be held in order to place one's self in a favorable light.

Socio-cognitive model of attitude A fully developed attitude consists of a label for the attitude object, an evaluation of the object, and knowledge and beliefs regarding the object and its evaluation; such attitudes can serve a knowledge and a self function.

ATTITUDE FORMATION refers to the creation and development of an attitude. An *attitude* is defined as an evaluation of an object, stored in memory; in other words, it is a relatively enduring cognition about the value of an object. People express attitudes by saying things such as "I like carrots, I dislike broccoli; free speech is good, totalitarianism is bad." As early as 1935, Gordon Allport declared the concept of "attitude" was indispensable to social psychology, and the amount of contemporary theory and research pertaining to attitudes suggests widespread support for that conclusion.

Understanding how attitudes form is important because attitudes are a pervasive influence in people's lives. People can have an attitude toward virtually any object (e.g., a chair, a person, a category of people, a political issue), and attitudes are formed very easily. Research has shown that when people judge an object—when they consider its various features—that process routinely includes evaluation of the object. Once formed, attitudes can be used as a simple rule-of-thumb for interpreting the social environment and used as a guide for behavior.

I. WHAT FORMS WHEN AN ATTITUDE FORMS?

According to the socio-cognitive model of attitudes, when someone holds an attitude, there are three types of information that can be stored in memory. First, there is an object label (e.g., the backyard, environmental extremist, Harry Houdini, the movie-rating system), along with rules for applying that label. Second, there is an evaluative summary of the object (e.g., the movie rating system is bad). Third, there can be an organization of knowledge about the object and its evaluation (e.g., movie ratings are not mandatory, the raters are concerned with sex and not violence). Not all attitudes are associated with a complex organization of knowledge. However, attitudinal knowledge may include arguments for or against a proposition, technical information about the object, guidelines for how to behave toward the object, and the social implications of adopting a belief. These beliefs may be factually correct or incorrect, and some beliefs may be more important than others.

II. SOURCES OF ATTITUDES

Attitudes (and supporting knowledge) can be acquired from many different sources. Although multiple sources can promote the same attitude, it is often the case that different sources promote different attitudes. (For example, parents and schools may endorse a negative attitude toward premarital sex while peers and the mass media may endorse a positive attitude.) Thus, it is difficult to predict the exact effectiveness of a particular source without knowledge of the larger context in which the attitude is formed. In the section below we describe 10 common sources of attitudes.

A. Culture

Every society has an integrated system of shared beliefs, actions, and artifacts. Research has shown that different types of cultures are associated with different attitudes. For example, most Asian and African cultures promote favorable attitudes toward collectivism, whereas most Western European and North American cultures promote individualism. A person raised in a given culture can adopt many attitudes without bothering to question the basis for them. For example, most North Americans would agree that "brushing your teeth is a good thing to do," and they would probably be amazed that anyone might dispute that statement. Research shows that such "cultural truisms" are relatively easy to change with plausible opposing arguments. In other words, if a favorable (or unfavorable) attitude is formed solely because it is the traditional thing to do, the attitude can be relatively unstable. One reason for this instability is that attitudes formed without any thought or opposition have little or no knowledge to support them.

B. Generational ("Cohort") Effects

People also grow up in a specific historical period, so the combination of local and world events that can influence attitudes will be different for each generation. For example, when people were asked in 1985 to report the most important national or world changes in the past 50 years, different generations recalled different events (usually events that occurred during their adolescence and early adulthood): people in their 60s mentioned World War II whereas people in their 30s mentioned the Vietnam War. When a new war seems imminent, people tend to think it in terms of the war most important to their generation. However, the same program of research showed only a weak relationship between memory for past political events and attitudes toward present political events. Apparently, the historical setting of a person's youth does make a lasting impression, but its influence can be diminished by other sources of attitudes.

C. Social Roles

Each person can perform many roles, such as parent, nature lover, shaman, New Englander, and each role is associated with a set of socially sanctioned attitudes. A natural experiment at an appliance factory illustrated how occupational roles can be the source of attitudes. Some factory workers were promoted to the position of foreman; they subsequently developed pro-management attitudes (compared to workers in a control group who maintained their pro-labor attitudes). When a recession caused some of the foremen to return to their old positions, their earlier, pro-labor attitudes returned. Since one person can perform many roles, there is a potential for conflict among role-based attitudes; the attitudes associated with the individual's more important and stable roles are more likely to persist.

D. Laws

Laws are a potential source of attitudes that have been hotly debated by politicians as well as social scientists. The traditional view is that "You can't legislate morality." It is unclear whether the passage of a law, by itself, can cause people to form certain attitudes. For example, research findings are equivocal regarding the effects of legalizing homosexual behavior on people's attitudes toward homosexuality. However, research shows that when laws are quickly implemented, and they are clearly and firmly supported by authority figures, people will develop attitudes consistent with the law. For example, when laws requiring school desegregation were quickly and strictly enforced, parents' and children's attitudes toward desegregation became more favorable, and the desegregation process went more smoothly.

E. Mass Media

The mass media are often cited as sources of attitudes, and research supports this notion. For example, consumer advertising has been shown to influence the purchase of everything from soup to nuts. Research conducted as early as the 1930s has shown that watching movies can influence attitudes toward various ethnic groups, as well as stereotypes for those groups. Many studies have linked viewing film and television violence with positive attitudes toward aggression, along with knowledge about how to aggress. The effects of such media messages are usually small, apparently because other sources of attitudes can be more powerful. Nevertheless, given the pervasiveness of the mass media, even small effects are important to society.

F. Total Institutions

This category includes organizations that can have virtually complete control over the information an individual receives (e.g., prisons, military units, cult or ethnic communes, rest homes, etc.). Total institutions often promote attitudes that will perpetuate the institution. For example, cults strive to induce members to form a positive attitude toward the cult (the in-group) while forming negative attitudes toward all nonbelievers (the out-group). Total institutions often produce immediate attitude formation and behavioral compliance, but these effects may be short-lived once the person is no longer in the institution (as in the case of kidnapped heiress Patty Hearst).

G. Schools

Schools dispense a large amount of knowledge that can be the basis of attitudes, including "citizenship training" that relates to many social and political issues. However, research indicates that public schools have primarily broad effects via subtle messages. For example, a math exercise involving calculation of an interest rate teaches not only certain math skills but instructs the student that the financial practice of borrowing and lending (a sin in the Middle Ages) is appropriate behavior. Public elementary schools have less impact on attitudes toward narrower issues (such as legislation regarding the availability of birth control). Some private schools that place a greater emphasis on a specific ideology may be a more potent source of specific attitudes.

H. Parents and Family

Parents are one of the most powerful sources of attitudes because they are the first source, they have

influence for a long period of time, and they can have extensive control over the information a young child receives (much like a total institution). Several investigators have found that children usually share their parents' attitudes toward, for example, political issues and premarital sex. As the child grows up (and is exposed to competing sources of attitudes), attitudes toward specific political and religious issues may deviate from those of the parents. However, surveys show that parents and children usually continue to belong to the same political party and the same religious denomination. Research has also shown that the relationship of parent–child attitudes is related to the strength of the child's attachment to his or her family. When children remain close to their parents, the children's attitudes usually remain similar.

I. Peers and Reference Groups

As a child grows older, he or she acquires friends and acquaintances who function as new sources of attitudes. A classic study from the 1940s showed what could happen when students who shared their parents' conservative attitudes became involved in the liberal campus community of Bennington College. Over the course of 4 years at college, the students' attitudes became increasingly liberal, and that liberalism was positively correlated with their popularity on campus. For many of these students, the attitudes acquired during college persisted 25 and 40 years later. This finding was especially common among students who had married college friends; that is, for those who formed a life-long reference group associated with their college experience.

J. Direct Experience

The strongest attitudes are usually formed when a person has direct experience with the attitude object. For example, being bitten by a dog has more impact than simply hearing about someone being bitten by a dog. Experiments have repeatedly shown that attitudes formed via direct (versus indirect) experience are more likely to persist in the face of opposing arguments, and are more likely to guide behavior.

III. PROCESSES OF ATTITUDE FORMATION

Attitudes can be formed in many ways, involving what we are born with, how we learn, how we think, and how we feel about ourselves. Thus, in addition to having multiple sources, attitudes can result from the multiple processes by which humans adapt to their environment. In the section below, 11 processes that contribute to attitude formation are described.

A. Genetics

There have been a few cases in which identical twins separated at birth were later found to have similar attitudes. For example, a pair of twin brothers, separated for 20 years, found they liked the same brand of beer, and both had become volunteer fire fighters. However, such evidence does not prove that individuals inherit specific attitudes—any two people selected at random are likely to share *some* attitudes. Research employing more rigorous methods suggests that people only inherit general behavioral tendencies that can lay the foundation for attitudes. For example, individuals born with a tendency to be highly active might, in a particular social environment, get into trouble more often and form a negative attitude toward authority figures. In such indirect ways, a heritable general tendency (or temperament) can interact with environmental influences and contribute to attitude formation.

B. Learning

Many studies have shown that attitudes—as well as beliefs and behaviors—are acquired ("learned") in various ways. The process of *classical conditioning* can occur when an attitude object is paired with another stimulus event. If the stimulus is pleasant then the person forms a positive attitude toward the object; if the stimulus is aversive then the person forms a negative attitude toward the object. For example, subjects in one experiment heard various slogans (such as "Workers of the world, unite"). The slogans were repeatedly presented along with a positive stimulus (a free lunch), a negative stimulus (unpleasant odors), or neutral stimuli. The results showed that subjects became more favorable toward slogans paired with a free lunch and more unfavorable toward slogans paired with unpleasant odors. [*See* CLASSICAL CONDITIONING.]

Another type of learning is *operant conditioning*—in which statements expressing an attitude are followed by either rewards or punishments. According to this theory, if a person expresses an attitude and gets rewarded then they are likely to maintain or strengthen that attitude. For example, students were asked a series of questions about their school's homecoming festivities: when some students said favorable things about homecoming, the experimenter responded by saying "Good"; other students got the same reward only when they said unfavorable things. As expected, the students' subsequent attitudes toward homecoming were strongly influenced by the earlier social reward and punishments. [*See* OPERANT LEARNING.]

A third learning process is *observational learning* (or modeling). Studies of the effects of models of attitude formation have supported the old saying that actions speak louder than words. For example, in one study children observed an adult who preached either charity or greed and who engaged in either charitable or greedy behavior. When the children were later asked to give money to a charity, the size of their donations was influenced more by what the model had *done* than by what the model had *said*. Other studies have shown that parental models have significant effects on children's attitudes toward gender roles and ethnic groups.

C. Mere Exposure

Research shows that people who are repeatedly exposed to an object come to like that object. In other words, people tend to have a positive attitude toward familiar things. In one study, college students were shown pictures of faces—some faces were shown two dozen times, others were shown once or twice. Later, the students expressed their attitudes toward all the faces: the more often the students had seen a face, the more they liked it. Common sense suggests that people might eventually get sick of seeing the same old thing over and over, but experiments have shown that the "mere exposure effect" is often surprisingly robust. Studies of advertising campaigns have shown that, at the very least, consumers become more familiar with frequently presented products, and they often prefer to buy what is familiar.

D. Labeling and Metaphors

The way an object is labeled often determines whether people form positive or negative attitudes. For example, an experiment showed that consumers liked ground beef more when it was labeled "75% lean" than when it was labeled "25% fat." Opposing sides in political disputes habitually choose labels with evaluative implications. For example, what the

British in 1770 labeled a "riot," the Americans labeled "the Boston Massacre." Each label emphasizes a particular feature of the attitude object at the expense of other features. "Riot" emphasizes the danger faced by the British guards and the disorganization of the people in the street—a reasonable person could form a positive attitude toward the British. "Boston Massacre" emphasizes the actions of the guards and implies that the community as a whole was attacked—an equally reasonable person could form a positive attitude toward the Americans.

Similarly, a metaphor can be used to define an event in such a way that the "correct" attitude toward the event is "obvious." For example, before the war in the Persian Gulf started in January of 1991, it was portrayed by supporters as an action necessary to stop the aggression of a new Hitler; while opponents described it as a potential quagmire similar to the Vietnam war. Researchers have found that people who used the Hitler versus the Vietnam metaphor for the Persian Gulf war (or hypothetical wars) tended to have attitudes consistent with that definition of the event.

E. Differentiation and Integration

Another way that attitudes can be formed is by changing the definition of the attitude object. This redefinition may involve either restricting the meaning of the object (differentiation) or expanding the meaning of the object (integration). For example, an advocate of Christianity, when faced with negative images of Christians (such as violent crusaders or lecherous ministers) may defend his or her attitude by using differentiation—dividing the category of "Christians" into true believers and false prophets. By forming a new (negative) attitude toward false prophets, the person can maintain his or her old (positive) attitude toward true believers. In contrast, integration is the process of lumping an attitude object in with other objects to make it appear more (or less) likeable. For example, Republican Presidential candidates (Reagan and Bush) tried to lump their Democratic opponents (Carter, Mondale, Dukakis, and Clinton) with the "tax and spend" approach to government. In this way, the Democratic candidate would cease to be an individual (a potentially positive attitude object) and would become a "tax and spend liberal" (a negative object).

F. Agenda Setting

By repeatedly presenting some issues and rarely (or never) mentioning others, the mass media influence which issues seem most important. For example, people's estimates of the prevalence of various diseases are strongly related to how often the diseases are mentioned in the media rather than their actual frequency of occurrence. An effect of agenda setting on attitudes was demonstrated by researchers who edited a series of evening news programs. One version of the programs featured a steady dose of news about the weaknesses of United States defense capabilities; another version featured various stories about pollution. After viewing all the programs, subjects reported that the problem presented to them most often was more important than problems that had not been presented. In addition, the subjects had more positive attitudes toward political candidates who took a strong position on the problem that had been emphasized in the news. Political leaders often try to control which issues will be discussed and which "facts" will (or will not) be widely distributed. In this way, the knowledge used to support attitudes can be biased. For example, by talking frequently about the threat of a cold war, politicians made such a war seem not only possible but likely, so a positive attitude toward increased defense spending seemed quite reasonable.

G. Expectancy–Value Judgments

Under some circumstances, people may form an attitude based on a thoughtful assessment of the pros and cons of the attitude object. Expectancy–value theories assume that people estimate the probability that an object will have certain attributes and place a value on those attributes. For example, going to a party can have several attributes (e.g., hearing loud music, being hung over the next day, meeting someone interesting). An individual can estimate the probability that those effects will occur (e.g., certain to hear loud music, might be hung over, probably won't meet anyone interesting), and the value of those effects (like loud music, hate being hung over, desperate to meet someone). All those subjective judgments are combined to produce the individual's attitude toward going to the party. Researchers have demonstrated expectancy–value processes by having subjects rate the probability a given object will have certain features and rate the value of each feature. When the probability ratings are multiplied by the value ratings there is a very strong relationship between the combined ratings and the subjects' overall attitudes toward the object.

H. Balance and Consistency Theories

Several theorists have assumed that people have a strong tendency to maintain consistency among their cognitions (to have "balanced" relationships among them). According to balance theory, we will like something (or someone) if liking it is consistent with our prior, important attitudes. For example, if Stalin strongly favors totalitarianism but Roosevelt, a new acquaintance, strongly opposes it, then Stalin is probably not going to like Roosevelt. It would be inconsistent to like someone who has the "wrong" attitude toward such an important issue. (If Stalin adopted a negative attitude toward totalitarianism then his liking Roosevelt would not be inconsistent.) Experiments have shown, for example, that subjects who are mistreated by an experimenter will subsequently form a favorable attitude toward a supervisor who severely criticizes that experimenter. In other words, the favorable attitude toward the new object (the supervisor) is psychologically consistent with the unfavorable attitude toward the old object (the experimenter).

I. Self-Perception

People can observe their own behavior and use that information to infer relevant attitudes. For example, a person may be eating brown bread at the dinner table and, when asked if he or she likes brown bread, is likely to say yes. There may be a variety of reasons for eating brown bread (e.g., it was the only type of bread being served; the bread was on sale). However, the person may ignore these background factors and use the most salient piece of information at hand—his or her own behavior—as evidence of a positive attitude.

This self-perception process can be used to explain the results of an experiment showing that children who had *not* been rewarded for playing with a puzzle subsequently played with it more (than children who had been rewarded) during a free period. The children who had not been rewarded had observed themselves playing with the puzzle without a compelling external cause for that behavior, so they inferred an internal cause—a positive attitude toward the puzzle. Further research has shown that people are likely to interpret their behavior as proof of an attitude only when their initial response to an object is weak or ambiguous.

J. Cognitive Development

As a young child matures, he or she develops new cognitive skills that can influence how an attitude is formed. One particularly important cognitive development is an understanding of the intent to persuade (in other words, being able to recognize that an advertiser or a parent is trying to get the child to form a certain attitude or belief). With regard to mass media advertising, children below the age of 6 often do not understand that advertisers are trying to persuade them to buy products; instead they uncritically accept what is presented as true. Around the age of 8, children begin to understand that not all of what is presented in advertisements is true and that they can argue against those messages. In this way, children become harder to persuade and they develop attitudes that are linked to knowledge of both supporting and opposing arguments. [*See* COGNITIVE DEVELOPMENT.]

K. Functional Value of Attitudes

According to the socio-cognitive model of attitudes, we form and maintain attitudes because attitudes help us to function in the social world. One such function of attitudes is the *knowing function* (also termed object-appraisal or instrumental function). Many theorists have noted that holding attitudes helps people to simplify the complex world in which they live. People can divide the world into good and bad objects, and then behave accordingly. If people have a positive attitude toward an object then they use strategies such as praising, approaching, or protecting; if people have a negative attitude they use strategies such as blaming, avoiding, or harming.

Pre-existing attitudes can guide the way people interpret new information. (Or, as Mark Twain put it, "Partialities often make people see more than really exists.") One study found the attitudes of Dartmouth and Princeton students influenced the way they perceived an especially violent football game. After viewing a film of the game, Dartmouth students "saw" most of the fouls being committed by Princeton players and Princeton students "saw" most of the fouls being committed by Dartmouth players. Attitudes can also influence the way people reconstruct past events. After a riot involving police and striking steel-workers, researchers found that people with pro-labor attitudes were likely to remember strikers as unarmed and peaceful whereas people with anti-labor attitudes remembered the same strikers as armed and dangerous.

Attitudes also perform a *self function* (variously termed social-adjustive, externalization, value-expressive, ego-defensive, or social identity function). One of the ways that people define who they are is by holding certain attitudes, and these attitudes can be used to produce positive self-regard. For example, when concerned with his or her relationship with other people, an individual can earn their approval by expressing attitudes that are agreeable to those people. When concerned with upholding personal values, an individual can generate self-esteem by expressing attitudes that are consistent with those values. When concerned with asserting or maintaining membership in a reference group, an individual can express attitudes that are widely held by group members. Advertisers make use of the self function of attitudes when they try to associate their products with certain personal attributes (e.g., Marlboro cigarettes are "macho"; Virginia Slims are for the "modern" woman). The implication of such messages is that consumers can present a certain image to others (and to themselves) by forming the "correct" attitude toward a certain product.

IV. ARE ALL ATTITUDES THE SAME?

All attitudes are *not* created equal. Research has shown that some attitudes can have strong, reliable effects on behavior whereas other attitudes have only weak, unreliable effects. The amount of influence attitudes will have on behavior is largely determined by *attitude accessibility*. Some attitudes can be easily retrieved from memory (they are "highly accessible"); other attitudes require more time and effort to retrieve (they have relatively low accessibility).

Experiments have consistently shown that highly accessible attitudes are more likely to guide a person's perception of events and actual behavior toward attitude objects. For example, about 5 months before the 1984 Presidential election, researchers asked people shopping in a mall to evaluate the two candidates (Reagan and Mondale). The speed with which the shoppers rated the two candidates was recorded, and the researchers assumed that *faster* responses indicated higher attitude accessibility. After the election, the shoppers were asked for whom they had voted. The researchers found that the shoppers with highly accessible attitudes 5 months before the election were more likely to actually vote for the candidate they had said they favored.

Attitude accessibility can be increased by repeated expression of the attitude. In one study, for example, subjects were given five types of intellectual puzzles to solve and then they stated their attitudes about those puzzles. Half the subjects stated their attitudes several times; the other subjects stated their attitudes only once. Then all the subjects were given a free period in which they could choose to work on any of the puzzles. The results showed that subjects with highly accessible attitudes were more likely to consistently work on puzzles they liked and to ignore puzzles they disliked, compared to subjects whose attitudes were less accessible.

Direct experience with the attitude object promotes high accessibility. For example, subjects who were only given a description of the puzzles mentioned above could not retrieve their attitudes toward those puzzles as quickly as subjects who actually had a chance to work on the puzzles. Researchers have suggested that direct experience increases attitude accessibility because the person observes his or her own behavior toward the object and that obvious behavioral information is given more weight than a person's subtle responses to a second-hand description of an object.

The nature of an attitude object can also influence the likelihood of the attitude being retrieved from memory. Objects that are prototypical—that include the essential and most characteristic features of a category of objects—are more likely to elicit the relevant attitude. For example, if a person likes dogs, then a Golden Retriever will easily elicit that favorable attitude, but a Great Dane might not ("That's not a dog, it's a horse!").

Bibliography

McGuire, W. J. (1985). Attitudes and Attitude Change. In "Handbook of Social Psychology" (G. Lindsey and E. Aronson, Eds.), Vol. 2. Random House, New York.

Oskamp, S. (1991). "Attitudes and Opinions," 2nd ed. Prentice Hall, Englewood Cliffs, NJ.

Petty, R. E., and Cacioppo, J. T. (1981). "Attitudes and Persuasion: Classic and Contemporary Approaches." Brown, Dubuque, IA.

Pratkanis, A. R., and Aronson, E. (1992). "Age of Propoganda: The Everyday Use and Abuse of Persuasion." Freeman, New York.

Pratkanis, A. R., Breckler, S. J., and Greenwald, A. G. (1989). "Attitude Structure and Function." Erlbaum, Hillsdale, NJ.

Pratkanis, A. R., and Greenwald, A. G. (1989). A socio cognitive model of attitude structure and function. In "Advances in Experimental Social Psychology (L. Berkowitz, Ed.), Vol. 22, pp. 245–285. Academic Press, New York.

Zimbardo, P. G., and Leippe, M. R. (1991). "The Psychology of Attitude Change and Social Influence." McGraw-Hill, New York.

ATTITUDE STRENGTH

Jon A. Krosnick and Wendy R. Smith
The Ohio State University

Glossary

Attitude A favorable or unfavorable orientation toward an object.
Attitude strength The degree to which an attitude is resistant to change and influences cognition and behavior.

ATTITUDES vary in the degree to which they are crystallized and consequential, and the notion of attitude strength is meant to capture this variation. Strong attitudes are resistant to change, are stable over time, and have powerful impact on information processing and behavior. A number of attributes differentiate strong attitudes from weak ones, including extremity, intensity, importance, and accessibility. We shall review the literature on the relations of 10 such attributes to crystallization and consequentiality.

I. INTRODUCTION

When social psychologists began their full-scale investigation of attitudes early in the century, they did so on the assumption that attitudes are enduring predispositions that exert strong forces shaping people's cognitive processes and behavior. To know whether a person likes and dislikes an object, it was presumed, was to be able to predict to some extent how he or she will think about and act toward that object over a long period of time. But as empirical studies of attitudes began to amass, it quickly became clear that this was often not the case. In many instances, people were found to think and behave favorably toward objects they disliked and to think and behave unfavorably toward objects they liked. Furthermore, the view of attitudes as stable qualities of individuals was shaken by studies demonstrating that attitudes shift frequently during the course of everyday life and can be changed quite easily by persuasive messages in laboratory settings.

Through continued investigations of these issues, social psychologists have come to recognize that all attitudes do not have the same qualities. Some resemble the classic view, in that they exert powerful influence on cognition and conation and are firmly crystallized. Others, however, have relatively little impact and are highly flexible, constantly shifting in response to daily experiences. In recent years, this distinction has been viewed as one of attitude *strength*, with the former attitudes being relatively strong and the latter being relatively weak.

At the same time, social psychologists have come to recognize that attitude strength is not a simple, unitary construct. Instead, an attitude can be strong in many different ways. Research on these issues is at a relatively early point, but much is already known about what we shall call the *dimensions* of attitude strength. In this article, we will begin by defining the most commonly studied dimensions of strength and review evidence regarding the relations among them. Then, we will summarize the literature demonstrating that these dimensions are all related to the crystallization and consequentiality of attitudes. Finally, we will summarize work on the causes of the dimensions and propose directions for future research.

II. DEFINITIONS AND MEASUREMENT

Our focus here is on 10 dimensions or attributes of attitudes that have been discussed frequently in the attitude literature in terms of their relations to strength: extremity, certainty, importance, intensity, latitudes of rejection and noncommitment, interest, knowledge, accessibility, direct experience, and affective–cognitive consistency. Here, we will describe each and enumerate how each has typically been measured in past research.

A. Extremity

Attitude extremity is the extent to which an individual likes or dislikes an object. The more extreme the individual's attitude is, the further it is from neutrality. Attitude extremity has typically been operationalized as the deviation of an individual's attitude rating from the midpoint of a dimension ranging from highly favorable to highly unfavorable.

B. Intensity

Some attitudes involve strong affective responses to objects, whereas others involve little or no emotional reaction. Attitude intensity has been measured routinely via self-perceptions: by asking people how strong or intense their feelings are toward an object.

C. Certainty

Attitude certainty refers to the degree to which an individual is confident that his or her attitude toward an object is correct. It has usually been measured by asking respondents how certain or sure they are of their attitudes, how easily their attitudes could be changed, or how confident they are that their attitudes are correct.

D. Importance

People consider some attitudes to be very important to them personally, and consequently they care deeply and are especially concerned about them. Attitude importance has generally been measured by asking people how personally important their attitudes are, how concerned they are about them, or how much they care about them.

E. Interest in Attitude-Relevant Information

Some people are very interested in attitude-relevant information, whereas others are not. This construct has usually been measured by asking people how closely they attend to information about an object, or how interested they are in information about the object.

F. Knowledge

Some attitudes are accompanied by a great deal of attitude-relevant knowledge in memory, whereas others are accompanied by little or no such knowledge. Amount of attitude-relevant knowledge has been measured by asking respondents to list everything they know about an attitude object, by examining answers people give to quiz-like questions, or by asking individuals to report how knowledgeable they feel they are about an attitude.

G. Accessibility

Attitude accessibility is defined as the strength of the link in memory between an object and an evaluation of it. It is presumably manifested as the ease with which an attitude comes to mind in the course of social perception. Accessibility has most often been measured by the length of time it takes people to report their attitudes toward an object. It has also been measured by the likelihood that people will mention the object in answering an open-ended question, by people's reports of how often they discuss the object with friends and family, or by reports of how often people think about the object.

H. Direct Experience

Direct experience includes both behavioral participation in activities related to an object and direct contact with the object itself. It has been measured by asking people the extent to which they have participated in activities related to the object, whether they have performed any of several types of actions with regard to the object, and whether they have had personal experiences involving the object.

I. Latitudes of Rejection and Noncommitment

Given a set of attitude statements ranging from very favorable toward an object to very unfavorable, a person's latitude of rejection includes those statements he or she finds unacceptable, and the latitude of noncommitment includes those statements he or she finds neither acceptable nor unacceptable. The more invested one is in the attitude object, the larger one's latitude of rejection is, and the smaller one's latitude of noncommitment is.

The sizes of individuals' latitudes of rejection and noncommitment can also be gauged using the "own categories method." For this, people are asked to sort a set of statements (that range from very favorable to very unfavorable) into groups, where statements in the same group represent the same stand on the issue. The fewer groups a person creates, the larger is his or her latitude of rejection, and the smaller is his or her latitude of noncommitment.

J. Evaluative–Cognitive Consistency

Attitudes vary in the degree to which there is consistency between overall evaluations of the object and cognitions about how the object is related to the attainment of valued goals. The measurement of evaluative-cognitive consistency has usually involved a multi-step approach. Individuals rate (1) their overall evaluation of the object, (2) the importance to them of various goals related to the object, and (3) the probabilities that the object would help achieve or block attainment of each goal. The importance ratings are multiplied by the instrumentality estimates, and the standardized sum of the products is subtracted from the standardized evaluation score. The absolute value of this difference is the measure of evaluative–cognitive consistency.

III. RELATIONS BETWEEN DIMENSIONS

These 10 dimensions have been defined and operationalized in ways that make them clearly distinct from one another. Some are attributes of the attitude itself (e.g., extremity and latitudes of rejection and noncommitment); some describe features of accompanying cognitive structures (e.g., knowledge and evaluative–cognitive consistency); some constitute subjective states (e.g., importance and certainty); some involve links in memory (e.g., accessibility); and some involve summaries of past events (e.g., direct behavioral experience). Thus, they seem likely to have unique origins and unique effects.

Despite these clear conceptual and operational distinctions, there have been many instances in the attitude literature where dimensions have been treated as interchangeable with one another. For example, a variety of investigators have presumed that intensity is equivalent to certainty, extremity, interest, or direct experience. Similarly, researchers have measured ego-involvement using intensity, importance, and latitudes of rejection and noncommitment.

Furthermore, a variety of investigators have presumed that these dimensions are indicators of higher-order constructs. For example, many researchers have measured the construct of "involvement" using questions assessing importance, interest, knowledge, and frequency or amount of thought, or the confluence of importance, frequency of thought, commitment, and social support. Others have argued that attitudinal "ego preoccupation" is a higher-order construct reflected by intensity, importance, and frequency of thought. Attitudinal "salience" has been measured by questions about importance and frequency of thought. And importance questions have been used to measure yet another construct as well: "personal relevance."

The most disagreement exists with regard to operationalizing the higher-order construct of "centrality." Questions about importance have frequently been used to gauge this construct, an approach that comes closest to the way most scholars have defined it. However, centrality has also been defined as the amount of mental time people spend thinking about an attitude object, which seems closer to the notion of accessibility. At the same time, others defined centrality as the extent of structural linkage among attitudes, yet direct measures of structural linkage have rarely if ever been employed in the attitude literature to operationalize this construct.

Thus, some attitude scholars have asserted that some of these dimensions are interchangeable with one another and reflect common, higher-order constructs. However, there is not complete agreement on exactly which dimensions reflect exactly which constructs.

In contrast to this view, many studies have assessed associations among these dimensions and have documented only low to moderate positive correlations. Furthermore, exploratory factor analyses of these dimensions have uncovered complex underlying structures that varied a great deal from study to study. And in the most recent investigations, structural equation analyses have shown that any models treating two or more dimensions as manifestations of the same underlying construct must be rejected. Consequently, it seems that these dimensions are best thought of as distinct from one another.

IV. EVIDENCE OF CRYSTALLIZATION

Despite the clear distinctions among these dimensions, they all share one remarkable set of attributes in common: they can all differentiate attitudes that are firmly crystallized and consequential from those that are not. Thus, they are all related to attitude strength. We will begin reviewing literature illustrating this by focusing on attitude crystallization, which has been shown to be associated with the attitude dimensions using nine sorts of approaches.

A. Persuasive Messages

One type of study has explored people's responsiveness to persuasive communications intended to change attitudes. Presumably, the stronger an attitude is, the less influenced it would be by such communications. To test this notion, one or more dimensions of strength have been measured in these studies, and respondents have been separated into groups high and low on those dimensions. As expected, less attitude change has been observed for attitudes that are more extreme, more important, more accessible, higher in interest, with larger latitudes of rejection and smaller latitudes of noncommitment, supported by more knowledge, or held with greater confidence.

A recent study demonstrated that direct experience also confers resistance to change, but this resistance can also be overcome. In this study, some subjects played with intellectual puzzles, while other subjects simply observed the puzzles without actually getting experience with them. Both groups of subjects were instructed to focus on the feelings the puzzles aroused in them and to report their attitudes toward the puzzles. When subjects were then exposed to emotion-focused arguments intended to change their attitudes, those people who had previously had direct experience with the puzzles were more resistant to change. However, when subjects were instead given informational counterarguments, attitudes based on more direct experience changed *more*. Thus, it seems that the direct experience strengthened the *affective* basis of the attitudes but left them vulnerable to cognitive attack.

The vast majority of persuasive communication studies have used messages that were counterattitudinal (i.e., advocating a viewpoint opposite to that held by subjects). However, one could also imagine proattitudinal persuasive messages, advocating a view consistent with that held by subjects but even more extreme. Individuals with strong attitudes would presumably be especially receptive and responsive to such messages. And indeed, more attitude change was observed recently in response to

such a manipulation among those individuals who had more direct experience. [See ATTITUDE CHANGE; PERSUASION.]

B. Leading Questions

A second approach that has been taken to testing the crystallization hypothesis involves examining people's responses to leading questions. Asking a leading question can induce people to generate cognitions consistent with the implications of the question and can thereby induce attitude change. If strong attitudes are more resistant to change, then people holding these attitudes should resist the persuasive impact of leading questions. As expected, researchers have found this to be the case with regard to certainty: people who were more certain about their attitude were more resistant to influence in this fashion.

However, one type of leading question was found to induce more attitude change among high certainty individuals than among low certainty individuals. In this case, loaded questions encouraged people to make statements that were consistent with but more extreme than their attitudes. Doing so led highly certain respondents' attitudes to become more moderate and had no effect on less certain respondents.

C. Explaining Reasons for Attitudes

A third set of studies has examined the impact of having people explain the reasons for their attitudes. This cognitive exercise often leads people to focus on reasons other than the true bases of their attitudes, and thinking about these reasons can in turn produce changes in attitudes. Consistent with the notion that weaker attitudes change more, the disruptive effect of explaining attitudes has been shown to be greatest among individuals with relatively little attitude-relevant knowledge.

D. Biased Autobiographical Recall

A fourth type of study examined attitude change caused by biased information retrieval. In one such study, some subjects were asked to recall pro-ecological behaviors they had performed in the past, and other subjects were asked to recall anti-ecological behaviors they had performed. This process led the former individuals to feel more pro-ecology and led the latter to feel less pro-ecology, thus changing attitudes. Not surprisingly, this attitude change was especially pronounced among subjects low in evaluative–cognitive consistency.

E. Essay Writing

In studies using a fifth method, attitude change was induced by having people write essays opposing their own attitudes. Composing such essays required subjects to generate ideas that challenged their current attitudes, which caused those attitudes to become more consistent with the positions advocated in the essays. This was particularly true among people low in evaluative–cognitive consistency.

F. Priming

Yet another technique used to change attitudes is priming. In this approach, a manipulation is executed to make one particular basis of an attitude especially salient to subjects; and consequently, attitudes change to become more consistent with that basis. For example, in one study of students' attitudes toward new university parking facilities, some subjects listened to a conversation that highlighted the relevance of environmental attitudes to the parking issue, whereas other subjects heard an irrelevant conversation. The former conversation succeeded in changing attitudes and behaviors on the parking issue to be more consistent with subjects' environmental protection attitudes, but only among people who had relatively little direct behavioral experience with the parking issue.

Other studies taking this approach had subjects watch television news coverage of a political issue, thus enhancing the accessibility of subjects' attitudes about how well the President was handling that issue. As expected, this caused subjects to change their overall job performance evaluations of the President to be more consistent with their assessments of his handling of the primed issue. However, this attitude change was concentrated primarily among individuals who were least knowledgeable about politics.

G. Repeated Exposure

A seventh type of study has examined attitude change caused by repeated exposure to objects. In one case, subjects were shown pairs of paintings and were asked to indicate which in each pair they preferred. The process of considering many such pairs led some subjects to change their attitudes toward some of the paintings, presumably because new features of the paintings became salient upon repeated viewings. The more accessible subjects' initial attitudes toward the paintings were, the less attitude change was caused by the repeated preference expression task.

H. Attitude Stability

The attitude change hypothesis has also been tested via an eighth type of study, assessing attitude stability over relatively long time periods during the course of everyday life. If stronger attitudes are indeed more resistant to change, they should show higher levels of stability. Consistent with this expectation, a number of studies have found more stability for attitudes higher in importance, extremity, evaluative–cognitive consistency, interest, and direct experience. Highly ambivalent attitudes have also been shown to be less stable over time.

I. Perceptions of Influenceability

Finally, a ninth type of study yielding results consistent with all the above has focused on people's *perceptions* of the crystallization of their own attitudes. In one case, investigators asked people about the impact that news media have in changing their attitudes on controversial political issues. The more important a person considered an attitude to be, the less he or she claimed the media influenced that attitude. Assuming that people's perceptions of their own influenceability are correct, this provides support for the notion that important attitudes are more resistant to change.

J. Resistance to Attitude-Relevant Behavior Change

One final sort of study we will mention examined not resistance of attitudes per se but rather resistance of attitude-relevant *behavior*. In one case, investigators explored the impact on one's own behavior of perceptions of others' opinions. When people perceive others to share their views on an issue, they are especially likely to express those views publicly. In contrast, when people perceive their opinion to be opposed by most other people, they tend not to express them. Thus, perceptions of others' attitudes shape attitude expression. Not surprisingly, this influence is more pronounced among individuals who attach less personal importance to the attitude involved. People tend to express their important attitudes publicly, regardless of whether they feel others agree or disagree with them on the issue. Thus, people are again less influenced when an important attitude is involved.

K. Mechanisms

In addition to documenting these associations between attitude dimensions and crystallization, past research has highlighted mechanisms likely to be responsible for increased resistance. For example, with regard to attitude importance, important attitudes become more polarized when people are told that they will be discussing an issue with someone with whom they disagree, whereas unimportant attitudes become more moderate. Thus, people apparently brace to protect important attitudes and prepare to be flexible when attitudes are unimportant. Second, more important attitudes are more likely to be consistent with other attitudes and with basic values. These other attitudes and values presumably lend stability to the target attitude in the face of attack. And finally, people for whom an attitude is personally important are especially likely to generate challenging cognitive responses to counterattitudinal arguments. This tendency toward biased cognitive elaboration also presumably enhances resistance to change.

L. Conclusion

Taken together, the studies reviewed above show that 9 of the 10 attitude dimensions are related to crystallization (with the exception of intensity). Whereas some such associations have been documented using only a single method for assessing crystallization, most have been shown using multiple methods. Therefore, it seems appropriate to maintain some significant confidence in these relations.

V. EVIDENCE OF GREATER INFLUENCE

Just as the 10 dimensions of attitudes are apparently related to attitude crystallization, they all appear related to the degree to which attitudes have impact on cognition and behavior. There is a great deal of such evidence available, and it addresses many phenomena: the impact of attitudes on behavior and perceptions of others' attitudes, the impact of attitu-

dinal similarity on social attraction, the impact of attitudes toward an object's individual attributes on attitudes toward the entire object, and the impact of attitudes on memory for attitude-relevant information. We review all this below.

A. Attitude–Behavior Consistency

As we mentioned, one of the most important goals of attitude research is to understand the causes of individual's behavior. Although it is well known that the attitude–behavior relation is typically weak, this relation is, by definition, strong in the case of strong attitudes and weak in the case of weak attitudes. Consistent with this notion, attitude–behavior consistency is greater for attitudes higher in direct experience, certainty, importance, knowledge, accessibility, extremity, and evaluative–cognitive consistency, and for attitudes with larger latitudes of rejection and smaller latitudes of noncommitment.

B. Perceptions of Events

Attitudes have long been thought of as serving functional purposes in people's everyday lives, one of which has been dubbed the knowledge function. The idea here is that some attitudes help people to make sense of the world and interpret ambiguous events. So, for example, if Bill has a positive attitude toward Jeanette, Bill will be inclined to interpret Jeanette's actions in a favorable, complimentary way. And if Bill's attitude toward Jeanette is negative, he will be inclined to view her behavior unfavorably. Thus, Bill needs only to recall an attitude to access an informational basis for making inferences. Presumably, strong attitudes are more likely to serve this function than weak ones.

The effect of attitudes on perceptions of others' behavior has been examined in a number of studies. One study examined the effect of people's attitudes toward a Presidential candidate on their evaluations of his debate performance. People who had a positive attitude toward the candidate should presumably be inclined to evaluate his or her debate performance more positively than that of his or her competitors. This was found to be so, especially among people whose attitudes toward the candidate were highly accessible and those whose attitudes were extreme.

Another experiment sought to determine if increasing the accessibility of attitudes toward a person increases bias in perceptions of his or her behavior. Some subjects were first asked to express their attitudes toward a particular famous person once; others were asked to express their attitudes many times; and still others were not asked to express their attitudes at all. The presumption here was that repeated expression of an attitude increases its accessibility. Consistent with this reasoning, subjects who had expressed their attitudes more often were more likely to evaluate an essay written by the famous person in a way consistent with their attitudes toward him.

Yet another study examined the impact of attitudes on political issues on evaluations of essays written about those issues. Presumably, essays supporting one's attitude on an issue should be evaluated positively, and essays opposing one's attitude should be evaluated negatively. This turned out to be so, especially among individuals whose attitudes on the issue were highly accessible.

One final bit of evidence here involves the impact of attitudes on thoughts generated about the attitude object. If one is asked to write an essay about an object, this presumably induces either favorable or unfavorable thinking about it, depending on the direction of one's attitude. And this should be especially true for individuals whose attitudes are strong. Consistent with this notion, the essay writing made people's attitudes more extreme, especially among those individuals who were high in evaluative–cognitive consistency.

C. Perceptions of Others' Attitudes

According to social judgment theory, actions and statements of attitudes are inherently ambiguous and require some degree of interpreting in order for a perceiver to specify precisely what another person's attitude is. This interpretation is accomplished partly through comparisons of the other person's behavior with one's own attitude, which acts as a perceptual anchor. And this comparative process is thought to bring about perceptual distortion: attitudes close to one's own are assimilated toward it, and attitudes clearly different are contrasted away from it.

Social judgment theory argues that stronger attitudes are more powerful anchors and therefore have more impact on perceptual processes. Thus, individuals with strong attitudes are thought to see others as primarily falling into one of two groups: those with whom they agree (at one end of the attitude continuum) and those with whom they disagree

sharply (at the other end). In support, researchers have found that voters who considered a political issue to be personally important perceived greater differences between the stands competing presidential candidates took on controversial issues. Similar findings regarding perceptions of individuals' and groups' attitudes have been reported with regard to attitude extremity: more extreme attitudes yield greater perceived differences between opposing individuals and groups.

Related evidence was reported in an experiment that explored perceptions of attitudes of social groups. Two sorts of groups were compared: those to which people belonged (i.e., ingroups), and those to which they did not belong and against which they competed for social status (i.e., outgroups). On issues people considered personally important, they exaggerated agreement with ingroups, and they exaggerated disagreement with outgroups. On issues that were not personally important to people, no such exaggeration occurred.

Analogous evidence was found in another study that varied the physical attractiveness of a target individual. On issues people considered personally important, they exaggerated perceived agreement between themselves and attractive others, and they exaggerated perceived disagreement between themselves and unattractive others. No such effects appeared for attitudes that subjects considered personally unimportant.

D. Similarity–Attraction Effect

Theories of cognitive consistency argue that people should be attracted to others who share their attitudes and repulsed by others who hold attitudes that conflict with their own. Consistent with this notion, a great deal of research has demonstrated that attitudinal similarity leads to interpersonal attraction. Presumably, this should be especially true in the case of strong attitudes as compared to weak ones. [*See* INTERPERSONAL ATTRACTION AND PERSONAL RELATIONSHIPS.]

There is much evidence in support of this expectation. A number of studies have shown greater correspondence between an individual's attitudes and his or her friends' attitudes on issues that are extreme or highly important. Similarly, attitude similarity is a more powerful determinant of attraction to strangers and to political candidates when the attitude involved is personally important. And finally, the more one knows about a particular attitude object, the more heavily he or she weighs self–other similarity in terms of attitudes toward it when evaluating others.

E. Part–Whole Attitude Consistency

According to various theories, people's attitudes toward objects are sometimes derived from their beliefs about the objects' attributes and their attitudes toward those attributes. Presumably, attributes toward which an individual has stronger attitudes have greater impact on one's overall attitude toward the object. And this enhanced impact is presumably reflected by a greater level of evaluative consistency between the overall attitude and attitudes toward the attributes.

Consistent with this reasoning, studies have shown that the attributes of cigarette smoking that individuals consider more important are also more strongly correlated with overall evaluations of smoking. Similarly, attitudes toward one's own body parts are more strongly correlated with overall attitudes toward one's body when attitudes toward the body parts are especially important. Analogously, individuals' self-esteem is more influenced by satisfaction with dimensions of self-evaluation that are more personally important to them and that were evaluated with greater certainty. Also, considerations of economic self-interest have more impact on presidential candidate preferences among people for whom economic issues are especially important.

F. Memory for Attitude-Relevant Information

According to cognitive dissonance theory, retaining information in memory that challenges one's attitude on an issue is uncomfortable. Therefore, people are presumably biased toward remembering attitude-consistent information and forgetting attitude-inconsistent information. This has been termed a "congeniality bias" in memory and is presumably stronger in the case of strong attitudes. Consistent with this expectation, recent results showed that attitude importance does indeed regulate the strength of this effect. Individuals who consider an issue to be more important are more likely to remember attitude-consistent information and less likely to remember attitude-inconsistent information than people who consider the issue to be unimportant. [*See* COGNITIVE DISSONANCE.]

A second hypothesis involving attitude strength and memory has also received some support. This hypothesis proposes that people should attend more closely to and think more deeply about information relevant to stronger attitudes. As a result, this information should be better remembered than information relevant to weaker attitudes. Consistent with this logic, studies have found that attitude importance is associated with better memory for attitude-relevant information. In addition, people who have more attitude-relevant knowledge and those more interested in the attitude object have better recall of attitude-relevant information. Also, perceptions of others' political attitudes are more accurate among people who considered the attitudes to be more personally important, presumably reflecting better memory for attitude-revealing behaviors or events.

Based on one particularly interesting set of findings, one might imagine that attitude accessibility would induce better memory for attitude-relevant information. In these studies, people were exposed to a set of objects simultaneously, and the researchers gauged how much attention people paid to each object. Interestingly, people were most likely to gaze at objects toward which they had highly accessible attitudes. If this is a general tendency, people presumably invest more effort in gathering information about such objects and therefore can recall such information better.

VI. CAUSES OF THE DIMENSIONS

In addition to the work we have reviewed above documenting the relations of attitude dimensions to crystallization and consequentiality, researchers have explored the causes or origins of some of the dimensions. This research is less well-developed, but there are some findings documented in this area that merit mention.

A. Extremity

One of the most elaborate research programs on the origins of attitude strength has explored the impact of mere thought on attitude extremity. According to this work, simply thinking about an attitude object often leads attitudes toward it to become more polarized. This is so because thinking leads people to revise the knowledge base underlying the attitude, generating attitude-supportive beliefs and eliminating attitude-inconsistent beliefs. The effect of thinking on attitude extremity can be reduced by confronting individuals with the attitude object about which they are thinking, thus making it more difficult to reinterpret its qualities. Also, the impact of thinking on extremity is reduced when one's beliefs about the object are complex and multi-dimensional.

Another documented cause of attitude extremity is repeated attitude expression. The more often a person expresses his or her attitude toward an object, the more extreme it becomes.

B. Certainty

Recent research has shown that mere thought about an attitude object also increases certainty in one's attitude toward it. Direct behavioral experience with an attitude object also enhances attitudinal certainty. Group discussions of an object increase individual's certainty about their attitudes toward it, particularly when a large fraction of the group shares the same attitude. And finally, attitudinal certainty can sometimes be increased by giving people the opportunity to think about how other people feel about the object in question. Individuals have a tendency to overestimate the number of others who share their views, and the resulting (and illusory) perceived social support enhances confidence in those views.

C. Accessibility

The accessibility of an attitude presumably reflects the strength of the link between the object and its evaluation in one's memory. Therefore, any process that strengthens this link would presumably enhance the attitude's accessibility. One such process is repeated expression or rehearsal. The more often one expresses an attitude, the more accessible it becomes. A second cause of accessibility is behavioral experience with the attitude object. The more such experience one freely chooses to undertake, the more accessible one's attitude toward the object becomes.

D. Importance

What leads people to attach personal importance to an attitude object? According to speculations offered by social scientists for many years, there are three categories of factors. First, people come to care about an attitude when they perceive the object to be relevant to their material self-interests—the behavioral rights and privileges they enjoy in living their daily lives. Second, importance may result

from social identification with a reference group or a reference individual. If that person or group's material interests are relevant to an attitude object, or if that person or group cares deeply about their attitude(s) toward the object, an individual's attitude importance may be enhanced. Finally, attitude importance can grow when an individual perceives an object to be related to his or her cherished values regarding how life should be lived. Recent research has lent support to all three of these proposed causes of importance.

E. Knowledge

According to a number of investigations, knowledge about an attitude object can develop through direct behavioral experience with it, through discussions with other people about the object, and through exposure to the media.

VII. CONCLUSION

So what do we know about attitude strength? First, we know that some attitudes are stronger than others, in that the former are more firmly crystallized and consequential. Second, we know that strong and weak attitudes can be differentiated using any of the 10 dimensions we have described. That is, extreme attitudes are stronger than moderate ones; important attitudes are stronger than unimportant ones; accessible attitudes are stronger than inaccessible ones; and so on.

Third, it seems that the various dimensions of attitudes we discussed are not all merely surface manifestations of a single underlying construct. Rather, they are each independent sources or aspects of strength. This conclusion is supported by evidence of weak correlations among the dimensions, as well as by findings from confirmatory factor analysis studies. It is also consistent with evidence of discrepancies between the dimensions in terms of their relations with other criteria. For example, whereas attitude importance, intensity, and certainty do not regulate the magnitude of question wording effects, evaluative–cognitive consistency and extremity do seem to exert such regulatory influences. Also, more frequent thought about a serious personal trauma is associated with decreased health, whereas more frequent discussion about a trauma is associated with increased health. Finally, although many of the 10 dimensions have been shown to be related to the stability of attitudes over time during daily life, accessibility (as measured by frequency of discussion) appears not to manifest that relation. Clearly, then, these dimensions do not always behave identically to one another and therefore merit being treated as distinct.

According to this perspective, any given attitude may be strong for any of a series of reasons (e.g., because it is important *or* intense *or* accessible). Furthermore, attitudes that have many sources of strength (e.g., importance *and* intensity *and* accessibility) may be particularly crystallized and consequential. That is, rather than merely being additive in enhancing strength, the various dimensions may combine interactively or synergistically in ways that magnify their independent effects. We look forward to future research exploring this possibility.

Some such work has been done and has yielded useful and quite plausible results. For example, one study showed that attitude-defensive biased processing of a persuasive message was most likely to occur among people high in knowledge and intensity. Interestingly, though, some investigations exploring interactions among these dimensions have turned up more complex patterns. For instance, an effect of question order on responses is most likely to occur among people who are low in certainty but consider an attitude to be personally important. Such findings, of course, reinforce the notion that these dimensions are not merely interchangeable with one another.

In addition to exploring these issues further, we expect future research on attitude strength to focus on controversies that have emerged in this literature only very recently. One controversial issue involves the distinction between attitudes that are important to an individual because of self-interest and those that are important because of value-relevance. Some researchers have argued that value-relevance induces resistance to attitude change under all circumstances, whereas self-interest induces openness to attitude change when one encounters compelling information justifying such change. In contrast, other researchers have proposed that both sources of importance yield the same result: openness to change in response to compelling information, but strong resistance to change thereafter. We expect to see much research exploring these matters in coming years.

Another controversy involves the question of whether self-perceptions are inferior measures of attitude strength when compared to other, more direct sorts of measures. According to some observers, self-perceptions are clouded by a variety of interfering forces, such as desires about the sort of person one would *like* to be. In contrast, measures such as response latency that do not rely upon subjects' perceptions of themselves may therefore be more reliable and valid. On the other hand, these latter measures are likely to be distorted by irrelevant constructs as well, such as how recently a person has thought about an attitude or how quick he or she is at making judgments generally. Consequently, it is always important to employ complex assessment procedures using multiple methods to overcome sources of error. It will be interesting to see whether once such procedures are implemented for self-perception dimensions and other sorts of dimensions alike, the dimensions differ in the magnitudes of their relations with attitude crystallization and consequentiality.

Yet another controversy involves the question of mediation. Some researchers have argued that accessibility may be a mediator of many or most of the effects of attitude dimensions on crystallization and consequentiality that we reviewed above. Thus, for example, attaching personal importance to an attitude might lead a person to think about it frequently, which might enhance its accessibility and thereby magnify its impact on cognition and behavior. Consequently, controlling for accessibility might reduce or eliminate effects of importance and other such dimensions. A very new view on this matter is that accessibility may play an important regulatory role only under some conditions, such as when decisions or behavior are executed effortless and automatically. Under these circumstances, which attitudes are most accessible and happen to come to mind will be the ones that have the most impact. In contrast, attitude dimensions such as importance may be the primary regulators of attitude effects when decisions are made carefully, effortfully, and involve extensive deliberation. Under these conditions, people presumably retrieve even relatively inaccessible attitudes if they are important.

Another controversy involves the question of how best to change a strong attitude. Some recent research suggests that the most effective way to do so is to directly attack the basis of its strength. So, for example, if an attitude is strong because it is based on an extensive body of information, it can best be changed by confronting the individual with new information that challenges what he or she already believes. To the contrary, other researchers have argued that the best way to change such an attitude is to provide a new basis of strength implying a different evaluation of the object. So, for example, an attitude that is strongly positive because of its information basis might be changed most effectively by arousing intense negative feelings toward the object. Some research has been reported supporting each of these two contradictory positions, and little is currently known about the conditions under which each perspective is most likely to apply.

As these controversies are addressed with empirical studies and as new controversies emerge, the literature on attitude strength will grow in volume and scientific significance. Thus far, work in this area has made it clear that an understanding of attitudinal processes requires theoretical and empirical attention to the many aspects of strength considered in this entry. Further work along these lines will no doubt broaden the value of the attitude literature and its applicability in the analysis and amelioration of significant social problems.

Bibliography

Abelson, R. P. (1988). Conviction. *Am. Psychol.* **43,** 267–275.

Converse, P. E. (1970). Attitudes and nonattitudes: Continuation of a dialogue. In "The Quantitative Analysis of Social Problems" (E. R. Tufte, Ed.). Addison-Wesley, Reading, MA.

Fazio, R. H. (1986). How do attitudes guide behavior? In "The Handbook of Motivation and Cognition: Foundation of Social Behavior" (R. M. Sorrentino and E. T. Higgins, Eds.), pp. 204–243. Guilford, New York.

Krosnick, J. A. (1990). Government policy and citizen passion: A study of issue publics in contemporary America. *Political Behav.* **12,** 59–92.

Petty, R. E., and Krosnick, J. A. (Eds.) (1994). "Attitude Strength: Antecedents and Consequences." Erlbaum. Hillsdale, NJ.

Raden, D. (1985). Strength-related attitude dimensions. *Soc. Psychol. Quart.* **48,** 312–330.

ATTRIBUTION

Gifford Weary, John A. Edwards, and Shannon Riley
The Ohio State University

I. Definitional Issues
II. Major Theories
III. Recent Theoretical Advances
IV. Special Topics
V. Conclusion

Glossary

Attribution An explanation or inference that a person makes about why he or she or another person behaved in a certain way or why an interpersonal event took place.

Causal schema Organized knowledge structures regarding causal relations that are stored in a person's memory.

Correspondent inference An attribution about an individual's dispositions that follows directly from or corresponds to his or her behavior.

Covariation principle The proposal that people tend to attribute effects to the causal factors with which they covary.

Dispositional attribution An attribution about a person's characteristics.

Noncommon effects Results of an action that are unique to that action (i.e., that would not occur if a different action were performed).

Responsibility attribution An attribution about the extent to which a person can be held accountable for some event.

Self-serving biases The tendency for people to make attributions that protect their self-esteem.

Situational attribution An attribution about the properties of a situation in which a behavior occurred.

Trait attribution An attribution about the extent to which a person has a certain enduring characteristic or disposition.

AN ATTRIBUTION is an explanation or inference that a person makes about why he or she or another person behaved in a certain way or why a certain interpersonal event took place. Attribution theories attempt to describe the kinds of attributions that people typically produce, the processes through which they arrive at these attributions, and the consequences that different types of attributions have for their mental and social lives.

I. DEFINITIONAL ISSUES

Psychologists have identified several different kinds of attributions. In this section, we will briefly describe some of the more widely used types.

Causal attributions are the most commonly studied attribution and will be the major focus of this article. Causal attributions are attributions regarding the properties of the person or the environment that might have caused the to-be-explained behavior. In order for an attribution to be "causal," the property it suggests must be (1) antecedent (i.e., logically prior) to the behavior and (2) sufficient for the occurrence of (i.e., capable of producing) the behavior. In general, a person attempting to make a causal attribution will be looking for stable structural properties of a situation or a person that might have led to the behavior, much as a scientist tries to explain phenomena by referring to invariant scientific laws.

Psychologists often classify causal attributions into two broad categories. Dispositional (or internal) attributions are inferences about a person's characteristics, such as his or her personality, ability, or effort. Situational (or external) attributions are inferences about the properties of the situation in which a behavior occurred. They are inferences about factors external to the person that might have elicited the behavior, such as luck, other peoples' actions, or a task the person has to perform. A person trying to explain a behavior might settle on either of these types of attributions. For instance, in trying to explain what caused Fred to hit Erma, we might decide that Fred is a hostile person (a dispositional attribution) or that Erma said something nasty to Fred (a situational attribution).

Attributions of responsibility identify the extent to which a person can be held accountable for some (usually negative) event. For a perceiver to make a responsibility attribution, he or she must decide whether several conditions existed. These include whether a dispositional attribution can be made; whether the actor intended to perform the behavior; whether he or she knew what the consequences of the act would be; and whether the actor understood the moral ramifications of the act. For example, Fred would be considered responsible for hurting Erma if it were decided that the impetus for the punch rested within him, that he intended to punch and therefore hurt Erma, and that he knew hurting others was wrong.

Once an attribution of responsibility is rendered, an attribution of blame can then be made. This will happen if the actor provides some excuse or justification for the event that the perceiver does not believe. For instance, Fred would be blamed for hurting Erma if he protested that the punch was an accident, but the perceiver did not believe him.

II. MAJOR THEORIES

Unlike some research topics in social psychology, there is no single, monolithic theory of attribution processes. Rather, there are several theories each with some similarities and differences to the others and each with substantial empirical support for its major propositions. However, all of the theories attempt to outline the conditions that presumably will lead a perceiver to decide that a behavior or event was produced by a dispositional property of the person involved, not by factors in the environment. The major theories will be presented briefly below, and an attempt will be made to highlight the theoretical points of convergence and divergence.

A. Heider's Naive Psychology

The originator of all attribution theories was Fritz Heider. He was concerned with how ordinary people understand events. How does an individual come to understand, for example, why his marriage failed, why she was hired for a particular job, why a friend seems to be constantly angry with his girlfriend, or why a mother abuses her children?

During Heider's prime years as a theorist, a major focus of inquiry for psychology was the role of the unconscious in producing adaptive and maladaptive behaviors. He felt a more fruitful approach, insofar as actions in interpersonal relations were concerned, would entail a systematic assessment of the common-sense, naive (nonscientific) conceptions people have about these relations. Indeed, Heider's main contribution, perhaps, was his analysis of the "unformulated or half-formulated knowledge of interpersonal relations as it is expressed in our everyday language and experience."

While recognizing that his naive analysis of action also often applies to oneself, Heider's major focus was on a perceiver's understanding of the actions of others. Consequently, the goal of attributional activities is to apprehend the dispositional or invariant properties inherent in others and in the social world. This search for invariances ultimately serves the goal of making the social environment more understandable, predictable, and controllable.

How do we search for the causal structure of interpersonal events? According to Heider, we do so by reliance upon attributions to the environment (external factors) or to something about the other person (internal factors). Specifically, Heider argued that action is a joint function of two conditions: personal and environmental forces. Personal force is a multiplicative combination of "trying" and "ability," and environmental force involves mainly "task difficulty." To produce an action outcome, the person's ability must exceed the difficulty of the task, the person must have the intention to perform the task, and there must be exertion in the direction specified by the intention. According to Heider, exertion varies directly with task difficulty. However, it varies inversely with "ability"; the more ability an individual has, the less exertion required to produce the outcome.

As an illustration of Heider's naive analysis of action, suppose that we observe a student excel in her classes. Our task, as social perceivers interested in understanding this student, is to ascertain whether her grades are due to something about her (e.g., her ability and intention to excel academically) or whether it is due to something about the environment, such as her very easy curriculum. Sometimes the conditions of action (task difficulty, ability, and trying—both intention and exertion) are quite clear and at other times they are not. If the data are sufficiently ambiguous, our own needs and wishes may influence our causal inference. For example, if we are in the same class as this student and if we are not doing as well as she, we may want to believe that she is getting a break from the teacher—that her task is not as difficult as ours. Finally, whatever our ultimate attribution of causality for her outstanding academic record, it will influence our understanding and evaluation of her, our expectations of her future behaviors, and our behaviors toward her.

B. Jones and Davis's and Jones and McGillis's Correspondent Inference Theory

Heider's naive analysis of action presented a system of terms important in the attribution of outcomes to personal and environmental forces. Correspondent inference theory addresses the important question of how social perceivers extract and analyze cues about these forces from the complex events they observe. More explicitly, the theory focuses on the factors that allow perceivers to attribute some action outcome to the intent and disposition of another individual.

In this theory, a correspondent inference is an inference about an individual's dispositions that follows directly from or corresponds to his or her behavior, and it is often defined as the confidence with which such an inference is held. It also may be defined as the amount of information gained regarding the probability or strength of an individual's disposition. For example, if we observe a political figure giving a pro-choice speech, we might confidently infer that the candidate intended to give such a speech and is personally pro-choice; the inference would correspond closely to the observed behavior. We might also, however, infer that the candidate was responding to strong external pressures to take such a position. In this instance, we would not be able to make a confident prediction regarding the strength of the candidate's personal beliefs on abortion rights.

How do we as social perceivers make this decision? How do we arrive at a decision about the correspondence of an observed behavior and a disposition? This is the main focus of the theory.

Correspondent inference theory first assumes that the individual had some foreknowledge of the consequences of his or her behavior, that there was an intention to bring about those consequences, and that the individual had the ability to translate the intention into successful performance. Second, the theory conceives of every action as a choice, a choice between alternative actions or between action and inaction. Third, the theory identifies a number of factors that allow perceivers to make decisions about the correspondence between actions and dispositions. These factors are the degree to which the behavior fits the perceiver's prior expectations about the outcomes that most people (category-based expectancies) and the target individual (target-based expectancies) desire, and the number of noncommon, or nonoverlapping, effects of the chosen action. According to the theory, if there are few noncommon effects and the departure from expectations is great, then perceivers will make highly correspondent inferences.

Returning to our politician, if we learn that the talk was given at a right to life convention, the assumed desirability or expected nature of the speech would likely depart greatly from what most perceivers would have expected to hear. Moreover, there would have been few common consequences for the politician of having chosen to give a pro-choice versus a pro-life speech in this particular setting. A confident inference that the politician's personal beliefs correspond to his or her behavior would be very likely; in this instance, we would have gained a great deal of information about the politician's beliefs and values.

C. Kelley's Model of Attribution Processes

While Heider emphasized and while Jones and his colleagues considered only processes involved in attributing causality for action outcomes to others, Kelley presented a model that expanded the focus to include attributions for one's own outcomes. He argued that perceivers consider the same factors when trying to link their own or another's outcomes to potential causes. Kelley outlined two basic models of attribution processes: one involves a complex analysis of the available information, and the other entails the use of cognitive structures that may be used when perceiver's do not have the time, opportunity, or motivation to engage in a great deal of cognitive work. Each of these models will be presented below.

In his model, Kelley assumes that social perceivers, in trying to understand and control their social environments, often operate in a very inductive fashion, much like scientists. That is, rather than going into situations with strongly held hypotheses or theories about the causes of various events, perceivers infer causality through the use of certain kinds of information.

More specifically, Kelley proposes that perceivers attribute effects to those potential causal factors with which they covary. The possible classes of causes include persons, entities, and times/modalities. An example may help to illustrate the meaning of these classes of causes. Let us say that the effect, or outcome that we are trying to explain is our enjoyment of a new film. The enjoyment could be due to something about us, it could be due to something about the time or circumstances surrounding our viewing of it, or it might have something to do with this particular film.

How do we arrive at a correct linking of potential cause and observed effect? According to Kelley, we use three kinds of information in analyzing the covariation of potential causes and effects: "consensus" over persons, "consistency" over time and modality, and "distinctiveness" over entities. Put another way, attributors ask three questions. Does everyone like this film or is the enjoyment particular to us? Do we always like the film or is our liking linked to a particular time or setting? Do we enjoy all films or do we particularly enjoy this one? Behavior that is low in consensus, high in consistency, and low in distinctiveness will be attributed to persons. In our example, we like the film and others do not, we like it wherever and whenever we see it, and we like all films; therefore, the attribution is to us—we like films. Behavior that is high in consensus, high in consistency, and high in distinctiveness, however, tends to be attributed to the entity.

While evidence indicates that people can make use of such complex combinations of information and can arrive at logical inferences using the covariation principle, there also are times when they are not motivated to, do not have the time to, or do not have the necessary information (e.g., a single instance observation) to engage in such a cognitive analysis. In such instances, rather than relying on the covariation principle, perceivers make use of their past experiences with and knowledge of the interaction of various causes in the production of an effect. This information is stored in knowledge structures referred to as causal schemata.

Kelley identified a number of such stored data patterns that allow us to make quick causal inferences. For example, he identified the multiple sufficient and the multiple necessary cause schemata, the compensatory cause schema, and the graded effects schema.

By way of illustration, let us consider the multiple sufficient cause schema. The information stored in this schema indicates that two (or more) causes can produce a given effect. Through experience, we may have learned that a politician can give a pro-choice speech because she believes in it and/or because she is addressing a pro-choice audience whose endorsement she badly needs. If, after observing such a speech, we are given information that the latter cause is present, then the presence of the former cause becomes unclear, and the behavior is discounted as a valid indication of the politician's true belief. This discounting principle, that the role of a given cause is discounted if other plausible causes are also present, is an important implication of the multiple sufficient cause schema. It also is quite similar to the noncommon effects analysis outlined above and, as such, provides an important point of convergence between correspondence inference theory and Kelley's model.

III. RECENT THEORETICAL ADVANCES

Recent theoretical work on attribution has taken a variety of tacks. In general, recent theories have attempted to explicate segments of the attributional process alluded to but left unanalyzed by the classic works of Heider, Jones, and Kelley. These theories can be roughly classified as information processing theories, perceptual theories, and interpersonal theories. These general approaches will be discussed below, along with representative examples of each approach. However, it should be recognized that there are other important theories left undiscussed.

A. Information Processing Theories

Information processing theories deal with the cognitive operations and processes that underlie the assignment of attributions. Some of these theories attempt to specify in a detailed way the information-processing stages that a perceiver goes through in arriving at an attribution. For instance, one model proposes five stages: (1) an acquisition stage, in which representations of the target's behaviors are formed in memory; (2) a causal reasoning stage, in which attributional schemata are constructed or retrieved from memory; (3) an information seeking stage, in which additional information regarding the attribution is sought from the environment or from memory; and (4) an output stage, in which the attribution is stored in memory.

Another model, the PEAT model, postulates that people store their observations about the world as probability statements, and assign attributions on the basis of these probabilities. For instance, if a perceiver knows that a certain creek is a good fishing hole (i.e., there is a high probability of catching a fish there) and that Fred is a bad fisherman (i.e., he has a low probability of catching a fish), then the fact that he caught a fish there will be attributed to the creek.

A second class of information processing theory deals with the types of knowledge people use when forming an attribution, and how this knowledge interacts with the available evidence concerning the actor's behavior to determine the attribution. For instance, the Abnormal Conditions Focus Model postulates that people use specific, detailed knowledge of what constitutes "normality" in a certain situation when forming an attribution. People compare this knowledge with the available information about the actor's behavior and situation in order to determine whether there was anything abnormal about the event. Elements of the behavior or situation that are abnormal are more likely to define a cause, and hence an attribution for a perceiver. Obviously, the way that a perceiver categorizes a situation will have a profound effect on what is considered normal or abnormal about the situation. For instance, if a person gets ill after eating collard greens late at night, the person who believes that eating collard greens is natural and enjoyable may focus on the lateness of the meal to explain why the person got ill, whereas a person who believes that eating collard greens is unusual may focus on the greens.

B. Perceptual Theory

Research on perceptual processes in attribution focuses on how the nature of information in the environment influences perceivers' perceptual and attributional processes. Proponents of the "ecological perspective" argue that people are innately attuned to certain types of information in the environment. Information of this kind directly produces a perception of causality in the perceiver, without the involvement of higher-order cognitive processes. There are several kinds of environmental cues that serve as these "basic determinants" of attribution, such as ordinal priority (earlier events are seen as

causal) and salience (the unique cue in a group of cues is seen as causal).

C. Interpersonal Theory

Recent work in attribution also has focused on the interpersonal context of the attribution. The Conversational Model starts from the premise that the attribution process is inherently interpersonal. That is, the attribution process usually takes place in the context of a real or potential communication with another person. Because of this, the rules of conversation have an effect on the types of attributions that people make. For instance, the sort of question asked by a questioner tells the perceiver what factors are relevant to the attributional judgment. The question "why did your friend choose this major in particular?" implies that the answer should be something about the major rather than something about the friend. [See INTERPERSONAL COMMUNICATION.]

IV. SPECIAL TOPICS

A. Motivation in Attribution

Research on the antecedents and consequences of attributional activity has traditionally focused on the perceptual and cognitive processes that occur during the formation of attributions. The role of motivations in attributions has not received as much attention in the literature. Motivation is, nevertheless, an important component of the attribution process. The central notion here is that people make attributions in order to satisfy certain needs, wishes, or motives. The two primary motives that have been observed operating in the attribution process are control motives and esteem motives. [See MOTIVATION.]

1. Control Motivation

No review of attribution theory and research would be complete without examining why people engage in attributional activity, and when they are most likely to do so. As previously noted, the dominant hypothesis is that people make causal inferences in order to satisfy a need for effective control. This control motivation–attributional activity hypothesis states that people make attributions to render the social world understandable, predictable, and controllable.

Control motivation has been described as a goal-directed state that leads to efforts to regain understanding and control. It is likely to be aroused when a person encounters evidence that calls into question his or her ability to predict and control the environment, or implies that he or she has an inaccurate understanding of the world. When control motivation is strong, people are more likely to be interested in forming attributions and engaging in effortful information-processing than when control motivation is weak.

Support for the control motivation–attributional activity hypothesis has been found in studies that have induced control motivation by exposing subjects to experiences that temporarily deprived them of control. This line of research has demonstrated that control deprivation leads to an increased utilization of available attribution-relevant information, an increased interest in forming attributions in subsequent settings, and a careful information-processing approach that, in turn, leads to enhanced memory for facts and inferences and to more accurate inferences.

Research with depressed individuals has provided convergent evidence for the operation of control motivation in attributional activity. Mildly and moderately depressed people comprise a naturally occurring population in whom control motivation is assumed to be chronically aroused. Depressed subjects have been found to show increased sensitivity to social information, heightened attributional complexity, and a willingness to seek out attribution-relevant information.

2. Esteem Motivation

In addition to satisfying a need for control, attributional activity may be the result of efforts to satisfy esteem needs. The major evidence for the operation of esteem motives in attributions is found in the self-serving biases that people display when making causal ascriptions for their own behaviors. Research has repeatedly shown that individuals make self-attributions for their own positive behaviors and external attributions for their own negative behaviors. The tendency to make self-serving attributions, to accept credit for positive outcomes and deny responsibility for negative outcomes, is thought to serve the purpose of enhancing or protecting self-esteem. [See SELF-ESTEEM.]

The self-serving bias is not, however, evident across all situations in which individuals make causal attributions for their own behavior. To explain the apparent inconsistencies in this area of research, some theorists have suggested that indi-

viduals' causal ascriptions for their own behaviors may be self-presentational strategies designed to gain approval from others and satisfy public esteem needs. It has been proposed that certain situational factors such as audience prestige and expertise or the expectation of future performance may act to moderate the use of self-serving attributions. In other words, where individuals' overly positive self-presentations could be invalidated by their own subsequent behaviors or by experts' assessments of their behaviors, people are likely to make modest attributions, often accepting responsibility for negative outcomes. However, when the public defensibility of positive self-presentations is not called into question or when subsequent behaviors are not required or likely to be evaluated by experts, individuals tend to display the self-serving bias in their causal attributions. Whatever an individual's choice of self-presentational strategy, the attributions made in these circumstances presumably serve to garner approval from others and to protect individuals' positive public images.

The operation of esteem motives in the causal inference process, then, is reflected in the generation of self-serving attributions. Such motives also may be evident in the use of causal attributions as self-presentational strategies. For example, causal attributions designed strategically to make the self look good in front of others can serve esteem maintenance and protection concerns.

B. Individual Differences in Attributions

1. Attributional Complexity

The dominant model in social cognition views people as cognitive misers whose thought processes are guided by fixed rules and riddled with biases. This model holds that when drawing causal inferences, people make simple and error-prone attributions. Some attribution research has found, however, that laypersons can and do make complex causal attributions for some human behavior. As we have seen in the discussion on motivations in attribution, there are certain situational conditions under which people can be driven to make complex attributions and to effortfully process social information. Some theorists have suggested that in addition to situational determinants, individual differences also may play a role in determining the complexity of attributions. One such individual difference is attributional complexity.

The Attributional Complexity Scale (ACS) was developed to measure individual differences in the complexity of attributional schemata and in the motivation to engage in attributional processing. It includes items designed to tap several different attributional dimensions. Individuals high in attributional complexity generally are more intrinsically motivated to understand and explain human behavior, prefer causal explanations that include more than a single cause, show more awareness about how much a person's behavior is a function of interaction with others, and tend to infer abstract and complex internal and external causes for people's behavior. These differences between complex and simple individuals are especially apparent in situations where there is abundant time and motivation to carry out attributional processing.

2. Desire for Control

Another individual difference that has been shown to affect attributional activity is the desire for control. Individuals high in desire for control display more extensive attributional processing than those low in desire for control. They also are more intrinsically motivated to understand the causes of human behavior because this information helps them exercise control over similar events in the future. In addition, people high in the desire for control attend to and use attributionally relevant information more than people low in this desire. Individuals with a high desire for control actively seek out attributionally relevant information, and generate a greater number of explanations and more complex explanations for human behavior than people with low desire for control. [See CONTROL.]

Desire for control not only affects the amount of attributional activity that individuals engage in, but it may also guide the kinds of attributions that people make. People high in desire for control are more likely to make self-serving attributions than people low in desire for control because they are more likely to attend to information that indicates that they can influence outcomes, thereby satisfying their need to see themselves in control of a situation. This same tendency to selectively attend to information that verifies their ability to control outcomes makes individuals with a high desire for control more susceptible to the illusion of invulnerability. The perception of being invulnerable to negative outcomes aids people in maintaining a sense of relative personal control.

3. Depression

Depression is yet another individual difference related both to the amount and to the style of attributional processing in which individuals engage. The relationship between depression and attributions is a complex one. While a negative attributional style may contribute to depressive affect, depression also may lead to certain kinds of attributions occurring more frequently. For example, depressed people have been shown to exhibit a depressogenic inferential style that entails a tendency to attribute negative outcomes to internal, stable, and global factors while attributing positive outcomes to external, unstable, and specific factors. Depressed people tend to accept blame for negative outcomes and refuse to take credit for positive outcomes. Nondepressed people, on the other hand, possess a more self-serving attributional style, tending to attribute negative outcomes to external causes much like individuals high in the desire for control. Such an attributional style is thought to be in the service of nondepressives' self-esteem maintenance or protection needs; the absence of such characteristic biases in depressives' attributions may reflect an absence of or inability to use such defenses. [See DEPRESSION.]

Depression also has been shown to be related to attributional complexity. This relationship resembles an inverted-U distribution with mildly and moderately depressed people showing high attributional complexity and nondepressed and severely depressed people displaying lower attributional complexity. Mildly and moderately depressed people report higher levels of motivation to engage in attributional processing and make more complex attributions when asked to determine the causes of outcomes. Although the causal direction between attributional complexity and depression still is unknown, it has been suggested that depressed people engage in more attributional activity because their expectations of uncontrollability and feelings of causal uncertainty provide them with increased motivation to engage in effortful information-processing.

C. Attributions in Close Relationships

The role of attributions in close relationships has received considerable attention in the attribution literature. The majority of the work in this area has examined attributions in marital relationships, focusing on such issues as the relationship between attributions and marital satisfaction.

Evidence suggests that the causal attributions that spouses make for their own and their partners' behaviors may influence the amount of marital satisfaction that spouses experience. Research with married couples has shown that distressed and nondistressed couples display different patterns of attributions when attempting to explain relationship outcomes. Specifically, distressed spouses attribute negative events to causes that are internal to the partner, stable, and global, while attributing positive events to causes that are unstable, specific, and located outside of the partner. Distressed spouses also tend to blame their partner for negative events and to view their partner as the cause of marital problems. Nondistressed spouses, on the other hand, show the opposite pattern of attributions for positive and negative events. These spouses also rate themselves as more responsible than their partners for marital problems, and they give more credit to their partners for positive events.

The tendency for distressed spouses to make attributions that heighten the impact of negative events and decrease the impact of positive events presumably contributes to the maintenance of distress and dissatisfaction in the marriage. Nondistressed couples' attributional patterns are thought to serve mainly a relationship-enhancing function.

While it may be premature to assume a direct causal association between attributions and marital satisfaction, convergent evidence for the influence of attributions on relationship satisfaction has been found in studies on dating relationships. This research found that subjects who rated both themselves and their partners as more responsible for positive outcomes and less responsible for negative outcomes reported the greatest amount of happiness, love, and commitment in their relationships. Additionally, subjects who attributed responsibility for negative behaviors to their partners reported being more unhappy.

Another area of investigation in the close relationship literature concerns when, during the course of close relationships, attributional activity is likely to be heightened. In the context of dating relationships, attributional activity has been shown to be enhanced at the beginning of the relationship when there is uncertainty about the status of the relationship, and at critical choice points when partners make important decisions about increasing their commitment to or terminating the relationship. In terms of marital relationships, people have been shown to produce complex attributions for human behavior during

marital separation or divorce. Presumably, it is the instability that characterizes these points in relationships that provides the motivation to engage in increased attributional processing. Indeed, research has shown that subjects report spending more time trying to understand their relationships and generate more spontaneous causal attributions when their relationships are perceived as unstable. The increased attributional activity at these points in a relationship may reflect efforts on the part of partners to regain a sense of control and understanding over their immediate social environment.

D. Attributions and Victimization

Reactions to victimization have been described as developing out of the desire for control and self-protection. A common strategy employed in response to victimization is the formation of attributions. By assigning causality, responsibility, and blame for a traumatizing event in ways that restore beliefs in an orderly, just, and controllable world, individuals can better cope with the experience of victimization. The role of attributions in victimization seems to be primarily that of a coping mechanism.

A primary issue investigated in the literature on attributions in victimization is the role of victims' attributions of "self-blame" in coping and adjustment. Victims' self-attributions have been hypothesized to foster improved coping by enhancing feelings of personal control and heightening the perceptions of the avoidability of future similar victimizing events. An important distinction must be made, however, between self-attributions to one's behavior and to one's characterological features; behavioral self-attributions allow individuals to perceive that future victimization can be controlled and avoided by a simple change in behavior, whereas characterological self-attributions enhance the perception that future similar events cannot be avoided. The former sort of self-attributions, then, may foster better adjustment, but the latter may not. Research with several groups of victims has provided support for the self-attribution–coping relationship. Studies concerning rape victims, victims of marital violence, and victims of physical injuries have revealed positive correlations between behavioral self-attributions and self-esteem, and negative correlations between characterological self-attributions and coping. [See COPING.]

Some inconsistencies do appear, however, in this line of research. Studies using breast cancer and arthritis patients and mothers of chronically ill children as subjects yielded no evidence of a positive relationship between self-attributions and coping. These studies found, alternatively, that feelings of perceived control and perceptions of avoidability of future similar outcomes were predictors of adjustment. It seems that not only behavioral self-attributions, but any attributions that signal the victim that he or she can control and avoid similar outcomes in the future lead to improved coping with victimization.

Research on attributions in victimization is not confined to victims. Nonvictims engage in attributional activity when confronted with the victimization of others and the potential victimization of themselves. Typically, nonvictims engage in what is known as "blaming the victim." The propensity of nonvictims to blame the victim for the negative event is thought to stem from the need for control and self-protection. By attributing responsibility for the negative event to the victim, people can maintain a belief that negative events are controllable, and they can insulate themselves from the possibility that they could be victimized in the future.

V. CONCLUSION

In this brief article, we have reviewed Heider's seminal analysis of the implicit, common-sense theories that people use in understanding the causes of their own and others' action outcomes. We also have examined the more systematic statements of attributional processes formulated by Kelley, Jones, and their colleagues. Additionally, we have taken a brief look at several of the more prominent, recent strands of theoretical and empirical work in this domain of inquiry. This work may be characterized by its predominant focus on either basic process issues or on applications of attributional ideas. These dual foci likely will characterize future attribution theory and research as well. In closing, we should note that the literature concerned with attributional processes is voluminous. Because we believe this volume of productivity speaks to the centrality of such cognitive activity to human social behavior, we believe that an attributional focus on basic social psychological phenomena will continue to flourish well into the next decade.

Bibliography

Bradbury, T. N., and Fincham, F. D. (1990). Attributions in marriage: Review and critique. *Psychol. Bull.* **107**, 3–33.

Harvey, J. H., and Weary, G. (1984). Current issues in attribution theory and research. *Annu. Rev. Psychol.* **35**, 427–459.

Harvey, J. H., and Weary, G. (Eds.) (1985). "Attribution: Basic Issues and Applications." Academic Press, Orlando, FL.

Hewstone, M. (1989). "Causal Attribution: From Cognitive Process to Collective Beliefs." Basil Blackwell, Cambridge, MA.

Ross, M., and Fletcher, G. J. O. (1985). Attribution and social perception. In "Handbook of Social Psychology" (B. Lindzey and E. Aronson, Eds.), Vol. II, 3rd ed. Random House, New York.

Shaver, K. G. (1985). "The Attribution of Blame: Causality, Responsibility, and Blameworthiness." Springer-Verlag, New York.

Weary, G., Stanley, M. A., and Harvey, J. H. (1989). "Attribution." Springer-Verlag, New York.

AUDITORY DISCRIMINATION

Earl D. Schubert

Stanford University

Glossary

Frequency modulation (fm) Continuous change in frequency of an ongoing tone. Frequently this takes the form of sinusoidal variation.

Harmonic Designating energy at a fequency of vibration that is an integral multiple of the fundamental frequency.

Hertz (Hz) The number of times a waveform is repeated in one second; cycles per second.

Intensity Used informally here as the strength of an acoustic signal. It is proportional to amplitude squared.

jnd The perceptually just noticeable difference in two signals presented to a sensory input.

Sine wave Amplitude variation that follows the form of orthogonal projection of uniform motion of a point on the circumference of a circle. $P = P_{max} \sin 2\pi ft$

Weber's law The rule that states the perceptually just discriminable change in a signal is a constant proportion of the signal magnitude.

IN GENERAL, by registering conditions and changes in the external world, certain senses aid in interfacing the organism with its environment. To the extent that the auditory system can register differences between sound sources and changes in their behavior, it contributes to the appropriate interaction of the organism with its surroundings.

I. UBIQUITOUS NATURE OF DISCRIMINATION

A. For Sensory Information in General

Primitive man is said to have held fanciful notions of how the world is revealed to us through our senses, for example the *aer internus* of earliest auditory theory—the idea that the air in the middle ear mirrored the happenings in the outside air. As rational explanation supplanted these picturesque postulated mechanisms, such views had to be gradually exorcised for more plausible descriptions, and eventually some form of sensory psychology became a useful area of study.

The key to understanding at least the major principles of our sensory orientation to our environment depends on recognition that a few key external dimensions furnish the adequate stimulus for the input to sensory channels. In most of those dimensions that link us to the environment—light, sound, pressure, passage of time, distance from recognizable objects, etc.—variation is continuous. To be of use to the organism, however, variation must be such as to effect a change in the sensory input. This can be taken as an operational definition of sensory discrimination. Discrimination of either discrete differences or continuing change in the relevant physical dimensions, then, is the primary operating principle that enables our interfacing successfully with the physical world. Physical changes that are too small to make any difference perceptually may frequently be registered by some other measuring device, but must be considered beneath our threshold of discrimination, and therefore not of sensory use. An understanding of the relation between physical variation and perceptual discrimination is central to the description of sensory performance.

B. Discrimination in Audition

In the auditory domain, examples of the usefulness of discriminating differences or changes are easily found: In listening to speech, only small differences in intensity characterize the accented as opposed to the unstressed syllable, but the difference is readily registered by the auditory system. Similarly, both obvious and subtle rhythmic acents in listening to music have their effect of the system. The small frequency change accompanying the speeding or slowing of a familiar mechanical device may tell us something useful about its state of health. The quickening or slowing of footsteps may on occasion be highly useful information. Changes in sound resulting from an increase in wind velocity are readily discriminated by the system, even though we may be indoors and might otherwise be unaware of such a change.

In most or all of these instances, we may not be directly aware on what physical dimension the variation—and by inference the resulting auditory discrimination—is taking place. The everyday function of the system is best accomplished not by any direct concern with these dimensions, but by using the incoming information to identify sound sources and recognize their behavior. It is primarily in our laboratory endeavors to structure our understanding of the system that we study its discrimination abilities along one selected dimension. This is a large part of the history of psychoacoustics, and much of our current knowledge of the operation of the auditory system depends on formalizing the parallels between the physical dimension and the psychological response.

II. LISTENING ACTIVITIES DEPENDENT ON AUDITORY DISCRIMINATION

A. Verbal Communication

By far the most frequently employed use of the auditory system for the typical individual relates to the processing of speech signals. Looking at the kaleidoscopic spectro-temporal changes suggested by the waveforms of running speech one might suppose the discriminating powers of the system would be taxed to the utmost. Actually, by the time language is learned probably very few fine discriminations are required. It is during the learning process, or in attending to unfamiliar sequences of speech sounds that the system is required to make fine distinctions. Most of the time the redundancy of the language and the stored linguistic knowledge about a familiar language permit us to operate not on individual dis-

criminations so much as on recognition of longer sequences—the "top down" processing familiar to workers formulating automatic speech recognition by computer programs.

It is this same ability to construct running speech from minimal cues that makes it possible to communicate in quite unfavorable noisy circumstances. It has been shown that in some environments—noisy restaurants, spectator crowds, high-level machine noise, etc.—only a few of the acoustic cues to speech are stronger than the surrounding noise, yet speech communication is still quite possible for the normal listener. Automatic speech recognizers, however, have still not solved this problem of operating in such poor signal-to-noise ratios.

B. Music Listening and Performance

The successful performance of music and the pleasure derived from listening depend rather heavily on a normally functioning auditory system. For performance, as with speaking, this dependence is heightened during the learning process involved in mastery of most instruments. Recognition of the desired frequency (being in tune) and the ability to recognize production of the acceptable tone quality are paramount and sometimes difficult in the initial stages. For seasoned performers and habitual listeners the process again becomes much more automatic, but still most performers on nonkeyboard instruments experience considerable difficulty playing acceptably if deprived of the auditory monitoring channel.

Music performers justifiably take pride in playing in tune, meaning they produce the frequency indicated by the score or some other predetermined pattern; but what few empirical studies are available indicate that frequently—especially in moving passages—auditory requirements are not truly strict. Admittedly, wandering beyond the accepted norms of variation is truly excruciating for the discriminating listener, but the listening ear does not demand performance close to the auditory just noticeable difference in frequency, to be described later.

Skillful performers may also use small deviations in frequency, intensity and spectrum for expressive purposes. These are of special interest to the student of the auditory system, for, though they frequently exceed the smallest difference perceptible by the system, they are responded to not as deviations on the relevant physical dimension, but as expressions of mood or intent. They are obviously registered at the input to the system, but in context are responded to more nearly cognitively than psychophysically.

Some listeners are especially insistent that the frequency range of reproduced music be as wide as possible, hence the long history of emphasis on high fidelity, meaning the faithful transmission of both the high and low end of the audible frequency range—not always easy except with expensive equipment. For some listeners extremely low distortion of the signal is also a basic requirement, i.e., no energy should be introduced into the signal, at any frequency, that was not present in the original signal. Definitive studies on how good the ear is at discerning infinitesimal amounts of such distortion in actual music listening are lacking.

C. Spatial Orientation

For persons with normal vision, the auditory apparatus is not of primary use in positioning us in our spatial environment. This is not true of the blind, who must employ auditory cues for creating much of their spatial world, and some of whom are incredibly skillful at doing so. Even for the sighted person, the auditory contribution to the awareness of sound outside the visual front arc can be very useful, and in some environments reassuring. If the invisible source merits close attention we frequently turn to place it in the visual field; thus, one could reason there has been little motivation to develop fine auditory localizing capabilities in either the front or the rear.

More importantly, the relative locations of sound sources and the tracking of their movement do create for us automatically an auditory spatial surround. We know immediately through the auditory channel something of the nature of the room we occupy: some hint of its size, the degree and adequacy of its sound-absorbing characteristics, and whether it has some unpleasantly intrusive modes of frequency enhancement (ringing). [*See* SPATIAL ORIENTATION.]

For listening to either speech or music, most listeners prefer an optimum balance of sound absorption and reflection. A room with too much reverberation interferes with the clarity of received speech, and a completely absorptive (dead) one requires more effort on the part of the speaker. For much of *recorded* sound, considerable care has been exercised in preserving the sense of the room "presence." Some listeners, in fact, appear to prefer some augmentation of the impression through such devices as wider spacing of the recording microphones or perhaps addition of artificial, electronically introduced reverberation.

III. DIMENSIONS OF ORGANIZATION OF THE AUDITORY WORLD

A. Intensity

1. The Sensitivity Curve

Probably the major dimension of use to the auditory system in recognizing differences among signals is the distribution of energy across the frequency range. This is because the system responds somewhat independently to different frequencies or rates of vibration, meaning it registers separately the amount of energy in the different parts of its frequency range. For very faint signals—those at or near threshold—this very seldom means differentiating between signal and silence, but rather recognizing whether energy in a given frequency channel is sufficiently above the ambient noise at that frequency. Characteristic patterns of energy distribution over the audible frequency range are recognized as peculiar to known sources, or as belonging together because of some cohering attribute—usually some form of temporal synchrony.

Even in an extremely quiet environment, it is not accurate to speak of signal vs silence over most of the frequency range. In the light of the extreme sensitivity of the system in its mid-range the organism itself must be considered physiologically noisy. For a normally sensitive system, such necessary functions as blood flow, breathing, and heart beat furnish a noise floor in the absence of an external signal. Furthermore, the nerves that course from the cochlea to the first neural relay in the brainstem fire somewhat randomly in the absence of external stimulation.

For these reasons it is not useful to think of auditory threshold as a fixed, discrete boundary. We can speak only of the probability that a given faint sound will be audible at a particular moment. Thus, a threshold value is defined as that intensity that has been shown to be audible some agreed-upon proportion of the time—usually 0.5 or 0.75, and in careful work this should be specified.

The usual frequency range of audibility is often conveniently characterized as 20 Hz to 20 kHz, but it is apparent from the sensitivity curve that it would be difficult to fix either end of the range precisely. Fundamental frequencies of musical instruments range as low as nearly 20 Hz, but, with the possible exception of 32-ft organ pipes, it is doubtful that they produce audible energy at that frequency—depending rather on energy in their harmonics in a manner explicated later. For most practical natural sources, production and radiation of energy at such low frequencies would be extremely difficult.

Presumably we favor or develop sources that produce most of their energy in the sensitive range of the system, a range that might most usefully be designated as 100 or 200 Hz to 3 or 4 kHz. The frequency range covered by the human voice is a good example. In fact, very likely any species that communicates through sound or vibration produces differentiable signals in their range of optimum reception. We have already suggested a parallel principle for the history of development and continued use of musical instruments.

With advancing age the ear gradually becomes less sensitive in the high-frequency range. If this hearing loss extends appreciably below 2000 Hz, difficulty in differentiating speech sounds can be appreciable. [See EARS AND HEARING.]

2. Discrimination of Discrete Intensity Changes

For sounds that are in the auditory area, i.e., above the threshold of hearing at any audible frequency, it is useful to discriminate differences in the sound's strength or intensity—defined for most auditory purposes as the square of the sound pressure. For predicting the behavior of the system it is instructive to know, for a sound of any combination of frequency and intensity, how much intensity change is required for the auditory system to recognize that a change has occurred. Again, because we are dealing with a system where other factors are bound to influence the response to small changes, this just noticeable difference in the intensity of the signal (jnd_I) can be defined only in a probability sense—usually the amount of change correctly registered in 75% of the trials presented. The size of this jnd_I has been mapped over most of the usable audible range.

Our usual perceptual responses are relative ones. We report, for instance, by what proportion some perceived phenomenon has increased or decreased when compared with another. We might expect, then that of the standard scales a logarithmic (ratio) scale fits the data more closely than a linear one. This is the case for many auditory phenomena, and the strength of auditory signals is usually specified on a scale of sensation level in decibels (dB), defined as

$$\text{units above threshold (SL}_{dB}) = 10 \log I/I_0$$
$$= 20 \log p/p_0,$$

where SL is sensation level; I is intensity of the sound in question; and I_0 is threshold intensity of a sound of that frequency. Similarly for sound pressure, p and p_0.

In specifying, then, the minimum detectable change in a sound, a similar expression

$$jnd_I \text{ in dB} = 10 \log I_2/I_1 = 20 \log p_2/p_1$$

suffices, where in this instance I_1 is the intensity of the original sound of the pair and I_2 is the sound sufficiently changed to elicit an auditory response of "different" the prescribed number of times. For additional clarity, I_2 is sometimes expressed as $I + \Delta I$.

A simple and attractive law in the description of those physical changes that are just perceptually detectable, known as Weber's law, states that the *proportional* amount of change required remains constant, i.e., that in this case $\Delta I/I = k$. This does not quite hold over the usable intensity range for just noticeable differences in intensity. Plotted as $\log(I + \Delta I/I)$ against SL, this minimum change in intensity required to hear a difference decreases linearly over a 75-dB range. For very faint sounds, the system requires about 1.5 dB to detect the change 75% of the time, but for sounds as much as 80 dB above auditory threshold, only about 0.5 dB is required. Because this slope is close to, but measurably different from, zero this is sometimes dubbed the "near miss" to Weber's law for intensity discrimination. How this discrimination is even possible at high levels where neurophysiological data indicate that most nerve fibers have reached the asymptote of their increase in firing rate with increase in signal level poses a puzzle. However, it has been convincingly demonstrated that discrimination occurs at high levels and it seems feasible that only a comparatively few fibers specific to high-level reporting can account for the phenomenon.

How much change is required depends somewhat on the way the intensity change is made. The linear relation described was derived by a process of comparing two discrete sinusoidal (single frequency) tones about $\frac{1}{2}$ sec in length. A much earlier, oft-cited study produced the requisite amplitude variation for comparison by a smooth sine-wave change to the new amplitude. It was done at an amplitude variation rate of 3/sec, which had been shown to be a rate to which the ear is very sensitive. Either of these two types of amplitude variation may, of course, occur in the functional sounds of everyday listening, so both types of data are useful. For this smooth type of variation the just noticeable difference did not conform to the same simple rule. It was, in general, larger at low and high frequencies than in the middle range, and it decreased quite rapidly with increasing sensation level over the low level range, $\geq$30 dB SL. At higher levels, $\approx$70–80 dB, the amount of change required as SL of the standard tone is increased changes at nearly the same rate as for discrete tones.

More recent studies, performed for only a narrow range of frequency and intensity, indicate that an abrupt intensity increment in an ongoing tone requires less amplitude change for discrimination than does the discrete comparison.

For nontonal signals, i.e., for noise bands of sufficiently broad spectrum to be practically aperiodic and very poorly pitched, the situation is much simpler. Such sounds nearly obey the previously described Weber's law in that it requires a little less than half a decibel to create a barely discernible difference in perceived intensity, and this holds over a wide range of levels. It is consistent that the law also holds for minimal intensity changes in a pair of clicks, since these are also broad-spectrum signals.

In functional listening we would seldom encounter these intensity changes in this comparatively pure form. Both complex periodic tones and those signals that are not so clearly tonal have much more complicated spectra than these controlled laboratory samples, and the pattern of amplitude or intensity variation can take many forms and occur at a variety of rates; and of course most of the useful changes will be larger than these barely perceivable ones. These jnds furnish at best a baseline guide to the lower limit of the system's ability to recognize that a change in the amplitude of a signal has occurred. In some instances such changes may be perceived directly as changes in loudness, in others they may denote something more specific to the current signal, as for example the accents of speech.

B. Frequency and Pitch

1. Determination of Tonal Frequency Range

Over what range of vibratory signals does the auditory system actually respond with perception of a pitch? A look at the sloping ends of the sensitivity (threshold) curve suggests the end of the range might be difficult to establish. A systematic attempt some years ago to fix experimentally the lower limit of *pitch* and the lower limit of *musical pitch* resulted in an estimate of about 20 Hz for the former and around 60 Hz for the latter. What might be considered the empirical determination of the lower musical limit, namely the lowest notes produced by conventional musical instruments, would indicate that 20 Hz might be the lower range for musical pitch, though it should be recognized that this may not mean energy in the range of 20 Hz, but rather waveform repetition rates of that order attributable to the spacing of successive harmonics, since, as noted earlier, it would be difficult for such instruments to produce above-threshold energy in that frequency region.

Most of the evidence we have—both anecdotal and formal—indicates that the pitch response persists to the upper limit of hearing. Where it ceases to be a *musical* pitch is a source of some argument. One of the simplest ways of establishing that a perceived pitch can be characterized as a musical pitch is to determine whether subjects can successfully set another pitch an octave above or below it. In something of an experimental anomaly, nonmusical subjects in one laboratory found it possible to make such octave settings as high as 10 kHz, whereas earlier in an independent study, musical listeners had found the task extremely difficult when the frequency reached 2500 Hz. This is of relevance in the current context since musical pitches have nearly always lent themselves to finer discrimination, i.e., more precise setting than less musical pitch sensations.

2. Smallest Perceptible Difference in Frequency

The change in frequency of vibration is probably the most interesting physical change registered by the auditory system, and the most widely studied. As with intensity, a large proportion of measurements have concentrated on the response to pure tones.

a. Discrete Changes

Most measurements have also used a pair of discrete tones, the observer being required to say which was higher or lower, with the difference between the two getting progressively smaller until it can be reliably reported only the requisite proportion of times. This difference is then the estimate of the just noticeable difference for frequency (jnd_f). Variation of the jnd_f

over the frequency range is not so simple as the case for intensity. Data from a comprehensive study are shown in Figure 1. The somewhat erratic behavior of the faintest tones (5 dB and 10 dB SL) is not too surprising; in fact some evidence exists that there is an essentially atonal (poorly pitched) interval extending about 10 dB above signal threshold. For levels above 20 dB SL the just noticeable difference in frequency appears to increase quite systematically as base frequency rises.

i. Mechanism of Pitch Perception A number of questions have been posed by auditory theorists about what particular operation of the system determines the fineness of pitch discrimination. Thoroughly indoctrinated *place pitch* theorists are convinced it must be mediated by slight shifts in the excitation pattern along the basilar membrane as the frequency changes slightly. In this case one might expect the just perceptible frequency change to be a constant fraction of the width of the auditory critical band filter. The dotted line in the figure suggests that this constant ratio may hold, since the slope of the line is nearly that of the jnd vs frequency plot at medium and higher levels. Others find it more reasonable to suppose the system would also use the temporal information afforded by the fact that neural impulses for a particular fiber tend to occur at the same phase of the signal on succeeding (not necessarily successive) cycles. This periodicity exists, then, in the neural signal and could in principle be used to register the frequency of the signal. With

these two possible mechanisms in mind, a closer look at the plot of Figure 1 might suggest revival of an old rule of thumb about pitch discrimination. At frequencies below about 1 kHz (possibly up to 2 kHz according to some studies) the data points do not follow the slope of the dashed line nearly so well as above. One might conjecture that in this frequency range the *number* of Hertz change required to register perceptually that a change has occurred remains more nearly constant, whereas at frequencies above that point the data points more closely follow the slope of the critical-band line. Such a pattern would suggest a counting type of mechanism in the range where locking to the phase of the signal is the rule, but the use of a filter mechanism where frequency rises to a rate where temporal locking to the signal rate begins to fade. Thus, the old rule of thumb referred to stated that one could discern a change of a constant number of cycles per second below about 1 kHz, but could detect a *proportional* frequency change above that frequency.

There are other reasons for emphasizing the proportional change in frequency required to make a minimum perceptual change. This quantity is of the same form as the musical scale in common use, where a constant change of around 6% represents the frequency change from one note on a keyboard instrument to the next higher one (a semi-tone). When the auditory jnd_f is expressed as a percentage, $\Delta f/f$, it is, of course, much smaller than the semi-tone. It is smallest over the range from about 500 Hz to around 2 kHz, having a value of around 0.2% in that range. For lower frequencies it increases to 0.5% at 200 Hz; for frequencies above 2 kHz it also increases (possibly linearly on a log–log plot) to around 1%. This result is for pure tones at 40 dB SL, which would be a comfortable listening level.

b. Continuous Change

The measurements discussed thus far are quite typical of those reported for sustained discrete tones. Two variations need to be noted for the sake of completeness. First, tonal variation can frequently take the form of a continuous glide, and on occasion these changes are important in practical everyday listening. It would seem the just noticeable difference for this form of frequency variation is registered differently in the auditory system, since it varies in quite a different way over the frequency range. As reported in Figure 1, it is larger than that for discrete tones in the low frequency range, i.e., below 2 kHz,

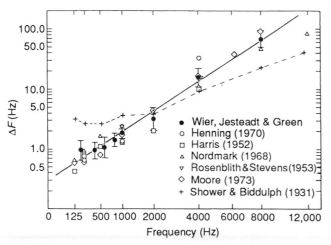

FIGURE 1   A composite portrayal of just noticeable differences in frequency reported by a number of investigators. [From Wier, Jestead, and Green, *J. Acoust. Soc. Am.* **61**, 178–184. Reprinted with permission.]

and somewhat smaller than the discrete-tone jnd for tones above that frequency. A better comparison is furnished by a number of studies that have used the same subjects for comparing discrete-tone and moving-tone (fm) discrimination. From such studies it appears that just noticeable differences for continuous frequency movement are about twice as large as those for discrete tones.

c. Short Tones

The second variation concerns the reaction to tones shorter than those generally used for establishing the just perceptible frequency change. As tones are shortened from a duration of about 200 sec, which would incidentally be a fairly short musical note, the frequency change required for a detectable pitch change increases practically linearly. A few studies, noting the relation between the frequency and temporal values, have suggested this may be a form of time-frequency uncertainty and that therefore the product of required change in frequency and duration of tone should remain constant($\Delta f \times d = C$). Variability between studies has been such that value of the constant C is a matter of some disagreement but the fact that an increase in required frequency change occurs with decreasing duration is well established.

d. Minimum Frequency Change for Complex Tones

We encounter something of a paradox in studying pitch responses in that, as noted, most of the reported measurements of the jnd_f have been made on pure tones, but most of the sounds we encounter in both musical and non-music-related everyday listening have complex waveforms, that is, they consist of a number of harmonic partials. We can, however, elicit a few useful principles regarding the just noticeable difference for complex tones even though the measurements of such are comparatively few. A number of studies have made comparisons between complex tones and pure tones of the same fundamental frequency. One problem is that investigators have labored over the choice of the complex waveform to be used. There is no agreed-upon prototypical complex waveform, so the studies range between a complex containing all partials of equal amplitude (at least prior to the transducer and the ear) and those waveforms that might be closer to those encountered in musical listening, e.g., sawtooth for strings and square wave for clarinet. In these instances of direct comparison, the just noticeable frequency change is generally smaller for complex tones than for sinusoids. It appears reasonable from such results that discriminability for the complex tones matches or slightly exceeds that for the most discriminable harmonic partial in the spectrum of the complex tone. Logic might suggest that the system, which separates out the lower seven or eight partials in the course of its frequency analysis, responds to that frequency—of those frequencies—where the change is most prominent. If more than one frequency channel has an equally small jnd_f, then the probability of detection of a change increases. This well-established principle of the separation of lower partials by the auditory system should not be taken to mean, however, that we hear separately the pitches of those partials in listening to a complex tone, since in most cases we do not. Some cases in which we do so will be part of another discussion.

One prominent theory of pitch perception postulates that precision in auditory identification of the fundamental pitch of a complex tone—a form of the jnd—can be estimated by summing the error for each of the partials, primarily the lower eight partials, since they are the ones presumably registered separately by the system. The rule could be roughly paraphrased by the expression

$$(\Delta f/f)\alpha \overset{k}{\Sigma} \Delta f_k/f_k,$$

where k is the identification of the individual partial.

This turned out to predict greater precision for the complex than is empirically the case and led to the conjecture that the jnd for a partial embedded in a complex tone is larger than for that same frequency as an independent sinusoid. As noted, partials in a harmonic complex are not normally heard separately; thus, in order to determine when a given partial changed audibly it was necessary to cue it in for the listener by sounding it separately a number of times before the jnd trials began. The results indicate that the jnd_f for a tone embedded in a harmonic complex is larger than for that same frequency in isolation. The obtained values range from $\approx 0.5\%$ for harmonics 1–4 to around 2% for harmonics 8–10. Using these values, the jnd_f for complex tones can be satisfactorily predicted.

Implied in these findings is the fact that not all harmonics in a complex tone contribute equally to the perceived pitch of the complex. This is verified by displacing each partial in turn from its canonical position in the harmonic series and noting the effect on the perceived pitch of the complex. For small changes in the frequency of a partial (±2–3%) the pitch of the complex does shift in the direction of the shift of the partial, the average change in the shift of the complex being, in these measures, roughly one-sixth of the frequency shift of the partial. These results have reinforced a long-held belief about the relative dominance of certain partials in determining the pitch of complex tones. The lower partials, those separated by the frequency analysis of the auditory system, carry greater weight, and within that group the partial with the smallest jnd_f (when heard within the complex) has the greatest influence. Which of the lower partials holds that distinction varies from one listener to another, and perhaps this is not surprising, since this specific auditory task lacks the benefit of a history of shared experience among subjects.

A corollary to this finding is that a harmonic partial that is stronger than others will exert a greater influence on the pitch of the complex, all other things being equal. This is of conceivable interest musically, since most tones of musical instruments—and for that matter many other complex tones encountered in everyday listening—consist of harmonic partials of different levels across their frequency spectrum.

If an individual harmonic partial is shifted by more than about 3% a different phenomenon occurs. The partial no longer has as great an effect on the pitch of the complex and with shifts of this magnitude and greater begins to elicit a pitch of its own. In other words it is no longer perceived as belonging to the series composing the complex. This is a matter of some interest in its own right, since one of the problems frequently encountered in everyday listening involves determining which energy concentrations across the frequency range belong to which of two or more simultaneous signals. A useful concept in this task has been the "harmonic sieve," a postulated special filter that, for a given frequency position, passes only frequencies within a given tolerance of the implied harmonic series for that position. Energies from other simultaneous signals are thus presumably excluded from the auditory synthesis of the preferred signal.

This implies an additional form of discrimination, a decision about how close a potential component frequency must be to be included in the harmonic synthesis that the auditory system performs on a complex signal subsequent to the initial spectral analysis. In order not to oversimplify the situation one should recall some related principles regarding the behavior of the auditory system. As noted earlier, listeners do not ordinarily hear a harmonic partial separately. Musicians who know the expected pitch of quite a number of the partials, given the pitch of the complex, can hear out such partials with very little effort. Other listeners have sometimes trained themselves to do this sort of analytical listening for special purposes. Detecting distortion products would be an example. But for the usual listener, hearing a particular harmonic requires some assistance. Recall that in these experiments on the discrimination of changes in a given harmonic, a pure tone of the same frequency as the partial in question was presented to the listener a number of times prior to beginning the experimental trials. It is something very close to the pitch of that sinusoid that separates out from the perception of the complex when the harmonic partial is mistuned by more than the "jnd for harmonic cohesion." Of wider relevance for auditory theory is that it furnishes an estimate of the widths of apertures in the proposed auditory harmonic sieve. From these measures that width would appear to be about ±3% of the center frequency of the aperture. This needs to be verified by other operations, but can be taken as a working estimate.

It has by now been amply demonstrated that the auditory system, presented with a periodic complex tone that has no energy in the lower (resolvable) harmonics, responds with a pitch that corresponds to that of the implied fundamental, i.e., the greatest common divisor of the frequencies present, corresponding also to the period of the repetition of the waveform. Because this does not present an easily distinguished place of stimulation along the basilar membrane but does feature easily identified time patterns it has been labeled a periodicity pitch, determined presumably by the temporal spacing of the envelope peaks resulting from the output of any critical band containing two or more partials. This is not a highly tonal pitch, nor a very precisely registered one. Its jnd_f is several times that of a comparable number of resolvable (lower) partials. This is of considerable interest for auditory theory, but probably of little consequence for practical listening since complex tones so constituted are not likely to arise from either natural sources or conventional musical instruments.

3. Discrimination of Frequency Ratios

The typical listener has a very useful short-term memory for pitch. This is evidenced by the fact that, with comparatively few exceptions, persons can produce, usually vocally or by whistling, the same or nearly the same frequency as they have just heard (or its octave equivalent if the tone is outside their reproducible range). By implication, this denotes storage of some physiological correlate of the pitch—either the proper setting of the tension of the vocal folds or shaping the mouth as the appropriate resonator. More remarkable, though from long practice it seems commonplace, is a memory for a prescribed *sequence* of pitches in the form of a stored melody. The latter is the more impressive in that it appears to be stored as a movable pattern of relative pitches, meaning that if the base pitch, or the key, is changed the same sequence of relative pitches is readily transposed to the new range.

We lack information almost completely regarding the form of storage of such a sequence. The trained musician can view it as a series of musical intervals, but viewed from the physics of sound these are most easily described as simple frequency ratios. Since as listeners, to either ourselves or others, or in any ensemble performance from impromptu harmonizing to formal presentation the recognition of the desired interval is required, i.e., we generally require the notes to be reasonably "in tune," the question of the jnd for frequency ratios or musical intervals is of some interest in auditory discrimination.

For even a partial understanding of this situation, one needs to note that in our culture—and in most—pitch sequences are framed in discrete steps, not the continuous glides of the laboratory oscillator or of the ubiquitous siren. A formal musical scale, anchored to a chosen base frequency (key note) can be constructed by properly combining simple ratios, but for reasons beyond our current interest this leads to difficulties in performing in other keys on a single keyboard instrument. The solution adopted many years ago was to build a musical scale of equal logarithmic steps, consisting of 12 steps (semi-tones) to the octave. Since we can start such a scale on any frequency, and since it needs to be specified for only one octave, a convenient description for our current purposes is

$$\text{frequency of scale note } n = 2^{n/12} f_s$$
$$n = 0, 1, 2, 3 \ldots 12,$$

where f_s is any arbitrarily chosen starting frequency, and n is the number of semi-tones above the starting frequency. The next octave can be covered by starting with the end of this span, namely, double the

starting frequency. A more generally useful expression for the laboratory for expressing the difference in octaves between two frequencies is

$$\text{octave difference } = \log_2 f_h / f_l,$$

and the expression for the difference in semi-tones between any two frequencies can be easily derived from this one, specifically

$$\text{difference in semitones } = 39.84 \log (f_h / f_l),$$

where f_h and f_l are the higher and lower bounds, respectively, of the interval to be expressed in semi-tones. For expressing finer frequency differences than the semi-tone, the cent, or 1/100 of the semi-tone is the standard.

There is good reason to expect some special response to simple frequency ratios. Because harmonic partials are integral multiples of the fundamental frequency, simple frequency ratios are the rule in the periodic sounds of speech, music, and other everyday signals. Thus, their patterns occur constantly in the auditory system from the presence of the resolved partials.

An easy definition of the simplicity of a ratio is the sum of the numerator and the denominator with the fraction reduced to its simplest terms. A little arithmetic shows that in tones with many partials the simpler the ratio the more frequently it will occur, all other things being equal.

Interestingly enough, this holds true not only for harmonic partials but tabulations show it to be true also for the ratios of the fundamental frequency of simultaneous notes in conventional western music, i.e., tabulation of the number of times each interval occurs shows that the simpler ratios occur most frequently. In musical terminology, the octave (2 : 1) occurs more frequently than the perfect fifth (3 : 2), the fifth more often than the perfect fourth (4 : 3), etc. One might predict that if exposure has its efficacy, simple ratios will be easily recognized by the auditory system.

But the path to an experimental determination of the jnd for frequency ratios is strewn with pitfalls. It is true that the periodic source, with only rare exceptions, produces harmonic partials that are very nearly exact multiples of the fundamental frequency. But since the primary focus in exploring recognition of true frequency ratios is musical, ratios of sinusoidal tones are of limited interest. Because of the emphasis, during musical training, on interval recognition, musicians are considered a separate population in these experiments. However, there are factors in their training and experience that do not foster the recognition of *exact* numerical frequency ratios. The equal tempered scale—as we have seen—foregoes exact ratios in favor of key flexibility, which may introduce some "fuzziness" in precise interval perception. Add to this that, in performance, intervals are stretched and compressed from their normal value for good and sufficient reasons related to musical expression. No premium is placed on exact conformance to numerical ratios. Finally, one aspect of musical training may serve to broaden the jnd for ratios. Music students, particularly vocalists, spend many hours in the rapid recognition of intervals—a necessary requisite in reading a part in ensemble performance. Thus, there is considerable emphasis on immediate categorization of an interval regardless of whether its ratio is exact. If, as has been shown in the differentiation of vowel sounds in speech, categorical perception of intervals is the rule and discrimination is sharpest at the borders between intervals rather than at the center, measures of jnds could well be affected.

One other aspect of listening to ensemble performance may also have some effect in the judgment of ratios. If the musical setting encourages a strong key sense, then the perceptual judgment about a mis-tuned ratio frequently is that one note or the other is out of tune—not a direct response to the adequacy of the ratio. This is a useful consideration in structuring an experiment on ratio jnd in such a way that the listener is not permitted to remain in the same key for a series of trials.

Despite these potential drawbacks there is at least reassuring agreement in the results of studies of the jnd for frequency ratios. Musicians cannot judge changes in the ratio with nearly the precision that they detect frequency variation in single tones, but they can reliably discern departures of less than 1%. Most of the ratio data available deal with octaves (2:1), fifths (3:2), and major thirds (5:4), those occurring most frequently in conventional music.

An attractive hypothesis regarding the mechanism for detecting departures of simultaneous complex tones from an exact ratio involves the detection of the beating of two harmonics of nearly identical frequency. Note that for two tones an octave apart there is potentially a coinciding harmonic in the lower tone for every harmonic in the upper tone. For the 3:2 ratio every third harmonic of the upper tone has a potential coinciding harmonic in the lower

tone, and so on. When the fundamental frequencies of such pairs of tones depart slightly from exact ratios these harmonics will differ slightly from exact coincidence and audible beating can result. The greater the mis-tuning the more rapid the beat rate.

This makes a very plausible explanation for the detection of departures from exact ratios of the fundamental. Fortunately with modern electronics it is testable. Tones can be easily synthesized omitting the "offending" partial from one tone of the pair, so that mis-tuning can occur without that particular source of beating. It is also easily possible to mistune *only* those coinciding pairs, leaving the ratio of the two tones otherwise intact, so that beating occurs without mis-tuning. One can, in brief, now vary mis-tuning and beating of coincident partials independently. One modern study that presented such synthesized pairs to analytical musical listeners found judgments of mis-tuning of ratios, as represented by musical fifths and major thirds, to be virtually unaffected by the presence or absence of beating partials. Listeners apparently can detect the change in the ratio without the aid of such beats.

Beats, however, can serve a desirable purpose in music listening. In a study of 3-tone chords—major and minor triads—subjects were asked independently for comparisons of *in tune*, *smooth*, and *pleasant* for pairs of chords. Among the group of musically trained listeners, some consistently judged the chord with the slightly mis-tuned center note to be more pleasant. Mis-tunings of 15 cents gave reliably different judgments, so again it appears that a departure of around 1% from the exact ratio is readily discernible.

4. Discrimination and Absolute Pitch

One form of pitch perception that might well be characterized as the prototypical example of categorical perception is the phenomenon of absolute pitch. This is the ability to place rapidly the pitch of a heard tone on a fixed scale of pitch—usually the letter names of keyboard instruments, though it could readily be transferred to identifying the vibration frequency of the tone if such associations are included in the possessors' experience. Why this ability occurs in some few listeners but is almost impossible for others to develop has been a fascinating question for some time, but is not within our purview here. The question of relevance here is whether absolute pitch ability is related to finer pitch discrimination in the form of the jnd_f. The question discussed previously of whether the tendency for immediate assignment into discrete categories influences finer distinctions along a continuum is the pertinent one. To the writer's knowledge, experimental data on this point are not available.

C. Spectrum and Quality, or Timbre

1. Discrimination of Spectral Profile Changes

One of the important contributions to the recognition and classification of acoustic signals, and thereby sources, is the shape of the excitation pattern of a sound on the basilar membrane or in the neural mapping of that pattern. The system responds to small differences in these spectral patterns. It has been known for decades that a change of 1 dB in one harmonic of a sustained complex tone (a shift of about 12% in its amplitude) can be detected as a discernible change in its quality or timbre. This was, at one time, in fact, part of a test for musical talent.

Recent more complete studies have been done on sets of sinusoids equally spaced logarithmically and of equal amplitude. The spacing is chosen to avoid familiar musical intervals, so the set usually sounds quite rough and poorly tonal. When the center component of this array is increased sufficiently over the others in amplitude the auditory system can detect a difference. Since this seems to be a comparison *across* the frequency range of the signal, the auditory response has been called profile analysis. When the components are very closely spaced undoubtedly masking operates strongly. When the spacing averages 23 Hz the center component must be raised by 5 dB for the change in profile to be detected. By the time the average spacing is increased to around 120 Hz the difference in profile can be detected when the center has been increased by 3 dB. By doubling this spacing the required increase drops to 2 dB. Thus, we are probably not so sensitive to changes in these non-musical sounds as in harmonic series.

2. Processing of Simultaneous Sounds

Considering how often we must listen in the presence of competing sounds, the ability to detect the presence of a familiar sound with minimal cues should be of considerable interest. It has been shown that if one starts with a harmonic series of 30 equal-amplitude partials and then for each of the three characteristic frequency regions of energy concentrations for a given vowel sound (the vowel formants) the two partials closest to the center of each such frequency region are increased by only 1–2 dB

the intended vowel sound will be recognized. Apparently recognition of a *familiar* sound requires very little change in the spectral profile, perhaps of the same order as the recognition that *any* change has occurred in the profile of an uncategorized sound. The relation of this finding to the hearing of speech in noisy situations or to the recognition of the sound of a clarinet or a trombone in a full orchestra is a matter for conjecture at this juncture.

A question of interest in both speech perception and music is the minimum separation of simultaneously present frequencies for which separate tones can be heard. If we ask the question for complex tones, the bulk of data comes from musical training. Music students are expected to hear the separate pitches of two notes a full tone apart (a major second) a separation that happens to be very close to the estimated width of proposed auditory (critical band) filters ($\approx$11% for young ears).

A laboratory study attacked the same question by asking listeners to identify the partials of a complex tone by noting whether a separately presented sinusoid was equivalent to a tone in the complex. The results showed that, although individual differences are great, on the average listeners could not reliably identify partials above the 6th, corresponding to a partial-spacing ratio of 6/5. This 20%, incidentally, is the equivalent separation of the tones of a musical minor third (1 : 2 : 1).

Perhaps more basic to auditory theory is the required separation for two single-frequency tones. On testing this turns out to be much closer to the estimated auditory filter width, namely 10%. Both the multi-partial and the two-partial estimates of minimum separation of tones were arrived at using both harmonic and nonharmonic tone complexes. In the only reported study that employed the same technique for musical and non-musical listeners to estimate minimal frequency separation for separate pitch perception the non-musicians fit the 20% estimate and the musicians 10%. Apparently with training the latter is the just noticeable difference in frequency for creating simultaneously perceived pitches.

D. The Time Dimension in Auditory Discrimination

1. Degree of Time Interval Resolution

In comparison to other sensory input channels, things happen rapidly in the acoustic channel. In rapid speech, linguistically separable elements may have durations anywhere from 10 msec (plosive sounds) to about 200 msec (sustained vowel sound) and an average pace for such elements of about 30/sec poses no problem for the auditory system. It follows that it must possess unusual capabilities for temporal discrimination. In interpreting such a statement, it should be remembered that the temporal pattern in any single channel (critical band) would be less rapid.

a. Click Separation

Seemingly basic to the analysis of the system's temporal capabilities is the limit of auditory separation of two of the shortest acoustic signals—namely a pair of clicks. At what temporal spacing does the auditory system first report a double image rather than a single? The problem with a straightforward answer to that question is that the auditory system, from its very useful habit of suppressing reflections, may fail to respond to the second click, so we may not get an accurate estimate of its actual minimum temporal resolution. A more objective method, and one that generalizes better to everyday performance, is to make use of a pair of waveforms like those labeled 1 and 2 in Figure 2. In the experiment on minimum discriminable time interval the listener hears a pair of such waveforms—sometimes 1 followed by 1 or 2 followed by 2, in which case the appropriate response is "Same." On other trials, chosen at random to represent half the trials on the average, the sequence is 1 followed by 2 or 2 followed by 1, and here the appropriate response is "Different." The spacing between the shorter and the taller spike in each waveform is varied until the listener can tell on 75% of the trials whether the members of the pair were the same or different. For the average listener this occurs when the spacing is 1.5 to 2 msec. This, then, is about the shortest temporal pattern that can be resolved by the auditory system.

b. Gap Detection

But in processing complex signals the ear encounters many temporal patterns more complex than this

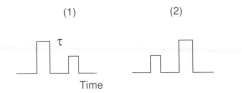

FIGURE 2   Schematic waveforms of click pairs used to establish minimum temporal separation of auditory events.

click pair, so we need to know its limits for other temporal sequences. One revealing measurement is how small a gap the system can detect in an ongoing signal. Because the sudden stopping and starting of a signal creates unwanted spectral cues, our most valid estimate of minimal gap detection is made with broad-band noise signals. These measurements indicate that a gap of 3–5 msec is detectable a reasonable proportion of times. Attempts to measure with octave bands of noise to get estimates for different frequency ranges indicate that progressively wider time gaps are required at lower frequencies, reaching 15–20 msec in the neighborhood of 1 kHz and nearly 50 msec around 250 Hz. Since octave bands get narrower in Hertz as center frequency is lowered, random fluctuations in the noise signal itself interfere with perception of the gap, so these low-frequency measurements are less useful.

2. Perception of Modulation

A frequently encountered pattern in complex signals is regular fluctuation in amplitude. Rates encountered may range from the amplitude vibratos of some musical instruments to the amplitude envelope rates that lead to perception of periodicity pitch discussed earlier. This has led to attempts to discover how sensitive the auditory system is to temporal changes in the form of amplitude modulation. Modulation of a *sinusoidal* "carrier" creates spectral changes that are not of interest in temporal investigation, so here again the signal of choice is modulated broad-band noise. At rates of amplitude modulation of such noise below about 60/sec the ear detects peak-to-valley changes of about 1 dB (modulation of 5%). This could be designated the just noticeable difference for noise modulation in this range. If the modulation rate is raised to about 100 /sec, just about the range where the ear begins to perceive a periodicity pitch for some signals, the peak-to-valley ratio must be at least 2 dB. At a rate as rapid as 500 modulations per second the peaks must be 6 dB above the valleys for the modulation of broad-band noise to be detected.

3. Perception of Temporal Order

There are many times when it is important to know which of two sounds occurred sooner. The auditory system is extraordinarily sensitive to the order of onset of brief signals. For very short tone bursts of sufficiently different frequency a difference in onset of 2–3 msec can be discerned. For the same kind of sounds that are closer in frequency—possibly meaning within the same critical band—greater onset disparity is required for the system to discern the correct order. This has not been extensively studied, but 10 msec is a preliminary estimate. For sounds of more practical duration, such as musical notes or acoustic signals, measurements show that a gradually greater onset disparity is required, reaching 20 msec for sounds 0.5 sec in length. We might ask whether this level of order discrimination serves well in such nonlaboratory pursuits as music listening or synchronization in ensemble performance. Determining exact synchrony for different instruments, or even different voices, is difficult since waveform envelopes of attack differ among different sound generators. For one reason or another, in musical performance there seems to be a permitted flexibility of about 30 msec, i.e., variation within that interval is common in skilled ensemble performance.

4. Perception of Temporal Regularity

Many of the periodic sources we listen to, for example orchestral instruments or the singing and speaking voice, are not actually rigidly periodic. Their waveforms exhibit small departures from exact periodicity—a characteristic referred to as jitter. Absence of this variation leads to the impression that instrumental tones or spoken vowels are no longer natural sounding. The ear is quite sensitive to this jittering of periodicity. In the laboratory, for complex tones of durations common in music and speech, the auditory system detects the presence of such jitter when departures from regularity are 0.6 to 1.0% of the period. Above the range of the most frequently occurring musical fundamentals sensitivity to jitter rises, reaching 0.1% at 3000 pulses/sec.

This might be designated as the system's sensitivity to irregularity in *micro-time* since the deviations are fractions of a millisecond. The auditory system is also quite sensitive to departures from regularity in longer periods such as those involved in music rhythms and cyclical events in mechanical devices. When observers are given a train of temporally punctate sounds with only one of the intervals of the series to be set by the listener most of the settings fall within 2% of the correct interval. In a related task—that of matching the duration of a single acoustic signal with no rhythm involved—the majority of errors fall within 6% of the correct duration.

IV. TIME, INTENSITY, AND SPECTRUM IN DISCRIMINATION IN AUDITORY SPACE

The localizing of sound sources in space is understandably a very difficult assignment for the auditory system. There is no simple way to map source locations onto the cochlea in the same point-to-point manner as spatial locations can be mapped onto the retina(s). The attractive view that interaural time differences and intensity differences between ears are combined with the interaural spectral differences occasioned by the acoustic shadow of the head falls short of a complete explanation. Although the binaural system can detect interaural time differences of a few microseconds, and although the intensity disparity occasioned by the sound shadow of the head reaches as much as 20 dB at 4 kHz and 35 dB at 10 kHz each of these clues by itself is highly ambiguous, i.e., more than one location is signaled by a given interaural difference. Yet the auditory system—though it by no means approaches the precision of the visual—does a fairly creditable job of registering the location of sound sources, even in somewhat reverberant environments. In the frontal region it gets considerable help from the visual system, which, engineered as it is for spatial resolution, exhibits discrimination 50–60 times better than the auditory in its most sensitive region.

A. Horizontal Plane

Localization in the ear-level horizontal plane is better than elsewhere. This is not surprising, since the combination of interaural time and intensity clues are somewhat less ambiguous here. Investigators have differed in their methods, and the results make it inadvisable to choose too precise a figure for just noticeable differences in location. Degree of resolution also differs systematically for several regions of auditory space and varies with the nature of the signal. In general broad-band signals are better localized than single-frequency tones, and interestingly enough, familiar signals are located more precisely than others. This could mean that the interaural spectral difference is more useful in processing familiar signals and possibly that a higher-level mechanism assists in localization.

Within the horizontal plane localization is best straight ahead of the listener, usually referred as zero azimuth. The just noticeable displacement from center runs from 1 to 2° for continuous speech, is 2 to 3° for broad-band noise, and is 1 to 4° for sinusoids. At extreme positions on either side, i.e., 90° right or left, performance is only about one-third as good. At the rear, performance is better than at the sides, about two-thirds of the precision measured at the front.

In addition to static change in position, minimum detectable *movement* of sources has also been measured in the horizontal plane. At the front, movement of 5° is detectable, whereas at the side 30° is required. Amount of change of position rather than the velocity of movement seems to be the determining factor. There is currently no convincing evidence for a separate mechanism for discerning source movement.

B. Median Plane

Localization in the median plane has also been extensively investigated. Here the primary clue has been shown to be the asymmetry of the placement of the ear canal in the pinna. In the input waveform, this amounts to a "delay and add" operation that leads to dips in the spectrum, and since the dimensions of the pinna are small the dips occur in the high-frequency end of the audio spectrum. It follows that high-frequency energy must be present in a signal for its source position to be successfully differentiated in the median plane. These dips change their frequency location as the source traverses the median-plane arc and furnish the position clue for the sound source.

Localization is not as good as in the horizontal plane. For continuous speech the source must be about 17° off center before its elevation can be reliably reported although for familiar speech only about 9° of elevation is required. It can be as little as 4° at this position for white noise. Accuracy decreases with greater elevation until the uncertainty is $1\frac{1}{2}$ to 2 times as large directly above the head.

In both planes, when visual clues are absent front–rear errors are fairly common. In everyday operation the rear hemisphere need serve only for gross localization, cueing the organism where to turn for better visual location.

C. Three Dimensions

One precaution in interpreting these measurements hinges on the fact that almost all studies of localization have aimed at isolating one facet of the process, and thus have placed the sources to be located in a single plane or restricted region of interest. Only a very few studies have placed the sources around the head in such a manner as to sample most of auditory space and thus be more generalizable to everyday behavior. When this is done with broad-band noise as the signal localization occurs within 2° in the horizontal dimension and about 3.5° in the vertical.

All in all, despite the acknowledged difficulty of the task the auditory system does create for the listener an immediately given and highly useful sense of auditory space. In addition, the degree to which the auditory system can improve its powers of spatial discrimination if the visual system is damaged is truly remarkable.

Bibliography

Bregman, A. (1990). "Auditory Scene Analysis." MIT Press, Cambridge, MA.

Green, D. (1988). "Profile Analysis: Auditory Intensity Discrimination." Oxford University Press, New York.

Handel, S. (1989). "Listening." MIT Press, Cambridge, MA.

Middlebrooks, J., and Green, D. (1991). Sound localization in human listeners. *Annu. Rev. Psychol.* **42,** 135–159.

Moore, B. C. J. (1989). "An Introduction to the Psychology of Hearing," 3rd ed. Academic Press, New York.

Yost, W., and Nielsen, D. "Fundamentals of Hearing," 2nd ed. CBS College, New York.

AUTHORITARIANISM

Bob Altemeyer

University of Manitoba, Canada

Glossary

Attitude A person's evaluative reaction to something.

Authoritarianism The covariation of attitudes of relatively high degrees of submission to some authority, aggression perceived to be sanctioned by that authority, and adherence to the conventions endorsed by that authority.

Ethnocentrism Belief in the superiority of one's "in-group" compared with various "out-groups."

Left-wing authoritarianism Authoritarianism challenging the established authorities in one's society.

Prejudice Prejudging someone unjustifiably.

Response sets A tendency causing a person consistently to make different responses to test items than he or she would have had the same content been presented in different form.

Right-wing authoritarianism Authoritarianism supporting the established authorities in one's society.

AUTHORITARIANISM, in general, can be defined as "often blind submission to authority as opposed to individual freedom" (*Webster's Third New International Dictionary*). Everyone submits to social authority daily, and the term does not apply to such mundane acts as stopping at traffic lights. But when people attack and kill innocents because some authority told them to ("I was only following orders") we are unquestionably discussing authoritarianism.

I. SITUATIONAL DETERMINANTS OF AUTHORITARIAN BEHAVIOR

The great lesson of social psychological research is that situational forces can often overwhelm individual predispositions. Striking evidence for this came from Stanley Milgram's famous experiments on obedience, which showed that almost everyone tested would inflict terrible electric shocks upon an unwilling victim at the orders of an experimenter. Most subjects in fact *completely* obeyed, to the point of administering shocks they had every reason to believe were fatal. People are apparently given far more training while they are growing up in obeying authorities than in deciding whether particular orders ought to be obeyed. [*See* OBEDIENCE AND CONFORMITY.]

The most dramatic evidence for the power of situational forces arose from two versions of Milgram's "team teaching" experiment, where the subject was combined with two confederates to administer the shocks as a team. In one condition, the two confederates defied the experimenter, and so then did 90% of the real subjects. But in another version the confederates were totally obedient, and so were 92% of the subjects. It thus made almost no difference who the subjects were: how well-educated, or religious, or altruistic. Behavior was almost completely controlled by the actions of the confederates, no matter who was "behaving."

Societies have in fact found it surprisingly easy to get ordinary people to attack, kill, and support the killing of others, by combining authoritative sanction and peer conformity. Sometimes people even realize the power that situations can have in producing authoritarian behavior. During the trial of Lt. William Calley for leading the My Lai massacre, pollsters found that most Americans said *they* would have obeyed orders to kill women and children in Viet Nam if they had been ordered to do so. Similarly, most of the Canadian soldiers in one study said that if a Prime Minister tried to seize dictatorial power, they would obey illegal orders to close the House of Commons, arrest Members of Parliament, and shoot protestors.

II. PERSONAL DISPOSITIONS FOR AUTHORITARIAN BEHAVIOR

If people grimly concede that they probably would have acted as Milgram's subjects and Lt. Calley's troops did, that does not mean they are total cardboard and completely interchangeable in all situations in life. Sometimes situational pressures are weak, or else conflict with one another. Then our predispositions as individuals become important. For example, many people refused to fight in Viet Nam. It sometimes matters a great deal who the actors are; their personal qualities *interact* with the situational pressures.

This was also demonstrated in Milgram's extensive studies. In some conditions, it was relatively hard to defy the experimenter because the victim was out of sight, in another room. Yet eventually, about 35% of the subjects refused to do any more shocking. In other conditions, the victim was seated right beside the subject, who sometimes even had to force the victim's hand onto a shock plate to hurt him. Only 35% of the subjects could do that to the end. What was the difference between these two groups, those who defied when it was hard to defy, vs those who completely obeyed when it was hard to obey? Not in mental health, as assessed by the MMPI. But the "obeyers" scored higher on another personality test, the "Fascism Scale," developed to measure authoritarian tendencies in individuals. Where did this scale come from?

A. The Authoritarian Personality

1. The "Berkeley Researchers"

Research on authoritarianism as a personality trait began during World War II because of the rise of fascism. Erich Fromm, Abraham Maslow, and Ross Stagner made seminal contributions. But the first important scientific step was taken by researchers at the University of California at Berkeley, organized by Nevitt Sanford. The group originally set out to study anti-Semitism. They found that persons who showed an extreme dislike for Jews on questionnaires were usually quite ethnocentric in general, glorifying their "in-groups" and disparaging almost everyone else. Guided by psychoanalytic theory, the "Berkeley researchers" tried to root out the personality of the bigot. What made him tick? What made her hate?

The resulting theory of the *authoritarian personality* became a landmark in psychology. Ethnocentrism, it was proposed, originated in early childhood experiences at the hands of harsh, cold, distant parents. Aggressive impulses against such parents had to be repressed, and hidden with a reaction-formation of abject submission and overglorification. Aggression could be directed, however, onto "safe" targets such as ethnic minorities, and rationalized through projected beliefs that these minorities were hostile. Thus, prejudice was the result of displaced hostility toward hated, but feared, authorities. [*See* PREJUDICE AND STEREOTYPES.]

Assuming (as Freudians do) that early modes of adjustment persist throughout life, the resulting adult personality would be very submissive to powerful authorities *and* on the lookout for safe groups to attack. Someone very susceptible to an Adolf Hitler, in other words. Sanford and his colleagues termed this personality "pre-fascist," "anti-democratic," and "authoritarian." While the researchers had not set out to understand the kind of destructive authoritarian submission Milgram would later investigate in his laboratory, the "prejudice trail" had led straight to it. Ethnocentrism and authoritarianism were seemingly but two sides of the same coin.

Formally, the authoritarian personality was defined as the covariation of *nine* traits (e.g., "destructiveness and cynicism," "projectivity," "exaggerated concern with sex"). This model was based upon interviews with highly ethnocentric persons, who seemed to have weak egos dominated by an unholy alliance between the id and the superego. The researchers developed a test to measure the covariation of these nine traits—the Fascism (or "F") Scale that would later distinguish between Milgram's "defiers" and "obeyers." Subsequent testing indicated these traits did indeed covary, and that this elaborate, pre-Fascist syndrome could be found in many Americans.

The authoritarian personality inspired profound admiration in some quarters, and intense criticism in others. The Berkeley researchers, it turned out, had made many technical mistakes in their investigations: they used very unrepresentative samples in pivotal studies; they did not keep analysts "blind"; they worded their questionnaires in such a way that response sets such as "yea-saying" could create inter-item correlations all by themselves—whether the nine traits actually covaried or not. A certain ideological bias was also noted, in that Communists could be as "anti-democratic" as Fascists.

A blizzard of research reports appeared during the 1950s and early 1960s appraising the theory. In the end there was *no* convincing evidence for the childhood origins, for the chain-reaction of ego defense mechanisms, or for the nine-trait definition of the authoritarian personality. The F Scale had only weak validity that inevitably produced a mountain of confusing results. Discouraged researchers turned away. Ironically, at this same time newspapers were carrying stories from Saigon, the Pentagon, My Lai, and Kent State.

2. Enduring Orientations

Because authoritarianism did not go away, research eventually resumed in the field, and it will be seen that the Berkeley researchers were eventually supported on several key points. Their work is also important because it gave certain "orientations" to the field that have continued to the present.

First, the Berkeley team concentrated on a *personality* variable of authoritarianism. That has continued to be the major thrust of research in this area, even though the best explanation will eventually come from understanding how personality interacts with situations to produce authoritarian behavior. Granting this, the scientific study of authoritarianism has still focused on understanding the people who need relatively *little* pressure to place the dictates of authority over human rights, i.e., "authoritarians."

Second, research has almost always concentrated on the potential "followers" in an authoritarian movement, rather than upon those who would lead it. This is partly because followers considerably outnumber leaders, and therefore lend themselves to powerful statistical analyses and defendable generalizations. But one also notes that without supporters, demagogues are just eccentrics in the park. So the focus has been, by analogy, upon the masses at the Nuremberg rallies, not the leaders on the podium.

Finally, research on authoritarianism has almost always studied North American whites. Very little information is available on authoritarianism among minorities in the United States and Canada, nor elsewhere in the world, especially in underdeveloped nations whose sometimes democratic governments appear most likely to be overthrown.

B. Right-Wing Authoritarianism

The first three of the nine traits listed in the Berkeley model were "authoritarian submission," "conventionalism," and "authoritarian aggression." These may have been the first things noticed about the personalities of ethnocentric people. Furthermore, the items on the Fascism Scale written to capture these sentiments covaried much better in the original studies than did the items tapping the other six traits in the model. This continued to be true in subsequent studies. When this was eventually noticed, in the late 1960s, it provided an inductive basis for a simpler approach to the subject.

Right-wing authoritarianism is defined as the covariation of three kinds of attitudes in a person:

1. Authoritarian submission—a high degree of submission to the authorities who are perceived to be established and legitimate in one's society;
2. Authoritarian aggression—a general aggressiveness, directed against various persons, that is perceived to be sanctioned by established authorities.
3. Conventionalism—a high degree of adherence to the social conventions that are perceived to be endorsed by society and its established authorities.

"Authoritarianism," it should be noted, has been qualified by the phrase "right-wing," which is used in a social psychological sense, not an economic one. Right-wing authoritarians are excessively submissive to the authorities they were socialized to consider legitimate. The submission is "right-wing" in that it is given to *established* authorities and conventions.

To illustrate, the neo-Nazis in South Africa, who want to maintain white dominance, and the perpetrators of the "dirty war" in Argentina would both be right-wing authoritarians. But so also would the "hard-liners" in Russia who sought to keep the Communist Party in power, and the Chinese who approved of the massacre in Tiananmen Square. Even though Communists are economic "left-wingers,'' they would be ''right-wingers'' in the so-cial psychological sense, since they wanted to pre-serve the established authorities in Russia and China.

There *could* as well be *left*-wing authoritarians, who would be submissive to ''authorities'' advocat-ing the *overthrow* of the established order. One re-calls the Mao-quoting radicals in North America dur-ing the early 1970s. However, while one can find dogmatic zealots in ''revolutionary'' movements to-day, researchers in North America at least have had difficulty finding many *authoritarians*-on-the-left. Perhaps this is because anti-establishment individu-als are usually too rebellious to submit to anyone's authority, while submissive persons naturally tend to uphold the authorities in their lives. In any event, little is known about left-wing authoritarians.

1. The RWA Scale

Right-wing authoritarianism, so conceived, is mea-sured by a 30-item attitude scale entitled the RWA Scale. The test, first used in 1973, has been revised often because items can lose their social relevance over time. Ten of the items from the 1992 version of the scale are reproduced in Table I.

TABLE I
Ten Items from the 1992 Version of the RWA Scale

1. Our country will be great if we honor the ways of our forefathers, do what the authorities tell us to do, and get rid of the ''rotten apples'' who are ruining everything.

4. People should pay less attention to the Bible and the other old traditional forms of religious guidance, and instead develop their own personal standards of what is moral and immoral.

5. What our country *really* needs, instead of more ''civil rights,'' is a good stiff dose of law and order.

7. There is nothing wrong with premarital sexual intercourse.

12. Obedience is the most important virtue children should learn.

15. Government, judges, and police should never be allowed to censor books.

19. Children should be taught to ask ''why?'' and to decide things for themselves, not simply to do what they are told.

26. The *real* keys to the ''good life'' are obedience, discipline, and sticking to the straight and narrow.

27. We should treat protestors and radicals with open arms and open minds, since new ideas are the lifeblood of progressive change.

28. More than anything else, our country needs a strong leader who will do *whatever* is necessary to cut out the malignancy that is ruining us.

Subjects are told the statements comprise a survey of general public opinion concerning a variety of social issues, and are asked to respond to each item on a -4 to $+4$ basis. Half the items on the test (e.g., Nos. 1, 5, 12, 26, and 28) are worded in the ''pro-trait'' direction, where agreement indicates authori-tarianism. For the remainder, the authoritarian an-swer is to disagree.

This balancing against direction-of-wording ef-fects cannot keep response sets such as ''yea-saying'' from affecting peoples' answers to each item. But it does keep such artifacts from influencing *summed* scores on the instrument. This is quite im-portant, because response sets can otherwise pro-duce more variance in scores on a psychological test than the trait supposedly being measured. This was one of the basic problems with the Fascism Scale, and affects many other instruments as well. Balanc-ing a test with con-trait items also helps disguise its purpose. Respondents can almost never tell what the RWA Scale is ''about'' or ''after.''

Which of the three defining elements is tapped by Item No. 1? Certainly submission to established authorities is advocated. But so also is convention-alism (''the ways of our forefathers''). And ''getting rid'' of the people ''who are ruining everything'' has definite aggressive connotations. So Item 1 seem-ingly taps all three of the defining elements. So also do many other statements on the test. This is consis-tent with the definition of right-wing authoritarian-ism, which specifies the *covariation* of the three attitude clusters. But it means one cannot produce three independent, ''pure'' subscores from the test.

a. Reliability of the RWA Scale

For a test covering many different topics, the RWA Scale has a relatively high level of internal consis-tency. The 435 inter-item correlations average about .20. This, combined with the scale's length, pro-duces an α-reliability of about .90. Test–retest reli-abilities, in turn, have ranged from .95 over 1 week to .85 over 28 weeks.

The internal consistency of responses to the RWA Scale has appeared in almost every population that has been sampled. The test was originally developed among Canadian university students, based upon earlier findings with the Fascism Scale and other measures. It was then discovered that the attitudes which covaried among these students also covaried among their parents. Then students across the United States responded with equal consistency, as did subsequent samples of the more general American public. The same pattern of responses showed up in South Africa and Australia. Surviving translation, it has also appeared in Germany and Russia.

It was not anticipated that attitudinal clusters which covaried in North America would covary elsewhere. Social attitudes ordinarily vary a lot from one society to another, and so could their organization. So the RWA Scale seems to measure a personality structure that is created in many places. But is that personality a ''right-wing authoritarian?'' Is the test valid?

b. Validity of the RWA Scale

A considerable amount of evidence indicates the RWA Scale measures right-wing authoritarianism, as defined above. Persons who score highly on the test (the top quartile of a distribution are labeled ''Highs'') have tended to support unjust acts by their governments, such as illegal searches, denial of the right to peaceful protest, and systematic police harassment. American Highs tended to support Richard Nixon to the end of the Watergate scandal, steadfastly choosing to believe him rather than the evidence that increasingly mounted against him. Afterward, they did not want Nixon put on trial for his deeds; nor have High RWAs wanted to punish police officers who beat prisoners, or military officers who authorized the deliberate killing of civilians during war.

On the other hand, Highs have been quite punitive toward ''common criminals'' when they were asked to ''play judge'' and pass jail sentences. And when subjects were given a chance to administer electric shocks (supposedly) to a peer during a fake learning experiment, right-wing authoritarians delivered significantly stronger shocks than did others.

The fundamental hypothesis of the Berkeley researchers has also been confirmed. High RWAs tend to be the most prejudiced people in the societies tested thus far. In South Africa, white Highs are quite hostile toward blacks. Russian Highs are prejudiced against the many minorities in their country. In North America, studies have revealed that High RWAs dislike Jews, blacks, Hispanics, Native Indians, West Indians, East Indians, Japanese, Chinese, Pakistani, Filipinos, Africans, Arabs, homosexuals, atheists, and feminists. (Men and women usually score equally on the RWA Scale.) Right-wing authoritarians appear to be ''equal-opportunity bigots,'' disliking most ''different'' people regardless of race, creed, or color. These prejudices tend to run alongside a streak of white supremacist belief akin to the Nazis' Aryan Superman myth.

Highs also have little love for democracy. In Russia they are against a free press, the ''dissidents,'' and democracy itself. In North America they often think they are more patriotic than anyone else; but they are susceptible to the argument that ''Americans have too much freedom, so the Bill of Rights should be repealed.'' And if the two central values of democracy are Freedom and Equality, research reveals almost everyone values Freedom highly. But High RWAs value Equality much *less* than other people do.

One series of studies asked participants whether they would be willing to someday help the government track down homosexuals, Communists, or ''radicals''—even have them tortured and executed. Most people said ''Absolutely not!'' But Highs said ''Possibly.'' This submission to authority, and potential for aggression in authority's name, is so strong in High RWAs that they were even more willing than most to join a ''posse'' to run down those ''who are too submissive to the established authorities, too aggressive in the name of authority, and too conventional'': That is, themselves.

The experiments that have painted this picture of Highs have drawn a very different picture of the bottom quartile of RWA distributions. ''Lows'' tended to object strongly to any abuse of power, no matter who was in control and who the victim was. They were inclined be moderate and even-handed in their recommended punishments for criminals, responding to the crime, not who the criminal was. Lows were usually less prejudiced than Highs, and quite opposed to suggestions to persecute any target group or ''repeal the Bill of Rights.''

This all appears very one-sided and biased, of course. But every statement above is based upon experiments in which the opposite outcome would have occurred, if it were true. No one has yet found anything very laudable about High RWAs.

How strong are the generalizations described above? The RWA Scale usually correlated .40 to .60 with these validity criteria—much better than the Fascism Scale and other measures can do. These rather solid relationships are attributable to the strengths of the individual statements on the test: ordinarily, every item on the RWA Scale—not just the summed score—correlated significantly with the criteria above. Hence, the test frequently exceeded the ''.40 ceiling'' that was widely believed in the 1970s to be the upper limit of explanation by personality tests.

But in absolute terms, correlations of .40 to .60 still leave most of the target variance unexplained.

One *cannot* say, therefore, that "prejudice and authoritarianism are just two sides of the same coin." The two are connected, but each has additional roots besides the other. Human behavior in general is usually too complexly determined, too influenced by situational factors, to be largely attributable to a single "individual difference" factor. But such factors undeniably play their roles at times.

III. THE ORIGINS OF INDIVIDUAL RIGHT-WING AUTHORITARIANISM

A. Genetic Factors

Why are some people more authoritarian than others? In general, psychologists say such personality traits result from the interaction of genetic and environmental determinants. One can advance a case for genetic factors here: submission to those higher in status is very common in animal societies. So humans may have inherited genes from their primate ancestors that (for example) affect the ease with which fear is experienced through the sympathetic nervous system, and hence submit to others. [*See* BEHAVIORAL GENETICS.]

Thus far, however, the search for genetic determinants of authoritarianism has proved inconclusive. A large investigation of fraternal and identical twins by the University of Minnesota "Twin Study Project" found RWA correlations were equally high (about .65) in both groups. If genetic factors played a role, identical twins should resemble each other more than fraternal twins do. However a second study by the same research team found equally high RWA correlations between identical twins reared apart and identical twins reared together. This argues *for* a genetic factor.

B. Environmental Factors

The evidence for environmental factors is more conclusive. One obvious hypothesis is that (say) college students learned the attitudes tapped by the RWA Scale from their parents. And many studies have found that, while parents have appreciably higher RWA Scale scores than their children, the more authoritarian the parents are, the more authoritarian their offspring tend to be. But the correlation is only about .40. Moreover the relationship with the authoritarianism of the students' best friends is yet lower. Certain kinds of religious training also tend to

produce authoritarianism, but not that many people receive such training nowadays. High school teachers do not seem to have much effect upon their pupils' attitudes. So where did the RWA Scale answers of university students come from?

The basic answer is, from their experiences in life, through the Law of Effect. If one knows such things as (1) the extent to which students have encountered unfair authorities, or dishonest ones, or foolish ones, and (2) their reaction to whatever unconventional people and minorities they have met, and (3) the outcome of whatever "forbidden" acts the students have done, then one can make fairly accurate guesses about what these students' scores will be when they answer the RWA Scale. In fact, answers to a 24-item "Experiences Scale" correlate in the .70s with RWA Scale scores obtained independently.

C. The Resulting Explanation

Research has therefore produced quite a different "environmental" explanation, from the Berkeley model, of why some young adults are quite authoritarian, and others are just the opposite. First of all, most children are taught to be broadly submissive to authority. During adolescence, however, many teenagers experience conflict with parental authority, the school system, etc. They may experiment with prohibited behavior, and meet new, different kinds of people. They may spot hypocrisy in church, in the police, in elected officials. Depending on the outcome of these experiences, some teenagers become markedly less authoritarian, most will drop a moderate amount, while some sail right on through and remain high in the trait.

To a certain extent, High RWAs "sail on" because of their *lack* of experiences. They tend to travel in "tight circles" of like-minded persons, and to read only those things that will confirm their ideas. They are much more likely to have *memorized* their philosophy of life, than to have searched and worked it out themselves. They positively avoid "other kinds" of people. For example, authoritarian students usually dislike homosexuals, but most of them say they have never (to their knowledge) known one personally.

D. Later Developments in Life

Higher education, especially in the liberal arts, lowers authoritarianism. The High RWAs in a secular university are most likely to benefit in this way from their educations, precisely because it exposes them to the diversity of human thought and experience they had previously missed. This exposure may take place as much in dorm "bull sessions" as in the classroom.

Furthermore, educational effects seem to persevere after college graduation, so long as one remains childless. But parenthood pushes RWA Scale scores back up again. One's response to the item "Obedience is the most important virtue children should learn" changes when one has a 3-year-old who wants to play in the street. Adolescence may be a particularly authoritarian time for parents as well. Hence, in what may be a time-honored cycle, the generations may spread apart in authoritarianism because of the mutual effects they have upon one another.

Societal events can also apparently raise RWA Scale scores. Several lines of evidence suggest that economic recessions increase authoritarianism. Upheavals in urban ghettos do too. So seemingly do violent "leftist" protest movements, especially compared with nonviolent ones. But if protestors are seen to be treated harshly by the authorities, it lowers authoritarianism scores, as Mahatma Ghandi and Martin Luther King Jr. understood.

Generally speaking though, populations seem "spring-loaded" to become more authoritarian during crises, not less so. Even the crimes of Richard Nixon and the 1970 "October Crisis" in Canada (when the government suspended democratic rights because of what was later shown to be a deliberately exaggerated threat of insurrection) had very short-term effects upon people's trust of authorities.

IV. THE PSYCHODYNAMICS OF RIGHT-WING AUTHORITARIANISM

A. Why Do the Three Attitude Clusters Covary?

The first question one might ask, in trying to understand how the authoritarian mind works, is why do authoritarian submission, conventionalism, and authoritarian aggression covary in the first place? It is easy to see why the first two go together: the established authorities in a society usually endorse, and enforce, the conventions of the social system in which they are the established authorities. Those who submit to these authorities will tend to be well-drilled in the accompanying conventions. But why should submissive, conventional people also be so *aggressive?*

There are many theoretical explanations of aggression. The psychoanalytic, Berkeley model of repressed hatred of authorities might be true. Or, since frustration sometimes produces aggression, perhaps submissive, conventional persons are more frustrated than others. Maybe they just have rather fast-firing "aggression mediators" in the limbic system in the brain. [*See* AGGRESSION.]

The explanation which best accounts for authoritarians' aggression, however, is based upon Albert Bandura's social learning theory. This theory holds that hostile acts are produced in two steps. First, they are *instigated* by some aversive experience. This makes people want to attack. But people have learned many inhibitions against hurting others while growing up (e.g., "Do unto others . . ."), which must be overcome somehow for aggression to occur. So the second step involves *disinhibiting* these social learnings.

What particularly instigates and disinhibits authoritarian aggression? It turns out that submissive, conventional people are usually more fearful than others are. They think it is more likely they will be killed by a drunk driver, or catch AIDS from incidental contact, than most people do. They are particularly likely to view society as degenerating into a violent, lawless world of "Mad Max." Fear, a very aversive stimulus, often puts the authoritarian's "finger on the trigger." (which is probably why recessions and urban violence increase RWA Scale scores.)

What releases "the safety?" Self-righteousness. Almost all of us think we are morally "better than average"—an example of the self-serving bias that has been found in many situations by social psychologists. But highly submissive, highly conventional persons usually think they are *much* better than others. Thus, when they feel like attacking someone, they can often rationalize the hostility with the thought that, after all, they are "the good people" attacking "bad people" on behalf of some authority. Many High RWAs believe they are God's designated hitters on earth.

Studies have found that High RWA students are just as likely to lie and cheat to get good grades as others are. But they feel *less* guilty about the bad things they have done than Low RWAs do, because they typically purge themselves of guilt through their religious practices. Ironically, this lack of guilt leads them to feel morally better than other people can feel, and this self-righteousness then makes it easier for them to attack others.

Experiments have thus shown that if one has measured (1) how much people are afraid of a "dangerous world," and (2) how self-righteous they are, one can explain most of the connections between RWA Scale scores and many kinds of authoritarian aggression. So, in conclusion, the three kinds of attitudes that define right-wing authoritarianism covary because (1) submission and conventionalism tend naturally to go hand in hand; and (2) the fear and self-righteousness that submissive, conventional people experience lead them to be aggressive when they think some established authority would approve.

B. The Cognitive Behavior of Right-Wing Authoritarians

1. Inferences and Important Beliefs

Authoritarians are just as smart as nonauthoritarians in most respects, if one controls for educational attainment. There is no correlation between RWA Scale scores and IQ among college students. And while Highs tend to major in "applied" programs at university, their grades are just as high as everyone else's in a general course such as introductory psychology. Still, their thinking shows certain weaknesses and vulnerabilities at times.

One researcher, Mary Wegmann, frustrated by serving on a jury with "authoritarian types" who seemed to her unable to make correct inferences from the trial evidence, studied people's abilities to reach correct conclusions when facts were not explicitly stated. As predicted, High RWAs had more difficulty doing so than most. For example, the subjects were told that only *two* factors had predicted success in an army arctic training experiment—a strong desire to participate, and knowledge of how to survive in the arctic. Highs still tended to believe that "soldiers having normal weight and blood pressure proved better." (It makes sense that such soldiers might be better, so even if it was *not* found to be true, Highs were ready to conclude it.)

Secondly, authoritarians are quite capable of demanding convincing evidence before reaching conclusions. But if the issue touches upon their central beliefs, they seem to put their critical reasoning ability into neutral. Thus, they correctly rejected the proposition "The fact that airplane crashes sometimes occur when the pilots' biorhythms are at a low point proves biorhythms affect our lives." But they agreed with "The fact that archaeologists have discovered a fallen wall at the site of ancient Jericho

proves the story in the Bible about Joshua and the horns."

2. The Fundamental Attribution Error

Authoritarians are similarly gullible when someone tells them what they want to hear. This is actually an example of the part of the fundamental attribution error that notes we tend to underestimate the impact of the situation upon other people's behavior; we instead attribute what they say and do to their personalities, to the "real them." [*See* ATTRIBUTION.]

Suppose a student, enrolled in a philosophy course that taught "how to make forceful arguments on any topic," wrote an essay on homosexual rights. The essay's conclusion, *which was assigned by the teacher,* was that homosexuals were not entitled to the same rights as others were. Would the essay necessarily reveal the student's own personal views? Of course not. But High RWAs, knowing all this, concluded that was how the student really felt. Highs were not, however, nearly so ready to reach the same conclusion about an assigned *pro*-homosexual essay; then they paid attention to the situational constraints.

Similarly, suppose a political candidate came out strongly for "law and order," but only *after* he had seen a poll showing this was what the vast majority of the electorate wanted. Does the politician really believe in upholding the law? Low RWAs doubted it. In fact, Lows doubted whatever a politician said after poll results were known. But High RWAs almost completely trusted the statement. (And historically, Adolf Hitler was carried to power in the 1932 German elections after running on a "law and order" platform, despite the fact that he himself had violently tried to overthrow the German government only a few years earlier.)

Authoritarians' vulnerability to deceivers who know which tune to sing is probably based upon the "social" foundation of their belief system. Compared with Lows, Highs do not believe things so much because they have made an independent examination of the evidence, but because that is what their authorities and the rest of their "tight circle" believes. A new person professing the same beliefs, even under very compromising circumstances, is welcomed because he confirms the beliefs. This however gets the new person into the "tight circle" effortlessly, where exploitation is easy—as many religious charlatans and flag-waving politicians know.

The authoritarian's reliance upon social confirmation can produce trouble when High RWAs interact only with one another. In 1987 Canadian students participated in an "international simulation" of European affairs in which five-person groups role-played NATO against a "Warsaw Pact" team programmed to behave as NATO did. The five NATOs were either *all* High RWAs or *all* Lows. By the end of an hour the authoritarian teams had threatened their opponents ten times as much as the Low teams had, and usually had brought "Europe" to the brink of war.

3. Social Identity Influences

Authoritarians are hardly unique in using acquaintances to confirm their beliefs and attitudes. Theodore Newcomb proposed many years ago that the need to "consensually validate" ideas was one of the mainsprings of human interaction. High RWAs just seem to rely upon such validation more than others, and to base it on a narrower range of acquaintances.

This helps explain their ethnocentrism. Henri Tajfel showed that, far from being a sign of mental illness, ethnocentrism was the result of a very common process whereby individuals enhance their self-esteem by boosting the groups to which they belong. This tendency is so automatic that when people are split into two arbitrary groups—even when they are told the categorization is random—they tend to think "their group" is better than the other. This is called the minimal group effect.

Right-wing authoritarians are particularly prone to such boosting. For example, classes of introductory psychology students, taught by the same professor and assigned to their time slots more or less at random, were asked on a survey at the very beginning of the term which class would prove the smarter. Most students said, sensibly, that there was no way of knowing. But each class also had its champions, who were over twice as likely to be High RWAs as Lows.

A consequence of Highs' emphasis upon their social identity is that they greatly desire cohesiveness and loyalty from members of their "in-groups." RWA Scale scores thus correlate .60–.70 with a Group Cohesiveness Scale invented by John Duckitt, which contains such statements as "Unity means strength, and a strong united nation is absolutely essential for progress and prosperity" and "For any group to succeed, all its members have to give it their complete loyalty." This emphasis upon "sticking together" and "being a good member" helps keep those tight circles tight.

4. Compartmentalized Thinking and Double Standards

Authoritarians' thinking also seems highly "compartmentalized," in that ideas which seemingly should be related to one another appear unconnected. This allows High RWAs to believe in contradictory notions (e.g., "A person can have lots of drive and determination but still *not* get very far in life because of discrimination against their race or sex;" and "If any poor person really wanted to, he could 'pull himself up by his bootstraps' ").

This ability to think out of both sides of their heads at once is again a common human ailment of which authoritarians seem to have an extra dose. As noted before, they do not seem to have critically examined what they believe, nor thought things through very much, but instead adopted a "saying for every occasion." Thus, their ideas are often unintegrated, just as their behavior itself often lacks integrity.

Experiments have found many situations in which High RWAs use double-standards in their judgments. When playing judge in mock trials, for example, they punished a panhandler who started a fight with an accountant significantly more than an accountant who started a fight in exactly the same way with a panhandler. Similarly they severely sentenced a gay leader who attacked an anti-gay protestor, but were relatively lenient when the roles were reversed. "Left-wing" governments that abused their power were condemned much more than "right-wing" governments that did exactly the same thing.

On the international scene, American Highs thought the Soviet Union had no right to invade its neighbors to ensure friendly governments, but they thought the United States could if it wished. (Russian High RWAs had the opposite double standard.)

North American authoritarians have also endorsed contradictory principles on the issue of religion in public schools. They favor having schools in their communities regularly teach Christian beliefs, Christian morals, and encouraging students to accept Jesus Christ as their personal savior. Most Highs, in this situation, endorsed the principle "the majority in a country has a right to have its religion taught in its public, tax-supported schools."

But if asked to imagine themselves living in Israel, or an Arab state, where the government decided to do the same kinds of things with Judaism/Islam in its public schools, almost all Highs said that this would be wrong. In these cases, they adopted the principle "minority rights should be respected, and no particular religion should be taught in public, tax-supported schools.''

C. Right-Wing Authoritarians' Awareness of Themselves

One can infer that right-wing authoritarians who are first in line to join a ''posse'' after right-wing authoritarians are not as self-aware as they might be. And this has been shown in many experiments. For example, if people who have answered the RWA Scale are then told what it measures, and asked to guess their scores, Lows usually guess they would score low, ''Middles'' usually guess they would be in the middle, but Highs almost always think they would be Middles or even Lows. Highs also think *''I'm not prejudiced.''*

To a certain extent, this is quite understandable in terms of social comparison processes. We basically infer relative standing on a trait by comparing ourselves to our acquaintances. If most of those acquaintances are pretty authoritarian, or prejudiced, it is easy to conclude one is ''average.''

But High RWAs also *want* to be ''average'' in most respects. They value being ''normal,'' as a goal in life, more than others do. And when persons who had answered an attitude scale were shown the average responses to each statement, and then invited to answer it again, Highs shifted more than twice as much toward the middle as Lows did. So High RWAs want to be normal, and this desire may help blind them to ways in which they are not.

There is additional evidence authoritarians are reluctant to ''face facts'' about themselves. If you ask university students to name anonymously three things they are reluctant to admit about themselves, Lows usually can do it, but Highs usually cannot. They go on to say there's simply nothing to report, because they are perfectly honest with themselves. Which would make them very rare human beings, if true.

However, in one experiment students who had answered a self-esteem scale were given (for a few minutes, until dehoaxed) false scores that made them very low, or very high in self-esteem. Then they were asked if they wanted information that proved high self-esteem scores predicted success in life. Most Low RWAs (about 65%) asked for this information, whether they had gotten good *or* bad news about their self-esteem. So did 73% of the High RWAs who had been told they had good self-esteem. But only 47% of the Highs who had gotten bad news wanted to learn about the implications.

Nevertheless, other studies have indicated some authoritarian minds have a more honest, if less ''available'' layer. If you ask Highs, on a −4 to +4 scale, if they believe in God, nearly all will answer ''+4'' and some will write down ''+5.'' But if you ask these same Highs the same question, *in very private, secret circumstances*, about a third of them will reveal they have doubts about God's existence, doubts they have never revealed to anyone else.

High RWAs are usually under considerable pressure to profess belief in their religion, so it is not surprising that they would keep any doubts about it in a very secret ''compartment.''

V. RIGHT-WING AUTHORITARIANISM AND RELIGION

Research has revealed many strong relationships between right-wing authoritarianism and religious variables. To begin, certain kinds of religious training apparently teach authoritarian submission, conventionalism, and authoritarian aggression, and thus produce authoritarianism. This helps explain the well-established finding that persons raised in no religion usually have lower RWA Scale scores than those who received religious training. Among the latter, persons raised in Judaism are typically less authoritarian than those from Christian backgrounds. Catholics and Protestants do not differ much overall, but within Protestantism those raised in ''liberal'' sects have lower mean RWA Scale scores than Baptists, Mennonites, Jehovah's Witnesses, and other ''conservative'' sects. As these differences remain when one controls for educational attainment, it seems likely some religions instill greater authoritarianism in their members than do others.

But if certain kinds of religious training produce authoritarianism, it also appears (predictably) that the more authoritarian one is, for whatever reason, the more one accepts one's home religion. Thus, for all faiths tested thus far, the authoritarian members tend to be the ''true believers.'' They are more orthodox in beliefs, they attend church more, they pray and read scripture at home more than others in their religion do.

Still, religious orthodoxy per se is *not* correlated with prejudice and the other more destructive aspects of right-wing authoritarianism. That is, scores on a Christian Orthodoxy Scale (that essentially measures belief in the Nicene Creed) do not correlate at all with prejudice scores, hostility toward homosexuals, willingness to join "posses," or being extra punitive when playing judge in mock trials. Just as there are many Christians who are Low RWAs, there are many Christians who believe the teachings of their faith and who are quite *unprejudiced*, etc. What is the religious difference between them and prejudiced, authoritarian Christians?

It turns out the difference does not depend so much upon the particular religious beliefs held, as upon a person's *attitudes toward those beliefs*. On the one hand, some people hold that their religious beliefs are the fundamental, essential, inerrant, God-given truth about humanity and deity, and all other beliefs are inferior. These people score highly on a Religious Fundamentalism Scale developed by Bruce Hunsberger, and they also score highly in authoritarianism *and* prejudice, readiness to join posses, and so on.

On the other hand other Christians, while having the same basic religious beliefs, do not see them in such absolute, ethnocentric terms. They score low on the Religious Fundamentalism Scale, low on the RWA Scale, and low in prejudice, etc. Such persons also score highly on a Religious Quest Scale developed by Daniel Batson, that measures the extent to which one sees religion as a way of asking "the important questions about life," and searching for the truth, whatever it may be, rather than memorizing what the authorities present.

VI. RIGHT-WING AUTHORITARIANISM AND POLITICS

Compared with religion, rather weak connections exist between people's RWA Scale scores and their political party preference. In Canada, High RWAs tend to support the Conservative Party, while Lows tend to vote for the New Democratic Party, or to be Independents. In the United States, High RWAs tend to be Republicans, and Lows either Democrats or Independents. But in both countries there are so many exceptions to these generalizations, that they predict little.

Of course, many people have no interest in politics, and no idea what the parties stand for. If one just looks at more interested, and knowledgeable citizens, much stronger tendencies (along the same lines above) emerge. And when one measures the authoritarianism of politicians themselves, very large differences appear. For example, in studies of four Canadian provincial legislatures in which lawmakers answered the RWA Scale, the correlation between their scores and being a New Democrat vs being a Conservative was .75. Usually, the New Democrat in a legislature with the highest RWA Scale score was still less authoritarian than the Conservative with the lowest score.

The difference between Democrats and Republicans in state legislatures is not so dramatic, but it is nonetheless solid. In a study of 40 Houses of Representatives and 9 Senates during 1990–1993, in which altogether 1233 lawmakers participated, the overall correlation between party affiliation and RWA Scale scores was .41. Republican caucuses almost always scored on the high end of the scale, while Democrats ranged enormously (with their high scores coming from the southern and southwestern states).

Party affiliations aside, these RWA Scale scores proved quite predictive of stands on many issues. Authoritarian legislators tended to have "conservative" economic philosophies: they believed the government should stay out of the economy, and that rich people should have their taxes lowered. They wanted to restrict abortion to cases of rape, incest, and threats to the mother's life—or not allow abortion in *any* cases. At the same time, they favored using and extending capital punishment.

High RWA lawmakers had very strong double standards about American and Russian actions. They favored legislation requiring Christian religious instruction in public schools. They were against imposing stiff fines upon companies that polluted the environment. They were opposed to stiffer gun control laws. They were against spreading the wealth of the United States much more evenly among the population. They were against the Equal Rights Amendment, and against affirmative action programs in hiring state employees. They favored a law that would have restricted anti-war protests "to certain sizes, times and places—generally away from public view."

The correlation between legislators' RWA Scale scores and their level of prejudice was .71—the largest relationship ever obtained between these two variables. The correlation between lawmakers' authoritarianism and their favoring legislation that would *reduce* freedom and equality in the United States was .84.

VII. PROTECTING SOCIETY FROM RIGHT-WING AUTHORITARIANISM

Can scientific research show ways to help reduce authoritarians' fears and prejudices, and help protect democratic institutions against their worst inclinations?

One is helped in this regard, both ethically and practically, by the fact that authoritarians themselves do not want to be so authoritarian. Experiments have found that when High RWAs learn they are High RWAs, they are upset and want to change. They do not usually want to become Lows, but they would like to be "average."

Highs are not apt to dwell upon their shortcomings, however, so one cannot simply give people the RWA Scale and tell them their scores—ethically and practically. But democratic societies can take steps to minimize the implicit threat posed by people who want "a strong leader who will do *whatever* is necessary."

For example, anti-discrimination laws can be quite beneficial. Authoritarians are more likely to obey laws they do not like than are nonauthoritarians, and such laws—when enforced—can bring Highs into equal-status contact with the different kinds of people they otherwise avoid in their tight circles. Thus, it has been found that authoritarian students who get to know a homosexual almost always become more accepting of gays and lesbians as a group.

Since secular higher education also expands Highs' orbits, a society that values its democratic institutions will make sure such education is as available as possible.

Newspapers that value freedom of the press will resist the temptation to overplay the "crime and violence" stories, which unnecessarily increase fear of a dangerous world in their communities.

Churches that value freedom of religion will move from a "fundamentalist" to a "quest" orientation. Dictatorships almost always close down churches, or get them under their control, as quickly as they seize the universities and media.

Reformers who value the right to protest will demonstrate nonviolently, and resist provocations to become violent. Outbursts of rage by reformers *increase* the sentiments in society they are trying to reduce.

The defense against the loss of democracy is twofold. Keep situational pushes toward dictatorship in check with solid institutional safeguards, such as the division of powers. And secondly, produce more persons who can be characterized by integrity, tolerance, and dedication to "liberty and justice for all."

Bibliography

Adorno, T. W., Frenkel-Brunswik, E., Levinson, D. J., and Sanford, R. N. (1950). "The Authoritarian Personality." Harper & Row, New York.

Altemeyer, B. (1988). "Enemies of Freedom." Jossey-Bass, San Francisco.

Christie, R., and Jahoda, M. (Eds.) (1954). "Studies in the Scope and Method of The Authoritarian Personality." Free Press, New York.

Duckitt, J. (1992). "The Social Psychology of Prejudice." Praeger, New York.

Stone, W. F., Lederer, G., and Christie, R. (Eds.) (1992). "Strengths and Weaknesses: The Authoritarian Personality Today." Springer-Verlag, New York.

AUTISM

Raymond G. Romanczyk
State University of New York at Binghamton

Glossary

Asperger's syndrome A developmental disability that may be related to autism. It is characterized by relatively good intellectual and language functioning, but in the presence of significant impairment of social interaction.

Autism A syndrome that is defined by behavioral deficits and abnormalities across all major areas of functioning. It is a developmental disability that typically occurs within the first 2 years of birth.

Echolalia The repetition of another person's verbalizations, in whole or in part, that may also be immediate or delayed in time. In the extreme form, even the speaker's intonation, pitch, and accent are mimicked very precisely.

Gaze aversion The active turning away from another individual so as to not make eye contact. This is an active process as opposed to the passive response of not making eye contact.

Self-injurious behavior Repetitive stereotyped behavior that due to its topography, frequency, location, or intensity produces physical damage. Examples include head banging, self-slapping, scratching, eye gouging, and self-biting.

Self-stimulatory behavior Repetitive and rhythmic behavior that appears to have no functional purpose with respect to the environment. Examples are body rocking, twirling in a circle, movement of fingers in front of the eyes, and hand flapping. Self-stimulation can also be much more subtle and may include such activities as swishing saliva in the mouth and subtle motor movements such as rubbing a particular spot on one's body.

AUTISM is a developmental disorder that typically affects all major areas of functioning, with severity between areas and across individuals having a broad range of expression. Historically it has been associated with early onset, typically appearing by age $2\frac{1}{2}$. It is not a disease entity but rather a syndrome defined by behavior characteristics and patterns, and therefore most probably has multiple etiologies rather than a single causative factor. Autism remains a controversial disorder with respect to diagnosis, etiology, and treatment strategies.

There are frequent examples of outrageous claims and distortions made by professionals, advocates, and the media. The tremendous gap between basic and applied research with typical clinical and educational practice, as well as treatment fads, places autism in a unique category. It often has severe impact upon individuals and families, is clinically complex, has an unusually large quantity of research relative to its prevalence, and is unmatched in the confusion, distortion, and fraud found in service delivery.

I. PERSPECTIVE

A. Historical Overview

Leo Kanner is credited with first defining the syndrome of autism in 1943. Kanner identified the syndrome and differentiated it from other severe disorders. As part of his work, it is perhaps unfortunate that he chose the term "autism," as this term is also associated with a description of social withdrawal in schizophrenia. However, Kanner appears to have actually had a slightly different perspective than the typical use of the term withdrawal. Indeed it is interesting that there still persists a popular image of individuals with autism being withdrawn and retreating from social interaction. Kanner used the description "aloof" which perhaps better describes the feeling of detachment one has in examining social interactions of individuals with autism.

Kanner identified a number of characteristics that he associated with the syndrome of "early infantile autism." They were: aloof, an intense desire to maintain sameness, normal–alert expression, avoids eye contact (gaze aversion), may appear deaf and/or blind, no anticipatory reaching out from infancy, does not initiate sounds or gestures for communication, does not use speech for communication, competency in use of objects, normal intelligence, normal motor coordination, and an apparent absence of common childhood behaviors such as bed wetting, thumb sucking, and nail biting.

In his description of the 11 children that he presented, he noted considerable variation in the number and severity of behaviors observed, but he conceptualized the syndrome as primarily an "autistic disturbance of affective contact" and later he utilized the term "early infantile autism." Importantly, however, he saw the primary feature as the inability to relate to other people and situations from the beginning of life. This emphasis on the presence of autism from birth was maintained by Kanner when he stated in 1971 that the primary characteristics for autism are "(a) the children's inability from the beginning of life to relate themselves to people and situations in the ordinary way, and (b) an anxiously obsessive desire for the preservation of sameness." However, as several researchers have commented, the effect of Kanner's evolving focus on social isolation and preservation of sameness reduced the number of salient characteristics thought to be part of the syndrome, and thus actually served to contribute to an overly broad diagnostic criteria.

B. Diagnosis

The diagnostic criteria for autistic disorder utilized by the *Diagnostic and Statistical Manual,* version III, revised, of the American Psychiatric Association (DSM-III-R) is the current *de facto* standard. The criteria are divided into three major areas and comprise a total of 16 items. The three areas are:

A. Reciprocal social interaction
B. Communication and imaginative activity
C. Limited repertoire of activities and interests

A diagnosis of autistic disorder may be made if 8 of the 16 items are present with the added stipulation that there are at least 2 of the 5 items from A, 1 of the 6 items in B, and 1 of the 5 items from C. It is critical to note that onset before 30 months of age

is *not* a necessary item for the diagnosis using DSM-III-R, but *was* a necessary item for DSM-III.

Since there is no specific test or quantitative measure associated with each item, there is latitude for judgment and interpretation that attenuates reliability of diagnosis. For example, item 5 from area A, "a gross impairment in the ability to make peer friendships," and item 5 from area C, "distinctively restricted range of interests and a preoccupation with a single, narrow interest," are illustrative of the intent to describe a set of behavioral characteristics, but also illustrate the degree of interpretation needed in each case. Further, none of the items are uniquely associated with autism, which highlights autism as a syndrome, a pattern of behaviors. The poor and changing criteria, as well as the presence of numerous other diagnostic systems and criteria, present severe challenges, clinically and methodologically, to the field, and require cautious interpretation of research and clinical findings. There is also an evolving effort to differentiate specific subgroups of autistic-like disorders within a broader clustering of developmental disorders which emphasize language and social interaction deficiencies. One such example is Asperger's syndrome, which is viewed by some as a distinct disorder very similar to autism except that intellectual functioning is only minimally impaired, and by others as an example of the heterogeneous range of autism.

It should not be surprising that poor diagnostic reliability for autism has been consistently observed. In 1971, DeMeyer *et al.* compared five different diagnostic systems for childhood schizophrenia and autism and concluded that while the diagnostic systems permitted good differentiation between what they termed "psychotic" and "nonpsychotic" groups, there was poor differentiation within the "psychotic" groups. They state that "in the absence of a well-proven biological indicator of the kind which identifies Down's syndrome or phenylpyruvic ketonuria, all authors must include careful descriptions of the subjects in clinical reports and research."

While DSM-III-R is without question the current standard for a diagnostic classification, it remains flawed with respect to providing an accurate diagnostic system for autism and each revision brings its own specific set of problems. There remain several other classification systems and diagnostic checklists which also have their strong and weak features. This once again underscores the difficulty of interpreting research and even descriptive studies concerning individuals with autism. This problem will no doubt continue to plague the field for many years to come.

C. Demographics

The prevalence rate for autism is a controversial topic. The Autism Society of America defines autism as a life-long developmental disability that "typically" is manifested by the age of 3 years and is presumed to be a neurological disorder. It is described as occurring in approximately 15 per 10,000 births. However, other estimates, place the rate at 1 per 20,000 to a rate of 27 per 10,000.

The central problem of course lies in the diagnostic criteria. There is a lack of a clear consensus and criteria have changed over time. While at the moment DSM-III-R is the *de facto* standard, the changes from DSM-III are significant, and further changes are forthcoming in DSM-IV. This difficulty in precisely defining and then measuring the syndrome results in profound difficulty in estimating prevalence, and also becomes a critical factor in evaluating etiological and treatment research. It is often the case in research on autism that the heterogeneity of the population and the poor diagnostic and subject selection criteria render cross-study comparisons most difficult.

Quite separate from diagnosis and related prevalence are systems used by individual states to identify children in need of special educational services. As an example, New York State uses a classification system of 11 "handicapping conditions," one of which is autism. The definition used for classification of autism is "A pupil who manifests a behaviorally defined syndrome which occurs in children of all levels of intelligence. The essential features are typically manifested prior to 30 months of age and include severe disturbances of developmental rates and/or sequences of responses to sensory stimuli, of speech, of language, of cognitive capacities, and of the ability to relate to people, events and objects." As of December 1991 there were 2,613,938 children in public schools and 469,058 in private schools in New York with 2,084 having been classified as having autism (these figures do not include preschool age children). This yields a rate of 6.6 per 10,000 children. Thus, depending upon one's point of view and which prevalence estimates one chooses, it could be argued that New York is using a reasonably accurate system of identification, or that children

with autism were being significantly over- or underestimated.

D. Primary Clinical Characteristics

The primary clinical characteristics of autism may be clustered into the broad domains of

(a) social behavior
(b) language
(c) cognitive development
(d) interaction patterns
(e) reaction to the environment
(f) behavioral repertoire

1. Social Behavior

Unusual or deficient social development is a hallmark of autism. Simple behaviors such as enjoying caresses or showing affection to a few individuals are often mistakenly taken out of context as an indicator that the child does not have autism. However, overall social development must be assessed rather than only a few specific behaviors. This includes making friendships with same-aged peers, playing games, rule-following and turn-taking, failure to initiate interactions and preferring isolate to social activities, poor emotion recognition and inappropriate or absent responding to another's emotional display, and poor anticipatory behavior to social interaction, such as an infant failing to reach out to a parent when the parent moves to pick up the child. Careful observation of interactions are critical to ascertain possible factors that if not recognized could obscure interpretation. Examples would be a child who apparently enjoys "cuddling" but is actually reacting only to specific tactile stimulation rather than the social aspects, or a child who might be described as enjoying simple games such as "patty cake" where in fact the child is simply engaging in self-stimulatory clapping and smiling in response to the hand movements and not the social interaction.

2. Language

Perhaps one of the areas of development that clearly illustrates the wide range of impairment for autism is language development. Approximately half of children with autism do not develop spoken language, while the remainder often develop isolated words and phrases but the communicative ability is weak. As an example, an individual with autism may have a reasonably large vocabulary and can be heard to imitate various conversations that have been overheard, but appears unable to engage in simple verbal social reciprocity such as saying "good morning" in response to the greeting of another person, or to make simple requests such as "pass the butter" or "please turn down the radio."

It is not unusual, however, both for verbal and nonverbal individuals to use a nonverbal means of indicating particular wants via taking one's hand and moving it toward the desired item. It is important to differentiate this type of "communication" from use of gestures as part of language and communication. In one sense, using another person's hand could be seen as a form of prompting, whereby the individual with autism is simply moving one's hand in the direction of an item and this relies on one's ability to guess what in fact the specific target it. Inaccuracies in guessing can often form the basis for very stressful interactions and can precipitate severe emotional outbursts on the part of the individual with autism and great frustration on the part of the individual attempting to understand the request being made. [See GESTURES; NONVERBAL BEHAVIOR.]

One may also observe what may be termed "language self-stimulation." That is, sounds, words, and phrases are repeated in rhythmic fashion and appear to serve no particular purpose other than providing simple sensory feedback. At somewhat more sophisticated levels, this can be observed in what may appear to be ritualistic behavior with respect to certain counting sequences, letters of the alphabet, or more esoteric sequences such as names of people or descriptions of events or memorization of almanac-type information. This is typically easily differentiated from the "special interest" activities of many typical individuals, such as baseball statistics, dinosaur names, flora or fauna identification, etc. That is, the individual with autism appears to engage in this repetitive and at times rhythmic activity in a very self-directed fashion that is quite different than the more socially directed or shared aspects seen in typical individuals.

3. Interaction Patterns

One striking characteristic of many individuals with autism is the pattern of interaction with other individuals and the physical environment. When interactions take place they are typically characterized by a highly stereotyped interaction that is of short duration. Because of the at-times apparent intense desire to maintain consistency in the environment, social interactions in particular can be very difficult and apparently anxiety provoking. This can extend to simple physical contact, physical proximity, the type of words and phrases used in a greeting, and even to the clothing and mannerisms of the interacting party. In contrast, one often observes good competency in the use of objects and devices in the environment. However, under close inspection, one may observe that in fact this competency stems from lack of distress over the rigidity of objects and devices. As an example, playing a simple video game over and over again or assembling and disassembling a toy can persist for extended periods of time. While on the surface it might appear constructive or normative, the enjoyment is more of a function of the repetition *per se* than the value of the activity.

One very striking aspect of interaction with many individuals with autism is the apparent lack of eye contact. It appears that this lack of eye contact is an active process in that eye contact is avoided. This can be seen in infants whereby if one holds the infant in front of one's face, the infant will turn to the side and if one repositions the infant's body again to make face to face contact, the infant turns away again. Thus, in educational and habilitative training programs it is quite typical to observe a strong component of attempting to teach the individual with autism to initiate and maintain eye contact. Interestingly, however, although this is a very frequently observed behavior deficit in autism, there is relatively little research that has been conducted. Research in our own laboratory is indicating that the actual frequency of eye to eye contact may not be deficient as much as it is the timing and context of the eye to eye contact which seems to separate individuals with autism.

4. Environmental Reactions

Although rarely quantified, common anecdotal reports of individuals with autism describe unusual reactions to environmental stimuli. One may observe an individual who is hypo- or hyperresponsive to sounds in the environment, is particularly uncomfortable in the presence of strong natural light, or is extremely reactive to tactile stimuli such as the texture of clothing or heat and cold. With respect to hyposensitivity, in some instances parents may suspected the child was deaf or blind because of lack of responsivity to auditory or visual stimuli. Thus, a child's lack of reaction may be so complete that it can mimic a severe sensory loss.

These unusual reactions often present a serious task for assessment in attempting to ascertain what the individual does and does not respond to and what aspects of the environment may or may not be causing distress. With respect to the former, a simple example may provide insight to the utilization of nonstandard assessment procedures. In an initial assessment of a young boy with autism whose parents believed him to have a severe hearing impairment, one could stand behind the child and take two wooden blocks and sharply bang them together and no startle response or reaction on the child's part was observed. However, it was also noted that when a staff member who was some distance behind the child opened a soda can with its characteristic pop sound, the child immediately oriented toward the source of that sound. The second aspect, that is ascertaining environmental events that may cause distress or unusually intense reaction, is typically a more difficult task. In particular it is important to tease apart the actual physical stimulus from the social interaction that is often confounded with such stimuli. For example, one might observe a child having an intense reaction to musical instruments being played and as part of "circle time" in a preschool program. One should not, however, necessarily assume that it is the instruments *per se*. For example, the reaction could be due to the fact that during circle time the teacher or teacher's aide typically sits near the child and may be in physical contact with the child to enhance participation, and thus the child is reacting more to the physical contact than to the musical instruments. This type of confounding is common and can often lead to false conclusions as it is subject to the biases of the observer with respect to what are presumed to be salient vs nonsalient stimuli.

5. Cognitive Development

Kanner noted that the original children in his sample looked normal and alert and he speculated that perhaps they were functioning at a near normative intellectual level. In fact, IQ assessment, as indexed by nonverbal assessments such as the form board, indicated relatively good functioning. Thus, on a number of performance measures, one may not see severe impairment and in fact often times individuals with autism may have some areas of particular skill or ability that may serve to provide the impression that functioning level is higher than it actually is. When a broad-based assessment that incorporates language elements and other symbolic and relational processing is used, it is clear that the majority of individuals with autism are significantly intellectually impaired. While there certainly are individuals with autism who function at the near normative intellectual level, this reflects probably less than 10% of the population. [*See* COGNITIVE DEVELOPMENT; INTELLIGENCE.]

6. Behavioral Repertoire

It is important to view maladaptive or unusual behavior in the context of the individual's complete repertoire. For example, humans (and primates for that matter) engage in many forms of self-stimulatory behavior (stereotyped, rhythmic actions that do not serve a functional environmental purpose but seem rather to only provide sensory input). However, while the individual with autism may display similar behavior, it is made significant because of the large proportion of the repertoire that it comprises. Many typical children engage in head-banging, temper tantrums, rocking, and attachment to certain objects, but for the individual with autism, these may represent a major proportion of their repertoire as opposed to the very small proportion for typically developing children.

For many individuals with autism their behavioral repertoire is characterized both by deficits in behavior, such as the absence of normative behavior, either specifically such as eye contact or more generally such as poor inhibitory mechanisms to modulate behavior, and by the presence of behavior excesses that can be extreme in nature. Self-stimulatory and self-injurious behavior are two common examples. Both self-stimulatory and self-injurious behavior may have strong self-reinforcement aspects as well as having a component that is functionally related to environmental variables. However, the clinical impression is often one of the persistent intensive behavior that is not environmentally regulated or motivated. Certainly examples of individuals who engage in severe head-banging to the point of retinal detachment, self-slapping, biting, and scratching that produces severe tissue damage all can reach an intensity and frequency such that environmental explanations appear to be not relevant. However, even given the strong possibility that certain of these behaviors may be physiologically mediated, such as through endorphin production, the role of environmental factors, although not often easily observable, has been demonstrated to play a very clear and significant role in the etiology and maintenance of such extreme behavior patterns.

II. ETIOLOGY

A. Psychogenic

The psychogenic hypothesis, that autism is caused by an emotional disturbance involving child/parent interactions, has been historically the dominant etiological theory. Indeed, this hypothesis is still expressed today and is the basis for numerous treatment strategies. This is quite ironic as Kanner was not a proponent of the psychogenic hypothesis, although he is mistakenly associated with it. In fact, Kanner has stated that "As for the all-important matter of etiology, the early development of the 11 children left no other choice than the assumption that they had "come into the world with an innate disability to form the usual, biologically provided contact with people." Kanner laments that he has erroneously been referred to as proposing a psychogenic origin for autism. In fact, Kanner has stated "One can now say unhesitatingly that this assumption has become a certainty."

Current research is unequivocal in its lack of support for the psychogenic hypothesis and it cannot be overstressed the degree to which perpetuation of this hypothesis does significant harm to families. The syndrome of autism is extremely serious and presents tremendous stress and challenge for families. The added burden of laying etiological blame at the foot of parents is inexcusable given the status of the last several decades of research. At this time clinging to the psychogenic hypothesis reflects clearly a biased and distorted view rather than an objective review of the research literature.

B. Neurobiological

The research evidence clearly points to a neurobiological basis for autism. In 1964, Rimland was the first to systematically describe the possible neurobiological processes that might contribute to the etiology of autism. Since that time, there has been steady and incremental work in this area. Unfortunately, it has been greatly hampered by the difficulties of diagnosis mentioned above. Thus, comparison across research studies is difficult and the continuing problem of defining appropriate control groups remains a hindrance to proper interpretation of research data. Nevertheless, the following are some of the major areas of research that attempt to address the neurobiological etiology of autism:

Neurochemical—dopamine, serotonin,
   epinephrine, norepinephrine, peptides,
   endogenous opioids
Neurophysiological abnormalities
Pre- and postnatal insult
Neuropathology
Immunological abnormalities

At first a review of the varied research on neurobiological etiology might lead one to conclude that the data are too inconsistent and too diverse to be of significant impact. In part this is true once again given the extreme problem with diagnostic consistency. However, by acknowledging that autism is in fact a syndrome and that one is necessarily going to have continued difficulty in definition if the criteria focus exclusively on behavior then much of the research on neurobiological aspects of autism can actually be seen as an attempt to find important biological markers to compliment the heretofore reliance on behavioral indicators. Indeed, one would expect to find in the not too distant future somewhat of a reversal of current research emphasis; rather than studying what are clearly heterogeneous groups of individuals with the diagnosis of autism in attempts to find common neurobiological factors, over time certain consistent neurobiological markers may be identified and then the behavioral similarities of individuals with these markers will be assessed. Thus, while at present it may be premature to speak of specific subgroups of autism, there is little doubt that this is the direction in which future research will lead.

C. Hereditary Factors

The role of genetics in autism has long been a topic of debate and concern. In attempts to understand etiological mechanisms, the complex role of genetics has received a great deal of attention. Clearly, the mechanism of inheritance is not simple mendelian transmission, and it is not a strong factor in terms of probability of inheritance. This complicates the pragmatic issue of genetic counseling for parents who have a child with autism and who wish to know the probability of having another child with autism.

Until recently, it has generally been estimated that approximately 2–3% of siblings are affected. If one uses the figure of 4.5 per 10,000 for the rate of autism, then it can be roughly estimated that families with a child with autism have a 50–100 times greater chance of having another child with autism as compared to nonaffected families. However, this is a complex area of research and involves parental decision to not attempt further pregnancies after the birth of a child with autism and, as has been mentioned previously, the critical nature of the diagnostic criteria utilized. In 1989, a research report by Ritvo *et al.* significantly increased the estimate of the probability of a second child having autism to a factor of perhaps 200–300 times greater than the norm. Further, when one looks beyond a strict definition of autism, but rather includes other disorders that affect cognitive and language functioning, there is now speculation that rates could be in the 25% range for families. At the moment, however, conclusions must remain tentative and large-scale research projects are required to establish these probabilities. However, as more and more emphasis is being placed upon hereditary factors and as methodological problems are being more adequately controlled, it appears that there may be a generalized inheritance for language and cognitive disorders that are expressed in various fashion and degrees, one of which is autism.

D. Summary

Research on etiological factors produces consistently inconsistent results. In discussing neurophysiological studies, some researchers reporting strong effects for prolonged brain stem transmission time, while other studies find no such effect for any of their subjects. Consistent neurobiological abnormalities are conspicuously absent.

III. TREATMENT CHALLENGES

Autism, to a degree unlike any other disorder, seems to be plagued by a continuing series of unsubstantiated treatments and interventions that at times border on the bizarre. This pattern of a new "cure" being found every year or two reflects the intense distress often found in families as they search for an effective intervention, and the poor state of the research literature and particularly diagnostic systems, so that reports of one or two individuals purportedly achieving significant treatment gains are then overgeneralized and capitalized upon.

It can be said with extreme clarity and confidence that there are no simple "miracle cures." It can also be said with confidence that the most effective strategy in providing significant habilitation for individuals with autism comes from an intensive and sophisticated behavioral/educational approach. However, this is not to be confused with typical special education services or the stereotype of behavior modification techniques. Rather, the requirement is for a comprehensive and highly choreographed intensive intervention that addresses directly the wide array of deficits displayed by the individuals with autism. It had been hoped by many researchers and clinicians that if significant impact could be made on one or two "key" deficit areas in autism then more generalized progress would follow in other areas. This has not been the case and speaks to the importance of providing an intervention program that directly teaches and maintains functional behavior across the many deficit domains previously discussed and directly addresses behavior excesses.

A. Maladaptive Behavior

One significant challenge that can have very serious consequences is the expression of maladaptive behavior by individuals with autism. Behaviors such as self-injury, self-stimulatory behavior, aggression, and extremely severe "temper tantrums" are not unusual and can be extremely difficult to attenuate or eliminate. Such behavior causes great distress, not only for the individual, but also for the family and others involved with the individual.

Historically, such behaviors have often been seen as "psychotic" or "irrational" and a direct result of an underlying psychopathology. However, with the benefit of several decades of intensive research, it is now clear that none of these behavior patterns is uniquely associated with autism (although the particular pattern of such maladaptive behavior and behavior deficits in autism continue to make intervention a complex and difficult process), and that such behavior patterns are indeed lawful and modifiable. Self-injurious behavior serves as a good example. At one level of analysis it seems paradoxical that an individual would produce direct physical harm to their own body. Self-injurious behavior in individuals with autism can take multiple forms including head-banging, self-biting, scratching and tearing at the skin, persistent repetitive rubbing of the skin, self-kicking, dropping forcefully to the floor on knees or elbows, etc. The range of topography is quite extensive but most often is focused upon the upper torso and head area as well as the hands and fingers. Thus, casual analysis leads to this paradox in that it is typically believed that organisms will not intentionally inflict pain upon themselves.

However, a more detailed behavioral analysis indicates striking parallels to what might be termed typical adult self-injurious behavior. For instance, when one looks past the topography of the specific behavior, such as the ingestion of extremely spicy foods that have as their base ingredients such as jalapeno peppers or certain strong forms of mustard or horseradish, they all produce very painful sensations and in fact if used in excess can cause tissue damage. Certainly the same type of analysis would hold for intense exercise that produces physical problems such as strains, bruises, and other tissue damage, and of course would include such behavior such as smoking and overeating. Perhaps one reason that such behaviors and the self-injury seen in autism are not often associated is because of the different temporal characteristics between the emission of the behavior and tissue damage, and the difference in the extensiveness of the repertoire displayed by different individuals. Thus, for most adults who would be seen to engage in "self-injurious behavior," they can provide a rationale and a justification, or more simply put, a cost–benefit analysis of their behavior. When confronted with a young child with autism who is banging his head against objects with such intensity that laceration and bleeding occur, it is difficult for most observers to ascertain any positive cost–benefit. Nevertheless, when one systematically analyzes environmental and social factors, there are very specific variables that contribute to the etiology and maintenance of self-injurious behavior which in turn can then be utilized in creating effective treatment programs. In particular, it is crucial to examine eliciting stimuli in the environment and the role of escape and avoidance mechanisms as maintaining factors for self-injurious behavior and numerous other maladaptive behaviors.

B. Language

Language development and communication are particularly problematic in autism. Even individuals who are able to speak and have a large vocabulary often do not use their speech for communicative purposes. Further, approximately half of individuals with autism are nonverbal. Certainly in the context of attempting to ameliorate maladaptive behavior, to assist the individual in modulating excessive reactions to the normally changing environment, and to attenuate the individual's desire for rigidity and sameness, language can be a very powerful therapeutic tool. Research begun in the late 1960s clearly indicated that speech and language could be taught to many individuals with autism utilizing operant learning procedures. This approach has been expanded over the last several decades such that a significant technology now exists, that when prop-

erly applied is highly successful. As an aside, however, it should be noted that this remains a controversial topic as it challenges certain schools of thought concerning language and its development. However, on the pragmatic side of therapeutic intervention, the results remain strong and consistent and will be described more fully at the end of this section.

Some of the anomalies seen in language for individuals with autism include pronomial reversal, wherein the pronoun "you" is substituted for the pronoun "I." Some have attributed lack of self-awareness and distortion of personality development to this avoidance of the use of I. However, a more parsimonious explanation has simply to do with word frequency and echolalia. The "echoing back" of speech can take several forms. The most common is partial echolalia in which bits and pieces of statements are repeated by the individual. As an example, if one were to say "Johnny would you like an apple?" the child might respond by saying "You like an apple?" Also common is delayed echolalia. This is a situation in which a child might repeat pieces of a conversation or television program from hours, days, or weeks previous. Another form of echolalia is termed full echolalia. In this more rare form the full content is echoed back including pacing and intonation. One might for instance observe an individual repeating sentences that not only are correct in their content, but also reflect the particular accents of the individuals involved.

C. Family

Parental stress is a significant factor when discussing autism. It should be noted that stress is a very different perspective than the historical view of parents of children with autism expressing greater levels of psychopathology and/or depression. This is not the case. Rather, when appropriate control groups are utilized, the factor that tends to stand out is the degree of stress parents of individuals with autism perceive that they are facing. In comparisons of stress levels of parents of autistic children to control groups, parents were found to have significantly elevated levels of stress, and parents and professionals agreed as to the relative impact of stressors although professionals overestimated family stress compared to that reported by the families. The items that were perceived as most severe in the context of its impact upon families were deficits in verbal language expression and inconsistencies in the child's abilities. [*See* STRESS.]

However, recent research has indicated that there are significant methodological problems in assessing stress and stressors in that often the two are not differentiated in many scales purporting to measure stress. That is, often items are contained that seek to determine whether a particular child behavior occurs or does not occur and then this is used to weight the total scores with respect to the assumed stress that a parent must be experiencing. Thus, while clinically there is great agreement that parents of children with autism experience significant levels of stress, it is clear that precise measurement remains at this time elusive.

In 1988, Stone and Rosenbaum examined beliefs about etiology, diagnosis, and symptoms of autism among parents, teachers, and specialists in the field of autism. They found that parents and teachers tended to over-estimate children's intellectual functioning (that is, to not view children with autism as having mental retardation) and that parents were least likely compared to the other two groups to agree that most children with autism have mental retardation. Unfortunately, both parents and teachers viewed autism as an emotional disorder with the etiology being emotional in nature. Thus, it was also the case that unlike the specialists, parents and teachers did not view autism as primarily a developmental disorder. Further, parents were more likely to believe that children would eventually outgrow their autism.

IV. OUTCOME

Outcome for individuals with autism is quite poor if one uses as the criterion independent functioning. Until quite recently, before there was as wide a range of living environments for adults with autism, estimates indicated that as many as 95% of adults with autism required residential care facilities. More recent estimates indicate that 1–2% of individuals with autism achieve what could be termed a normative adjustment and paid employment, with upward of three-fourths of individuals with autism having very poor adjustment. However, such figures need to be put into historical context with respect to the evolving range of services for individuals with autism, including educational opportunities, a diversity of living environments, supportive employment, and attempts at early intervention. Nevertheless,

even given this progress that has enhanced outcome, if one uses absolute markers of progress, rather than environmental compensation, then outcome for autism remains very poor. This is often a point of great debate and misunderstanding in that altering the environment to compensate for an individual certainly can result in a good outcome for that particular individual with respect to standard of living and satisfaction. However, this must not be confused with direct amelioration of autism. For such assessment one must use normative environments and standardized assessment instruments as the evaluation criteria.

One of the most important research projects conducted on autism established a new marker with respect to the degree to which normative functioning is achievable for individuals with autism.

In 1987, Lovaas provided at least 40 hr of one-to-one behavioral treatment per week to a group of autistic children less than 48 months of age. Two control groups received either 10 hr or less of one-to-one behavioral treatment per week or were left untreated and used to control for referral biases. As part of the treatment strategy, specific areas were targeted for intense focus. These included:

self-stimulation and other maladaptive behavior
compliance to simple verbal requests
discrimination training
imitation of nonverbal and verbal toy play
training family members as co-therapists
expressive language
abstract language
interactive play
expression of emotion
preacademic tasks
observational learning

The outcome results were striking. There was essentially no difference between the two control groups. This was perhaps somewhat surprising as most service delivery professionals would consider 10 hr of one-to-one treatment per week as high. However, for the experimental group, 47% achieved normal intellectual functioning (average 30 IQ point gain compared to control groups) and were being promoted through the normal educational system. That is, they were not placed in special education classrooms nor did they require supportive services. Also, the majority of the remainder of the children in the experimental group were participating in classrooms and programs for children with aphasia, perhaps indicating continued difficulty with language but who otherwise were making good progress in the social/emotional domain. [*See* APHASIA.]

Thus, these results mark a radical change in what must be considered as possible outcome for individuals with autism. On the cautionary side, this type of intensive treatment intervention is enormously costly with respect to personnel. It also requires great expertise to choreograph such intensive intervention, as it is not simply the application of various teaching techniques and procedures. Rather, a highly individualized and integrated series of events, strategies, and curricula must be brought together that bear upon motivational and learning deficits. Replication research is needed to clarify what are the essential components that would allow equally effective intervention that is less costly.

Bibliography

American Psychiatric Association (1987). "Diagnostic and Statistical Manual of Mental Disorders," 3rd ed., revised. Washington, DC.

Berkell, D. E. (Ed.) (1992). "Autism: Identification, Education, & Treatment." Erlbaum, New Jersey.

Cohen, D. J., Donnellan, A. M., and Paul, R. (Eds.) (1987). "Handbook of Autism & Pervasive Developmental Disorders." Wiley, New York.

Dawson, G. (Ed.) (1989). "Autism: Nature, Diagnosis, & Treatment." Guilford, New York.

DeMeyer, M. K., Churchill, D., Pontius, W., and Gilkey, K. (1971). A comparison of five diagnostic systems for childhood schizophrenia and infantile autism. *J. Autism Child. Schizophrenia* **2,** 359–377.

Frith, U. (1989). "Autism: Explaining the Enigma." Blackwell, Boston.

Kanner, L. (1943). Autistic disturbances of affective contact. *Nerv. Child* **2,** 217–250.

Kanner, L. (1971). Follow-up study of eleven autistic children originally reported in 1943.

Lovaas, O. I. (1987). Behavioral treatment and normal educational and intellectual functioning in young autistic children. *J. Consult. Clin. Psychol.* **55,** 3–9.

Maurice, K. (1993). "Let Me Hear Your Voice: A Family's Triumph over Autism." Knopf, New York.

Rimland, B. (1964). "Infantile Autism." Appleton-Century-Crofts, New York.

Ritvo, E. R., Jorde, L. B., and Mason-Brothers, A. (1989). The UCLA-University of Utah epidemiologic survey of autism: recurrence risk estimates and genetic counseling. *Am. J. Psych.* **146,** 1032–1036.

Schopler, E. and Mesibov, G. B. (Eds.) (1992). "High-Functioning Individuals with Autism." Plenum, New York.

Stone, W. L., and Rosenbaum, J. L. (1988). A comparison of teacher and parent views of autism. *J. Autism Dev. Disorders,* **15**(3), 403–414.

Wing, L. (1989). The diagnosis of autism. In "Diagnosis and Treatment of Autism" (C. Gilberg, Ed.), pp. 5–22. Plenum, New York.

AUTOBIOGRAPHICAL REMEMBERING AND SELF-KNOWLEDGE

Craig R. Barclay
University of Rochester

Glossary

Affect Affects (feelings) are essential biological emergents needed for the establishment and regulation of interpersonal relationships.

Autobiographical memory Memory for self-knowledge and self-referenced information.

Autobiographical remembering Constructive and reconstructive cognitive processes used to justify contextualized affect which renders specific and generic autobiographical memories in the present that serve some adaptive function.

Emotions Socially and culturally constructed fuzzy concepts that organize and facilitate the expression of affect in language.

Image-schemata Cognitive representations that are not as abstract as propositions (subject–verb clauses) or as concrete as mental images. They funcion as schemata, which are generic representations of recurrent activities, but they also have properties of images in that their generic properties can be visualized in concrete ways, e.g., container which has an inside, outside, and a boundary between.

Implicit theories Schematic mental structures of beliefs about the stability of some personal attribute together with rules that specify potential causes of personal transformations.

Internalization A growth process or mechanism that transforms experience into a form that is mentally represented.

Internal working models Cognitive–affect representations of early caregiving relationships that mediate children's expectations for comfort or rejection during infancy and early childhood (these models may be operative throughout the lifespan).

Intersubjectivity The mutual, and reciprocally controlling, affective flow emerging between people, especially between mothers and infants that forms the basis of attachments.

Objectification The process of making conscious and externalizing personal thoughts and feelings.

Protocultures Cultures in the making.

Provisional self Emergent selves contingent on contexts and activities.

Self-knowledge Knowledge acquired through (a) direct perception and interaction with objects, and others in the world, together with the affordances associated with each and (b) remembering, reflecting, reasoning, and the creation of meaning to form prototypic concepts of self.

Subjectification Internalizing (through speech, language, and movement) thoughts and feelings that emerge in the social, public sphere.

Transcendental self A cognitive and affective structure that exists prior to experience.

Transitional objects Symbols of internalized self-objects which are progressively elaborated introjections of caregiving figures.

AUTOBIOGRAPHICAL REMEMBERING and its relationship to self-knowledge is conceptualized within two complementary formulations. First, autobiographical memories are memories of self-referenced information and second, such recollections are knowledge acquired through varied experiences that become personally significant because they are embedded in affective, interpersonal, sociocultural, and historical contexts. In the first formulation it is assumed that *a self* exists prior to the acquisition of knowledge. Here, autobiographical memories are constituted by a *transcendental self* that gives meaning to everyday experience. Without such an entity no memories would be autobiographical. In the second, selves are composed and recomposed as emergents of remembering activities used to justify feelings and objectify past experiences. The reconstructive cognitive processes used to justify affect infuse memories with personal significance and meaning which makes memories autobiographical. On this view *provisional selves* are constituted in memories that are contingent on context and used for certain adaptive purposes.

The root metaphoric projection leading to the concept of a transcendental self is that *a self is an entity*, e.g., a mental structure like a theory or identity, whereas the metaphor for provisional selves is grounded in embodied, felt experiences and projected as *self is an emergent property of improvisational activities*, e.g., the Japanese notion of "jen" or the interpersonal context within which psychosocial equilibrium is maintained. A specific, but prototypic, metaphor for provisional selves is that *selves are vapor:* the image–schematic projection to the metaphoric source domain (known) is a container from which vapor is produced, e.g., a teapot, and the target domain (unknown) is selves. Imagine a teapot filled with boiling water. As the water boils it gives off steam or vapor. The actual patterning of the emerging vapor depends on the amount of heat, kind of teapot, especially the shape of the spout, and the environmental context the vapor enters. For instance, if there is a slight breeze, the vapor field will be different (unstable) than if there is no breeze (stable).

In traditional approaches to Western cognitive psychology, autobiographical memory is most often defined as memory for an episode from the past that is located in time and space: that is, autobiographical memory is episodic memory of the personal past. The primary theoretical concern here is with determining the accuracy with which one can temporally and spatially locate some verifiable experience. [*See* EPISODIC MEMORY.]

Alternatively, ecological approaches concerned with the adaptive uses of memory in the present are less concerned with the accuracy of memory as an archive of the past, but more with the authenticity and adaptive function of autobiographical memories in the present. There is greater concern for the verisimilitude of autobiographical reconstructions than verity. However, autobiographical memories can be reconstructed with great accuracy depending on their purpose; clearly there are certain experiences we cannot forget.

Autobiographical memory and self-knowledge conceived by an entity metaphor has led to the reification of both knowledge and self. Examples include notions of a stable self-concept and identity achieved as a commitment formed around interpersonal relationships and personal ideology as a resolution to an identity crisis. However, if autobiographical memories are seen as objectifications of reconstructive processes aligned with affect, sociocultural and historical contexts, then selves are continuous adaptive becomings. This notion is associated with a theory of existence rooted in the fundamental capacities of the subject, e.g., consciousness, affect, deep motivations, embedded with contextual factors like learned motive, culturally based ritual activities, class, race, gender, and ethnicity. Thus, autobiographical memories and self-knowledge are constituted when needed for interpersonal, e.g., the formation of friendships and other intimacies, and psychological reasons, e.g., coping with stress.

I. ACQUISITION AND REPRESENTATION OF AUTOBIOGRAPHICAL MEMORIES AND SELF-KNOWLEDGE

The perspective on autobiographical memories and self-knowledge adopted in this chapter are (a) autobiographical memories are objectifications of single and repeated embodied experiences in symbolic (language and thought), imaginable, or motoric (movement) forms that have (b) acquired personal significance through the contextualized affective tone justified by reconstructive remembering processes which lead to the acquisition and structuring of self-knowledge. Accordingly, an important acquisition mechanism underlying the cognitive construction and reconstruction of autobiographical memories is contextualized affect. Taken from a developmental viewpoint on attachments or object relations, autobiographical memories and self-knowledge emerge in comforting relationships with others that meet our deep motivational need for relatedness. In turn, such memories are subjectified as internal working models, i.e., cognitive–affective image-scehmatic representations of caregiving relationships, or transitional objects, e.g., internalized self-objects or caregiving substitutes.

Although the objectification and subjectification of autobiographical memories are initially consequences of affect, with age and experience affects (as culturally shaped concepts of emotions) are consequences of cognition as well. The existential activities of everyday life result in emergent meaningful memories used adaptively: these memories are self-knowledge which become an essential affective–cognitive matrix characteristic of an individual which is shaped and reshaped by continuous being with the world and cultural experts. Therefore, autobiographical remembering and self-knowledge creation are more processes of becoming than entities that are called up from long-term (episodic or semantic) memory when needed. The cognitive representational system must embody enactive, imaginable, and symbolic forms that are co-constituted with feelings. This means that propositions, schemata, image-schemata, and physical movement cannot be deconstructed and analyzed separately from other aspects of personness.

Evidence supporting these claims comes largely from research on affect–cognition relationships in memory for everyday autobiographical events, and studies of collective remembering done in psychology and anthropology (discussed in the next section), especially work on the acquisition of narrative skills used to reconstruct the past.

Examples demonstrating the nature of representation and acquisition of autobiographical memories are found in diary studies of everyday autobiographical memory. In the typical study, subjects are asked to keep diaries of at least two memorable events a day for extended time periods e.g., 2 months. These records are then used to construct recognition memory tests presented after short- and long-term delay intervals, e.g., 24 hours to $2\frac{1}{2}$ years, following the completion of data collection.

Each recognition test usually contains four types of test items. Three of these item types are drawn from the participant's diaries (items using either the subject's actual records or paraphrased diary entries yield replicable findings). In most studies, original items (O) are replications in meaning and descriptive information of the subject's actual diary records; meaning is held constant by not manipulating the evaluative function, i.e., the affective terms and intensifiers, of diary entries. Three types of foil (F) items are also used: evaluation (FE), description (FD), and other (FO). Evaluation foils are created by changing the evaluative function which results in test items that vary in semantic similarity (meaning) to the actual diary records from which they are derived. Descriptive foils are test items created by changing some nonevaluative, informational aspects of actual records, and OF items are taken from the diaries of a person not participating in the study.

The characteristic recognition memory response pattern is that O items are correctly identified as actual memorable events at rates approximating 94% correct following delays up to 2 years. Accuracy on these test items declines to nearly 80% after $2\frac{1}{2}$ years, but remains significantly above chance performance. Interestingly, recognition accuracy on FO items varies around a mean performance of approximately 76% correct: thus, 24% of the time subjects are claiming that memorable events reported by another person are their own. Chance performance is obtained on FD items within 24 hours following data collection and remains so for as long as recognition memory tests are given. However, FE items are correctly rejected as nonevents within 24 hours and performance is consistently above chance following 3-month delays. It therefore appears that people are much more sensitive to meaning changes than to changes in details.

In subsequent analyses it has been demonstrated that meaning changes can be scaled along a dimension of "semantic similarity," and that the correct rejection of FE items varies over time such that items high in semantic similarity are falsely identified as acutal events within 24 hours and up to delay intervals of 3 months following the completion of data collection: items low in similarity are correctly rejected following a 24-hour delay and only gradually become falsely identified as actual events over a 12-month period.

These recognition memory findings have been replicated and are consistent with the theoretical perspective taken here. Specifically, autobiographical memories are memories constituted within a cognitive–affective matrix and are represented in schematic forms. Autobiographical memories are schematized over time, and this acquisition process is governed by the meaning of everyday experiences.

It is noteworthy that in a recognition memory paradigm information is presented that creates a feeling of familiarity for the subject coupled with some degree of uncertainty that the presented information is a representation of an actual event. Incorrect responses (false alarms—verifying that an FE or FD test item is an original memory, identifying an FO item as an actual event or failing to correctly identify an original event) can result because subjects import prior knowledge to the test situation that may bias their judgment; furthermore, subjects set subjective criteria for making a decision to accept or reject a test item as an actual memory. The biases and criteria operative during a test lead subjects to make plausibility or likelihood judgments about the authenticity of each test item rather than judgments based on absolute certainty.

In addition to the pattern of recognition performance described above, subjects studied thus far tend to report greater confidence in their memory accuracy than is warranted by the data. That is, even on foil items falsely identified as actual records, subjects indicate that they are highly confident (e.g., means of 5.5 on a 7-point scale with 7 being absolute certainty) that these items represent their memory of actual events that occurred in their everyday lives. It is argued that this overconfidence coupled with the kinds of inaccuracies found in recognition studies is engendered by a culturally acquired value that one's sense of self is stable over long periods of time. One means we have for offering evidence of this value is to remember our personal history in some canonical narrative form that structures personal recollections. Stated differently, since Western culture emphasizes the achievement of a stable self-concept, especially during adolescence, people adapt to this task by assimilating narrative structures that are used as scaffolding for the reconstruction of self. Since these structures are relatively stable over time, people come to believe that their sense of self is also stable. Obviously, from the data reported above, this belief is not wholly well founded, and may be dependent upon implicit theories (i.e., schemata representing beliefs and heuristics about the condition leading to change) individuals hold regarding the stability or instability of human development. For instance, one might hold a tacit theory about the nature of lifespan development as either stable or unstable; depending on which theory is held conceptions of self as stable or unstable will result.

II. PSYCHOSOCIAL AND CULTURAL FUNCTIONS OF AUTOBIOGRAPHICAL REMEMBERING

The literature suggests that autobiographical remembering serves at least three important functions: *intrapsychic, interpersonal,* and *cultural–historical.*

These functions also reveal one of the most powerful knowledge acquisition mechanisms, namely the social–linguistic origins of knowledge. In particular, knowledge most generally is created through comparison among persons, objects, or activities on a "social plane." Initially, less knowledgeable people (novices), e.g., children, engage interactively with more knowledgeable others (experts) in goal-oriented activities, e.g., going to bed, eating. Experts provide information and structure needed to remember as well as a comfortable affective (intersubjective) "space" for interaction to occur. Early interactions of this kind involve social speech acts initiated first by the expert and then used by the novice. With increasing language abilities, novices internalize social speech acts on a "psychological plane" which becomes a base from which individually initiated productive activities can occur. One of the earliest observations of this phenomenon is in mothers speech to their nonverbal infants, and subsequently the conversations that parents have with children about what is important to remember and why, i.e., parents mark the significance of remembering certain events, and what inferences children can make from what is remembered. These kinds of activities seem to account for the early beginnings of autobiographical memories which children can use to comfort themselves when their primary caretakers are not available, or to establish new interpersonal relationships.

Accordingly, one important intrapsychic function of autobiographical remembering is comfort: remembering personally significant events can reenact soothing interpersonal relationships, and thereby function as transitional objects. Another function is reassurance: that is, through autobiographical remembering a person can reconstruct evidence that he or she is the same person (subject and self) today as in the past. Reassurance can cause a reduction in anxiety as well as a substitute for boredom. Accordingly, autobiographical remembering can structure attention in ways that facilitate the enjoyment of everyday life.

Clearly, these intrapsychic functions are not the only ones. For instance, in cases where individuals have subjectively experienced extreme trauma, autobiographical remembering can result in horrifying reenactments that increase anxiety, e.g., memories associated with panic disorders, involuntary and intrusive memories, or in extreme cases, multiple personalities. Furthermore, psychopathologies of this order seem to be associated as well with hypervigilence and psychological and emotional numbing (containment). One specific pathological process of this kind receiving increasing attention is post-traumatic stress disorder (PTSD) found among many war veterans, rape victims, and Holocaust survivors. [*See* POST-TRAUMATIC STRESS DISORDER.]

Even though the study of psychopathology is one avenue for investigating the psychosocial and cultural–historical functions of autobiographical remembering, focusing on adaptive functions instead makes it possible to explore in greater detail how intimate relationships are established and maintained, and how culture is transmitted.

Two examples illustrate the interpersonal functions of autobiographical remembering as a psychosocial processes. One is the manner in which mothers talk to or with their children about shared experiences; the other is the way parents mark what is worth remembering and impart an explanatory system that provides the interpretation of recollections, their meaning, and how they should be understood within a family.

In longitudinal studies of young children's autobiographical memories researchers have found that many mothers elaborate, e.g., verbally extend or fill in details given what the child remembers, conversations they are having with their children in the process of remembering a shared novel experience. Other mothers do not elaborate. In delayed follow-up testing by a trained interviewer, those children whose mothers were elaborative were able to provide more information, temporal organization, and narrative density, while contextualizing experiences and expressing what the experiences meant through the use of more affective terms, than were children whose mothers were not elaborators. These findings suggest that the transmission of narrative structure is in the quality of social and language interactions cultural novices have with cultural experts.

Other researchers have shown that parents (mothers usually) identify for young children what information is worth remembering from a past event and what kinds of inferences that can be made from tokens marking those events. For instance, when looking through family photo albums of pictures from shared experiences, e.g., a family picnic, parents, together with their children, will often identify people, objects, and activities in a picture and construct reasons and explanations of what was occurring and why. Frequently, these remembering sessions will lead to elaborations that are prompted by pictures which unpack for children much of their family history and the personalities and characteristics of their relatives. This process is akin to the kinds of conversations families have at reunions, e.g., during holiday gatherings, where individuals take interactive turns describing and explaining what they do, where they have been or the kinds of work they have been doing. Objectifying this kind of information in the context of a family allows other members to reflect and comment, describe and interpret their own experiences, give advice, or evaluate what has been said. Through this conversational process, individual histories are composed, analyzed, and reassembled leading to the assimilation of individual histories into existing family histories. Accordingly, this process facilitates the co-construction of collective personal and family memories.

Consider next how autobiographical remembering functions to create, change, and preserve culture and history. Many cultural anthropologists are interested in ritual activities that sustain community as in the case of stuides of the OK mountain peoples of Inner New Guinea and Shinhala Buddhist "religious virtuosos" (female ascetics) in southern Sri Lanka. "Ritual experts" in these cultures are responsible for remembering and performing rites of passage and religious ceremonies of many kinds, e.g., transition from boyhood to manhood. The ultimate goal of the expert is to bring the inductee to a point of emotional and psychological rapture such that the person believes he or she has been essentially transformed. If the expert fails to create this experience, he or she looses face and status among colleagues (other ritual experts) and clients alike.

In preparation for a prescribed ritual, for instance, word travels among the OK peoples living in different villages that a ritual will take place, and oftentimes ritual experts from different villages gather together before the ceremony and collectively reconstruct the ritual procedures, especially if the ritual being performed does not occur frequently. In this way, cultural practices are maintained in an oral tradition, and passed from generation to generation through the witnessing of ceremonies. Furthermore, an apprentice ritual expert can be introduced gradually to different practices, and privileged knowledge communicated so as to continue established ritual traditions. Interestingly, in oral traditions in particular, culture changes with repeated performances of the same rituals because the individual and collective reconstruction of ritual procedures change from performance to performance in much the same way that variations occur in epic songs performed by Bards. In this way, culture is always becoming:

stated differently, ritual reconstructions create protocultures which can be concretized in word, song, dance, art, or architecture.

III. GET A SELF, GET A STORY: CONSTRAINTS ON THE NARRATIVE CONSTRUCTION OF SELF

One of the central tenets of developmental psychology, and other subdisciplines within psychology, anthropology, or sociology, is that living systems are self-organizing systems that maintain unstable equilibration. In developmental psychology the assumption of self-organization ("agency") is coupled with one of adaptation, i.e., through the interdependent processes of assimilation and accommodation (structural change). While the human tendencies to organize and adapt may be invariant across cultures, the means of organization vary as a function of socially and culturally transmitted skills individuals need to know to be productive community members.

A major skill learned via sociocultural transmission mediating the construction and reconstruction of autobiographical memories, as well as transcendental and provisional selves, is the capability to narrate or tell "good life stories." Good stories reflect the integration and interpretation of life experiences within a causal–explanatory structure embedded in a spatial–temporal framework, e.g., school structures like grade and the organization of grades into primary, junior, and senior high school, or annual, recurrent religious rituals. Given these structural features, good stories about one's life are recognized widely as reflecting a stable and well-formed sense of self. However, the subjective perception of stability of self probably reflects more the stability of the institutions one affiliates with, the quality of relationships one develops over time, and the kinds of narrative skills acquired through experience, than a stable mental and emotional self-structure.

Narrative accounts of life experiences take many forms, e.g., progressive, stable, regressive, shaped by different emotional scenarios played out psychologically and in relationships. The particular form used to reconstruct a life story at one time may vary over time both within and between individuals and change the overall interpretations of a life lived. For instance, a "romantic-saga" (grounded in metaphors like *life is an adventurous journey*) consists of alternating objectifications and subjectifications of progressive (positively evaluated life experiences)

and regressive (negatively evaluated experiences) evaluations of personal experiences over the lifespan, whereas a "tragic-comedy"—a common form for "soap operas" and situational comedies—begins with a postivie, progressive affective tone; over time as the plot develops, the affective evaluation of experiences becomes increasingly negative as unfolding events become problematic. A negative tone is maintained until a climax is reached associated with a precipitating event. Following the climax, the evaluation of subsequent experiences gradually becomes more and more positive as problems are resolved, shared understandings are created, or forgiveness of a moral transgression occurs. Such stories usually end on a high positive note ("I Love Lucy" and "The Bill Cosby Show" are prototypes of this narrative form).

Regardless of the particular narrative technique employed most socially and culturally legitimated life histories take a canonical story form in Western thought. Life stories have a beginning, middle, and end, with some trouble (existential stress) that arises which needs to be resolved in order to reestablish cognitive, emotional, interpersonal, and sociocultural equilibrium. For example, an inexperienced and uneducated youngster who is taken advantage of by older more knowledgeable adults may recognize the unevenness of the power-authority relationship and unfairness of a particular situation, e.g., "Young Boys Incorporated" were under-age youth recruited by adults in Detroit to sell street drugs, and if they were caught they were arrested and adjudicated. In this way the people they worked for were able to resist arrest. This awareness can potentially produce stress that motivates younsters to (a) change the nature of their relationship with adults and (b) generalize their experiences by recognizing that they are not the only youth being mistreated. If youth conceptualize their own existential problems as generalizable phenomena affecting others, then effective coping strategies and solutions are more likely to be found or constructed. In this way, the carrying out of possible solutions can lead to the development of themes that represent the conceptual (semantic) organization of everyday experiences, e.g., "survivor," "provider–caregiver," "wanderer" or "hero." These themes can become a person's life work since they help to organize past experiences and predict possible future events. The emergence of themes can redirect the trajectory of a peron's life since the resolution to a good life story can reflect an adaptive and productive response to existential stress.

Accordingly, in narrative terms the perceived coherence of one's life is a reflection of the coherence of the narrative structure used to reconstruct the past in the present. The elements of coherent narratives include the amount of information given, i.e., persons, places, objects, and attributes of each, narrative density, i.e., the number of propositions (subject–verb clauses) used, and narrative organization. Narrative organization includes (a) temporal–spatial organization evidenced in the frequent use of temporal and spatial terms as well as the number of causal–conditional terms used and (b) narrative functions. Three narrative functions are found in most coherent life stories. These are an orientation function, or context-setting, referential function, i.e., a remembered event or episode, and an evaluative function that conveys the meaning of life experiences by telling, through the use of affect terms and intensifiers, how experiences should be interpreted and understood.

Of the narrative elements mentioned above, the temporal organization and evaluative function are perhaps the most important in conveying a coherent life story in our culture. The extent to which the person is aware of external and internal explanatory systems, i.e., commonly held knowledge about how the world and interpersonal relations work, organizing experiences, impacts greatly on how those experiences are remembered and conveyed. If an explanatory system is known, then the person will be able to reconstruct a coherent past in the present; if, however, the person cannot generate an explanatory system, especially if an external one is unavailable, then the reconstruction of the past will appear as incoherent. Experiences will be remembered and reported, but they will not be systematically placed in time and space. Furthermore, without access to an explanatory system, it is difficult for the person to construct meaning at the time seemingly unexplainable events occur. In remembering such events, a paucity of affect terms are used since the person does not have the "language" to convey how the experiences should be understood.

Clear cases of incoherence in life stories reconstructed in autobiographical recollections and self, which reveal the limits of narrative structures, come from the memories of people who have experienced extreme trauma: for instance, women who have been raped, people who are the victims of random violence, and Holocaust survivors. (Note however that many people experience trauma, e.g., chemotherapy for the treatment of cancer, yet are still able to integrate their traumatic experiences into a coherent life story because the reasons for the treatment [trauma] are obvious, chosen, and agreed upon. Also, everyone who experiences trauma does not necessarily develop clinical psychopathologies.)

Consider, for example, the dissociative phenomenon termed "doubling" experienced by many Nazi concentration camp survivors. In a sense these people today live two parallel lives embodied in the same person: the life remembered from the camps and life in the present. When Holocaust survivors are asked to tell their personal histories, which includes their entire life history and not just their memories from the camps, in terms of their autobiographical memories they most often provide a canonical life history that follows conventional story forms. Their experiences during the war are included as "trouble," but in the context of their entire life they are frequently able to place those experiences in a clear temporal–spatial framework by using the beginning (e.g., invasion of Poland) and end dates (e.g., liberation) of the war. For instance, one survivor interviewed began her personal history by saying, "My life is divided into four phases." She then goes on to elaborate those phases from childhood to the present. However, when specifically asked to remember her war experiences she begins [sic], in a changed voice, "You know, my life is really just a series of episodes. I can't tell you exactly when things occurred or where: it seems that there were moments of intense fear, which are still vivid to me today, followed by long periods of boredom. I have no memory for what I did or where I was when I was bored." When pointedly asked about her sense of the past and future during the war, whether she could explain why she experienced what she reported and give meaning to her war experiences at the time they happened, she replied simply that these were rational questions and made no sense to her.

In sum, relative to the coherence found in a life history, memories of war experiences in the concentration camps are most often incoherent from a narrative perspective. This phenomenon has led me to distinguish between *momentary selves* and *narrative selves*. Momentary selves emerge when no explanatory system is available to the person. Momentary selves can be the root of much human suffering in the sense that the memories constituting them appear and reappear involuntarily, e.g., as nightmares; these memories or intrusive thoughts are reenactments of traumatic experiences that cannot be understood by the victim or by witnesses to the victims memories. Holocaust survivors have no language to convey the meaning of "extermination" to others or to themselves. The full meaning of the atrocities they experienced are hidden from public view; only empathetic approximations to understanding can be achieved by those of us who did not physically share their horrors.

IV. CONCLUSION

Autobiographical memories are memories that acquire meaning through the embodiment of affect that emerges in interpersonal, sociocultural, and historical contexts. These memories are made public through a process of objectification where they can be socially legitimated and examined for authenticity (true to life) and accuracy (true in fact). Subsequently, autobiographical memories are internalized through a process of subjectification grounded at first in social speech acts produced in interaction with others. Linguistic competence (in speech, writing, and movement) becomes the means through which personal recollections are used to establish and maintain intimacies and to comfort ourselves during periods of anxiety.

Autobiographical remembering creates provisional selves that over time become the essential features of an existential sense of self, or self-knowledge. The release of autobiographical memories into consciousness and the public sphere is accomplished through metaphoric projections of image-schemata acquired through actual physical experiences. These projections, however, can take only a limited number of socially acceptable forms; more specifically, in any culture at a particular historical time, there are a finite number of possible selves available. In part, this is because there is a fixed set of narrative forms available through which selves can be composed. On this view, coherent and incoherent personal histories and selves are formed depending upon the degree to which explanatory systems are known to the individual and would give structure and meaning to life experiences.

Certain forms of psychopathology, for instance, dissociative disorders like post-traumatic stress disorders may be associated with an individual's functional narrative strengths and weaknesses. Reenactments in the form of intrusive memories, hypervigilance, and containment (psychic and emotional numbing) may result because certain experiences cannot be explained, interpreted, and meaningfully understood given their lack of narrative organization.

Bibliography

Barclay, C. R. (in press). Autobiographical remembering: Narrative constraints on objectified selves. In "Reconstructing the Past: An Overview of Autobiographical Memory." (D. C. Rubin, Ed.), Cambridge University Press, New York.

Barth, F. (1987). "Cosmologies in the Making: A Generative Approach to Cultural Variation in Inner New Guinea." Cambridge University Press, New York.

Conway, M. A., Rubin, D. C., Spinnler, H., and Wagenaar, W. A. (Eds.) (1992). "Theoretical Perspectives on Autobiographical Memory." Kluwer, The Netherlands.

Eakin, P. J. (1985). "Fictions in Autobiography: Studies in the Art of Self-Invention." Princeton University Press, Princeton, NJ.

Holland, D., and Quinn, N. (Eds.) (1987). "Cultural Models in Language and Thought." Cambridge University Press, New York.

Johnson, M. (1987). "The Body in the Mind: The Bodily Basis of Meaning, Imagination, and Reason." University of Chicago Press, Chicago.

Lakoff, G. (1987). "Women, Fire, and Dangerous Things: What Categories Reveal about the Mind." University of Chicago Press, Chicago.

Middleton, D., and Edwards, D. (Eds.) (1990). "Collective Remembering." Sage. London.

Neisser, U., and Fivash, R. (Eds.) (in press). "The Remembered Self." Cambridge University Press, New York.

Obeyesekere, G. (1981). "Medusa's Hair: An Essay on Personal Symbols and Religious Experience." University of Chicago Press, Chicago.

Rubin, D. C. (Ed.) (1986). "Autobiographical Memory." Cambridge University Press, New York.

BEHAVIORAL GENETICS

Craig T. Nagoshi
Arizona State University

Glossary

Allele One alternate form of a gene at a particular place (locus) on a chromosome.

Dominance The ability of one allele (the dominant) to override the phenotypic expression of another allele (the recessive).

Epistasis Nonadditive effects of the combined actions of two or more genes, i.e., gene–gene interaction.

Gene A segment of a chromosome (deoxyribonucleic acid or DNA) that codes for some aspect of protein synthesis.

Genotype The genetic composition of an individual.

Heritability The proportion of phenotypic variability that can be accounted for by genetic factors.

Inbreeding Matings between genetically related individuals.

Linkage The extent to which two genes near each other on the same chromosome are transmitted together instead of segregating and independently assorting.

Phenotype The apparent, measureable characteristic or trait.

Pleiotropy Multiple phenotypic effects of the same gene.

BEHAVIORAL GENETICS, as the name indicates, is the interdisciplinary research area concerned with determining if and how genetic factors influence any of the phenomena studied in the behavioral sciences, especially psychology. Behavioral geneticists apply the concepts and methodologies of molecular, population, and quantitative genetics to behavior as the phenotype of interest.

I. INTRODUCTION

The idea that behavior, particularly human behavior, might be determined by genetic factors has been controversial throughout human history and the history of psychology. Aristotle proposed that humans had a "human soul" possessing consciousness and free will, which was different from the biologically determined "animal soul" of other creatures. Judeo-Christian theology and Descartes' mind–body dualism emphasized that the most "human" behaviors, such as intelligence and morality, were products of a conscious mind removed from biological mechanisms. Thus, even though animal breeders had known for thousands of years that behaviors could be selected and bred for, it was still possible for behaviorism to be founded at the beginning of this century and to dominate psychological thinking, while minimizing the importance of biological/genetic processes in understanding human behavior.

Two readily apparent, related aspects of human behavior, however, make a compelling case for the need to study genetic influences. These are stability and variability.

If a behavior, e.g., scoring high on tests of intelligence, is consistently manifested by an individual across time and across many different situations, then the stability of this behavior must be due to some consistent set of physical determinants.

Through consistent reinforcement and/or punishment of certain behaviors, plus generalization, a stable behavior could have been established by environmental influences on the individual. On the other hand, the behavior could be a manifestation of some consistent "hard-wired" physiological process, e.g., greater efficiency of the connections in the brain's neural network. Since all physiological/biological processes ultimately begin from some genetic code, it could be inferred that the stable behavior is the result of the individual having inherited some gene or genes for the behavior.

In turn, both the lack of variability and the presence of variability in stable behaviors also require the influence of some set of consistent physical determinants. For example, all physiologically normal humans raised among other humans acquire the ability to use language. The lack of variability in this behavior among humans, plus the absence of this behavior in this form in other animal species, is consistent with the supposition that all normal humans inherit a set of genes that code for the physiological structures that are required for language. Other stable behaviors, such as performance on intelligence tests, are characterized by great variability among humans, and this variability is maintained despite historical and social changes in the environmental factors thought to influence the behaviors. Since each individual is genetically unique, stable individual differences in behavior are also consistent with the supposition that genetic determinants may be involved.

Although behavioral genetics is concerned with establishing the genetic determinants of behavior, the discussion above makes clear that genes, in fact, do not directly cause behavior. Figure 1 reiterates the idea that genes are basically just a biochemical

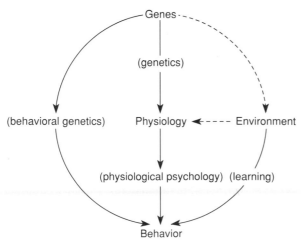

FIGURE 1　Relationship of genes to behavior.

process for coding the synthesis of proteins which, in turn, are assembled into the physiological structures and processes of the organism. These physiological structures then become one of the determinants of behavior, and the study of this process is the realm of physiological psychology. Thus, any finding from behavioral genetics of significant genetic influences on behavior automatically implies that some physiological mechanism is the more proximal determinant.

Behavior can also be influenced by the environment through learning, and one dotted line in Figure 1 shows the physical monist/physiological psychology presumption that ultimately learning operates by modifying the physiology of the organism. It should thus also be noted that genetic influences always operate on physiology within the context of some set of environmental influences. The other dotted line presents the possibility (discussed below) that genetic factors can affect environmental influences.

In Figure 1, the understanding of how genetic processes are translated into physiology is noted to be the realm of genetics. Molecular genetics is concerned with the sequence and operation of biochemically defined genetic material (the DNA basepairs described below) in transcribing, transmitting, and implementing the code for the synthesis of physiological structures and processes. Quantitative genetics estimates the relative influence of genetic vs environmental influences on a variable trait by comparing differential resemblances or patterns of differential variability among individuals of different degrees of genetic relatedness. Population genetics bridges molecular and quantitative genetic approaches by seeking to relate gene frequencies and degree of genetic influence with particular traits for populations of organisms operating within particular environmental contexts.

Since behavioral genetics is basically simply the application of genetics to a special set of traits, behavior, much of this article will be an overview of genetic concepts and methodologies. Issues of particular relevance to the study of behavior will be emphasized toward the end of the article, which will also briefly describe some of the major findings from human behavioral genetics studies. We begin with a discussion of Darwin's theory of evolution by natural selection and of Mendel's work on the logic of genetic transmission.

II. EVOLUTION AND MENDELIAN GENETICS

The evolutionary theory of Charles Darwin (1809–1882) had a profound impact on Western thought. Even though it provides a basis for a unified understanding of all biological phenomena, the theory was and remains controversial. In psychology, it was integrated into the concepts of 19th century physiological psychologists, became a major inspiration for William James' school of functionalism (the school which, somewhat ironically in this context, led to John B. Watson's behaviorism) and Sigmund Freud's school of psychoanalysis, and through the work of Darwin's cousin Francis Galton, also was the starting point for the scientific study of individual differences and genetic influences on human behavior.

Darwin's theory, first published as *On the Origin of Species by Means of Natural Selection* in 1858, has three major components, each of which has important implications for the understanding of human behavior:

1. *Induction of variation* proposes that members of a species differ from each other at birth and through maturation along a multitude of different trait dimensions and that biological processes continually create these individual differences. As will soon be apparent, not only are such differences ubiquitous for any species, they are absolutely essential for the survival of the species in the face of relentless changes in environmental conditions. One obvious implication of this for psychology is that, in contrast to the ideas of several early behaviorists, individual members of a species, including humans, are biologically unique and should not be expected to respond to the same environmental influences on behavior in exactly the same way.

2. *Maintenance of variation* proposes that individual differences in the traits that vary within a species are biologically transmissible from one generation to the next. Again, this is absolutely essential for the survival of the species. This idea leads to the immediate inference that behavior must also be biologically transmissible, since stable patterns of behavior are undoubtedly essential aspects of species survival. This idea was clearly consistent with the results of thousands of years of animal breeding, noted above, when applied to non-human animals. The implications of the third component of Darwin's theory led to the controversies that still flare today.

3. *Natural selection* assumes that there are always more members of a species born at any one time than will ever survive to reproduce.

Darwin proposed that environmental conditions at a particular time, e.g., availability of food, nature of predators and parasites, climate, etc., tend to give some individuals born with one set of traits an advantage in being able to survive, reproduce, and rear offspring to maturity over other individuals with different levels of these traits. Over several generations of this natural selection, more individuals with the advantageous characteristics are born with and transmit these characteristics, while there is a decreased incidence and transmission of the disadvantageous characteristics. Darwin argued that over a sufficient number of generations, particularly in response to some major change in the environment, the members of a species may now possess such different traits from the starting population that they constitute a new species.

As noted above, Darwin's theory clearly reinforces the importance of genetic transmission and biologically based individual differences as determinants of the characteristics of organisms, including behavioral characteristics. The theory also implies that all species, including humans, are biologically related on some level to every other species. The similarities and differences between and within species could be understood solely in terms of the interactions between the genetic endowments of a species and the selection pressures in the environment. Research into the determinants of behavior in other animal species in order to understand human behavior is justified, because other animals and humans have some of the same or similar physiological structures and processes that determine behavior. Other implications include the expectation that humans retain physiological structures that were once adaptive or neutral in value in natural environments, but which may be maladaptive in rapidly changing modern societies. Another implication is that even those "higher" aspects of human behavior and mental processes that supposedly differentiate us from other animals can be related to genetically transmitted physiological functions that resulted from natural selection.

Although natural selection was the most parsimonious and successful proposed mechanism for accounting for species change, at the time Darwin published his theory the way that traits were biologically transmitted was poorly understood. Darwin himself realized that the then current concept that parents gave off biological particles ("gemmules") that merged and blended in the offspring would, in fact, invalidate his principles of induction and maintenance of variation. Generations of blending traits would result in all individuals having the same averaged trait, i.e., no variation. It was only after the work of Mendel and the beginning of modern genetics that a mechanism for the maintenance of variation was established.

Gregor Mendel (1822–1884) studied the types and frequencies of plant characteristics that resulted when members of a species possessing one kind of charactristic were crossed with members having a different characteristic. For his most famous work on pea plants, such characteristics included green vs yellow pea color, smooth vs wrinkled pea form, long vs short plant stem, etc. The results of his cross-breeding studies led him to infer two principles for genetic transmission.

The *law of segregation* stated that every character (the phenotype) is determined by the combination of two elements (genes), one from each parent. These elements split off cleanly (segregate) from each other in the production of the sex cells and are transmitted intact to the offspring. Since it is possible for one form of the gene (a dominant allele) to prevent the expression of the other form (the recessive allele), a process called dominance, the same phenotype could result from different combinations of genetic elements (the genotype). For example, a green pea would result whether the genotype consisted of both alleles coding for green color (homozygous dominant) or a genotype with both green and yellow coding alleles (heterozygous), since the green allele was dominant. This was apparent when Mendel crossed "pure" green and "pure" yellow pea plants and found that the next generation all had green peas. When this second generation was crossed with each other, however, Mendel found that one-fourth of the succeeding generation again manifested yellow peas. Thus, the yellow alleles were not blended, and the variability of the genes determining green vs yellow pea color was maintained.

The *law of independent assortment* stated that different genes determined different characteristics. These genes were randomly combined in the sex cells and, hence, independently transmitted to the offspring. Mendel found that when he looked at the results of crossing plants for two different traits, for example, green pea color/long stem with yellow pea color/short stem plants, the odds of a plant possessing green vs yellow peas were completely independent of the odds of the plant having a long vs a short stem. This was also important for Darwin's theory, since it meant that one trait could be selected for without affecting some other trait.

As it turned out, modern genetic findings have turned up several exceptions to Mendel's laws. Many traits determined by single genes (one pair of alleles) do not show dominance, such that heterozygous genotypes may result in phenotypes intermediate between phenotypes resulting from the two homozygous genotypes. Heterozygous genotypes may produce more extreme phenotypes (overdominance). Recent findings suggest that parents in a few genetic systems may be able to determine the expression of both alleles of an offspring (uniparental disomy and imprinting). With regard to independent assortment, it is now known that genes that are close to each other on the same chromosome are often transmitted together (linkage) and that single genes can have multiple phenotypic effects (pleiotropy). Nevertheless, Mendel's laws more than adequately accounted for observations of genetic transmission at the phenotypic level long before the biochemical nature of genes was understood.

Although Mendel presented his findings at a scientific meeting in 1865, they were "lost" until 1900, when several biologists rediscovered and started widely applying the laws. In the meantime, Darwin's cousin Francis Galton (1822–1911) was using the theory of evolution to establish the science of behavioral genetics.

Galton immediately inferred from Darwin's theory that all human behaviors had a biological/genetic basis and were the result of natural selection. With his book *Hereditary Genius: An Inquiry Into Its Laws and Consequences* (1869), he asserted that social eminence (reflective of intelligence) was genetically determined. He demonstrated this by showing how the incidence of eminence in the male relatives (fathers, sons, uncles, cousins, etc.) of eminent men was a strict function of the degree of biological relatedness between the probands and the relatives. He developed the idea of the twin research design, when he studied more physically similar twins vs less similar twins and asserted that the former's greater similarity on psychological traits also indicated a genetic basis for psychological as well as physical characteristics. He established laboratories for the systematic measurement of thousands of individuals on physical (height, weight, etc.) and psychological (acuity of eyesight, acuity of hearing, reaction time, etc.) traits in hopes of establishing the large data bases he knew were required to delineate genetically based distributional characteristics, social class differences, developmental trends, and familial resemblances.

Besides his enormous contributions to psychology in establishing ways of measuring psychological phenomena of all sorts, Galton's quest for ways to demonstrate genetic transmission in relatives led to the development of new statistical techniques. His student, Karl Pearson, developed the correlation coefficient to quantify familial resemblances in some standardized fashion, and genetic questions have continued to be one of the spurs for the development of statistical procedures commonly used in the social sciences (e.g., Fisher's chi-square and F tests).

Thus, much of the logic and methodologies of modern behavioral genetics had been laid down by Galton and his students by the time Mendel's ideas were rediscovered. Ironically, it took some time and controversy to reconcile Galton's ideas, that accumulations of genetic elements of some sort produce continuous, typically normal distributions of traits, such as intelligence, with Mendel's ideas about discrete traits under the control of only a few combinations of alleles. The reconciliation involved the recognition that the random combination (consistent with independent assortment) of several discrete genetic elements, all of which have some influence on the trait, would produce the continuous, normal distributions Galton saw. It is still important, though, to distinguish between traits thought to be under the control of a single gene vs those under the control of several genes. [See TRAITS.]

Although Darwin's ideas were important for the school of functionalism established in the United States by William James and others at the end of the 19th century, and Galton's ideas were the starting point for trait theories of intelligence and personality, genetic explanations for behavior were largely eclipsed by behaviorism throughout the first half of this century. There was also a great amount of philosophical resistance in the general public to the idea of biological/genetic determinants of human behavior. For instance, there was considerable public controversy following the publication of Arthur Jensen's 1969 paper, from which readers inferred that, due to the high heritability of intelligence, educational programs would have only minimal effects in ameliorating race differences in IQ.

Several historical developments have led to the much greater acceptance today of behavioral genetics in both mainstream psychology and the general public. The discovery of the structure of deoxyribonucleic acid (DNA), the fundamental molecule of heredity, by Watson and Crick in 1953 spurred the vast expansion of knowledge in recent years on the biochemical characteristics and processes of what had up to then been only a hypothetical genetic mechanism. Discoveries about the biochemical workings of genes and gene products continue and will continue to be among the most exciting findings in science. The findings from physiological psychology and neuroscience have greatly expanded our understanding of the biological processes that determine behavior, while the idea of learning as the sole basis for behavior no longer has ascendancy. Meanwhile, the accumulation of findings from pedigree, twin, and adoption studies has provided compelling evidence for the significant heritability of intelligence, personality, schizophrenia, alcoholism, etc. We shall return to these findings, after an overview of molecular, population, and quantitative genetics.

III. MOLECULAR GENETICS

The DNA molecules in every living cell consist of two strands of phosphate and deoxyribose sugar groups held at a fixed distance from each other by pairs of nitrogenous compounds called bases. Each of the four bases is attached to one strand and can only pair with the corresponding base on the other strand in a particular combination: adenine with thymine and guanine with cytosine. The molecule itself is held together by its double helix structure, as discovered by Watson and Crick. When the molecule is "unzipped," each strand thus is a mirror-image of the other strand and can be used as a template for the construction of proteins and enzymes, when 3-base ribonucleic acid (RNA) units carrying amino acids link up with the DNA strand in the order dictated by the exposed basepairs.

Through this transcription and replication mechanism, each cell programs the synthesis of the structures and chemicals needed to maintain itself, and the DNA in the cell's nucleus carries the program to create new cells. Also through this mechanism multicellular organisms transmit the program for the creation of new organisms. These strands of nuclear DNA are called chromosomes and a gene is simply a segment (locus) of the chromosome that codes for some protein or enzyme. In sexually reproducing organisms, the "blueprint" for the organism resides in one or more pairs of chromosomes (26 pairs in humans), and each parent transmits one half of each pair of chromosomes in the sex cells to the offspring. Thus, the biochemical basis for Mendel's hypothetical genes and alleles was established.

Autosomal genes are those that are on the "normal" chromosomes not involved in determining gender. When the gene (allele) from one parent pairs up with the gene from the other parent at a locus, one gene may biochemically "turn off" the transcription mechanism of the other gene. This is what Mendel observed as dominance.

Chromosomes that determine gender are often different from the other chromosomes in that both members of the pair may not be equivalent in size and, hence, amount of genetic material. In humans, normal females carry one pair of so-called X-chromosomes, while normal males carry an X-chromosome paired up with a much smaller Y-chromosome. The Y-chromosome carries almost no genetic information other than to turn on the process for altering the developmental course of the embryo to become a male. Whatever traits are coded for by genes on the X-chromosome in males (which is transmitted by the mother) will thus be expressed, including traits determined by recessive genes that might otherwise have been inactivated by a dominant gene on the other X-chromosome that females receive from the father. As will be discussed below with regard to population genetics, deleterious traits tend to be expressed by recessive genes. The results of so-called X-linkage are seen, for example, in the higher incidence in males of the relatively common form of congenital mental retardation called the fragile-X syndrome, where a piece of the X-chromosome is "loose" or broken off and the genes on that piece are presumably inactive.

One theme that emerges from an understanding of the mechanisms of genetic transmission is the Darwinian idea of the importance of maintaining variability in a species. Sexual reproduction itself, although costly to the organism in terms of energy use, lost opportunities for food gathering, and vulnerability to predation, is clearly meant to create new genetic combinations in the offspring by combining genes from both parents. The process of splitting the chromosome pairs for the sex cells also involves recombination of genetic material, as the members of the pair cross over each other and exchange genes. Mutations that spontaneously occur as a result of transcription errors or environmental insults can alter the transmitted genes.

Another theme that emerged early on from molecular genetics was that some human behaviors and aspects of behaviors, particularly mental retardation, were clearly the result of simple genetic mechanisms (note, though, that not all instances of mental retardation have simple genetic explanations). Errors in chromosomal replication and division at times result in missing or duplicated chromosomes in the sex cells transmitted to the offspring. The offspring then end up with a missing member or piece of a member of a chromosome pair or with an extra chromosome (trisomy). These chromosomal defects are usually fatal for the fetus, when they occur on the larger chromosomes, and usually result in some degree of mental retardation when they occur on the smaller chromosomes of a viable offspring. Besides the fragile-X syndrome noted above, another common form of mental retardation is Down's syndrome, which is caused by a trisomy on chromosome 21.

Another good example of a simple genetic mechanism responsible for mental retardation is phenylketonuria, which is caused by a recessive autosomal gene that fails to code for the synthesis of an active enzyme responsible for the breakdown of the amino acid phenylalanine. The build-up of phenylalanine in the infant depresses other amino acid levels and hinders normal nervous system development. The pleiotropic effects of this genetic defect include hyperactivity, irritability, and moderate to severe mental retardation. This syndrome is also interesting in demonstrating that genetically determined traits can be modified by the environment. Infants who are detected early with the double recessive genotype can be put on a low phenylalanine diet, and this diet has been shown to be effective in greatly reducing the deleterious effects of the gene.

A technique called linkage analysis is used to confirm that a trait is under the control of a single gene and to identify the particular chromosome the gene resides on. This involves identifying several large family pedigrees (two or more generations, with large numbers of siblings in each generation) or large numbers of sibships with a high incidence of the trait of interest (e.g., some form of mental retardation). Each individual in a pedigree is assessed for the occurrence or absence of the trait, and the pattern of transmission of the trait through the pedigree can be tested against the pattern expected by different kinds of Mendelian single-gene transmission modes, for example, autosomal dominant, X-linked recessive, etc. In addition, each individual is also tested for the co-occurrence of some other trait (a linkage marker), for example, a blood group type, known to be controlled by a single gene at an approximate locus on a particular chromosome. If the trait of interest consistently co-occurs with the linkage marker, i.e., there is a genetic correlation, then the traits are not independently assorting and must be close to each other on the same now-identified chromosome. The deviation from expected Mendelian ratios for independent assortment, indicative of linkage, is expressed as a so-called LOD (logarithmic odds) score.

Molecular genetic techniques developed over the last 20 years now allow for the possibility of identifying the exact location of a gene on a chromosome and determining not only the sequence of the gene's basepairs, but also the particular protein or enzyme synthesized by the gene. These recombinant DNA techniques include restriction enzymes for slicing the DNA strand at particular basepair sequences, polymerase chain reactions for multiplying the particular DNA segments to be studied, radioactive labeling and Southern blotting for observing variations (restriction fragment length polymorphisms (RFLP), variable number tandem repeats (VNTR)) in the DNA sliced by the restriction enzymes, restriction maps of overlapping segments of DNA sliced by different restriction enzymes to determine basepair sequences, and cloning to insert DNA segments into cells to determine the gene products. Cloning also offers the possibility (the first such treatment studies are now under way) of correcting an individual's genetic defects by inserting active cells with the correct genes.

Linkage analyses in behavioral genetics now often involve attempts to genetically correlate behavioral traits with specific genes identified through molecular genetic techniques. For example, several groups have recently sought to demonstrate a pleiotropic relationship (by definition the most extreme form of linkage) between alcoholism and a gene that codes for one form of the neural receptor for the neurotransmitter dopamine. Current proposals for the mapping of the entire human genome will greatly facilitate such linkage analyses in the future.

IV. POPULATION GENETICS

As noted above, population genetics seeks to understand the frequencies and relative influence of genes on particular traits for a group of organisms operating within a particular environmental context. An important starting point for population genetics

was the statistical derivation of the Hardy-Weinberg-Castle equilibrium, which showed that, in the absence of influences that produce disequilibrium (discussed below), the relative frequencies of alleles (dominant vs recessive, etc.) and genotypes homozygous dominant, heterozygous, etc.) for a phenotype remain at a constant ratio over generations. This was basically just a restatement of Darwin's idea of maintenance of genetic variation, but in this case it was derived through mathematically following the logic of genetic transmission defined by Mendel.

Population geneticists have identified four major forces that can change allelic frequencies, i.e., the relative frequencies of one form of a gene vs another, in a population:

1. *Migration* can change allelic frequencies if individuals who move into or out of a population differ from the original population in their allelic frequencies. For example, it can be argued that the waves of immigrants who came to the United States throughout its history were more likely to carry genes for such traits as adventurousness, hardiness, rebelliousness, etc., compared to the populations left behind.

2. *Random genetic drift* can affect small populations, when chance causes some alleles and not others to accumulate over several generations.

3. *Mutation* is the ultimate source of inducing genetic variations, as alleles are altered by errors in genetic replication and transmission and by environmental influences. The spontaneous mutation rate, however, is thought to be quite low, and the effect of mutation on allelic frequencies in most cases is minor compared to natural selection.

4. *Natural selection* is, of course, the prime basis for genetic change described by Darwin. It should be remembered, however, that natural selection operates on the basis of the phenotypes that give an organism some advantage or disadvantage (relative fitness) in surviving to reproduce offspring who, in turn, will pass on the genes that determine the phenotype. If a trait, such as schizophrenia, is selected against by the environment, i.e., the trait reduces the reproductive success of the individual, and is determined by a dominant allele, then both homozygous dominant and heterozygous genotypes will be selected against. In this case natural selection will rapidly decrease the

frequency of the dominant allele. If, however, the maladaptive trait is coded for by a recessive allele, as was the case for phenylketonuria, then only homozygous recessive genotypes will be selected against, and large numbers of heterozygotes (carriers) will continue to transmit the "bad" allele to some of their offspring. This process tends to ensure that adaptive traits are coded for by dominant alleles, while maladaptive traits are carried and maintained on recessives in populations. This picture becomes more complicated when there is not complete dominance for a gene. In the extreme case, selection may eliminate all but one form of a gene for an adaptive trait in a population or species, and this trait then becomes a species characteristic (i.e., there is no variability for the trait).

Natural selection may also act to maintain or even increase the variability of a phenotype in the population, creating a so-called balanced polymorphism. For example, sickle-cell anemia is a typically fatal medical condition in individuals of African ancestry. The disease is caused by an autosomal recessive gene; thus, homozygous recessive genotypes are selected against. Heterozygotes, however, manifest a greater resistance to malaria in malarial environments than homozygous dominants, and both alleles are maintained in the population, despite the deleterious effects of the recessive gene by itself. Predator–prey and parasite–host relationships also often manifest balanced polymorphisms, as natural selection for adaptations in one organism are constantly being compensated for by corresponding natural selection for adaptations in the other organism.

Since characteristics that increase the probability of being chosen as a mate also directly affect reproductive success, sexual selection is a special form of natural selection and can produce many of the same effects described above. On the other hand, the phenotypes chosen by mates may not be consistent with those resulting from natural selection, i.e., as a result of sexual selection, species may come to manifest traits that appear to be maladaptive.

Besides forces that change allelic frequencies, population geneticists also consider two forces, inbreeding and assortative mating, that change genotypic (but not allelic) frequencies by increasing the similarity of the genes that both parents transmit to their offspring. This is important, because such parental similarities in the genes they transmit would increase the relative frequencies of homozygous dominant and recessive genotypes, while decreasing the proportion of heterozygotes. This, in turn, typically has the effect of increasing the variability of the phenotype in the offspring generation, since there would be higher frequencies of the extreme genotypes. This increased variability might counter the reduction in variability resulting from some types of natural selection.

Inbreeding is the mating of genetically related individuals and, as described above, causes parents to be more similar in the genes they transmit to offspring. Since recessive alleles often code for deleterious traits but are not expressed, due to their being paired with a dominant, the increased incidence of homozygous recessive genotypes resulting from inbreeding often results in decreased fitness for the offspring of such matings (inbreeding depression). The counterpart to this is the increased fitness (hybrid vigor) found when more genetically unrelated individuals are mated. Some evidence for both inbreeding depression effects on intelligence have been found in studies of offspring from cousin marriages, while hybrid vigor effects have been found in studies of offspring from cross-ethnic group marriages. [*See* INBREEDING.]

Assortative mating is where mates are similar in their phenotypes, whether due to mate choice or environmental factors. There are three different ways that assortative mating may occur.

In genetic similarity, mates select each other or are selected for each other on the basis of having similar genes, and the effects of this on offspring genotypic frequencies are similar to the effects for inbreeding. This phenomenon has been demonstrated in some animal species, but whether humans select mates on the basis of genetic similarity is controversial.

In phenotypic assortment, mates select each other on the basis of similarities in observable characteristics. Phenotypic assortment can only produce greater genetic similarity between the parents if there is a significant relationship between the genotype and the phenotype, i.e., if the characteristic is heritable. In fact, many human behaviors, such as intelligence, personality, attitudes, some psychopathology, etc., have been shown to produce moderate to high spouse correlations indicative of phenotypic assortment.

In social homogamy, mates are similar in their phenotypes simply because the environments in which they meet and mate only have individuals possessing certain characteristics. In a highly stratified society, social class differences can cause human mates to be highly similar in several behaviors relative to possible mates from other classes, even when there is no active phenotypic assortment at the level of individuals. Social homogamy can only produce greater parental genetic similarity if the phenotypes of interest are heritable and there is a significant gene–environment correlation (discussed below) across social classes.

One important offshoot of population genetics is sociobiology, which seeks to determine the evolutionary significance (i.e., fitness value) of behavioral systems. For example, sociobiologists are interested in the environmental conditions, physiological characteristics of the organism, and available genetically transmissible behaviors that cause one animal species to be characterized by altruistic behaviors, while other otherwise similar species are not altruistic. While behavioral geneticists generally attempt to determine the relative influence of genetic factors on variations in behavior within a species, sociobiologists thus tend to look at the influence of such factors on variations in behavior across species.

V. QUANTITATIVE GENETICS

Up until the recent widespread availability of new molecular genetic methodologies, much of behavior genetics was simply concerned with the issue dealt with by quantitative genetics, assessing the relative contribution of genetic vs environmental factors (nature vs nurture) in determining individual variations in traits within a species or population. Since only the phenotypes are measured, and the genetic bases for the familial resemblances discussed below only assumed, quantitative genetics relies heavily on various statistical techniques to arrive at its conclusions.

The starting point for quantitative genetics is variability. As discussed at the beginning of this article, stable individual differences in behavior or any other trait must be the result of genetic and/or environmental processes that are both unique for each individual and consistent in their effects across time. Heritability is defined as that proportion of the variability of a phenotype that can be accounted for by genetic factors or $h^2 = V_G/V_P$, where V_G and V_P are the genetic and phenotypic variabilities, respectively. Traits without any variability, such as the ability to use language in humans, may be entirely under genetic control, but the lack of variability for the trait precludes any statistical tests to determine the relative influence of genes and environment.

The counterpart to the assumptions about variability is that, if relatives resemble each other (i.e., do not vary) for some trait, it must be because they share the same genetic and/or environmental determinants of the variability of the trait. By comparing the relative degrees of resemblance (correlations) for the phenotype of interest across relationship types that theoretically differ in their underlying shared genetic and environmental determinants, the quantitative geneticist can infer the extent to which variability in genetic vs variability in environmental factors accounted for the variability of the phenotype.

For the commonly used study of twins reared together, first described by Galton, identical (monozygotic or MZ) twins are known to share all of their genetic variability (they literally have the same genes), as well as sharing the same family environment. Fraternal (dizygotic or DZ) twins are like nontwin siblings in only sharing half of their additive (additive vs nonadditive genetic effects are discussed below) genetic variance, but they are like MZ twins in sharing the same family environment. Hence, if MZ twins are more alike than DZ twins, it is assumed that this is because the former share twice as much genetic variability as the latter. Thus, doubling the difference between the MZ and DZ correlations should estimate the heritability. For example, MZ twins reared together typically correlate around .75 on tests of intelligence, while DZ twins reared together correlate around .50. Thus, the heritability would be $h^2 = 2(r_{MZ} - r_{DZ}) = 2(.75 - .50) = .50$, or 50% of the variability in intelligence is accounted for by genetic factors. Fifty percent heritability means that part of the MZ resemblance of .75 is still unaccounted for. This part, .25 or 25% is presumably due to the effects of shared family environment.

In fact, there are several more kinds of genetic and environmental processes that can produce resemblances among relatives. Genetic influences can be classified as additive or nonadditive. Additive effects are analogous to the idea of "gene dosage," in that for polygenetically determined traits familial resemblances are predicted from the extent of the linear accumulation of shared genes. For example, each parent shares on average 50% of the additive genetic variability for a phenotype with his or her offspring by transmitting half of the offspring's genome. Siblings share with each other on average 50% of the additive genetic variability, because for each of the two parents the probability is 25% that the same genes were transmitted to both siblings (50% to one sibling × 50% to the other). Additive genetic variability is important in that it determines the extent to which a trait can be changed in a population through natural or artificial selection.

The two types of nonadditive genetic effects, dominance and epistasis, can be thought of as being analogous to statistical interactions. The dominance effects described above for single genes are an inter-allele interaction, where the effect of one allele cannot be predicted without knowing the effect of the other allele. Thus, parents and offspring do not share any dominance genetic variability, since dominance effects require particular combinations of alleles from both parents. Siblings, on the other hand, do share 25% of dominance genetic variability, since that is the probability of both siblings receiving the exact same combination of alleles from both parents.

Epistasis is an inter-gene interaction, where the effect of one gene cannot be predicted without knowing the effect of some other gene or genes. Only identical twins share a high degree of epistatic genetic variability, since they inherit not only the same genes, but also the exact same combination and ordering of the genes. Siblings will share some epistatic genetic variability only if 2 or 3 genes are considered.

Environmental effects can be classified as shared (common), special twin, and unshared (specific). Shared environmental variability represents the assumption that individuals growing up in the same family may resemble each other because they are influenced by the same environmental determinants of the phenotype. Adoptive siblings and adoptive parents and their offspring provide strong tests of shared environmental effects, since presumably this is the only factor that would create any familial resemblances. Special twin environmental variability is a special form of shared environmental effects that assumes that twins may share more similar environments, perhaps due to being of the same age, than non-twin siblings.

Unshared environmental effects make family members different from each other. This may be due to idiosyncratic events in a person's life and differential treatment of siblings by parents. Measurement unreliability will also typically be manifested in the unshared environmental component of quantitative genetic models. Differences between identical twins reared together must be due to un-

shared environmental variability, since that is the only factor MZs do not have in common.

Genetic effects may also be correlated with environmental effects. Gene–environment correlations can be passive, where the child is born into a family environment in which environmental conditions created by the parents are consistent with the parents' and the offspring's genotype. They can be reactive, where the environment changes in response to the offspring's genotype, or active, where the offspring's genotype causes him or her to change the environment to make it more consistent with his or her genotype. Positive gene–environment correlations can presumably magnify genetic effects, while negative gene–environment correlations can diminish them. Gene–environment correlations also create the possibility that measures of the family environment used by psychologists, such as parents' socioeconomic status, may in fact be confounded by genetic factors.

Finally, there is the possibility of gene–environment interactions, where genetic effects cannot be predicted unless the environmental conditions are known. For example, genes determining intelligence may not have the opportunity to be expressed if a child is raised in a severely deprived environment.

Table I presents the theoretical extents to which the factors presented above can cause relatives to resemble each other across various relationship types. Quantitative genetic studies typically compare phenotypic resemblances across two and occasionally more relationship types, and some of the most commonly used designs will be dscribed below. For several of these factors, the differences across relationship types are too small to reliably detect their effects. For instance, it can be seen that dominance and epistatic genetic effects are difficult to distinguish. Gene–environment correlations are confounded with pure genetic effects, and gene–environment interactions may be confounded with within-family environmental effects.

Before describing quantitative genetic designs used to estimate heritabilities for human behavior, animal behavioral genetic studies should be mentioned. To the extent that, due to evolutionary reasons, other animal species, such as drosophila (fruit flies), nematodes, mice, and rats, share with humans the same physiological processes that determine behavior, animal genetic studies have a number of advantages in providing information about the genetic determinants of human behavior. Unlike human adoption studies, in research with animals prenatal

TABLE I
Components of Shared Variance for Different Familial Relationships

	Genetic			Environmental			Gene–environment	
	Additive	Dominance	Epistatic	Twin	Shared	Specific	Correlation	Interaction
Identical (MZ) twins	1.00	1.00	1.00	1.00	1.00	.00	1.00	1.00
Fraternal (DZ) twins	.50	.25	.00	1.00	1.00	.00	<.50?	<.50?
Non-twin siblings	.50	.25	.00	.00	1.00	.00	<.50?	<.50?
Parents/offspring	.50	.00	.00	.00	1.00	.00	<.50?	<.50?
Half-siblings	.25	.00	.00	.00	1.00	.00	<.25?	<.25?
Uncles–aunts/ nephew–nieces	.25	.00	.00	.00	0.00?	.00	<.25?	<.25?
First cousins	.125	.00	.00	.00	0.00?	.00	<.125?	<.125?
Adoptees	.00	.00	.00	.00	1.00	.00	.00	.00

environments can be controlled by transplanting fetuses across animals with different genotypes. Rearing environments can be controlled to eliminate differences across relationship types or manipulated to test for gene–environment interactions. Inbred strains of genetically identical animals can be used to control for genetic variability. Heritabilities can be estimated by assessing the phenotypic response to selective breeding for extremes on the trait.

Family studies with humans involve obtaining parent/offspring and/or sibling correlations. As can be seen in Table I, such studies cannot disentangle the effects of genetic influences from shared environmental influences, although they can provide an "upper limit" for heritability. The extension of a family design to the examination of large pedigrees can provide evidence for the Mendelian transmission of a trait under the control of a single gene.

Comparisons of reared-together identical vs fraternal twin resemblances can provide an estimate of heritability, but cannot always disentangle additive vs nonadditive genetic effects. As can be seen in Table I, MZs may resemble each other more than DZs also due to greater shared gene–environment correlations and interactions. In addition, these comparisons assume that greater MZ than DZ resemblances for a trait are not the result of MZs being treated more alike than DZs. A few studies have validated this "equal environments" assumption for intelligence and personality, but it remains untested for other phenotypes.

Adoption studies involve some combination of comparing resemblances of biological parents with their adopted-away offspring vs the resemblances of the adoptive parents with the offspring or comparing

adoptive vs nonadoptive sibling resemblances. Such designs have the advantage of theoretically separating additive genetic and shared environmental influences, although pre- and neonatal environmental effects cannot be controlled for. Attempts by adoption agencies for the sample to match adoptive parents with the biological parents (selective placement) could confound the analyses. This effect has been found to be at times appreciable in studies of intelligence (but not for personality). If the biological parents of the adopted-away offspring are tested, then selective placement can be controlled for.

In order to illustrate two other important aspects of quantitative genetic analysis, Figure 2 presents a path model for the genetic transmission of two different phenotypes (subscripts x and y) from fathers (subscript F) and mothers (subscript M) to their biological offspring (subscript O). In the model, each phenotype P is determined by a genetic factor G and an environmental factor E. The Gs of the parents are linked to the Gs of the offspring by one-half, reflecting the 50% of shared additive genetic variability of parents and offspring, which in this case is confounded by shared environment.

The first additional aspect of note are the arrows connecting the Ps at the top of the figure. These represent phenotypic assortative mating between fathers and mothers and, as can be seen, these arrows allow for greater similarity of the genetic variability transmitted by both parents to the offspring. For instance, mother's transmission of G_{Mx} to G_{Ox} is augmented by an additional path from father's G_{Fx} through the assortative mating path to G_{Mx}. This must be accounted for in estimating the heritability h^2.

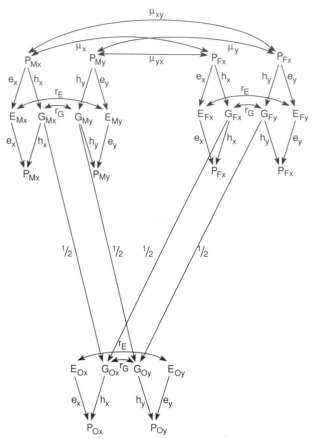

FIGURE 2 Path model of bivariate parent–offspring genetic transmission.

heritability is dependent on high phenotypic variability. As discussed in the section on population genetics, however, high phenotypic variability is associated with traits that have not been highly selected for, i.e., are not important for biological fitness, unless there is a balanced polymorphism. With these caveats in mind, we will now present a few thumbnail sketches of behavioral genetic findings in some domains of human behavior.

A. Intelligence

Since the work of Galton, intelligence has been the most studied phenotype in behavioral genetics. Numerous family, twin, adoption, and, more recently, separated identical twin studies have generally produced estimates of 50 to 80% heritability and about 15 to 25% shared environmental influences on performance on intelligence tests. In keeping with the caveats noted above, despite the high genetic influence on variability in intelligence, mean scores on IQ. tests have risen from one-half to over one standard deviation in Western societies since World War II, a trend indicative of significant environmental influences (probably the increased availability and quality of education in these countries). [*See* INTELLIGENCE.]

B. Personality

Behavioral genetic studies of personality have been almost as numerous as those for intelligence. In general, these studies have yielded heritability estimates of around 50% for most traits, with some evidence for differential heritability for different traits and many traits showing strong nonadditive genetic effects. The most controversial finding from this domain has been the almost complete lack of shared environmental influences found in adoption studies for personality measures. Family environments appear not to make siblings alike in any way, and the importance of family environment in personality development has been questioned. This has spurred developmental research on differential treatment of offspring in families. [*See* PERSONALITY DEVELOPMENT.]

C. Schizophrenia

Schizophrenia has been the psychological disorder that has received the most behavioral genetic attention. Pedigree, family, twin, and adoption studies have all found significant heritabilities for schizo-

The other aspect of note is the r_G arrows connecting the G_xs and G_ys. These represent the genetic correlations discussed above with regard to linkage and or pleiotropy. As can be seen in Figure 2, these genetic correlations are shared genetic effects, and they may be indicative of functional genetic relationships. For example, a significant genetic correlation between performance on tests of verbal ability and performance on tests of spatial ability would indicate some common physiological/genetic process for these abilities.

Before leaving quantitative genetics, several important caveats should be noted. Heritabilities reflect the relative influence of genetic factors on the variability of a trait for just the particular sample of individuals studied and the particular environmental conditions in which they are living. Heritability estimates may not generalize to other populations, and they may greatly change if environmental conditions change. Similarly, high heritabilities do not preclude a trait from being influenced by the environment. Another caveat refers back to the idea that high

phrenia, and this has been consistent with various theories about some kind of physiological basis, probably involving the dopamine system, for the disorder. On the other hand, the 20 to 50% rate of discordance (nonresemblance) between identical twins for schizophrenia indicates a significant specific environmental influence. Linkage studies have failed so far to consistently identify any single gene associated with the disorder, and the accumulated behavioral genetic evidence suggests that there are multiple genetic determinants possibly leading to multiple, etiologically distinct subtypes of schizophrenia. [See SCHIZOPHRENIA.]

D. Affective Disorders

Behavioral genetic studies of affective disorders have been important in making the case for the etiological separation of major depression from bipolar disorder (manic depression). Twin studies of major depression indicate a moderate heritability for the disorder and a strong shared environmental influence. The higher incidence of the disorder in women than men also indicates an environmental effect. The few behavioral genetic studies of bipolar disorder have obtained much higher heritabilities than for major depression. [See DEPRESSION.]

E. Alcoholism

The results of large-sample adoption studies conducted in Denmark and Sweden during the 1970s convinced many researchers and the general public that alcoholism was mostly under the control of genetic determinants. This helped to spur the infusion of resources into studies of the physiological/neurochemical responses of organisms to alcohol. As discussed earlier, there have been attempts recently to identify an "alcoholism gene" by linking alcoholism to a gene known to code for a particular receptor for dopamine. The latest reports suggest that the effects of this gene are not specific for alcoholism. Meanwhile, the accumulated behavioral genetic evidence still suggests that the disorder is influenced by many different genes, as well as by significant environmental factors.

VII. BEHAVIORAL GENETICS AND PSYCHOLOGY

After a contentious start, behavioral genetics has become an accepted part of mainstream psychology. For behavioral domains whose heritability has been well-established, such as schizophrenia, future research will involve linkage analyses and molecular genetic methodologies to identify specific genes and the physiological processes associated with the genes. This holds the promise of being able to more specifically target these processes that determine a behavior. Other behavioral domains, such as attitudes, have not been well-explored by behavioral genetics, and basic heritability analyses from twin and adoption studies will continue to be important.

Finally, one theme that was apparent in the overview of behavioral genetic findings above was that behavioral genetic designs often provide important insights into environmental influences on behavior. The study of gene–environment correlations and interactions clearly will provide opportunities for the greater integration of behavioral genetics and mainstream psychology and the consequent enrichment of both.

Bibliography

Dixon, L. K., and Johnson, R. C. (1980). "The Roots of Individuality: A Survey of Human Behavior Genetics." Brooks/Cole, Monterey, CA.

Plomin, R., DeFries, J. C., and McClearn, G. E. (1990). "Behavioral Genetics: A Primer," 2nd ed. Freeman, New York.

Plomin, R., and Rende, R. (1991). Human behavioral genetics. *Annu. Rev. Psychol.* **42,** 161.

Willerman, L. (1979). "The Psychology of Individual and Group Differences." Freeman, San Francisco.

BEHAVIORAL MEDICINE

James K. Luiselli
Psychological & Educational Resource Associates

Glossary

Behavior therapy Psychological therapy based upon learning theory principles derived from classical and operant conditioning.

Biobehavioral Interaction between biological processes and behavior.

Health psychology Field of psychology that relates to health enhancement, disease prevention, and rehabilitation.

Primary prevention Therapeutic efforts to prevent the occurrence of disease or pathophysiological condition.

Secondary prevention Therapeutic efforts (a) to promote early detection and prompt treatment of disease and (b) to eliminate behavioral risk factors.

Tertiary prevention Therapeutic efforts for the purpose of symptomatic relief.

BEHAVIORAL MEDICINE represents the combination of medical and behavioral sciences for the treatment, management, and prevention of disease, pathophysiological conditions, and health risks. Many definitions have been presented that describe the field of behavioral medicine, relevant foci, methodologies, and exclusion criteria. Although there are similarities in definitions, descriptions are not uniform and, in fact, different interpretations of the scope and content are common. In many ways, behavioral medicine is a field that is still evolving, with consensual boundary conditions yet to be defined.

I. DEFINITIONS

In 1978, the Yale Conference on Behavioral Medicine was convened for the purpose of defining the newly emerging field, current status, and future directions. The seminal definition produced from that conference was as follows: "Behavioral medicine is the field concerned with the development of behavioral science knowledge and techniques relevant to the understanding of physical health and illness and the application of this knowledge and those techniques to prevention, diagnosis, treatment, and rehabilitation. Psychosis, neurosis, and substance abuse are included only in so far as they contribute to physical disorders as an end point."

The Yale Conference definition stressed an interdisciplinary focus that encompassed behavioral, biomedical, and social sciences. Other definitions of behavioral medicine emphasize a more restricted interpretation, particularly with regard to theoretical orientation. The term "behavioral," for example, is linked to the disciplines of behavior therapy, behavior modification, and experimental analysis of behavior that are characterized by the clinical applications of respondent and operant conditioning principles. Furthermore, multiple definitions have been offered that differentiate subcategories of behavioral medicine. One specialization, behavioral health, addresses disease prevention and health maintenance in otherwise nonafflicted persons. Health psychology represents an area that focuses on psychological processes as applied to disease prevention, compliance with health-care routines, and therapeutic adherence. Finally, behavioral pediatrics entails preventive and therapeutic practices that apply specifically to children and adolescents.

Although different definitions of behavioral medicine exist, there is general agreement that the field entails the interrelationship among multiple variables that affect illness and health. Genetic factors play a role in predisposing an individual toward a particular condition and in the existence of specific congenital anomalies. Cognitive processes in the forms of thoughts, beliefs, and attributions influence opinions about disease, coping strategies, and self-control capabilities. Many environmental factors impact the expression of disease and these variables can occur as physical pathogens or life style stressors. And an individual's overt behavior patterns related to consummatory responses, vocational practices, self-care routines, and general "daily living" all combine to affect health and well-being. Within behavioral medicine, these and related variables are seen as reciprocal influences which both affect and are affected by one another.

II. INFLUENCES AND HISTORICAL FOUNDATIONS

The evolution of behavioral medicine as a field of scientific inquiry and clinical practice appears to be a function of several historical trends that emerged during the 1960s. First, there began to develop a closer alliance among physicians and behavioral scientists that yielded new conceptualizations concerning the influence of environmental variables on the expression of disease, illness, and risk factors. The presence of cardiovascular disease, as an example, was closely linked with influences such as sedentary life style, high-cholesterol diets, and cigarette smoking. Clinical specialists began to investigate life-style management approaches that could reduce these and similar risk factors. The critical impact of personal life-style factors also was influenced by changes in the epidemiology of disease namely, a shift from the threat of acute, infectious disease to the management of chronic illness.

The emergence of biofeedback technology was another important development that shaped the evolution of behavioral medicine. Biofeedback is a process whereby the body's bioelectrical potentials are detected, amplified, and transformed into an analogue display that permits an individual to gain control over blood pressure, neuromuscular responding, heart rate, and electroencephalographic (brainwave) activity. The ability to establish self-regulation of these and other physiological responses led to clinical applications of biofeedback for the treatment of various medical disorders. Examples of biofeedback approaches in behavioral medicine include the treatment of hypertension, migraine headache, irritable bowel syndrome, Raynaud's disease, and motor dysfunction associated with cerebral palsy and cerebrovascular trauma (stroke).

Behavioral medicine also was influenced by characteristics and limitations of traditional medical practice. The enormous financial costs associated with surgeries, long-term health care, and extensive medical procedures could be off-set by teaching individuals how to prevent the onset of potential health-threatening conditions and to cope more effectively with illness. Many patients showed a preference for "nonmedical" approaches to therapeutic care. It also was apparent that psychological or behaviorally based treatment would be associated with fewer side effects when contrasted with invasive physical procedures or protracted pharmacological regimens.

III. INTERVENTION PERSPECTIVES

Despite differences in definitions, there appear to be three common intervention perspectives that comprise the field of behavioral medicine. *Tertiary prevention* deals with the treatment and care of individuals who have an acquired illness or dysfunctional condition. The primary focus in this regard is one of symptomatic relief. To illustrate, a patient who is afflicted with chronic rheumatoid arthritis might receive biofeedback, relaxation, cognitive imagery, and problem-solving training in conjunction with primary medical interventions in the forms of physical therapy and pharmacological management. The behavioral medicine treatment would be intended to teach the patient self-regulation skills to attenuate and preempt the experience of pain. Tertiary prevention also encompasses interventions to reduce discomfort and distress associated with invasive medical procedures such as nausea that accompanies chemotherapy treatment for cancer and acute pain that is experienced during skin debridement for chronic burn patients.

Secondary prevention has been defined to encompass two areas within behavioral medicine. First, the term describes measures for the early detection and subsequent treatment of physical disorders. Secondary prevention efforts would include the implementation of public health monitoring programs that are made available through mass-screening projects for hypertension, diabetes, and breast cancer. These and similar interventions are intended to cure and slow the progression of disease, halt the transmission of infection, and limit disability.

The second category included within secondary prevention has been termed behavioral risk reduction and is directed at eliminating factors that are associated with the development of physical illness. There are many examples of health risk factors in contemporary society. Cigarette smoking, high-fat diets, and sedentary life style all have been shown to contribute to coronary heart disease. If an individual has one or more of these known risk factors, behavioral medicine intervention in the form of secondary prevention would occur by attempting to remove or eliminate these influences. Thus, treatment would be instituted to eliminate cigarette smoking, to consume low-fat foods, and to establish a regular schedule of physical exercise.

The area of *primary prevention* concerns efforts to prevent the occurrence of disease or pathophysiological risk factors. Typically, primary prevention interventions encompass methods to initiate and maintain routine practices such as dental care, physical exercise, and well-child care (e.g., immunization, developmental monitoring). A related area is to teach persons how to select and prepare more nutritionally sound meals and avoid high-fat/high-calorie food items. Accident prevention through the application of seat belts and safety-seats in vehicles and comprehensive home-safety practices also would be target areas subsumed under primary prevention. It should be pointed out that the difference between primary and secondary prevention rests with the existence of risk factors. To return to a previous example, teaching an individual to reduce and ultimately refrain from smoking cigarettes would be an example of secondary prevention. The presentation of anti-smoking media to deter an individual from ever engaging in cigarette consumption (i.e., developing a risk factor) would be an example of primary prevention.

IV. CHARACTERISTICS

There are several characteristics that comprise clinical practice and research experimentation in behavioral medicine. First, the integration of physical and behavioral sciences, by definition, presumes an interdisciplinary approach to prevention and treatment. An interdisciplinary perspective requires that professionals work in a coordinated fashion and that all members of a treatment team are knowledgeable concerning each other's clinical specialities. Within behavioral medicine it is essential that psychologists

are familiar with basic concepts of anatomy, biochemistry, neurology, and physiology. Similarly, physicians must be acquainted with fundamental principles of learning, cognition, and socioemotional development. Medicine, psychology, psychiatry, sociology, education, and epidemiology represent primary disciplines that are integrated within a comprehensive behavioral medicine approach.

Behavioral medicine focuses equally on both basic and clinical research endeavors. Basic processes relate to underlying mechanisms that are implicated in the etiology of disease and restoration of health. Biochemistry and electrophysiology are relevant medical domains in this regard. The interrelationship between basic biological processes and therapeutic management is evident for many clinical disorders. In the treatment of obesity, for example, relevant target measures would include a reduction in weight, increased energy expenditure, and improved range of motion. At the same time, positive changes in these overt clinical indices would be supplemented by covarying measures related to serum triglycerides, high- and low-density lipoproteins, and blood pressure. Similarly, the interrelationship between electroencephalographic activity and the presence of seizures would be studied in the treatment of epilepsy. In effect, basic processes are studied to determine their role in causality and in response to clinical treatment.

Behavioral medicine treatment and research rely heavily on empirical assessment to evaluate the effects from clinical interventions, preventive strategies, and experimental manipulations. This emphasis on objective measurement is a fundamental characteristic that is integral to behavior modification and behavior therapy treatment approaches. When assessment is conducted, particular measures of clinical relevance are quantified and recorded. These measurements can include overt motor responses, physiological activity, or cognitive processes. As it relates to a patient with a seizure disorder, for example, assessment could be performed to document the frequency of seizures (motor–behavioral measure), the pattern of electroencephalographic activity (physiological measure), and the individual's self-statements concerning the affliction (cognitive measure). Behavioral medicine assessment attempts to quantify the interrelationship between these three categories of dependent measures to demonstrate convariation among response units. That is, it may be possible to affect change in one area while simultaneously producing similar changes in another. Or, the positive influences of treatment on motor responding may have no effect, or perhaps an opposite reaction, on physiological or cognitive responding. The objective measurement of motor, physiological, and cognitive indices is defined as tripartite assessment.

Treatment methodology in behavioral medicine includes diverse procedures and methodologies. Many individualized techniques represent standard interventions that were developed by psychologists for the clinical practice of behavior therapy. One common procedure, relaxation training, is intended to train patients to reduce and control muscle tension that contributes to psychophysiological disorders such as migraine headache, hypertension, and irritable bowel syndrome. Patients who receive relaxation training are taught to induce tension-reduction through the progressive tightening and releasing of muscle groups, the assistance of portable biofeedback devices (e.g., electromyography, skin temperature), or the use of mental imagery. A second category of individualized therapy methods includes cognitive–behavioral control strategies. These methods enable a patient to change negative self-statements and attributions as a means to improve coping skills and reduce their impact on the maintenance of a clinical disorder. For example, a patient with obesity who engages in self-defeating comments (e.g., "I'm fat, I'll never lose weight") would be taught how to eliminate these statements in favor of a greater sense of self-efficacy (e.g., "I can do it, I'll work hard and overcome this problem!"). Relaxation, cognitive–behavioral, and related training procedures typically are introduced during individualized sessions between a patient and therapist. The ultimate objective from treatment is to enable the patient to gain self-control of a therapeutic regimen. [*See* COGNITIVE BEHAVIOR THERAPY; RELAXATION.]

Other behaviorally oriented treatment strategies are designed to be implemented by significant others who have direct contact with a patient, for example, parents, teachers, nurses, and so on. Treatment of this type frequently is instituted for pediatric disorders since, as contrasted to adults, many children are unable to acquire proficient self-management skills. Similarly, persons with developmental disabilities usually are unable to benefit from self-control training due to intellectual and cognitive impairments. The treatments implemented by significant others are geared toward increasing health-enhancing behaviors, removing conditions that maintain a presenting disorder, and generalizing therapeutic effects within multiple environmental settings. A pediatric pain patient, as an example, might be taught pain-coping strategies by a psychologist that subsequently could be encouraged and reinforced by parents. The child's parents also might work with their child in reducing the frequency of administration of analgesic tablets and increasing performance of therapeutic activities. In such a case, the child might earn specified rewards for adhering to a treatment plan and gradually achieving prescribed goals.

On a larger scale, many behavioral medicine interventions are applied to affect the performance of persons under group conditions, typically from a primary or secondary intervention perspective. The concern for motor vehicle safety represents one area that has received extensive program and research evaluation. These projects have included interventions to increase use of seat belts and car-seat devices and have included discrete monetary rewards for "buckling-up," visual cues to prompt restraint behaviors, and corrective feedback during highway travel. Other applications have addressed preventive-behavior practices such as reducing the risk of skin cancer by limiting exposure to the sun and increasing energy expenditure by promoting use of stairs vs escalators in shopping centers. These large-scale projects are described as behavioral community interventions.

V. ADDITIONAL CLINICAL DOMAINS

As noted previously, the field of behavioral medicine encompasses a number of specialty areas that target primary, secondary, and tertiary preventive outcomes. In addition to some of the clinical disorders already cited, several other areas of specialization are noteworthy. The area of behavioral pediatrics covers an extensive amount of treatment and preventive practices that relate to children's medical problems, psychosocial development, and adjustment to illness. Like behavioral medicine as a whole, the subspecialty of behavioral pediatrics has been defined differently by a number of theorists and alternative terms such as biosocial, psychosocial, and developmental pediatrics have been proposed. The realm of clinical treatment in behavioral pediatrics includes chronic pain, asthma, neurological disorders, oncology, and cardiology. Interventions also are developed frequently to prepare children for surgery, teach self-care procedures (e.g., self-catheterization), and establish adherence to therapeutic regimens. A more recent focus is on the social and emotional factors involved in normal growth and development or, so called, ambulatory pediatrics.

Behavioral medicine treatment and research have particular relevance for persons with developmental disabilities such as mental retardation, autism, and specific syndromes that are characterized by cognitive, intellectual, and neurological impairments. Many persons with developmental disabilities, for example, evince problems with bladder and bowel incontinence, seizures, and neuromuscular functioning and, as a result, can benefit from the combination of medical and behavioral treatments. Certain syndromes are associated with behavioral and medical disorders such as obesity in persons with Prader-Willi syndrome and motor deterioration in Hurler, Hunter, and Rett syndrome. Among persons who are developmentally disabled it is very common to encounter the presence of health-threatening behaviors such as self-injury, vomiting, food refusal, and pica (ingestion of nonedible substances). From a primary prevention perspective, treatment objectives include establishing healthier life styles by promoting a regular schedule of physical exercise, eating nutritious foods, and maintaining personal care and hygiene routines.

Behavioral pharmacology concerns the treatment of physical disorders, learning responsiveness, and varied clinical conditions with medication that is used singularly or in combination with behavioral methods. Behavioral assessment techniques are employed frequently to assist physicians in determining the therapeutic effects from medications and in identifying optimal dose ranges. Assessment also is crucial to evaluate the interactive effects from multiple medications. In addition to measuring the positive influence of medication, behavioral pharmacology assessment focuses on potential negative side effects that can occur during treatment. [*See* BEHAVIORAL PHARMACOLOGY.]

There perhaps is no greater challenge to the discipline of behavioral medicine than overcoming the devastating epidemic of acquired immune deficiency syndrome (AIDS). AIDS represents a variety of end-stage illnesses that are sequelae to human immunodeficiency virus (HIV) infection. Because HIV is transmitted via specific bodily fluids (e.g., blood, semen, vaginal secretions) that must contact directly the bloodstream rather than through airborne or insect-borne pathways, AIDS can be prevented by engaging in behaviors that eliminate the possibility of infection. Behavior-change interventions and community-based preventive efforts in AIDS treatment are intended to eliminate high-risk practices among the population. Relevant approaches include the dissemination of AIDS informational brochures that describe features of the disease, high-risk influences, and behavior-specific prevention strategies related to sexual activity and intravenous drug use. Many communities have adopted AIDS-outreach programs that provide preventive educational and treatment services. Public programs that test for the presence of HIV have been established as another community effort toward risk reduction. Although progress continues in the development of an effective vaccine for AIDS, the immediate availability of a medical cure is not likely for some time. Therefore, the development of large-scale behavior-change interventions remains an area of essential primary prevention research.

VI. CONCLUSION

Behavioral medicine continues to evolve as an area of clinical practice and research. The abundant diversity of theory, application, and experimentation underscores the many features and functions of this field. It is clear that the broad foci that characterize behavioral medicine are why an unequivocal definition remains elusive. As such, it perhaps is best to view behavioral medicine as a general orientation toward the psychological and environmental treatment of disease and promotion of health rather than a complete compilation of principles and procedures.

Bibliography

Dahlquist, L. M., and Czyzewski, D. I. (1989). Pediatric behavioral medicine. In "Innovations in Child Behavior Therapy" (M. Hersen, Ed.). Springer, New York.

Dishman, R. K. (Ed.) (1988). "Exercise Adherence: Its Impact on Public Health." Human Kinetics, Champaign, Il.

Kelly, J. A., and St. Lawrence, J. S. (1988). "The AIDS Health Crisis: Psychological and Social Interventions." Plenum, New York.

Luiselli, J. K. (Ed.) (1989). "Behavioral Medicine and Developmental Disabilities." Springer-Verlag, New York.

Meyers, A. (Ed.) (1991). Interactive models in behavioral medicine. *Behav. Ther.* **22,** 129.

Russo, D. C., and Kedesdy, J. H. (Eds.) (1988). "Behavioral Medicine with the Developmentally Disabled." Plenum, New York.

Williamson, D. A. (Ed.) (1987). Recent advances in behavioral medicine. *Behav. Modification* **11,** 259.

BEHAVIORAL PHARMACOLOGY

William A. McKim

Memorial University of Newfoundland, Canada

Glossary

Classical conditioning A phenomenon first studied by Pavlov in which a previously neutral stimulus is paired with a stimulus that elicits a reflexive response. Eventually the neutral stimulus will elicit the reflexive behavior.

Discriminative stimulus A stimulus that signals the availability of reinforcement.

Drug receptor Most drugs produce changes in physiological processes by interacting with specific receptors in the body. These receptors are large protein molecules embedded in membranes of cells and are different for different classes of drugs. A drug interacting with a receptor site is often described as being similar to a key operating a lock.

Operant behavior Behavior that is maintained by its past consequences rather than elicited or evoked by a stimulus or antecedent condition.

Physical dependence The state in which withdrawal symptoms will occur when the use of a drug is reduced or discontinued.

Reinforcement An event such as the delivery of food or water which will increase the frequency of an action that immediately precedes it.

Schedule of reinforcement This term describes the relationship between the delivery of a reinforcing stimulus and operant response or responses it follows. There are many different schedules, but the most common ones are ratio schedules where the reinforcer is delivered when a number of responses have been emitted, and interval schedules where the reinforcer is delivered after a response on the basis of the passage of time.

Skinner box A chamber of a type invented by B. F. Skinner used to study operant behavior in laboratory animals. The chamber is isolated from external stimulation and contains devices activated by responses of the animal which permit delivery and recording of reinforcements.

Tolerance A lessening of the effect of a drug when the same dose is repeatedly administered, or conversely, the necessity of giving a higher dose with repeated administrations in order to achieve the same effect.

BEHAVIORAL PHARMACOLOGY may be defined in one of two ways. The term was initially used by Peter Dews of Harvard Medical School to refer to the analysis of drug effects using operant analysis of behavior as developed by B. F. Skinner. More recently the term is used in a broader sense to refer to the study of the effects of drugs on behavior using any of the experimental techniques of modern behaviorally oriented psychology. The key word here is "behavior," since this expansion in definition does not extend to include mentalistic concepts such as emotion, motivation, or cognition unless they are defined in terms of observable behavior. Before Dews suggested the term "behavioral pharmacology" in the 1950s, research in this area was commonly referred to as "psychopharmacology"—a combination of the fields of psychology and pharmacology. "Psychopharmacology" is still used, but is generally taken to include all research involving any aspect of psychology, including the mentalistic, and is used particularly to refer to the study of drugs in the treatment of mental illness or psychological disorders. "Psychopharmacology" is also commonly used to describe any research involving psychoactive drugs, including neurophysiological and neurochemical research.

It is important to note that there may be several aims of research in behavioral pharmacology. As Travis Thompson and Charles Schuster, the authors of the first text in the field, put it, "The behavioral pharmacologist is not only interested in observing behavioral changes produced by drugs, but analyzing the mechanisms of the drug's effect." In addition, Peter Dews has pointed out that not only are behavioral techniques useful in helping analyze the behavioral mechanisms through which drugs alter behavior, but just as often, drugs may be used as tools to help untangle complex problems in the analysis of behavior.

I. HISTORY OF BEHAVIORAL PHARMACOLOGY

Humans have always been curious about substances that alter the mind. Alcohol, cannabis, and opium have been used for millennia. Aristotle commented on the effects of alcohol, and the analgesic effects of opium were noted by the very earliest Greek and Egyptian physicians. Up until the beginning of the 20th century, however, investigations of these substances involved only verbal descriptions of the effects of the drug on the subjective experience, more often with literary rather than scientific intent. Such descriptions as DeQuincey's *Confessions of an English Opium Eater* and Gautier's *La Club des Hachichins* were fascinating descriptions of the drug experience, but were of limited value to science.

Systematic studies of the effects of these substances had to await two developments. First, there was the development of modern chemical techniques in the 19th century that permitted the isolation of drugs from natural substances and the synthesis of substances that do not occur naturally.

The second important development was a precise, systematic and replicable means of describing, recording, and analyzing behavior. Three such systems were developed. In Russia the Nobel Prize–winning physiologist Ivan P. Pavlov discovered and explored what we now call classical conditioning. In his laboratory in St. Petersberg caffeine and other drugs were administered to dogs and their effects on acquisition and extinction of conditioned reflexes were observed. In addition, Pavlov also successfully conditioned the effects of drugs to previously neutral stimuli. His work produced interesting results, but Pavlov did not pursue this line of research further. [*See* CLASSICAL CONDITIONING.]

In North America Thorndike and the followers of the behaviorist John B. Watson used the techniques of instrumental learning, i.e., mazes, runways, etc., to investigate learning and behavioral processes in laboratory animals. In the 1920s Macht acquired a maze from Thorndike and in a series of studies investigated the effects of a number of different drugs on rat behavior. Once again, this work did not immediately stimulate much further investigation.

Also in North America, B. F. Skinner and his co-workers developed the techniques known as the operant analysis of behavior. Skinner and his students developed a technology whereby the behavior of an animal in an isolated environment could be manipulated by altering the schedule of reinforcement, i.e., by precisely controlling the contingency between performance of a specific action such as pressing a lever and the delivery of a reinforcer such as food. Using these techniques, the rate and pattern of responding of experimental animals, usually rats and pigeons, could be controlled with a precision not previously possible and remained stable throughout lengthy experimental sessions and over repeated sessions. Skinner and Heron recognized early that this technique could be particularly useful in studying the effects of drugs because it created a stable behavioral baseline and gave the researcher some measure of control over the responding of the animal. In 1937 they published a paper describing the effects on *dl*-amphetamine and caffeine on the behavior of rats. In this paper, Skinner and Heron acknowledge that their research was derived from studies conducted earlier in Pavlov's laboratory. Their study was published in the psychological literature rather than in a pharmacology journal and it appears not to have been noticed by pharmacologists. [*See* OPERANT LEARNING.]

After Skinner and Heron there were other attempts to investigate the effects of various drugs using operant techniques, but up until the 1950s such studies were sporadic and uncoordinated.

During the time psychologists were becoming interested in the effects of drugs on behavior, there was a growing interest among pharmacologists in drugs that affected the central nervous system. However, most pharmacologists were unaware of the techniques developed by psychologists. Behavioral research carried out by pharmacologists did not involve very sophisticated behaviors. For the most part such studies merely involved observing laboratory animals after they had been given a drug, and quantifying total amount of activity in an unstructured situation. If spontaneous motor activity increased it was taken to indicate that the drug was a central nervous system "stimulant"; if it decreased, the drug was a "depressant."

Even though both psychologists and pharmacologists were doing behavioral research with drugs, up until the 1950s there could not be considered to be a separate discipline of behavioral pharmacology. The impetus to develop such a field came in the early 1950s and arose largely from two events. The first was the tremendous therapeutic and commercial success of chlorpromazine and other antipsychotic drugs, and the second was the compelling demonstration by Peter B. Dews of the usefulness of Skinner's operant techniques to study drug effects.

A. Chlorpromazine

Chlorpromazine was marketed by the French pharmaceutical company Rhône-Poulenc as an antipsychotic drug in 1952. Initially it was used to prevent surgical shock, but it was soon discovered that it was also effective as an antipsychotic—it was the first drug useful in treating the specific symptoms of schizophrenia and other psychoses. This demonstrated the tremendous economic potential of behaviorally active drugs and an intensive search for new drugs and new medical applications of older drugs began.

In the development of chlorpromazine, behavioral techniques had been used to confirm that chlorpromazine and other phenothiazines had antipsychotic properties. In fact, one of the techniques used to identify the important behavioral properties of the phenothiazine antipsychotics was a rope climbing task developed by Macht in the tradition of instrumental learning. It became obvious that there was a need for a better understanding of how drugs altered behavior, and that the synthesis of pharmacology and behavioral techniques would be useful, not only to pharmaceutical companies wanting to develop and test new compounds, but as a separate field of investigation that could lead to a better understanding the interaction of drugs and behavioral processes.

B. Operant Technology

In 1955, Peter Dews began publishing a series of papers in pharmacology journals in which he reported using Skinner's operant technology to demonstrate some remarkable and surprising drug effects. Dews was trained as a physician in England and came to the United States where he worked for Burroughs Wellcome Co. and later earned a Ph.D. in physiology from the University of Minnesota. In 1952 he took a position at Harvard Medical School. Earlier in his career he had attempted to study the effects of THCs on behavior (THC is one of the active ingredients in cannabis), but had given up in frustration because ". . . there were no promising techniques in pharmacology for studying behavioral effects." He went on to do experiments on the effects of histamines and antihistamines on isolated smooth muscles of guinea pigs and blood pressure of cats. These techniques involved the continuous recording of responding of the preparation in real time on a polygraph.

When he arrived at Harvard, Dews went across the river to Cambridge

. . . to see B. F. Skinner who introduced me to C. B. Ferster who in turn took me into their laboratory. And there they were recording something they called operant behavior as ups and downs of a continuous line in real time. I was at home at once and was determined to follow the lead of Skinner and Heron fifteen years before and to apply the techniques to behavioral pharmacology.

Of particular appeal to Dews was the fact that operant techniques recorded a steady-state behavior for an extended period of time during which the effects of a pharmacological treatment could be continuously monitored and recorded. Comparisons between drug and control conditions were made for each individual animal between different sessions. This was in the tradition of pharmacology familiar to Dews. Operant technology represented a departure from the methods used earlier by psychologists in the instrumental learning tradition who tested animals using very brief discrete trials in a runway or a shuttle box and based their conclusions on the mean performance of large groups.

Figure 1 is from Dews's 1955 paper. It shows the effect of different doses of pentobarbital on the rate of key pecking of pigeons responding for food on two different schedules of reinforcement. Pentobarbital had a distinctly different effect depending on the schedule in effect when the drug was administered. At doses of 1.0 to 2.0 mg/kg the drug *increased* response rates if the pigeon was responding on a

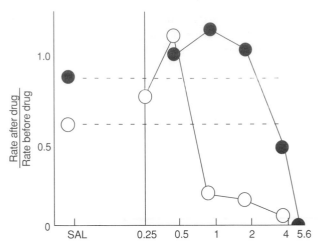

FIGURE 1   The log dose–effect curves for pentobarbital on the relative response rate of pigeons responding on FI 15-min (open circles) and FR 50 schedules (closed circles). The dotted lines indicate response levels after a control injection of saline. [From Dews, P. B. (1955). *J. Pharmacol. Exp. Ther.* **113**(4), 393–401.]

fixed ratio 50 schedule (FR 50—every 50th response was followed by an exposure to food), but *decreased* responding if a 15-min fixed interval was in effect (FI 15 min—the first response after 15 min had elapsed was followed by an exposure to food).

Dews showed that pentobarbital altered the behavior of the pigeon in a different manner depending on the schedule of reinforcement in effect at the time the drug was given. This showed convincingly that drug effects depend on the type of behavior that is occurring rather than simply "depressing" or "stimulating" all behavior. This paper and several more like it were published in the pharmacology journals. Operant techniques finally captured the attention of pharmacologists.

In addition to the work of Dews, in the mid and late 1950s Joseph V. Brady established the first university-related laboratory using operant technology for the study of drug–behavior interactions at Walter Reed Army Medical Center and later at the University of Maryland. Brady stimulated the development of behavioral pharmacology by urging the pharmaceutical industry and the federal government of the United States to support this new field.

In 1956 a conference was held on "The Techniques for the Study of the Behavioral Effects on Drugs" sponsored by the New York Academy of Science. It was chaired by Dews and Skinner and the participants included D. S. Blough, Richard Herrnstein, H. F. Hunt, Neil Miller, William Morse, Murray Sidman, and many others who had made

significant contributions at that time. Also in 1956, Skinner made a formal call for the development of a new science of behavioral pharmacology. The new science got its formal start when the Behavioral Pharmacology Society was founded. In about 1955 a group interested in pharmacology started having informal evening dinner meetings during the annual meeting of the Eastern Psychological Association. The Society evolved a year or two later. In 1989 the journal *Behavioral Pharmacology* was founded, the first journal specifically devoted to the area.

Early interest in the behavioral analysis of drug effects was not confined to North America. In Britain, interest in the field was stimulated by a pioneering symposium held in London sponsored by the Ciba Foundation in 1963. It was attended by many prominent European researchers of the time as well as those from North America including Len Cook and Peter Dews. The proceedings were edited by Hannah Steinberg and published in 1964. Since that time, researchers such as D. E. Blackman, David Sanger (now in France), Susan Iverson, Trevor Robbins, and Ian Stolerman and their students have had an extensive impact on the field.

The operant tradition of behavioral analysis of drug effects also spread to the continent. Marc Richelle, after spending a year at Harvard with B. F. Skinner returned to Belgium in 1959 where he set up a behavioral pharmacology laboratory and began publishing in European journals. Other prominent Belgian behavioral pharmacologists include C. Niemegeers and F. Colpaert. Other European pioneers in the field include R. Dantzer in France, J. Slangen in Holland, and Daniel Bovet, G. L. Gatti, and Georgio Bignami in Italy. The continued expansion of behavioral pharmacology in Europe was marked by the founding of The European Behavioral Pharmacology Society in 1986.

Most researchers in behavioral pharmacology come from one of two backgrounds; either they have been trained as psychologists and acquired an understanding of pharmacology or they have been trained as pharmacologists and taught themselves the techniques of behavioral analysis. Recently, however, a number of graduate programs have been developed which combine training in both traditions.

II. ENVIRONMENTAL INFLUENCES ON DRUG EFFECTS

In the years since Dews's early studies, many behavioral pharmacologists have explored the complex interaction between environmental factors and the effect of various drugs. In addition to schedule of reinforcement, these factors include rate of responding, extent of stimulus control, the nature of the reinforcer, and the past behavioral and pharmacological history of the organism.

A. Schedule of Reinforcement

Dews's 1955 study showed that the effects of a barbiturate depend on the schedule of reinforcement. It has been demonstrated that each class of drugs has a unique pattern of effects on various schedules. Drugs such as cocaine and amphetamine, for example, have effects quite different from barbiturates. When various doses of amphetamine are administered to animals responding on a FI and FR schedule similar to those used in the Dews experiment, a dose range is encountered where FI responding is increased considerably above control levels and FR responding is nearly eliminated—exactly the opposite of the barbiturates.

B. Rate of Responding

The rate at which an operant response is emitted has traditionally been the primary dependent variable analyzed by operant psychologists, and early in the development of the field it was discovered that response rate had a pervasive influence on the effect of many drugs. In one of his early experiments with amphetamine, Dews noticed that the drug seemed to be interacting specifically with the rate of responding. He noticed that the drug increased low rates of responding, while at the same time it decreased responding in situations that normally engendered high rates. This phenomenon has become known as the rate dependency effect. It appears to be responsible for the observation described earlier that responding on FI (which normally engenders comparatively low rates of responding) is increased, and responding on FR (which normally engenders high rates) is slowed by amphetamine. In fact, it is likely that drugs often affect different schedules differently because different schedules produce different base rates of responding.

The rate dependency effect has wide generality and can account for the effect of many drugs in many different behavioral situations. For example, responding on FI schedules is normally characterized by a range of response rates. Organisms normally pause immediately after a reinforcement, but

as the time for the next reinforcement approaches, response rates increase until the organism is responding at a fast rate when the next reinforcement is due. Careful analyses of the different rates of responding during a FI have clearly shown that the rate dependency effect applies to these different rates; responding early in the interval which is normally slow is speeded by amphetamine, but the fast responding later in the interval is slowed by the same administration of the drug. Figure 2 shows the traditional method of reporting rate dependent effects. This shows that not only the direction, but also the amount, of change in rate caused by the drug is directly related to the control rate, i.e., the rate that the animal would be responding without the drug.

Rate dependent effects are caused by many different drugs in many different species responding on a wide variety of tasks. At one point, in fact, rate dependent effects were thought to be so universal that many researchers were more interested in exceptions to rate dependent effects than in rate effects themselves.

C. Other Factors

Many other environmental influences have been shown to interact dynamically with drug effects but the pervasiveness of rate has made it necessary to eliminate the influence of rate before the role of these other factors can be demonstrated. For example, different reinforcing events must be presented in such a manner that they engender identical rates and

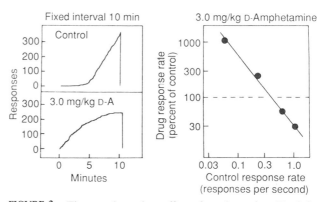

FIGURE 2 The rate-dependent effect of amphetamine. The left panels show the cumulative records of a pigeon responding on a FI 10-min schedule for food under control conditions and after being given 3 mg/kg d-amphetamine. In the right-hand panel drug-induced changes in response rate are shown as a percentage of control rate of responding. [From Bartlett, J. (1980). *Trends Pharmacol. Sci.* **1**, 215–218.]

patterns of behavior before it is possible to show that in some cases a drug will differentially alter behavior controlled by different reinforcers. James Barrett trained monkeys to respond on an FI 5-min schedule. The reinforcing event was either food or a brief electric shock. (Shock can serve as a reinforcer if the organism has a suitable history of responding.) Responding on both schedules was identical in terms of rate and pattern, but the effect of several drugs was different depending on whether the reinforcing event was food or shock. Pentobarbital, for example slowed the food reinforced performance, but created a considerable increase in the shock reinforced behavior.

Other factors have been demonstrated to influence the effect of drugs even when schedule and rate are held constant. These factors include the degree of discriminative control and the behavioral and pharmacological history of the organism, i.e., whether it had previous experience with the same or other drugs.

As James Barrett has put it,

> . . . a drug is not simply a molecule with static unitary behavioral effects. The same dose of a drug can exert an array of effects on behavior depending on the immediate consequences of responding, the prior experience of the organism and the total environmental context in which the behavior takes place.

III. DISSOCIATION AND DISCRIMINATIVE PROPERTIES OF DRUGS

One branch of contemporary behavioral pharmacology deals with drugs as discriminative stimuli. This branch of the field has it origins outside traditional operant analysis, but is now considered to be an integral part of behavioral pharmacology. Investigations into the discriminative properties of drugs originated with research in the instrumental learning tradition and the early neurophysiological theories of Donald Hebb at McGill University.

A. Dissociation

It had always been believed that information acquired during a drugged state was not readily available for recall when the organism was undrugged and vice versa. This phenomenon is called *dissociation* or *state-dependent learning*. In the 1930s Girden

and his co-workers found that a conditioned leg flexion response in dogs acquired while under the influence of a centrally acting curariform drug did not occur to the conditioned stimulus when no drug was present, but did so again when the drug was readministered. These findings were explained by the neurophysiological model developed by Donald Hebb. Hebb's model proposed that learning was a result of changes in the synaptic interconnections of neurons which caused particular patterns of discharge called phase sequences. Phase sequences formed during a time when a drug has altered neural functioning will be different from phase sequences developed in a no-drug state. Thus, when the drug wears off, the neurons will not be able to recreate the appropriate phase sequence and the learned material will not be available for recall. It is only when the drug is given again that the appropriate phase sequences can be reinstated and the information be recalled.

Donald Overton, then a graduate student at McGill University's Psychology Department, did a series of experiments to determine whether state-dependent learning could be demonstrated using other centrally acting drugs and a more traditional learning task than Girden had used. Overton used a T-maze with an electrified floor. The rat was placed on the apparatus and removed when it entered a safe area at the end of one of the arms. In order to escape the shock as quickly as possible the rat had to make the correct turn at the choice point. Overton was easily able to demonstrate that rats that learned the maze when drugged with pentobarbital were unable to behave appropriately when given a placebo and vice versa.

B. Drug State Discrimination

To explore the extent of dissociation, Overton wanted to determine whether information learned on drug days (turn right) would interfere with information acquired on saline days (turn left) and vice versa. On alternate days, the rats were administered pentobarbital and one arm led directly to safety. On other days they were given a saline placebo and the other arm was safe. Overton discovered that the rats very quickly learned to make the appropriate response depending on whether they were drugged or not. He also found that rats would learn to make the appropriate response at doses much lower that those required to cause complete dissociation. In other words, he showed that rats would very quickly learn to treat the presence or absence of the drug as a discriminative stimulus which indicated the direction they should run at the choice point of the maze.

Since Overton's early experiments, research on the discriminative stimulus properties of drugs has rapidly expanded, and the electrified T-maze has been replaced with the Skinner box. Herbert Barry III, then at Yale and now at the University of Pittsburgh, is generally credited with applying operant techniques to the field. Rather than using the older, discrete trials approach of instrumental learning, Barry trained experimental animals to press a lever for food in a two-lever Skinner box. On days when a drug is administered, presses on one lever are reinforced, and on saline days the other lever is reinforced. Two methods have been used to eliminate the possibility that the food–lever correlation rather than the drug state is controlling lever pressing. In one, the researcher introduces brief extinction sessions when neither lever is reinforced. On these sessions the correct lever is not signaled by the immediate delivery of food and the animal must depend on its ability to detect the presence or absence of the drug in its system to control its behavior. Another technique is to deliver food on the correct lever on an FR 20 schedule so that the first 20 responses in a session provide an indication of whether the discrimination has been acquired. The advantage of the operant technique is that it is more sensitive than the electrified T-maze, and by taking the percentage of responses on each lever, it is possible to establish the extent to which the drug stimulus is controlling behavior. This is not possible with the T-maze where responding is entirely one way or the other on any given trial. In addition, fewer research subjects are needed.

Using these techniques it has been demonstrated that most centrally acting drugs have discriminative stimulus properties, although some classes of drugs such as the barbiturates appear to be more easily discriminable than other classes. Such drugs can acquire discriminative control at least as rapidly, and in some cases more rapidly, than more conventional stimuli like noises and lights. It has also been shown that as well as discriminating between a drug and saline, laboratory animals can discriminate between different doses of the same drug and between different drugs.

It has not yet been established for any drug what aspect of the drug's effect is exerting the stimulus control, but it is known that the control does not originate from any effect drugs have on the peripheral sense organs, nor does it appear to have anything to do with effects on the peripheral nervous system. The control appears to arise from a drug's effect on the central nervous system and, at least for drugs with known receptor sites, the discriminative effect can be eliminated by blocking the drug's receptors. The discriminative stimulus seems equivalent to what we would term the subjective effect in humans. In fact, experienced drug users usually classify drugs in categories similar to categories established using laboratory animals.

In addition to determining whether a drug can act as a discriminative stimulus, behavioral pharmacologists have also been able to test for generalization between drugs. In this situation, an animal is trained to discriminate between saline and a drug and then is tested with another drug, a technique similar to generalization. Animals will usually generalize responses between drugs of the same pharmacological class. Animals trained to discriminate morphine from saline, for example, will make morphine-like responses when tested with other opiate drugs. The morphine response, however, will not generalize to other classes such as amphetamines or barbiturates.

Drug discrimination techniques are also widely used in neurochemical investigations of the mechanism of action of many drugs. For example, it is possible to block the discriminative properties of morphine by pretreating the animal with selective opiate antagonist like naloxone, showing that the stimulus properties of morphine require functioning μ-receptors. The effects of morphine are not blocked by antagonists of other drug classes. Furthermore, it is possible to locate the site of action of many drugs in the brain. Minute amounts of drugs injected directly into specific parts of the brain can also have discriminative stimulus properties and block the properties of other drugs.

IV. DRUGS AS REINFORCERS

A. Research with Non-humans

Early research was generally not able to demonstrate that laboratory animals would administer drugs to themselves in the same manner humans do. Most of these studies involved the oral administration of drugs, usually alcohol, and even though some studies showed that animals could demonstrate a preference for some drugs, they were seldom ever able to show that animals would make themselves physically dependent on a drug, i.e., voluntarily consume enough drug that withdrawal symptoms would develop if the drug were discontinued. Physical dependence was believed to be the defining characteristic of addiction at the time. Also, these studies were not able to demonstrate the compulsiveness usually associated with human drug-seeking behavior. Because of these failures and other widespread beliefs about the nature of drug addiction it was generally believed that drug addiction was restricted to humans.

In 1962, three groups of researchers announced at a meeting of The Committee on Problems of Drug Dependence in Ann Arbor, Michigan, that they had developed the now classic technique which permits laboratory animals to administer drugs to themselves intravenously. The technique involves implanting a cannula into a vein of an laboratory animal and attaching the cannula to a motor-driven pump. The pump is connected to programming apparatus so that it can be operated by the animal when it depresses a lever. Thus, the animal can administer an intravenous injection to itself. Using this method Travis Thompson and Charles Schuster of the University of Maryland, and Gerald Deneau, Tomoji Yanagita, and M. H. Seevers at the University of Michigan showed that monkeys would self-administer morphine, and James Weeks and James Collins demonstrated that rats would self-administer morphine.

The importance of these experiments was that they demonstrate quite clearly that the administration of a drug can be a reinforcing event in the same manner as food to a hungry animal or water to a thirsty one. They showed that there is nothing special or different about drug taking and that the general principles that have been learned about operant behavior are applicable to drug self-administration. Furthermore, they showed that drug use is not a result of a pathology or a disease and is not independent of normal psychological processes.

One of the earliest important findings using this technique was that physical dependence is not necessary for drug self-administration. Travis Thompson and Roy Pickens demonstrated that drugs like cocaine would be self-administered even though they do not normally induce physical dependence. This made it clear that drugs are self-administered because of their positive effects rather than because they delayed or relieved unpleasant withdrawal symptoms.

In the years since these early studies much has been learned about the self-administration of drugs.

It has been shown that most of the classes of drugs consumed by humans are also self-administered by non-humans. These include alcohol, nicotine, caffeine, barbiturates, opiates, tranquilizers, and amphetamines, but there are a couple of notable exceptions: THC and hallucinogenic drugs such as LSD. In addition, laboratory animals will work to avoid infusions of some drugs that humans do not like to consume: for instance the antipsychotic chlorpromazine. [*See* SUBSTANCE ABUSE.]

It is also clear that the patterns of behavior generated by different schedules of drug reinforcement are similar to those generated when more traditional reinforcers are used, and that other phenomena like extinction, discriminative stimulus control, chaining, second-order schedules, etc., are also observed.

Drug administration patterns over time appear to be very similar for humans and non-humans. For example, a human volunteer drinking alcohol in a research ward in a hospital and a rhesus monkey self-administering ethanol through a cannula both show an erratic pattern of intake and abstinence with occasional self-inflicted withdrawal symptoms: a pattern very similar to that shown by alcoholics in the natural environment. As well, both humans and animals administering opiate drugs show a smooth gradual increase in intake from day to day without severe daily fluctuations, and the cocaine pattern in both humans and animals involves cycles of intake and abstinence when the drug is freely available.

The drug self-administration technique has also been used to answer some interesting questions about drug use. For example, which drugs are the most reinforcing? Several methods have been used to answer this question. In one, known as the progressive ratio schedule, the schedule demand increases as the session progresses. For example, a drug may be available on a FR 25 schedule, meaning that the animal must make 25 responses for an infusion. After the first infusion, however, the schedule changes to an FR 50 and then to an FR 100 and so on. Eventually the schedule value will reach a point where responding will not continue. This is known as the breaking point. Drugs that are highly reinforcing would be expected to have high breaking points. Experiments such as these generally show that cocaine and amphetamine have higher breaking points than other drugs. Analogous results have been found in choice experiments where the animal must make a choice between two levers, each of which delivers an infusion of a different drug or a different dose of the same drug.

The choice procedure has also been used to present animals with a choice between a drug and food or some other reinforcer. Generally it can be shown that consumption of a drug will be reduced when the opportunity to respond for a drug is made to compete with responding for other reinforcers in this manner. This observation may well explain why drug abuse appears to thrive in environments where there is unemployment, poverty, and boredom, i.e., environments where there are few other sources of reinforcement to compete with drugs as reinforcers of behavior.

Another line of research has shown that neutral stimuli like lights and sounds can also become reinforcers through association with drug administration. Stephen Goldberg of the United States National Institute on Drug Abuse was the first to use second-order schedules in self-administration research. In a second-order schedule drug infusions are paired with a distinctive stimulus, usually a light. Throughout the session, the organism responds on a short schedule, often an FR 10 for the light alone. Each of these FR 10s, however, is treated as a single response in a different schedule reinforced with the light and drug combination, an FI 60-min for example. On such a schedule, the animal would be reinforced with a light after every 10 responses, and would only get the drug–light combination after completing the first FR 10 after 60 min. In other words there would be only one drug administration per hour. On second-order schedules, the light appears to acquire powerful reinforcing properties and these schedules generate vast amounts of behavior even though the drug administrations are relatively infrequent. There can be little doubt that such situations are analogous to the way drugs control behavior as reinforcers in real life situations. Drug tastes and smells and often the environment where the drug is consumed become associated with a drug and acquire motivating properties of their own. Second-order schedules also help explain long chains of behavior which culminate in one infrequent drug administration.

B. Neuroanatomy of Drug Reinforcement and Addiction

Years of neuroanatomical studies have shown that the brain contains pathways which appear to be responsible for reinforcement. That is, the function of these pathways is to cause an organism to repeat behaviors which occurred just prior to their stimulation. These pathways are normally activated when the organism engages in activities such as eating and sexual behavior, and thereby cause the behavior of

each organism to adapt to different environments because they ensure that activities that contribute to the survival of the individual or the species will be repeated. Some believe that drugs directly stimulate these reinforcement circuits in the brain through their effect on brain neurochemistry and as a consequence, behavior that is followed by the administration of such drugs is very likely to be repeated.

C. Research with Humans

Because of the precise control that can be achieved over the environment and behavior in an Skinner box, it has been possible to learn a great deal about drug use of laboratory animals. In the early 1960s it was widely believed that non-humans would not consume drugs, but because of these technical advances, we know more about drug taking by laboratory animals than we know about drug use by humans. A number of very successful attempts have been made, however, to apply operant learning techniques to the study of human drug taking. Pioneers in this field are Jack Mendlelson and Nancy Mello. At The Massachusetts General Hospital and later at McLean Hospital in Belmont, Massachusetts, they studied drug self-administration of human volunteers living on a research ward. Volunteers, all with previous drug experience, could earn drugs by performing some activity such as riding an exercise bicycle or pushing a button. Using these techniques it is possible to meet the scientific standards achieved previously with laboratory animal subjects and also satisfy ethical and safety standards required by governments and institutions.

Drugs studied in such situations include heroin, methadone, cocaine, diazepam, barbiturates, THC, nicotine, and caffeine. In general, such studies indicate that human and non-human drug self-administration is controlled by similar factors and obeys similar laws. These studies have also made it possible to observe the effects of drugs on mood and human social behavior, and provide a model to evaluate drug abuse treatment strategies.

V. CONDITIONED DRUG EFFECTS

One area of research of modern behavioral pharmacology has its origin in classical or respondent conditioning rather than operant analysis of behavior. This involves the study of the conditioning of drug effects. Many years ago a student of Pavlov's laboratory in Leningrad gave a dog an injection of apomorphine and then sounded a tone when the drug began to have its effect of causing the dog to salivate. After a few pairings of the tone and the drug, the tone by itself caused the dog to exhibit this effect of the drug, i.e., it caused the dog to salivate. In Pavlov's terminology, the drug was the UCS (unconditioned stimulus), the salivation was the UCR (unconditioned response), the tone was the CS (conditioned stimulus), and the salivation produced by the tone was the CR (conditioned response).

Since that time there have been many demonstrations of conditioned drug effects. Shepard Siegel of McMaster University in Hamilton has shown that in many cases, the CR is in fact, opposite to the UCR. In other words, if the effect of the drug is in one direction, an increase in body temperature for example, the conditioned effect of the drug is in the opposite direction, a decrease in body temperature.

Siegel and other researchers have shown that this conditioned effect in the opposite direction, called a *conditioned compensatory effect*, follows the principles of classical conditioning. Siegel also demonstrated that in many cases this compensatory response is responsible for the development of tolerance for drugs. If a stimulus reliably precedes the delivery of a drug, the conditioned compensatory response will occur in response to the stimulus. Because this response is physiologically opposite to the effect of the drug, the normal drug effect is diminished. This lessening of the drug effect after repeated administrations is a type of tolerance. Siegel has shown that tolerance to many effects of drugs will disappear if the stimulus condition normally present when the drug is taken is no longer present, i.e., there is no stimulus to evoke the conditioned compensatory effect.

This is an example of an effect referred to as *behavioral tolerance* to distinguish it from other types of tolerance that arise from metabolic and physiological mechanisms. Behavioral tolerance can also occur when the effect of a drug is diminished because an organism learns to alter its behavior to compensate for the behavioral changes the drug normally causes.

As mentioned above in the discussion of second-order schedules, it appears that the reinforcing effects of a drug can also be conditioned to environmental stimuli. Sights, sounds, and even places that have reliably been associated with drug administration can acquire reinforcing properties that can also

control behavior in the same manner as the drug. Animals will not only bar press for lights that have been paired with a reinforcing drug, but will actively seek out and return to places where they have experienced the effect of the drug in the past, an effect called *place conditioning*. Place conditioning techniques have been used to investigate the reinforcing effects of many drugs. It has shown for example that amphetamine is reinforcing in species such as chickens and goldfish.

VI. FUTURE DEVELOPMENTS

A. Behavioral Toxicology

Just as operant technology has provided a means of analyzing the effects of drugs on behavior, it is also proving useful in assessing the effects of various toxins on behavior. The work of Bernard Weiss and Victor Laties at the University of Rochester has stimulated the development of behavioral toxicology. Researchers in this new field have been able to demonstrate behavioral changes caused by various environmental and industrial pollutants and provide data useful in assessing risks and in establishing acceptable standards.

B. Behavioral Teratology

It has been known for some time that exposure to drugs and toxins in the uterus is capable of causing physiological and anatomical changes in the offspring. Applying techniques of behavioral pharmacology and behavioral toxicology to the study of the long-term behavioral effects of exposure to substances *in utero* is a new area of research called behavioral or functional teratology. It has shown that exposure to substances in the uterus is capable of altering behavior throughout the adult lifespan even when there are no detectable anatomical anomalies.

Bibliography

Goldberg, S. R., and Stolerman, I. P. (eds.) (1986). "Behavioral Analysis of Drug Dependence." Academic Press, Orlando.
Journal of the Experimental Analysis of Behavior (1991). Special Issue on Behavioral Pharmacology, Volume **56**(2), 167–423.
McKim, W. A. (1991). "Drugs and Behavior: An Introduction to Behavioral Pharmacology," 2nd ed. Prentice-Hall, Englewood Cliffs, NJ.
Stolerman, I. (1992). Drugs of abuse: Behavioural principles, methods and terms. *Trends Pharmacol. Sci.* **13**(5), 170–176.

Behavior Measurement in Psychobiological Research

Martin M. Katz and Scott Wetzler

The University Hospital for the Albert Einstein College of Medicine

Glossary

Behavior Manner of acting, reacting, functioning, or performing. Usually refers to the action of the individual as a unit. In a more general sense, refers to the process of perception, thinking, emotion, and action. The science of behavior is the science which investigates the nature of such psychological phenomena across species.

Componential approach An orientation based on the assumption that all psychological states can be conceived of as patterns of perceptual, thought, emotional, and behavioral components. The components that make up the structural pattern are conceived of as independent, or partially so, and should be measured as separate factors in themselves

Emotion A complex and usually strong subjective response such as love or fear. The response involves physiological changes as a preparation for action. The part of the consciousness that involves feeling and sensibility.

Medical model A model or an orientation based on the assumption that disorders or illnesses are whole entities with distinct configurations of characteristics, qualitatively different from each other. In psychiatry, the unit of measurement is usually the disorder itself and not a single type of behavior or emotion.

Mental disorder Conceptualized as a clinically significant behavioral or psychological syndrome that occurs in an individual and that typically is associated with either a painful symptom (distress) or impairment in important areas of functioning (disability). In addition, there is an inference that a behavioral, psychological, or biological dysfunction exists and that the disturbance is not confined to relationship between the individual and society.

Multivantaged approach An approach to psychological assessment which recognizes that measurement of many of the components of psychological functioning is still at an early stage of development and is subjective in quality and therefore requires more than one perspective. The recommended approach to measurement of such cognitive, behavioral, and emotional components uses self-reports, performance tests, and multiple observers making behavioral ratings in different settings.

THE DISCIPLINE OF PSYCHOBIOLOGY is concerned with the interaction of neural processes and psychological functioning and includes studies of the actions of psychotropic drugs on human behavior. Great advances have been made over the past 30 years in identifying discrete neurotransmitter systems within the central nervous system, and attempts have been made to link their functioning to that of specific emotions such as anxiety. At the same time, basic investigations in psychopharmacology determine how drugs bring about rapid recovery from such complex mental disorders as severe depression. It is necessary in all such research to apply measures of cognition, emotion, and behavior which are as precise and valid as those which measure biological factors. This article deals with how psychologists define behavior, how they approach problems of measurement, and various instruments for measuring the relevant components of psychological functioning. Examples are then provided of research in which such methods are applied to the investigation of the interaction of biology, drugs, and behavior.

I. ROLE OF BEHAVIOR IN BIOLOGICAL RESEARCH

A. Introduction

Developments in biology during the past three decades have radically changed our views of the causes of the major mental disorders and of the bases of normal human behavior. We now have psychotropic drugs which can control and, in some cases, completely resolve such serious, formerly intractable, disorders as mania, severe depression, and schizophrenia. These discoveries have contributed to advances in the understanding of central nervous system functioning, particularly the identification of distinct neurotransmitter systems and their roles in these disorders and normal emotions.

Despite these advances in knowledge about the new drugs, little has been learned about the underlying links between their behavioral actions on the one hand and specific drug–neurochemical interactions on the other. The future of research on the roots of the mental disorders lies with our capacity to identify the links between the functioning of neurobiological systems and human behavior.

B. "Medical" and "Componental" Models

Given the advances in biological technology, it may appear unusual that more progress has not been made in establishing these links. The fact is, however, that in the field of mental disorder, the major mode of thinking tends to be in terms of *classes* of illness, referred to as the "medical model." This model is based on the assumption that disorders or illnesses are whole entities with distinct configurations of characteristics, qualitatively different from each other, which appear and disappear as whole entities. The unit of measurement, therefore, is the disorder itself, and researchers try to establish links between the entire disorder and neurochemical systems. The unit is not a single type of behavior, or type of emotion. We believe that although useful in the clinical framework, this categorical or holistic model of thinking tends to impede rather than advance research.

Establishing the presence of a specific disorder in a patient is a complex judgmental process based on clinical history and patterns of behavior, emotions, and cognition and therefore makes linking with precisely measured biological factors quite difficult. When an association between a disorder and a biological factor is demonstrated, there is still great difficulty in identifying which of the many aspects that make up the complex disorder are responsible for the relationship.

This model, as noted, is a traditional one in medical research; it has on occasion been successfully applied in psychiatric research and has succeeded even more frequently in other specialities of medicine. If the primary goal is clinical, i.e., discovering new treatments, then it is understandable that medical research takes illness as its point of departure. If, however, the goal is to uncover the specific behavioral mechanisms underlying the disorder or to determine how drugs which prove to be efficacious bring about significant changes in these disorders, then more basic questions are involved. These questions would focus, for example, on uncovering which behaviors, emotions, and cognitions are linked specifically with the functioning of those neurotransmitter systems that are directly affected by these drugs.

We therefore conclude that to advance the science for investigating biological–behavioral interactions in normal and abnormal states, we must apply an alternative or complementary model which we identify as the "componental approach." In this latter strategy, we assume with the medical model that all human psychological states can be conceived of as patterns of perception, thinking, emotion, and behavior. For the purposes of scientific investigation, however, the components that make up this complex structure are conceived of as independent, or partially so, and thus should be measured as separate factors in themselves. The units in this approach are, therefore, components which describe the various aspects of the disordered state and permit their independent measurement. This permits a quantitative approach, resulting in precise and articulated measurement, more suited to the main problems of uncovering the relationships between biological and psychological factors. In the next section we present the background of this approach in psychology and then describe a system for accomplishing its aims.

C. Applying the Componental Approach

The measurement of psychological attributes, many of which are subjective in nature, is difficult, and the field is in a continuing state of development. Psychologists find it useful when considering issues of measurement to categorize psychological functions such as perception, emotion, cognition, and social behavior.

The area of emotion exemplifies the multiform problems of measurement. Emotions are, by definition, experiential or subjective states—states that only the person experiencing them can "know," even if he or she does not always have the words with which to describe them. Through the use of inventories of descriptors, psychologists try to present the person with the right words, but these terms can only be approximations of what any patient is likely to feel. When the person's own report is used as a vehicle, there are other barriers to attaining accurate measurement of a "feeling" state. It turns out that subjects may have constraints of various types that prevent them from providing a frank picture of their internal state. For example, additional complications arise when dealing with disturbed patients, who may in many cases be unable to indicate how they feel.

Investigators, therefore, seek other ways of assessing emotional states. In most instances of clinical research, they will ask experts to examine the patient and then, on the basis of these observations, to judge the extent to which a given state (e.g., anxiety or depression) exists. The experts in this case are psychiatrists, psychologists, and nurses who see the patients in different interview and ward settings. Psychologists will also use other instruments, a self-report or performance measures, in the course of their studies to assist them in gauging the intensity of a particular affect, such as anxiety. [*See* ANXIETY AND FEAR.]

D. The Multivantaged Method

The use of several perspectives acknowledges that from not one of these vantages is it possible to obtain a comprehensive and reliable estimate of the depth and extent of an affect or emotional state. Validity and reliability of measurement of the state are therefore enhanced by combining these perspectives. In addition, combining such measurements assumes that the more intensive or severe a state, such as anxiety, the more likely it is that it will be manifested in more situations. It also assumes the converse—that is, to the extent that the state is only mildly present, it will be less likely to appear in all situations and may be detectable only in one or two of those to be described.

In measuring psychological qualities, we also use such terms as "constructs." A construct is an abstraction; it implies that from a physical or objective standpoint the quality itself may not be directly measurable but that there are aspects of it in the subject's overt behavior or in his or her description of that state that appear to occur together and that help to define it. Thus, "anxiety" is something that we cannot actually see but that we believe exists because there are a number of aspects occurring together (e.g., subjective fear, uncomfortable physical feelings, restlessness) that help to define it. From the multiperspective approach, a patient can usually describe the fear, but it requires outsiders to observe the agitation and the other aspects of its physical expression.

Many of the constructs we use in psychopathology are, in addition, overinclusive and thus quite complex. Clinicians, for example, use such terms as "cognitive impairment" to describe serious thinking disorders. In examining aspects of this construct, we note the inclusion of such varying disturbances as difficulties in concentration and in memory, loss of insight, confusion, and poor judgment. Some of these impairments can only be discovered by examining the performance of the patient, others only by expert observation, and still others only by the patient's own report.

Thus, in all of these areas of psychological functioning, we find it necessary to rely on a multiperspective approach to attain both validity and comprehensiveness, since in regard to the latter, certain characteristics of the construct can only be measured by applying a certain type of instrument. Before we indicate how the multivantaged approach is applied, we provide an overview of the types of methods that are used to measure the various aspects of these and other psychological constructs.

II. METHODS FOR MEASURING EMOTION, BEHAVIOR, AND COGNITION

A. Self-Report Tests

The subject's or patient's own description of his or her psychological state or attitudinal set is a crucial vantage for the assessment of human behavior. He or she has unique access to his or her internal feelings—states which outside observers can only infer. While this information may be subject to various biases, it is also the most truly "phenomenological" of all vantages. It conveys how the subject views his or her psychological state; the subject is presumed to know his or her feelings and attitudes better than anyone else. Thus, self-report tests must be included in any kind of comprehensive assessment approach.

Self-report tests consist of lists of simply worded items or questions to which the subject responds in a true/false (e.g., "I like mechanics magazines"), yes/no (e.g., "Do you enjoy meeting new people?"), or numerical rating (e.g., "How much were you distressed by feeling sad during the past week, rated on a 0–4, not at all to extremely, scale?") format. They may be relatively brief, covering only 15 items (e.g., the Beck Depression Inventory) or as many as 566 items (e.g., the Minnesota Multiphasic Personality Inventory-2). In general, items are then summed together to create dimensional scores. These total raw scores are then converted to *standardized scores* based on normative data. For example, a standardized *T* score of 70 on a depression scale would mean that the subject was 2 standard deviations above the mean (or in the top 3% of the population) and that he or she may be described as being significantly clinically depressed.

There are hundreds of different self-report tests which may be used to measure feelings, behavior, and attitudes in psychobiological research. It is beyond the scope of this article to outline them all or to describe any in great detail. Brief summaries of the most popular tests will give an impression of the wide range of item content. The first decision in test selection is determining whether the aim is to study *normal or abnormal behavior.* A single psychological test is rarely able to focus on both kinds of human behavior. One of the most widely used tests of normal behavior is the California Psychological Inventory, which measures socially desirable qualities on 20 scales (e.g., sociability, tolerance, flexibility). Another is the Personality Research Form, which measures 15 personality traits relevant to an individual's functioning (e.g., impulsivity, dominance, nuturance).

Within the domain of abnormal behavior or psychopathology, there are three kinds of tests: (1) psychiatric symptom and mood checklists which measure *transient clinical states,* (2) questionnaires which measure *long-standing personality dysfunction,* and (3) inventories which measure *maladaptive behaviors.* The most widely used self-rating scale in psychopathological and psychopharmacological research is the Symptom Checklist 90, which mea-

sures the distress caused by 90 common psychiatric symptoms scoring on nine dimensions of psychopathology (e.g., depression, anxiety, hostility, psychoticism). Related to the symptom checklists are mood scales which measure disturbed affects. For example, one of the most sensitive indicators of change during a psychotropic drug treatment study is the Profile of Mood States, which measures six affective dimensions (e.g., tension/anxiety, vigor, fatigue). The Symptom Checklist 90 and the Profile of Mood States both provide multidimensional profiles of a patient's clinical status. Other symptom and mood checklists (e.g., the Beck Depression Inventory, the Taylor Manifest Anxiety Scale) may focus on only one critical emotion and thus provide a single unidimensional score.

The Minnesota Multiphasic Personality Inventory is one of the oldest self-report personality questionnaires, measuring 10 dimensions of psychopathology (e.g., hysteria, schizophrenia, hypochondriasis). A revision with new norms has recently been established (MMPI-2). Another personality questionnaire which has been recently developed and is widely popular in both research and clinical settings is the Millon Clinical Multiaxial Inventory-II. This test measures 11 personality disorder (e.g., narcissistic, schizoid) and 9 clinical syndrome (e.g., anxiety, thought disorder) scales. Finally, advances in behavior theory and behavior therapy based on models of conditioning have generated a number of behavioral inventories such as the Attributional Style Questionnaire, which measures a subject's tendency to have a depressive world view (e.g., pessimistic, helpless). [*See* Clinical Assessment; Personality Assessment.]

B. Observational Rating Scales

When the focus in an investigation is on a construct (e.g., anxiety) rather than merely on an individual's own perception of his or her state, then it would be a mistake to rely solely on the self-report vantage. The self-report vantage has intrinsic weaknesses when behavior is at issue, for example the patient's potential lack of insight concerning the nature of his or her own behavior. Other vantages (e.g., doctor, nurse, family) may offer more valid information on particular facets of functioning or, at least, offer additional information. Behavior may be observed and rated in a variety of settings. A number of different observers with different qualifications may be enlisted to observe and rate behavior in those settings. The wider the range of settings and the greater the number and kind of observers, the more valid the measurement of that particular construct.

We have identified three kinds of observers with different qualifications who make their ratings in specific settings. Of particular interest are rating scales completed by a doctor based on an interview with the patient (either live or viewed on videotape). These ratings are considered to be from the *"expert's" vantage,* based on the doctor's accumulated clinical knowledge of psychopathology and prior experience with psychiatric patients. However, these interviews are relatively brief (1–2 hours) and therefore are based on little contact with the patient. For psychiatric inpatients, *nurses' ratings* of ward behavior are based on more extended direct observation of the patient's functioning and are made by professionally trained staff. Finally, for psychiatric outpatients, *family ratings* of the patient's behavior in the community are also based on direct observation (although by untrained observers) and are the most ecologically valid of the three kinds of observation. That is to say, observations of behavior during a brief interview or in a psychiatric hospital are less useful predictors of behavior in the community than is the direct observation of behavior in the community. Needless to say, it is much more difficult for professional raters to observe behavior in the community, a task which is delegated to family members.

The most commonly used structured interviews and observational rating scales are the Schedule for Affective Disorders and Schizophrenea (SADS) and the Structured Clinical Interview DSM-III-R (SCID), which generate diagnoses for the major psychiatric syndromes. With proper training, these diagnoses are made in a highly reliable fashion, and ratings define homogeneous patient populations for inclusion in a research study. Another popular observational rating scale is the Hamilton Depression Rating Scale, which provides an example of this type of methodology when applied to a single syndrome. It covers the full range of depressive symptoms and measures the severity of a depressive disorder. One example of a nurses' rating scale is the Global Ward Behavior Scale, which measures general features of a patient's functioning (e.g., agitation, retardation). Finally, the Katz Adjustment Scale is a family rating instrument which is completed by a well-informed source (e.g., parent, sibling, child, significant other) and measures the patient's social behavior and func-

tioning in the community (e.g., withdrawal, belligerence, bizarreness).

C. Objective Performance Instruments

Both self-report tests and observational rating scales require a subjective evaluation of feelings, attitudes, and behavior. Ideally, we would like to have objective measures of these constructs as well. For example, the objective measurement of galvanic skin response represents one component in the assessment of a construct such as anxiety, or the measurement of finger tapping speed as a component of psychomotor retardation. In general, it is possible to measure an individual's objective performance on a number of cognitive and motor tasks and draw conclusions about certain components of human behavior. These measures of objective performance may then be integrated with the subjective rating described above to provide a fuller picture of each construct.

Significant advances in cognitive and experimental psychology now permit the accurate and objective measurement of many different functions. In addition, a new field has developed, called "neuropsychology," which emphasizes brain–behavior relationships. While the reader is best directed to standard texts in these fields for a more in-depth description of assessment strategies and methods, suffice it to say that neuropsychological tests are commonly used in conjunction with sophisticated radiological techniques for the determination of how brain structure and function are related to specific neuropsychological abilities and functions.

Three multipurpose test batteries have been developed which cover many different intellectual, cognitive, and neuropsychological functions: Wechsler Adult Intelligence Scale—Revised, Halstead–Reitan Battery, and Luria–Nebraska Neuropsychological Battery. In addition, to these comprehensive test batteries, there are more than a hundred tests which measure specific cognitive functions. In this brief overview, six areas of cognitive functioning and examples of neuropsychological tests which measure those functions are mentioned: (1) sensation and perception, (2) motor speed and coordination, (3) language, (4) memory, (5) higher integrative functions, and (6) general intellectual functioning. Representative tests include the Speech Sounds Perception Test and the Line Bisection Test for sensation and perception; the Finger Tapping Test and Purdue Pegboard Test for motor speed and coordination; the Western Aphasia Battery for language; the Wechsler Memory Scale—Revised for memory; the Trailmaking Test and Wisconsin Card Sorting Test for higher integrative functions; and the Wechsler Adult Intelligence Test—Revised for IQ scores and for general intellectual functioning.

III. EXAMPLES OF THE MULTIVANTAGED APPROACH IN PSYCHOPATHOLOGY

To illustrate how the componential or multivantaged approach is applied in biobehavioral research, we draw illustrative examples from the Collaborative Study of the Psychobiology of Depression sponsored by the National Institute of Mental Health (NIMH). That study was designed to test hypotheses which implicated disturbances in central nervous system chemistry as the basis for depressive disorders. It involved study of a diverse sample of patients and normal control. In the course of that research, two ancillary issues were addressed:

1. Investigating relationships between neurochemical variables and emotions associated with the disorder of depression
2. Examining the psychological changes brought about by effective tricyclic drugs in the treatment of depression

These issues are of basic importance in understanding the mechanisms underlying serious psychopathology and determining the ways in which drugs bring about improvement in biological and behavioral pathology.

A. Associating the Functioning of Neurotransmitter Systems with Specific Emotions or Behaviors

One of the most influential biological theories of the nature of a specific mental disorder in recent years has been the "catecholamine" theory of depression. It postulated a deficiency in the nervous system of certain monoamine neurotransmitters at the central synapses as responsible for depression and an excess as responsible for mania. A great deal of inferential evidence and results from small studies provided early support for this intriguing theory. Later, however, conflicting evidence appeared, some studies reporting higher, others normal concentrations of

monoamine metabolites in depressed patients. [*See* CATECHOLAMINES AND BEHAVIOR; DEPRESSION.]

It is now accepted that a substantial proportion of severely depressed patients have higher than normal concentrations. Such findings leave open the question of whether the differences in monoamine metabolite levels between depressions and normals are due to a specific emotional state such as depressed mood or anxiety, both closely associated with the disorder, or result directly from the biochemical pathology of the illness itself. Determining the possible relationships among the emotional states of depressed mood, anxiety, and hostility as a function of central monoamine neurotransmitters was an important focus of the NIMH Collaborative Study of the Psychobiology of Depression. The study examined the relationships (before treatment) between behavioral and emotional measures, hypothesized to be associated with the functioning of three brain monoamine neurotransmitters, norepinephrine, dopamine, and serotonin. [*See* SYNAPTIC TRANSMITTERS AND NEUROMODULATORS.]

Measuring the associations between these emotions and the principal metabolites of these neurotransmitter systems might indicate whether the behavioral differences can be accounted for by the biochemical differences between depressed patients and normals. Such studies also suggest ways in which specific emotions can be traced directly to the pattern of functioning of specific neurotransmitters in the central nervous system.

Adopting the componential approach, it was possible to test several hypotheses in this study concerning the relationships of anxiety and depressed mood to specific neurotransmitters and their metabolites. The study example included 233 subjects (134 depressed, 19 manic patients, and 80 normal controls) from six hospital settings. During an initial 2-week period before the initiation of treatment, 174 had had complete analyses of cerebrospinal fluid metabolites and the set of components measuring behavioral and emotional states. Although the results showed modest relationships between the metabolite (MHPG) from the norepinephrine system with both depressed mood and anxiety, more extensive analyses led to the conclusion that concentrations of this neurotransmitter metabolite were significantly related to an anxiety–agitation factor which included such somatic aspects of that factor as sleep disorder. This relationship, which was highly significant in depressed patients, was also found in urinary MHPG–behavioral analyses conducted within the smaller sample of manic patients whose behavior is, in most respects, quite opposite to that of depression. There is strong reason, therefore, to suggest that the norepinephrine neurotransmitter system may be a neural structure for "anxiety" or alarm states in severely mentally ill patients rather than being specific to "depressive" illness.

The findings support also, as do other results in this study, the suggestion that differences in the functioning of neurotransmitter systems are more likely to be traced to variations in specific emotional states, rather than to "whole" disorders. Given these promising results in linking emotions and monoamine neurotransmitter concentrations, it would appear that applying the componential approach to these problems would be a highly effective strategy in developing a sound scientific base for further work.

B. Evaluating the Effects of Drugs on Behavior and Emotions

One of the most remarkable findings over the past 30 years in the field of psychopharmacology is the discovery that tricyclic drugs, specifically imipramine and amitriptyline, are highly effective in the treatment of a large proportion of the severe depressive disorders. These disorders, which can extend over months, sometimes years, and were thought to be due mainly to psychological factors, were found in upward of 50% of cases to be resolved or nearly resolved after 4–6 weeks of drug treatment.

Despite many years of study of the clinical and biological mechanisms underlying the process of recovery brought about by these drugs, the basic mechanisms remain obscure. Much has been learned about the process of neurochemical change in the central nervous system effected by the drugs, which precedes recovery; very little is known about the psychological changes that accompany these neurochemical effects. The imbalance of research effort appears to have come about as a result of the assumption that the drugs are specific for the state of depression, making it appear unnecessary to investigate their specific actions on certain of the other affective components known to be present in most depressive disorders, notably anxiety and hostility.

Further, more recent theory about the bases of depression suggests that the core of the illness may lie in certain cognitive attitudes about life, rather than in the pattern of emotional functioning. For these reasons, more recent studies have begun to examine the nature of drug effects very early in the treatment of patients in an attempt to identify their specific actions on the emotional, cognitive, and behavioral components of the state of depression.

Recent studies, one of which followed from the already described NIMH Collaborative Program on the Psychobiology of Depression, were able to differentiate between actions of the drug which appear to affect all patients, whether or not they will eventually recover, and those effects which appear to occur in the drug responders only. For example, it was clear from several studies that the sleep problems associated with the depressive disorder are markedly reduced by the drugs in all patients, regardless of whether they eventually get better. Early reductions in anxiety, hostility, and cognitive impairment, however, only occurred in those patients who would later recover within the 4-week treatment period. These changes in the drug responders were effected quite early, before there was much evidence of overall improvement in these patients. Thus, such early effects appear to be the "triggering" actions of the drugs, those that initiate the recovery process.

It is difficult in such studies, however, to distinguish the effects actually due to the drugs from those in the responders which may be due to placebo factors or simply to being in the hospital. Current research is now utilizing new methods and additional control groups to identify those actions which are due specifically to the tricyclic drugs. The findings currently make it appear, for example, that the drugs are more specific to anxiety than to depression, in accord with other clinical research which shows the drugs to be equally effective for generalized anxiety disorders. Such results have many implications for further work in psychopharmacology and for the treatment of mental disorder.

The components of psychopathology, such as anxiety, depression, and hostility, pervade almost all the serious mental disorders. The componential approach permits the linking of behavioral elements with specific changes in the functioning of the critical neurotransmitter systems. The results from drug–behavioral studies then, in conjunction with what is already known about the sequence of drug actions on the functioning of neurotransmitter systems in the central nervous system, will contribute to uncovering the mechanisms through which these drugs bring about their remarkable effects in the depressive disorders. Such studies will then make possible more effective planning in psychopharmacology as investigators in that field seek new drugs for the wide range of serious mental disorders for which we still do not have effective treatments. [*See* PSYCHOPATHOLOGY.]

Bibliography

Hersen, M., Kazdin, A. E., and Bellak, A. S. (1991). "The Clinical Psychology Handbook," 2nd ed. Pergamon Press, New York.

Katz, M. M. (1987). The multivantaged approach to the measurement of affect and behavior in depression. In "The Measurement of Depression" (A. J. Marsella, R. M. A. Hirshfeld, and M. M. Katz, Eds.), pp. 297–316. Guilford, New York.

Lezak, M. (1983). "Neuropsychological Assessment," 2nd ed. Oxford University Press, New York.

Maas, J. W., Koslow, S., Davis, J., Katz, M. M., Mendels, J., Robins, E., Stokes, P., and Bowden, C. (1980). Biological component of the NIMH Clinical Research Branch Collaborative Program in the Psychobiology of Depression. I. Background theoretical considerations. *Psychol. Med.* **10,** 759–776.

Mitchell, J. V. (Ed.) (1985). "Ninth Mental Measurements Yearbook." Buros Institute Mental Measurements, Highland Park, NJ.

Wetzler, S., and Katz, M. M. (Eds.) (1989). "Contemporary Approaches to Psychological Assessment." Brunner/Mazel, New York.

◆

BILINGUALISM

Fred Genesee
McGill University, Canada

Glossary

Compound bilingualism A form of bilingualism in which two sets of linguistic signs are associated with the same meanings; this is usually associated with a common context of acquisition.

Coordinate bilingualism A form of bilingualism in which corresponding linguistic signs (e.g., words) from two languages are associated with different meanings; this is usually associated with different contexts of acquisition.

Integrative/instrumental motivation An integrative motivation is the desire and motivation to learn a language in order to understand or become like members of the target language group; an instrumental motivation is the desire and motivation to learn a language in order to benefit socially, economically, or materially from knowledge of and/or the ability to use the target language for pragmatic purposes.

Matched-guise technique A research technique in which subjects are asked to listen to and give their impressions of speakers of different languages on the basis of prerecorded language samples only; generally used to assess people's attitudes toward different language varieties and language groups. Unknown to the subjects, the language samples have been provided by bilinguals so that each speaker is presented in different but matched language guises.

Universal grammar A theory (or theories) that defines and limits what a human language can be like; as well, a theory of the knowledge about human language which is thought to be innate and essential for the learning of human language.

BILINGUALISM includes those phenomena related to knowing, learning, or using more than one language. It can encompass cases of multilingualism—knowing, using, or acquiring more than two languages—and cases that involve spoken and signed languages. In general terms, the study of bilingualism can be broken down into research that focuses on individuals and that which focuses on societies, groups, or nations. Studies of individual and societal bilingualism are characterized by somewhat distinct disciplinary perspectives, with psychology and linguistics being the primary perspectives in the study of individual bilingualism, and sociology, anthropology, education, and political science being concerned with societal aspects of bilingualism. Although this distinction is somewhat arbitrary, it, nevertheless, is useful in organizing an extensive body of research and knowledge.

I. INDIVIDUAL BILINGUALISM

Individual bilinguals can differ in a number of respects. Most obviously, they differ with respect to which skills (e.g., speaking, reading, writing, listening) they have in each language and their level of proficiency in each skill area. In addition to language proficiency, bilinguals can be described and differentiated with respect to the following characteristics: (a) age of acquisition (e.g., early versus late bilinguals, or successive vs simultaneous); (b) the relationship between the languages (e.g., compound—interdependent systems; co-coordinate—independent systems); (c) context of language acquisition (e.g., instructed or naturalistic); (d) the status of the languages (e.g., minority and majority group bilinguals); and (e) the motivational orientation of the individual (e.g., instrumental vs integrative). Although these features of bilingualism have been described dichotomously, in fact, each represents a continuum of variation so that, for example, age of acquisition can be subdivided into different ages of acquisition and not simply early versus late. Thus, individual bilingualism is best viewed as multidimensional, and researchers and theoreticians have found it useful and necessary to make these kinds of distinctions in their search to better understand and explain aspects of individual bilingualism.

A. Becoming Bilingual

Bilingualism can be achieved by learning two or more languages simultaneously during infancy or by learning a second language after a first language has already been acquired (successive bilingualism). Research on people learning more than one language, simultaneously or successively, is concerned with the same basic issues as research on people learning only one language—namely, the pattern and rate of language development and the processes which underlie acquisition. At the same time, however, there are a number of research questions which, while of some interest to first language acquisition researchers, are of major interest to researchers of second language acquisition. For example, second language acquisition researchers are interested in explaining the evident individual differences in rates of learning and ultimate levels of proficiency which often characterize second language acquisition after a first language has been acquired; such variation is less evident, at least in the domains of speaking and listening, among monolinguals. Factors associated with age, aptitude, cognitive style and maturity, personality, and type and amount of exposure to the second language have been invoked as possible explanations of individual differences in second language proficiency. Second language acquisition is also subject to important attitudinal and motivational factors that can influence both the effort expended in learning a second language and the ultimate level of proficiency achieved. A comprehensive social psychological theory of second language acquisition has been proposed by Robert Gardner to take account of these kinds of factors in second language learning, in both classroom and nonclassroom settings. [See LANGUAGE DEVELOPMENT.]

Another issue that has received attention among second language acquisition researchers is input. Whereas theories of first language acquisition have tended to view input as playing a largely supportive role in language development, some theories of second language acquisition view it as serving a primary causal role. The focus on input in studies of second language acquisition can be attributed, in part, to an interest in classroom-based or instructed learning and to processes related to second language teaching which, by definition, involve the manipulation and control of input in order to promote second language learning. Also in the context of classroom-based learning, researchers have examined the role of attitudes, motivation, learning strategies, and affective variables, such as classroom anxiety, as predictors of second language achievement. This work is of considerable theoretical and practical importance given the prevalence of second language learning in classroom settings.

Concerning the issue of age, there is much controversy as to whether there is a "critical period" for learning a second language. It has been argued that language learning, first and second, becomes difficult and limited after an innately determined critical period, generally associated with the loss of neural plasticity in the brain. When first formulated, the critical period was thought to occur around puberty, but researchers now believe that it might occur earlier and, moreover, that there is not one but many critical periods during which native-like proficiency in different aspects of language can be achieved—the sensitive period hypothesis. Empirically, the picture that seems to be emerging is that older learners (i.e., postpubertal) make faster progress acquiring a second language in the short term than young learners, but that in the long term younger learners are much more likely to ultimately attain native-like levels of proficiency than older learners. Although it is difficult to identify individuals who have acquired native-like competence in a second language even though they began to learn the language after puberty, such cases do exist. The question that remains to be answered is whether the evident differences in proficiency that are often associated with age of second language learning are due to maturational changes in the ability to learn language or, alternatively, whether they implicate other factors of a nonlinguistic nature, such as cognitive ability, attitudes, or the nature of the learning situation itself, for example.

Perhaps the most pervasive issue in research on second language acquisition has been whether the patterns and processes underlying second language acquisition (either simultaneously with or successively after acquiring a first language) are the same as those that characterize monolingual acquisition. Answering this question is complicated by the possibility that the particular combination of languages being learned (e.g., Spanish + French versus Spanish + Thai) may influence the patterns of acquisition and the processes which account for those patterns. In the case of successive second language acquisition, early theories stressed the dependence of second language acquisition on first language acquisition. These theories argued that it is relatively easy to learn those aspects of a second language which are similar to the first language but difficult to learn those features that are different from the first language. Known as the *Contrastive Analysis Hypothesis,* this theory was complemented by then current notions of general learning which stressed habit formation, in the behaviorist tradition of B. F. Skinner. Accordingly, second language learning was viewed as a process of overcoming the habits of the first language in order to master the new language.

Explanations based on contrastive analysis and habit formation were severely criticized and gave way to theories of second language learning which emphasized developmental aspects of acquisition. According to this perspective, second language learners cognitively construct rules about the target language in much the same way as first language learners; in fact, this is sometimes referred to as the "identity hypothesis" (or developmental hypothesis) because it essentially equates first and second language acquisition. Also the subject of critical analysis, this perspective has given way to yet another point of view which emphasizes structural properties of the target language and of the learning system. Accordingly, it is thought that the learner passes through a series of "interlanguages" or "approximative systems" which, on the one hand, are based on properties of the target language and, on the other hand, are idiosyncratic and represent the products of a variety of creative constructive strategies learners use to master the language. This perspective presently enjoys wide currency.

There is also currently considerable interest in the possibility that second language acquisition, especially after acquisition of a first language, is constrained by innate properties of the mind which are specific to language learning and which influence language development in significant ways. Noam Chomsky's theory of universal grammar has received the lion's share of attention here. Some theorists argue that these language-specific constraints become inaccessible with age or are accessible only through their instantiation in the first language and that, therefore, second language acquisition is different from first language acquisition and perhaps even limited; others argue against such a position. Al-

though this debate is unresolved, recent evidence suggests that age effects in second language acquisition are not necessarily due to inaccessibility of innate language-specific acquisition constraints.

Work on simultaneous acquisition of two or more languages during infancy has also been motivated by issues concerning the relationship between the languages being learned. More specifically, much of the research on simultaneous bilingualism has been directed at the question of whether bilingually raised children differentiate between their developing languages from the beginning or, alternatively, whether they initially have a unitary system comprised of elements and rules from both languages and only subsequently come to differentiate between them. In fact, most studies of bilingually raised children have observed that they mix elements (phonological, morphological, lexical, and syntactic) from their developing languages in the same utterance or stretch of conversation. Mixing of this sort is reported to be relatively more frequent in the early stages of acquisition and diminishes over time until approximately the third year when differentiation between the languages is noted to occur quite often.

Frequently, these results have been interpreted in support of the *unitary language system hypothesis.* However, there are methodological problems which challenge this interpretation. Most serious, researchers have not systematically examined bilingually raised children's use of their languages in contexts where differential use of the languages is called for. Recent research which addresses this issue suggests that bilingually raised children are able to use their languages differentially in the appropriate contexts. Because most of the extant research has used cross-sectional or very limited longitudinal designs, detailed descriptions of the phonological, lexical, and syntactic development of bilingually raised children are at present unavailable. There are a number of factors associated with bilingual acquisition that might be expected to influence the acquisition of two languages: (a) the degree and type of bilingual mixing by caregivers, (b) structural similarities in the languages being learned, (c) the context of language acquisition, (d) continuity in exposure to the target languages, and (e) socio-affective factors. This remains an interesting and relatively unexplored aspect of bilingualism.

B. Bilingual Education

Education has been a major contributor to individual bilingualism. Historically, schooling through the medium of languages of imperialist countries was commonplace, witness the spread of English, French, and Spanish in the 19th century. Although the goal of such education was not explicitly to promote individual bilingualism, in effect it did. In many countries around the world today, education through the medium of nonindigenous languages which are of some economic, political, or cultural importance continues to be a major source of individual bilingualism. Contemporary forms of bilingual education take a variety of forms and aim to achieve a diversity of goals: for example, to unify a multilingual country, to assimilate members of minority groups into the mainstream of society, to enrich the education of the majority group, to spread and maintain the use of colonial and international languages, and to preserve and strengthen ethnic and religious traditions.

There has been extensive debate among educators, researchers, and politicians in many communities concerning the effectiveness of educating children through the medium of a second language. A distinction between additive and subtractive forms of bilingualism, proposed by Wallace Lambert, is useful here. Lambert argues, on the one hand, that education through the medium of a second language can be an additive bilingual experience for children from majority ethnolinguistic groups because it does not threaten the maintenance and development of their home language or culture. On the other hand, he argues, schooling in a second language only is a potentially subtractive bilingual experience for children from minority language groups (e.g., Spanish-speaking children educated in English in the United States) because it often portends displacement of the home language and culture by the second language and, thus, implicates social psychological costs that can impede effective education. He proposes that use of the home language and positive support for the home culture in school programs for these children can dispel the socio-cultural threat that often accompanies schooling in a second language only, thereby transforming a potentially subtractive bilingual experience into an additive one. In a related vein, Jim Cummin has argued that developing academic language skills in minority language children's home language first supports and facilitates their acquisition of English as a second language for purposes of schooling. Indeed, there is considerable evidence for this. It has been argued on pedagogical grounds that if special provisions are not made to adapt instruction to take account of the

kinds of language skills and out-of-school experiences of minority language children, then instruction in a second language within the context of the majority cultural group can be inaccessible and meaningless to such students. Instruction in and through the home language is one way of making the cultural adaptations that are called for.

Relevant to this debate are bilingual education programs, known as "immersion," which were developed in Canada to provide majority group English-speaking Canadian children with an opportunity to learn Canada's other official language, French; these programs are examples of additive bilingualism. In early total immersion programs, children receive all instruction, including math, science, and social studies for example, through the medium of French during the first several years of elementary school. In the middle and later grades, both English and French are used to teach the curriculum. Alternative forms of immersion currently exist: delayed immersion (beginning in the middle elementary grades), late immersion (beginning in the senior elementary grades or beginning grades of secondary school), partial immersion (with only 50% of instruction being offered through the second language), and double immersion (with instruction through two second languages). The program has been adopted in many communities and countries around the world and for a variety of second languages, such as Mohawk, Hebrew, Hawaiian, Chinese, Spanish, and German. In comparison to its original Canadian goal of supporting official bilingualism, immersion programs now serve a number of additional educational, social, and political goals, including educational enrichment for majority language children, the promotion of important ethnic languages, the survival of endangered indigenous languages, and the educational integration of students from different linguistic and cultural backgrounds.

Extensive evaluations of immersion programs in Canada, the United States, and elsewhere indicate that the participating children develop advanced levels of functional proficiency in the target language and, at the same time, demonstrate the same and in some cases superior levels of first language development and academic achievement in comparison with children educated entirely through their first language. Evaluations indicate further that even children who are otherwise at academic risk acquire superior levels of second language proficiency while showing the same gains in first language development and academic achievement as similarly at-risk children educated entirely through their first language. It is important to emphasize that in every case, the children participating in these programs are members of the dominant ethnolinguistic group in the community, English or otherwise.

In contrast to the documented success of English-speaking children in second language immersion programs in North America, children from minority language backgrounds who either lack or have limited proficiency in English often experience subtractive bilingualism and disproportionately high rates of academic failure when educated in English-only schools—so called "submersion." Additive forms of bilingual education in which such children receive initial academic and literacy instruction in their home language followed by instruction through English have been developed for these children. In some cases, termed maintenance programs, use of the home language for instructional purposes is continued throughout the elementary grades along with English in order to develop bilingual competence in the children. In other cases, termed transitional programs, the home language is used only in the early grades of school until the children have acquired sufficient English to make the transition to instruction entirely in English; bilingualism is not a goal of these programs. Hybrid bilingual-immersion programs have been developed which offer instruction in both the minority and majority language to both majority and minority language children in the same classrooms.

Evidence concerning the effectiveness of bilingual-immersion programs is as yet unavailable. Numerous evaluations of transitional and maintenance bilingual programs have been conducted in the United States. The results of many of these studies are inconclusive owing to methodological problems in their design or to difficulties conducting the evaluations. The results of well designed studies and of meta-analyses of extant research which take into account methodological and programmatic factors indicate that instruction through minority languages can be an effective form of education for minority language children. These studies indicate that extended use of the children's home language and continuous provision of quality instruction are correlated positively with program outcomes. Moreover, contrary to opponents of bilingual education who claim that use of minority children's home language will retard their acquisition of English and their integration with majority language children, there is no evidence of these effects.

That the results of such innovative educational programs might be complex and at times seemingly contradictory is not surprising, on the one hand, in view of the diverse linguistic and socio-cultural backgrounds of minority language students and, and, on the other hand, in view of the complex relationship between language, culture, and schooling. Researchers are exploring these relationships to better understand the factors which can influence the outcomes of bilingual education. This has been and is likely to continue to be a controversial form of education because it challenges conventional assimilationist models of education in the United States and elsewhere. Indeed, developed countries around the world are engaged in similar educational and socio-political debates as they seek to accommodate increasing numbers of immigrant children in their schools.

C. Cognitive Consequences of Bilingualism

Theoreticians have long been fascinated with the relationship between language, intelligence, and cognition in general. This has led to some strong claims about the relationship between bilingualism and cognition. Some researchers have argued that bilingualism, especially during infancy and early childhood, leads to intellectual inferiority as well as linguistic deficiencies; others have argued to the contrary that bilingualism enhances certain aspects of cognitive development. Findings in support of both positions have been reported. Some of this inconsistency can be accounted for in terms of lack of methodological rigor, especially in early research which generally reported intellectual and linguistic deficiencies among bilinguals. The results from the Canadian immersion programs indicate quite clearly that impaired cognitive or linguistic abilities do not necessarily accompany bilingualism. To the contrary, the results from immersion and other recent research indicate a variety of positive cognitive concomitants of bilingualism, including greater cognitive flexibility, metalinguistic awareness, general intelligence, and even linguistic competence. [See COGNITIVE DEVELOPMENT.]

Jim Cummins has argued that, notwithstanding methodological factors, the effects of bilingualism on cognition and intelligence might be expect to vary depending on the individual's level of proficiency in the languages—positive cognitive consequences are likely to result only when high levels of proficiency are attained in both languages; otherwise no or negative consequences are likely to result. Negative consequences are thought to result from poorly developed linguistic skills because this impairs the developing child's interactions with his or her environment, especially when it comes to schooling. In comparison, positive consequences are thought to result from high levels of proficiency because of enhanced analytic skills that come from mastering two languages. It turns out that research which reports negative side-effects of bilingualism has often been conducted with children in subtractive bilingual situations whereas reports of positive effects involve children in additive bilingual situations. Although not without its shortcomings, the *threshold hypothesis,* as this explanation is known, is useful because it can account for the disparate results which have been reported. It also has important implications in educational settings where second languages are being used for instructional purposes—namely, that it is necessary to aim for extensive use and proficiency in the second language if the cognitive advantages of bilingualism are to be realized.

D. Psycholinguistic Aspects of Bilingualism

As noted earlier, a recurrent theoretical issue in work on bilingualism is the interdependence of the bilinguals' languages. At issue, simply stated, is how is it that, on the one hand, bilinguals manage to keep their languages separate when speaking and writing while, on the other hand, they are able to switch between languages and process information in two languages accurately and without apparent effort? Bilinguals' ability to use language in these ways raises important questions about how they (1) organize and represent language, and (2) access and process language.

Uriel Weinreich proposed that language representation in bilinguals can take one of three forms: compound, coordinate, or subordinate. Compound bilinguals were hypothesized to have fused or interdependent language systems; coordinate to have independent language systems; and subordinate to represent their weaker language with reference to their stronger language. Weinreich hypothesized further that the context of language learning was responsible for the nature of a particular individual's language representation, with compound bilingualism being associated with acquisition of both languages in overlapping contexts; coordinate bilingualism being associated with acquisition in distinct contexts; and subordinate bilingualism being associated with a predominance of one language over the other in most contexts of acquisition.

This theory was seminal and insightful. It not only recognized that bilingualism is not a homogeneous phenomenon, as noted earlier, but it also identified context of acquisition and level of proficiency as important dimensions along which bilinguals can and should be differentiated. The distinction between compound and coordinate bilinguals has been the object of extensive experimentation and has undergone a number of theoretically motivated modifications. Although there has been some empirical support for the distinction, it is evident that a simple distinction between compound and coordinate types, or other categorical distinctions, cannot be made unequivocally. It has been found that different aspects and subcomponents of an individual bilingual's language systems can be of one type while other components are of the other type—for example, particular domains of the lexicon may be overlapping in both languages while other domains are separated by language. The degree of overlap may depend on structural similarities between the languages as well as on how much the person's experiences with each language overlap. To the extent that this is true, it becomes impossible to classify language representation in individual bilinguals in any simple unitary way. Interestingly, this was a possibility that Weinreich discussed in his original writings, but it was subsequently ignored.

In a related vein, researchers have examined the neurophysiological organization of language in bilinguals versus monolinguals. It has been well established that there is topographical representation of different language functions in the brain in monolinguals. The question arises is language represented in the same areas in bilingual brains as in monolingual brains? It has been suggested on theoretical grounds that there might be greater right hemispheric involvement in language representation and processing in bilinguals than monolinguals and that this depends on the age, manner, and stage of second language acquisition. It is also possible that structural characteristics of either the written or spoken forms of language might influence where and how they are processed in the brain; for example, languages with idiographic (e.g., Chinese) as opposed to alphabetic written forms (e.g., Spanish) might involve the right hemisphere more.

Research findings based on a variety of research techniques have been varied and intriguing. While the results for bilinguals often resemble those for monolinguals, there are numerous cases which do not. It is not clear whether these dissimilar cases reflect artifacts related to methodology, subject selection, or normal variation among individuals, or whether they represent true and systematic variation which offers important insights about language representation in bilingual brains. In any case, at present, there appears to be no consensus on the neuroanatomical organization of language in bilinguals. However, this remains a fascinating line of research and, with the development of very sophisticated, noninvasive neurophysiological recording techniques, it may yet be possible to extend our knowledge in this domain further.

To explain the lack of interference between languages during production and comprehension in proficient bilinguals, early researchers postulated the existence of language switches which made one language accessible, during either input or output, while the other was inactive and, therefore, noninterfering. Variations on this theoretical notion have been proposed in response to evidence that earlier versions were inadequate. Researchers' preoccupation with switching mechanisms reflected their focus on the ability of bilinguals to function in each language independently of the other. However, they generally ignored other aspects of language processing in bilinguals which are equally compelling, namely, their ability to automatically process input presented in both languages and their ability to switch between languages rapidly and without errors during production. These abilities are clearly inconsistent with the notion of simple on/off switches.

It is now generally agreed that, on the one hand, proficient bilinguals are able to keep their languages independent during comprehension and production, but that, on the other hand, this probably does not require specialized switching mechanisms. An alternative explanation is that in most cases both language systems are active but, depending on context and other cues, one will be selected for on-line processing. Inefficiencies in the monitoring system which serves to select the appropriate language for processing could account for the rare interferences that occur during bilingual processing. This explanation has the advantage of being able to account for both the relative lack of interference in bilingual processing and the efficient interactions between languages which also characterize bilingual usage. Moreover, it is compatible with similar processes thought to characterize monolingual language processing and, therefore, is more parsimonious.

II. SOCIETAL BILINGUALISM

The reference point for the study of societal bilingualism is the group, be it a nation–state or country, territories or language communities within nation–states, or particular ethnolinguistic groups. Generally speaking, societal bilingualism is associated with contact between speakers of different languages or language varieties. There are a number of historical factors that have led to such contact and, over time, to societal bilingualism: (a) military conquests, occupation, or annexation; (b) political marriages and succession arrangements; (c) colonization; (d) migration and immigration; and (e) federation. Contemporary factors play an ongoing role in the development of societal bilingualism: (a) neocolonialism in the form of economic, military, and political dependency; (b) current immigration and migration of labor from less to more developed countries; (c) internationalization for economic, cultural, educational, scientific, or political reasons; and (d) government policies which seek to promote or stifle the development and use of particular languages.

Societal bilingualism can take a variety of forms and has been described in a variety of ways. No single way of describing societal bilingualism is generally accepted as the best or only one and, indeed, certain descriptive rubrics are more useful for some theoretical or research purposes than others and for some social situations than others. Some countries are officially monolingual (e.g., Japan, Jordon), while other countries are officially bi- or multilingual (e.g., Canada, Switzerland); yet other countries have no official language policy (e.g., England, United States). Designation as an official language usually means that a language is used in all official government documents, for the conduct of government business (during legislative meetings and in the courts), in education, and in public media. Although not officially bilingual, many countries include bilingual regions or subgroups within their population—for example, the United States, France, and China. Indeed, it is rare to find a completely monolingual country.

In most bilingual countries or communities, one language enjoys more prestige, use, and power than the other(s); the former is generally referred to as the majority or dominant language while the less prestigious, powerful, and used language is referred to variously as the minority, regional, or vernacular language. In a now classic series of studies, known as the matched-guise studies, Wallace Lambert and his colleagues at McGill University showed that individuals with native-like proficiency in two languages are likely to be judged more negatively when heard using their less prestigious language than when using the more prestigious one. It seems that bilinguals are assumed to be members of the social group whose language they are heard using and that, as a result, they are stereotyped or viewed in the same way as the group as a whole. While other researchers have reported results and interpretations that are more complicated than this, generally speaking, these results indicate that language is more than a medium of interpersonal communication; it can also be an important socio-cultural marker with significant consequences for the way one is perceived and perhaps treated by others. [*See* INTERPERSONAL COMMUNICATION; PREJUDICE AND STEREOTYPES.]

A. Language Use in Bilingual Communities

A number of functional models of societal bilingualism have been proposed by sociolinguists to describe the patterns of language use found in bilingual communities. One of the earliest of these was that of Charles Ferguson. Ferguson coined the term "diglossia" to describe situations in which there is functional specialization of high and low forms of a language. Examples are the use of classical and local colloquial forms of Arabic in the Middle East or North Africa and French and Haitian Creole in Haiti. The high form of the language is preferred for formal, public occasions and the low form of the language is used primarily for oral communication among intimates for informal, private communication (e.g., the use of high German versus Switzerdeutsch in Switzerland). This conceptualization has been broadened to include functional specialization of different languages, and not just varieties of a given language.

There have been attempts to identify more precisely the specific social domains in which particular languages or language varieties are used in a particular community; most notable here is the pioneering work of Joshua Fishman. On the basis of systematic observation and interviews with residents of the Puerto Rican community in New York City, Fishman and his colleagues identified five domains which carried different expectations with respect to the use of English and Spanish; they were family, friendship, religion, employment, and education. The list of possible domains is unlimited and attempts have been made to define the significant features of do-

mains to provide a simpler integrative schema. Among other characteristics, domains have been differentiated in terms of participants, place, and topic or purpose of communication. What are thought to be the significant features of each of these aspects of domain have also been described. For example, participants have been described in terms of their age, sex, role; place in terms of public/private and individual/group; and topic in terms of such features as personal/impersonal. Identifying the specific features of social situations in this way is important since it is on the bases of these specific features that sociologists seek to link up the use of particular languages with specific social situations.

This approach to describing language use in bilingual communities is largely normative and deterministic. It does not recognize the deliberate choices that interactants make when using language nor does it address the issue of how different features of social situations figure in such choices. More dynamic, decision-making models have been proposed to address these issues. One possibility is that speakers' language choices are based on a series of considerations that are hierarchically organized. In other words, speakers consider each feature of a situation and weigh the language choices that are possible; situational features themselves are hierarchically ranked according to their relative order of importance. Representing language use in bilingual situations in the form of a decision tree such as this can, in principle, not only predict but also, to some extent, explain some language choices. It also recognizes that not all features of a situation are equally important and that bilingual speakers actively assess the possibilities in social situations and make choices from among those possibilities.

Speakers do not always make the language choice expected according to structural features of the situation: the so-called unmarked choice. In fact, speakers sometimes choose to use a language that violates situational expectations: that is, they select the marked choice. According to Howard Giles's language accommodation theory, language choices can be explained in terms of social psychological motivations or intentions. In simplified terms, speakers can choose to use the language variety of their interlocutor in order to express liking for and a willingness to cooperate with the other. In cases where the interlocutor is a member of a different ethnolinguistic group, choosing to use the other's language can also be an expression of affinity or respect for the speakers' social group and, therefore, the speaker; this pattern is termed "convergence." "Divergence" or choosing to use a language that is not that of the interlocutor can be an indication of lack of intergroup affinity or respect as well as an expression of the speaker's ethnolinguistic distinctiveness.

It follows that bilinguals can make use of their language skills to convey their social identity as well as their attitudes and intentions toward their interlocutors as individuals or members of different social groups. Anthropologists also highlight the role of social identity and intergroup factors in their work on interpersonal communication in bilingual communities. For example, Carol Myers-Scotton has argued that selecting the unmarked language choice indicates acceptance of the role relationships and social identity associated with that situation; selecting the marked language choice signals rejection of that identity and a desire to negotiate a different identity.

An important implication of this work is that the social meaning conveyed by language in bilingual situations can lie as much, and in some cases more, in how and what language is used rather than in what is explicitly said. The social significance of language choices in such situations arises from the importance of language as a social marker. An additional important implication of this line of work is that language choices are not simply made in reaction to external situational factors, but rather particular choices serve to create particular social situations. In other words, social situations are brought into being by language choices irrespective of the referential meaning conveyed by the interlocutors. Taken together, these different lines of work indicate that patterns of language use in bilingual communities reflect the importance of a number of different factors—social situational, social psychological, intergroup, and interpersonal.

B. Language Maintenance and Shift

Language maintenance refers to situations where patterns of language use in a community are stable over time. *Language shift* refers to the redistribution of languages or language varieties over certain domains or with respect to certain functions within a language community. Language shift can take several forms. Shifts from one form of monolingualism to another form of monolingualism have been the most frequently studied. This form of shift can take place in long established language communities (e.g., from Welsh to English in Wales, and from Basques to French in France) or in groups with less extensive residence in a community (e.g., from German to English among German immigrants to the United States, from Algerian to French among Algerian immigrants to France). Such shifts from one form of monolingualism to another are usually associated with a transitional bilingual stage when both languages are used, often in a diglossic fashion. This process usually requires several generations and is characterized by progressive spread of the new language into new functional domains. Signs of shift usually appear first among younger generations of speakers. With time, however, the bilingualism of the younger generation leads to monolingualism in the new language among their offspring. A number of indepth observational studies have been conducted in several communities which have experienced such a shift and have resulted in detailed descriptions of the process (in Oberwart, Austria, by Susan Gal, for example).

While language shift can occur in monolingual communities, as noted above, it is of particular interest in bilingual communities since the distribution of languages is often unstable and there is a tendency to shift from using one language to another. In these cases, government policies to maintain the status and use of particular languages and legislative intervention to put these policies into action may be deemed necessary; issues related to language planning will be discussed in the next section. Systematic efforts by a social group at maintaining the status or use of its language in the face of instability often reflects the importance that a social group attaches to its language as a marker of ethnic distinctiveness or nationalism.

Language shift can lead to language attrition and even loss or "death" if the language which is lost to the community is not spoken by another language community. For example, acquisition of English and the resulting loss of Mohawk (an indigenous Amerindian language) in the northeastern region of North America would result in the death of Mohawk since it is not spoken anywhere else in the world. Similar cases are Hawaiian in Hawaii, Welsh in Wales, and Basque in Spain. There is a language shift worldwide toward the use of international languages, such as English, French, and Spanish; this is often accompanied by loss and death of indigenous minority languages.

Cases of shift from monolingualism to bilingualism without language loss are evident where countries encourage the learning and use of additional languages. This can involve the spread of languages which have wider international utility or internal national use (such as English in India, where government business is frequently conducted in English as a lingua franca). Or, it can involve the adoption of an indigenous language (such as Swahili in Tanzania) as a national lingua franca along with other commonly used regional languages.

Numerous factors have been identified as contributing to language shift. Howard Giles' notion of "ethnolinguistic vitality" is relevant here. Ethnolinguistic vitality is defined as that which makes a group likely to behave as a distinct and active collectivity in intergroup situations. Groups with high levels of vitality are likely to survive while groups with little or no vitality are at risk of extinction. It follows that the languages of minority groups that enjoy high levels of vitality are more likely to survive in comparison with those of groups with relatively low levels of vitality. Vitality comprises three general categories of factors—status, demographic, and institutional support, each of which comprises more specific factors. Languages with high status (including economic, social, language, and sociohistorical status) are more likely to survive because of the utility, prestige, or power associated with them. Demographic factors include the number of speakers of the language, their geographical distribution, migration patterns, and urban–rural differences. These are all factors which entail contact between speakers of minority and majority group languages, generally resulting in a shift toward use of the majority or more prestigious language. Finally, institutional support includes the availability of mass media, governmental services, religion, and education in the language, all of which serve to strengthen a language and contribute to its use and survival.

C. Language Planning

Language planning is most often undertaken by new nations that seek to establish, change, systematize, and/or rationalize matters related to language in their jurisdictions. Thus, for example, when the state of Israel was established in 1948, Hebrew was adopted as the national language because of its obvious historic link with the Jewish people. But, because Hebrew had been largely unused for some time, steps were undertaken to expand and modernize it so that it could be an effective medium of communication in running the affairs of the country. Language planning is also undertaken by nations

with established language histories in response to changing linguistic circumstances in the country or internationally. For example, in 1968 the U.S. Congress passed legislation which permitted and, at the same time, encouraged instruction through languages other than English in order to respond to the educational needs of growing numbers of limited-English-speaking children.

As these examples illustrate, language planning is concerned with both the symbolic function and the practical utility of language within a society. These are referred to as *corpus* and *status planning,* respectively. *Corpus planning* refers to systematic changes in the language itself that are brought about through planning activities; for example, it could include changes to the orthography, syntax, or lexicon to modernize the language; it could be the creation of a written form of a language which exists only in oral form, sometimes referred to as graphization; or it could involve standardization of the language—the selection and codification of a variety of the language to be used as the norm for the language community.

Status planning includes those planning decisions and activities that are intended to enhance or diminish the status of a language and/or to promote or restrict the acquisition and use of a language. Examples of status planning intended to enhance use of a language are the selection of national or official languages, provision of government services through a language, the creation of government agencies or departments to oversee the use and development of a language (such as the Academie Francaise in France), legislation which provides for the use of a language for instructional purposes in public schools, and the provision of mass media (television or radio services) in a language. Ideally, there are four stages to language planning: (1) initial fact-finding during which pertinent demographic and social information is collected; (2) the actual planning stage, which includes the identification of objectives and the articulation of activities to attain the objectives; (3) implementation of the plan; and (4) evaluation of the effectiveness of the interventions. In actuality, all of these stages are not always undertaken.

Because of its association with nationalism, ethnic identity, and power, language planning is seldom neutral. To the contrary, it is often ideologically motivated and provokes political and social conflicts. It is not uncommon to find language planning at the center of heated political and social debates—witness the cases of Quebec and Belgium, which have sought to reconcile the needs and concerns of different language groups in the same communities. Because of the importance of language as a symbol of socio-political power and as a medium of communication, language planning can be a tool for domination and control or it can be a tool for promoting equality and collaboration among language groups.

Acknowledgments

I thank G. R. Tucker, E. Nicoladis, M. Swain, and C. Hoffman for helpful comments on an earlier draft of this manuscript.

Bibliography

Appel, R., and Muysken, P. (1987). "Language Contact and Bilingualism." Edward Arnold, London.

Cooper, R. L. (1989). "Language Planning and Social Change." Cambridge University Press, New York.

Genesee, F. (1987). "Learning Through Two Languages: Studies of Immersion and Bilingual Education." Newbury House, Rowley, MA.

Grosjean, F. (1982). "Life with Two Languages: An Introduction to Bilingualism." Harvard University Press, Cambridge, MA.

Hakuta, K. (1986). "Mirror of Language: The Debate on Bilingualism." Basic Books, New York.

Hamers, J., and Blanc, M. H. (1989). "Bilinguality and Bilingualism." Cambridge University Press, Cambridge.

Hoffmann, C. (1991). "Introduction to Bilingualism." Longman, London.

Larsen-Freeman, D., and Long, M. H. (1991). "An Introduction to Second Language Acquisition Research." Longman, London.

Paulston, C. B. (1988). "International Handbook of Bilingualism and Bilingual Education." Greenwood Press, Westport, CT.

Romaine, S. (1989). "Bilingualism." Basil Blackwell, Oxford.

◆

BIOFEEDBACK

John P. Hatch
The University of Texas Health Science Center at San Antonio

Glossary

Classical conditioning The formation of a conditioned reflex through the temporal pairing of an unconditioned stimulus, which reflexively elicits a response, and a neutral conditioned stimulus. After the pairing the formally neutral conditioned stimulus acquires the ability to elicit a response similar to the one elicited by the unconditioned stimulus.

Operant conditioning The presentation of a stimulus dependent on the occurrence of a response for the purpose of modifying the strength or frequency of the response.

Reinforcer In operant conditioning any stimulus which when presented or removed dependent on the occurrence of a response results in the modification of the response. In classical conditioning the presentation of a conditioned stimulus and an unconditioned stimulus in close temporal proximity.

BIOFEEDBACK is the technique of using electronic equipment to display to people some aspect of their biological functioning, usually in the form of auditory or visual signals, for the purpose of teaching them to modify some physiological event. The physiological event to be modified can be either the normal or the abnormal activity of an organ or system. The first step in the biofeedback process is the detection of the physiological signal with an appropriate transducer. The detected signal is then amplified and converted into a form that is accessible to the external senses. Finally, the signal is fed back to the person who then uses the information in his or her attempts at gaining voluntary control over the targeted physiological event. Usually, the targeted physiological event is one that is normally not available to conscious awareness such as blood pressure level or brain wave activity. However, biofeedback also may be used in modifying a normally voluntary function over which the person has lost voluntary control because of disease or injury. Although the psychological mechanisms involved are not fully understood, it generally is assumed that the development of voluntary physiological control with biofeedback represents a learning process.

I. UNDERLYING LEARNING THEORY

Learning theorists traditionally have distinguished between two types of learning. One type, called *classical conditioning*, involves the pairing in close temporal proximity of two stimuli. One of the two stimuli, known as the unconditioned stimulus, normally elicits some reflex behavior such as salivation, eye blink, or change in skin conductance. The other stimulus, known as the conditioned stimulus, is neutral prior to the pairing but acquires the ability to elicit a response similar to the unconditioned response after the pairing process. The second type of learning recognized by learning theorists is known as *operant conditioning*. In operant conditioning the response is generally thought of as emitted on a more or less voluntary basis, rather than being reflexively elicited by any particular stimulus. Also, the operant conditioning process involves the pairing of a stimulus dependent on the occurrence of a response. The paired stimulus is known as a positive reinforcer if its presentation leads to an increase in the frequency or magnitude of the response, and it is known as a negative reinforcer if its removal leads to an increase in the frequency or magnitude of the response. [*See* CLASSICAL CONDITIONING; OPERANT LEARNING.]

Between 1928, when the two types of learning were formally distinguished, and the early 1960s it was generally assumed that operant and classical conditioning were mutually exclusive processes. All voluntary skeletal motor behavior was assumed to be subject to operant conditioning, while visceral and glandular responses mediated by the autonomic nervous system were assumed to be involuntary and modifiable only through classical conditioning. It was thought impossible that salivation to a light stimulus could be operantly reinforced by food. This view was retained until the early 1960s when groups of researchers in the Soviet Union, Canada, and the United States began a series of experiments designed to show that responses mediated by the autonomic nervous system can in fact be brought under voluntary control through techniques that closely resemble operant conditioning.

II. EARLY DEVELOPMENT

A. Experiments on Humans

It was first shown that human subjects could learn to voluntarily dilate blood vessels of the finger in order to avoid or escape an electric shock if they were provided with visual information about their vasomotor activity. Subjects provided with an amplified auditory representation of their heart beat also were trained to accelerate their heart rate in order to avoid an electric shock to the ankle. Other responses generally considered involuntary were brought under voluntary control by providing subjects with feedback information about the targeted response and some form of operant reinforcement. Studies conducted in the 1960s also demonstrated operant conditioning of the skin conductance response and brain wave activity. Voluntary control over the firing of single motor units was demonstrated by providing subjects with auditory and visual displays of individual myoelectric potentials recorded from fine wire intramuscular electrodes.

B. Experiments on Animals

At about the same time that voluntary control of autonomically mediated behavior was being demonstrated in humans parallel lines of research were in progress using various animal species. For example, thirsty dogs were trained to increase and decrease the flow of saliva using water as a reinforcer. Bidirectional changes in heart rate and blood pressure were also shown to be subject to operant conditioning in monkeys and rats.

III. SOMATIC MEDIATION

The results of the human and animal studies described above were replicated many times, and the conclusion that autonomically mediated responses can be brought under voluntary control through operant conditioning is now firmly established. However, needed information about the biological mechanisms involved in such learning was not available, and the question of whether autonomic responses were being directly controlled or whether they were being indirectly affected by some change in somatic responding was hotly disputed. For instance, in the early studies involving heart rate and vasomotor conditioning in humans the subjects were frequently observed to alter their respiration or muscle tension level. It could not be determined from these studies whether subjects were learning to control their heart rate directly or whether they were learning to alter their respiration or their level of muscular exertion, which in turn caused their heart rate to change in the appropriate direction.

A. Experiments on Curarized Animals

In order to address the issue of somatic mediation, a series of studies were carried out on animals, which had their skeletal muscles paralyzed with the drug *d*-tubocurarine. This experimental preparation was believed to control for changes in skeletal motor or respiratory activity that might be mediating the physiological response. Using direct electrical stimulation of the brain as a positive reinforcer and escape from electric shock as a negative reinforcer, operant conditioning of many autonomic responses was demonstrated in over 20 experiments. Soon, however, the magnitude of the results gradually declined to the point where the original experiments could no longer be replicated. Although a total of 2500 additional rats were studied under curare, the original experiments could not be replicated, and the reasons for the failure to replicate were never discovered. Therefore, the existence of operantly conditioned autonomic responding by rats under curare must be considered unproved at this time.

B. Specificity of Biofeedback Effects

Despite the difficulties in proving that operant conditioning of autonomic responses is not somehow mediated by somatic responding, research on the voluntary control of autonomic responses has continued. Under the rubric biofeedback much has been learned about the ability of human beings to voluntarily alter many aspects of their biological function. Some of these voluntary visceral acts achieve a high degree of response specificity, which suggests that they are not simply a part of a more general somatic activation response. For example, when patients paralyzed from the neck down were trained with biofeedback to raise their blood pressure most did so without significant alteration in heart rate. Normal subjects also were trained to alter heart rate without affecting blood pressure and to alter blood pressure without affecting heart rate. Subjects also were trained to raise and lower heart rate and blood pressure together or in opposite directions simultaneously. In biofeedback studies designed to train people to modify hand temperature it was found that people can reliably produce a difference in the temperature of the two hands, and that as training progresses they can control the temperature of increasingly specific areas of skin. If these responses were secondary to somatic activity then such a high degree of response specificity would be unexpected.

Studies in which somatic activity in the form of gross movement, muscular electrical activity, or respiratory activity has been recorded and correlated with change in the targeted physiological response have produced mixed results. Some studies showed parallel changes in somatic and operantly conditioned visceral responses while others did not. It also was shown that subjects can alter their heart rate with biofeedback even while pacing their respiration rate to a frequency set by the experimenter. On the whole, the available evidence suggests that somatic responding and visceral responding often show parallel change during biofeedback training, and some change in somatic behavior may be necessary for voluntary visceral responding to occur; however, changes in somatic responding do not appear to be a sufficient explanation for changes in visceral responding that occur during biofeedback training.

The extent to which somatic responses are involved in the voluntary regulation of visceral functions remains an important theoretical question. However, to view the somatic and autonomic nervous systems as independent would be to take a narrow view of the physiology involved. Neither somatic nor autonomic responses occur in a vacuum, and it probably is the case that neither type of response can be well understood without considering the other type as well.

IV. COGNITIVE MEDIATION

Questions also were raised about possible cognitive mediation in biofeedback studies with human subjects. Because people have voluntary control over their cognitive processes and because certain types of thoughts, images, and emotions are known to affect physiological function, it was considered possible, for example, that a subject who was operantly conditioned to increase and decrease heart rate could do so by creating exciting or relaxing mental images.

In contrast to the issue of somatic mediation the question of cognitive mediation of visceral responding has received relatively little research attention. In a number of investigations subjects were simply asked what they were thinking about at the time that they demonstrated the desired response. In general, subjects did tend to report more active and arousing images during training to speed heart rate and more relaxing and passive images during training to slow heart rate. However, when subjects were asked to engage in arousing or relaxing imagery, the corresponding changes in physiological functioning were rather small compared to those observed during biofeedback. These limited findings would suggest that, like somatic mediation, cognitive mediation is probably not a sufficient explanation for the voluntary control that has been achieved with biofeedback training.

Although biofeedback research has been strongly influenced by operant conditioning there are other theoretical models that have influenced the field. One such model is the *ideomotor model*. According to this theory, voluntary acts are mediated by mental images stored in the brain of the movements to be carried out. An issue that continues to be debated is the question of whether the biofeedback signal should be conceptualized as a reinforcing stimulus or as a source of information that the subject uses in establishing voluntary control. The two points of view are not mutually exclusive since a reinforcer always conveys some information, and the presentation of information under the right circumstances can reinforce behavior.

The most well-developed version of the ideomotor theory in the field of biofeedback is the conceptualization of learned heart rate control. According to this model, the repeated occurrence of a response results in the establishment of a motor image of the response. When a person later performs the act he does so by constantly comparing the immediate sensations consequent upon the response with the stored image of that act. This theory would predict that as a response is learned the learner would develop a greater ability to sense the occurrence of the response. The ideomotor theory has spawned a considerable amount of research on the discriminability of heart rate with biofeedback training, but the evidence does not strongly support the hypothesis that biofeedback enhances the discriminability of heart beats.

V. BIOFEEDBACK PARAMETERS AFFECTING LEARNING

Studies have also focused on the various parameters that affect the acquisition and performance of voluntary visceral responding with biofeedback. Many of the factors that affect learning with biofeedback also affect the learning of other voluntary motor acts. Either visual or auditory signals may be used as the feedback stimulus, and no clear advantage has been found for either type. A distinction also can be made between binary and analogue feedback. With *binary biofeedback,* the information presented indicates only whether the magnitude of the target response is above or below some threshold level. For example, a tone may be turned on whenever hand temperature equals or exceeds 90°F and turned off whenever it falls below that temperature. The subject is informed only whether the response meets the criterion at any moment. With *analogue biofeedback,* the feedback signal varies proportionately with the magnitude of the target response. For example, hand temperature might be continuously displayed on a meter so that the subject receives information not only about the direction of the response but also about the magnitude and the form of the response. Many studies have demonstrated superior performance of subjects with analogue feedback as compared to binary feedback, but there are exceptions. For instance, binary feedback can produce as large a decrease in heart rate as analogue feedback. Almost all current studies use some form of analogue feedback signal, some of which can become quite elaborate with the use of computerized graphics displays.

Another feedback parameter that affects learning is the immediacy of the feedback signal with respect to a change in the target response. Similar to the reinforcer in operant conditioning, any change in the biofeedback stimulus should occur as soon as possible following a change in the target response for optimal learning. Feedback that is delayed by only a few seconds is not as effective as immediate feedback.

Sometimes the feedback signal is the only form of reinforcement used in biofeedback training, but tangible reinforcers such as money or prizes for appropriate performance may also be used. For most subjects the knowledge of results provided by the biofeedback plus their own desire to master the task is sufficient to motivate learning. However, an additional motivational effect of tangible reinforcers has been shown.

VI. BIOLOGICAL MECHANISMS

Relatively little is currently understood about what changes occur in the biological mechanisms that underlie biofeedback assisted voluntary control of visceral responding. The available evidence suggests that during biofeedback assisted heart rate speeding there is both a decrease in cardiac parasympathetic neural tone and an increase in sympathetic neural tone. Voluntary heart rate slowing, however, seems to be primarily dependent on an increase in cardiac parasympathetic activity. It also has recently been discovered that the vasodilation produced during biofeedback assisted hand temperature warming is mediated through a nonneural, β-adrenergic mechanism. The vasoconstriction that accompanies voluntary hand temperature cooling, however, is mediated by an efferent sympathetic, nervous pathway.

VII. CLINICAL APPLICATIONS

As soon as it was discovered that autonomically mediated responses could be brought under voluntary control great interest was generated over possible clinical applications of biofeedback. It was speculated that patients who demonstrated dysfunction of various response systems might be trained to regulate their physiological functioning in a direction of improved health. Although large-scale, controlled clinical trials are lacking, there have been a large number of small studies that support the clinical efficacy of biofeedback therapy for a variety of disorders.

In general, there are two rather broad philosophies that are followed in the clinical application of biofeedback therapy. One attempts to take advantage of the specific effects that can be produced in a response system. Following this approach, the therapist attempts to teach the patient to reverse specific symptoms of illness. For instance, sinus tachycardia patients were trained to slow their heart rate with biofeedback. The second philosophy contends that biofeedback can be used to promote voluntary control over a general psychophysiological state, which is thought to result from physical or psychological stress. Because many common disorders are believed to be caused or aggravated by stress, biofeedback is used to teach patients to relax, and cope more effectively with stress. For example, biofeedback often is used to teach migraine headache sufferers to raise their hand temperature. Even though warming of the hands is not known to directly or specifically alter the pathophysiology of migraine headache, several studies demonstrated a reduction in headaches using this technique. It is assumed that the hand warming response assists the patient in achieving a state of deep relaxation, which in turn somehow interferes with the relationship between stress and headache.

Biofeedback has been applied to the treatment of a wide variety of medical disorders. Within the cardiovascular system heart rate biofeedback is used in the treatment of sinus tachycardia, cardiac arrhythmias, and anxiety. The vasodilation response that accompanies biofeedback assisted hand warming is beneficial in the treatment of Raynaud's disorder, which involves the painful constriction of blood vessels in the hands and feet. Thermal biofeedback also is used in the treatment of migraine headache and hypertension. Direct blood pressure biofeedback has been used in the treatment of hypertension with limited success, but it has met with greater success as a treatment for orthostatic hypotension in patients who have suffered spinal cord injury.

Feedback of skeletal muscle activity in the form of electromyographic biofeedback is used in treating many stress related disorders. Electromyographic biofeedback is widely used in the treatment of patients with muscle contraction headache, temporomandibular joint disorders, and low back pain. Electromyographic biofeedback also is extensively applied as part of a physical rehabilitation program in the treatment of patients suffering from cerebral palsy, spinal cord injury, stroke, and spasmodic torticollis. As a component of a generalized relaxation training program electromyographic biofeedback is used in treating chronic pain syndromes, hypertension, asthma, irritable bowel syndrome, and many other stress related or psychosomatic disorders.

One of the most successful clinical applications of biofeedback is the use of manometric feedback from the anal sphincter to restore voluntary control in patients with fecal incontinence. Manometric biofeedback is assumed to operate by increasing the strength of the external anal sphincter muscle, by teaching the patient to coordinate external and internal anal sphincter activity, and by assisting the patient in learning to recognize the sensations associated with rectal distention.

Biofeedback of brain wave activity is used in treating epilepsy. Epileptic patients provided with biofeedback information about their production of 12–14 Hz (sensory-motor rhythm) activity can selectively augment their production of this brain wave. Patients treated in this way often show a reduction in the frequency of their epileptic seizures. [*See* EPILEPSY.]

Bibliography

Basmajian, J. V. (1989). "Biofeedback: Principles and Practice for Clinicians," 3rd ed. Williams & Wilkins, Baltimore.

Engel, B. T., and Schneiderman, N. (1984). Operant conditioning and the modulation of cardiovascular function, *Annu. Rev. Physiol.* **46,** 199.

Finley, W. W., and Jones, L. C. (1992). Biofeedback with children. "Handbook of Clinical Child Psychology" (C. E. Walker and M. C. Roberts, Eds.), 2nd ed. Wiley, New York.

Gatchel, R. J. (1988). Clinical effectiveness of biofeedback in reducing anxiety. In "Social Psychophysiology and Emotion: Theory and Clinical Applications" (H. L. Wagner, Ed.). Wiley, Chichester, England.

Hatch, J. P., Fisher, J. G., and Rugh, J. D. (Eds.) (1987). "Biofeedback: Studies in Clinical Efficacy." Plenum, New York.

Miller, N. E. (1978). Biofeedback and visceral learning, *Annu. Rev. Psychol.* **29,** 373.

Rosenbaum, L. (1989). "Biofeedback Frontiers: Self-Regulation of Stress Reactivity." AMS Press, New York.

Schwartz, M. S. (1987). "Biofeedback: A Practitioner's Guide." Guilford, New York.

BIRTH ORDER, EFFECT ON PERSONALITY AND BEHAVIOR

Russell Eisenman

McNeese State University

Glossary

Anxiety A great fear, usually in the person's mind and not objectively real.

Birth order The order of birth of a child into a family such as the first child is the first born, the second child is the second born, etc.

Creativity Originality plus usefulness.

Only child A child without any siblings, i.e., no brothers or sisters.

Scientific Using the scientific method to gain knowledge; includes hypothesis testing of things which can be publicly verified.

BIRTH ORDER can have important effects on one's personality and behavior. How could the order in which one is born into a family have such an effect? The child's order of birth may influence how the parents treat the child and this treatment, in turn, can produce personality differences. It should be recognized that birth order is a demographic variable, like social class or area of residence. We should not expect birth order or other demographic variables always to have an effect, but sometimes they will. Often the effect is due to the demographic variable and other things in what statisticians call an interaction. That is, birth order may exert an effect on the person only if something else is also present, e.g., being a first born and having middle-class parents.

Most research has focused on comparing the first born child with all other later born children. Thus, most of what we know about birth order has to do with ways in which first borns and later borns are different, although I will mention some of my research on the middle child, and some findings about last borns. But, most of this article will focus on first borns vs later borns. Only children will also be mentioned. Either they are like first borns, since they are the first (and only) child born, or they are sometimes different, as will be later explained.

I. ANXIETY

Parents tend to be overly anxious with regard to their first child. The birth of their first child is a major event in their lives, and it is also somewhat of a threatening event. They have never been parents before, and they do not know what they should do in many instances. Thus, parents tend to be overly restrictive with their first child, having many fears of the terrible things which will happen if they do not monitor and care for their child constantly. This anxiety influences the personality of the child. First borns grow up to be more anxious than later borns. By the time the parents have a second, third, or fourth child, etc., they know better how to care for children and know that they do not have to be so overly concerned with protecting their child from every imaginable harm. Thus, they let up some, and allow the later born children (those after the first child) more freedom. But, their treatment of the first born child results in someone who grows up with more than the average anxiety. First borns, thus, tend to be more anxious than later borns. This is likely the basis of an old joke which says that parents should have 10 children and throw away the first 3. The idea is that anxious parents make many mistakes before learning how to be a parent without undue worry. [*See* ANXIETY AND FEAR.]

It should be made clear that we do not mean that every first born child is more anxious than every later born child. Students often misunderstand what scientists mean when they make their generalizations. We mean there is a tendency, greater than could be expected by chance, for first borns to be more anxious than later borns. There will be many exceptions, instances where a first born is not anxious or where a later born is.

II. INTELLECTUAL OR ADULT ATMOSPHERE

When the first born child is growing up, until the birth of a sibling, the child has the parents all to himself or herself. This probably accounts for many personality difference of first borns relative to later borns, especially if the parents are intelligent, or oriented toward learning. First borns tend to score higher than later borns on intellectual measures. When the later born children come the parents will probably spend less time with them than they did with the first child, and the later born child will have as its model the other children in the family. But, the first child had adults to model after, and thus may acquire a more adult-like interest in things and therefore score higher on intellectual measures. The child also develops more interests in adult-like things. This may account, in part, for the fact that first borns achieve at a greater rate than later borns. For example, there are more famous first born scientists, for their proportion in the population, than would be expected by chance. First borns also often have charge of the younger children. In many families, the first born child is made to act like a junior adult, taking care of the younger siblings. This probably teaches responsibility to the first born. The first born child learns to be a responsible, reliable person to a much greater extent than any of the later borns. Thus, the later born children are less burdened with responsibility, but this may be harmful when they have to assume responsibility, as in the classroom or in the workplace. The early training in responsibility may give the first born a greater likelihood of suc-

cessful achievement in situations where responsibility is called for. On the other hand, later borns may know how to have fun better, or at least not be so burdened with concerns of what is the right thing to do.

III. RISK TAKING

Another difference in personality has to do with the kinds of risks first borns or later borns will take. First borns often have a tendency to avoid situations which involve physical injury, such as dangerous sports like football. First borns will take risks if they believe they can handle the situation safely, but will be less likely to engage in behavior which exposes them to potential injury. Thus, first borns are less likely than later borns to be college football players. Football is a violent sport and injury is unavoidable no matter how skilled one is. On the other hand, first borns are overrepresented among astronauts and aquanauts. Aquanauts are the Navy's explorers of the ocean, in contrast to astronauts who explore space. These would seem to be potentially dangerous occupations, but first borns probably figure that they can avoid harm via good training and high quality skills. Thus, the issue may be perceived harm: first borns may believe that they can avoid harm as astronauts or aquanauts, due to training and ability, while it is impossible to believe this about an inherently violent sport, such as football.

In one study, first borns were found to be more likely than later borns to risk their semester grade on one test. This would seem to go against the idea that first borns do not like to take risks. In fact, it is probably the case that first borns do not like the likelihood of physical injury. But, if they feel competent to avoid the possible harm, then they will risk their semester grade on one test, become an astronaut or aquanaut, etc. So, the idea which some have gotten that first borns do not like to take risks is a bit misleading. They do not like to risk physical injury, but they will chance it if they believe they have a good chance of avoiding it. Like many things in life, it is what the person perceives which motivates their behavior. Thus, we have to look at it from the phenomenological standpoint of the individual. That is, we have to put ourselves in their shoes and think like them if we want to understand human behavior. A so-called "objective" view may be misleading, since it leads us to assume that a person would make a decision based on reasons which we perceive to be the objective truth. But, to that person, another viewpoint may be most crucial.

IV. CREATIVITY

Some interesting differences in creativity between first borns and later borns have been found. First borns tend to be higher in creativity, at least among males, but it may be the opposite for females: later born females may be higher in creativity than first born females. Thus, to understand the relationship between birth order and creativity, we have to consider sex differences as well. It is only by looking at both birth order and gender that the creativity results become clear. First born males tend to score higher on creativity measures than do later born males. Creativity can be defined as the combination of originality and usefulness, and there are tests developed to measure this. When we come to females, the results are the opposite: later born females score higher on creativity than first born females. How can this be explained? It may go back to how parents treat their first born child and also how parents treat their female children. Regarding the first born child, if it is a girl, (a) the parents may be anxious and restrictive because she is a first born, but (b) parents are also likely to restrict female children more than they do their male children. Thus, the first born girl would be the most restricted of all the birth order/ sex groupings. Other researchers have found that the first born female tends to grow up with traditional values. Traditional beliefs may be all right in many instances, but would tend to restrict creativity, which often is aided by a radical challenging of the views of the greater society. That is, the creative person is often something of a rebel, at least as far as thoughts about traditional, accepted beliefs are concerned. A person will most likely be creative if society's conventional belief system is questioned. Sometimes the creative person is a rebel in behavior, too. But, of course, this does not mean that being a rebel makes one creative. It may merely make one anti-social without producing anything original and useful. However, the history of creativity shows that many creative people were anti-social in both bad ways and good ways. [See CREATIVE AND IMAGINATIVE THINKING.]

V. MIDDLE CHILDREN

While there is much speculation about the middle child, there is very little solid research. Some re-search has suggested that middle children, whether male or female, tend to be low in creativity. This could possibly be due to the fact that middle children are, by definition, later borns, but part of it seems due to the roles they play in the family. Middle children are often given much more freedom than the first child, and they often rebel against the strict supervision of the little-adult first born whom the parents put in charge. While rebellion could lead to creativity, it can also simply lead to a defiant attitude which does not facilitate the production of any useful products. Why this should be specifically true for middle children as opposed to other later borns is not clear, and the findings must be considered as speculative. Perhaps future research will throw some light on what it means to be a middle child.

VI. LARGE-GAP LAST BORNS

If the child is a last born, but there is a large gap between the birth of the child and the sibling preceding it, then the child is often raised more like a first born. Thus, large-gap last borns often come out in personality as more like the first born. The parents may spend much time with the large-gap last born, thus inducing the adult-like orientation in this child which was true of the first born. Recall that the first born had the parents exclusively to himself or herself, until the birth of the second sibling. If the other children are sufficiently older and independent, or have moved away from the house, the large-gap last born is treated much as the parents treated the first born. Of course, absent would be the parental insecurity. So it may be that the large-gap last born has many of the personality characteristics of the first born except for the high anxiety.

VII. THE ONLY CHILD

In early research, only child subjects were combined with first borns, and researchers sometimes mentioned the category of "first born and only children." This is a mistake, although sometimes the only child is like the first born. For example, the adult orientation of the only child is similar to that of the first born. And, the parental anxiety with the first child would be there, too. So, in many ways, only children will be like first borns. However, only children tend to be more popular with their peers than do first borns. Possibly what is occurring here is that first borns, having been put in charge of the younger siblings, run into conflicts with peers when they try to dominate. The dominating attitude may serve the first born well in many situations where confidence and assertiveness are called for. But it will likely lead to conflicts at school and at play with other children, who do not recognize the first born child as having a legitimate right to dominate. The only child, not being in charge of siblings, does not learn this attitude, so does not have this conflict with peers. Thus, the only child tends to be more popular with other children than does the first born child.

One reason that researchers were tempted to include first born and only children together in their data analysis is that there are not many only children in the population. If one surveys a classroom of, say, 50 children, less than a handful are likely to be only children. There are just not that many only children in any sample. Since a large number of subjects from a given category are needed to do statistical analysis, the researcher typically has less than enough only children. Thus, it is tempting to combine them with first borns. While this is all right in some instances, in other cases, as shown by the peer popularity data, it is not justifiable. Thus, those who want to study the only child need to sample a large number of subjects.

VIII. BIRTH ORDER AND NEED FOR RECOGNITION

First borns seem to have a greater need for public recognition than do later borns. This may explain their greater achievement. It also helps bring together such findings as that of Richie Zweigenhaft that first borns are more likely to be members of congress but also overrepresented among women who are strippers. Zweigenhaft points out that both result in public recognition, although of very different kinds. But, if first borns want public recognition, then there are many paths to the same goal, some socially acceptable and some deviant (which means different, often with a negative connotation).

IX. ARE FIRST BORNS CONSERVATIVES?

Psychoanalyst Alfred Adler said that the first born is the little king of the family until dethroned by the birth of the second sibling. Thus, said Adler, the first born is always looking back to the past, to the good ole days when things were better. Adler said that this makes the first born a conservative. There is very little research done to support or reject this notion. If first born males are more creative than later born males, it would seem some evidence against the alleged first born/conservatism link, since extreme conservatism would seem to lead to inhibition and acceptance of things as they are. This would hardly be conducive to creativity.

However, Frank J. Sulloway of the Program in Science, Technology, and Society at Massachusetts Institute of Technology has come up with some evidence which supports Adler's view, at least in part. Sulloway looked at birth order and support for major innovations in the history of science. He found that first borns tend to be opposed to the radical innovations when they occur, and later borns are more likely to favor them. Take, for example, the Darwinian Revolution. To support the revolutionary views of Charles Darwin and their implications, one had believe that (a) evolution occurs; (b) natural selection is an important cause of evolution; and (c) human beings are descended from lower animals. The descent from lower animals is based on natural as opposed to supernatural causes. Sulloway studied the views toward Darwinian theory of 300 scientists between 1859 and 1870. He also had data on their birth order. First borns tended to oppose and later borns support the Darwinian Revolution. Further, Sulloway finds this birth order effect to be true for other major scientific innovations throughout history. Thus, the first born seems to resist change, just as Adler would have predicted.

Such findings seem inconsistent with the earlier-mentioned research about the greater creativity of first born males, and the greater achievement in life of first borns, who are more likely to achieve eminence than are later borns. Perhaps first borns demand more certainty, so that new, revolutionary theories are looked upon with skepticism. This demand for certainty helps them achieve, wherein they pursue things to their utmost, but may make them too skeptical when it comes to innovative scientific theories. Incidentally, first borns are better than later borns at opposing what turn out to be crackpot scientific theories, such as phrenology (determining intelligence and other traits by counting bumps on the head) or some of the nonsense about hypnosis.

The greater achievement and creativity of first borns could be due to the above-mentioned need for recognition. Both achievement and creativity could lead to recognition. Perhaps this partly can explain how first borns can be both creative and achieving on the one hand, and opposed to innovative scientific discoveries on the other.

X. THE CONTRIBUTIONS OF ADLER AND SCHACHTER

Alfred Adler (1870–1937) was a psychoanalyst who was a follower of Sigmund Freud, the inventor of psychoanalysis. But, Adler, like several of Freud's early followers, felt that Freud neglected the social context of things, and broke away and established his own school of psychology, individual psychology. Among the many concepts which formed the basis of his approach was Adler's belief that birth order is worthy of study. He speculated in detail about how the ordinal position of the child affected the child's personality.

For many years, research psychologist did not study birth order to any extent. Part of the problem is that birth order is a demographic or actuarial variable, like age, gender, or social class, and psychologists did not see it as worthy of study in and of itself. However, in 1959 Stanley Schachter published his book *The Psychology of Affiliation,* in which he showed that birth order was an important variable. He found that first borns tended to be more anxious than later borns, and under conditions of stress desired to affiliate with other subjects experiencing stress. Later borns under stress often preferred to be alone. Many other researchers started looking at birth order in their studies. Sometimes, they had little understanding of what birth order should mean, but it was easy to ask subjects to list their birth order.

As we have gained a greater understanding of birth order, it is possible now to do research which is based on what we know, and not just throw in birth order as another variable, as some of the earlier researchers did. I recall that when I was a graduate student, doing my doctoral dissertation on birth order, I was told of a professor in another department who was also studying birth order. I made an appointment to see him, to find out what he knew about birth order. This was at the University of Georgia, which is a rather large campus. I walked a great distance to meet him, only to learn that he knew almost nothing about birth order. It turned out that he was using a computer card which had spaces for 10 variables. He was interested in 9 things, and since he had a 10th space, he threw in birth order, just to see what might come out. While this strictly empirical approach to research is acceptable, it is much better to be guided by theory and previous findings. Research in recent times has done just that, so that we have a better understanding of what birth order means for both behavior and personality. Future research, building upon what is known and exploring new areas, should help us understand even more about birth order and how it relates to characteristics of the person. It may seem strange that the order of one's birth can have such a strong effect on personality and behavior, but, as the above discussions show, it often does. It would be a mistake to assume that birth order always has a given effect. What may be true in one case may not be true in another. As mentioned in the introduction, the interaction with other factors may be very important. Also, we need to take into account such things as the spacing between siblings, the sexes of the other siblings, and many other situational factors which may affect the birth order findings. In some instances there will be no birth order effect, but this does not negate all the positive findings which have been established. Birth order remains an intriguing variable worthy of future study.

Bibliography

Adler, A. (1958). "What Life Should Mean to You" (A. Porter, Ed.). Capricon Books, New York.

Blake, J. (1989). "Family Size and Achievement." University of California Press, Berkeley/Los Angeles.

Eisenman, R. (1991). "From Crime to Creativity: Psychological and Social Factors in Deviance." Kendall/Hunt, Dubuque, IA.

Leman, K. (1987). "The Birth Order Book." Dell, New York.

Schachter, S. (1959). "The Psychology of Affiliation." Stanford University Press, Stanford.

Sulloway, F. J. (1993). "Born to Rebel: Radical Thinking in Science and Social Thought." In press.

BODY IMAGE

Madeline N. Altabe and J. Kevin Thompson
University of South Florida

Glossary

Body image A generic term used to describe a variety of specific phenomena that relate to an individual's perception of their body.

Body image disturbance A specific type of disturbance that involves a type of dissatisfaction or misperception of size that is related specifically to an individual's physical appearance.

Cognitive–behavioral therapy The empirically supported intervention approach for the treatment of appearance-related body image concerns.

Developmental theory A theory that focuses on pubertal issues (menarcheal timing) or traumatic events related to an individual's body (i.e., teasing) as a cause of body image disturbance.

Sociocultural theory A theory of body image disturbance which relates its occurrence to prevailing societal views of ideal or acceptable physical appearance characteristics.

BODY IMAGE is a construct that has been used to understand everything from phantom limb phenomenon (sensations from amputated limbs) to the motivation behind eating disorders (physical appearance disparagement). It has been conceptualized as a simple umbrella term for several different phenomena with affective cognitive, behavioral, and physio-logical manifestations. It has also been defined as a mind's eye view of the body, sort of a singular mental representation of the physical self, that may be modified by experience.

I. OVERVIEW OF "BODY IMAGE"

To understand body image, as the term is used today, one must evaluate the many contexts in which the construct is studied. Psychology has moved through many different approaches to understanding human behavior, and these have each contributed to our understanding of body image. The two perspectives which initially demonstrated the most theoretical interest in body image were the psychoanalytic and social psychological models. Psychoanalysts were interested in body experience as a reflection of personality processes. For example, when it was demonstrated that schizophrenics overestimated the size of parts of their bodies, psychoanalytically minded theorists hypothesized that this was reflective of a poor boundary between their sense of self and the external world. [*See* SCHIZOPHRENIA.]

A second, quite different, wave of interest was engendered by social and personality psychologists in the 1950s. These researchers were interested in attitudes and behaviors that individuals related to the self and the social world. Body experience was seen as a subcategory of the self. This approach opened up the door to understanding gender differences in body image and led to the development of questionnaire measures to assess some aspect of body image.

The relevance of applied or clinically relevant issues also aroused interest in body image, particularly in the areas of neuropsychological problems and eating disorders. Neurologists were stimulated by the unusual body experiences of patients with certain types of brain disease or injury. For instance, some patients reported symptoms of anosognosia, in which they failed to perceive that a part of their body (i.e., an arm) was connected to the rest of their body. The area of eating disorders has perhaps had the greatest impact on the overall field of body image, with its research documenting the physical appearance component as a cardinal symptom of anorexia nervosa and bulimia nervosa. Currently, the relevance of physical appearance concerns to a diversity of groups, from adolescents to older adults, has broadened the study of appearance-related body image from the realm of eating disorders into the area of "normal" populations.

Thus, like many psychological phenomena, body image has been defined, studied, and conceptualized from multiple perspectives. In this article, we review some of the primary movements, but largely focus on the currently dominant area of body image research and theorizing—the physical appearance component. In this section, we will review the different manifestations of the appearance definition, assessment methods, and intervention strategies, including psychologically based treatments. First, however, we offer a more comprehensive background coverage of the history of body image.

II. HISTORICAL UNDERPINNINGS

The onset of interest in body image can be traced to its relationship to neurological disorders. In the late 1800s, clinicians became interested in the phantom limb phenomenon and other aspects of altered body perception that accompanied brain insult or injury. These neurologists, along with Gestalt psychologists, concluded that there might be an internal mental representation of body information, which they termed body image. Head was one of the most important of the researchers at this time. He observed that sensory changes accompanied brain lesions and is credited with coining the term "body schema." He believed that an individual's representation of their body could even extend to their clothing. Schilder offered one of the best early definitions, defining body image as "the image of the human body means the picture of our own body which we form in our mind, that is to say the way in which the body appears to ourselves."

The early psychoanalysts' interest in this area was primarily based on the writings of Freud who conceptualized the development of the ego as a result of an infant's early interactions with the world. It was believed that children learned about the role of objects in the world by comparing them to their own bodily functions. Of course, much of the early work in this area dealt with psychosexual development. Fisher was one of the pioneers who transformed the psychodynamic study of the body to one that focused on the body of a boundary between the self and external world. The symptoms of schizophrenia, as well as other disorders, were thought to partly relect these poor boundaries.

Finally, the early work in the field of eating disorders served as the basis for much of the recent focus on the empirical study of a physical appearance component of body image. Lasegue, in 1873, was perhaps the first individual who connected this aspect of body image to eating disorders, noting that an anorexic patient stated that she was "neither changed no thinner" when confronted with the fact that her food intake could not support an infant. Bruch, in 1962, was the first researchers to propose that appearance issues were one of three symptoms necessary for the development of anorexia nervosa. She also believed that a cure for the disorder was not possible without "a corrective change in the body image."

A wealth of research in the field of eating disorders has substantiated the important role of body image in the etiology and treatment of these problems. In the new revision of the Diagnostic and Statistical Manual of Mental Disorders, which is used for the classification of all psychiatric/psychological disorders, a body image criterion is required for the diagnosis of anorexia nervosa and bulimia nervosa. In addition, there is a singular disorder devoted exclusively to body image—*body dysmorphic disorder*. This disorder consists of an extreme disparagement of some aspect of appearance that interferes significantly with an individual's social or occupational functioning. Finally, although often ignored as a feature of obesity, researchers demonstrated over 30 years ago the importance of body image to an understanding of individuals with excessive weight. Therefore, it is obvious that body image is seen as an important clinical issue by psychologists and psychiatrists.

In recent years, the focus on an appearance aspect of body image has gone beyond the domain of eating disorders. Research has now begun to focus on the investigation of many basic issues in body image, including developmental, assessment, and treatment parameters. Several books and chapters have been offered to synthesize the current knowledge in this area and research is moving at a rapid pace. We now turn to an overview of the research in this burgeoning field.

III. BODY IMAGE DISTURBANCE: OVERVIEW

We now introduce a new phrase to describe the physical appearance aspect of body image. *Body image disturbance* is generally agreed upon by researchers because most of the work in this area has focused on elevated levels of some aspect of appearance concern, which investigators believe is problematic and possibly related to other psychological problems. It is important to note that this definition is not synonomous with *dissatisfaction* with some aspect of physical appearance. Indeed, dissatisfaction is only one manifestation of body image disturbance, albeit a very common associate of some weight and eating problems. However, there are many aspects to the construct of body image. An understanding of the many types, and definitions, of this important variable is a crucial first step in any discussion of theories, assessment methods, or interventions.

Body image disturbance is any form of affective, cognitive, behavioral, or perceptual disturbance that is directly concerned with an aspect of physical appearance. In addition, many measures of body image are *generic* indices of overall dissatisfaction, which do not further refine the appearance concern into an affective, cognitive, behavioral, or perceptual domain. In the next section, we focus primarily on these composite indices, because they have been used almost exclusively to report on general levels of appearance dissatisfaction in various surveys.

IV. BODY IMAGE DISTURBANCE: EXTENT OF DISSATISFACTION

The most comprehensive study of body dissatisfaction was conducted in 1986 by Cash and colleagues for *Psychology Today* and found that females were more concerned with their appearance than men. In addition, this survey noted that very few individuals (18% of men; 7% of women) were not concerned with their looks.

Other researchers have also documented the presence of greater body dissatisfaction in females. One such study found that 85% of women wanted to lose weight, while only 40% of men felt they were too heavy. Forty-five percent of the men wanted to gain weight. These findings have been replicated and indicate an interesting situation—many men may be dissatisfied for an entirely different reason than women, because they are not as heavy as desired. It should be noted, however, that almost no research has been conducted with older adults, and these findings may be limited to college-age individuals.

Figure 1 contains the schematic figures used for studies of dissatisfaction. As noted in the caption to these figures, individuals are often asked to rate their current size—based on how they "think" they look or "feel" most of the time—and also select the figure they believe is the societal ideal. The difference or discrepancy between these ratings is often used in body image research as an indicator of overall dissatisfaction. As discussed shortly, a variety of these figural ratings are available, including stimuli for research with adolescents.

Body dissatisfaction is not confined to adult samples. Adolescent girls also have been shown to have a great deal of discomfort with their present body size. One investigation found that less than 4% of a sample of British female adolescents were overweight by the standard height/weight charts, but over 10 times that many wanted to lose weight. These findings have also been replicated and other researchers have documented the strong relationship between adolescent body dissatisfaction and levels of psychological dysfunction, such as depression and low self-esteem.

It has also been suggested that many groups may be at-risk to develop excessive body image concerns because of their vocational activities. Ballet dancers, models, and athletes (particularly weightlifters, wrestlers, and individuals involved in gymnastic activities) have all been found to suffer from elevated concerns with appearance. In addition, it has been suggested that girls who experience early menarche, commonly defined as onset of menses prior to age 11, may have elevated levels of physical appearance dissatisfaction. These findings led one group of investigators to state that "maturing faster than her peers may place a girl at risk for bulimia."

In summary, there are a number of individuals without an accompanying eating disorder, who experience elevated levels of body dissatisfaction. Be-

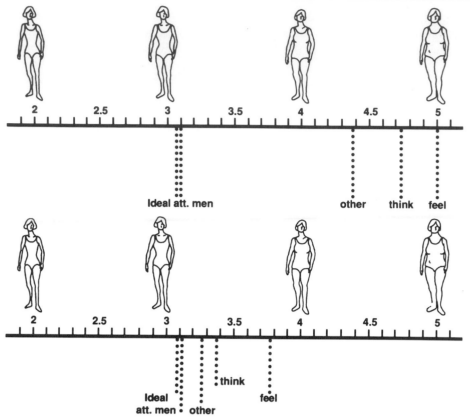

FIGURE 1   Figure ratings for eating-disturbed (*top*) and asymptomatic (*bottom*) subjects. Ratings are for ideal, attractive to men, other—how they look to others, think—how they think they currently look, and feel—how they feel most of the time. [From J. K. Thompson (1991). *Int. J. Eating Disorders* **10**, 196. Copyright © 1991 John Wiley & Sons; reprinted with permission.]

fore dealing with the many measures available for the assessment of body image disturbance, we now offer a brief review of the emerging theories offered for its occurrence.

V. THEORIES OF BODY IMAGE DISTURBANCE

Most researchers agree that a sociocultural factor is perhaps the most powerful influence on individuals' feelings about the acceptability of their physical appearance. Throughout history, women have altered or modified their physique based on the prevailing cultural "ideal." As Striegel-Moore and colleagues noted, in recent years, the social message has been that "what is fat is bad, what is thin is beautiful, and what is beautiful is good." Figures 2 and 3 illustrate some of the surveys that have documented this increasing trend toward thinness in our society.

Other theories are less well developed; however, emerging evidence suggests that developmental events may play a role in body image. The role of menarcheal timing has been posited as an important

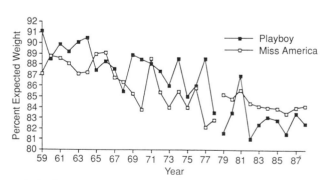

FIGURE 2   Average percentage of expected weight of Playboy centerfolds and Miss America contestants, 1959–1978 and 1979–1988. [From C. V. Wiseman *et al.* (1992). *Int. J. Eating Disorders* **11**, 87. Copyright © 1992 John Wiley & Sons, Inc.; reprinted with permission.]

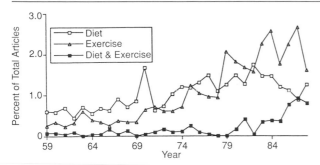

FIGURE 3   Number of articles as a percentage of total articles in six women's magazines. [From C. V. Wiseman *et al.* (1992). *Int. J. Eating Disorders* **11**, 88. Copyright © 1992 John Wiley & Sons, Inc.; reprinted with permission.]

pubertal event that may have lasting effects on body image. It has been found that adults who had been early maturers (generally defined as the onset of menarche prior to age 11) were shorter, but had 8.8% more body fat than later maturers. Thompson and colleagues have documented the presence of teasing about physical appearance as an early event that is associated with current body dissatisfaction in adolescents and elevated adult concerns with appearance.

Perceptual theories have also been offered to account for the tendency of many individuals to overestimate the size of certain body sites. Thompson and colleagues found that size overestimation was associated with visuospatial deficits on neuropsychological tests. They also compared size matched groups of anorexics and non-eating-disturbed controls and found no difference in size overestimation. Both groups overestimated size to a greater degree than a randomly selected, larger-sized, group of controls. They concluded that a general tendency toward the overestimation of smaller stimuli might account for much of the research suggesting that anorexics view their body in a distorted fashion, i.e., overestimation of body size.

The investigation of theoretical models of body image disturbance is still in its infancy. One new hypothesis which has gathered a good deal of attention revolves around the issue of social comparison. In a series of studies, Thompson and colleagues have documented the role of engaging in an evaluative comparison process, in terms of physical appearance, with other individuals, as an important correlate of body satisfaction. Future research will no doubt compare the role of each of the above theories as an explanation for the development of body image disturbance. We now turn to an overview of measurement issues.

VI. ASSESSMENT OF BODY IMAGE DISTURBANCE

There are a number of different types of *figural* stimulus materials for the assessment of overall satisfaction. For example, Stunkard and colleagues developed a widely used set of nine female schematic figures that range from underweight to overweight (four of which are depicted in Fig. 1). Generally, subjects are asked to rate the figure based on the following instructional protocol: (a) current size and (b) ideal size. The difference between the ratings is a *discrepancy* index, and is considered to represent the individual's level of dissatisfaction. Thompson and colleagues have found that the current size rating may be affected by the particular way that this instruction is worded. Specifically, affective ratings (based on how the subject feels) are larger than current size ratings based on cognitive instructions (based on how subjects thinks they look). In fact, Altabe and Thompson found that the discrepancy between affective and cognitive ratings is significantly related to level of eating disturbance.

The great majority of figural measures are designed to document overall size satisfaction for adult samples. However, a measure created specifically for children/adolescents was recently introduced by Collins. In addition, Thompson and Tantleff constructed a figural stimulus which allows for the assessment of breast and chest size preference. Using the same rating protocol described above for the overall figure methods allows for a determination of dissatisfaction with breast or chest size.

There are a large number of questionnaire measures that assess a generic aspect of body satisfaction. One of the most widely used in the Body Dissatisfaction subscale of the Eating Disorder Inventory. This instrument uses a six-point scale to measure satisfaction with nine different body sites. The Body Areas Satisfaction Scale of the Multidimensional Body Self-Relations Questionnaire also captures satisfaction with specific body sites. There are also a number of measures of a more global appearance satisfaction, including the Body Shape Questionnaire.

Researchers have also designed scales designed to measure an anxiety component of body image disturbance. The Physical Appearance State and Trait Anxiety Scale (PASTAS) taps into the anxiety component associated with weight and overall appearance concerns. There are two subscales of eight items each: weight (W) and nonweight (NW) factors. In addition, there are two versions—the Trait version is designed as a measure of general or characterological body image anxiety and the State version assesses current or immediate level of anxiety. The State version was created for repetitive use, to index transient changes in anxiety, such as might occur immediately after a treatment session targeting body image issues.

The Physical Appearance Evaluation scale of the Multidimensional Body Self-Relations Questionnaire is also a measure of the affective component of body image. The Mirror Distress Rating involves an individual's self-evaluation while gazing at body features for 30 seconds while standing in front of a mirror. Subjects make a rating based on a Subjective Units of Discomfort (SUDS) index, which has a range from 0 (absolute calm) to 100 (extreme discomfort).

Yet another subscale of the MBSRQ provides a measure of the cognitive component of body image. The Appearance Orientation scale is an eight-item measure that indexes a cognitive "attentional" aspect of body image. The Bulimia Cognitive Distortions Scale also contains a Physical Appearance subscale that deals specifically with cognitive distortions related to physical appearance.

There are two types of procedures for the assessment of a behavioral aspect of body image. The first method involves a self-report of avoidance of body image-related situations. Rosen and colleagues developed the Body Image Avoidance Questionnaire (BIAQ) which contains four scales: clothing, social activities, eating restraint, and grooming/weighing. Importantly, the scores on this scale converge well with ratings made by observers (roommates). The second type of procedure is the direct observation of body image related behaviors. This is probably the least developed area in the assessment of body image disturbance. However, there are some interesting procedures that could prove useful as additions to an overall body image assessment protocol. For instance, as noted above, Rosen and colleagues found that roommates' ratings correlated well with subjects' self-report of avoidance behaviors.

Thompson and colleagues reported on the Physical Appearance Behavioral Avoidance Test (PA-BAT), a procedure that requires subjects to approach their own image in a mirror, from a 20-foot distance, in 2-foot intervals. Subjects evaluate the image for a period of 30 seconds at each interval

and also make a SUDS rating (0–100) similar to that discussed above for the Mirror Distress Rating. Subjects are informed that they can discontinue the process if a level of "extreme discomfort" is reached. Thus, the behavioral measure is the point of termination. SUDS's ratings can be used as an index of the affective component of body image.

There are a wealth of technologies, some quite sophisticated, for the assessment of the perceptual component of body image disturbance. The procedures can be divided into two broad categories: single-site methods and whole-image adjustment methods. The single-site measures provide for the assessment of size perception accuracy at individual body sites. For instance, the Image Marking Procedure requires subjects to estimate the width of body sites by marking on white paper attached to the wall. Ruff and Barrios developed the Body Image Detection Device (BIDD), which projects a beam of light onto an adjacent wall; subjects adjust the light to a width that matches their conception of the width of a particular body site. Thompson and Thompson modified the design of the BIDD to allow for the simultaneous presentation of four light beams, reflecting the cheeks, waist, hips, and thighs. This procedure is called the adjustable light beam apparatus (ALBA).

Alternatively, using the *whole-image adjustment* procedures, the individual views a whole-body image, via pictorial, mirror, or video presentation. The images can be modified to represent an image smaller or larger than actual size. Subjects are generally asked to match the image to their conception of actual size. An index of over- or underestimation is computed from the matching process.

In summary, there exists a wealth of measures for the assessment of some aspect of body image disturbance. These indices are important for the documentation of existing disturbance, but also integral to the determination of an effective treatment program. In the next section, we briefly review the treatments which have been offered to lessen an individual's concern with physical appearance.

VII. TREATMENT OF BODY IMAGE DISTURBANCE

There are few empirically validated studies on the treatment of body image disturbance. Although a number of strategies have been advocated, from art and dance classes to confronting individuals with videos of their emaciated bodies, the only empirically supported techniques include cognitive–behavioral strategies. In particular, Cash and Rosen have targeted an evaluation of these procedures and Cash has created a manual to be used as a guide for the therapist and patient.

Among the cognitive–behavioral procedures that have been shown to be effective are desensitization techniques, cognitive-restructuring, and relaxation exercises. The exposure-based desensitization requires an individual to confront her image concerns by evaluating problematic body sites in a mirror. The cognitive procedures challenge irrational beliefs about appearance, such as "I must be thin to be special." Rosen has also found that homework assignments, consisting of *in vivo* exposure exercises, in which individuals confront avoided social situations that involve appearance evaluation, are also effective. [*See* COGNITIVE BEHAVIOR THERAPY.]

Only recently have researchers attempted to integrate body image treatment methods into comprehensive treatment programs for eating disorders. In all likelihood, the future will reveal an increasing trend toward the evaluation of intervention procedures, including methods other than cognitive–behavioral techniques.

VIII. CURRENT TRENDS IN BODY IMAGE RESEARCH

In recent years, the investigation of body image has been undertaken in previously relatively ignored populations. For instance, the following areas are now active avenues of inquiry: individuals with congenital deformities or physical appearance changes subsequent to injury or accident, persons electing cosmetic surgery to modify naturally occurring physical characteristics, the variation of appearance concerns across diverse ethnic groups, and the importance of early sexual abuse in the formation of adult body image disturbance.

In Pertschuk's comprehensive review of reconstructive surgery, cleft lip and palate, craniofacial malformations, and craniofacial trauma are discussed, in addition to other problems of congenital deformity or injury/disease related malformations. Shontz also offers a review of physical disability and body image, along with an organizing theory for the findings in this research area. The area of breast cancer has received a good deal of attention and researchers agree that surgical alteration of the breast has a significant effect of a woman's body image. One review noted that changes in body image, along with depression and sexual problems, were associated with breast surgery.

Pruzinsky offers a review of the psychological effects of cosmetic surgery and notes that there is a lack of clear consensus provided by the extant literature, which reveals the possibility of negative as well as positive outcomes. There is no doubt that there is an increasing use of this method to objectively modify physical appearance. Future research is likely to parallel the accelerated utilization of cosmetic surgery.

Although the bulk of research in the area of body image has been on caucasian females, recent trends indicate a focus on diversity. It has been found that the Western societies' excessive valuation of thinness does not generalize to other cultures, but focus on women's beauty does. Specific comparisons across cultures have yielded interesting findings. Scottish and American women are quite similar in appearance evaluation, although American women may have more differentiation in satisfaction across body sites. One research group found that Muslim men preferred heavier women than Judaic-Christian men. White British females had more concern about appearance than black or Asian groups. Notably, research with African-American and other non-Caucasian females suggests that conforming to a predominantly Caucasian group puts them at risk for body image disturbance.

One rapidly expanding area of inquiry involves the effect of early sexual abuse or precocious sexualization (experience at an early age with sexual matters) on the formation of body image. Researchers are investigating the potential long-lasting effects from these types of traumas. In particular, the negative effects on body image may also be paralleled by a greater risk for the development of eating disorders. Importantly, findings suggest that the deleterious effects may show up in children shortly after abuse.

Overall, there is an increasing emphasis on the investigation of individuals with diverse backgrounds among clinicians and researchers in the area of body image. In addition, it now seems apparent that body image issues are critical aspects for individuals with congenital malformations, physical transformations as a result of trauma, or the desire to modify appearance via cosmetic surgery. Finally, the role of early sexualization episodes, including sexual abuse, is receiving research attention.

IX. SUMMARY AND CONCLUSIONS

"Body image" has been used for hundreds of years to describe a variety of phenomena that differ radically in their specific manifestation. In this article, we have reviewed some of the major areas of research and clinical work for psychologists that have included some aspect of body image. Although most of the recent work has involved the investigation of a physical appearance component of body image, in all likelihood, if the past is any indicator of the future, body image will evolve and take on new and different definitions, dimensions, and domains.

Bibliography

Cash, T. F., and Pruzinsky, T. (1990). "Body Images: Development, Deviance, and Change." Guilford, New York.

Fisher, S. (1986). "Development and Structure of the Body Image." Erlbaum, Hillsdale, NJ.

Strober, M. (Ed.). *International Journal of Eating Disorders*, Vols. 1–15. Wiley, New York.

Thompson, J. K. (1990). "Body Image Disturbance: Assessment and Treatment." Pergamon, Elmsford, NY.

Thompson, J. K. (1992). Body image: Extent of disturbance, associated features, theoretical models, assessment methodologies, intervention strategies, and a proposal for a new DSM IV category—Body Image Disorder. In "Progress in Behavior Modification" M. Hersen, R. M. Eisler, and P. M. Miller Eds.), pp. 3–54. Sycamore, Sycamore, IL.

BORDERLINE PERSONALITY DISORDER

Jerome Kroll
University of Minnesota Medical School

Glossary

As-if personality A type of personality lacking a stable core identity, which then takes on characteristics of persons in the environment.

Cluster B The grouping of four personality disorders (narcissistic, borderline, histrionic, and antisocial) in Axis II of DSM-III-R.

Dissociation An altered state of consciousness that appears split off from one's ongoing sense of awareness and self-consciousness.

Rejection-sensitive dysphoria A transient form of depressed mood brought on by perception of rejection by others.

BORDERLINE PERSONALITY DISORDER is a term that identifes a heterogeneous group of patients with serious character pathology and behavioral disturbances. The main features of this disorder are behavior that is implusive, dramatic, and often self-destructive; moods that are labile and reactive to life circumstances; interpersonal relationships that are stormy; and a sense of self-identity that is fragile and contradictory.

I. HISTORICAL DEVELOPMENT OF THE CONCEPT

More than one decade after the development and publication of DSM-III, borderline personality disorder (BPD) remains the most controversial category in the nomenclature. Disagreement persists regarding the term itself, the particular diagnostic criteria established for BPD by DSM-III and DSM-III-R, the scope of applicability, and the extent of overlap with Axis I and other Axis II disorders. Ultimately, this degree and intensity of dispute reflect both the range of difficulties in identifying and working with those persons designated as borderline, as well as the more basic question of validity: whether the BPD construct describes a meaningful unitary syndrome that corresponds to an actually existing state of affairs. While this latter question can certainly be asked of any of the personality (Axis II) disorders, something about the borderline concept seems to have engendered the strongest controversy.

At least one major reason for the ongoing disputes is the fact that the very concept of borderline was born out of attempts to explain the clinical observation that certain patients seemed to do very poorly in psychodynamic psychotherapy. Thus, from the very first, this category was used to describe a disparate group of patients who had two things in common: they responded to psychotherapy by developing transient psychotic symptoms and they did not meet classical definitions of schizophrenia. It is not that they did not necessarily improve; many obsessional patients, for example, did not improve with psychotherapy. Rather, it is that these patients worsened in psychotherapy with a fairly specific pattern of acting out that showed up most dramatically in the development of severe transference problems. The difficulty confronting the predominantly psychoanalytic theoreticians and skilled therapists was how to fathom the nature of these patients who gave promise of being good psychotherapeutic cases, yet deteriorated during the course of a psychotherapy. Thus, the very origins of the borderline concept arose in the context of a clinical puzzle.

The solution to the puzzle, keeping in mind that American psychiatry held a much more encompassing concept of schizophrenia in the 1940s and

1950s than at present, was to conceptualize these patients who became worse in psychotherapy as having a schizophrenic core underlying the neurotic facade. This notion was given concrete expression in a paper by Hoch and Polatin in 1949 describing the new category of pseudoneurotic schizophrenia. The construct fit neatly into a psychoanalytic model that postulated a spectrum of psychopathology based upon increasing primitiveness of defense mechanisms, extending in an unbroken chain from mild neurotics at one end to deteriorated schizophrenics at the other. The pseudoneurotic patient served as the missing link, bridging neurosis and psychosis, and thus serving as visible proof of the continuity connecting mild and severe psychiatric disorders. [*See* DEFENSE MECHANISMS; SCHIZOPHRENIA.]

The problem with the pseudoneurotic schizophrenia construct was that the patients did not go on to develop the more classical symptoms of hallucinations and delusions nor the deteriorating course that is the usual outcome of schizophrenia. Nevertheless, the observation that there existed a group of patients who appeared neurotic, but worsened with intensive psychotherapy, was a valid finding that outlived the misleading label attached to it. The focus of what might be wrong with these difficult-to-treat patients shifted away from schizophrenia to consideration of severe character pathology, described as borderline states by Knight in 1953 and as the psychotic character by Frosch in 1964. In addition, the joint U.S.–U.K. diagnostic studies carried out in the mid-to-late 1960s demonstrated convincingly that many patients diagnosed as schizophrenic by American psychiatrists fit much better with manic–depressive and personality disorder symptoms and outcome. This diagnostic realignment tightened the diagnostic criteria for schizophrenia, thereby further emphasizing the differences between borderline conditions and schizophrenia.

In 1968, Grinker and colleagues published the results of their study of 58 hospitalized patients who fell into a broadly defined notion of borderline syndrome. These patients had difficulties in interpersonal relationships, transient losses of reality testing under stress, angry and depressive affects, and deficient self-identities. Cluster analyses of the data, primarily of measurements of ego functions, produced four major clusters. There was a "core" borderline group, two groups defined as bordering upon the pyschoses and neuroses, and a fourth group embodying certain "as-if" features, most notably absence of a core self-identity. Grinker's study, the first to utilize psychometric instruments and statistical analyses, moved the borderline concept away from the realm of schizophrenic spectrum disorders and provided the basis for future empirical studies that continued the attempt to define the still vague borderline syndrome.

It is instructive that in the next series of studies carried out by Gunderson and Singer in 1975, the primary diagnostic concern was still to demonstrate that borderlines were different than schizophrenics. At the same time that empirical studies were focusing on narrowing the construct of borderline, Kernberg developed a broader notion of borderline, based upon a fusion of ego psychology and object relations theory, to designate a form of personality organization that was characterized by the use of primitive ego defenses (denial, splitting, projective identification), intact reality testing (with transient regressions under stress), and identity diffusion. Kernberg's construct of borderline personality organization includes the milder as well as the more severe forms of character pathology, and, in essence, encompasses most of the patients presently grouped under the Cluster B (dramatic, unstable) personality disorders: histrionic, narcissistic, borderline, and antisocial.

This was the state of affairs in 1976–1980 while the DSM-III committee developed inclusion and exclusion criteria for the personality disorders. There were four competing and overlapping concepts of borderline, and the final result represented some degree of compromise between the various groups. Since ideological and economic considerations, in addition to empirical studies and clinical lore, influenced the final product, it is important to define these considerations in some detail. The four overlapping concepts of borderline were as follows: (1) A residual model based upon the schizophrenic spectrum concept, using the term borderline to designate those persons, usually relatives of schizophrenics, who displayed odd, eccentric thinking and schizoid interpersonal relationships; this group was given the term schizotypal personality disorder in DSM-III. (2) An affective disorder model, which considered BPD as an affective spectrum illness displaying prominent features of mood instability with a predominance of depression, anger, and preoccupations with suicide. (3) An empirically derived model based primarily on the research of Gunderson, with diagnostic symptoms placed into five major groupings: impulse/action patterns (including self-destructive behaviors);

ego-dystonic, transient psychotic episodes; mood instability with primarily negative affects; disturbed but intense interpersonal relationships; and an unstable sense of self. (4) A psychoanalytic concept based primarily on the work of Kernberg, but encompassing theoretical formulations by Mahler relating to difficulties in the separation/individuation phase of child development.

The final configuration of BPD adopted for DSM-III was most influenced by Gunderson's work, but nevertheless showed the strains inherent in a compromise between points of view that are ideologically very divergent. The results were the creation of several new personality disorders within Axis II, not based upon empirical studies, but with each reflecting to some extent components that were once loosely connected to the borderline concept. Essentially, in dividing the broad territory of the borderline syndrome, as this concept evolved during a 40-year span, the cognitive disturbances that had long been noticed were placed in the schizotypal personality disorder, the milder dramatic and attention-seeking traits were placed into the histrionic personality disorder, self-centeredness and entitlement became the core of the narcissistic personality disorder, and the affective symptoms of mood instability and negative affectivity (depression, anger, anxiety), along with impulsivity, were given prominence in the borderline personality disorder.

Borderline personality disorder was defined by DSM-III-R as a condition marked by a pervasive pattern of instability of mood, interpersonal relationships, and self-image, beginning by early adulthood and present in a variety of contexts, as indicated by at least five of the following:

1. A pattern of unstable and intense interpersonal relationships characterized by alternating between extremes of overidealization and devaluation.
2. Impulsiveness in at least two areas that are potentially self-damaging, e.g., spending, sex, substance use, shoplifting, reckless driving, binge eating.
3. Affective instability: marked shifts from baseline mood to depression, irritability, or anxiety, usually lasting a few hours and only rarely more than a few days.
4. Inappropriate, intense anger or lack of control of anger, e.g., frequent displays of temper, constant anger, physical fights.

5. Recurrent suicidal threats, gestures, or behavior, or self-mutilating behavior.
6. Marked and persistent identity disturbance manifested by uncertainty about at least two of the following: self-image, sexual orientation, long-term goals or career choice, type of friends desired, preferred values.
7. Chronic feeling of emptiness or boredom.
8. Frantic efforts to avoid real or imagined abandonment.

The revision of DSM-III-R into DSM-IV was completed by late 1993. Although the BPD construct did not undergo any major alterations, several changes were instituted which served to correct the overemphasis in DSM-III on the close relationship between BPD and the affective disorders and the omission of cognitive deficits. Criterion 3 (Criterion 6 in DSM-IV), which outlined the affective symptoms seen in BPD was changed to reflect reactivity of mood; this serves to emphasize the difference between the mood disturbances seen in BPD and the relatively situation-independent mood disturbances characteristic of the endogenous affective disorders (major depression and manic–depressive illnesses). Complementing this more accurate delineation of the type of mood disorder seen in BPD was the inclusion of a new criterion to reflect the specific cognitive disturbances of BPD. The DSM-IV draft calls for a ninth criterion as follows: Transient stress-related paranoid ideation or severe dissociative symptoms. There were a few additional changes to the original eight criteria, but these are relatively minor, either reflecting grammatical alterations in the interest of clarity or the result of low sensitivity/specificity ratings for a few items on further field testing. Thus, the description of the identity disturbance in Criterion 6 was reworded and the construct "boredom" was dropped from Criterion 7.

II. CORE SYMPTOMS AND CHARACTER STYLE

The clinical description of a psychiatric disorder does not correspond exactly to that disorder's diagnostic criteria in DSM-III. The main reason for this is that a clinical description needs to be a full and rich portrayal of the condition under question, whereas the requirements for diagnostic criteria are vastly different. Diagnostic criteria must aim for those characteristics of an illness that capture a few of its core symptoms while avoiding overlap with neighboring conditions. For example, as indicated above, while boredom may very well be a characteristic mental state in BPD, it was also found in histrionic and narcissistic personality disorders and therefore was of little specific diagnostic value. It did not help discriminate between BPD and other Cluster B personality disorders. In addition, diagnostic criteria must have acceptable validity and reliabiltiy. The issue of validity of psychiatric disorders, especially of personality disorders, is a troublesome one, since there are not external validators. The construction of DSM-III had paid major attention, some would say excessively so, to reliability issues. For example, certain factors that most workers would agree are characteristic of a disorder, such as the psychological defense of splitting in BPD, were not included in the diagnostic criteria because of a preference for behavioral rather than psychological phenomena, presumably because assessment of behaviors permits greater agreement as to whether they are present or not as compared to psychological constructs.

As indicated at the beginning of this article, there remains considerable controversy about the core characteristics and boundaries of BPD. Workers in the field have tended to bring to the evaluation of BPD their own theoretical and clinical perspectives in the evaluation of borderlines. In addition, some of the core characteristics of BPD, such as an increase in dissociative phenomena, appear to be changing in the past decade, a possibility that raises the question of the cultural influences and even faddish quality of some of the symptoms.

Most workers would agree that BPD is a relatively severe personality disorder, seen primarily in young adults, that presents with a characteristic cognitive style, mood disturbances, problematic interpersonal relationships, negative and deficient sense of self, and a variety of dramatic and impulsive behaviors usually of a self-injurious nature. These diagnostic features represent points distributed on a continuum of personality traits with somewhat arbitrary use of social norms to determine cut-off scores separating normal from pathological. Because of this, some workers in the field have advocated use of a dimensional rather than categorical model for the personality disorders, but a categorical model has always been adopted because it is easier to use in clinical work.

The cognitive style seen in borderline individuals encompasses three overlapping features. First, bor-

derlines tend to have altered states of consciousness; these are usually referred to as dissociative states, and vary in intensity, density, and duration. They run the gamut from brief periods of self-absorption to fugue states lasting hours. The person may be partially or fully amnestic for some of the dissociative episodes. Second, borderlines tend to split their universe into good and bad, black and white. They have difficulty conceptualizing a person, including themselves, or an event, as encompassing positive and negative features. They tend to swing between the opposite poles of idealization and devaluation in their affections toward others. Third, borderlines tend to have impressionistic and global rather than precise and focused perceptions. They tend to be intolerant of unpleasant thoughts and images and to interrupt these processes with impulsive action, dissociation, and drug and alcohol use. There is a tendency toward imprecision and exaggeration, with a loss of salient detail. All of these disturbances are increased under conditions of stress.

The affective disturbances are characteristically mood instability or lability. Mood is typically reactive to environmental circumstances, but this must be taken to include the borderline's own thought processes too. Negative affects, such as sadness, anger, and anxiety predominate the emotional landscape, but too literal adherence to this description would belie the positive affects and interpersonal warmth that borderlines can exhibit.

Problematic interpersonal relationships are a hallmark of borderlines. Their relationships are characteristically intense, stormy, and conflictual. Dependency needs, power struggles, and the idealization/ devaluation swings described earlier tend to complicate most meaningful relationships. Victimization and entitlement themes in which the borderline alternates between being exploited by others and demanding reparations from others for damages incurred are frequent patterns seen in this disorder.

Borderline individuals tend to have a deficient sense of self, and what enduring image of themselves they may have is usually negative. A deficient sense of self refers to the absence of a stable sense of core identity, of knowing who you are. A certain degree of this is expected in adolescents and young adults in Western culture, but the borderline problem with identity, by definition, must go beyond the norm for this age group. Borderlines will take on different roles and personality characteristics, depending upon the dominant features of the group they are associating with. This has been referred to as the ''as-if'' personality, first described by Helene Deutsch in 1942. When not caught up in a persuasive group identity, borderlines tend to have very negative notions about themselves, ranging from dislike to contemptuous loathing.

Finally, borderlines characteristically are dramatic and impulsive in their actions. The patterns of impulsivity include directly self-injurious behaviors as well as an assortment of either ill-considered or risk-taking behaviors that also may be seen as self-destructive. Alcohol and drug abuse, bulimic eating disorders, promiscuity, and attraction to predatory partners are among the impusive actions seen in borderlines. As with the other core features of borderlines, the self-injurious behaviors range from infrequent and mild delicate cutting of the wrists to deep cutting of the limbs, torso, and genitals, as well as occasional ingenious use of cigarettes, lighters, caustic solutions, and hot irons to burn themselves. Suicide threats and attempts are also hallmarks of borderlines, most frequently but not exclusively with prescription as well as nonprescription medication overdoses. There are many more threats and gestures than serious attempts, leading to the use of the term ''parasuicide'' to describe these provocative actions of borderlines, but often the differentiation between manipulative and serious attempts is not at all clear.

III. DEMOGRAPHIC AND DATA-BASED STUDIES

There are no accurate measures of the prevalence of BPD in the community. Most estimates range from 0.5 to 1%, but may go higher as a broader concept of borderline, such as that used by Kernberg, is applied. The prevalence of the disorder in clinical settings is influenced by the type of clinical population under consideration. An average across studies indicates that the general prevalence of BPD is 10–15%, in inpatient settings about 20%, among outpatients with a personality disorder 30–35%, and among inpatients with a personality disorder 60–65%. Prevalence figures alone may be deceptive; it is possible that borderlines in an inpatient setting may have little similarity to outpatients who have never needed hospitalization. In most studies, excepting those done in VA and prison settings, 60–75% of BPD are women.

Although DSM-III diagnostic rules do not permit differential weighting of the different criteria, most studies have demonstrated that several items contribute disproportionately to diagnostic efficiency. The presence of two, or at most three, specific criteria (impulsivity, unstable–intense interpersonal relationships, and self-injurious behaviors) predict most strongly the diagnosis of BPD, although once again, the type of clinical setting (inpatient or outpatient) will influence this finding.

There is considerable overlap (20–60%) between BPD and the other personality disorders, especially those of Cluster B, as well as schizotypal and dependent personality disorders. This finding continues to raise the question of whether personality disorders are discrete entities truly different from each other or reflect points on a continuum of serious character pathology. There are several Axis I disorders that have substantial overlap with BPD. These are alcohol and substance abuse disorders, bulimia, and the mood disorders, primarily dysthymia and major depression. To some extent, this finding reflects overlapping criteria (e.g., substance abuse is listed as a criterion for BPD), the heterogeneity of the BPD concept, and the fact that traits such as impulsivity and mood lability do express themselves in a wide array of behaviors. [*See* PERSONALITY DISORDERS.]

IV. ETIOLOGY AND RELATIONSHIP TO OTHER DISORDERS

Since it appears that BPD is not a unitary disorder, and since diagnostic threshold can be met in a polythetic system by fulfilling any five of eight (or nine, under DSM-IV) criteria, it is highly unlikely that a unitary etiology will be found for this or other Cluster B personality disorders. Theories about the etiology of BPD tend to follow major trends of interest in the behavioral sciences in general. Thus, the predominance of psychoanalytic constructs as explanatory hypotheses of human health and illness has given way to a variety of biological–genetic models in the past decade. Even the recent robust correlations between childhood sexual abuse and adult BPD symptoms are increasingly explained more in terms of long-lasting neurophysiological alterations of stress–response systems rather than in terms of psychodynamic mechanisms. The major theories of the etiology of BPD are as follow:

A. Psychoanalytic model of stage-specific
   difficulties
   1. Deficit model (Masterson; Adler)
   2. Conflict model (Kernberg)
B. BPD as an affective spectrum model
C. BPD as post-traumatic stress disorder secondary
   to childhood sexual and physical abuse
D. BPD as an impulse spectrum disorder

A. Psychoanalytic Hypotheses

Based upon Mahler's theories of the importance of
successful resolution of the rapprochment subphase
of the separation/individuation processes in toddlerhood (ages 15–30 months), several overlapping
psychodynamic hypotheses were advanced to explain those BPD features that were thought to represent the consequences of rapprochment failure.
These features were the mental operation and defense of splitting, identity diffusion, and deficiencies
in object constancy and object relationships. Differences of opinion and emphasis exist between various
psychodynamic theories: Masterson has suggested
that the mother of the borderline is herself borderline
and establishes emotionally impossible conditions
for the toddler to achieve age-appropriate separation
and individuation, thereby resulting in the development of a borderline personality in the child. Adler
has emphasized the borderline child's inability, under circumstances similar to those described by
Masterson, to form internalized soothing, holding
introjects, such that the borderline child (and adult)
lacks basic ego functions such as frustration tolerance, stable self-object relationships, and methods
for calming itself during periods of stress. Kernberg
has postulated the likelihood of an excessive aggressive drive in the infant that interferes with the fusion
of sexual and aggressive drives; Kernberg's model
therefore sees borderline pathogenesis as the result
of a complex interaction between infant and caregiver rather than as unilaterally caused by a "not-
good-enough" mother.

The basic problem with the psychoanalytic
hypotheses regarding etiology of BPD is shared by
psychodynamic explanations of behavior in general:
first, difficulty in operationalizing and thereby in
testing various theories and second, a lack of specificity whereby certain postulated mechanisms at
best appear to be general risk factors (e.g., parental
psychopathology) rather than the specific and inevitable cause of a particular outcome. This latter problem, of course, applies to all unitary theories of etiology. Finally, the nature of the psychodynamic
hypotheses are such that supportive evidence comes
primarily from retrospective rather than prospective
studies, and from individual case studies in which
the investigator testing the hypothesis is also the
therapist commited to the hypothesis.

B. BPD as an Affective Spectrum Disorder

The observation that borderline patients are frequently depressed, and the prominence of mood instability in the symptom picture, have led to the
hypothesis that an affective disorder underlies the
borderline condition. Attempts to validate this hypothesis examined a variety of biological markers,
familial patterns, follow-up data, and pharmacological responses. The initial findings, varying somewhat from study to study, were that from 20 to 60%
of borderline patients met diagnostic criteria for an
affective disorder, usually major depressive episode. This was not particularly surprising since the
diagnostic criteria for BPD were slanted toward affective type symptoms. The studies have shown that
patients with depression and borderline patients who
were concurrently depressed resembled each other
in regard to several biological markers of depression,
such as the dexamethasone suppression test, REM
latency time, and thyroid stimulating hormone response to thyrotropin, but the resemblances fell
away with "pure" borderline patients, i.e., borderline patients who were not depressed. [See DE-
PRESSION.]

Similar results were found in the family pedigrees
of borderline patients. Borderline patients with concurrent depressions had a greater prevalence of relatives with affective disorders. However, this finding
is true for most of the Axis II disorders, namely, that
there is a higher prevalence of depressed persons in
the families of patients with any personality disorder
and depression. On the other hand, borderline patients without depression tend to have increased familial linkages to other disorders, namely, borderline and antisocial personality disorders, and
alcoholism and drug abuse. Studies of pharmacological efficacy with borderlines have demonstrated
minimal benefit from antidepressants, even with depressed borderlines, except for some amelioration
of depressive symptoms. Lithium therapy has not
proven valuable in treating BPD. There have been
some indications that monoamine oxidase inhibitors
are effective in reducing core borderline symptoms,
thereby supporting the atypical depression model of

BPD, but these findings have never been sufficiently replicated to be more than suggestive. Finally, the long-term follow-up studies have shown that most borderline patients do not go on to develop depressive syndromes, again arguing against a causal linkage between BPD and affective disorders.

Despite the fairly clear evidence that BPD is not a variant of affective disorders, most studies do show that a certain percentage of borderline patients have a recurrent affective disorder (either depressive or bipolar type II, i.e., depressions and hypomanias) and evolve into a typical affective disorder pattern after the dramatic borderline symptoms recede in the 30s. Thus, it seems likely that a subclass of borderlines has a primary affective disturbance.

C. BPD as Post-Traumatic Stress Disorder Secondary to Childhood Sexual and Physical Abuse

There has been a increasing awareness of the frequency of childhood sexual abuse in the life history of many psychiatric patients. This awareness has paralleled a growing public consciousness of domestic violence of many types. The question remains unresolved as to whether child abuse and other forms of violence have indeed become more common recently, reaching epidemic proportions, or whether the social taboos that maintained silence over such assaults have been lifted, with the result of greater casefinding and reporting of such episodes. Among psychiatric patients, rates of childhood sexual abuse range between 25 and 80%, depending on the population surveyed and the survey methods. Surveys from such varied locations as state hospitals, community hospitals, outpatient clinics, and emergency rooms have been consistent in these findings. Reported rates are highest for borderline personality disorder, in the order of 50–80%. In the borderline population, there also appears to be a correlation between severity of certain types of symptoms, such as self-injurious behaviors and dissociative episodes, and the severity of the childhood sexual abuse experiences, as judged by age of first abuse, frequency and duration of abuse, degree of force and violence employed, and absence of ameliorative factors in the life of the child. The correlations between abuse and borderline symptomatology have been robust enough to lead several workers to hypothesize that most patients who have been diagnosed BPD are really suffering from PTSD and that

this latter diagnosis makes better scientific and social sense, removing the stigma that has been attached to a BPD label. The case is strengthened by the logic of borderline symptoms, such as dissociation, as a learned response of the abused child to the horrors of the abuse experience, a response that was once adaptive, but has now become generalized as a response to all emotional flooding. In a similar way, self-injurious behavior seems to make sense as an expression of the self-hatred that the abuse victim directs inwardly. [See CHILD ABUSE; POST-TRAUMATIC STRESS DISORDER.]

There are several obvious problems to the linear causal chain that links childhood abuse to borderline symptomatology. The major problems relate to specificity between abuse and outcome. Patients with many psychiatric diagnoses, as well as many persons who do not have psychiatric symptoms have histories of childhood sexual abuse. Only a percentage of abused persons develop the BPD or PTSD picture. Conversely, not everyone with BPD has a history of childhood abuse. In addition, the abused child was most likely raised in a chaotic home with many other disturbing features, such that it is not valid to single out the experience of sexual abuse as the cause of adult problems. There are also considerable methodological problems related to the very sensitive nature of the topic and the fact that most of the research and clinical work are based upon retrospective reports of abuse in childhood. The methodological problems slice both ways; there are persons who have been abused and who deny it, and there are patients who may distort, exaggerate or invent abuse histories. There is no easy resolution to these issues, but, in general, the detailed reports by patients about their abuse appear to have credibility and are accepted by most researchers and health care workers. The particular diagnostic question discussed here about the overlap of BPD and PTSD, however, is less an issue of data than definition of causal relationships in human behavior. Thus, it appears that childhood sexual abuse and the disturbed environment in which the abuse occurred function as general risk factors predisposing to increased severity of many types of psychiatric and physical illnesses. Within the BPD population, there does appear to be a large subgroup whose symptoms and personality styles were profoundly affected by the experiences of childhood sexual abuse and whose symptoms can be understood as a form of PTSD. It needs to be kept in mind that PTSD is still a fairly vague concept encompassing many types of traumas and responses, and that most persons suffering from PTSD do not show borderline symptoms.

D. BPD as an Impulse Spectrum Disorder

Although it sounds tautological to say that a syndrome characterized by impulsivity may be an impulse spectrum disorder, more is implied in the statement than meets the eye. Essentially, such a hypothesis raises the question of whether there is a group of disorders that share some common features in addition to impulsivity, such as familial linkage, associated psychiatric disorders, and underlying neurophysiological mechanisms. Family studies have shown an increased rate of alcoholism, substance abuse, and antisocial personality in the relatives of borderline personality. Other disorders considered related to problems with impulsivity include compulsive gambling, bulimia, intermittent explosive disorder, and the other Axis II personality disorders within Cluster B (histrionic and narcissistic). Studies are presently under way to investigate serotonergic and dopaminergic mechanisms that may have some linkage to impulsive behaviors.

It is well recognized that the notion of "impulsivity" is very vague, such that the various conditions being considered as impulse disorders may turn out to have very little in common beyond surface appearances. Conceptual clarification concerning what the terms "impulsive" and "compulsive" mean, and how these relate to the notion of "addiction," will be necessary if the hypothesis regarding impulse spectrum disorder is to be of any practical use.

V. COURSE OF BORDERLINE PERSONALITY DISORDER

The initial delineation of borderlines as encompassing a group of difficult treatment cases combined with the finding of a poor outcome on short-term follow-up led to a fairly pessimistic outlook for patients with this diagnosis. Patients who were diagnosed in their late teens or early 20s as borderline were still doing poorly 2 to 5 years later, with ongoing self-injurious behavior and suicide attempts leading to multiple hospitalizations. It was not until the late 1980s that follow-up studies covered the 10- to 20-year period after initial hospitalization. Surprisingly, the outcome was much more favorable than the early studies indicated. In several independent

studies from different parts of the country, it became clear that between 50 and 60% of BPD patients were doing fairly well as they moved into their 30s. Another 30–40% of patients showed varying levels of disability. Suicide rates ranged from 8 to 15% on 10-year follow-up. The largest follow-up series of patients was reported by Stone, who traced 502 of 550 patients (of whom 193 met DSM-III criteria for BPD) who had been hospitalized on an intensive long-term psychotherapy ward at New York State Psychiatric Institute during the years 1963–1976. As judged by Global Outcome Scores (GAS), 63% of the BPD patients were in the good to recovered categories, another 16% had made a fair adjustment, 12% were doing poorly, and 9% suicided. Less favorable outcome was correlated with the presence of major affective disorder, antisocial personality, and a pattern of alcohol and drug abuse. Poor outcome was not correlated with self-mutilative behaviors in the early years of the illness. Patients with a history of childhood neglect or sexual abuse tended to do less well than patients without these histories. Finally, there was not a good overall correlation between outcome and psychiatric treatment; some patients with very good outcomes had minimal treatment following index hospitalization and some patients with extensive treatment had poor outcomes. It is possible that averaging the outcome data washes out a treatment effect, but this remains to be demonstrated.

VI. TREATMENT OF BPD

There has been as much controversy about the treatment of BPD as there has been about the diagnosis. To a large extent and with some overlap, treatment modalities have tended to follow etiological hypotheses. As one might expect with a condition that drew its initial delineation from a group of difficult-to-treat patients, no single modality has yet demonstrated clear-cut superiority or even effectiveness. Studies designed to evaluate treatment of BPD have been plagued by the usual problems of therapy outcome research: differing characteristics of the patient population, despite use of DSM-III criteria; difficulty in determining what constitutes evidence of improvement; difficulty in establishing control groups.

Psychodynamic psychotherapy has been the standard and accepted form of treatment of BPD, despite the many problems that arise in this form of treatment. In a sense, the BPD population, comprising primarily young verbal adults who are dysfunctional but nonpsychotic, have appeared to be the obvious if not ideal candidates for psychotherapy. Close to 50% of psychotherapy patients seen in private practice and at most outpatient clinics will have a diagnosis of BPD or a related Axis II Cluster B (narcissistic or histrionic) disorder. While there has been no canon defining a specific therapeutic protocol for BPD (or any other disorder), the work of Kernberg has been most influential in guiding the theory and practice of psychotherapy with borderlines. The therapy has tended to be a mix of supportive and exploratory work, with special attention paid to avoiding becoming enmeshed in ill-advised rescue attempts and other acting out features that are the hallmarks of borderline patients. The outcome results of the Menninger psychotherapy project reported by Wallerstein and Stone's follow-up study suggest that it is impossible to predict, from patient characteristics alone, which patients would benefit most from supportive and which from exploratory psychotherapy, nor is there evidence that ultimate outcome is better with exploratory than supportive psychotherapy. A single study by Stevenson and Meares employing a 12-month psychotherapy regimen that utilized a written protocol based upon self-psychology demonstrated significant improvements across a broad range of measurements. Patients served as their own controls (pre- and post-treatment measures); a separate control group of patients was not used.

There has been increasing interest in cognitive–behavioral treatment (CBT) modalities for BPD. The essence of these modalities is a focus on recognizing and eliminating the factors that reinforce self-injurious behaviors, and learning and practicing new behaviors that will enhance the quality of life of the patient. Therapy is not directed toward underlying psychodynamic causes, since the assumption of CBT is that self-injurious behavior is a learned behavior that has become relatively independent of the specific causes that originally inspired it. CBT is done individually and in groups. Techniques that are taught and practiced include behavioral skill training, contingency management, cognitive restructuring, exposure to emotional cues, distress tolerance, interpersonal skills, and emotional regulation. Linehan and colleagues reported significant improvement in self-injurious and parasuicidal behaviors in a group of SIB borderlines in CBT compared to a group receiving treatment as usual. The improvements were not accompanied by changes in severity of reported depression, suicidal ideation, or reasons for living. [*See* COGNITIVE BEHAVIOR THERAPY.]

The relationship of BPD to PTSD in those borderlines who experienced sexual abuse in childhood suggests that a PTSD-oriented treatment program should be helpful. To date, this has not been the case, most likely because no overall effective program for the treatment of PTSD has been demonstrated. The treatment of PTSD usually includes group therapy, desensitization techniques, and pharmacological agents. There has been a proliferation of incest and sexual abuse treatment groups, some of which seem to be very helpful and some of which have a deleterious effect on some group members. No controlled studies have been reported. Pharmacological treatment of PTSD is in its infancy; different medications have been reported to be effective with particular components of PTSD, especially the sleep disturbance and depressions that accompany PTSD, but no agents appear to interrupt the flashbacks and intrusive imagery that form the hallmark of this disorder.

The pharmacological treatment of PBD is widely used, but relatively disappointing. Tricyclic antidepressants are effective only in alleviating depressive symptoms in those borderlines who are also depressed. Monoamine oxidase inhibitors have been reported to reduce the target symptom of rejection-sensitive dysphoria, but a controlled study is still wanting. There have not been controlled studies of the efficacy of the specific serotonin reuptake blockers to date. Lithium has not appeared to be of special benefit. There are mixed reports on the benzodiazepine anti-anxiety agents; there may be some benefit to the anti-anxiety properties, but several studies have reported a worsening of impulsive behaviors in BPDs taking these agents. In addition, long-term use of benzodiazepines would not be indicated in patients with significant alcohol or drug abuse histories. The single class of medications that has demonstrated significant short-term effectiveness in several key borderline symptoms has been low-dose anti-psychotics, but here the benefits must be weighed against the serious long-term side effects of these agents. A study of Soloff and associates in 1993 failed to replicate the positive findings of their earlier study reporting improvement in borderline patients with the use of antipsychotic medications.

There has been a recent trend away from long hospitalizations for borderline patients. While much of the driving force toward brief hospitalizations in all medical fields has been concern about rising medical costs, there has also been growing awareness of the deleterious rather than helpful effect of prolonged hospitalization of borderlines. Although there are undoubtedly some patients who benefit from a controlled hospital environment that prevents major self-destructiveness, the general experience has been that borderline patients continue their self-injurious behaviors in the hospital. This behavior sets up major conflicts with staff regarding proper responses to patients who challenge staff to prevent them from hurting themselves. Placing patients on one-to-one or constant observation has seemed to encourage rather than discourage self-injurious acts. The broad, but not unanimous consensus recently is that hospitalizations should be kept as brief as possible within the boundaries of responsible patient care, with the option of brief rehospitalizations seen as preferable to lengthy hospital stays.

Bibliography

Druck, A. (1989). "Four Therapeutic Approaches to the Borderline Patient." Jason Aronson, Northvale, NJ.

Gunderson, J. G. (1984). "Borderline Personality Disorder." American Psychiatric Press, Washington, DC.

Herman, J. L. (1992). "Trauma and Recovery." Basic Books, New York.

Kernberg, O. (1984). "Severe Personality Disorders." Yale University Press, New Haven, CT.

Kroll, J. (1988). "The Challenge of the Borderline Patient." WW Norton, New York.

Kroll, J. (1993). "PTSD/Borderlines in Therapy: Finding the Balance." Norton, New York.

Linehan, M. M., Armstrong, H. E., Suarez, A., Allmon, D., and Heard, H. L. (1991). Cognitive–behavioral treatment of chronically parasuicidal borderline patients. *Arch. Gen. Psychiatry* **48,** 1060–1064.

Links, P. S. (1990). "Family Environment and Borderline Personality Disorder." American Psychiatric Press, Washington, DC.

Paris, J. (1992). "Borderline Personality Disorder: Etiology and Treatment." American Psychiatric Press, Washington, DC.

Soloff, P. H., Cornelius, J., George, A., Nathan, S., Perel, J. M., and Ulrich, R. F. (1993). Efficacy of phenelzine and haloperidol in borderline personality disorder. *Arch. Gen. Psychiatry* **50,** 377–385.

Stevenson, J., and Meares, R. (1992). An outcome study of psychotherapy for patients with borderline personality disorder. *Am. J. Psychiatry* **149,** 358–362.

Stone, M. (1990). "The Fate of Borderline Patients." Guilford, New York.

Wallerstein, R. S. (1986). "Forty-Two Lives in Treatment. Guilford, New York.

BRAIN

Bryan Kolb and Ian Q. Whishaw
University of Lethbridge, Canada

Jan Cioe
Okanagan University-College, Canada

Glossary

Action potential Brief electrical impulse by which information is conducted along an axon. It results from short-lived changes in the membrane's permeability to sodium.

Amnesia Partial or total loss of memory.

Aphasia Defect or loss of power of expression by speech, writing, or signs, or of comprehending spoken or written language caused by injury or disease of the brain.

Cerebral cortex Layer of gray matter on the surface of the cerebral hemispheres composed of neurons and their synaptic connections that form four to six sublayers.

Hippocampus Primitive cortical structure lying in the medial region of the temporal lobe; named after its shape, which is similar to a sea horse, or hippocampus.

Neuron Basic unit of the nervous system; the nerve cell. Its function is to transmit and store information; it includes the cell body (*soma*), many processes called *dendrites,* and an *axon.*

Neurotransmitter Chemical released from a synapse in response to an action potential and acting on postsynaptic receptors to change the resting potential of the receiving cell; chemically transmits information from one neuron to another.

THE BRAIN is that part of the central nervous system that is contained in the skull. It weighs approximately 1450 g at maturity and is composed of brain cells (neurons), as well as support cells, that are organized into hundreds of functionally distinct regions. Neurons communicate both chemically and electrically so that different brain regions form functional systems to control behavior. Measurement of brain structure, activity, and behavior has allowed neuroscientists to reach inferences regarding the mechanisms of the basic functions, which include (1) the body's interactions with the environment through the sensory systems (e.g., vision, audition, touch) and motor systems, (2) internal activities of the body (e.g., breathing, temperature, blood pressure), and (3) mental activities (e.g., thought, language, affect). By studying people with brain injuries it is possible to propose brain circuits that underlie human behavior.

I. ANATOMICAL AND PHYSIOLOGICAL ORGANIZATION OF THE HUMAN BRAIN

A. Cellular Composition

The brain is composed of two general classes of cells: neurons and glial cells. Neurons are the functional units of the nervous system, whereas glial cells are support cells. Estimates of the numbers of cells in the human brain usually run around 10^{10} neurons and 10^{12} glial cells, although the numbers could be even higher. Only about 2–3 million cells (motor neurons) send their connections out of the brain to animate muscle fibers, leaving an enormous number of cells with other functions. [*See* GLIAL CELLS.]

There are numerous types of neurons (e.g., pyramidal, granule, Purkinje, Golgi I, motoneurons), but they share several features in common. First, they have a cell body, which like most cells contains a variety of substances that determine the function of the cell. Second, they have processes called *dendrites,* which function primarily to increase the surface area on which a cell can receive information from other cells. Third, they have a process called an *axon,* which normally originates in the cell body and transmits information to other cells (Fig. 1). Different types of neurons are morphologically distinct, reflecting differences in function. These various types are distributed differentially to the many regions of the brain reflecting regional differences in brain function.

Neurons are connected with one another via their axons; any given neuron may have as many as 15,000 connections with other neurons. These connections are highly organized so that certain regions of the brain are more closely connected to one another than they are to others. As a result, these closely associated regions form functional systems in the brain, which control certain types of behavior.

B. Gross Anatomical Organization of the Brain

The most obvious feature of the human brain is that there are two large hemispheres which sit on a stem

(i.e., the brainstem). Both structures are composed of hundreds of regions; nearly all of them are found bilaterally. Traditionally, the brain is described by the gross divisions observed phylogenetically and embryologically as summarized in Table I. The most primitive region is the hindbrain, whose principal structures include the cerebellum, pons, and medulla. The cerebellum was originally specialized for sensory-motor coordination, which remains its major function. The pons and medulla also contribute to equilibrium, balance, and the control of gross movements (including breathing). The midbrain consists of two main structures, the tectum and the tegmentum. The midbrain consists primarily of two sets of nuclei, the superior and inferior colliculi, which mediate whole body movements to visual and auditory stimuli, respectively. The tegmentum contains various structures including regions associated

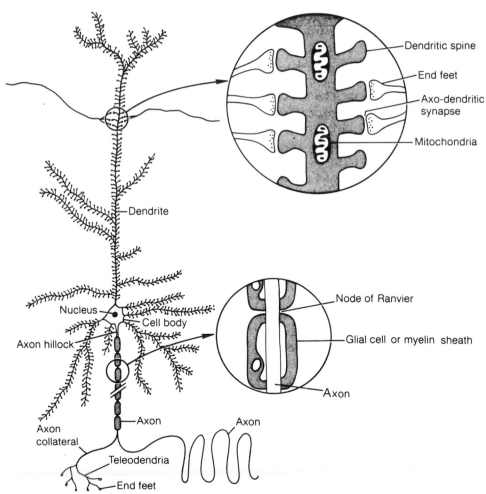

FIGURE 1   Summary of the major parts of a stylized neuron. Enlargement at the top right shows the gross structure of the synapse between axons and the spines on dendrites. Enlargement on the bottom right shows the myelin sheath that surrounds the axon and acts as insulation. [From Kolb, B., and Whishaw, I. Q. (1990). ''Fundamentals of Human Neuropsychology,'' 3rd ed. Freeman, New York.]

TABLE I
Divisions of the Central Nervous System

Primitive divisions	Mammalian divisions	Major structures
Prosencephalon (forebrain)	Telencephalon (endbrain)	Neocortex Basal ganglia Limbic system Olfactory bulb Lateral ventricles
	Diencephalon (between brain)	Thalamus Hypothalamus Epithalamus Third ventricle
Mesencephalon (midbrain)	Mesencephalon (midbrain)	Tectum Tegmentum Cerebral aqueduct
Rhombencephalon (hindbrain)	Metencephalon (across brain)	Cerebellum Pons Fourth ventricle
	Myelencephalon (spinal brain)	Medulla oblongata Fourth ventricle

with (1) the nerves of the head (the so-called cranial nerves), (2) sensory nerves from the body, (3) connections from higher structures that function to control movement, and (4) a number of structures involved in movement (substantia nigra, red nucleus), as well as a region known as the reticular formation. The latter system plays a major role in the control of sleep and waking. [See CEREBELLUM.]

The forebrain is conventionally divided into five anatomical areas: (1) the neocortex, (2) the basal ganglia, (3) the limbic system, (4) the thalamus, and (5) the olfactory bulbs and tract. Each of these regions can be dissociated into numerous smaller regions on the basis of neuronal type, physiological and chemical properties, and connections with other brain regions.

The neocortex (usually called the *cortex*) is composed of approximately six layers—each of which has distinct neuronal populations. It comprises 80% of the human forebrain by volume and is grossly divided into four regions, which are named by the cranial bones lying above them (Fig. 2). It is wrinkled, which is nature's solution to the problem of confining a large surface area into a shell that is still small enough to pass through the birth canal. The cortex has a thickness of only 1.5–3.0 mm but has a total area of about 2500 cm^2. The cortex can be subdivided into dozens of subregions on the basis of the distribution of neuron types, their chemical and physiological characteristics, and their connec-

tions. These subregions can be shown to be functionally distinct. [See NEOCORTEX.]

The basal ganglia are a collection of nuclei lying beneath the cortex. They include the putamen, caudate nucleus, globus pallidus, and amygdala. These nuclei have intimate connections with the neocortex as well as having major connections with midbrain structures. The basal ganglia have principally a motor function, as damage to different regions can produce changes in posture or muscle tone and abnormal movements such as twitches, jerks, and tremors.

The limbic system is not really a unitary system but refers to a number of structures that were once believed to function together to produce emotion. These include the hippocampus, septum, cingulate cortex, and hypothalamus, each of which have different functions (Fig. 3). [See LIMBIC SYSTEM; HYPOTHALAMUS.]

The thalamus provides the major route of information to the neocortex, and different neocortical regions are associated with inputs from distinct thalamic regions connected with the neocortex. The different thalamic areas receive information from sensory and motor regions in the brainstem as well as the limbic system.

C. Physiological Organization of the Brain

Like other cells in the body, the neuron has an electrical voltage (potential) across its membrane, which results from the differential distribution of various ions on the two sides of the membrane. In contrast to other body cells, however, this electrical potential is used to transmit information from one neuron to another in the nervous system, which is accomplished in the following way. Neurons have a resting potential across the membrane of the dendrites, cell body, and axon, which remains relatively constant at about −70 mV. If the membrane permeability for different ions changes, the electrical potential will also change. If it becomes more negative the cell is said to be hyperpolarized, and if it becomes less negative (i.e., more positive) it is said to be depolarized. When the membrane of a neuron is perturbed by the signals coming from other neurons or by certain external agents (e.g., chemicals), the voltage across the membrane changes, becoming either hyperpolarized or depolarized. These changes are normally restricted to the area of membrane stimulated, but if there are numerous signals through many synapses to the same cell, they will summate, altering the membrane potential of a larger region of the cell.

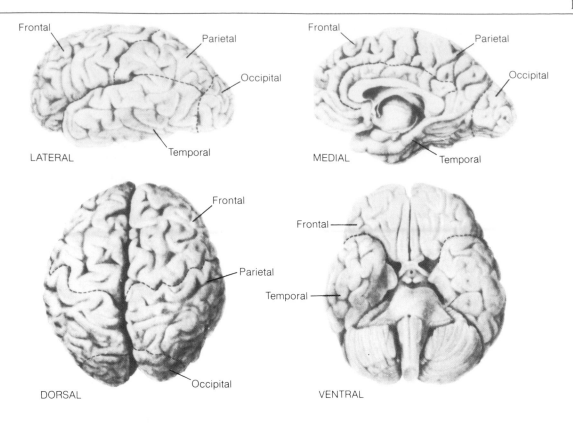

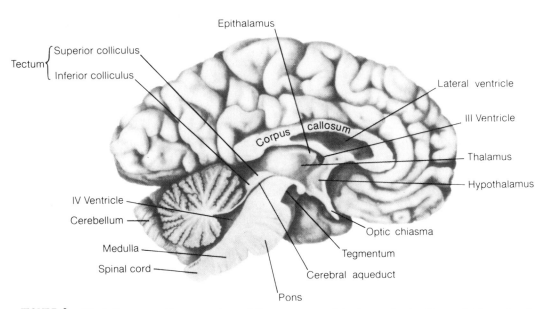

FIGURE 2   (Top) Summary of gross regions of the neocortex of the human brain. (Bottom) View of major structures of the brain. [From Kolb, B., and Whishaw, I. Q. (1990). "Fundamentals of Human Neuropsychology," 3rd ed. Freeman, New York.]

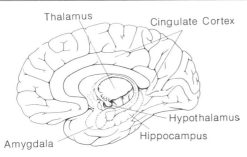

Thalamus Cingulate Cortex

Hypothalamus

Hippocampus

Amygdala

FIGURE 3 Medial view of the right hemisphere illustrating positions of limbic structures. Anterior is to the left.

If the excitation is sufficient to reduce the membrane potential to about −50 mV, the membrane permeability for positive Na^+ ions changes. The influx of ions raises the potential until it becomes positive (e.g., +40 mV). This change in membrane potential spreads across the cell and if it reaches the axon, it travels down the axon, producing a self-propagating signal. This change in permeability is quickly reversed by the cell in about 0.5 msec, allowing the cell to send repeated signals during a short period of time. The signal that travels down the axon is known as an action potential (or nerve impulse), and when it occurs, the cell is said to have fired. The rate at which the impulse travels along the axon varies from 1 to 100 m/sec and can occur as frequently as 1000 times/sec, depending on the diameter of the axon; the most common rate is about 100/sec.

D. Chemical Organization

Once the nerve impulse reaches the end of the axon (the axon terminal), it initiates biochemical changes that result in the release of a chemical known as a neurotransmitter into the synapse. Although the action of transmitters is complex, their effect is either to raise or to lower the membrane potential of the postsynaptic cell, with the effect of making it more or less likely to transmit a nerve impulse.

Dozens of chemicals are known to be neurotransmitters, including a variety of amino acids [e.g., glutamic acid, glycine, aspartate, and gamma-aminobutyric acid (GABA)], monoamines (e.g., dopamine, norepinephrine, serotonin), and peptides [e.g., substance P, β-endorphin, corticotrophin (ACTH)]. Any neuron can receive signals from neurotransmitters through different synapses. The distribution of the various transmitters is not homogeneous in the brain as different regions are dominated by different types. Because drugs that affect the brain act by either mimicking certain transmitters or interfering with the normal function of particular transmitters, different drugs alter different regions of the brain and subsequently have different behavioral effects. [*See* SYNAPTIC TRANSMITTERS AND NEUROMODULATORS.]

II. FUNCTIONAL ORGANIZATION OF THE BRAIN

A. Principles of Brain Organization

The fundamental principle of brain organization is that it is organized hierarchically such that the same behavior is represented at several levels in the nervous system. The function of each level can be inferred from studies in which the outer levels have been removed, as is summarized in Figure 4. The principal idea is that the basic units of behavior are produced by the lowest level, the spinal cord, and at each successive level there is the addition of greater control over these simple behavioral units. At the highest level, the neocortex allows the addition of flexibility to the relatively stereotyped movement sequences generated by lower levels, as well as allowing greater control of behavior by incorporating complex concepts such as space and time. Although new abilities are added at each level in the hierarchy, it remains difficult to localize any process to a particular level because any behavior requires the activity of all regions for its successful execution. Nonetheless, brain injury at different levels will produce different symptoms, depending on what functions are added at that level.

B. Principles of Neocortical Organization

The cortex can be divided into three general types of areas: (1) sensory areas, (2) motor areas, and (3) association areas. The sensory areas are the regions that function to identify and to interpret information coming from the receptor structures in the eyes, ears, nose, mouth, and skin. The motor complex is the region involved in the direct control of movement. The association cortex is the cortex that is not ascribed specific sensory or motor functions.

Distinct regions of the sensory cortex are associated with each of these sensory systems, and each region is made up of numerous subregions which function to process a specific type of sensory information. For example, in the visual system separate regions are devoted to the analysis of form, color,

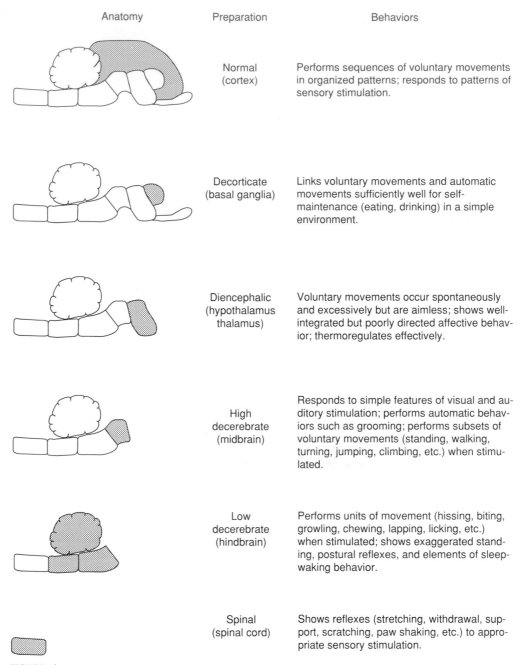

Anatomy	Preparation	Behaviors
	Normal (cortex)	Performs sequences of voluntary movements in organized patterns; responds to patterns of sensory stimulation.
	Decorticate (basal ganglia)	Links voluntary movements and automatic movements sufficiently well for self-maintenance (eating, drinking) in a simple environment.
	Diencephalic (hypothalamus thalamus)	Voluntary movements occur spontaneously and excessively but are aimless; shows well-integrated but poorly directed affective behavior; thermoregulates effectively.
	High decerebrate (midbrain)	Responds to simple features of visual and auditory stimulation; performs automatic behaviors such as grooming; performs subsets of voluntary movements (standing, walking, turning, jumping, climbing, etc.) when stimulated.
	Low decerebrate (hindbrain)	Performs units of movement (hissing, biting, growling, chewing, lapping, licking, etc.) when stimulated; shows exaggerated standing, postural reflexes, and elements of sleep-waking behavior.
	Spinal (spinal cord)	Shows reflexes (stretching, withdrawal, support, scratching, paw shaking, etc.) to appropriate sensory stimulation.

FIGURE 4   Summary of the behavior that can be supported by different levels of the nervous system. Shading indicates highest remaining functional area in each preparation.

size, movement, etc. Damage to each of these regions will produce a distinct loss of sensory experience. In each system there is a region of sensory cortex that produces an apparent inability to detect sensory information such that a person will, for instance, appear to be blind, unable to taste, or have numbness of the skin, etc. In each case, however, it can be shown that other aspects of sensory function are intact. Thus, a person who is unable to "see" an object may be able to indicate its color and position! Similarly, patients may be able to locate a place on the body where they were touched while being unable to "feel" the touch. Regions of sensory cortex producing such symptoms are referred to as primary sensory cortex. The other regions are known as unimodal association regions, and damage to them is associated with various other symptoms. Thus, in every sensory system there are regions of cortex that, when damaged, result in an inability to understand the significance of sensory events. Such symptoms are known as agnosias. For example, although able to perceive an object (e.g., toothbrush) and to pick it up, a person may be unable to name it or to identify its use. Similarly, a person may be able to perceive a sound (e.g., that of an insect) but be unable to indicate what the sound is from. Some agnosias are relatively specific (e.g., an inability to recognize faces or colors).

The motor cortex represents a relatively small region of the cortex that controls all voluntary movements and is specialized to produce fine movements such as independent finger movements and complex tongue movements. Damage to this region prevents certain movements (e.g., of the fingers), although others (e.g., arm and body movements) may be relatively normal. Although the motor cortex is a relatively small region of the cortex, a much larger region contributes to motor functions, including some of the sensory regions as well as the association cortex. For example, a person may be unable to organize behaviors such as those required for dressing or for using objects as a result of damage to this larger region. Such disorders are known as apraxias, which refers to the inability to make voluntary movements in the absence of any damage to the motor cortex.

The regions of the neocortex not specialized as sensory or motor regions are referred to as association cortex. This cortex receives information from one or more of the sensory systems and functions to organize complex behaviors such as the three-dimensional control of movement, the comprehension of written language, and the making of plans of action. The principal regions of association cortex include the prefrontal cortex in the frontal lobe, the posterior parietal cortex, and regions of the temporal cortex. Although not neocortex, it is convenient to consider the medial temporal structures, including the hippocampus, amygdala, and associated cortical regions, as a type of association cortex. Taken together, damage to the association regions causes a puzzling array of behavioral symptoms that include changes in affect and personality, memory, and language.

III. CEREBRAL ASYMMETRY

One of the most distinctive features of the human brain is that the two cerebral hemispheres are both anatomically and functionally different, a property referred to as cerebral asymmetry.

A. Functional Asymmetry

The clearest functional difference between the two sides of the brain is that structures of the left hemisphere are involved in language functions and those of the right hemisphere are involved in nonlanguage functions such as the control of spatial abilities. This asymmetry can be demonstrated in each of the sensory systems, with differences in left-handed and right-handed persons. We will first consider the common case of the right-handed individual. In the visual system the left hemisphere is specialized to recognize printed words or numbers, whereas the right hemisphere is specialized to process complex nonverbal material such as is seen in geometric figures, faces, route maps, etc. Similarly, in the auditory system the left hemisphere analyzes words, whereas the right hemisphere analyzes tone of voice (prosody) and certain aspects of music. Asymmetrical functions go beyond sensation, however, to include movement, memory, and affect. In the control of movement, the left hemisphere is specialized for the production of certain types of complex movement sequences, as in meaningful gestures (e.g., salute, wave) or writing. The right hemisphere has a complementary role in the production of other movements such as in drawing, dressing, or constructing objects. Similarly, the left hemisphere has a favored role in memory functions related to language (e.g., written and spoken words), whereas the right hemisphere plays a major role in the memory of places and nonverbal information such as music and faces. With respect to affect, the right hemisphere is superior to the left for recognizing emotional aspects of stimuli and seems to play an important role in the comprehension of humor.

B. Anatomical Asymmetry

The functional asymmetry of the human brain is correlated with various asymmetries in gross brain morphology, cell structure, neurochemical distribution, and blood flow. Differences in gross morphology and cell structure are most easily seen in the regions specialized for language, including the anterior (Broca's) and posterior speech areas (Fig. 5). For example, one region in the posterior speech area, the planum temporale, is twice as large on the left hemisphere in most brains, whereas a re-

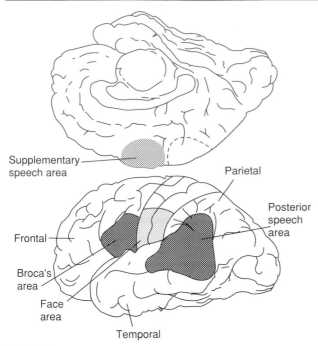

FIGURE 5 Schematic diagram showing the anterior speech area (Broca's area) in the frontal lobe, the posterior speech area (including Wernicke's area) in posterior temporal and parietal regions. Shaded region between speech areas is the motor and sensory cortex controlling the face and tongue. [From Kolb, B., and Whishaw, I. Q. (1990). "Fundamentals of Human Neuropsychology," 3rd ed. Freeman, New York.]

gion involved in the processing of musical notes, Heschl's gyrus, is larger in the right temporal lobe than in the left.

C. Variations in Cerebral Asymmetry: Handedness and Sex

There is considerable variation in the details of both functional and anatomical asymmetry in different people. Two factors, handedness and sex, appear to account for much of this variation. First, left-handers have a different pattern of anatomical organization than do right-handers. For example, left-handers appear to have a larger bundle of fibers connecting the two cerebral hemispheres, the corpus callosum, which implies that the nature of hemispheric interaction differs in left- and right-handers. Similarly, left-handers are less likely to show the large asymmetries in the structure of the language-related areas than are right-handers. Functionally, the organization of the left-handed brain shows considerable variation: Language is located primarily in the left hemisphere in about two-thirds of left-handers, in the right hemisphere in about one-sixth,

and in both hemispheres in about one-sixth. Left-handers with different speech organization than right-handers do not simply have reversal of brain organization, however, although the nature of their cerebral organization is still poorly understood. Second, males and females also differ in functional and structural organization. For example, the corpus callosum of females is larger relative to brain size than that of males, and females are less likely to show gross asymmetries or to have reversed asymmetries. Animal studies have shown a clear relation between anatomical organization and the presence of the perinatal gonadal hormones present at about the time of birth, suggesting that these hormones differentially organize the brain of males and females. Functionally, the effect of brain damage in males and females differs as well, although in complex ways that are poorly understood. It does appear, however, that frontal lobe injuries in both human and nonhuman subjects have differential effects in the two sexes, with larger behavioral effects of frontal lobe injury observed in females. Other factors are also believed to influence the nature of cerebral asymmetry, especially experience, interacting with both sex and handedness. [*See* HANDEDNESS.]

IV. ORGANIZATION OF HIGHER FUNCTIONS

Complex functions such as memory or emotion are not easily localized in the brain, as the circuits involved include vast areas of both the cerebral hemispheres and other forebrain structures. Part of the difficulty in localizing such functions is that they are not unitary things but are inferred from behavior, which in turn results from numerous processes. Nonetheless, it is possible to reach some generalizations regarding such functions.

A. Memory

Memory is an inferred process that results in a relatively permanent change in behavior, which presumably results from a change in the brain. Psychologists distinguish many types of memory, each of which may have a distinct neural basis. These include, among others, (1) long-term memory, which is the recall of information over hours, days, weeks, years, etc.; (2) short-term memory, which is the recall of information over seconds or minutes; (3) declarative memory, which is the recall of facts that are accessible to conscious recollection; (4) procedural memory, which is the ability to perform skills that are "automatic" and that are not stored with respect to specific times or places (e.g., the movements required to drive); (5) verbal memory, which is memory of language-related material; and (6) spatial memory, which is the recall of places or locations. [*See* MEMORY.]

The neural basis of human memory can be considered at two levels: cellular and neural location. Thus, changes in cell activity and structure are associated with processes like memory, which may occur extremely rapidly in the brain, possibly in the order of seconds or at least minutes. Further, there is a variety of candidate regions for memory processes, the region varying with the nature of memory process. One structure that plays a major role in various forms of memory is the hippocampus. Bilateral damage to this structure leads to a condition of anterograde amnesia, which refers to the inability to recall, after a few minutes, any new material that is experienced after the damage. There is only a brief period of retrograde amnesia, which refers to the inability to recall material before the injury. The relatively selective effects of hippocampal injuries in producing anterograde but not retrograde amnesia suggests that different brain regions are involved in the initial learning of information and their later retrieval from memory. As a generalization, it appears that the temporal lobe is involved in various types of long-term memory processes, whereas the frontal and parietal lobes play a role in certain short-term memory processes. Damage to these regions thus produces different forms of memory loss, which are further complicated by whether the injury is to the left or right hemisphere. [*See* AMNESIA; HIPPOCAMPAL FORMATION; MEMORY, NEURAL SUBSTRATES.]

B. Language

Damage to either of the major speech areas (Broca's or the posterior speech zone, which is sometimes referred to as Wernicke's area) will produce a variety of dissociable syndromes, including aphasia (an inability to comprehend language), alexia (an inability to read), and agraphia (an inability to write). There are various forms of each of these syndromes that relate to the precise details of the brain injury. A number of other forms of language disturbance result from damage outside the speech areas, including changes in speech fluency [i.e., the ability to generate words according to certain criteria (e.g., write down words starting with "D"; give the name of objects)], spontaneous talking in conversation,

the ability to categorize words (e.g., apple and banana are fruits), and so on. It appears that nearly any left hemisphere injury will affect some aspect of these language functions, as does damage to some regions of the right hemisphere. [*See* APHASIA.]

C. Emotional Processes

Like memory processes, emotional processes are inferred from behavior and include many different functions including autonomic nervous system activity, "feeling," facial expression, and tone of voice. Certain subcortical regions (hypothalamus, amygdala) play a major role in the generation of affective behaviors, especially the autonomic components such as blood pressure, respiration, and heart rate. In addition, damage nearly anywhere in the cortex will alter some aspect of cognitive function, which in turn will alter personality and emotional behavior, but damage to the right hemisphere produces a greater effect on emotional behavior than similar damage to the left. Moreover, the frontal lobe plays a special role as well, possibly because it has direct control of autonomic function as well as of spontaneous facial expression and other nonverbal aspects of personality. Thus, damage to the right hemisphere, or the frontal lobe of either hemisphere, is likely to lead to complaints from relatives regarding a change in "personality" or "affect." The control of emotional behavior may not only be relatively localized to different regions of the brain, but also related to specific neurotransmitter systems in the brain. For example, one dominant theory of the cause of schizophrenia proposes that there is an overactivity of the dopaminergic neurons (i.e., neurons that use dopamine as neurotransmitter) in the forebrain, likely in the frontal cortex (hence, the dopamine hypothesis of schizophrenia). Similarly, the dominant theory of depression is that it is related to low activity in systems that employ norepinephrine or serotonin as neurotransmitters. Because there are asymmetries in the cerebral distribution of these transmitters, it is reasonable to expect that depression may be more related to the right than left hemisphere, which is consistent with the dominant role of the right hemisphere in emotion. [*See* DEPRESSION; SCHIZOPHRENIA.]

D. Space

The concept of space has many different interpretations, which are not equivalent. Objects (and bodies) occupy space, move through space, and interact with other things in space; we can form mental representations of space, and we have memories for the location of things. It is difficult, therefore, to define space or to know how the brain codes spatial information. Damage to different parts of the cerebral hemispheres can produce a wide variety of spatial disturbances including the inability to appreciate the location of one's body, or even the location of one's body parts relative to one another. It is generally accepted that the right hemisphere plays the major role in spatial behavior, but there can also be spatial disruptions from left hemisphere damage, especially if the behavior involves verbalizing space. The major region in the control of spatial behavior is the parietal cortex, although the hippocampus is also involved. [*See* SPATIAL ORIENTATION; SPATIAL PERCEPTION.]

E. Conclusions

One of the key features of the brain is the localization of function. We have seen that certain brain structures are critical for a number of the higher human functions and that damage in specific locations on one particular side of the brain can result in the loss of behaviors which are not seen when the other side is injured. This localization of function results from the unique inputs and outputs of the subregions of the brain. Nevertheless, the hierarchical organization of the brain guarantees that control of a specific behavior is seldom restricted to a single area. There are multiple representations of the different cognitive functions in the different levels of neural organization but they are not simply backup circuits. Each level adds its own unique contribution which ultimately produces a degree of complexity that makes it possible for humans to behave flexibly in a changing environment.

Bibliography

Kolb, B., and Whishaw, I. Q. (1990). ''Fundamentals of Human Neuropsychology,'' 3rd ed. Freeman, New York.
Nauta, W. J. H., and Feirtage, M. (1986). ''Fundamental Neuroanatomy.'' Freeman, New York.

BRAIN CHEMICALS

Efrain C. Azmitia
New York University

Glossary

Astrocyte A star-shaped neuroglial cell that is important for ionic and energy metabolism in the brain. Cells contain and release a number of neuronotrophic factors. Contains Ca^{2+} and K^+ but no Na^+ channels. These cells can divide and increase in number as the brain ages.

Monoaminergic neurons Neurons that produce neuroactive substances by hydroxylation and then decarboxylation of either tryptophan or tyrosine. These compounds are degraded by the action of the enzyme monoamine oxidase. The cell bodies found in the brainstem regions and processes extend throughout the brain. Examples include serotonin (5-hydroxytryptamine), dopamine, and norepinephrine.

Neuron A specialized neuroepithelial cell that has Na^+, Ca^{2+}, and K^+ channels and does not divide after differentiation. These functional units maintain a voltage potential that permits conduction of electrical signals and cytoskeleton, which enables transport of proteins to and from the cell body.

Neuronotrophic factors Protein molecules that can increase the survival, growth, or maturation of a neuron usually by activation of or by internalization through a specific membrane receptor. Neuronotrophic factors are often made and released by astrocytes. Examples include proteins such as S-100β, nerve growth factor, and BDNF.

Neuropeptides Small molecules consisting of two or more amino acids that are made, stored, and released by certain neurons. Their postsynaptic action is usually very long lasting due to tight association with the postsynaptic receptor. Examples include corticotrophin, enkephalin and substance-P.

Neurotransmitter A chemical substance that is made and stored in a pre-synaptic process and can be released by depolarization to effect the ionic balance or metabolic activity of a postsynaptic cell usually by acting at a specific membrane receptor.

Release A process by which neurotransmitters are delivered from the inside of the neuron to the extracellular space. Release can occur by a Ca^{2+}-dependent mechanism from membrane-bound organelles called vesicles or directly from the cytoplasm, using the reuptake transporter molecule acting in reverse.

Reuptake A process by which chemical substances are taken up from the extracellular space through a specific transporter protein that functions by exchange diffusion and is driven by the Na^+ gradient. A common mechanism to remove neurotransmitters from the synaptic cleft to terminate their postsynaptic action.

Transtrophins Chemical substances that are released by the neuron as neurotransmitters and which act on astrocytes to release a neuronotrophic factor. These substances may also act directly on immature neurons to effect their survival, growth, or maturation.

HUMAN BEHAVIOR is the outward manifestation of neuronal cell activity in the brain. Neurons are organized into discrete nuclei and develop pathways connecting with other clusters of neuronal cells. These connections comprise the organization of the brain and enable chemicals to be secreted in precise target areas (most molecules cannot travel through the circulatory system into neural tissue because of the blood–brain barrier). Although messages traveling along neuron pathways are electrical, chemicals are necessary for the final leap between neurons. These chemicals (e.g., serotonin, acetylcholine, GABA, dopamine, and norepinephrine) interact with specific receptors on the postsynaptic neuron. After interaction with the receptor, the electrical message is quickly terminated either by breakdown of the chemical (e.g., acetylcholine esterase or monoamine oxidase) or by reuptake of the chemical into the presynaptic neuron. Signal transduction occurs after the activation of the receptor as a result of changes in the levels of cyclic-AMP and inositol phosphates or the modulation of specific ionic channels. These will produce a response in the postsynaptic cell that is then transmitted to yet another cell until either hormonal secretion or muscle movement occurs.

Brain chemicals serving an organizing and directing role during early development are termed neurotrophic factors. Most of these neurotrophic factors actually appear to behave as neurotransmitters since they are synthesized, stored, and released, and produce postsynaptic actions through specific receptors. Therefore, the distinction between neurotransmitters and neurotrophic factors may be semantic. A novel concept is to consider the chemical forces operating in the design and maintenance of the brain as "transtrophins."

I. INTRODUCTION

This article on brain chemicals discusses neurotransmitters and neurotrophic factors. Specifically, the author argues that certain molecules found in the brain both provide the means for transmitting information signals that direct behavioral responses and serve as trophic factors that design and shape brain circuits.

Behavior is the outward expression of brain activity that comprises the coherent firing of organized neurons. The cellular study of brain activity has been dominated by principles established in the late 19th century in neuroanatomy and neurophysiology. These principles assume that brain neural networks are fixed, immutable, and represented by connections between an afferent neuron and its target. Neurophysiology, making use of the easily accessible neuromuscular preparation, laid the framework for interpreting the actions of chemicals in the brain.

These chemicals, termed "neurotransmitters," cross the gap between the presynaptic terminal and the postsynaptic cell containing the receptor. Activation of the receptor enable the action potential to move the electrical charge down the postsynaptic neurons and complete the connection as predicted by the neuroanatomical circuit. At each major step, from the synthesis of neurotransmitters to signal transduction in the postsynaptic cells, multiple regulatory mechanisms are superimposed to ensure that chemicals are produced and released in sufficient quantities at those sites where they are needed to influence the target neuron to alter its membrane potential. [See SYNAPTIC TRANSMITTERS AND NEUROMODULATORS.]

Neurotransmitter chemicals travel along pathways which connect one group of cell bodies with a target region which can be distant. The axons of neurons supply a unique chemical to cells that they may not otherwise be capable of producing. Therefore, neurotransmitters can be viewed as reagents in a chemical reaction, the product of which is neuronal activity (change in membrane potential) and, ultimately, a behavioral response.

Other intervening products of these chemical reactions do not conform to our concepts of a neurotransmitter. The cellular and molecular responses can involve long-lasting shifts in cell metabolic rate, reorganizing the cytoplasmic scaffolding (cell skeleton), fluctuations of receptor availability, and modification of neuronal morphology. These long-term changes produced by neurotransmitters often occur during early development, before the brain pathways are firmly established. Furthermore, many neurotransmitter receptors are in place prior to neuronal innervation; and in many systems the highest levels of neurotransmitter receptors are seen during the prenatal stage. A further complication in designating the chemicals in the brain is that the target cells of neurotransmitters are often nonneuronal. For example, astrocytes, microglial or radial glial cells, endothelial or ependymal cells, and endocrine or muscle cells all possess neurotransmitter receptors. Yet none of these cells are neurons.

The concept of a chemical crossing a synapse does not fit into neuronal–glial interactions that do not comprise the neuron–neuron interactions that originally served to illustrate the functions of "neurotransmitters." The reaction of the target to the neurotransmitter is not too dissimilar from the consequences of exposure to neurotrophic factors.

II. NEUROTRANSMITTER FUNCTION

The most extensively studied aspect of neurotransmitters is their ability to influence the membrane potential of a target neuron. Most known neurotransmitters can be classified into three temporal-based categories: *fast, intermediate,* and *slow.* Fast neurotransmitters include acetylcholine (Ach), γ-aminobutyric acid (GABA), excitatory amino acid neurotransmitters (e.g., glutamate, aspartate, and glycine), and purines. The newly discovered gaseous transmitters (nitrous oxide and carbon monoxide) would be also included in this category. Intermediate neurotransmitters include the monoamines (serotonin and catecholamine) and histamine. Finally, slow neurotransmitters include neuropeptides and neurosteroids.

A. The Fast Classification

Ach, GABA, and amino acid transmitters (e.g., glutamate and aspartate) can be considered to be fast neurotransmitters (Table I). Ach is an excitatory neurotransmitter that acts at the neuromuscular junction. The motoneurons which secrete acetylcholine are densely myelinated to help promote a fast signal down the axon to the terminal. Ach is released from synaptic vesicles into a specialized neuromuscular junction. The synapse area of the postsynaptic side is indented to increase the surface area exposed to the released neurotransmitter. Ach interacts with a specific nicotinic receptor that has a fairly low affinity for the neurotransmitter which allows very rapid disassociation after binding, minimizing the time of receptor occupation. The nicotinic receptor is an anion channel which permits Na^+ and K^+ movement that produces a rapid depolarization in the muscle fiber. The enzyme cholinesterase, located in the synaptic space, rapidly metabolizes Ach to choline. Choline is taken up by a specific uptake system to quickly replenish the presynaptic neuron's content of Ach. The enzyme choline acetyltransferase produces up to 200 nmol/g/min of Ach. Thus, every step of the operation in controlling the movement of a muscle is adapted to ensure that a signal can be transmitted and terminated at an extremely rapid rate.

An example of an inhibitory fast neurotransmitter is GABA, the most common neurotransmitter in the brain. GABA-ergic fibers are usually myelinated. GABA is the principal neurotransmitter in the cerebellar circuitry that is concerned with the coordination of fine motor movement. GABA synthesis occurs via a single step from the abundant chemical glutamic acid by glutamic acid decarboxylase and can produce approximately 20 nmol/g/min. The binding to the receptor is fairly low affinity which permits rapid disassociation. GABA produces a di-

rect inhibitory response by opening a Cl^- channel which is an integral part of the receptor. GABA action is terminated by a reuptake process into either neurons or glial cells, and is broken down by the enzyme GABA transaminase.

B. The Intermediate Classification

Monoaminergic neurotransmitters may be considered intermediate on the temporal scale (Table I). These neurons have a normal firing tonic rates in the range of 0.5–4/sec, although they can increase to as rapid as 20/sec or remain silent for hours at a time. They have a number of monoaminergic receptors subtypes associated with them having a fairly wide range of affinities (10^{-9} to $10^{-5} M$). In addition, they can be either myelinated or unmyelinated depending on the species (e.g., rat versus human).

Dopamine, an excitatory neurotransmitter, is synthesized from tyrosine first by a hydroxylation and then a decarboxylation step. The synthesis of other catecholamines requires additional enzymes. These enzymatic reactions utilize molecular oxygen, reduced-biopterin, pyridoxal phosphate, and iron. They proceed at a fairly slow rate of 0.2 nmol/g/hr. The release of the monoamines can occur from at least two distinct pools: (i) synaptic vesicles after membrane depolarization and Ca^{2+} influx or (ii) the cytoplasm by a Ca^{2+} independent mechanism. The dopaminergic fibers travel from the substantia nigra to striatum as well as frontal cortex. Dopamine interacts with its main receptors with a high affinity that produces a modest disassociation rate and may contribute to the fairly long postsynaptic actions that have been reported (up to 400 msec). The dopamine receptor activation is linked via a well-established second-messenger system to activation of adenylate cyclase which then secondarily is transduced to changes in ion channels by activation of phosphorylation mechanisms. Other linkages to additional second messenger systems are probable but less well established. The action of dopamine at the synapse is terminated principally by a reuptake mechanism back into the dopaminergic terminal. Dopamine is then inactivated principally by the A-form of monamine oxidase (MAO-A), which has a high affinity for dopamine.

Serotonin (5-HT) has mainly inhibitory responses on its forebrain target neurons. The serotonergic neurons have a slow firing rate and are not as excitable as the catecholaminergic neurons. The synthetic rate of 5-HT is nearly identical to that of dopamine; in fact the enzymes tryptophan hydroxylase

TABLE I

Temporal Scale of Transmitters

Class	Substance	Location	Response	Turnover	Receptor	Deactivation
Fast (millisecond)	Acetylcholine	Neuromuscular	Excitatory Fast-firing rate—100/sec	Choline + Acetyl CoA = Ach (200 nmol/g/min)	Nicotinic 10^{-6}–10^{-8} M	Cholinesterase reuptake
Myelinated fibers	GABA	Cerebellum	Inhibitory Fast-firing rate	Glutamic acid = GABA + CO_2 (20 nmol/g/min)	5×10^{-5} M	Transaminase reuptake
Intermediate (100 msec)	DA	Caudate	Excitatory 1/sec	Tyrosine $\rightarrow$ DOPA (0.2 nmol/g/min) $\rightarrow$ Dopamine	10^{-9} M	MAO-A reuptake
Unmyelinated fibers	5-HT	Hippocampus	Inhibitory 1/sec	Tryptophan $\rightarrow$ 5-HTP $\rightarrow$ 5-HT (0.02 nmol/g/min)	10^{-9} M	MAO-B reuptake
Slow (minutes)	Substance P	Dorsal root ganglion	Excitatory Large Pulse	Prohormone $\rightarrow$ Substance P Endopeptidase	10^{-12}–10^{-15} M	*Proteolytic enzymes* Endo & exopeptidase diffusion
Unmyelinated fibers	Enkephalin	Spinal cord	Inhibitory	Prohormone $\rightarrow$ Enkephalin Endopeptidase	M receptor 10^{-12}–10^{-15} M	*Proteolytic enzymes* Endo & exopeptidases diffusion

and tyrosine hydroxylase are structurally similar and believed to have evolved from a common ancestral protein. The synthesis of serotonin proceeds from tryptophan, which is the least common of all amino acids. Tryptophan hydroxylase has a slower rate than tyrosine hydroxylase. The release of 5-HT occurs by both vesicular and nonvesicular mechanisms which are Ca^{2+} dependent and Ca^{2+} independent as mentioned above. The interaction with its receptors and its principal metabolic routes are similar to dopamine. However, serotonergic neurons contain the B-form of monoamine oxidase, which has a much lower affinity for 5-HT than the A-form. Thus, the 5-HT sequestered by serotonergic neurons by reuptake will be relatively protected from the degradative actions of MAO-B until the cytoplasmic levels of 5-HT are high. The inhibitory actions of 5-HT on the high-affinity receptors (5-HT-1 family) are generally mediated by an inhibition of cyclic-AMP formation. Thus, as described above, the association with the receptor is tight and the signal transduction mechanism on ionic fluxes is indirect.

This is a good place to emphasize that individual neurotransmitter system can span more than one temporal scale. For example, one of the 5-HT receptors (5-HT$_3$) is linked to an ion channel. The affinity of 5-HT for this receptor is about $100\times$ higher than occurs at the receptor of the 5-HT-1 family. Furthermore, 5-HT fibers that are largely unmyelinated in the rodent brain can become myelinated in the primate brain. Finally, certain 5-HT neurons can display much faster rates of firing than normally seen in the majority of cells in the rodent raphe nuclei. Therefore, 5-HT can also be considered as a member of both the fast and slow neurotransmitter classification of neurotransmitters depending on the species and the receptor properties.

C. The Slow Classification

Neuropeptides are examples of chemicals that almost always function in the slow neurotransmitter category (Table I). Peptides can be any length from 2 to 100 amino acids long. Most of the work in this area has shown that the peptides are synthesized in the cell body area as much longer prohormones. These prohormones are believed to be stored and transported to the terminal areas in dense core vesicles. The prohormones are broken down into the appropriate peptide by specific endopeptidase enzymes. Thus, the synthesis of neuroactive peptides is complex and very slow when compared to transmitter substances in the fast and intermediate neuro-

transmitter categories. In addition, the release of the peptides from dense core vesicles is believed to involve a sustained depolarization and is Ca^{2+} dependent.

The nerve fibers that contain a neuropeptide normally also contain either a fast or intermediate neurotransmitter. This commonly observed colocalization is believed to enable the peptide action to modify, usually by amplification, the response of the other nonpeptide neurotransmitter.

There are examples of neuropeptides that are either excitatory (substance-P in the dorsal root ganglia) or inhibitory (enkephalin in the spinal cord). These peptides have very high affinities with their postsynaptic receptors, usually on the order of 10^{-12} to 10^{-15} M. The peptide would therefore bind very tightly to the receptor and produce a long-lasting action. The clearance of the peptide from the synapse is also believed to be slow and occurs principally by diffusion out of the cleft and eventual degradation by proteolytic enzymes. Thus, the peptides are not suited for transmission of rapid information but convey signals about state that are long term in duration. Neurosteroids may be another family in this group of slow neurotransmitter substances.

III. NEUROTROPHIC FUNCTION

Neurotrophic molecules can increase the survival, growth, and/or maturation of neurons. These substances are almost always produced by nonneuronal cells such as astrocytes, radial glial cells, and epithelial cells. Neurotrophic compounds are small soluble protein molecules such as nerve growth factor (NGF), epidermal growth factor (EGF), platelet-derived growth factor (PDGF), brain-derived growth factor (BDGF), insulin, and S-100β. The notion that nonneuronal cells affect neuronal cells is a major direction of neuroscience research and would encompass the cytokines (tumor necrosis factor, interleukins, and interferons) made and released by macrophages, microglia, and fibroblasts. The main action of the cytokines is to stimulate proliferation of nonneuronal cells. However, there is evidence that both growth factors and cytokines can have acute actions on the membrane potential of the target neurons and change cell firing rate. In general, neurotrophic molecules have a molecular weight of 10 to 20 kDa and have complex synthetic pathways and tertiary structures. These cells are most active during early development or after injury. There is extensive post-translational modifications such as glycosylation, phosphorylation, and ion binding that are required for the proteins to achieve their active forms. The trophic proteins are not released as discrete packages. There is considerable evidence that Ca^{2+} is usually required to effect release. Interestingly, the neurotrophic actions of NGF on certain neurons and neuroblastoma cell lines can be replaced if the cells are grown in a high concentration of K^+, which depolarizes them. The association of neurotrophic molecules with their target cells occurs through very high-affinity receptor binding. Receptor occupancy by neurotrophic molecules produces changes in cyclic-AMP and Ca^{2+} fluxes. These changes are frequently long lasting. In conclusion, one could argue that neurotrophic molecules fit into the neurotransmitter category with a very slow temporal response time.

IV. TRANSTROPHINS

If the classical growth factors and cytokines are classified as *very slow neurotransmitters* because of their effects on signal transduction mechanisms, then neurotransmitters may in turn be classified as neurotrophic factors. There is good evidence that neuropeptides function as growth factors. Thyrotropin-releasing hormone and substance-P, colocalized with serotonin, sometimes have trophic effects on serotonergic fibers. Adrenalcorticotrophic factor (ACTH) and corticotrophin factor are peptides that have neurotransmitter properties, but also function as positive trophic factors. Likewise, enkephalin has a negative trophic action on a variety of neuronal systems in the brain. The effective doses for neurotransmitter and neurotrophic effects are similar, although it appears the trophic properties are most easily demonstrated in the developing or damaged brain, while neurotransmitter action predominates in the more "stable" environment of the adult brain.

There is evidence that intermediate and slow neurotransmitters also have trophic functions. The serotonergic systems illustrate how monoaminergic neurons can function as neurotrophic molecules, and there is also evidence that dopamine, GABA, Ach, and glutamate can alter the morphology of their target structures. Serotonin is an ancient chemical related to the plant growth hormone, auxin. During early development, 5-HT has been detected in embryo before the neural tube has formed. In the brain, 5-HT-producing cells are among the very first neu-

rons to complete neurogenesis. The serotonergic system is the first brainstem system to innervate both the forebrain and spinal cord.

These large multipolar neurons have their cell bodies largely confined to the midline (raphe) area of the brainstem, a part of the reticular formation which is phylogenetically the oldest part of the brain. It contains a number of systems involved in centrally regulating basic functions such as heart rate and respiration. All serotonin found in the brain comes from a relatively small number of neurons. In the adult human raphe there are less than 300,000 neurons. However, these neurons send out fibers that innervate the entire forebrain using multiple pathways. Indeed, virtually every cortical neuron is in close proximity to a 5-HT fiber. The forebrain target cells contain 5-HT high-affinity receptors for 5-HT which are present at their highest levels before the arrival of the 5-HT producing fibers. Reduction of the serotonin innervation of the neonatal cortex causes a delayed maturation of cortical neurons. This delayed maturation would occur by decreased activation of receptors either on the cortical neurons themselves (direct) or on astrocytes which make and release growth factors (indirect).

Astrocytes produce and release the cortical growth factor S-100β when stimulated with a 5-HT$_{1A}$ antagonist. S-100β is also a potent growth factor for spinal cord motoneurons, dorsal root ganglion neurons, and serotonergic fibers themselves. A feedback mechanism exists, since the 5-HT activation of astrocytes also produces changes in glial morphology and a decrease in the 5-HT$_{1A}$ receptor density. The S-100β molecule has a variety of actions on neurons, which include neurite extension of axons, maturation of dendrites, and enhanced survival of neurons depending on the assay conditions. Astrocytes also have specific receptors for S-100β and cytokines, which result in increased proliferation of these cells (Fig. 1).

Thus, 5-HT acts as a "transtrophin" by acting on a glial receptor to release S-100β; which in turn will effect the appropriate target cells. Interestingly, norepinephrine interacts with the β-adrenergic receptor to produce the release of NGF from the appropriate astrocytes. Thus, astrocytes can be induced to release a number of their neurotrophic molecules upon activation of specific membrane-bound neurotransmitter receptors. Furthermore, neurotransmitter receptors on neurons can also produce direct trophic actions by altering the membrane potential, in a manner analogous to the effect achieved by exposing neurons to high K^+ levels. Thus, brain chemicals

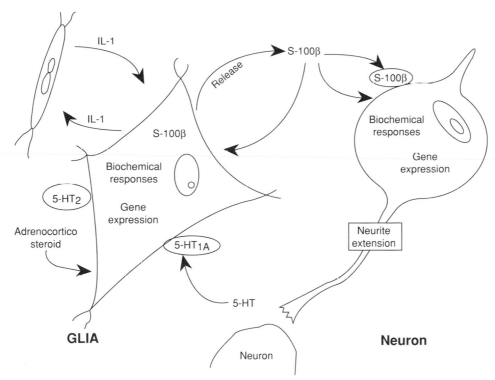

FIGURE 1   A schematic diagram of the possible astrocytic and neuronal interactions as related to
S100β and serotonin. S100β is produced in astrocytes and can be released via serotonin stimulation
of the astrocyte 5-HT$_{1A}$ receptor. Extracellular S100β has actions on both neurons and astrocytes.
The interactions may be modified by cytokines (IL-1) secretion from microglial cells or by circulating
adrenosteroids. [From Azmitia *et al.* (1992). *Progress in Brain Research* **94**, 459–473.]

which have been traditionally viewed as acting as
neurotransmitters for relaying information can also
be considered as neurotrophic factors that change
morphology. We propose that both functions, transmission and morphology change, are normally integrated. This dual role can be termed "transtrophins." The brain may use "transtrophins" to
cultivate an afferent–target cell connection and then
utilize this circuitry for behavioral expression.

Bibliography

Azmitia, E. C. (1991). Awakening the sleeping giant: Review of
the anatomy and plasticity of 5-HT in the brain. *J. Clin.
Psych.* **52** (*Suppl.* 12), 4–16.

Azmitia, E. C., Whitaker-Azmitia, P. M., and Bartus, R. (1988).
Use of tissue culture model to study neuronal regulatory trophic and toxic factors in the aged brain. *Neurobiol. Aging* **9**,
743–758.

Cooper, J. R., Bloom, F. E., and Roth, R. H. (1991). "The
Biochemical Basis of Neuropharmacology," 6th ed. Oxford
University Press, Oxford.

Davila-Garcia, M. I., and Azmitia, E. C. (1990). Neuropeptides
as positive or negative neuronal growth regulatory factors:
Effects of ACTH and Leu-enkephalin on cultured serotonergic neurons. In "Molecular Aspects of Development and
Aging of Nervous System," (Jean Lauder *et al.*, Eds.), pp.
75–92. Plenum, New York.

Jacobs, B. L., and Azmitia, E. C. (1992). The structure and
function of the brain serotonergic system. *Physiol. Rev.* **72**,
165 229, 1992.

BRAIN DEVELOPMENT AND PLASTICITY

Marian Cleeves Diamond
University of California at Berkeley

Glossary

Basal ganglia Masses of nerve cells in the "base" of the cerebral hemispheres.

Cerebral cortex The "gray" matter of the cerebral hemispheres constituting 3–4 mm of nerve cell bodies and their processes which are responsible for higher cognitive processing.

Dendritic spines Small synaptic projections from the dendritic shaft receiving over 75% of the input to the dendrite.

Epigenetic Environmental influences.

Glioblasts Precursors of glial cells.

Neuroblasts Precursors of nerve cells.

Plasticity Cellular changes due to their responsiveness to the environment.

DEVELOPMENT OF THE BRAIN and the rest of the nervous system requires two kinds of cells, neurons (nerve cells) and neuroglia (glial cells). During neuronal development their prolific origin, migration, and eventual targeting to distant cells is taking place at an explosive rate while at the same time massive neuronal death is occurring, as much as 50% before birth. In the process of migration, cell adhesion molecules play an important role in determining eventual locations of nerve cells. Both the internal and the external environment are constantly modifying the development of the nervous system, a procedure defined as plasticity which can continue in some parts of the nervous system throughout the lifetime of the individual. The brain and spinal cord constitute the central nervous system and are embryologically derived from a neural tube. The peripheral nervous system receives contributions from both the neural tube and the neural crest as does the autonomic or visceral nervous system. In the adult nervous system the cerebral cortex demonstrates plasticity or modifications very readily, in fact more so than other parts of the nervous system. Some factors which easily alter the structure and chemistry of the cerebral cortex include enriched or impoverished living conditions, gonadal and adrenal steroidal hormones, and nutritional influences such as protein deficiency.

I. INTRODUCTION

The development of the human nervous system is one of the most miraculous and complex biological processes that exist. Once formed, various regions of the nervous system are constantly being modified or are demonstrating "plasticity" in response to the ever-changing environment. Whether controlling factors involved during prenatal development are identical to those during postnatal plasticity is not completely understood. To know the numerous coordinated mechanisms of action taking place at all times during development and plasticity of the nervous system will be the continued challenge for investigators during the 21st century.

Both structurally and functionally the divisions of the nervous system are essentially inseparable. But for didactic reasons it is divided into three main systems: the central nervous system (CNS), the peripheral nervous system (PNS), and the autonomic or visceral nervous system (ANS or VNS). The CNS includes the brain and spinal cord; the PNS, the cranial and spinal nerves and their ganglia; and the ANS or VNS, nerve cells and their fibers innervating smooth muscle, cardiac muscle, and glands. Developmentally all systems are undergoing changes, but at different rates and in different areas of the body. It is not clear that one set of laws governs all patterns of formation and morphogenesis.

II. NEURONS AND NEUROGLIA

A. Origin

A network of epigenetic factors controls the spatial pattern of gene expression that determines differentiation of cells and their organization into a nervous system. There are two major sources of neurons and glial cells, the ventricular zone of the neural tube and the neural crest. Neurons and neuroglia that form the brain and spinal cord develop from the neuroepithelial walls of the neural tube. At 23 days of age the neuroepithelia are found between the lumen and outer limiting membrane of the neural tube and alternate in activity cycles between cell division and synthesis of DNA. Once the cycles cease, differentiation of the neuroepithelia into neuroblasts begins. [*See* GLIAL CELLS.]

The neuroblasts break their attachments and migrate away from the ventricular zone adjacent to the lumen to form a new, mantle layer at about 35 days of age. Within this mantle layer the neuroblasts mature into neurons, which constitute most of the gray matter of the brain and spinal cord. Proliferation of germinal neuroepithelial cells and initial differentiation of neurons occurs normally in the absence of peripheral organs. Cellular position is a major determinant of early development because neighboring cells and tissues are important in determining cell fate. Changing the environment of cells alters what they become.

The outermost or marginal layer of the neural tube is formed from the extension and migration of axons from the developing neurons. This layer becomes the white matter of much of the brain and spinal cord.

About the time the newly formed neuroblasts begin to migrate out to form the mantle layer, glioblasts (primitive glial cells) lengthen by maintaining their attachments to the lumen surface and the outer limiting membrane as the neural tube thickens. Some of these glioblasts become radial glia and serve as guides along which neuroblasts migrate to the mantle layer. A relatively small number of radial glia remain attached to the surface of the lumen to become ependymal cells which will line the surface of the ventricles of the brain and the central canal of the spinal cord. The majority of glioblasts round up within the mantle layer to become mature neuroglia: protoplasmic and fibrous astrocytes and oligodendrocytes. Some of which will migrate into the marginal layer to form myelin and act as structural and metabolic support cells for the neuronal processes.

B. Migration and Targeting

During the development of the CNS and PNS massive cell migration occurs in which inductive cell to cell interactions are necessary for specification of cell fates. A number of influences act together to assure accurate navigation. Neurons make adhesive contacts at a leading edge and pull themselves forward. The extension of the processes occurs at growth cones. Cell adhesion molecules (CAMS) are important for cell migration. CAMS hold cells together for mechanical stability and to allow for interaction by means of other molecules. There are three families of N-CAMS (Neuron-CAMS): those whose adhesiveness depends on calcium (cadherin family), those whose adhesiveness does not depend on calcium (immunoglobulin super family), and integrins (receptors for extracellular matrix molecules). All are defined by base sequences in the DNA and amino acid sequences in proteins. Most molecules fit into these three classes, but there are a number of novel molecules that do not. All adhere to cell surfaces and extracellular matrix molecules. Heterogeneity is shown by differences in immunoreactivity of subpopulations of nerve cells. Behavior can be modulated by changes in surface receptors and CAMS. Migration can be regulated by such extracellular materials as fibronectin, laminin (a major component of the basement membrane of epithelia), tenascin, and collagen type I.

C. Death

Neuronal death during the course of normal development of the nervous system was discovered as early as 1896. In 1926 it was noted that overproduction of neurons was followed by a significant loss during development when at least three forms of neuronal death occur: (1) disintegration of tissues that develop transiently (e.g., tail of the human embryo); (2) at regions of separation, fusion, folding, and cavitation (e.g., going from the neural plate to the neural tube); (3) remodeling after an initial period of overproduction (e.g., basal ganglia, cerebral cortex, cerebellum, sympathetic ganglia, etc.). Nerve cell survival depends upon both afferent transneuronal trophic support and retrograde trophic support. Trophic support from hormones in the blood and glial cells plays an important role.

The existence of neurons depends upon a balance between access to neurotrophic factors and the strength of lethal mechanisms. Cell death can occur because of competition at the level of target innervation with failure to obtain a factor(s) produced by the target. Neurons affect properties of targets and targets affect properties of nerve cells. One of the neurotrophic factors may be nerve growth factor, but it is only one of many possible trophic agents. Nerve growth factor is required for survival and neurite growth of cholinergic neurons in the basal forebrain, sympathetic postganglionic neurons, and sensory ganglion cells from the neural crest.

If the neuron is deprived of a synaptic target, it dies. Cells that die are neither intrinsically defective nor preprogrammed to die. If cells have more than one trophic support, they can survive. As many as 50% of the neurons are lost in the anterior horn of the spinal cord, in the retina, and the IVth nerve nucleus, as examples.

III. DEVELOPMENT OF THE NERVOUS SYSTEM

A. Formation of the Neural Tube

The formation of a human being takes place in the reproductive system of the female where the fertilized ovum divides into two daughter cells to form a 2-cell embryo within the first 24 to 30 hours following conception. By the 32-cell stage, within the ball of cells, develops a central cavity containing an inner cell mass attached to one pole of the outer wall of the cavity. The mass will form the embryonic disc consisting of the three basic germ layers, ectoderm, mesoderm, and entoderm, collectively being responsible for the development of the entire body. But the entire nervous system will form from only one germ layer, the ectoderm.

At about 16 days of age, within the ectoderm, a midline thickening of newly differentiated cells forms a neural plate, induced by the underlying notochord. The neural plate is the smallest unit of tissue that alone can form the entire nervous system. The biochemical mechanisms of neural induction and the mechanisms of determination of cell type in the neural ectoderm are not at present known. For induction, second messengers, mobilization of intracellular calcium, and activation of protein kinase A are all possibly involved. A deepening midline groove in the neural plate creates the flanking neural folds, with continued deepening ultimately leading to the fusion of the folds to form the neural tube. This tube detaches from the surface ectoderm to become the future brain and spinal cord.

The open ends of the undeveloped neural tube are called anterior and posterior neuropores. If normal closure is not achieved, malformation of the nervous system results. Failure of anterior closure causes anencephaly (lack of brain formation) which is fatal. Improper closure of the posterior neuropore can result in such abnormalities as amyelia (absent lower cord) or an exposed cord (spina bifida) to the more benign but often painful pilonidal sinus (cyst) over the coccyx.

B. Formation and Derivation of the Neural Crest

A special group of cells breaks off from the neural folds before the closure of the neural tube to form the neural crest cells which cluster alongside the lengthening tube. Their migration is dependent upon the maturation of the extracellular matrix. The derivatives of the neural crest cells are all the neurons and glial cells within the PNS except sensory nerve cells forming cranial nerve ganglia which arise from cranial placodes, neurons and glial cells in the ANS or VNS, neurons in the CNS forming the mesencephalic nucleus of V, and the adrenal medulla.

C. Derivatives of the Neural Tube

By the end of 4 weeks the tube is essentially closed. In the cranial third of the tube the future brain develops into three distinct, spherical vesicles, the forebrain (prosencephalon), midbrain (mesencephalon), and hindbrain (rhombencephalon), with each of these three vesicles forming bilateral structures with few exceptions such as the pineal gland of the forebrain. The prosencephalon further divides into the telencephalon which expands into the massive cerebral hemispheres accounting for 80 to 90% of the total mass of the brain and also into the diencephalon. The diencephalon transforms into the epithalamus, thalamus, and hypothalamus from which the optic stalks grow out to expand into the optic cups, giving rise to the retina and optic tracts.

The mesencephalon does not undergo further visible division, but its walls form structures such as the superior and inferior colliculi, the cerebral peduncles, and substantia nigra. The rhombencephalon divides into a more rostral metencephalon, forming the cerebellum and the pons, and more caudally, the myelencephalon or the future medulla oblongata. [See CEREBELLUM.]

The central canal of the neural tube forms the ventricles of the brain. The lateral ventricles are found in the telencephalon, the third ventricle in the diencephalon, with the aqueduct in the mesencephalon, and the fourth ventricle in the met- and myelencephalon. The choroid plexus, within the lateral, third, and fourth ventricles, produces the cerebrospinal fluid, as much as 700 cc per day, which is reabsorbed into the venous system.

The outer few millimeters of gray matter covering the cerebral hemispheres are called the cerebral cortex (bark). On the basis of evolutionary age, the cortex is subdivided into three areas: archi- (ancient), paleo- (old), and neocortex (newest). The neocortex, a six-layered structure, is the largest and fastest-growing cortical area, expanding anteriorly to form the frontal lobes, upward and posteriorly to form the parietal and occipital lobes, and downward and anteriorly to form the temporal lobes. The insular cortex, a cortical island, is covered over by portions of the frontal, parietal, and temporal lobes. The paleocortex refers mainly to the olfactory brain or rhinencephalon and is sometimes called a transitional cortex with five to six layers. The archicortex, a three-layered cortex, arises on the medial wall of each hemisphere and at an early stage is called the hippocampal ridge (hippocampus = sea horse). Bulging into the lateral ventricles, the neuronal cell bodies of the ridge migrate posteriorly and then arc around into the temporal lobes to form the dentate gyrus and hippocampus. The clusters of hippocampal cells leave a trail of axons called the fornix in their path from the medial wall of the hemisphere to the temporal lobe. The archicortex deals with such functions as emotional and sexual behavior, spatial mapping, and recent memory processing. [See HIPPOCAMPAL FORMATION; NEOCORTEX.]

The corpus striatum begins as a thickening in the base of each hemisphere just below the lateral ventricles and to either side of the third ventricle. Due to its position in the base of the hemispheres, the corpus striatum is often called the basal ganglia. The corpus striatum consists of the caudate and lentiform nucleus, the latter being a composite of the putamen and globus palidus, and the amygdaloid nucleus. The latter is the first part of the corpus striatum to appear; it is also the most complex part of that body. As the temporal lobe forms, the amygdala fuses to the tail of the caudate and finally settles at the rostral end of the temporal lobe above the tip of the inferior horn of the lateral ventricle.

D. Cranial Nerves

Twelve pairs of cranial nerves transmit information to and commands from the brain. The complex receptor organs associated with some of these nerves in the head and neck are not found in the rest of the body. Cranial nerves are each associated with a specific region of the embryonic brain. Cranial nerve I arises from the telencephalon, cranial nerve II from the diencephalon, cranial nerves III and IV from the mesencepahlon, and cranial nerves V through XII from the met- and myelencephalon. The function of the cranial nerves are as follows:

1. olfaction
2. vision
3. external eye movement, closure of pupil, changes in the diameter of lens
4. external eye movement
5. sensory from face, cornea, mucus membrane of nasal and oral cavities; motor to muscles of mastication
6. external eye movement
7. muscles of facial expression, submaxillary and sublingual salivary glands, lacrimal gland, taste buds of anterior two-thirds of tongue
8. auditory and vestibular
9. muscles of pharynx and larynx, taste buds posterior one-third of tongue, parotid salivary gland
10. thoracic and abdominal viscera, taste buds on epiglottis, skin around ear, muscles of pharynx and larynx
11. trapezius and sternocleidomastoid muscle and muscles of pharynx and larynx
12. muscles of the tongue

IV. DEVELOPMENT AND PLASTICITY OF THE CEREBRAL CORTEX

A. Introduction

The cerebral cortex has three divisions, the neo-, paleo-, and archicortex. Each division has its own developmental pattern. Both the neo- and paleocortex have almost their full complement of nerve cells at birth. Any further growth in size is due to the explosive postnatal development of the branches of the nerve cells as they are making their synaptic contacts. In the rat the neocortex thickness reaches its peak of growth 1 month after birth and then slowly declines throughout life. In the human neocortex, the deoxyglucose uptake is greatest in the first 2 years after birth, then continues more slowly until about 10 years of age when it reaches its peak of activity.

In contrast to the neo- and paleocortex, in the rat, the archicortex continues to grow slowly, but steadily during the entire lifetime. The granule cells in the dentate gyrus of the archicortex continue to divide after birth and can even be influenced to increase division in adulthood by stimulation introduced through an enriched living environment.

B. Experiential Environmental Influences

The neurons in the neo- and paleocortex exhibit an impressive amount of plasticity. Every layer of cortical neurons in area 18, an area responsible for visual integration, responds to our experiential environment, with the outer layers, II and III, showing the greatest changes. Every part of the nerve cell from soma to synapse alters its dimensions in response to the environment. The enlarged nerve cells with their more numerous glial support cells are apparently utilized by the rat to solve maze problems more effectively than rats without such modified cells. In 4 days area 18 can significantly change its structure in response to environmental stimuli. By 30 days all areas of the neocortex have changed measurably.

It is just as important to stress the fact that decreased stimulation will diminish a nerve cell's dendrites as it is to stress that increased stimulation will enlarge the dendritic tree. Studies have shown that structural differences can be detected in the cerebral cortices of animals exposed at *any* age to different levels of stimulation in the environment. Measurable changes have been demonstrated in prenatal as well as early postnatal rat brains up until an age equivalent to a 90-year-old person.

Original studies on brain neuronal loss with aging included too few samples, and inadequate information was available about the living conditions prior to autopsy. Apparently, neuron loss with aging varies from one area to the next, but the healthy stimulated neocortex does not lose a significant number of cells with aging. Both hemispheres appear to respond to the enriched and impoverished conditions equally.

The archicortex is not as plastic as is either the neo- or paleocortex. But neurogenesis has been shown in the dentate granule cells of the adult rat as a consequence of a stimulating environment.

Environmental enrichment has the potential to enhance brain development following injury; the amount of injury, the location of the injury, and the degree of enrichment are important variables in influencing rehabilitation.

C. Hormonal Influences

Thyroid hormones, adrenal glucocorticoids, and sex steroid hormones all influence neural development. The thyroid begins to function at 10–12 weeks in the human fetus allowing for a long period during gestation to influence brain development. Children with thyroid abnormalities exhibit a high incidence of congenital mental deficiency. If such individuals are treated from birth with thyroid hormone, the IQ can be raised to within normal range.

In the rat reduction of thyroxine in the early postnatal period brings about failure of growth and maturation of the cerebral cortex. Neonatal thyroidectomy in rats reduces the volume of nerve cells, not the number, in some parts of the brain but not others. A critical period exists for the development of dendritic spines on apical dendrites of cortical pyramidal cells. In a thyroid deficient animal, if thyroid treatment is begun before Postnatal Day 13, normal spine development takes place. If treatment begins on or after Day 15, the spine reduction is irreversible.

During the neonatal period glucocorticoids retard cell differentiation and inhibit proliferation of neurons and glial cells. Adrenalectomy in neonatal rats on Postnatal Day 11 increases brain growth and total brain DNA. Glucocorticoid receptors are detected in the rat brain on Prenatal Day 17 and increase to adult levels by Postnatal Days 15–30.

The sex steroid hormones play an important role in brain development. At birth both male and female brains have estrogen receptors. Within 5 days after birth, the enzyme aromatase acts on testosterone, converting it to estrogen, which acts on estrogen receptors in the hypothalamus to change the female brain into a male brain. The estrogen receptors in the cerebral cortex apparently play a role in determining the patterns of left–right asymmetry. The male brain shows a right hemisphere being significantly thicker than the left. The female brain for the most part does not show significant asymmetry differences. When she does, the left cerebral cortex is thicker. After birth there is more neuronal death in the female brain than in the male.

D. Nutritional Influences

Studies show there is a critical period from birth to 2 years of age when the human nervous system is most vulnerable to malnutrition and when it is most responsive to nutritional therapy. The biological mechanisms of dysfunction caused by malnutrition in humans are not well understood. Nutrients are essential for growth factors, trophic factors, and hormones. The nervous system is affected both directly and indirectly. As examples, severe malnutrition affects heart muscle which reduces the blood supply to the brain. Reduced plasma proteins alter the osmotic pressure and can cause edema in the brain. Anemia reduces the oxygen supply to the brain.

Nutritional deprivation has a maximum effect when the developmental processes are most active. That is, if neuron production and growth are very active, malnutrition causes a severe deficiency in the production of neuron number and processes. The cortex of the cerebellum and cerebrum develops rapidly in the neonatal period and is very vulnerable to neonatal malnutrition. Myelination occurs mostly postnatally in rats and humans so experimental results can be compared closely. The CNS myelination process is greatly reduced with malnutrition as are the number of oligodendrocytes.

Other comparisons between species should be made at times of activity not time of birth. A low protein diet in rats during pregnancy and lactation causes a significant reduction in cerebral cortical dendritic growth in the terminal branches in the offspring. Enriched environments in the early postnatal period do not overcome this neuronal deficiency caused by protein deficiency. Providing a high protein diet plus an enriched environment will rehabilitate the cerebral cortical dendrites immediately after weaning of the protein deficient rats.

In the cerebral cortex, the most striking effects of malnutrition at all ages are the reduction of dendritic spines and a deficit in the number of synapses per neuron. Malnutrition for 2–3 weeks after birth results in a deficit of about 30% of synapses/neuron in layers II–IV in the rat visual cortex. Nutritional therapy for 200 days will increase the number of synapses by 20%. Social and nutritional deprivation are additive in bringing about detrimental effects on synaptogenesis. Similarly, enriched environments combined with protein rehabilitation are beneficial to cerebral cortical development early in life.

Bibliography

Cowan, W. M., Fawcett, J. W., O'Leary, D. D. M., and Stanfield B. B. (1984). Regressive events in neurogenesis. *Science* **225**, 1258–1265.

Diamond, M. C. (1988). "Enriching Heredity." Free Press, New York.

Gibson, K. R., and Peterson, A. C. (1991). "Brain Maturation and Cognitive Development." Aldine de Gruyter, New York.

Huttenlobher, P. R., Courten, C., Garey, L., and Van der Loos, D. (1982). Synaptogenesis in human visual cortex: Evidence for synapse elimination during normal development. *Neurosci. Lett.* **33**, 247–252.

Jacobsen, M. (1991). "Developmental Neurobiology." Plenum, New York.

Kalil, R. E. (1989). Synapse formation in the developing brain. *Sci. Am.* **261** (6), 76–85.

Rakic, P. (1987). Principles of neuronal migration. In "Handbook of Physiology" (W. M. Cowan, Ed.). American Physiological Society, Bethesda, MD.

Winick, M. (1989). "Nutrition, Pregnancy, and Early Infancy." Williams and Wilkins, Baltimore, MD.

Yakovlev, P. I., and Lecours, A. R. (1967). The myelogenetic cycles of regional maturation of the brain. In "Regional Development of the Brain in Early Life" (A. Minkowski, Ed.). Blackwell, Oxford.

Brain Electric Activity

Vasudeva G. Iyer
University of Louisville School of Medicine

Glossary

Brain mapping Technique of recording and displaying brain electric activity in the form of a topographic map in the time or frequency domain using gray or color scale.

Depolarization Physiological process in which the negative resting membrane potential of a neuron is reversed by the inflow of positively charged ions.

Dipole Concept of an electrical field with positivity on one end and negativity on the other, similar to the poles of a bar magnet.

Electroencephalogram (EEG) A record of brain electric activity. Electroencephalograph is the device used for recording EEG.

Epileptiform activity Abnormal EEG pattern that accompanies epileptic seizure activity in the brain.

Evoked potentials (stimulus-evoked responses) A record of brain electric activity, induced by specific stimuli, e.g., flashes of light, sound clicks, electric pulses, etc.

Polysomnography Recording of multiple physiological parameters, e.g., EEG, EMG (electromyogram), EOG (electrooculogram), respiration, EKG (electrocardiogram), etc., during sleep.

Spike An electric event in EEG that stands out of the background with a pointed top and a duration of 20–70 msec. A sharp wave has a similar configuration but a longer duration, up to 200 msec.

Spindle A cluster of rhythmic waves showing a gradual increase and then decrease in amplitude. A typical example is the sleep spindle seen in Stage 2 sleep.

Synaptic (postsynaptic) potential (PSP) Electrical change in the postsynaptic membrane of a neuron, induced by liberation of neurotransmitter at the synapse (contact point between two nerve cells), resulting from arrival of incoming nerve impulses. Postsynaptic potentials may be excitatory (EPSP) or inhibitory (IPSP).

BIOELECTRIC ACTIVITY accompanies the various physiological processes that occur in the brain. A record of this activity, which can be obtained through electrodes placed over the scalp, is called an electroencephalogram (EEG). At the inception of EEG, there was great expectation that typical bioelectrical abnormalities would be identified in different mental disorders. However, it was soon realized that routine visual analysis of EEG failed to document consistent changes or specific patterns in such disorders. Further research led to the development of EEG as a valuable clinical tool in the diagnosis and management of organic neurological disorders, most notably in the field of epilepsy. Recent innovations in technology such as computer-based acquisitions and analysis, and topographic brain mapping have kindled renewed interest in the EEG correlates of behavior and of psychiatric disorders.

I. HISTORICAL ASPECTS

Richard Caton in 1875 reported the presence of spontaneous electrical activity in animal brains; he also was able to detect electrical changes in response to visual stimulation with flickering light. Hans Berger of the University of Jena in Germany in 1929 was the first to report human brain electrical activity, "da elektrenkephalogramm." His finding was later confirmed by Adrian and Matthews from England. Berger described many features of the electroencephalogram including alpha and beta rhythms and certain abnormalities seen in seizure disorders. Following Berger's work there was exponential increase in knowledge about brain electrical activity; some of the major contributors include Gibbs, Davis, Lennox, Lindsley, Jasper, and Grey Walter.

II. PHYSIOLOGICAL BASIS OF EEG

The EEG consists of continuously changing electrical potentials over a wide range of frequencies. The waveforms are similar whether recorded over the scalp or directly from the brain surface except for a fourfold decrease in voltage over the scalp. It is believed that the EEG reflects field currents set up by ionic fluxes occurring in the brain, close to the surface. The ionic fluxes are most likely the result of graded potentials like the synaptic potentials rather than the action potentials which have a much shorter duration. Summation of synaptic potentials of many neurons is necessary, in order to obtain recordable voltage changes over the scalp. Identical polarity over a sufficiently large area most likely results from underlying groups of vertically oriented dipoles. The cortical pyramidal neurons with large number of synapses over the apical dendrite and the basal cell body are ideally placed to evoke field currents with such dipolar configuration. The prevailing theory is that the EEG reflects field currents set up by summated excitatory and inhibitory postsynaptic potentials (EPSP and IPSP) occurring in the vertically oriented pyramidal neurons in the cerebral cortex.

III. RECORDING OF BRAIN ELECTRIC ACTIVITY

Routine EEG recordings are done by placing electrodes, usually metal discs that pick up electrical potentials, over the scalp; to assure equal distance between electrodes, and correlation to the topography of the underlying brain, a standard system of head measurement and electrode placement has been developed. This is called the 10–20 system of electrode placement; electrodes are placed over the scalp at points that correspond to 10 or 20% of the

distance between specific bony landmarks of the skull. Standard clinical technique uses 21 electrodes with an additional ground electrode, which are all attached to the skin using an electroconductive paste.

The electrodes are connected to an EEG machine (electroencephalograph) which in essence amplifies the voltage difference between any given pair of electrodes. It is crucial to visualize the electrical activity occurring in many electrode pairs simultaneously in order to locate the site of origin of such activity in specific portions in the brain. A minimum of 16 simultaneously amplified measurements are recommended, given the complexity and the large area of the underlying cerebral cortex. Recent advances in technology allow up to 64 channels of recordings. Unwanted electrical signals generated by muscles, eyeballs, and other structures around the head (artifacts) are partially eliminated by using specific filters.

While the scalp electrodes are excellent for most recordings, there are some instances where they are insufficient. Thus, they may not show events that take place in the deeper areas of the brain such as the mesiotemporal or the orbitofrontal cortex. Such recordings need either a nasopharyngeal electrode (placed through the nostril) or sphenoid electrode (wire electrodes placed close to the base of skull through a needle). Certain clinical situations may necessitate recording directly from the brain surface after removal of portions of skull bone (electrocorticography) or depth using surgically implanted probes, e.g., during remedial surgery for epilepsy.

The electrodes are connected together in different combinations (montages) to facilitate rapid visual interpretation of the waveforms. In general, the electric potential of each electrode is either measured against a common electrode (referential montage) or measured between electrode pairs connected together in chains, front to back or side to side (bipolar montage). As a rule recording is obtained while awake and asleep. Overbreathing for 3 min (hyperventilation) and stimulation with flashes of light (photic stimulation) are also undertaken to "activate" certain normal and abnormal patterns.

IV. DISPLAY, ANALYSIS, AND STORAGE OF EEG DATA

The multichannel amplified brain electric activity may be stored and displayed in different ways. The conventional technique uses paper recording systems. For clinical studies 20–30 min of EEG is recorded in a continuous folded paper at standard paper speed, e.g., 30 mm/sec with time in the X axis and voltage in the Y axis. The paper has background markings so that the duration and amplitude of the waveforms can be determined easily. For any given patient the actual recording may run to 200–300 pages or more. The interpretation of such a recording consists of visual assessment of amplitude and frequency of the electrical activity and comparison to the known normal range, as well as quick recognition of abnormal waveforms. Thus, pattern recognition is a crucial aspect for visual EEG analysis and many of the recording and display techniques are geared to enhance the speed of visual interpretation. Paper recording is simple and easy to interpret, but the disadvantage is that the data cannot be redisplayed or manipulated offline after recording. Often microfilming is done to make storage of data from paper-recorded EEG practicable.

The EEG data may also be digitized using an analog to digital converter, stored on electromagnetic tape and displayed over a cathode ray oscilloscope. Some of the newer machines are equipped with storage systems such as rewritable optic discs and large monitors which can display 32–64 channels of EEG. Massive volumes of reanalyzable EEG data could be stored with such devices. These systems also allow offline analysis of a particular waveform under many different montages and also use techniques such as spectral analysis, digital filtering, etc.

V. NORMAL PATTERNS WHILE AWAKE AND ASLEEP

The normal EEG shows predictable patterns depending upon the state of alertness of the patient, i.e., whether awake, drowsy, or asleep (Table I). It

TABLE I
Behavioral Correlates of EEG

State of alertness	Typical EEG pattern
Awake and relaxed	Alpha rhythm
Awake and attentive or anxious	Low voltage tracing; alpha rhythm disappears
NREM sleep	V waves, K complexes, and sleep spindles on a slow background of theta or delta frequency
REM sleep	Alpha frequency background, "sawtooth" waves, rapid eye movements, atonia of skeletal muscles

also shows typical maturational changes appearing at a very early age and reaching the adult pattern toward the latter part of adolescence. There are also subtle changes in the EEG pattern in the last two decades. Ever since the initial recording by Berger in 1920, numerous studies of brain electrical activity under different behavioral states and conditions have been undertaken by many different workers, leading to definition of acceptable normal patterns. These are described below.

A. Awake State

In an awake adult, the most prominent feature of the EEG is the rhythmic activity noted over the back of the head corresponding to the occipital electrodes. This is the alpha rhythm described by Berger. It has a frequency of 8–13 Hz and is most prominent in the state of relaxed wakefulness with eyes closed (Fig. 1). Most adults show a frequency of 9–11 Hz, which, once established, remains fairly constant for an individual. The mean amplitude is about 50 μV and this tends to wax and wane. Opening the eyes or mental activity, such as arithmetic, will attenuate or block the alpha rhythm.

There have been numerous studies to link the alpha rhythm and psychophysiological patterns. Initial attempts at linking alpha index (percentage time that alpha rhythm is present) to personality did not reveal consistent correlations. Most investigators also failed to show a link between IQ scores and the alpha rhythm.

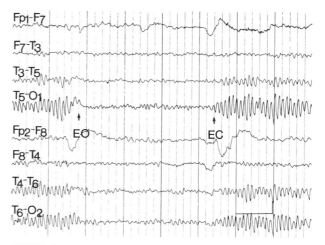

FIGURE 1   EEG showing blocking of alpha rhythm with eye opening. EO, eyes opened; EC, eyes closed. Filters: low frequency, 1 Hz; high frequency, 70 Hz. Calibrations: horizontal, 1 sec; vertical, 50 μV.

TABLE II
EEG Wave Forms and Frequency Bands

Frequency band	Frequency range	Comment
Alpha	8–13 Hz	Common examples are alpha rhythm, mu rhythm, REM sleep background, etc.
Beta	>13 Hz	Subvigil beta during drowsiness; drug-induced beta (e.g., barbiturates)
Theta	4–7 Hz	Stage 1 sleep; early age groups while awake
Delta	<4 Hz	Stages 3 and 4 sleep; early age groups while awake

The origin and significance of the alpha rhythm have been debated over the past many years. Rhythmic activity in general is believed to result from the interaction between the thalamic and cortical neurons. Studies on dogs which also exhibit an alpha rhythm have demonstrated that these waveforms are generated approximately 1 mm below the surface of the occipital cortex.

Other features that may be observed in waking stage include the mu rhythm which has a comblike shape and is best seen over the central electrodes corresponding to the motor–sensory (Rolandic) area and beta rhythm which has faster frequency (more than 13 Hz) seen best over the anterior areas corresponding to the frontal electrodes. Table II summarizes the usual frequency bands seen in conventional EEG tracings.

B. Asleep State

The EEG pattern during sleep is remarkably different from that seen in wakefulness. Different stages of sleep are recognized based on EEG pattern. In an adult, when wakefulness gives way to drowsiness, the alpha rhythm gradually disappears and is often replaced by low voltage theta activity. Increase in beta activity may also occur at this time (subvigil beta). Later some sharply contoured waves are noted over the vertex region bilaterally and symmetrically (V waves); larger biphasic waves may also be seen in a wider distribution (K complexes). The most striking feature of stage 2 sleep is the sleep spindle (Fig. 2). It is seen most prominently over the vertex. Each spindle lasts for about a second and may recur at frequent intervals. The deeper stages of sleep are characterized by decrease in sleep spindles and the occurrence of delta activity in a diffuse distribution. [*See* SLEEP: BIOLOGICAL RHYTHMS AND HUMAN PERFORMANCE.]

The rapid eye movement stage of sleep (REM), which has been correlated with dreaming, occurs in a cyclical fashion appearing for the first time around 80–90 min after sleep onset. It is characterized by the occurrence of rapid eye movements and an alpha frequency background; skeletal muscle tone is markedly decreased during the REM sleep. A routine EEG recording done in the laboratory during daytime seldom shows REM sleep. It is more often recorded in newborn infants and in nocturnal sleep.

VI. CERTAIN ABNORMAL EEG PATTERNS

EEG is perhaps the only simple, inexpensive, and noninvasive clinical test available for evaluation of brain function other than regular bedside examination. It is extensively used in the evaluation of patients with a wide variety of neurologic disorders, most importantly seizure disorders. Some of the common abnormalities are discussed below.

A. Seizure Disorders

Epileptic seizures result from abnormal electrical activity of the cerebral neurons. Depending upon

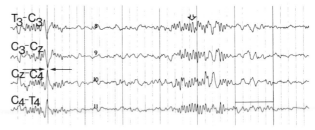

FIGURE 2   EEG showing stage 2 sleep. Open arrow points to sleep spindles and closed arrow to a V wave. Filters: low frequency, 1 Hz; high frequency, 70 Hz. Calibrations: horizontal, 1 sec; vertical, 50 μV.

the part of the brain from which they originate and how they spread, different clinical phenomena may occur during a seizure. The EEG pattern is often crucial in categorizing the type of seizure, determining appropriate medications, and assessing the prognosis in patients with suspected seizure disorders. [*See* EPILEPSY.]

In the usual clinical situation, the EEG is recorded at a time when the patient is not actually having a seizure. Such recordings are called interictal recordings. Recordings during a seizure are called ictal recordings. Since seizures are unpredictable in their time of occurrence, it is often possible to obtain only an interictal recording. Such recordings may provide the physician with clues pertaining to the site of origin of seizures and the potential for recurrence. The epilepsy-prone brain shows EEG abnormalities called spike discharges, which are very sharp-looking waveforms that stand out from the background (Fig. 3). Usually the spikes are surface negative and are easily localized when appropriate montages are used. Sometimes each spike may be followed by a large slow wave, the spike and wave complex. The ictal pattern often consists of rapid spiking of low amplitude followed by a decrease in rate and an increase in amplitude.

In patients suspected of having seizures a number of measures are undertaken to enhance the probability of recording interictal and ictal patterns. Patients are often asked to keep awake during the previous night (sleep deprivation) which enhances the probability of recording spontaneous sleep in the lab (without sedatives); this measure is also is said to improve

the chances of recording interictal spikes. Spikes may appear more often during certain stages of sleep; e.g., early stages of NREM sleep. In addition, the patient is also subjected to hyperventilation for 3–5 min which is often a potential stimulus for bringing out 3 per sec spike and wave discharges of absence (petit mal) seizures (Fig. 4). Hyperventilation may also enhance abnormal focal slowing. Another routine test performed is photic stimulation using flashes of light. This may induce an unusual response called photoparoxysmal response or may provoke actual seizures in susceptible patients. In certain types of seizures such as the partial complex seizures which often originate from the more medial parts of the temporal lobe, one may need special electrodes such as the sphenoid electrodes for successful recording of focal spikes.

When there is diagnostic uncertainty about seizures, it is often necessary to record the EEG and clinical phenomena simultaneously (seizure monitoring) over several days. This is done with special monitoring equipment incorporating electrophysiological and video recordings. Such recordings can often determine whether recurrent behavioral phenomena are manifestations of epileptic seizures. It is also useful in the evaluation of patients who are refractory to medical treatment to determine whether there is a surgically resectable epileptic focus.

B. Dementia

The EEG is a valuable tool in the diagnosis of conditions which cause dementia such as Alzheimer's dis-

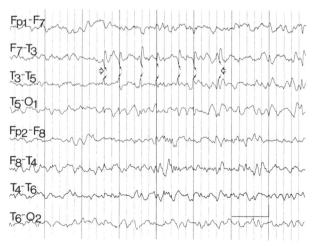

FIGURE 3 Horizontal arrows point to a cluster of spike discharges. The oblique arrow points to individual spikes. Filters: low frequency, 1 Hz; high frequency, 70 Hz. Calibrations: horizontal, 1 sec; vertical, 50 μV.

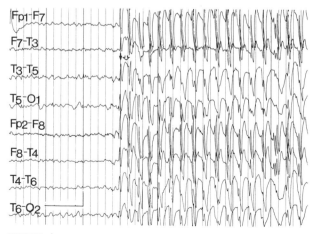

FIGURE 4 Three per second generalized spike and wave discharges of absence seizure. Closed arrow points to the spike and open arrow to the wave component. Filter: low frequency, 1 Hz; high frequency, 70 Hz. Calibrations: horizontal, 1 sec; vertical, 75 μV.

ease. When there is diagnostic uncertainty between pseudodementia, especially from depression, and true dementia, EEG may be helpful in making the distinction. Slowing of background activity is a feature of dementia but not of depression. In certain types of dementia such as Creutzfeldt-Jakob disease the EEG shows certain typical patterns, which may be the first and the only clue to the diagnosis. [*See* EEG, COGNITION, AND DEMENTIA.]

C. Brain Death Determination

Although it is not legally necessary to have an EEG confirmation for determination of brain death, an EEG is often requested for confirming brain death. Special techniques of recording are necessary. It is often important to document that the electrodes are indeed attached to the patient and that the whole recording system is working normally. One looks for electrocerebral silence (ECS) which is defined as no brain electric activity of more than 2 μV in amplitude.

VII. POLYSOMNOGRAPHY

The recording of multiple physiological data such as respiration, airflow, oxygen saturation, and leg movements, along with EEG, muscle tone (EMG, electromyogram), heart rate (EKG, electrocardiogram), and eye movements (EOG, electrooculogram), during sleep is called polysomnography. The technique is useful in the diagnosis of certain conditions such as breathing disorders of sleep (sleep apnea syndrome), nocturnal seizures, REM behavior disorder, etc. In the evaluation of narcolepsy the patient is given opportunities for napping four to five times during daytime at 2-hr intervals with recording of EEG, EOG, and chin EMG (multiple sleep latency test, MSLT); daytime sleepiness is quantified based on sleep latency, i.e., the time interval between going to bed and falling asleep during the naps. The normal mean sleep latency is more than 5 min. A short sleep latency and the presence of more than one nap with REM sleep during the MSLT suggest narcolepsy, provided the previous night's sleep pattern was normal.

VIII. VISUAL, AUDITORY, AND SOMATOSENSORY EVOKED POTENTIALS

Unlike the EEG which is a recording of spontaneous electrical voltage changes, the evoked potentials represent bioelectric activity that occur in response to specific stimuli. While it is theoretically possible to stimulate any receptor in the body and record from the brain a change in electric activity, to be useful in a clinical setting and to be able to do the tests quickly and efficiently the stimuli must be easily quantifiable. The recording also poses logistic problems as the electric activity evoked by stimuli are often smaller in amplitude than the spontaneously occurring EEG activity. Hence, the technique of signal averaging which enhances a time-locked response and attenuates random electric activity is utilized. In the early days simple superimposition was used to record evoked activity but with the availability of powerful computers it is possible to digitize the signals and measure voltage at specific time intervals from the onset of the stimulus for a large number of responses and average them. This has made possible the high resolution and noise reduction necessary for recording of evoked potentials in clinical settings.

There are three varieties of evoked potentials that are recorded in clinical practice (Table III). These are the visual, auditory, and somatosensory evoked potentials. In the case of visual evoked potentials (VEP), the retina, in particular the macula, is stimulated using either flashes of light or a pattern reversal stimulus (black and white checkerboard pattern on a TV screen); the electrical activity generated in the retina (electroretinogram) and over the occipital cortex (VEP) are recorded by averaging a large number of traces. The typical VEP shows a prominent positive wave at a mean latency of 100 msec (P100 response), best recorded over the occipital area.

The recording of the response in the case of pattern reversal stimuli depends on the patient being able to continuously focus on the changing pattern on the screen. Hence, if one becomes drowsy or inattentive the response may be lost. In the case of photic flash stimulation the advantage is that the patient does not have to be looking at a screen. A response could be obtained even when the patient is asleep or under anesthesia. However, the responses to pattern reversal are much more constant in latency and more reliable for clinical interpretation.

The P100 response will be slow to appear if there is a delay in conduction of signals in the optic pathways. Thus, pressure on the optic nerve from a tumor could lead to a delayed and diminished P100 response. The most common clinical situation where the visual evoked potential is of diagnostic value is

TABLE III
Evoked Potentials

Type	Stimulus	Response
Visual (VEP)	Flashes of light or pattern reversal	Positivity over occipital areas at 100 msec (P100)
Brainstem auditory (BAEP)	Clicking sounds	Waves 1–5 representing passage of signal through the auditory nerve and brainstem auditory pathways
Somatosensory (SEP)	Electric stimulation of peripheral nerves	Series of responses representing passage of signal through the nerves, nerve roots, and central somatosensory pathways and arrival at the sensory cortex

in multiple sclerosis, in which demyelination of the optic nerve occurs. Myelin which is an insulating material around the nerve fiber is crucial for rapid conduction and hence when there is a demyelination the signal conduction is slowed leading to a delayed P100 response.

In the case of the brainstem auditory evoked potential or response (BAEP or BAER), the inner ear (cochlea) is stimulated using sound clicks at 60 or 70 dB above the hearing threshold, delivered through a headphone, and the resulting electrical activity is recorded. Using special ear electrodes one could also record the electric activity of the cochlea (electrocochleogram). The BAEP shows a series of waveforms (positive and negative) corresponding to conduction of signals through the auditory nerve and different portions of the brainstem auditory pathway. The positive peaks are numbered waves 1–5. The BAEP could be recorded irrespective of whether the patient is awake, sleep, or under anesthesia.

The BAEP could reliably detect abnormal conduction in the auditory nerve or in the brainstem auditory pathways. It is useful in the early diagnosis of tumors that affect the 8th nerve, such as the acoustic neurinoma and hemorrhage and demyelination.

Another type of evoked potential in clinical use is the somatosensory evoked potential (SSEP). In this test either the median or the tibial nerve is stimulated, and the responses are recorded as they go through the spinal cord and the brainstem to the somatosensory cortex. It should be noted that abnormalities of peripheral nerve conduction could influence SSEP and hence simultaneous nerve conduction studies may also have to be done.

Conduction abnormalities in the somatosensory pathways are diagnostically significant in conditions like multiple sclerosis and spinal cord tumors. They are also useful as indices for monitoring the spinal cord function while surgical procedures like correction of scoliosis are undertaken. Such intraoperative monitoring could alert the surgeon to early spinal cord dysfunction so that immediate remedial measures could be taken to avoid permanent damage and paraplegia.

IX. COGNITIVE EVOKED POTENTIAL

While there are a number of techniques available to the psychologist to evaluate learning and memory, objective measurement of these functions using bioelectric phenomena has always been difficult. A technique that has been explored in the past several years is the recording of what is known as cognitive evoked potential. Other names include endogenous evoked potential, event related potential, and P300 response. Most studies use a series of exactly similar stimuli interspersed with randomly occurring dissimilar stimuli (usually visual or auditory). Changes in brain electric activity in response to both the similar and dissimilar stimuli are separately averaged. The recognition of the dissimilar stimulus is accompanied by the occurrence of a large positive wave over the vertex at about 300 msec from the presentation of the stimulus (hence the term P300 response). The response tends to appear less pronounced as the person becomes inattentive or drowsy. The latency is prolonged in patients with cognitive defects particularly in those with different forms of dementia including Alzheimer's disease.

The site of origin of the P300 response is unclear. While the temporal lobe is considered to play an important role in the generation of the cognitive evoked potential, it is suspected that the scalp-recorded vertex-prominent P300 probably has a multiregional origin.

X. FUTURE TRENDS

In the early days of EEG, it was hoped that study of brain electric activity would provide much-needed objectivity to the study of mind–body relationship. However, the EEG developed into a clinical tool for diagnosis of neurological disorders, as the EEG changes noted by traditional visual analysis were inconsistent in many mental disorders. The recent development of techniques for computer-based acquisition, display, storage, and analysis of EEG and evoked potentials has made it possible to extract vast amounts of information that could be quantified and analyzed in much greater detail. Study of a large number of normal volunteers and patients with different psychiatric disorders is being undertaken in many centers. Software programs are being devised that will make statistical comparison between a given subject's EEG and the data base, providing diagnostic probabilities. With large data bases and reliable statistical programs it is hoped that the interview-based psychiatric diagnosis will be substantiated by the documentation of diagnostic bioelectric patterns. Choice of appropriate medications, e.g., anxiolytics, antidepressants, etc., may also gain much more precision when normalization of bioelectric abnormalities is targeted.

Bibliography

Aminoff, M. J. (1992). "Electrodiagnosis in Clinical Neurology," 3rd ed. Churchill Livingstone, New York.

Bickford, R. G. (1989). EEG color mapping (topography)—Advantages and pitfalls, clinical and research perspective. *Am. J. EEG Tech.* **29,** 19–28.

Daly, D. D., and Pedley, T. A. (Eds.) (1990). "Current Practice of Clinical Electroencephalography." Raven Press, New York.

Duffy, F. F., Iyer, V. G., and Surwillo, W. W. (1989). "Clinical EEG and Topographic Brain Mapping." Springer-Verlag, New York.

Hughes, J. R., and Wilson, W. P. (1983). "EEG and Evoked Potentials in Psychiatry and Behavioral Neurology." Butterworth, Boston.

John, E. R., Pricheps, L. S., Fridman, J., and Easton, P. (1988). Neurometrics: Computer-assisted differential diagnosis of brain dysfunctions. *Science* **239,** 162–169.

Markand, O. N. (1990). Alpha rhythms. *J. Clin. Neurophys.* **7**(2), 163–189.

Neshige, R., and Luders, H. (1992). Recording of event-related potentials (P300) from human cortex. *J. Clin. Neurophys.* **9**(2), 294–298.

Niedermeyer, E., and Lopes da Silva, F. (1993). "Electroencephalography: Basic Principles, Clinical Applications and Related Fields," 3rd ed. Williams and Williams, Baltimore.

Zappulla, R. A., LeFever, F. F., Jaeger, J., and Bilder, R. (Eds.) (1991). Windows on the brain: Neuropsychology's technological frontiers. *Ann. NY. Acad. Sci.* **620,** 1–101.

BRAINWASHING AND TOTALITARIAN INFLUENCE

Dick Anthony
Graduate Theological Union

Thomas Robbins
Santa Barbara Center for Humanistic Studies

Glossary

Brainwashing A pattern of interrogation and indoctrination to which Western prisoners of war were exposed during the Korean War; more generally, a coercive style of persuasion which allegedly radically alters beliefs against the will of the individual through the induction of primitive states of consciousness in which the person is powerless to resist new ideas.

Thought reform The historical process of indoctrination in totalitarian ideology utilized for the coercive re-education of non-Communists by the Chinese; more generally, refers to the attempt to transform personal identities through intensive or stressful indoctrination in the context of a totalistic ideology.

Totalism An all-encompassing ideology which interprets the world in terms of a comprehensive set of polarized, black versus white categories, typically designed to legitimate a totalitarian state. The term also refers to the pattern of psychological characteristics that predisposes individuals to enthusiastically submit to totalitarian ideologies, social movements, and governments.

Totalitarianism A comprehensive organization of a nation state and total society in terms of a militant totalist ideology.

BRAINWASHING has been used to denote the actual historical experience of the indoctrination of Western prisoners of war in Korea and the methods of influence employed by their Communist captors. More generally the term denotes an extreme mode of indoctrination which allegedly is qualitatively different from normal social influence and other modes of indoctrination in that it is supposedly derived from scientific research and capable of overwhelming free will.

Brainwashing supposedly undermines subjects' true political and religious beliefs and the sense of identity based upon them. It is alleged to coercively substitute sharply contrasting beliefs and a false self. The variables which determine the efficacy of influence are assumed to be esoteric and technical, such as the use of drugs, hypnosis, and distinctive conditioning procedures based upon scientific research. These factors allegedly involve the creation of a distinctive, altered state of consciousness within which the subject is highly suggestible and in which alternative beliefs and an alternative identity are coercively implanted. The predisposing characteristics of subjects are not considered salient. Physical coercion is not considered essential to the process.

An alternative perspective, which focused on personality and motivational factors determining the attraction of persons to totalitarian ideologies and groups, emerged at roughly the same time that the notion of brainwashing developed. This perspective emerged from within a general interdisciplinary analysis of totalitarianism, and was used to interpret the indoctrination of Westerners within Communist prison of war camps and prisons by, among others, Edgar Schein and Robert Lifton.

The latter approach, which we will refer to in this paper as the analysis of totalitarian influence, found that such influence was not capable of causing the involuntary substitution of false beliefs for true ones, nor of supplanting a person's real self with an inauthentic one. The appearance of involuntary alteration of beliefs and identities, according to this perspective, was created primarily by prisoners' simple behavioral compliance to their captors wishes because of extreme physical coercion, resulting in no real change in belief. The small amount of real change in belief by Westerners in Communist prisons, on the other hand, was based upon characterological and ideological predispositions and did not result from novel or distinctive techniques of influence.

I. EMERGENCE OF THE BRAINWASHING MODEL

The "brainwashing" idea developed during World War II when both Nazi and American intelligence services became interested in developing techniques to more effectively interrogate prisoners and, optimally, to transform enemy prisoners and internal subversives into "deployable agents" who would be enthusiastic converts to general political attitudes diametrically opposed to the ones which their interrogators found objectionable. The intelligence services had in mind a variety of uses for such converts, such as using them as secret agents who, because of their pasts, would be more likely to escape detection than more conventional agents. Additional goals for the brainwashing process included improving the capacity of soldiers to resist hostile interrogation and developing more effective wartime propaganda techniques.

The feasibility of "brainwashing" or the radical psycho-political re-education of persons whose will was to be overwhelmed was suggested to German and American intelligence services by the Moscow show trials in the late 1930s. At these trials high Soviet officials confessed implausible crimes relating to allegedly counterrevolutionary activities. The Stalinists were at that time presumed by many journalists, social scientists, and Western public officials to have discovered the key to the scientific conquest of the human will.

Most informed scholars now believe that physically coerced behavioral *compliance* and not some mode of inner *conversion* was operative in both the Moscow show trials of the 1930s and later Communist trials in Eastern Europe, such as that of Cardinal Mindzenty, who made a sensational confession. However, in the 1940s and 1950s the brainwashing explanation of such confessions was taken very seriously by German and American officials, and both countries funded ambitious research programs to develop brainwashing techniques. The German program was conducted by the S.S. and the Gestapo, and the American program was conducted by the Office of Strategic Services [OSS], the World War II predecessor of the Central Intelligence Agency, and later by the CIA itself.

Most of the CIA funded research was carried out under the auspices of two supposedly independent philanthropic foundations which served as front organizations disguising the CIA origin of the funding. The research was conducted by American and Canadian psychiatrists, psychologists, and other social scientists, many of them very prominent. (Some may have remained ignorant of the CIA sponsorship of these projects.)

In many attempts to replicate the apparent overwhelming of the wills of Stalin's victims, the scientists working on the issue assumed that an essential prerequisite to authentic brainwashing was a *deconditioning* process to eradicate subjects' prior mental patterns. This was in part the rationale for the use of powerful psychedelic drugs such as Mescaline and LSD which were viewed as potent deconditioning agents. Scientists believed that once a person's mind was wiped clean by such drugs, or by other deconditioning agents such as sensory deprivation or electroshock therapy, new political attitudes and a new sense of self could then easily be implanted by conditioning techniques or by hypnosis. The American research program, which eventually became heavily involved in experiments with LSD, was influenced by earlier Nazi work with Mescaline. In general, the key elements of government research programs were (1) drugs, (2) sensory deprivation and isolation, (3) hypnosis, (4) conditioning procedures, and (5) physical debilitation. Electric shock, psychosurgery, and insulin shock were occasionally employed.

The Nazi research program, which was less ethically inhibited than the American program, had a significant death rate among subjects, although CIA sponsored research in the United States and Canada also produced casualties in terms of mental breakdown and disorientation. Civilian psychologists and psychiatrists who collaborated in these programs were also concerned with finding methods of curing mental illness which were more effective and less time consuming than Freudian talk therapy. Thus, the research, which was not successful in terms of its original goals, nevertheless impacted psychotherapy in terms of drug therapy, behavioral conditioning, and electroconvulsive therapy.

It is important to note that intelligence officials regarded traditional methods involving physical coercion and threat as having some serious limitations. It was difficult to discern whether persons who were compliant out of fear were being truthful when they answered questions or expressed beliefs. Advanced scientific techniques were regarded as promising to improve upon crudely coercive tactics and prolonged incarceration in this respect.

To some degree *deception* was regarded as the basic alternative to physical constraint: subjects were sometimes told they were simply being treated for emotional and mental problems, and they were not aware of the nature of the drugs they imbibed, nor of the coercively indoctrinational intent of the conditioning procedures that were applied to them. In some cases subjects were administered strong psychedelic drugs without even being informed that they were being given any drugs at all.

Despite the scope and ambitiousness of these German and American mind control research programs (the American research program went on for over 25 years), in terms of their original goals of improving interrogation and coercive indoctrination tactics beyond that obtainable with physical coercion or other traditional methods, they were complete failures. The German program produced many deaths but no reliable alternatives to extreme brutality and terror in interrogation and indoctrination procedures and was never able to convert enemies into deployable agents.

The American program also had some serious casualties. For instance, the covert administration of psychedelic substances caused some psychotic episodes and on at least one occasion led to the suicide of a subject. In addition, one large project, which involved a combination of drugs, electroshock, conditioning procedures, and sensory deprivation resulted in (1) the mental breakdown and disorientation of some subjects; (2) over 60% of its subjects suffering severe memory problems for up to 10 years; (3) some cases of permanent brain damage.

As we have indicated, despite the intensity and severity of these methods the American program never learned how to change people's minds about their political orientations or to force them to reveal deeply held secrets. The most that could be said for the methods evaluated is that they could drive people crazy or make them mentally defective, but even such casualties became no more sympathetic to political opinions with which they disagreed, and would have been too disabled to be useful even if

they had. After 25 years of dedicated effort and the involvement of the cream of American psychiatry and psychology, the American CIA had become no more capable of coercively creating deployable agents than it had at the beginning.

II. IMPACT OF CHINESE POW CAMPS

Some of the CIA sponsored research we have referred to actually was conducted in the 1950s during or after the Korean War. During this period the notion of "brainwashing" had become popular with the public largely because it seemed relevant to explaining the grim experiences of American soldiers in Communist prison camps in Korea. Although few if any soldiers were converted to Communism, some American POW's were induced by their captors to make statements critical of American policy and supportive of Communist allegations that American forces were employing germ warfare. These performances troubled many Americans but stimulated writers and movie makers, who presented an extreme scenario of traumatically induced psychosis and mind control, the movie *The Manchurian Candidate* being the best known entertainment product.

The research supported by the CIA on how to achieve mind control described above was not actually influenced by the POW ordeals. Knowledgeable researchers and officials were aware that the Chinese were not employing advanced scientific methods or attempting systematic radical deconditioning and the transformation of thought patterns. However, the agency conducted a disinformation campaign aimed at exploiting the brainwashing idea to reassure Americans that germ warfare allegations made by POW's were not true, that captured American soldiers were not traitors or weak, and that no competent (i.e., unbrainwashed) person could voluntarily accept Communist ideology, which was assumed to be inherently implausible to a rational person.

Central to this effort was the publication by Edward Hunter, a propaganda expert employed by the CIA who worked undercover as an American journalist, of *Brainwashing in Red China*. This volume explained the apparent success of the Chinese thought reform programs in terms of sinister but advanced science-based techniques much like the ones which the CIA-sponsored research program in the United States had so far been unsuccessful in creating. Hunter coined the term brainwashing in this volume because of its sinister overtones of over-powered human will and falsely claimed that the term was a translation of a Chinese term for thought reform. Thus, not only the process of brainwashing but also the very term itself was a sham constructed for propaganda purposes.

The Communist thought reform programs, Hunter claimed in a later volume, were capable of transforming a person into a "puppet" or "human robot" and of inserting new beliefs and thought processes into a captive body. Hunter formalized what we will term the "robot" or "brainwashing" model of psychologically coercive social influence. As portrayed by Hunter and those writers whom he influenced, brainwashing is a sinister psycho-technology assumed to be highly effective in overpowering human will through means of deception, induced hypnotic states, and Pavlovian conditioning, which undermine resistance to persuasion. Initial individual dispositions are simply overwhelmed and are thus not major factors in predicting who will be influenced by the process.

The "robot" mind control paradigm was expressed in various works by writers such as Hunter, William Sargent, Joost Van Meerloo, Aldous Huxley, Farber *et al.*, and others. Several of these works credited the Russian scientist I. Pavlov, working with dogs, with discovering a way of inducing a primitive mental state in which both animals and humans exhibit an enhanced susceptibility to conditioning. A primitive trance state of high suggestibility could thus, it was thought, be induced by various means, e.g., hypnosis, in which individuals could more easily be programmed by scientific conditioning procedures.

Some writers maintained that this primitive state of consciousness was rare in the United States where reason and education prevailed, but was the normal state of consciousness in other, especially Oriental and preliterate cultures, and was moreover associated with religious rituals, including, in one formulation, early Methodist revivals. The connection between the brainwashing model and religion thus did not begin with recent "cults."

With respect to totalitarian societies also, the robot perspective was frequently expanded from the analysis of coercive indoctrination in prison situations to a general model of totalitarian control of whole societies. According to authors utilizing this paradigm, the general public within totalitarian societies were controlled by technical innovations in communication techniques, such as hypnosis and conditioning which allegedly operated by means of mass rallies and propaganda. As with the analysis

of interrogation situations, the robot perspectives focused upon supposedly irresistible techniques that overwhelm free will and downplayed the fear of the coercive apparatus of the state or the voluntary acceptance of totalitarian ideologies by people who were attracted to them for their own reasons.

At least with respect to coercive indoctrination and interrogation situations, the available data on approximately 7000 Korean War American POW's does not support the robot model. More than 30% of the prisoners died but approximately 4500 were ultimately repatriated. Of these only 21 POW's refused repatriation, and of these 10 subsequently changed their minds. Thus, only 11 out of 4500 persons, approximately one-fifth of 1% of those who survived imprisonment, arguably accepted anti-American perspectives.

Comparison with turncoat rates of American POW's in former wars indicates that the rate during the Korean War was the lowest in our history. Thus, these data indicate that the alleged overpowering brainwashing techniques of the Chinese and Korean Communists not only were completely ineffective, but if anything they actually encouraged continued allegiance to American ideology and policies.

Despite the lack of effectiveness of Chinese indoctrination techniques revealed by these statistics, the government nevertheless hired researchers to study returning POW's and to evaluate the nature of Communist brainwashing. Edgar Schein, Robert Lifton, and Albert Biderman each headed projects on POW brainwashing funded by the armed forces and given armed forces cooperation. The reports of their research on Communist POW's by Lifton and by Schein foreshadowed their later, more ambitious research studies on the nature and effect of the attempted Chinese Communist thought reform of Western civilian prisoners in China.

The CIA appointed Cornell University psychiatrists Lawrence Hinkle and Harold Wolff to conduct its own secret study of all the different varieties of alleged Communist brainwashing, e.g., Russian show trials, Chinese Communist thought reform of their own countrymen as well as of imprisoned Westerners in China, and of Korean War POW's. The Hinkle and Wolff project was given access to all the CIA secret files and they conducted interviews which the CIA arranged with former Communist interrogators and prisoners alike.

A declassified version of the Hinkle and Wolff CIA sponsored study was eventually published and was considered by other experts to be the definitive U.S. government work on the subject of Communist brainwashing. In addition to Hinkle and Wolff's own research, this report summarized the results of the government funded research on Korean War brainwashing by Schein, Lifton, Biderman, and others. In general, according to Hinkle and Wolff, the Maoist techniques were not novel or extraordinary or based on advanced science. There was no evidence of the use of hypnotic processes or induced altered states of consciousness.

Compared to Soviet methods, the Chinese Communists did innovate in their emphasis on fervently propagandizing military captives. Constant propaganda was combined with the alternation of long isolation with peer group pressures, severe debility, torture, and extreme threat and total uncertainty about the future. In re-educating dissidents and deviants, the Chinese departed from the Soviet preference for one on one, interrogator–interogatee interaction (the "Darkness at Noon" model) to emphasize peer group dynamics and a managed interpersonal environment.

With respect to the effectiveness of Communist methods, Hinkle and Wolff confirmed the impression conveyed by the failure of the CIA's own brainwashing research projects. That is, no known brainwashing techniques, whether German, Communist, or American, have been capable of indoctrinating people with political or social attitudes conflicting with ones to which they are naturally attracted. Specifically, Hinkle and Wolff argued that the Communists have not been successful in converting Americans to Communist doctrine in either of the two well-known situations—American POW's in Korea or American civilians imprisoned in Communist China—in which brainwashing theorists such as Hunter argued that coerced conversions had occurred.

In addition to the fact that very few American POW's refused repatriation, Hinkle and Wolff pointed out that even those few who did refuse did so for reasons other than conversion to Communism, e.g., fear of punishment for collaborative activities that they had engaged in for practical rather than ideological reasons. With respect to Western civilians imprisoned in China who upon their release issued statements to the press which sounded sympathetic to Communism, Hinkle and Wolff's repudiation of a brainwashing explanation was, if anything, even more unequivocal.

According to Hinkle and Wolff, who claimed to have access to intensive research on a number of American civilians allegedly brainwashed in China, all of those studied were sympathetic to Chinese Communism and antipathetic to American values *before* their imprisonment by the Chinese. Conse-

quently, the Communist values that they expressed upon their release were little different from the ones that they had long been committed to before the thought reform experience. Contrary to the sensationalistic accounts of their supposedly brainwashed viewpoints by the American press and by authors such as Hunter, Sargent, and Meerloo, no substantial change in their viewpoints had occurred under the impact of brainwashing.

The Chinese thought reform methods were also demystified by Edgar Schein, a social psychologist, whose well-known volume, *Coercive Persuasion*, pronounced the attempted thought reform of Western civilian prisoners by the Chinese to have been a relative failure. Only one or two of Schein's 15 subjects who had undergone Chinese thought reform showed any substantial degree of positive attitude change toward Communism, and even in these isolated instances such change stopped well short of conversion to Communism. The rest of his subjects showed only behavioral compliance to the demands of their captors, without significant ideological change. Schein also criticized the elements of brainwashing analyses which emphasized dissociative states, conditioning, suggestibility, and defective thinking. Schein found that such altered states and exotic techniques were not at all characteristic of Chinese thought reform.

Schein emphasized that rather than such alleged brainwashing techniques, the physically coercive setting and methods of Chinese thought reform define Communist coercive persuasion, which involves a setting from which there is no escape. On the other hand, Schein affirms the presence of the purely psychological, i.e., nonphysical, elements of coercive persuasion in conventional American institutions such as reputable religious orders, fraternities and sororities, rehabilitation organizations, etc.

Furthermore, according to Schein, the purely psychological techniques used in Communist coercive persuasion, and in many normal American institutions as well, are not inherently objectionable. Such techniques should be judged, he claims, according to the nature of the values which they are intended to promote, not because they, when judged simply as methods of influence, are inherently inimical to human freedom.

III. INVESTIGATING THE "PSYCHOLOGY OF TOTALISM"

An alternative to the "Robot Model" of extremist indoctrination emerged out of the concern of many intellectuals and scholars about proliferating totalitarian movements and governments and their interest in the kinds of persons who are attracted to totalitarianism.

Although the Mussolini regime began in the 1920s to use the term "totalitarianism" in a positive sense to denote monolithic national unity, many intellectuals were troubled by the rise of Fascism and dedicated themselves to the study of totalitarian states, parties, and ideologies. This intellectual phenomenon became the basis for a large and multi-faceted genre of "totalitarian studies," a part of which dealt with the psychology of totalitarian movements. Initially in the 1930s such studies focused primarily upon the analysis of developments in Fascist states, e.g., Italy, Germany, and in some interpretations Spain, Japan, and Rumania. After the Second World War, Communist states such as the Soviet Union and Communist China were also generally included in most analyses.

The most influential general analyses of totalitarianism as a uniquely modern political phenomenon appeared in books by Hannah Arendt (1950) and Carl Friedrich and Zbigniew Brzezinski (1956). These books synthesized more specialized studies by other scholars of totalitarianism into overall interpretations of the phenomenon. In addition, a seminal conference on the nature of totalitarianism was held by the American Academy of Arts and Sciences in Boston in 1953. The committee planning the conference was chaired by Carl Friedrich and those attending included the creme of scholars in totalitarian studies including Arendt, Alex Inkeles, Else Frenkel-Brunswick, Erik Erikson, George F. Kennan, and many others. The papers delivered at the conference were published in a book edited by Carl Friedrich.

These general analyses by Arendt and by Friedrich and Brzezinski, and most of the papers in the conference volume, shared a common framework of assumptions about totalitarianism which had developed in the previous 20 years of scholarship, and were, especially Arendt's, immensely influential with other scholars as well as the educated general public.

The books by Arendt and by Friedrich and Brzezinski, as well as most other general analyses within totalitarian studies, include the following criteria as characteristic of totalitarianism as a mode of ideological societal reconstruction: (1) Totalitarian *ideology* is apocalyptic and millenarian and identifies a holy remnant or vanguard elite that will lead the world into a utopian new age. Totalitarian ideology is basically manichean, i.e., it poses absolute black and white alternatives for human kind, society, and the individual. The state is identified as the key agent of a purposive, revolutionary historical process. (2) A thorough *structural reorganization of society* is implemented to re-shape all significant social institutions in terms of the messianic ideology and the state assumes an unprecedented degree of control over all social institutions. (3) The state maintains a monopoly over all media of communication and all communication must conform to ideological tenets. (4) The systematic use of *terror* and extreme physical coercion serves as the essential device to maintain social control. (5) Certain social groups are designated as the carriers of evil and are considered to be beyond redemption. No limits are imposed upon the measures which should be taken in combatting and destroying such internal and external enemies. (6) Totalitarian societies have unlimited expansionist intentions, i.e., they intend to use force to establish worldwide domination of other societies.

This view of totalitarianism does not involve the theory that commitment to totalitarian ideologies and practices are involuntary except in the mundane sense that behavioral conformity is coercively enforced by harsh physical means. A certain percentage of the population is viewed as being sincerely committed to a totalitarian view of the world, but such people have converted to the millenarian viewpoint because of their own inner motives. Another segment of the population are opposed to totalitarian beliefs, but are coerced into behavioral compliance through physical force. Many people are intermediate between these two extremes, being neither clearly in favor of nor clearly opposed to the goals and beliefs of the revolution, but they conform to its demands because of a mixture of fear of the consequences of disobedience and sincere but half-hearted belief in its possible value. Contrary to the brainwashing paradigm, none of these groups have lost their inner free will in any novel ways that are unique to totalitarian societies.

A. Pre-existing Motives for Conversion to Totalitarian Social Movements

Fascist and Communist social movements existed within the societies they eventually came to control prior to the point at which such control was achieved. Members of such movements, or people like them, become the segment of the population in totalitarian societies who are "true believers" once totalitarian domination has been achieved.

Research shows that motivational predispositions to join totalitarian social movements exist prior to any actual contact with such movements. The determination of who actually joins such movements results from the interaction of individual totalitarian, or authoritarian, motives with the extreme dualistic absolutism and apocalypticism of the totalist ideology which satisfies such yearnings.

A distinctive "totalist" psychology, that is the psychological dimension of totalitarian societies, ideologies, and individuals, was described by Robert Lifton in his book *Chinese Thought Reform and the Psychology of Totalism*. Lifton's book reported the results of an interview study of people who had undergone the thought reform process in China, the process that Hunter and other brainwashing theorists considered to be the most clear-cut example of brainwashing. Lifton explicitly attempted to evaluate the brainwashing concept in his study, and finished by repudiating both the brainwashing term and the concept of overwhelmed will which it signified.

Lifton replaced the brainwashing concept with the concept of "totalism" in describing the thought reform process. Both the term and the concept of totalism were originally defined by Erik Erikson in a 1953 article (Wholeness and Totality—A Psychiatric Contribution) which constituted his contribution to the volume of papers resulting from the historically important 1953 conference on totalitarianism sponsored by the American Academy of Arts and Sciences that we described above.

Erikson later expanded on the totalism concept in his 1958 book *Young Man Luther,* in which he also further developed the concepts of "negative identity" and "negative conscience" which are constituent elements of totalism as he defines it. Lifton draws upon both of these discussions of totalism in his use of Erikson's concept in his book, and upon related passages in Erikson's other books and articles as well.

In the article in which he originated the concept of totalism, Erikson maintained that persons with certain personality characteristics are particularly attracted to movements, governments, and ideologies which manifest a characteristically totalitarian ideological and persuasive style. He defined totalism as "man's inclination, under certain conditions to undergo . . . that sudden total realignment and, as it were, co-alignment which accompanies conversion to the totalitarian conviction that the state may

and must have absolute power over the minds as well as the lives and the fortunes of its citizens." (p. 159).

Both Erikson and Lifton are psychoanalysts, and the concept of totalism involves an application of psychoanalytic conceptions of child development to the issue of the types of persons who are attracted to totalitarianism. Erikson's formulation of the psychology of totalism was strongly influenced by a tradition of the psychoanalytic analysis of totalitarian influence which originated in the study of the types of persons attracted to Fascist political orientations. Leading authors in this tradition include Wilhelm Reich, Eric Fromm, and the co-authors of the landmark study *The Authoritarian Personality,* Theodore Adorno, Daniel Levin, Else Frenkel-Brunswick, and Nevitt Sanford.

According to this tradition of thought, people attracted to Fascism are also ethnocentric, i.e., prejudiced against cultural, religious, and racial groups different from their own. Such people are also strongly attracted to hierarchically organized social systems which rigidly control the lives of those caught up in them. According to the authors of *The Authoritarian Personality,* these tendencies result from being reared in circumstances in which children are rigidly controlled and forbidden to express aggression towards their parents.

People reared in these circumstances, according to authors in this tradition, tend to have a polarized self-sense in which a precariously maintained, unrealistically positive self-concept is always on the verge of being overthrown by a powerful but largely unconscious negative self-image. Such a child becomes "extra-punitive," i.e., always on the lookout for someone else to blame when things go wrong.

Totalitarian ideologies appeal to such people because they rigidly divide the world into the saved and the damned, and thus support the maintenance of unrealistically positive self-concepts by encouraging the projection onto scapegoats of unconscious negative self-images. Totalitarian social systems also reproduce on a larger scale the rigidly hierarchical structure characteristic of authoritarian family systems and thus appeal to people who have difficulty functioning in circumstances that require more individual creativity and personal responsibility than they are used to.

Although Erikson's concept of totalism was influenced by this tradition of thought, and shares its key assumptions, Erikson himself had earlier strongly influenced the theory of authoritarianism described in *The Authoritarian Personality*. Early in the Second World War, Erikson published a now classic article upon the development of Hitler's own authoritarianism and the general cultural and fmilial circumstances that created widespread authoritarianism in Germany. The conception of the relationship between authoritarian child-rearing practices and the development of an authoritarian personality expressed in the book *The Authoritarian Personality* owes much to Erikson's earlier article.

Erikson's later concept of totalism broadens the concept of authoritarianism from Fascist to Communist types of totalitarianism, and to other types of totalitarian influence as well. Erikson's thought on the relationship between personality formation and attraction to totalitarianism both contributed to and drew from the larger psychoanalytic tradition concerned with these issues. Neither Lifton's nor Erikson's use of the totalism concept can be properly understood outside of its relationship to this larger tradition of thought and research.

As indicated above, Lifton's book interpreted the experiences of his subjects, who had undergone Communist thought reform, in terms of Erikson's concept of totalism. (He extensively interviewed 25 Westerners and 15 Chinese who were subjected to Chinese Thought Reform. The Westerners were imprisoned during the process.) Following Erikson, Lifton stated "By this ungainly phrase [ideological totalism] I mean to suggest the coming together of immoderate idology with equally immoderate individual [totalist] character traits—an extremist meeting ground between people and ideas." (p. 419)

In analyzing influence within the thought reform environment as resulting from an interaction between individual predispositions toward totalitarianism and the characteristics of totalitarian ideology, both Erikson and Lifton locate the psychology of totalism approach squarely within the perspective of general totalitarian studies. By showing that Erikson's concept of individual totalism as a characterological gestalt accounts for the variation in responsiveness to totalitarian ideology, even within thought reform prisons, Lifton persuasively repudiates the brainwashing theory that thought reform consists of specialized communication techniques that convert people to totalitarian ideology against their will or their intrinsic predispositions.

Parenthetically, Schein, in his book *Coercive Persuasion,* which described his research upon the thought reform of Western civilians in China, was also influenced by the theoretical tradition concerned with discovering the inner motives for conversion to totalitarianism, of which Erikson's concept of totalism was a part, as well as by general totalitarian studies. He discusses the views of Fromm, Erikson, Adorno *et al.*, and Hoffer upon predispositions to totalitarianism in a chapter of Coercive Persuasion entitled "A Passion For Unanimity," wherein he also discusses more general analyses of totalitarianism such as that of Friedrich and Brzezinski. (The title of this chapter is probably taken from a chapter subsection from the Brzezinski book entitled "The Terror and the Passion for Unanimity".) Psychological predispositions to totalitarianism are also discussed by Schein in his chapters "The Special Role of Guilt in Coercive Persuasion" and "A Socio-Psychological Analysis of Coercive Persuasion."

Insofar as Lifton's book involves a description of conversion to totalitarian ideology, it is more a speculative application of Erikson's concept of totalism than it is an empirically grounded scientific study. Only 2 of Lifton's 25 Western subjects and none of his Chinese subjects substantially changed their political and social opinions and attitudes as a result of their thought reform experience. (Neither of the 2 subjects who were influenced converted to Communism, but they did become somewhat more sympathetic to Chinese Communism than they had been at the beginning of their thought reform experience.) Lifton could scarcely have generated a description of the general characteristics of the psychology of totalitarianism based upon the experiences of only 2 subjects, neither of whom actually converted to Communism.

Insofar as it was actually an empirical study at all, then, Lifton's project was more a demonstration of the failure of thought reform to influence the 38 of his 40 subjects who did not appreciably change their attitudes, than it was of the nature of conversion to totalitarianism. Lifton thus confirmed earlier studies, e.g., Hinkle and Wolff, as well as the failure of the American research to create deployable agents, which had also indicated little or no evidence that people substantially change their political opinions primarily as a result of attempted brainwashing.

Moreover, as we have indicated, Lifton found that each of his two subjects who were influenced by thought reform had strong totalistic predispositions prior to their experience. In this respect, also, Lifton's results confirm the results of earlier studies, e.g., Hinkle and Wolff's, which indicated that those who emerge from thought reform sympathetic to

Communism already have totalistic characteristics prior to their participation in the process. Lifton's overall results thus confirm the results of earlier studies which indicated that the Communists possessed no capacity to convert people against their will to Communist ideology.

In the years since the publication of Lifton's book, his phenomenological description of the eight psychological themes that constitute totalistic ideological influence is sometimes treated, particularly in a popular or journalistic context, as equivalent to a general formulation of the characteristics of brainwashing, that is as characterizing a process that coercively changes people's political or religious opinions against their will. The misinterpretation of Lifton's description of the general features of totalitarian influence as being equivalent to a brainwashing explanation of involuntary political or religious conversion has probably been partly due to the cold war anti-communist climate which prevailed when his work was published. The misinterpretation also probably owes something to the cultural ubiquity and dominance of the robot or Manchurian Candidate view of the nature of totalitarian influence that emerged after the Korean War.

However it developed, the interpretation of Lifton's analysis of the general features of ideological totalism as equivalent to an endorsement of the concept of involuntary brainwashing is clearly mistaken. Lifton uses the term "brainwashing" in several places, yet he tries to demystify the term, which, in his view, has acquired a misleading connotation of "an all-powerful, irresistible, unfathomable and magical method of achieving total control over the human mind." Such usage "makes the word a rallying point for fear, resentment, urges for submission, justification for failure, irresponsible accusation, and for a wide gamut of emotional extremism."

By the end of the 1960s, then, two different models of extreme social influence and manipulative indoctrination associated with totalistic groups had emerged, the robot/brainwashing model on the one hand and the totalitarian influence model on the other. The two models have distinctly different emphases in terms of four partly interrelated issues.

1. The brainwashing process as sought after by Nazi and American government researchers and as described by Edward Hunter and others with regard to Korean POW's, Chinese thought reform, and Soviet show trials is viewed by its proponents as a very effective psycho-technology which overrides the will of helpless, passive victims. This conceptualization is not born out of by the studies of Schein, Lifton, Hinkle, and Wolff, and others who found that Communist indoctrination was ineffective in coercively altering the political and social opinions of people opposed to Communist ideology.

2. Adherents of the totalitarian influence approach tended to see extreme physical coercion as intrinsic to Communist social control in general and to the thought reform process in particular. From this point of view, physical coercion is the sole means by which Communist societies and the thought reform process produce involuntary compliance. Brainwashing approaches on the other hand maintain that Communist societies and the thought reform process produce involuntary compliance primarily through the involuntary alteration of political opinions and identities. From the brainwashing perspective, physical coercion is not essential to producing involuntary compliance in Communist societies.

3. From the standpoint of brainwashing theory, the inescapable potency of this psycho-technology renders individual predilections irrelevant. Scholars within the totalitarian influence tradition, on the other hand, contend that those who convert to totalitarian ideologies and movements are predisposed to do so because of pre-existing personality characteristics and ideological preferences.

4. Finally, the robot brainwashing model draws a sharp line between indoctrinated totalists and the rest of the population, particularly freedom-loving Americans. The latter are viewed as being innately opposed to totalism but as unable to resist it if they encounter brainwashers because of their omnipotent technology of mind control. In contrast, Fromm, Adorno, Erikson, Lifton, Schein, and others do not sharply differentiate between indoctrinated cadres and members of a Western culture which is itself permeated by proto-totalist themes, as are many of its social groups.

From the point of view of Adorno *et al.*, Erikson, Lifton, and the other theorists of the totalitarian influence approach, individuals in Western culture experience in varying degrees the tensions which fuel totalist movements, and most participate in conformist social groups, e.g., religions, college fraternities, the armed services, dysfunctional families, which are totalistic to one degree or another. This prophetic critique of conventional society is an intrinsic part of the totalitarian influence approach to explaining totalistic conversion, and it tends to blur the boundary between pervasive authoritarian conformism in the culture and the totalitarianism of extremist groups.

IV. CONTROVERSIES OVER CULTS

After the Korean War and the furor over the treatment of POW's subsided, popular media and even scholarly interest in brainwashing declined. There was a resurgence in the mid-1970s, which was initially associated with the criminal career and trial of Patricia Hearst.

Beginning in the middle 1970s, an intensive anticult movement began to form which adopted the brainwashing argument as a central dimension of its ideology. This movement worked to oppose the apparent popularity of esoteric religious or religio-therapy movements ("cults") such as The Church of Scientology, The Unification Church, Hare Krishna, or The Children of God, which had initially at least gained most of their converts from the 1960s counterculture. According to anticult ideology, such counterculture religions employ brainwashing techniques to beguile and enslave participants and to enable the latter to be ruthlessly exploited.

Initially the primary social practice adopted by the anticult movement for combatting alleged cultic brainwashing was "deprogramming." Deprogramming is an intensive influence practice whereby individuals are removed from residence in religious groups and subjected to counterindoctrination. Deprogramming usually transpires under conditions of forcible restraint following a kidnapping, sometimes involves legally mandated incarceration imposed under conservatorship laws, and occasionally occurs through the voluntary agreement of the convert.

Deprogramming was designed to free converts from the alleged psychic imprisonment caused by cultic brainwashing. Sometimes it was successful in convincing people to withdraw from the religious group, sometimes not. When it was not successful litigation often ensued, either kidnapping charges or disputes over the use of conservatorship laws in support of deprogramming.

Although litigation over deprogramming persists, by the early 1980s, legal reverses had led to less reliance upon coercive deprogramming as the primary anticult tactic. The anticult movement had switched its emphasis to civil actions against cults for fraud, infliction of emotional distress, false imprisonment, and other legal causes of action. These claims are buttressed in court by testimony about the effects of psychologically coercive cultic conditioning in radically undermining the personal autonomy and responsibility of participants and disorienting and psychologically damaging the latter. Similar claims have arisen in a variety of other legal areas including child custody cases, prosecutions against members or leaders of certain groups for various crimes (e.g., child abuse), and prosecutions of former members who seek to base defenses of insanity or diminished capacity on claims about mind control and disorienting trauma.

Throughout the 1980s, litigants' legal briefs and supportive expert testimony and depositions tended to refer to "brainwashing," "coercive persuasion," and "thought reform" and often to the "foundational" work in this area by Edgar Schein, Robert Lifton, and Hinkle and Wolff. Margaret Singer, a clinical psychologist, and Richard Ofshe, a sociologist, were the most active anticult witnesses, and they also co-authored articles formulating their version of anticult brainwashing theory. Singer and Ofshe also played leadership roles in the anticult movement itself, serving on the boards of anticult organizations and publications, and giving talks at their conferences.

Although anticult witnesses claim to be using the theories of totalitarian influence developed by Schein, Lifton, and Hinkle and Wolff, their actual testimony bears the hallmarks of the brainwashing arguments developed by Hunter, Sargent, Farber *et al.*, and others. Anticult witnesses claim that cultic brainwashing regularly produces involuntary acceptance of ideologies and memberships which bear no relationship to converts predisposing motives and true beliefs. In some cases, the identity displayed by converts is described as, in effect, a dissociated false self while the true self is allegedly suppressed by cultic manipulations.

Anticult witnesses typically allege that such mental enslavement is produced by "hypnotic" processes, which are allegedly constituted by normal religious activities, e.g., meditation, repetitive chanting, guided imagery or boring lectures, as well as practices which allegedly induce "primitive" states of consciousness through other means such as pseudo-psychotherapeutic emotional arousal or physiological debilitation supposedly resulting from poor diet or too little sleep.

Anticult witnesses testify that such altered states of consciousness constitute a primitive condition of mind in which suggestibility is enhanced and in which the "conditioning" procedures of cults are more effective. They insist that physical coercion is not an essential factor in totalitarian influence. They also insist that there is a clear dividing line other than physical coercion between the influence tactics of totalitarian groups and cults, on the one hand, and those of conventional institutions such as the Catholic Church, the army, college fraternities, mental hospitals, and so on. (They have considerable difficulty articulating what that dividing line consists of, however. The only criteria that they have come up with are exceedingly imprecise, e.g., the alleged "intensity and pervasiveness of cultic conditioning procedures.")

In several important cases, the robot brainwashing paradigm of Farber, Harlow, and West was explicitly used as the framework for describing the conditioning of the former cultic allegiances and attitudes of the plaintiffs. The altered states allegedly induced by cultic rituals are said to produce intense sensations which gurus and prophets falsely interpret in persuasive terms which manipulate the practitioners to submit to the group and its leadership.

Richard Delgado, in a series of law review articles, has articulated the basic legal rationale for heightened control of religious movements by the government, e.g., civil suits such as those described above, laws regulating religious practices, and conservatorships for the purposes of involuntary deprogramming. Delgado's analysis is designed to explain why the constitutional protection of freedom of religion does not apply where cults are concerned. Basically what his argument boils down to is that if conversion to a religion is involuntary, than prohibitions against governmental regulation of religion do not really apply.

Delgado argues that state intervention is legitimate when a person joins a group under conditions in which consensuality (or voluntariness) is not present. Delgado's formulation of what such involuntariness or loss of free will at the hands of cults actually consists of is heavily dependent upon robot brainwashing conceptions, however. He avoids citing any of the methodologically superior studies on conversion to new religious movements that have failed to confirm the brainwashing analyses.

Delgado's formulation, which has influenced a number of appellate court outcomes, treats deception as a functional equivalent of physical coercion

in terms of bringing the indoctrinee onto the premises and keeping him or her there pending application of the high powered brainwashing psychotechnology. In 1988, a California Supreme Court decision influenced by Delgado's point of view abridged the constitutional protection which would otherwise be accorded even to religious speech acts constituting "coercive persuasion" in the special case in which a group has concealed its identity. The legal strategy of those making claims of destructive psychological manipulation against cults is to expand the boundary condition of concealment of the identity of the organization to include conduct such as not warning recruits of controversial anticult allegations that group practices and rituals such as meditation or chanting produce dangerous dissociative states and heightened suggestibility.

The anticult strategy of basing civil suits upon robot brainwashing testimony was initially, in the late 1970s and early to middle 1980s, very effective. Juries were almost without exception responsive to this line of testimony and were for the most part not persuaded by contrary testimony put on by defense experts which pointed out the scholarly deficiencies of brainwashing analyses. Survey evidence indicates that the general public widely accepts the accuracy of cultic brainwashing analyses, and the widespread acceptance of such theories is apparently too deeply ingrained for scientific witnesses for the defense to be able to penetrate it.

Several cases resulted in judgments for the plaintiffs in the 20 to 30 million dollar range. One of these judgments required a number of state organizations of the Hare Krishna movement to go into receivership and put the continued existence of this movement in the American context in peril. Some knowledgeable observers contended that as a result of these events the separation of church and state in the United States was in greater doubt than it had ever been.

Recently, i.e., from 1985 until the present, the legal pendulum seems to be swinging the other way, primarily because of the judicial application of rules with respect to the necessity that expert testimony must meet general scientific standards of acceptability before it can be presented to a jury. Several important decisions have been overturned on appeal on the grounds that the robot brainwashing paradigm is not generally accepted as valid in the relevant scientific community, i.e., in psychology and sociology, and therefore should not be used as a basis for the circumvention of governmental guarantees of freedom of religion. (Margaret Singer was the primary witness in two of these cases.)

Moreover, several courts have held in advance of the actual trials in anticult brainwashing cases that anticult brainwashing witnesses could not testify because their theories were not generally accepted in the academic world. In two of these cases, Margaret Singer's and Richard Ofshe's testimony was specifically excluded upon the grounds of its lack of scientific acceptance, and also because their testimony did not represent an accurate interpretation of its claimed theoretical foundation, i.e., Lifton's and Schein's theories of totalitarian influence.

A. Scientific Problems with Anticult Brainwashing Testimony

For the most part, crude and sensational robot/brainwashing, "Manchurian Candidate" theories such as flourished in the 1950s and early 1960s are currently not taken seriously in the academic world, although they appear in popular volumes with evocations of cultists "snapping" in and out of states of mind control. As we have indicated, models which are utilized in claims of psychological coercion made against cults tend to veer in the "robot" direction, particularly in the form in which such theories are presented in court testimony and depositions.

Formulations that veer in the robot direction tend to have the following characteristics. (1) Cultist mind control is seen as very effective. (2) Predisposing motivational factors are either denied or are trivialized as mere buttons pushed by manipulative indoctrinators. Predisposing factors are definitely not viewed as evidence that participation in cults is voluntary. (3) Dissociative states, hypnotic processes, and altered states of consciousness are emphasized, as well as consequent patterns of defective or impaired thinking. (4) Indoctrinees are presumed to thoroughly lose their capacity to make decisions, i.e., there is a definite loss of free will. (5) "Mind controlling" organizations are regarded as utilizing techniques of influence which are qualitatively distinct from those used in mainstream institutions. These five emphases are attributes of robot brainwashing arguments which are contradicted by the theories of totalitarian influence developed by Lifton, Schein, Erikson, Adorno *et al.,* and others.

In addition to the incompatibility of robot brainwashing testimony with its claimed theoretical foundation, it also is generally incompatible with almost all of the research upon the question of brainwashing

in cults which has been published in mainstream scientific journals. There has been abundant research upon "new religions" or "cults" in recent decades. A number of trends have emerged in these findings which appear to be incompatible with brainwashing models but may be more consistent with a theory of interaction between motivational factors and the properties of totalitarianism.

1. Research has indicated that there is considerable interest in exotic religious groups among young persons that is not explainable in terms of coercive influence. Many students indicate that they would be interested in associations with alternative groups even before they have ever had actual contact with one. It is not, therefore, a matter of initially hostile persons (such as POW's) who may subsequently face an overriding of their will and radical alteration of their ideas through thought reform. There is a pool of pre-converts with pre-existing orientations compatible with involvement in some esoteric or controversial groups.

2. A number of studies have examined the process of induction into controversial and stigmatized movements such as the Unification Church ("Moonies"). Such conversion usually consists of several stages of increasingly more intensive involvement occurring over several weeks or months, rather than being a simple all or nothing decision. It is apparent from such studies that only a small percentage of persons who go through each stage of influence actually go on to the next stage of the process.

Those who actually complete the process and become full-fledged members are a very small fraction of those who are initially contacted by the movement. The process, therefore, cannot reasonably be portrayed as overwhelmingly effective in overriding individual predilections. Moreover, questionnaires and interviews administered at each stage of the process indicate that the people who continue at each stage are being persuaded by theological arguments and symbols rather than being mindlessly responsive to suggestion because of being in a primitive state of consciousness.

A careful study of the Unification influence process by Eileen Barker, an English sociologist, rejected the notion that an overwhelming external stimulus from the influence procedures themselves accounted for the (few) conversions which were affected. Her book reporting this study won an award for distinguished scientific achievement by the leading professional association in the sociology and psychology of religion.

3. Numerous studies have indicated that most converts do not remain long in high-demand, marginal religious groups, particularly highly stigmatized communal groups such as the Unification Church. Such high-demand groups appear to be somewhat like "revolving doors," with persons continually coming and going. The average length of membership in the Unification Church, for instance, is 2 years.

Moreover, most people leave such groups voluntarily rather than through involuntary deprogramming or through other contact with the anticult movement. This pattern of sporadic affiliation and disaffiliation seems more consistent with the typical voluntary, bidirectional influence process between individuals and groups in a pluralistic society than it does with a totally unidirectional process in which an individual is a helpless captive of overwhelmingly external influence.

On the other hand, groups such as the Meher Baba movement, which are not totalistic, not communal, and which are compatible with other social involvements and normal career tracks appear to keep their members over a longer period. The latter type of groups do not generally tend to be controversial or to attract allegations of brainwashing.

4. There are a number of clinical studies that indicate that involvement in certain demanding and controversial groups produces a sense of well-being or "relief from neurotic distress" on the part of many converts. This is quite consistent with the psychology of totalism approach, which has shown that totalitarian or authoritarian movements tend to reduce conscious emotional pain resulting from pre-existing identity confusion or negative identities. The findings that alternative religions reduce neurotic distress are incompatible with brainwashing analyses, on the other hand, which insist that such involvements have a uniformly negative impact upon mental health.

Other clinical studies have indicated an absence of serious psychopathology in some highly stigmatized groups, although depth psychological factors such as those intrinsic to totalitarian influence approaches such as those of Fromm, Adorno *et al.*, Erikson, etc., have usually not been dealt with in these studies.

5. A number of studies have indicated that ex-devotees are much more likely to attest that they had been "brainwashed" by and to strongly recriminate against a group if they had been forcibly removed from the group and if they had substantial subsequent contact with "anticult" networks which conduct deprogramming and other "rehabilitation" programs, e.g., "exit counseling," ex-member support groups, etc. The vast majority of ex-members, on the other hand, who leave groups voluntarily and have no substantial contact with the anticult movement tend to view their experiences with these groups much more favorably and do not see themselves as having been brainwashed.

Authors of these studies tend to interpret these findings as indicating that the brainwashing view of cultic membership results from indoctrination by the anticult movement, which itself has some of the characteristics of a totalistic social movement, rather than being an objective empirical description of the experience.

6. There are a number of well-designed studies indicating cognitive competence among devotees of certain controversial groups. This would seem to disconfirm the more lurid robot brainwashing analyses which maintain that members of totalistic groups subsist during their tenures in such groups in primitive, dissociated states of consciousness.

7. Some research has evaluated the existence of personality factors predisposing individuals to join totalistic religious movements. Anthony and Robbins conducted participant observation studies of the Unification Church and reported some qualitative impressions and phenomenological analyses of the conversion process in terms of the conversion of negative to contrast identities along the lines described by Erikson and Lifton. Another researcher published a study which interpreted the conversion process in a Jesus movement commune in terms of a totalistic conversion process. Anthony and his research team at the Graduate Theological Union, one of whom was Nevitt Sanford, one of the co-authors of *The Authoritarian Personality*, evaluated the incidence of authoritarianism in a variety of alternative religious movements. They administered an updated version of the F scale, which is designed to measure the personality syndrome underlying attraction to authoritarian movements. The average scale score did vary widely from movement to movement, indicating that variation in individual totalism may indeed be a factor in explaining why people join specific movements and are not attracted to others. In the typology of new religious movements published in the book *Spiritual Choices*, Anthony and Ecker report that one group of alternative reli-

gions, which includes the People's Temple and Synanon, is characterized by authoritarianism and contrast identities among their members.

In addition to these few studies on psychological totalitarianism in alternative religions, considerable research has been done over a period of 40 years indicating that some traditionally conservative religious groups attract people who score highly on various measures of totalitarianism, e.g., the F scale or Rokeach's Dogmatism scale. Such people also tend to score highly upon measures of ethnocentrism. (Some of the most important research of this sort is reported in the books upon "right-ring authoritarianism" by Bob Altemeyer.)

It seems likely that these results upon certain Christian groups would generalize to alternative religious movements or cults, as many of them have theological and social beliefs that seem similar to those in some fundamentalist denominations. These results are also compatible with Lifton's insistence that fundamentalist religious movements are totalistic, and with the few studies specifically evaluating totalism in new religions. In general, then, there is some intriguing evidence supporting a totalitarian influence explanation of conversion to alternative religions, and this would seem to be a fruitful direction for further exploration. The same research tends to contradict brainwashing explanations for conversion, however, because proponents of the latter paradigm insist that people who join cults do so only because of external influence and not because of personality characteristics that predate contact with the group.

In the legal arena the outcomes of claims pressed about cults in various kinds of cases have been mixed. Nevertheless, in recent years those critics of cults who employ a brainwashing model have consistently experienced key setbacks. Certain legal weaknesses of the model have emerged: (1) Brainwashing theories have been seen to challenge the authenticity and truth of devotees' faith in a manner which elicits the constraints of the first amendment. Attempts to explicitly legalize the coercive deprogramming of adult converts through guardianships or conservatorships issued to parents fell afoul of this objection. (2) Absent the objective standard of physical restraint or threat, experts wanting to testify about cultic thought reform have had difficulty in credibly "drawing the line" between influence procedures which allegedly are and those which are not so overwhelmingly coercive as to incapacitate

converts such that their commitment becomes involuntary.

Given some degree of emotional intensity, group solidarity, and experiential ritual behavior such as meditation, almost any group can be accused of using psychological coercion by virtue of alleged hypnotic trance states, emotional manipulation, and pressure for group conformity. Physical constraint or threat, which might provide some objective criteria for line drawing, has been explicitly rejected by cultic brainwashing theorists since the groups being considered clearly do not use physical coercion as a characteristic mechanism of social control or indoctrination.

Decisions in a series of cases have found that Lifton's theory of thought reform may not be used as the basis for brainwashing testimony in the absence of extreme physical coercion. Several courts have found that in the absence of scientifically credible criteria for drawing the line between groups that brainwash and those that do not, brainwashing testimony expresses a constitutionally impermissible attempt to restrict the freedom of religious belief.

The lack of scientific criteria for drawing the line was one reason why in 1990 a federal judge barred the testimony of Margaret Singer and Richard Ofshe about alleged brainwashing in support of a diminished capacity defense of an ex-Scientologist being prosecuted for mail fraud.

Some courts making procedural rulings to bar testimony about psychological coercion in cults were explicitly influenced by the action of the American Psychological Association in rejecting a report which had been authored by a task force appointed by the APA to report on alleged coercive persuasion in cults and other groups. Originally appointed by the APA, and chaired by Margaret Singer who was the senior author of its report, the task force was composed primarily of scholars and clinicians who are active in advocacy against cults and in court cases. After receiving evaluations of the task force's report by several outside reviewers, the APA rejected the report and declined to issue it as an official APA document because it did not meet the APA's standards of scientific acceptability. The rejection of the report was cited as proof that the anticult brainwashing theory is not generally accepted in the relevant scientific community in procedural rulings in the two cases in which Margaret Singer's and Richard Ofshe's testimony was forbidden in advance of the trial.

In the light of the sequence of cases in which anticult brainwashing testimony has been excluded as unscientific, and/or unconstitutional, it seems likely that judges will no longer permit such testimony in most courtrooms. The proposed use of thought reform research as a basis of testimony with respect to cults makes it likely that a witness will not be allowed to testify at all, or will have his testimony severely limited. Consequently, such experts are seeking other theoretical grounds for criticizing allegedly coercive conversion processes in new religious or therapeutic movements.

Recently a number of "experts," including Richard Ofshe in several cases, who were testifying or proposing to testify about psychological pressure in religious or therapeutic groups, specifically denied that their testimony would be based upon research with respect to brainwashing, coercive persuasion, or thought reform, or to POW research and the work of Schein and Lifton, etc.

V. VIOLENCE AND VOLATILITY

It is conceivable that in the aftermath of the shocking apparent collective suicide of members of a "cult" in Waco, Texas, in April of 1993, the robot/brainwashing model, which has suffered legal setbacks, may recover some of its prestige. It is ironic that tragic events such as Waco and the 1978 mass suicides in Jonestown should be popularly viewed as supportive of brainwashing perspectives. Sympathetic discussions of such theories as applied to cults often appear to depict cult leaders as motivated by selfish and material interests. Why then should such "con men" consider suicide to be in their interest? A more promising avenue of inquiry might consider Erikson's notion of the relationship between "negative identity" and totalism. Individuals with polarized identities find in apocalyptic sects a meaning system which can alleviate emotional distress by projecting negativity onto scapegoats and demonic outsiders while constructing a "purified self" for the leader as well as the members. But such resolutions are always precarious such that the group and its individual members may be highly volatile. Threats to the "boundary" of the group are met with paranoia and militant defensiveness.

The raid on the Davidian Waco compound by federal agents in February of 1993 apparently appeared to confirm leader David Koresh's violent apocalyptic visions, but on another level it threatened to disconfirm his beliefs, i.e., if he were captured or gave himself up peacefully and the world went on as before his totalist system of psycho-ideological reconstruction would collapse. What Robert Lifton has called "revolutionary immortality" was imperilled, and consequently revolutionary suicide provided a way out.

The tragedy which ensued in Waco in April of 1993 may be more explicable in terms of the psychology of totalism rather than brainwashing theory. The further development and application of the former analytical perspective might ultimately be conducive to the development of *strategies of mediation* which might be more effective than the confrontational tactics sometimes favored by those persons influenced by brainwashing notions.

Bibliography

Adorno, T., Frenkel-Brunswick, E., Levinson, D., and Sanford, N. (1950). "The Authoritarian Personality." Norton, New York.

Anthony, D. (1990). Religious movements and brainwashing litigation. In "In Gods We Trust" (T. Robbins and D. Anthony, Eds.), 2d ed. Transaction, New Brunswick, NJ.

Anthony, D., and Robbins, T. (1991). Law, social science and the "brainwashing" exception to the first amendment. *Behav. Sci. Law* **10** (1), 5.

Arendt, H. (1979). "The Origins of Totalitarianism." Harcourt Brace Jovanovich, San Diego.

Barker, E. (1984). "The Making of a Moonie: Choice or Brainwashing?" Blackwell, Oxford.

Bromley, D., and Richardson, J. (1983). "The Brainwashing–Deprogramming Controversy." Edwin Mellen, New York/Toronto.

Bromley, D., and Hadden, J. (Eds.) (1993). "Handbook of Cults and Sects in America," Vols. 3–4. J.A.I. Press, Greenwich, CT.

Erikson, E. (1942). Hitler's imagery and German youth. *Psychiatry* **5**, 475–493.

Erikson, E. (1953). Wholeness and totality—a psychiatric contribution. In "Totalitarianism: Proceedings of a Conference Held at the American Academy of Arts and Sciences." Harvard University Press, Cambridge MA.

Friedrich, C., and Brzezinski, Z. (1956). "Totalitarian Dictorship & Autocracy." Praeger, New York.

Hinkle, L. E., Jr., and Wolff, H. E. (1956). Communist interrogation and the indoctrination of "enemies of the states." *A.M.A. Arch. Neurol. Psych.* **76**, 117.

Hunter, F. (1951). "Brainwashing in Red China." Vanguard, New York.

Lifton, R. (1989). "Chinese Thought Reform and the Psychology of Totalism." University of North Carolina Press, Chapel Hill.

Marks, J. (1980). "The Search for the Manchurian Candidate." Random House, New York.

Singer, M., and Ofshe, R. (1992). Thought reform programs and the production of psychiatric casualties. *Psychiatric Ann.* **20** (4), 188.

CAFFEINE: PSYCHOSOCIAL EFFECTS

Joseph P. Blount
Widener University

W. Miles Cox
North Chicago Veterans Affairs Medical Center
The Chicago Medical School

Glossary

Caffeinism The official diagnostic category for excessive caffeine consumption to a point of intoxication.

Double blind A type of research design in which neither the subject nor the experimenter (but only some third party) knows whether the subject has received a drug (e.g., caffeinated coffee) or an inert substance (e.g., decaffeinated coffee). The advantage of this design is that it allows the investigator to isolate the pharmacological effects of the drug from the psychological effects.

DSM-III-R The current diagnostic manual of the American Psychiatric Association.

Ergogenic aid A substance that helps an athlete generate increased force or endurance.

State-dependent learning A drug-induced effect on memory that occurs when information that is learned in one drug state is later more accurately recalled when the individual is in the same drug state rather than a different one.

Statistical significance The assurance, through a statistical test, that an observed data pattern is genuine rather than having occurred by chance.

Theobromine A xanthine closely related to caffeine that is found especially in cacao beans and chocolate.

Theophylline A xanthine closely related to caffeine that is found in tea leaves.

Withdrawal symptoms Symptoms that occur when a person suddenly stops taking a drug that he or she is accustomed to taking. Headache and fatigue are the most common symptoms associated with withdrawal from caffeine.

CAFFEINE is a psychoactive drug that occurs naturally in many foods and beverages (e.g., coffee, tea, cocoa) and is added to many commercial products (e.g., soft drinks, analgesics). Caffeine is closely related chemically to theophylline and theobromine; all three compounds are methylated xanthines. Coffee contains caffeine, tea contains both caffeine and theophylline, and cocoa contains both caffeine and theobromine. Caffeine is used very widely, often in high doses, and it has been the subject of much research. Four major questions have been raised regarding caffeine and its effects: (1) What are its physical and mental benefits? (2) What are the possible harmful effects of caffeine from single doses or chronic use? (3) Is caffeine consumption a social problem? (4) What are the short- and long-term mechanisms that cause its physiological and behavioral effects? Scientific studies have given us considerable understanding of the mechanisms by which caffeine has its effects and have clarified much of the speculation about potential health risks. Biomedical results are not discussed in detail here, but a summary (Blount and Cox, 1991) and an evaluative review (James, 1991) are listed in the references. Research results on psychological well-being and behavioral effects of caffeine have greatly increased our understanding of the complex ways in which caffeine can produce beneficial effects in one individual but harmful effects in another, or different effects in the same individual at different times. Given the current state of knowledge, mild caution about excessive use of caffeine is prudent for the general population, reduced intake is indicated for certain clinical populations, and further research is needed in particular areas.

I. INTRODUCTION

According to more than one legend, caffeine was introduced to humans through divine intervention. The existence of such legends indicates the important role caffeine has had in society throughout the ages. One of the more interesting legends appears geographically correct. An Arabian goatherd noticed that the beans made his goats energetic and unable to sleep, and he decided to try some himself. He became happy, danced and whirled and leaped and rolled about on the ground. In today's terminology this might be called the first coffee trip. A holy man joined the goatherd's orgy and took instructions from Mohammed to boil the beans and have monks drink the liquid to stay awake longer and continue their prayers.

In the 10th century A.D., an Arabian medical book suggested that coffee was a cure for almost everything including measles and excessive lust. By the 15th century, coffee plants were being cultivated and transported, and coffee consumption spread in the Islamic world. In the 17th century, Dutch cultivation spread coffee to Europe (in greenhouses), to the East Indies, and eventually to the more favorable climate in Latin America. Coffeehouses and coffee consumption and the method of using ground beans spread rapidly in England and France.

The women in England reacted with a petition against coffee, calling it an enfeebling liquor. The real problem was not reducing lust, but social change: The coffeehouses were a place to relax, do business, or learn the news of the day, and people were spending a lot of time there. Old social patterns were being challenged. In Mecca, this activity was seen as competing with attendance at mosques. Coffee bean supplies were burned, and the use of coffee was outlawed. Of course, illegal coffee channels grew up, and soon the prohibition was lifted. In England, Charles II feared seditious plots would originate in coffeehouses; therefore, he outlawed them—only to have to withdraw his ruling 11 days later. By the 18th century, coffeehouses were functioning as "penny universities" where anyone could learn from great literary and political figures. The famous insurance company, Lloyd's of London, began in Edward Lloyd's coffeehouse around this time.

Caffeine consumption has always been closely intertwined with financial issues. In 17th century France there was competition between coffee establishments and wine establishments. In the English colonies in the new world, tea at first served as a cheaper and more readily available alternative to coffee. However, a British tea tax reduced some of this economic advantage and was credited with contributing to political separation and with shifting the new nation's habits from tea to coffee. Technological improvements and marketing seem to have contributed to industrial growth across the 19th century. Roasting of coffee beans improves the flavor of the drink and commercial roasting increased convenience by eliminating the necessity for home roasting. At the turn of the century, vacuum packing permitted indefinite storage of commercially roasted and ground coffee. In 1892, the first commercial combination of different beans was introduced. The success of Maxwell House was probably not due to "superior" flavor or association with a famous hotel. Rather, the blend introduced a new level of consistency in taste for which preferences could be developed and brand loyalty cultivated.

Societal factors outside the coffee industry seem to have had large impacts on coffee consumption. When alcohol prohibition was imposed in the United States in 1920 coffee consumption increased 40% in 1 year alone and fears were expressed that it had reached a threshold of abuse. Coffee did not seem to be serving merely as a social substitute for alcohol. When prohibition was repealed, coffee consumption continued to rise. During World War II, consumption reached a peak about double its prohibition level; perhaps the war effort and work schedules created the need to use coffee for its stimulating effects. Consumption then declined during the 1950s (no war effort, price increases in coffee), 1960s (competition from soft drinks), and 1970s (health-consciousness and changes in lifestyle).

Empirical research has shown a logical association between beliefs and consumption: those who "always" or "usually" select noncaffeinated beverages believe that such beverages are habit forming, increase nervousness, and contribute to medical conditions such as ulcers, high blood pressure, and cancer. Those who "rarely" or "never" select noncaffeinated beverages believe the beverages give people more energy, help them to relax, and help them to feel better. The coffee industry has responded as if beliefs are important determinants of caffeine consumption, in part with increased marketing of decaffeinated coffees and in part by sponsoring research to show that caffeine has only benign effects (Dews, 1984). Industry support of scholarly research is to be commended; however, selective reporting and interpretation of results in ways favorable to the industry are to be condemned and guarded against. Industry fears of a net loss of markets have not occurred: the decline has leveled off and consumption has remained constant across the 1980s and early 1990s. Current per capita consumption is higher than what it was just before Prohibition. It is difficult to ascertain how much of this leveling is due to new marketing techniques, such as the promotion of drip grinds, gourmet blends, espresso methods of preparation, and iced coffees. The fear is that users of decaffeinated products will temporarily maintain consumption but then drink fewer cups per day because decaffeinated products lack caffeine's taste-enhancing action and tendency to produce physical dependence (see below). The level of concern in the industry is represented by a multi-component marketing technique used in Australia. Caffeine is added to flavored milk so that milk's healthy image will overcome caffeine's negative one. The beverage is targeted at children in the hope that they will become life-long consumers of caffeine. The advertisements try to capitalize on the allure of the drug counterculture and on the public's new awareness of the psychoactive properties of caffeine by inviting consumers to obtain "the maximum hit." Coffee is an important worldwide commodity of trade second only to oil. Hence, even a small reduction in consumption could have a sizable impact on international relations, capital investments, and job dislocations.

In a 1984 sociological analysis, Troyer and Markle compared coffee drinking to cigarette smoking. They suggested that coffee drinking was an emerging social problem and that society's future attitude toward the problem would be largely decided by biomedical experts. Like smoking, health risks could lead to societal constraints against the industry and consumers' behavior. One danger is that certain organizations could bias the experts by emphasizing ill effects, or others by portraying the caffeine as safe. The debate over what caffeine-related conditions to include in the American Psychiatric Association's revised version of the *Diagnostic and Statistical Manual of Mental Disorders* takes on many of the characteristics that Troyer and Markle pointed out (see Addiction below). Another danger is that scientists would be deterred from working with caffeine for fear of media-fanned public outcry about results that went against established patterns of behavior. Although individual scientists have expressed discomfort at organizational, media, or public pressures, in the last 9 years, there has been a wealth, not a lack, of research. Because the objective results have remained mixed, the medical community has not yet put caffeine in the same category as alcohol and nicotine. The remainder of this article summarizes the current state of the field with regard to caffeine and human behavior.

II. PSYCHOPHARMACOLOGY

Caffeine is an alkaline compound in the family of naturally occurring derivatives of xanthine. Although most other alkaloids are insoluble in water, caffeine is slightly soluble and becomes still more so in the form of complex double salts. After oral ingestion in humans, caffeine is rapidly absorbed in the gastrointestinal tract and distributed into all parts of the body, including in the case of pregnant women, the mother's milk and her fetus. Peak blood plasma levels of caffeine are reached within about 30 minutes after ingestion of tea or coffee, and within about 1 hour for Coca Cola (and presumably other soft drinks). That rates of caffeine absorption are slower for soft drinks than for coffee is a surprising finding because of the fact that the rate of absorption of alcohol is increased by carbonation.

Caffeine primarily acts as a central nervous system stimulant. Moderate doses of 200 mg (about two cups of coffee taken close together) activate the cortex; higher doses activate the spinal cord or autonomic nervous system. Single caffeine doses decrease heart rate during the first hour after administration and increase heart rate and cardiac output during the following 2 hours. Caffeine dilates systemic blood vessels, but constricts cerebral blood vessels. Caffeine causes a slight increase in basal metabolic rate (10%). Caffeine increases the secretion of stomach acids, increases the respiratory rate, and slightly increases the production of urine. It acts as a bronchodilator by relaxing the smooth muscles. On the other hand, caffeine strengthens the contraction of skeletal muscles.

About 95% of a dose of caffeine is metabolized by the liver into other products and excreted by the kidneys. Very small portions may be excreted in pure form or through other channels, such as in saliva, semen, or breast milk. About 97% of a dose of caffeine is eliminated in 15 to 30 hours. Many factors may cause the rate of clearance to vary. For example, clearance is much slower among smokers, persons with liver disease, women who are pregnant or use oral contraceptives, and infants (because infants lack certain enzymes). When a chronic adult user abruptly discontinues all use of caffeine, complete removal of caffeine from the body can take up to 7 days.

III. PREVALENCE OF CAFFEINE CONSUMPTION

Caffeine intake can be calculated as the product of a person's consumption of food, beverages, or other products containing caffeine times the caffeine content of these products. Such data can be obtained by having people keep diaries of what they consume or retrospectively report what they remember consuming or by having a third party record what they consume. There is substantial agreement among these different methods of collecting data. Furthermore, there is close agreement between these methods and certain measures of caffeine production, such as the amount of coffee imported per capita. These intake data reveal interesting patterns. For instance, the most prominent source of caffeine in Britain is tea, but in the United States, it is coffee. The shift in preference from tea to coffee in the United States has been attributed to the British tax on tea in the 1700s. The U.S. peak of more than three cups of coffee per day per capita in 1962 fell to less than two cups in 1983, a shift that has been variously attributed to poor advertising and/or a decline in the quality of coffees in the 1960s. Currently in the United States, females drink more coffee than males, and the younger generation gets its caffeine

primarily from soft drinks. Caffeine consuming habits also change with age. For example, those 35–64 years old drink more coffee than younger or older age groups. On the other hand, tea consumption shows no difference across ages, and soft drink consumption declines.

The second factor necessary to calculate caffeine intake is the amount of caffeine in a source. The amount of caffeine depends on both methods of commercial production and personal methods of preparation. Tea is especially variable, ranging from 8 to 91 mg per serving. Due to such variation and to differences in the definitions of serving size (and sometimes definitions are not reported), various au-

TABLE I
Levels of Caffeine in Common Foods and Beverages

Beverage/food	Serving size (oz)	Approximate mg caffeine/serving
Coffee		
Drip	5	150
Percolated	5	110
Instant, regular	5	50–100
Instant, flavored mix	5	25–75
Decaffeinated coffee	5	1–6
Tea		
Black		
1-min brew	5	20–35
3-min brew	5	35–45
5-min brew	5	40–50
Green		
1-min brew	5	10–20
3-min brew	5	20–35
5-min brew	5	25–35
Instant	5	30–60
Cocoa beverage	5	2–20
Soft drinks		
Jolt	12	70
Caffeinated cola drinks	12	30–65
Mountain Dew, Mello Yello, Sunkist Orange	12	40–50
7-Up, Sprite, RC-100, Fanta Orange, Hires Root Beer	12	0
Chocolate		
Cake	1/16 of 9-inch cake	14
Ice cream	2/3 cup	5
Mr. Goodbar	1.65	6
Special Dark, Hershey	1.02	23

thors report different data on caffeine content. Nonetheless, it is useful to have representative values for the caffeine content of major dietary sources, and these are given in Tables I and II. Many people believe that the dark color of soft drinks indicates which ones contain caffeine. In actuality, caffeine forms a white powder, a yellow residue (caffeine is a xanthine and xanthine is the Greek word for "yellow"), or a clear solution. Note that root beer is dark and contains no caffeine, whereas Mountain Dew is clear and contains caffeine.

Despite this variability, a number of authors have used the figures for caffeine content to calculate the average person's daily caffeine intake. For American adults (consumers and nonconsumers) a representative average including all sources, not just coffee, is 200 mg (3 mg/kg body weight) per day. Adults who are considered heavy consumers ingest 500 mg (7 mg/kg) per day or more. A 27-kg child who consumes three soft drinks and two chocolate bars would have equivalent body levels of caffeine and could therefore also be considered a heavy consumer! Some adults who consume 2000 mg/day have sought professional help to reduce their intake. Note that laborers consume more caffeine than others; college students consume more caffeine when preparing for examinations than at other times. Several segments of society consume less than these figures: Pregnant women appear to consume about 2.1 mg/kg, although the data are limited and pregnancy-related weight gains have not always been taken into account. Children under 18 (both consumers and

TABLE II
Levels of Caffeine in Common Drugs

Drugs	Standard adult dose	Approximate mg caffeine/std. dose
Prescription painkillers		
Darvon compound capsule	1	32
Cafergot tablet (migraine)	1	100
Nonprescription (over-the-counter)		
Painkillers		
Anacin, Midol, Vanquish	2	65
Plain aspirin	2	0
Cold/allergy		
Dristan	2	30
Coryban-D, Sinarest, Triaminicin	1	30
Stimulants		
No-Doz	2	200
Vivarin	1	200

nonconsumers) ingest about 37 mg (1 mg/kg) per day. The health code of the Mormons, as well as that of certain other religious groups, prohibits all use of stimulants.

IV. COGNITIVE TASKS

The popularity of coffeine is probably due to its stimulant action. Many people report that caffeine increases their mental arousal, and it is widely believed to improve actual performance. Researchers have attempted to objectively assess the effects of caffeine on attention, speed of reaction, memory, and/or the flow of thoughts.

At the perceptual level, acute caffeine ingestion lowers visual luminance threshold, and improves auditory vigilance. On visual vigilance tasks, caffeine increases alertness and speeds up responding while reducing attention to detail. Chronic caffeine users show enhanced sensitivity (d'), but increased errors on visual vigilance tasks. Regarding reaction time, small to moderate amounts of caffeine (i.e., 32 to 200 mg) help speed reactions to simple, routinized tasks, such as indicating whether an even or odd digit was presented, pressing buttons corresponding to bulbs lit in a circular pattern, or watching for strings of three even numbers. Conversely, when habitual caffeine users abstain for 2 days, their reactions are slowed and their attention is impaired. (The physical indicator of impaired attention is less anticipatory heart-rate deceleration.) For novel or slightly more complex tasks, it is difficult to predict whether caffeine will improve or impair performance. For example, whereas visual reaction times are often improved by caffeine, caffeine seriously impairs performance on the Stroop test. The Stroop test involves naming a color of ink while ignoring an incompatibly spelled color (e.g., the word "red" printed in green ink). The impairment is understandable if one realizes that the drug cannot selectively speed one kind of processing. By enhancing both word reading and color naming, the interference between them is increased and performance impaired.

Because to a large extent driving a car is routinized, the improvements in auditory vigilance and visual reaction time would seem to imply benefits for late-night driving—if not counteracted by loss of fine motor coordination (see effects on physical performance below). No researcher seems to have carefully tested the net effects of caffeine on driving performance. It is noteworthy, though, that several researchers have used laboratory tasks to test the common belief that caffeine counteracts the effects of alcohol, and have found that coffee further impairs rather than improves performance. For example, a person who has consumed enough alcohol to be close to the legal level of intoxication and then drinks a cup and a half of coffee (150 mg of caffeine) has even slower reaction times than if only the alcohol had been consumed. In short, consuming coffee after consuming alcohol may make one more prone to accidents rather than less so. On the other hand, more recent research has found some indication that caffeine may counteract the effects of alcohol, but the amount of "antagonism" is surprisingly small. The practical importance of this issue calls for careful research that uses doses of caffeine typical of social use (instead of using only excessive doses), pairing wider ranges of alcohol and caffeine doses, adjusting both kinds of doses to subjects' body weights, taking into account subjects' typical patterns of alcohol and caffeine use, and including as part of the experiment a demonstration that caffeine alone actually improves performance.

Many people believe that arousal produced by caffeine is beneficial to learning and retention. At the simplest level of habituation (e.g., to an aversive noise or to the demands of a visual vigilance task), acute caffeine ingestion reduces the rate of habituation. Chronic caffeine users seem to have a modified habituation process. At the level of learning and memory, some research has, in fact, shown beneficial effects. However, many studies involving short-term memory have shown no effect or impaired performance due to caffeine. It has been proposed and partially demonstrated that this lack of consistency can be resolved by disentangling the complex interactions among personality type (extrovert/introvert and/or high/low impulsivity), diurnal rhythm of arousal, task requirements (e.g., sustained information transfer, short-term memory), dosages matched to body weights, and the curvilinear relationship with arousal level (moderate arousal enhances performance, whereas excessive arousal hinders it). For example, coffee may improve an extrovert's performance on a particular task in the morning, but impair the same person's performance on the same task in the afternoon. Conversely, coffee may hinder an introvert in the morning, but facilitate that person in the afternoon.

Another kind of drug-induced effect on memory is state-dependent learning. It occurs when information learned in one drug state is later recalled better when the individual is in the same drug state rather than a different one. An example of state-dependent learning is the alcohol drinker who while sober forgets what he or she did while intoxicated, but recalls it again when next intoxicated. In the experimental laboratory, state-dependent learning with alcohol has been demonstrated with social drinkers. However, several attempts to demonstrate state-dependent learning in the laboratory with caffeine have been unsuccessful. One possible cause for the latter negative results is that the "drug" and "nondrug" states that were supposed to be different actually were not. The experimenters assumed that the drug state involved a high level of arousal because caffeine was consumed, and that the other state involved a low level of arousal because a placebo (i.e., no caffeine) was consumed. However, subjects in the later condition may have also been aroused, because, for example, they had been challenged to perform well on the experimental task, or they were excited by being in an unfamiliar setting and in the presence of a stranger. The first explanation is especially plausible because many people find that having to take any kind of a test causes them to be anxious. Assuming that alcohol reduces test anxiety would account for the state-dependent learning that was found in one study that, from the learning to the test phase of the experiment, shifted subjects from a combined alcohol/caffeine state to (a) the same state (which produced no decrement in performance), (b) an alcohol-only state (which produced a performance decrement), (c) a caffeine-only state (which produced small decrement), or (d) a no-drug state (which produced maximal decrement). In short, at the present time, it is not entirely clear whether caffeine does or does not produce state-dependent learning. It seems that there is a good chance that caffeine does produce state-dependent learning, but that this effect will be difficult to isolate.

Many people report that caffeine helps them think more clearly and creatively. In the public stereotype, creative persons use drugs to excess. Survey research has shown that, contrary to the stereotype, writers, artists, and musicians do not use drugs, not even caffeine, to excess. In fact, most creative people say they learned early in their career that drugs interfere with the creativity process. When they do use caffeine, it is only to counteract the effects of lack of sleep. [*See* CREATIVE AND IMAGINATIVE THINKING.]

Whether ordinary people's more mundane cognitive performance improves while they are under the influence of common levels of caffeine has been tested using a variety of tasks, ranging from simple subtraction, to identifying errors in written passages, to taking the Graduate Record Examination (among many others). A very wide range of positive results have been found. In a number of cases, the results have been replicated. However, a large number of inconsistent findings have also turned up. One explanation for the inconsistencies was that caffeine cannot enhance performance in normal situations, but can merely restore degraded performance in situations of fatigue or boredom. In response to these suggestions, a number of researchers took fatigue-based results, tested them in nonfatigue contexts, and found true caffeine enhancement. A second attempt to explain the inconsistencies was a model of arousal that involved personality characteristics of the subjects and the time of day that they were tested (see the discussion of memory above). This approach seemed especially promising because there were a wide variety of supportive results. However, recently there have been a number of findings inconsistent with this model and alternative theoretical accounts have focused on "postlunch dip" rather than diurnal rhythm. A third attempt to explain the inconsistencies was to examine the information processing components of the task. This was done in the case of the Stroop test discussed earlier above. Humphreys and Revelle have analyzed tasks in terms of information transfer versus short-term memory functions. The problem is that there is no agreed upon set of principles by which to analyze the processing components of a given task. In summary, the problems described here are a classic example of the complex contextual nature of social science research in contrast to the searches for simple, universal laws that are common in the physical sciences.

An important criticism of many of the positive findings is that they used doses of caffeine much larger than those common in everyday life. Only a few studies have directly compared such dose sizes. Often, these studies have found statistically significant effects with large doses but weak or nonexistent effects with everyday doses. If this pattern of results can be interpreted as a threshold effect, then moderate consumption can be recommended. However, if this pattern is interpreted as a linear dose–response relationship, then complex tradeoffs must be considered in deciding how much caffeine a given individual should consume.

One particularly interesting inconsistent result is a study that reported high caffeine intake among college students was associated with *low* academic grades. It is impossible to conclude from this association that coffee drinking is the cause of the low grades. It could be that low grades cause coffee drinking or that a third variable causes both. Because this report is frequently cited, it should be replicated and cause and effect relationships should be investigated. Furthermore, it would be important to have more studies of other "real-world" forms of thinking, such as reading comprehension and problem solving. Studies that compared fatigued or bored subjects with alert ones would help resolve the issue of whether caffeine actually improves performance generally or is largely confined to restorative effects. Do the benefits of caffeine occur at the expense of impaired performance later in the day? Is the period of increased stimulation/metabolism followed by a restorative period of decreased stimulation/metabolism? Researchers do not seem to have addressed these simple, practical questions.

V. PHYSICAL PERFORMANCE

In addition to mental arousal, people report that caffeine increases their physiological arousal. Assuming these subjective impressions reflect underlying physiological changes, one would expect effects on fine motor coordination, spontaneous gross motor activity, and athletic endurance. In fact, hand steadiness has been shown to be about 25% worse after consuming 200 mg of caffeine (about two cups of strong coffee). Furthermore, there have been a number of empirical reports of caffeine impairing motor skills which involve delicate muscular coordination and accurate timing. Unlike the cognitive measures discussed above, hand steadiness is a very sensitive measure and there is great consistency in the findings. For these reasons, it should be included in all studies as a standardized index of the behavioral effects of the doses used.

Animal studies have consistently found that caffeine increases activity without producing the "locomotor stereotypy" or persistent repetitive movements produced by amphetamine. There are only a few studies with humans; those using high dosages have found increases in gross motor activity for both children and adults. Some studies have found no increases in activity, but only decreases for high consumers who abstain in order to take part in the study and then are in a no-caffeine condition. Careful naturalistic observation studies with doses the size of two-thirds of a soft drink have failed to find any changes in activity for 5 year olds.

Many people believe that caffeine is an ergogenic aid, a substance that helps an athlete generate increased force or endurance. Witness the coffee drinking rituals preceding marathons or the use of coffee to get through the daily grind of training. Empirical studies have shown improved work production in trained cyclists, runners, and cross-country skiers, for example, extending mean cycling time to exhaustion by 20% when cycling at 80% of maximal capacity. Such ergogenic effects occur only during prolonged work and not during short-term work episodes. When the work conditions have been varied or when dosage or caffeine habits are not sufficiently accounted for, effects have been equivocal (although none have been in the reverse direction). Caffeine seems to delay deterioration in performance due to fatigue through both psychological and physical effects. It decreases perceived exertion, perception of fatigue, and drowsiness. It increases self-reported alertness and motivation.

An athlete concerned about the use of caffeine should realize that there is a great range of variability in responses to caffeine. For example, in contrast to others, more sensitive individuals may become overstimulated and show performance decrements. To obtain a beneficial effect while avoiding acquiring tolerance, the athlete might consider abstaining from caffeine for several days before a major event and then consume a moderate serving of coffee (e.g., two cups) 1 hour before competition. For some activities, the diuretic effects of caffeine may be a problem if maintaining hydration is important and difficult. Regular, heavy use throughout training may reduce benefits during competitive performance and may increase blood cholesterol and the risk of heart attack or other medical problems. Finally, the athlete should realize that the International Olympic Committee has banned caffeine when its values are greater than 15 μg/ml in a urine test.

VI. MOOD

One of the most frequent things people report about caffeine is that it affects their mood, and the great majority of research supports these claims. How these mood changes are described depends upon the wording of the questionnaire the researcher uses. In general, consuming moderate quantities of caffeine increases self-reports of alertness, vigor, content-edness, clarity of mind, energy, and efficiency. What counts as a moderate quantity depends on one's personality, habits, and current blood plasma level of caffeine. Higher doses increase reports of nervousness, anxiety, anger, and tenseness, while reducing relaxation or boredom. Finally, it should be noted that the subjective effects are not as strong in the elderly. These subjective effects seem related to the reinforcing properties of caffeine. For example, when give a choice between color-coded capsules without being told which contains caffeine, those who choose the caffeine capsules are those who report positive mood changes. Those who do not are the those who report negative mood changes.

VII. PERCEPTION

Can consumers of a caffeinated beverage perceive the presence or absence of caffeine in the beverage based on immediate sensory qualities at the time of consumption? Apparently they cannot at normal levels of concentration in colas, tea, or coffee; however, when concentration reaches 200 mg per cup of coffee, the presence of caffeine can be reliably detected. At medium and high concentrations, elderly women (67–77 years old) are less sensitive (have larger Weber ratios) to caffeine than younger women (18–25 years old). Ability to rate the intensity of caffeine is unrelated to ability to taste thiourea. Neither acute nor chronic caffeine ingestion appreciably affects other taste thresholds.

One rationale for adding caffeine to foodstuffs is that it enhances flavor. Experimental results have failed to show any enhancement for a variety of substances, even when "whole mouth" procedures are used. In a mixture with sucrose, taste suppression is the most common finding. [*See* TASTE.]

Caffeine has been reported to reduce the kinesthetic after-effect in highly impulsive subjects. Higher caffeine users who also use oral contraceptives show poorer color discrimination than nonusers of oral contraceptives for the yellow-through-blue portions of the color spectrum. According to anecdotal reports, caffeine increases synesthesia. Olfactory hallucinations triggered by 500 mg injections have been reported.

Can a person who ingests a caffeine or placebo capsule perceive the presence or absence of caffeine later (30 minutes to 2 hours has been tested in various studies) on the basis of pharmacological effects? Various researchers have found that untrained observers can make this discrimination reliably at 300, 200, or 100 mg. With training, most people can make the discrimination at 56 mg, a fraction at 18 mg, and only a few at 10 mg. That physiological and subjective effects are present at these low doses is noteworthy. In these studies, different people rely upon different cues, and there are wide individual differences in sensitivity to caffeine. It is not clear to what extent the discrimination is controlled by direct effects of caffeine versus suppression of withdrawal effects.

VIII. ADDICTION

Is caffeine really an addictive drug? By the criteria used in the 1970s, a drug of addiction must have psychoactive properties, must have reinforcing properties, and must result in withdrawal symptoms when its use is abruptly discontinued. Caffeine is psychoactive: witness the stimulating effects people report. Caffeine is reinforcing according to people's reports as well as carefully controlled experimental studies. Does removing caffeine produce withdrawal symptoms? The adverse effects are well documented. When caffeine users abstain, they experience such symptoms as dysphoria, drowsiness, yawning, poor concentration, disinterest in work, runny nose, facial flushing, headache, fatigue, irritability, and anxiety. The symptoms typically begin between 12 and 24 hours after the person discontinues use of caffeine. The symptoms vary from individual to individual; they can be mild to extreme, peak within 20 to 48 hours, and last for a week. Headache, for example, is reported by about one-fourth of the heavy users who abstain. In a few cases, the symptoms have been reported to appear when caffeine intake was gradually reduced over several weeks rather than abruptly. Even someone who is a relatively light user, habitually consuming as little as 200 mg of caffeine per day, may experience some withdrawal symptoms. Nonusers can become quickly addicted—within as little as 6 to 15 days, if high doses are consumed. Drugs of addiction tend to upset the homeostasis of the body. Addicts would, in fact, be in constant disequilibrium except for the fact that they develop compensatory responses, i.e., physiological changes the opposite of those induced by the drug. Furthermore, these compensatory responses become conditioned to the cues that precede drug use. In short, the body prepares itself for the drug assault. Caffeine users, like users of other addictive drugs, develop compensatory responses that become conditioned to the stimulus cues associated with caffeine consumption. For example, the sight of coffee inhibits salivation in chronic users of caffeine, a response that compensates for the increase in salivation produced by caffeine. Note that decaffeinated coffee provides the same visual and gustatory cues as caffeinated coffee, thereby also inhibiting salivation. Clearly, then, caffeine is a drug of addiction by these standards. [*See* HOMEOSTASIS; SUBSTANCE ABUSE.]

More recent discussions of the "abuse liability" of drugs emphasize drug use properties that maintain self-administration despite other drug-use properties that interfere with fulfilling life's responsibilities or with healthy bodily functions. Additional clinical criteria include unsuccessful efforts to control use, continued use despite knowledge of a problem caused by use, and tolerance to the behavioral effects of the drug. With regards to these criteria, caffeine has not maintained self-administration behavior as reliably as classic drugs of abuse such as cocaine or *d*-amphetamine. One study found 100- or 200-mg caffeine capsules acted as positive reinforcers and maintained self-administration, but that study gave subjects an unusual kind of additional support: when the subjects chose between capsules, the experimenters reminded them of their own subjective responses to each kind of capsule during past administrations. In this study, 400- and 600-mg doses acted as punishers. Other studies have varied the caffeine conent of available capsules or coffee to see if self-administration varies. There is some evidence for daily regulation of caffeine intake, but compensation is very imperfect. There are some intriguing initial results that show one respect in which caffeine is stronger than alcohol: placebo responses to caffeine include motor and cognitive behavior, not just social and affective behaviors. Because caffeine generally has weaker functions or has effects only in more limited situations, some authors have suggested (reasonably) that it has less dependence potential than, say, *d*-amphetamine. Others have gone further to suggest that caffeine withdrawal but not caffeine abuse be included in a newly revised *Diagnostic and Statistical Manual of Mental Disorders*. Others have (unreasonably) suggested that caffeine is not capable of promoting dependence.

A. Tolerance

When an individual has developed tolerance to a drug, larger dosages are required than previously to achieve a given effect. This pattern of decreasing effects can cause drug users to increase dosages in order to compensate for the decrease. With chronic caffeine use, it takes larger dosages to achieve the same (mild) diuretic and salivary effects. Caffeine users show smaller blood pressure increases than nonusers with the same caffeine dosage. There is some evidence to suggest that these different levels of tolerance develop after only a few days of chronic use and are lost within a day, although one would like to see this research replicated. On the other hand, less tolerance seems to develop for the stimulating effects of caffeine on the central nervous system. Furthermore, for many individuals, increases in caffeine dosage would be self-limiting because higher doses exacerbate undesirable symptoms (nervousness, anxiety, restlessness, insomnia, tremors, gastrointestinal disturbances, and feelings of uneasiness).

B. Toxicity

In contrast to the high toxicity of theophylline, caffeine is not very toxic. Nevertheless, caffeine can produce symptoms that require medical consultation. For example, sudden increases in consumption have been associated with a variety of adverse effects, such as delirium, abdominal cramps, vomiting, high levels of anxiety and hostility, and psychosis. More gradual increases may not show toxicity because tolerance develops. Higher doses of caffeine can cause convulsions and still higher doses can cause death from respiratory failure. A lethal dose in adults appears to be 5 to 10 g, the amount of caffeine in approximately 200 cola beverages. There is little concern that death could occur from beverage consumption because gastric distress and vomiting would prevent concentrations from reaching life-threatening levels. Although similar principles would seem to apply to over-the-counter caffeinated drugs, at least seven deaths from ingested caffeinated medications were reported between 1959 and 1980. One death after injection of 3.2 g has also been reported.

IX. PSYCHOPATHOLOGY

Many years ago, the well-known psychologist Harry Stack Sullivan observed "incipient depression and neurasthenic states" in a client after "unwitting denial of the accustomed caffeine dosage." He surmised that "there might be times when a cup of coffee would delay the outcropping of a mental disorder." Recent concerns reflect the opposite point of view, namely, that consumption of caffeine might lead to caffeine intoxication, that it might exacerbate other psychological disorders, or that its symptoms might be misdiagnosed as another disorder.

A. Caffeinism

Caffeine consumption to the point of clinical manifestations is termed "caffeinism" or "caffeine intoxication." The *Diagnostic and Statistical Manual* (DMS-III-R) defines three diagnostic criteria: (1) recent consumption in excess of 250 mg (2 to 4 cups of strong coffee), (2) at least five somatic symptoms, and (3) no diagnosis of another covering physical or mental disorder. Because health professionals have traditionally ignored patterns of caffeine consumption (cf. the anecdote about Sullivan above), this diagnostic category performs the useful function of drawing attention to caffeine and helping prevent misdiagnosis. Nonetheless, all of the criteria are open to criticism. The 250-mg threshold may be too low in that the majority of the population exceed this level on any given day. The 12 candidates for somatic symptoms is an imprecise collection troubled by subjective terms, duplications, omissions, and overlap. The third criterion provides no way to eliminate competing hypotheses.

B. Anxiety Disorders

The relationship between caffeine and emotional health has been most often studied in terms of generalized anxiety disorder (GAD) and panic disorder (PD). Several biologically plausible mechanisms for anxiogenic (anxiety-producing) effects of caffeine have been studied, but definitive results have not yet been obtained.

The idea that caffeine consumption should correlate positively with anxiety level is too simplistic. Population studies have found positive, null, and negative correlations. The most persuasive studies have shown moderate *negative* (about −.25) correlations between caffeine consumption and anxiety. One explanation is that anxious people avoid caffeine because of its stimulant effects. Note that this explanation depends on the original presumption that acute caffeine doses cause increases in anxiety; furthermore, this explanation makes it impossible to predict even the direction of a population correlation. That direction depends upon what proportion of the people recognize the link between caffeine and anxiety and self-regulate their intake.

In laboratory studies that use low doses, some healthy people interpret the stimulation provided by caffeine as a pleasant, general elevation in mood, whereas others find it unpleasant. After consuming moderate amounts of caffeine (200 mg), many people report increased feelings of restlessness, tension, and anxiety. Larger doses (300 mg) can lead to further anxiety, hostility, and depression. Similar induction of anxiety has been found in animals. Although the human data indicating these effects were obtained from self-reports, they have been corroborated by objective observers. In double-blind experiments, observers were able to reliably see the increased restlessness and "drug effect" of caffeine on users. In even larger doses, the symptoms may be indistinguishable from anxiety disorders. Reductions in daily caffeine level can reduce anxiety, although sudden withdrawal can increase it.

Most laboratory studies have shown that caffeine increases anxiety for normals and that patients with panic disorders are particularly sensitive to the anxiogenic effects of caffeine. In addition to the usual symptoms, they show palpitations, nervousness, fear, nausea, and tremors. They show clear dose-response effects. A 480-mg dose is enough to create a panic attack in these patients, although a much larger dose would be required to create similar panic in a normal person. In contrast to these studies, one study found caffeine injections of 250 mg increased state anxiety for normals but not for GAD or PD patients. This "failure" may have been due to overshadowing effects from the injection procedure, the paper and pencil dependent measure, or the small dose size. In summary, additional studies are needed to establish the true physiological mechanism by which caffeine affects anxiety and to corroborate the interpretations of the behavioral data proposed above. In the meantime, all the available data strongly reinforce the clinical wisdom that patients with anxiety disorders should avoid caffeine-containing foods and beverages. [*See* ANXIETY DISORDERS; PANIC DISORDER.]

C. Depressive Disorders

One theory is that caffeine interferes with the hypothalamic-pituitary-adrenal axis and thus plays a role in major depression. At present, there is no physiological evidence for this. A contrasting theory

is that during depressive episodes, patients self-medicate with caffeine to raise themselves out of their depression. Either theory implies a positive correlation between level of depression and level of caffeine consumption. One population study found such a positive correlation, but a weak one. Some laboratory studies have found that caffeine increases feelings of depression and exacerbates manic-depressive symptoms; furthermore, reducing daily caffeine intake can improve mood. Caution must be used in applying this finding clinically. For example, in two cases of bipolar affective disorder who were on lithium treatment, reduction of caffeine intake increased lithium tremors.

In contrast to the studies with positive results, several have found null results. At this time, the relationship between caffeine and depression, if any, is unclear.

The role of low-dose oral or i.v. caffeine in electroconvulsive therapy (ECT) presents a much clearer picture. When ECT is indicated for major depression patients, it is often difficult to achieve desired seizure duration and to hold settings within desired ranges. Pretreatment with doses from 100 to 125 mg of caffeine can maintain duration and settings and achieve equivalent therapeutic outcome with no cardiac complications, cognitive side effects, or additional complications. One note of caution: patients can respond differently on different trials; hence careful monitoring on every trial is necessary. As chemists invent new xanthine derivatives, there is some chance that they will find one without unwanted side effects and with more selectivity for adenosine receptors thus allowing more circumscript pharmacological intervention. [*See* DEPRESSION.]

D. Schizophrenic Disorders

Schizophrenic patients have been observed to drink 20 cups of coffee a day, wear coffee-brown "mustaches," and snort instant-coffee crystals. Populations studies have shown that they chronically consume more caffeine than the general public (although some studies have failed to find this difference). Caffeine ingestion has been shown to exacerbate schizophrenic syndromes as evidenced in paper-and-pencil self-reports as well as in nurses' observations. Both case studies and hospital floor studies have shown that caffeine removal reduces schizophrenic symptoms, in particular, aggression. One of these studies on aggression is difficult to interpret because in the same time period, a nearby state hospital showed the same decline in aggressive patient acts without any change in caffeine consumption! Other studies have failed to find any effect of caffeine removal. Some authors have tried to explain seemingly contradictory results by saying the effects occur for only certain subgroups of schizophrenic patients (those who are impulsive and those who are hypersensitive to caffeine). Different proportions of these subgroups could account for different outcomes. [See SCHIZOPHRENIA.]

Note that while chronic caffeine consumption is associated with increased aggression, acute consumption decreases aggression. There is a plausible physiological mechanism for acute effects: benzodiazepine elicits maternal-like aggression in virgin rats and causes disinhibition in humans; caffeine is a benzodiazepine antagonist and hence should decrease aggression. Laboratory data with both rats and humans show this decrease in overt aggressive behaviors. Just as with anxiety, the opposite relationships for acute and chronic consumption should not be viewed as a paradox. Rather, different complex sets of factors contribute to the difference in relationships.

E. Clinical Precautions and Conclusions

Two issues are important for their practical implications, although there has not been a lot of research related to them. (1) Clinicians working with anorexics may want to monitor their patients' caffeine intake. In their striving to be thin, anorexics have been observed to consume large quantities of diet colas or coffee, apparently because these beverages have few calories but suppress the appetite. (2) Clinicians working with patients who are taking psychotropic medication should be aware of potential drug–caffeine interactions. Diazapam has antagonistic and synergistic interactions with caffeine, although the exact nature of these interactions is controversial. Presumably other benzodiazepines have similar interactions. Coffee and phenylpropanolamine have been reported to produce manic psychosis. Coffee and tea both form flaky, insoluble precipitates with antipsychotic drugs. One case study reported caffeine consumption increased step by step with increased medication. Conversely, with caffeine abstinence, the symptoms disappeared and so did the need for medication.

The relationship between caffeine and psychopathology is an important but confusing area. Intoxica-

tion among inpatients is probably much more common than has been realized; therefore, routine assessment of patterns of consumption is advisable. The use of "coffee groups" in therapy needs to be considered carefully, case by case. The results reported above and the simplicity of restricting caffeine recommend trying the restriction in many cases. Nonetheless, blanket condemnation of caffeine intake is unwarranted. What is detrimental for some appears beneficial for others. Furthermore, restricting one intoxicant (e.g., caffeine intoxication) may lead to others (e.g., water intoxication).

X. OTHER ISSUES

A. Sleep Disturbance

It is commonly believed that the ingestion of caffeine, particularly in the form of drinking coffee close to bedtime, interferes with sleep. Indeed, there is evidence (both in the form of questionnaire and experimental studies) that caffeine has adverse effects on sleep. Caffeine can interfere with both the quantity of sleep (e.g., a delay in sleep onset) and quality of sleep (e.g., adverse effects on the depth of sleep). However, definitive conclusions are difficult to draw, because the effects of caffeine on sleep can be modified by such factors as the time when caffeine is ingested, an individual's habitual pattern of caffeine intake, and individual differences in sensitivity to caffeine. Moreover, caffeine can have adverse consequences on sleep without the individual being aware of such effects. [See SLEEP: BIOLOGICAL RHYTHMS AND HUMAN PERFORMANCE.]

B. Heritability

To what extent is caffeine consumption influenced by genetic factors? During the 1980s and early 1990s, the media reported "astonishing successes" in the field of behavior genetics in identifying genes underlying such crippling diseases as cystic fibrosis or Huntington's disease, and more complex traits, such as manic–depressive disorder and alcoholism. The influence of genetics has been sought even for such seemingly personal choices as cigarette smoking and coffee drinking. One common research technique is to look for stronger patterns of inheritance in twins than in brothers and sisters or in adopted siblings. The calculated heritability is the degree to which the trait stems from genetic factors. Studies of male twins have reported an unadjusted heritability estimate for coffee drinking of 46% that drops to 36% when the confounding factor of cigarette smoking is adjusted for. That the heritability estimate remains sizable and highly statistically significant supports the conclusion that coffee drinking is, in part, genetically determined. However, this result must be interpreted cautiously. These estimates are confounded by other sources of variance in the data, such as age and sex, that have not been adjusted for. The estimates are based on self-reports that may not be as reliable as desired, and involve substance use, not addiction or caffeinism that may have different estimates. Causal inerpretations cannot be made directly from the heritability estimate. For example, viral diseases may show the same patterns of incidence in families—not because the virus is inherited, but because susceptibility is.

C. Premenstrual Syndrome

The media have given what appears to be premature coverage to a purported link between caffeine consumption and severity of premenstrual syndrome. Only one researcher has reported a connection, and that in poorly controlled studies. Another researcher has failed to find a connection. [See PREMENSTRUAL SYNDROME.]

D. Headache and Migraine

There is a debate over whether caffeine has independent analgesic effects equivalent to acetaminophen. Several researchers have found promising indications that sumatriptan relieves migraine headaches more quickly, effectively, and with fewer side-effects than caffeine compounds (or aspirin compounds). There is one interesting report that shows the relevance of personality variables to biomedical research: for introverts, caffeine in combination with analgesics may potentiate pain stimulation.

E. Treatment for Obesity

Although neither caffeine alone nor ephedrine alone leads to effective weight loss, the compound seems effective through anorexia (75%, diminished appetite) and increased thermogenesis (25%, heat production). Newer selective β-agonists should be compared against this reference.

XI. CONCLUSIONS

Because caffeine consumption involves both pharmacological effects and behavior, both behavioral and biomedical science are needed to fully understand its impact on health. The research to date has discounted some but not all of the potential concerns about negative health consequences. Caffeine has both beneficial and adverse effects on physical and mental performance, but these are not well-established because of the intricacies of the research methodology. There is much more to be learned about the mechanisms by which caffeine produces its effects. Researchers have come to opposite conclusions on many of the issues, and in the process have revealed extraneous variables that must be taken into account. It is important that there be future research to resolve these issues, and that the studies be well-designed and well-controlled, taking these new variables into account.

Some organizations have used the research on caffeine to advocate that caffeine consumption be considered a social problem. This level of alarm is inappropriate; however, more education of the general public regarding caffeine is warranted. Educational efforts should cover known and probable health risks, misconceptions that caffeine counteracts the effects of alcohol, misconceptions about sources of caffeine, becoming aware of one's actual intake, and ways to reduce one's intake. Those who want to reduce or eliminate caffeine intake may do so on their own by reducing the concentration of caffeine in the foods or beverages that they consume (e.g., by steeping tea 1 minute instead of 5, mixing caffeinated and decaffeinated coffee), substituting noncaffeinated products for caffeinated ones (e.g., carob for chocolate, drinking fruit juice during coffee breaks, noncaffeinated for caffeinated over-the-counter medications), gradually eliminating occasions on which caffeine is consumed (e.g., coffee with the evening meal), and by organizing a support group of friends or co-workers. Some individuals may find it hard to reduce their intake of caffeine because they lack motivation, because of social pressure to consume, or because they do not want to give up the stimulating effects of caffeine. Such individuals may want to seek the help of health-care professionals who use systematic multi-component interventions that have been shown to be successful. In short, in order for individuals to decide to continue or change their caffeine habits, they must be informed.

Bibliography

American Psychiatric Association. (1987). *DSM-III-R: Diagnostic and Statistical Manual of Mental Disorders,* 3rd. ed., revised. American Psychiatric Association, Washington, DC.

Benowitz, N. L. (1990). Clinical pharmacology of caffeine. In "Annual Review of Medicine: Selected Topics in the Clinical Sciences" (W. P. Creger, C. H. Coggins, and E. W. Hancock, Eds.), Vol. 41. Annual Reviews, Inc., Palo Alto, CA.

Blount, J. P., and Cox, W. M. (1991). Caffeine. In "Encyclopedia of Human Biology" (R. Dulbecco, Ed.), Vol. II. Academic Press, San Diego.

Blount, J. P., and Cox, W. M. (1985). Perception of caffeine and its effects: Laboratory and everyday abilities. *Percept. Psychophys.* **38,** 55–62.

Bruce, M. S., and Lader, M. H. (1986). Caffeine: Clinical and experimental effects in humans. *Hum. Psychopharmacol.* **1,** 63–82.

Dews, P. B. (Ed.) (1984). "Caffeine: Perspectives from Recent Research." Springer-Verlag, Berlin.

Griffiths, R. R., and Woodson, P. P. (1988). Caffeine physical dependence: A review of human and laboratory animal studies. *Psychopharmacology* **94,** 437–451.

Fudin, R., and Nicastro, R. (1988). Can caffeine antagonize alcohol-induced performance decrements in humans? *Perceptual and Motor Skills* **67,** 375–391.

Hughes, J. R., Oliveto, A. H., Helzer, J. E., Higgins, S. T., and Bickeal, W. K. (1992). Should caffeine abuse, dependence or withdrawal be added to DSM-IV and ICD-10? *Am. J. Psych.* **149,** 33–40.

Humphreys, M. S., and Revelle, W. (1984). Personality, motivation, and performance: A theory of the relationship between individual differences and information processing. *Psychol. Rev.* **91,** 153–184.

James, J. E. (1991). "Caffeine & Health." Academic Press, San Diego.

Revelle, W., Humphreys, M. S., Simon, L., and Gilliland, K. (1980). The interactive effect of personality, time of day, and caffeine: A test of the arousal model. *J. Exp. Psychol. Gen.* **109,** 1–31.

Troyer, R. J., and Markle, G. E. (1984). Coffee drinking: An emerging social problem? *Soc. Problems* **31,** 403–416.

Watson, R. R. (1988). Caffeine: Is it dangerous to health? *Am. J. Health Promot.* **2**(4), 13–22.

◆

CALCULATION

Michael McCloskey and John Whalen
Johns Hopkins University

Glossary

Acquired dyscalculia Impairment in calculation or other numerical processing occurring as a result of brain damage.

Arithmetic fact A learned association between a basic arithmetic problem and its answer, such as $8 \times 7 = 56$.

Arithmetic rule A learned generalization applying to a class of basic arithmetic problems, such as $N + 0 = N$, $N \times 0 = 0$, or $N \times 1 = N$.

Backup strategy An alternative problem-solving strategy applied when the preferred method cannot be used (e.g., solving $7 + 4$ by counting when the fact $7 + 4 = 11$ cannot be retrieved from memory).

Calculation algorithm A learned sequence of steps for solving multi-digit arithmetic problems.

Nonuniform impairment The finding that brain-damaged patients with deficits in arithmetic fact retrieval usually show variation across problems in extent of impairment, even for problems comparable in problem size (e.g., intact performance on 8×9 in the presence of impaired performance on 7×9, 8×8, and 9×9).

Operand One of the numbers in an arithmetic problem. For example, in $9 + 3$, $9 - 3$, or 9×3 the operands are 9 and 3.

Operand error A multiplication fact retrieval error in which the incorrect response is correct for a problem that shares an operand with the stimulus problem. For example, in the error $6 \times 4 = 18$, the answer is correct for 6×3.

Proactive interference Difficulty in learning or remembering information caused by information learned previously.

Problem-size effect The finding of longer reaction times and higher error rates for simple problems with large operands (e.g., 8×6) than for problems with small operands (e.g., 3×2).

Retroactive interference Difficulty in remembering previously learned information occurring as a consequence of subsequent learning.

CALCULATION, as used in this article, refers to the solving of simple arithmetic problems through application of mathematical operations. Psychological research on calculation has been aimed at elucidating the cognitive representations and processes underlying arithmetic problem-solving, and the acquisition of these representations and processes.

I. COMPONENTS OF CALCULATION SKILL

Arithmetic calculation involves a wide range of cognitive processes. Consider the following multiplication problem:

$$\begin{array}{r} 309 \\ \times 28 \\ \hline \end{array}$$

Solving this problem requires various general numerical processes, such as recognizing and writing digits. Also implicated, however, are cognitive processes specific to calculation. These include retrieval from memory of arithmetic "table" facts such as $8 \times 9 = 72$, and perhaps also application of arithmetic rules such as $N \times 0 = 0$. Furthermore, the problem-solving process must be guided by a calculation algorithm that specifies an ordered series of steps for arriving at an answer (for example, start with the rightmost column, and retrieve from memory the product of the digits in this column; then write the ones digit of the product beneath the column, and hold the tens digit in working memory as a carry; and so forth). Cognitive research on calculation has explored a variety of issues concerning arithmetic facts, rules, and algorithms, with the bulk of the effort focusing on arithmetic fact retrieval. [*See* MEMORY; PROBLEM SOLVING.]

II. ISSUES AND METHODS IN THE STUDY OF CALCULATION

A. Fundamental Issues

Studies of calculation have centered around two related sets of theoretical issues. One set concerns the nature of the cognitive representations and processes underlying skilled calculation. Among the questions of current interest are, In what form are arithmetic facts stored in memory? How are these facts retrieved in the course of performing a calculation? Are some simple problems, such as 8×1, solved by application of a rule (e.g., $N \times 1 = N$) rather than by retrieval of a specific stored fact? Can differences among multi-digit arithmetic problems in speed and accuracy of solution be interpreted in terms of the number of component steps required in executing the appropriate calculation algorithm?

The second major set of issues concerns the acquisition of calculation skill. In this realm the specific questions include, How are arithmetic facts, rules, and algorithms learned in the early years of schooling? By what means do children perform calculations before they have fully learned these facts, rules, and algorithms? To what extent are phenomena observed in skilled calculation performance (e.g., variation in retrieval time among arithmetic facts) determined by experiences during learning?

B. Research Methods

Several research methods have been applied in addressing these theoretical issues. Studies of skilled calculation performance have typically involved presentation of single-digit (e.g., 6×7) or simple multi-digit (e.g., 59×43) problems to normal adult subjects. In production tasks the subject generates the answer to the problem (e.g., stimulus, 6×7; response, "forty-two"); in verification tasks the problem is presented with an answer, and the subject indicates whether the answer is correct (e.g., stimulus, $6 \times 7 = 48$; response, "no"). The dependent measures of principal interest are speed and accuracy of responding and, in production tasks, types of errors (e.g., $6 \times 7 = 35$ *versus* $6 \times 7 = 13$).

Recently, questions concerning normal skilled calculation have also been addressed through single-case studies of brain-damaged patients with various forms of calculation deficits (acquired dyscalculia). The rationale for this work is that the ways in which a cognitive process breaks down may reveal much about its normal structure and functioning. In using calculation deficits as a basis for inferences about normal calculation, researchers ask, What must the normal calculation processes be like such that disruption of these processes could result in the various observed patterns of impairment? For instance, analyses of patterns of impaired performance in patients with deficits in memory for arithmetic table facts have motivated conclusions about normal arithmetic fact retrieval.

Issues concerning acquisition of calculation skill typically are addressed through studies of children learning arithmetic. For example, developmental changes in speed of responding to single-digit arithmetic problems have offered insights into the process of learning arithmetic table facts; and analyses of children's errors in solving multi-digit problems have shed light on the nature and acquisition of calculation algorithms.

Despite the diversity of issues addressed and methods employed, the goal in research on calculation is to develop theoretical frameworks encompassing normal adult calculation, the acquisition of calculation skill, and the disruption of this skill by brain damage.

III. ARITHMETIC FACTS AND RULES

A. Cognitive Representations and Processes

1. Arithmetic Facts

Studies of arithmetic performance in normal and brain-damaged subjects have yielded several phenomena that speak to the representations and processes underlying arithmetic fact retrieval. In producing or verifying answers to single-digit arithmetic problems, both children and adults typically show longer reaction times and higher error rates for problems with large operands (e.g., 8×6) than for problems with small operands (e.g., 3×2). This problem-size effect is also observed in brain-damaged patients with deficits in memory for arithmetic facts: Problems with large operands typically show greater impairment than problems with small operands.

The studies of brain-damaged patients have also revealed that extent of impairment may vary considerably across problems. The nonuniform impairment is apparent even among problems comparable in operand size. For example, one reported patient showed very high rates for the multiplication problems 9 × 7, 8 × 8, and 9 × 9, yet was always correct for 8 × 9.

Analyses of error types in studies using production procedures have shown that arithmetic fact retrieval errors are highly systematic. For example, in multiplication the vast majority of errors are operand errors (also referred to as table-related errors), in which the incorrect response is correct for a problem sharing an operand with the stimulus problem. For example, in the error 8 × 7 = 48, the response is correct for 8 × 6. In most operand errors the incorrect response is correct for a problem that not only shares an operand with the stimulus problem, but also is close in magnitude with respect to the other operand. For example, given the problem 8 × 7, erroneous responses like 48 (correct for 8 × 6) and 63 (correct for 9 × 7) are far more common than errors like 16 (correct for 8 × 2) or 21 (correct for 3 × 7). This phenomenon has been labeled the operand distance effect.

Finally, studies with normal adults have revealed various priming effects in which responding to a problem influences speed or accuracy on subsequent problems. For example, producing the correct answer to a problem (e.g., 8 × 4 = 32) increases the likelihood that this answer will occur as an error to a related problem presented subsequently (e.g., 9 × 4 = 32). This phenomenon is referred to as error priming.

Several models of arithmetic fact retrieval have been proposed in attempts to account for the available phenomena. Table search models posit that arithmetic facts are stored in a table-like structure, as illustrated in Figure 1. Each row and column of the table is headed by a node representing a problem operand, and answer representations are stored at the intersection of the appropriate row and column. When a problem is presented, the appropriate row and column operand nodes are activated (e.g., the 8 row and 9 column nodes for 8 × 9; see Fig. 1). Activation then spreads across the row and down the column via associative links between nodes, until an intersection occurs at the node representing the correct answer. Time required to retrieve an answer

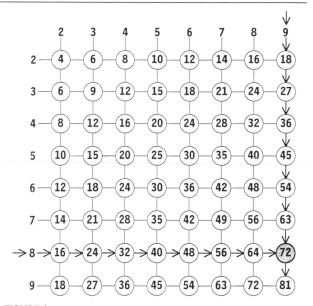

FIGURE 1 Table-like representation for multiplication facts postulated by table-search models. [Reproduced from McCloskey, M., Harley, W., and Sokol, M. S. (1991). *J. Exp. Psychol. Learning, Memory, Cog.* **17**(3), 377–397.]

is assumed to be simply the time required for the activation spreading across the row to intersect with the activation spreading down the column.

Table search models were motivated primarily by the finding of slower reaction time for small problems than for large problems, and offer a straightforward interpretation of this problem-size effect: Activation must spread farther through the table for large problems such as 8 × 9, than for small problems such as 4 × 3. However, recent studies have shown that the problem-size effects are less regular than required by table search models. Whereas the models predict a steady increase in reaction time as problem size increases, the data show several departures from this pattern. For example, tie problems—that is, problems with two identical operands, such as 7 + 7—show faster reaction times than expected on the basis of problem size, and 5's multiplication problems are typically found to be faster than 4's problems.

Table search models also have difficulty explaining the nonuniform impairment across problems observed in brain-damaged patients with deficits in memory for arithmetic facts. For example, it is unclear how disruption to a table-like representation such as that shown in Figure 1 could yield a performance pattern in which 8 × 9 was consistently correct while 9 × 7, 8 × 8, 7 × 9, and 9 × 9 showed severe impairment. Finally, researchers proposing table search models have not offered specific assumptions about how errors come about, or how priming effects might occur.

Figure 2 illustrates a somewhat different model of arithmetic fact retrieval, Ashcraft's network retrieval model. This model posits a memory network in which two sets of operand nodes (one for the first operand in a problem, and one for the second operand) are linked directly to answer nodes. For example, the first-operand 8 node and the second-operand 4 node are linked directly to a node representing the answer 32 (rather than being indirectly linked via other answer nodes, as in table search models). The model assumes that when a problem is presented, the corresponding operand nodes are activated, and activation then spreads to the connected answer nodes. The answer nodes for all multiples of the problem operands will receive some activation—for example, presentation of 6 × 3 will activate not only 18, but also 12, 24, 30, 42, and so forth. However, because only the correct answer node receives activation from both activated operand nodes, this answer is usually activated more strongly than the various other multiples of the problem operands.

The network retrieval model assumes that time to retrieve a fact is determined by the strength of association between the relevant operand nodes and the node for the correct answer. Associative strength is assumed to be a function of frequency of exposure to a problem, such that problems encountered more frequently have stronger associations in the memory network.

According to the network retrieval model, the problem-size effect occurs because small problems are encountered more often than large problems, and thus have stronger associations in memory. (In support of this assumption about variation in frequency with problem size, several studies have found that small problems have a higher frequency of occurrence than large problems in arithmetic textbooks.) Because exposure frequency need not be perfectly correlated with problem size (e.g., 5's multiplication problems may be encountered more frequently than 4's problems), the model is not embarrassed by findings showing irregularities in the problem-size effect.

Nonuniformity of impairment across problems in brain-damaged patients may also be interpreted, given the assumption that operand nodes are linked directly to answer nodes. For example, intact performance on 8 × 9 could occur in the presence of impairment on 7 × 9 and 8 × 8 if the associative links to the 63 and 64 answer nodes were disrupted by brain damage while the links to the 72 node were spared.

Like the table search models, Ashcraft's network retrieval model does not speak directly to error types or priming effects. However, the model could perhaps be elaborated to address these matters. For example, the predominance of operand errors in multiplication (e.g., 3 × 7 = 28) might be interpreted by reference to the assumption that when a problem is presented, the answer nodes for incorrect multiples of each operand are activated to some extent.

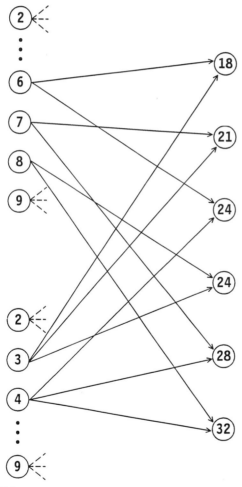

FIGURE 2   A representative portion of the arithmetic fact network postulated by Ashcraft's network retrieval model. The nodes in the upper left of the figure represent the first operand in a problem, the nodes in the lower left represent the second operand, and the nodes on the right represent answers. [Reproduced from McCloskey, M., Harley, W., and Sokol, M. S. (1991). *J. Exp. Psychol. Learning, Memory, Cog.* **17**(3), 377–397.]

A somewhat different conception of arithmetic fact representations and retrieval processes has been advanced by Siegler and colleagues. As illustrated in Figure 3, their distributions of associations model assumes that in the course of learning arithmetic facts, problem representations become associated with both correct and incorrect answers. Whenever the correct answer to a problem is studied or generated, a problem-to-correct-answer association is strengthened. However, if a student arrives at an incorrect answer to a problem (e.g., 8 × 7 = 48) then the association between the problem and this wrong answer is strengthened. According to the distribution of associations model, incorrect answers often occur as a result of errors in the use of backup strategies, methods for calculating an answer when it cannot be retrieved from memory. For example, a child who cannot retrieve the answer to 8 × 7 may solve the problem by repeated addition, adding 7 8's or 8 7's. If the child errs in performing the repeated addition—for example, by adding only 6 8's, or by making an addition errors such as 8 + 8 = 14—then the resulting incorrect answer

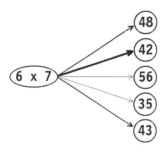

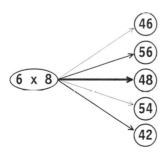

FIGURE 3   An example of fact representations postulated by Siegler's distribution of associations model, illustrating association of problems with correct and incorrect answers. Thickness of association lines indicates strength of association. [Reproduced from McCloskey, M., Harley, W., and Sokol, M. S. (1991). *J. Exp. Psychol. Learning, Memory, Cog.* **17**(3), 377–397.]

will increase in its strength of association to the problem.

Speed and accuracy of fact retrieval are assumed to be a function of the associative strength of the correct answer relative to the associative strength of incorrect answers. If a problem is much more strongly associated to the correct answer than to incorrect answers, then retrieval is assumed to be fast and accurate. On the other hand, if one or more erroneous answers have significant associative strength, then the correct answer may be retrieved slowly, or one of the associated incorrect answers may be retrieved instead. Thus, it is assumed that incorrect associations established during learning of arithmetic facts may continue to affect performance into and through adulthood.

The distribution of associations model provides novel accounts of several phenomena. The problem-size effect is interpreted by noting that errors in application of backup strategies are more likely for large problems than for small problems. For example, solving 8 × 7 by adding 7 8's is more likely to result in an error than solving 4 × 2 by adding 2 4's. As a consequence, associations to incorrect answers will usually be stronger for large than for small problems, leading to slower reaction times and higher error rates for the former.

Associations to incorrect answers also play a central role in the model's interpretations of error types. For example, the predominance of operand errors in multiplication is interpreted as follows: A common error in repeated addition is adding an operand too many or too few times (e.g., adding 7 6's or 9 6's when attempting to solve 6 × 8 by adding 8 6's). These errors will strengthen associations between problems and incorrect multiples of their operands (e.g., associations between the problem 6 × 8 and the answers 42 and 54). Subsequent retrieval of these incorrect associations will result in operand errors (e.g., 6 × 8 = 42, 6 × 8 = 54). Note that this interpretation also accounts for the operand distance effect, the finding that an operand error is usually the correct answer to a problem that not only shares an operand with the stimulus problem, but is also close in magnitude with respect to the other operand. A student using the repeated addition strategy is unlikely to err by more than 1 or 2 in the number of times an operand is added. For example, in attempting to add 8 6's a student might erroneously add 7 or 9 6's, but is unlikely to add 3 6's. Thus, errors in repeated addition may result in association of 6 × 8 with 42 and 54, but are unlikely to associate 6 × 8 with 18.

Although the distribution of associations model accounts well for some error type results, observed error patterns may not conform entirely to the predictions of the model. For example, children using repeated addition frequently make simple adding mistakes (e.g., $45 + 9 = 53$ in solving 9×6 by adding 6 9's), and these mistakes should lead to errors such as $9 \times 6 = 53$ in adults. However, these sorts of errors are quite uncommon in adult arithmetic fact retrieval performance.

Because the distribution of associations model assumes a separate representation for each problem in memory (see Fig. 2), the model allows for the possibility that brain damage may disrupt the representations for some problems while leaving other problem representations intact. Thus, the model can account for the finding of nonuniform impairment across problems in brain-damaged patients (e.g., impairment on 8×8 and 7×9 with intact performance on 8×9).

Priming effects, however, are not readily accommodated. Because each problem is assumed to have a separate representation in memory, responding to a problem (e.g., 8×4) should not affect problem–answer associative strengths for other problems (e.g., 9×4). Thus, the model cannot account for phenomena in which responding to a problem affects subsequent performance on other problems (e.g., increased likelihood for the error $9 \times 4 = 32$ caused by prior presentation of 8×4).

Finally, we consider briefly the network interference model proposed by Campbell and colleagues. This model combines many of the representational and processing assumptions of Ashcraft's network retrieval model and Siegler's distribution of associations model. For example, the network interference model posits operand-to-answer associations (as in the network retrieval model), as well as associations of whole-problem representations to correct and incorrect answers (as in the distribution of associations model). Thus, for many phenomena the network interference model can offer interpretations similar to those of derived from the other two models. For example, the problem-size effect is assumed to result in part from higher presentation frequency, and thus stronger associations in memory, for small problems than for large problems.

However, Campbell's network interference model places special emphasis on interference effects occurring during arithmetic fact learning and retrieval. For example, the problem-size effect is assumed to result not only from differences in pre-sentation frequency, but also from interfering effects of facts learned early in training on subsequent learning of other facts. Small facts such as $4 \times 3 = 12$, it is argued, are learned earlier than large facts such as $9 \times 8 = 72$, and hence the former cause proactive interference in learning of the latter. Similarly, in characterizing processes occurring during retrieval of a fact, Campbell's model emphasizes interference in retrieval of the correct answer caused by prior or concurrent activation of incorrect answer representations. For example, presentation of the problem 8×4 will result in strong activation of the answer mode for the number 32. This node may remain sufficiently activated for some time to result in errors like $9 \times 4 = 32$.

2. Arithmetic Rules

Several researchers have proposed that whereas most simple arithmetic problems are solved by retrieval of specific facts (e.g., $7 \times 4 = 28$), some problems may be solved by reference to rules applying to classes of problems. For example, all 0's addition problems may be solved by reference to the rule $N + 0 = N$, and the rule $N \times 0 = 0$ may underlie responses to 0's multiplication problems. Perhaps the clearest evidence in favor of this proposal comes from studies of brain-damaged patients with impairments in arithmetic fact retrieval. As discussed above, impairment is typically nonuniform across problems that are presumed to be solved by retrieval of specific facts (e.g., 7×9 and 9×9 may be impaired while 8×9 is intact). However, performance is usually found to be uniform within sets of problems that may be solved by rule. For example, extent of impairment is usually found to be the same for all 0's multiplication problems. Similarly, whereas re-training a patient on individual problems like 8×7 usually leads to little or no improvement on related problems like 8×6 or 8×8, re-training on one of a set of rule-based problems may lead to recovery for the entire set. For example, in patients who are uniformly incorrect on 0's multiplication problems, training on a single problem (e.g., 6×0) may lead to recovery on all of the 0's problems.

B. Acquisition

1. Arithmetic Facts

Learning of arithmetic table facts is a gradual process occurring over several years of schooling. For example, studies of elementary school children in the United States suggest that although instruction in addition begins in the first grade (if not before), addition facts are often not well-learned until the third or fourth grade.

Prior to and during the learning of arithmetic facts, children make extensive use of backup strategies in solving simple problems. Addition problems (e.g., 3 + 5) are usually solved by counting. Typically, the child starts with the maximum operand, and counts up from that operand a number of times equal to the minimum operand (e.g., for 3 + 5, counting up 3 from 5 to obtain 8). This min counting hypothesis is supported by results showing that first graders' response times for single-digit addition problems increased linearly with the minimum operand (as would be expected if each counting-up operation contributed a constant to the overall response time).

Children also use counting strategies in solving subtraction problems, either counting down from the first operand a number of times equal to the second operand (in which case the answer is the final value obtained), or counting down from the first operand to the second operand (in which case the answer is the number of counting-down steps required). For example, 8 − 5 may be solved by counting down 5 from 8 to obtain 3, or by counting down from 8 to 5 and noting that 3 counting-down steps were required. Some evidence suggests that children usually choose the strategy that minimizes the number of counting-down steps (e.g., solving 8 − 5 by counting down from 8 to 5, but solving 8 − 3 by counting down 3 from 8).

In the case of multiplication, the most common backup strategy used prior to learning of the table facts is repeated addition, in which one operand is added a number of times equal to the other operand. For example, 8 × 5 may be solved by adding 8 5's or 5 8's.

As might be expected, these sorts of backup strategies are relatively slow and prone to error. For example, one study found that third graders solving single-digit multiplication problems by repeated addition required an average of 23 seconds per problem, and arrived at the correct answer only about 60% of the time. Thus, memorization of arithmetic table facts is a crucial step toward achieving fast and accurate arithmetic problem solving.

As children begin to learn the table facts for an arithmetic operation, a gradual shift occurs from backup strategies to retrieval of memorized facts (e.g., retrieving the fact 5 + 3 = 8, rather than counting up 3 from 5). Early in learning, most prob-

lems are solved by backup strategies, with fact retrieval occurring only occasionally (usually for problems with small operands, such as 4 + 2, and tie problems such as 3 + 3). As learning progresses, reliance on backup strategies gradually decreases, and fact retrieval comes to predominate. However, some recent evidence suggests that even in many adults, backup strategies may be used for some particular facts the individual has found difficult to memorize. Also, backup strategies are frequently observed in brain-damaged patients who have retained their understanding of arithmetic operations, but are impaired in retrieval of table facts.

The various models of arithmetic fact retrieval offer somewhat different perspectives on the learning of arithmetic facts. Ashcraft's network retrieval model views the learning process as one of gradually strengthening associations between representations of the problem operands, and the representation of the correct answer (e.g., for the fact 8 × 7 = 56, strengthening associations between the 8 and 7 operand representations, and the 56 answer representation). On this account a fact has been learned when the operand–answer associations are sufficiently strong that the correct answer representation is activated to at least some threshold level when the problem is presented.

Whereas the network retrieval model focuses on operand-to-correct-answer associations, Siegler's distribution of associations model considers associations of problem representations to both correct and incorrect answers. Studying or generating an answer to a problem is assumed to strengthen the association between the problem and answer representations in memory, whether the answer is correct or incorrect. Usually, correct answers are encountered or generated more often than incorrect answers, and so the associative strength of the correct answer gradually increases relative to the strength of association for incorrect answers. However, incorrect answers resulting from common errors in use of backup strategies may accrue significant associative strength. As discussed in the preceding section, the associations to incorrect answers are assumed to be an important determinant of retrieval speed and accuracy not only in childhood but also in adulthood.

Finally, Campbell's network interference model emphasizes effects of learning a fact on acquisition of other facts. As previously noted, this model assumes that the problem-size effect occurs in part because facts introduced early in schooling (usually facts involving small operands, such as 2 + 2 = 4) cause proactive interference in acquisition of facts introduced later (usually facts involving large operands, such as $8 + 6 = 14$). The network interference model does not consider interfering effects of later-learned facts on memory for facts learned earlier. However, such retroactive interference effects may also play a significant role in arithmetic fact learning and retrieval. For example, one recent study found that student's performance on addition fact retrieval deteriorated temporarily but substantially when the students began learning multiplication facts.

2. Arithmetic Rules

Whereas a considerable amount of research has explored acquisition of arithmetic facts (e.g., $8 \times 7 = 56$), learning of arithmetic rules (e.g., $N \times 1 = N$) has received little attention. Counts of the frequency with which particular problems appear in arithmetic textbooks suggest that problems potentially solvable by rule (e.g., 6×1) typically occur less frequently than problems for which individual facts must be learned (e.g., 6×3). This finding presumably reflects the fact that instruction for the rule-based problems involves explicit teaching of the rules, with a reduced emphasis on drill of individual problems.

Some results suggest that whereas certain arithmetic rules are easily acquired, others are not. For example, two studies conducted over 50 years ago assessed the relative difficulty of individual arithmetic problems in school children. In the case of addition the 0's problems (e.g., $7 + 0$, $0 + 5$) proved to be among the easiest for children to solve, suggesting perhaps that the $N + 0 = N$ rule is readily acquired. Similarly, $N - 0$, $N - N$, and $N \times 1$ problems were among the easiest in their respective operations, suggesting that the rules $N - 0 = N$, $N - N = 0$, and $N \times 1 = N$ are also easy to learn. In contrast, multiplication-by-0 problems (e.g., 6×0, 0×3) were found to be among the most difficult multiplication problems. This finding, and other more recent results, suggest that the $N \times 0 = 0$ rule is for some reason difficult to learn. One speculation is that as a result of learning the $N + 0 = N$ and $N - 0 = N$ rules, children induce the more general but incorrect rule $N \ op \ 0 = N$, where op is any arithmetic operation. The resulting expectation that N is the correct answer to a problem of the form $N \times 0$ may create difficulty in learning the correct rule $N \times 0 = 0$. Consistent with this account, errors on 0's multiplication problems in children and adults virtually always take the form $N \times 0 = N$.

IV. CALCULATION ALGORITHMS

A. Cognitive Representations and Processes

Like arithmetic rules, calculation algorithms (i.e., procedures specifying the steps required to solve multi-digit arithmetic problems) have been studied less extensively than arithmetic facts. However, several basic findings have emerged from recent research. First, studies of brain-damaged patients have shown that knowledge of calculation algorithms may be disrupted while knowledge of arithmetic facts remains intact, and vice versa. For example, a patient with preserved calculation algorithms but impaired arithmetic fact retrieval may successfully execute all of the steps involved in solving a multi-digit multiplication problem, while at the same time erring on one or more of the arithmetic table facts (e.g., answering 2484 rather than 3284 to 821×4, due to the fact retrieval error $4 \times 8 = 24$). These results suggest that cognitive representations of calculation algorithms are functionally and neuroanatomically separate from the representations of arithmetic facts.

A second basic finding, obtained in studies with normal adults, is that reaction times for solving multi-digit arithmetic problems vary meaningfully with the number of component steps assumed to be involved in applying the relevant calculation algorithm. For instance, problems requiring a carry operation (e.g., $34 + 28$) systematically take longer to solve than problems that do not require carrying (e.g., $26 + 43$). Findings such as these accord with intuition in suggesting (a) that execution of a calculation algorithm involves carrying out a sequence of component steps, and (b) that the algorithms provide for variation in the particular steps depending upon the nature of the problem being solved (e.g., whether or not carrying is required).

Finally, research with brain-damaged patients suggests that calculation algorithms may include special-case procedures that apply to certain classes of problems. For example, patients who are severely impaired in solving single-digit multiplication-by-zero problems may nevertheless process 0's flawlessly in the context of multi-digit problems. For example, a patient who consistently responds 3 to 3×0 or 0×3 may nevertheless answer 906 and not 936 to 302 × 3. This finding suggests that for at least some individuals, 0's in multi-digit multiplication problems are not treated like other digits, but rather are handled by special procedures. Thus, the problem 302 × 3 may be solved not by multiplying 3 × 2, then 3 × 0, and then 3 × 3, but rather by multiplying 3 × 2, then applying a special-case procedure to the 0 (e.g., when a 0 is encountered in the top number, bring down the 0 or the current carry value if there is one), and then multiplying 3 × 3.

B. Acqusition

Children in the process of learning calculation algorithms frequently err in solving multi-digit arithmetic problems. The errors are not random, but rather appear to reflect systematic "bugs" in the children's algorithms. For example, a child who has not fully mastered the subtraction algorithm may consistently subtract the smaller number in a column from the larger numer, regardless of which number is on top (e.g., obtaining 33 for 53 − 26 as well as 56 − 23). In this instance the child's subtraction algorithm includes the "subtract-smaller-from-larger" bug, which leads to predictable errors on any problem requiring borrowing. A large number of procedural bugs have been identified through studies of children's error patterns on multi-digit arithmetic problems, and the specific bugs evident in a child's performance have been found to vary across individuals (as well as within individuals as learning of an algorithm proceeds).

Children's procedural bugs may arise at least in part from attempts to "repair" incomplete calculation algorithms. Consider, for example, a child whose subtraction algorithm does not include procedures for borrowing, but rather specifies only that the bottom number in each column should be subtracted from the top number. When a situation requiring borrowing is encountered (e.g., the right-hand column in 53 − 26), the incomplete algorithm simply does not specify what should be done, because (as far as the child knows) a larger number cannot be subtracted from a smaller number. Thus, the child is said to be at an *impasse*. The impasse may trigger a *repair* process in which the incomplete algorithm is modified in such a way that it can now be applied to situations of the sort that created the original impasse. In the present example, the subtraction algorithm may be modified to specify that the smaller number in each column is subtracted from the larger number. The modified algorithm is more complete than the original, because it now applies to problems like 53 − 26 as well as to problems such as 56 − 23. However, the repair has introduced the "subtract-smaller-from-larger" bug, and hence will result in errors on problems that require borrowing.

Bibliography

Ashcraft, M. H. (1992). Cognitive arithmetic: A review of data and theory. *Cognition* **44**, 75–106.

Campbell, J. I. D. (Ed.) (1992). "The Nature and Origins of Mathematical Skills." Elsevier, Amsterdam.

McCloskey, M., Harley, W., and Sokol, S. M. (1991). Models of arithmetic fact retrieval: An evaluation in light of findings from normal and brain-damaged subjects. *J. Exp. Psychol. Learning, Memory, Cog.* **17**, 377–397.

McCloskey, M. (1992). Cognitive mechanisms in numerical processing: Evidence from acquired dyscalculia. *Cognition* **44**, 107–157.

Siegler, R. S. (1988). Strategy choice procedures and the development of multiplication skill. *J. Exp. Psychol. Gen.* **117**, 258–275.

vanLehn, K. (1990). "Mind Bugs: The Origins of Procedural Misconceptions." MIT Press, Cambridge, MA.

CAREER DEVELOPMENT

Samuel H. Osipow
The Ohio State University

Glossary

Congruence The fit between work environment and personal type.

Correspondence The fit between work requirements and work personality.

Psychology of careers The description of career lives (after Super).

Psychology of occupations Requirements for success in an occupation (after Super).

Self-efficacy Expectancy of performing a task to a successful outcome.

Vocational maturity Individual level of mastery of vocational developmental tasks.

Vocational psychology Combines the psychology of occupations and the psychology of careers (after Super).

CAREER DEVELOPMENT reflects the sequence of career decisions and activities of an individual over the course of their career life to date. Implied in that definition is the notion that careers can be enhanced (thus, developed) by self-aware activities of the individuals themselves, counselors, human resource personnel, educators, and others who have the potential to significantly touch the work lives of people. This definition not only describes one's career but also describes the interventions that may improve that career progression. Both of those components are discussed in this article.

I. HISTORY OF THE FIELD

The psychology of career development is a relatively new subject area, having its origins near the begin-ning of the 20th century in the work of Frank Parsons (1909). Parsons, concerned with the difficulties encountered by many young men in finding a suitable means for entering the work force, developed a program, called the Breadwinners College, offered through the YMCA in Boston, designed to help identify personal skills and abilities and match them to careers. From this modest beginning, a complex set of professional services and procedures has resulted.

While Parsons is usually credited as providing the first career services, the roots of thought about careers as a systematic process can be traced to much earlier times. Notions of work as necessary and often onerous are seen in Biblical writings, e.g., the story of Adam and Eve's expulsion from the Garden of Eden includes the need to labor for one's sustenance. According to Williamson's historical analysis of the field, during the Renaissance work was seen to have the potential to be intrinsically meaningful, and Martin Luther later introduced the idea of the vocation as a calling to use one's potential in their life's work.

The need to develop formal concepts and procedures to aid in decisions about career entry and progress only came about when society created structures that differentiated work activity, because of industrialization, and when policy included the conception of individual choice in work. If no options exist either because work is homogenous or because an individual's work is preordained by virtue of their family and/or birth order, then there is no need to create understandings about careers and their development.

Other events early in the 20th century also promoted concepts and practices now known as the field of career development. World War I saw the first mass psychological testing program, the Army alpha testing of millions of newly mobilized men, in order to permit improved training and assignment decisions. The success of this program led to the creation of agencies to develop large numbers of new industrial tests all throughout the 1920s and 1930s, including a wide range of Minnesota abilities tests. Also, the early work on interest assessment was started by Strong in the 1920s and Kuder in the 1930s.

The depression era saw more significant career programs developed: the ground work for the General Aptitude Test Battery and the basis for the Dictionary of Occupational Title were laid during this period, and set the stage for yet another substantial growth spurt in the use of tests driven by the World War II human resource assignment needs. The testing and assessment tools developed in the first 40 years of the century were then widely implemented in training and assignment issues affecting the lives of millions of people.

However, it was not until after World War II that general recognition of the need for a conceptual basis for understandings about careers occurred. This was largely stimulated by the development of vocational guidance centers to help veterans make the transition from the military to civilian life. The GI Bill created educational opportunities previously denied to them for millions of men and women that made the issue of career choice as opposed to job choice relevant to many for whom careers had been an elusive or impossible goal. Whereas previous career counseling efforts had been designed primarily to aid students in making entry level decisions, such as postsecondary training or not, the concept of careers involved a more ambitious level of planning than previous vocational guidance efforts. [*See* VOCATIONAL CHOICE.]

Consequently, in the late 1940s and 1950s, two elements came together to create our contemporary conception of career development: the tools of career assessment combined with the efforts of a few pioneers attempting to sketch theoretical ideas about how careers unfold. This wedding created the beginning of the efforts now described as career development, which is part of the field of vocational psychology. According to Super, a leading figure in the field over more than half a century, vocational psychology consists of two subfields: the psychology of occupations, which describes the characteristics required for success in various fields of work, and the psychology of careers, which describes the career lives of individuals.

II. IMPORTANT THEORETICAL CONCEPTIONS

In discussing the theories that have had a major impact on understandings of career development it must be noted that most of them, if not all, have sought to describe career processes and seek to identify potentially useful interventions. The early attempts to provide a conceptual basis for understanding career development include a number of approaches: Super's developmental theory, Roe's parent–child interaction theory of careers, Holland's person–environment approach, Ginzberg, Ginsburg, Axelrad, and Herma's developmental theory, and a variety of psychodynamic theories (e.g., Bordin, Nachmann, and Segel).

More recently, the theories can be usefully grouped into person–environment theories, which include Holland's theory and the theory of work adjustment of Dawis and Lofquist; developmental theories, still including the active theory of Super and more recently developed theoretical statements by L. Gottfredson and Vondracek, Lerner, and Schulenberg; and finally, social learning theory applied to career development, the most notable example being the work of Krumboltz, Mitchell, and Jones, The most active contemporary theories are Holland's, Dawis and Lofquist's, Super's, and social learning theory. Psychodynamic theories are still sometimes used, but have generally diminished in importance in the career area, and the theories of Roe and of Ginzberg *et al.* have faded largely because of weak empirical support and/or superseded by similar but more powerful theories.

Holland's theory, one of the two major person–environment theories, is very influential, serving as the basis for considerable research and practice in the field of career development. Holland proposes that six personal orientations to the world exist, namely realistic, investigative, artistic, social, enterprising, and conventional, each of which represents a distinctive approach to perceiving and responding to the world. Briefly summarized, realistic people are practical and take a concrete stand toward matters. They are often individuals in fields such as agriculture, police and military work, and various technical fields at all levels. Investigative individuals are rational problem solvers who are attracted to fields focusing on systematic inquiry such as the sciences, but also engage in trouble shooting. Artistic people focus on aesthetic matters. Social people emphasize supportive interpersonal activities, such as found in teaching, and the various helping professions. Enterprising people also emphasize interpersonal activities but in a more self-serving manner, such as in sales and law. Finally, conventional people focus on routine, repetitive, systems work, such as accounting or routine clerical activities. The Holland system provides methods for assigning individuals to the types. Of course, people are too complex to easily categorize as one type, so Holland suggests that two or three digit type codes be used to classify people.

Holland's system includes a similar method to analyze environments. Each work setting reflects one of the types that characterizes the work environment, again, coded into three digits representing three of the six typologies. The essence of the theory is that individuals seek congruence between their personal typology and their work environment typology. Where that congruence is high, the theory predicts high levels of satisfaction, persistence, and productivity. Where that congruence is low, satisfaction, persistence, and productivity will be poor. Workers seek congruence.

A second major person–environment theory is the theory of work adjustment, developed by Dawis and Lofquist at the University of Minnesota over a period of more than 35 years. Like Holland's theory, this theory also emphasizes the importance of the person–environment fit in predicting worker satisfaction and productivity, but the specific variables are somewhat different. Here, the worker is not categorized as a member of a type, but instead, is described in terms of personality characteristics such as achievement orientation, need for autonomy, etc. Dawis and Lofquist, like Holland, provide a series of methods to use in assessing these characteristics. In addition, the theory is concerned with job performance, and uses a structured method to assess supervisor judgments of worker productivity. Finally, the work setting is characterized by its potential to satisfy various psychological needs, called reinforcers. Where the work setting provides needs important to the worker's personality, satisfaction is seen to be high; where the worker performs in a manner highly consistent with the supervisor's requirements, the worker is seen to be satisfactory; where both variables are high, the outcome is a high level of correspondance, a desirable condition. Workers seek correspondance. One important difference between the theory of work adjustment and Holland's theory is in the emphasis given by the theory of work adjustment to descriptions of how the individual's work personality (e.g., needs requirements and performance attributes) comes about, while Holland's theory provides much less attention and detail to that issue.

A number of developmental theories exist, the most notable being Super's approach. Building on the idea that careers are developmental, Super proposed that individuals pass through a variety of stages in their lives, each of which requires the mastery of a distinctive set of vocationally related behaviors. Mastery of these behaviors reflects the individual's degree of vocational maturity. Efforts are expended by individuals and institutions to foster growth in the vocational developmental tasks for the relevant age level, in order to facilitate vocational maturity. This maturity underlies the vocational behaviors and decisions required by one's life state are made. In addition to vocational maturity, however, a personal maturation occurs in which the self-concept emerges and shapes the content of appropriate career decision-making. Consequently, progress through vocational developmental tasks leads the individual to develop the skills required to make decisions regarding career entry, adjustment, and progress. The specific content of these decisions is seen to reflect the accuracy of the individual's ability to implement the self-concept in their choice of work. Thus, career choice and development is seen to reflect the adequacy of self-concept implementation. This concept is similar to Holland's congruence concept, and to the theory of work adjustment concept of correspondence.

The final major theoretical approach to career development is the social learning theory. This approach is substantially different from those described earlier. This theory attempts to predict and describe the process of career development and decision-making rather than the timing and the content of the decisions. It is built on the notion that career development reflects a series of individual variables such as genetic background, learning experiences, and skills, as well as variables describing social context, such as the economy, the political climate, educational resources, etc. Social learning theory would see variables such as career self-efficacy to be critically important outcomes of the variables mentioned previously, which in their turn have an important impact on the way people go about making important career decisions that have developmental implications. Furthermore, career decision process is seen to be life long, implying that career issues wax and wane. This variability in individuals' level of focus on career issues results in a very interactive view of how careers unfold. The similarities and differences between these theories were the topic of a recent conference on the issue of theory convergence in career development.

III. CONTEMPORARY ISSUES IN CAREER DEVELOPMENT

Since the study of career development has a very practical and immediate aspect in human affairs, a number of applied issues have emerged for study. Some of the most significant of these are discussed below. These issues are usefully organized in terms of life stages defined in terms of career entry, career adjustment and maintenance, and career departure and retirement.

A. Problems in Career Development

Campbell and Cellini attempted to devise a developmentally based taxonomy to classify career problems with the goal of creating problem-specific interventions. Career counseling and program interventions have existed literally since Parson's early work. A few writers, notably E. G. Williamson and H. B. Pepinsky, made early attempts to classify career problems and relate them to counseling. However, the attempts were necessarily very rudimentary, given the knowledge based that existed to understand career development issues. Campbell and Cellini's taxonomy was an attempt to build a complex system to sort out adult career problems, based upon an extensive data base, that would be specific enough to lead others to devise assessment procedures and interventions and, thus, impel the field toward some necessary standardization in both research and practice. Their work was based upon developmental models of career issues, and reflects the concept that career problems emerge over the lifespan in ways that are predictable by life stage.

The Campbell and Cellini taxonomy divides problems into four major categories. The first category describes problems in career decision-making, further subdivided into getting started, information gathering, generating, evaluating, and selecting alternatives, and formulating plans for implementing decisions. Each of these within the first problem category is yet further divided to an even more concrete level. Categories 2, 3, and 4 describe, in turn, problems in implementing career plans, problems in organizational/institutional performance, and problems in organizational/institutional adaptation. Once again, each category is subdivided, and subdivided once again. So, for example, category 3.2B includes problems in organizational/institutional performance (3), in the personal factors subcategory (3.2), and most specifically as debilitating physical

and/or emotional disorders (3.2B). Thus, individual issues in career development can be very specifically defined and described. While each category is not yet open to adequate psychometric assessment, the categories do provide a useful general guide to many of the issues of importance to us in describing and understanding career development.

B. Career Entry

Long recognized as a problem for young people about to enter the labor market, career decision and indecision has more recently been seen to be an issue for older individuals who also need to make changes in their work lives because of both internal issues (e.g., poor initial choices) or external issues (e.g., labor market issues). However, most of the research and assessment of career indecision has focused on late adolescents or early adults.

Two major approaches to examining career indecision are commonly taken. The first is an empirically derived measure called the Career Decision Scale identifying sixteen potential reasons people have difficulty in deciding about their careers. The CDS has been used to identify problems for intervention, and also as a criterion for assessing the outcome of programmatic interventions designed to resolve career indecision. The second approach is called My Vocational Situation, which also attempts to assess antecedents related to career indecision, such as vocational identity, information, and barriers.

The creation of these measures has generated considerable interest in research and practice in dealing with career indecision. One resulting observation is that a certain amount of career indecision is relatively common and normal, and when present at certain life stages and to a moderate degree, may even facilitate the career development process. When career indecision persists, however, or is present to an extreme degree, it is called career indecisiveness, and suggests a more basic, underlying set of personal problems and issues that must be resolved in order for the individual to function effectively. Career indecisiveness can create serious problems in career entry, which, carried on too long, can impair the career development process.

C. Career Adjustment Issues

Using the lifespan approach to examining career development, the primary task suggested for the major part of the lifespan consists of a series of work adjustment issues. Among the tasks included are adjustment to work upon entry, issues related to career advancement and career satisfaction, and the transition to retirement.

In addition, a number of career adjustment issues deal with what might be called "deviations" in the process or special considerations, such as mental health issues associated with work. These latter include factors such as occupational stress, the impact of unemployment, and barriers imposed by membership in a particular social class or ethnic group, or by virtue of gender.

Generally speaking, adjustment to career immediately upon entry involves acquiring behaviors and attitudes that are effective in learning the formal and informal work rules of the employment setting. It is commonly noted that among the most likely causes of job termination is the individual's failure to maintain good interpersonal relationships with co-workers and supervisors. Even when performance may be less than desired, many employers will be slower to terminate the services of someone who "fits into" the work place. Thus, the new worker's task includes a strong emphasis on interpersonal adjustment as well as job performance.

As time goes on, however, career development requires the worker to become aware of those behaviors that will permit advancement. These include self-knowledge and information about career ladders and the behaviors and skills necessary to move up on those ladders. In addition, the worker needs to become knowledgeable about the ways to shift from one career path to another that may increase the satisfaction of more of the individual's goals, by job changes, more education and training, and even changes in organization and field of work.

Most workers mark their career progress in one or more of several ways. Some use the frequency and size of salary or income increases. Others use job titles and supervisory roles as markers. Still others find access to job functions more to their personal liking as indicators of their career development, and some use regularity in employment as a sign of success. Workers generally use some combination of all these to reflect their progress in career development. Professional, managerial, skilled, and unskilled workers probably emphasize different combinations of markers to assess their career progress, but the principle of using the achievement of some goals, intrinsic or extrinsic, applies to all. Some individuals are less likely to be aware of these markers, and, consequently, may manage their careers less effi-

ciently. In addition, some employment situations do not permit the worker as easy access to controlling and achieving their work goals as do others.

At some point, the rate of frequency of appearance of these markers slows down, and the individual begins to reach a career plateau in which it may become increasingly obvious that maximum career growth has been achieved. At this point, workers begin to make their transition to retirement. For some, this transition may occur over a long period of years. Others are more abruptly exposed to the need to plan for retirement. Individuals who have health problems that occur rapidly or who work in industries downsizing by encouraging older workers to retire before they reach planned retirement ages are among those who have less time in transition to retirement.

D. Career Adjustment Problems

Arising out of these issues of achieving optimum career development are a number of potential problems for workers. Some are related to career satisfaction and dissatisfaction. When the career markers are not achieved to the workers satisfaction, or if the worker is so unaware of these markers as to fail to recognize progress, some dissatisfaction can occur. Also significant in producing worker dissatisfacton are poor relationships with co-workers and supervisors.

Generally, satisfaction and dissatisfaction can occur in response to levels of pay, job duties, supervisory relationships, and co-workers. Some investigators have also observed that perceived equity in rewards and treatment in the workplace plays a large role in job satisfaction. All these variables combine to produce overall job satisfaction levels. These levels are not constant or stable over time, but vary, probably as the perception of the variables noted above change.

Individuals use various devices to deal with dissatisfaction on the job. Obviously, seeking job changes is a common strategy, but some workers try to alter the circumstances of their workplace to improve satisfaction, while others merely continue in unsatisfactory work situations.

It should be noted that there is a difference between job satisfaction and career satisfaction. Noting that a job is situation specific and a career represents a series of positions of employment over time, it is easy to see how one may experience fairly wide variations in job satisfaction as a function of the specific situations surrounding each job one holds, but that career satisfaction levels are likely to be more stable because they represent events occurring over longer periods of time. Occasionally one observes individuals who occupy only one or two jobs over their career, but it is more common for individuals to have many jobs over a lifetime. These jobs may have more or less in common with each other.

Another kind of career adjustment problem occurs in connection with occupational stress. Most investigators of occupational stress use the Selye formulation assuming that stress represents the disruption of homeostasis. Applied to work settings it is expected that in the normal course of events, people will experience a variation in the demands of their work situation whose parameters fall within some predictable range of experience. When that range is abruptly expanded, the individual is placed under "stress" until the necessary behavioral adjustments are made to resolve the cause and effects of the expansion of the parameters. This conception does not view stress as necessarily undesirable, in that stress may provide the opportunity to develop new responses and to grow. What makes stress undesirable at times is the individual's inability to respond appropriately because of the lack of response capacity or because the stressors themselves exceed the existing maximum capacity needed to resolve them possessed by the individual. [See STRESS.]

Clearly, the work environment possesses many potential sources of stress. Osipow and Spokane have described these sources of stress in their model of occupational stress as overload, responsibility, insufficiency, ambiguity, boundary spanning, and physical environment. The Osipow and Spokane model proposes that individuals may experience stress in their work environment from the sources noted above and attempt to resolve the stress by means of the use of various coping resources such as recreation, self-care, social support, and rational–cognitive procedures. The adequacy of their coping responses may be seen in the degree of strain that results, as reflected in psychological, interpersonal, vocational, and physical outcomes. Reduction of strain, the undesirable outcomes, may be achieved through coping resources, modification of the stressors in the work environment, or some combination of the two. Workers who have chronic difficulties in reducing occupational strain to acceptable levels ordinarily voluntarily move to different job situations or develop behavioral patterns that interfere so significantly with their work adjustment and/or productivity that they cannot continue in their work.

Occupational stress is but one manifestation of the mental health correlates associated with career development. Clearly, individuals who are highly stressed in their work over long periods of time are likely candidates for various psychological disorders. These may include anxiety, depression, phobic responses, sleep disorders, and substance abuse, to name a few common problems that may be associated with career stressors over time.

It has also been established that there are other connections between overall mental health and career development, ranging from problems in early career decisions seen in individuals with mental disturbances, the reduced ability of interest measures to predict careers in individuals with deviant Minnesota Multiphasic Personality Inventory profiles, and the interactive nature of substance abuse problems in career lives. Recent studies, for the most part carried out in Great Britain, reveal a connection between abrupt unemployment and mental illness. Since most of the early reactions to unemployment by social agencies focus exclusively on gaining reemployment for the worker, the psychological consequences are usually ignored, and can lead to even more disruptive career behavior if they are not treated promptly. Thus, for example, the unnoticed effects of depression can further impair the job-seeking behaviors necessary for the worker to obtain employment.

E. Career Assessment

The assessment of career development has assumed considerable importance in helping individuals make sound decisions as well as in testing aspects of theory about career development. There appear to be two major ways career assessment takes place. The first has to do with the measurement of the individual's interests, abilities, and personality. This process is used to increase the ability to make career entry and maintenance decisions based on information that relates to the fit between the individual and various career settings.

For these purposes an entire industry devoted to career measurement has grown. There are dozens of widely used instruments to measure and predict interest satisfaction. These approach the task either by comparing the interests of one individual to those of various criterion groups chosen because their interests are distinctive and related to satisfaction in a particular career. Of these the two best known are the Strong Interest Inventory and the Kuder Occupational Interest Survey.

The other major approach is what might be called a process method in which the content of the individual's interests is assessed for purposes of identifying the career directions that might satisfy the manifest interests of the individual. A good example of this approach is Holland's Self-Directed Search.

Abilities assessment is an essential part of determining career potential. It seems obvious that the mastery of certain skills, or the potential to master them efficiently, is important to career success. Thus, the measurement of abilities can help point to those careers most compatible with sets of skills that the individual possesses. The most comprehensive of these measures is the General Aptitude Test Battery, which measures abilities along a variety of abstract and concrete dimensions and which is connected to the world of work through Occupational Aptitude Profiles that have been developed in concert with the Dictionary of Occupational Titles. Various combinations of scores have been determined to predict success in training for or the performance of certain occupations. This information can aid one in selecting a family of jobs for which to train. Other ability measures have been developed for use with younger individuals, these including the Differential Aptitude Test, which measures different abilities and is generally used in high school academic settings to help students make curricular choices.

Finally, personality measures are also often used to sharpen the career development process. While some recommend the use of instruments with a psychopathology base, such as the Minnesota Multiphasic Personality Inventory, most would recommend instruments that measure personality traits or styles, such as the Minnesota Importance Questionnaire, which measures psychological needs, or the NEO, the California Psychological Inventory, or the Sixteen Personality Factors Questionnaire, all of which measure major personality styles in terms that can intuitively be related to job and career tasks. Since there are little data that indicate that certain personality styles and traits are directly related to certain occupational directions, most career development professionals use personality data as context and background information for helping individuals understand their prospects and work style. [*See* TRAITS.]

The second major way that assessment plays a part in careers development has to do with the developmental aspect of careers. Various instruments have been devised to assess an individual's life stage with respect to careers. The two major instruments are the Career Development Inventory, created by Super and his colleagues, and the Career Maturity Inventory by Crites. These measures can identify the level of career maturity possessed by an individual, at least through the early stages of career development. These results are used to enhance the identification of potential barriers the individual may be facing in terms of acquiring career development behaviors necessary to effective career progress.

F. Career Barriers

In addition to the barriers to career development described by limitations in one's abilities, interests, and personality as noted above, three other categories of events often raise barriers to career access. These include gender issues, social class, racial, and ethnicity issues, and economic conditions.

1. Gender Barriers

Sex-role stereotypes have long played a role in limiting the career development of women, and to a smaller extent, that of men as well. The socialization process women and men go through culturally teaches people that certain roles and values are more suitable for one sex than for the other. Stereotypically, women are expected to be nurturant, passive, and submissive in their relations with others, while men are taught to be dominant, assertive or even aggressive, and competitive in their interpersonal relations. Furthermore, women have traditionally been expected to be home oriented and child care focused at the expense of work outside the home, while men have been expected to emphasize their work and financial success. Paid employment that is pursued by women has been expected to incorporate these personal and role requirements and characteristics. The result has been that women's careers have been intermittent to permit childbearing and child-caring activities. Thus, careers in teaching, nursing, and clerical activities have been seen to be not only appropriate but also convenient for women to pursue if they work outside the home at all. Men, on the other hand, have had nearly (but not completely) a free choice in their career aspirations. The only limitations were those imposed by personal qualities influencing their career access, and, to a small extent, sex-role stereotypes that kept men limited to small numbers in certain females stereotyped fields such as nursing, social work, elementary teaching, and secretarial jobs, for example.

This has changed significantly since the 1970s because of the advent of the resurgent feminist movement. Women have demanded and gained access to the fuller range of career prospects, and most sex-role stereotypes associated with employment have been assailed, although considerable sex-role bias and stereotyping continue to exist. Most occupations reflect sex segregation in membership to some extent and in income to a more significant degree. However, the career differences between men and women have been significantly reduced in the past generation, it is clear that much change has occurred, and many of the sex-based barriers have been permeated.

2. Social Class, Race, and Ethnicity

Matters of social class, ethnicity, and especially race, have created barriers for certain groups in our society, notably African Americans, Hispanic Americans, American Indians, and Asian Americans. Issues of racial discrimination and racial tension have worked to limit access to certain careers based on personal qualities for racial minority groups members. These have resulted in significant income differences between those groups and the majority groups. Social class issues confound the issue, since race and ethnicity seem disproportionally related to poverty, which, in turn, impairs access to the high-quality education needed for entry to and success in many desirable career fields. As is so for women, these barriers have been permeated, but so many problems related to career access remain for minority groups that career development

processes and outcomes remain impaired and are very different than for majority culture males.

3. Economic Barriers

Career development occurs in the context of economic issues. When the economy is expanding and the demand for workers of all kinds is high, individuals tend to experience satisfactory career development and progress. Conversely, when the economy is weak, people lose their jobs and seek whatever employment they can find. Usually, these new jobs represent discontinuities in career development, and even worse, regression. Career development specialists have been required to pay more attention to these nonpsychological matters in understanding how career development occurs and can be enhanced.

Bibliography

Betz, N. E., and Fitzgerald, L. F. (1987). "The Career Psychology of Women." Academic Press, New York.
Brown, and Brooks, L. (1991). "Career Counseling Techniques." Allyn-Bacon, Boston.
Dawis, R., and Lofquist, L. (1984). "A Psychological Theory of Work Adjustment." University of Minnesota Press, Minneapolis, MN.
Holland, J. L. (1985). "Making Vocational Choices: A Theory of Careers, 2nd ed. Prentice-Hall, Englewood Cliffs, NJ.
Lent, R., and Savickas, M. (Eds.) (1994). "Convergence in Career Development Theories: Implications for Science and Practice." Consulting Psychologists Press, Palo Alto, CA.
Osipow, S. H. (1983). "Theories of Career Development, 3rd. ed. Prentice-Hall, Englewood Cliffs, NJ.
Spokane, A. R. (1991). "Career Intervention." Allyn-Bacon, Boston.
Walsh, W. B., and Osipow, S. H. (Eds.) (1988). "Career Decision Making." Erlbuam, Hillsdale, NJ.
Walsh, W. B., and Osipow, S. H. (Eds.) (1990). "Career Counseling." Erlbaum, Hillsdale, NJ.

CATECHOLAMINES AND BEHAVIOR

Arnold J. Friedhoff and Raul Silva

New York University Medical Center

Glossary

Antidepressant drugs These medications are used to treat a variety of conditions such as depression, panic attacks, and obsessive–compulsive disorder. Generally speaking there are three different groups: the tricyclic antidepressants, which include imipramine and related agents, amitriptyline, and nortriptyline; the monoamine oxidase inhibitors (MAO inhibitors) such as tranylcypromine and phenelzine; and the newest group, the serotonin reuptake blockers, which include clomipramine, fluoxetine, sertraline, and paroxetine.

Antipsychotic drugs These medications are also used in a variety of conditions. The name is derived from the improvement they produce in certain psychotic behaviors such as delusions and hallucinations. The first such agent, chlorpromazine, was synthesized circa 1950. Examples of the classical antipsychotic agents are haloperidol and chlorpromazine. New atypical agents include clozapine and risperidone. These medications are also called neuroleptics.

Catecholamines There are three endogenously produced substances (epinephrine, norepinephrine, and dopamine) called catecholamines. These compounds serve as neurotransmitters.

Limbic system These are a group of structures located in the brain that are involved in regulating emotion and its association with behavioral and mental functioning.

Neurotransmitters These are compounds that are released into interneuronal junctions called synapses. They are released from the axon of a presynaptic neuron and impact on the receptors of the postsynaptic neuron, the nerve cell on the other side of the synapse. This is the chemical means by which the transfer of information occurs in the brain.

CATECHOLAMINES are powerful chemicals that can be found in neurons throughout the body. The effects of these compounds are responsible for the functioning of the brain even during the early fetal stages of life. They help regulate an endless number of functions ranging from thinking and mood to motor control. In this article we review the structure, the anatomical distribution, and the role these substances have on functioning and behavior.

I. NATURE OF THE CATECHOLAMINERGIC SYSTEMS

A. Introduction

Catecholamines are relatively small organic molecules that function in the brain and elsewhere in the body, primarily in a regulatory or modulating role, to keep various systems functioning smoothly in response to demands of the internal and external environment. The most familiar of the three natural catecholamines is adrenaline, or epinephrine. Its effects have been experienced by all of us, in response to a frightening experience, for example. Its release from the adrenal gland and from nerve cells or neurons regulating heart rate and blood pressure help to put us into a readiness state for fight or flight. Norepinephrine, the closest chemical relative of epinephrine, is more prominently localized in the brain than epinephrine, but is also found in so-called peripheral neurons (those neurons found outside of the brain). In the brain norepinephrine regulates mood and level of emotional arousal and alertness. Dopamine, the third catecholamine, is prominently involved in regulating motor or movement functions, and also in the coordination of associative thinking and integration of sensory motor function. Thus, key volitional acts such as movement and thinking are fine-tuned, integrated, and given emotional coloration through the actions of the three catecholamines.

Understanding the role of catecholamines in normal and pathological behavior is important in understanding the structural organization and functional aspects of this system in the brain. The relationship of the catecholaminergic system to behavior has been deduced largely by using drugs to alter the function of various components of the neural networks that make up the system.

B. Neurotransmission

Information transfer in the brain is carried on mainly by synaptic transmission, or the passage of a message across synapses or gaps between communicating cells. This occurs through a combination of electrical transmissions which take place within a neuron and the release of a chemical or neurotransmitter which crosses the synaptic gap and then acts on a postsynaptic neuron via specialized detection sites called "receptors"; however, there are some exceptions to this general model. For example, some neurons, not catecholaminergic, relate to each other entirely by change in electrical potential. In many cases involving the catecholaminergic system, other substances are co-released with the neurotransmitter which modify or modulate its effect. The nature of the effector response can vary depending on the type of receptor, location of the membrane and nature of the neuromodulators. For example, the stimulation of β-3-adrenergic receptors located in adipose tissues will stimulate the breakdown of fats (lipolysis). This can be contrasted with the stimulation of different α-2-adrenergic receptors, one of which may inhibit the release of certain neurotransmitters at the presynaptic level of adrenergic nerve cells thereby causing inhibition of norepinephrine release. Meanwhile, stimulation of another α-2-adrenergic receptor located on the membranes of the β cells of the pancreas will cause a decrease in insulin secretion. [See SYNAPTIC TRANSMITTERS AND NEUROMODULATORS.]

The synapse is an important locus for the action of drugs that modify behavior. By blocking reuptake of transmitters the effect of the transmitter can be enhanced or exaggerated. Conversely by blocking receptors on postsynaptic cells, transmitter effect can be reduced. A third possibility, which has been exploited pharmacologically, is the modification of the ion exchange involved in electrical transmission. This too can have effects on motor and mental activity.

C. Biosynthesis of Catecholamines

The starting point for the synthesis of all the catecholamines is L-tyrosine, which is a nonessential amino acid that can be found in the diet. L-Tyrosine is hydroxylated (gains an OH group) to form dihydroxy-L-phenylalanine, which is also known as levodopa or L-dopa. The enzyme responsible for this transformation is tyrosine hydroxylase. In dopaminergic neurons, L-dopa is metabolized to dopamine by means of the enzyme dopa decarboxylase. This enzymatic process occurs in the cytoplasmic component of neurons. In noradrenergic nerve cells and in the adrenal medulla, dopamine is transformed to norepinephrine. It has been estimated that approximately 50% of the dopamine synthesized in neuronal cytoplasm of noradrenergic cells is metabolized to norepinephrine. Norepinephrine can then be transformed to epinephrine by the addition of a methyl group (CH3) to its amino group, through the action of the enzyme phenethanolamine-N-methyltransferase. This last step occurs in certain neurons of the brain and in the adrenal medulla (graphic and schematic representations of the biosynthesis and breakdown of catecholamines can be found in many of the references listed at the end of the article). In general the enzymes described in this section are produced in the neuronal cell bodies and are then transported via axoplasmic flow and stored in nerve endings. Therefore, the process of catecholamine biosynthesis takes place within these terminals. The catecholamines synthesized are then taken up and stored in vesicles (chromafin granules) of the nerve terminals which are located near the cell membrane. During neural transmission catecholamines are released from these vesicles into the synaptic cleft. Although certain precursors of catecholamines (such as L-dopa) penetrate the blood brain barrier the catecholamines do not. Thus, all of the catecholamines found in the brain are produced there.

The amount of catecholamines that exist within the adrenal medulla and the sympathetic nervous system is generally constant. Initial changes that occur in the synthesis of these substances in response to changes occur in minutes, while slower adaptational changes occur over much longer periods, even days in some cases. Catecholamines in the body are maintained at constant levels by a highly efficient process that modulates its biosynthesis, release, and subsequent inactivation.

When an appropriate signal is received by a catecholaminergic neuron it is transmitted down the axon to the presynaptic terminal where it initiates the release of quanta of neurotransmitter into the synaptic cleft. The transmitter acts on receptors in follower cells, resulting in the activation or inhibition of these cells.

D. Inactivation of Catecholamines

There are two major means for catecholamine inactivation; reuptake and enzymatic degradation. The reuptake system is fast and highly efficient. It operates through a rapid reuptake of released transmitters back into the presynaptic terminal. The involved transporter reuptake protein has two functions: (1) it rapidly inactivates transmission by removing transmitter from the synapse and (2) it conserves transmitter by re-storing that which is not used in signal transmission. Catecholamines made in the neuron but not stored in terminal vesicles are catabolized by a series of isoenzymes known as monoamine oxidases (MAO) which are located in most living tissues. Another enzyme important in the breakdown of catecholamines released into the synapse is catechol-O-methyltransferase. Discussion of all of the metabolic steps in degradation of catecholamines is beyond the scope of this chapter; however, it is important to note that drugs that increase catecholamine levels in the synapse, particularly norepinephrine, are successful antidepressant medications. The concentration of norepinephrine can be altered by two types of drugs: reuptake blockers which prolong the life of norepinephrine in the synapse by preventing its re-entry into the presynaptic neuron and monoamine oxidase inhibitors which interfere with breakdown by monoamine oxidase.

From observations of the action of these drugs it has been proposed that depression is the result of low levels of norepinephrine in the brain; however, direct evidence for this proposal has not been found. In support of the proposal, the antihypertensive drug reserpine, which depletes norepinephrine and the other catecholamines, sometimes causes serious depression. Curiously, drugs that increase levels of serotonin, a noncatecholamine found in the brain, are also antidepressants. [See DEPRESSION.]

Norepinephrine and epinephrine also act as hormones when released from the adrenal medulla. Epinephrine is the principal catecholaminergic hormone produced in the medulla. Norepinephrine is the primary neurotransmitter in all postganglionic sympathetic neurons except for those that supply the vasodilator blood vessels of the skeletal muscular system and the sweat glands. The sympathetic nervous system, along with the parasympathetic nervous system, makes up the autonomic nervous system which helps regulate the visceral functions of the body. The autonomic nervous system has control centers which are located in the spinal cord, hypothalamus, the reticular formation of the medulla oblongata, and other regions of the brain stem. The centers located in the spinal cord and in the brain stem are regulated by the hypothalamus which also communicates with the pituitary and cerebral cortex. This interconnection enables the complex orchestration of multiple somatic, visceral, and endocrinological functions. [See HORMONES AND BEHAVIOR.]

The nonadrenergic system has two major areas of origin in the brain: the locus coerulus and the lateral tegmental nucleus. The projections of this system extend to all regions of the brain. As explained earlier, dopamine is the precursor in the synthesis of norepinephrine and epinephrine. In addition to this, dopamine has its own complex system and specialized function. The dopamine system is composed of three subdivisions. These are the mesocortical, mesolimbic, and nigrostriatal systems. The mesocortical system extends from ventral tegmentum to a variety of areas such as the olfactory tubercles, the accumbens, and the prefrontal cortex. The neurons of the mesolimbic system originate in the substantia nigra and the ventral tegmentum, and project to the accumbens, amygdala, and olfactory tubercle. It is believed that the limbic system is probably more involved in regulating certain mental processes. The nigrostriatal system extends from the substantia nigra to the neostriatal regions. In addition to other functions, the nigrostriatal system is involved in motor movement. Disturbances of vital structures in this area are related to illnesses such as Parkinsonism. [See LIMBIC SYSTEM.]

E. Catecholaminergic Receptor Sites

Catecholamine receptors are proteins imbedded in the plasma membrane of a neuron. Activation of these receptors by catecholamines can produce excitatory and/or inhibitory responses. Receptor number, in many cases, is increased or decreased as an adaptive response. For example, blockage of dopamine receptors by antipsychotic drugs, which are dopamine receptor antagonists, often results in a compensatory increase in the number of receptors. There are a number of types of catecholamine receptors which respond to one of three catecholamines, dopamine, norepinephrine, or epinephrine.

1. Dopaminergic Receptors

Five types of dopamine receptors have been identified. They are all called dopamine receptors because they all respond to dopamine and are relatively homologous in structure; however, two types, D1 and D2, can be discriminated pharmacologically by both agonists and antagonists. It is very likely that drugs selective for the other three types will also be found. The ability to selectively activate or inactivate different aspects of the dopaminergic system with drugs that act on one receptor type has made it possible to explore the role the D1 and D2 dopaminergic system plays in behavior.

1. D1 receptors are found in the caudate nucleus and cortex. There are a variety of extraneural sites where these receptors are located, including the vascular structures of the brain, heart, renal, and mesenteric systems.

2. D2 receptors have been identified in the putamen, caudate nucleus, striatum, as well as in limbic structures and in low density in the cortex. There have been two subtypes of D2 receptors identified (D2a and D2b) but differences in anatomical location and physiological properties have not been worked out.

3. D3 receptors have been identified in the limbic system.

4. D4 receptors have been recently identified in the frontal cortex, basal ganglia, medulla, midbrain, and the amygdala.

5. D5 receptors have also recently been identified in the caudate, putamen, olfactory bulb, and tubercle as well as in the nucleus accumbens.

2. Adrenergic Receptors

There are two types with subdivisions within each.

a. α-Adrenergic Receptors

1. α-1-Adrenergic receptors are located on postsynaptic effector cells such as those on the smooth muscles of the vascular, genitourinary, intestinal, and cardiac systems. Additionally, in humans these receptors are located within the liver.

2. α-2-Adrenergic receptors inhibit the release of certain neurotransmitters. For example, at the presynaptic level in certain adrenergic nerve cells these receptors inhibit norepinephrine release, while in cholinergic neurons they are responsible for inhibiting acetylcholine release. α-2-Adrenergic receptors are also located in postjunctional sites such as the β cells of the pancreas, in platelets, and in vascular smooth muscle. Although there are at least two subtypes of both α-1 and 2-adrenergic receptors, the details concerning the actions and localization that would differentiate these particular subtypes have not been worked out.

b. β-Adrenergic Receptors

1. β-1-Adrenergic receptors have been located in the heart, the juxtaglomerular cells of the kidney, and the parathyroid gland.

2. β-2-Adrenergic receptors have been identified in the smooth muscles of the vascular, gastrointestinal, genitourinary, and bronchial structures. Additionally, β-2-adrenergic receptors have been located in skeletal muscle and in the liver as well as on the α cells of the pancreas which are responsible for glucagon production.

3. β-3-Adrenergic receptors are reported to be located in adipose tissue.

F. Plasma Catecholamines

The three catecholamines, when found intact in plasma, do not come from the brain because they cannot cross the blood–brain barrier; however, their metabolites can. Thus, metabolites in plasma originate both in brain and in peripheral tissues. Study of these metabolites has provided certain insights into the role catecholamines play in behavior. However, direct study of catecholamines in living human brain tissue has not been possible. Fortunately, the new imaging technologies such as PET scanning, NMR, and SPECT open up possibilities for visualizing catecholaminergic function in live conscious human subjects during waking hours. There are a variety of methods available for measuring catecholamines in plasma.

II. IMPACT OF CATECHOLAMINES ON BEHAVIOR

Most of the information that is available concerning the functions of catecholamines in regulating human behavior directly results from the use of a group of medications often called psychotropic drugs, and antidepressant medications called thymoleptics. Other medications include psychostimulant medication such as the dextroamphetamines, methylphenidate (most commonly known by its trade name, Ritalin), and L-dopa (which has been used to treat Parkinsonism) as well as a medication that was initially used to treat high blood pressure, reserpine. Most of these drugs impact on more than one system (for example dopaminergic, noradrenergic, or serotonergic systems). Catecholamines have been proposed as mediators of most psychiatric illnesses including schizophrenia, Tourette's syndrome, depression, autism, pervasive developmental disorders, attention deficit–hyperactivity disorder, stereotypic movements, and tremors. Unfortunately, to date no definitive evidence for their role in any of these has been forthcoming. What is definite, however, is the role catecholamines play in mediating the action of mood-altering, mind-altering, and other types of psychotropic drugs. Antipsychotic drugs that block dopamine receptors reduce the more classical psychotic symptoms (delusions and hallucinations). There is some speculation about which dopamine receptors these agents block in order to produce improvement, but the prevailing view is that the more traditional agents block D2 receptors while the newer atypical agents (such as clozapine) may also block D4 receptors. The fact that agents that block dopamine receptors produce improvement in schizophrenia has led to the proposal that schizophrenia is caused by overactivity of the dopaminergic system. In support of this so called "dopamine hypothesis," at least one group has reported an increased density of D2 receptors in brains of schizophrenic patients using a relatively new imaging technology called positron emission tomography (or PET scanning). Increased density of these receptors in postmortem brain tissue from patients with schizophrenia has also been reported. Most patients, however, have received neuroleptic treatment which, itself, can cause these changes. Thus, it is not clear whether this increased density is an effect of the pathophysiology or the result of treatment. It is well established that reducing dopaminergic activity with neuroleptics inhibits hallucinatory activity and normalizes delusional or paranoid thinking. It seems probable that the dopaminergic system, particularly the D2 system, has a physiological role in keeping thinking and level of suspiciousness in bounds. Curiously, patients who respond well to antipsychotic medication have a decrease in plasma HVA, the principal metabolite of dopamine, during treatment, whereas nonresponders do not. What is odd about these findings is that most plasma HVA does not come from the central nervous system.

Antipsychotics improve certain other symptoms associated with schizophrenia such as impaired thought processes and attentional problems. Thus, it seems that the dopaminergic system may also regulate associative processing and attention. Drugs that improve psychotic symptoms have one more important effect. They produce emotional blunting or so called "flat affect." Inasmuch as these drugs reduce dopaminergic activity, it seems that dopamine may play a role in affect regulation.

Another illness that may illuminate the role of dopamine in regulation of behavior is Tourette syndrome. This is an illness with onset usually between the ages of 4 and 8 years of age; however, it can occur at any time. It is characterized by rapid, repetitive movements known at motor tics, which can be as simple as eye blinking or as complex as assuming contorted body positions. In addition to these movements, vocal tics occur—ranging from repetitive coughing and throat clearing to shouting obscene words. These utterances can be a great source of embarrassment to the affected individuals. Both the vocalizations and the motor tics respond to antipsychotic drugs which are, of course, dopamine receptor blockers. This effect on Tourette symptoms occurs even though the patients are not psychotic. Although dopamine is known to play a role in integrating motor movements, there is a distinct possibility it may also inhibit socially undesirable movements and vocalizations.

It seems that Tourette syndrome is in some way related to obsessive–compulsive disorder (this latter illness being particularly prevalent in families of Tourette patients). Obsessive–compulsive disorder is often responsive to drugs that increase serotonergic activity. Thus, there appears to be a complex interaction between the serotonergic and dopaminergic systems in the regulation of psychomotor activity. [See OBSESSIVE–COMPULSIVE BEHAVIOR.]

The study of psychological depression and its treatment can also help to illuminate the role of catecholamines in the regulation of behavior. Drugs like the tricyclic antidepressants and the monoamine oxidase inhibitors, both of which increase norepinephrine in the synapse, are useful in treating depressed patients. As a result of those observations it was first concluded that depression resulted from abnormally low activity of the noradrenergic system. It now appears, however, that increasing norepinephrine levels via drug treatment, serves to compensate for unknown pathology in depression. Additionally, all of the drugs useful in treating depression affect other transmitters beside norepinephrine.

These observations are, nevertheless, informative. It seems probable that norepinephrine, by regulating its own activity, in concert with other transmitters, plays a role in the relief and prevention of depression if not in the cause of depression. Norepinephrine may regulate mood, level of emotional arousal, sleep/wakefulness states, and appetite (all of which are often disturbed by depression).

Autism is a serious psychiatric condition that begins in infancy or early childhood. It is characterized by a qualitative impairment in interaction and socialization. Autistic children appear to be oblivious to their surroundings but, ironically, can react with a temper tantrum if a single toy is moved from its usual location. They are often lacking verbal and nonverbal communication skills. Speech may be limited to repeating a word over and over, and they may not even point to something they want in order to obtain it. Autistic individuals exhibit a restriction of activities and engage in a variety of odd behaviors such as sniffing, twirling, and spinning, and inordinate interest in the single function of an object (i.e., staring at a wheel spinning on a toy car for hours). They also sometimes present with violent or self-injurious behavior and temper tantrums. Some of these patients may possess striking talents beyond their apparent cognitive capacity (often referred to as cevante-like traits). A few can masterfully play the piano without ever receiving instruction or memorize an entire city's bus routes. [See AUTISM.]

The pervasive developmental disorders are illnesses that may vary in presentation. They may present with only one feature of autism or most of the features (but by definition not all). Though elevated serotonin levels in whole blood seem to be the most consistent finding in autism, there have been reports of increased norepinephrine levels in the plasma of these children when compared to normal control groups. Additionally, the effectiveness of dopamine-blocking neuroleptics on attention and improvement of certain behaviors in autistic children cannot be ignored. One investigation of biologi-

cal markers in children with pervasive developmental disorder reported that the group that responded to treatment had lower initial plasma levels of HVA (the principal metabolite of dopamine.)

Attention deficit–hyperactivity disorder, or ADHD, is characterized by overactivity, fidgetiness, impulsivity, and distractibility. It is more frequently seen in males and there is usually a family history of the disorder. The illness begins early in life but often is not diagnosed until the child is in school, as its pathology becomes more evident when more controlled behavior is required. There is strong evidence for involvement of the catecholaminergic systems in this illness. Prevailing theories propose a decrease in turnover of both dopamine and norepinephrine. Findings include decreased norepinephrine metabolites in the plasma of these individuals and treatment involves the use of drugs that have norepinephrine-like effects. Oddly, increases in noradrenergic activity in the activating systems of the brain produces emotional arousal and many of the attendant symptoms of ADHD. In addition, adults given the psychostimulants used to treat ADHD in children have the expected activating effects. Perhaps then the function of the noradrenergic system may be developmentally regulated. [See ATTENTION-DEFICIT HYPERACTIVITY DISORDER.]

III. CONCLUSIONS

Catecholamines in the brain act at the highest levels of mental function. Although their role in specific mental disorders is not entirely clear, there is little doubt that they modulate, if not mediate, functions like processing of associations, integration of thought processes with movement and speech, emotional tone or affect, mood, appetite, arousal, and sleep/wakefulness state. Most of these functions have not been successfully modeled in non-human species, leaving their study to be carried out in living humans. This limitation has made more than inferential conclusions as to behavioral and mental function impossible.

New technological advances in functional brain imaging and in studies of gene expression in accessible human cells have opened new windows into the brain, but definitive studies await further advances.

Bibliography
Axelrod, J. (1987). Catecholamines. In "Encyclopedia of Neuroscience" (G. Adelman, Ed.) Vol. I, 1st ed. Birkhauser, Boston.

Davis, K. L., Khan, R. S., Ko, G., and Davidson, M. (1991). Dopamine in schizophrenia: A review and reconceptualizaton. *Am. J. Psych.* **148**(11), 1474–1486.

Friedhoff, A. J. (1991). Catecholamines and Behavior. In "Encyclopedia of Human Biology" (R. Dulbecco, Ed.), Vol. II. Academic Press, San Diego.

Friedhoff, A. J. (Ed.) (1975). "Catecholamines and Behavior." Vols. I & II. Plenum, New York.

Gilman, A. G., Rall, T. W., Nies, A. S., and Taylor, P. (Eds.) (1990). Goodman and Gilman's: The Pharmacological Basis of Therapeutics," 8th ed. Pergamon, New York.

Kaplan, H. I., and Sadock, B. J. (Eds.) (1989). "Comprehensive Textbook of Psychiatry/V", 5th ed. Williams & Wilkins, Baltimore.

Silva, R. R., and Friedhoff, A. J. (1993). Recent advances in research into Tourette's Syndrome. In "Handbook of Tourette Syndrome and Related Tic and Behavioral Disorders" (R. Kurlan, Ed.). Marcel Dekker, New York.

Wilson, J. D., Braunwald, E., Isselbacher, K. J., Petersdore, R. G., Martin, J. B., Fauchi, A. S., and Rood, R. K. (Eds.) (1991). "Principles of Internal Medicine." McGraw-Hill, New York.

CATEGORIZATION

Eleanor Rosch
University of California at Berkeley

I. The Classical View of Categorization
II. Challenges and Alternatives to the Classical View
III. Minimodels and Critiques of Graded Structure
IV. Categories as Theories
V. Summary

Glossary

Attribute/feature An aspect of a category member that can be isolated from the whole by perception or conception (e.g., parts, color, shape).

Category Two or more distinguishable objects or events which are treated equivalently (e.g., given the same name).

Concept Hypothetical mental structure underlying a category.

Defining features Attributes/features thought to be necessary and sufficient for an item to be a category member.

Exemplar A member of a category.

Graded structure (also called goodness of example, representativeness, prototypicality, typicality) Judgments of how well category members fit subjects' idea or image of the category.

CATEGORIZATION, the process by which distinguishable objects or events are treated equivalently, is one of the most basic functions of living creatures. Humans live in a categorized world; from household items to emotions to gender to democracy, objects and events (although unique) are treated as members of classes. There are three basic questions for categorization research: why do we have the particular categories that we do and not others; how are categories acquired, stored, and used by the mind; and what is the relation between categories in the mind and the objects, cultural forms, and contingencies in the world? Research on these issues has undergone roughly four phases: (1) The classical view (the

1920s–1960s). Categories, as part of general learning theories, were simply assumed to have defining features. (2) Challenges and alternatives to the classical view (the 1970s). Categories were argued to have a graded rather than defining structure and to originate as nonarbitrary reflections of world/perceiver contingencies. (3) Mathematical models and critiques of graded structure (mid-1970s–mid-1980s). (4) Categories as theories (mid–late 1980s). Each of these periods contains an implicit or explicit philosophical position, characteristic types of experimental research, and implications both for the development of categories in children and for the relation of language to categories. These will be discussed in turn.

I. THE CLASSICAL VIEW OF CATEGORIZATION

Research in psychology tends to reflect prevailing philosophical viewpoints. Categorization is the area in psychology which deals with the ancient philosophical problem of universals, that is, with the fact that unique particular objects or events can be treated equivalently as members of a class. Although philosophers since Plato have disagreed concerning whether universal classes exist outside the mind (realism) or are the product of concepts (conceptualism), there was general agreement that when one knew something, it was the universals that one knew. That is to say, experience of particulars as it comes moment by moment through the senses was deemed unreliable; therefore, only stable universal categories could function as actual *objects of knowledge*. In Plato these objects were the Platonic Forms; in Aristotle, the formal causes of the categories, i.e., their definitions in terms of genus and differentia. For the British empiricists (who followed Aristotle in this respect), concepts consisted of a *connotation* (meaning, intension), which was a specification of the qualities that a thing must have to be a member of the class, and a *denotation* (extension), which was just those objects in the world which belonged to the class.

Because categories were objects of knowledge (and of names), they had to have certain properties: (1) They had to be exact rather than vague; that is, boundaries had to be clearly defined. One cannot have vague knowledge. (2) Category members had to have something in common; after all, that was the object of reference. And that which the members had in common had to be the necessary and sufficient conditions for membership in the category. (3) Following from the other properties, all members of a category were equally good with regard to membership; either they had the necessary common features or they did not. Thus, categories were seen as a common set; all positive instances should manifest the common characteristic(s) defining membership, and negative instances should lack it. This is not simply a western view of the logic of categorization; the same issues appear in the Indian Sanskritic tradition and may in other philosophical traditions as well.

In psychology, behaviorism was the dominant view during the first half of this century, particularly in the United States. The central theoretical issue was learning, normally studied through the experimental techniques of classical and operant conditioning. It is somewhat paradoxical that the issue of categorization did not enter explicitly into experimental psychology until the 1950s. The natural analog of the philosophical problem of universals in the conditioning paradigm is stimulus generalization—an organism is conditioned to a single stimulus yet generalizes his response to other "similar" stimuli. However, none of the behaviorists appeared to make this connection nor to speak of generalization gradients as relevant to concepts or categories. One might speculate that this was due not only to the mentalistic flavor of the word *concept* but also to the fact that generalization gradients violate all of the requirements for a proper category in the classical view as outlined above.

The work of Jerome Bruner and his associates in the 1950s brought concept learning explicitly into experimental psychology and argued for the active role of the learner in forming hypotheses. It is in the design of experiments within this tradition that we can see a reflection of the prevailing philosophical assumptions about the nature of categories. Stimulus arrays typically consisted of items which represented all possible orthogonal combinations of an arbitrary set of attributes. For example, there might

be forms which were squares and circles, each one of which was either red or blue and each one of which had one or two borders. The concepts which subjects learned were defined by specific attributes combined by a logical rule; for example, *red, blue and square, round or blue*. For such concepts, once the subject had learned the rule(s) defining the positive subset, boundaries of the concept could only be well-defined and any instance which fit the rule(s) was equivalent to any other. Theoretical interest was focused on how subjects learned which attributes were relevant and which rules combined them. In developmental psychology, input from the traditions of Piaget and Vygotsky combined with the concept identification paradigm outlined above. The emphasis was on mapping how children's ill-structured, often thematic, concepts differed from the logical adult mode. The relationship between language and concepts appeared unproblematic, at least at one level; words simply referred to the defining features of the concepts, and it was the job of semanticists to work out a suitable formal model that would show how this relationship could account for features such as synonymy and contradiction. In short, within the classical view, there was consistency between the prevailing philosophy, research paradigms in psychology, understanding of child development, and the role conceived for language.

II. CHALLENGES AND ALTERNATIVES TO THE CLASSICAL VIEW

A. Color Categories

Consider the example of color categories such as *red* and *blue*. Though often used as attributes in the classic concept identification experiment, these are categories in their own right. But do they fit the requirements for a proper category? Is there some precise place on the continuum of variations in hue, brightness, and saturation where a color is definitely and repeatedly classified as *red* whereas its nearest just noticeably different neighbor is classified as something else? What is it that all red things have in common that forms the necessary and sufficient conditions for something to be red? Is everything that we call *red* as good or true a red as any other thing (is red hair as true a red as a red fire engine?) And are color categories arbitrary, to be carved out of the physical color space at the will of cultures or experimenters?

During the period of the classical view, color categories were indeed considered to be arbitrary and to vary without restraint across cultures such that when a relationship between color names and the cognitive variable of memory was found in a classic study by Brown and Lenneberg, it was interpreted, without second thought, as an effect of language on thought. In 1969, two anthropologists, Berlin and Kay, suggested that there were a limited number of basic color terms across languages and that while the boundaries of those color categories fluctuated widely between, and even within, both languages and speakers, there was a great deal of agreement (even between languages) on which colors were the good examples of those terms. Following this, Rosch showed that it was the universal best examples of color terms which were responsible for the supposed effect of language on thought. Most strikingly, in the Dani, a New Guinea people who lacked the full complement of basic color terms, these best example colors were better remembered than other colors. Furthermore, color categories were far easier for the Dani to learn when they were structured in a normal way with the good examples of the colors central to the category than when they were structured in a distorted fashion with the good examples on the periphery. The same pattern emerged in Dani memory and learning of the form categories *circle*, *square*, and *triangle*. The best examples of the four primary colors correspond to the physiologically determined unique hue points for these colors which were discovered by De Valois and Jacobs in the late 1960s, and similar physiological mechanisms might be envisaged for geometric figures. The new image of categorization which this suggested was one in which at least some categories form universally around perceptually salient areas of perceptual domains, such as color and form, then generalize (by the hitherto neglected process of stimulus generalization) to other similar stimuli. It was a model in which categories such as colors might have as their center a kind of physiological Platonic Form but no analyzable criterial attributes, no formalizable definitions, no definite boundaries, and graded rather than uniform membership in the category.

B. Graded Structure of Categories

Might this nonclassical view of categories extend to categorization as a whole? Might many (or all) common categories have unknown or unanalyzable (supposedly criterial) attributes, fuzzy boundaries, and/or graded structure? An extensive research program initiated by Rosch and her associates and added to by many has established a core of empirical findings. In the first place, all categories show gradients of membership; that is, if asked to rate how well a particular item fits one's idea or image of a category, subjects have no trouble in making such judgments. Reliability scores (subject's agreements with each other and consistency with themselves over time) range from the low .50s to the high .90s depending upon the stimulus items, the instructions, and the statistics used. (For example, virtually everyone agrees that an *apple* is a better example of *fruit* than is *fig* but the ordering of *pineapple* and *strawberry* fluctuates.) What is robust and uncontrovertible is the rapidity, ease, and feeling of meaningfulness with which people make judgments of goodness of example for members of the most diverse kinds of categories: perceptual categories such as *red*, semantic categories such as *furniture*, biological categories such as *woman*, social categories such as *occupations*, political categories such as *democracy*, formal categories that have classical definitions such as *odd number*, and ad hoc goal derived categories such as *things to take out of the house in a fire*.

Of itself such ratings of goodness of example, representativeness, or typicality within categories would be of limited interest. However, such ratings have been found to affect virtually all of the major dependent variables used as measures in psychological research.

1. Speed of Processing

Reaction time, often taken as a royal road to measurement of the organization of mental processes, has been extensively investigated in category verification tasks. Subjects are usually asked to verify statements of the form "An [exemplar] is a [category name]" as rapidly as possible. The better (more representative/more typical) an exemplar has been rated, the faster the reaction time to verify its membership. This finding is robust under a variety of experimental paradigms and under a full range of types of category, both naturally occurring and artificial. (Accounts of *why* these variables act as they do are referred to under Section III.)

2. Effects of Advance Information/ Priming/Set

Another established technique in experimental psychology is to observe the effects on performance produced by varying subject's prior expectations. When subjects are presented a category name in advance of making some speeded judgment concerning a category member or members, performance with good (representative/typical) members of the category is found to be facilitated and performance with poor (nonrepresentative/atypical) members hindered. This has been used to argue that the (not indisputable) point that the actual cognitive representation of the category is in some way more like the better than the poorer exemplars.

3. Order and Probability of Exemplar Production

When subjects are given a category name and asked to produce names of members of the category (e.g., to list *tools*), better exemplars are more likely to be produced and they are produced with greater frequency. When subjects are asked to draw examples of categories which do not have easily named exemplars, the drawings approximate typical more than atypical items.

4. Ease of Learning

Goodness of example/representativeness/typicality gradients show two basic effects on the learning of categories. For a variety of artificial categories containing pre-established differences in representativeness, subjects learn better examples earlier than poorer examples. There is also naturalistic evidence from child development that category names are acquired first for better category examples. The second effect of typicality gradients is that categories can be acquired more easily when better examples are presented first, a finding with implications for education.

5. Inferential Reasoning

In inductive reasoning tasks, subjects appear to infer from more to less representative members of categories more readily than in the reverse order. For example, when told that robins on an island have a new disease, subjects are more likely to infer than ducks will catch it than that robins will catch a disease from the ducks. Young children generalize from humans to other animals but not vice versa. [*See* REASONING.]

6. Probability Judgments

Kahneman and Tversky have demonstrated extensively that people use representativeness to judge probability, a heuristic which leads to a variety of responses considered errors in normative models of probability judgment. Base rates are ignored; e.g., a person thought typical of a particular profession will be judged likely to have that profession regardless of the rarity of members of the profession. Sample size bias is also ignored in the face of more typical but smaller samples. Effects more representative of their causes (such as a long random looking sequence of coin tosses) are judged more probable than are actually more probable shorter sequences. And the conjunction of two events will be judged more probable than either event alone (even though that violates a fundamental axiom of probability) when the conjunction appears more representative of actors or conditions.

7. Natural Language Indicators of Graded Structure

Natural languages themselves contain various devices which acknowledge and point to graded structure. Thus, in English we may say "A robin (but not a penguin) is a *true* bird" and "A penguin (but not a robin) is *technically* a bird." When subjects are given sentence frames such as "$\{x\}$ is virtually $\{y\}$," they reliably place the more representative member of a pair in the referent $\{y\}$ slot. Furthermore, representativeness ratings for members of superordinate categories (such as *bird* or *furniture*) predict the extent to which the member term is substitutable for the superordinate word in sentences. (For example, *robin* but not *penguin* is substitutable for *bird* in "The *bird* was perched on a branch.") A final point may be very important for the development of category terms in the history of language. American Sign Language for the deaf generally lacks superordinate category terms; such categories are signed by a short list of exemplars—and only the most representative exemplars are used!

8. Asymmetry in Similarity Ratings

Similarity is the universal dimension (the glue) appealed to in accounts of generalization, learning, inference, and categorization. There is no adequate theoretical account of similarity, but similarity relations are normally assumed to be symmetrical and reversible like physical space. However, similarity relations are found to be asymmetric when applied to graded membership in categories; less good exemplars are often considered more similar to good exemplars than vice versa (e.g., a slanted line is judged more similar to a vertical line than the vertical is to the slanted). This finding would seem to underlie various anomalies in the learning, generalization, and inference literature.

We have been speaking of goodness of example/representativeness/typicality simply in relation to the empirical gradients obtained from people's judgments of how well an item fits their idea or image of a category. Do we know what underlies such representativeness judgments? From experiments and common sense, a number of different sources of goodness of example have been proposed:

1. Central tendencies
   a. Means of quantifiable attribute dimensions (e.g., the best examples of the category animal are those at the mean for the dimensions of size and predacity).
   b. Family resemblances (named after Wittgenstein). Items are best examples that have most attributes in common with most other members and least attributes in common with nonmembers. The term can apply both to (i) categories with isolatable nameable attributes and (ii) categories with nonquantifiable gestalt configurational properties.
   c. Frequencies (statistical modes). Goodness of example is based on frequency of encounter with exemplars. (Actually, frequency tends to determine typicality only in the absence of structural variables.)
2. Prototypes. Goodness of example is determined by similarity (closeness in metric or nonmetric psychological space) to a standard. (*Prototype,* in its most generic sense, simply means the standard to which items are compared.)
   a. Ideals
      i. Salient stimuli. Some stimuli in the category space are made salient by physiology (as with colors, forms, and perhaps facial expressions of emotion), by social structure (president, teacher), or by formal structure (multiples of 10 in decimal system mathematics).
      ii. The extremes of attribute dimensions (e.g., the largest cities tend to be judged most representative of *city.*)
      iii. Cultural ideals that are explicitly taught (such as *saints*).
      iv. Goal derived ideals (*celery* best exemplifies *low calorie foods to eat on a diet.*)
      v. Ideals derived from causal theories (as with sequences that "look" random).
   (Note that ideals may also be central tendencies if the category forms around the ideal.)
   b. Prototypes as abstractions. Though the prototype may be based on central tendency in any of its forms, it is the abstracted prototype which serves as a standard.
   c. Exemplars as prototypes. Here it is a particular item(s) which has been encountered that serves as the standard.
      i. First learned items. Primacy effects are not readily found in the laboratory in category learning but may be very important in the emotive real life situations of child development.
      ii. Salient items such as those that are particularly emotionally charged, vivid, concrete, meaningful, or interesting.
      iii. Most recently encountered items. (Would you buy a particular brand of car *the day after* hearing a horror story about that brand?)
      iv. Items most similar (in some respect(s)?) to the currently encountered one. (Kahneman's norm theory asserts this to be a very important process in making everyday judgments.)
      v. All items. This is the limiting case of exemplars as prototypes; there is some evidence for categorization based on the retention of all items in particular laboratory tasks.

Note that all of these factors are types of or aspects of the graded structure of categories. Graded structure, is at times, summarily dismissed by classificatory slight of hand: for example, by identifying it with only one of its types (such as an abstracted prototype) and showing that this type does not account for a class of experimental findings. Definitions may also be misleading; if graded structure effects are called *probabilistic,* they may be critiqued on the basis of certain statistical issues in the study of probabilistic cues (the requirement of linear separability) which obscures the range of issues involved in the understanding of graded structure research. On the other hand, it would be naive to think that all measures of graded structure are equally reasonable, and there are a number of critiques of various measures in the above list—each based on its own assumptions about the study of categorization (for example, see Medin and Palacios). The above categories of graded structure represent a complex mixture of causal, representational, and processing assumptions which afford far more than cursory consideration.

Taken as a whole, the findings concerning the graded structure of categories would seem to offer a challenge to the classical views of child development and of language (as well as philosophy). If categories are not actually logically bounded sets with necessary and sufficient criteria for membership, what happens to the view of children as developing toward an understanding of categories as such sets? And if just such universal classes were taken as the meanings of words, how now account for word meaning? These issues will be discussed further in the succeeding sections of the paper.

C. Nonarbitrariness and Coherence of Categories

Where do categories and category systems come from in the first place? Why are chairs chairs and a different category from tables or sofas? Why does this object on which I am now sitting seem to be truly a *chair* (its real name as children say) rather than a *piece of furniture, material object,* or *desk chair?* Why does the category of *gray chairs weighing between 1.3 and 2.9 lbs.* seem neither basic, coherent, nor likely?

The sets of stimuli used in traditional laboratory concept attainment tasks were unstructured sets of equiprobable co-occurring attributes; these provide no clue as to the ecological conditions of real world category evolution. Rosch proposed that under natural conditions there is a great deal of correlational structure in the world of perceptions, actions, and life activities. Basic level categories were proposed to be the most abstract level at which that structure could be informatively mapped. *Chair,* for example, is the level of abstraction at which the perceived parts and properties that we consider attributes of the object (back, legs, seat), the simple mental codability of the object in terms of an image, the motor movements involved in using the object, and the use of the object in daily life activities all come together in a maximally structured and coherent grouping. In a series of experiments, Rosch and her associates demonstrated that for taxonomies of common objects, basic object categories were the most inclusive categories whose members (a) possessed significant numbers of cognitively salient attributes in common—as measured by asking subjects to list attri-

butes; (b) invoked similar motor sequences when the object was used or interacted with in its usual manner; (c) possessed similar shapes—as measured by a correlation of shape; and (d) could be identified from averaged shapes of members of the class thus allowing the class to be represented by an image.

The basic level so defined was shown to have implications for many other areas. There was evidence that it had perceptual priority; objects appear to be first recognized at the basic level, then either searched further perceptually to make subordinate classifications or explored conceptually to derive superordinate inferences.

It would seem reasonable that the basic level is the first level of categorization learned. Various experiments have demonstrated this using artificial categories in which the basic level has been defined by clusters of correlated attributes. It would seem equally reasonable that in natural contexts, the basic level is the first developed by children. This is a complex story, not yet resolved. Many experiments have confirmed that young children both sort and name objects at the basic level which is equivalent to the adult basic. Indeed, 3 and 4 year olds will sort objects categorically at the basic level—a cognitive feat of which young children had been judged incapable in studies that had used only items from superordinate categories. Mervis has shown, with naturalistic observation, that children may first develop child basic categories which are different from the adult basic. There is debate about whether preverbal children, observed as to the order in which they manipulate objects, are categorizing at the adult basic level (Gopnik) or in much more general groupings (Mandler).

With respect to linguistic issues, it is the basic level at which objects are almost invariably named by both adults and children in free naming situations (of course naming can always be manipulated by context). Longitudinal studies of child language development have shown children first using basic level names; these were also the names used by adults to the children (as observed by Roger Brown long ago). Markman has shown that the use of names for categories makes it much more likely that young children will sort categorically rather than thematically, suggesting that children may have a very general hypothesis linking language use and categorization. Regarding the historical linguistic issue of what categories are coded first in a language, there is evidence that American Sign Language, which has a restricted vocabulary for nouns, has single signs almost entirely and exclusively at the basic level. From historical linguistics there is evidence that words often first refer to concrete nouns and bodily actions, later generalizing to abstractions.

The concept of basic level should not apply only to categories of concrete objects and artificial categories, and it has been extended to other domains, most successfully to events and to personality trait language. There is some indication that it is at the basic level of description that objects fill slots in scripts of daily activities (one *gets dressed in the morning,* a script, by putting on one's *pants, shirt,* etc., basic level items). However, most research on basic level has dealt with attributes and micro-level activities; exploration of the basic level in its larger social/cultural context is yet to come.

Taken together the work on graded membership in categories and on nonarbitrary basic level categorizations provides a challenge to the classical view of categories. The following sections show what has resulted.

III. MINIMODELS AND CRITIQUES OF GRADED STRUCTURE

This period saw the elaboration of a variety of critiques of graded structure and the development of a number of alternative mathematical minimodels for the categorization process which would account for graded structure effects.

A. Models

If categories are not represented in the mind as a set of criterial defining attributes, then how are they represented? And by what procedures does one go about classifying new instances of a category? The empirical facts of graded structure just reviewed do not constitute a completed information processing account of the phenomenon. Many researchers turned to mathematical models for greater specificity. Artificial categories were once again the stimuli but were now constructed so as to mimic the graded structure of natural categories. That is, they did not have defining features, included better and worse examples, and exemplar frequency varied.

The main issue of theoretical debate was the level of abstraction and/or detail that is preserved in the category representation. Extreme prototype-as-abstraction models (Homa, Reed, Posner) assert that only the summary representation preserving the central tendencies among category exemplars is necessary. Fairly extreme exemplar views (Brooks, Medin) argued that the memories for all individual exemplars are combined whenever a category judgment is made. Other investigators (Holyoak, Hayes-Roth) modeled the category representation in the form of a frequency distribution which preserves not only the central tendency, but also some information about the shape of the distribution and the extent of variability among exemplars. Still other investigators use abstractions of features rather than of prototypes: e.g., in the inclusive two-stage feature comparison model of Smith, Shoben, and Rips, matches of a new item to a category are first attempted on the basis of features that are *characteristic* of the category; if this fails, *defining* features are invoked (thus incorporating the classical view as a stage of processing). One popular exemplar model (the context-cue model of Medin and Schaffer) proposed that subjects compare a new item to all or some exemplars from each category, rather than to the prototypes only, and compute similarity of the new item to each of the retrieved exemplars individually. Similarity values are combined multiplicatively rather than additively thus incorporating effects of correlations among attributes.

Each of these models (and many more variations) predict results well in some experiments (with certain stimuli and instructions) but fail under other (counter example) conditions. (It is this experimental contextual specificity that led to our appelation *mini*models.) Furthermore, it became apparent that any set of data could be modeled either in a prototype fashion by making it part of the evoked memory representation or in an exemplar fashion by making it part of the momentary situation-specific computation. This led Barsalou to argue that abstractionist and exemplar models could not be distinguished on the basis of empirical evidence since each model of storage is always presented with complementary processing assumptions which allow it to match any kind of experimental data. At present this frenzy of modeling has partially given way to some new issues about categorization which will be outlined in the final section on categories as theories. (The latest form of models, connectionist models of categorization, such as Kruschke's, will be introduced in the following section.)

B. Critiques of Graded Structure

Attempts to specify and model categorization processes on graded structures were mirrored by efforts to specify and critique the meaning and possible importance of this new view of categories. The critiques are largely based on the assumption that graded structure should provide the same kind of stable and certain object of knowledge and object of semantic reference that the classic view was supposed to provide.

1. Formal Semantic Conditions

Graded structure effects do not of themselves constitute a formal semantic model. However, given the prevailing classical "essentialist" attitude in philosophy and linguistics, it was taken as obvious that if some aspect of graded structure (such as an abstracted prototype or an ideal) was to substitute for criterial attributes as the object of knowledge and/or the meaning of words, then such a structure (prototypes, etc.) would have to fulfill the requirement of a formal semantic model; for example, account for synonymy, contradiction, and conjunctive categories. In an influential tour de force, Osherson and Smith modeled prototype theory using Zadeh's system of fuzzy set logic, in which conjunctive categories are computed by a minimization rule, and showed that prototypes do not follow this rule; for example, *guppy*, which is not a very good example of either the category *pet* or the category *fish*, is an excellent example of the category *pet fish*. (This has become known as "the pet fish problem.") After several other demonstrations of the failure of Zadeh's fuzzy logic in this context, Osherson and Smith conclude that graded structure, while it may apply to the way category members are recognized, has nothing to do with the inherent logic of categories or the real meaning of category terms.

2. Graded Structure/Typicality Effects Are Too Universal

As we have already pointed out, graded structure effects are universally found in the most diverse kinds of categories including those such as *odd number* for which people agree there is a standard formal classical definition. This has been taken as a refutation of the importance, or even meaningfulness, of graded structure effects. (This may be the only case on record where the robustness of a finding is considered its downfall.) By what logic could such a judgment have been generated? If the classical definition of a category is taken as the meaning to which the category name refers, and if the prototype or other graded structure variable is taken as that which fulfills the same function as the classical definition, i.e.,

is the meaning to which the name refers, then no category can have both a classical definition and a graded structure prototype; to do so would give the (nonpolysemous) word two contradictory meanings.

3. Core Concept and Processing Heuristics

One solution offered to both of the above critiques is embodied in a class of models of categorization in which the actual meaning of category terms is a classical definition onto which is added a processing heuristic or identification procedure which accounts for graded structure/typicality effects. In this way *odd number* can "have" both a classical definition and a prototype. By this two-tiered system, graded structure models are consigned the task of accounting for data, while the classical view, decoupled from empirical referent, is left to fulfill its original philosophical mandate.

4. Context Effects and the Instability of Graded Structure

If an object of knowledge were to change with every whim of circumstance, it would not be an object of *knowledge*. By the same view, the *meaning* of a word must not change with conditions of its *use*. One of the great virtues of the criterial attribute view is that criterial attributes are just that which is unchanging over contexts. If prototypes or other aspects of graded structure are to fulfill this function, they must be unaffected by context. However, as Barsalou has demonstrated, context effects on graded structure are ubiquitous. For example, when American college students are asked to take the point of view of a Chinese citizen in rating the goodness of example of animals, then *swan* and *peacock* are given as the best examples, both atypical animals in the American context. In the context *secretaries taking a break*, the beverage *tea* is rated more typical than *milk;* however, the order reverses in the context *truck drivers taking a break*. Even in the same context (or a default no-context condition), agreement between subjects is not perfect (the extent of agreement varies widely both with the experimental design and with the statistics used in the analysis), so one cannot argue for a uniform cultural order of goodness of example. And reliability of the same individual person over time is also not perfect, making it problematic to think of individual minds as having unchanging representations. Furthermore, people show perfectly good category effects complete with graded structure for ad hoc goal derived categories for which we surely would not want to posit prestored unchanging representations (e.g., *things that might fall on one's head.*)

The critiques of graded structure demonstrate how difficult it is to contrive accounts in which prototypes or other graded structure variables fill the functions which, of necessity, criterial attributes fulfill in the classical view. One response to this is to downgrade the role of graded structure, the other might be to challenge classical essentialist assumptions. On its most specific level, the challenge suggests that category information/meaning/referent does not exist *as such* in either the culture or the mind. Barsalou suggests that categories are computed from other kinds of information anew "on the fly" in each situation and that we should think of context effects as the *flexibility* not *instability* of graded structure.

On a more general level, in current cognitive science, there is a whole class of computer models known as connectionist (parallel distributed processing) models specifically designed to violate certain essentialist assumptions. Representation of a particular entity, such as a category, is modeled as a state of activation defined over the entire memory system rather than as an invariant component of memory retrieved from a particular location. Knowledge and word meanings are states of activation of the system; there is no question of invariant objects. On a more general level still is the suggestion of philosophers, notably Wittgenstein and his successors, that knowledge and language are not matters of referring to anything at all, but rather should be considered forms of life—thus suggesting a reworking of the entire classical view.

IV. CATEGORIES AS THEORIES

The approaches to categorization reviewed so far have tended to emphasize perception as a starting point; similarity, correlated attributes, etc., were treated as things perceived. In information processing terms this constitutes a *bottom up* approach. In recent years, perhaps not surprisingly in light of the growing domination of the computer metaphor of the mind, some researchers have switched to a *top down* view, arguing that categories are actually theories which determine perception. (Medin is a major proponent of this view in cognitive psychology, Keil and Carey in developmental psychology, Lakoff in linguistics.) The theories approach offers

a number of contributions to the understanding of categories.

A. Critique of the Use of the Concept of Similarity

Both prototype and exemplar models assume matches to a standard, based on similarity. Yet we have no adequate account of similarity. Tversky's popular model, which uses weighted common and distinctive features, does not actually explain similarity since assignment of the weights is done outside the model; e.g., a zebra would be more similar to a barber pole than to a horse if *striped* was sufficiently weighted. In fact, Carey has found that young children classify a live human with a live worm rather than with a toy monkey although the human and monkey have many more nameable common features. The argument is that it is children's developing biological theories which provide the basis for weighting attributes and perceiving similarities.

B. Critique of the Concepts of *Attributes* and *Features*

Categorization research talks continuously of attributes and features, but what is to count as one? For example, the number of features that *plums* and *lawnmowers* have in common could be infinite: both weigh less that 1000 kg; both are found in our solar system; both cannot hear well, etc. Most of the attributes used in the stimuli in artificial categories or listed by subjects for natural categories have the following (long acknowledged) problems: they are often definable only in relation to their category (we call parts of a chair *back* and *seat* because they are parts of a *chair*); they are themselves categories not primitives (parts, colors, shapes); and they are properly attributes of the category only if combined into the appropriate structures (the wings and feathers of a bird have to be properly assembled into a bird structure). The attributes that are seen in an object depend upon prior information about the object (subjects list different attributes for children's drawings if told they are drawn by city versus farm children, creative versus retarded children). And finally, there are many experimental demonstrations that correlations of attributes may not be seen without appropriate causal theories that link them, and that illusory correlations may be seen when dictated by theory. In short, as in the case of similarity, a major building block for theories of categorization has been attacked. (But note also that no alternative theory has been offered.)

C. Theories May Preserve Classical View of Concepts and Word Meaning while Also Accounting for Graded Structure Effects

A bachelor is by classical definition an unmarried man. Poor examples of the category (homosexuals, the pope, Tarzan) do not require us to posit fuzziness in the category itself; they are simply the result of the lack of fit between our folk theories (our idealized cognitive models) about bachelorhood and conditions in the world.

D. A Causal Theory of Natural Kind Terms

In contrast to the classical view of meaning, the philosopher Kripke (elaborated by Putnam) has suggested that natural kind terms (*gold, skunk*) require a causal theory of meaning; items are named, and identity of the category preserved by historical continuity while experts discover the actual category attributes. Keil has discovered analogous causal theories in children who, while conceding that a coffee pot could be remade into a birdfeeder, staunchly maintained that a desacked and repainted skunk would still be a skunk.

E. The Classical View as a Theory

Finally, the classical view itself may be considered a theory, a tenacious theory which, as we have seen, can survive much data. It is a theory which children develop; Keil calls it the characteristic to defining shift. Children who were once content to classify a man as an *uncle* or a weather condition as *rain* on the basis of characteristic features become little lawyers in their efforts to find defining features which will unequivocally determine borderline cases.

Is the theory of categories as theories a new claim of substance, or is it only a battle cry? On the one hand, it comes as a refreshing recognition of the larger context in which categorization always occurs—which it is hoped will provide an antidote to the minimodel mentality. However, the theories view is remarkably silent on all positive issues one might expect it to address. What is meant by a theory? (Explicit statements that can be brought to consciousness? Any item of world knowledge? The complete dictionary and encyclopedia? Any expectation or habit?) How does the theory view, beyond criticizing other accounts, itself account for similarity—a problem at least as old as the problem of universals? Likewise for the problem of attributes—given a theory, how are we to derive or predict attributes from it?

It is hard to escape the impression that at present absolutely anything can count as a theory and that the word *theory* can be invoked as an explanation of any finding about similarity or attributes. If perceptual constraints are in evidence, one talks of perceptual *theories* (and invokes evolution)—somewhat like the proliferation of *instincts* and *drives* in an earlier psychology. It is interesting that many of the arguments used to support a theory view (e.g., examples that require one to bring world knowledge into one's explanation) are the very kind of issue used in the Heideggerian phenomenological tradition to argue *against* theories and in support of the necessity of positing a nontheory based background of habits and skills which underlies the categories and activities of human life. Clearly, the theories view has a very interesting challenge ahead of it.

V. SUMMARY

Categorization research has gone through several stages. The classical view was that categories had criterial attributes and clear boundaries. This was challenged by evidence that many categories have no criterial attributes and indefinite boundaries, and that *all* categories seem to have graded structure. The following period was marked by minimodels and critiques of graded structure. One present trend is toward an understanding of the role of theories in categorization; it is hoped that this will serve to place categorization research in the larger context of forms of human life.

Bibliography

Carey, S. (1985). "Conceptual Change in Childhood." MIT Press, Cambridge, MA.

Keil, F. C. (1989). "Concepts, Kinds, and Cognitive Development." MIT Press, Cambridge, MA.

Lakoff, G. (1987). "Women, Fire, and Dangerous Things: What Categories Reveal about the Mind." University of Chicago Press, Chicago.

Markman, E. M. (1989). "Categorization and Naming in Children." MIT Press, Cambridge, MA.

Mervis, C. B., and Rosch, E. (1981). Categorization of natural objects. *Annu. Rev. Psychol.* **32,** 89–115.

Nakamura, G. V., Taraban, R. M., and Medin, D. L. (Eds.) (in press). ''The Psychology of Learning and Motivation: Categorization by Humans and Machines,'' Vol. 29. Academic Press, San Diego, CA.

Neisser, U. (Ed.) (1987). ''Concepts and Conceptual Development: Ecological and Intellectual Factors in Categorization.'' Cambridge University Press, Cambridge.

Rosch, E., and Lloyd, B. B. (Eds.) (1978). ''Cognition and Categorization.'' Lawrence Erlbaum, Hillsdale, NJ.

Rosch, E., Mervis, C. B., Gray, W. D., Johnson, D. M., and Boyes-Braem, P. (1976). Basic objects in natural categories. *Cognitive Psychology* **8,** 382–439.

Smith, E. E., and Medin, D. L. (1981). ''Categories and Concepts.'' Harvard University Press, Cambridge, MA.

CENTRAL AUDITORY DISORDERS

F. Eustache, J. Lambert, and B. Lechevalier
Université de Caen
Institut National de la Santé et de la Recherche Médicale

Glossary

Amusia Neuropsychological disorder consisting of impaired musical reception (receptive amusia) or production (productive amusia) after brain damage.

Auditory agnosia Inability to recognize (to variable degrees) environmental sounds, speech, and music that the patient still can hear.

Auditory evoked potentials Sequence of positive and negative waves of invariable latency following an auditory stimulus, reflecting sequential or parallel activity of several anatomical structures involved in auditory perception.

Cortical deafness "Feeling of deafness" with alteration of vocal audiometry but largely spared pure tone audiometry, resulting from cortical or subcortical brain damage.

Dichotic listening Experimental procedure in which two different messages are simultaneously presented to each ear.

Hemianacousia "Deafness of one of the cerebral hemispheres" demonstrated by audiological and neuropsychological techniques.

Pure word deafness Inability to understand spoken language, to repeat and to write to dictation, with no other sign of aphasia.

CEREBRAL LESIONS may result in disorders of auditory perception. These can be studied with audiological and neuropsychological techniques aimed at distinguishing them from peripheral deafness or other disturbances. Clinical syndromes vary greatly according to the cause and extent of brain damage. Both clinical case reports and experimental studies provide information about neuronal structures involved in central mechanisms of auditory perception.

I. TERMINOLOGY AND METHODOLOGICAL ISSUES

Description and classification of central auditory disorders have long given rise to terminology difficulties. Several concepts, corresponding to distinct syndromes, were described around the turn of the century. However, the terms of cortical deafness, auditory agnosia, and pure word deafness have progressively been misused. In the early 1980s, electrophysiological criteria have been proposed to differentiate these concepts. Auditory evoked potentials (AEPs) are lost in case of cortical deafness, whereas they are normal or nearly normal in auditory agnosia and pure word deafness. A new syndrome, hemianacousia or "unilateral hemipheric deafness," described by Michel and Peronnet, consists of unilateral loss of AEPs and contralateral auditory extinction as shown by the dichotic listening test.

Apart from these discussions about terminology, the early descriptions of central perception disorders of hearing showed that the first cases were more than quantitatively different. The authors stressed the selective or, at least, predominant features of auditory impairments. The terms *pure word deafness, auditory agnosia,* and *sensory amusia* thus underscore the selective involvement of one sector of the sound environment. Descriptions of Wernicke's aphasia with spared musical perception and production also supported this dissociation.

One way to try to understand how disorders of auditory perception may be dissociated is to make a structural analysis of sound perception. Are the perception of pitch, duration, rhythm, and tone selectively affected? Do these "structural" disturbances involve the perception of a particular type of sound? This type of approach, more and more accurate in recent studies, has provided evidence that central auditory disorders may be extremely selective, involving only one of the precited parameters. The purpose of this article is to describe the clinical, audiological and neuropsychological tools used to analyze a central disorder of auditory perception. The main syndromes are then presented. Although most data come from single cases, the results of several serial studies are also given. Finally, anatomo-clinical correlations will be considered, and the resulting hypotheses about the functional role of central auditory areas and pathways in man are proposed.

II. AUDIOLOGIC AND NEUROPSYCHOLOGIC EXAMINATIONS

Other than a few details that will be considered later, the examination of a central auditory disorder may be systematized in the following way. The mode of onset should be carefully assessed. The presenting symptoms may be mistaken for aphasia, acute psychosis, or peripheral deafness. A past history of stroke may be of value, as the auditory impairment often becomes clinically obvious after a second cerebral infarction involving the contralateral temporal lobe. Once the central origin of the disturbance has been demonstrated, three questions must be answered. Is the patient able to categorize auditory stimuli (e.g., distinguish speech from musical or environmental sounds)? Is the patient impaired in the analysis of sound parameters (pitch, intensity, tone, duration, rhythm)? Is he or she able to identify stimuli?

A. Audiometry

Audiologic investigations consist of both psychoacoustic tests and objective measurements of auditory perception. These are mandatory for the distinction between peripheral and central disorders. Tonal audiometry assesses auditory thresholds at several frequencies from the subject's responses to calibrated sound stimuli. In central auditory syndromes, the results are typically normal, since pure sounds used in tonal audiometry are perceived at the level of the medial geniculate bodies. In some cases, however, pure tone thresholds may be transiently or permanently raised, due to a retrograde degeneration of the geniculate bodies. In vocal audiometry, the subject is asked to repeat words uttered at varying intensities. In the case of internal ear deafness, the results are homogeneous at all tests. Inconsistencies may appear in nerve deafness. Dissociations are most obvious, however, in cortical deafness and auditory agnosia, where unintelligibility may be complete despite normal pure tone audiometry. In these cases, objective testing of middle and inner ear and auditory nerve function, i.e., impedancemetry and electrocochleography, gives normal results.

B. Auditory Evoked Potentials (AEPs)

Evoked cortical responses following sound stimuli consist of three main phases. Early potentials, or brainstem auditory evoked responses (BAERs), occur within 10 msec after the stimulus and reflect neuronal activity in auditory pathways and nuclei in the brainstem from the distal part of the auditory nerve to the mesencephalon. Five waves can be individualized, and correspond theoretically to different anatomical structures, although a single wave may probably be accounted for by several structures. Wave V corresponds to the medial geniculate body.

Middle latency AEPs are recorded between 10 and 70 msec and reflect the activity of temporal lobe structures. The two main waves are Na and Pa, generated subcortically and cortically, respectively. Long latency AEPs occur later than 70 msec and consist mainly of a negative wave culminating at 100 msec (wave 100 or N_1), partly generated in the auditory cortex of the supratemporal plane. These long latency AEPs are abolished when the primary auditory cortex is damaged. When Na and Pa are abolished, long latency AEPs usually are abolished as well, but may exceptionally be spared. One possible cause of error in presence of a unilateral temporal lesion is the false recording of ipsilesional cortical potentials generated by the contralateral cortex.

Electrophysiological testing is necessary to explore cortical and subcortical auditory areas, in order both to confirm the central origin of the disorder of auditory perception and to delineate the features of the syndrome. These electrophysiological measurements are especially informative in association with dichotic listening tests.

C. Dichotic Listening Tests

This technique was first used by the English psychologist Broadbent to study auditory attention in air traffic controllers. It consists of simultaneously delivering, to both ears, two different stimuli within the same sound category (e.g., words) with the same intensity, by means of a tape recorder and stereophonic headphones. Stimuli are usually verbal, but musical dichotic listening tests have also been used in several studies. The dichotic stimulation creates a perceptual conflict in order to disclose central auditory disorders which could otherwise go undetected. The greater part of central auditory pathways are crossed (i.e., auditory stimuli delivered to one ear project onto the contralateral temporal cortex), so that a hemispheric lesion often results in contralateral ear extinction. Most aphasics with left hemispheric damage have right-sided dichotic extinction. Left ear extinction, however, is most frequently encountered among brain-damaged subjects. In this case, patients fail to repeat messages reaching their left ear during dichotic stimulation. Such an extinction often results from lesions in the right sylvian area. Sometimes this extinction will reveal rather precisely a lesion in the primary auditory cortex of the temporal lobe or surrounding areas. In this instance, cortical ipsilesional AEPs are also abolished (contralateral to the extinguished ear): this characterizes *hemianacousia*. Hemianacousia may be right or left sided according to the side of cerebral damage. Another possible cause for left-ear extinction is a lesion of the corpus callosum that results in interruption of auditory stimuli as they pass from right auditory areas to left-sided language areas. Finally, demented patients often have left-ear dichotic extinction, the reasons for which are still unclear.

Besides its clinical relevance in patients, the dichotic listening test has been extensively used to study auditory perception in normal subjects. The results may be summarized as follows. Right-handers usually have right ear dominance (i.e., they repeat first the right-sided message), except for a few individual cases. This dominance still holds true in left-handers but to a lesser extent. The very few individuals in whom right hemispheric dominance for language has been proven by the Wada test (transient hemispheric narcosis induced by intracarotid amobarbital injection) usually have dichotic left ear dominance. These asymmetries observed in normal subjects do not preclude the interpretation of dichotic listening tests in patients, since pathological extinction is much more clear-cut than physiological right/left differences.

D. Psychoacoustic Tests

The aim of these tests is to detect subtle impairments in auditory perception which are beyond the reach of simple clinical and audiologic examinations. Lüsher's test consists in the presentation of sounds of decreasing intensities. Normal subjects can perceive intensity differences as low as 0,7 to 2 dB, whereas some patients with pure verbal deafness can only discriminate intensities differing by 5 dB. Temporal discrimination is tested by counting or fusion of clicks. A normal subject can count as many as 9 to 11 clicks per second. This score may be not greater than two in a case of pure verbal deafness. The click fusion test consists in decreasing the time interval between two clicks until only one click is perceived. Normally, one can still perceive two clicks separated by 1 to 3 msec. All these tests may be carried out by either binaural or monaural stimulation. These psychoacoustic measurements may be completed by investigating the subject's ability to localize sounds in space.

E. Neuropsychological Testing

Neuropsychological tests use stimuli of calibrated intensities and frequencies recorded on a magnetic tape in order to specifically explore the auditory perception of environmental, musical, and speech sounds. Together with the tests described above, neuropsychological tools help differentiate central auditory disorders from aphasia, peripheral deafness, confusional states, and psychiatric disturbances. In addition, they allow a greater delineation of the auditory impairment. A recording of various types of sounds first gives an assessment of the subject's ability to discriminate environmental, musical, or verbal sounds from each other. A within-category study may then be undertaken. The subject is given pairs of environmental sound sequences lasting 10 sec each which he has to discriminate. He is then asked to identify sound sequences, either orally or in writing, or by a multiple-choice questionnaire, the stimulus being presented in conjunction with several pictures representing the response alternatives.

Musical and verbal sounds may be tested in the same way. These two types of sounds lend themselves to further refinements of tests, specially in the structural analysis of stimuli. While recognizing music as such, a subject may, for instance, fail to appreciate specific features such as pitch, duration, rhythm, tone, intensity, or even esthetic quality. The relevance of responses depends very much on the premorbid level of musical education. Wertheim and Botez proposed a battery designed to assess musical abilities, which is useful but lengthy and difficult to use. They classify subjects into four categories according to their musical level: (1) persons who like music but lack musical education; (2) professionals with no formal musical education; (3) amateurs or professionals with extensive musical education and culture; (4) people who lack even basic musical abilities and knowledge. The same authors also elaborated a ''battery to investigate musical functions,'' which is only suitable for musically educated people. Special tests are needed to explore amusias as well as some auditory agnosias. The subject is given pairs of musical sequences differing by one or more of the following features (pitch, intensity, duration, rhythm) and has to say whether they are same or different. He may also be asked to detect errors in well-known melodies, and to reproduce rhythms. Other tests need specialized laboratories (perception of a musical sound without a fundamental frequency). At a different level, the subject is asked to identify well-known melodies. This test may disclose an isolated disturbance with sparing of other musical abilities. The investigation of musical abilities also includes discrimination of music categories (religious, military), musical reading and writing, singing either by imitation or from the title of the melody. The assessment of amusia thus explores both musical perception and production.

The study of auditory perception of speech sounds includes several tests of phonemic perception. Speech sounds, or phonemes, result from the combination of multiple physiological parameters. They are generated by the vibrations of expired air through the larynx and are modified in supralaryngeal resonance cavities (pharynx, nose, mouth, lips). Uttered sounds vary greatly from one individual to another, and between regions. Phonetico-acoustic description thus stresses some features of the phonological structure of a given language. As a matter of fact, phonemes are individualized not only by specific phonetic or acoustic features, but also by opposition relationships from one to another within the phonological system. Phonemic perception is assessed by having a subject identify or discriminate phonemes differing only by a single feature. Most studies use stop consonants (p, b, t, d, k, g), which

carry the greatest perceptual difficulties because of their shortness, while fricatives are of longer duration (f, v, s, z). Analysis usually focuses on two features: voice and place of articulation. The feature voice depends on the time interval between the relaxation of articulators and contraction of the vocal cords. This time is less than 20 msec in voiced consonants (b, d, g) and more than 40 msec in voiceless ones (p, t, k). In psychoacoustics, this duration is termed voice onset time (VOT). The feature place is the point where speech organs occlude or constrict the expired air column. Anterior consonants /p, b, m/ are in a low frequency range (500 to 1000 Hz), coronal consonants /t, d, n/ in the high frequencies (2500 to 3500 Hz), while back ones /k, g/ occupy the mean frequencies (1500 to 2000 Hz). Perception of consonants is always studied in the setting of a syllable (C/V), most often with the vowel ''a,'' since transition formants C-V or V-C are essential clues for perception.

It is possible, from the phonetic characteristics of a language and using a speech synthesizer, to propose either identification or discrimination tests. These two terms and the processes they underlie have sometimes been mistaken in earlier studies. In phonemic identification tasks, the subject is given a spoken item and responds by pointing one of several possible answers in a multiple choice. In phonemic discrimination, he is presented with a pair of successively spoken syllables and has to say whether they are the same or different. Patients may be impaired in both tests. Discrimination is sometimes better than identification, while the opposite is less common.

Using the synthesizer, one can artificially modify the VOT continuously, from a voiced (e.g., /b/) to a voiceless (e.g., /p/)phoneme. In normal subjects, there is a clear-cut boundary between sounds identified as /b/ and those identified as /p/. Items with a VOT below 20 msec are identified as voiced, whereas those with a VOT above 40 msec are perceived as voiceless. Sounds produced with a VOT between 20 and 40 msec are randomly identified either as voiced or voiceless. These results may vary, however, according to the language and other parameters, including the speech rate. Similarly, the identification of place of articulation may be studied by manipulating other acoustic features linked to the spectral characteristics of phonemes. For occlusive consonants, the variation may be the angle of transition of the second formant. Both for voicing and for place, the basic result from psychoacoustic studies in normal individuals is the existence of a clear-cut boundary between two given phonemic categories. When one asks a subject to discriminate sound pairs, he or she always discriminates between stimuli which have already been identified as pertaining to distinct phonemic categories. Discrimination scores are thus similar to identification scores and may be inferred from the latter. For such reasons, the perception of phonemes is referred to as being categorical. This categorical aspect of phonemic perception compensates the variations of acoustic parameters in the speech signal. Categorical perception facilitates the extraction, from the sound signal, of distinctive features relevant to its classification into one phonemic category. There is no exact correspondence between the acoustic signal properties and our perception of speech sounds. In other words, perceiving a word requires converting a continuous acoustic signal in a discrete phonetic–phonological representation. Acoustic differences within one phoneme do not seem to be taken into consideration by our perceptual system. The categorical dimension of speech perception strongly supports the distinction between a common auditory processing of verbal and nonverbal sounds on one hand, and specific processing of linguistic sounds. These models of auditory information processing have been particularly developed by Liberman and associates at the Haskins laboratories. The common auditory system is thought to process acoustic information according to the spectral and temporal structure of signals, and would notably carry out the analysis of fundamental frequency, intensity, and signal duration. The linguistic process is hypothesized to consist of various analysis levels: (1) phonetic analysis, to convert acoustic parameters into distinctive features of phonemes; (2) phonologic analysis, to filter phonetic or allophonic variation; (3) higher level processes involving lexical access as well as semantic and syntactic processing. The auditory and phonetic processing levels could be differently implicated in speech analysis. According to some authors, different brain lesions could impair either selectively or simultaneously these two processing levels.

III. PRINCIPAL CLINICAL SYNDROMES

A. Cortical Deafness

In most cases, patients with cortical deafness feel deaf to all auditory stimuli. This "absolute deaf-ness" is usually transient. The patient soon becomes aware of noises or conversation. Auditory inattention is all the more significant when the sensation of deafness is important. Cortical and/or middle-latency AEPs are abolished, which means that auditory information fails to reach primary auditory areas because of bilateral cortical or subcortical lesions. As for other syndromes described below, etiologic considerations include stroke, trauma, tumors, infection or degenerative diseases.

B. Hemianacousia

First described by A. Meyer at the turn of the century, and "revisited" by F. Michel, hemianacousia is, in fact, difficult to demonstrate, and corresponds to a half-cortical deafness, or deafness of one cerebral hemisphere. Because of bilaterality of auditory afferences, hemianacousia is much less disabling than hemianopia (half-visual field defect). The "hemianacousic" patient is seldom aware of his auditory defect. He may feel auditory discomfort in situations corresponding to dichotic conditions, e.g., telephoning while talking to someone else, or listening to different instruments of an orchestra. The diagnosis of hemianacousia is based on dichotic listening tests and AEP recordings. Hemianacousia is associated with contralesional ear extinction and absence or near absence of ipsilesional long latency AEPs. The lesion involves auditory radiations and/or the auditory cortex. In addition to the above-cited causes, hemianacousia may be a symptom of multiple sclerosis.

C. Syndromes of Verbal Deafness

Pure verbal deafness is the failure to understand spoken language, to repeat, and to write to dictation in the absence of any other sign of aphasia. Pure verbal deafness is very uncommon, and its reality has even been questioned. Most published cases include associated impairments, e.g., defective perception of nonverbal sounds (noise and/or music), or other features of aphasia. Patients are impaired in conversation but may rely on contextual cues, such as knowledge of the subject or lip reading. Repetition is the most difficult task because no contextual help is available and coexisting, even slight, speech disturbances may increase the difficulties. The mechanisms of this "auditory agnosia specific for speech sounds" have been largely debated. In most cases, tonal audiometry shows raised thresholds, but this is usually considered insufficient to explain the verbal integration defect. BAERs and middle latency AEPs are spared. Long latency AEPs may be impaired, sometimes with an asymmetry of amplitude consistent with the extent of brain damage. A number of studies have led to the proposition that impaired temporal resolution is a critical mechanism of the verbal comprehension deficit. Defects in temporal resolution may be demonstrated through click fusion or click counting tests. Other psychoacoustic disturbances, however, may be implicated in the pathogenesis of verbal deafness, such as impaired discrimination of pitch or intensity.

One of the major characteristics of pure verbal deafness is the gross impairment of phonemic perception. Testing consists in looking at whether certain phonetic features are less well perceived than others. Vowels are presented in isolation and consonants are associated with the vowel /a/ in a C/V or C/V/C context. According to the theories discussed above, the general auditory process allows the identification and discrimination of some linguistic components such as vowels. The perception of vowels would be possible through their acoustic attributes: they are more stable than consonants and of longer duration. The general auditory process is better adapted to phonemic discrimination than to accuracy of identification. At this level of processing, voice is also better discriminated than place of articulation. Conversely, the second, linguistic type of auditory processing would encompass identification of all consonant phonemes.

According to these criteria, Auerbach and his collaborators differentiated in 1982 two types of pure verbal deafness. In their first category, phonemic perception is selectively impaired for short, occlusive phonemes and particularly for place of articulation. This disorder, labeled prephonemic in their terminology, indicates a defect in the general auditory system. They propose it stems from subtle psychoacoustic derangements, in particular in the domain of temporal acuity. This type of pure verbal deafness is associated with bilateral temporal lobe damage. In the second category, the disorder of phonemic perception would be less specific, involving both place of articulation and voice. In this case, word deafness is thought associated with left temporal lobe lesions, and temporal resolution defects would play no particular role in its pathogenesis.

This classification has been widely accepted as far as the opposition auditory vs phonetic disorder is concerned. However, the dichotomy auditory–bilateral vs phonetic–left unilateral has been questioned, notably by Praamstra and colleagues in 1991. According to them, interaction of auditory and phonetic levels of involvement is important, if not necessary, to generate pure verbal deafness. They describe a patient who experienced pure verbal deafness following two consecutive brain lesions, left- then right-sided. Studies of phonemic perception showed that both types of deficit were associated. The view that pure verbal deafness is a result of associated general auditory and phonetic deficits is consistent with the topography of brain lesions which affect both cortical auditory areas, either by direct damage in bilateral lesions or by disconnection in left-sided ones.

D. Auditory Agnosia

Auditory agnosias may be defined either in a wide or in a restricted sense. In its extended meaning, auditory agnosia concerns all auditory stimuli, including oral language. It is the proportion of verbal agnosia, defined as verbal deafness, and of environmental sound agnosia that distinguishes pure verbal deafness from auditory agnosia. In its restricted sense, when there is impairment of verbal comprehension, the term "pure verbal deafness" should be preferred. Strictly speaking, auditory agnosia only affects environmental sounds. Language may be perceived in a distorted manner, but it is always understood. In most published cases, auditory agnosia affects several types of environmental sounds, or is not described with sufficient accuracy to exclude other disturbances.

Some auditory agnosias are complete, the patient being unable to recognize the nature of sounds. These global forms are often associated with auditory inattention. Sometimes, appreciation of pitch and intensity is spared, while perception of rhythm and duration is impaired. There are also dissociated cases of auditory agnosia. Clinical syndromes are very varied. A verbal message may be understood while voice appears distorted and unusual. The impossibility to recognize a speaker from his voice is named phonagnosia, and auditory affective agnosia refers to a neutral perception, without prosody, of all voices.

Auditory agnosia may result either from right-sided or bilateral damage to the temporal lobes. These lesions are usually infarctions, occurring in two steps, and may be cortical or subcortical. Cortical AEPs are normal or moderately impaired, but normally not abolished.

E. Amusias

The term "amusia" refers to disorders of musical perception and/or expression. The most striking examples of dissociation in musical abilities are in fact "negative" cases. These patients, usually professional musicians, retain their premorbid musical abilities despite marked Wernicke's aphasia with jargonaphasia and impaired comprehension from extensive left-sided brain damage. On the other hand, well-documented cases of pure amusia with subtle disorders of perception of tone, pitch, intensity, and musical esthetics, with no other auditory disorder, are extremely rare. Impaired musical perception associated with auditory agnosia or pure verbal deafness is much more frequent. Although amusia is often associated with a right temporal lobe lesion, it would be too simplistic to oppose the left hemisphere responsible for language to the right hemisphere subserving music. Disorders of musical perception may be seen following left-sided lesions, especially when they consist of difficulties in the identification of musical pieces or in rhythm perception. With regard to melody perception, Peretz distinguishes an analytic perception of pitch sited in the left hemisphere from a holistic perception of the melodic outline, that depends on the right hemisphere.

F. Diversity of Clinical Syndromes

The main syndromes that have been outlined indicate that different sound domains (noise, music, language) may be selectively affected by auditory perception disorders. The data from human neuropsychology thus suggest that there are several recognition systems, specialized for each type of sound stimulus. Very selective disturbances have been described for music or speech perception. Dissociations may also occur between cognitive strategies, whatever the type of auditory stimuli. We published two cases to support this view. The first patient had a slight impairment of verbal comprehension and was poor at melody identification, while all discrimination tests were correct, including those with complex material. The other patient was able to name and identify presented items, but was impaired at sound discrimination. Neither had important difficulties in the structural analysis of auditory stimuli, nor agnosia beyond the auditory domain. These results suggest that discrimination and identification of auditory stimuli involve different mechanisms in auditory processing and both may be selectively affected in brain damaged subjects.

IV. NEUROPSYCHOLOGY OF AUDITORY PERCEPTION

Beyond the syndromes discussed above and their anatomo-clinical correlations, we shall now consider disorders of auditory perception in various clinical settings: (1) impaired auditory perception in aphasia or dementia; (2) Landau–Kleffner's syndrome, a cause of acquired aphasia in children frequently associated with auditory agnosia; (3) studies of auditory perception in patients with unilateral brain damage.

A. Impaired Auditory Perception in Aphasia

Luria was among the first to suggest that comprehension disorders in aphasia could be caused by impaired perception of the phonetic features of verbal sounds. According to his view, Wernicke's aphasics have lost "phonemic perception," i.e., they are unable to perceive the distinctive features of language sounds. Blumstein and her collaborators have shown that the difficulty at phoneme discrimination in aphasic patients was correlated to phonetic distance, i.e., the number of features by which two phonemes differ. Aphasics are thus more likely to make discrimination errors between two phonemes that contrast by a single feature than when they differ by two or more features. They also make more errors in consonant discrimination when these contrast by place of articulation than by voicing. Quantitative variations may occur, but no correlation has been found thus far with either the type of aphasia or the location of brain lesions. Phonemic perception is thus more impaired following left- than right-sided brain lesions, but, contrary to Luria's hypothesis, there seems to be no correlation with comprehension deficits in aphasia. [See APHASIA.]

The hypothesis of a disturbance in the processing of acoustic dimensions of verbal sounds has been questioned. As we shall see below, difficulties to discriminate the place of articulation cannot be ascribed to an audiologic deficit, as they are not alleviated by lengthening of formant transitions. This issue has been further addressed in several studies of categorical perception that involve both phonemic identification and discrimination tasks. A study of VOT perception by Blumstein gave rise to three score patterns. A group of aphasics scored as well as normal subjects both at discrimination and identification. In the second group, patients were impaired in both tasks. The third group of patients showed a characteristic dissociation between spared discrimination and impaired identification. This author also studied the perception of place of articulation by means of a procedure close to that of VOT. This enabled her to test discrimination and identification of phonemes "b, d, g" by manipulating the formant transition along a continuum. Again, aphasic patients scored better in discrimination than in identification tasks. This dissociation, supported by several studies, suggests that aphasics have no difficulties to the perception of the acoustic dimensions of language, since they still can discriminate phonemes. Rather, they might suffer from an instability of the links between phonologic representation and identification. To identify a stimulus requires a stable phonologic representation. The alteration of verbal sound perception in aphasics is more likely to be due to their inability to maintain a stable phonologic representation than to a disruption in conversion from acoustic parameters into a phonetic representation.

The dissociation between phonemic identification and discrimination performances is consistent with the theoretical concepts elaborated from case studies of pure verbal deafness. A difficult issue is the vulnerability of perception of place of articulation in aphasia, including in the discrimination tasks. One explanation could be found in its acoustic properties, since it is characterized by steep spectral changes. Several authors have investigated the hypothesis that in aphasia one is unable to resolve these spectral modifications because of their rapidity. Discrimination and identification have thus been studied with stimuli of various duration of formant transitions. Artificially lengthening formant transitions did not improve performance. In fact, scores were even worse for the formants of the longest duration. Maintaining the phonetic quality of stimuli does not thus improve its perception. Blumstein further assessed this point by proposing discrimination tasks including nonlinguistic sounds with acoustic properties identical to syllables /da, ga/ and with similar contrasts. The purpose of this experiment was to test the following hypothesis: if the general auditory system subserves language sound processing, perception performances of verbal and nonverbal sounds

should be correlated. The experiment showed that this is not the case. The discrimination of verbal and nonverbal sounds are independent abilities. It is thus unlikely that a deficiency of general auditory processes explains the difficulties of aphasics to discriminate place of articulation.

Aphasics are more impaired at discriminating place of articulation than voicing features. However, as we have seen, this cannot be ascribed to an audiologic deficiency since lengthening the formant transitions results in no improvement. Moreover, in aphasia, discrimination is usually better than identification. These results support the view of two levels in language sounds integration: a first, "prelinguistic" level, spared (or relatively spared) in aphasia, and a second, "linguistic" level, disturbed in aphasia. These disturbances in phonemic perception would not be significantly different according to the type of aphasia and could not explain impairments in comprehension in aphasics.

While the dissociation of auditory vs phonetic levels in phonemic perception is supported by experimental results, several data provide evidence for multiple relationships between these levels as well as with other language processes. In aphasics, there is an interaction between phonologic and semantic factors. Increased semantic requirements result in decreased abilities of phonologic discrimination and vice versa. Further, some perceptual impairments only become obvious with demanding semantic tasks. This suggests that speech perception interacts with higher level lexical and semantic processes.

B. Auditory Perception Disorders in Dementia of the Alzheimer Type

Dementia of the Alzheimer type (DAT) is associated with diffuse degenerative changes of the cerebral cortex. Although temporal cortical lesions may result in impaired auditory perception, this issue has been surprisingly little investigated. Most studies have used standard audiometric tests, and have shown the existence of an auditory handicap. Its prevalence appears significant when performances of DAT patients are compared with those of age-, sex-, and educational level-matched controls. Some authors have found a correlation between auditory loss and severity of dementia, and suggested that the auditory impairment could be a predictive clue for the rate of cognitive decline. Other investigators have reported a correlation between dichotic performances and atrophy and metabolism limited to the temporal lobes. Relationships between left temporal lobe metabolism and right-ear scores at dichotic listening tests have been found. Additionally, reduced dichotic performance in both ears was seen when there was metabolic asymmetry with hypometabolism in the left temporal lobe. [*See* ALZHEIMER'S DISEASE.]

The first study of the identification of environmental sounds in DAT was carried out by Rapcsak and co-workers. Patients were asked to match an environmental sound stimulus with a picture in a multiple choice that included acoustic, semantic, and unrelated distractors. The authors interpreted their results in terms of auditory agnosia. The qualitative analysis disclosed predominant acoustic errors in demented but nonaphasic patients, while demented subjects with aphasia made both semantic and acoustic errors. In a recent study of identification of verbal sounds (phonemes and words), nonverbal sounds (noises), and known melodies in DAT patients, we found lower scores in patients than in controls. Unlike previous studies, these results could not be explained in terms of peripheral auditory loss, as both groups had similar performances on standard audiometric tests. Both controls and DAT patients made more errors with nonverbal than verbal stimuli, but with a different pattern of errors. DAT patients were more likely to choose unrelated items. These results lend further support to the presence of a central auditory perception impairment in DAT.

C. The Landau–Kleffner Syndrome

Most reported cases of auditory agnosia and of central auditory deficit have been observed in adults. However, auditory agnosia also exists in children and may be caused by the Landau–Kleffner syndrome. This includes acquired aphasia, epileptic seizures, and behavioral and psychomotor changes, together with EEG disturbances that comprise paroxysmal spikes and spike wave complexes in a changing evolutional pattern. Since the first description by Landau and Kleffner in 1957, approximately 100 additional cases have been reported, two-thirds of which are boys. Acquired aphasia, associated with spike and wave complexes, is found in all cases. EEG abnormalities predominate in temporal and temporo-parieto-occipital regions and are activated by sleep.

Aphasia occurs before the age of 7 in 75% of cases. Most characteristic are comprehension distur-

bances. They may begin suddenly or progressively. They are often severe, and may extend beyond language. Auditory agnosia may affect perception of environmental sounds, voices, tone of instruments, and nursery songs. These disturbances, together with auditory inattention and aphasia, stand in contrast with normal or near-normal results at standard audiometry tests. This indifference to auditory messages should not be mistaken for autistic behavior. Spontaneous speech progressively decreases while perseveration, stereotypies, and phonemic paraphasias appear. Written language may be affected as well. Intellectual abilities are usually preserved. Hyperkinesia is reported in half of the cases, and may be associated to personality changes.

A number of cases thus include true auditory agnosia together with disorders of speech. This syndrome has sometimes been referred to as acquired verbal auditory agnosia. Evolution can only be assessed after several years, but some reported cases lack sufficient follow-up time. Recovery is likely to be better when the language impairment starts after the age of 6. However, outcome is very variable, either good or deteriorating to severe behavioral disorders.

D. Studies in Patients with Unilateral Brain Damage

The development of neuropsychology of auditory perception has benefitted from studies in large series of patients, carried out with appropriate statistical methods and designed to assess possible correlations with the lateralization of brain damage. The Italian Neuropsychological School has undertaken many such studies and has specifically investigated agnosia for environmental sounds. Vignolo and his colleagues found that right brain damaged patients were impaired at discriminating sequences of meaningless sounds. On the other hand, left brain damaged subjects failed to identify meaningful environmental sounds. The basic result of these studies is that right-sided lesions result in discrimination difficulties (aperceptive agnosia) while left-sided lesions give rise to identification impairment (asemantic agnosia).

Van Lancker and his co-workers carried out similar studies in the domain of voices. They found that either left or right brain damaged patients poorly discriminated unknown voices, whereas only right brain damaged patients had trouble identifying familiar voices.

These two groups of studies that investigated sound and voice perception lead to distinct conclusions. In addition to a hemispheric specialization for cognitive strategies (discrimination vs identification), the stimulus type must also be taken into account (meaningless vs environmental sounds; unknown vs familiar voices). In these studies, the experimental paradigms included variations in both the task strategy and the type of material proposed but did not manipulate them separately. The nature of the stimuli (e.g., voice, environmental sounds), as well as their familiar or nonfamiliar character, is likely to be correlated to the side of the brain lesion.

Robert Zatorre, at the Montreal Neurological Institute, studied patients with unilateral brain lesions following surgery for epilepsy. He focused on the role of the temporal lobe structures in the processing of various musical parameters. Right-temporal surgical excisions led to impaired perception of pitch and tone, while left temporal lesions resulted in impaired perception of rhythm and time parameters. Left temporal lesions were also associated with disorders of phonemic perception.

V. CEREBRAL REGIONS INVOLVED IN HEARING AND NEUROPATHOLOGY

The auditory cortex occupies the upper aspect of the first temporal gyrus (T1). It includes Heschl's gyrus, and, posteriorly, the planum temporale. Galaburda and Sanides described its architectonics. Areas 41 and 42 form the primary auditory cortex. They are made of granular cortex or koniocortex, divided into two regions: medial (KAm) and lateral (KAlt). This primary area is surrounded by associative cortex, or parakoniocortex, of distinct architectonics, including medial, lateral, rostral, and caudal areas. The medial area is separated from the insula by a thin strip of prokoniocortex. The posterior area extends to the parietal operculum. Anteriorly, the rostral part is close to the orbito-frontal cortex. The lateral part, thought to be particularly involved in musical perception, occupies a part of area 22, on the lateral side of T1. Consequently, the lateral area is linked by associative fibers to pathways from visual areas through the inferior temporal lobe, and to sensory pathways. Callosal fibers terminate in KAm. A specific area, described by Galaburda and Sanides, area TPt, sits astride the sylvian fissure, on the parietal and temporal cortices. It belongs to the posterior part of area 22 and could be selectively involved in language processes on the left side.

Additional functional data are given by two sets of procedures: (1) intracerebral electrode recordings and (2) brain functional imaging, particularly, positron emission tomography. Cortical electrode recordings are more accurate than AEPs and provide functional correlates to cytoarchitectonic data. Intracerebral AEPs include several waves that are segregated anatomically according to their latencies. Short-latency waves reflect thalamo-cortical pathways and are recorded selectively at the posterior-dorsal-medial end of Heschl's gyrus. Middle latency components are spread over the lateral part of the primary area (area 41) and the secondary area (area 42). The analysis of AEPs according to tone frequencies of the stimulus shows that AEPs are recorded medially for high frequencies and laterally for low frequencies. Activation studies with positron emission tomography in normal subjects showed the respective roles of left and right cerebral hemispheres in phonetic and pitch perception. While passive hearing of syllable pairs activated primary and secondary auditory areas bilaterally, a superimposed cognitive tasks resulted in activation of specific lateralized systems. Thus, a phonetic test such as a rhyme judgment activated Broca's area of the left hemisphere, whereas a pitch judgment activated the right prefrontal cortex.

In most cases, the brain lesions responsible for central auditory disorders are uni- or bilateral cortical–subcortical infarctions, often asymmetrical. Usually, this is the result of repeated infarctions. Other lesions include hemorrhages, ruptured aneurysms, sequelae of purulent meningitis, tumors, or trauma. Broadly speaking, bitemporal lesions, cortical, subcortical (involving the temporal isthmus, external capsules, medial geniculate bodies), or mixed, result in auditory agnosia, cortical deafness, or pure verbal deafness (bilateral brain damage type). Right-sided temporal or temporo-parietal lesions may give rise to amusia, mainly but not exclusively of the semantic type, pure verbal deafness (unilateral lesion type), or right hemianacousia.

Beside single case reports, the studies of patient series have shed light on general mechanisms relevant to the clinical presentation of brain lesions, such as the role of the left cerebral hemisphere in identification strategies. Such serial studies also have improved our knowledge of the anatomical correlations in several disorders of the processing of musical parameters.

Bibliography

Blumstein, S. E. (1990).Phonological deficits in aphasia: Theoretical perspectives. In "Cognitive Neuropsychology and Neurolinguistics: Advances in Models of Cognitive Function and Impairment" (A. Caramazza, Ed). Erlbaum, Hillsdale, NJ.

Eustache, F., Lechevalier, B., Viader, F., and Lambert, J. (1990). Identification and discrimination disorders in auditory perception: A report on two cases. *Neuropsychologia,* **28,** 257.

Lechevalier, B., Lambert, J., and Eustache, F. (1992). Agnosies auditives et syndromes voisins (surdité corticale, surdité verbale pure). Editions techniques, Encycl. Méd. Chir. (Paris-France), Neurologie, 17021 B[20].

Liegeois-Chauvel, C., Musolino, A., and Chauvel, P. (1991). Physio-anatomical localization of the primary auditory area in man. *Brain* **114,** 139.

Praamstra, P., Hagoort, P., Maassen, B., and Crul, T. (1991). Word deafness and auditory cortical function. *Brain* **114,** 1197.

Zatorre, R. J., Evans, A. C., Meyer, E., and Gjedde, A. (1992). Lateralization of phonetic and pitch discrimination in speech processing. *Science* **256,** 846.

CENTRAL NERVOUS SYSTEM

Ronald T. Brown
*Emory University School
of Medicine*

Mary K. Morris
Georgia State University

I. Neuroanatomy
II. Neurophysiology
III. Behavior

Glossary

Amnesia Partial or total loss of memory; antero-grade amnesia refers to the inability to remember events subsequent to some disturbance of brain function such as head injury, electroconvulsive shock, or degenerative disease, while retrograde amnesia refers to the inability to remember events that occurred prior to the onset of amnesia.

Aphasia Defect in the expression and/or comprehension of language due to injury or disease of the brain.

Attention A complex psychological construct which includes arousal (overall level of receptivity to incoming stimuli), selective attention (changes in responsivity that are brought about by a subset of stimuli which are biologically significant), and motor intention (readiness of the motor systems within the central nervous system to react to the environment).

Central nervous system The brain and spinal cord.

Cerebral lateralization The process whereby functions come to be located primarily in one cerebral hemisphere.

Executive functions The ability to evaluate a problem, plan a response, carry out that plan, and assess the adequacy of the response within the context of ongoing environmental cues.

Neuron The basic unit of the nervous system or the nerve cell; these cells are specialized for conduction of electrochemical signals that transmit and store information; the neuron includes the cell body (soma), dendrites, and an axon.

Neurotransmitters Substances which are released from axon terminals, diffuse across synapses, and excite or inhibit receptor sites on adjacent cells to chemically transmit information from one neuron to another.

Perception The process of becoming aware of, modulating, integrating, and interpreting sensory information, resulting from cellular activity in sensory regions of neocortex beyond primary sensory cortex; sensation refers to the process by which peripheral receptors transmit information to primary sensory cortex.

Synapse A narrow gap between the end of the axon and an adjacent neuron. The point of functional connection between two neurons; it is at the synapse that biochemical transmission occurs.

THE CENTRAL NERVOUS SYSTEM (CNS) consists of the brain and the spinal cord, and is distinguished from the peripheral nervous system which includes all of the neural tissue external to these two structures. The first two sections of this article review the basic neuroanatomy and neurophysiology of the CNS. The final portion focuses on behavior since the CNS is the basis of both reflexive and voluntary behaviors. Several behavioral domains will be discussed including sensation, perception, motor activity, attention, language, memory, executive functions, and emotion.

I. NEUROANATOMY

A. Basic Structures

The individual cells that comprise the CNS are divided into two broad classes: neurons, which are the cells that conduct information, and glial cells, which provide a variety of support functions to neurons. The CNS also can be divided into regions of gray matter, where the cell bodies of neurons predominate, and white matter, where the long processes of neurons termed axons are located. Axons connect individual neurons and are covered with a layer of glial cells called myelin that gives these regions their characteristic white color. The myelination of axons continues throughout development into early adulthood and facilitates the conduction of nerve impulses along the axon. [*See* GLIAL CELLS.]

The brain is surrounded by three membranes known as the meninges. The tough, outermost layer, called the dura mater, is closely attached to the inner surface of the skull. The second membrane, the arachnoid mater, is thin and delicate and has a web-like appearance. The third layer or pia mater is transparent and closely follows the convolutions on the surface of the brain, referred to as gyri (ridges) and dips down into the fissures or sulci (valleys) which separate them. Between the arachnoid and pia maters is the fluid-filled subarachnoid space which is part of the cerebrospinal fluid system.

B. Neural Tube and Ventricular System

An embryonic structure called the neural tube is the basis for the entire CNS. Differential growth along the walls of the neural tube during development gives rise to the primary subdivisions of the embryonic brain: (1) the prosencephalon (forebrain), (2) the mesencephalon (midbrain), and (3) the rhombencephalon (hindbrain). As the fetus develops, the prosencephalon divides to form the telencephalon and diencephalon, and the rhombencephalon develops into the metencephalon and the myelencephalon. The spinal cord develps from the most caudal (toward the rear) portion of the neural tube.

The rudimentary tubular structure of the CNS is still evident in the ventricular system. The ventricles are a set of interconnected or communicating spaces that are filled with cerebrospinal fluid (CSF). Each cerebral hemisphere contains a lateral (toward the side) ventricle. The paired lateral ventricles communicate with singular third and fourth ventricles located at midline. Cerebrospinal fluid acts as a buffer to protect the brain and the spinal cord. It is present not only in the ventricles but also in the central canal of the spinal cord and in the subarachnoid space that surrounds the brain and spinal cord. CSF is continually being produced and reabsorbed as it circulates through this intricate system. It is primarily produced by the choroid plexus in the walls of the lateral ventricles and then drains into the circulatory system through the permeable arachnoid granulations located in the sinuses of the cerebral venous system.

C. Major Subdivisions of the Brain

1. Telencephalon

The telencephalon includes the cerebral cortex and the subcortical basal ganglia. In humans, most of the cerebral cortex is six-layered neocortex. A few cortical areas, such as the hippocampus and olfactory cortex, are composed of more primitive three-layered cortex. Cerebral cortex includes the left and right cerebral hemispheres, separated by the median longitudinal fissure. Although these hemispheres appear superficially to be mirror images, significant anatomical and functional differences are present. [*See* NEOCORTEX.]

The relationship between gray and white matter in the cerebral cortex can be easily seen in a cross-sectional sample. The outer-most surface of the cortex is made up of gray matter. Beneath this outer layer is a larger area of white matter that contains all of the axonal fibers that provide input to and output from the cortical gray matter. Three types of fibers can be identified: (1) commissural fibers, which connect the two hemispheres; (2) projection fibers, which connect cortical and subcortical structures; and (3) association fibers that interconnect cortical areas within the same hemisphere.

The neocortex can be divided into four lobes, primarily by reference to specific sulcal landmarks (see Fig. 1). The frontal lobe is that part of the hemisphere above the lateral sulcus and in front of the central sulcus. It contains several subregions that are involved in the initiation of movements, from the actual control of the musculature to the highest levels of planning and intentionality. The parietal lobe is bounded in front by the central sulcus and below by the lateral sulcus, which untimately turns upward to form the posterior (toward the rear) boundary of this lobe. The parietal lobe contains somatosensory areas, as well as association areas critical for cross-modal integration and symbolic and spatial representation. The occipital lobe is located in the most posterior portion of the hemisphere and is involved in visual perception. The temporal lobe includes the area inferior (toward the bottom) to the lateral sulcus and anterior (toward the front) to the occipital lobe. It is involved in auditory perception, language comprehension, higher-order visual processing, and memory. Deep cortical structures include the hippo-

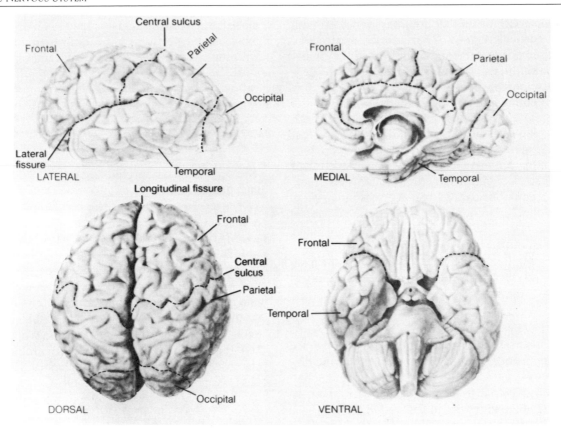

FIGURE 1   The location of the frontal, parietal, occipital, and temporal lobes of the human brain. [From Bryan Kolb and Ian Q. Whitshaw. ''Fundamentals of Human Neuropsychology.'' Copyright © 1990 by W. H. Freeman and Company. Reprinted with permission.]

campal formation which is folded within the parahippocampal gyrus on the medial (toward the midline) surface of the temporal lobe, an area that is critical for memory function. The cingulate gyrus also is located on the medial aspect of the hemisphere, superior (toward the top) to the large white matter bundle known as the corpus callosum, that connects the two hemispheres. The amygdala is a complex of nuclei located in the dorsomedial portion of the temporal lobe, just in front of the anterior end of the hippocampus. The basal forebrain is composed of several contiguous structures in the ventromedial frontal lobe, inlcuding the septal nuclei, the nucleus basalis of Meynert, and the diagonal band of Broca. All of these regions contribute to an extensive network of structures called the limbic system that is involved in emotion. [*See* HIPPOCAMPAL FORMATION; LIMBIC SYSTEM.]

The basal ganglia include the caudate nucleus, the putamen, and globus pallidus, which are also called the corpus striatum. These structures are connected to numerous cortical regions, especially in the frontal lobes, and serve to modulate the output of these regions. Recent studies have documented the existence of parallel, functionally segregated loops that interconnect discrete areas of the basal ganglia with discrete cortical zones and allow the basal ganglia to influence cortical function in a highly specific and localized manner.

2. Diencephalon

The diencephalon is buried deep within the cerebral hemispheres and encloses the third ventricle. It can be divided into four major subdivisions, the thalamus, the hypothalamus, the subthalamus, and the epithalamus. The thalamus is the largest division and plays an integral role, in conjunction with the cortex, in sensory, motor, and limbic fucntions. Virtually all sensory information ascending to the cortex synapses first in portions of the thalamus. The pathways by which the basal ganglia and cerebellum influence the cortex also involve a thalamic relay. The thalamus can be divided into three cell masses, anterior, medial, and lateral, each of which contains several discrete nuclei that are interconnected with specific cortical regions. The anterior and medial cell masses are the thalamic division of the limbic system, and the lateral cell mass belongs to the sensory and motor systems.

The hypothalamus is located at the base of the diencephalon. Extensive interconnections with both limbic structures and the autonomic nervous system allow it to play a central role in maintaining homeostasis. The hypothalamus is involved in a wide range of homeostatic fucntions, including energy and temperature regulation, water balance, cardiovascular function, sleep, reproduction, and emotional behavior. The subthalamus and the epithalamus are small divisions of the diencephalon, involved in the motor functions of the basal ganglia and the control of circadian rhythms, respectively. [See HOMEOSTASIS; HYPOTHALAMUS.]

3. Brainstem

The brainstem is derived form multiple subdivisions of the embryonic brain: (1) the mesencephalon, which gives rise to the midbrain; (2) the metencephalon, which gives rise to the pons; and (3) the myelencephalon, which gives rise to the medulla. The brainstem contains all the ascending and descending pathways between the cerebral cortex and the spinal cord. Most of the cranial nerves also travel through the brainstem. The cranial nerves provide sensory and motor function for the head, convey information from peripheral sensory receptors to the brain, and are involved in the control of the viscera.

The midbrain can be divided into the tectum and the tegmentum. The tectum contains the four colliculi, protrusions that are visible on the dorsal (toward the back) surface of the brainstem. The two anterior "bumps" are the superior colliculi, involved in orienting reflexes of the eyes and head. The posterior "bumps" are the inferior colliculi which are included in the ascending auditory pathway. The tegmentum is located on the ventral (toward the belly) surface and contains the substantia nigra and the red nucleus, which contribute to motor function. The cerebral peduncles, bundles of motor fibers on their way to the spinal cord, also pass through the ventral brainstem.

The pons can be seen as a bulge in the ventral brainstem. It contains a portion of the reticular activating system, a complex mixture of nuclei and fiber tracts that stretches form the diencephalon through the hindbrain to multiple regions in the forebrain, brainstem, and spinal cord, and is involved in the modulation of arousal. The medulla oblongata is the most caudal portion of the brainstem, continuous with the rostral (toward the front) end of the spinal cord. It also contains a portion of the reticular activating system, including nuclei that control vital respiratory and cardiovascular functions.

D. Cerebellum

The cerebellum is derived from the embryonic metencephalon and forms much of the roof of the fourth ventricle. The surface of the cerebellar cortex has a distinctive appearance with numerous narrow folds or folia. Underneath this cortex is a large central mass of white matter containing several nuclei which project to the cerebellar cortex, an organization analogous to the cerebral cortex and the thalamic nuclei. The cerebellum acts with the rest of the motor system to monitor and adjust the correspondence between intended and actual movements. Recent research has suggested that the cerebellum may also play a role in learning and memory. [See CEREBELLUM.]

E. Spinal Cord

The spinal cord is included in the CNS. Its principal functions are to distribute motor fibers to the effectors of the body (i.e., muscles and glands) and to collect somatosensory information to be relayed to the brain. A transverse section through the spinal cord reveals a central canal which is part of the ventricular system, although this is not patent in the adult. The central canal is surrounded by a region of gray matter that has the general shape of a butterfly. The dorsal "wings" of the butterfly are referred to as the dorsal horns and subserve sensory function; the ventral "wings" or ventral horns subserve motor function. This central gray matter is surrounded by a zone of white matter where the axons of the neurons in the dorsal and ventral horns travel. Motor axons exit the spinal cord ventrally; sensory axons enter the spinal cord dorsally. The spinal cord can be divided into 31 segments; 8 cervical, 12 thoracic, 5 lumbar, 5 sacral, and 1 coccygeal. Each segment of the cord is linked with the organs and musculature of a specific body segment, called a dermatome. Because of this segmental organization, it is possible to infer the location of spinal cord damage with substantial accuracy from changes in sensory-motor function in a different body parts.

II. NEUROPHYSIOLOGY

A. Structure of a Neuron

The neuron or nerve cell is the foundation for mental processes and behavior. These cells are specialized for the conduction of electrochemical signals that transmit information from one part of the body to another. Neurons vary in structure, depending upon their specific function and location within the CNS, but all have three major components, the soma, dendrites, and axon. The soma, also referred to as the cell body, is where the cell's metabolic activities occur. Dendrites, branches which extend from the cell body, receive information from adjacent neurons and transmit it to other neurons via the axon. Axons vary both in number of collaterals or branches and in length. Further, the axons of most neurons, particularly those that are large in diameter and fast-conducting, are surrounded by a myelin sheath, a fatty covering that serves as an insulator. Myelin protects the axon from mechanical damage and insulates it from extraneous electrical noise. The myelin sheath is interrupted at intervals by nodes of Ranvier, or areas where myelin is either absent or very thin. The presence of these nodes allows impulses to leap from node to node increasing conduction speed. This process is referred to as saltatory conduction.

There are three types of neurons which transmit information between the CNS and the sensory organs, muscles, and glands. Sensory or afferent neurons transmit information from the peripheral parts of the nervous system such as the sensory organs to the spinal cord or brain. Motor or efferent neurons carry signals from the brain or spinal cord to the periphery of the nervous system where they intersect with effectors of behavior such as the various muscles and glands. Interneurons connect afferent and efferent neurons and integrate their activities.

B. Synaptic Transmission

Progagation of impulses between neurons is referred to as synaptic transmission. The point or site of connection between neurons where this transmission occurs is referred to as the synapse or synaptic cleft, which is a narrow gap between the end of the axon and an adjacent cell. While the majority of synapses occur between axons and dendrites, axon–soma and axon–axon connections also exist.

The transmission of impulses within and between neurons combines both electrical conduction and chemical transmission, in a complex electrochemical process. In short, the body's fluids contain electrically charged particles or ions. The neuron's semipermeable membrane selectively regulates the passage of particular ions into and out of the cell. When the neuron is in a "resting state," its membrane allows potassium (K^+) and chloride (Cl^-) to enter the cell, while exluding sodium (Na^+) ions. The result of this uneven distribution of ions is that the fluid inside the cell is negatively charged and the fluid outside of the cell is positively charged. This process is referred to as polarization and the electrical imbalance across the cell membrane is referred to as the resting potential. This uneven balance is maintained by both the passive process of membrane permeability and a more active process by which the neuron takes in potassium (K^+) and pumps out sodium (Na^+).

Electrical, chemical, and physical events can all lead to changes in voltage across the cell membrane. In the presence of these specific stimuli, the resting potential can be increased or decreased. Increased potential, referred to as hyperpolarization, represents a state of inhibition. Reduced potential, referred to as depolarization, represents a state of excitation. Both hyperpolarization and depolarization involve a change in the cell membrane's permeability which commences at the point of stimulation.

During depolarization, the membrane changes to allow sodium ions to rush into and potassium ions to rush out of the cell. This results in the cell's interior becoming positively charged, while the exterior fluid becomes negatively charged. At approximately -50 mV, the cell membrane suddenly becomes completely permeable, allowing Na^+ to rush in. This abrupt change in the distribution of ions is referred to as the action potential. An action potential typically begins at the junction of the soma and the axon. Excitation spreads to adjacent areas in the neuron so that the action potential, sometimes referred to as a nerve impulse or spike, eventually travels the full length of the axon. Action potentials do not vary in size. Rather, it is theorized that they maintain the same magnitude throughout their axonal journey. Thus, information in the nervous system is not encoded in terms of variations in size of action potentials, but rather by changes in their frequency, patterning, and destination. For example, a bright light does not cause larger action potentials in the neurons of the visual system than does a dim light. Rather, the brighter light results in action potentials being generated in these neurons at a greater frequency.

C. Neurotransmitters

Communication between synapses is typically chemically mediated, in contrast to the electrical conduction process within a single neuron. When the action potential or spike reaches the axon terminal, it stimulates the release of a chemical substance or neurotransmitter which diffuses across the synaptic cleft and activates or inhibits the receptor site in the adjacent cell. Neurotransmitters produce depolarization or hyperpolarization in the postsynaptic cell by, respectively, "opening up" or "closing up" the pores of the cell's membranes, thereby affecting the flow of ions across the membrane. Depending upon the nature of the transmitter and the nature of the receptor site, the postsynaptic potential at any particular synapse will be either depolarizing (excitatory) or hyperpolarizing (inhibitory). The former is referred to as an EPSP; the latter as an IPSP. EPSPs and IPSPSs vary in magnitude, depending upon how much neurotransmitter substance is received at the receptor site. Several EPSPs must accumulate and reach a specific magnitude in order for an action potential to occur in the postsynaptic cell. It also should be noted that EPSPs and IPSPSs which occur simultaneously can negate each other's effects. [*See* SYNAPTIC TRANSMITTERS AND NEUROMODULATORS.]

A number of neurotransmitter substances have been identified. The first to be isolated, and perhaps the best understood, is acetylcholine (ACH), an excitatory neurotransmitter substance found throughout the CNS, which mediates neuromuscular transmission and parasympathetic arousal. ACH is found in various parts of the peripheral nervous system (e.g., between motor neurons and skeletal muscles), the spinal cord, and specific areas of the brain. Those neurons releasing ACH are referred to as cholinergic neurons. Another class of neurotransmitters, the catecholamines, include norepinephrine, epinephrine, and dopamine. These neurotransmitters have been found to be involved in personality, mood, and drive states. Serotonin is the neurotransmitter implicated in the suppression of arousal, regulation of hunger and temperature, sexual behavior, aggression, and the onset of sleep in the sleep–waking cycle. Other neurotransmitters include γ-aminobutyric acid (GABA), the most common inhibitory transmitter in the CNS, and the endorphins (e.g., enkephalin), naturally occurring opiates which appear to be involved in the inhibition of pain. [*See* PAIN.]

In recent years, the neurotransmitters have been important in the understanding of human behavior and treatment of psychiatric disorders. For example, identifying the function of neurotransmitters at various receptor sites has provided physicians with an increased understanding of how specific pharmacologic agents exert their effects. Drugs which block the action of acetylcholine (e.g., curare) may result in fatal muscle paralysis. Excessive dopamine has been posited in the development of schizophrenia. Low levels of GABA in the motor region of the brain have been associated with Huntington's chorea, while insufficient dopamine in the basal ganglia is believed to be etiologic in Parkinson's disease.

Recent evidence suggests that learning and memory occur at the level of the synapse. Repeated electrical stimulation of neural pathways appears to lead to long-lasting increases in the strength of synaptic response that may last from days to even months. This structural modification is referred to as long-term potentiation. This phenomenon has been clearly demonstrated in the hippocampus and its connections, areas that have been shown to be core components of learning and memory.

III. BEHAVIOR

A. Cerebral Lateralization

Several broad schemes exist for dividing the brain into functional subsystems. Anterior regions, responsible for behavioral output, can be distinguished from posterior regions, responsible for the analysis and integration of information from the environment. Cortical regions interact with subcortical regions via a complex network of excitatory and inhibitory connections to permit both stimulus-driven and volitional behaviors. However, the functional division of cerebral laterality (i.e., left and right hemisphere) is probably the best known schema.

Although the left and right cerebral hemispheres appear quite similar, detailed examination reveals numerous anatomic differences that are thought to support functional asymmetries. For example, the superior temporal aspect of the planum temporale, a cortical region posterior to auditory cortex, is larger on the left in the majority of individuals; this is believed to reflect left hemisphere specialization for language.

Converging evidence from studies of patients with lateralized brain lesions, commissurotomy (i.e., split brain) patients, and normal individuals evaluated under specialized laboratory conditions suggests differential hemispheric contributions to cognitive function. The left hemisphere is specialized for processing linguistic stimuli while the right hemisphere appears to be specialized for processing complex configural information such as spatial orientation, music, and faces. Although the two hemispheres may be specialized for different types of stimuli, it might also be that each hemisphere has a characteristic processing style that is best suited for analyzing those stimuli. For example, the left hemisphere may process information in a serial, sequential manner, conducive to the analysis of language. In contrast, the right hemisphere has been described as a parallel, holistic processor, more appropriate for handling complex configurations.

Although the majority of individuals fit this functional model of lateralization, individual variability is clearly present and is related to factors such as handedness and gender. Some degree of functional asymmetry appears to be present from birth. Newborns can accurately discriminate speech from nonspeech sounds and demonstrate greater activation of the left hemipshere in response to human speech.

B. Sensation and Perception

Sensation is the process of receiving stimulation through specialized sensory organs, while perception refers to the process of becoming aware of, modulating, integrating, and interpreting that information. Perception represents the modification and organization of incoming stimuli. Specialized cells, referred to as receptors, convert sensory energy (e.g., light waves) into neural activity in the form of either graded potentials or action potentials. The process is referred to as transduction. The various sensory systems include vision, audition, taste, and smell (olfaction).

1. Visual System

Light enters the eye through its tansparent outer covering, the cornea. It subsequently passes through the pupil, an adjustable opening in the iris (the pigmented portion of the eye), is focused by the lens, and finally falls on the light-sensitive area of the eye, the retina. The outer layer of the retina contains two types of receptor cells: rods and cones. Rods are visual receptors that are sensitive to low-intensity light and are involved in night and peripheral vision; cones are receptors found mainly in the central region of the retina and permit color vision.

The rods and cones synapse with bipolar cells which in turn synapse with ganglion cells. Axons of the ganglion cells gather together to form the optic nerve which carries visual impulses from the retina to the visual processing areas of the brain. Prior to entering the brain, however, the optic nerves partly cross, forming the optic chiasm, with approximately one-half of the fibers from each eye crossing to the other side of the brain. The fibers which cross come from the nasal portions of both retinas. As a result, information from each eye reaches both sides of the brain, with signals from the left visual field terminating in the right hemisphere and signals from the right visual field being sent to the left hemisphere. Finally, these optic tracts travel to the thalamus and ultimately to the primary visual cortex of the occipital lobe. [See VISUAL PERCEPTION.]

2. Auditory System

Sound waves enter the outer ear and travel through the auditory canal which is sealed at its inner end by a thin membrane known as the tympanum or eardrum. The sound waves cause the eardrum to vibrate, which in turn moves the three tiny bones or ossicles of the middle ear: the malleus, incus, and stapes. The ossicles amplify the motion set off by the eardrum and transmit the vibration to the oval window (the membrane which separates the middle and inner ear). The amplified vibration received by the oval window is transmitted through the fluid of the inner ear to the spiral shaped cochlea. Attached to the basilar membrane of the cochlea is the organ of Corti which contains the auditory receptor cells, the hair cells. The hair cells are sandwiched between the basilar membrane and the tectoral membrane. Fluid movement in the cochlea moves these two membranes in a way which distorts and bends hair cells, thus giving rise to neural impulses in the adjacent auditory nerve. The pathways from the cochlea travel via a series of nuclei to the thalamus and ultimately to the primary auditory cortex in the temporal lobe. The auditory system is bilateral, with each ear projecting to both sides of the brain. [See EARS AND HEARING.]

3. Taste and Smell

Taste and smell (olfaction) are both chemical senses which respond only to molecules in solution. The sensory receptors for taste are located in the taste buds which are sensitive to four basic taste qualities: bitter, sweet, sour, and salt. Other tastes are considered to be a combination of these four qualities and/or a mixture of taste or smell. Signals from the taste buds are transmitted to the brain by three different cranial nerves which unite to form the tractus solitarious in the medulla. At this nucleus solitarious, these fibers cross the midline and continue, via the thalamus, to the insula and the somatosensory cortex (tongue area). A second branch of the tractus solitarious projects to the lateral hypothalamus and the amygdala, areas that are involved in feeding. [*See* TASTE.]

The sense of olfaction is relatively insensitive in humans compared to other animals. The receptor cells of olfaction lie within the olfactory epithelium, the membrane which lines the roof of the nasal cavity. The axons of these olfactory receptor cells synapse in the olfactory bulb. From there the olfactory nerve passes through the pyriform cortex and subsequently to the thalamus and to the orbital frontal cortex. Olfactory receptor cells are not specific to single odors. Rather, it is believed that the pattern of activity across many receptors leads to the experience of a particular odor. [*See* SENSE OF SMELL.]

4. Somatosensory System

The somatosensory system includes the cutaneous or skin senses: touch/pressure, pain, temperature, and position sense. The qualities of skin sensations are due both to the mechanical and thermal properties of the tissue in which the sensory nerves terminate and to variations in temporal and spatial patterns of neural discharge of those sensory nerves. The axons of the cutaneous receptor cells are organized into two systems in the spinal cord, the medial lemniscal system and the spinothalamic system, both of which ascend to the posteroventral nuclear complex of the thalamus which, in turn, sends projections to the somatosensory cortex. The medial lemniscal system is involved in touch/pressure and position sense while the spinothalamic system mediates the sensation of pain and temperature. The arrangement of these projections in the postcentral gyrus generally represents the body parts topographically, with the legs at the top and the hand at the bottom of the gyrus. [*See* TACTILE PERCEPTION.]

C. Motor System

The motor system consists of a number of subsystems including the spinal cord, the brainstem, the cerebellum, the basal ganglia, and the neocortex. These structures are interconnected and are organized in both parallel and hierarchical systems. The

brainstem and cortex can each influence the spinal cord autonomously for the purpose of invoking movements, but also are interconnected, permitting them to influence each other. The cerebellum is important in balance and posture and, together with the basal ganglia and motor cortex, is essential to the performance of coordinated and refined motor movements. Generally, the cerebellum tends to be largest and most developed in humans, who are capable of more graceful and precise movements than are other species. Damage to the cerebellum can result in ataxia, a condition producing severe tremor, a loss of balance, and gait disturbance. The basal ganglia are important in the initiation and control of voluntary movements and particularly in the regulation of muscle tone. [*See* MOTOR CONTROL.]

There are two major descending pathways from the motor cortex, allowing each hemisphere to control the trunk of the body of the same side and the arms and legs of the opposite side; these are referred to as the lateral and ventromedial systems. Both pathways ultimately synapse with motor neurons located in the nuclei of the cranial nerves and in the ventral horns of the spinal cord. The motor neurons are the final link in the pathway, projecting directly to the muscles. The lateral system projects from both cortex and brainstem in one hemisphere to the spinal cord of the opposite side. The corticospinal component of this system connects directly with motor neurons and is involved in the movement of distal musculature (i.e., fingers and hands) on the contralateral side of the body. The rubrospinal component connects first with interneurons, and then with motor neurons that control the musculature of the shoulders, arms, and hand. The ventromedial system projects to interneurons of the spinal cord from the cortex and brainstem of the same side before synapsing with motor neurons that control the musculature of the trunk.

For both motor and sensory cortex, a topographical relationship exists between body parts and parts of the neocortex. This relationship is often demonstrated schematically by cartoon men or homunculi drawn over the motor and sensory areas to represent this type of organization. The face and the hands of the homunculi are larger as they are capable of finer perceptions and movements than are other body areas and thus require proportionately more neocortex to represent them.

D. Language

The discovery of an association between damage to the left hemisphere and language disturbance is commonly attributed to the French neurologist, Paul Broca. He described a pattern of langauge impairment, primarily involving speech production, that was correlated with damage to a region in the left frontal lobe, that has come to be known as "Broca's area." Subsequently, Karl Wernicke described a different pattern of language deficits associated with damage to the left temporal-parietal region, later termed "Wernicke's area." These early descriptions of subtypes of acquired language disorder or aphasia were the first attempts to characterize distinct aphasia syndromes and relate them to specific neuroanatomic substrates. [See APHASIA.]

Aphasias can be classified into syndromes based on patterns of sparing and impairment in different language processes. Patients may exhibit disorders of language comprehension for either auditory (i.e., speech) and/or visual (i.e., written) material. They may also exhibit disorders of language production that can affect articulation, fluency, word finding, syntax, repetition, or writing. For example, the syndrome of Broca's aphasia is characterized by (1) relative sparing of auditory comprehension, (2) sparse, effortful speech output that is "telegraphic", (i.e., limited to content words such as nouns and verbs), (3) phonemic paraphasias, (i.e., speech errors in which one sound is incorrectly substituted for another), and (4) impairments in reading and writing.

The brain regions involved in language have been identified both by clinical investigations of patients with brain lesions and by the use of cortical stimulation during neurosurgery. The cortical regions involved in language include the classical areas of Broca and Wernicke in the left hemisphere, the sensory and motor regions for the face bilaterally and the supplementary motor area bilaterally.

Although the study of aphasia has empahsized the identification of cortical language zones in the left hemisphere, there has been a growing appreciation for the role of other brain regions. Lesions of subcortical structures, particularly the left posterior thalamus, are associated with disturbances of speech and language. The right hemisphere also appears to have some language capabilities. Studies of split brain patients suggest that the right hemisphere has considerable auditory comprehension skills, but limited speech and understanding of grammar. Patients who have had the left hemisphere removed in early childhood develop considerable language competence, suggesting that the right hemisphere is able to subserve some language functions; however, deficits in higher order linguistic skills and often behavior are present in these patients.

E. Attention

Over the past several years, there have been significant advances in the study of attention and how this process is mediated by the CNS. Attention is an intricate physiological and psychological construct which consists of three distinct components: arousal, selective attention, and motor intention. Arousal delineates the overall level of receptivity to incoming stimuli, while selective attention refers to changes in responsivity that are elicited by a subset of stimuli which are biologically significant. Finally, intention refers to the readiness of the motor systems to react to the environment.

Several electrophysiological studies have supported the belief that the reticular activating system is pivotal in the first process of attention, that of arousal. In support of this notion, several seminal studies with animals have demonstrated that lesions of the mesencephalic reticular formation induce a state of severely diminished arousal. The posterior parietal cortex has been posited as the brain region associated with selective attention. In several studies employing both humans and monkeys, it has been demonstrated that specific neurons within the parietal cortex heighten their activity when the animal is attending to a novel stimulus. Lastly, the dorsolateral frontal lobe appears to regulate intentional activity as demonstrated by increased activity in this area when animals are ready to make movements. Animals with dorsolateral frontal lobe lesions have contralateral limb akinesia, a failure to use one limb to respond to a meaningful stimulus which is not attributable to weakness of the limb or inattention.

Electroencephalographic (EEG) (brain wave activity) and positron emission tomographic (PET) (metabolic activity) studies have suggested that the right hemisphere is dominant for attention. From a clinical perspective, attentional and intentional disorders accompany right more frequently than left hemisphere lesions. Attentional disturbances are pervasive symptoms for a number of neurological, psychiatric, and learning disorders for both adults and children. For example, many learning disabled children with deficits in attention and excessive motor activity are viewed as having an organically based deficit localized in the midbrain, which affects their capacity to maintain arousal and to focus and sustain attention. These children ahve been found to demonstrate slower reaction times, different EEG responses, and decreased neurophysiological activity when compared to their normally developing peers. [See EEG, COGNITION, AND DEMENTIA.]

F. Memory

Disturbances in memory are typically associated with damage to three neuroanatomic regions: (1) the medial temporal lobes (including the hippocampus and possibly the amygdala); (2) the diencephalon (including the dorsomedial nucleus of the thalamus and the mammillary bodies; and (3) the basal forebrain, particularly those regions involved in producing the neurotransmitter acetylcholine. Memory deficits can involve the ability to learn and retain new information, referred to as anterograde amnesia, and/or the ability to recall previously learned information, referred to as retrograde amnesia. [See AMNESIA.]

Patients who underwent bilateral temporal lobectomies to control intractable seizures have provided the clearest evidence of the critical role of the hippocampus in learning and recalling new information. Following surgery, these patients exhibited profound and permanent anterograde amnesia. The degree of memory impairment was directly related to the amount of hippocampus that was removed.

Unilateral temporal lobectomy results in a more circumscribed memory impairment that is material-specific and related to hemispheric specialization. Left temporal lobectomy patients have more difficulty recalling verbal material such as word lists or stories. In contrast, right temporal lobectomy patients have difficulty recalling nonverbal material (e.g., faces, musical passages or geometric designs).

Amnesia secondary to diencephalic damage has been demonstrated in patients with Korsakoff's syndrome and in a handful of case studies with focal lesions of the medial thalamic area. Korsakoff's syndrome is a neurodegenerative disease, secondary to chronic alcoholism. Although anterograde amnesia is present, the deficits of Korsakoff patients distinguish them from patients with damage to medial temporal structures. For example, unlike medial temporal lobe patients, Korsakoff patients exhibit extensive loss of past memories, confabulation, and apathy. Cerebral atrophy extends beyond the diencephalon to the frontal lobes in these patients, suggesting that many of their deficits may be secondary to frontal lobe damage rather than aspects of their memory disturbance.

Historically, it has proven helpful to distinguish between different types of memory. Earlier models focused on the distinction between immediate memory (attention span), short-term memory (lasting up to 30 seconds), and long-term memory. More recently, considerable attention has been focused on the distinction between declarative memory or memory for facts that can be consciously recalled (e.g., what you ate for breakfast) and procedural memory, the recall of motor skills and automatic routines (e.g., riding a bicycle). Amnestic patients frequently exhibit spared procedural memory, in conjunction with severely impaired declarative memory. A growing body of evidence suggests that these two memory systems are distinct and are subserved by different neural systems. [See MEMORY.]

G. Executive Functions

Executive functions refer to the ability to evaluate a problem, plan a response, carry out that plan, and assess the adequacy of the response within the context of ongoing environmental cues. These functions are thought to be mediated by the prefrontal cortex. They are quite complex, rather subtle when operating effectively, and appear to be developmental, maturing with age, particularly during early adolescence. Because the prefrontal cortex is a later myelinating area of the brain, some recent studies have suggested that performance on tasks hypothesized to be sensitive to frontal lobe functions demonstrate rather dramatic developmental changes during adolescence.

Patients with executive function deficits frequently perform within the average range on standardized tests of intelligence. However, their deficits are often detected on sensitive neuropsychological measures and are apparent in these patients' daily functioning. Executive function deficits can include motor abnormalities, cognitive deficits, and personality change. Motor abnormalities may include problems with gait, abnormal reflexes, motor slowing (bradykinesia), and decreased initiative and spontaneity. Cognitive deficits are generally manifested by mental inflexibility and difficulties shifting attention from one task to another. Perseverative behavior, or the inability to inhibit a response once it has begun, is common. Finally, memory may be disrupted by increased distractibility and failure to use appropriate strategies to aid recall.

Patients who have sustained damage to the prefrontal cortex frequently demonstrate changes in personality functioning with both overexaggerated and apathetic responses reported in the clinical literature. Thus, impairment in executive function occurs when behavior increasingly is under control of external environmental stimuli rather than autonomous self-regulation.

H. Emotion

Changes in emotional behavior are among the most frequently described consequences of brain injury. Unfortunately, we know much less about these behaviors than we do about cognitive function since they are difficult to measure objectively. Early attempts to localize emotional processes in the brain focused on subcortical structures. In 1937, Papez hypothesized that a group of interconnected structures, referred to as the limbic system, was the neuroanatomic substrate of emotion. In 1939, Kluver and Bucy described a behavioral syndrome in monkeys, associated with damage to the amygdala and anterior temporal lobe, which included striking aberrations in social and emotional responsivity, including a loss of the fear response to previously threatening stimuli. This syndrome has subsequently been described in humans with damage to similar brain regions.

More recent studies have focused on the contribution of cortical areas to a variety of emotional behaviors. Studies of both patients with unilateral lesions and normal individuals have indicated that the right cerebral hemisphere is specialized for interpreting nonverbal emotional signals, such as facial expression and prosody (i.e., tone of voice). The right hemisphere may also be dominant for the production of these same nonverbal signals. Physiologic arousal in response to emotional stimuli (e.g., changes in heart rate or galvanic skin response) can also be altered by brain injury. Reduced galvanic skin responses to emotionally arousing visual material and to mild electrical shock have been reported following right hemisphere damage.

Other investigators have focused on the experiential aspects of emotion such as mood. Patients with right hemisphere lesions are often described as indifferent or even euphoric, while patients with left hemisphere damage often exhibit depression. Studies of normal subjects have reported that positive mood states are associated with activation of the anterior regions of the left hemisphere and negative mood states with right anterior activation. In combination, these observations raise the possibility that both hemispheres are involved in the mediation of mood states but contribute differentially, depending on the valence of the experienced emotion.

Bibliography

Carpenter, M. B., and Sutin, J. (1983). "Human Neuroanatomy," 8th ed. Williams and Wilkins, Baltimore.

Cooper, J. R., Bloom, F. E., and Roth, R. H. (1986). "The Biochemical Basis of Neuropharmacology." Oxford University Press, New York.

DeArmond, S. J., Fusco, M. M., and Dewey, M. M. (1989). "Structure of the Human Brain: A Photographic Atlas," 3rd ed. Oxford University Press, New York.

Ellis, A. W., and Young, A. W. (1988). "Human Cognitive Neuropsychology." Erlbaum, Hillsdale, NJ.

Heilman, K. M., and Valenstein, E. (1985). "Clinical Neuropsychology," 2nd ed. Oxford University Press, New York.

Kandel, E. R., Schwartz, J. H., and Jessell, T. M. (1991). "Principles of Neural Science," 3rd ed. Elsevier, New York.

Kolb, B., and Whitshaw, I. O. (1990). "Fundamentals of Human Neuropsychology," 3rd ed. Freeman, New York.

Luria, A. R. (1980). "Higher Cortical Functions in Man." Basic Books, New York.

Mountcastle, V. B. (1987). "Handbook of Physiology: The Nervous System," Vol. V. American Physiological Society, Bethesda, MD.

Walsh, K. W. (1978). "Neuropsychology: A Clinical Approach." Churchill Livingstone, New York.

◆

CEREBELLUM

M. I. Botez
University of Montreal

I. Anatomy, Physiology, and Neurochemistry of the Cerebellum and Its Pathways
II. The Cerebellum and Motor Behavior
III. The Cerebellum and Nonmotor Behavior
IV. Conclusions

Glossary

Asynergia Disturbance of coordinated movements in which the range, direction, and force of muscle contractions are inappropriate.

Cerebellar cortex Formed by three cellular layers: the molecular, Purkinje, and granular layers.

Cerebellar nuclei Structures lying in the cerebellar white matter: dentate, emboliform, globose, and fastigius nuclei.

Cerebellum Structure in the posterior cranial fossa consisting of a central part (vermis) and two lateral hemispheres. Each hemisphere is connected to the brainstem by three peduncles.

Frontal-like syndrome with cerebellar lesions Deficits in programming and planning of daily activity.

Ideagraphy The identification, by metabolic or circulatory positron emission tomographic (PET) scan studies, of human brain activation caused by events that are simply ideational and are not coupled to any sensory input or motor output. Cerebellar structures are activated during such cognitive tasks.

Main neurotransmitters in the cerebellum Brain amines (serotonin, noradrenalin, dopamine) and amino acids (glutamate, aspartate).

Parietal-like syndrome with cerebellar lesions Deficits in visuospatial organization for a concrete task.

Reaction time Time taken for a response to a visual, proprioceptive, or auditory stimulus.

THE ROLE of the cerebellum in nonmotor behavior, i.e., in cognitive behavior, is a fascinating subject which became "a hot one" during the last few years. To understand the role of the cerebellum in human behavior, we use a multidisciplinary approach, including clinical, radiologic, metabolic, and neurochemical studies in humans as well as some pertinent neuropsychological and neurochemical data in animals.

I. ANATOMY, PHYSIOLOGY, AND NEUROCHEMISTRY OF THE CEREBELLUM AND ITS PATHWAYS

A. Gross Anatomy

The cerebellum is a symmetric structure lying in the posterior fossa. Its major subdivisions are the centrally positioned vermis and the paired lateral cerebellar hemispheres.

The cerebellum is attached to the brainstem by three paired cerebellar peduncles, namely: (i) the inferior or restiform body to the medulla; (ii) the middle or brachium pontis to the pons; and (iii) the superior or brachium conjunctivum to the higher levels of the neuraxis.

Structurally, the cerebellum consists of: (i) a superficial gray mantle, the cerebellar cortex; (ii) an internal white mass, the medullary substance; and (iii) four pairs of intrinsic nuclei embedded in the white matter. Embryologically and functionally, the cerebellum can be divided into three parts: the archicerebellum, the paleocerebellum, and the neocerebellum. The archicerebellum, i.e., the oldest part of the cerebellum, comprises the nodulus, the paired flocculi, and their peduncular connections. Archicerebellum, i.e., the flocculonodular lobule, is closely related to the vestibular system (Fig. 1). The paleocerebellum, i.e., the anterior lobe, receives impulses from stretch receptors via the spinocerebellar tracts and is concerned mostly with muscle tone.

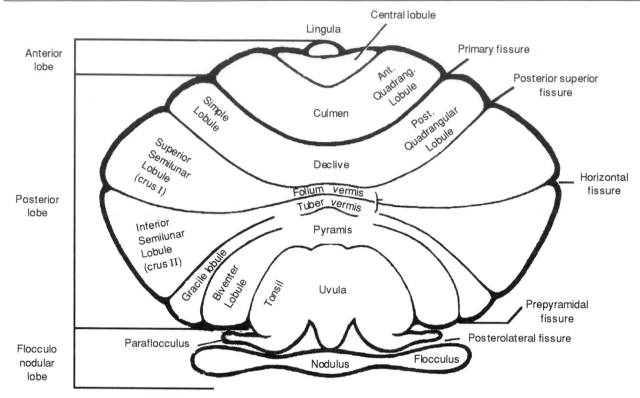

FIGURE 1   Schematic diagram of the fissures and lobules of the cerebellum.

The neocerebellum, i.e., the posterior lobe (Fig. 1), is the largest and phylogenetically newest part of the cerebellum. It receives inputs from the contralateral cerebral cortex via relays in the pontine nuclei. During phylogenetic evolution, the cerebral cortex and the neocerebellum were enlarged dramatically. Classically, the neocerebellum was considered to be mostly concerned with the coordination of somatic motor functions. During the last few years, it became evident that the lateral aspects of the cerebellar hemispheres are involved in some nonmotor, i.e. cognitive, functions. [*See* BRAIN.]

B. Histology

The cerebellar cortex is composed of three cellular layers from the surface: the molecular layer, the Purkinje cell layer, and the granular layer (Fig. 2). Cells found in the molecular layer are outer (superior) stellate cells and basket (inferior) stellate cells. Their axons make synaptic contact with the Purkinje cells.

The Purkinje cells give rise to dendritic trees in the molecular layer whereas their axons synapse with neurons in deep cerebellar nuclei.

The granular layer formed by granule cells also contains Golgi type II cells, which form intricate connections with the mossy fibers and dendrites of granule cells.

The mossy fibers contain afferents to the cerebellar cortex from the pontine, vestibular, reticular, and trigeminal nuclei as well from the spinal cord. These afferents terminate in the internal granular layer. The granule cells send their axons in the molecular layer to become parallel fibers.

Climbing fibers arise from the inferior olivary nucleus and reach the dendrites of the Purkinje cells. Collaterals from both mossy and climbing fibers reach the deep cerebellar nuclei. There are four cerebellar nuclei: the dentate, emboliform, globose, and fastigius nuclei. The emboliform and globose nuclei are collectively referred to as interposed nuclei.

Afferents to the dentate nucleus arise from the pontine nuclei via Purkinje cells, from inferior olivary nuclei, from the locus ceruleus, raphe nuclei, and reticulotegmental tracts. Efferent fibers from the dentate are cerebelloolivary, dentothalamic, and dentorubral fibers.

The emboliform nucleus receives olivocerebellar afferents and sends cerebellorubral fibers. The glo-

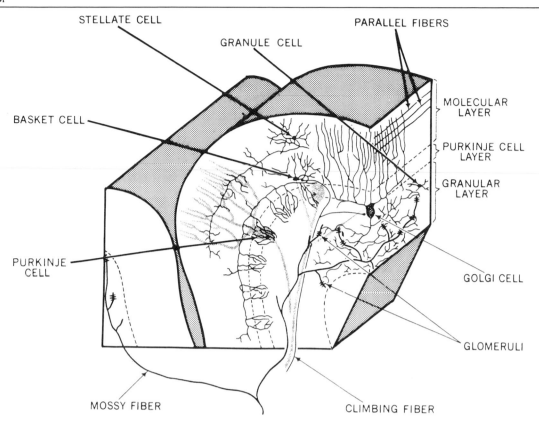

STELLATE CELL

GRANULE CELL

PARALLEL FIBERS

BASKET CELL

MOLECULAR LAYER

PURKINJE CELL LAYER

GRANULAR LAYER

PURKINJE CELL

GOLGI CELL

GLOMERULI

MOSSY FIBER

CLIMBING FIBER

FIGURE 2   Section of the cerebellum showing the branching of nerve cells.

bose receives afferents from the red nucleus and sends efferent cerebellothalamic fibers.

The fastigial nucleus receives spinocerebellar, reticulocerebellar, and tectocerebellar projections; the efferents are cerebelloreticular, cerebellospinal, and cerebellovestibular.

Proprioceptive and exteroceptive efferents to the cerebellum course ipsilaterally in the dorsal spinocerebellar tracts and enter the cerebellum through the inferior cerebellar peduncle. Afferent fibers from contralateral muscle, skin, and joint receptors that ascend in the ventral spinocerebellar tracts enter the cerebellum through the superior cerebellar peduncles and synapse in the cerebellar cortex and deep nuclei. Efferents from deep cerebellar nuclei account for many of the fibers in the middle and superior cerebellar peduncles.

Axons innervating the dentate nucleus come from the lateral part of the cerebellar hemispheres. A smaller intermediate zone sends axons to the small globose and emboliform nuclei, and the midzone, i.e., the vermis, sends axons to the fastigial nucleus.

C. Cerebellar Circuitry

As demonstrated by Kemp and Powell, there are two main classic cerebro-cerebellar loops underlying motor control (Fig. 3). The first neural circuit is the cortical → pontine (and olivary) → cerebellar cortex → dentate (parvocellular part) → ventral lateral and ventral anterior thalamic nuclei → cerebral cortex. From the dentate nucleus (magnocellular part), motor control is exerted on the spinal cord via the red nucleus. Output from the globose nucleus reaches the Darkschevitch nucleus in the higher brainstem and output from the emboliform nucleus reaches the centromedian intralaminar nucleus of the thalamus. The second loop involves the striatum → globus pallidus → ventrolateral thalamic nuclei → motor cortex (Fig. 3).

The input and output systems of the cerebellum which could be related to nonmotor behavior are shown in Figures 4 and 5. Frontal lobe projections to the pons originate from both motor and associative areas. Motor projections derive from primary, i.e., rolandic 4, areas as well as from the supplementary motor area and area 6, whereas association projec-

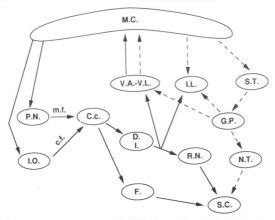

FIGURE 3   Cerebro-cerebellar loops underlying the motor behavior. M.C., motor cortex; V.A.-V.L., ventralis anterior and
ventralis lateralis thalamic nuclear complex; I.L., intralaminar
nuclei; S.T., striatum; G.P., globus pallidus; C.c., corpus cerebelli; P.N., pontine nuclei; I.O., inferior olivary nucleus; D, dentate nucleus; I, interpositus nucleus; F, fastigial nucleus; R.N.,
red nucleus; N.T., tegmental nuclei; S.C., spinal cord. The cortico-cerebellar loops are crossed; cerebellar lesions give rise to
ipsilateral deficits (see text).

tions come from premotor and prefrontal areas (8
through 12 and 44 through 47). Broca's area could
be included in the association areas.

The pontine nuclei receive heavy projections from
association areas of the frontal neocortex, from the
posterior parietal cortex and the superior temporal
sulcus. Paralimbic and autonomical projections to
the pons derive from the limbic lobe (especially from

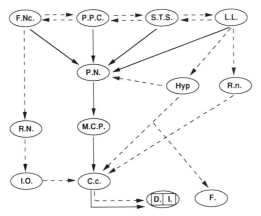

FIGURE 4   Cerebellar afferents. F.Nc., frontal neocortex;
P.P.C., posterior parietal cortex; S.T.S., superior temporal sulcus; L.L., limbic lobe; R.N., red nucleus; I.O., inferior olivary
nucleus; P.N., pontine nuclei; Hyp, hypothalamus; M.C.P., middle cerebellar peduncle; m.f., mossy fibers; c.f., climbing fibers;
D, dentate nucleus; I, interpositus nucleus; F, fastigius. The
cortico-cerebellar projections are mainly contralateral.

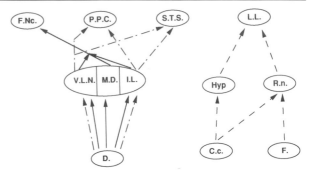

FIGURE 5   Cerebellar efferents. F.N.C., P.P.C., S.T.S., and
L.L.: frontal neocortex, parietal posterior cortex, superior temporal sulcus, limbic lobe. V.L.N., M.D., I.L.:n. ventralis lateralis, medial dorsal, intralaminar thalamic nuclei. Hyp, hypothalamus; R.n., reticular nuclei; D, dentate; C.c., corpus cerebelli;
F, fastigii; R.N., red nucleus; I.O., inferior olive. The cerebellar
efferents projects mainly on the contralateral thalamic nuclei and
on the contralateral cerebral cortex.

the cingulate gyrus), the hypothalamus, and mamil-
lary bodies (Fig. 4).

Projections from the cerebellum back to the cerebral association areas are less known than the
cortico-pontine projections (Fig. 5). Dentate nucleus
projections via the thalamus to the association cortices include medial dorsal, ventrolateral, and intralaminar thalamic nuclei (Fig. 5). Parts of the
centrolateral and intralaminar nuclei (particularly
the central lateral nucleus) have strong projections
to the posterior parietal cortex and superior temporal sulcus (Fig. 5). On the other hand, reciprocal
hypothalamic connections to the cerebellar cortex
and fastigial nucleus have also been found.

The various cortico-cerebellar–cortical loops involving not only motor cortical areas but also associative areas provide the anatomical background for
information-processing mechanisms. The cerebellum, like the basal ganglia and thalamus, receives
information from the cerebral cortex for processing
and sends the results of this processing back to the
cortex, to both sensory motor and association areas.
In turn, these areas can send information back to
the cerebellum for further processing.

D. Neurochemistry

Table I shows the main localisation of neurotransmitters in the cerebellum. [*See* SYNAPTIC TRANS-
MITTERS AND NEUROMODULATORS.]

It should be remembered that the sources of noradrenalin, serotonin, dopamine, and acetylcholine
are the locus ceruleus, the raphe nuclei of the brain-

TABLE I
Main Neurotransmitters in the Mammalian Cerebellum

Structures	Neurotransmitters
Granule cell layer and molecular layer	Glutamate, aspartate, serotonin, γ-aminobutyric acid (GABA), dopamine, noradrenalin
Purkinje cells	Glutamate, aspartate, kainate, quisqualate, GABA, serotonin, dopamine, noradrenalin
Inferior olive and climbing fibers	Glutamate, aspartate, serotonin, noradrenalin
Mossy fibers	Acetylcholine, serotonin, excitatory amino acids (glutamate, aspartate)
Dentate, interpositus, and fastigial nuclei	Glutamate, serotonin dopamine, noradrenalin
Pedonculus cerebellaris superior	Noradrenalin from locus ceruleus

stem, substantia nigra, and nucleus basalis of Meynert, respectively.

If there are physiological subcortical–cortical loops, we have to underline: (i) the existence of neurochemical subcortico-cortical loops and (ii) an interdependence between various neurotransmitter systems.

Serotonin from mossy fibers is excitatory to target neurons. Serotonin itself could induce Purkinje cell inhibition. It could also potentiate the inhibitory action of GABA.

Electrical stimulation of the locus ceruleus has been shown to depress Purkinje cell firing rates. There is direct evidence that locus ceruleus norepinephrine-containing cells have a direct inhibitory effect on Purkinje cells in the cerebellum.

The modulatory actions of noradrenalin on neural circuits are complex and exerted in both cerebral and cerebellar cortices.

At a low threshold, noradrenalin appears to enhance GABA, the inhibitory transmitter of cerebellar interneurons.

In the mammalian cerebellum, the dopaminergic system is distinct from the noradrenergic system. It has recently been demonstrated that the subcortical dopamine system is regulated by the prefrontal cortex; noradrenalin/dopamine interactions in the prefrontal cortex can have a definite influence on social and cognitive behavior. Recently, it has been demonstrated that cerebellar noradrenalin infusion in rats facilitates recovery after sensorimotor cortex injury.

GABA induces depressant responses from Purkinje cells. Glutamate, aspartate, kainate, and quisqualate are excitatory in both Purkinje cells and climbing fibers.

In the rat cerebellum, the glutamate/glutamine ratios are highest in the molecular layer and mossy and climbing fiber boutons, the ratios are intermediate in granule cell bodies dendrites, and in putative GABAergic cells (Purkinje, basket, and Golgi cells), and are lowest for glial cells (Bergmann glia, astrocytes in the granule cell layer, and oligodendrocytes).

In the rat cerebellum, cerebellar mossy fibers use glutamate as a transmitter. The release of glutamate can be inhibited via presynaptic heteroceptors of the 5-HT2 type receptor agonist of serotonin localized on mossy fiber terminals.

Dopaminergic/glutamatergic balance may be important for both akinetic motor disorders and psychosis. Recent animal experiments suggest that glutamate plays a fundamental role in the control of psychomotor activity.

Interactions between the noradrenergic and dopaminergic systems have been proven in rats by the suppression of nigrostriatal and mesolimbic dopamine release *in vivo* following brain noradrenalin depletion.

Spontaneous alternative behavior in a Y maze in rats is disrupted by lesions of dopaminergic terminals in the lateral septum. In the same rats, the suppression of noradrenergic innervation by destroying noradrenalin efferents from the locus ceruleus passing through the pedonculus cerebellaris superior compensates the behavioral deficit induced by lesions of domaminergic terminals.

Floccular injections in rabbits of the GABAA agonist muscimol and of the GABAB agonist baclofen have similar effects, namely, a reduction of vestibulo-ocular response (VOR) and optokinetic response (OKR) reflexes. This effect is presumably explained by an inhibition of Purkinje cells.

Recent experimental findings in rabbits have revealed that adaptive changes of the vestibular and possibly other motor control systems are strongly facilitated by noradrenergic innervation of the flocculus, which is normally provided by the locus ceruleus.

Cholinergic and noradrenergic stimulation in the rabbit flocculus has synergistic facilitatory effects on optokinetic responses.

Watson and McElligott motor learning tasks have been demonstrated to be dependent upon cerebellar norepinephrine in both young rats depleted of central stores of noradrenalin by 6-hydroxydopamine lesions and old normal rats.

Extracellular recordings in the paraflocculus of Long–Evans rats have been made to determine how noradrenalin iontophoresis affects the responsiveness of individual Purkinje cells and interneurons to presentations of visual stimuli within their visual receptive fields. Noradrenalin iontophoresis improves visually evoked responses. It seems that an important aspect of the noradrenergic action within local cerebellar circuits is the redefinition of receptive field properties of individual neuronal elements, thereby improving information flow through the cerebellum. [*See* BRAIN CHEMICALS.]

II. THE CEREBELLUM AND MOTOR BEHAVIOR

A. Functional Considerations

Many years ago Holmes suggested that there are three elementary motor functions of the cerebellum: initiation of movement, compound movement (regulation), and feedback control (correction). These three components represent cerebellar participation in the three successive phases of movement.

Classically, the cerebellum is concerned with the coordination of somatic motor activity, the regulation of muscle tone, and mechanisms that influence and maintain equilibrium. Although cerebellar damage does affect simple movements, it is the execution of more complex sequential movements or the decomposition of movement which is the cardinal sign of cerebellar damage. Each movement requires the coordinated action of a group of muscles. The agonist is the muscle that provides actual movement of the part; the antagonist is the opposing muscle that must relax to permit movement. Other muscles must fix, or stabilize, certain joints in order to facilitate the desired movement. Such synergistic motor activities require not only complex reciprocal innervation but also the coordinated control of muscle tone and movement. The cerebellum provides this control for the somatic motor system in close connection with the motor and premotor cortices (see Fig. 3). [*See* MOTOR CONTROL.]

B. Motor Disturbances Occurring with Cerebellar Lesions

1. Archicerebellar Lesions

Lesions involving the posterior cerebellar vermis (nodulus, uvula, flocculus) produce the archicerebellar syndrome, i.e., disturbances of locomotion and equilibrium bilaterally. The patient is unsteady in the standing position. The gait is uncoordinated and resembles that of a drunken individual.

2. Paleocerebellar Lesions

Classic experimental studies have shown that both inhibitory and facilitatory effects upon muscle tone can be obtained by stimulating the anterior lobe of the cerebellum, depending on the electrical parameters of stimulation. In clinical neurology, hypotonia (i.e., the diminution of muscle tone) has been attributed to paleocerebellar lesions.

3. Neocerebellar Lesions

Lesions of the cerebellar hemisphere and of the dentate nucleus, i.e., of the cortico-pontocerebellar loop, give rise to symptoms ipsilateral to the cerebellar lesions.

Delays in the initiation of movement have been observed both in humans with cerebellar disorders and in animals with cerebellar lesions. Neurons in the cerebellar cortex and dentate nucleus change their discharge frequency prior to the activation of motor cortical neurons and the movement-related responses of these cortical neurons are delayed when there is dentate function. Disturbances of coordinated movements are referred to as asynergia, in which the range, direction, and force of muscle contractions are inappropriate. Cerebellar asynergia can be demonstrated by tests of precise movements to a point; distances are frequently improperly gauged (dysmetria) and fall short of the mark or exceed it (hypermetria). Hypermetria is accompanied by asymmetric velocity profiles and by prolonged agonist and delayed antagonist electromyographic activity necessary to brake movements. Diadochokinesia is tested by rapid successive movements, such as alternately supinating and pronating the hands and forearms. Dysdiadochokinesia occurring with cerebellar lesions could be explained by delays in movement initiation, dysmetria at the end of movement, as well by abnormalities of movement velocity and acceleration. Other disorders occurring with cerebellar lesions are movement decomposition and the "intention" tremor. Cerebellar tremors occur during voluntary and associated movements and are not present at rest.

Cerebellar ataxia is an asynergic disturbance particularly involving the axial muscles. The disturbance is evident during walking; the gait is broad-based and the patient reels, lurches, and stumbles. The nystagmus consists of an oscillatory pattern in which the eyes slowly drift in one direction and then rapidly move in the opposite direction to correct the drift. In cerebellar lesions, the nystagmus is considered to be an expression of asynergia. Speech disturbances, i.e., slurring of speech and the tendency to utter some words in an explosive manner, are common.

C. Role of the Cerebellum in Motor Programming and Motor Learning

Actual physiological data show that fast complex movements are supposed to be preprogrammed prior to execution. The basic structure of a motor program (e.g., muscle groups involved, sequence of muscles activated) is not generated exclusively within the cerebellum. Cerebellar patients are still able to perform complex motor tasks, although execution is slow and ataxic.

Motor programming has been investigated in normal subjects and patients with cerebellar disorders who were instructed to execute movement sequences to a simple reaction signal. Each to-be-executed sentence consisted of single, two, or three key-press components. Evidence of anticipatory motor programming in normal subjects was reflected in the pattern of onset time and interkey-press time. Normal subjects and patients with mild cerebellar dysfunction showed increases in response onset time as the sequence length increased from a single movement to two or three consecutive finger movements. In contrast, patients with severe cerebellar symptoms had abnormally long response onset times and no further increases in their initial response time with the number of finger movements to be performed. Furthermore, cerebellar dysfunction was associated with significantly slower interkey-press response times. These results indicate that anticipatory motor programming critically depends on cerebellar integrity. Recent neurophysiological findings indicate that cerebellar patients are even able to use prior information to improve their disturbed motor performance.

1. Time Perception

Timing is an essential feature of repetitious movements like finger tapping or movements in which fast changes in either direction of movement or force are needed. In a series of recent studies, it has been shown that in contrast to patients with Parkinson's disease, those with cerebellar lesions present increased variability when attempting to produce periodic intervals in an index finger tapping task. Analysis of these tapping data was based on a theoretical model of timing; this model assumes that the variability of inter-response intervals may be due to variability of a central time keeper system ("clock") and/or a motor implementation system which executes the command. Some studies in patients with circumscribed lesions indicate that the cerebellar hemispheres are critically involved in the operation of a central timing process, whereas the medial regions of the cerebellum are associated with the execution of these responses. These studies await confirmation from other laboratories as to the role of the cerebellum as a "clock" of motor behavior.

2. Role of the Cerebellum in Motor Learning

Studies on the role of the cerebellum in motor learning have focused on the acquisition and retention of simple reflexes or responses, adaptation of the vestibulo-ocular reflex, and, in few cases, more complex behavior involving visuo-motor adaptation by humans. The Marr-Albus theory suggests that climbing fiber inputs to Purkinje cells, originating in the inferior olive, provide "teaching" signals and that mossy fiber inputs originating in the pontine nuclei provide important contextual information to form new associations based on climbing fiber inputs to the Purkinje cells. Motor learning in patients with cerebellar dysfunction was assessed by performance of two tasks. The first consists of repetitive tracing of an irregular geometric pattern with the hand under normal visual guidance, and the second involves repetitive tracing of a different geometric pattern with mirror-reversed vision. Cerebellar patients are impaired in the skilled performance of movement in the normal vision task probably because of a failure of motor adaptation. Patients with combined cerebellar and brainstem atrophy show a deficit in the mirror-reversed vision task which can be considered as a failure in motor skill learning. The anatomical background of this phenomenon is probably altered information processing to the cerebellum via the climbing and mossy fibers. It can be concluded that: (i) the cerebellum contributes to the learning of movement skills; and (ii) structure inputs to the cerebellum are critical in this process.

Voluntary movements of the fingers or hand either as part of a motor paradigm or as part of a somatosensory exploration of objects increase regional cerebral blood flow and regional cerebral metabolism mainly in the lateral part of the anterior lobe of cerebellum.

III. THE CEREBELLUM AND NONMOTOR BEHAVIOR

To Franz Joseph Gall, the founder of phrenology, the cerebellum was nothing less than the primary anatomic locus of love. Since then, and especially during the last 30 years, some papers have pointed to an association between cerebellar damage and some psychiatric symptoms, but a definite cause–effect relationship between neuropsychological performance and cerebellar lesions in humans was proved only in 1985.

Multilateral animal studies, clinical pathologic correlations, sophisticated neuropsychological testing, and PET scan observation of cerebellar activity have served as sources of information on the role of the cerebellum in nonmotor, i.e., cognitive, functions.

A. Animal Models

It has been observed that monkeys and chimpanzees trained to discriminate weights totally failed to do so only if both the brachium conjunctiva and medial lemniscus have been sectioned. More recent animal studies have investigated the role of the cerebellum in associative learning. A simple form of associative learning was investigated in rodents by classic conditioning of an adaptive response to a noxious stimulus, such as the blink of an eyelid in response to a puff of air or an electric shock. When a unilateral lesion was produced in the interpositus nucleus of the cerebellum, a conditioned response could not be elicited or learned by the animal, on the affected side. The cerebellar lesion completely and selectively abolished a previously learned response in trained animals, and prevented the learning of a conditioned response by such animals. Such an effect has been noted in humans as well.

In four species of mutant mice with maldevelopment of the cerebellum, degradation of nonmotor activities was found, including deficits in spontaneous alternation activity, visuospatial learning, discrimination learning, and perseveration.

B. Clinical Neuropsychology

Neuropsychological studies have been conducted on patients with chronic bilateral cerebellar damage as well as on patients with unilateral cerebellar lesions. Thirty-three outpatient epileptics with normal CT scans and 31 others with cerebellar and brainstem atrophy were evaluated neuropsychologically. There were no statistically significant differences between groups with regard to age, education, and number of grand mal and other seizures. Neuropsychological assessment revealed lower performances by the atrophic group on the following measures: full IQ scale, verbal IQ scale, performance IQ scale, information, arithmetic, block design, object assembly, digit symbol, and Stroop test forms I and II. No significant differences were observed between the two groups for the remaining five subtests of the WAIS scale (comprehension, digit span, similarities, picture arrangement, picture completion), for the immediate recall and delayed recall subtests belonging to the Wechsler memory scale. Visual and auditory reaction time (RT) and movement time (MT) were measured separately with a Lafayette apparatus, using the method of Hamsher and Benton.

Analyses of the composite scores of neuropsychological performance showed that the cerebellum interfered with the following complex behavioral functions: (1) visuospatial organization for a concrete task, a function related to the cerebello-parietal loops, as demonstrated by deficient performances on the object assembly, digit symbol, and block design subtests; (2) planning and programming of daily activities, a function related to the cerebello-frontal loops. Deficient performance on the Stroop test was relevant in this matter. The last function to be impaired was the speed of information processing: visual and auditory RT performances were deficient in the atrophic patients whereas MT showed no significant differences between the two groups. These findings confirmed the fact that MT performances reflecting motor abilities are independent from RT performances reflecting the speed of information processing (SIP).

Fifteen patients with olivopontocerebellar atrophies (OPCA) and 15 patients with Friedreich's ataxia (FA) compared with pair-matched controls were evaluated neuropsychologically. The OPCA cases had significantly lower performances on the Standard Progressive Matrices of Raven (SPMR), Rey's complex figure, Trail B, similarities, and block design (timed and untimed version) with a tendency toward significant differences in the Hooper visual organization test. No impairment was found in visual memory (copy of Rey's complex figure), digit span forward and backward, picture arrangement, and immediate memory learning. The FA patients were impaired on SPMR, Rey's complex figure, and block design (untimed version). No impairment was apparent in FA patients on digit span forward and backward, similarities, picture arrangement, Hooper's visual organization, and immediate memory learning tests. Both visual and auditory RTs were lengthened in Fa and OPCA patients. Multiple choice task RTs were also measured in OPCA patients and revealed significant lengthening in comparison to their controls. There was a significant relationship between the SPMR and RT performances.

Neuropsychological assessments, including simple visual and auditory RT determinations, did not reveal any cognitive impairment in patients with chronic unilateral cerebellar infarcts as compared to their controls.

Positron emission tomography (PET) and single photon emission computed tomography (SPECT) studies showed decreased metabolism in contralateral cerebellar structures following unilateral frontoparietal infarcts; this *cerebro-cerebellar diaschisis* is the result of remote transneuronal metabolic depression of the corticopontocerebellar pathways. Using SPECT, a reverse phenomenon was demonstrated, i.e., *cerebello-cerebral diaschisis;* reduced cerebellar hexamethylpropyleneamine oxime (HMPAO) uptake was invariably accompanied by a diminution of HMPAO in the contralateral basal ganglia and frontoparietal cortex. Diaschisis was observed even 15 years after the stroke.

In conclusion, despite the presence of cerebellocerebral diaschisis in unilateral cerebellar infarcts, no impaired neuropsychological or RT performances were noted.

In two *acute* unilateral cerebellar infarcts, involving both posterior-inferior cerebellar and superior cerebellar arteries, we found—5 and 10 days, respectively, after the stroke—markedly lengthened RTs and low performance on SPMR. After 3 months, performance was in the normal range compared with the controls.

A series of experimental findings support data showing an absence of RT or some other neuropsychological deficits in patients with chronic unilateral cerebellar infarcts. Unilateral experimental dentate lesions in monkeys lengthened auditory RT in the immediate postlesion period; auditory RT gradually declined over about 20 days postoperatively, approaching normal values.

Furthermore, unilateral lesions of the right dentate and interpositus nuclei in monkeys produced severe movement dysfunction of the ipsilateral limb which recovered in 10 to 15 days. After recovery, left cerebellar nuclei were lesioned, which caused a deficit in the left arm and in the right contralateral arm that had recovered from the previous lesion inflicted on the right side. In a monkey in which the middle cerebellar peduncle was destroyed unintentionally by a stereotaxic lesion aimed at the dentate nucleus, it was observed that besides ataxia and dysmetria, the animal displayed marked inattention on the side of the lesion during the first postoperative days. The transient nature of this inattention was also characteristic of unilateral lesions of association areas of the cerebral cortex in monkeys. These experimental findings and our observations of humans converge to the same conclusion: there is some functional relationship between both sides of the cerebellum which could compensate for both motor and cognitive behavior.

Our bilateral cerebellar-damaged patients with epilepsy, Friedreich's ataxia, or olivopontocerebellar atrophies presented slower RT and MT than their controls. Significant differences in MT reflected motor (i.e., coordination) deficits per se, whereas RT (a test of cognition) measured the SIP. Besides experimental studies on monkeys showing RT lengthening after cerebellar lesions, it has been found that in human epileptics whose treatment included implantation of electrodes in the cerebellar cortex, stimulation increased RT to visual stimuli presented tachistoscopically.

The role of subcortical structures in SIP has already been recognized; recent findings clearly indicate that subcortical structures do not simply serve as pathways linking the two hemispheres but play an essential coordinating role in the integration of hemisphere activity.

Our studies suggest that the cerebellum is directly involved in SIP, thus showing that it is engaged in rapid motor and cognitive information processing. Second, the cerebellar patients—as compared to the controls—generally had slower intellectual abilities, as reflected by lower SPMR performance. Third, mild frontal-like and parietal-like syndromes were observed in all groups of patients studied. The cerebellum and its pathways interfere with visuospatial organization for concrete tasks as well as with the planning and programming of daily activities.

Frontal-like syndromes in cerebellar patients have been also demonstrated by using delayed alternation tasks as well as the tower of Hanoi, a nine-problem task that requires cognitive planning. The role of the cerebellum in these syndromes is mainly indirect, through various cerebello-cortical, anatomophysiological and neurochemical pathways (see Figs. 4 and 5, and Table I).

A possible role for the cerebellum in language skills has also been postulated. It is certain that the cerebellum participates in triggering or starting speech but there is no clinical evidence of language comprehension disorders or naming difficulties in adult cerebellar patients. Concerning memory, there are memory retrieval difficulties and a diminution of the global memory quotient in bilateral cerebellar damaged patients. [See LANGUAGE DEVELOPMENT; MEMORY.]

If some affective disorders were observed in experimental neuropsychology, no firm evidence of affective disorders occurring with cerebellar disorders has yet been presented. The cerebellar–limbic loops have been emphasized as eventually being responsible for such symptoms.

Besides the anatomical–physiological cerebello-cortical two-way loops possibly interfering with non-motor behavioural disorders related to cerebellar damage, one must consider some neurochemical subcortical–cortical loops.

It has been suggested that some frontal lobe-type cognitive changes occurring with cerebellar lesions, i.e., deficits in delayed alternation tasks in OPCA patients, could be a consequence of a loss of cholinergic innervation to orbital and possibly temporal areas. However, replacement therapy based on the cholinergic theory has been proven to be ineffective in cerebellar heredodegenerative ataxias.

As an alternative hypothesis we therefore believe that the significantly lower RT performances of cerebellar patients could be due—at least in part—to a dopaminergic deficiency. It has been found that go and no-go tasks as well as RT in experimental animals are dependent on dopamine levels in the brain or more exactly on dopamine–noradrenalin balance. Dopamine depletion definitely impairs RT performance in experimental animals. Other data which favor a dopamine deficiency in RT performance are the following: (i) dopaminergic innervation of the cerebellum has recently been demonstrated; (ii) our FA and OPCA patients had low levels of cerebrospinal fluid (CSF) homovanillic acid; (iii) visual and auditory RTs were improved by amantadine hydro-

chloride administration in OPCA patients as shown in a previous open clinical trial; however, the beneficial action of amantadine cannot be explained solely on the basis of its dopaminergic impact since it also has an inhibitory effect on N-methdyl-D-aspartate (NMDA) receptors. Glutamate neurotoxicity in rat cerebellar granule cells is mediated by NMDA receptors.

CSF 5-hydroxyindoleacetic acid, the serotonin metabolite, is low in some ataxic patients. Serotonin has specific inhibitory effects on glutamate excitatory activity; the motor improvement observed in some ataxic patients after the administration of serotonin precursors may be due to its inhibitory action on glutamate excitotoxicity.

The neuroradiological correlates of RT and MT measurements in OPCA patients were evaluated. Those with severe versus mild–moderate atrophy as assessed by three neuroradiological measures, i.e., brainstem, brachium pontis, and fourth ventricle ratios, presented few significantly lengthened RT and MT performances. In contrast, patients with severe atrophy revealed by the midbrain ratio had significantly lengthened simple visual and auditory RT and MT performances on all eight measures. This could be explained by the fact that atrophy at the midbrain level involves dopaminergic, noradrenergic, and glutamatergic structures and pathways.

There is some distinct evidence that dysfunction of glutamatergic, dopaminergic, noradrenergic, and perhaps serotonergic pathways underlies the impairment of SIP and probably of some other neuropsychological performances in cerebellar disease. The behavioral neurochemistry of cerebellar disease is in its infancy.

C. PET and SPECT Studies

Recent advanced activation techniques using PET measurements of cerebral blood flow have made it possible to address concerns relevant to clinical neuropsychology with a precision not previously available. PET enables the demonstration of activated neuronal populations in the human brain by measuring regional cerebellar blood flow (rCBF) and regional glucose and oxygen metabolic rates coupled to neuronal activity.

Ingvar and associates introduced the term ideagraphy, which is the identification, by either metabolic or circulatory PET scan studies, of humain brain activation caused by events that are simply ideational and not coupled to any sensory input or motor output.

The so-called mental simulation of movement (MSM) may be defined as an imagined rehearsal of a motor act with the specific intent of learning and improving it, without any simultaneous sensory input or any overt input, i.e., any muscular movement. It constitutes a pure cognitive activity. MSM has been investigated as a cognitive model of a motor act which requires several components, such as motivation, attentional resources, visual and kinesthetic imagery. Various MSM tasks are used: the subjects are asked to imagine tennis movements or graphic movements, or to visually project that they are walking along a well-known route in their home town, silently counting a.s.o.

By measuring Xenon rCBF, normal subjects imaging a graphic movement with either the right or left hand were studied. Regions corresponding to the prefrontal cortex, the supplementary motor area, and the cerebellum were activated significantly. SPECT revealed a significant bilateral rCBF increase in the cerebellum ($p<.001$) as well as in the basal ganglia ($p<.01$) during mental simulation of tennis training in normal volunteers. Similar forms of activation were noted during silent counting.

When somatosensory discrimination of shape, i.e., of rectangular parallelipeda with the right hand, was studied, PET data demonstrated a significant metabolic increase in the left sensorimotor hand area, bilaterally in the premotor cortex, the left supplementary motor area, left ventral posterior thalamus, right anterior lobe of the cerebellum, and right dentate nucleus. In general, during learning of a motor task, cerebellar activation was restricted to the anterior lobule. Tactile learning increased rCBF in the posterior lobule of the cerebellum. It therefore appears that the cerebellum participates in learning of somatosensory information.

PET studies of single word processing were also carried out. Of the tasks used the simplest was visual fixation alone on a color TV monitor. The inferior lateral occipital cortex striate, extrastriate, and left putamen were activated. The second task was passive observation of the word presented either visually or auditorily; different classical cortical areas were activated. The third task was to speak each presented word loud; in this output task, besides cortical area activation, the superior anterior cerebellum was also activated. The fourth task was to generate a semantically appropriate verb aloud in response to each noun presented. Only cortical areas were activated. Two other association-monitoring tasks were used: (i) in a semantic monitoring task, the subjects noted members of a semantic category (dangerous animals); and (ii) in a rhyme-monitoring task, they judged whether visually presented pairs of words rhymed. On these two association tasks, in addition to specific cortical areas, the anterior, posterior, and inferior lateral cerebellum were activated. It therefore seems that word association activates the lateral and posterior lobules of the cerebellum.

Recent PET data on tasks which produced changes in rCBF and rCMR in the cerebellum can be summarized as follows: the lateral part of the anterior lobe is activated by vibration, flexion, extension of the hand, fingers, and motor sequences, motor sequence learning, tactile learning, tactile recognition, somatosensory discrimination, preparation for reading repeating words, and spontaneous speech. Lateral and posterior lobe activation is observed during tactile learning, somatosensory discrimination, route finding, and word association. The dentate nucleus is activated mainly during somatosensory discrimination. It has to be emphasized that cerebellar activation is accompanied by activation of classical (and even nonclassical) cortical elementary and associative areas.

What is the practical value of cerebellar activation during cognitive tasks? As mentioned earlier in this article, reverse cerebello-cerebral diaschisis in patients with chronic unilateral cerebellar infarcts does not induce neuropsychological deficits. We believe that the findings of these fascinating studies have to be interpreted cautiously from the practical–clinical point of view.

IV. CONCLUSIONS

During the last several years, some progress has been made in the field of both motor and nonmotor functions of the cerebellum. Cerebellar functions have to be approached in a multidisciplinary manner. Classic data on the role of the cerebellum in motor behavior have been completed with new findings on its involvement in motor learning. The cerebellum acts as a "learning machine." Bilateral cerebellar lesions in man induce frontal-like and parietal-like syndromes through anatomophysiological and neurochemical cerebello-cortical loops; among other subcortical structures, the cerebellum is involved in the control of SIP. The role of the cerebellum in the initiation of language skills is well known, but its participation in language comprehension remains to be proven (if it exists at all) in cerebellar patients. A slowing of general intellectual abilities has been documented in cerebellar patients. Some memory retrieval difficulties occurring with bilateral cerebellar lesions have been found. Unilateral cerebellar infarcts seem not to be followed by major neuropsychological deficits and are well compensated. The role of the cerebellum in the control of timing sense has been documented.

A series of experimental animal studies in our laboratory and elsewhere have confirmed the role of the cerebellum in behavioral processes in the fields of classical conditioning, spatial learning, emotion, and motor coordination.

Fascinating SPECT and PET experiments have demonstrated cerebellar activation during various cognitive tasks; cerebellar activation is however accompanied by activation of classical cortical areas. Clinical and PET investigations support the fact that new posterior and lateral, phylogenetically developed cerebellar areas are especially related to cognition. Future research on cognitive functions of the cerebellum should not be confined only to anatomo-physiological, clinical neuropsychological, and even PET and SPECT approaches, but should include neurochemical and pharmacological measures in both humans and animals.

Bibliography

Botez, M. I. (1992). The neuropsychology of the cerebellum: An emerging concept. *Arch. Neurol.* **49,** 1229.

Botez, M. I., Botez, Th., Elie, R., and Attig, E. (1989). Role of the cerebellum in complex human behavior. *Ital. J. Neurol. Sci.* **10,** 291.

Botez, M. I., Léveillé, J., Lambert, R., and Botez, Th. (1991). Single photon emission computed tomography (SPECT) in cerebellar disease: cerebello-cerebral diaschisis. *Eur. Neurol.* **31,** 405.

Botez, M. I., Pedraza, O. L., Botez-Marquard, Th., Vézina, J. L., and Elie, R. (1993). Radiologic correlates of reaction time measurements in olivopontocerebellar atrophy. *Eur. Neurol.* **33,** 304.

Decety, J., Sjoholm, H., Ryding, E., Stenberg, G., and Ingvar, D. H. (1990). The cerebellum participates in mental activity: tomographic measurements of regional cerebral blood flow. *Brain Res.* **535,** 313.

Diener, H. C., Hore, J., Ivry, R., and Dichgans, J. (1993). Cerebellar dysfunction of movement and perception. *Can. J. Neurol. Sci.* **20** (suppl. 3), 562.

Ito, M. (1993) Synaptic plasticity in the cerebellar cortex and its role in motor learning. *Can. J. Neurol. Sci.* **20** (suppl. 3), 570.

Lalonde, R., and Botez, M. I. (1990). The cerebellum and learning processes in animals. *Brain Res. Rev.* **15,** 325.

Lechtenberg, R. (Ed.) (1993). "Handbook of Cerebellar Disease." Dekker, New York.

Leiner, H. C., Leiner, A. L., and Dow, R. S. (1991). The human cerebro-cerebellar system: Its computing, cognitive and language skills. *Behav. Brain Res.* **44,** 113.

Schmahmann, J. (1991). An emerging concept: The cerebellar contribution to higher function. *Arch. Neurol.* **48,** 1178.

CHILD ABUSE

Vicki Carlson
Washington University, St. Louis

Glossary

Benign neglect The practice of withholding nutrition from a weak, ill, or unwanted child. The practice is often accompanied by parental pity rather than malice, in a context of poverty.

Educational neglect The failure to provide for a child's cognitive development including failure to conform to state legal requirements regarding school attendance or failure to attend to special education needs.

Emotional abuse Verbal or emotional assault, threats of physical assault, humiliation, actions that cause extreme fear or anxiety, active rejection, deliberate deprivation of basic necessities as punishment, or economic exploitation. Exposure to extreme marital violence is sometimes classified as a form of emotional abuse.

Emotional neglect Failure to provide the psychological nurturing necessary for a child's psychological growth and development; passive rejection or ignoring of a child; the failure to provide minimally sensitive and responsive caregiving. Economic exploitation can also be a form of emotional neglect.

Foundling A nameless, deserted child who has been taken in by another caregiver or institution.

Munchausen syndrome by proxy A rare psychiatric disorder in which an adult fabricates a history of illnesses and symptoms for their child, often directly inducing symptoms in the child through poisoning or other means. The children in these cases are subjected to unnecessary tests, hospitalizations, medications, and treatments that can be painful and damaging. The name comes from a famous 18th century German teller of tall tales.

Nonorganic failure to thrive A growth rate that is below the fifth percentile and is not due to physical abnormalities such as intestinal absorption disorders or disease. The growth retardation is due to caregiving behavior (whether intentional or unintentional) and stressful environmental conditions. Children with this condition often show rapid growth gains when hospitalized.

Physical abuse Acts, intentionally committed by parents or responsible caretakers, such as striking, shaking, beating, burning, suffocating, and the like, which are very likely to inflict pain or injury on a child. What constitutes a physically abusive act varies with the developmental characteristics of the child. Young infants can suffer fatal brain injuries or broken bones due to shaking or twisting, actions that would not cause such injuries for older children.

Physical neglect The failure of a parent or responsible caregiver to meet the basic needs of the child (when the parent has the capacity to make such provisions). Subtypes include abandonment, nutritional neglect, exposure to the elements, medical neglect, and inadequate supervision.

Sexual abuse Sexual contact between a child (usually defined as under 18 years of age) and an adult or person at least 5 years older than the victim for the purpose of the sexual gratification of the perpetrator. Contact may include: forcible rape, genital intercourse or contact, oral–genital or oral–anal contact, fondling, forced touching of the adult's body, exposure to or coerced observation of sexual activity whether live or in photographs or film, or the use of a child to create pornography. Perpetrators have been described as either "regressed" or "fixated" offenders. Regressed offenders are said to have attained age-appropriate sexual functioning in the past but have become attracted to a child, often one within the family during a time of stress. Fixated offenders or pedofiles consistently prefer children. Recent studies indicate there are not as many purely regressed offenders as had been previously thought.

WITHIN EACH CULTURE, at any point in time, there are standards, legally formalized or informal, as to the limits of acceptable behavior toward the youngest members of the group. Child maltreatment includes acts of omission and commission which are believed to expose children to an inappropriate risk of physical or emotional pain and suffering and/or may lead to seriously diminished development in any area of life. In current usage there is a focus on harms intentionally caused by parents and responsible caregivers. A broader use of the term includes suffering caused by institutional and social practices, the inequitable distribution of resources, and violent conflict from the local to the international level.

I. DEFINING THE PROBLEM OF CHILD ABUSE

A. Cultural Differences

Child-rearing practices considered normal and healthy in one society may seem abusive to members of another group. The common American practice of housing a baby in a separate bedroom and letting her cry herself to sleep is viewed as severe emotional abuse by Native Hawaiians who view close contact as critical for infant well-being. There is wide variation in opinion on the role of punishment in education and in parental discipline. The United States is ranked very high among Western nations in the amount of physical violence directed toward children. Physical punishment is an almost universal method of discipline in the United States. In contrast, parental spanking was outlawed in Sweden in 1979.

Beyond differences in child rearing and techniques of discipline are differences in the culturally meaningful institutions and activities. For example, a variety of rituals and procedures mark maturation and acceptance as an adult member of the community. Westerners react with horror at non-Western initiation rites, such as preadolescent or adolescent circumcision for young men, facial scarring, or deprivation of basic needs. Even broader criticism exists against the practices of female clitoridectomy and infibulation. These practices are painful, often done without anesthesia, and can result in infection and death. International health conferences have called for the elimination of such practices, yet individuals who value these traditional ways view the prevention of their participation in such procedures as its own form of mistreatment.

B. Within-Culture Deviations from Standards of Behavior Regarding Children

A second level of definition includes standards reflected in public consensus, legal definition, and professional opinion within a culture. Here major deviations from common standards of care are labeled abusive. The term "child abuse" usually denotes this level of definition.

Controversy exists over the best ways to define the various subtypes of maltreatment. Different definitions serve different ends. For research and treatment purposes, maltreatment may best be described as a continuum ranging from less than adequate to criminally reprehensible. Within the contexts of social policy and criminal justice, there is a need for categorical definitions. There must be a line between less than ideal but adequate caregiver behavior and practices so harmful they warrant coercive intervention.

C. Abuse at the Societal Level

Conditions such as poverty, racism, female gender devaluation, poor health care, politically induced famine, international economic inequities, and the terror and disruption of warfare produced more suffering and death among the young than individually inflicted harms. Public and private international relief efforts, religious and charitable agencies, child advocacy groups such as the Children's Defense Fund in the United States, national governments, and international leagues such as The United Nations work to eliminate suffering at this level.

The 1987 Draft United Nations Convention of the Rights of the Child is an update of the 1924 Geneva Declaration of the Rights of the Child and the 1959 U.N. Declaration of the Rights of the Child. It represents an international effort to define and specify the "special care and assistance" to which children are entitled. Included among the many rights specified in the Draft are the right to adequate nutrition, housing, recreation, and medical services; freedom from punishment for parents' or relatives opinions and beliefs; parental care without separation unless abuse or neglect makes separation necessary; the right to parental and state care that is "in the child's best interest"; the right of disabled children to special care and protections; "the right to the highest attainable standard of health and medical and rehabilitation facilities"; the right to a "standard of living adequate for the child's physical, mental, spiritual, moral, and social development"; the right to education; the right to be protected from exploitation and from work "that is likely to be hazardous or to interfere with the child's education or to be harmful to the child's health or physical mental spiritual, moral or social development"; the right to protection from "all forms of sexual exploitation and sexual abuse"; the right to protection "against all other forms of exploitation prejudicial to any aspects of the child's welfare." Relatively few children in the world currently enjoy the fulfillment of all the rights outlined in the Draft.

II. A RECENT HISTORY OF CHILD MALTREATMENT

A. The Evolution of Beliefs and Practices Related to Children

The mistreatment of children has been documented throughout written history. The tale of suffering is interspersed with periods of reform and efforts to improve the plight of children. First, there is the progression from children as property to children as individuals with personal rights. When treated as property, children have been prostituted, sold as slaves, worked to the point of disability or death, or killed at the discretion of their parents/owners. Efforts to move children from the status of property to that of person have resulted in less abusive treatment of children.

Second, there is progress in meeting the challenge of managing reproductivity. Neonaticide, infanticide, and benign neglect of toddlers have all served as consciously or unconsciously sanctioned methods of after the fact family planning, all at high cost in pain and suffering to the children involved and often to parents as well. These methods of limiting reproduction can be replaced by technological and social alternatives including birth control, abortion, adoption, foster care, and foundling homes or or-

phanges (the first of which was established in Milan in A.D. 787). The moral and pragmatic values of various methods of birth control and especially abortion continue to be debated.

Third, cultures and historical eras have differed in attitudes toward appropriate discipline in the service of education. Beating students seems to have been common in ancient Greece, Rome, and medieval Europe. The Children's Petition of 1669 was the first time in Britain that legal limits were placed on corporal punishment in schools. It had no influence on common practice. In the United States, New Jersey was the first state to ban corporal punishment in the schools in 1867. In 1980, corporal punishment was legal in 40 states although individual cities and towns may have outlawed it. The U.S. Supreme Court has consistently supported schools' use of corporal punishment even over parental protest. A 1986 Department of Education survey revealed over 1,000,000 instances of school paddlings during the previous year; 80% of them occurred in the South. Parents and Teachers against Violence in Education, founded in Australia in 1978, organized a U.S. chapter in 1983. They seek to use voluntary citizen influence to further limit the practice of corporal punishment, in all its forms, in schools.

Finally, the history of human religious and ritual practices includes child sacrifice in various forms, burial of newborns in building foundations to improve the durability of the structure, uncomfortable ritual practices, painful discipline for religious purposes, and emotionally disturbing depictions of the horrors of being incorrect in religious belief or lax in religious practice. Debates continue concerning the boundaries between legitimate religious freedom and medical, physical, or emotional maltreatment of children.

B. The Progressive Era

1. Societies for the Prevention of Cruelty to Children and The American Humane Association

During the 19th century a number of influences served to increase child suffering. These included child labor in factories and increased numbers of families living in crowded urban poverty. Early attempts at reform were often made from a religious perspective. They were aimed at limiting the public consequences of individual parental failings. A common intervention was the removal of troubled children to foster care, orphanages, or reformatories established to prevent negative moral development. Civil codes and statutes were later developed to manage these activities on behalf of "dependent" children.

There was a turning point in 1873, one of a number of times the popular media has played an important role in altering child-related social policy. That year a New York social worker discovered Mary Ellen Wilson, an 8 year old, who had been beaten, chained, and starved by her foster parents. The laws at the time prevented the child's removal from the family until the caregivers had been found guilty. The case was brought to trial largely through the efforts of leaders in the Society for the Prevention of Cruelty to Animals. Little Mary Ellen was removed to an orphanage and her foster mother served a prison term. The next year the Society for the Prevention of Cruelty to Children was founded in New York. Throughout the rest of the century 160 other Societies were formed, and in 1877 they organized nationally under the name of The American Humane Association. For the next 80 years this organization was at the forefront of child abuse treatment and prevention. Initially, the Societies also served in investigative and enforcement capacities. They advocated the legislative reforms that culminated in the establishment of the Juvenile Courts in many cities during the early 1900s. The Juvenile Courts freed the Societies to return to providing voluntary, direct social services for families who were struggling to cope, yet had not caused enough harm to their children to be the focus of court intervention.

C. Increase in the Federal Role in Child Protection

The U.S. Children's Bureau, in the Department of Commerce and Labor, was formed in 1912 as a result of the 1909 White House Conference on Children. The Children's Bureau organized the first registration of infant births and deaths, an important step in addressing infant mortality. In 1921, it sponsored the Sheppard-Towner Infancy and Maternity Act, the first major U.S. program to provide nutritional and health care assistance to mothers and infants in need, and it was instrumental in the eventual prohibition of child labor in 1938. The Social Security Act of 1935 marked an even greater expansion of federal involvement, authorizing federal funds to augment state efforts to provide basic needs and medical care for "dependent children."

D. Medicine's Rediscovery of Child Abuse

Advances in pediatric radiology, during the 1940s, had allowed physicians to review full skeletal X-rays with new precision. Subdural hematomas were detected in combination with multiple long bone fractures, damage at the joints, and injuries to cartilage in various stages of healing. After unsuccessful attempts to define some strange new bone disease, the reality of inflicted injury, perpetrated by caregivers, could not be overlooked. In 1946, John Caffey named the phenomenon the "parent–infant traumatic syndrome" (PITS). Relatively little attention was paid to this syndrome at the time.

If one were to ignore the fields of History, Antrhropology, and Social Work, and focus solely on the Psychological and Medical literature in the United States, it might appear that child abuse began in the 1960s. Attention from the medical profession, extensively covered by the popular media, propelled physical child abuse into the national spotlight in 1962.

In 1962, Henry Kempe and his colleagues brought extensive media and professional attention to physical child abuse by coining the term "battered child syndrome" in an American Association of Pediatrics symposium and in a related article in the *Journal of the American Medical Association*. There followed a tremendous professional and public response to the depiction of serious injuries, even death, perpetrated by the very individuals responsible for the children's care.

E. Legislation and Reporting Laws and Protective Services

In 1963, the Children's Bureau produced guidelines for establishing state-level child abuse reporting laws. The laws required physicians and professionals in direct contact with children to report known cases of abuse or neglect to designated state agencies. Failure to report known cases carried the risk of fines and imprisonment. To offset mandated reporters' concerns about retribution from reported individuals, the reporting statutes included immunity from charges of libel.

Between 1963 and 1967, all states enacted legislation mandating physicians and many other child professionals to report cases of child abuse. The reporting process plus extensive media education efforts were responsible for an explosion of official reports. Designated agencies were hard pressed to investigate, process, and to serve the avalanche of cases produced by the new policies. Funding had to be provided and then increased to meet the need for services created by the reports.

The Courts have served as arbiters in cases where unwilling parents or children face coercive intervention due to charges of child abuse and neglect. Legal professionals work to ensure due process for accused perpetrators, and to develop evidence gathering and court procedures appropriate for young children. Representation for the children, Guardians *ad Litem* give legal voice to the child's unique perspective. Innovations in evidence and procedure, such as videotaped child testimony and exceptions to hearsay rule, have been developed to prevent further injury to the child at the hands of the legal processes designed to ensure fair hearing to alleged perpetrators. Research to document these effects is under way.

In the midst of this tremendous expansion of the public role in evaluating child-rearing quality, advocates have argued for extreme caution in overriding parental rights, urging that coercive intervention be used in only the most severe situations. They have argued that a mandated report to an inadequate overwhelmed, underfunded child protective agency, resulting in a poorly managed intervention with openended separations of children from their families, can produce its own unacceptable harms.

Protective service workers face some of the most difficult demands imaginable. The work is emotionally draining and annual staff turnover rates of 85% are not uncommon. State, federal, and private funding levels determine the degree to which effective programs can be implemented and maintained. The field continues to evolve and improve in investigation, communication with families including clearly delineated treatment plans, and implementing an expanding range of effective case management, treatment, and prevention services. Despite these efforts, critics have come forth to argue that current social policy goes too far to protect children from potential maltreatment and fails to adquately protect adults from false accusations of abuse and neglect. A movement has emerged to substantially limit child protection efforts. Alleged perpetrators of abuse who felt they had been damaged by false reports and the investigatory processes that ensued have organized support and advocacy groups such as VOCAL, Victims of Child Abuse Reporting Laws, founded in 1984. They describe stigma, financial loss incurred in long legal battles, and damage to family relationships. They opposed the acceptance of anonymous reports and urged the rapid expungement of records and reports not substantiated after investigation.

F. Federal Funding of Child Abuse and Neglect Programs

Throughout the first half of the 20th century, state and federal governments passed legislation aimed at eliminating child suffering caused by societal level neglect. In 1974, one hundred years after Mary Ellen Wilson inspired the founding of New York's Society for the Prevention of Cruelty to Children, the U.S. Congress acknowledged the need for federal involvement by passing The Child Abuse Prevention and Treatment Act. In it child abuse and neglect were defined as "the physical or mental injury, sexual abuse or exploitation, negligent treatment, or maltreatment of a child by a person who is responsible for the child's welfare under circumstances which indicate that the child's health or welfare is harmed or threatened thereby, as determined in accordance with regulations prescribed by the Secretary." Persons responsible for the child's welfare includes "any employee of a residential facility; and any staff person providing out-of-home care." Sexual abuse is defined as "the employment, use, persuasion, inducement, enticement or coercion of any child to engage in or assist any other person to engage in, any sexually explicit conduct or simulation of such conduct for the purpose of producing a visual depiction of such conduct: or the rape, molestation, prostitution or other form of sexual exploitation of children, or incest with children." The law authorized the establishment of the National Center on Child Abuse and Neglect (NCCAN) which (1) coordinates studies of the prevalence of child abuse; (2) contracts research on causes, identification, treatment, and prevention of child abuse and neglect; (3) funds demonstration projects to support treatment and prevention efforts; and (4) provides a clearinghouse to disseminate information.

G. Expansion of the Scope of Child Maltreatment

In the early 1980s, the Reagan administration considered eliminating the federal role in child abuse. A National Child Abuse Coalition formed to urge Congress to continue federal involvement. Federal involvement did continue and in 1984 the law was amended to expand the definition of maltreatment.

1. "Baby Doe" Cases

Technological advances in the care of very small, impaired newborns were accompanied by new medical and ethical dilemmas. In 1984, the Child Abuse Prevention and Treatment Act was amended to include the following definition of a new form of child abuse.

> "withholding of medically indicated treatment" means the failure to respond to the infant's life-threatening conditions by providing treatment (including appropriate nutrition, hydration and medication) that in the treating physician's or physicians' reasonable medical judgement will be most likely to be effective in ameliorating or correcting all such conditions. The term does not include the failure to provide treatment (other than appropriate nutrition, hydration or medication) to an infant when in the treating physician's or physicians' reasonable medical judgement (A) the infant is chronically and irreversibly comatose; (B) the provision of such treatment would merely prolong dying, not be effective in ameliorating or correcting all of the infant's life-threatening conditions, or otherwise be futile in terms of the survival of the infant; or (C) the provision of such treatment would be virutally futile in terms of the survival of the infant and the treatment itself under such circumstances would be inhumane.

Interpreting this law is an ongoing challenge and, as yet, no parents have been punished for withholding extraordinary care.

2. Fetal Damage

Some pregnant women have been charged with child abuse in response to their behavioral choices during pregnancy, especially, illegal drug use. A few have been imprisoned in an effort to protect their fetuses. This approach has been strongly criticized. While considerable evidence implicates prenatal smoking and alcohol use as detrimental to the infant outcome, especially for their contribution to low birth weight, the long-term effects of prenatal illegal drug exposure have yet to be established. Illegal drug use is often accompanied by a variety of environmental risk factors, such as poverty, stress, poor nutrition, and the legal use of tobacco and alcohol. A grave concern is that reporting in these cases would deter women with substance abuse problems from ob-

taining the early and consistent prenatal care they and their babies need. Balancing the rights of parents and their offspring and defining the division between individual and societal responsibility continue to challenge our best thinking in clinical practice and public policy.

3. Expanding Concern for Sexual Abuse

The number of sexual abuse cases increased severalfold from 1977 to the early 1980s, as the topic of sexual abuse made a significant move from secrecy into the domain of public discourse. In March of 1984, allegations of sexual abuse of hundreds of preschoolers, involving ritualistic abuse, were made against teachers and staff at the McMartin Preschool in southern California. The case received tremendous media coverage for years, becoming the most expensive trial in U.S. history before ending with acquittals for all alleged perpetrators. Allegations in other child care settings followed. The threat of sexual abuse had come closer to the thousands of parents using out-of-home child care.

New research revealed the importance of adolescent perpetrators. Over 50% of molested boys and 15–20% of sexually abused girls had adolescent perpetrators. The number of specialized treatment programs for adolescent offenders grew from 20 in 1982 to 520 in 1988.

Ritualistic abuse, one of the most secretive of all forms of abuse, became the focus of new attention. The Los Angeles–based Resource and Education Network on Ritualistic Abuse estimates that 1 to 5% of all sex abuse cases involve ritual abuse. In a 1988 review of sexual abuse reports in daycare settings, David Finkelhor reported 13% of the cases to be ritualistic in nature. Three types of ritualistic abuse were observed, (1) cult-based where the sexual abuse was in the service of a larger goal, (2) pseudo-ritualistic cases where the sexual experience was really the goal, and (3) psychopathological where the perpetrator was clearly experiencing a psychiatric disorder.

4. Efforts to Characterize Psychological Mistreatment

Clearly all the aforementioned types of maltreatment carry with them profound emotional effects. In the mid 1980s, James Garbarino pioneered efforts to define independent forms of emotional abuse and neglect. By 1991 an entire issue of the journal *Development and Psychopathology* (Dante Cicchetti, editor) was devoted to a state of the art review of legal, clinical, research, and social policy perspectives concerning psychological maltreatment.

Current classifications include caregiver behavior which is: rejecting, degrading, terrorizing, isolating, missocializing, exploiting, or denying of emotional responsiveness. Another approach to definition emphasizes the documentable emotional and psychological effects upon the children including low self-esteem, fearfulness, anxiety, depression, and excessive aggression toward self or others.

III. Incidence and Prevalence of Child Maltreatment in the United States

A. Reported Cases

The American Humane Association tracked the number of U.S. child maltreatment reports from 1976, when 669,000 reports were estimated, through 1986, when over two million reports were recorded. This represents a 212% increase in a decade. In 1990, when the National Center for Child Abuse and Neglect's newly established tracking system made its first estimate, 2.7 million children were named in 1.7 million child abuse and neglect reports. Thus, in 1976 an estimated 1% of the U.S. population under the age of 18 years was reported as maltreated. In 1990 the estimate was closer to 3%. There is generally agreement that the number of reports considerably underestimates the true instances of maltreatment.

Neglect was the most common charge (45%). Twenty-five percent of the cases were reported for physical abuse, 15% for sexual abuse, and 6% for emotional mistreatment. The few remaining cases could not be classified into these categories. Children often experience multiple types of maltreatment. Boys and girls were reported at the same rates except for sexual abuse where 85% of the reports were on female victims. Blacks and whites were reported at similar rates but more whites were reported for physical and sexual abuse while more blacks were reported for neglect.

In 1990, an estimated 42% of reported cases were substantiated after investigation. Lack of substantiation does not necessarily mean the child named in the report did not experience maltreatment. Available evidence may not have been sufficient for a judgment to have been made. Intentional false charges of maltreatment are not common. These may involve custody disputes or disputes between neighbors in which the reporting mechanism is used as a means of harassment. Approximately 2 to 10% of custody disputes include changes of sexual mistreatment of the contested child.

A much greater problem than false reports is that of true cases of maltreatment which go unreported. Research in the area indicates two-thirds of child abuse and neglect cases *known* to mandated professionals go unreported. There are many barriers to reporting; lack of certainty, embarrassment, fear of retaliation, and fear that the reporting and subsequent intervention may bring stigma and cause more harm than good. Therapists and others in a helping role sometimes believe their continued work with the family would do more good than making the report.

B. Measuring Unreported Maltreatment: The NCCAN National Incidence Studies

The National Center of Child Abuse and Neglect has produced two national scale incidence studies, one in 1980 and a follow up in 1986. They employed innovative methods to deal with the problem of professional underreporting. In addition to reported cases, the researchers counted cases known to relevant professionals whether or not they had been reported. Strict confidentiality made this technique possible. In the 1986 study, only 44% of the cases serious enough to meet study criteria had been reported and assessed in as in need of protective services.

1. Increasing Rates

Cases resulting in demonstrable harm increased by 66% between 1980 and 1986. Abuse increased more than neglect. Physical abuse went up by 58% and sexual abuse tripled. The percentage of fatal or serious injuries did not increase, but moderate injuries did. Levels of neglect and emotional abuse did not rise significantly between the two studies. Table I gives the rates for specific types of maltreatment estimated for 1986.

2. Demographics of Known Maltreatment

Sixty-three percent of known cases were neglect, with boys and girls experiencing similar rates. Girls were more likely to experience abuse than boys (13.1 cases per 1000 children versus 8.4 cases per 1000, respectively). The girls' rate of sexual abuse was four times the boys' rate. Boys were twice as likely as girls to have been emotionally abused.

TABLE I

Rates of Specific Types of Maltreatment Reported to Child Protective Service Agencies and/or Known to Professionals in Relevant Child-Related Fields, 1986

All types	22.6 cases/1000 children
Abuse	9.4 cases/1000 children
Physical abuse	4.9 cases/1000 children
Sexual abuse	
Intrusion	0.8
Genital molestation	1.1
Other/unknown	0.6
Total	2.1 cases/1000 children
Emotional abuse	
Close confinement (tying, binding)	0.2
Verbal or emotional assault	2.3
other or unknown	1.0
Total	3.0 cases/1000 children
Neglect	14.6 cases/1000 children
Physical neglect	
Refusal of health care	1.1
Delay of health care	0.6
Abandonment	0.3
Expulsion	0.7
Other custody issues	0.5
Inadequate supervision	3.0
Other physical neglect	3.5
Total	8.1 cases/1000 children
Educational neglect	
Permitted chronic truancy	3.5
Failure to enroll/other truancy	1.1
Inattention to special education needs	.1
Total	4.5 cases/1000 children
Emotional neglect	
Inadequate nurturance/ affection	0.8
Chronic/extreme spouse abuse	0.4
Permitted drug/alcohol abuse	0.7
Permitted other maladaptive behavior	0.4
Refusal of psychological care	0.4
Delay in providing psychological care	0.4
Other emotional neglect	0.9
Total	3.2 cases/1000 children

Source: "Study Findings: Study of National Incidence and Prevalence of Child Abuse and Neglect," published in 1988 by the National Center on Child Abuse and Neglect, Children's Bureau, Administration for Children, Youth, and Families, Office of Human Development Services, U.S. Department of Health and Human Services HE 23.1210: IN 2/2.

Babies under the age of 2 were less likely to have experienced abuse but when they did, the consequences were more likely to be fatal. Older children were at greater risk for all kinds of abuse and to have a moderate injury as a result.

Children from larger families, defined as four or more children, were more likely to experience maltreatment than children from homes with fewer children. This was especially true for neglect, where children from larger families were more than twice as likely to be neglected as children from smaller families.

Type and severity of maltreatment were similar for urban and rural counties in the study. Rates of known maltreatment did not differ significantly by child's race. This finding stands in contrast to findings based on *reported cases* in which minorities are reported at a rate greater than that expected given their proportion of the population.

Poverty was an important correlate of abuse and neglect. Overall maltreatment rates for children with family incomes of less than $15,000 were more almost seven times as great as rates for children with family incomes above $15,000 (see Table II.) The connection between low family income and the onset of abuse is strongest for infants and young children. Low income does not seem to be as important as a risk factor for physical abuse beginning in adolescence or for sexual abuse.

TABLE II

Difference in Rates of Maltreatment (per 1000) Based on Family Income in the 1986 National Incidence Study[a]

Category	Less than $15,000	$15,000 or more	Relative risk
All maltreatment	54.0	7.9	7
All abuse	19.9	4.4	4.5
Physical abuse	10.2	2.5	4
Sexual abuse	4.8	1.1	4
Emotional abuse	6.1	1.2	5
All neglect	36.8	4.1	9
Physical neglect	22.6	1.9	12
Educational neglect	10.1	1.3	8
Emotional neglect	6.9	1.5	5
Fatal injury/impairment	0.03	0.01	3
Serious injury/impairment	6.0	0.9	7
Moderate injury/impairment	30.9	5.5	6
Probable injury/impairment	5.4	0.9	6
Endangered	11.7	0.6	20

Source: "Study Findings: Study of National Incidence and Prevalence of Child Abuse and Neglect," published in 1988 by the National Center on Child Abuse and Neglect, Children's Bureau, Administration for Children, Youth, and Families, Office of Human Development Services, U.S. Department of Health and Human Services HE 23.1210: IN 2/2.

Note: Definitions include cases of endangerment as well as cases of documented harm, therefore rates are higher than those in Table I.

[a] The relative risk column has been added.

C. Self-Report Studies of the Extent of Child Maltreatment

1. Physical Abuse

When individuals are asked in confidence to report acts of violence they have perpetrated, estimates of the prevalence of child abuse are considerably higher than estimates derived from official reports or counts of cases known to professionals. In Murray Straus and Richard Gelles' national representative study of family violence conducted in 1985, parents reported an annual rate of at least one instance of serious abuse for 3% of the boys and 2% of the girls. Blue-collar parents reported twice as much abuse as white-collar workers.

2. Sexual Abuse

Estimates of sexual abuse over the full span of childhood range from 9 to 52% for females and from 3 to 9% for males. The best estimate of female incest comes from a random sample of 930 San Francisco women. Seventeen percent of women who had spent a major part of childhood with a stepfather were molested by them, compared to 2% father–daughter incest among women reared by their biological fathers. One-tenth of a percent of the cases involved a biological mother as perpetrator and there were no cases of incest perpetrated by step-mothers. There is added stigma for males who have been sexually abused so the current estimate of 5 to 15% of male victims may be an underestimate. The first national conference on male survivors was held in 1988. Increased awareness of the issue may improve our understanding of its pervasiveness.

IV. ETIOLOGY

A. Progression from Single Cause to Integrative Models

In Kempe's "syndrome" of child abuse, etiological emphasis was on parental psychopathology and personality disorder frequently passed on from parent to child, which would result in abusive behavior under conditions of increased stress. This psychiatric model dominated research in the 1960s.

In the 1970s, sociologists countered that such a model ignored the ways in which maltreating parents were themselves victims of greater forces. They supported this "sociological model" with reviews of reported abuse cases which documented the correlation between child abuse and chronic poverty and unemployment, shrinking labor markets, dysfunctional family processes, and other forms of social stress.

Also during the 1970s, causal models in developmental psychological theory were expanded in two directions beyond main effects parental influence models to include child and environmental contributors to child outcomes. Children's effects on their caregivers were added to theories about the origins of child personality and mental health characteristics. Studies began to reveal child characteristics that were associated with increased risk of maltreatment. In addition, Urie Bronfenbrenner's "ecological theory of child development" influenced child maltreatment theory with its emphasis upon layers of causal influence, including individual family, neighborhood, and cultural characteristics. James Garbarino first applied these ideas in 1976 in an integrated "ecological perspective" on child maltreatment. Jay Belsky's *Ecology of Child Maltreatment* published in 1981 described causal influences at four levels: the individual parent psychology, family system, proximal environmental context, and overall cultural levels.

In 1981, Dante Cicchetti drew on the "organizational perspective" of development and principles from developmental psychopathology in another integrative model of child maltreatment. He described enduring and temporary characteristics in the parent, child, and environmental domains that continuously transact to influence the quality of caregiving and in extreme cases lead to child maltreatment. He argued that an adequate model had to include both risk and protective factors in order to effectively account for maltreatment's occurrence. In the real world maltreatment cannot be predicted by simply adding up the negatives.

B. The Search for Risk Factors for Maltreatment

High levels of income and available social resources act as buffers to stress. Additional protective factors have been identified such as having a warm relationship with a capable adult during childhood, good learning and problem solving skills, and appealing interpersonal or physical attributes. Efforts continue to identify additional protective factors. The bulk of studies accomplished to date have emphasized negative influences or risk factors for maltreatment.

1. Parent Characteristics

Parents of physically abused children tend to be younger at the birth of their first child, unmarried, and relatively less educated than nonabusive parents. Physically abusive parents have been shown to have some distinct biological characteristics such as greater autonomic reactivity (as measured by skin conductance and respiration rates) to children's emotional expressions. They report experiencing both positive and negative social interactions with children as more aversive and stressful than nonabusive parents. Maltreating parents have more health problems and handicapping conditions. Some of these illnesses may have psychological origins.

Retardation and lack of information may be related to neglect; however, deficient general intelligence does not seem to be a risk factor for physical abuse. There is evidence for deficiencies in specific abstract reasoning abilities related to child management, coping and problem solving, and limited skills in providing structure and discipline. Abusive parents exhibit overly high expectations and they tend to get caught up in ever escalating, coercive cycles of discipline and negative child reaction. Neglecting parents are characterized more by unresponsiveness and lack of availability. Low self-esteem, low ego strength and resiliency, and external locus-of-control have been found to be characteristic of abuse and neglect. Physically abusive parents tend to have negative perceptions of their children, attributing more behavior problems to them than independent observers see. In addition, they impute intentionality to their children's misbehavior.

Many abusive parents, especially perpetrators of emotional and sexual abuse, experienced maltreatment at the hands of their own parents. It is a major risk factor. However, the "cycle of abuse" is far from inevitable. Many maltreated individuals become adequate, nonmaltreating parents. The current estimate is 33% of physically abused children repeat the abuse with their own children. Rates of intergenerational transmission of psychological maltreatment and sexual abuse may be somewhat higher.

Studies indicate that the parents who do *not* repeat the cycle are characterized as having very clear memories of the mistreatment they suffered accompanied by strong emotional responses to it. They are more likely to have supportive interpersonal relationships and the opportunity to confide in at least one other person. As children they were likely to have established a warm and trusting relationship with at least one adult.

The marital relationships of physically abusive parents frequently are marked with conflict, especially violent conflict. Abusive family interactions are more negative and less positive than comparisons. Maltreating parents have less supportive social networks beyond their families. Neglecting parents are more likely to be isolated while abusive parents' networks tend to consist of short-term, conflictual relationships. [See MARITAL DYSFUNCTION.]

Despite the early emphasis on parental psychopathology, less than 10% of abusive parents have diagnosable psychological disorders as defined by the American Psychiatric Association standards. Included within the 10% are cases of (a) Munchausen syndrome by proxy, a rare thought and behavioral disorder, named after a famous 18th century German teller of tall tales, in which an adult fabricates a history of illnesses and symptoms for his child, often directly inducing symptoms in the child through poisoning or other means in order to experience the attention of the medical response to the child's disorder. The child is subjected to unnecessary tests, hospitalizations, medications and treatments. (b) Antisocial personality disorder, a disorder in which the individual has consistent difficulty operating within the social norms for conflict resolution, honesty and property rights, work, and family responsibility. Child abuse and neglect are defining characteristics. (c) Postpartum psychosis, a rare disorder with a prevalence of one or two cases per thousand births, in which delusions, distorted thinking, and mood states can result in loss of control and harm to the child or the mother. (d) Schizophrenia and manic depression, disorders which include periods during which contact with reality and decision making are diminished. During such times an individual who does not have buffering resources to take over child responsibilities may be neglectful of a child's needs. Distorted thinking and feeling states can be disturbing. These inadvertent consequences of the disorders are a greater risk to children than are direct assaults which are relatively rare. [See ANTISOCIAL PERSONALITY DISORDER; DEPRESSION; SCHIZOPHRENIA.]

Abuse and dependence upon alcohol, and illegal drugs are important risk factors for maltreatment. Depression and dysthymia, mood disorders, are characterized by persistent low mood or irritability, accompanied by problems with sleep and eating, and disruption in the ability to fulfill role functions such as child management. Depression is particularly common among neglecting parents. [See SUBSTANCE ABUSE.]

Physical abusers are characterized by difficulties with impulse control and constructive channeling of angry and frustrated emotions more than by full scale psychopathological disorders. They are relatively isolated from other individuals and community agencies which could assist. For sexual offenders the isolation from age-appropriate contacts, combined with a sexual attraction to young children, leads to an increase in the probability that the sexual desires will be acted upon.

2. Child Characteristics

Children are not responsible for their own mistreatment. However, there are child characteristics which are associated with increased probability of maltreatment. Some child characteristics are associated with increased child care demands. Prematurity and low birth weight, colic, illness, accidents, and physical and behavioral handicapping conditions all make child care more difficult. Temperamental characteristics such as irritability, persistence, and high activity, especially in combination with maternal depression or high levels of environmental stress, also increase the risk of physical maltreatment.

Mentally retarded individuals are more at risk for maltreatment, especially sexual abuse, than their nonretarded peers. They are viewed as easier targets by perpetrators, and they often spend at least some of their lives in institutional care by nonparental adults. They may not have adequate abilities to defend themselves or report wrongdoing. A recent NCCAN report gave 83% as the estimated lifetime prevalence of at least one instance of some form of sexual abuse in this group. [*See* MENTAL RETARDATION.]

Aspects of child appearance may increase the probability of maltreatment. Some children remind their parent of another disliked individual. Maltreatment can be an unintended result of the resemblance. Careful measurements of the facial characteristics of physically abused and control children have revealed that the physically abused children as a group have facial dimensions more characteristic of older children. This could contribute in subtle ways to inappropriate caregiver expectations.

Numerous studies have documented behavior problems in maltreated children, both within the family and with peers. Some of these studies were based upon parent reports and thus were due to negative parental attributions toward a disfavored child. Teachers and independent observers have also reported elevated levels of behavior problems. Whether or not these problems preceded the maltreatment or are the results of maltreatment, they can contribute to subsequent acts of maltreatment.

Being a stepchild is a risk for maltreatment. Being male is associated with increased risk for physical abuse, and by far most sexual abuse victims are female. Female children continue to be at risk for infanticide or poor care in societies where females are valued less.

Certain developmental phases are harder for parents to cope with than others. The helplessness of infancy is a delight for some parents and a drain for others. Toddlerhood, in which the normal healthy individual experiments with his or her own autonomy, becoming willful and at times contrary, is also the developmental phase during which toilet training is accomplished. This phase can tap the resources of the most patient parent, and it is a high-risk time for toddlers who are in the care of step-parents or whose parents suffer impulse control problems or severe stress levels.

Adolescence is another developmental transition generally considered to be a challenge to the family system. The family has to make room for a new member who has new physical, cognitive, and sexual capacities, is increasingly costly to support, and is increasingly moved by outside influences. The potential for conflict is great. Adolescents experience proportionally more abuse than younger children, especially psychological and sexual abuse. At least half of known abused adolescents were not maltreated during their childhood years, but began to experience abuse during adolescence. Stepparents are even more likely to be part of adolescent onset abuse than is the case for younger children. The etiology of adolescent onset maltreatment differs from the etiology of child onset maltreatment. Poverty and environmental stress are not as important. Parents who begin to maltreat during adolescence are less likely to have a history of maltreatment in their own childhood. [*See* ADOLESCENCE.]

3. Environmental Characteristics That Increase the Probability of Child Maltreatment

By comparing census tract data with maltreatment report data, James Garbarino found a number of socio-demographic characteristics that characterize neighborhoods with high levels of abuse and neglect reports. They are: (1) a high percentage of families living below the poverty level, (2) high unemployment, (3) a high percentage of female headed households, (4) overcrowded housing, (5) a large proportion of racial minorities, (6) low levels of education,

(7) frequent moves, and (8) a low percentage of affluent residents. In addition, community leaders describe neighborhoods with particularly high rates of maltreatment as "socially impoverished" as well. They lack a sense of unity. Professional networking is weaker and residents experience less positive neighboring and more stressful day to day interactions.

Some child-related institutional settings have elevated rates of maltreatment. In a 1988 review of reported cases of sexual abuse in child care settings, David Finkelhor discovered that the risk for sexual abuse was lower in day care settings than in a child's own household. The risk was lowest in centers with many teachers and children and in centers where parents were free to come and go easily. Forty percent of these perpetrators were female and only 8% of the perpetrators had been arrested previously for sexual abuse.

V. THE CONSEQUENCES OF MALTREATMENT

A. Death

In 1990, at least 1200 American children died as the result of maltreatment. Twenty-five percent of them were active protective service cases at time of death. Deaths were not distributed uniformly but clustered around the youngest and oldest ages. As with other child abuse estimates this is an underestimate and no one knows just how great an underestimate it is. No standard protocol exists to differentiate deaths caused by natural illness, accident, or maltreatment.

B. Injury, Handicap, or Impairment

Violent physical acts often produce harm. Other types of maltreatment can also have physical consequences. Neglect produces inadequate growth patterns, infections, diseases, and accidental injuries due to poor supervision. Sexual abuse is often discovered when a child presents with veneral disease or injuries to the sexual organs. Emotional mistreatment can also produce physical sequelae. In psychosocial dwarfism or failure to thrive, inadequate caloric intake combines with inadequate parental attention or environmental stresses to produce children below the fifth percentile in size. Upon discovery and hospitalization these children's growth rates

rapidly improve. Table III gives the range of injury and impairment associated with the cases of maltreatment described in NCCAN's 1986 National Incidence Study.

C. The Developmental Psychopathology of Maltreated Children

Early studies of maltreatment's consequences to the children lacked control groups, and were based upon clinical judgment rather than systematic and objective observation. Recent studies have employed improved methods and have been theoretically guided. As in other areas of child abuse work our assessments of the effects of maltreatment are underesti-

TABLE III

Injury/Impairment Resulting from Abuse and Neglect in the 1986 National Incidence Study

Severity level	Percentage of reports	Estimated rate per 1000 children in the population
Fatal	0.1%	0.02
Serious	10%	2.3

"involved a life-threatening condition, represented a long-term impairment of physical, mental, or emotional capacities, or required professional treatment aimed at preventing such impairment. Examples of serious injuries/impairments include: loss of consciousness, stopping breathing, broken bones, schooling loss which required special education services, chronic and debilitating substance abuse, diagnosed cases of failure to thrive, third degree burns or extensive second degree burns, and so forth."

Moderate	60%	13.9

Those which "persisted in observable form (including pain or impairment) for at least 48 hours. For example, bruises, depression or emotional distress (not serious enough to require professional treatment) and the like."

Probable	11%	2.4

There were cases in the study in which given the characteristics of the maltreatment, it seemed likely that moderate or serious injury/impairment had occurred, yet it was not specifically mentioned. These cases were labeled as *probable* injuries/impairment.

Endangered	19%	4.0

Cases in which damage had not yet resulted from the maltreatment, but the respondent rated the situation as having a very high potential for harm.

Total	100%	22.6

Source: "Study Findings: Study of National Incidence and Prevalence of Child Abuse and Neglect," published in 1988 by the National Center on Child Abuse and Neglect, Children's Bureau, Administration for Children, Youth, and Families, Office of Human Development Services, U.S. Department of Health and Human Services HE 23.1210: IN 2/2.

mates. The maltreated children observed in outcome studies have almost all received some intervention, from reporting and investigation to extensive individual and family therapy. Ethical standards of research preclude studying maltreated children who have not been afforded whatever level of services are available in their communities, therefore the consequences of maltreatment reported are those that remain after at least some degree of professional intervention, the duration and quality of which are rarely specified.

1. Poverty

Commonsense would suggest and research, especially that summarized by Leory Pelton, has confirmed that poverty has profound negative effects on child development. Since a disproportionate number of maltreated children live in poverty, researchers examining the developmental consequences of maltreatment have had to employ demographically matched comparison groups in order to discover maltreatment's unique contributions to negative outcome. Longitudinal studies have demonstrated convincingly that maltreatment does have psychosocial consequences beyond those expected as the result of an upbringing in poverty. Not every abused child experiences these negative effects. The research is not a definite prediction for any one maltreated individual. Group studies can only reveal an increased probability of negative outcome. Buffering and protective factors do exist and they allow some maltreated children to emerge as relatively well adjusted.

2. Cognitive Competence

Prospective studies have documented progressively poor performance on IQ tests among maltreated youngsters and increasing learning disabilities. Neglect and psychological unavailability are particularly detrimental to intellectual development. Maltreatment alters other aspects of cognition as well, altering the very way the victims perceive the world, producing hypervigilence and heightened responsiveness to perceived danger in their surroundings. [See COGNITIVE DEVELOPMENT; INTELLIGENCE.]

3. Attachment

Maltreated infants are very likely to develop insecure or "disorganized/disoriented" attachment relationships with their caregivers. An insecure attachment makes successful resolution of subsequent developmental challenges more difficult, e.g., successful negotiation of peer relationships and the ability to relate effectively with care providers and teachers.

4. Communication

Maltreated children show language delays, especially in the ways they talk about experiences beyond the here and now and express their inner states and feelings. [See INTERPERSONAL COMMUNICATION.]

5. Behavior Problems

Maltreated children are described as having more behavior problems than their nonmaltreated peers by parent reports, teacher reports, and objective observation. Parents in maltreating families overreport behavior problems, perhaps as a rationalization for the abuse. Teacher reports and direct observations have shown abused children to be more physically aggressive and verbally abusive to others, both adults and peers.

6. Peer Relationships

Studies of children's friendship formation indicate that children who approach new friends with inappropriate aggression tend to be not just ignored but also rejected by those peers. These difficulties, once established, become stable, leading to adjustment problems and isolation in adulthood. [See PEER RELATIONSHIPS AND INFLUENCES IN CHILDHOOD.]

7. Conduct Disorders: Running Away, Delinquency, and Eventual Criminality

Most maltreated children do not become delinquent and an even smaller number of them advance to criminality. Looking in the other direction we find that juvenile delinquents report much higher rates of abuse and neglect than nondelinquents. Maltreatment contributes to delinquency in a number of ways. It disrupts relationship formation, making the process frustrating and unsatisfying for many children. It sets up a harsh and unfair world view, within which deviant actions and breaking social rules for immediate gain make some sense. Physically abused children are at risk to repeat the aggression. Many runaways leave home to escape maltreatment, especially physical and sexual abuse. Other children's departures from home are involuntary. They are rejected by parents no longer willing to offer even minimal care. Once on the street the probability of illegal involvement, especially prostitution, increases. [See CRIMINAL BEHAVIOR.]

D. Psychopathology and Mood Disorders

1. Anxiety and Depression

Elevated levels of anxiety and depression among maltreated children have been reported during the childhood years. The depression continues for many children and for others it emerges anew in adulthood. Depression produces its own level of suffering and in addition it sets the stage for subsequent difficulties in fulfilling role demands, especially those of parenting. [*See* ANXIETY DISORDERS.]

2. Post-Traumatic Stress Disorder

Children who have experienced severe violence or sexual abuse may show the signs of post-traumatic stress disorder (PTSD), including a pervasive sense of fear, sleep disorders, flashbacks, and reenactments are similar to the experiences of victimization. Some victims of sexual abuse do not experience PTSD because the abuse itself was not a "sudden trauma," but more of a situation, climate, or context. Very young children may have been slowly "groomed" or set up for the abuse in such a way as to reduce the elements of sudden trauma. For these children the impact of their misuse unfolds over a number of years as they become aware of their exploitation. [*See* POST-TRAUMATIC STRESS DISORDER.]

3. Dissociative Disorders and Multiple Personality Disorder

Dissociative disorders represent some form of mental escape from painful/traumatic experiences. In dissociation certain perceptions and memories are separated from affect, compartmentalized out of the mainstream of psychic life. These defenses may save the individual from the full immediate impact of a traumatic experience; however, they do so at a price. The dissociation delays or prevents the working through of the experience, producing feelings of confusion and helplessness and, in extreme cases, a fragmented or "multiple personality." This very severe disorder entails a disruption of memory and identity. Two or more personalities, each of which has distinct characteristics and a separate memory of a life history, alternate control of the body. The different personalities often act to compartmentalize different ranges of emotions. The person is not usually out of touch with reality but has periods of amnesia or blackouts and becomes increasingly maladjusted over time. Child victims who have a biopsychological predisposition to dissociate come to use this ability in the context of unpredictable extreme trauma at the hands of a person who is at other times a nurturing caregiver. Histories of extensive maltreatment, usually physical or sexual, are present in almost all known cases of multiple personality disorder. Most of the abuse is sexual. [*See* DISSOCIATIVE DISORDERS.]

4. Alcohol and Drug Abuse

Sexually and physically abused individuals are at greater risk for later abuse and dependence of alcohol and drugs.

E. The Effects of Sexual Abuse

Victims of sexual abuse, both male and female, often exhibit stress-related symptoms at the time of the abuse or its disclosure including: fear, anxiety, sleep disturbances, depression, aggression, and inappropriate sexual behavior such as explicit words or acts which reveal abnormal sexual knowledge. Long-term effects include anxiety, depression or dysthymia, feelings of isolation and stigma, poor self-esteem, and problems in trusting and in establishing satisfying sexual relationships. In some cases these difficulties emerge years after the abuse, after seemingly effective adjustment in the intervening years. Both male and female victims have an increased risk of experiencing sexual dysfunction; however, there is more risk that male victims will become perpetrators of sexual abuse in the next generation.

In addition to the consequences of maltreatment which are directly felt by the victims over the years, is another set of consequences which serve to set up the same risk conditions such as poverty and disrupted family relationships that caused the maltreatment in the first place. A 1989 study of two groups of very poor women (homeless vs those with housing) revealed no difference between the groups concerning history of physical and sexual abuse. Approximately 86% of both groups had been maltreated.

VI. TREATMENT AND PREVENTION

A. Treatment to Stop Current Abuse

Treatment, or efforts to prevent the recurrence of maltreatment once it has already occurred, is also called "tertiary prevention." Different etiological theories and developmental approaches to parenting guide approaches to treatment.

1. Behavioral Approaches

Specific behavioral therapies derived from learning theory focus on family learning histories and the retraining of effective parenting skills. In cases of physical abuse, education concerning escalating coercive patterns of conflict and sound disciplinary alternatives are offered. In addition, self-control skills, especially those directed at anger control, have been shown to be effective in equiping formerly abusive parents with skills to recognize potential conflict situations, contain their anger through deep breathing or other relaxation techniques, and choose different behavioral responses.

The principles of classical conditioning have been employed in the treatment of sex abuse offenders. The goal in these programs is to override sexual responsiveness patterns and to redirect them to more appropriate targets. Broadly defined parent training approaches are designed to improve parents' coping repertoires especially in the context of child management.

For neglectful parents, behavioral interventions are aimed at increasing the problem solving, organization, and social interactional skills in order to support independence and to develop and maintain support systems in the future.

2. Treatment from the Perspective of Attachment Theory

Therapies within this framework have as their goal the reworking of existing mental models of relationships in order to build more effective ones, either with an individual therapist or in supportive group work. Major treatment goals are to reduce the profound loneliness and isolation, to facilitate a more positive self-evaluation, to provide a hearing for feelings about the individual's relationship with her child, and to offer concrete suggestions on new ways to interact. The comfort, acceptance, and support that develop within the therapeutic relationship become the model for the parent's interaction with her child and family.

Treatments focused on the value of social support include Parents Anonymous for physical abuse and Parents United which addresses sexual abuse. Both these organizations employ many self-help principles. Parents United offers specialized groups for perpetrators, spouses, victims, and siblings, acknowledging that their feelings and perspectives differ.

3. Comprehensive Approaches

Integrative, ecological theories of abuse lead to multifaceted approaches such as family preservation. This is an intense, comprehensive involvement which begins when a family is in crisis. It continues for 6 weeks or so. A counselor, with a case load of only one or two other families, is on call 24 hours a day. Intervention is tailored to address the strengths and weaknesses of each family, at the individual, family, and environmental levels. Help in obtaining basic resources such as food, housing, transportation, and medical and legal services is central. The goal is to address the real needs of the family to determine if they can provide adequate care. If they cannot make progress with this intense support, then alternative placements for the child are considered.

The most extensively evaluated treatment approach for abuse and neglect is Project 12-Ways. It, too, is a comprehensive approach which addresses the many sources of difficulty in maltreating families. Treatment includes training in stress reduction, self-control, constructive uses of leisure time, child development basics, and job search strategies. Integration with local substance abuse treatment and employment resources are included. The unique needs of single parents are also addressed.

4. Criminal Justice System

In its own way the criminal justice system offers an important approach to treatment. Some perpetrators of severe harm are removed from the home through a restraining order or removed from the community through imprisonment. Such action reinforces societal values of nonviolence and the special protection requirements of young children. In less dangerous situations the courts are moving toward alternative sentencing especially treatment which allows a perpetrator to remain in the community and provide support for his or her family. Students of spouse maltreatment have advocated the use of criminal charges and often imprisonment for individuals judged guilty of battering their spouses. Child advocates generally have urged a less criminal approach to addressing child maltreatment. Recognizing that spouse and child abuse often occur in the same households, what is needed is a more comprehensive approach to treating family violence in its different forms.

B. Treatment to Remediate the Suffering of Maltreatment's Victims

Art therapy, imagery, body work, play therapy, individual therapies, and group therapies are employed to reduce the suffering and reduce future negative outcomes among victims. Treatment goals include assisting clients in regaining a sense of control over their lives, improving the sense of self-worth, and teaching new skills for interpersonal relationships. Support groups for survivors work to reduce the sense of loneliness and ''damaged goods'' feelings that are often a part of the victim experience.

C. Prevention of Maltreatment

Treatment approaches are time intensive and costly. It takes tremendous effort to undo the variety of damage caused by child maltreatment. Much of it cannot be undone. All agree it would be better to prevent maltreatment before it happens. In 1980, few prevention programs received NCCAN funding. By 1990, 50% of NCCAN funding went to prevention. Contributions for preventive programs from individuals and corporations continue to increase as well.

Effective new funding approaches combine private and public resources. Between 1980 and 1990 forty-nine states established ''Children's Trust Funds,'' which collectively spent 28 million dollars on prevention programs. The monies come from small fees added to marriage or other licenses and check off boxes on state income tax forms. Federal dollars matched those collected by the states. There has been substantial growth in private efforts to prevent abuse and neglect. Corporations, the media, and private organizations have mounted numerous prevention programs.

1. Secondary Prevention

Two levels of prevention are aimed at parents who have not yet maltreated. Secondary prevention refers to efforts aimed at identified high-risk populations, e.g., families living in poverty, single parents, parents dealing with unexpected or unwanted pregnancies, parents with impulse control problems, depression, or substance abuse, and families in economic or emotional crisis. Specific approaches include: helplines and hotlines for parents in stress; other forms of crisis support such as crisis nurseries in hospitals; ongoing family support services such as assistance with day care, medical care etc.; and self-help support groups such as Parents Anonymous which provide social support and some specific behavioral management techniques to address anger that threatens to go out of control.

Home health services such as early and regular contact with visiting nurses after the birth of a child have been shown to reduce subsequent child abuse and neglect reports during infancy. Evaluation research of such a program designed by David Olds and his colleagues, also revealed enhanced parenting skills such as the expression of affection and providing structure and positive discipline. Visited mothers, especially the youngest, single teen mothers, showed more successful adjustment and satisfaction with their infants than did mothers in a matched control group. In follow-up assessments the visited mothers were the focus of fewer child abuse and neglect reports were less restrictive and punishing with their children and provided more appropriate play materials than similar mothers who had not participated in the program. Babies in the intervention group tended to have higher developmental quotients than the comparison babies and participating mothers waited longer to have their next child than mothers who had not been visited.

Treating victimized children is another approach to secondary prevention. Providing an opportunity to acknowledge past suffering, teaching effective interpersonal problem solving and planning strategies, and offering situations in which abused and neglected children can increase their self-esteem can serve to reduce the probability of maltreatment in the next generation. Considerable research has been directed at refining methods of assessing adults' child abuse potential in order that direct prevention services could be directed to the individuals in most need.

2. Primary Prevention

Primary prevention includes activities that exert a positive influence on the whole system, thereby increasing healthy family functioning and eliminating some of the risk conditions that contribute to maltreatment. Included in the scope of primary prevention are; policies that improve educational and employment opportunities for parents; the promotion of family planning in order to avoid unwanted births or births that are too closely spaced; prenatal care for pregnant women in order to reduce the number of premature and low birth weight babies; policies which support new parents during the perinatal period, such as ''rooming in'' during the hospital stay, and parental leave with job security; early education interventions such as Head Start with its comprehensive approach to services including parent education and mental health components; economic improvements such as reduction of unemployment through job training programs and placement services; efforts to reduce the overall level of violence in the society such as the promotion of violence-free problem solving in general, alternatives to corporal punishment in schools and in homes.

3. Prevention Aimed at Potential Victims

A growing number of preventive efforts, especially those designed to reduce sexual abuse, are now focused on training potential victims to stop or report the abuse. School-based curricula, plays and films, comic books, define "good touch" and "bad touch," and describe self-protection approaches. They warn children that secrets that make them feel bad are not to be kept. They urge children to seek help from an adult they trust and to persist if they are not believed, urging them to tell and tell again until they find an adult who does hear what they are saying. Evaluation studies of these efforts reveal limited effectiveness in preventing victimization especially among preschoolers who present particular challenges to the creators of these programs. The developmental needs of these young potential victims have not yet been adequately met. Some would argue that we need to direct more prevention efforts toward potential abusers, attacking their misconceptions about the potential for harm their actions entail.

4. Education

Explicit public education campaigns describe child maltreatment, stressing that it is preventable and treatable. The National Committee for the Prevention of Child Abuse, directed since 1972 by Anne Cohn Donnelly, has produced some of the most extensive public education campaigns. They have used television spots, print, and brief pamphlets directed at parents and children. Their public service ads are aimed at revising American attitudes toward violence in childrearing with such messages as:

"It shouldn't hurt to be a child."
"Child abuse hurts us all."
"When big and little stresses of life build up and you are just about to lash out at your child, stop. Take time out. Don't take it out on your kid."

"Words can hurt like a fist."
"Children believe what their parents tell them. Watch what you say."
"Stop using words that hurt. Start using words that help."
"We all have a role to play in preventing child abuse. If you know of a parent having trouble, reach out and offer some help."

and a new message aimed directly at *perpetrators* of sexual abuse:

"Stop, you don't have to molest that child."

Bibliography

American Association for Protecting Children, A division of The American Humane Association. (1988). "Highlights of Official Child Neglect and Abuse Reporting: 1986." The American Humane Association, Denver.

Belsky, J. (1980). An ecology of child maltreatment. *Am. Psychol.* **35,** 320–335.

Braun, B. G. (1990). Dissociative disorders as sequelae to incest. In (Richard P. Kluft, Ed.) "Incest-Related Syndromes of Adult Psychopathology." American Psychiatric Press, Washington DC.

Cicchetti, D. (Ed.) (1991). Special issue; Defining psychological maltreatment. *Dev. Psychopathol.* **3,** 1–119.

Cicchetti, D., and Carlson, V. (1989). "Child Maltreatment: Theory and Research on the Causes and Consequences of Child Abuse and Neglect." Cambridge University Press, New York.

Donnelly, A. C. (1991). What have we learned about prevention: What we should do about it. *Child Abuse and Neglect* **15,** 99–106.

Clark, R. E., and Clark, J. F. (1989). "Encyclopedia of Child Abuse." Facts on File, New York.

Drotar, D. (Ed.) (1985). "New Directions in Failure to Thrive: Implications for Research and Practice." Plenum, New York.

Garbarino, J., Schellenbach, D., Sebes, J., and Associates (1986). "Troubled Youth, Troubled Families." Aldine, New York.

Giovannoni, J. (1989). Definitional issues in child maltreatment. In (D. Cicchetti and V. Carlson, Eds.) "Child Maltreatment: Theory and Research on the Causes and Consequences of Child Abuse and Neglect." Cambridge University Press, New York.

Milner, J. S., and Chilamkurti, C. (1991). Physical child abuse perpetrator characteristics: A review of the literature. *J. Interpers. Violence* **6,** 345–366.

National Center on Child Abuse and Neglect (1992). National Child Abuse and Neglect Data System, Working Paper 1, 1990 Summary Data Component. DHHS Publication No (ACF) 92-30361.

Sedlak, A. J. (1991). National Incidence and Prevalence of Child Abuse and Neglect: 1988. National Center on Child Abuse and Neglect, Children's Bureau, Administration for Children, Youth, and Families, Office of Human Development Services, U.S. Department of Health and Human Services. Washington, DC.

Spiegel, D. (Section Ed.) (1991). Section II: Dissociative Disorders. In "American Psychiatric Press Review of Psychiatry." (A. Tasman and S. M. Goldfinger, Eds.), Vol. 10. American Psychiatric Press, Washington, DC.

Wolfe, D. A. (1987). "Child Abuse: Implications for Child Development and Psychopathology, Vol. 10 of the Developmental Clinical Psychology and Psychiatry Series. Sage, Newbury Park.

CHUNKING

Francis S. Bellezza
Ohio University

Glossary

Bit A unit of information indicating one of two possible alternatives.

Cognitive unit A mental structure made up of a small amount of information not interrelated strongly enough to form a chunk. A protochunk or soft chunk.

Conscious memory Contains the limited amount of information of which we are immediately aware.

Mental structure A representation in memory of interrelated information created by our perceptions and thought processes.

Permanent memory Information available to us in memory which may not be currently conscious.

Rehearsal The process by which information is maintained in our conscious memory.

Semantic memory That information in memory which is well-learned, not easily forgotten, and not associated with a particular event.

A CHUNK can be defined as a well-learned cognitive unit made up of a small number of components representing a frequently occurring and consistent perceptual pattern.

I. THE CHUNK AS A MENTAL STRUCTURE

In a paper published in 1956 George Miller made the chunk the quintessential concept of the new cognitive, that is, mental, psychology. The chunk represented mental structure. Miller proposed the chunk as a mental construct interceding between environmental stimuli and the organism's responses to those stimuli. Certainly, mental events, such as experienced ideas, images, and concepts, had been proposed by philosophers hundreds, if not thousands, of years earlier. But among psychologists of the mid-20th century, mental events were not considered scientific constructs. To explain what occurred in the organism, one relied on stimulus–response conditioning or on neurological mechanisms. For example, the behaviorist Clark Hull had argued that implicit stimuli and responses occur in the organism. These implicit stimuli and responses allowed enviromental stimuli and the overt, behavioral responses of the organism to be connected in a manner more flexible than the direct connections mandated by the ideas of classical and operant conditioning. Similarly, a neurologically oriented psychologist, Donald Hebb, proposed that neural circuits become activated and strengthened when learning takes place, and these neural circuits allow for sophisticated relations to develop between stimuli and responses. Neurologically based arguments were also made by the gestalt psychologists. Wolfgang Köhler suggested that perceptual fields were paralleled in the brain by corresponding neurological fields.

However, Miller's notion of a chunk was different from these examples of intervening structure. A chunk does not deal with implicit stimuli or responses, nor does it deal with neural activity. A chunk represents *information*. The 1950s saw the rise of information theory and the spreading influence of the digital computer as a model of human cognition. Computers did not deal with stimuli and responses, and computers did not deal with neural activity. Computers processed information, and, as a consequence, *information-processing theories* of cognition were born. A chunk can be thought of as representing information: a symbol. And as a language symbol, the chunk could be manipulated and used in the human information-processing system much like programming-language symbols could be processed by a computer program. Cognitive psychologists began speaking less and less of the associating or conditioning of stimuli and responses and began speaking more and more about the encoding, storage, and retrieval of information. [*See* MEMORY.]

But what is a chunk? Information theory had a unit of information called a *bit,* named after binary digit. A bit of information is the amount of information representing the choice between two alternatives. The sequence of binary digits 10011101 comprises eight bits of information because each digit represents one of two alternatives. A sequence of letters such as *kuxzpthm* comprises more than eight bits because each letter represents one of 26 alternatives. In fact, if we assume each letter is equally likely to appear in the string, then each letter represents 4.7 bits. So, in this case the eight-letter sequence *kuxzpthm* represents 37.6 bits of information. If we analyze the information content of strings of text, the computations are somewhat more complex because various letters occur with different frequencies, and letters follow other letters with different frequencies. But we will not bother with these details here. The point Miller made was that in our cognitive systems the eight-letter string *kuxzpthm* is fundamentally different from the eight-letter string *elephant* because *elephant* is a familiar pattern of letters and represents a chunk of information, whereas *kuxzpthm* does not represent a chunk. A chunk is a familiar pattern of information that has a representation in our cognitive system. As far as our memory system is concerned, given the letters e-l-e-p-h-a-n-t, the spoken word "elephant" follows with a probability value close to 1. Similarly, the spoken word "elephant" is decoded into the letters e-l-e-p-h-a-n-t with a probability close to 1. For someone illiterate there would be no orthographic chunk, that is, written word, for elephant. For a literate person who had never heard of an elephant, there would be neither a chunk of orthographic nor a chunk of phonetic information in memory. For chunks to be available in memory, learning must have taken place.

II. CHUNKING AS A MENTAL PROCESS

A second reason why the term chunk became so important is that it represented a mental process as well as a mental structure. Not surprisingly, this process has been called chunking. Because chunks represent familiar patterns of perceived information, the question naturally arises how an unfamiliar pattern of information becomes familiar. How do the elements of the pattern get chunked? In his 1956 paper George Miller described a chunking experiment reported by Sidney Smith. When people are presented strings of binary digits such as 101000100111001110010, where each successive digit is presented for a brief period of time, they can immediately recall only about nine of the digits. With longer strings people make recall errors. Smith trained himself to change strings of binary digits (0 or 1) to strings of octal digits (0 to 7) by changing each set of three binary digits into one octal digit. In this transformation 000 becomes 0, 001 becomes 1, 010 becomes 2, and so on, up to 111 which becomes 7. As the binary digits were presented singly, Smith grouped them in his mind by threes, so he thought of 101-000-100-111-001-110-010 as 5-0-4-7-1-6-2. By doing this Smith changed 21 binary digits into 7 octal digits. He was able to remember the 7 octal digits and, when it was time to recall, decode them back into the original 21 binary digits. So now, instead of remembering only 9 binary digits he could, using this recoding process, recall 21 binary digits. What was happening here?

Smith's results make a number of important points. The first point is that we can keep in mind only about 7 chunks of information at one time. This important fact led to the title of George Miller's well-known 1956 article, "The Magical Number Seven, Plus or Minus Two." If we want to discuss how much we are aware of, that is, how much information is in consciousness at any given time, we must talk in terms of chunks of information, not bits of information. If binary digits are thought of in terms of 0s and 1s, both familiar symbols, we can hold about 7 plus or minus 2 symbols in memory. If octal digits are thought of in terms of the familiar symbols 0, 1, 2, 3, 4, 5, 6, 7, we still can hold about 7 plus or minus 2 octal digits in memory. This is true even though each octal digit represents three bits.

The second point made by Smith's results is that the advantages of chunked information come about through the process of learning. What Smith learned to do was recode the sequences of 0s and 1s into shorter sequences of octal digits. Hence, he was able to use his 7-chunk capacity of conscious memory to hold a greater number of bits of information than he could without recoding. However, this increase in capacity came at a cost. Smith had to make the sets of three binary digits familiar to him. He had to expend time and effort to learn. He had to learn to label, at a fast rate, 101 as 5, 000 as 0, 100 as 4, and so on. So chunking is the process by which we learn repeated patterns of information so that they become familiar. Often, we give a verbal label to each pattern so we can talk about the patterns of information using their shorter labels or symbols. When necessary, we can decode the labels back into the multiple components of the patterns. A common form of this chunking process is learning to read words and to spell words. Children learn to pronounce the letter sequence s-c-h-o-o-l as "school" and also learn to spell "school" as s-c-h-o-o-l. Other levels of analysis are possible. For example, spoken words can be represented by more primitive phonemes. Also, individual letters can be pronounced and also be analyed into curved and straight-line segments.

A. Chunks Exist in Our Minds

Chunks do not exist in the environment. Chunks are mental structures. In a clever experiment the psychologists Gordon Bower and F. Springston presented people with strings of letters which then had to be recalled. Sometimes the letters were grouped such as YMC-AFB-ITW-ONB-CPHD, and sometimes the same letters were grouped slightly differently, such as YMCA-FBI-TWA-NBC-PHD. People could remember the second grouping better than the first grouping, because in the second grouping they recognized familiar patterns. This result is important because it demonstrates that familiar patterns must be recognized. That is, their corresponding chunks must be activated in memory. Sometimes chunks are not activated even when the perceptual patterns they correspond to seem to be occurring in the environment. Hence, the activation of a chunks in memory depends on a process called *pattern recognition*. [*See* PATTERN RECOGNITION.]

B. Individual Differences

The number and kinds of chunks a person has in his or her mind depends on experience and training. For example, if chess masters are allowed to look at a chess game for 5 to 10 seconds, they can usually reproduce the positions of the 20 to 25 pieces involved without error, even if they have never seen the game before. Ordinary players will be able to reproduce only about six pieces. Why the differ-

ence? The reason is that chess masters have become familiar with a large number of patterns of chess pieces that reoccur in game after game. These patterns act as chunks in memory. When the chess master looks at a game, he or she sees six chunks, not 20 to 25 separate pieces. This is not true for the nonexpert, who sees many separate pieces with the location of each piece being a chunk of information. The fact that the chess master's ability is dependent on perceiving familiar patterns can be demonstrated by placing chess pieces on a chess board in a random manner. Then, both the chess masters and novices after a brief look will be able to place only about half a dozen pieces correctly. The arrangement of pieces no longer corresponds to the chunks available in the chess master's memory. Herbert Simon has estimated that a chess master has in memory 25,000 to 100,000 chunks of familiar arrangements of pieces. This "chess vocabulary" is roughly the same size as the vocabulary of an educated adult in his native language.

III. CHUNKING, CONSCIOUS MEMORY, AND REHEARSAL

In his 1890 volumes *Principles of Psychology* William James made the distinction between primary and secondary memory. Primary memory contains the information that we are immediately aware of, information that is in our consciousness. There is only a limited amount of information that we can think of at one time. Secondary memory contains information that we are not immediately aware of but, nevertheless, is accessible to us if we need it. If you are asked "What is your mother's maiden name?" you can probably respond in a short period of time, even though you probably were not thinking of your mother's maiden name when asked the question. You were able to retrieve the information from your secondary memory and make it conscious. Psychologists have a number of names for secondary memory; it has been called permanent memory, *long-term memory,* and long-term store, just as they sometimes call primary memory conscious memory, *short-term memory,* short-term store, or *working memory.* Separate sensory memories of very short duration have also been proposed. There are some subtle but important differences proposed for the memory systems described by these different terms, but for our purposes I will lump them all into just two memory systems called conscious memory and permanent memory.

William James' distinction between conscious memory and permanent memory was ignored during the period, roughly between 1910 and 1960, when behaviorism was the dominant theory in American psychology. In the 1960s, however, a number of theorists, including Richard Atkinson and Richard Shiffrin, revived the theory. The 7-chunk capacity discussed by George Miller obviously was not a characteristic of permanent memory, so there must be a conscious memory whose capacity was limited to about 7 chunks. It should be kept in mind that as models of memory have developed, theorists have argued whether the capacity of conscious memory is best described as 7, 5, or even 3 chunks. For the sake of simplicity I will stick with 7 chunks.

What was the purpose of having these two memory systems? Well, the two memory systems seem to have evolved to deal with the problem that our neurological system cannot process information as fast as it receives it. Information cannot be stored in permanent memory at a fast rate. Nor can information always be retrieved from permanent memory quickly. We all wish that we could simultaneously attend to a great deal of information and promptly remember most of it when needed, but we cannot do this. Conscious memory acts as a buffer system that holds and organizes information from the environment so that it can be sifted, organized, and possibly stored in permanent memory. Similarly, conscious memory holds information retrieved from permanent memory until we have all the information we need to remember and are ready to use it. Chunks are created in conscious memory somewhat like bricks in a mold and then stored in permanent memory. When they are needed they become active in conscious memory again.

Information, especially language information, is transmitted to us in a serial manner. If we did not have conscious memory, we would be forgetting information almost as soon as we heard it. For this reason dual-storage theorists, including Atkinson and Shiffrin, suggested that although conscious memory has a limited capacity for information, the chunking process can occur by the process of *rehearsal,* even when information is no longer available in the environment. We can store only a small number of chunks of information in conscious memory but with rehearsal maintain it there so that larger chunks can be formed. Atkinson and Shiffrin further proposed that conscious memory is primarily audi-

tory–verbal–linguistic. That is, conscious memory, which they referred to as short-term store, represents information linguistically so that it can be rehearsed over and over. The rehearsal process can result in the information in conscious memory becoming unitized into a chunk.

To illustrate the process of rehearsal and chunking, let us use the example of a child who can recognize and say each letter of the alphabet but cannot recite all the letters in their correct order. Each letter is represented by a phonetic chunk and an orthographic chunk because orthographic and phonetic patterns representing each letter are familiar to the child. Let us consider what happens if the child is hearing the recitation of the alphabet for the first time. He or she hears the sequence "abcdefghijklmnopqrstuvwxyz" but can only keep in conscious memory about 7 chunks, maybe the sequence "a, b, c, d, e, f, g" which the child may rehearse over and over. With sufficient rehearsal this becomes a chunk. With practice, additional alphabet chunks will be formed, like "h, i, j, k." In fact, when listening to children sing the alphabet, as they do on children's programs, one can hear approximately 6 chunks, somewhat like "abcdefg-hijk-lmnop-qrs-tuv-wxyz." The letter chunks or symbols have been chunked into larger strings of what we might call superchunks. These superchunks are linked together to form the alphabet.

Although disagreements and controversies have developed regarding the nature and function of rehearsal, these cannot be explored here. But I will make one more point. Rehearsal is not necessary for chunking. For example, we learn complex visual patterns by looking at them repeatedly, not by rehearsing them in conscious memory. A radiologist, like the chess master discussed above, learns patterns of visual information by repeated viewing so they become chunks in his or her memory. The same is true for the art expert learning the styles of different painters. This repeated viewing is necessary because there is some question as to how well we can rehearse visual information in conscious memory. We probably can, but to only a limited extent.

A. Chunks, Chunk Labels, and Pointers

The *dual-storage memory system,* comprising conscious memory and permanent memory, has to have a way to share information. Although the chunking process is constrained by the capacity of conscious memory, the contents and labels for chunks are transferred to permanent memory as the chunks are formed. This chunked information can then be retrieved from permanent memory when pattern recognition occurs. In pattern recognition permanent memory is quickly and automatically searched to determine if a chunk exists whose content matches the perceived pattern. When a familiar pattern is perceived, it is recognized by its correspondence with a chunk in permanent memory. However, the components of the chunk may not be transferred into conscious memory. Rather, a verbal label for the chunk may be placed in conscious memory. After reading ''elephant'' we may think of its pronunciation but not its spelling. This verbal label can then be rehearsed. This is one of the things our language is able to do for us. Does every chunk have a verbal label? Chunks include words and familiar numbers. However, we can have chunks that do not have verbal labels. For example, there are probably a great many faces we can recognize, such as faces of celebrities. However, for some of these faces we may not remember names or, perhaps, never have learned the names. Furthermore, people who are experts in chess, reading x-ray photographs, or repairing automobile engines may recognize many different diagnostic patterns in their area of expertise but not have verbal labels for them. Every chunk may not have a verbal label, but every chunk has a *pointer.* Psychological researchers have borrowed the term pointer from computer science to describe how chunks are represented in conscious memory even when they do not have verbal labels. A pointer is the chunk's *address* in permanent memory. That is, the pointer indicates where in permanent memory is stored information about the components of the chunk.

Some psychologists have suggested that conscious memory be thought of as that part of permanent memory containing pointers and labels that are currently active. Activation decays with time, so information is ''lost'' from conscious memory unless it is continually presented to us or we rehearse it. This interpretation of conscious memory seems to many psychologists to be more natural than proposing two computer-like memory systems where information is continually transferred from one to the other and back again.

B. Hierarchy of Chunks

Chunks form a hierarchy in permanent memory. For example, letters of the alphabet are chunks because they are familiar visual patterns and also have names. Digits are chunks for the same reason. But letters can be formed into words which are also chunks. Digits can be formed into familiar numbers such as 1492 or 1776. Furthermore, words can be formed into familiar sayings, such as ''A penny saved is a penny earned.'' These sayings are also chunks. Longer memorized passages may also be chunks. The pledge of allegiance, memorized poetry, prayers, and words to songs may all be chunks made up of chunked phrases and sentences. Information tends to be represented in conscious memory using chunks representing the largest amount of information. For example, when reading the lines of a familiar poem, we may think of the title of the poem. However, a chunk may be broken into its component parts in conscious memory. An example of this is when school children are asked to spell out words given to them in a spelling bee. Therefore, conscious memory can hold information while new chunks are being created, hold chunk labels or pointers, or can hold the component parts of chunks.

IV. DEFINING A CHUNK

Mental structures store information in permanent memory. In addition there are *mental processes,* such as *storage* and *retrieval,* that act upon these mental structures. But these processes can only be mentioned here. Chunks are not the only kind of mental structures. What makes a chunk unique? To define a chunk, there has to be some procedure for determining its content. A chunk representing a spoken word can be pronounced as a series of phonemes. A chunk representing a written word can be spelled. If the chunk is a visual symbol or a geometric figure, it can be drawn. If it is a pattern of chess pieces, it can be assembled on a chess board. But determining the content of a chunk is often difficult. For example, what if a chunk represents a familiar face? If a person says ''I can clearly picture her face in my mind,'' how can the features of that face be determined? Can the person draw the face? Those with special skills can. How can we be sure that the features of the face are really in conscious memory? There is a well-known example of the ambiguity of seemingly clearly experienced subjective events. Many people are certain that they can form a mental picture of a zebra. But when asked to count its stripes, they cannot do so. For a mental structure to be evaluated as a chunk, there must be a way to determine its contents. This problem of validation makes difficult some attempts to determine the content of a chunk.

Keeping in mind the requirement that the contents of an activated chunk must be verifiable, the necessary properties of a chunk are the following: (a) First, a chunk is made up of a limited amount of information; usually a small number of other chunks, the number depending which theorist one consults. This property follows from the capacity limits of conscious memory. (b) Second, a chunk is activated in memory if some critical number of its memory components are activated. That is, a chunk is available in memory. Furthermore, this availability does not greatly decrease with time. There is little forgetting of chunks. (c) Third, a chunk is unvarying in content over time. The dictionary defines a chunk as a thick mass or lump of anything. When a chunk is activated, its contents should be reported with little or no variation. Chunks are not units whose contents vary from one activation to the next.

Almost all theorists would probably agree with requirement (a). There are a number of theorists who would not agree with requirements (b) and (c), but I believe that they are necessary properties of a chunk. These requirements are discussed in more detail below.

A. Chunks Contain Perceptual Information

Mental structures can be divided roughly into *perceptual codes* and *conceptual codes*. Perceptual codes are mental structures created by our repeatedly perceiving stereotypic stimulus patterns in our environment, and conceptual codes are mental structures we create by combining information using thinking processes. For example, the conceptual code for vehicle is a concept we develop over time by understanding that there exists a class of objects that are used for transporting other objects in physical space. The printed word vehicle is, of course, a perceptual code but our concept of vehicle is a conceptual code.

The three necessary properties of a chunk listed above lead to the conclusion that chunks are primarily perceptual codes. The reason for this is that perceptual information is repeated both frequently enough to be very well-learned and therefore resistant to forgetting. Also, perceptual information is repeated stereotypically enough to define the contents of a chunk with little variability. Patterns of information generated by our thinking processes, along with many of the patterns we perceive in our environment, do not occur frequently enough or stereotypically enough to be represented by chunks in memory. Below I discuss which types of perceptual codes are chunks.

1. Which of Our Perceptions Form Chunks?

Many chunks represent language information such as printed and spoken words. Some chunks represent other symbols such as squares, circles, and crosses. Some chunks, however, represent stereotypically appearing natural objects such as faces, hands, apples, and dogs. Also, chunks represent stereotypically appearing man-made objects such as plates, forks, glasses, and bricks. Because of the necessary properties of a chunk outlined above, representations of all these types of events in memory must be limited in the number of their perceptual components. Furthermore, these events must be frequently occurring so that their chunks are not easily forgotten. Finally, these events must be constant in their appearance.

Although the contents of a chunk should be perceptually constant, there is a limit to how much constancy we can expect. Orthographies for words vary, but we learn to read various fonts and letter sizes and come to consider them to be so similar as to be interchangeable. In a similar manner, we often find that we can read notes and letters even if they are in unusual handwriting. But this problem of variability becomes acute when we consider chunks representing the visual appearance of physical objects. Although most physical objects have a word representation in memory, the visual appearance of any physical object represented by that word may not be represented by a chunk. Common words like tree, trousers, automobile, and sandwich do not represent a particular physical object but rather a class of objects. We may have a chunk for the visual appearance of a particular tree, a particular pair of trousers, a particular automobile, or a particular type of sandwich because each represents a familiar, frequently occurring physical object. The chair we sit at every day in our office may be represented by a chunk in memory. That chunk representing a particular chair is associated in memory to the concept chair and also associated with the chunk representing the spoken word chair and the written word chair. However, we may not have a representational chunk for a class of objects such as tree, trouser, automobile, sandwich, or chair. On the other hand, some classes of objects may be so stereotyped in appearance that we have a chunk for the appearance of the object associated with its label. This may be true for an object such as a fork, which is simply a handle with four tines at the end. But do all chairs look similar enough to have a representational chunk? Probably not.

B. Concepts Are Not Chunks

Keep in mind that we have a mental representation called a concept for each class of objects, such as chairs or cars. But we do not necessarily have a chunk representing the physical features of that class of objects. The concept chair contains a vast amount of information relevant to chairs, but we may not have a chunk representing a stereotypic visual representation of a chair. We may be able to draw a prototypical chair, but that prototype may correspond to few or none of the chairs that we regularly perceive. The *prototype* is not a chunk based on perception but is a mental inference based on our experience with a wide variety of chairs over our lifetime. This point has been made by the psychologist Eleanor Rosch who discusses the importance of prototypes in categorization decisions. The perceptual components of a chair may not be perceptually experienced by us in a way stereotypic enough to form a chunk. Chunks are percepts not concepts. [*See* CATEGORIZATION.]

Even though we may not have chunks in memory representing the appearance of object classes, we have pattern recognition processes that allow to identify objects. In a process called *perceptual categorization* an object we perceive is categorized as representing a familiar concept. Sometimes this is a difficult process. Is an object a cup or a bowl? Is an object a chair or a stool? A chunk may exist for the spoken and written representations of these classes objects and even for the perceptual features of a particular object in the class but not for the perceptual features of the object class itself. We may be able to correctly identify a newly designed chair as a chair, although we never saw it before.

C. Definitions of Objects Are Not Chunks

The results of our thinking processes are not stereotyped enough to form chunks. I demonstrate this by a simple example. If we do not have chunks to represent the perceptual features of common classes of objects, can we have some other information in

memory regarding these objects that does form a chunk? Does the information in a linguistic definition of a common object form a chunk of information? To determine this, I performed an experiment in which college students listed the features of eight common objects: apple, car, cat, chair, doll, gun, hammer, and robin. They then did exactly the same task one week later. The mean number of features listed for the objects was about 7.5, which is approximately the number of components in a chunk. However, for each object the average student listed only about 55% of the same features from one week to the next. That is, about half the features of an object he or she gave one week was given the other week. Although our knowledge of the defining features of a common object expressed in language is reasonably stable, it is not stable enough to be considered as a chunk of information.

D. Categories Are Not Chunks

If verbal descriptions of common classes of objects do not form chunks, what about larger mental structures such as superordinate categories of objects? An apple is a fruit, a car is a vehicle, a cat is a four-footed animal, a chair is an article of furniture, and a hammer is a tool. Do definitions of superordinate categories form chunks? In the same experiment as described above for definitions of objects, I asked students to define eight categories of objects using lists of features. These categories were articles of clothing, human dwellings, fish, flowers, insects, stones, trees, and vegetables. The results were pretty much the same as for the object classes. An average of 6.6 features were given for each category, but the average student listed only 46% of the same features for a category from one week to the next. Like mental structures containing definitions of objects classes, the knowledge representing definitions of categories expressed in language is not stable or unitized enough to be considered a chunk.

Categories can be defined both intrinsically, as above when defining features were listed, and also extrinsically by listing instances of the category. Do these extrinsic definitions of categories form a chunk? This is doubtful because the number of instances people can give of a category seemed beyond the capacity of conscious memory. However, to verify that lists of category instances do not comprise a chunk, I asked a group of college students to write down all the instances they could of 12 common categories such as four-footed animals, birds, articles of furniture, and so on. They had plenty of time to do this, and they had to do exactly the same task one week later. As expected, they typically generated anywhere from 12 to 40 items, depending on the category. This is obviously too much information for one chunk. Also, for any category the typical student listed one week only about 69% of the instances he or she listed the other week. The rest of the instances were unique to the session. Category instances are too large and unstable a set of information in memory to form a chunk. If we assume that chunks are derived primarily from perceptual information, this result makes sense. For example, people do not experience all four-footed animals together to provide a perceptual basis for the formation of a category. Rather, instances of a category are associated to the category label singly or in small numbers over a period of time. Because of this process, the instances of a category may not be particularly well-defined. As Eleanor Rosch has suggested, many categories have fuzzy boundaries. For example, is a kangaroo a four-footed animal, or is a chimpanzee a four-footed animal? People are often not sure about what instances belong in a category.

Although categories do not seem to be chunks, George Mandler has proposed that categories are organized hierarchically such that subcategory groupings exist which are chunks and contain about five category members each. Verbal labels are not necessary for these chunks, but in the category of four-footed animals one may think of farm animals (cow, pig, horse, goat, sheep), savanna animals (lion, elephant, giraffe, hyena, zebra), and so on, as comprising possible chunks. One of the ways in which Mandler has investigated these subcategories is to have a person name as many items as he or she can from some category. Researchers have found that after every five or so instances the person pauses. This pause indicates that an interrelated group of category instances has been retrieved from permanent memory and the person has finished naming them. During the pause the person searches permanent memory for another group of category items. Mandler has proposed labeling these category subunits as chunks. But are they chunks according to the definition being used here? Mandler and Arthur Graesser performed an experiment in which they asked people to name items from various categories. They asked people to do this task twice. During each generation session they used interresponse times to determine which generated instances belong to the same grouping. Mandler and Graesser found that

two category instances occurred in the same grouping from session to session only 72% of the time. Having the same group of three, four, or five instances occurring in the same grouping would be a value much lower than 72%. These values indicate that information in subcategory units is not interrelated to the extent needed to make the unit a chunk.

E. Chunks Are Part of Semantic Memory

In 1972 Endel Tulving made an important distinction between two kinds of permanent memory. First, there is memory for well-learned knowledge such as vocabulary meanings, correct grammar, well-known facts, basic mathematical skills, and so on. This kind of memory Tulving called *semantic memory*. This is memory for information that we know very well. We know this information so well and have used it so often that we usually cannot remember the exact time or place when we first learned it. The other kind of memory is *episodic memory*. This is our memory for events in our lives. Associated with memories about events is information that gives us some idea of when and where these events occurred. Tulving pointed out that for many years psychologists had been performing experiments believing that they were changing semantic memory. For the most part, however, laboratory experiments involved episodic memory, because new experiences were created for the participants who were later tested to determine how much they remembered about these particular events. After the experiment, these experiences would be mostly forgotten with little permanent effect on the participant's semantic memory. [*See* EPISODIC MEMORY; SEMANTIC MEMORY.]

Considering the requirement that chunks be stable over time, I suggest that chunks be considered part of semantic memory. This point of view is not shared by all researchers. In his renowned 1956 article George Miller mentioned the work of William Bousfield. In some of his experiments Bousfield presented people a list of words such as "dog, apple, sofa, truck, banana, airplane, cat, table, ship, chair, lamb, peach, lamp, bicycle, pear, cow." When asked to recall the list, people tended to groups the words together in clusters according to what category the word belonged, such as dog, cat, lamb, cow; apple, banana, peach, pear; sofa, table, chair, lamp; and truck, airplane, ship, bicycle. A number of psychologists have suggested that people were "chunking" the words. Why might we consider these sets of four words chunks? First, the sets represent a small number of components. Second, the components are highly related; they belong to a common category. Also, they tend to be recalled together after the list is presented. I suggest, however, these memory units are not chunks because they represent episodic events whose representations in memory are transient in nature. They do not represent a frequently occurring perceptual pattern. The representations of the groupings in memory represent an event that has occurred in a particular time and place and are associated with that time and place. The units formed are part of episodic memory, not part of semantic memory. If the word combination dog, cat, lamb, cow co-occurred very frequently in our culture, like north, south, east, and west, then it might be represented as a chunk in memory. But the interassociations among the words dog, cat, lamb, cow result from the fact that (a) they happen to have occurred in the same word list together, and (b) they belong to the same semantic category of animals. The same is also true for the other word groupings. Just because a set of words are experienced once and are all instances of the same semantic category, they are not necessarily formed into a chunk.

To further make the point that this representation in episodic memory is not a chunk, consider the following thought experiment. It is possible that the Bousfield procedure mentioned above could be performed every day using the same college students. Every day they would be presented a list of words from the same four categories and they would have to recall the words, which they might do quite well, clustering words from the same category. However, some of the words could be repeated from day to day, but some new words from the same categories could also be introduced. This procedure could be repeated for 100 days. Would new chunks be formed each day using different combinations of repeated and nonrepeated words? I suggest not. These memory structures are better considered as representing events in episodic memory that are usually forgotten with time.

V. THE CONTINUUM OF MENTAL STRUCTURES

I have suggested that chunks are primarily perceptual codes not conceptual codes. But I would like to go further and make a distinction among three types of mental structures ranging from the most stereotypically organized in memory to the least ste-reotypically organized. These I will label chunks, cognitive units, and knowledge structures, with cognitive units and knowledge structures representing types of conceptual codes. These three types of mental structures should not be thought of as forming discrete and well-defined categories. Rather, chunks are at one end of a continuum, representing small amounts of stable and well-defined perceptual information, and knowledge structures are at the other end, representing large amounts of weakly interrelated information.

A. Chunks

A chunk represents familiar and repeated perceptual patterns. A distinction is not always made between the mental content of a chunk and the physical stimulus it represents, and this error emphasizes the point that chunks result from perception. The information in chunks is highly integrated because the sensory components upon which those chunks are based are highly integrated, and those components consistently co-occur in the same temporal and spatial pattern.

B. Cognitive Units

A *cognitive unit* is much like a chunk. A cognitive unit is a mental structure in which the information in memory is limited in quantity, being able to fit in conscious memory and is interrelated. As in a chunk, information in a cognitive unit tends to be learned at the same time. Also, all the information in a cognitive unit tends to be recalled from memory at the same time. However, the information in a cognitive unit is not as highly interrelated as in a chunk. The information in a cognitive unit is more easily forgotten than information in a chunk because it is not as frequently experienced. A cognitive unit may be thought of as a temporary chunk, a soft chunk, or a protochunk. The subunits formed and recalled from the categorized word lists presented by Bousfield might be considered cognitive units. If a cognitive unit with consistent components is experienced often enough, it will become a chunk in memory.

John R. Anderson has evaluated a variety of mental structures as cognitive units. One of these is the *proposition*. Not only do we have concepts such as father, but we organize these concepts into memory representations of propositions, such as "John Adams was the father of John Quincy Adams." In addition to propositions, *frames* may be cognitive units. Frames include co-occurring features of classes of objects. Many automobiles look very similar, but we know that automobiles are not stereotypic in their appearance. But automobiles do have components in stereotypical spatial and mechanical relations to one other. Automobiles have a horizontal chassis suspended on four wheels carrying a power source, steering controls, a body, and so on. As demonstrated in an experiment discussed above, we can list these attributes with only a fair amount of reliability, indicating that frames are not chunks.

Another possible cognitive unit is a *script*. Scripts have been proposed as a mental structures by Roger Schank and Robert Abelson. A script is a set of stereotyped activities in which we engage in certain situations, such as eating in a restaurant, traveling on a commercial airline, or preparing in the morning for our daily activities. Scripts and frames are sometimes referred to as types of *schemas*. Are scripts chunks? I did an experiment on generating scripts like the experiments described above in which college students generated activities for 10 scripts one week and then did the identical task one week later. Students generated approximately 16 to 20 actions in each script, too much information for a chunk. As in previous experiments, the content of scripts was not found to be reliable. Only about 50% of the actions of a script listed one week were listed the other week. Scripts might be made up of smaller units called scenes. There is little information as to whether scenes are chunks.

C. Knowledge Structures

A *knowledge structure* is any set of interrelated information in memory. This interrelated information may be composed of chunks, cognitive units, and other knowledge structures. Knowledge structures are loose but extensive collections of information in memory representing such topics as politics, intelligence, recreation, human relations, and so on.

VI. THE INTERRELATEDNESS OF MENTAL STRUCTURES

I have discussed how chunks are formed by repeatedly experiencing stereotypic perceptual patterns. How are the other mental structures formed? Many, if not most, of our mental structures are the result of thought processes not under the strict control of environmental events. Thinking can result in the organization or interassociation of information in memory where that information does not represent stereotypical perceptual patterns. The purpose of much of our thinking is to overcome the restrictions of organizing information based only on perception. In thinking we manipulate symbols, which sometimes representing chunks but sometimes representing other types of knowledge structures, to produce knowledge that goes beyond perceptual information. Thinking is a process that includes the manipulation of symbols whose perceptual content is often not very well defined and whose perceptual content may vary from one instance of its use to the next.

Mental structures such as chunks, cognitive units (propositions, frames, scripts, and some concepts), and knowledge structures are all interrelated in memory. This is not the place to discuss the nature of these relations or the processes by which these interrelations are used in *cognitive processes*. However, in a number of cognitive theories a mental structure once stimulated will stimulate another mental structures though the flow of mental *activation*. This activation flows through the associative links established among the various mental structures.

A. Integration versus Elaboration

The notion of a chunk presented here fits in with the distinction that has been made between activation of a particular chunk in memory versus activating mental structures associated with that chunk. These two processes have been given various labels such as intra-code processing versus inter-code processing. Intra-code processing is the way a chunk is activated. Activation is automatic, that is unintentional, and all the components of the chunk become activated in memory. Intra-code processing takes place on a particular perceptual code, that is, on a particular chunk and does not extend beyond that chunk. George Mandler has called this intra-code processing integration and has suggested that integration occurs automatically because the very strong connections among the features of the chunk carry the activation to all its components very easily. In contrast to this process, Mandler calls the process of inter-code activation elaboration because elaboration requires some conscious intention. The relations among chunks and among other mental structures are not strong enough for activation to spread

589

automatically. Inter-code processing depends on the person intentionally thinking about other memory structures to which the chunk may be related in memory. This process is not automatic, and which of the other mental structures are to be activated is not easily predictable. Inter-code processing takes place among mental structures, including among chunks.

Bibliography

Anderson, J. R. (1980). Concepts, propositions, and schemata: What are the cognitive units? "Nebraska Symposium on Motivation" In H. E. Howe, Jr., and J. H. Flowers, Eds.), Vol. 28, pp. 121–162. University of Nebraska Press, Lincoln.

Bellezza, F. S. (1988). Reliability of retrieving information from knowledge structures in memory: Scripts. *Bull. Psychonom. Soc.* **26,** 11–14.

Mandler, G. (1975). Memory storage and retrieval: Some limits on the research of attention and consciousness. In "Attention and Performance" (P. M. A. Rabbit and S. Dornic, Eds.), Vol. 5, pp. 499–516. Academic Press, New York.

Mandler, G. (1989). Memory: Conscious and unconscious. In "Memory: Interdisciplinary Approaches" (P. R. Soloman, G. R. Goethals, C. M. Kelley, and B. R. Stephens, Eds.), Springer-Verlag, New York.

Miller, G. A. (1956). The magical number seven, plus or minus two: Some limits in our capacity for processing information. *Psychol. Rev.* **63,** 81–97.

Simon, H. A. (1974). How big is a chunk? *Science* **183,** 482–488.

Tulving, E. (1972). Episodic and semantic memory. In "Organization and Memory" (E. Tulving and W. Donaldson, Eds.), pp. 381–403. Academic Press, New York.

CLASSICAL CONDITIONING

Robert L. Thompson
Hunter College, City University of New York

Glossary

Conditioning The operation of arranging contingencies within or between stimulus classes and response classes with the intent of behavior modification or analysis. The process by which behavior is thereby modified.

Contingency A predictive relationship among events. A common quantitative expression of contingency is some mathematical function of the conditional probability of one event given the other and given the absence of the other. Terms such as pairing and contiguity do not capture all that contingency does. Paired or contiguous events may or may not be contingent.

CLASSICAL CONDITIONING refers to the modification of behavior by stimulus–stimulus contingencies. The first systematic treatment of many of the phenomena of what is now called classical conditioning was elaborated by the Russian physiologist Ivan P. Pavlov (1849–1936) in collaboration with many students and colleagues. Since the publication of his conditioning work in English (1906, 1927, 1928) and its endorsement by a number of distinguished American psychologists in the first three decades of this century, the range of species and responses on which the principles have been demonstrated has grown enormously, as has research on the mechanisms, complexities, interpretation, and areas of application to human concerns.

I. TERMINOLOGY, BACKGROUND, AND BASIC CONCEPTS

Let us start with a mechanistic/materialistic conception of the living organism as moving through time as the locus of a stream of behavior. This view is not incompatible with some kinds of cognitive/computational/information-processing thinking, or even with William James' stream of consciousness, depending upon how we conceive of consciousness. The present view is not dualistic. It requires that we recognize that ultimately we know the world through our senses and our actions, however voluntary or involuntary our actions may be.

The behavior stream may be represented as a nexus of concurrent input and output events, traditionally called stimulus and response events, but in large part ultimately abstractable with reference to the independent and dependent variables in the scientific study of behavior. Of the continuous stream of input (sensory, afferent, stimulus, S) events, some are relatively constant and some changing. Some originate from constant or variable features of the environment, some from the organism's own behavior or from the consequences of its behavior in the environment, external or internal. They enter the various processing stages of the nervous system through exteroceptive, proprioceptive, and interoceptive channels. Of the stream of output (efferent, response, R) events through muscles and glands, some are relatively stable (as are those originating in held postures) and some are changing from moment to moment. Some S and R events are punctate, some extended in time. Some are recurrent, some not. Many Ss and Rs will determine the Ss and Rs that follow in the environment or from the organism (variously because of its dynamic processing capacity or its "hard wiring" or its plasticity). An experimenter deliberately intrudes well-specified stimulus events into the behavior stream at well-specified intervals and in well-specified relations to each other or to S and R events in the behavior stream. Some Ss and Rs are more vivid or salient, some more important biologically or socially. Whether their significance is innate or acquired is not important here. What is important are correlations or contingencies among the S and R events that arise "naturally" or by contrivance: Two-term contingencies as in R–R, S–R, S–S, and R–S; three-term contingencies as in S–R–S, S–S–S, etc.; and still higher order contingencies.

Even the two-term contingencies are not as simple as they seem. Just about all Rs produce Ss as feedback. (That is how the brain "knows" that they have happened.) Whether a part of the stream of behavior is called an S or an R depends on where we look for it, how we measure it, and what we do with it. However arbitrary, the classes of Rs and Ss provide one set of logical categories for an analysis of behavior. Correlations among R classes (R–R) direct us to the "structure" of actions. Reflex relationships are indicated by S–R correlations, and as we pursue them we encounter all the phenomena, all the processes and laws of the reflex that came to light in the 18th, 19th, and 20th centuries. Habituation, the decline in response properties with repeated presentations of the stimulus, is one such process that figures importantly in a perspective on learning.

In S–S relations we must contend with the consequences of one class of stimuli being associated with another class, and ask which go together "naturally" (redness and ripeness, dark clouds and rain, lightning and thunder) and which by contrivance (the dinner bell and opportunity to eat), and what this does to the stream of behavior. These are the problems of classical conditioning. On the other hand, response–outcome relations (R–S, sometimes written as R–O) direct our attention to the consequences of actions and we enter the rich field of instrumental or operant learning.

The careful observer soon recognizes many complications. In one of our S–S examples lightning is followed by a thunder clap. But the stream of S and R events is continuous and ever changing. Some Rs occur more often, some less often. We say that we learn to anticipate the thunder, but that means that we do something such as covering our ears, or tensing our neck. Rs intervene in the S–S sequence, attenuating the loudness and surprisingness of the thunder. Other Rs such as those comprising nonchalance are punished by the thunder clap and become less frequent. What started as an S–S contingency became an S–R–S contingency having operant

(R–S) features as well as S–S features. The final S in the three-term contingency, its "value" somehow modified by the anticipatory response, is an outcome (O) of that R as well as as an outcome of the initial S, the lightning. In the classic Pavlovian preparation to be described in more detail later, conditioned salivation made the food powder more palatable and facilitated its ingestion. Without arguing the case further, every stimulus–stimulus contingency potentially gives rise to intervening (conditioned) Rs which have a sometimes functional, sometimes adventitious instrumental outcome. It is difficult to talk about the S–S contingencies of classical conditioning without considering the consequences that conditioned responses may have, i.e., operant conditioning, but let us try.

Classical conditioning is also widely known as Pavlovian conditioning, respondent conditioning, or reflex conditioning. In the early literature it was also called Type I, Type S, associative shifting, or simply, conditioning. Classical conditioning is distinguished from operant or instrumental conditioning in which behavior is modified by response–outcome contingencies. Both kinds of contingencies may be elaborated in various and complex ways, e.g., by being in effect only in certain contexts or in the presence of other signals (stimuli), or by being quantitatively modulated according to environmental conditions or states of the organism. How these two kinds of contingencies interact, how they are to be conceived theoretically, and what kinds of neural processes participate in their expression are among the continuing questions that inspire research on basic processes in behavior.

Much of the modern study of classical conditioning is also concerned with experimental analysis of the properties of the relevant stimuli and the limits of their effectiveness, the kinds of relationships among stimuli that are successful or unsuccessful in changing behavior, the classes of behavior that can be changed by these procedures, the kinds of changes that occur, and the relative permanence of the changes. Behavior modifications may occur in either direction; they may be excitatory or inhibitory. It is just as important to ignore or not respond or to stop responding to certain signals as it is to start responding to others. It has also come to be appreciated that stimuli do not exist in a vacuum. Every stimulus occurrence is in some context or setting. The context or some aspect of it enters into a kind of compound with the explicitly manipulated stimulus, and this must be taken into account in studying the functions of the stimulus. Further, the individually manipulated stimulus itself is multidimensional. A tone has among its psychological attributes, pitch, loudness, duration, and dimensions that reflect how often it has occurred and the intervals between occurrences. Not all of these attributes are likely to share equally in whatever "value," signaling power, or associative strength the tone may acquire.

The term classical conditioning refers to both an operation and a process. As an operation or procedure its defining property is the occurrence of what are typically two stimulus events in some specifiable temporal or spatial order, and without regard to anything the subject organism may be doing. For example, at regular intervals the sound of a buzzer may be followed by the delivery of food. This is called a response-independent procedure. The specifiable order is called a contingency, a special kind of correlation. Each event is called a stimulus; the plural form is stimuli. The stimuli are presumed to be discriminable by (within the sensory capabilities of) the participating subject organism—human or nonhuman. Usually the sequence of events can be repeated, but this is not necessary. It does not matter whether the events in point occur in or out of the laboratory, or whether they are experimentally arranged or occur "naturally." Strictly speaking, it does not matter if there is no behavioral effect of the procedure. The occurrence of the stimulus sequence so that it is at least potentially detectable by the subject constitutes a classical conditioning "trial." Of course, we are most interested in those stimulus pairings that have an effect on behavior, and in those that ought to have an effect but seem not to.

As an inferred process of behavioral change resulting from the pairing of stimulus events, classical conditioning is an elementary if not essential process in learning. In the prototypical case, the second member of the stimulus pair reliably evokes instances of a strong (high probability, high magnitude, short latency, low threshold) response class or several such classes. In Pavlov's well-known investigations, a hungry dog, adapted to the laboratory routine, when presented with food or a signal for food such as the sounding of a metronome for, say, 30 seconds, might lunge toward the source, make various head, mouth, tongue, and swallowing movements, and salivate copiously. (By diverting the duct of one of the several pairs of salivary glands externally through a small surgical incision in the cheek, Pavlov could measure automatically a representative sample of the total salivary flow with little interference with the normal responses to food.) Given the motor and secretory activities, Pavlov chose to measure only salivation because, at the time, it was easier to measure quantitatively and could be taken as representative of the entire pattern of alimentary activity, even including stomach secretions. The second member of our prototypical stimulus pair, the stronger stimulus, food in the mouth in this case, Pavlov called the unconditioned stimulus (US). More likely, a better translation of his Russian term is thought to be unconditional stimulus because the strong response that it evoked was an unconditional response (UR), it was virtually certain to occur. The correlation between the UR and the antecedent US was called an unconditional reflex. The first member of the stimulus pair, the sound of the metronome in this case, the to be conditioned stimulus, typically did not initially evoke anything like the degree or kind of response(s) that the US did. Rather, the first stimulus probably evoked an investigatory or orienting response of small magnitude. After one pairing, but almost always after several more pairings (trials), the first stimulus came to evoke responses other than the orienting response. These new responses may or may not have features in common with the URs, but they were conditional upon the pairing with the US, so they were called conditional responses (CRs) and the first stimulus was now a conditioned or conditional stimulus (CS), a member of a new stimulus–response correlation called a conditional reflex. The change in behavior resulting from the process of systematic pairing of two stimuli, CS and US, in that order, was the increase in probability of a class of responses, salivary secretions, evoked by the initially ineffective CS. There is more that should be noted. Salivation was not the only conditional response. Movements and postures of the dog's head and body also occurred in the period before food delivery. Pavlov did not ignore these, but still emphasized the salivary secretions as representative of all that went on. Later investigators made much of the motor aspects of Pavlov's procedure. Suitable control procedures (some of which followed only decades later) were necessary to show the CRs to be conditional upon the contingency between US and CS, not simply that they were contiguous or paired. These conditional responses (CRs) are learned responses.

Conditioning is called a learning process. If it is *the* learning process or if there are many learning processes cannot be answered easily. In need of a definition, learning is an abstraction that refers to a class of behavioral changes, a class whose borders are inevitably vague. The class called learning refers to relatively long-lasting changes in the probability of certain behavior as a result of experience. But only certain kinds of experience are relevant. For instance, changes in behavior due to fatigue are ruled out as a learning experience. Sometimes a distinction is made between associative and nonassociative learning. The latter embraces sensitization and habituation. but these sometimes receive associative treatments. To illustrate changes in behavior attributable to the experiencing of stimulus–stimulus contingencies we can take examples from a virtually inexhaustable number of instances: learning to fear the dentist's drill, feeling relief when a dental procedure is seen to be over, coming to anticipate a tasty meal in a certain restaurant, having a sensation of nausea on tasting a food that once made us sick, expecting to hear a loud clap of thunder after seeing a nearby lightning flash, having a mental image of a friend when his name is mentioned. In the first of these examples, the sight, sound, and thought of the drill has been paired with painful stimulation from the drill as it was applied to one's tooth. In the second case, the dentist's setting aside of his instruments signals that the treatment procedure during which one has felt uncomfortable and stressed is just about over. The reader should be able to construct an account of the other examples. Psychologists long ago abandoned attempts to assemble a catalog of all possible reflexes. Because of the facts of conditioning, the list might never end.

At first glance the examples above all appear to deal with feelings of anticipation or expectation, emotions, private events in general. But commonly, feelings and emotions interact with whatever else an individual may be doing, and in that way become indirectly observable, or at least inferable. Moreover, feelings and emotions are accompanied by outer activity, muscular tension, restlessness, facial expressions, scanning to look for the restaurant in one of our examples. (Some theorists would say that the motor activity *is* the feeling. At least, it is not always clear which comes first, the muscular activity or the private feeling.)

The reach of classical conditioning extends beyond feelings and emotions to include large-scale motor activities such as the approach to or tracking and manipulation of signals or objects predicting the imminent availability of biologically significant or otherwise valued substances or events. And physio-

logical events of all kinds have been held to work according to Pavlovian rules. In the fields of psychoneuroimmunology and behavioral medicine, suppression and enhancement of the activity of the immune system are lively topics essential to the understanding of factors conducive to health and disease. The regulation of cardiovascular processes, appetites and addictions, placebo effects, and, of course, digestive processes are finely tuned through conditioning principles. In the realm of cognitive science, associative/computational/connectionistic models of thought processes, perceptual phenomena, mental imagery, and the act of remembering are illuminated by the modern understanding of the complex texture of event relationships that emerge from conditioning experiments. In many cases the data and their interpretation are still controversial, and just how much activity under the skin we will accept as in the province of behavior analysis is itself arguable. From the present perspective, any activity of any part of an individual—a cell, an organ, a muscle group, the entire organism—that can be observed and measured and shown to systematically vary with other observable and measurable events can be considered as behavior. To speak of behavior, then, is not simply to speak of what a creature or part of it is doing, but also why it is being done, i.e., to include the responsible independent variables.

Lest we put too much emphasis on internal events, note that perhaps the first American scientific report of conditioned responses appeared in 1902 as a Ph.D. thesis from the University of Pennsylvania. Edwin B. Twitmyer authored *A Study of the Knee Jerk.* Knee jerks were systematically observed to occur to a signal preceding a strike to the patellar tendon. American psychologists were not interested then, and for a long time thereafter. Even after Pavlov's work was well known, many psychologists believed that it was applicable mainly to activities principally controlled by the autonomic nervous system acting on the internal organs (i.e., smooth muscles and glands) and not to the skeletal musculature which was thought to be amenable only to operant or instrumental conditioning (response–outcome contingencies). A body of work on the conditioning of motor responses such as limb flexion in humans and animals was advanced by another Russian and former colleague of Pavlov's, V. M. Bekhterev. Bekhterev's work was taken up by a number of American behaviorists since it was accessible in a French translation in 1913, well before the main body of

Pavlov's work was available in translation from the Russian. Theorists came to see Bekhterev's procedures as confounding the distinction between stimulus–stimulus and response–outcome contingencies. It was not until after 1968 when Brown and Jenkins described autoshaping or sign-tracking, the conditioning of skeletal muscular responses (often part of a consummatory complex) by stimulus–stimulus contingencies, that the applicability of Pavlovian procedures to motor learning and performance was widely accepted.

Autoshaping was not the only issue that brought up questions of the usefulness of the classical/instrumental distinction. One of Pavlov's basic conditioning procedures was called temporal conditioning. A US alone occurred at regular intervals and subjects came to respond as the time for the US was near. Time was said to act as the CS. Similarly, B. F. Skinner introduced a procedure which he called superstitious conditioning (now called a fixed-time schedule). An operant reinforcer, food, a prototypical US, was delivered at regular intervals without regard to a response contingency. Again, subjects came to respond differentially as the time for food was near. Skinner focused on motor responses, and Pavlov on the salivary glands. The superstition experiment was replicated and extended by several researchers. Without belaboring the results, it was clear that this was another paradigm in which an operant or a Pavlovian analysis seemed a somewhat arbitrary choice. A contemporary view holds that the distinction between classical and instrumental conditioning is valid only on operational grounds. It does not say anything about a difference in learning processes. Formally, stimulus–stimulus contingencies are response-independent procedures, but they inevitably give rise to intervening responses or are intruded upon by intervening response components of the behavior stream. Similarly, response–outcome procedures must occur in a context (one cannot press a lever for food unless a lever is present), so at the very least, the context is inevitably paired with the outcome, i.e., a stimulus–stimulus contingency is built into the response-outcome operation. Discrimination training procedures make this explicit in creating a three-term contingency between a signal, instances of a selected response class, and an outcome.

Classical conditioning is said to be the prototype of learning about signals, or what is associated with what. For Pavlov, it was an empiricist's solution to the philosopher's problem of how associations are acquired, strengthened, and maintained. Viewing classical conditioning as a fundamental process in associative learning, Robert Rescorla, a prominent research scientist in the area, is concerned with identifying the associative relations that emerge in conditioning experiments. For him, three questions claim attention in any conditioning experiment: What is actually learned, how the learning is expressed in performance, and what conditions are responsible for learning. Other investigators emphasize other questions, e.g., what is the role of classical conditioning in the successful survival of the individual and the species.

Rescorla's view, widely accepted, is that classical conditioning amounts to learning the relations among events as a means of some kind of representation of the environment. Behavior changes appropriately, but what actually is learned? Is it enough to speak only at a behavioral/descriptive level? The question of what is actually learned is an old and enduring one, although it certainly has its critics. Must it have a concrete physical/physiological answer or will theoretical abstractions, metaphors, or analogies do? Is it a specific glandular secretion or muscular movement or act; an expectancy or anticipation of an upcoming stimulus event; a preparatory response appropriate to the event; a mental representation of the event or events in the environmental context; a set of associations as neural traces bonded in some manner? Does the CS come to substitute for the US? (One of the clearest conclusions from modern research is that the stimulus substitution hypothesis simply will not do.)

And how shall the learning be translated into behavior? Will salivation occur to a signal for food even if the Pavlovian dog is not hungry? How is the expectancy of a painful hypodermic injection realized as a change in blood pressure and heart rate? Can new experimental procedures reveal learning when conventional measures ruled it out? And inevitably we must ask about the necessary and sufficient conditions for bringing about this learning, however we characterize it. What determines an effective contingency? Is contiguity in space and/or time essential? Do the requirements for learning change at different stages of learning? Numerous books collecting research reports and reviews, dozens of scientific journals, and serial publications such as *The Psychology of Learning and Motivation,* the *Annual Review of Psychology,* and the *Annual Review of Neuroscience* address these and many more issues at the forefront of conditioning.

II. BEHAVIORAL PROCESSES

A minimum understanding of an individual's actions must deal with their acquisition, maintenance, and elimination. A full account must go further and address the source (provenance) of a class of behavior, its initiation and strengthening, its spatial organization and locus, its integration and modulation, its maintenance (including aspects of memory storage and retrieval), its weakening, termination, and elimination. The great range of variables affecting any one class of actions or processes may seem unmanageable except in the controlled conditions of the laboratory. The perspective can be enlarged still more to take into account the functional significance of each class of behavior (its biological fitness or survival value), its ontogeny (development), and evolution.

Pavlov and his co-workers explored these themes, elucidating the many properties of CS–CR–US–UR relations. Since that time, research has greatly enlarged the depth and extent of our knowledge of basic behavioral processes in general and of classical conditioning in particular. Almost any textbook on learning has sections on such processes as:

1. Acquisition—the so-called "learning curve" in which systematic changes in the probability, magnitude, latency, and other measures of the conditional response (CR) are tracked in the course of conditioning trials. Acquisition may occur in one trial as in certain cases when a flavor is paired with a substance causing illness, or may be protracted over a large number of trials. The quality and intensity (magnitude) of the CS and US under consideration, their temporal and contingent relations, the history of the individual subject (both recent and phylogenetic), the presence of competing contingencies with other USs, and other variables will determine the course of acquisition and its final, asymptotic level. (Conditioning does not go on forever. Each combination of variables can support some ultimate level which is approached more and more gradually as the number of trials increases. Later trials may add little or no "associative strength" to the CS. For some cognitive theories, this is because the US is reliably "expected" or is no longer "surprising.")

2. Pseudoconditioning—the phenomenon of sensitization, an increase in the strength of the UR or of responses to the CS as a result of US occurrence alone. Sensitization is usually considered a nonassociative process, even more "primitive" than classical conditioning. A critical consideration in the design of experiments intending to demonstrate classical conditioning is to provide a control to evaluate the possible contribution of sensitization to the CS–CR relation, i.e., to distinguish associative from nonassociative factors in conditioning.

3. Habituation—effects of pre-exposure of the subject to CS or US presentations on the magnitude of the responses they evoke, and the impediments to acquisition of CRs that may follow. Over repeated presentations of CS or US alone, sensitization effects, if any, dissipate, and the orienting response to the CS and the UR to the US weakens.

4. Extinction—the operation in which US is withheld following CS occurrences, and the process by which CRs are rendered less likely or eliminated thereby. Resistance to extinction is a useful index of the strength of conditioning.

5. Spontaneous recovery—in which CRs weakened by extinction or orienting responses reduced by habituation regain strength after the passage of time.

6. Reconditioning—in which rapid reestablishment of CRs is effected when once again US is contingent upon CS following a period of extinction.

7. Generalization—in which stimuli having properties in common with those of the original CS, but not identical to it, will now evoke the CR, the effect decreasing as the stimulus difference increases.

8. Discrimination learning—in which US occurrence is made contingent upon some particular property of the CS (CS+, e.g., the diameter of a circle) and withheld when that property is absent (CS−, e.g., circles having a different diameter). This is one way in which differences in environmental conditions are made significant. Discrimination learning may also occur within a stimulus presentation as when a CS of, say, 30 seconds duration comes to evoke a CR only in the final few seconds. In this temporal discrimination, the first part of the CS, being unaccompanied by the US, functions like a CS− while only the final part may function as CS+. Discrimination learning is the method of choice for assessing sensory capacity. In Pavlov's laboratories, attempts to train very fine

discriminations occasionally led to behavioral disturbances characterized as "experimental neuroses" and which had later relevance for Pavlov's forays into psychiatry.

9. Induction—in which properties of the CR may be enhanced on a CS+ trial immediately preceded by a CS− trial or trials (positive induction), or diminished on a CS− trial that closely followed a CS+ trial or trials (negative induction).

10. Overshadowing—in which when CSs are presented in combination (called a compound CS), say an odor and a tone together signal the presentation of a morsel of food, only one member of the compound may become effective in evoking the CR. The more "salient" stimulus, the one for which the individual may be better "prepared" biologically or experientially, overshadows the other stimulus.

11. Blocking—in which prior conditioning of one member of a stimulus compound prevents the second member from becoming an effective CS. The informativeness of the first stimulus appears to be sufficient, and the second stimulus, because it is redundant, may be effectively ignored.

12. Context effects—the environment in which CSs and USs occur serves as a stimulus source or context which enters into a compound with CSs and is a predictor of the frequency of USs. Context effects are topics for much contemporary research which indicates their importance in analysis of the dynamics of the conditioning process.

13. Second-order conditioning—in which the CS from a set of CS–US contingent pairings functions like a US in contingent pairings with a new CS. For example, a tone is established as a CS by repeated pairing with a US. Next, a light is established as a CS by pairings with the tone alone. The light has become a second-order CS. Pavolv discussed such higher-order conditioning as the key to the wide applicability of conditioning processes to complex social behavior. However, his second-order conditioning results were seldom stable, and his attempts at third-order conditioning were less successful yet. Today, more stable second-order conditioning has been established, and the procedure provides a valuable tool for probing the associative relations among stimulus events.

14. Conditioned inhibition—in which a CS− presented in combination with an established CS+ suppresses the CR or impedes conditioning to a new CS+. The conditioned inhibitor, CS−, may be established separately, as in conventional discrimination training, or in compound with a CS+. In the latter case, trials with the compound CS are not "reinforced" by US occurrence, while trials, with CS+ alone are followed by US.

15. Sensory preconditioning—in which two neutral stimuli, say a light and a tone, are systematically paired. If next the tone is established as a CS by pairing with a US, the light may exhibit CS properties as well, although it has never been paired with the US. The procedure for sensory preconditioning and the procedure for second-order conditioning are similar except for the stage in training when the two stimuli (light and tone in the present examples) arc paired.

Whenever some experimental factor resulted in a decrease in CR or UR magnitude or probability, Pavlov postulated an active inhibitory process. For example, the process of extinction built up internal inhibition. The disruptive effects of an extraneous (uncontrolled) stimulus on the eliciting of a CR by a CS was attributed to a process of external inhibition. (The orienting or investigative response evoked by the extraneous stimulus was preemptive.) The phenomena of conditioning represented for Pavlov the interplay of excitatory and inhibitory processes in the brain, particularly in the cerebral cortex. Pavlov's neurophysiology has not survived the test of new research, but the empirical character of the behavioral operations and resulting phenomena remain as core concepts of conditioning. Moreover, the processes discussed above in the context of classical conditioning have analogous expressions in operant conditioning. [See OPERANT LEARNING.]

III. PROCEDURES AND CONTINGENCIES

A. The Subjects

Classical conditioning has been demonstrated in every vertebrate species tested and in just about every invertebrate tested and having some kind of nervous system. The mollusks *Aplysia*, *Hermissenda*, and *Limax* have been favored subjects for neurophysiological research on the cellular mechanisms in learning. Aneural organisms such as the protozoan *Paramecium* appear on the borderline of convincing evidence of true associative learning. Prenatal and neonatal mammals, including humans, have evidenced classical conditioning.

B. The US

It is generally agreed that for efficient conditioning, the US should be sufficiently intense to reliably elicit a strong response. Common USs in laboratory studies include food, acidic liquids, or water delivered directly into the mouth or into a receptacle close to the mouth eliciting salivation, gastrointestinal activity, and for palatable substances, approach to the food source or the CS signalling food delivery; a puff of air delivered to the cornea eliciting eyelid responses; electric shock or other momentarily painful events eliciting withdrawl movements, locomotion, vasomotor and respiratory changes, interference with ongoing operant behavior, etc.; sudden loud noise eliciting startle; drugs eliciting a variety of physiological effects including responses of the immune system; ingested sugar eliciting secretion of insulin by the pancreas; ingestion of quantities of water eliciting diuresis; and many other stimulus events including the turning on of a heat lamp in a cold space, the opening of a door to a social space, and the presentation of a sexual partner. The list is very long.

USs are commonly classified in layman's terms as desirable or undesirable, satisfying or annoying. Pavlov and some European workers speak of alimentary and defensive conditioning. The terms commonly in use in the West are appetitive and aversive, and they are usually operationally defined in the context of operant conditioning as positive and negative reinforcers, respectively. Positive reinforcers increase the probability of responses that produce them or preserve their presence; negative reinforcers increase the probability of responses that terminate or avoid them. USs that do not readily lend themselves to classification as appetitive or aversive are sometimes classified according to their route of administration or principal receptor site—external (exteroceptive) or internal (interoceptive).

C. The CS

CSs are ordinarily chosen for their neutrality with respect to the CRs of interest, but complications often arise. Orienting responses, which in effect are URs to weak stimuli, may have multiple components, some of which confound measurement of CRs. If one attempts to eliminate the orienting responses through habituation, stimulus pre-exposure

effects may interfere with the course of subsequent conditioning.

Novel stimuli are usually more effective than familiar stimuli. As noted earlier, even the simplest stimuli are likely to be embedded in compounds with the context. Individual and species differences in sensory sensitivity have to be reckoned with. Species differences loom large in consideration of the "belongingness" of certain CS–US combinations. Pavlov supported an equipotentiality principle wherein any stimulus, properly paired with any US, could be established as a CS. But equipotentiality has been a troublesome claim. In one of many experiments after Pavlov's time, rats were shown to acquire CRs to tone–shock pairings more readily than to taste–shock pairings; but, conversely, the rats more readily acquired CRs to taste–drug pairings than to tone–drug pairings. On the other hand, the results are not all in. When additional procedures are used to test for CS effectiveness, learning is sometimes revealed in one context while it was not detected in another.

D. CS–US Relations

The temporal relations between CS and US have received a major share of the research efforts to identify the variables that influence classical conditioning and to provide optimal arrangements for a particular application of conditioning. From Pavlov's time and until the 1960s, temporal contiguity, CS closely followed in time by US, was taken as the critical feature. A standard terminology was applied to the various arrangements in use: When CS begins several seconds or more before US and continues to at least US onset, the procedure is called *delayed conditioning*. In *simultaneous conditioning,* Cs and US onsets coincide, although in the older literature, CS–US delays of a fraction of a second up to 2 seconds or more were sometimes called simultaneous. In *trace conditioning,* CS begins and terminates before US onset. (The interval between a brief CS and a later US in trace conditioning was used as a test of the "span of attention" in some early research with animals. The appearance of CRs indicated that an association could be formed between events separated in time.) In *backward conditioning,* CS follows termination of US. (The evidence for successful backward conditioning is mixed. At best, it is less likely to succeed than forward conditioning using any reasonable CS–US relation.) When no explicit CS is used and US occurs at regular intervals, the procedure is called *temporal conditioning*. (See Part I for mention of temporal conditioning as the interface of distinctions between classical and operant conditioning.) Not every occurrence of CS need be accompanied by US, giving rise to procedures called *intermittent* or *partial reinforcement*. When two (or more) CSs occur in sequence before US onset, the term *serial conditioning* is applied.

CS–US intervals of the order of 0.5 to 2 seconds were generally thought of as optimal for many procedures, but exceptions are many. The so-called conditioned emotional response (CER) procedure imposes a CS–shock interval of 30 seconds to 3 minutes on an ongoing baseline of positively reinforced operant behavior. Conditioning is assessed by suppression of the operant responding. Taste (flavor) aversion procedures demonstrate successful conditioning with interstimulus intervals (ISI) of several hours. Autoshaping studies with pigeons usually employ CS–US intervals of 6 to 10 seconds. Recent research with the autoshaping procedure has shown the intertrial interval (ITI) to be an equally influential variable. The ITI may also be thought of as the US–US interval. Efficient excitatory conditioning depends on the ratio of the ISI to the ITI, small ratios of the order of 0.1 or less being optimal in the autoshaping case. There is a suggestion that inhibitory conditioning occurs at those ratios which do not support excitatory conditioning. Therefore, an optimal ISI interval has little meaning by itself. The identification of optimal parameters for conditioning depends upon the response system selected for study and the particular measures (dependent variables) to be used.

As a rule, the Pavlovian tradition almost exclusively studied CS–US relations in which the stimuli were paired and USs never occurred in the absence of CS. In one or another form, the 1960s saw the question raised of whether successful conditioning needed only CS–US contiguity. What would happen if USs occurred also in the ITI? The upshot of a great deal of research saw the emergence of the concepts of predictiveness, informativeness, and a more mathematical version of contingency applied to CS–US relations. To be conditioned, a potential CS must reliably predict or inform the subject of an upcoming US. The subject learns about CS–US relations. If the conditional probability of US given CS is greater that the conditional probability of US in the absence of CS, excitatory conditioning should occur. A graded series of such positive contingen-

cies should yield a graded series of CS–CR strengths by some appropriate measure. If the conditional probability of US given CS is less than that given the absence of CS, then inhibitory conditioning should result with CS predicting the absence of US. If the conditional probabilities are equal or nearly so, the subject learns that CS and US events are truly random, there is no predictive or informative power in CS, and there is no conditioning to CS. Of course, the subject may still learn something about the rate of US occurrences. Note, however, that the phenomenon of blocking discussed earlier means that while contingency may be necessary for conditioning, it may not be sufficient. Contingency does not give a complete account of informativeness. In a different vein, note too that noncontingent arrangements in response–outcome relations are relevant to the circumstances called *learned helplessness*.

While most studies employ a forward conditioning procedure wherein an appetitive or aversive US follows a CS, other arrangements are possible. Given the presence of an appetitive or aversive state of affairs in which USs occur periodically on some schedule, a CS could signal the termination of that state of affairs. There is then a fourfold set of procedures that can be visualized in a two by two table having appetitive vs aversive USs occurring at some rate along one edge, and CSs that predict the onset or offset of the US condition along the adjacent edge. It was suggested by O. H. Mowrer that these arrangements define a basic set of emotional states evoked by the CS. The prediction of an appetitive state of affairs gives rise to joy or pleasure; the prediction of its termination gives rise to disappointment. The prediction of an aversive state of affairs gives rise to fear or anxiety; the prediction of its termination to relief. These emotional states were said to have motivational properties and to modulate ongoing operant behavior.

A considerable amount of analysis and discussion has been given to conscious awareness and language processes interacting with conditioning procedures in human subjects. Experimental strategies attempt to evaluate such effects, to circumvent them, or to manipulate them directly. And further, some associative structures within language are themselves established and analyzed as conditioned relations.

E. Has Conditioning Occurred?

A great deal has been written about methods for assessing whether a procedure has resulted in some kind of learning. In the present matter, does the CS have different properties as a result of the experience of the subject? The conditioning procedure itself is subject to a variety of control procedures to determine what about the CS–US relation, if anything, has resulted in associative learning. If a response of the same form as the CR occurs "spontaneously" as do eye blinks, the baseline level of the response must be measured. It must be shown that neither the CS alone nor the US alone, nor their occurrence in some explicitly unpaired manner increases the likelihood of a CR given the CS. (Of course, over time, the explicitly unpaired procedure would be expected to produce inhibitory conditioning.) Usually, independent groups of subjects serve in the various control conditions. Further, when a large number of conditioning trials are used, it should be shown that a truly random (noncontingent) occurrence of an equal number of CS and US occurrences over the same time period does not affect CR in the same way. It is important to recognize that the concept of contingency (and noncontingency) as a statistical relation requires a large sample of trials. In a truly noncontingent procedure, some CS and US events must be contiguous.

Acquired changes in the evocative power of the CS are customarily measured in terms of the magnitude, latency, rate, probability, or resistance to extinction of the CR. Measures such as recruitment (the rate at which the magnitude of the response changes) are used in some psychophysiological work. Depending on the particular temporal relations, it is often the case that CR strength is assessed only on trials on which the US is omitted. In either case the subject may learn that the CR has an effect on the US, modifying its effect or sometimes causing its omission.

Response form (topography) is sometimes used as a criterion to distinguish CRs from other spontaneous or "voluntary" responses. According to the stimulus substitution view of classical conditioning advanced by Pavlov, a true CR must have features in common with the UR. It is now recognized that this need not be the case, and from an oerational perspective, whatever response changes occur as a result of an S–S contingency are considered conditioned changes.

Acquired changes in CS functions are now often assessed by means of transfer tests and summation tests. The former involves application of the CS to new training arrangements; the latter tests for CS effects when it is put in compound with other CSs or stimuli having still other functions. For example, a stimulus suspected of being excitatory with respect to a food US could be combined with another excitatory CS. An enhanced response to the CS combination would be consistent with the suspected excitatory effect. However, it would be necessary to have a control procedure to evaluate the effect of the addition of a simply novel stimulus to the known excitatory stimulus.

Still another present day technique for assessing stimulus functions uses a US devaluation procedure. If a subject can be suspected of "knowing" that a CS predicts delivery of a certain food rather than merely responding automatically, the food can subsequently be made to cause gastric discomfort (e.g., nausea). When later the CS is presented, a strong response would suggest the automatic reaction, while a weak response would suggest that the CS evokes some "representation" of the food as an undesirable event.

IV. SUMMING UP

1. The essential fact of classical (Pavlovian) conditioning is that experiencing a contingent relation between two stimulus events may produce changes or modifications in behavior, depending on the choice of stimuli, and many other variables. The Pavlovian terms CS and US, CR and UR, and the simplified relation called "pairing" are commonly used in discussing classical conditioning.

2. The conditioned response (CR) that results from successful pairing of a CS with a US may emerge rapidly or gradually. It will weaken or disappear if CS is presented alone sufficiently often. Many other processes can determine when and in what form the CR may appear.

3. A vast range of organisms, stimulus events, simple and complex stimulus relations, physiological functions, and overt actions that can be made more or less likely comprise the scope of classical conditioning. The form of the CR may be independent of the form of the UR. The view of classical conditioning as stimulus substitution is applicable in a very limited number of cases.

4. CS–US pairing or contiguity alone is not sufficient to produce conditioning in many cases. Pairings always occur in a context which

introduces other stimulus relations. For excitatory conditioning to occur, US must be contingent upon CS, and CS must be informative regarding US occurrence. Conditioning may not occur if CS is redundant (blocked by or overshadowed by other CSs). For inhibitory conditioning to occur, US must be contingent upon the absence of the CS in question.

5. In many procedures, excitatory conditioning depends on the ratio of the CS–US interval to the intertrial interval. In a cognitive interpretation, it is as if the CS must be worth attending to because the US does not occur relatively often enough to make undifferentiated attention to the context worthwhile.

There are many important topics in classical conditioning that have been barely mentioned or overlooked in this essay. Principal among them are the many practical clinical applications of classical conditioning and the many physiological phenomena that can be illuminated through conditioning principles. There is also a large literature on the rapidly developing neurophysiology of conditioning. Several ingenious experimental techniques have been developed to explore the stimulus and response relations produced in conditioning procedures. Finally, several theoretical models of the conditioning process and conditioning phenomena have been advanced and are being tested and modified constantly.

The reader is referred to the following bibliography for enlightenment.

Bibliography

Ader, R., Felten, D. L., and Cohen, N. (Eds.) (1991). "Psychoneuroimmunology," 2nd ed. Academic Press, San Diego.

Ader, R., Weiner, H., and Baum, A. (Eds.) (1988). "Experimental Foundations of Behavioral Medicine: Conditioning Approaches." Erlbaum, Hillsdale, NJ.

Atkinson, R. C., Herrnstein, R. J., Lindzey, G., and Luce, R. D. (Eds.) (1988). "Stevens' Handbook of Experimental Psychology." Vol. 2, Part I, 2nd ed. Wiley, New York.

Bower, G. H. (Ed.) (serial publication, 1970–present). "The Psychology of Learning and Motivation." Academic Press, San Diego.

Davey, G. (Ed.) (1987). "Cognitive Processes and Pavlovian Conditioning in Humans." Wiley, New York.

Gibbon, J., Berryman, R., and Thompson, R. L. (1974). Contingency spaces and measures in classical and instrumental conditioning. *J. Exp. Anal. Beh.* **21,** 585–605.

Gormezano, I., Prokasy, W. F., and Thompson, R. F. (Eds.) (1987). "Classical Conditioning," 3rd ed. Erlbaum, Hillsdale, NJ.

Pavlov, I. P. (1927). "Conditioned Reflexes" (translated by G. V. Anrep). Oxford University Press.

Pavlov, I. P. (1928). "Lectures on Conditioned Reflexes" (translated by W. H. Gantt). International, New York.

Pavlov, I. P. (1941). "Conditioned Reflexes and Psychiatry" (translated by W. H. Gantt). International, New York.

Rescorla, R. A. (1988). Pavlovian conditioning: It's not what you think it is. *Am. Psychol.* 43, 151–160.

Rescorla, R. A. (1992). Hierarchical associative relations in Pavlovian conditioning and instrumental training. *Curr. Directions Psychol. Sci.* **1,** 66–70.

Turkkan, J. S. (1989). Classical conditioning: The new hegemony. *Behav. Brain Sci.* **12,** 121–179.

CLINICAL ASSESSMENT

Eileen Gambrill

University of California at Berkeley

Glossary

Antecedents Events that immediately precede behavior and influence its frequency.

Behavior Any measurable or observable act or response. Behavior is defined broadly in some perspectives to include cognitions, feelings, and physiological reactions which, although they are not directly observable, are defined so that they can be measured.

Behavioral Approaches to understanding behavior in which learning histories and current environmental contingencies of reinforcement are emphasized. Behavioral approaches differ in the relative degree of attention devoted to thoughts and images.

Clinical inference Assumptions about the causes of a problem.

Cognition Internal events such as thoughts (beliefs, self-statements, attributions) and images.

Consequences Events that follow behavior and influence its frequency.

Contingency The relationship between a behavior and the events that follow (consequences) and precede (antecedents) the behavior.

Diagnosis A label given to a client with particular characteristics that is assumed to reflect etiology and to have intervention implications.

DSM-III-R Official classification system of mental disorders published by the American Psychiatric Association.

Psychodynamic Approaches to understanding behavior, in which unconscious mental and emotional processes (e.g., motives and conflicts) stemming from early childhood experiences are emphasized. Approaches differ in attention given to interpersonal processes, biological factors, and the cultural context.

Validity The extent to which a measure measures what it was designed to assess. There are many different kinds of validity (e.g., predictive, content, concurrent, construct).

CLINICAL ASSESSMENT involves the clarification of presenting problems and related factors including identification of outcomes that will be focused on. It should offer guidelines for selection of intervention methods.

Goals of assessment include describing clients, their problems and desired outcomes as well as their life situations, understanding why problems occur (inferring causes), deciding on what methods are most likely to achieve desired outcomes, and obtaining a base from which to evaluate progress. Assessment requires the search for and integration of data that are useful in deciding how to remove complaints. It involves (1) detecting client characteristics and environmental factors related to problems; (2) integrating and interpreting data collected; and (3) selecting outcomes to focus on. It should indicate what situational, biological, or psychological factors influence options, create demands, or cause discomfort. Decisions must be made about *what* data to collect, *how* to gather this, and *how* to organize it. Assessment should indicate the specific outcomes related to complaints, what would have to be done to achieve these outcomes, how these could most effectively be pursued, and the potential of attaining them.

The assessment methods that are used differ because of differences in theoretical perspectives which influence the kind of data collected as well as the uses and functions of these data. Clinical inferences vary in how closely they are tied to concrete evidence. Carrying out an assessment is like unraveling a puzzle or locating the pieces of the puzzle. Certain pieces of the puzzle are sought rather than others depending on the clinician's theoretical orientation and knowledge, and puzzle completion may be declared at diverse points. Issues of practicality also arise. The aim of all methods is to yield data that are useful, reliable, and valid. Specialized knowledge may be required and critical thinking skills are needed to weigh the value of evidence and examine the soundness of assumptions. Although decisions must typically be made on the basis of incomplete data, without a sound assessment framework, opportunities to gather useful data may be lost and ineffective or harmful plans may be suggested. Data should be gathered that are of value in helping clients. Collecting irrelevant data wastes time and money and increases the likelihood of incorrect decisions. Assessment should offer clients more helpful views of problems and a more helpful vocabulary for describing problems and options.

There is general agreement that an individualized assessment should be conducted which considers cultural differences. This does not mean that this is indeed done and practice perspectives differ in what is focused on. Individualized assessment avoids the patient uniformity myth in which clients (or families, or groups) are mistakenly assumed to be similar. Behavior consists of different response systems, which may or may not be related depending on the unique history of each individual: (1) overt behavior (for example, avoidance of crowds) and verbal reports (verbal descriptions of anxiety); (2) cognitions (thoughts about crowds); (3) physiological reactions (for example, increased heart rate when in crowds). Each person may have a different pattern of responses in a situation. Only through an individualized assessment can these unique patterns and related situations be discovered. Suicidal potential should be assessed as relevant. Recognizing the signs of pathology is important anytime this would be helpful in understanding what can be accomplished and how it can be accomplished. A clear agreement between clinicians and clients about the focus of helping efforts increases the likelihood that intervention will focus on outcomes that are of concern to clients.

I. THE GUIDING ROLE OF PRACTICE THEORIES

How problems are structured is a key part of clinical decision-making. Assessment frameworks differ in what is focused on, the kinds of assessment methods used, and how closely assessment is tied to selection of intervention methods. Preferred practice theories influence what clinicians look for and what they notice as well as how they process and organize data collected. Practice theories favored influence beliefs about what can be and is known about behavior and how knowledge can be developed. Dimensions along which theories differ include the following:

◆ Unit of concern (individual, family, community)
◆ Goals pursued (e.g., explanation and interpretation alone or understanding based on prediction and influence)
◆ Clarity of goals pursued
◆ Criteria used to evaluate the accuracy of explanations (e.g., consensus, authority, scientific)
◆ Range of problems addressed with success
◆ Causal importance attributed to feelings, thoughts, and/or environmental factors
◆ Range of environmental characteristics considered (family, community, society)
◆ Causal importance attributed to biochemical causes
◆ Attention devoted to past experiences
◆ Degree of optimism about how much change is possible
◆ Degree to which a perspective lends itself to and encourages empirical inquiry (finding out whether it is accurate)
◆ Degree of empirical support (evidence for and against a theory)
◆ Attention given to documenting degree of progress
◆ Ease with which practice guidelines can be developed
◆ Degree of parsimony

Practice frameworks differ in the value given to observation of interactions in real-life settings, in whether significant others are involved in assessment, and how directive clinicians are. They differ in degree of attention paid to cognitions (thoughts), feelings, environmental characteristics (such as reactions of significant others), genetic causes, and/ or physiological causes. Different frameworks are based on different beliefs about the causes of behavior. Beliefs about behavior, thoughts, and feelings, and how they are maintained and can be changed influence what data are gathered and how data are weighted and organized. History shows that beliefs can be misleading. For example, trying to assess people by examining the bumps on their head was not very fruitful. However, for decades many people believed that this method was useful.

Problems can be viewed from a perspective of psychological deficiencies or from a broad view in which both personal and environmental factors are attended to. For example, a key point of feminist counseling is helping clients to understand the effects of the political on the personal, both past and present. Frameworks that focus on psychological characteristics are based on the view that behavior is controlled mainly by characteristics of the individual. In interactional perspectives, attention is given not only to the individual but to people with whom he or she interacts. The unit of analysis is the relationship between environmental events and psychological factors. It is assumed that both personal and environmental factors influence behavior. Interactional views differ in how reciprocal the relationship between the individual and the environment is believed to be and in the range of environmental events considered. In contextual, ecological perspectives, individual, family, community, and societal characteristics are considered as they may relate to problems and possible resolutions. A contextual framework decreases the likelihood of focusing on individual pathology (blaming the victim), and neglecting environmental causes and resources. Practice perspectives that focus on individual causes of personal problems may result in "psychologizing" rather than helping clients. Assessment frameworks differ in the extent to which they take advantage of what is known about behavior, factors related to certain kinds of problems, and the accuracy of different sources of data.

Forming a new conceptualization of presenting problems, one that is shared by both the clinician and the client that will be helpful in resolving problems is an integral aspect of assessment. The kind of conceptualization suggested will depend on the theoretical orientation of the clinician. It is important to arrive at a common view of the problem, as well as agreement as to what will be done to change it. This common view is a motivating factor in that, if clients accept it and if it makes sense to clients, there will be a greater willingness to try out procedures that flow from this account. Mutually agreed-on views are fostered in a variety or ways, including questions asked, assessment procedures used, and rationales offered. Focused summaries help to pull material together within a new framework. Identifying similar themes among seemingly disparate events can be used to suggest alternative views.

II. SIGN AND SAMPLE APPROACHES

Traditional assessment is based on a sign approach in which observed behaviors are viewed as indicators of more important underlying (and unobserved) personality dispositions (typically of a pathological nature) or traits. Traits can be defined as a general and personally determined tendency to react in consistent and stable ways. Examples are "aggression" and "extraversion." Inherent in sign approaches such as psychoanalytic approaches is the assumption that observable behavioral problems are only the outward signs of some underlying process, which must be altered to bring about any lasting change. A focus of change efforts on the behavior itself, according to this model, would not succeed, because no change has supposedly been brought about in underlying causative factors. A clinician may conclude that a child who has difficulty concentrating on his school work and sitting in his seat is hyperactive. The observed behaviors are viewed as a sign of an underlying disorder. The underlying hypothetical constructs are viewed as of major importance in understanding and predicting behavior. Dispositional attributions shift attention away from observing what people *do* in specific situations to speculating about what they *have*. Inconsistencies in behavior across situations are not unexpected within this approach because it is assumed that underlying motives, conflicts, wishes may be behaviorally manifested in many different ways. [*See* INDIVIDUAL DIFFERENCES IN TEMPERAMENT; TRAITS.]

The interactions between wishes, the threats anticipated if wishes are expressed, and the processes used to cope with or defend against conflictual situations are of interest in psychodynamic frameworks. Important elements in such processes are believed to be beyond conscious recognition of the individual experiencing them even when they may be recognized or inferred by others. The concepts of "positions" (developmental stages) and "mechanisms" (psychological processes such as defense mechanisms) are central concepts. Defensive aims, processes, and outcomes are of interest. Defense mechanisms include suppression, undoing, repression, role reversal, projection, and regression. The defenses are believed to be heightened under conditions of high emotion, stress, and conflict. Motives include the wish to avoid unpleasant, overwhelming, or out-of-control states. Some unconscious processes anticipate such outcomes. Classification of phenomena is in terms of deflections from volitional consciousness and rationally intended actions: as intrusions and omissions. For example, recurrent dysfunctional alterations in self-esteem and interpersonal behavior (such as those seen in the personality disorders) are viewed as involving both intrusive, inappropriate schemas and omissions of realistic learning of new schemas. It is assumed that the "dynamic unconscious" constantly undergoes symbolic changes which in turn affect feelings and behavior. Other aspects of psychoanalytic approaches include an emphasis on verbal reports concerning early histories and efforts to alter innder processes by verbal means. Compared to behavioral assessment, less attention is devoted to environmental variables that may influence behavior because of the assumed core relevance and stability of underlying dispositions. [See DEFENSE MECHANISMS.]

There are many different kinds of psychodynamic assessment frameworks. For example, there are variants of object relations theory, each of which may have a somewhat different approach to assessment. The nature of a client's past interactions with their parents is viewed as central. However, there are differences in what is focused on by clinicians of different psychodynamic persuasions. In object relations theory, the concepts of mirroring and self objects are key ones. Attention is given to internal mental representations of the self and significant others. It is assumed that how we feel about ourselves and act toward others is a reflection of internal relationships based on experience. The term "object relations" refers to the interplay between the images of self and others. This interplay results in wishes, impulses, thoughts, and feelings of power (or its lack). Ego psychology emphasizes identification and support of strengths and working within the "defenses" rather than breaking them down. Proponents consider resistance to change natural and work with and support adaptive strengths. Defense mechanisms, such as rationalization of actions and projection of feelings onto others are identified but not necessarily discussed. [See OBJECT RELATIONS THEORY.]

Behavioral assessment involves a sample approach. In a sample approach, direct observation of behavior in real life settings (or, if this is not possible, in situations that resemble these) is valued. A behavioral approach is based on an interactional view in which it is assumed that behavior is a function of both organismic variables (genetic history and physiological states) and the environment. Labels are used as summarizing categories rather than as terms indicating some underlying characteristic (usually a

disorder). Unlike in sign approaches where the cause of behavior is assumed to be underlying dispositions, the cause of behavior is assumed to lie largely in environmental differences. Behavioral frameworks differ in the relative amount of attention devoted to thoughts and environmental contingencies. Differences in focus are so marked that they have resulted to the formation of different journals and societies. Differences in emphasis are related to the role attributed to thoughts in influencing behavior. This role varies from a causal to a mediating role. In the former, reflected in cognitive–behavioral frameworks, thoughts are presumed to cause changes in feelings and behavior. In the latter, reflected in applied behavior analysis, thoughts are assumed to influence feelings and behavior in a mediating (not causal) manner. It is assumed that one must look to past and present environmental contingencies to account for both thoughts and feelings.

In cognitive–behavioral methods, attention is devoted to thoughts as well as behaviors. Thoughts of interest include attributions for behavior, feelings, and outcomes, negative and positive self-statements, expectations, and cognitive distortions. Attention is devoted to identifying the particular kinds of thoughts that occur in problem related situations. Cognitive–behavioral approaches differ in their assumptions about the kinds of thoughts that underlay behavior. However, all share certain assumptions such as the belief that individuals respond to cognitive representations of environmental events rather than to the events per se. It is assumed that learning is cognitively mediated and that cognition mediates emotional and behavioral dysfunction. [See COGNITIVE BEHAVIOR THERAPY.]

In applied behavior analysis, environmental contingencies are focused on. A contingency analysis requires identification of the environmental events that occasion and maintain behavior. There is an interest in describing the relationships between behavior and what happens right before and after as well as "metacontingencies"—the relationships between cultural practices and the outcomes of these practices. There is an emphasis on *current* contingencies. Attention is directed toward the change of "deviant" environments rather than the change of "deviant" client behaviors. There is an interest in identifying functional relationships. A behavioral analysis includes a description of behaviors of concern as well as evidence that specific antecedents and consequences influence these behaviors; it requires a functional as well as a descriptive analysis.

Although there are differences, all behavioral approaches share many characteristics that distinguish them from sign approaches. Assessment is an ongoing process in behavioral assessment. This contrasts with some traditional assessment approaches in which assessment is used to "diagnose" a client in order to decide on treatment methods. What a person *does* is of interest in behavioral approaches rather than what she *has*. Behavior is of great interest, especially the behaviors of individuals in real-life contexts. Identifying variables that influence the frequency of behaviors of interest is a key assessment goal. Behavior is assumed to vary in different contexts because of different learning histories and different current contingencies as well as different levels of deprivation and fatigue. There is an emphasis on clear description of assessment methods as well as clear description of problems and outcomes. It is assumed that only if complaints are clearly described can they be translated into specific changes that would result in their removal. The emphasis on behavior and the influence of environmental contingencies call for the translation of problems into observable behaviors and the discovery of ways in which the environment can be rearranged. Clients are encouraged to recognize and alter the role they play in maintaining problems. For example, teachers and parents often reinforce behaviors they complain about. Assessment is individualized; each person, group, family, organization or community is viewed as unique. Data about group differences do not offer precise information about what an individual does in specific situations and what cues and consequences influence their behavior.

The focus on behavior has a number of implications for assessment. One is the importance of observing people in real-life contexts whenever feasible, ethical, and necessary to acquire helpful data. A range of assessment methods is used including observation in real-life settings as well as role plays. Multiple assessment methods are also called for because of the lack of synchrony between overt behavior, physiological reactions, cognitions (thoughts), and feelings. Assessment and treatment are closely related in a behavioral model. It is assumed that assessment should have treatment utility. There is an emphasis on the use of validated assessment methods. The principles of behavior are relied on to guide assessment and intervention. There is a preference for limited inference and a focus on constructing repertoires (on helping clients to acquire additional knowledge and skills that will increase opportunities for reinforcement). Clients are viewed in terms of their assets rather than their deficiencies. The preference for enhancement of knowledge and skills requires a focus on behaviors that are effective in real-life contexts. In a task analysis, the specific behaviors that are required to achieve an outcome are identified. For each step, performance is clearly described as well as the conditions in which it is expected to occur.

A. Some Important Distinctions

The form of a behavior (its topography) does not necessarily indicate its function (why the behavior occurs). Identical forms of behavior may be maintained by very different contingencies. Just as the same behavior may have different functions, different behaviors may have identical functions. The distinction between motivational and behavioral deficits is also important. If a desired behavior does not occur, this may indicate either that the behavior exists but is not reinforced on an effective schedule or is punished (a motivational deficit) or that the behavior is not present in the client's repertoire (a behavior deficit). Motivational deficits are often mistaken for behavioral deficits. Motivational and behavioral deficits can be distinguished by arranging conditions for performance of a behavior. For example, clients could be requested to role play behaviors and asked whether similar or identical behaviors occur in other situations. Behavior surfeits are often related to behavior deficits. For example, aggression on the part of a child may be related to a lack of friendship skills. It is also important to distinguish response inhibitions from behavior deficits. Emotional reactions such as anxiety may interfere with desired behavior.

B. Past History

Although the past is viewed as important in influencing current behavior in just about all perspectives, assessment frameworks differ in how much attention is devoted to the past and what is focused on. Past experiences are a major focus in psychodynamic assessment frameworks. Knowledge about past circumstances may be of value when it is difficult to identify current maintaining factors and may be helpful in preventing future problems. Information about a person's past may provide valuable information about unusual social histories related to problems. An understanding of how problems began can be useful in clarifying the origins of what seems to be puzzling reactions. New ways of viewing past events may be helpful to clients. Information about the past can be useful in encouraging clients to alter present behaviors and may help clients understand the source of current reactions. Demographic indicators about a client's past behavior in certain contexts may be better predictors of future behavior than personality tests or clinical judgments.

Information about the past offers a view of current events in a more comprehensive context. Major areas include medical history, educational and work history, significant relationships, family history and developmental history. Helpful coping skills may be discovered by finding out what clients have tried in the past to resolve problems. Research concerning autobiographical memory suggests that memories change over time, making it difficult to know whether reports are accurate. From a psychodynamic perspective, accuracy would not be an issue. Rather, the client's memories of events, whether accurate or not, are the substance of import. It is assumed in fact that memories may be distorted by unconscious motives/conflicts and so on. Excessive attention to past troubles may create pessimism about the future and encourage rationalizations and excuses that interfere with change, especially if this is not fruitful in selecting effective plans.

C. What about Psychiatric Labels?

Labels are used in assessment in two main ways. One is as a shorthand term to refer to specific behaviors. The term hyperactive may refer to the fact that a student often gets out of his seat and talks out of turn in class. A counselor may use "hyperactive" as a summary term to refer to these behaviors. Labels are also used as a diagnostic category which is supposed to offer guidelines for knowing what to do about a problem. Here, a label connotes more than a cluster of behaviors. It involves additional assumptions about the person labeled which should be of "diagnostic" value. The *Diagnostic and Statistical Manual of Mental Disorders* (1987) (DMS-III-R) of the American Psychiatric Association describes hundreds of terms used to describe various disorders.

Methodological and conceptual problems connected with the use of diagnostic categories include lack of agreement about what label to assign clients and lack of association between a diagnosis and indications of what intervention will be effective. Psy-

chiatric labels have been criticized for being imprecise (saying too little about positive attributes, potential for change, and change that does occur, and too much about presumed negative characteristics and limits to change). Both traits and diagnostic labels offer little detail about what people do in specific situations and what specific circumstances influence behavior. There is no evidence that traits have dispositional properties. Little cross-situational consistency has been found in relation to "personality traits." Some behaviors may appear "trait-like" in that they are similar over time and situations because of similar contingencies of reinforcement. Degree of consistency should be empirically explored for particular classes of clients and behavior rather than assumed. Acceptance of a label may prematurely close off consideration of promising options. The tendency to use a binary classification system (people are labeled as either having or not having something, for example, as being an alcoholic or not), may obscure the varied individual patterns that may be referred to by a term. Critics of the DSM highlight the consensual nature of what is included (reliance on agreement rather than empirical criteria) and the role of economic considerations in its creation. Some argue that psychiatric classification systems encourage blaming victims for their plights rather than altering the social circumstances responsible for problems.

Labels that are instrumental (they point to effective interventions) are helpful. For example, the understanding of anxiety disorders has advanced requiring the differential diagnosis among different categories (simple phobia, generalized anxiety, panic attacks and agorophobia). Failure to use labels that are indeed informative may prevent clients from receiving appropriate intervention. Labels can normalize client concerns. Parents who have been struggling to understand why their child is developmentally slow may view themselves as failures. Recognition that their child has a specific kind of developmental disability that accounts for this can be a relief.

III. SOURCES OF INFLUENCE

Influences on behavior include other people's actions, the physical environment, tasks and materials, physiological changes, thoughts, genetic differences, and developmental factors. Material and community resources and related political, economic, and social conditions influence options. It is important to obtain an overview of the client's current life as this may relate to problems, including relationships with significant others, employment, physical health, recreational activities, and community and material resources available. Antecedents of behavior, like consequences, have a variety of sources. In addition to proximal antecedents (those that occur right before a behavior), distal antecedents may influence current behavior. Past or future events may be made current by thinking about these. These thoughts may then influence what we do, feel, and think. *Setting events* are antecedents that are closely associated with a behavior but are not in the situation in which behaviors of concern occur. For example, an unpleasant exchange with a teacher may influence how a child responds to his parents at home. The earlier event alters the likelihood of given reactions in subsequent situations. Preferred practice theories influence the attention given to various sources. Problems vary in the complexity of related factors. Problems may be complex because significant others lack needed skills, have interfering beliefs, or are threatened by proposed changes. Distinguishing between problems and efforts to resolve these will avoid confusion between the results of attempted solutions and effects of the original concern. Expected role behavior in a certain culture may limit change. Ongoing discrimination against a group may limit opportunities. Clients may lack needed information or skills. A *behavior deficit* may exist (the client may not know how to perform a given behavior).

A. Other People/The Nature of the Client's Social Relationship

With any presenting problem, the possible influence of significant others in the maintenance of a problem should be explored. Behavior occurs in a context. How significant others respond makes up an important part of our environment. Significant others are those who interact with clients and influence their behavior. Examples include family members and staff in residential settings. Significant others are often involved in assessment. For example, in family therapy, family members participate in assessment. Understanding relationships among family members is a key part of assessment in family therapy. Interactions between couples is closely examined in relationship counseling. Clients may lack social support such as opportunities for intimacy,

companionship, and validation or the opportunity to provide support to others. Social interactions may be a source of stress rather than a source of pleasure and joy. It is important to assess the nature and quality of client's social network and social support system.

B. The Physical Environment

The influence of the physical environment should be examined. Physical arrangements in residential and day care settings influence behavior. Unwanted behaviors may be encouraged by available materials. For example, toys that are visible to children may distract them from educational tasks. Temperature changes affect behavior as do degree of crowding and noise level. Characteristics of the community in which clients live that may influence complaints and possible intervention options should be assessed. Neighborhood quality influences wellbeing. For example, children who live in lower quality environments (e.g., there is little play space, housing is in industrial neighborhoods, upkeep of streets is poor) are less satisfied with their lives, experience more negative emotions, and have more restricted and less positive friendship patterns. There is a relationship between number of nonaccidental injuries to children and the physical conditions of the home which is related to socioeconomic status.

C. Tasks and Activities

The kind of task confronting an individual may influence the rate of problem behavior. Particular tasks or activities may be high-risk situations for unwanted behavior. Many studies have found a relationship between the kind of task and deviant behavior such as self-injury. Problems may occur because a task is too tedious or difficult or because an individual is uncomfortable or bored, or is told to do something in an unpleasant manner. In these instances, altering antecedents may correct the problem.

D. Bio-physiological Factors

Presenting problems may be related to neurological or biochemical factors. Such factors may place boundaries on how much change is possible. Malnutrition, hypoglycemia, and allergic reactions have been associated with hyperactivity, learning disabilities, and mental retardation. Biochemical abnormalities are found in some children with serious behavior disturbances such as those labeled autistic. However, this only establishes that abnormalities in biochemistry are present, not that they cause a certain disorder (e.g., cause certain behaviors). Biochemical changes may be a result of stress related to social conditions such as limited opportunities due to discrimination. Drugs, whether prescribed or not, may influence how clients appear and behave. Certain kinds of illness are associated with particular kinds of psychological changes.

Drugs, alcohol, environmental pollutants, and nutritional deficiencies may influence health and behavior. Accidents may result in neurological changes which result in concomitant psychological changes. Even when brain damage can be shown to exist, this does not show that it causes any particular behavior. Premature acceptance of biophysical explanations will interfere with discovering alternative explanations that yield intervention knowledge. Behavior changes may be due to brain tumors. Hormonal changes associated with menopause may result in mood changes which may be misattributed to psychological causes. On the other hand psychological changes may be misattributed to hormonal changes. There are gender differences in return of diffuse physiological arousal (DPA) to baseline levels; men take longer to return to baseline levels. These gender differences have implications for understanding and altering aggression among family members. Whenever physiological factors may be related to a problem as, for example, with seizures, depression, fatigue, or headaches, a physical examination should be required. Overlooking physical causes including nutritional deficiencies and coffee, alcohol, or drug intake may result in incorrect inferences. [See HORMONES AND BEHAVIOR.]

E. Cognitive–Intellectual Characteristics

People differ in their intellectual abilities which may influence problems and outcomes. Genetic differences have been found in intelligence as well as in shyness, temperament, and conditioning susceptibility. The importance of assessing what people say to themselves in relevant situations is emphasized in many assessment frameworks. For example, in cognitive–behavioral approaches, clients' internal dialogues (what they say to themselves) and the way this relates to complaints and desired outcomes is explored and altered as necessary. Certain thoughts may occur too much, too seldom, or at the wrong time. A depressed client may have a high frequency of negative self-statements and a low frequency of positive self-statements. In a radical behavioral perspective, thoughts are viewed as covert behaviors to be explained, not as explanations for other behaviors, although it is assumed they can serve a mediating function and influence both feelings and behaviors. The thoughts and feelings in a situation are assumed to be a function of the contingencies experienced in this situation or in situations that are similar or associated in some way. A causal role may be misattributed to thoughts because the histories related to the development of thoughts is overlooked. The role of thoughts can be examined by varying certain ones and determining the effects on behavior.

F. Feelings

When feelings are presented as a problem or are related to a problem, associated personal and environmental factors must be identified. Assessment frameworks differ in the role attributed to feelings and in factors sought to account for feelings. Some emphasize the role of thoughts in creating feelings. Others emphasize the role of unconscious conflicts and motives related to early childhood experiences. Other frameworks focus on the role of environmental contingencies in influencing emotional reactions. For example, in a radical behavioral approach, feelings are viewed as by-products of the relationships between behavior and environmental events. Feelings can be used as clues to contingencies (relationships between behavior and environmental events). Changing feelings will not make up for a lack of required skills, or rearrange contingencies required to attain desired outcomes.

G. Cultural Differences

Cultural differences may affect both the problems that clients experience as well as the communication styles and assessment and intervention methods that will be successful. An individualized assessment requires attention to cultural differences that may be related to problems and potential resolutions. Culturally sensitive practice requires knowledge of the values of different groups and their historical experience in the United States, and now these differences may influence the client's behavior, motivation and view of the helping process.

Different groups may prefer different problem-solving styles and have different beliefs about the causes of problems. The norms for behavior vary in different groups. It is important to be knowledgeable about cultural differences that may be mistakenly viewed as pathology. The degree of acculturation (the process of adaptation to a new or different culture) is important to assess. This influences drop-out rate, level of stress, attitude toward clinicians, and the process and goals that are appropriate. Knowledge of problems faced and preferred communication styles of people in different generations will be useful. Bicultural individuals, are members of two or more ethnic or racial groups.

H. Developmental Considerations

Assessment requires knowledge about developmental tasks, norms, and challenges. Information about required behaviors at different ages and life transitions can be helpful in assessment. Knowledge of what is typical behavior at different times (developmental norms) can be useful in "normalizing" behavior—helping clients to realize that reactions they view as unusual or "abnormal" are in fact common. Knowledge about typical changes in different phases of the life cycle (e.g., adolescence, parenthood, retirement) allows preventative planning. The following kinds of information will be helpful: (1) norms for behavior in specific contexts; (2) tasks associated with certain life-situations such as parenthood and retirement; (3) the hierarchical nature of some developmental tasks (some behaviors must be learned before others can be acquired). Different kinds of norms may be used in the selection of outcomes. Criterion referenced norms rely on what has been found to be required to attain a certain outcome through empirical analysis. Another kind of norm is what is usual in a situation. However, what is usual may not be what is desirable. For example, although it may be typical for teachers to offer low rates of positive feedback to students in their classroom, it is not optimal. The similarities of contingencies for many people at a given age in a society may lead one to assume incorrectly that biological development is responsible. The role of similar contingencies may be overlooked. Acceptance of a stage theory of development may get in the way of identifying environmental factors that can be rearranged.

I. Reviewing Resources and Obstacles

Assessment involves identification of personal assets and environmental resources that can be used to help clients attain desired outcomes, as well as personal and environmental obstacles. Personal resources and/or obstacles include cognitive–intellectual abilities and deficiencies, physical abilities and handicaps, social skills and social-skill deficits, vocational and recreational skills, financial assets, and social support systems. Clients differ in their "reinforcer profile" and in degree of motivation to alter problematic circumstances. Environments differ in opportunities for certain kinds of experiences (see discussion of physical environment). Resources such as money, housing, vocational training programs, medical care, or recreational facilities may be unavailable. Limited community resources (such as day care programs, vocational training programs, recreational centers, high-quality educational programs, parent training programs) and limited influence over environmental circumstances may pose an obstacle. Child maltreatment is related to poverty. Unemployment is related to substance abuse and spouse violence. Agency policies and practices influence options. Lack of coordination of services may limit access to resources. Clients may receive fragmentary, overlapping, or incompatible services.

IV. SOURCES OF INFORMATION

Sources of data include interviews, responses to written or pictorial measures, data gathered by clients and significant others (self-monitoring), observation in the interview as well as in role play or in real-life settings, and physiological indicators. A variety of electro-mechanical aids are available for collecting data such as wrist counters, timers, biofeedback devices, and audio- and videotape recorders. Familiarity with and knowledge about different methods, as well as personal and theoretical preferences and questions of feasibility influence selection. Preferred practice theories strongly influence selection of assessment methods. For example, in individually focused psychodynamic approaches, self-report and transference effects within the interview may be the main source of data used.

In behavioral approaches, self-report is supplemented whenever possible by other sources of data such as observation in real-life settings, role play, and/or self-monitoring. (Clients keep track of some behaviors, thoughts, or feelings and surrounding circumstances in real-life). Some sources, such as self-report in the interview, are easy to use and are flexible in the range of content provided. However, accuracy varies considerably. The question is: what methods will offer a fairly accurate description of reactions or conditions of concern and related events? Individual differences will influence a client's willingness to participate in a given manner. Accuracy of decisions can be improved by using multiple methods, drawing especially on those most likely to offer accurate relevant data.

Self-report is the most widely used source of information. There are many different types of self-report including verbal reports during interviews and answers on written inventories. Interviews also provide an opportunity to observe clients. Advantages of self-report include ease of collecting material and flexibility in the range of material that may be gathered. Structured interviews have been developed for both children and adults in a number of areas. These may be completed by the clinician, the client, or significant others. The accuracy of self-reports depends on a number of factors including the situation in which data are collected and the kinds and sequence of questions asked. Helpful questions in assessing the accuracy of self-reports include the following: (1) Does the situation encourage an honest answer? (2) Does the client have access to the information? (3) Can the client comprehend the question? (4) Does the client have the verbal skills required to answer questions? Special knowledge and skills may be required when interviewing children. Play materials and storytelling may be used to gather data about children's feelings and experiences.

Measures that have uniform procedures for administration and scoring and that are accompanied by certain kinds of information are referred to as *standardized measures*. Thousands of standardized questionnaires have been developed related to hundreds of different personal and/or environmental characteristics. Standardized measures are used for a variety of purposes including: (1) describing populations or clients, (2) screening clients (for example, making a decision about the need for further assessment or finding out if a client is eligible for or likely to require a service), (3) assessing clients (a more detailed review resulting in decisions about diagnosis or assignment to intervention methods), (4) monitoring (evaluating progress), and (5) making predictions about the likely futures of clients (for example in relation to use of a particular intervention method). As always, a key concern is validity. Does a measure assess what it is presumed to assess? Reliability must also be considered. How stable are responses on a measure given a lack of real change? Unstable measures are not likely to be valid. How sensitive will a measure be to change?

Personality tests may be used to collect assessment data. *Objective tests* include specific questions, statements, or concepts. Clients respond with direct answers, choices, or ratings. *Projective tests* such as the Thematic Apperception Test, incomplete sentences test, and the Rorschach Inkblot Test are purposefully vague and ambiguous. It is assumed that each person will impose on this unstructured stimulus presentation unique meanings that reflect his or her perceptions of the world and responses to it. Psychoanalytic concepts underlay use of most projective tests. These tests focus on assessing general personality characteristics and uncovering unconscious processes. Tests are used not as samples of the content domain (as in behavioral approaches), but as signs of important underlying constructs. Whereas content validity is of great concern in a behavioral perspective, this is not so within a traditional approach. In fact, items may be made deliberately obscure and vague.

Valuable information can be obtained from data clients collect (self-monitoring). As with any other source of data, not all clients will be able or willing to participate. Observation of relevant interactions in real-life settings offers a valuable source of information. This is routinely used in applied behavior analysis. If observation in real-life settings is not possible, observation in role plays may provide a useful alternative. Physiological measures have been used with a broad array of presenting problems including illness such as diabetes and dermatitis and problems such as smoking, anxiety, sexual dysfunction, and rape. Measures include heart rate, blood pressure, respiration rate, skin conductance, muscle tension, and urine analysis. Physiological measures are useful when verbal reports may be inaccurate. Certain kinds of desynchronies between verbal reports of fear and physiological measures may provide useful assessment data. Whenever presenting problems may be related to physical causes, a physical examination should be obtained. Failure to do so may result in overlooking physical causes.

V. ASSESSING THE VALUE OF DATA

Assessment methods differ in their accuracy. For example, self-report of clients or significant others may not accurately reflect what occurs in real life.

Observers may be biased and offer inaccurate data. Measurement inevitably involves error. One cause of systematic error is social desirability; people present themselves in a good light. Criteria that are important to consider in judging the value of assessment data include: (1) reliability, (2) validity, (3) sensitivity, (4) utility, (5) feasibility, and (6) relevance. *Reliability* refers to the consistency of results (in the absence of real change) provided by the same person at different times (time-based reliability), by two different raters of the same events (individual-based reliability) as in inter-rater reliability, or by parallel forms of split-halfs of a measure (item-bound reliability). Reliability places an upward boundary on validity. For example, if responses on a questionnaire vary from time to time (in the absence of real change), it will not be possible to use results of a measure to predict what a person will do in the future.

Validity concerns the question: Does the measure reflect the characteristic it is supposed to measure? For example, does behavior in a role play correspond to what a client does in similar real-life situations? Assessment is more likely to be informative if valid methods are used—methods that have been found to offer accurate information. *Direct* (e.g., observing teacher–student interaction) in contrast to *indirect* measures (e.g., asking a student to complete a questionnaire assumed to offer information about classroom behavior) are typically more valid. Validity (accuracy) is a concern in all assessment frameworks; however, the nature of the concern is different in sign and sample approaches. In a sign approach, behavior is used as a sign of some entity (such as a personality trait) that is at a different level. The concern is with *vertical* validity. Is the sign an accurate indicator of the underlying trait? *Horizontal* validity is of concern in a sample approach. Different levels (e.g., behavior and personality dispositions) are not involved. Examples include: (1) Does self-report provide an accurate account of behavior and related circumstances? (2) Does behavior in role play reflect what occurs in real life? Different responses (overt, cognitive, and physiological) may or may not be related to an event. For example, clients may report anxiety but show no physiological signs of anxiety. This does not mean that their reports are not accurate. For those individuals, the experience of anxiety may be cognitive rather than physical.

The *sensitivity* of measures is important to consider; will a measure reflect changes that occur? The *utility* of a measure is determined by its cost (time, effort, expense) balanced against information provided. *Feasibility* is related to utility. Some measures will not be feasible to gather. Utility may be compromised by the absence of empirically derived norms for a measure. *Norms* offer information about the typical (or average) performance of a group of individuals and allow comparison of data obtained from a client with similar clients. The more representative the sample is to the client, the greater the utility of a measure in relation to a client. *Relevance* should also be considered. Is a measure relevant to presenting problems and related outcomes? Do clients and significant others perceive it as relevant?

VI. THE SOCIAL CONTEXT OF ASSESSMENT

Assessment takes place in the context of a helper–client relationship. The nature of this relationship is considered important in all practice frameworks. Influence of the clinician on the client has been found even in very nondirective approaches. The role of the relationship is viewed differently in different practice perspectives. Great attention is given to the diagnostic value of transference and countertransference effects in psychodynamic therapies and the relationship itself is viewed as the primary vehicle of change. Traditionally, transference has been viewed as a reenactment between the client and the counselor of the client's relationship with significant others in the past, especially parents. Countertransference effects refer to feelings on the part of helpers toward their clients. Transferences are distinguished from therapeutic or working alliances within psychodynamic perspectives. Understanding and analyzing how the client relates to the clinician are of major importance. The way the client relates to the clinician is considered to be indicative of the client's past relationships with significant figures in the past and is thus viewed as a key source of information about the client. Within other perspectives such as cognitive–behavioral approaches, the relationship is viewed as the context within which helping occurs. The interpersonal skills of the clinician are viewed as essential for facilitating a collaborative working relationship, validating and supporting the client, and encouraging clients to acquire valued behaviors.

There is a continuing need throughout assessment to explain the roles and requirements of the client and the counselor, the process that will occur, and the rationale for this. Introductory explanations include an overview of mutual responsibilities and of the framework that will be employed. Because different client behaviors may be required during different phases of assessment and intervention, this "socialization" of the client is an ongoing task. Behavioral clinicians tend to be more directive than psychoanalytically oriented clinicians. They more frequently give instructions, provide information, influence the conversation, and talk more. Clinicians may err by being too directive or too nondirective. Overly directive clinicians may not recognize the need to help clients to explore and to understand their behavior. In contrast, nondirective counselors may err by assuming that self-understanding is sufficient to achieve desired outcomes (when it is not).

VII. COMMON ASSESSMENT ERRORS AND THEIR SOURCES

Errors may occur in any of the three steps involved in assessment: (1) detection of characteristics of the client and his or her life situation that are related to problems and desired outcomes; (2) integration and interpretation of data gathered; and (3) selection of outcomes to pursue in order to remove complaints. Errors made in the first two steps will result in errors in the third step. Examples of common errors are noted below. They result in incomplete or misleading assessment. Some errors involve or result in inappropriate speculation—assuming that what is, can be discovered simply by thinking about the topic.

◆ Hasty assumptions about causes (failure to search for alternative accounts)
◆ Speculating when data collection is called for
◆ Confusing the form and function of behavior
◆ Using misleading and/or uninformative labels
◆ Confusing motivational and behavior deficits
◆ Focusing on pathology and overlooking assets
◆ Collecting irrelevant material
◆ Relying on inaccurate sources (e.g., anecdotal experience)
◆ Being unduly influenced by first impressions
◆ Being mislead by superficial resemblances of a client to other clients in the past or to a stereotype

Errors in detection include inadequate selection of modalities (e.g., confining attention to thoughts),

inadequate selection of data collection methods (e.g., reliance on the interview alone), and errors in the data collection method itself (e.g., observer bias). Inaccurate or incomplete accounts of problems and related factors may occur because attention is too narrowly focused on one source (for example on thoughts or feelings). The fundamental attribution error is made when behavior is attributed to internal dispositions of the individual, overlooking the role of environmental causes. Sources of error in integrating and interpreting data include focusing on consistency rather than informativeness of data, hasty generalization based on limited samples, and inadequate conceptualization of problems due to theoretical biases (e.g., focus only on environmental factors) or superficial knowledge of practice frameworks. Another source of error at this stage is use of vague language that is not informative (e.g., psychological jargon). Errors in selection of outcomes to focus on may occur due to error in the first two phases.

Studies on clinical decision-making indicate that decisions are made on the basis of quite limited data. Even though a great deal of data are gathered, only a small subset is used. Clinicians tend to gather more data than are needed and, as the amount of data gathered increases, so does confidence in its usefulness, even though accuracy may not increase. Clinicians have a tendency to confuse consistency of data with informative value. Irrelevant as well as relevant data may be influential. Clinicians, like other individuals, are affected by limited information-processing capacities and motivational factors. As a consequence, they do not see all there is to see. Because of preconceptions and biases, things that are not actually present may be reported and events that do occur may be overlooked. There is a behavior confirmation tendency. Data are sought that are consistent with preferred theories and preconceptions, and contradictory data tend to be disregarded.

It is easy to recall bizarre behavior and pay excessive attention to this, ignoring less vivid appropriate behavior. The frequency of data that are available is overestimated. Many factors that are not correlated with the true frequency of an event influence estimates of its frequency and how important it seems (such as how visible it is, how vivid it is, and how easily it can be imagined—that is, how available it is). Chance availability may affect clinical decisions—that is, certain events may just happen to be available when thinking about a problem, and these have an impact on what is attended to. Clinicians in given settings are exposed to particular kinds of clients, which may predispose them to make certain assumptions. For example, a psychologist who sees many severely depressed individuals may be primed to attend to signs of depression. Base rate data that are abstract tend to be ignored, which increases the probability of inaccurate inferences. A lack of concern for sample size and sample bias can lead to incorrect judgments. General predictions about a person that are based on tiny samples of behavior in one context are not likely to be accurate, especially when behaviors of interest occur in quite different situations. Not distinguishing between description and inference may result in incorrect assumptions. Use of multiple methods in a contextual practice framework provides the greatest opportunity for sound assessment.

VIII. ETHICAL ISSUES AND FUTURE DIRECTIONS

Lack of assessment competencies may result in the selection of ineffective and/or harmful intervention methods. It is thus incombatant on clinicians to use valid methods that are useful in selecting effective intervention plans. This may require training. There are great stakes in how problems are framed and considerable resources are devoted to influencing how people think about problems. Many problems once viewed as sins were then seen as crimes and more recently are considered to be mental disorders. Explanations influence how people are viewed. In past years, pathology was often attributed to housewives who wanted to work. Incorrect explanations of problems often harm clients. Knowledge about social, political, and economic factors that influence the very definition of personal and social problems will help clinicians to consider problems in their social context and decrease the likelihood of pathologizing clients.

A discussion of clinical assessment would not be complete without noting the increased attention given to evolutionary influences. It is easy to lose sight of the fact that humans are the result of a long evolutionary process and that we carry anatomical,

physiological, and psychological characteristics related to this history. An evolutionary perspective adds a valuable dimension to understanding aggression and caregiving in society, whether directed toward family members or strangers as well as defeat states such as depression and the experiences that may be responsible. Computers will play an increasing role in helping clinicians to handle the many different kinds of data that must often be integrated. There has been considerable interest in the integration of different approaches to clinical practice. Some have explored the possible integration of behavioral and psychoanalytic approaches. Others have investigated the relationship between classical psychodynamics and object relations perspectives. Discussions here concern the nature of inferred conflict and how mental phenomenon of interest are formed. Accurate descriptions of assessment perspectives will increase the likelihood that points of convergence and differences are correctly identified. Continuing research efforts are needed to identify valid assessment methods and indicate assessment frameworks that are most likely to help clients. Increased interest in clinical reasoning bodes well for enhancement of assessment competencies.

Bibliography

Bellack, A. S., and Hersen, M. (Eds.) (1988). ''Behavioral Assessment, 3rd ed. Pergamon, New York.

Bergen, J. R., and Kratchowill, T. R. (1990). ''Behavioral Consultation and Therapy.'' Plenum, New York.

Ciminero, A. R., Calhoun, K. S., and Adams, H. E. (1986). ''Handbook of Behavioral Assessment, 2nd ed. Wiley, New York.

Gambrill, E. (1990). ''Critical Thinking in Clinical Practice.'' Jossey-Bass, San Francisco, CA.

Gilbert, P. (1989). ''Human Nature and Suffering.'' Erlbaum, Hillsdale, NJ.

Goldstein, M., and Hersen, M. (Eds.) (1990). ''Handbook of Psychological Assessment.'' Pergamon, New York.

Howowitz, M. J. (1987). ''States of Mind: Configurational Analysis of Individual Psychology, 2nd ed. Plenum, New York.

Kirk, S., and Kutchins, H. (1992). ''The Selling of DSM: The Rhetoric of Science in Psychiatry.'' Aldine de Gruyter, Hawthorne, NY.

Nay, W. R. (1979). ''Multimethod Clinical Assessment.'' Gardner, New York.

Wetzler, S., and Katz, M. M. (1989). ''Contemporary Approaches to Psychological Assessment.'' Brunner/Mazel, New York.

COGNITIVE BEHAVIOR THERAPY

Jacqueline B. Persons
University of California at San Francisco

Glossary

Applied behavior analysis The use of procedures based on operant conditioning to solve clinical problems; most commonly used in working with severely disturbed patients in settings where the therapist has extensive control over the patients' environment.

Classical conditioning A form of learning in which a previously neutral stimulus, the conditioned stimulus (CS; e.g., a bell), is paired repeatedly with an unconditioned stimulus (UCS; e.g., food). After repeated pairings, the CS elicits a response similar to that elicited by the UCS (e.g., the bell elicits salivation). The organism learns the relationship between the two stimuli. Also called Pavlovian conditioning.

Operant conditioning A form of learning in which a reinforcer (e.g., food) is given to an organism only after it produces a certain response or behavior. The organism learns the relationship between the response and the reinforcer. Also called instrumental conditioning.

Radical behavior therapy The conceptual framework described in the writings of B. F. Skinner. Skinner viewed behavior as controlled by environmental contingencies and focused on approaches to changing behavior that involve modifying behavioral contingencies through operant conditioning.

Schema A belief, or set of beliefs; in Beck's cognitive theory, schemas guide an individual's perception of the self and the world, and, when dysfunctional, predispose individuals to psychopathology.

Social learning theory A learning theory that proposes that learning can occur by watching others and modeling their behavior. The terms modeling, vicarious learning, and observational learning describe aspects of this phenomenon.

COGNITIVE BEHAVIOR THERAPY is a type of psychotherapy that emphasizes direct, active interventions to solve psychological and other difficulties by making direct changes in cognitions (thoughts) and behaviors.

I. HISTORICAL ORIGINS AND THEORETICAL UNDERPINNINGS

Modern cognitive behavior therapy has many roots. Perhaps the earliest is Greek Stoic philosophy, which proposes that one's *view* of one's world, rather than the external world *per se,* determines moods and behavior. Epictetus wrote: "People are disturbed not by things, but by the views which they take of them."

Ivan Pavlov's classical conditioning theory is another root of current-day cognitive behavior therapy. Pavlov demonstrated that if a bell repeatedly sounded immediately before food was presented, a dog *learned* to salivate in response to the bell. That is, the dog learned that the bell predicted, or was associated with, food. This notion underlies many cognitive behavioral interventions. [*See* CLASSICAL CONDITIONING.]

For example, cognitive behavior therapists treating insomnia often suggest the rule, "Beds are for sleeping." That is, they recommend that insomniacs stop reviewing computer printouts, reading exciting novels, ruminating about problems at the office, or any other activity in bed except sleeping and sex. The rationale for this rule stems from classical conditioning theory. If a person habitually spends hours in bed ruminating, then the bed and other stimuli associated with bedtime become paired with ruminating and come to elicit anxiety—which does not facilitate sleep.

Classical conditioning theory also contributed to Joseph Wolpe's pioneering development of systematic desensitization as a treatment for phobias in the 1950s. Wolpe treated phobias by teaching patients to imagine brief scenes of their phobic situation or object while deeply relaxed. In this way, he hoped to teach a new pairing (phobic object–relaxation) to replace the old pairing (phobic object–anxiety). Wolpe used the term "reciprocal inhibition" to describe the psychological mechanism underlying systematic desensitization. Outcome studies have shown that systematic desensitization is an effective treatment for phobias, but experimental studies have not supported Wolpe's view that reciprocal inhibition is the mechanism underlying the treatment. Studies have shown, for example, that patients benefit from systematic desensitization even if relaxation is omitted. What appears to be key, however, is exposure to the feared stimulus.

A simple story illustrates the approach. Imagine that you take your child horseback riding and the child falls off the horse and is frightened. What would you do to help the child overcome the fear? Most of us answer this question by saying something like, "I'd take the child up to the horse, hold her while she pats it, and gradually help her get back on the horse." This folk treatment has in it the central idea underlying most cognitive behavioral treatments for anxiety disorders: to overcome a fear, it is necessary to expose oneself to the feared situation. If the phobic patient repeatedly exposes him or herself to the feared situation, the fear will gradually extinguish. [See Anxiety and Fear.]

Wolpe's systematic desensitization also involved exposure to the feared situation, of course, and behavior therapists have speculated that exposure is in fact the active mechanism underlying systematic desensitization. Modern methods of treating anxiety emphasize exposure therapy and involve repeated, prolonged exposures, in imagination or in real life (*in vivo*), to feared situations, often by beginning with less feared situations and moving gradually to more feared ones.

Exposure treatments can also be understood in cognitive terms. For example, the child who is frightened of horses is probably having cognitions like, "Horses are dangerous; if I approach them, I'll get hurt." The behavioral exposure treatment allows the child to acquire new information that disconfirms this belief and leads to the development of new beliefs, which might include, "Horses are big but I probably won't get hurt," and "I can cope with scary situations."

Edward Thorndike's operant conditioning theory and later developments in the theory by B. F. Skinner also played an important role in the development of cognitive behavior therapy. Operant conditioning theory posits that responses which are reinforced (that is, followed by a pleasureable consequence) will be strengthened and are likely to be repeated, whereas behaviors that are not followed by pleasureable consequences will be weakened and are less likely to be repeated. [See Operant Learning.]

Operant learning theory is widely used by behavior therapists; behavior therapists who utilize operant methods exclusively term themselves "radical behavior therapists." Operant methods are used most frequently by clinicians who work with severely disabled children and adults. This branch of behavior therapy is called applied behavior analysis and emphasizes manipulation of the contingencies in the patient's environment to strengthen desirable behaviors and weaken undesirable ones. Thus, many residential treatment centers for children and adults utilize a point system of rewards for completing household tasks, good grooming, appropriate dress, and appropriate behavior. All of us, of course, utilize strategies from operant conditioning on a daily basis. Most of us receive a paycheck at the end of each week or month of work. How long would we continue to work if we didn't receive that check?

Social learning theory has also made important contributions to behavior therapy. Social learning theorists, perhaps most prominently Albert Bandura of Stanford University, point out that much learning occurs in situations that do not involve conditioning processes. Language learning, for example, is difficult to explain in conditioning terms but often seems to involve observational learning—watching what others do and imitating their behavior. Modeling is often used, for example, in assertiveness training and social skills training approaches to treatment, in which the patient learns a new behavior by watching the therapist model the behavior and then imitating it.

Other roots of modern cognitive behavior therapy include cognitive psychology (including Gordon Bower's associative network theory of mood and memory, George Kelly's notion of "personal constructs,'' Martin Seligman's learned helplessness theory, and Richard Lazarus' notion of the role of cognition in emotional and behavioral change) and developmental psychology (including Bowlby's theory of attachment).

II. FEATURES OF COGNITIVE BEHAVIOR THERAPY

A variety of theoretical models and clinical interventions have been developed by cognitive behavior therapists (many are described below). Although these models and strategies differ in important respects, all share certain features common to all cognitive behavioral approaches to treatment.

A. An Empirical Approach

The cognitive behavior therapist takes an empirical approach to clinical problems, in at least two senses. First, the therapist uses therapeutic strategies that have been shown empirically to be helpful. This is not strictly possible, of course, as each patient's problems are unique, and the efficacy of a particular set of strategies with a particular patient in a particular therapist's office at a particular point in time has not yet been studied. However, within these limitations, cognitive behavior therapists stress empirical verification of their procedures.

Second, the therapist adopts an empirical approach within the therapy itself. At the beginning of treatment, one of the therapist's first tasks is to develop a model of, or way of understanding, the patient's difficulties. This case conceptualization is a hypothesis, as it cannot be verified objectively. For example (after collecting some information about the patient's current difficulties and early life history), the therapist might propose to a young woman suffering from panic attacks that her panic results from the juxtaposition of a very demanding set of life stresses and certain dysfunctional attitudes, or cognitions, such as, ''I must be self-sufficient,'' ''I cannot rely on others,'' ''If I call on others for help, they will not respond.'' If this hypothesis seems plausible to the patient, the therapist will use it to develop treatment interventions. In this case, the therapy would involve several types of interventions: helping the patient examine the accuracy and utility of her beliefs that she must do everything herself and cannot rely on others (including her husband and the therapist) for assistance, assertiveness training, and couples therapy to assist the patient and her husband to develop new patterns of communicating and interacting. All these intervention strategies are based on the hypothesis about the nature of the psychological mechanisms (in this case, cognitions), causing and maintaining the panic. Thus, the success of the interventions can be seen as an indirect test of the hypothesis on which they are based. If these interventions are ineffective, the therapist might revise the hypothesis about the mechanisms driving the patient's problems and test the efficacy of new interventions based on the new hypothesis.

In order to proceed with this an hypothesis-testing approach to treatment, it is important to develop a clear set of treatment goals and some ways of measuring progress, so that an objective assessment of the benefits (or harms) of treatment can be obtained. For example, a depressed patient might be asked to complete a standard measure of depressive symptoms on a weekly basis. In a successful treatment, depressive symptomatology generally begins to lessen within a few weeks; if it does not, the therapist and patient might want to discuss and reevaluate the treatment, perhaps adding a medication treatment or making some other change. Thus, an empirical, hypothesis-testing approach is a hallmark of cognitive behavior therapy.

B. Problem-Focused and Goal-Oriented

Cognitive behavior therapy is problem-focused and goal-oriented. Patients seek treatment because they have problems they want to solve and goals they wish to reach. The cognitive behavior therapist focuses in a direct way on these concrete problems and goals. Problems might include depression, angry outbursts, overeating, drug or alcohol abuse, conflict with the spouse or boss, difficulties managing an oppositional adolescent, and so on.

The therapist works with the patient to identify the problems, decide which ones to work on in therapy, and determine some objective, concrete ways of measuring progress. The primary goal of treatment is to solve the concrete problems. For example, in the case of the young lady with panic attacks described earlier, the primary goal of treatment is to eliminate her panic. A second goal of treatment is to modify her dysfunctional beliefs and cognitions about herself and others so that she is not vulnerable to a later episode of panic when life stresses accumulate.

C. Collaborative

Cognitive behavior therapy is collaborative, with patient and therapist communicating in a direct, straightforward manner to discuss problems, make treatment goals, and develop strategies for attacking the problems to reach the goals. Although the therapist is, in an important sense, the expert, the patient shares actively in the treatment process throughout. The therapist does not simply ''fix'' the patient or solve the problems; the therapist and patient work together to find solutions to the patient's difficulties.

Of course, some patients seek treatment because they have difficulty collaborating with others—including therapists! In this case, it will be difficult to achieve a truly collaborative patient–therapist relationship. The cognitive behavior therapist might address this difficulty by attempting to obtain a collaborative understanding with the patient that collaboration is difficult and that this problem will be addressed in the therapy.

D. Therapist Is Active, Directive

The cognitive behavior therapist plays an active role. Patients come to therapy because they are confronting problems they feel unable to solve on their own. The therapist's role is to provide some active, direct assistance. This is not as simple as it might at first seem, of course. For example, a patient with an anxiety disorder might feel unable to drive across town to the therapist's office due to (irrational, dysfunctional) cognitions like, ''I can't trust myself to drive alone.'' The therapist who solves this problem by driving to the patient's home would not be helping this patient very much. Instead, a more helpful role would involve working with the patient to challenge her beliefs that she cannot drive alone.

E. Homework Is Central

Homework is a central feature of cognitive behavior therapy. The role of homework is consistent with the active, teaching role of the therapist. That is, cognitive behavior therapy is viewed as a place where patients learn new skills and try new behaviors. New skills require practice, and homework supplies that practice. In addition, a key part of cognitive behavior therapy involves learning new behaviors, and many of these cannot be done during the therapy session; therefore, homework assignments provide a structure for carrying out new be-

haviors outside the therapy session. Homework assignments are ideally arrived at in a collaborative way, with the therapist making some suggestions about things the patient might do to take a step ahead on his/her problems, and the patient making a final decision about what he/she feels able to do and believes would be helpful. Typical homework assignments might include asking a young woman for a date, approaching a previously avoided freeway driving situation, initiating a discussion with the spouse about some financial problems, or jogging twice during the week.

F. Focused on the Present

Cognitive-behavior therapy is focused primarily on present-day matters, not on the past. Most of the time in the therapy session is spent discussing current problems and working on solutions to them.

There is an important role, however, for discussions of the past. An understanding of the origins of problems can often be helpful in developing strategies to solve them. For example, Sam, a depressed young man, described his parents as critical, demanding people; on several occasions when, as a child, he did not measure up to his parents' expectations, they threatened to abandon him at the orphanage down the street. An understanding of this early learning history will help Sam's therapist develop a hypothesis about the psychological underpinnings of his current depression that will lead to some treatment interventions. For example, it might be suggested that Sam is depressed because he's avoiding taking on challenging projects at work; as a result, he feels bored and dissatisfied, receives poor performance reviews from his boss, and feels worthless and incompetent. He may avoid taking on challenging projects at work because he's afraid of making a mistake and being fired. This understanding of Sam's depression, which was found in his early history, suggests several treatment interventions, including

- helping Sam evaluate his belief, ''If I make a mistake, I'll be abandoned,'' in his current situation (is his boss really going to fire him if he makes a mistake?)
- alerting Sam to the types of situations which activate this belief
- teaching Sam to identify situations he avoids because of this belief

◆ teaching Sam strategies for responding to the thought, "I'm going to get fired," so he can approach feared situations more comfortably

III. SEVERAL MODELS OF COGNITIVE BEHAVIOR THERAPY

Drawing on the theoretical traditions described earlier, cognitive behavior therapists have developed a variety of models to explain psychopathological behavior in cognitive and behavioral terms. These models, in turn, have led to intervention strategies. Several of these models are presented briefly here.

A. Peter Lewinsohn's Behavioral Model

Peter Lewinsohn, at the University of Oregon, drawing on B. F. Skinner's earlier behavioral analysis, developed, in the late 1960s, a behavioral model of depression. Lewinsohn proposed that depression is the result of environmental changes that reduce the individual's ability to obtain positive reinforcements. Because reinforcers have been withdrawn, many of the individual's usual behaviors extinguish and the individual becomes passive, inactive, and depressed. Lewinsohn's theory emphasizes the role that social reinforcements play in depression, hypothesizing that individuals with deficient social skills become depressed because they experience reduced rates of interpersonal reinforcement. [See Depression.]

Lewinsohn developed a behavioral treatment for depression based on his model. The chief components of the treatment involve teaching the depressed patient to take action to increase his/her pleasant activities and to improve social skills; both strategies, of course, have the goal of increasing the positive reinforcements the depressed person receives. The model has been revised to add some cognitive components that were missing from the original model, including the proposal that depressed individuals have a heightened sense of failure to live up to internal standards and/or to change the current state of affairs, and increased self-critical behaviors. The treatment, however, has remained primarily a behavioral one. Outcome studies have demonstrated that treatment interventions based on Lewinsohn's behavioral model are clearly more effective than no treatment, and apparently equal in efficacy to other treatments.

B. Rational-Emotive Therapy

Albert Ellis developed rational-emotive therapy (RET) in the 1950s; his first of dozens of books on RET, *Reason and Emotion in Psychotherapy*, appeared in 1962. Ellis proposed that irrational beliefs about the self and the world are a major cause of human misery. RET also focuses on behavioral change but, at least in Ellis' hands, emphasizes cognitive persuasion and disputing of irrational beliefs. Ellis views the development of RET as directly related to his early experiences as a sex therapist; sex therapy was by necessity quite pragmatic and behaviorally oriented, even in the 1940s—in contrast to the psychodynamic orientation of other types of psychotherapeutic work. Ellis has devoted his energy to writing books about RET for the lay public and for clinicians; although a few empirical studies examining the efficacy of RET and studying its mechanisms have been conducted, more are needed. [See Psychotherapy.]

C. Aaron T. Beck's Cognitive Therapy

Aaron T. Beck, a psychiatrist at the University of Pennsylvania, has played a central role in the development of cognitive therapy. He published a cognitive theory of depression in the 1960s and subsequently published many books and articles describing cognitive models of anxiety, marital difficulties, and other disorders, as well as intervention strategies for treating these problems.

Beck's ideas originated in his clinical experience with depressed patients; he noticed that these patients experienced a stream of negative thoughts about themselves, others, and the future; he labeled this "the cognitive triad." These thoughts were so ever-present and automatic that often the patient, unless asked to focus on them, was not aware of them; Beck labeled these "automatic thoughts" because they appeared to arise automatically, without any effort or attention. Automatic thoughts can often be elicited by asking, "What thoughts are you having that are causing you to feel depressed?" The depressed patient might respond, "My boss didn't smile at me in the hall this morning," "This means he's angry at me," "He feels I didn't do a good job at that presentation I made last week," "He's planning to fire me," and "No one will respect me after this."

Beck also described a second type of cognition, which he labeled dysfunctional attitudes or schema.

Schemas are beliefs the individual holds about himself and the world, such as, "I'm weak and vulnerable and I can't cope with demanding situations," and "A catastrophe may happen at any moment." (These particular beliefs, according to Beck, are common in patients with anxiety disorders.) These beliefs are usually not easily retrieved, and the individual may not be able to report them. However, according to Beck's theory, they determine the individual's interpretation of daily events and the individual's behavioral, cognitive, and emotional response to these events. For example, a person who believes, "I'm weak and vulnerable and I can't cope with demanding situations," is likely to become quite anxious when he gets in his car and finds his battery is dead. He may have the automatic thought, "I can't handle this, I don't know what to do," and may handle the situation poorly, interrupting his wife in a business meeting to solicit her help instead of taking action himself to solve the problem. Beck observed that in patients suffering from depression, anxiety, and other problems, both types of cognitions (automatic thoughts and dysfunctional attitudes) tend to be distorted and unrealistic.

A large amount of empirical work has been done to test Beck's theory, much of it supportive of the model. Beck and his colleagues also developed a therapy, cognitive behavior therapy, drawn directly from the theory. Cognitive behavior therapy has been applied to depression, anxiety, marital difficulties, substance abuse, eating disorders, and a wide variety of clinical problems. Outcome data have shown that it is an effective treatment—superior to waiting list control conditions and equal to other treatments, including antidepressant medication. A small amount of evidence suggests that cognitive behavior therapy may be superior to other psychotherapies in the treatment of anxiety disorders. [See ANXIETY DISORDERS.]

D. Problem-Solving Therapy

Problem-solving therapy (PST) had its formal origins in a paper published in 1971 by Thomas D'Zurilla and Marvin Goldfried. It rests on assumptions that psychopathology and maladaptive behavior are inversely related to effective problem solving and that training in problem solving can ameliorate and/or prevent psychopathology and maladaptive behavior. [See PROBLEM SOLVING.]

To develop PST, D'Zurilla and Goldfried outlined a model of effective problem solving that includes five components:

1. problem orientation, or the ability to recognize that a problem exists and to arrive at some initial ideas about the cause and significance of the problem
2. problem definition and formulation
3. generation of alternative solutions
4. decision making
5. solution implementation and verification

The treatment teaches these five components of effective problem solving. D'Zurilla and Goldfried suggest that PST is useful in cases where assessment indicates that at least one source of an individual's difficulties is a deficit in problem-solving skills. Of course, a particular clinical problem (e.g., substance abuse) may also result from other deficits as well, and interventions in addition to problem-solving ones may be needed and can be integrated into a comprehensive case-specific treatment package. PST emphasizes social, or interpersonal, problem solving but also addresses other types of problem as well—such as finding a new apartment or handling a car repair.

Empirical studies have shown that PST is helpful in the treatment of a variety of disorders and problems, including depression, anxiety, and marital and family problems. PST has been used both to treat psychopathology and to help nonpatients function at a higher level. PST has been used with adults, children, and adolescents, and to help individuals, groups, and families.

E. Self-Management Therapies

There are several types of self-management theories and therapies. All rest on the assumption that individuals can "stand outside themselves," observe their behavior, and work to change it. Therefore, the general therapeutic strategy common to all self-management therapies is one of teaching individuals principles they can use to manage, or control, their own behavior. The three most important self-management models are Albert Bandura's self-efficacy model, Frederick Kanfer's self-control model, and Donald Meichenbaum's self-instructional model.

Albert Bandura proposes that perceived self-efficacy is a major determinant of human behavior. Perceived self-efficacy is a person's estimate of his/her ability to successfully carry out a certain behavior. Empirical studies have shown that performance and perceived self-efficacy are related; the direction of causality is unclear, however. Perhaps performance (successfully carrying out a behavior) leads to increased self-efficacy; perhaps increased self-efficacy leads to better performance. Bandura has not developed a formal set of treatment procedures based on his model. He proposes that psychological treatments of *any* sort are therapeutic in part because they increase the patient's sense of self-efficacy. [*See* SELF-EFFICACY.]

Frederick Kanfer's approach to treatment is based on a model of self-regulation he developed with his colleagues. The model was further elaborated by Lynn Rehm, who developed what he called a self-control model for depression. The focus of treatment based on the model is on training self-regulatory behaviors and increasing motivation to use those behaviors. Self-regulatory behaviors include self-monitoring, self-evaluation, and self-reinforcement. Several studies have shown that components of the model are helpful in the treatment of a variety of clinical problems, including depression, alcoholism, social evaluation anxiety, and children's problems, among others. Unfortunately, however, studies of self-control treatment for depression show that treatments utilizing single components of the model are as effective as treatments utilizing multiple components. These findings are disappointing from a theoretical point of view, as the model predicts that a treatment that includes all of the components ought to be more effective than a treatment that includes only one or two.

Donald Meichenbaum's self-instructional training had its origins in developmental psychology. Research studies suggested that children develop the ability to control their behaviors in a predictable set of stages over time. A child's behavior is first directed by parental speech, then shifts to the child's overt, then covert speech, and is finally internalized (thoughts). Meichenbaum developed a treatment to train people to progress through these stages.

Meichenbaum's model rests on the assumption that behavior is directed by internal self-instructions and that behavioral problems (inhibitions, excesses) are due to deficits in this internal self-instructional process. For example, the student preparing for an exam who uses the internal "self-instruction" "I'm going to fail" will not be very successful in preparing for the exam. The therapist using the self-instructional model will work with the student to develop some more adaptive ways of talking to him/herself, perhaps including, "I'm going to do the best I can," and "I'll focus on the material instead of my fears about the exam."

Self-instructional methods have been shown to be helpful in reducing impulsivity in children and in assisting adults with a variety of problems, including anger, anxiety, and pain. Many of the cognitive behavioral models described earlier include a self-instructional component, including the exposure approaches to fear and social skills training.

F. Multimodal Therapy

Arnold Lazarus developed his own approach to behavior therapy, which he labeled "multimodal therapy." Multimodal therapy views human misery and problems as having multiple causes and dimensions, and therefore views effective treatment as having multiple components as well. The acronym BASIC ID summarizes the aspects of problems that require assessment and intervention in Lazarus' model: *B*ehaviors, *A*ffective processes, *S*ensations, *I*mages, *C*ognitions, *I*nterpersonal relationships, and biological functions (*D*rugs and other biological interventions).

A strength of Lazarus' approach is that it avoids the unidimensional focus that some behavioral treatments appear to have (e.g., Ellis seems to focus only on beliefs). Its primary weakness is that few outcome studies have examined its efficacy.

G. Radical Behavior Therapy

The term "radical behavior therapy" refers to treatment procedures based on Skinner's operant learning model. The term "radical" derives from the Latin word "radix," meaning "root." Radical behavior therapists try to get to the "root" of problematic behaviors by searching for and manipulating the environmental contingencies that control the behaviors.

Radical behavior therapists label themselves "behavior therapists" but do not generally label themselves "cognitive behavior therapists" because they reject the usual view of cognitions adopted by cognitive behavior therapists. Radical behavior therapists reject the view of cognitions as having a special status. Instead, the radical behavior therapist views a cognition as simply a type of behavior. According to this view, cognitions, like other behaviors, can be understood only within the context of the contingencies controlling the behavior.

For example, a patient might offer effusive thanks to his therapist. The meaning of this piece of verbal behavior, according to the radical behavior therapist, is not determined by the meanings of the words in the patient's declaration; instead, it depends on the context in which the behavior occurs. For example, the patient's statement might be an attempt to reinforce the therapist for not focusing on last week's uncompleted homework assignment, or it might be an attempt to reinforce the therapist for confronting the patient about his substance abuse problem.

As described earlier, the first applications of operant methods to clinical problems involved the use of the operant methods in treating severely disabled patients, where the therapist has a good deal of control over the patient's environment. Newer developments in radical behavior therapy have led to attention to other types of clinical problems. Steven Hayes and Robert Kohlenberg have adapted operant principles to the treatment of depression, anxiety, and the typical types of problems seen in patients seeking outpatient psychotherapy.

Steven C. Hayes recently described a therapeutic approach he labels "comprehensive distancing." He states that it is useful for patients who view their difficulties as due to certain private behaviors that the patient is not controlling effectively. One example is the patient who says, "I avoid driving on the bridge because I'm anxious, and I have to control my anxiety in order to be able to drive." In Hayes' model, anxiety is a private behavior that the patient believes must be controlled in order to solve the driving problem. However, Hayes points out that attempts to control anxiety generally backfire: the attempt to control anxiety generally leads to increased anxiety. Therapy focuses on teaching clients to let go of the struggle to solve problems by controlling private behaviors like anxiety.

Robert Kohlenberg and Mavis Tsai recently described a radical behavioral approach to treatment they call "functional analytic psychotherapy." Functional analytic psychotherapy focuses on the behaviors that generally occur in therapy sessions, particularly interpersonal behaviors that would be expected to occur in the context of the patient–therapist relationship. Thus, they view their therapeutic approach as particularly helpful to patients who have interpersonal difficulties—and of course, many, if not most, psychotherapy patients meet this description. The functional analytic psychotherapist treats interpersonal difficulties by directly eliciting and rewarding, in immediate and nonarbitrary ways (e.g., smiles and expressions of caring), improvements in the patient's interpersonal behaviors. Although the therapist does attempt to work on generalization of

gains to relationships outside that of the patient–therapist, this therapy takes place nearly entirely within the patient–therapist relationship, which therefore becomes quite intense.

Both comprehensive distancing and functional analytic psychotherapy are new approaches, so virtually no outcome data examining the efficacy of these approaches are available. However, they are fascinating new applications of behavioral principles to clinical problems.

H. Developmental Cognitive Therapies

Two new approaches to cognitive behavior therapy fall under the rubric "developmental cognitive therapies": the developmental cognitive therapy described by Michael Mahoney, and "structural psychotherapy," developed in Rome by Vittorio Guidano and Gianni Liotti. Both models emphasize the unitary nature of self-knowledge, rather than focusing separately on cognition, behavior, and emotion. They adopt the constructivistic view that the mind actively constructs the individual's reality, rather than simply recording environmental inputs, and, drawing on John Bowlby's attachment theory, they view early attachment experiences as contributing importantly to the development of the sense of self.

The goal of the developmental cognitive therapies is not to correct distortions in thinking that prevent the individual from seeing the external world as it "really is" but instead on helping the individual construct an adaptive, satisfying view of self and world. Treatment interventions differ from traditional ones in placing more emphasis on early experiences that shaped the patient's views of self and world. For example, the therapist might encourage a chronological review of early experiences that the patient views as supporting the current, maladaptive view of the self and the world. The goal of this review is to collect new evidence, previously ignored or discounted, that will allow the patient to construct a new, more adaptive, productive, and happier view of the world and the self. The developmental therapies are a new development in cognitive behavior therapy; as a result, no empirical studies examining the efficacy of these approaches are yet available.

IV. EFFICACY OF COGNITIVE BEHAVIOR THERAPY

Cognitive behavior therapists place a high value on the empirical demonstration of the efficacy of their intervention strategies. Literally hundreds of published studies demonstrate the efficacy of cognitive-behavioral therapies; most are published in the *Journal of Consulting and Clinical Psychology, Behavior Therapy, Behaviour Research and Therapy, Cognitive Therapy and Research,* and *Archives of General Psychiatry,* among others. Additional outcome studies are published daily.

Controlled outcome studies indicate that cognitive behavior therapy (as compared to no treatment) is effective in the treatment of a wide variety of disorders and problems, including anxiety disorders, depression, marital difficulties, sexual disorders and dysfunction, insomnia, chronic pain, substance abuse, eating disorders, and children's problems (e.g., enuresis, hyperactivity, autism), among others. Cognitive behavior therapy has also shown to be helpful in treating medical problems like irritable bowel syndrome, headaches, and hypertension. Cognitive behavior therapy has also been shown to be helpful to medical patients who have difficulty adhering to a demanding medical regimen (e.g., those suffering from diabetes) or who must undergo stressful medical procedures, including chemotherapy.

Although a substantial body of data indicates that patients receiving cognitive behavior therapy fare better than patients in a waiting-list (untreated) control condition, data generally do not support the assertion that cognitive behavioral therapies are superior to other active treatments. However, it would be fair to say that more evidence supports the efficacy of cognitive behavior therapy than supports the efficacy of other psychotherapies; this statement is true simply because the efficacy of other psychotherapies (particularly the traditional, long-term psychodynamic therapies) has rarely been studied empirically.

V. CURRENT ISSUES

A major current issue within cognitive behavior therapy is the tension between cognitive and noncognitive behaviorists. Many noncognitive behaviorists left the major professional association, the Association for Advancement of Behavior Therapy (AABT), and formed the Association for Behavior Analysis (ABA). This split reflects a theoretical schism; ABA members tend to be radical behavior therapists and to reject the view that cognitions have special status.

Related to the cognitive/noncognitive schism is a renewed interest in the role of environment. Researchers are now giving more attention to the life events that influence the development of and appear to activate symptoms and problems. The "cognitive revolution" in cognitive behavior therapy shifted behaviorists' attention from external environmental contingencies, which were seen as controlling behavior, to internal variables (cognitions). The pendulum is now swinging the other way.

Another current issue is the gap between research and practice, commonly called the scientist–practitioner gap. The gap is frequently blamed on clinicians' reluctance to read the research literature. However, several researchers have pointed out that clinicians may not read the literature because researchers do not study questions that are of interest to the practicing clinician.

Controlled outcome studies are a good example of the scientist–practitioner debate. In the typical controlled outcome study, patients receive a standardized treatment package; that is, each patient receives the same treatment. However, clinicians rebel against this approach to treatment, insisting that each patient is unique and needs an individualized treatment plan. In fact, the models of cognitive behavior therapy are consistent with clinicians' views that before problematic behaviors can be changed, the therapist must develop a hypothesis about the nature of the contingencies or cognitions that cause and maintain the behaviors. However, individualized assessment and treatment are abandoned in the usual controlled outcome study. The author recently described a new model for outcome research, suggesting that the approach to treatment adopted by clinicians in their daily work (individual assessment followed by individualized treatment based on the results of the assessment) be adopted by outcome researchers.

VI. FUTURE DIRECTIONS

Several future directions are apparent. First, cognitive behavior therapists, like many other psychotherapists, are interested in the possibilities of psychotherapy integration. The psychotherapy integration movement, formalized in the recent formation of the Society for Exploration of Psychotherapy Integration (SEPI) and by the appearance of a new journal, the *Journal for Psychotherapy Integration,* reflects the new interest in the idea that psychotherapies may be more alike than different. Cognitive behavior therapists are now considering questions like: "what techniques from psychodynamic psychotherapy might improve cognitive-behavior therapy?''

Second, new theoretical developments are on the horizon, with the radical behavior therapists returning to the traditional roots of behavior therapy in operant conditioning, and the developmental cognitive therapists ranging farther afield, toward developmental psychology and cognitive psychology.

A third direction of development for the future is the expansion of cognitive behavioral approaches to the treatment of new problems, particularly problems commonly seen by physicians, such as pain and headache. Behavioral interventions are increasingly important in the development of strategies for preventing serious medical problems; interventions to change risky sexual behaviors and prevent AIDS are quite important in this regard.

Finally, cognitive behavior therapists continue to emphasize empirical verification of the efficacy of their strategies, and researchers will continue to work to enhance the efficacy of strategies currently available, and to develop new, even more effective, intervention strategies.

Bibliography

Beck, A. T., Rush, A. J., Shaw, B. F., and Emery, G. (1979). ''Cognitive Therapy of Depression.'' Guilford, New York.

Dobson, K. S. (Ed.) (1988). ''Handbook of Cognitive-Behavioral Therapies.'' Guilford, New York.

Jacobson, N. S. (Ed.) (1987). ''Psychotherapists in Clinical Practice.'' Guilford, New York.

Kazdin, A. E. (1975). ''Behavior Modification in Applied Settings.'' Dorsey Press, Homewood, IL.

Persons, J. B. (1989). ''Cognitive Therapy in Practice: A Case Formulation Approach.'' Norton, New York.

COGNITIVE DEVELOPMENT

Marvin W. Daehler
University of Massachusetts at Amherst

Glossary

Analogical transfer The ability to employ a principle or procedure effective in one domain to achieve success on a problem in a new domain.

Cardinality The rule that the size of an array is identical to the number last assigned when items are counted accurately.

Cognitive development The wide array of changes in representing and processing information observed from infancy to adulthood that contributes to increasingly mature thinking and behavior.

Concept A representation that preserves common features or shared functional relationships of a set of specific stimuli, events, or other kind of information.

Context The broad social and cultural conditions that bear upon and influence goals, purposes, and values along with the setting, related knowledge, and skills associated with reasoning and problem solving.

Egocentrism An orientation in which one's own perspective dominates and in which another's perspective may not even be recognized.

Habituation The gradual decline in responding associated with the repeated or lengthy occurrence of a stimulus.

Intermodal perception Coordination of information arising from two or more sensory modalities to perceive and make inferences about an entity.

Metacognition An individual's awareness and knowledge of his or her own cognitive capacities and processes.

Object permanence The understanding that objects still exist and occupy space even though no longer within the visual field.

Recall memory The ability to retrieve or reproduce a previously encountered stimulus or event that is no longer perceptually present.

Recognition memory The ability to determine whether a currently available stimulus or event is identical or similar to one previously encountered.

Scheme In Piagetian theory, the mental structure which is the basis for systematic behavior extended to similar objects and situations.

COGNITIVE DEVELOPMENT is concerned with those changes that take place in thinking and knowing during an individual's earlier years, particularly from infancy to young adulthood. The ability both to accumulate enormous knowledge of our physical, social, and mental environs and to perform complex reasoning in these various domains helps to set apart human intellectual and behavioral competencies from those observed in other animals. Not surprisingly, the development of representations, structures, and processes underlying such capacities has been of considerable interest in research on infants, children, and adolescents.

I. DEFINING ASPECTS OF COGNITIVE DEVELOPMENT

A central tenet of theories of cognition and cognitive development is that the mind is able to process and represent information obtained through various sensory receptors such as eyes, ears, nose, and skin. A representation is something that stands for something else. In other words, it is a kind of model, map, label, or symbol for some entity that is to be represented. Psychologists assume that the nature of mental representations, the structures of the mind that serve to construct and organize these representations, and the processes that incorporate, store, arrange, and retrieve them undergo important modifications, especially during the first and second decade of an individual's life.

Consider, for example, how we might represent the sight of another's face. At a physiological level, impressions received via visual receptors must necessarily be preserved through some quality or state involving the neurons, cells within the nervous system designed to transmit messages electrochemically. This neurophysiological level of representation may assist us in learning how the brain works, but cognitive researchers are primarily interested in the mind and how it serves as the basis for thinking and knowing. At the level of the mind, we must consider what meaning the representation possesses for an individual. For example, would a very young infant who can perceptually process the basic features and elements comprising eyes, ears, nose, and mouth be able to appreciate this array as a configuration depicting someone's face?

Even if the baby recognizes a human face, is his or her representation of that face the same as that created by the older child or adult? In the preverbal infant, representations may be constructed and stored in the form of dynamic procedures that are exhibited behaviorally as sets of sensorimotor actions. Perhaps at a very early age representations can also take a form like images that encompass and retain information which closely parallels the spatial qualities of the observed face. The older child, on the other hand, might possess more arbitrary and abstract representational forms similar, perhaps, to such verbal propositions as "That is a face!" Important developmental questions emerge concerning whether these various kinds of representations are available to children of different ages and how each type might influence the capacity to think about and behave toward the surrounding world. A further intriguing possibility is that these different kinds of representations are associated with and distributed over large numbers of neural paths and connections so that meaning is achieved through many components of the mind working together.

Other developmental questions arise concerning the structures and processes associated with thinking and knowing. Do infants and young children possess the same kind of memory as adults? Does the size or organization of the memory system change with development? Do the ways in which information is attended to, how it is stored and retrieved, and how it is evaluated undergo revisions and if so, what implications do such changes have for the development of thinking?

Describing the mind of the infant, child, and adult is an important objective in research on cognitive development. Another central purpose, however, is to explain how any observed change comes about. Numerous theories have been proposed to provide explanations of change. However, one issue that must be addressed by all of these theories concerns the contribution of nature and nurture to cognitive development. Are infants born with certain abilities? Although the answer to this question remains controversial, at least some basic sensory, learning, and memory processes must be available in newborns to permit them to eventually become skilled and competent intellectual beings. However, determining exactly which capacities babies initially exhibit remains a major research challenge.

A closely related issue confronting theories of cognitive development is how and to what extent experience modifies these early capacities. When development takes place, is it the result of maturation, the gradual unfolding over time of genetically based programs? Or are particular experiences, training, or opportunities to act upon the environment essential to intellectual progress? Few would hold to the view that cognitive development simply unfolds. Thus, to a considerable extent, the nature, sequence, and timing of experience is assumed to play an important role in intellectual growth. However, extensive debates among caregivers and throughout society more broadly about how much and what kinds of learning opportunities to make available to young children prior to and during the formal school years underscore the many different positions that can be taken on the role of experience in cognitive development.

Still another central issue with respect to cognitive development pertains to whether changes exhibit stage-like qualities, that is, proceed through periods in which fundamentally distinctive, qualitatively different ways of thinking are displayed, or whether developmental differences are the outcome of more gradual, cumulative transformations. Is the thinking of 2 year olds compared to the thinking of 10 year olds truly distinctive in that different structures and processes are involved? Or are observed differences the aftermath of increased speed or efficiency with which those structures and processes operate or an outgrowth of access to greater amounts of information? While intellectual capacities undergo dramatic transformations from infancy to adulthood, the underlying mechanisms responsible for these changes may be more continuous than observable behavior suggests.

One additional example of the kind of problems challenging our understanding of cognitive development concerns the universality of the changes that are observed. Although all intellectually competent individuals must possess basic representational capacities and a set of cognitive structures with which to process them, individual differences in cognition may evolve within and between various cultures. Efforts have increased in recent years to explore whether the historic and social context in which thinking originates can have a significant bearing on cognitive development.

II. HISTORICAL AND THEORETICAL INFLUENCES

The earliest systematic efforts to understand the development of cognition originated in attempts to define and measure intelligence. In 1905, Alfred Binet and Theodore Simon devised an extensive battery of problem solving, verbal reasoning, and logical thought tasks for children. They did so in response to an invitation by French government authorities to establish a test that would distinguish children who could benefit from the regular school curriculum from those who could not. Their efforts provided the foundation for many of the kinds of intelligence tests with which we are familiar today. Although intelligence tests can yield a wealth of information about the cognitive capacities of children, they rarely have been effective in doing so largely because of their emphasis on differences in performance rather than on establishing an inventory of the basic properties which underlie thinking and complex behavior. [See INTELLIGENCE.]

A somewhat more direct historical contribution to the study of cognitive development can be found in the research of learning theorists. A central assumption in most learning theories is that events, sensations, or ideas become associated when they occur together. Such associations, established through classical and operant conditioning, are hypothesized to serve as the cornerstone for memory, knowledge, and complex human thought. [See CLASSICAL CONDITIONING; OPERANT LEARNING.]

Learning unquestionably provides an important means by which the contents of an individual's rep-

resentations become altered. However, one impediment to most learning theories has been the absence of a language for describing the structures and processes that evoke representations. Another limitation has been the frequent assumption that the mind is a passive receptacle of associated experiences, an assumption which runs counter to an increasingly more popular interpretation of the mind as an active information processor.

Dissatisfaction with learning theory explanations of cognitive development increased in the 1960s and early 1970s as two other theoretical orientations, Piaget's theory of cognitive development and information-processing perspectives, began to influence psychologists. Jean Piaget, a Swiss psychologist originally trained in biology, initiated an extensive program of research on the development of knowledge beginning in the 1920s.

In Piaget's theory, thinking is conceptualized as a kind of biological adaptation which undergoes considerable modification during infancy and throughout the childhood years. As a consequence, cognition becomes more systematic and organized with development. The basic mental structure, the *scheme,* serves to instate and extend a behavior across similar objects and situations. Schemes change with experience. In fact, the newborn exhibits only a few reflexive schemes such as sucking. But as the infant exercises this and other reflexive behaviors, his or her schemes are transformed by the constraints imposed by the external environment. Experience repeatedly modifies schemes and forms the basis for more functionally adaptive behaviors. As schemes become integrated and organized and are eventually enacted with accompanying external motor activity, they function as the basic modules making up thinking and reasoning. Piaget further theorized that these more advanced, effective schemes are *constructed* by the child; they are not the product of forces working on the passive mind. Thus, infant and child are active participants in their own cognitive development.

Probably one of the most widely publicized features of Piaget's theory is its delineation of four stages in cognitive development. Some of the chief characteristics of thinking associated with the four stages—sensorimotor, preoperational, concrete operations, and formal operations—are summarized in Table I.

Each successive stage in Piaget's theory marks a qualitatively different level of thinking that permits more effective means of reasoning, problem solving,

TABLE I
Piaget's Stages of Cognitive Development

Stage (and approximate age range)	Major cognitive structures	Behavioral achievements
Sensorimotor (birth until 18–24 months)	Schemes are tied to motor actions which initially begin as reflexes but which develop into complex, coordinated ways of acting upon the environment.	Reflexive sucking, grasping, looking, etc., are transformed into refined acts such as reaching for and manipulating objects. Practical knowledge of space, causality, and means to solve problems emerge.
Preoperational (18 months–7 years)	Mental symbols are constructed and begin to be employed, but thinking is intuitive rather than logical, and egocentric, that is, biased by the child's perspective and centered on limited perceptual qualities of objects and events.	Children are now able to use language, engage in imaginative activities such as pretend play, and understand drawings. However, ability to reason about classes, relations, space, time, and causality is restricted and prone to systematic errors.
Concrete operational (7–11 years)	Mental schemes are organized into coherent structures that yield logical reasoning, but thought remains limited to concrete objects, events, and relationships.	Children can reason effectively about classes of objects and their relationships and about spatial, temporal, and causal phenomena.
Formal operations (11 years and above)	The object of thought can extend beyond the physically present and observable to include the abstract and hypothetical.	Children can engage in systematic reasoning about possibilities as well as reality. Morality, religion, politics, and other highly conceptual subjects including the self can become the focus of thought and reflection.

and engaging the environment. Nevertheless, each succeeding stage incorporates and integrates aspects of earlier stages; thus, there is continuity despite the qualitative differences. Every child proceeds through the stages in the same order; their acquisition is hypothesized to follow an invariant sequence. Moreover, the stages are considered to be universal although the age at which a child reaches each and how completely the final stage of thinking is exhibited depends on cultural and experiential influences.

Piaget's encompassing theoretical views and his frequently surprising claims about both the limits and strengths of infant and child cognition have led to a wealth of studies investigating the development of representational and thinking capacities. Although his emphasis on the active nature of thought met with widespread acceptance, Piaget's notions about stages in cognitive development have been criticized severely. As a result, various information-processing perspectives, popular throughout much of cognitive psychology, have beome increasingly attractive to developmental researchers in their recent efforts to understand changes in thinking and knowing.

A central assumption in information-processing viewpoints is that the human mind, like the computer, has a limited capacity to operate on information. Not surprisingly, in infants and children compared to adults, that capacity may be even more limited. For example, various memory systems could store fewer units of information in children than in adults. Additionally, plans, procedures, rules, and strategies created to circumvent limitations in storing, retrieving, and organizing information could undergo substantial developmental modifications.

Another characteristic of information processing that very likely changes with development and experience is the amount of attention or energy that must be allocated to various cognitive activities. Engaging in a new conceptual task may demand considerable concentration. Once mastered, however, that activity may be performed automatically, that is, with very little attention paid to it. As an example, consider the preschooler's earliest challenges in learning to read. At first, distinguishing the markings of the individual letters of a text may usurp all the child's resources. With practice, this level of encoding may proceed more rapidly and routinely so that attention can be allocated to deciphering the pattern of letters that form words. In the more proficient reader, processing words seems to require relatively few cognitive resources; attention can be directed to comprehending the meaning of the string of words. Concept learning, problem solving, and many of the mental operations relying on the knowledge that we possess can gain enormous benefits from this process of automatization.

Information-processing approaches have come to dominate explanations of cognitive development in recent years. For the most part, the child's improving capacity to take in information more efficiently, to process it more automatically, to implement more powerful strategies, and to generalize these capacities more broadly have been offered as prominent explanatory mechanisms for the differences in thinking that are observed from infancy to young adulthood.

One frequent criticism of information-processing perspectives is that cognitive abilities, rather than a reflection of a general capacity, are often closely tied to what an individual understands about a particular domain of knowledge. As a result of this observation, researchers have begun to consider more fully the contexts and conditions under which cognitive development takes place. Context, narrowly defined as an analysis of the knowledge and demands required in a specific task, has long been of interest in information-processing approaches. However, the broader view of context embraces the purposes, goals, and values of thinking and problem solving, aspects of cognition which are often defined by social and cultural factors.

The tasks a child confronts (e.g., learning to read, acquiring the skills to weave cloth or herd animals, gaining knowledge of the constellations to navigate the open seas, solving physics problems), the tools and resources provided (e.g., written alphabets, computers, formal schools), and the strategies and approaches promoted by a community for engaging in these tasks are made available and are broadly governed by historical and cultural achievements. Moreover, the acquisition of specific cognitive tasks in younger members of the community is typically monitored and regulated by parents, teachers, even informal mentors.

Given that thinking and problem solving are embedded within a social context, consideration of the role that others play in cognitive development has taken on increasing importance. An essential principle of Lev Vygotsky's sociohistorical theory of cognitive development is that infants and children adopt ways of thinking and solving problems that are informally modeled as well as culturally prescribed.

Much of cognition is a social phenomenon, transmitted to younger, less competent members of the community by those who are more skilled or knowledgeable in the use of intellectual tools and ways of thinking. For example, when parents reserve time to read to their preschoolers, they are not only proclaiming to their children the importance of literacy, but also demonstrating and encouraging the distinctive skills and capacities allied with it. Thus, from Vygotsky's perspective, others serve as an interdependent resource for an individual's construction of knowledge and ways of thinking.

III. MAJOR SPHERES OF CHANGE

The newborn is able to see, hear, smell, taste, and feel (even well before birth) although these sensory and perceptual capacities undergo substantial refinement especially during the first few weeks and months after delivery. For example, vision, the most extensively researched perceptual system in babies, improves dramatically during the first 6 months of infancy because sensory receptors proliferate in the retina and neurons grow extensively in the subcortical and cortical regions of the brain associated with visual processing during this time. But newborns are far from blind and they show preferences for attending to contours (edges or dark–light transitions in patterns), movement, and visual stimuli of moderate brightness. Thus, babies busily process information visually and via other receptor systems. [See PERCEPTUAL DEVELOPMENT.]

A. Attention

Infants less than 1 or 2 months of age often fail to scan visual arrays systematically, especially the internal features of a complex stimulus such as the eyes or mouth of a human face; their attention is caught instead by some outer component such as chin or hairline. Not surprisingly, then, infants' preferences for looking at more detailed stimuli over less complex visual arrays or at faces rather than stimuli of similar complexity and detail are not clearly evident until about 2 months of age when they begin to scan displays far more thoroughly.

By 3 months of age, perhaps even before, infants begin to display behaviors suggesting an understanding of unity and coherence for objects; they can infer, for example, from the correlated motion associated with visible end segments that an occluded middle portion of a rod also exists to connect the ends. These data have led some researchers to propose that infants are already beginning to make inferences and *expect* certain things about their environment based on the limited visual information that is available.

Other evidence that infants expect particular relationships can be found in work on *intermodal perception,* the coordination of information arising from two or more sensory modalities. By 4 months of age infants will direct more of their looking to visual events that match accompanying auditory sequences in rhythm and tempo; they also will soon link approaching and retreating visual events with sounds that signal the same progressions. Within a few weeks of birth, babies may even recognize an object visually that has only been explored with their mouth.

Attention undergoes several kinds of change during early childhood. One trend, especially prominent between the ages of 1 and 6 years, is an increased ability to focus on a task or set of materials. This heightened focus permits greater learning about any specific task. Another notable developmental change extending into the school years is the ability of older children to deploy their attention more systematically. For example, when comparing two pictures, older children are more likely to explore each efficiently and thoroughly, and not surprisingly, to make more accurate judgments about their similarities and differences. A further indication of change is found in the ability to attend more selectively to relevant aspects of a situation and to ignore distracting features.

B. Memory

An extremely important component of cognition is memory. Even newborns show habituation, a reduction in responding to the repeated or lengthy occurrence of a stimulus, one indicator of basic memory capacity. But when do more traditional signs of memory such as the ability to recognize or recall an event emerge? Recognition memory, that is, the capacity to identify something briefly experienced before, is demonstrated by babies within weeks of birth and may be possible even earlier. The capacity to recall information, that is, to retrieve or reproduce a stimulus or event no longer perceptually present, is readily apparent by about 1 year of age and most likely begins several months before this time. For example, infants less than a year old have been ob-

served to search in the correct location for a hidden toy or in a specific bureau drawer for an article of clothing. [*See* MEMORY.]

Cataloging the early appearance of basic memory capacities constitutes only a small part of the story associated with its development. As children mature, they display striking changes in the amount of information they can remember. This observation has led to considerable research concerned with how memory improves over childhood. For the most part, developmental differences do not appear to stem from major changes in the availability or capacities of sensory, short-term (or working), and long-term memory, structures commonly theorized to be important in remembering. One exception to this claim bears upon the operational efficiency of the various memory systems; the speed and proficiency with which information is processed may increase with development to permit the allocation of a greater proportion of limited resources to storage and retrieval and less to encoding. Thus, for younger children, a greater proportion of effort may be needed to register information whereas for older children, a greater proportion of effort can be allocated to processes that help to organize and retain that information.

Just as significant are the expanding abilities of children to implement memory strategies and processes, to foster encoding, maintenance, and retrieval of information. As children mature, they begin to execute a variety of strategies to help them recall things. Among them are *rehearsal,* that is, repeating a list of items over and over (such as the numbers to dial in making a telephone call), a technique that maintains information in short-term memory over a brief period of time. Children in western societies spontaneously begin to display this tactic around 6 or 7 years of age and as they become older, engage in it more competently. While younger children can also be trained to rehearse, they have difficulty actively maintaining rehearsal even though it improves their recall.

A second strategy facilitating memory bears upon the *organization* of information, that is, conceptualizing it to fit some category or grouping familiar to the individual. For example, memory for things to be purchased for a party can be improved if the items are grouped into food, decoration, and entertainment categories. Preschoolers are much less likely than are older children to cluster items in this way.

Another strategy assisting memory is called *elaboration.* This technique involves associating an item with something that can be easily remembered or creating a connection among things to be remembered in such a way that the items form a conspicuous configuration. To help remember, a child asked to bring a stuffed bear, an umbrella, and an old pair of glasses for the school play the next day might imagine the bear wearing thick glasses and holding a large umbrella while walking in the pouring rain. The mnemonic verse "Thirty days hath September" is another example of elaboration, in this case, a poem designed to help remember the number of days in each month of the year. Elaboration emerges as a spontaneous strategy fairly late in development, typically not until the adolescent years, and even adults often fail to engage in it systematically in their efforts to remember.

There are other strategies such as providing *retrieval cues* to facilitate search (e.g., placing category labels on boxes containing groups of items to identify what is in each). The point to be emphasized, however, for all of these memory strategies is that younger children are less likely than older children to initiate them spontaneously, to perform them efficiently, and to maintain them after training despite their benefits to performance on memory-related tasks. This latter handicap may stem from a limited understanding of *metacognition,* that is, an individual's awareness and knowledge of his or her own cognitive capacities and processes and how they aid one's behavior. Young children seem less able to reflect upon cognitive processes, including those related to memory, that are beneficial to thinking and problem solving. [*See* Metacognition.]

Still another major factor contributing to improved memory abilities is the rapidly expanding knowledge base created as a result of experience. Infants and very young children simply do not have a lot of content knowledge; they have not had enough experience to learn very much about their world. However, the general knowledge an individual acquires and has available in long-term memory can have substantial consequences for recall. For example, children who are expert chess players can reconstruct briefly seen arrangements of legitimately positioned pawns, knights, rooks, and so forth on a chess board far more effectively than adults who are novice chess players. Preschoolers who know a great deal about dinosaurs are often able to remember a list of their names better than adults.

With repeated experiences, humans typically formulate *scripts,* expectations about commonly encountered activities (such as the things a child does before going to school—get dressed, eat breakfast, brush teeth, put on coat to go outside, etc.). These scripts serve as additional organizational frameworks for storing and retrieving specific memories. Thus, increases in content knowledge may be a factor that promotes processing efficiency and enhances strategic and metacognitive abilities. The knowledge base is clearly an important component of memory development.

C. Concepts

Individuals remember and reason about concepts. Concepts are representations that preserve common features or functional relationships shared by a set of specific stimuli, events, or other kind of information. A vigorous research effort is focused on the kinds of concepts infants and young children possess and how their concepts develop. The inclination, for humans, even babies, to form concepts is unquestionably a basic requirement for development; otherwise we would treat each new example of a stimulus or event as if it belonged to a category totally different from anything experienced before. How concepts are established has been a major issue for both cognitive and developmental psychology.

When infants and children first form a concept, remembering specific instances that are members of the category could be especially important. From these exemplars, the child may eventually come to appreciate the correlated or defining features that serve to distinguish one concept from another. Exactly how this process takes place remains puzzling but children, even infants, very likely initiate essentially informal theories about things that look, function, or otherwise relate to each other in similar ways to form their initial concepts. [*See* Categorization.]

When most of us are asked to consider examples of a concept, we typically think *about* specific classes of things, e.g., dogs, mothers, planets, or perhaps some abstract notion such as justice. But many important concepts relate to broad and pervasive facets of physical and social reality such as time, space, number, and even the mind and self. For example, very young infants do not exhibit the concept of *object permanence,* an understanding that objects continue to exist even when no longer visible. Piaget claimed that knowledge of object permanence appeared in rudimentary form about 9 months of age and continued to undergo developmental progression throughout the first 18 months of life. However, more recently, researchers have provided intriguing evidence to suggest that object permanence possibly emerges sometime around 3 or 4 months of age. In fact, within months after birth, perhaps even sooner, infants may start to wrestle with concepts related to causality as well as the existence of objects, knowledge essential for understanding how the everyday physical world operates.

Understanding basic principles that are part of many important concepts begins very early in development. For example, by 4 months of age infants discriminate numerical differences among small sets of items, an essential component of understanding number and quantity. Discriminating among larger sets of numbers and a complete understanding of *cardinality,* that is, recognizing that the final number in a counted set can refer to the total number in the array, occurs probably by 3 to 4 years of age. Between 4 and 6 years of age, children reach yet another level in understanding the concept of number when they come to realize that only transformations involving addition to or subtraction from an array of items affect their cardinality.

Knowledge of *ordinal* properties, that numbers often contain information about relative order (first, second, etc.) or magnitude (more, less, etc.), is also acquired during the preschool years. Of course, cardinality and ordinality are just a few of the essential qualities of number that must be understood before the child can begin to engage in mathematical reasoning involving, first, basic arithmetic in the elementary school years and, ultimately, more abstract mathematics including algebra and calculus in the adolescent and adult years.

Acquiring competence in mathematics demands mastery of the procedures involved in numerical reasoning, understanding the principles that govern the implementation of these procedures, and appreciating when such principles and procedures apply to a specific task or problem. Not surprisingly, inability to coordinate and integrate all of these competencies may be a primary reason why proficiency in mathematics undergoes a lengthy developmental course. Mastery of any other complex domain (e.g., reading, writing, scientific problem solving, etc.) is likely to show an equally prolonged pattern of development for similar reasons. [*See* CALCULATION.]

Infant concepts of space reveal another element of immature thinking; their notions are often initially egocentric, that is, organized by their own frame of reference. By 6 months of age infants can begin to use *landmarks,* distinctive external locations or cues, to influence their search for objects and to regulate their physical movement. By the preschool years, landmarks are represented conceptually and begin to be organized into *route mappings,* sequences of directional shifts at specific locations. By 10 years or so, children can create and understand configurations of spatial symbols such as those depicted on a map.

Sweeping reductions in egocentrism take place during the early childhood years. Between 1 and 2 years of age children begin to realize that others do not see things exactly the same way as they do; others can and will have a different visual perspective depending on their location. Throughout the preschool and school years, children become increasingly effective in deciphering the particular perspective of others, not only with regard to what others can see, but also with respect to the knowledge, feelings, and beliefs others may hold and that must be considered in order to carry out effective communications and interactions with them. All of these changes indicate that the child is gaining a greater appreciation of the mind, both of others and of their own.

The origin of children's understanding of the mind probably begins with the realization that they and others are capable of causing things to happen. Some things occur for accidental or physical reasons (a ball will roll down an incline), but others occur because someone specifically initiates and makes them happen (such as rolling a ball up an incline). This sense of intentional control or agency and the realization that they, themselves, and others "think," occurs sometime during or shortly after the second year of life and signals the beginning of an emerging theory of mind. Children's language now includes references to mental activity ("know," "think," and "imagine"). Sometime during their third year, children begin to understand that such mental events as dreams, thoughts, and images have a different source than concepts originating from physical experiences through the sensory receptors. Out of these distinctions, typically around 4 to 6 years of age, children come to realize that they and others can have different beliefs, even false beliefs, influencing their behavior.

The expanding knowledge of the mind, both of one's own and of others, has enormous implications for social interactions and relationships. Much of our own behavior is governed by what we believe to be the reactions, desires, and goals of parents, peers, and others whether in our play or at work. Indeed, it is possible that just prior to adulthood, thinking takes on a new kind of egocentrism by becoming excessively preoccupied with the mental reactions of others. Adolescents seem to feel as if they are constantly on center stage in the thoughts of peers, parents, and others, an interpretation which supports the popular image of teenagers as unusually self-conscious in their actions and deeds.

D. Reasoning

Another impressive feature of human thinking is the ability to construct hierarchies of concepts and to engage in reasoning utilizing these hierarchies. For example, a specific cat holds membership in subordinate classes (e.g., Siamese cat) as well as in superordinate classes (e.g., animal). Yet this hierarchical organization is not immediately evident when infants and young children initially acquire concepts. Very young children have difficulty comprehending that an object can belong to several hierarchically arranged classes simultaneously. As a consequence, they may be reluctant to credit an object with more than a single label. They may also have difficulty concluding that since animals embrace the subordinate class of cats, there must necessarily be at least as many animals as there are cats in any collection of animals, an example of reasoning involving *class inclusion*. [*See* REASONING.]

A formal reasoning ability that parallels class inclusion in its development is the capacity to perform *transitive inferences*. If informed that A is greater than B and that B is greater than C, then A must also be greater than C. This logical conclusion, although observed under certain circumstances in 4 year olds, is not routinely exhibited until children are several years older.

Reasoning involving various forms of *logical necessity* improves over a long developmental period and may not be demonstrated until the adolescent years, especially when premises do not conform with experience. For example, children may emphatically reject the conclusion that "cats are bigger than sheep" when told to assume that "cats are bigger than cows, and cows are bigger than sheep." Children have difficulty separating the formal logical inference from the content of the information in the premises and are likely to rely upon their experience to draw a conclusion. By the adolescent years, when able to think within abstract and hypothetical frameworks, logical necessity begins to override practical

experience although research with adults reveals that logical thinking is not always displayed or easy to carry out even then. Although adolescents and adults may be able to logically conclude, given the above example, that cats must be bigger than sheep, reasoning under more complex circumstances is often influenced by factors other than the premise information.

E. Problem Solving

Cognitive processes, whether engaged in identifying something around the corner, in remembering the next item to be purchased, or in reaching a satisfactory resolution to a puzzling dilemma, share the common purpose of solving a problem. Indeed, problem solving is what motivates and organizes much of cognition. Not surprisingly, then, performance in solving problems often improves with development. [*See* PROBLEM SOLVING.]

One characteristic of complex problems is that they require *planning*, that is, establishing a sequence of subgoals to be completed before reaching a solution. Sometime between 6 and 12 months of age, infants demonstrate planning; for example, they execute the subgoal of reaching for a string to pull a desired toy toward them when the toy cannot be directly obtained. But important developmental changes take place in the number, complexity, and efficiency of the subgoals represented by children of different ages in their planning to solve problems. Older children are more likely to enlist a larger number of subgoals. They are also more capable of including responses that initially move them farther away from the solution and to plan their routes to the solution more efficiently and with less backtracking. [*See* PLANNING.]

To solve many kinds of problems involving novel situations, we often resort to experiences with which we are more familiar. The ability to utilize a principle or procedure familiar in one domain to solve a problem in a new domain is called analogical thinking. When we use our knowledge of how a computer functions to help us theorize about how the human mind works, we are using an analogy. [*See* ANALOGICAL REASONING.]

Even toddlers and preschool children engage in analogical thinking. But children at all ages, as well as adults, frequently have considerable difficulty in reasoning analogically. For example, both children and adults regularly fail to notice that a principle may be applied to a different problem unless features, even some as irrelevant as a character's name or the thematic setting, are shared to assist in noticing the relevant source information or unless the individual is instructed to think back to a particular prior situation. Of course, when superficial features are similar, the potential for negative transfer increases as individuals attempt to apply a principle or procedure simply because the problem looks similar. This kind of difficulty can often confront teachers in their efforts to help children transfer what they have learned in mathematics, science, and other kinds of disciplines. Because younger children have more limited knowledge, are less able to represent solution principles abstractly, and may display a greater tendency to rely on superficial features to apply a principle, they are generally less successful in analogical thinking than are older children and adults.

IV. THE PROCESSES AND MECHANISMS CONTRIBUTING TO CHANGE

Whereas Piaget emphasized the reorganization of thought into increasingly abstract and logically ordered cognitive structures as children advance through various stages of development, information-processing perspectives have focused on four main kinds of explanations for cognitive development: changes in basic capacities, the implementation of increasingly powerful strategies, the emergence of metacognition, and the expanding knowledge base. Each may play a role. Furthermore, progression in one realm may have momentous consequences for the operation of any other.

Basic capacities to perceive, discriminate, categorize, learn, and retain information over brief periods of time are functioning already at or shortly after birth. However, the speed and efficiency with which these activities are carried out, including the extent to which they are performed automatically and perhaps in parallel rather than sequentially, undergo substantial change throughout development. These refinements in basic capacities not only facilitate attention and memory but also enable the compiling of strategic procedures that have dramatic analytic repercussions. Strategies assist in tasks ranging from the recall of information to planning and problem solving with respect to both the physical and social environment.

Children's growing awareness of mental capacities, their own and those of others, along with observations of and reflections upon the repercussions of their own emerging strategic skills, can further promote reasoning and problem solving. Metacognitive abilities related to an understanding of the strengths and limits of memory and of other intellectual proficiencies may kindle the establishment and use of instruments and tools to assist in thinking and problem solving. Add a flourishing base of knowledge to these other changes and the end result is the remarkable disparity between the professed immature thinking and behavior associated with infants and the rational, mature reasoning and conduct regularly identified with adults.

To emphasize the disparity between the thinking capacities of infants and adults, however, can also be somewhat misleading. Where deficiencies are observed in the cognitive abilities of young children, surprising competencies are often soon displayed. The capacity to represent information, a rudimentary understanding of basic concepts of objects, space, and causality, and adaptive problem solving indisputably emerge within the first year. Limited strategic behaviors appear in the second year. The rudiments of logical reasoning are already exhibited by preschoolers, probably even by toddlers. Much of cognitive development involves the extension and application of these early simple proficiencies to more complex and demanding situations. Substantial differences between the thinking of younger and older children exist, but the initial competencies of infants and young children along with powerful means of building upon and strengthening them lead to rapid developmental changes in cognition.

V. NEW DIRECTIONS AND FUTURE CHALLENGES

Researchers remain puzzled by many aspects of cognitive development. Work on putting the pieces together continues at a rapid pace. One issue concerns the extent to which cognitive development can be explained in terms of domain-general rather than domain-specific changes. Most research efforts have focused on possible domain-general shifts such as the speed of processing information or the ability to acquire more abstract representations to explain cognitive development. Yet recent efforts have revealed that the particular knowledge acquired or the strategies implemented in a specific domain often provide a fairly good account of both the strengths and limitations of cognitive abilities, but only for that domain.

New theoretical ideas imported from *connectionist* models are also becoming increasingly helpful in explaining cognitive development. Connectionist models attempt to simulate cognition by using the computer and assume that thinking depends on a complex array of interconnecting processing units. When some kind of input is provided and a response is produced, various levels of these processing units become strengthened or weakened as a result of the pattern of positive and negative feedback that follows. Connectionist models can be surprisingly powerful in demonstrating transformations in behavior as a result of changes in the weightings of the various units. Moreover, the units may bear some conceptual similarity to the architecture of the brain, specifically, its neuronal organization.

An additional related challenge for the future is to map the various changes associated with thinking and reasoning to changes that occur in the brain throughout development. For example, shortly after birth, a rapid proliferation of connections among the billions of neurons in the brain takes place. Becoming more knowledgeable about the causes and consequences of this growth along with neural changes associated with specific kinds of experience presents fertile territory for future research.

Finally, our knowledge of how social factors affect cognitive development remains sketchy and theoretical attempts to incorporate such contexts are limited. The cultural setting unquestionably affects the content of children's thinking, that is, the kinds of things they think about. The knowledge base of children from one culture to another can certainly differ substantially. But the more critical issue is whether these social differences also modify the process of cognitive development. For example, does the thinking of children in cultures and families which require them to engage in work in order to survive differ from the thinking of children encouraged to play and to explore their physical and social environment? Does the spatial reasoning of children exposed to extensive hours of video games differ from those not so engaged? What is the impact of exposure to music or art, or to hand's-on problem-solving experiences compared to knowledge acquired through text examples? We have much more to learn about the impact of these kinds of factors for cognitive development.

Bibliography

Bukatko, D., and Daehler, M. W. (1992). "Child Development: A Topical Approach." Houghton Mifflin, Boston.

Flavell, J. H., Miller, P. H., and Miller, S. A. (1993). "Cognitive Development" (3rd Ed.). Prentice Hall, Englewood Cliffs, NJ.

Mandler, J. M. (1992). How to build a baby. II. Conceptual primitives. *Psychol. Rev.* **99**, 587–604.

Markman, E. M. (1989). "Categorization and Naming in Children: Problems of Induction." MIT Press, Cambridge, MA.

Rogoff, B. (1990). "Apprenticeship in Thinking: Cognitive Development in Social Context." Oxford University Press, New York.

Rumelhart, D. E., and Norman, D. A. (1988). Representation in memory. In "Stevens' "Handbook of Experimental Psychology" (R. C. Atkinson, R. J. Herrnstein, G. Lindzey, and R. D. Luce, Eds.), 2nd ed., Vol. 2, pp. 511–587. Wiley, New York.

Siegler, R. S. (1991). "Children's Thinking." Prentice Hall, Englewood Cliffs, NJ.

Spelke, E. S., Breinlinger, K., Macomber, J., and Jacobson, K. (1992). Origins of knowledge. *Psychol. Rev.* **99**, 605–632.

Wellman, H. M. (1990). "Children's Theories of Mind." MIT Press, Cambridge, MA.

Wellman, H. M., and Gelman, S. A. (1992). Cognitive development: Foundational theories of core domains. *Annu. Rev. Psychol.* **43**, 337–375.

COGNITIVE DISSONANCE

Mary E. Losch
University of Iowa

Glossary

Affect The positive or negative emotional response to a stimulus.
Arousal An energized state typically accompanied by measurable increases in physiological responses such as heart rate or palmar sweating.
Consonance Psychological state resulting from consistency between or among thoughts and beliefs or between thoughts/beliefs and behavior.
Dissonance Psychological state resulting from inconsistency between or among thoughts and beliefs or between thoughts/beliefs and behavior that motivates the individual to regain consistency.
Paradigm A basic experimental design or procedure used for exploring a research question.

COGNITIVE DISSONANCE theory has played a major role in social psychology for more than three decades. The central hypothesis in the original theory states that individuals experience inconsistency in thoughts and/or actions as a negative affective state and seek to reduce such "dissonance" and restore consistency. Numerous empirical tests of the theory have served to clarify the necessary conditions under which dissonance occurs and have provided insight into specific psychological and physiological processes that are associated with the state of dissonance. Cognitive dissonance theory, even

as it has evolved to incorporate new findings provided by hundreds of investigations, has retained its position as one of the most important theories in social psychology. Its power to explain attitude-discrepant behavior and the ways in which we deal with psychological inconsistency is impressive even today.

I. FESTINGER'S THEORY OF COGNITIVE DISSONANCE

In the late 1950s Leon Festinger put forward what has proven to be one of the most enduring theories in social psychology. Basing his hypotheses on the notion that individuals strive for consistency in their knowledge, beliefs, attitudes, and behavior, Festinger posited that when people are unable to quickly resolve inconsistencies, a psychologically uncomfortable state (dissonance) results. He hypothesized that (1) this negative feeling would motivate the person to try to reduce the inconsistency and return to the more comfortable state of "consonance" or consistency, and (2) the dissonant state would result in active avoidance of information or situations which might heighten the feelings of dissonance.

Because we are frequently presented with information that is at odds with some of our attitudes, it is important to specify when such logical inconsistencies might result in a great deal of dissonance and when they might not. For example, as postulated in the original theory, the magnitude of the dissonance is a function of the importance of the inconsistent cognitions to the individual. Clearly, there is some inconsistency in our lives every day. Reading a novel rather than cleaning out a closet or mowing the lawn results in some measure of dissonance; however, because the dissonant elements are relatively unimportant, the amount of dissonance in these instances is quite low. On the other hand, reading the novel rather than meeting an important business deadline would (for most of us) result in much greater levels of dissonance.

A specific application of dissonance theory comes in the area of decision-making. In Festinger's view, decisions virtually always result in some level of dissonance. As with other situations, the more important the decision, the higher the level of dissonance. In addition, if the alternatives are equally attractive, the choice will result in higher levels of dissonance than if they are not equally appealing. This intuitive notion is easily illustrated when thinking about, for example, deciding between automobiles, each of which has appealing features. Upon choosing one of the cars, one's attitude toward the chosen alternative might become more positive, and hence, reduce the potentially high levels of dissonance that resulted from choosing between equally attractive alternatives. [See DECISION MAKING, INDIVIDUALS.]

This motivation to reduce or remove the negative affective state is a key aspect of cognitive dissonance theory. The more dissonance, the more motivation to reduce it. Reduction in dissonance can occur through behavioral changes, cognitive changes, and/or active exposure to new (more consonant) information and opinions. An example of a behavioral change to restore consonance would be modifying one's diet in accordance with new dietary guidelines to reduce the incidence of disease. Cognitive changes most frequently manifest themselves in attitude change as illustrated in the automobile example above. Festinger also hypothesized that seeking new information to "outweigh" the dissonant information is another effective means of reducing dissonance.

II. EMPIRICAL TESTS: PREDICTIONS AND PARADIGMS

Dissonance theory spawned hundreds of experiments in the years immediately following its publication and a host of paradigms were developed to test its predictions. A few of the paradigms employed most often are discussed below.

A. Forced/Induced Compliance Paradigm

The most popular paradigm and the one used in some of Festinger's own dissonance studies is known as forced or *induced compliance*. In this design, dissonance is produced by inducing respondents to comply with a counterattitudinal request through the use of an incentive. For example, individuals might be paid different amounts of money to perform a task or behave in a way that is counter to their privately held beliefs or attitudes. According to the theory, the inconsistency between the behavior and the attitude should result in dissonance. Moreover, the magnitude of the dissonance should be inversely related to the magnitude of the incentive offered, because a large reward could be thought of as a strong justification or reason for engaging in the behavior. One means of reducing the dissonance would be for the individual to change his or her attitude in the direction of the behavior.

The theory gained substantial support from studies showing that agreeing to make counterattitudinal statements in return for incentives does in fact lead to attitude change, with the magnitude of the change being greater under conditions of low incentive rather than high incentive. These data have been replicated not only using money as the incentive, but also by varying the strength of a persuasive appeal or the likeability of the experimenter making the appeal. This finding that attitudes could be affected by behavior provided strong support for the theory of cognitive dissonance. [See ATTITUDE CHANGE.]

As the studies of cognitive dissonance continued, it became increasingly clear that several qualifications were necessary for an accurate portrayal of the dissonance concept. Within the induced compliance paradigm, multiple studies indicated that dissonance (as measured by attitude change) occurred only under certain conditions. Specifically, attitude change in favor of the behavior is evident only when individuals: (1) perceive that they have freely chosen to behave in a counterattitudinal fashion; (2) believe that the attitude-discrepant behavior will lead to an unwanted or negative outcome; (3) believe the aversive event to be foreseeable at the time of the behavioral commitment; and (4) perceive a threat to their self-concept. For example, if individuals feel that they were forced into the behavior, then no dissonance is aroused. Also, if the counterattitudinal behavior has no negative consequence, then there is no accompanying change in attitudes. In addition, if there was no way for them to know that they might bring about a negative event, they do not change their attitudes. Finally, data indicate that dissonance is more likely to occur when the counterattitudinal behavior is in violation of a person's self-concept. That is, because most people have positive self-concepts, freely choosing to bring about a negative event will bring about more dissonance than behaviors that are not inconsistent with one's self-concept. These qualifications have added predictive clarity to the original theory as it was addressed in the induced compliance paradigm.

B. Effort Justification Paradigm

A second related paradigm developed to test predictions of cognitive dissonance theory is known as *effort justification*. In this application, it is posited that the more we suffer in a particular behavior, the higher the level of dissonance and hence, the greater the attitude change. This hypothesis has been supported in a number of experiments wherein subjects are asked to engage in activities that required effort levels ranging from low to high in order to participate in a future task. Later ratings of the subsequent task were directly related to the difficulty of the preliminary activities. These findings are consistent with anecdotal accounts of the power of extremely difficult or humiliating initiations into clubs or other groups. As predicted by dissonance theory, to the extent that we voluntarily choose to engage in the behavior, the harder we work to achieve something, the more we value it subsequently.

C. Free-Choice Paradigm

Postdecisional dissonance has been explored using what is known as the free-choice paradigm. As noted earlier, dissonance is a potential outcome of numerous decisions and the likelihood that it will occur is magnified if the choices are perceived as equally attractive. Studies that ask subjects to choose between or among equally desirable items consistently find postdecision attitude change in favor of the chosen alternative, higher levels of confidence in choices, or desire for information consonant with their decision—all of which are predicted by the theory of cognitive dissonance.

III. COMPETING THEORIES: SELF-PERCEPTION AND IMPRESSION MANAGEMENT

Two major theoretical challanges to cognitive dissonance have been mounted to account for the data supporting dissonance theory as it manifests itself in induced compliance paradigms. The first of these is Daryl Bem's *self-perception theory* and the second

is the *impression management theory* developed by Tedeschi and his colleagues in the early 1970s.

A. Self-Perception Theory

Basing his analysis on Skinner's model of behaviorism, Bem argued that we gain insight into our own attitudes and notions of self much the same way we gain information about others—we observe behavior. In the case of the induced compliance paradigm, Bem argued that when asked about their attitudes, subjects in low-incentive conditions simply reflected on their recent, salient behavior and reported a view consistent with that behavior. For those in the high-incentive condition, the behavior was viewed to have an external or environmental cause and was attributed to that source. His later formulations of the theory were grounded in an attributional framework dealing with this issue of self-knowledge.

Numerous experiments examining the role of the importance of individuals' initial attitudes were conducted in an attempt to distinguish between the approaches of Festinger and Bem. A rather confusing array of conflicting predictions and arguably uninformative findings resulted. In the final analysis, it was the role of arousal that proved to be the factor distinguishing between the theories.

To be specific, if attitude change were simply a matter of self-perception, then arousal should play no role in the process. Investigations into the role of arousal in dissonance (which are discussed in more detail in later sections) revealed that arousal was an important component of the dissonance process in induced compliance paradigms. These findings were not easily incorporated into the self-perception model. In applying the two approaches, it has been argued that self-perception processes may be operating when behaviors are not sufficiently counterattitudinal to arouse dissonance.

B. Impression Management Theory

The second significant account to challenge cognitive dissonance theory was impression management theory. The central point in this theory is that the attitudes that subjects report to experimenters in the context of an induced compliance paradigm are not a candid reflection of their true beliefs. The apparent attitude change is viewed not as a result of any arousal state or need to reduce inconsistency, but is instead considered an attempt to *appear* consistent to the experimenter or other high-status person.

Studies designed to distinguish between the theories have yielded mixed results, some supporting impression management, others dissonance predictions. To tip the scales in favor of dissonance theory, however, some studies have used unobtrusive measurements of attitude change; these studies have reported attitude shifts lasting well beyond the time of the experiments. This finding runs counter to impression management theory which would predict that "true" attitudes never changed, only the public reports of them did so. Hence, measurements of target attitudes subsequent to the experimental session should find attitudes similar to those expressed prior to the counterattitudinal behavior. These results have cast serious doubt on the ability of impression management theory to account for all attitude changes in induced compliance paradigms.

IV. AROUSAL, NEGATIVE AFFECT, AND THE "PILL PARADIGM"

Given the motivational core of dissonance theory, one of the major questions about the state of dissonance has been whether physiological "arousal" is a necessary component. Given that other arousal states such as fear typically result in the facilitation of simple tasks and the impairment of complex tasks, dissonance should produce similar effects on performance. Consistent with this prediction, several investigators have found that individuals' performances were improved on simple tasks and impaired on difficult tasks when they freely chose to engage in counterattitudinal behavior.

A second line of research has also provided insight into the importance of arousal to dissonance phenomena. Based on Schachter and Singer's theory of emotion, it was argued that like other emotional states, pressure to change one's attitudes results from a neutral arousal state that is labeled negatively because of one's responsibility for bringing about a negative event. In these experiments which also utilized an induced compliance paradigm, subjects were induced to write counterattitudinal essays under conditions of high or low choice. In addition, subjects were led to believe that a pill they had ingested would cause them to feel either tense or relaxed or it would have no side-effects at all. It was hypothesized that subjects in the "tense" condition would misattribute any dissonance arousal to the pill and hence they would experience no motivation to change their attitudes. The results revealed that

as expected, subjects in the "no side-effects" condition showed the usual attitude change whereas subjects in the "tense" pill condition did not.

Several other experiments have provided conceptual replications of these original misattribution findings. For example, dissonance effects have been attenuated by the threat of shock, unpleasantly small surroundings, and fluorescent lighting that the subjects were told caused uncomfortable feelings. Although this evidence does not provide any direct assessment of physiological arousal, the findings suggest that subjects do perceive some sort of arousal state following dissonance inductions in induced compliance paradigms.

Some of the most direct evidence suggesting that arousal is a necessary component of dissonance comes in an experiment that revealed that tranquilizers attenuated attitude change and amphetamines accentuated attitude change in a standard induced compliance paradigm. One interpretation is that subjects in the sedative group experienced little physiological arousal and hence little motivation to change in their attitudes. On the other hand, subjects in the amphetamine group experienced extremely high levels of arousal which they misattributed to the dissonance; therefore, these individuals were motivated to change their attitudes a great deal. Of course, a major problem with these findings is that the drugs alter not only undifferentiated arousal, but valenced affect as well. Rather than experiencing high levels of arousal as neutral, it is possible that the sudden onset of symptoms characteristic of amphetamine effects could be construed as negative. Subjects in the tranquilizer group on the other hand might have experienced dampened negative affect or less "psychological discomfort," which led to their lower attitude change scores.

Although many of these induced compliance investigations were based on the assumption that the arousal that was mediating the attitude change was physiological in nature, no direct measures of physiological responding were employed. Even though published reports of the physiological effects of dissonance in other contexts existed in the late 1960s, they had methodological shortcomings or resulted in findings which were difficult to interpret. More recent studies have focused on assessment of physiological responses which occur during dissonance in induced compliance paradigms. In these instances, subjects in high-choice (i.e., dissonance) conditions showed an increased frequency of spontaneous electrodermal responses (measures of palmar sweating indicative of the activation of the sympathetic branch of the autonomic nervous system) over subjects in low-choice (i.e., nondissonance) conditions. Hence, dissonance, as experienced in induced compliance paradigms, does appear to be associated with higher levels of sympathetic nervous system arousal. Accepting that arousal is a component of the dissonant state, an additional line of inquiry centered around the question of whether this state was neutral or was in fact an aversive or negative state as suggested in the original theory.

Using misattribution "pill" paradigms, several studies attempted to determine whether dissonance is an aversive state as Festinger originally proposed and additionally, whether the negative state rather than arousal is the critical factor mediating attitude change. In one such study, the paradigm included four descriptions representing the presence or absence of arousal and the presence or absence of positive or negative feelings. The descriptions of the pill's side-effects included pleasant excitement (positive/arousal), relaxation (positive/no arousal), tension (negative/arousal), and unpleasant sedation (negative/no arousal). Results indicated that, consistent with the conception of dissonance as a negative but not a psychologically arousing state, subjects in both of the pleasant conditions evidenced more attitude change than subjects in the two unpleasant conditions. In addition, subjects in the arousal conditions changed their attitudes more than subjects in the nonarousal conditions. Based on these findings, it was concluded that the unpleasantness and not the arousal per se is the critical perception in the dissonance state.

Others have challenged this conclusion in light of the results of a study which suggests that dissonance can be misattributed to positive as well as negative cues. For half of the subjects in the study, a humorous cartoon was presented immediately after they agreed to write a counterattitudinal essay. Given the timing of the cartoon, the authors believed that it would serve as a positive misattribution cue. For the other subjects, the cartoon was presented after the postcommitment attitude measure; and according to the authors, the cartoon should not be available as a misattribution cue. As predicted, high-choice subjects who viewed the cartoon immediately following their behavioral commitment rated the cartoon as funnier and changed their attitudes less than the subjects viewing the cartoon later. The authors concluded that freely choosing to behave in a counterattitudinal fashion results not in a negative state but in general physiological and felt arousal which is neutral with regard to affective tone and can be attributed to either a positive or a negative cue.

Alternatively, it may have been the case that subjects viewing the cartoon before they expressed their attitudes may have been more distracted from their dissonant cognitions and hence, less likely to experience much dissonance. It has also been argued that subjects who viewed the cartoon first, and who were presumably experiencing dissonance, may have attended to and thought more about the cartoon in order to avoid thinking about other negative feelings they were experiencing and, hence, rated the cartoons as funnier than did other subjects. This interpretation is consistent with other research indicating that merely thinking about an issue can polarize attitudes. In addition, viewing the pleasant cartoon in a dissonant state (assuming dissonance is unpleasant) may have produced a contrast effect leading both to more positive perceptions of the cartoons and relief from their negative affective state. As indicated in the discussion of the reformulated version of cognitive dissonance theory presented next, the debate about cognitive dissonance processes is still unresolved and continues to spark research studies and lively debate in contemporary social psychology.

V. A REFORMULATION OF DISSONANCE THEORY

The most recent iteration of cognitive dissonance theory posits an alternative interpretation of the data suggesting that dissonance is negative. Instead, this new theoretical argument separates dissonance into two components: dissonance arousal and dissonance motivation. In addition, in contrast to Festinger's premise, inconsistency is no longer considered the spark for dissonance; instead, it is argued that dissonance arousal results from acting with personal responsibility to bring forth a negative event. That is, the aversive consequence is critical, not inconsistency between thought and action.

In the early 1980s Cooper and Fazio argued that in misattribution experiments utilizing the pill paradigm, there is no way to determine what interpretation of their feeling state subjects engaged in prior to misattribution to the pill. Further, they argued that subjects may have first experienced a general, neutral state of arousal which was then labeled as negative because they believed they were ingesting an experimental pill with potential side-effects. The argument states that this negative context may have provided a cue which subjects could use to label any general arousal resulting from freely choosing to engage in counterattitudinal behavior. Because the pleasant excitement condition does not provide a plausible explanation for negative feelings, only cues providing an unpleasant component can be used as misattribution cues. To clarify, it is argued that the negative context of the experiment (i.e., ingesting an experimental pill) prevents a true test of dissonance because misattribution of feelings of general arousal may occur in the "unpleasant" conditions.

In the reformulation of the theory, "dissonance arousal" is distinguished from "dissonance motivation." Specifically, it is suggested that dissonance arousal is a "general and undifferentiated state of arousal" which, when labeled positively, prevents dissonance motivation (aversive pressure to change one's attitude). Dissonance motivation is also believed to be prevented if dissonance arousal is labeled negatively but is attributed to some external source. Only in the case where dissonance arousal is interpreted negatively and attributed to freely choosing to engage in a counterattitudinal act is dissonance motivation present, according to this reformulation. Therefore, attitude change occurs not because of the preliminary arousal (dissonance arousal) but because of the negative labeling of this arousal (dissonance motivation) resulting from attributing the arousal to one's freely choosing to behave in a manner that will bring about a negative consequence. Without arousal, it is argued, no labeling would occur.

Central to this thesis are the affective responses of an individual following the agreement to freely engage in a counterattitudinal act. On the other hand, the original theory argued that psychological discomfort (i.e., a negative state) is the state that leads to attitude change in the induced compliance paradigm and this argument has been supported by a number of studies such as those discussed earlier. Embracing other findings which suggest that the dissonance arousal can be attributed to positive cues, the new formulation requires the existence of two states for attitude change to occur: an affectively neutral state of diffuse and perceptible physiological arousal followed by an affectively negative state.

This aspect of the new formulation has received some limited support in recent studies whereas other data have contradicted the notion that the arousal is neutral. Instead, the results suggest that dissonance is an inherently negative state. Addressing criticisms of earlier studies that used a pill paradigm, this design utilized a neutral misattribution cue (wearing plastic prism goggles) within the standard induced compliance paradigm. Subjects freely choosing to engage in counterattitudinal behavior in this study evidenced arousal (as measured by physiological responses) in both the positive and negative cue conditions. However, rather than attributing the arousal to the positive cue and therefore circumventing "dissonance motivation" to bring their attitudes in line with their behavior as predicted by the reformulated theory, those in the positive cue condition did in fact change their attitudes in the direction of their behavior whereas those in the negative cue condition did not. These data are consistent with the earlier notions that dissonance is in fact experienced as a negative state.

As noted earlier, the second major departure from the original theory lies in the reformulated theory's shift from the view that dissonance arises from inconsistency to one where dissonance arousal results instead from behaviors that produce aversive consequences. More exactly, it is argued that causing a foreseeable negative outcome results in dissonance arousal. Inconsistency is neither necessary nor sufficient to produce dissonance in the new formulation. However, the overlap between the two notions (i.e., inconsistency and causing an aversive outcome) is so great, particularly within the induced compliance paradigm, that testing this aspect of the theory will be difficult. Indeed, knowingly causing a negative consequence *is* an inconsistency for most individuals who would view such a behavior as contradicting their view of themselves as "good" people. This is the central point of earlier arguments of the importance of self-concept as a mediator of dissonance effects. Alternatively, circumstances in which inconsistency does not lead to attitude change may instead result from a lack of importance (as postulated in the original theory but never defined) rather than from the lack of an aversive outcome. Perhaps only when the outcome is perceived as important can it be construed as valenced: either positive or negative. Otherwise, the elements of inconsistency may simply be viewed as irrelevant, and hence, no dissonance would be aroused. In any case, separating importance from aversive consequences in order to test the reformulated theory poses formidable methodological challenges.

VI. COGNITIVE DISSONANCE THEORY TODAY

Although certainly not the force it once was in social psychology, research into the processes of cognitive dissonance is not as passe as some might be led to believe. Articles extolling the virtues of the theory as an enduring, synthesizing model and calling for the invocation of the theory as an important explanatory mechanism for new findings have been published quite recently. In addition, debate about Cooper and Fazio's reformulated theory of cognitive dissonance has already begun to spur new investigations designed to test the predictions generated by their model.

In sum, despite the impressive theoretical challenges that have been mounted, dissonance theory has yet to be displaced as a powerful explanatory approach to a host of social behaviors. Indeed, coinciding with social psychology's recent movement from almost exclusively "cold" cognitive approaches to understanding social cognition in the 1970s and 1980s to one that embraces more motivational or emotional (i.e., "hot") mediators, cognitive dissonance may again play a major role in helping explain fundamental aspects of our social behavior.

Bibliography

Aronson, E. (1992). The return of the repressed: Dissonance theory makes a comeback. *Psychol. Inquiry,* **3**(4), 303–311.

Berkowitz, L., and Devine, P. (1989). Research traditions, analysis, and syntheses in social psychological theories: The case of dissonance theory. *Pers. Soc. Psychol. Bull.* **15**(4), 493–507.

Cooper, J., and Fazio, R. H. (1984). A new look at dissonance theory. In "Advances in Experimental Social Psychology" (L. Berkowitz, ed.) Vol. 17, pp. 229–266. Academic Press, Orlando, FL.

Tedeschi, J. T. (1981). "Impression Management Theory and Social Psychological Research." Academic Press, New York.

COGNITIVE MAPS

Kim Langfield-Smith
Monash University, Australia

Glossary

Artificial intelligence The study of how human knowledge is structured and processed, in order to build computer models that mimic human information processing.

Beliefs Understandings that represent relationships between objects, properties, and ideas. These may range from core beliefs, for example about the nature of the world, to more specific beliefs.

Cognitive structure Any mental representation used to organize knowledge, beliefs, values, or other data whether hypothetical or neurological.

Domain An area of interest that may form the focus for a cognitive map of decision making.

Hippocampus The region of the brain thought to be associated with spatial memory and exploration.

Spatial relationships These relate to the distance and direction between objects within a spatial cognitive map.

COGNITIVE MAP is a term that is used to describe several different forms of representations of an individual's cognitions. Initially, these were representations of objects and attributes in a spatial environment, but the term has also been used to describe representations of causal beliefs, decision processes, and knowledge. Closely related terms include mental maps, schemas, and cognitive structures.

I. THE ORIGINS OF COGNITIVE MAPS

The term "cognitive map" was used by Tolman in 1932 when he conducted experiments with rats and proposed that they formed cognitive maps of their local environment. Cognitive maps were developed by the rats learning the spatial relationships between places and objects. These cognitive maps enabled the rats to move around a maze, even when the structure of the maze was changed, and to eventually achieve their goal. It was theorized that these maps were not simply routes to a goal, but allowed the animals to develop behavior strategies. The idea of the existence of a cognitive map was an alternative to the stimulus–response model; however, it was still asserted by some subsequent researchers that the behavior of the rat was a result of stimulus–response learning. Cognitive maps were used metaphorically to explain certain behavior and it was not claimed that these maps actually existed in the same form within the brain.

Since those early experiments "cognitive maps" have been used in research in a variety of disciplines including psychology, education, geography, management, and marketing. The original conception of a cognitive map was to represent spatial relationships between objects in an environment, but later applications extended the idea to representing other types of knowledge, language structures, causal beliefs, and decision processes.

A. Schemas and Other Cognitive Representations

The term "mental map" is a more general term than cognitive map and has been used to describe representations of environments of geographic space, drawing on both psychology and geography. Other forms of representations include knowledge structures such as schemas, scripts and frames, and semantic networks. The similarities are that they are all theories of cognitive structure.

A schema can be described as a knowledge structure that people use to organize and to make sense of social and organizational information or situations. Schemas have implications for interpretations, expectations, and human behavior, and are assumed to operate at the subconscious level. The origins of schema theory can be traced to the work of Bartlett and Piaget. Bartlett hypothesized that schemas are complex knowledge structures held in the subconscious. Bartlett developed hypotheses that relate to schema processing, that is, to the way in which new knowledge is integrated with old data within a schema. Schemas are hypothesized to be general models which contain standard sequences of events, actions, and variables. Thus, schemas can be used to interpret sensory input and to guide action. For example, an individual may hold schemas for a cat. There may be standard general information about the number of legs, tail, and shape of ears. However, the schema would also include variables concerning color and length of fur. Thus, the contents of this schema would allow a person to identify a cat. There may also be sub-schemas that detail possible eye shapes, or behavioral characteristics of cats.

Scripts are schemas which contain context-specific knowledge of conventional behavior and event sequences and enable people to categorize the situation and to choose suitable behavioral alternatives. Scripts are held prototypically, and are generated to fit predictable and frequently encountered situations. People are assumed to hold a repertoire of scripts to suit a variety of settings that they would commonly encounter. Scripts can be thought of as forming a hierarchical structure: metascripts lack detail, are stored at a high level of abstraction, and provide the outline for the development of subordinate scripts or script tracks. A common example is the restaurant metascript, which would contain the sequence of activities that usually take place when visiting a restaurant—such as ordering food, eating the food, and leaving the restaurant. This script acts to guide the appropriate behavior and interpretation for all situations that involve the purchase and consumption of food in a public place. From this metascript, subordinate scripts may be constructed which relate to eating in specific types of restaurants. These could include the self-serve restaurant script or the eating-in-a-restaurant-in-China script.

Weak scripts serve merely to organize a situation and aid in the understanding of the behavior of the self and others, but lack strong sequencing between the elements. These weak scripts have also been described as frames and as prototypes. Strong scripts contain the exact sequencing of events, and detail the relationships between script items. Scripts for formal meetings could be described as strong scripts.

The processing of a script refers to the activation of that script to gain an understanding of the specific situation, and to perform the appropriate behaviors contained in the script. Automatic script processing takes place where familiar situations can be handled with little conscious processing, and controlled script processing which is used in novel situations where people consciously choose appropriate behavior. Controlled processing would occur in less familiar situations. The move from automatic to controlled processing would occur as certain situations become more frequently encountered by a person.

Experiments in psychology have provided evidence that supports the existence of scripts. The reliance on scripts explains why people may have difficulty in accurately recalling the details of certain situations. For example, eye witnesses to events such as motor vehicle accidents often "gap fill" the details. That is, they assume that certain details occurred according to the expected sequence of events contained in their script, but when they are questioned have difficulty in determining whether all the expected events actually did occur. [*See* Eyewitness Testimony.]

II. SPATIAL COGNITIVE MAPS

Spatial cognitive maps can be viewed as essential for everyday functioning and for long-term survival. Human spatial behavior is dependent on the existence and content of a cognitive map of a particular environment. When a cognitive map exists an individual can develop several strategies for behavior.

It is convenient to visualize a person's cognitive map as similar to a geographer's map. However, while in many ways a cognitive map may function as a map, this does not necessarily imply that it has the same physical properties of a map. An unresolved question is whether the representation of an environment is analogue or propositional, or both. In an analogue representation the actual distances between objects and directions in the real world are preserved within the cognitive map. There is also evidence that mental images may be stored in a nonvisual, nonverbal manner. These abstract representations can be thought of as providing meaning to certain aspects of a map, or to the map itself, and are called propositions.

A spatial cognitive map contains information about an environment that includes locations and attributes of phenomena. Locational information includes distance and direction. Information about distances between objects in an environment helps us to plan behavior strategies. Direction can be thought of as relative or relational. For example, objects may be located relative to other objects—a phone box is to be found 10 feet to the left of the fire station. An example of a relational location is "the phone box is to be found about 2 miles to the east of my current location." By constructing and understanding these relations, people can navigate certain routes and locate certain objects. Attribution information provides knowledge of what can be found in certain locations and why the individual would want to find that object. This knowledge will be objective (neutral) or will be affective. For example, in locating the phone box, the objective attributes may consist of a "6-foot glassed-in booth containing a telephone," while the affective attributes may be "dangerous after sunset" and "easy to drive to." Thus, we can envisage objects in a cognitive map having location and attribute information.

Cognitive maps contain subjective knowledge of the environment. Thus, different individuals' maps of the same physical environment will vary in terms of the relevant objects, distance, and attributes that are included. Individuals may exclude various objects from their cognitive maps, not only because they are not aware of their existence, but also because those objects have little or no significance for the person. Distances between objects may differ, and points of relativity and relevant attributes are a function of individual preferences and the limits of available cognitive categorizations. The affective attributes of objects will also differ. Thus, an individual's spatial cognitive map of an environment is incomplete and distorted, and the contents may be abstract and highly selective. However, there would be some similarities between individuals' maps due to common experiences and backgrounds.

A. Development of Spatial Cognitive Maps

In the same way that cognitive maps are not merely visual maps, spatial learning is different from visual learning. Information in spatial cognitive maps is acquired through both visual and sensory inputs. For example, the Chinatown area of a city may be recognized by the interaction of distinctive restaurant smells as well as certain visual characteristics. In an individual's cognitive map of a city, Chinatown

is represented as a certain location, and in terms of its visual and olfactory attributes.

Individuals' cognitive maps undergo a continual process of construction and modification driven by the motivation of curiosity, not biological needs. The initial direct experiences that individuals have of objects may be unreliable and are corrected, elaborated, and reinforced through spatial behavior (repetitive experiences). In particular, attributes of objects, especially affective ones, may be added and revised following repeated experiences. This learning that occurs during experiences of navigating in the real-world environment is termed primary spatial learning. Secondary learning occurs when spatial memories are acquired symbolically. Impressionistic representations often occur when direct experiences are not available. For example, many people have cognitive maps of London without having directly experienced the city. These maps are gained through experiences such as viewing travelogs and films, reading books, and listening to friends' travel experiences. Obviously by many people's standards, these maps will be incomplete and fairly inaccurate.

The degree of direct interaction with an environment provides more detailed and elaborate cognitive maps. For example, the depth of knowledge of a particular environment where experiences are visual (experiences from a car, or a travelog) is less than if people actively experience an environment (through walking or living in it).

The influence of personality and information-processing variables cannot be ignored when considering how cognitive maps develop. Selective perceptions, the need for cognitive consistency and simplicity, and individuals' various attitudes and values will filter the type of information that is stored in cognitive maps. Prior associative processes and the contents of cognitive maps of other related environments may influence what objects are attended to and the nature of location and affective attributes.

There are several views concerning the order in which the content of cognitive maps is developed. Key landmarks in an environment may be positioned within a map and then routes connecting those landmarks may be constructed. Alternatively, routes may form the initial framework for the map, and landmarks may then be positioned.

Much of the evidence for how cognitive maps develop and change comes from research that studies children and animals. A difficulty in this area of research is that cognitive maps cannot be observed directly but their existence must be inferred. While there is little question that the contents of cognitive maps derive from experiences, the question of whether the conception of space and distance in cognitive maps is innate or learned is less clear.

B. Neurophysiology and Cognitive Maps

The evidence for the existence of cognitive maps has largely been behavioral. However, in the area of neurophysiology evidence for the physical existence of spatial cognitive maps has been presented. Cognitive maps have been considered part of the neural structures that are part of the hippocampus in the brain. Figure 1 shows the position of the left rat hippocampus. In this figure, all the forebrain structures except those at the mid-line have been removed. Cognitive maps are seen as providing spatial representations of psychological space for certain familiar environments. The main evidence for the existence of cognitive maps in the hippocampus is based on research that observes the effect of lesions on function in that brain area. [*See* HIPPOCAMPAL FORMATION.]

These cognitive maps consist of a mapping space and a locative (exploratory) mechanism. The mapping space acts as a memory system and contains information about places in an environment, their spatial relations, and the existence of certain objects in specific places. Thus, individuals (and other organisms) can locate themselves in familiar environments and move around the environment without further inputs. Different environments may be linked together conceptually even when they have not been experienced at the same time. The mapping space is assumed to consist of a matrix of neurones, where each one represents a place in a particular environment. Input to the matrix can take two forms: inputs that provide sensory information about the environment, and inputs that provide information that the animal is changing its position in space, to sample inputs from a different part of space.

The locative mechanism allows cognitive maps to be built and subsequently updated. Individuals hold cognitive maps for a variety of environments, and on entering a new environment will bring forth potential place representations. The choosing of a particular location will determine how the other locations within an environment will be represented in the new cognitive map. The map is gradually built up through sensory and motor inputs that provide information about distances. Revisions to cognitive maps occur when an inconsistency is detected between a sensory input and a place representation and the predicted sensory input. Old maps are not discarded, but are maintained in some form of representation—this is termed the ''misplace.'' Information contained within a cognitive map of an environment can be used to alert a person to problem situations. For example, danger may be associated with particular places within an environment, and detours can be taken when certain paths become unavailable. Layering, or embedding of maps, allows for multiple affective and locational information to be stored with objects.

Cognitive maps are a result of learning and ongoing learning. Individuals can use their cognitive mapping system to select and test strategies to solutions. This is achieved through reference to other neural systems.

III. COGNITIVE MAPS AND DECISION MAKING

Cognitive maps have been used to analyze individual and group decision making. These maps differ from spatial maps as they are often abstract representations of beliefs about certain environments or decision contexts. In some situations the cognitive maps are used to explain decision makers' behavior (that is, their actions and decisions) or to help predict

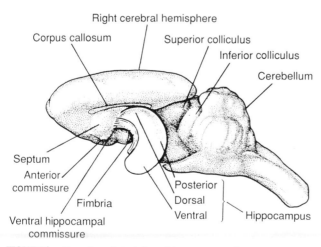

FIGURE 1   Drawing of the left rat hippocampus. [From O'Keefe, J., and Nadel, L. (1978). ''The Hippocampus as a Cognitive Map.'' Oxford University Press, Oxford; reprinted by permission of Oxford University Press.]

subsequent decision making behavior. [*See* DECISION MAKING, INDIVIDUALS.]

A. Foreign Policy Decision Makers

In the 1970s, cognitive maps began to be used by researchers at the University of California at Berkeley in the field of political science, to represent the beliefs and causal assertions of key policy makers concerning particular policy domains. For example, a cognitive map of the causal beliefs of a middle-eastern leader about a recent crisis would include beliefs about the possible causes of the crisis, important interactions between competing parties, individual and neighboring nations, alternative actions that the leader might have taken, and the consequences of these actions. The beliefs that are referred to range from general beliefs about nature and the world, which may be described as core beliefs, to specific beliefs about narrow decision-making contexts.

Cognitive maps of foreign policy makers were drawn as directional graphs that represent the deci-

sion maker's causal assertions as points and arrows. These points were the policy alternatives, the causes and effects, goals, and utilities of the decision maker. The purpose was to derive inferences from the maps and to see whether a decision maker made policy choices that were consistent with the causal assertions in their cognitive map. In the main, these maps were derived by researchers content analyzing policy documents or transcripts of speeches. Thus, the maps represented the espoused beliefs of the decision maker and are not necessarily consistent with the personal or actual beliefs of the policy makers. They are maps of what people publicly assert, but not necessarily what they think.

B. Cognitive Maps and Managerial Decision Making

In the area of management decision making cognitive maps have been used to provide a link between thinking and observed behavior, and to provide a tool for facilitating problem solving and decision making within organizations. These maps are often

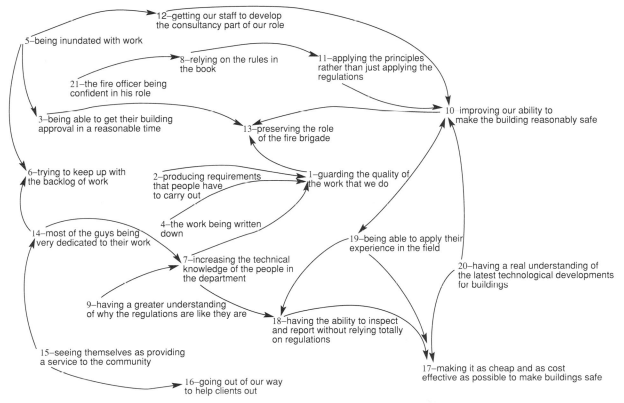

FIGURE 2   A simplified cognitive map showing causal beliefs. [From Langfield-Smith, K. M. (1992). *J. Management Studies* **29**(3), 349–368. Reprinted by permission of Blackwell Publishers.]

visually represented as networks of causal beliefs about a certain problem area, or domain of interest. In management consulting practice, individual managers' cognitive maps have been used as interactive tools to help in improving decision making: to focus attention on important issues, to trigger memory, to reveal gaps in knowledge, and to highlight key factors.

Figure 2 contains an example of a manager's cognitive map. This manager is a member of a fire brigade involved in enforcing fire protection standards in buildings. The map is an abstraction and a simplification of the manager's specific beliefs concerning that particular domain of fire protection. The lines connecting the written elements in the map represent causal relationships. For example, the manager believes that "being able to get their building approval in a reasonable time" leads to "preserving the role of the fire brigade," which leads to "improving our ability to make the building reasonably safe." The contents of this map were developed during a series of interviews between the manager and researcher. It is assumed that his perceptions, or beliefs, about

that specific part of his world are filtered through, and develop from, his more general core systems of beliefs and values. The specific beliefs contained in the map may not directly guide action but along with other inputs may shape and constrain decision-making behavior—providing a boundary for that behavior—and help to explain subsequent actions and decisions.

IV. OTHER APPLICATIONS OF COGNITIVE MAPS

In the field of marketing, the "means–end" theory of cognitive maps has been used to represent consumers' choices and behavior. These maps derive from cognitive psychology. It is assumed that individuals' personal values drive the choice of criteria that they use to select alternative consumer products and cause them to behave in certain ways. Individuals are considered to have cognitive maps that help them to categorize stimuli in a complex

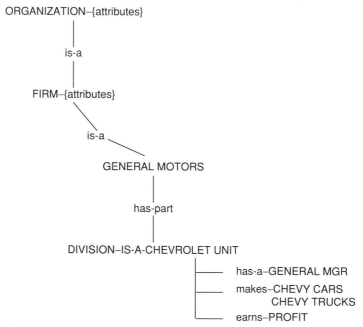

FIGURE 3 Hierarchical form of semantic rule network. A hypothetical semantic network about General Motors that illustrates some of the more common network arcs. IS-A arcs (General Motors *is-a* firm), HAS-PART arcs (General Motors *has-part* division), and heuristic knowledge arcs (Chevrolet *makes* cars). Arcs can also represent other logical connections such as conjunction, disjunction, quantification, and possible worlds. [From Stubbart, C. I., and Ramaprasad, A. (1990). In "Mapping Strategic Thought" (A. S. Huff, Ed.), pp. 251–288. Wiley, New York. Reprinted by permission of John Wiley & Sons, Ltd.]

world. These maps are similar to the schemas that were described in an earlier section. The types of categorizations that may be found in these maps are influenced by an individual's value systems. For example, a consumer may be driven by values of environmental conservation and thrift. Thus, cleaning products may be categorized by attributes such as high biodegradability, value for money, and minimum of harmful chemicals. These cognitive maps can be used by marketing analysts to help explain individuals' decision processes and buying behavior.

Cognitive maps have been a topic for research in the artificial intelligence area since the 1980s. The focus is to obtain insights into human information processes that can be used to build into artificial intelligence software and machines. Cognitive maps have been used to map the reasoning that individuals use to solve a problem, to represent how people connect images and propositions, and to study how people organize knowledge.

Early research into artificial intelligence mapped individuals' knowledge structures and processing using a wider range of relationships than just causal assertions. Semantic networks are used to represent the hierarchical relationships between concepts of natural language and knowledge. Figure 3 demonstrates a semantic network that relates to General Motors. The connecting lines represent relationships between the various concepts nodes. For example, the concepts "General Motors" and "firm"

are linked by "is-a." Thus, in reading this network it tells us that "General Motors is a firm" and consequentially has all of the attributes of a firm. The Chevrolet unit has three concepts attached which describe attributes of that division.

Bibliography

Cossete, P., and Audet, M. (1992). Mapping of an idiosyncratic schema. *J. Management Studies* **29**(3), 325–437.

Huff, A. S. (Ed.) (1990). "Mapping Strategic Thought." Wiley, New York.

Kesner, R. P. (1991). The emergence of multi-dimensional approaches to the structural organization of memory. In "Perspectives on Cognitive Neuroscience" (R. G. Lister and H. J. Weingarnter, Eds.), pp. 218–228. Oxford University Press, New York.

Langfield-Smith, K., and Wirth, A. (1992). Measuring differences between cognitive maps. *J. Operational Res. Soc.* **43**(12), 1135–1150.

O'Keefe, J. (1991). The hippocampal cognitive map and navigational strategies. In "Brain and Space" (J. Paillard, Ed.), pp. 273–295. Oxford University Press, Oxford.

Schacter, D. L., and Nadel, L. (1991). Varieties of spatial memory: A problem for cognitive neuroscience. In "Perspectives on Cognitive Neuroscience" (R. G. Lister and H. J. Weingarnter, Eds.), pp. 165–185. Oxford University Press, New York.

Thinus-Blanc, C., Save, E., Bohot, M.-C., and Poucet, B. (1991). The hippocampus, exploratory activity, and spatial memory. In "Brain and Space" (J. Paillard, Ed.), pp. 334–352. Oxford University Press, Oxford.

Wallace, R. (1989). Cognitive mapping and the origin of language and mind. *Curr. Anthropol.* **30**(4), 518–526.

Yeap, W. K. (1988). Towards a computational theory of cognitive maps. *Artificial Intelligence* **34**, 297–360.

COMPETITION

Robin S. Vealey
Miami University of Ohio

I. The Competition Process
II. Antecedents of Competitive Behavior
III. Outcomes from the Competitive Process
IV. Summary

Glossary

Aggression A form of behavior directed toward inflicting harm or injury onto another person.

Competition Social comparison process whereby individuals compare their performance with some standard in the presence of other individuals who can evaluate the comparison process.

Competitive anxiety Tendency to feel apprehension and tension in competitive situations.

Competitiveness Personality disposition that reflects the intensity or energy directed toward achieving success in competition.

Cooperation A situation in which all rewards to individuals depend upon the mutual interactive behavior of two or more individuals.

Extrinsic motivation Motivation derived from rewards external to the competitive experience such as social approval and trophies.

Intrinsic motivation Motivation derived from rewards inherent in the competitive experience such as feelings of pride and mastery.

Rivalry A form of competition that usually elicits emotion in which the performance standard is to best a specific opponent.

Zero sum game Term used to indicate that competition requires one competitor to fail for every one who is successful.

COMPETITION is a social comparison process whereby individuals compare their performance with some standard in the presence of other individuals who can evaluate the comparison process. The main antecedent of competitive behavior is the basic undifferentiated human need to be competent which is then differentiated into competitive behavior in specific achievement contexts via the socialization process. Research has examined several outcomes from the competitive process including anxiety, aggression, motivation, character, and human performance. From a social psychological perspective, competition is neither good nor bad. Rather, competition is a social evaluation process in which the positive or negative consequences of engaging in competitive behavior are determined by the nature of the social context in which the competition occurs.

I. THE COMPETITION PROCESS

A. Definition of Competition

Competition is a social process that is especially pervasive in Western culture. The concept of competition often elicits emotional discourse as proponents and opponents of competition debate its value to society. However, to debate the pros and cons of competition from an intuitive perspective is fruitless as no one bothers to clearly define competition. To understand the antecedents and consequences of competition, it is imperative to define competition from a social psychological perspective.

Rainer Martens was the first to define competition so as to differentiate between competitive and noncompetitive activities. He defined competition as a social comparison process whereby individuals compare their performance with some standard in the presence of other individuals who can evaluate the comparison process. Thus, competition is a social evaluation achievement process because most psychologists agree that achievement involves the evaluation of performance in comparison to a standard. The standard can be another person's performance, the individual's own past performance, or

Encyclopedia of Human Behavior, Volume 1

some idealized performance level. However, self-comparisons in the absence of evaluative others, or nonsocial comparisons, are not considered to be competition. For example, if a person played a round of golf by herself attempting to better her previous score, this would be considered a self-evaluative achievement situation, but not competition. Thus, not all achievement situations can be labeled as competition because competition requires that at least one other person must be involved to make competition a *social* achievement situation. [*See* SOCIAL COMPARISON.]

B. Competitive as a Social Evaluation Achievement Process

Competition is not a single event or a set of conditions but rather a process. This process is graphically represented in Figure 1 as having four interrelated stages that are influenced by personal attributes of the individual as well as by external factors in the environment. Each stage is discussed below.

1. Objective Competitive Situation

The first stage of the competitive process is the objective competitive situation (OCS) with which the person is confronted. The OCS simply refers to those factors in the physical and social environment that meet the criteria of a competitive situation. As stated in the above definition, the OCS must include the comparison of performance to a standard and at least one other person who can evaluate the comparison. The OCS specifies the type of task, the difficulty of the opponents, the playing conditions, the playing rules, number of spectators, and the available extrinsic rewards. Thus, the OCS defines the environmental and social conditions for the person who is considering engaging in the competitive process.

2. Subjective Competitive Situation

How the person perceives, interprets, and appraises the OCS is the second stage of the competitive pro-

cess which is called the subjective competitive situation (SCS). The SCS is mediated by such factors as personality dispositions, attitudes, and motives for participation. Most studies of competition have assumed that the OCS is perceived identically by everyone, although common sense suggests that this assumption is false. To improve our understanding of how people behave in competitive situations, we must understand individual differences in how they perceive the same situation. Because the SCS describes a process that occurs within the person, it cannot be directly measured and can be inferred only from other behavioral indices.

3. Response

During the subjective appraisal that occurs at the SCS stage, individuals decide whether they will continue in the competitive process. That is, they decide to either approach or avoid the OCS. If individuals decide to approach the OCS, then the third stage of the competitive process occurs which is the response stage. The response stage includes behavioral responses such as performance or aggression, psychological responses such as feeling anxious or confident, and physiological responses such as increased heart rate or sweating. How a person responds to the OCS is largely determined by the SCS. Another important factor related to a person's response is her or his ability level relative to the task demands of the OCS.

4. Consequences

The final category of the competitive process is the consequences arising from the comparison of the person's response to a standard. Consequences may be positive, negative, or neutral. Importantly, it is how the person perceives the consequences of the comparison that determines how significant these consequences are to her or him. In competition, the consequences are frequently viewed in terms of success and failure, with success normally perceived as a positive consequence and failure as a negative consequence. If a tennis player loses a match but perceives that she played well, the consequences may be positive for her rather than negative. As seen in Figure 1, the consequences stage in the model is linked back to the OCS and SCS to complete the competitive process. These links indicate that an individual's history of consequences in competitive situations will determine that person's attitudes about competition and whether she or he chooses to approach or avoid subsequent competition. This

FIGURE 1   Martens' model of the competitive process.

completes the framework of competition as a complex social evaluation achievement process.

C. Terms Related to Competition

Several different terms are used to describe psychological constructs related to competition. These terms include cooperation, rivalry, competitive behavior, and competitiveness. The distinction between these terms, although subtle, is important.

1. Cooperation

Early research defined both competition and cooperation in relation to the distribution of rewards. Competition was defined as a situation in which rewards to individuals were distributed unequally on the basis of performance. Often the term "zero sum game" was used to indicate that competition by nature requires at least one competitor to fail for every one who is successful (the sum of winners and losers is zero). In contrast, cooperation was defined as a situation in which the rewards to individuals were distributed equally based on mutual interactive behavior between individuals. In a cooperative situation an individual obtains a reward only if all individuals obtain it, whereas in a competitive situation if one or a limited number of individuals obtain a reward, the remaining individuals do not.

The reward definition of competition was found lacking by researchers for many reasons, and one important reason was that when viewed this way competition and cooperation are seen as polarities. Competition is not the opposite of cooperation. Instead, nearly all competition involves cooperation of some type. Cooperation is necessary within teams as they work together on strategies, and cooperation is even needed between opponents as they abide by mutual rules and attitudes. It is the very essence of competition that demands competitors to cooperate so as to challenge each other to achieve optimal performances. Interestingly, the term competition is derived from the Latin verb meaning "to seek together" which implies the importance of cooperation as an integral part of competition.

2. Rivalry

Just as competition is not simply the opposite of cooperation, competition should be distinguished from rivalry. Rivalry is a popular term often used when describing competitions that elicit a great deal of emotion. This is because the focus in a rivalry is on the specific opponent with the object being to best this opponent with one's own performance as a secondary concern. This is different from competition in which the focus is on the attainment of a goal or achievement of a specific performance standard. Obviously, sport competition lies on a continuum from an emphasis on opponent-centered goals (rivalry) to an emphasis on performance-oriented goals (competition). However, it is important to note that the definition of competition is performance-oriented and does not necessarily imply a person-centered rivalry.

3. Competitive Behavior

Competitive behavior is defined as the manifestation of an overt, observable response that an individual makes to the OCS. Thus, competitive behavior occurs at the response stage of the competitive process. Examples of competitive behavior would include signing up to run in a road race as well as performing vigorously during the course of the race.

4. Competitiveness

Competitiveness is a term used widely to describe the intensity with which a person behaves when competing. However, competitiveness is a personality disposition which predisposes an individual to act in a certain way. Competitiveness, then, is a personality disposition that reflects the intensity or energy directed toward achieving success in competition. Actually, competitiveness is a specific form of the broader and more general achievement disposition within all individuals. As discussed previously, the main difference between a typical achievement situation and competition is that the latter specifies that someone must be present to evaluate the performance. Thus, competition is a specific form of an achievement situation in which social evaluation is present, and competitiveness may be thought of as a disposition to achieve *and* be evaluated. Because competitiveness is a personality disposition, it falls within the SCS in the competitive process and occurs in the process temporally prior to the actual response or competitive behavior.

II. ANTECEDENTS OF COMPETITIVE BEHAVIOR

Competition has been defined as a social evaluation achievement process that is multi-stage and interactive. Every day, millions of individuals engage in competition to test and evaluate their abilities via social comparison with others. However, the question arises as to where this behavior comes from? Is it instinctual or is it learned? In this section, the antecedents of competitiveness and competitive behavior are examined to understand how people become attracted to competition and why they seek out opportunities for social comparison and evaluation.

A. Competence Motivation

Because competition is a form of achievement, the literature on the development of achievement motivation provides information regarding the antecedents of competitiveness and competitive behavior. Psychologists generally agree that the motive to achieve is intrinsic in humans meaning that motivation is derived from within the individual and the rewards are inherent in the activity itself. Several prominent psychological theorists including Robert White, Jerome Kagan, Richard deCharms, and Edward Deci indicate that the achievement motive is developed from the broader-based motive to be competent.

Competence is defined as the ability of individuals to engage in successful transactions with the environment to enhance self-growth and human development. That is, all humans are born with a basic intrinsic need to be competent or to be able to deal effectively with the environment. Toward this end, individuals engage in repeated mastery attempts in an attempt to gain competence and have an effect on their environment. If these mastery attempts result in successful or competent performance outcomes, feelings of efficacy and inherent pleasure are experienced which increases subsequent intrinsic or competence motivation. The ultimate goal of this competence motivation and mastery striving is autonomy or the ability to govern one's self. According to theorists, autonomy can be achieved only through competence which results as the individual achieves success in progressive interactions with the environment in a gradual learning process. Effective child-rearing practices such as mastery and independence training are essential for the development of competence motivation and autonomy.

These early theorists proposed that the innate motive to deal competently with the environment is a broad-based, undifferentiated motive. However, this early innate motive gets channeled into specific achievement contexts through early socialization experiences of children. For example, Susan Harter has demonstrated that competence motivation is specific to physical, cognitive, and social contexts, and that children's perceptions of competence and motivation differ across these domains. Thus, although the undifferentiated motive to be competent is innate, the directions into which it is channeled are learned via socialization practices. Thus, the motive to achieve success through competition, termed competitiveness, is developed by channeling children's competence motivation into competitive activities, usually through competitive sport participation. This differentiation process is where competitiveness becomes extrinsically motivated as children are externally rewarded via praise from significant others and tangible rewards such as trophies rewarded for success in competition. Thus, competitiveness and competitive behavior result from the socialization of children into competitive situations (OCS) in which they engage in successful mastery attempts in socially evaluative situations and obtain extrinsic rewards for their successful performance.

B. Development of Competitiveness

The work of Joseph Veroff supports the development of competitiveness as being learned via the differentiation process that channels the competence motive into sport competition. Veroff theorizes that there are actually two achievement motives. The intrinsically based achievement motive is termed autonomous achievement motivation and involves only internalized personal standards of evaluation. It does not involve social comparisons. The second motive, called the social achievement motive, is identical to the competitiveness construct. Individuals high in the social achievement motive are motivated to obtain information about themselves through social comparisons so as to evaluate their abilities and hence improve their competency (an intrinsic motive) or to obtain social approval (an extrinsic motive). These two functions of social achievement motivation are termed informative function and normative function. The informative function provides the information necessary to accommodate one's failures and to evaluate whether personal aspirations are realistic or unrealistic in comparison with others. This function is intrinsic and is crucial to the development of the sense of competence. The normative function involves social approval or disapproval from significant others as well as the world at large. This function is extrinsic in that enhancement of self-esteem is often sought rather than evaluation or accurate self-assessment.

The development of achievement motivation, according to Veroff, involves mastering these two achievement motives sequentially. First, children must master the autonomous achievement stage and then they must be successful in social comparisons. Once they have successfully mastered these stages, they then move to the third stage known as the integrated achievement motivation stage. This third stage is simply an integration of the first two stages in which individuals have acquired the ability to know when to make social comparisons and when to use their own personal standards for evaluation.

The autonomous achievement motive first appears in the preverbal stage of early childhood when children initiate behaviors intended to increase their competence. During the early school years, successful autonomous achievement motivation facilitates the evolution of social achievement motivation. At this stage, the pressure and desire to compare socially develops. The important thing is that children must feel adequate as a person in comparison to their significant others. Not everyone progresses through the three stages of achievement motivation. Individuals who successfully master the autonomous stage but are unsuccessful in social comparison are unlikely to become competitive or engage in competitive behaviors. These individuals might work hard in achieving personal goals, but they probably would avoid competition.

C. Socialization of Competitive Behavior

The development of competence motivation, autonomy, and successful social comparison has been shown to be important precursors of competitiveness and competitive behavior. However, it is clear that very young children cannot compete, rather they strive for autonomy and their interest in competition develops during socialization into a specific social context. The work of Carolyn Sherif supports that competitiveness develops in a social context in which parents, siblings, and peers are important in structuring the standards and goals to which children compare their performance. Research also indicates that physical and athletic ability are particularly valued attributes among children of elementary and secondary school age. Thus, as social comparison motivation strengthens during the elementary school years, an increasing number of children seek out

sport opportunities to develop and assess their athletic skills relative to their peers.

The major factor influencing the type and amount of involvement in competition is the process of socialization. Socialization is a process whereby individuals learn skills, values, attitudes, and norms associated with the performance of socially defined roles. The family has been found to exert the most pervasive influence on the involvement of children in competitive sport. This socialization often begins when the child is in early infancy and is based on the encouragement of competitive play behaviors and the selection of competitive toys for children. Also, differences observed in parental treatment of young male and female children have been associated with the greater involvement in sport by males in society. Specifically, family members provide social support for competitive behaviors exhibited by children such as providing encouragement for competitive behavior, making competitive opportunities available to children, and acting as models by engaging in competition.

The influence of the family as a socializing agent for the development of competitiveness and competitive behavior appears to decline at adolescence. At this stage, children's peer groups and significant others in the schools and community become more influential. However, these opportunities and support are still considerably greater for males than females, again emphasizing the importance that society places on competitive behavior for males. [See PEER RELATIONSHIPS AND INFLUENCES IN CHILDHOOD.]

Environmental factors also influence the socialization of competitive behavior especially in terms of opportunity. Regional and neighborhood location, often reflecting social class differences, influence the types of opportunities available to young people. Also, the scope of available opportunities for participation are usually greater in urban as compared to rural settings. Clearly, for individuals to successfully engage in social comparison with peers in competition, they must have the opportunities to do so. Another environmental influence on the socialization of competitive behavior is the availability and visibility of competitive role models. In particular, male role models are extremely visible through the popular media and the competitive behavior and attitudes of young people are often influenced by the actions of these models. For example, research has shown that violence and aggression in ice hockey is influenced mostly by the viewing of aggressive models that are highly visible in the sport. Overall, the coverage of competitive sport in the electronic and print media provides powerful messages to young individuals as to what constitutes acceptable and even expected competitive behavior.

Research has identified cultural differences in competitive behavior supporting the point that the environment plays a crucial role in channeling achievement and competitive behaviors. Linda Nelson and Spencer Kagan found that American children were much more competitive than Mexican children as the American children were irrationally competitive to the point of giving up the chance to get rewards for themselves in order to keep other children from getting similar rewards. Similar differences were found between urban and rural children, with urban children displaying more of the intense competitive behaviors. Terry Orlick found similar results in that Canadian children were less likely to respond positively to cooperative noncompetitive games when compared to Inuit children. Joan Duda also found these results when comparing Anglo and Navajo children, with Anglo children exhibiting much more intense competitive behavior. Overall, these observed cultural differences in competitive behavior suggest that social environmental factors play a major role in determining to what degree competitiveness develops.

III. OUTCOMES FROM THE COMPETITIVE PROCESS

Competition has been defined as a social evaluation achievement process and the developmental antecedents of competitiveness and competitive behavior have been overviewed. It is also important to examine the outcomes of competition. Using the competitive process model as a framework, it seems important to understand the responses (behavioral, psychological, physiological) and consequences that occur as a result of competition. In this section, several outcomes that result from competition are examined including anxiety, aggression, character, motivation, and performance.

A. Anxiety

All individuals have experienced feelings of anxiety or apprehension when placed in competitive situations. Anxiety is a typical response to competitive situations because individuals perceive these situations as threatening to their self-esteem. That is, individuals fear failure in competitive situations that are important to them and respond with competitive anxiety manifested as nervousness, negative thoughts, and apprehension. [*See* ANXIETY AND FEAR.]

Anxiety is pervasive in competition and can be considered within the context of the model of the competitive process described previously in this text. As depicted in Figure 2, the objective competitive situation (OCS) defines the environmental factors that create competitive anxiety. Competitive trait anxiety is a personality disposition that describes a person's tendency to perceive competition as threatening and to respond with apprehension or tension. The OCS and competitive trait anxiety combine to create a perception of threat which may be thought of as occurring within the subjective competitive situation (SCS) of the competitive process model (see Fig. 1). Research indicates that characteristics of competition that induce perception of threat include fear of failure, fear of evaluation, ego threat, outcome certainty, negative outcome certainty, external control, and perceived importance of the competition. Also, high competitive trait-anxious individuals perceive greater threat in competition than low competitive trait-anxious individuals. This perception of threat creates the response of state anxiety which is a current emotional state characterized by feelings of tension and apprehension. Thus, trait anxiety is a disposition or tendency to feel anxious, while state anxiety involves the actual feelings of tension and apprehension that result from specific situations. [*See* TRAITS.]

One factor within the competitive situation that has been shown to influence the level of anxiety experienced by individuals is the type of activity. Individual sport activities such as wrestling and gymnastics have been shown to elicit higher anxiety levels than competitive team sport activities such as softball and basketball. This seems to be due to the higher evaluation potential inherent in individual activities in which no diffusion of responsibility can

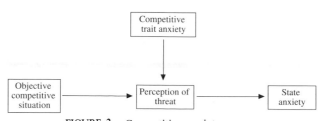

FIGURE 2   Competitive anxiety process.

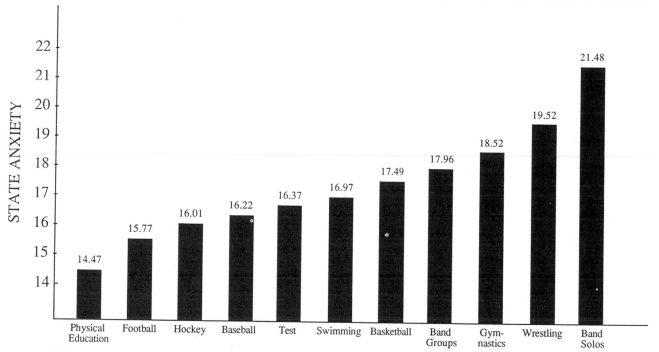

FIGURE 3   Children's state anxiety in sport and nonsport competitive activites (state anxiety range is 10 to 30). [From Simon, J., and Martens, R. (1979). *J. Sport Psychol.* **1**, 165.]

occur as when compared to being surrounded by teammates in a team competitive situation. Interestingly, this phenomenon carries over to competitive nonsport activities as well. As depicted in Figure 3, research by Julie Simon and Rainer Martens has shown that competitive band solos created more anxiety in young individuals than competitive sport activities. However, as previously discussed, the individual competitive sports of wrestling and gymnastics followed the band solos in terms of eliciting anxiety and were more anxiety inducing than competitive band groups and competitive team sports. These findings indicate that anxiety experienced as a result of competition is similar in both sport and nonsport competitive activities. The key factor in eliciting anxiety seems to be the social evaluation potential of the situation.

Another factor within the competitive situation that elicits anxiety responses is the importance of the competition to the individuals. As the criticality or the importance of the competitive outcome increases for the individual, the greater the anxiety response. Also, greater anxiety is experienced by individuals during competition when they feel they are not being successful as compared to individuals who perceive they are succeeding in the competition. Overall, it seems that there are several factors

inherent in the nature of competition that serve to elicit anxiety in individuals within competitive situations.

B. Aggression

Another outcome of competition is aggression which is very visible in competitive situations, especially sport. Aggression is defined as a form of behavior directed toward inflicting harm or injury onto another person. The main source of aggression in competitive situations is the inevitable presence of frustration. Frustration often results when a person's goals are thwarted and in competition, especially competitive sport, the main objective is to block the goal achievement of the opponent. Theoretically, humans are thought to have a predispostion to respond to frustration with aggression; however, that predisposition can be modified through the learning process. Thus, frustration may not always result in aggression, but clearly the presence of frustration increases a person's readiness to aggress. [*See* AG-GRESSION.]

Most social learning theorists agree that aggression is a learned behavior that develops as a result of modeling and reinforcement. Clearly, aggressive responses are modeled and reinforced in competitive sport. Ice hockey players are glorified for slamming opponents into the boards and even fighting, while baseball players are encouraged and even expected to charge the mound and aggress against the pitcher as a result of being hit by a pitched ball. Research indicates that children socially learn aggressive behaviors in competition at an early age.

Research has supported the link between frustration and aggression in competitive situations. In fact, many situational factors inherent in competitive situations seem to elicit aggressive responses. Losing teams have been shown to demonstrate more aggressive responses in competition as compared to winning teams. Also, aggression increases as the competition proceeds temporally and also increases as the performance differential between competitors increases. This seems to occur because when the performance differentials increase, competitors may engage in aggression without seriously affecting the competitive outcome. Similar to the findings on anxiety in competition, the importance of the competition and the saliency of available rewards in the competitive situation also increase the probability that aggression will occur.

A classic experiment examining the relationship between competition and aggression was conducted by Sherif and colleagues at a summer camp for boys. The experiment involved three stages. The first stage was very informal in which the campers were allowed to participate fully in all camp activities. In the second stage, the boys were separated into two groups within which they participated in the camp activities. In the third stage, the two groups engaged in competition and were faced with many frustrating situations designed by the experimenters. The results indicated that only minimal aggressive responses occurred during the first and second stages of the experiment. However, high levels of aggression occurred during the third stage which escalated to the point that aggression occurred outside of the actual competitive events and the groups had to be disbanded. This experiment demonstrated that the effects of competition on aggressive responses can extend far beyond the specific context of the competitive event.

It is a popular belief that competition reduces aggressive impulses in humans by providing a release or purging of aggression (called catharsis) so that aggression will not occur in nonsport settings. Proponents of this belief claim that competitive sport can reduce the destructive behaviors in the larger society. However, the theoretical and empirical evidence does not support this claim. For both competitive participants and competitive spectators, aggressive tendencies actually increased after competing in or watching a competitive event. Thus, both actual competitive participation and vicarious competitive participation do not serve as a catharsis for aggressive responses. Instead, the literature indicates that competition increases aggression for both participants and spectators. An example of this is the increasing violence that occurs in cities in the aftermath of a major sport championship such as the World Series or Super Bowl.

C. Character

Similar to the popular belief that the competition acts as a catharsis for the acceptable release of aggression, it is also popularly believed that competition builds "character" or socially valued personality characteristics. However, this belief has not been substantiated in the research literature. In fact, research indicates that competition serves to reduce prosocial behavioral tendencies such as helping and sharing and serves to increase antisocial tendencies. Furthermore, both of these effects are magnified by losing. Research also indicates that fairness as a competitive value becomes subordinate to competence and winning as age and experience in sport competition increases. Most researchers agree that personality characteristics associated with character in individuals are probably established before they begin involvement in competition. That is, character is seen as more influenced by child rearing and early socialization than by participation in competition. Research examining personality changes in college athletes across their 4 years of participation found no significant changes which substantiates the position that competition does not build character.

D. Motivation

As discussed in the previous sections, competition elicits anxiety, aggression, and other anti-social behaviors in individuals. But what about motivation? That is, does competition increase the motivation of individuals to achieve? Clearly, the study of motivation is extremely broad and thus all the facets of motivation are beyond the scope of this discussion. However, it seems important to include some examination of the effects of competition on the motivational responses of individuals. [*See* MOTIVATION, EMOTIONAL BASIS.]

One aspect of motivation is continuing motivation or persistence which in competitive sport is illustrated by whether individuals continue to participate. It is estimated that approximately 40% of American children withdraw from competitive sport each year. What is it about competition that causes this attrition rate? Research indicates that there are several aspects of the competitive process that influence children's decisions to drop out of competitive sport. The most prevalent finding seems to be that children discontinue competition as they dislike the competitive emphasis on winning which creates lack of enjoyment, fear of failure, psychological stress, and disapproval from significant others.

Overall, this research indicates that when the underlying achievement goals of children are not met in the competitive situation, they discontinue participation. The achievement goals most often cited by children as reasons to enter into competition include enjoyment, affiliation, skill development, and excitement and personal challenge. Thus, children discontinue competitive participation when it is not enjoyable, when they are not able to engage socially with friends, when they do not develop competence at skills, and when it is not exciting and challenging.

Many people draw the conclusion that competition is bad for young people as it develops antisocial behavior and does not fulfill their needs. However, it is important to remember that competition is simply a socially evaluative comparison process—it is neither inherently good or bad. The research on motivation to continue competitive participation emphasizes the need to structure and adapt the competitive process to meet the achievement needs of young developing individuals. For example, sport competition for youth should be structured so that children have fun, learn skills, develop physical competence at their own pace, and affiliate with peers. The first place to intervene in the competitive process to make it more positive and rewarding for people is at the objective competitive situation (OCS) stage. The OCS can be structured and modified to meet the needs of all diffferent types of individuals who want to engage in competition.

Another outcome of competition related to motivation is the development of intrinsic and extrinsic motivation. Competition always contains at least two potential outcomes—the intrinsic reward of feeling competent (intrinsic motivation) and extrinsic rewards such as social approval or money (extrinsic motivation). Most theorists agree that intrinsic motivation is more powerful as it is personally con-

trollable and satisfies the basic human need to be competent and self-determining. The question arises as to what is it about competition that elicits both types of motivation?

Most individuals begin participation in sport competition for intrinsic reasons such as enjoyment and personal satisfaction. However, extrinsic rewards are common in competition such as trophies, scholarships, and even large salaries in professional sports. Research indicates that extrinsic rewards given in competition may serve to weaken or undermine existing intrinsic motivation. Edward Deci's cognitive evaluation theory explains how this process occurs. Extrinsic rewards may affect intrinsic motivation in two ways: controlling and informational. If the extrinsic rewards associated with competition are perceived as controlling by individuals, then intrinsic motivation decreases as individuals feel less self-determining. However, if the extrinsic rewards given in competition are perceived as informational, individuals feel more competent and self-determining which then enhances their intrinsic motivation for competition. Research has demonstrated that scholarships that were perceived as controlling by college athletes decreased these athletes' intrinsic motivation for sport competition, while scholarships that were perceived as providing information about competence increased athletes' intrinsic motivation. The key point is that extrinsic rewards associated with competition do not always weaken intrinsic motivation, but that they have the potential to do so if seen as controlling by individuals. Competition should be structured to minimize the controlling aspects of rewards and to use rewards to emphasize information about improvement and competence.

E. Performance

Perhaps the most interesting outcome associated with competition is performance. That is, does competition serve to make individuals perform better than they can perform on their own? The very first scientific experiment in social psychology by Triplett in 1898 examined this question. Triplett examined cycling records by comparing unpaced, paced, and competitive race times. He found that paced times were faster than unpaced and that competitive times were the fastest of all. Triplett then set up an experiment with a winding task and again found that subjects performed faster in pairs than when alone. Triplett asserted that the presence of others aroused one's competitive drive and released additional energy that boosted performance.

Research supports that competition improves performance on simple or well-learned skills as well as speed, strength, and endurance tasks. Although the research is equivocal, there is some evidence that competition is detrimental for tasks that emphasize accuracy. Evidence also indicates that high-ability individuals performed better on complex motor tasks in competitive conditions, but low-ability individuals performed better in noncompetitive conditions. The research in this area emphasizes the fact that the influence of competition on motor performance is quite complex and additional research is needed to account for the various aspects of competition that influence individual performance.

It is also interesting to examine whether competition within groups serves to enhance or decrease the performance of the groups. Individual members of competitive sport teams are often in competition with each other for certain positions within the team. Even when groups are formed for cooperative, reasons, subtle competition generally takes place between group members. The literature indicates that the type of task influences whether competition within the group facilitates group performance. If the task can be carried out independently by group members, intragroup competition can enhance performance. However, competition within groups has been shown to decrease performance on highly interdependent, interactive tasks. Thus, constant competition within teams whose members must constantly interact with each other such as volleyball or hockey can prove detrimental to group performance.

IV. SUMMARY

Competition is a complex social evaluation process in which the positive or negative consequences of engaging in competitive behavior are determined by the nature of the social context in which the competition occurs. Competition is neither good nor bad, rather it is an inert process whereby individuals can assess their competencies in relation to others. Both the negative outcomes of competition such as anxiety and aggression and the positive outcomes of intrinsic motivation and enhanced performance are

a result of the way that competition is structured and experienced. Socialization practices should be followed that allow children to develop autonomy and gain perceived physical competence to engage in successful social comparisons. The informative nature of social comparison should be emphasized so that competition is sought out to provide information about one's skill development in relation to others. The rivalrous, normative nature of competition that focuses on the enhancement of self-esteem by beating others should be de-emphasized. Also, competition should be structured and modified to fit the specific needs of individuals. For example, competitive baseball for children should be structured very differently from professional baseball. The emphasis in competition for children should be enjoyment, skill development, and social affiliation as opposed to winning and specialization. Competition should be viewed by all individuals as a challenging arena for the assessment of self-competence.

Bibliography

Deci, E. L., and Ryan, R. M. (1985). "Intrinsic Motivation and Self-Determination in Human Behavior." Plenum, New York.

Duda, J. L. (1986). A cross-cultural analysis of achievement motivation in sport and the classroom. In "Current Selected Research in the Psychology and Sociology of Sport" (L. Vander-Velden and J. Humphrey, Eds.), pp. 117–131. AMS, New York.

Gill, D. L., Dzewaltowski, D. A., and Deeter, T. E. (1988). The relationship of competitiveness and achievement orientation to participation in sport and nonsport activities. J. Sport Exercise Psychol. 10, 139–150.

Horn, T. S. (Ed.) (1992). "Advances in Sport Psychology." Human Kinetics, Champaign, IL.

Martens, R., Vealey, R. S., and Burton, D. (1990). "Competitive Anxiety in Sport." Human Kinetics, Champaign, IL.

Passer, M. W. (1988). Determinants and consequences of children's competitive stress. In "Children in Sport" (F. L. Smoll, R. A. Magill, and M. J. Ash, Eds.), 3rd ed., pp. 203–227. Human Kinetics, Champaign, IL.

Roberts, G. C. (Ed.) (1992). "Motivation in Sport and Exercise." Human Kinetics, Champaign, IL.

Scanlan, T. K. (1988). Social evaluation and the competition process: A developmental perspective. In "Children in Sport" (F. L. Smoll, R. A. Magill, and M. J. Ash Eds.), 3rd ed., pp. 135–148. Human Kinetics, Champaign, IL.

Sherif, C. W. (1976). The social context of competition. In "Social Problems in Athletics" (D. Landers, Ed.), pp. 18–36. University of Illinois Press, Champaign, IL.

Veroff, J. (1969). Social comparison and the development of achievement motivation. In "Achievement-Related Motives in Children" (C. P. Smith, Ed.), pp. 46–101. Russell Sage Foundation, New York.

CONFLICT BEHAVIOR

Adrian Parker and Trevor Archer

University of Göteborg, Sweden

Glossary

Cognitive factors Higher-order psychological factors relating to intellect, reasoning, belief, and construct systems which may have an influence on lower-order events such as learning, perception, and conflict resolution.

Cognitive unconscious Information presented at a speed too rapid for conscious recognition nevertheless establishes some kind of memory trace. This information is subsequently learned more quickly than nonpresented information. The designation ''cognitive'' is added to emphasize that the effect is in the area of learning and perception and has not as yet been shown to have a motivational or an emotional influence on behavior—as is alleged to occur with the Freudian unconscious and with subliminal perception.

Conflict A perceptual state involving the executive function of the organism where the immediate choices in the organism's repertoire, together with the outcome of these choices, are seen to involve incompatible motives and needs.

Constructs A term promoted by the American psychologist George Kelly to describe the belief systems which individuals use to divide persons (and the world in general) into specific categories such as pleasant–unpleasant, attractive–repulsive, honest–dishonest. Constructs are usually bipolar and characteristic of the individual.

Coping skills The skills, including those known as defense mechanisms, for dealing with the demands (especially those which are psychologically threatening) of the environment. The term is more neutral in not committing the user to a belief in psychodynamic concepts.

Defense mechanism The description of the various ways which consciousness is said to defend itself against potential anxiety by distorting the perception of the situation to become a less or nonthreatening one. The usual defense mechanisms are denial, projection, displacement, sublimation, and rationalization.

Gestalt psychology Literally the study of how the whole is greater than the sum of the parts. An approach within psychology which emphasises that a basic principle in facilitating learning, perception, and even psychotherapeutic change is to create a whole and meaning image from its components. Conflictual aspects are resolved by combining their inherent polarizations or promoting a dialogue between them.

Life events The specification of stress-related events such as divorce, separation, job loss, immigration, which are thought to interact culminatively to determine the occurrence of illness or psychological disturbance to which the individual may be biologically predisposed.

Perceptual defense The study of how certain taboo or unpleasant words, descriptions, and pictures have lower thresholds for perception than those of a neutral character.

Psychoneuroimmunology The study of the way psychological factors interact via neural and chemical messengers (hormones) with the body's immune system, thereby providing a pathway for psychological factors to have determining effects on illness.

Social identity theory Social identity is composed of several different identities corresponding to the social groups of which we are a member. The more positive the images of these groups, the more positive is our self-esteem, and we strive to increase the status of our group membership by creating a series of in-groups and out-groups. This becomes a basis for social prejudice and group conflict.

State-specific memory Memory that is specific to a particular state of consciousness and is not retrievable or only partially retrievable in other states. For example, events which a person recalls in a drug-induced state may not be recalled in the normal waking state and vice versa.

Stroop effect A technique for studying the effect of perceptual bias on recognition time and learning by using words for colors written in colors which are incongruous with their meaning. The word *red,* for instance, written in blue.

CONFLICT can be defined as a perceptual state involving the executive function of the organism where the immediate choices in the organism's behavioral repertoire, together with the outcome of these choices, are seen to involve incompatible motives and needs. The conflictual state can have emotional, motivational, and cognitive components. Conflict is integral to all human behavior and its attempted resolution can be seen as a major part of man's effort toward mastery of his environment. As such the concept of conflict behavior must occupy therefore a central position in psychological science. Indeed, the study of conflict follows the history of psychology where each area of sectarian research has tended to claim a monopoly on knowledge. Three areas of research can easily be identified; the psychobiological approach highlighting ethological and behavioral aspects of conflict, the psychodynamic approach stressing the role of unconscious motives in conflict, and the humanistic approaches which emphasize the importance of conflict and crisis for promoting growth and change. Only in the present time are there real signs of a consensus between these approaches beginning to emerge. With this, an interest is also emerging for the study of conflict in wider contexts such as the role of conflict and stress in physical illness and in the study of large-scale group conflict.

Axiomatic to the psychobiological approach is the view first put forward by the philosopher of science John Dewey: "the brain is primarily the organ of a certain type of behavior, not an organ of knowing the world." This is to acknowledge that with respect to evolutionary demands, the human psyche would seem to be best equipped for handling straight decision making in the face of practical conflicts and then carrying out these choices. The brain may not be designed to give any successful resolution of abstract philosophical and ontological problems. This apparent truism may explain not only why existential conflicts are the most intractable but why behavioral conflicts appear to be the most readily amenable to psychological intervention.

Indeed in a similar vein, early psychologists initially chose to study simple paradigms of conflict situations, often attempting to determine the variables governing their resolution or persistence in the form of symptoms. The approach known as behavioral psychology emerged from this with its foundations in the study of how rat behavior is determined by simple laws relating to the contingency and frequency of noxious and rewarding reinforcers. In contrast, the early psychoanalytic approach focused on the dynamic forces and defenses governing emotional conflict. Historically (with exception of gestalt psychology and a few partisan approaches such as Jungian psychology), it was much later that therapies and theories developed to take into account the unique nature of the human species: his ability to be conceptualize the environment and enter into existential conflicts. Recent developments are, however, giving this aspect a central role in illness. Unresolved psychological conflict with its resulting long-term stress appears to be an important and sometimes a crucial determining factor not only in psychological disturbance but also in the genesis of a wide range of illness. Indeed, it is a contemporary preoccupation to produce a more flexible and integrated psychology that does justice to the enormous range of human conflict and its effects on both mind and body. In pursuit of this we must look at the various contributions made by the behavioral, psychoanalytic, and phenomenological approaches.

I. THE CONTRIBUTION OF BEHAVIORAL PSYCHOLOGY

Despite or perhaps because of its simplicity, the behavioral approach made rapid progress. However, in the study of conflict, much of this progress was, ironically, owed to the incorporation of concepts derived from the sole representation of the existential and holistic approach, that of gestalt psychology. One of its most influential figures, Edward C. Tolman, introduced constructs such as expectancies, signs, and cognitions as intervening variables in the simple stimulus–response analysis of behavioral psychology. For Tolman, even rats were cognizant of the salient features of their environment. Another gestalt psychologist, Kurt Lewin, proposed what is now regarded as the classic analysis of conflict in terms of conflicting goals. This was of the trilogy of approach–approach, approach–avoidance, and avoidance–avoidance goal conflict.

In *approach–approach conflict,* both goals are accredited equal positive values and a choice naturally entails loss of one. Analogies are easy to find in the human situation when we are faced for example with a choice between equally attractive job offers or equally attractive roles, such as in career fulfillment and in parenthood.

Approach–avoidance conflict involves by definition an aspect of punishment or loss in achieving the desired goal and evokes fear or anxiety. Challenges by their nature often entail fears and contemporary fears may not be only of physical harm but of psychological annihilation or humiliation, for instance as often experienced by the challenge of and risks involved in the public performance of a skill. Many life crises, from the first step the child makes to his first date, can be seen as conflicts of overcoming anxiety. Their attempted resolution creates the learning experience for future skills and confidence in dealing with the demands of the environment.

Avoidance–avoidance conflict is often regarded as the most deleterious of conflict paradigms since behaviorally the organism cannot avoid punishment. Some conflicts can be of relatively minor significance: hard work or the prospect of exam failure. Other conflicts of this type can, however, have serious effects: a monotonous yet stressful work situation against the demeaning prospect of being out of work. (The situation is not helped by accumulating evidence of a rising incidence of myocardial disorders with this type of job.) The conflict can be one between physical harm and psychological damage. Consider the anxiety evoked by and the consequences involved in the choice between risking death or physical harm in war or alternatively refusing to take arms in war and undergoing group rejection and imprisonment.

Nonresolution of all types of conflict in terms of an outcome in making behavioral choice (or at least some form of behavioral action) necessarily implies stress. Stress, independent of whether it is of a chronic nature, can produce a variety of behavioral and, as will be discussed later, physiological symptoms.

Whereas the above conflict analysis can be regarded as a contribution from gestalt psychology, the behavioral approach using animals resulted in some exact lawful relationships. For instance, in observations of animal behavior, whether in the laboratory or in a natural setting, we may speak of conflict between two incompatible types of behavior if tendencies for these two behaviors are simultaneously present. To say that an animal has a *tendency* to behave in a particular manner implies that we have some evidence to suggest that this animal is likely to do so. Thus, certain causal factors for the behavior in question ought to be present. Causal factors for a given type of behavior may be present even when the behavior is unlikely to appear: a hungry rat in the presence of food may not consume the food if both rat and food are placed in a strange, novel setting. The occurrence of two incompatible behaviors in conflict may be illustrated by certain aspects of flock behavior. In the case of a flock of Great Tits the stimulus defined by one individual toward another may produce either approach or withdrawal. The distance between individuals in a flock is dependent upon the approach–avoidance balance whereby balance is achieved when both tendencies are present but are in conflict and mutually inhibit each other. When the flock moves these individuals are influenced both by factors normally eliciting feeding behavior and by factors inducing following behavior. Thus, conflict is not used to refer to a hypothetical or physiological state, but to incompatible response probabilities. An approach–approach conflict involves two tendencies in conflict approaching two different objects some distance apart, which implies that the incompatibility is a physical one. Here, the animal may reach a point in-between where there exists a balance between the tendency to be drawn to each object. The position of this point will be unstable as the tendency to approach either goal increases with its proximity. Any departure from the point of balance toward one goal increases the tendency to approach the other goal with a concomitant decreased tendency to approach the other. In avoidance–avoidance conflict an animal is confronted by two objects it attempts to avoid. The tendency to avoid either goal is likely to increase with its proximity. Therefore, any movement toward either object is then likely to result in a return to the point of balance.

While behavioral psychologists initially studied these situations in terms of animal behavior, they eagerly sought parallels in humans. The Russian psychologist I. P. Pavlov described the behavior of his dogs when they were unable to discriminate between competing but similiar stimuli as a basis for a choosing one of them. He coined the term *experimental neurosis:* to describe how they yelped, bit aggressively, or lay down and gave up the task. Many years later the American psychologist, Martin Seligman, focused on behavior in the avoidance–avoidance paradigm and described a condition he termed *learned helplessness.* Seligman's dogs, on successively receiving electric shocks at whatever end of the cage they chose to move to, finally gave up in their efforts to avoid the shocks and became passive and behaved as if they were resigned to their fate. This passivity continued even when the experimental paradigm changed and the active behavior of the animal would have removed it from the noxious stimulus. Theoretically, the learned helplessness condition assumes altered responding in at least three major categories of behavior: emotional, motivational, and cognitive. In the laboratory, all three categories are eminently testable and, mainly for this reason, the concept of learned helplessness remains the laboratory analogue for depressive states that, arguably, enjoys a unique status of validity. Seligman and his co-workers assume parallels here with the kind of reactive depression in humans that results from the culminative effects of negative life events. By this account one develops the strategy of giving up in the face of apparently irresolvable conflict, becomes depressed, and loses the belief that own actions can change outcomes. This simple observation has become the cornerstone of a group of therapeutic approaches known as cognitive therapy(ies). The underlying principle here is to teach the human patient alternative ways of viewing his environment, create new choice situations, and thereby encourage activities which may lead to positive reinforcement, either in purely behavioral or in conceptual (cognitive) terms. [*See* COGNITIVE BEHAVIOR THERAPY; LEARNED HELPLESSNESS.]

Behavioral psychologists made a lasting and important contribution in the area of fear and anxiety as a learned drive. O. H. Mowrer described a *two-stage theory of avoidance behavior.* The first stage being pure avoidance behavior as described in terms of classical conditioning: the organism shows fear and associated behaviors in a punishment situation. It may, however, learn to escape in terms of operant choices and this escape learning is the second stage in which fear as a learned or secondary drive has its roots. There are competing models of the latter

behavior. Hans Eysenck for instance emphasizes that the persistence of neurotic behavior is due to avoidance of the feared object—by always running away at the first possible opportunity. For Eysenck it is the first physiological signs of anxiety, increased pulsation of the heart or increased rate of breathing, that induce this behavior rather than fear as a learned drive. Others such as Dollard and Miller have seen fear as an acquired drive in its own right. In a classic experiment, rats learned to work hard at pedal pressing for the "reward" of being released from a cage they associated with electric shocks. Dollard and Miller regarded the dependency effects of drugs such as barbiturates as due to their reinforcement of drug-using behavior via fear reduction. Even cats placed experimentally under stress prefer a mixture of alcohol and milk rather than milk. [*See* ANXIETY AND FEAR.]

Theorists such as Mowrer together with the Dollard and Miller team provided linkages with the other major approach to conflict behavior, that of psychoanalytic and psychodynamic psychology. These behavioral psychologists saw conscience as a major determinant of behavior, but conscience for them, rather that being a subjective and phenomenological concept, could be explained in terms of conditioning which occurred according to the reinforcement and contingency laws of learning or else through imitation as a basic form of social learning. In these terms neurosis is seen then as an internal conflict between conscience and drives. Only a few theorists such as Tolman influenced by the gestalt school of psychology, went one stage further and attempted to extend the behavioral approach to look at the internal sources of conflict as occurring within the subjective perspective of the organism. The impact of this was only to come in contemporary times.

II. THE PSYCHODYNAMICS OF CONFLICT

There is little doubt that the major contribution of the psychoanalysis, and in particular that of Freud, is in having provided a rich catalogue of *experiential* means as well as behavioral means of dealing with conflict between drives and the demands of reality or social learning (the super-ego). These are the classical *defense mechanisms* originated by the ego as strategies to defend it against the ensuing anxiety. Their common feature is that they result in an initial amelioration of the conflict by distorting the perception of reality to fit in with the needs of the individual.

While some behavioral psychologists tend to object to such formulations, a more innocuous terminology in the form of renaming defense mechanisms, *coping strategies,* usually proves acceptable.

In 1991, Phebe Cramer made a convincing case for defense mechanisms explaining a wide range of behavior. She noted how each mechanism has its own developmental history from early childhood onward. Denial, as the most primitive of defenses, appears first and then declines in the frequency of its use from 5 years onward. It is then gradually replaced by more sophisticated defenses such as projection, intellectualization, reaction formation, and identification. Some experimental verification of this model has been found. [*See* DEFENSE MECHANISMS.]

But what biological function do defenses serve? In some senses they clearly can be both maladaptive and adaptive. Taking the adaptive aspect first, defense mechanisms may be regarded as the strategies an individual learns to enable personality to function in the face of conflict from the environment. Regression, for instance, often operates in situations where efforts at problem solving or conflict resolution, based on current learning, are blocked and frustration results. The individual then regresses to a behavior repertoire which may have earlier given successful solutions.

In the case of other defense mechanisms such as the denial of the conflict or its projection onto others, the price for their operation is a distortion of reality, and this is often in the long run clearly maladaptive. An accurate perception of reality—and one which includes the individual's own motives and behavior—is important from the point of view of successful conflict resolution and ultimately for the harmonious functioning of personality.

Nevertheless, the primary function of defense mechanisms, as the term implies, is to protect the executive function of personality from threat and breakdown. Experimentally, there are techniques which demonstrate how defenses operate. Many years ago Postman and Bruner coined the term *perceptual defense* to describe the higher recognition threshold required for the identification of emotionally loaded words that were tachistoscopically presented (rapidly flashed) on a screen. The acceptance of such a phenomenon as perceptual defense nevertheless entails a paradox: How can the perceptual process be a process of both knowing and avoiding knowing at the same time?

To demonstrate this convincingly one needs techniques that circumvent the problem of response bias:

it might be that individuals recognize the emotionally taboo words but refuse to say them or even admit that they see them. One of the techniques that can demonstrate that genuine subliminal conflicts do occur makes use of *the Stroop effect.* In the Stroop effect subjects are asked to read the names of various colors that are printed in colors that conflict with the meaning of the word, for instance the word RED is printed in green. Normally, this interferes with the naming of the colors by delaying the naming response. The Stroop effect can be shown to operate even subliminally, that is below the threshold for conscious recognition. Subjects report that they are unaware of whether such a word is being presented but an interference on their performance can nevertheless be demonstrated if they were required to say the meaning of color words. Such experiments have led many authorities to reject the notion that perception is a unitary and accept that degrees of perceptual processing or at least perceptual registration of events can occur without full conscious awareness. As we shall see later cognitive psychologists of nonanalytic persuasion prefer the term *the cognitive unconscious* to describe this process. Although there is clearly evidence that information can be cognitively registered in this way as subliminal perception, there is little evidence for its dynamic effect in influencing behavior or decision-making processes at an unconscious level.

This is, however, not to say that defenses cannot have profound effects on human behavior in the face of threat, conflict, and stress. These considerations are taken account in a series of recent publications by Miranda Olff using what has been acclaimed as the most reliable and promising method of studying defenses, *the defense mechanism test* (DMT). The rationale behind the DMT was developed by Kragh and Smith at University of Lund to specify the type of distortions that occur while tachistopically (in part subliminally) viewing a picture with a potentially threatening content. Of particular interest is how defenses distort the development of the emerging perceptual image. The degree and form of defensiveness in individuals as assessed by the DMT has recently been found to interact with a multitude of psychobiological factors, many of which are recognized stress indicators such as adrenal hormones, immunoglobulins, and lymphocyte activity.

As has been described above, defenses are not just a liability but can also serve, at least in a limited way, a positive function in enabling the individual to cope with conflicts that would otherwise be overwhelming. It is then not surprising that several styles of coping have been identified which show differing relationships to mental and physical health. What are the "healthy" ways of coping with stress and conflict? Olff's work suggests that both a *goal-oriented* and an *emotionally reactive* way of dealing with threats may be effective strategies. Both these strategies of handling threat show a positive relationship to indices of a healthy immune system. Indeed it would seem natural that a low level of defense to stress and conflict would, in some personalities, also demand a high level of emotional reactivity in order to cope. In contrast, there is a style of handling conflict and threat which is identified as *cognitive defense* and is characterized by internalization and intellectualization of the conflict. Cognitive defense generally showed as expected negative correlations with the indices of immune response, but there appeared to be also a higher level of immune response occurring in individuals operating under conditions of constant high stress. Such a finding may well reflect the potential protective aspect of certain kinds of defense in dealing with long-term conflict occurring at a constant level. [*See* COPING.]

A fourth means of handling conflict is described by Olff as *defensive hostility,* which involves projection outward of hostility, related only negatively to psychosomatic health. Indeed, it appears likely that this means of defense, involving as its does the projection of threat and hostility, can hardly be considered to be adaptive as its effect would be most likely self-reinforcing, thereby leading to only more stress and conflict.

III. THE EFFECTS OF CONFLICT ON THE BODY

The earlier mentioned studies of the use of various defence mechanisms in handling threat and conflict indicate that stress is not just a mental and behavioral event but also has in some cases a profound and lasting physiological impact. Indeed, *stress* can be defined in terms of this threat (where the stimulus can be of an internal and/or external origin) to the psychophysiological integrity or well-being of the organism. Generally, chronic stress has profound deleterious effects on psychophysiology through increased release of corticosteriod hormones and catecholamines. Under normal conditions the body is programmed to provide short-term muscular responses to stress situations. The short-term effects of the above hormones are vasoconstriction, and the

increased mobilization of fat and protein provide energy to the tissues in order to meet the demands of conflict. However, these same mechanisms, if long-term, through the action of the hormones lead to hypertension and vascular disorders. In addition, a significant reduction in lymphocyte number and activity occurs, an effect which may explain the now well-established finding that chronic stress leads to increased susceptibility to a wide range of illnesses. [*See* STRESS; STRESS AND ILLNESS.]

The immune system is almost certainly phylogenetically older than the central nervous system and therefore is accredited as having the primary role of defending the organism against, as well as adapting it to, the environment. Like the nervous system, the immune system is also capable of learning, so much so that the term *psychoneuroimmunology* is now used to describe study of how various components of the immune system learn to respond to conditioned stimuli. Stimuli that are consistently and associatively paired with those that previously induced a stress response come also to have a stress-inducing effect when presented alone. The significance of this can hardly be overstated since it implies a direct link between illness, hormones, and psychological factors. Already two adaptive systems have been described. Allergic reactions can be seen as overreactions analogous to the nervous system's anxiety states, and auto-immune diseases can be regarded as an analogy with depressive states in that the response becomes internalized and self-destructive. To quote the actor cum director Woody Allen: "I don't get depressed, I develop a tumor."

IV. COGNITIVE AND UNCONSCIOUS DETERMINANTS OF CONFLICT

Conflict can be analyzed not only in terms of external demands on the organism but also in terms of its "internal" demands. These include a variety of psychological constructs such as conscience, needs, drives, social and cultural roles, and self-representations. The question concerning how much of this occurs at a so-called unconscious level has been frequently debated and deserves some comment since the notion of *unconscious conflicts* is fundamental to psychodynamic explanations of how phobias arise. The classical example that Freud gave is that Hamlet's neurosis is due to the Oedipus complex re-evoked by the killing of his father. Generally, symptoms occur due to overactive defenses which are evoked to deal with the threatening aspect of the conflict by distorting its perception. Naturally such a process has its cost. It is easy to see how the fear of the forbidden and desired person, along with the disruptive nature of the impulses aroused, can on this analysis lead to a phobia.

While some aspects of this approach may be intuitively appealing, the notion of the dynamic manipulation of the contents of consciousness by an all powerful Unconscious lurking beneath its surface, has never been accepted by mainstream psychology. Nevertheless, a concept known as the *cognitive unconscious* has very recently come into vogue on the basis of experimental findings from the study of memory and perception. This notion describes how perceptions and learning can occur without the individual being cognizant of the information involved but nevertheless showing evidence of its acquisition in his or her behavior. This is still a long way from the psychodynamic unconscious with its dynamic steering of the individual's choices and it is still very unclear as to the degree of complexity that such information processing can involve—in short, "how smart or how dumb" the cognitive unconscious is in processing information. It is possible that the information processing involved is of a very limited nature. It may simply be, for instance, that what are termed perceptual defenses are learned responses, activated by signs of threat and conflict, and leading to "looking away" or interpreting the stimuli in set ways which reduce anxiety. As one reviewer put it, we do not need to read junk mail to throw it away.

Another concept from cognitive psychology that has been frequently applied to the study of conflict is attribution. The notion of attribution concerns the type of rationalizations that are given by individuals as explanatory hypotheses for their behavior. The attribution of behavior due to environmental causes and therefore beyond the control of the individual is said to be externally determined whereas the attribution of personal responsibility for behavior is said to be internally determined. Research indicates that the type of attributions individuals make predicts behavior. For instance, externally determined patients are reported to score higher on scales of depression and hopelessness and to more frequently show suicidal behavior in the face of conflict. [*See* ATTRIBUTION.]

V. THE PHENOMENOLOGY OF CONFLICT AND DEFENSE

The third force or phenomenological approach in psychology is the study of the subjective interpretation of situations and their meaning for the individual. This approach necessitates the postulation of organizing structures such as "the self" and its associated roles. The issue which naturally arises here concerning so-called unconscious roots of behavior is the supposition that not all the contents of experience and perception are represented in the self-concept. Perceptions which are in conflict with how the person has been taught to view himself and behave are either re-interpreted in accordance with this or denied and therefore not given verbal identification. They are nevertheless said to be represented in the form of so-called nonverbal feelings.

While the principles involved in this process appear similar to those postulated by psychodynamic theory, the descriptive language is clearly different in terms of being a more humanistic and existential one. Defenses are thus seen as styles for handling perceptual data and arise in order to enable the self, as the organizing principle in consciousness, to cope with the demands of the environment. Defenses arise when the more biological side of personality (temperament) is in conflict with the "conditions of worth," that is the conditional demands from the environment governing the expression of love and care toward the individual. These demands lead naturally to the learning of self-concepts, social skills, and roles but, in doing so, lead also to the dissociation of the incongruous, nonaccepted self-experiences that are in conflict with the learned role.

How can this approach deal with the problem that has beset psychoanalysis: the dubious ontological status of the unconscious? If we follow the phenomenology cum functionalism of William James and Carl Rogers, the solution may be to simply accept that consciousness exists in many different forms. Some of these are dissociated from one and another, and the various forms may utilize different languages of symbolic representation for memories and ranges of experiences. Supporting this conceptualization are the now well-established findings relating to *state-specific memories,* and the study of altered states of consciousness and dissociated states sometimes reveal that these memories are organized as distinct and conflictual self-representations.

According to this view, conflict and anxiety can then have a positive function since there is assumed to be a *force for growth* existing as a biological principle. This drive operates during the opportunity for change—in a crisis or in a therapeutic context—and strives after creating the re-integration of experiences and split-off parts of the self. Indeed, dissociated and altered states of consciousness have often been claimed to be associated with creative problem solving and therapeutic change. Much of these reports are, however, anecdotal and there is little in the way of well-controlled research.

The question of how emotional and dissociated states relate to brain functioning, although of enormous importance, is still a muted problem. It is true that much has been written in the popular literature concerning differences in the two brain hemispheres and thought processes (the right hemisphere being said to be more intuitive and concerned with spatial relations while the left hemisphere being more specialized in logical verbal problem solving). Most of the research findings indicate, however, that these differences are at best relative and occur as statistical tendencies rather than absolute functional specializations. There is, however, some current interest in the way hemispherical specialization may determine emotional learning experiences which result in aversion. Given that the right hemisphere has a preference for the handling of visuo-spatial information that occurs with emotional arousal, it has been suggested that this specialization may underlie aversive conditioning and explain how such fears of snakes and spiders not only defy logic but show great resistance to extinction.

VI. CONFLICT AND THE NATURE OF PSYCHOLOGICAL DISTURBANCE

For many years a medico-psychiatric view dominated clinical psychology and the findings from behavioral research had an explanatory input limited to anxiety and phobic states. Even psychoanalytic categorizations were based on an essentially 19th century Kraeplin system of medical classification. During the 1980s, although retaining the spirit of the Kraeplian system of category thinking, there has been an attempt to produce a theory-free system known as DSM-III. While the scientific validity of DSM-III has been severely criticized, it is nevertheless generally agreed that the system has incorporated a more sophisticated view of how predispositional and situational factors interact. The consensus view amongst psychologists appears to be that long-term conflicts in the form of stress related events—so-called *life events*—interact with biological (predispositional) factors to produce the variety of psychotic and neurotic disorders.

A refreshingly new approach which allows clinical and healthy psychology to build an alternative model to the medical one for the study of mental disturbance is currently being developed. This approach combines the behavioral work on cognitive functioning with the phenomenological in the form of constructs relating to the self-concept and self-esteem. Since some research findings in psychology seriously question the unity and homogeneity of such disorders as schizophrenia and neurotic disorders an alternative way of viewing these is as degrees of psychological dysfunction.

The specific form of dysfunction is decided by the interaction between the biologically determined predispositions in personality and cognition in relation to stress factors in the environment. The aim is to use this model to develop a profile of all the areas of psychological functioning and specify with respect to life events how certain patterns of dysfunctioning or "symptoms" come to develop. Self-esteem and self-concepts are clearly part of the executive functioning of the organism and along with cognitive variables attain an important part of this profile. Self-esteem is seen as closely connected to the (above-mentioned) process of attribution. Using these concepts it has been shown that patients with depressive "symptoms" have excessive *internal attributions* in the form of being fixated on negative events relating to themselves and will tend to interpret events to conform to their preconceived self-concepts. In contrast, deluded patients make excessive *external attributions* in the form of persecutory ideas, perhaps as a defense against impending depression and low self-esteem by blaming others for negative events. [*See* SELF-ESTEEM.]

VII. THE APPLIED PSYCHOLOGY OF CONFLICT RESOLUTION

The type of therapeutic solution to conflict offered by psychological science has up to the present been severely restricted by the particular focus of each theoretical orientation. Behavioral psychology has, in terms of behavior therapy, focused on the disabling effects of conflict. As a technology it attempts to promote new learning experiences by changing the reward contingencies. In later years with the emergence of construct theory and cognitive psychology, importance was given to how the individual perceives and conceives himself and his environment. The aphorism is: change the person's constructs and you can change his behavior. The reverse is also said to be also true if one follows the principle of attribution.

Representative of the so-called third (humanistic) force in psychology is gestalt therapy which has traditionally worked with dramatizations and polarizations of the views that different possible scenarios of conflict resolutions represent for the individual. Generally the humanistic approach attempts to provide a therapeutic relationship in the context of which re-integration of experience and new learning can occur. Conflict and crisis are the vehicles for change.

Like humanistic psychology, psychoanalytic therapy in its contemporary form of psychodynamic theory also aims at forming a working alliance with the healthy, functioning aspects of personality. However, the technique is by therapeutic interpretations, to render unconscious defenses assessable to consciousness. In contrast to behavioral psychotherapy, the aphorism here is that insight and working through of conflicts lead to change in behavior.

While it is a long way from the study of rat behavior and the psychoanalytic couch to the resolution of internal and group conflict, already during the 1960s psychologists were becoming interested in the application of theories about group identity to social behavior. Muzafer Sherif and his co-workers carried out what is now regarded as a classic experiment in the resolutions of group conflict. Working with boys at a summer camp, the researchers followed the process of how group identity and rivalry arose. Different codes of behavior evolved and with it conflict and opposition. Open hostility developed between the groups. At this stage various techniques for intervention and conflict resolution proved successful. One of these was the formation of superordinate goals that required the co-operation of both groups in order to resolve an externally imposed threat. Another was the introduction of methods to promote interaction and contact between the groups.

There are a few examples of psychological intervention in real group conflict. One well-known example, albeit almost on an anecdotal scale, was the successful involvement of Carl Rogers in facilitating openness and communication between members of a small group of Catholics and Protestants in Northern Ireland. Rogers relied on creating a therapeutic atmosphere of empathy, acceptance, and warmth.

For many years practical solutions to racial and group conflict were influenced by Gordon Allport and his suggestions for reducing conflict by increasing contact between groups and focusing on similarities between individuals. However, with the recent development of the approach known as *Social Identity Theory*, the emphasis has now shifted away from the individual toward dealing with intergroup differences and promoting an understanding of the need to maintain these in the face of threat and discrimination.

While the above holds promise for promoting resolution of group conflict, it must be said that in the international political arena, despite its potential value and the obvious need for it, psychological expertize has had only limited, virtually nonexistent application.

Bibliography

Archer, T., and Nilsson, L. (Eds.) (1989). "Aversion, Avoidance, and Anxiety." Erlbaum, NJ.
Bentall, R. (1991). Explaining and explaining away insanity. In "The Pursuit of Mind" (R. Tallis and H. Robinson, Eds.), Chapt. 8, Carcanet Press, Manchester.
Brenner, C. (1982). "The Mind in Conflict." Paterson, Colchester, UK.
Cramer, P. (1991). "The Development of Defense Mechanisms. Theory, Research, and Assessment." Springer-Verlag, Heidelberg.
Hentschel, U., Smith, G. J. W., Ehlers, W., and Draguns, J. G. (1993). "The Concept of Defense Mechanisms in Contemporary Psychology." Springer-Verlag, New York.
Hinde, R. A. (1970). "Animal Behavior. A Synthesis of Ethology and Comparative Psychology." McGraw–Hill, New York.
Loftus, E., and Klinger, M. (1992). Is the unconscious dumb or smart? *Am. Psychol.* **47,** 761–765.
Olff, M., Godeart, G., and Ursin, H. (Eds.) (1991). "The Quantification of Human Defense Mechanisms." Springer-Verlag, Heidelberg.
Parker, A. (1977). "States of Mind." Taplinger, New York.
Solomon, G. (1990). Emotions, stress, and immunity. In "The Healing Brain: A Scientific Reader." (R. Ornstein and C. Swencionis, Eds.). Guilford, New York.

CONFLICT COMMUNICATION

Dudley D. Cahn

State University of New York College at New Paltz

Glossary

Conflict A difference or incompatibility between people.

Conflict communication behavior Observable interaction that occurs when people attempt to resolve a difference or incompatibility.

Conflict communication strategy A cognition; a mental or psychological state; a disposition; a preference for a way of responding to a source of conflict.

Mediated conflict communication A dispute in which a neutral third party intervenes to facilitate communication between the parties involved.

CONFLICT may be defined as a difference or incompatibility between people. This difference has behavioral, cognitive, and social aspects that are communicative in nature. Three different types of communication account for a great deal of research on conflict in personal relationships. They are as follows:

1. *Specific disagreements*—a specific communication act or interaction, namely, an argument over a particular issue. Sometimes this disagreement is referred to as a complaint, criticism, difference of opinion or view, hostile/coercive response, defensive behavior, or unpleasant action.

2. *Problem-solving discussion*—an encompassing communication situation known as a problem solving discussion concerning an ongoing problem that consists of more than one contested issue.

3. *Unhappy/dissolving relationships*—a general pattern of communication characteristic of dysfunctioning couples, stormy marriages, and couples who report that they are dissatisfied, unhappy, maladjusted, or seeking counseling.

Whatever the type, conflict communication may be viewed as a process that includes antecedents and consequences. Antecedents occur at an early stage of *potential* conflict communication wherever a difference or incompatibility exists or is thought to exist. Conflict communication becomes an *actuality* when interaction reveals that the partners are attempting to resolve their differences. Consequences occur at a final stage of development when the conflict *threatens the relationship* because the partners perceive that significant and unwanted sacrifices must be made to satisfy the other.

According to researchers, there are at least three ways in which conflict may get out of hand and do harm. First, the more excited and heated the conflict (in terms of physiological arousal, especially for the men), the more likely partners were to disengage from their relationship during the next few years. Second, some patterns of conflict were more disastrous to the relationship in the long run even if they appeared more desirable at the time. Third, certain nonverbal behaviors during conflict (e.g., woman's disgust, man's miserable smile, etc.) predicted relationship breakups later. The fact that certain communication behaviors and ways of dealing with conflict are associated with relationship dissatisfaction and breakups necessitates a better understanding of conflict communication. [*See* CONFLICT BEHAVIOR.]

To the extent that the study of conflict communication is important in the development of personal relationships, a better understanding of the subject is achieved by placing relevant theory and research within a particular research perspective or tradition.

This is no easy task for two reasons. First, when attempting to pull together empirical findings on the subject of conflict communication, one discovers that the extensive research on conflict in personal relationships appears disorganized. Numerous empirical studies are the products of researchers in several related disciplines, such as psychology, communication, and family studies, and published research reports appear to reflect different orientations to doing research, use different types of measures, and reflect the jargon of their particular disciplines. The first step then is to identify the major perspectives on gathering data and to organize the relevant studies along the lines of these major research approaches.

A second problem is that more than one research perspective or approach appears to dominate the study of conflict in personal relationships. The nature of conflict communication is viewed differently by scholars depending on their particular research approach. Therefore, this article describes conflict communication and its role within the context of three different research approaches.

I. THE SYSTEMS-INTERACTIONIST RESEARCH APPROACH TO THE STUDY OF CONFLICT COMMUNICATION BEHAVIOR

According to the systems-interactionist research approach, conflicts exist in varying degrees and complexity for partners in personal relationships. As a conflict increases in degree and complexity, however, it goes beyond differences regarding a specific problem, issue, or argument because of the emotional nature of many close relationships. In its most negative form, conflict is expressed as an emotionally charged communication pattern that typically involves anger and hostility, escalates, and harms the personal relationship.

A. On the Nature of Conflict Communication

Conflict communication from this perspective may be viewed as verbal and nonverbal interaction between persons expressing opposing interests, concerns, or opinions. Partners' conflict communication is categorized as constructive and destructive according to whether it escalates and harms the partners' emotional ties.

B. Research Question Asked by This Approach

Researchers who work within the systems-interactionist paradigm have invested considerable time and effort attempting to answer the following question: How can partners solve their problems without doing (more) harm to their personal relationship? This research approach is useful for examining the role played by concrete communication behaviors in a dyadic model and the effects of these behaviors on the outcome of the conflict.

C. Typical Case for Data Collection

Usually, researchers who illustrate this approach to the study of conflict in personal relationships focus on dyadic interaction and typically recruit married couples, create a conflict situation, audiotape or videotape their interaction, and compare the conflict communication patterns of those who are satisfied with their marital relationship with those who are not. Recording partners in conflict appears to be useful for subsequently examining the interaction and for identifying constructive and destructive dyadic communication patterns.

D. Relevant Theories and Key Concepts

Relevant theories view communication and conflict processes as *stochastic,* where the data for research take the form of a series of events that occur in a sequential pattern in which preceding events constrain the probabilities of subsequent ones. Partners' conflict communication may be compared to a game where the move of one partner constrains the alternatives available to the other thereby reducing uncertainty in predicting subsequent moves or plays. Because of the interdependent nature of behaviors during conflict communication (where antecedent behaviors influence the probabilities of subsequent behaviors), the systems-interactionist approach is particularly useful for examining communication behaviors that are linked to one another in an escalating process.

E. Sources of Dyadic Conflict

A partner's behavior is said to be problematic when it produces conflict communication. From the systems-interactionist perspective, problematic behaviors are of interest because they fit the assumption that subsequent behaviors (i.e., conflict communication) are dependent on preceding behaviors (sources of conflict). Because one way to deal with conflict is to eliminate the behavior that leads to it, it is necessary to first identify the problematic behavior.

Efforts to identify problematic behaviors in personal relationships have produced lengthy lists. Moreover, the same behaviors are not always perceived as problems by both men and women and different behaviors appear to be perceived as problems at different stages in relationship development.

Once the conflict is under way, behavioral interaction measures are useful for observing and recording the interrelated behaviors that occur during conflict and lead to escalation.

F. Measuring Instruments for Collecting Data in Dyads

A number of dyadic measures are available for observing the stochastic nature of conflict communication behavior. These measures typically enable observers or raters to classify a particular verbal or nonverbal behavior according to a predetermined set of conflict communication categories. Hops, Wills, Patterson, and Weiss developed the Marital Interaction Coding System (MICS) that consists of the following six general behavior categories:

1. problem-solving statements
2. neutral statements
3. positive statements
4. negative statements
5. nonverbal behaviors that facilitate communication
6. nonverbal behaviors that impede communication.

Another measure, the Couples' Interaction Scoring System (CISS) developed by Gottman consists of eight verbal behavior or content codes (disagreement, agreement, mind reading, communication talk, proposing a solution, summarizing other, summarizing self, feeling, or problem information) and three nonverbal behavior or affect codes (positive, negative, or neutral). Interestingly, with the exception of agreement, verbal behaviors (content codes) did not discriminate between dissatisfied and satisfied couples, although nonverbal behaviors (affect codes) did generally discriminate between the two types of couples.

Viewing conflict interaction as an exercise in dominance, whereby spouses attempt to influence each other toward incompatible goals, Koren, Carlton, and Shaw created four categories of verbal and nonverbal behavior.

1. *Solution proposal:* factual arguments, solution proposals (e.g., "Let's talk more often").
2. *Criticism·* critical comments (e.g., "You never listen to me").
3. *Inquiry:* seeking facts, opinions, or feelings of the other (e.g., "what happened then?" "How do you feel about that?").
4. *Responsiveness:* conveying acknowledgment, agreement, or acceptance of the other's influence attempts (e.g., "I realize that"; "I agree"; "Let's do that").

Based on the claim that verbal communicative acts are key determinants of marital satisfaction, Ting-Toomey provides the Intimate Negotiation Coding System, or INCS, for measuring videotaped partners' conflict communication behaviors. The measure focuses on three types of verbal behavior, including a descriptive category: *integrative,* confirming, coaxing, compromising and agreement statements; and *disintegrative,* confronting, complaining, defending, and disagreement statements.

Sillars, Pike, Jones, and Redmon have created an interaction coding scheme as a measure of conflict communication that includes avoidance behaviors. They tape recorded discussions of marital issues at the subjects' homes and later coded speaking turns in terms of verbal behaviors into three general verbal categories, one of which represents avoidance.

1. *Avoidance acts:* denial, discontinuity, switching topics.
2. *Distributive acts:* faulting, rejection, hostile statements.
3. *Integrative acts:* information giving/seeking, description, disclosure, problem solving, support.

By listing specific, concrete verbal, nonverbal, affect, dominance, and avoidance behaviors, these measuring instruments provide a clear conception of what systems-interactionists mean by conflict communication behavior and enable them to objectively observe the escalation of conflict in personal relationships.

G. Research Findings

Negative conflict communication is characterized by negative affect, coercive/controlling, escalating, rigid messages, and conflict avoidance.

1. Negative Affect

When engaged in conflict, dissatisfied partners rely more on a type of communication called negative affect (or punishing, aversive) messages. The measuring instruments described above have revealed the following negative characteristics of conflict communication:

Dissatisfied partners display higher rates of aversive behaviors, express more criticisms/blame/accusations, are less responsive, and display fewer problem-solving behaviors and reinforcers than satisfied partners.

Dissatisfied partners are more likely than satisfied partners to use cross-complaining and counter-complaints and less likely to engage in validation sequences.

Compared to satisfied partners, dissatisfied partners are more likely to begin a conflict by directly attacking one another with criticism and negatively loaded statements, followed by attempts to justify oneself and blame the other.

Affect codes rather than content codes discriminated marital distress.

2. Coercive/Controlling Behaviors

Researchers have revealed that coercive and controlling behavior during conflict interaction (as well as at other times) is associated with dissatisfying marital relationships. Moreover, a personal relationship often refers to an intimate male–female relationship in which there appears to be sex differences in the use of controlling messages. In conflict interactions that were behaviorally coded, men assumed a more coercive stance toward their intimate partners, while women took an affiliative or accommodating position.

3. Escalation: Negative Reciprocity

Once hostility is expressed by either partner, it is likely to escalate in frequency over the course of the interaction. In both dissatisfied and satisfied partners, negative communication behavior is more likely to be reciprocated than positive. Of course, there is greater negative reciprocity for dissatisfied partners than for happy ones.

Early research findings indicate that reciprocity of negative affect is symmetrical. However, Levenson and Gottman detail different types of negative affect messages and reveal that most of the husband's negative affect consists of anger and contempt, while only a little of the wife's negative affect is anger and contempt. Most of her negative affect is whining, sadness, and fear. While a husband may reciprocate his wife's anger, she does not reciprocate his. Instead, the wife responds with fear to her husband's anger suggesting that their relationship is not symmetrical or fairly balanced.

According to Gottman, dissatisfied partners appear to respond verbally with complaints and criticism in the first conflict phase and nonverbally with hostile behaviors in the second phase. In the third phase, dissatisfied partners find it difficult to agree on a solution.

4. Rigidity

Research shows that interactions of dissatisfied partners show a higher degree of structure and more predictability of one spouse's behaviors from those of the other than is found in the interactions of satisfied partners.

5. Conflict Avoidance

One way to manage a conflict is by using indirect methods such as teasing and humor for expressing unacceptable emotions on threatening or embarrassing topics. Because these methods serve to remind partners of their bonding, they can promote solidarity, reestablish intimacy, and excuse a slight. Not all jokes are equal, however. Benign humor consists of jokes about the self, about the relationship, or about the partner in a gentle manner. Hostile humor includes jokes about the partner in a negative way, particularly with sarcasm. Researchers report that more satisfied couples use humor not to resolve sources of conflict, but to bring a verbal disagreement to an end on a playful note.

Other avoidance behaviors include denials of conflict, changing topics, contradictory statements about the presence of conflict, statements that direct the focus of conversation away from the conflict issues, and abstract, noncommittal, and indirect statements. Researchers have observed that a strong reciprocity tendency in partners' interaction in that avoidance behaviors were typically followed by other avoidance behaviors. They also found that less satisfied couples engaged in fewer avoidance behaviors than more satisfied partners. At least one researcher reports that conflict avoidance in marriage is a complex topic in that different types of married couples use conflict avoidance to different degrees and in different ways as either hostile or friendly.

There may be a difference in the way men and women engage in conflict avoidance behavior. According to Gottman, men show a larger autonomic nervous system (ANS) response to stress, respond more readily, and recover more slowly than do women. If extreme ANS response is viewed as harmful, unpleasant, and undesirable, then men might be more inclined than women to avoid situations that would be associated with repeated ANS activation. Thus, men may become more conciliatory and are likely to avoid conflict or terminate it by withdrawing.

Other researchers observed that both husbands and wives are more likely to be demanding when arguing over a change they wanted in the other and more likely to be withdrawing when arguing over a change their partner wanted them to make. Although neither sex indicated that it would be more demanding than the other sex, data revealed that the men were overall more withdrawn than women.

H. Conflict Training: Helping Couples Resolve Issues and Improve Their Intimate Relationships

Some behaviors lead to more positive outcomes than others—i.e., some behaviors de-escalate emotional outbursts. To prevent the escalation of conflict and to restore homeostasis, de-escalation behaviors need to be identified and encouraged. For example, discussion that focuses on resolving a problem is less emotionally upsetting than name calling and partner blaming. Thus, the couple as an interpersonal system may redirect itself in pursuit of a more positive and constructive goal. To accomplish this goal, behavior modification is used to reinforce positive behaviors but not negative behaviors.

In addition to behavioral modification, research has shown that training in conflict communication skills enhances the effectiveness of couples' training. The teaching of effective conflict communication skills is directed toward enhancing emotional ties within the personal relationship. By observing their own concrete verbal and nonverbal behaviors on videotape, partners learn how they convey either interest or disinterest, and warmth or coldness, as well as attraction or repulsion.

The systems-interactionist approach accounts for many empirical research studies on conflict in personal relationships. In addition to its productiveness as a research paradigm, it has also generated many useful techniques for helping partners improve their personal relationship by encouraging positive, constructive, and integrative conflict communication.

II. THE RULES-INTERVENTIONIST RESEARCH APPROACH TO MEDIATED CONFLICT COMMUNICATION

The notion of mediation as conflict communication may at first appear novel. Although opportunities for interaction seem limited by the presence of an outsider (a mediator), disputing partners may exchange information, influence one another, and develop mutual agreements. However, mediation may not be appropriate for every dispute. Where effective, mediation facilitates communication between partners, is future oriented, and often includes renegotiation of the personal relationship. Thus, mediation is a unique form of conflict communication in which partners may participate in a more formal conflict resolution process than they normally encounter in their everyday lives.

A. On the Nature of Conflict Communication

The rules-interventionist approach views conflict communication as mediation in which a neutral third party creates and enforces certain rules that enable partners to resolve their dispute. The introduction of the mediator as an interventionist emphasizes the partners' inability to resolve disputes by themselves. Mediation is normally seen as an alternative to adjudication where a judge imposes a decision upon the disputing parties. Mediated conflict emphasizes the development of reasonable outcomes for all concerned.

B. Research Question Asked by Rules-Interventionists

The rules-interventionist approach to the study of mediated conflict has generated studies designed to answer the question: What role does a third party play in helping partners restore communication for the resolution of issues? This research approach is useful for incorporating the actions of an impartial third party or mediator along with those of the conflicting partners in a triadic model to determine the effects of the mediator and the partners on the outcome of the mediation process.

C. Typical Case for Data Collection

Understandings that define relationships for partners and that govern their interaction develop over time. For some, however, these understandings may no longer hold, resulting in a breakdown in communication. Researchers who take a rules-interventionist approach to the study of mediated conflict call attention to the role of a third party in helping partners communicate, resolve disputes, and restore or redefine their relationship as the typical case involving partners in personal relationships. For example, mediators may help divorcing spouses legally dissolve the marriage, restructure the family, and create new relationships in which former spouses can cooperate with each other (on matters such as custody and visitation) long after the divorce.

D. Relevant Theories and Key Concepts

Because mediated conflict presents an entirely different context or type of relationship from dyadic conflict communication as discussed above, the study of mediation appears to need a different research approach. The rules-interventionist approach is particularly useful because it is designed for three interacting individuals—two partners and a mediator—and each person's effect on the outcome.

Unlike the systems-interactionist approach where stochastic probability governs the outcome of interaction, in the rules-interventionist approach the mediator intervenes to place interaction under the control of *rules* designed to limit emotional conflict, reduce uncertainty and surprises, and encourage open communication, cooperative problem solving, and equitable treatment.

Successful mediators begin mediation by laying down communication rules. The rules enforced by the mediator go beyond explaining the process and legality of mediation. The mediator places limits on the agenda and the tone of the discussion. The mediator rules out such common tactics as name calling and dwelling on the irrelevant issues. Less successful or less skilled mediators are usually unwilling to enforce communication rules during the sessions. These rules help the mediator achieve a more successful outcome of the mediation process rather than letting the partners' interaction alone determine the outcome.

Mediation theorists view personal relationships as complex, private systems and as delicate entities that must be respected. Therefore, they assumed that partners are in the best position to decide for themselves with minimal intervention by others. However, while partners determine issues and make decisions for themselves, the mediator ensures that her/his rules regarding interaction are observed.

E. Sources of Mediated Conflict

There is a difference between the sources of conflict that give rise to particular behavioral dyadic interaction patterns and those that give rise to mediation. Compared to private conflicts that tend to occur in the privacy of one's own home or involve only the partners themselves, mediated conflict is seen more as a social or public event because of the introduction of the third party. Moreover, whereas the sources of conflict in behavioral dyadic interaction are partners' problematic behaviors that turn out to be quite numerous, the latter may be reducible to five types.

Control over resources: money, property, space, children, and so forth that may be viewed as not sharable.
Preferences and nuisances: activities of one person impinge on another's sensibilities, preferences, or sensitivities.
Values: concerning what should be—e.g., religious and ideological issues.
Beliefs: concerning what is—e.g., facts and reality.
The nature of the relationship: repair and redefinition of personal relationships.

Mediation may be rated and evaluated by using triadic interaction measures to observe and record conflict communication. Two of the most common are discussed below.

F. Measuring Instruments for Collecting Data in Triads

Donohue and his colleagues developed a measure for coding partners' and mediators' verbal acts. They distinguished between two types of verbal acts: cues to subsequent utterances and responses to prior utterances. In addition, the partners' verbal acts were identified according to the following categories:

Attacking: personal accusations; negative evaluations.

Defending: presenting proposals, providing information, requesting information or clarification, or providing a rationale for one's position.

Integrating: any utterance that agreed with the prior utterance, demonstrated support for a proposal or position.

Finally, Donohue and his colleagues added the following categories to code the mediator's interventions.

Structuring: identifying and enforcing interaction rules.

Reframing: helping to restructure disputants' own proposals; pointing out areas of agreement.

Expanding/requesting: requesting proposals; requesting clarification of proposals; requesting reaction to proposals.

Slaikeu and his associates developed the Mediation Process Analysis (MPA) to code both spouse and mediator verbal and nonverbal (affect, tone) conflict communication. The instrument consisted of the following eight *content* codes.

Process: statements or questions regarding mediation issues; relevance of remarks or suggestions regarding mediation actions.

Information: factual information about the mediation process and its alternatives, the children, and the spouses.

Summarize other: restatements/rephrasing other's statements.

Self-disclosure: statements indicating agreement or disagreement, expression of feelings, empathic statements.

Attributions: statements attributing attitudes or actions to the spouses, children, and others.

Proposed solution: solutions regarding either party or both; problems with the solution.

Agreements: statements of agreements made before, during, and toward the end of mediation; statements regarding disputes that could arise in the future.

Interruptions: including who was interrupted and who did the interrupting. (Only when a broken statement was not resumed was it coded as an interruption.)

Slaikeu and his colleagues also included the tone (affect) of the verbal statements. Therefore, in addi-

tion to the eight content codes, the MPA also required that the coders assign to each unit one of the following three tone codes.

Positive: The tone of voice denotes warmth, cooperation, understanding, humor, encouragement, or enthusiasm.

Negative: Tone indicates irritation, lack of cooperativeness, anger, sarcasm, or threat.

Neutral: Tone conveys no obvious pleasure or displeasure.

By applying both Donohue's and Slaikeu's coding schemes to recorded mediation, one might better understand the role of the mediator and how her or his actions help to settle disputes.

G. Research Findings

Separate groups of researchers have applied different interventionist measures on essentially overlapping data derived from 80 audiotapes of divorce mediation. Using these tapes for coding triadic interaction, researchers found that successful mediators were more likely than unsuccessful mediators to use more intense structuring and reframing interventions in response to attacks. The more successful mediators were also more likely to rephrase negative comments into more positive ones. Researchers have shown that more successful mediators were more in control of the mediation, used more interventions to involve the divorcing partners in finding the information necessary for agreement, and distributed more of these interventions fairly and consistently between disputants. [*See* DIVORCE.]

Other researchers report that the most important difference between cases that settled successfully and those that did not was the amount of time mediators were expected to spend discussing the final settlement. In the successful cases, mediators not only felt obligated to spend more time discussing the terms of the final agreement, but they also were expected to spend more time discussing possible solutions in general. They were not expected to spend much time explaining the mediation process to the spouses, requesting disclosure of feelings, and making statements about the parties' attitudes.

In all, researchers discovered the following patterns of actions implying that rules are operating:

Speaker time was fairly evenly distributed among the two spouses and the mediator.

Whereas mediators tended to address both spouses, husbands and wives usually directed their remarks to the mediator.

Mediators tended to ask more questions than did either of the parties.

Mediators expressed statements on procedural issues three times more than did the parties. Mediators conveyed more information on what mediation is and made more statements regarding the process itself than did the parties.

Mediators, made the most statements summarizing the spouses' comments.

Spouses emitted more emotionally toned statements than did the mediator.

One-third of the statements made by both spouses were self-disclosures. A number of statements were about the attitudes, motives, and actions of others, usually the other spouse.

Perhaps in an effort to establish rapport and encourage the spouses to share their feelings, mediators' statements showed more empathy than did those uttered by the spouses.

Mediators attempted to balance proposals by specifying how both parties could be involved, while each spouse tended to specify what he or she could do.

Very few statements were classified as interruptions (where the thought was not resumed).

Divorce mediation sessions that ended in agreement appeared to progress from differentiation to integration through three phases: information exchange, problem solving, and finally resolution actions. Based on a version of the MPA, results revealed that mediation that did not end in agreement never progressed beyond the first stage. Such sessions were characterized by a continuing emphasis on information exchange throughout and by a de-emphasis on problem solving and resolution actions.

H. Structured Mediation: Helping Partners Settle Disputes

In general, the rules-interventionist approach views conflicts of interest as mixed motive—a mixture of cooperative and competitive interests where a variety of outcomes is possible, such as mutual loss, gain for one and loss for the other, and mutual gain. To help both parties emphasize cooperation and gain something from mediation, third party interventionists need a thorough understanding of mediator goals

and tactics that include structuring the process of mediation, reframing the disputants' positions, and expanding the information resource.

III. THE COGNITIVE-EXCHANGE RESEARCH APPROACH TO THE STUDY OF CONFLICT COMMUNICATION STRATEGIES

When thinking about the topic of conflict communication in personal relationships, one probably envisions partners engaged in a verbal disagreement. Cognitive-exchange researchers take an entirely different view of conflict communication as mental (cognitive) strategies that range from preferences for direct confrontation to conflict avoidance. Since these strategies are internal (mental, psychological), the process nature of conflict communication is not as easily discernable to outside observers as it is when overt behaviors are observed. From the cognitive-exchange perspective, to view conflict communication as a process means that one must ask partners' to give their own retrospective reports on the perceived sources of conflict that resulted in the selection of conflict communication strategies that in turn influenced the development of their personal relationships.

A. On the Nature of Conflict Communication

The cognitive-exchange approach views conflict communication as strategies that are internal responses to perceived sources of conflict. Because some conflict communication strategies involve intending to avoid open confrontation, conflict communication may exist even when partners are not engaging in overt disagreement.

B. Research Questions Asked by This Approach

Questions of interest asked by cognitive-exchange researchers are among the following: What antecedent conditions influence one's choice of conflict communication strategy? What alternative strategies are best for dealing with different sources of conflict? This research approach is useful for examining the role played by internal predispositions in the form of conflict communication strategies in a broad, general model of relationship development and the effects of these strategies on the outcome of the conflict.

C. Typical Case for Data Collection

Cognitive-exchange research typically focuses on developing relationships (including romantic partners, friends, and roommates) as the typical case for data collection. Researchers have identified at least two important characteristics of relationship development: *satisfaction*—positive affect or attraction to the relationship—and *commitment*—the tendency to maintain the relationship and to feel psychologically "attached" to it. Research typically asks the relationship partners to fill out subjective measures known as self-reports in the form of questionnaires (i.e., paper-and-pencil tests).

D. Relevant Theories and Concepts

One of the distinguishing features of the paradigm is the notion of social exchange—in which human behaviors are viewed in terms of their utility and are associated with *rewards and costs*. Partners in a relationship are thought to engage in behaviors that have consequences for each other, and different behaviors have different consequences or outcomes. While the value of behaviors is not universal, positive consequences such as pleasure and gratifications are usually seen as rewards, whereas negative outcomes such as undesirable effort and social embarrassment are likely to be interpreted as costs.

Presumably relationship partners try to maximize profits and minimize costs, although they may forego short-term profits for long-term gains. In theory, a rewarding relationship is expected to continue, while a costly one is supposed to deteriorate in time. Thus, the constructive resolution of a conflict due to a positive conflict communication strategy could be perceived as a reward, while the inability to resolve issues due to a negative strategy could be perceived by the partners as a cost.

Some researchers take the position that the value of rewards and costs is in "the eye of the beholder," which is influenced by attribution processes and efficacy expectations. Attribution refers to the process of assigning reasons or motivations for particular behaviors, while an efficacy expectation refers to the belief that a problem can be solved by confronting it. They argue that attributions of blame or intent give rise to hostile behavior such as retaliation. However, they go on to argue that regardless of one's attribu-

tions of cause, responsibility, and blame, given low efficacy expectations, a partner is unlikely to engage in efforts to resolve the conflict and will choose to avoid it or withdraw from it. Given high efficacy expectations, however, the person is likely to undertake such efforts and confront the problem. In such cases, resolution attempts are directed toward that which is perceived as most easily changed and likely to produce satisfactory results.

E. Sources of Conflict in Developing Relationships

Perceived imbalance in the resources of exchange, perceived inequity, and perceived unequal distribution of power in a relationship likely lead to feelings of relationship dissatisfaction which, itself, may be a source of conflict. When studying relationship dissatisfaction in general as a source of conflict, researchers use self-report techniques to assess the degree of dissatisfaction in the relationship. In this approach cognitive variables like relationship dissatisfaction are believed to be capable of producing other effects. Thus, self-reported relationship dissatisfaction may be seen as a cognition that influences the selection of particular confrontation and conflict avoidance strategies.

To measure general dissatisfaction with a romantic relationship, researchers have devised questions and scales like the following for use on self-report measures:

How much do you like your partner? (1 = I like him/her very much; 9 = not at all)
To what extent are you attracted to your partner? (1 = not at all; 9 = extremely attracted to him/her)
To what degree are you satisfied with your relationship? (1 – extremely satisfied; 9 = not at all)

F. Measuring Instruments for Collecting Data in Developing Relationships

In an attempt to examine cognitive responses to sources of conflict, Rusbult and her colleagues devised the following typology of strategies as perceived responses to sources of conflict.

Exit: breaking up, separating, or divorcing.
Voice: attempting to change the relationship, discussing problems, compromising, working

things out, and adopting a problem-solving orientation.

Loyalty: accepting of minor problems, highly committed to maintaining the relationship, and assuming that conditions will improve.

Neglect: ignoring the partner, not caring about the relationship, and allowing conditions to worsen.

As so often happens when researchers attempt to devise a typology, there were mixed cases in which partners preferred strategies typical of more than one category.

Rusbult's typology relates to social exchange theory in the following ways. When partners are satisfied with their relationship (rewards outweigh costs) and perceive no superior alternatives to their primary relationship, partners prefer to be loyal or give voice as alternative cognitive responses to perceived sources of conflict. The greater the satisfaction and the more inferior the alternatives, the more the partners are committed to the relationship, and the more likely they will respond with voice rather than loyalty.

However, where partners are not satisfied with their relationship (costs outweigh rewards) and perceive superior alternatives to their primary relationship, partners prefer to neglect or exit from the relationship as alternative cognitive responses to perceived sources of conflict. The lesser the satisfaction and the more superior the alternatives, the less the partners are committed to the relationship, and the more likely they will respond by exiting rather than with neglect.

Building on Rusbult's typology of responses to conflict, others argue that partners may progress through different types of cognition as dissatisfaction grows. At first, they might prefer loyalty as a strategy, hoping that things will get better soon. They may turn to the strategy of giving voice when the situation does not improve, then decide to neglect the partner when that fails, and eventually choose to exit the relationship. By combining the notion of progression with social exchange theory, it might be argued that newly formed couples would prefer loyalty because they fear losing their partner who is not fully committed to the relationship. However, after commitment takes place, they prefer to give voice to their dissatisfaction; but if conditions only worsen, then they prefer neglect. Finally, when superior alternatives appear, they prefer to exit. Longitudinal research could be designed to study cognitive responses to sources of conflict over time.

Other researchers have created different lists of responses to sources of conflict. For example, Canary and Spitzberg used a measure with seven conflict communication strategies: integrative (e.g., "I sought a mutually beneficial solution"), personal criticism of the partner (e.g., "I criticized an aspect of his or her personality"), showing anger (e.g., "I shouted at him or her"), sarcasm (e.g., "I was sarcastic in my use of humor"), topic shifting (e.g., "I avoided the issue"), semantic focus (e.g., "I focused on the meaning of the words more than the conflict issue"), and extended denial (e.g., "I denied that there was any problem or conflict"). Canary and Spitzberg found that the partners most readily recalled one another's use of two conflict communication strategies, anger and criticism.

One line of research on alternative strategies for managing conflict in intimate relationships actually grew out of business administration/management research and a concern for supervisor–subordinate conflicts in industrial organizations. Rahim proposed a typology for the management of organizational conflict, consisting of the following five strategies: dominating (forcing, competing), integrating (confronting, collaborating), obliging (smoothing, accommodating), avoiding, and compromising (give and take) styles that reflected either a high or low degree of concern for oneself and concern for the other (e.g., partner).

These conflict communication strategies may be related to social exchange theory in terms of rewards and costs.

Avoiding (lose–lose): Seeing nothing to gain by engaging in conflict, individuals avoid it. Consequently, both parties lose out on obtaining any rewards.

Obliging (lose–win): Individual perceive that they have nothing to gain by continuing a conflict and that the other party can receive rewards if they simply give in. Thus, they acquiesce.

Dominating (win–lose): Individuals perceive that they can gain an advantage over the other party through conflict and compete until they win.

Compromising (win and lose): Individuals perceive that they must make trade-offs (sacrifice some rewards to gain others) when in conflict; so they settle for a compromise.

Integrating (win–win): Individuals perceive that engaging in conflict will result in both parties getting the rewards they want.

Since the Rahim measure used business executives as respondents when developing the instrument, he recommended that the measure be used to diagnose styles of handing conflict only among members of business organizations. Thus, using the Rahim measure to collect data in intimate relationships may be a questionable practice. In cases where researchers have used his measure in intimate relationships (e.g., parent–child, friends, and siblings), they discovered that the respondents did not differentiate between integrating and compromising as much as they did between the other conflict communication strategies. Thus, when collecting data in nonorganizational settings, they recommend modifying Rahim's instrument by combining the items used to measure integrating and compromising strategies into a single strategy.

G. Research Findings

There appear to be important *male–female differences* that affect partners' perceptions of rewards and costs and their role in conflict. Men appear to differ from women in the way they perceive conflict that in turn affects their relationship satisfaction. At least one researcher has asked dating partners to keep daily observation records of conflicts over a 2-week period. Such research reveals that the perception of many unresolved conflicts is most salient to women's perceived relationship satisfaction, whereas the perception of a large number and the stability of conflicts (i.e., the same issues coming up again and again) are most salient to men's relationship satisfaction.

Other male–female differences in *perceptual processes* have been found to have an impact on conflict in intimate relationships by distorting the intent of the message sent. For instance, the behavior of dissatisfied spouses compared to that of satisfied spouses is perceived more negatively by partners than intended. This confirms an earlier finding that dissatisfied husbands are more inclined than those who are satisfied to attribute "negative connotations" to their wives' attempts to communicate affection, happiness, and playfulness.

There is evidence that partners may tend to prefer the strategy of avoidance—a tendency in personal relationships like marriage for partners to avoid dealing with conflicts. Yet, a number of research findings support open confrontation as a constructive conflict communication strategy. For example, at least one study reports that black couples and white couples who believe in avoiding conflicts reported lower marital happiness in the first year of marriage and again 2 years later than those spouses who both believe in confronting conflicts.

A number of factors that contribute to preferences for open confrontation or conflict avoidance strategies have been observed. People are more likely to confront when they are committed, equal in power, prepared for confrontation, and when the issue is important. Men are more likely than women to blame their mates for problems, avoid emotional involvement, and select coercive conflict communication strategies or neglect and exit as their way of dealing with conflict. Some personality types are more prone to open confrontation, while others to avoidance. Culture and immediate social context are also influencing factors. For example, there is a tendency among male and female managers to prefer more competitive strategies of conflict resolution when dealing with workers and more accommodating strategies with their partner at home.

H. Educating Partners about How to Manage Conflicts

Some of the sources of conflict result from faulty perceptions or inferences. Training in cognitive restructuring helps partners deal with sources of conflicts and improve their relationship. Essentially, cognitive restructuring is a means of increasing relationship satisfaction by relabeling faulty cognition—i.e., misperception and unwarranted inference. Of particular interest are perceptions of undesirable behavior and inferences made from them. Cognitive restructuring includes helping partners see the connection between their behavior and a partner's feelings, identifying myths and accepting reality, emphasizing the positive aspects of their relationship, training in empathy, and learning strategies of accommodation.

In conclusion, this article cuts across disciplines, relevant research perspectives, and theoretical concerns to emphasize the dominant research approaches as frameworks for organizing and better understanding the many research studies of conflict in personal relationships.

Bibliography

Cahn, D. (Ed.) (1990). "Intimates in Conflict: A Communication Perspective." Erlbaum, Hillsdale, NJ.

Cahn, D. (1992). "Conflict in Intimate Relationships." Guilford Press, New York.

Chusmir, L. H., and Mills, J. (1989). Gender differences in conflict resolution styles of managers: At work and at home. *Sex Roles* **20**, 149–163.

Crohan, S. E. (1992). Marital happiness and spousal consensus on beliefs about marital conflict: A longitudinal investigation. *J. Soc. Pers. Relationships* **9**, 89–102.

Donohue, W. A. (1991). "Communication, Marital Dispute, and Divorce Mediation." Erlbaum, Hillsdale, NJ.

Folberg, J., and Milne, A. (Eds.) (1988). "Divorce Mediation: Theory and Practice." Guilford Press, New York.

Gottman, J. M. (1991). Predicting the longitudinal course of marriages. *J. Marital Family Ther.* **17**, 3–7.

Graham, S., and Folkes, V. (Eds.) (1990). "Attribution Theory: Applications to Achievement, Mental Health, and Interpersonal Conflict." Erlbaum, Hillsdale, NJ.

Storaasli, R. D., and Markman, H. J. (1990). Relationship problems in the early stages of marriage: A longitudinal investigation. *J. Family Psychol.* **4**, 80–98.

CONSCIOUSNESS

Bernard J. Baars and Katharine McGovern
The Wright Institute

Glossary

Blindsight Damage to primary visual cortex leads to a condition in which the victim can be coaxed to respond to objects and their features without reporting any conscious experience of the object. There is much evidence to suggest that such individuals continue to have unconscious visual representation of the objects.

Consciousness The state of consciousness, as opposed to deep sleep or coma, has massive behavioral, neurophysiological, and anatomical correlates. The contents of consciousness can be defined as those events that can be reported with verifiable accuracy and which are claimed to be conscious. Conscious contents are either *qualitative,* such as percepts, images, and feelings, or *nonqualitative* such as conscious concepts, beliefs, and intentions.

Context One of the three major constructs in global workspace theory, operationally defined as a knowledge structure that shapes and constrains conscious contents without itself being conscious.

Contrastive analysis Analysis of pairs of psychological events which differ from each other only in that one is conscious and the other not, much like an experiment in which consciousness is the independent variable. Many sets of contrastive pairs are already well established empirically: e.g., attended vs nonattended streams of speech, habituated vs novel stimuli, perceptual vs pre-

perceptual models of a stimulus, etc. The set of unconscious–conscious contrasts constrains any theory of consciousness.

Decontextualization Unconscious contextual assumptions may become consciously accessible when they are violated by current experience. In stepping into a small rowboat, we experience a tossing of the horizon, which, we quickly realize, reflects the movements of the boat. Thus, our underlying assumption about our visual field relative to the normal horizon is objectified: turned from context into an object of conscious contemplation.

Epiphenomenalism The claim that consciousness is nothing but a by-product of brain processes, with no causal role of its own.

Fixedness In any kind of problem-solving, being blind to solutions that are obvious to an outsider. Examples range from Gestalt effects, hidden figures, disastrous military decisions, culture shock, and the inability of scientists to understand a novel paradigm. In global workspace theory, fixedness is treated as the result of a dominant context which unconsciously confines the problem search space.

Global workspace A domain that can be accessed by numerous specialized processors in the nervous system, whose contents are widely broadcast or distributed to all other specialists in the system. One of three main constructs in GW theory, together with *specialized unconscious processors* and *contexts*—unconscious knowledge structures which shape conscious experiences.

Limited capacity mechanisms Consciousness is associated with a central "bottleneck" in human information processing, as shown by selective attention effects, dual-tasks interference, and the very narrow limits on immediate memory.

Orienting response (OR) The neurophysiological reaction to novel stimuli, first explored by I. P. Pavlov. The OR includes orienting of receptors, desynchronization of the EEG, changes in the P300 component of the cortical evoked potential, pupillary dilation, and changes in heart rate, skin conductivity, and vasodilation or constriction.

Priming Facilitation or inhibition of responses to one stimulus (as measured by reaction time, shifts in interpretation, recall, or recognition) due to prior presentation of a related stimulus which is no longer present.

Qualia The subjectively experienced properties of mental contents; for example, one's personal experience of the color red.

Threshold (or zero-point) problem The difficult problem of specifying whether phenomena near the threshold of conscious experience are actually conscious or not; examples include subliminal perception, learning without awareness and blindsight. It is often possible to circumvent the problem by using contrastive analysis focusing on clearly conscious and clearly unconscious cases.

THOUGHT regarding the nature and role of consciousness in human affairs has ancient roots. Modern scientific psychology has accumulated considerable evidence about conscious and unconscious processes that can be studied by contrasting matched conscious and unconscious phenomena. This approach serves to define a demanding set of constraints on theories of consciousness. Global Workspace Theory accounts for many of these constraints by viewing consciousness not as a module or single step in an information-processing system but rather as a system-wide integration and dissemination capacity. The theory thus draws together in one framework the many functions of consciousness in perception, thinking, and action.

I. INTRODUCTION

Systematic thought about conscious experience goes back as far as we can trace it, to the roots of Western philosophy in Plato and Aristotle, and in Eastern thought to the Upanishads and early Buddhism. By comparison, scientific work on the topic is quite recent, though it is noteworthy that Wilhelm Wundt, the institutional founder of modern experimental psychology, was deeply influenced by Arthur Schopenhauer, who in turn borrowed heavily from the then recently translated Sanskrit Vedas. Consciousness was indeed the main topic of 19th century psychology, but with the dawn of the 20th century,

physicalistic philosophies in the form of behaviorism and logical positivism mounted a devastating critique. For the first time in written history, consciousness and related topics like volition and self were excluded from respectable scholarship. This exclusion lasted until quite recently. While cognitive psychologists of the 1960s and 1970s returned to almost all the main topics of 19th century psychology—memory, imagery, selective attention, perception, and language understanding—the scientific study of conscious experience *as such* was delayed another decade or two.

Current philosophy of mind is still much concerned with conscious experience. The mind–body problem, which goes back to the beginnings of written thought, continues to be debated, and while most scientists are no doubt physicalists, serious arguments continue to be advanced for the two other classical positions, mentalism and dualism. Controversy continues on the problem of qualia (is your experience of "red" the same as mine?), the question of first-person phenomenology (in Thomas Nagel's words, "What is it like to be a bat?"), and whether robots can in principle be conscious. Philosophers continue to debate whether consciousness has any causal role at all, or whether it is "epiphenomenal," a mere side-effect of brain functioning.

The scientific study of consciousness, fortunately, does not have to await answers to these perennial philosophical debates. Reliable scientific evidence bearing on consciousness has been mounting for decades, quite independent of the philosophical predilections of the scientists who collected it. This includes I. P. Pavlov's work on the orienting response, the massive neurobehavioral reaction to a novel or significant stimulus, and C. Cherry and D. A. Broadbent's pioneering research on "selective attention," the fact that of two simultaneous, dense streams of perceptual information, we can be conscious of only one at a time, though the unconscious stream is partly processed. The accumulated evidence clearly places empirical constraints on any theory of consciousness, as we shall see.

II. EVIDENCE TO BE EXPLAINED

Consider the massive behavioral and neural difference between someone who is in deep sleep or coma compared to one who is awake and alert. No alien space visitor could fail to observe that vertebrates, including humans, cease any purposeful movement for a third of the earthly day, and that human beings can report no memory of inner or outer events that occur in deep sleep. This stunningly obvious behavioral cycle corresponds exactly to massive electrophysiological changes throughout the brain, as the fast, irregular, and low-amplitude activity characteristic of wakefulness is replaced by the regular, slow, high-amplitude waves of deep sleep. It also happens to correspond exactly to reports of conscious experience.

The neuroanatomical structures necessary for the state of consciousness are well known: they include the brainstem reticular formation, the outer shell of the thalamus (its reticular nucleus), and the fountain of nonspecific neurons that projects widely from the thalamus to all parts of the cortex (Fig. 1). Absent any of these structures, humans and animals lapse into coma. In contrast, any part of the great cerebral cortex and most subcortical structures can be lost without impairing conscious wakefulness. Thus, the *state* of consciousness has well-established behavioral, neurophysiological, and anatomical correlates.

An adequate theory of consciousness must clearly deal with the *contents* of consciousness as well, since, when awake, we can experience an indefinite number of distinct conscious contents, including percepts and images in all sensory modalities, memories, fantasies about possible futures, and the like. In addition, we can gain conscious access to a vast range of abstract concepts, intentions, expectations, and actions.

To find evidence bearing on conscious contents *as such*, it is helpful to perform a "contrastive analysis" between mental events that are clearly conscious—those that people report as conscious, can talk about, distinguish, remember, and act upon—and very similar ones that are *not* conscious. Some everyday experiences illustrate this point. Everyone surely knows of redundant stimuli fading from consciousness; the repeated noise of a refrigerator pump is a favorite example. Sometimes, when such a highly predictable train of events suddenly stops, the *absence* of the stimulus becomes conscious. We know something has changed, even though we were not aware of the train of stimuli before. Scientific students of such habituation phenomena such as Russian psychologist Sokolov suggest that the nervous system must maintain a rather accurate, unconscious representation of the repetitive stimulus, since a change in *any* parameter of the stimulus (spectral distribution, amplitude envelope, temporal pattern, spatial location, or even the complete absence of the stimulus) may bring it to consciousness. Similarly, while reading a book, if a friend makes some remark, one's first impulse may be to ask, "What did you say?"—but suddenly, the memory of what was said comes to mind. The words must have been represented unconsciously, or they would not be remembered a few seconds later. More commonly, we can recall an image of an earlier conscious episode, such as this morning's breakfast: it is widely believed that such an episodic memory must have been represented unconsciously in some form *before* it was brought to mind. [*See* EPISODIC MEMORY.]

All such contrasts between comparable conscious and unconscious representations raise the question, "why is one event conscious, and the closely matched comparison, unconscious?" Psychologists are increasingly performing such a "contrastive analysis" in precise, carefully controlled experimental situations.

Table I shows a set of contrastive pairs comparing matched conscious and unconscious percepts and images. Above, we illustrated the cases of habituated vs novel stimuli; accessed memory episodes vs those still in memory; immediate auditory memory before and after recall; and selective attention to one out of two possible dense streams of stimulation such as speech. In addition to these contrastive pairs, there is much evidence that perceptual stimuli

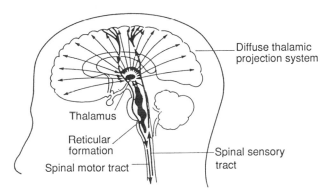

FIGURE 1 The ERTAS: A neural global workspace? Brain structures most closely associated with conscious experience include the reticular formation of the brain stem and midbrain, the outer shell of the thalamus, and the set of neurons projecting upward diffusely from the thalamus to the cerebral cortex. Together these structures can be labeled the extended reticular-thalamic activation system (ERTAS). Stimulation of a number of neurons throughout this system causes cortical activation. The ERTAS as a whole can be interpreted as a functional global workspace.

TABLE I
Contrastive Evidence in Perception and Imagery

Conscious events	Comparable unconscious events
1. Perceived stimuli	1. Processing of stimuli lacking in intensity or duration or centrally masked stimuli
	2. Pre-perceptual processing of stimuli
	3. Habituated or automatic stimulus processing
	4. Unaccessed versions of ambiguous stimuli
	5. Contexts of interpretation for percepts
	6. Unattended streams of perceptual input
7. Images in all sense modalities	7. Unretrieved images in memory
8. Newly generated visual images Automatic images that encounter some difficulty	8. Automatized visual images
9. Inner speech: words currently rehearsed in short-term memory	9. Inner speech: currently not rehearsed
	10. Automatized inner speech?

in general are processed for a fraction of a second before they become conscious, suggesting the existence of unconscious "pre-attentive" or "pre-perceptual" representations. Next, perception and comprehension often involve stimuli that can be experienced in more than one way. Of the alternative interpretations of an ambiguous word (and a glance at a dictionary should persuade anyone that virtually all words can be ambiguous) only one is conscious at any given time, though there is much evidence that alternative interpretations are processed unconsciously. A word shown to one eye can be masked by a competing stimulus presented to the other eye, so that the marked word is not experienced directly; yet the unconscious word can still facilitate perception of a related stimulus presented immediately afterward. Finally, there are numerous types of contextual knowledge which shape perceptual experience without being currently conscious. For example, the visual system makes the unconscious assumption that light comes from above, as indeed it does in our normal environment. But present a

photograph of mooncraters with the sunlight shining from below, and we experience the craters as hills, and vice versa. Thus, the unconscious contextual assumption that light comes from above is easily revealed. Hundreds of context effects have been studied in vision, hearing, touch, language comprehension, action control, and the like, suggesting that all conscious perception, comprehension, and action control are shaped by such unconscious contextual elements. There is a natural contrast between the unconscious contextual information and the conscious experiences which it shapes.

Similar contrastive pairs exist for experiences of purely internal origin. We can compare visual images, inner speech, kinesthetic images, and emotional feelings with equivalent representations that have become unconscious through repeated use or which are not currently available in immediate memory. Consciously available beliefs and short-term action plans can be compared to similar processes that are unconscious. Most of the fundamental, long-term beliefs that guide our actions and judgments appear to be unconscious most of the time, even when they continue to have observable effects. They are *presupposed* in conscious contents, "taken for granted." Likewise, in the control of action, we can compare novel, relatively conscious actions to highly rehearsed and predictable ones, which are automatic and largely unconscious.

Spontaneous problem-solving tasks show the three classical components of conscious problem assignment, unconscious incubation, and conscious display of the results (the aha! experience). This triplet is often reported in advanced creative problem solving in mathematics, art, and science, but in these cases it is unfortunately difficult to be sure that incubation is indeed wholly unconscious. But the same three stages occur in simple memory retrieval (what is your mother's maiden name?), mental arithmetic, finding hidden perceptual figures, and so on. In these short-term tasks we can be reasonably sure that the problem is posed consciously, processed unconsciously, and that the answer is once again conscious. [*See* PROBLEM SOLVING.]

An adequate theory of conscious experience must account for *all* of the above pairs of conscious–unconscious contrasts, and is therefore highly constrained.

A vast body of evidence can be summed up by saying that consciousness is *serial, limited in capacity,* and *internally consistent,* while unconscious processes may operate *in parallel,* have *very great capacity* when taken together, and allow for the co-existence of mutually *inconsistent* representations. We will consider these general facts in turn.

Consider first the seriality of conscious experiences vs parallel processing of unconscious events. Seriality is of course expressed by the traditional metaphor of a "stream of consciousness." It has been known since the 19th century, for example, that simultaneously competing, potentially conscious stimuli can only become conscious serially, one after another. Such mutual competition for conscious access exists with stimuli as short as 100 msec.

Parallelism of unconscious processes is most obviously shown by the brain itself: It is a huge organ, on the order of 100,000,000,000 nerve cells, each firing on the average 40 times per second, each connected with up to 10,000 others. We now know that transmission between cells depends upon a large number of chemical neurotransmitters, each of which can activate multiple receptors that serve very different functions. Relatively small populations of specialized neurons are known to serve quite specific ends, which are of course unconscious in their details, though the biofeedback literature suggests that they can be influenced by immediate conscious feedback. Such feedback is probably rare in normal brain functioning. [*See* SYNAPTIC TRANSMITTERS AND NEUROMODULATORS.]

A second general fact is that *conscious capacity is limited while unconscious processes, taken together, have very great capacity.* Three phenomena may be cited for capacity limitations associated with consciousness. They are (1) selective attention, (2) dual-task interference, and (3) the narrow limits on immediate memory.

A. Selective Attention

When we watch a baseball game on television, we cannot simultaneously experience a football game projected on the same screen, nor can we follow a friend's conversation. Colin Cherry and D. A. Broadbent recognized this limitation of conscious experience in the 1950s in their pioneering experiments on the "cocktail party phenomenon," the fact that we can follow only one coherent stream of speech out of the many that may be available at a crowded cocktail party. In a typical selective attention experiment, two coherent streams of speech are presented to the two separate ears. While we are fully conscious of one at a time, the other is largely

unconscious. However, it can be shown that semantic processing can be carried out unconsciously in the nonattended ear, since people will become conscious of their own name presented in that ear. Unconsciously, listeners can make use of words presented in the unattended ear to resolve ambiguities in the attended ear. If the conscious sentence is "we stood by the bank," the interpretation of the ambiguous word "bank" is influenced by the word "river" or "money," presented simultaneously in the unconscious ear.

Selective attention effects are not dependent on having two physically separate channels, such as the two ears. One can rapidly alternate the two narratives between the two ears without changing the basic fact that one coherent of stream of language is conscious and the other, unconscious. As pointed out above, the conscious stream can be a football game, shown on the same screen as a baseball game. Or different sense modalities can compete against each other for access to consciousness, as when an auditory narrative excludes a visual tracking task. It appears therefore that selective attention effects are due to conscious availability of coherent content over time, rather than location, pitch, amplitude, sense modality, or other purely physical parameters.

B. Dual-Task Interference

In pure selective attention phenomena we are conscious of only one stream of coherent information, while the other is mostly unconscious. This holds true for dense and coherent streams of information where the attended and unattended streams are presented simultaneously, such two coherent spoken narratives. In this general case, unconscious processing does not significantly degrade conscious experience. However, there are many other situations in which two tasks are "time-shared," as in carrying on a conversation while driving a car. When consciousness must alternate between two tasks, there is often interference and mutual degradation of performance. If we are about to drive a car into busy traffic, conversation will typically be interrupted. If the conversation, on the other hand, becomes highly significant and unpredictable in content, we may have to stop the car.

No such limitations are known to occur between two entirely unconscious processes, such as the highly purposeful eye movements we make in reading and simultaneous syntactic analysis of the sentences being read. These two highly complex processes co-occur routinely without mutual interference.

C. Immediate Memory

The third major line of evidence for the limited capacity of consciousness is that *immediate memory* can hold only three or four separate, unrehearsed, and unrelated items. If subjects have the opportunity to rehearse the items, short-term memory capacity can increase to seven or nine items. This handful of items is readily available to consciousness, even while other very similar material may be stored in long-term memory, so that it is not retrievable without additional information and effort. [*See* MEMORY.]

The limits on conscious processing capacity are so narrow and Procrustian that they seem paradoxical: why does the brain, with its enormous size, capacity, complexity, and sophistication, limit consciousness so severely? It is surely not due to a general limit on biological information processing, because unconscious processes, such as the analysis of multiple levels of language, proceed quickly and efficiently without any problem. We will explore one answer to the limited-capacity paradox in the theoretical section below.

We can now proceed to the third general contrast: *conscious contents are internally consistent, while unconscious representations may coexist even when they are mutually contradictory.* Conscious inputs that are not mutually consistent will be either kept out of consciousness or fused into a single, consistent percept. This is the case, for example, when binocular rivalry is created by presenting different stimuli to each eye. The separate stimuli fuse into a single conscious experience only if they are mutually consistent in time, spatial location, and content. If not, they will alternate, or one will suppress the other altogether.

Unconsciously, however, many different and mutually inconsistent processes can coexist, in abstract knowledge as well as perceptual input. The following puzzle illustrates the coexistence of mutually contradictory "islands" of unconscious knowledge. Imagine an observer standing on a mountain top at dawn, pointing to the first rays of the sun just as they show over the horizon. Staying rooted to the spot all day, the observer again points to the sun just as it is sinking below the horizon at dusk. Two lines can be drawn to the sun from the observer at dawn and dusk: where do the two lines intersect? Most educated people believe that the lines meet in the observer, which is obviously false when we consider that the earth, along with the mountain and the observer on top, has rotated perhaps 180 degrees between sunup and sundown!

Why do educated people fall for this simple puzzle? It seems that most people have not one but two separate "islands" of knowledge about the relative movements of earth and sun. From an earth-dweller's point of view, the sun seems to move around the flat, stable surface on which we live. But educated people have been persuaded that the earth rotates on its axis relative to the sun. They only betray their earth-bound perspective in this kind of puzzle, where the two kinds of knowledge come into conflict. Of course there is nothing wrong with the earth-bound perspective. It is quite useful for local orientation and navigation. The puzzle simply shows that we have more than one way to think about our planet, and that the two islands of knowledge are quite dissociated.

In recent years, cognitive scientists working on expert knowledge have come to the realization that knowledge is likely to consist of dissociated islands. Only when we become *conscious* of contradictions between the separate cognitive islands do we realize the dissociation. If they are both unconscious, they can coexist quite happily.

Consciousness, it appears then, based on a vast body of evidence, is *serial, limited in capacity,* and *internally consistent.* Unconscious processes may operate *in parallel,* have *very great capacity* when taken together, and allow for the coexistence of mutually *inconsistent* representations.

What could explain these very general findings?

III. THEORETICAL VIEWS OF CONSCIOUSNESS

With the rise of an information-processing approach to scientific psychology we have seen vastly more sophisticated theories of human functioning. But until very recently modern theories did not refer to consciousness explicitly, using instead terms and mechanisms that are closely associated with it, such as "attention," "short-term memory," and the like.

None of these terms does justice to conscious experience as such. Since the 1950s the term "attention" has emphasized the process of selection between alternative streams of information, and the distinction between conscious and unconscious streams has been discussed primarily as a kind of "filtering" of the unconscious stream. The filter metaphor has been plagued with difficulties, as experiments demonstrated higher and higher levels of analysis in the unattended channel. Further, the focus on "filtering" of the unattended stream of information tells us nothing about the attended, conscious stream.

Selective attention is of course very important, and is intimately associated with conscious experience. Major progress has been made recently in clarifying the complex neural networks involved in the control of attention. We believe that the word "attention" is best used to mean "control of access to consciousness," both because of the research tradition on selective attention and because commonsense psychology employs "attention" very much like "access control." We can *call someone's attention* to a television program, and the person in question will become conscious of it. However, we do not *call someone's consciousness* to anything. People just *are* conscious of some event, after their "attention" is drawn to it.

Short-term memory, or working memory, is also closely connected with consciousness, as noted above. But it is not the same as consciousness. Not all items in short-term memory are conscious at any given time; of the seven digits of a new telephone number that we can mentally rehearse, only one or two are conscious at any single moment. Thus, short-term memory is not identical to consciousness, though it is closely related.

The domain of visual imagery, the "mind's eye," has been explored intensively in recent years, and it too, has a great overlap with consciousness. Visual imagery is one of several internally generated domains of conscious access and experience, including inner speech, anticipatory emotional feelings such as hope and anxiety, and current goals. The mind's eye is a crucial part of the conscious domain, but it is not the whole. Thus, none of the major research topics that are associated with consciousness is quite the same as consciousness.

The most widespread ideas about consciousness can be stated in terms of five hypotheses, each with its pros and cons. A complete model must incorporate at least these five ideas.

The *activation hypothesis* suggests that mental representations must reach some threshold value to become conscious. This is most obvious in the case of sensory experience. Fechner's influential work early in the 19th century on the absolute threshold of stimulation was explicitly conceived as an effort to define the minimal energy needed to "enter" consciousness. "Threshold of recall" phenomena can also be conceived in the same way, but here of course we cannot talk about a physical energy threshold. Instead, psychologists, including Herbart and Freud, have suggested some *internal* "threshold of activation." It is easy to show "fan effects" in memory, where multiple recall cues can together activate a target memory which will become conscious if their joint activation exceeds a certain threshold.

For example, so-called "remote associates" are often evoked by the following word triplets.

(a) cookies sixteen heart _____
(b) poke go molasses _____
(c) surprise line birthday _____
(d) elephant lapse vivid _____

The most popular answers are "sweet," "slow," "party," and "memory." One can now go back to the stimulus words, and imagine how spreading activation from each word could overlap at the target word, until activation at the target exceeded a certain threshold and came to consciousness. External stimulation or internal images or intentions can activate memories, or even novel conscious experiences. The view of memory as driven by activation is currently attractive, since it fits well with connectionist network models of memory, but it has a long history in which activation was primarily defined as the probability of target access to consciousness.

A simple activation hypothesis fails as an adequate account of consciousness, however, because of problems in dealing with redundancy effects: Stimuli or behaviors which are repeated and predictable become unconscious. This includes habituation of perceptual events and mental images, skills practiced to the point of automaticity, and semantic satiation for repeated meaningful words. If activation is needed to enter consciousness, we are left with the paradoxical result that, after some point, additional activation causes conscious contents to become *un*conscious. Apparently simple "activation" cannot be used to explain *both* the likelihood of a stimulus coming to consciousness *and* the fact that repeated stimuli tend to habituate and become unconscious. We need something more.

The *novelty hypothesis* represents another common idea. It claims that consciousness is drawn to novel, unexpected, or nonhabitual events. It is largely true as far as it goes, but it does not explain many facts, such as the threshold phenomena described above, or the capacity limitations of consciousness. Further, significant stimuli, such as the crying of an infant, periodic hunger, sexual interest, persistent pain, and the like, do not habituate even after many repetitions. The novelty hypothesis is a piece of the puzzle, but not the whole.

The *highest level of integration hypothesis:* Several psychologists suggest that conscious contents involve the highest level of integration in some hierarchical view of the nervous system. We know, for example, that sensory systems involve increasingly integrated and sophisticated anatomical maps of the sensory receptor surface. Points of light and contrast at the level of the retina are integrated at the level of the thalamus, which is in turn mapped at a higher level in the primary visual cortex into lines, orientations, and simple shapes, proceeding to at least another 20 increasingly complex and integrated visual maps, until finally we obtain such high-level constructs as three-dimensional object constancy, moving bodies, faces, kinetic representations of object movement, and whole integrated multi-sensory scenes. Consciousness can access such high-level information.

This view seems true as well, as far as it goes. Certainly there is evidence consistent with it, such as the fact that adults most of the time attend to the *meaning* of speech, rather than lower levels of analysis such as sound, phonemes, morphemes, single words, syntax, and the like. But it does not account for the fact that we can be conscious of only a single star on an entirely dark night, even though the tiny amount of light from the star may activate only a single retinal receptor cell. Consciousness is marked, among other properties, by its *flexibility* in ranging up and down perceptual and motor hierarchies. If we encounter a problem in communicating our meaning to a listener, we can quickly restate the same idea in a very different form. But we can equally well change the very fast and complex movements of the tongue in order to be able to talk while avoiding touching a painful tooth. While we can have conscious access to quite high levels of perceptual and conceptual analysis, consciousness does not seem to be limited to high level of analysis.

The *tip-of-the-iceberg hypothesis* states that consciousness is only a small peak emerging from the vast mass of unconscious events. Psychoanalysis popularized this idea beginning about 1900. We have already cited much psychological and neuroscien-

tific evidence along those lines. As before, the iceberg hypothesis is no doubt true as far as it goes, but it does not cover all the facts. Like the other hypotheses, they are only pieces of the puzzle.

Finally we have the *theater hypothesis*. In this view, the mind is like a darkened theater, in which only one actor can occupy the brightly lit stage of consciousness at any given time. The audience is unseen, though it exists and has observable effects. Directors, playwrights, and costume designers operate behind the scenes, invisible except through the actions of the players on stage. To reach the stage, any actor must compete against others who desire publicity. The audience only attends to the action on stage, though, in some models, they can whisper privately to each other, without access to the stage.

Historically, Plato's allegory of the cave and Aristotle's "common sense" are versions of the theater hypothesis. More recently, it has emerged in the searchlight hypothesis of F. H. C. Crick and others, varieties of a blackboard hypothesis, and global workspace theory. Some version of the theater hypothesis may be able to incorporate the four claims discussed above. Global workspace theory attempts such an integration.

IV. THE RELATIONS BETWEEN CONSCIOUS AND UNCONSCIOUS PROCESSES

Conscious processes cannot be understood apart from unconscious ones. It is unhelpful to view the two as separate domains, as if the unconscious were in a compartment separate from consciousness. The idea of a compartmentalized unconscious is often attributed to psychoanalysis, but Freud probably did not intend his theoretical metaphor to be taken quite so literally.

Conscious and unconscious processes should not be divorced, in part because they are needed to define each other. In science as elsewhere, a phenomenon is defined by noticing the effects of its presence and absence. Thus, conscious and unconscious processes cannot even be conceptualized *as such* if they are kept entirely separate. Further, there is robust evidence for the closest imaginable interplay between conscious and unconscious events at all times. The reader's current conscious experience is shaped in part by unconsciously controlled but very precise eye movements, by complex syntactic and lexical analysis, and by conscious thoughts about the topic of consciousness which may have occurred long ago, but which continue to influence the reader's experience in the present. Thus, conscious events influence unconscious ones, and vice versa, in continuous interaction.

Given this amount of interaction, it is surprising that existing models tend to focus on either conscious or unconscious processes. There is a curious dichotomy between limited-capacity models, which attempt to explain phenomena like immediate memory, selective attention, and the like, and work on massively parallel "societies" of highly detailed, specialized, and presumably unconscious processors.

Brain damage can be especially revealing of unconscious, parallel, highly specialized processing. Highly localized brain damage may selectively impair speech production, facial recognition, each of the specific sensory systems, color perception, short-term memory functions, voluntary control, reading, homeostatic control of vital functions, specific emotions, the ability to direct attention, very specific conceptual domains, and the like. Neuropsychological models have only recently begun to deal with this level of complexity. A new perspective, involving parallel distributed networks, sometimes called a "society model" of the nervous system, suggests that the great bulk of information processing is performed by local networks that are unconscious, complex, representational, adaptive, operate in parallel, and are normally very efficient. In such a distributed society of sophisticated processors, the question now becomes, what is the role of the limited-capacity bottleneck that is so closely tied to consciousness?

V. GLOBAL WORKSPACE THEORY

Global workspace theory is the most detailed effort to date to provide an integrated conception of consciousness and its role in the nervous system. This approach starts with a simple, first-approximation model, building up to increasingly complex and adequate models until it provides at least a qualitative model of much conscious and unconscious functioning. It begins by viewing the nervous system as a society of intelligent, specialized processors or "experts" which can communicate with each other and arrange cooperative strategies through the use of a central information exchange, the global workspace (GW). The audience of experts itself is therefore highly distributed, comparable, in some ways, to a market economy. The global workspace in this architecture is much like a blackboard on the podium of a scientific meeting. The audience is filled with "experts" who can talk to each other directly, and who may wish to address the society as a whole in certain cases. Since only one global message can be broadcast to the assembly at one time, experts with different messages to send must compete for access to the global workspace. Global messages may serve to inform, recruit, or control other experts, especially when some novel problem needs to be solved, for which the appropriate expert, or coalition of experts, is not known ahead of time. Experts which receive global messages may act individually or in coalition with others to accomplish a goal, or they may find the message irrelevant. One encouraging sign is that GW theory converges quite well with computational theories based on entirely different sources of evidence.

Applied to the problem of consciousness, GW theory suggests that conscious experiences may act much like messages in a neural global workspace architecture. While only one internally consistent message can occupy the global workspace at a time, messages will change from moment to moment and vary in content depending on the specialty of the processor which has access. Unconscious processors operate autonomously until they encounter a problem (novelty, ambiguity, or degraded stimulus conditions) and require converging input from another source. At that point, access to the global workspace is sought so that the problem can be broadcast globally and other processors recruited to solve it.

In addition to the notions of global workspace and specialized, intelligent processors, global workspace theory makes use of a third construct, called *context*. Contexts are defined as unconscious knowledge structures which evoke, shape, and constrain conscious contents without themselves becoming conscious. They represent knowledge that is called into play during the conscious perception and understanding of current events. Contexts are similar to a number of other constructs such as schemas, scripts, frames, and semantic networks, with the major difference that contexts are explicitly defined to be unconscious, though they define and shape conscious experiences.

Figure 2 shows a graphic formalism for the three major constructs in global workspace theory—the global workspace, specialized processors, and con-

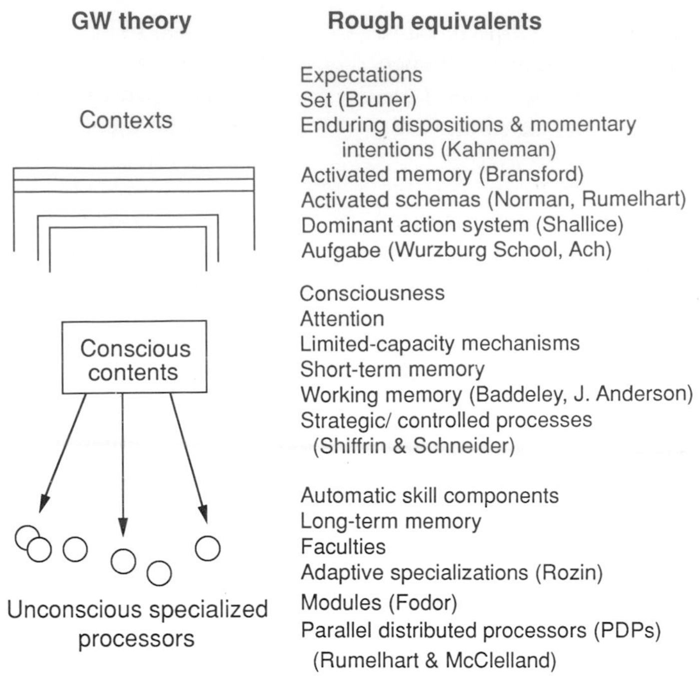

GW theory   Rough equivalents

Contexts   Expectations
                             Set (Bruner)
                             Enduring dispositions & momentary
                                intentions (Kahneman)
                             Activated memory (Bransford)
                             Activated schemas (Norman, Rumelhart)
                             Dominant action system (Shallice)
                             Aufgabe (Wurzburg School, Ach)

                             Consciousness
                             Attention
                             Limited-capacity mechanisms
Conscious   Short-term memory
contents   Working memory (Baddeley, J. Anderson)
                             Strategic/ controlled processes
                                (Shiffrin & Schneider)

                             Automatic skill components
                             Long-term memory
                             Faculties
                             Adaptive specializations (Rozin)
Unconscious specialized   Modules (Fodor)
processors   Parallel distributed processors (PDPs)
                                (Rumelhart & McClelland)

FIGURE 2   Similarities between global workspace (GW) theory and other widespread concepts. The concepts defined in this article are modern variants of ideas that have been widely used elsewhere. However, they are specifically defined in GW theory in terms of conscious and unconscious functioning.

texts—along with comparable concepts from other psychological theories.

VI. CONTEXTS OF EXPERIENCE

Various types of context shape our experience of perceptual, conceptual, and goal-related information. We can speak of *perceptual contexts,* such as knowledge that light typically comes from above, which allow us to "see" mooncraters rather than hills in photographs of lunar landscapes. In word comprehension, contexts may determine which of a word's many meanings is selected. "I'm going to the bank" will be understood differently when one is holding a fishing rod rather than a checkbook. *Conceptual contexts* represent our stable framework of abstract beliefs about the world and other people. Such conceptual contexts facilitate everyday understanding and communication, though they can suddenly become the source of interpersonal and intercultural misunderstanding when we transport these largely unconscious assumptions to new domains of experience where they may not apply. Finally, *goal contexts* are future-directed representations about

action outcomes, which serve to trigger subgoals and plans, and which help guide effector movements. Thought sampling studies show that the stream of consciousness is usually occupied with thoughts and images about unsatisfied goals and wishes, and emotions are widely believed to result from appraisal of our current state compared to our goals.

Contexts may be relatively fleeting, as in word comprehension in an ongoing conversation, or quite long term, as with one's enduring goals to survive, exercise social influence, defends against threats, and care for one's family. Goal contexts are organized in a significance hierarchy, which may, of course, change over time. Low-level goal contexts can change quite quickly. Thus, the reader may pursue an interest in human consciousness in many different ways; reading the present article is but a short-term subgoal of the more general and long-lasting goal. Notice that such goals and subgoals often continue to be effective even when they are not consciously acknowledged as goals.

Evidence about contexts (as defined here) in shaping conscious contents comes from several sources: from *priming effects, fixedness,* the role of *top-down expectations* in perception and comprehension, and the phenomenon of *decontextualization* by context violation. First, studies of priming effects demonstrate that a conscious experience often sets the stage for later input, influencing our understanding of new situations when the stage-setting experience is long gone. In the short term, we can bias one meaning of a word with an associate of one meaning: consider the example of "arrest: book" vs "volume: book." Over longer durations, there is a great deal of recent evidence for long-term effects of profound, life-changing conscious events, such as traumas. Our major way explanation of the extensive effects of conscious events on later processes, without conscious recall of the original event, is by means of complex, enduring unconscious knowledge structures which influence subsequent conscious experience—and this is, of course, the definition of "context" proposed above.

One counter-argument to the role suggested here for conscious priming is the strong evidence for subliminal priming. However, current research suggests that unconscious priming is limited to simple stimuli, whereas conscious priming is often complex and far-reaching in its effects.

A second source of evidence for contexts is *fixedness* or "being blind to the obvious." Here are cases where unconscious contexts shape our experience so strongly that we cannot see alternatives which may be obvious to an outsider. There are well-known "garden path" sentences, which rely on the automatic inference made by most English speakers that the first verb in a sentence will be its main verb. One famous example is "The horse raced past the barn fell." This sentence is usually difficult to understand, although, given a clarifying context, it becomes easy: "Two horses entered the race, one running past the pond, the other past the barn. The horse raced past the barn fell." Fixedness appears to be a universal phenomenon in problem-solving, in everyday life as well as in the laboratory. Creativity is often viewed in terms of an ability to break a fixed set. [*See* CREATIVE AND IMAGINATIVE THINKING.]

Third, largely unconscious *expectations* are known to shape our experience of ambiguous, degraded, vague, or noisy sources of information, which are very common in everyday perception, language, and interaction with other people. In all these cases, active but unconscious structures and processes determine which of several interpretations will become conscious.

A fourth source of evidence for contexts is *decontextualization* due a mismatch between a context and input: Strong violations of context may become consciously accessible. The reader's own experience of the "garden path" sentence cited above may well provide a good example.

These examples show why "context"—the unconscious shaping of conscious experience—is a central construct of GW theory. Conscious experience is believed to be a joint function of global input and the current dominant context hierarchy. Events are experienced differently given a different perceptual, conceptual, or goal context.

Global workshape theory treats consciousness as a major *architectural* characteristic of the nervous system, not as a single, localized phenomenon. Conscious contexts are disseminated throughout the nervous system. The seriality, limited capacity and internal consistency characteristics of conscious experience may derive from the need to address the system as a whole for certain purposes.

VII. FUNCTIONS OF CONSCIOUSNESS

William James wrote that "The *particulars of the distribution of consciousness,* so far as we know them, *point to its being efficacious . . .* the study of consciousness shows it to be exactly such as we might expect in an organ added for the sake of steering a nervous system grown too complex to regulate itself" [italics in the original]. This view contrasts markedly with epiphenomenalism, which, in the words of T. H. Huxley, views conscious experience much as the "steam whistle which accompanies the work of a locomotive [but which] is without influence upon its machinery."

The evidence sketched above militates strongly against epiphenomenalism. Indeed, if consciousness is a major biological adaptation, it may have not just one but several functions.

The evidence suggests at least the following:

1. *Definitional and context-setting functions.* By relating global input to its contextual conditions, the system underlying consciousness acts to define a stimulus and remove ambiguities in its perception and comprehension.

2. *Adaptational and learning function.* The more novelty the nervous system must adapt to, the more conscious involvement is required for successful learning and problem solving.

3. *Prioritizing and access control function.* Attentional mechanisms exercise control over

what will become conscious. By consciously relating some event to higher-level goals, we can raise its conscious access priority, making it conscious more often and therefore increasing the chances of successful adaptation to it. By persuading smokers that the apparently innocuous act of lighting a cigarette is life-threatening over the long term, the medical profession has raised the smokers' conscious involvement with smoking, and created the possibility for more creative problem solving in that respect.

4. *Recruitment and control of thought and action.* Conscious goals can recruit subgoals and motor systems in order to organize and carry out voluntary actions.

5. *Decision-making and executive function.* While the global workspace is not an executive system, executive access to the GW creates the opportunity for controlling any part of the nervous system, as shown by the extraordinary range of neural populations that can be controlled with conscious biofeedback. When automatic systems cannot resolve some choice-point in the flow of action, making it conscious helps to recruit knowledge sources able to help make the proper decision. In the case of indecision, we can make a goal conscious to allow widespread recruitment of conscious and unconscious resources acting for or against the goal.

6. *Error-detection and editing function.* Conscious goals and plans are monitored by unconscious systems which will act to interrupt execution if errors are detected. Though we often become aware of making an error in a general way, the detailed description of what makes an error an error is almost always unconscious.

7. *Reflective and self-monitoring function.* Through conscious inner speech and imagery we can reflect upon and to some extent control our conscious and unconscious functioning.

8. *Optimizing the trade-off between organization and flexibility.* Automatized, "canned" responses are highly adaptive in predictable situations. However, in facing unpredictable conditions, the capacity of consciousness to recruit and reconfigure specialized knowledge sources is indispensible.

In sum, consciousness appears to be the major way in which the nervous system adapts to novel, challenging, and informative events in the world.

VIII. RECENT DEVELOPMENTS

The last 10 years have seen a major increase in psychological and neuroscientific efforts aimed at solving the puzzle of conscious and unconscious functioning. In addition to work discussed above, a great deal of research has been devoted to defining the threshold of subjective experience, on phenomena of subliminal priming, feature integration in conscious perception, neuropsychological studies on intact and damaged persons, and the problem of voluntary control. In general, there is increasing research in psychology and neuroscience comparing cases of very similar conscious and unconscious processes, much like the contrastive analyses discussed in the beginning of this article.

Special attention is currently being paid to neuropsychological studies of lesions that affect conscious functioning. Damage to the primary visual projection area of the cortex (Area V1) produces localized blindness in the corresponding part of the visual field. Patients with such "blindsight" report no conscious visual experience in the last part of the visual field. However, some information is unconsciously available to these patients: they can answer questions and act appropriately with respect to objects presented in the blind area, and can unconsciously process stimulus location, movement, speed, direction of movement, orientation, flicker, and size. Blindsight patients can conform their hands to the size and shape of unseen objects that they are asked to reach for and can use the meaning of unseen words flashed in their blind field to select words flashed later in their intact visual fields. Similar evidence for unconscious processing comes from studies of abilities that remain intact for people suffering from amnesia and agnosias, such as the inability to recognize familiar faces, and neglect syndromes.

The role of "fringe consciousness"—the many experiences which people cannot describe exactly, but about which they report with very high confidence, such as feelings of familiarity, "rightness" of a fleeting stimulus, emotional feelings, or even artistic beauty—was described by William James late in the 19th century. Recent theoretical developments suggest that fringe consciousness is an efficient means of representing nonconscious contextual information in consciousness in a radically condensed, partial form. Thus, for example, all of one's memories of childhood may remain unconsciously stored as one enters one's old neighborhood; but the contextual role of these memories and their shaping of perception and experience are represented in consciousness by the feeling of familiarity. Fringe conscious information often seems to act as cue or "handle" for accessing unconscious material. Such developments have implications for understanding the interaction of conscious and nonconscious processes in everyday perception and problem solving as well as in neuropsychological phenomena such as "blindsight" and in clinical situations involving emotional feelings.

Presently, there is no consensus on a general theory of consciousness. The new field of cognitive science offers promise in dealing with the conceptual issues by bringing together researchers from a diverse collection of fields, including experimental psychology, neuroscience, computer science, and philosophy. We believe that the coming debate will center more and more on the apparent dichotomy between limited-capacity mechanisms intimately tied to consciousness and the enormous family of unconscious systems that governs the fine details of our mental processes.

Bibliography

Anderson, J. R. (1983). "The Architecture of Cognition." Harvard University Press, Cambridge, MA.

Baars, B. J. (1988). "A Cognitive Theory of Consciousness." Cambridge University Press, New York.

Baars, B. J. (Ed.) (1992). "Experimental Slips and Human Error: Exploring the Architecture of Volition." Plenum, New York.

Crick, F. (1984). Function of the thalamic reticular complex: The searchlight hypothesis. *Proc. Nat. Acad. Sci. USA* **81,** 4586–4593.

Dennett, D. C. (1991). "Consciousness Explained." Little, Brown, Boston.

James, W. (1890/1983). "The Principles of Psychology," reprint. Harvard University Press, Cambridge, MA.

LaPolla, M. V., and Baars, B. J. (1992). A psychologically implausible architecture that is always conscious, always active. *Behav. Brain Sci.* **15**(3), 448–449.

Mangan, B. (1993). Taking phenomenology seriously: The "fringe" and its implications for cognitive research. *Conscious. Cognit.* **2**(2), 89–108.

Marcel, A. J. (1983). Conscious and unconscious perception: Experiments on visual masking and word recognition. *Cog. Psychol.* **15,** 197–237.

Newell, A. (1990). "Unified Theories of Cognition." Harvard University Press, Cambridge, MA.

Posner, M. I., and Rothbart, M. K. (1992). Attentional mechanisms and conscious experience. In "The Neuropsychology of Consciousness" (A. D. Milner and M. D. Rugg, Eds.) Academic Press, London.

Rumelhart, D. E., McClelland, J. E., and the PDP Group. (1986). "Parallel Distributed Processing: Explorations in the Microstructure of Cognition." Vol. I, "Foundations." Bradford/MIT Press, Cambridge, MA.

Searle, J. (1992). "Rediscovery of the Mind." Bradford/MIT Press, Cambridge, MA.

Shallice, T. (1988). "From Neuropsychology to Mental Structure." Cambridge University Press, Cambridge, UK.

Singer, J., and Pope, K. S. (1978). "The Stream of Consciousness: Scientific Investigations into the Flow of Human Experience." Plenum, New York.

Sokolov, E. N. (1963). "Perception and the Conditioned Reflex." MacMillan, New York.

Velmans, M. (1991). Is human information processing conscious? *Behav. and Brain Sci.* **14,** 689–690.

Weiskrantz, L. (1986). "Blindsight: A Case Study and Implications." Oxford University Press, Oxford.

CONSERVATISM/LIBERALISM

William F. Stone
University of Maine

Glossary

Attitude A set of positive or negative beliefs and feelings about a particular social object or practice, as exemplified by the statement: "She has a positive attitude toward socialized medicine." Attitudes are enduring aspects of personality; they are made up of beliefs and feelings about, together with tendencies to behave in positive or negative ways toward the object of the attitude.

Elites The groups of people who are most informed, active, and influential in a society. Members of elite groups tend to dominate public affairs.

Greens Political groups, such as the Green Party in Germany, whose primary focus is on environmental preservation. Although Germany is alone in having Green Party members in its parliament, groups with similar aims are active in many countries.

Humanist In Tomkin's theory, the personality characterized by sensitivity to one's own and other people's feelings. The humanist advocates social change and innovation, and accepts liberal ideology.

Ideology A shared set of ideas about how society should function and how people should relate to one another. An ideology usually involves utopian goals and assumptions that are basically matters of opinion.

Left Generic term for liberal and socialist ideologies and parties.

Libertarian Adherent of an ideology that advocates liberty in thought and conduct. The libertarian stresses minimal government, maximal freedom, and the rule of self-interest.

Norm A shared rule of conduct or belief that each member of a social group is expected to follow.

Normative In Tomkin's theory, the personality characterized by distrust of one's own and other's emotions. The normative person is strongly supportive of norms and traditions, and is attracted to conservative ideologies.

Right Generic term for ideologies and parties on the conservative end of the political spectrum.

THE TERMS *conservative* and *liberal* are much misunderstood. The confusion surrounding their meanings has several origins. They can be considered either as individual personality dispositions or as historically grounded ideologies. A conservative person is one who is devoted to the status quo and who accepts authority and the norms of society. A liberal is change-oriented and places great emphasis on individual freedom, being opposed to the external imposition of authority. In reality, neither people nor philosophies are that simple and unalloyed. They are all mixtures, to some degree, of opposing tendencies. The great psychologist William James attributed people's conservative tendencies to *habit:*

> Habit is thus the enormous fly-wheel of society, its most precious conservative agent. It alone is what keeps us all within the bounds of ordinance, and saves children of fortune from the envious uprisings of the poor. It alone prevents the hardest and most repulsive walks of life from being deserted by those brought up to tread therein. . . . It dooms us all to fight out the battle of life upon the lines of our nurture or our early choice, and to make the best of a pursuit that disagrees, because there

is no other for which we are fitted, and it is too late to begin again.

However, the conservative psychological tendencies observed by James are counteracted by others that include curiosity, sensation-seeking, adventuresomeness, and like characteristics that we group under the heading "liberal." We will speak of these liberal and conservative personal tendencies as "humanism" and "normativism," respectively. [*See* HABIT.]

Conservative and liberal are also terms that commonly apply to political philosophies. As a political ideology, conservatism has come to mean favoring governmental supervision of personal morals and opposition to regulation of business and trade. Liberals support civil liberties, personal privacy, and governmental planning and regulation of the economy.

I. IDEOLOGY: CONSERVATIVE–LIBERAL, RIGHT–LEFT

The meanings of liberal and conservative ideology have changed over the last 200 years. What is now referred to as "classical liberalism" originated with philosophers such as John Locke. Conservatism's prophet was Edmund Burke, whose contemporary supporters were appalled by the French Revolution's call for "Liberty, Equality, and Fraternity." One source of confusion about these concepts is that some ideas, originally liberal (such as Locke's emphasis on individual freedom), are now shared by liberals and conservatives in the United States. A second source of confusion is that members of the lay public often hold simplified conceptions of terms that in actuality refer to complex social–political philosophies and practices. The casual use, by reporters and popular writers, of the terms liberal and conservative and of left and right contributes to the confusion about their meaning.

A final source of confusion is that lay people are often less consistent in their political beliefs than members of political elites; a person can be socially liberal (in favor of abortion, birth control, an cohabiting before marriage) but economically conservative. Let us examine what social scientists mean by the terms today.

A. Liberal/Conservative: Definitions

Liberalism and conservatism are ideologies that specify goals and means for political systems. Some

writers attribute the origin of the term *liberal* to the Spanish "Liberales," a party that favored adoption of a constitution similar to the French constitution of 1791. Social scientists define contemporary liberalism as an ideology that emphasizes freedom of the individual, constitutional democracy, the rule of law, open discussion and tolerance of different points of view, social progress and change, equality and minority rights, religious freedom, and rational approaches to remedy social deficiencies and to improve human welfare, often through governmental action. Liberal political platforms emphasize concern for others and cooperative relationships among people.

Conservatives emphasize tradition and stability in preference to change. They advocate freedom, religion, and patriotism, and believe that there are differences among individual people that make them inherently unequal. Conservatives are more distrustful of human nature and less certain about progress than liberals.

Conservatives from the time of Plato have distrusted democratic rule and tend to believe that some individuals are better suited to govern than others. They endorse individualism, free markets, the sacredness of private property, and the centrality of business and manufacturing to society. The conservative emphasizes the competitive character of human relationships, and tends to be distrustful of others. Some observers have commented on the conservative's fear of change, uncertainty, and people different from themselves. By and large, conservatives identify with strong leaders and national symbols. Both conservative and liberal ideologies endorse freedom; the conservatives emphasize economic freedom and unrestricted use of property. Liberal ideology emphasizes freedom of thought and speech, equal access to education, and the prerogatives of democratic citizenship.

B. Left and Right

Today, left and right are generally understood to be synonyms for liberal and conservative. Although the terms appear frequently in the media, American voters seldom use the terms. In Europe, *left* and *right* are frequently used in preference to *liberal* and *conservative*. The European usage is more inclusive: Continental parties include, on the left, liberal, socialist, and communist parties. The right includes moderate capitalists, staunch conservatives, and extreme right-wing parties. In the Scandinavian countries, the media routinely refer to the socialist (left) parties and the nonsocialist (right) parties. In Norway, for example, the socialist parties include the Communists, the Socialist Left, and the Labor Party. Norway's nonsocialist parties include the Center Party, the Conservative Party, and the Christian Folk Party.

C. Change versus the Status Quo

Because the liberal–conservative meanings of issues change over time (free public education through high school, once a liberal idea in the United States, is now noncontroversial), it has been suggested that these labels be defined in terms of readiness for change. Rather than defining liberals as supporters of welfare and less defense spending, one could characterize them as people who readily accept and even advocate change. Viewed in this light, the conservative is a person who wants to keep things as they are, to maintain the status quo, the established norms and ways of doing things. The social psychologist Charles Bird defined liberal, conservative, and reactionary in terms of change:

> The reactionary is regarded as one who prefers not the existing, but a past state of an institution; the conservative is assumed to have an attachment to things as they are: the liberal is said to prefer modifications of the *status quo* when they permit a building of the new into the pattern of the old; and the radical approves of and seeks drastic changes in the existing order. (1940, pp. 174–175)

These preferences may be shown in the holding of some attitudes in keeping with liberal, conservative, or reactionary tendencies, or in the adoption of entire ideologies. Scholars who disagree that conservatism can be equated with support for the status quo point out examples of conservative leaders who have been strongly change-oriented. Margaret Thatcher, former British Prime Minister, is given as an example. It can be argued, however, that Thatcher's activism was in the service of reaction as defined by Bird.

II. LEFT AND RIGHT IN HISTORICAL CONTEXT

Left and right as political referents are said to have their origin in the French National Assembly of the late 18th century. There, two membership constituencies were represented. To the king's left were seated the intellectuals and representatives of the new liberal merchant class. On his right sat the members of the waning aristocracy, the nobles whose loyalty was to things as they were or as they had been at an earlier time.

Historically, "left" and "right" have carried emotional overtones. When people are asked for their associations to these words, *left* is often associated with "negative" words such as bad, dark, forbidden, and weak, whereas *right* connotes good, light, correct, and sacred. These connotations are found in many languages. In science, *dextral* (from the Latin *dexter,* right, favorable) refers to the right side of the body, and *sinistral* (from the Latin and Middle English, *sinister;* on the left hand or side, hence unfavorable, injurious) pertaining to the left side of the body. The French word for left, *droche,* also signifies ungainly or awkward, and the Norwegian word for right, *hoyre,* means literally higher. Such examples could be multiplied many times over.

Research has shown repeatedly that for many people, *left* represents change, risk, and threats to the status quo. *Right,* on the other hand, suggests order, stability, and a devotion to existing policies and institutions. The association between left and liberal seems to have given "liberal" a slightly negative aura, such that the "L-word" has been used as an epithet. In recent election campaigns in the United States, such feelings have been exploited by conservative political campaigners who use "liberal" as a scare-word.

III. LIBERAL AND CONSERVATIVE ATTITUDES

Conservatism and liberalism refer to individual attitude clusters as well as to widely shared political ideologies. Since the invention of attitude scaling about 1920, and the initiation of public opinion polling in the 1930s, social psychologists have sought to measure and study these attitudes. [*See* ATTITUDE CHANGE; ATTITUDE FORMATION; ATTITUDE STRENGTH.]

A. Measuring Conservatism/Liberalism

There are two ways of assessing personal conservatism–liberalism. One is simply to ask the person to identify him or herself as liberal or conservative. Public opinion pollsters often adopt this approach, classifying their respondents on a 7-point scale ranging from Very Conservative to Very Liberal. This approach, however, has limited value because many respondents have little understanding of the terms. Another approach frequently used by poll takers is to assess the person's liberal and conservative stands on various issues. Survey researchers often ask their respondents about beliefs concerning economics, the role of government, and lifestyle issues. At the time of this writing, for example, liberals endorse a woman's "freedom of choice" and waiting periods for hand gun purchases, while conservatives tend to oppose abortion and gun controls.

The scales employed by social psychologists incorporate many items or "statements." Examples of attitude statements that we have used in research on liberalism and conservatism are statements modified from those used in the 1940s by Eysenck. Liberal positions are represented by statements such as

♦ Ultimately, private property should be abolished and complete socialism introduced.
♦ Men and women have the right to find out whether they are sexually suited before marriage (e.g., by living together).
♦ Our treatment of criminals is too harsh; we should try to cure them, not to punish them.

Conservative statements are exemplified by the following:

♦ Production and trade should be free from government interference.
♦ "My country right or wrong" represents a fundamentally desirable attitude.
♦ We should believe without question the teachings of our religion.

Attitude scales are generally made up of 20 or more such statements; for each, the responses are on graded answer categories, Agree Very Much, Disagree Slightly, and so on. This is the Likert method of attitude scaling. Respondents are typically given seven answer categories from strong agreement to strong disagreement. The responses, from 1 to 7 on each statement, are then added up (scoring answers to liberal statements negatively) to arrive at a single conservatism score for that person.

It is not necessary to assume that liberalism and conservatism form a unidimensional scale; it has been pointed out that everyone has some conservative and some liberal impulses. That is, we all trea-

sure certain things from the past and value familiar practices and routines (conservative), and we all have ideals and things about out lives that we would like to change (liberal). Therefore, some researchers (e.g., Kerlinger) have investigated the possibility of giving everyone two scores, a liberal and a conservative score. There is some evidence in support of this approach, since answers to liberal and conservative statements are sometimes unrelated. Given many different areas of concern, it is possible to hold both liberal and conservative attitudes at the same time. People who are highly ideological, however, are consistently liberal or conservative in their beliefs.

B. Conservatism in the United States: Survey Data

Because of measurement problems and the changes in the left–right connotations of different issues over time, assessing the proportion of liberals and conservatives in the population of a country is problematic. Using the self-designation method, the Gallup Poll found in 1987 that 30% of Americans described themselves as liberal, and 43% considered themselves conservative. However, when asked about specific issues, it is clear that members of the American public are much more liberal than the Gallup poll statistics indicate. Analyses of public opinion suggest that many of the Americans who are philosophical conservatives are operative liberals, in that they favor many liberal programs.

The answers given by Americans to public opinion poll questions over the last four decades indicate that they are liberal on many issues. Questions concerning abortion, racial tolerance, feminism, family, and religion all elicit predominantly liberal responses and recent trends have been toward greater liberalism. One of the strongest liberal trends centers on equal rights, especially for women and minorities. There have been conservative shifts on economics and other issues. Support for the death penalty, for example, began to increase in the 1960s and in the 1990s commands majority support in the United States. A number of observers have documented periodic swings in opinion between conservative and liberal attitudes, in addition to some long-term trends.

Generally speaking, more Americans designate themselves conservative than liberal. However, the majority are liberal as judged by their issue positions. The trends suggest that the "Reagan revolution" was more an expression of President Reagan's personal magnetism than a conservative ideological movement.

1. Social, Political, Economic, and Religious Conservatisms

It seems useful to distinguish different kinds of conservatism. We have mentioned abortion rights as an issue which polarized the United States's electorate in the 1990s. The "pro-choice" side on this liberal–conservative issue enjoyed majority support. Some people on the "liberal" side of the abortion issue are conservative on economic issues such as balancing the budget. Thus, it makes sense to distinguish liberal and conservative stands within restricted issue domains like economic policy, welfare and health care, and sexuality and reproduction. Political activists show greater consistency across issues than people who have less interest in the broad issues. Public opinion theorists refer to this consistency as greater "constraint" in the political attitudes of opinion leaders.

2. Ideology and Voting

Surveys generally show that some political parties can be characterized as liberal, others as conservative. In the United States, the Democratic and Republican parties each have both conservative and liberal members (one survey of state legislators found both the most liberal individual and the most conservative individual to be Democrats). Nevertheless, on the average the Democrats are clearly the liberal party and the Republicans constitute the conservative party.

Ideological influences vary significantly from election to election. Thus, the salient issues may be different in each election period. At one time, the public's concerns may focus on question of war and peace which may be nonideological. Another election may find voters most concerned about the economy or about crime or attempts to restrict abortion. Voters in the United States are less ideological than citizens in many other countries, that is, the Americans tend not to distinguish between candidates on liberal–conservative grounds.

C. Cross-Cultural Comparisons

It is difficult to generalize across cultures that vary greatly in historical circumstances and forms of government. However, a comparison of ideology in Great Britain and the United States contrasts two countries with very close historical and linguistic ties.

1. Conservatism in the United States and Great Britain

The political spectrum in the Untied States is significantly to the right of that in Great Britain. This difference can be traced to the long history of democratic socialism in Britain, now represented by the Labour Party. As an economic and political movement, socialism failed to gain a foothold in the United States. Universal health care, for example, is just beginning to be discussed in the United States as a real possibility, whereas throughout the lengthy tenure of the Conservatives as the ruling party in Britain, socialized medicine has been retained. Another factor leading to greater liberalism in Britain is the existence of multiple parties, where three major parties share the vote: Labour (socialist), Conservative, and Liberal. Citizens' political attitudes are shaped by differences in the political system in which they live. Their expectations regarding stability and change are based in large part on their own experiences within the system.

2. Russian Communism: Liberal or Conservative?

The uncertain meanings of *conservative* and *liberal* are nowhere better illustrated than in the political situation of Russia following the demise of communism and the breakup of the Soviet Union. The free-market reformers, according to contemporary political definitions, are conservative. Communism is a left-wing or extreme liberal ideology. Yet, as of this writing, the reformers are seen by the world as leftists, advocating change, and the communists are considered the conservatives! These impressions have been supported by surveys that show support for communism in Russia today represents support for the former status quo. Such observations strengthen the conception of liberals as change-oriented and conservatives as proponents of things as they are or were.

IV. CONSERVATISM–LIBERALISM AND CONTEMPORARY IDEOLOGIES

Many theorists have discerned liberal and conservative beliefs in other religious and political ideologies. Here, we discuss the existence of such beliefs in the ideology of contemporary Christian sects and in socialism, fascism, libertarianism, and the green parties.

A. Religion

Religious liberals and conservatives differ concerning their beliefs in the proper source of guidance for behavior. The religious right appeals either to scripture (Protestant Christianity) or to infallible authority (Catholic Christianity). Religious liberals place much more emphasis on human reason and upon human feelings. Liberals advocate a relativistic morality dependent on contemporary social conditions. Conservatives are more absolute, and liberals more relativistic about questions of right and wrong.

B. Socialism and Social Democracy

Socialism refers to the social democracy currently practiced, for example, by the governments of France and Spain as opposed to the authoritarian socialisms exemplified by Stalinist Communism. The Scandinavian countries—Denmark, Norway, and Sweden—also have strong socialist parties which often form governments. Democratic socialism is basically a liberal ideology, but with a stronger emphasis on community, equality, and the need for government planning for resource allocation as opposed to market mechanisms. Welfare liberals have much in common with socialists. Liberals, however, tend to oppose the broad government ownership of basic industries that is favored by socialists.

C. Fascism

Adolph Hitler's party was called National Socialism, but it was oriented toward a partnership between the government and the large corporations rather than between government and governed. Because of its extreme emphasis on inequality, fascism is much more closely aligned with conservatism than with liberalism. The rise of neo-Nazi parties in Europe has raised anew questions about authoritarianism, the presumed psychological characterisitic of people attracted to fascism, and its relation to conservatism.

D. Libertarians and Greens

The libertarian places extreme emphasis on freedom of the individual to do what he or she likes, without government interference. This emphasis places libertarianism closer to conservatives than to liberals; their emphasis on *liberty,* however, pertains to personal conduct as well as to property and commerce. Although this doctrine has broad appeal, its attraction is reduced upon recognition of libertarianism's extreme emphasis on self-interest. Conservatives generally are more in favor of laws to protect the weak from the strong than are libertarians.

Greens represent a growing force in Western societies and have gained seats in the German parliament. The Green parties' major emphasis on the conservation of the natural environment has attracted some conservatives to their cause. However, the movement has increasingly attracted liberals since conservatives have a relatively greater preference for economic growth over environmental preservation.

V. TEMPERAMENTAL CONSERVATISM AND LIBERALISM: NORMATIVISM AND HUMANISM

In his libretto for the comic opera *H.M.S. Pinafore,* W. S. Gilbert had an actor voice the opinion that "every boy and every gal that's born into the world alive is either a little Liberal and or a little Conservative." Since this idea was advanced in the 1880s, a number of attempts have been made to link temperamental differences with attraction to liberal or conservative ideologies. One theory that suggests such a relationship is Silvan Tomkin's theory of ideological scripts. According to this theory, the acceptance of conservative or liberal ideology is partly dependent on one's emotional make-up, whether one has a *normative* or a *humanistic* personality.

A. Normative Personality

A normative person tends to deny his or her feelings and to be annoyed or embarrassed by emotional expression by others. They are oriented more to negative emotions such as anger, disgust, and fear than to positive emotions such as happiness, interest, and surprise. Normatives tend to emphasize absolute standards of right and wrong. The normative person's guides to life are "norms"—shared rules of behavior, written or unwritten. Anger is directed at those who break the rules, not toward oppressive authority. The normative person, in common with the conservative, is uncomfortable with change. New ideas, new political movements, and suggestions that the status quo is wrong create anxiety for the normative person.

B. Humanism

Humanism is the name given by Tomkins to a personality whose concerns center on human needs and pleasures rather than on rules and authorities. Humanists are emotionally more positive than normatives, and are attracted to positive feelings in others. They relish novelty, and are critical of practices based on long usage or arbitrary authority. People with humanistic personalities are attracted to liberal ideologies, while those with normative personalities are attracted to conservative ideas and beliefs.

There is some evidence that these temperamental differences are established in childhood, in part because of the parents' attitudes toward discipline, play, and child development. Parental modeling of attitudes also seems important, but according to Tomkins normative and humanist personalities differ primarily in emotional constitution. Both inborn constitutional differences and the emotional interaction between parents and child are seen as important to the development of these temperaments.

VI. CONCLUSION: WHAT "CONSERVATIVE" AND "LIBERAL" MEAN TODAY

Conservative and liberal refer to ideologies whose definitions depend upon specific historic and geographical loci. The "classical liberalism" identified with John Locke and the authors of the U.S. Constitution was concerned with individual rights against royal and aristocratic authority. Present-day conservatives and liberals in the United States share parts of this heritage. Conservatives continue to emphasize individual freedoms but mainly in the commercial world: Government should not regulate business, should favor free trade, and the like. Liberals much more than conservatives favor democracy, civil liberties for all citizens, and the intervention of government to solve social ills. The clear opposition between liberalism and conservatism as we know it today in the United States began in the 1930s with support for and opposition to the activism of government under Democrat Franklin D. Roosevelt's New Deal program. However, modern liberalism can be traced to the progressive politics of FDR's Republican cousin, President Theodore Roosevelt, at the beginning of the 20th century.

Despite their opposition to liberalism, American conservatives have assimilated most of the New Deal reforms such as controls over banking, unemployment insurance, and the Social Security system. However, the conservative administrations of Presidents Reagan and Bush decreased government controls over business and opposed proposals for a universal health care system.

Bibliography

Barash, D. P. (1992). "The L Word." William Morrow, New York.

Bird, C. (1940). "Social Psychology." Appleton-Century, New York.

James, W. (1983). "The Principles of Psychology." Harvard University Press, Cambridge. (Originally published in 1890.)

Kerlinger, F. N. (1984). "Liberalism and Conservatism: The Nature and Structure of Social Attitudes." Lawrence Erlbaum, Hillsdale, NJ.

Knight, K. (in press). Measures of liberalism and conservatism. In "Measures of Political Attitudes," (J. P. Robinson, P. R. Shaver, and L. W. Wrightsman, Eds.), revised ed. Academic Press, San Diego, CA.

Lipsitz, L. (1986). "American Democracy." St. Martin's Press, New York.

McFarland, S., Ageyev, V., and Abalakina, M. (1993). The authoritarian personality in the U.S.A. and U.S.S.R.: Comparative studies. In "Strength and Weakness: The Authoritarian Personality Today" (W. F. Stone, G. Lederer, and R. Christie, Eds.), Chapt. 8. Springer-Verlag, New York.

Milbrath, L. W. (1989). "Envisioning a Sustainable Society: Learning our Way Out." State University of New York Press, Albany, NY.

Rossiter, C. (1962). "Conservatism in America," 2nd ed. Vintage Books, New York.

Smith, T. W. (1990). Liberal and conservative trends in the United States since World War II. *Public Opinion Quart.* **54**, 479–507.

Stone, W. F., and Schaffner, P. E. (1988). "The Psychology of Politics," 2nd ed. Springer-Verlag, New York.

Tomkins, S. S. (1991). "Affect Imagery Consciousness: The Negative Affects: Anger and Fear," Vol, III, Springer, New York.

CONSUMER PSYCHOLOGY

Thomas J. Page, Jr.
Michigan State University

Glossary

Affect Liking, as in affection.
Attitude A learned predisposition to behave in a consistently favorable or unfavorable manner toward an object or class of objects.
Attribute A feature or characteristic of an object or person.
Behavior The actions or conduct of a person.
Scale A means of measuring some attribute of a person or object.

CONSUMER PSYCHOLOGY is the study of behavior engaged in by consumers. A consumer is an individual who identifies a need or desire that she wants to satisfy. (Note that organizations as consumers are not discussed in this article.) These needs or desires can be quite far ranging, from the need to get to and from work everyday to the desire to take a vacation in some exotic location. The behavior that an individual engages in to satisfy these needs or desires is much more than just purchasing some good or service. These behaviors include information search, evaluation of alternatives, decision making, purchase, use, postpurchase evaluation, and eventual disposal of the good or service. Thus, the study of consumer behavior is the study of how an individual (i.e., the consumer) goes about satisfying (i.e., behavior) his or her needs and desires.

I. INTRODUCTION

Consumer behavior is studied in order to gain an understanding of the consumer, which allows businesses to offer goods and services in accordance with the consumer's desires. Consumers do not always behave in predictable or understandable ways, hence the need to study consumer behavior. For example, consumers often equate higher prices with higher quality even for identical goods, leading to a positive-sloping demand curve.

The other major factor leading to the development of consumer behavior as a discipline was the post World War II economy. Prior to World War II, the U.S. economy was pretty much a seller's market. That is, producers could sell what ever they produced, and consumer input was given little, if any, attention. "You can have any color car you want as long as it is black," was not an empty statement. Following the war, there was tremendous pent up demand for consumer goods that had not been available because of the war. By the early 1950s, however, this demand was largely satisfied, and the market place began to shift from a seller's market to a buyer's market. Business began to realize that in order to stay in business and be competitive, they were going to have to start paying more attention to the consumer. In other words, business had to increase its understanding of the individual's needs and desires, and how the consumer went about satisfying them; it had to study consumer behavior.

Consumer behavior could be considered an offshoot of marketing, which in turn could be considered an offshoot of economics. Indeed, much of the early consumer behavior research had a strong economic flavor. However, as research in the discipline has grown, numerous other disciplines have made significant contributions to the field of consumer behavior. Perhaps one of the largest contributors to the development of consumer behaviors is psychology. Psychology, particularly social psychology, deals with behavior. Since consumer behavior is a special type of behavior, it made sense for researchers studying consumer behavior to borrow theories developed in social psychology and apply them to consumer behavior questions. Notable contributions from psychology include information-processing theories, theories of attitude and the relation of attitude to behavior, and the decision-making process. Not only has consumer behavior borrowed from psychology, but also from economics, sociology, anthropology, geography, political science, and philosophy. In fact, consumer behavior is perhaps one of the most interdisciplinary fields in which research is being conducted, and it is still evolving.

A. Topics to Be Discussed

While the field of consumer behavior is still relatively young, it has developed a considerable body of research. This research has examined a wide variety of topics, some in more detail than others. Even though many of these topics are vitally important, obviously in an article of this length, choices have to be made as to what topics will be discussed. Therefore, the choice of topics to be discussed in this article is based on the widespread interest of researchers in the field of consumer behavior in conducting research on these particular topics. The three main areas to be discussed here are: (1) information processing, (2) attitude and attitude behavior relations, and (3) consumer decision making.

Information processing has been a primary area of interest to consumer behavior researchers for many years. The main focus of research in this area is on how consumers obtain, process, store, and use information relevant to making a decision that satisfies a need or desire. Research in this area has ranged from how many pieces of information a consumer can actively keep track of at one time on the theoretical side, to what is the best way to present per unit price information (e.g., price per pound) on a grocery store shelf on the practical side.

Research on attitudes has also been a major thrust in consumer behavior. Consumer researchers have investigated the structure of attitudes, how attitudes are formed and changed, and the relationship of attitudes to other constructs such as purchase intention and actual purchase behavior. Theoretical research in this area has looked at such questions as how to effectively measure and model a person's attitude and how effectively one's attitude predicts one's intentions to perform a particular behavior. Practical research on attitudes has looked at such questions as how does a person's attitude toward a television commercial affect his attitude toward the product advertised in the commercial, and how to change a person's attitude to make them more likely to recy-

cle waste material. [*See* ATTITUDE CHANGE; ATTITUDE FORMATION; ATTITUDE STRENGTH.]

Consumer decision making examines how the consumer makes a choice among all of the available alternatives. In other words, once a consumer reaches the stage in which a purchase is to be made, what processes does he go through to arrive at a final decision of which good or service to purchase. Research in this area has focused mainly on the development of models that explain how attributes of the objects under consideration (e.g., price, quality, warranty, color, etc.) are evaluated in order for the consumer to choose the good or service that best statisfies her needs or desires. [*See* DECISION MAKING, INDIVIDUALS.]

All three of these areas, information processing, attitudes, and decision making, have benefitted greatly from research in psychology. Each has engendered a considerable body of research and no attempt is made in this article to provide an in depth treatment of these areas. Instead, what follows is a general overview of each area designed to provide a brief introduction to the topic.

II. INFORMATION PROCESSING

As stated above, information processing concerns how individuals obtain, process, store, and use information relevant to making a decision that satisfies a need or desire. Information processing forms the link between the outside world and the consumer's decision-making process. For example, does a consumer considering the purchase of a new car examine few or many sources of information about potential cars to purchase, and does the consumer store this information in memory or rely on printed brochures? Does the consumer examine all of the attributes of a particular model before considering the next model, or does he consider one attribute (e.g., price) across all models and then go on to the next attribute (e.g., gas mileage)? Understanding these processes is vitally important to businesses in order for them to develop effective means of conveying information to consumers.

Before an individual can process information, they must be exposed to it. Being exposed to information, however, does not necessarily mean that the individual will process it. It simply means that the consumer has had the opportunity to process it if she desires to. There are numerous factors that influence what information gets processed out of all the information one is exposed to. It would be impossible to process all of the information an individual is exposed to through the five senses. Indeed, even trying to do so would be impractical and dysfunctional. For example, try reading all of the signs and billboards the next time you drive down a busy street. For this reason, individuals have developed what is termed selective perception. To the consumer, this means that he will engage in further processing only of selected pieces of information.

What determines which pieces of information are ignored and which are processed further is a complex question. Basically, it comes down to which pieces of information are relevant to satisfying the consumer's needs or desires, and which are not. The consumer is more likely to pay attention to information that can help him or her make a decision. For example, a consumer in the market for a new car is more likely to notice advertisements for cars in magazines or on television than is a consumer who is not in the market for a new car.

Once the individual becomes aware of the information (i.e., pays attention to it), he must perform some sort of mental operation on it if he desires to comprehend the information. This comprehension involves interpreting and assigning meaning to the contents of the information. This process is strongly affected by three major factors: individual characteristics, stimulus (i.e., message) characteristics, and situational characteristics.

A. Individual Characteristics

There are numerous individual characteristics that affect the interpretation of a piece of information. Perhaps the two most important factors are the individual's level of involvement with the topic of the message, and her prior knowledge about and experience with the topic. An individual that is highly involved in purchasing a new car is likely to read magazine ads and brochures about automobiles in detail, and perhaps read them several times, whereas a person that is just thinking about purchasing a new car (i.e., moderately involved with the topic) may just glance at them and make a mental note of the brand name and model. A person that is not interested in purchasing a new car (i.e., not involved with the decision) may flip through the magazine without even pausing at the new car advertisements.

A person's prior knowledge about and experience with a topic also determine how he interprets information. A person with a great deal of knowledge about a particular topic may find it easier to interpret a piece of information about the topic than an individual who has very little knowledge about the topic. For example, an auto mechanic is more likely to understand detailed information about a car's engine (e.g., compression ratios, torque curves, and displacement) than someone without such expert knowledge.

If the consumer without a great deal of prior knowledge is highly involved with a particular purchase decision, she is likely to actively attempt to comprehend the information by asking someone with expert knowledge to explain it to them. In this case, learning takes place. In a consumer context, learning occurs when an individual acquires the knowledge or experience necessary to make a decision that satisfies his or her needs or desires.

B. Stimulus Characteristics

Stimulus characteristics also determine how an individual processes information. Stimulus characteristics include source and message characteristics. Source characteristics include source credibility and the attractiveness of the source. Messages from credible sources are more likely to be believed than messages from noncredible sources. Credibility is based on expertise, objectivity, and trustworthiness. If you were buying a used car from someone you did not know, you would be more likely to believe a mechanic that you have dealt with for a long time if he tells you the car is in good condition than you are the person trying to sell you the car.

The attractiveness of the source also affects how the message is processed. Attractiveness can be based on physical appearance or on social status. A message from a physically attractive source is more likely to be processed than is one from an unattractive source. It is not an accident that people appearing in advertisements are generally physically attractive. Social status refers to the person's notoriety and reputation. A message from someone that is well known and highly respected is more likely to be processed than a message from someone that is not well known or respected. For this reason, celebrities are often used to endorse products even though the product is not related to their claim to fame (e.g., Joe DiMaggio and Mr. Coffee).

C. Message Characteristics

Message characteristics are basically concerned with how the information is presented. The most basic characteristics are whether the message is verbal, visual, or some combination of the two. Visual messages tend to be processed differently from verbal messages. Visual messages generally try to create a feeling in the individual whereas verbal messages generally try to create knowledge or change beliefs (however, this is not always the case).

Within verbal messages, there are several characteristics that influence how the message is processed and what is learned from it. These characteristics include whether an argument should be one-sided or two-sided, a conclusion should be drawn, and a competitor's product should be mentioned. One-sided arguments present only one side of an issue (e.g., only the good features of a particular make of automobile). This can cause the individual to form his or her own counter-arguments to those presented in the message (e.g., if the car has all of those features, it must cost a lot of money) thereby reducing the persuasive effectiveness of the message. However, if both sides of the argument are presented, the individual may not develop counter-arguments and may find the message more persuasive. Of course, the effectiveness of presenting both sides of an argument depends on the nature of the arguments and the product. [*See* PERSUASION.]

Messages that explicitly draw a conclusion lessen the possibility that the individual will miss the point of the message. However, it is often the case that an individual will be persuaded more strongly by a message that does not explicitly draw a conclusion. In these cases, the individual processes the message and arrives at a conclusion based on his or her own thought processes. People are generally more likely to be persuaded by the results of their own thinking than they are by what somebody tells them. For example, a message about a car that stresses its safety features, but does not explicitly say that the car is safe, will allow the consumer to conclude on his or her own that the car is safe, and this belief may be held more strongly than if the message had just said the car is safe. Of course, this strategy runs the risk of having the individual draw the wrong conclusion.

Explicitly mentioning a competitor's product in a message can have both advantages and disadvantages. For a superior product, it may be advantageous to directly compare it against the inferior rivals. Obviously, such a strategy would be disadvantageous for inferior products. For well-known brands, it may not be advantageous to compare the brand against lesser known rivals since doing so increases awareness of the rival brands. New brands, however, may find it quite useful to explicitly position themselves as similar or superior to well-known brands. The area of comparative advertising is complex, and lately has come under close scrutiny from the courts because of potentially misleading or false statements made about a competitor's product.

D. Situational Characteristics

Situational factors can affect the way a person processes information. These factors include the emotional state, or mood, of the individual, and the physical environment in which the individual processes the information. For example, a person in a sad or lonely mood is quite likely to process a message differently from a person in a happy mood. The person in the sad mood may react negatively to the message, whereas the person in the happy mood may react positively to the message. The effects of the physical environment on information processing are fairly obvious. A person that is distracted from processing the information is not likely to process the information as thoroughly as a person that is not distracted.

E. Memory

Once the information has been processed, the individual must decide whether to retain it or discard it. If the information is to be retained, then it must be transferred to long-term memory. There are several models of memory, but the most popular one characterizes memory as having a short-term and a long-term storage component. The short-term memory store is where incoming stimuli are processed. (This does not mean that there is a physical location in one's head called short-term memory; it is just a convenient way of representing mental processes.) Short-term memory is characterized as having a limited capacity for handling information. The typical individual can actively keep track of about five to seven "chunks" of information at one time. A chunk is merely a combination of pieces of relevant information. For example, the consumer processing information about automobiles could keep track of about five to seven brands and some associated attributes (e.g., price and gas mileage). If the consumer attempts to process more information, he is likely to become confused. [*See* CHUNKING; MEMORY.]

If the individual wishes to retain the information, it must be transferred from short-term memory to long-term memory. To do this, the individual must first rehearse the information. Rehearsal involves mentally repeating the information so that it can be kept in short-term memory long enough to be encoded. If the information is not rehearsed, it is quickly lost from short-term memory. Encoding the information means that the individual assigns a phrase or image to the information so that it can be stored in long-term memory. Storage involves organizing the information in long-term memory. Long-term memory is generally viewed as having unlimited capacity for storing information. Once the information is stored in memory, if the individual wishes to use it, it must be retrieved into short-term memory, and, if necessary, go through the entire process again.

One interesting point about long-term memory is that forgetting is generally not viewed as a loss of information from long-term memory, but rather a failure to retrieve it. That is, the individual still retains the information in memory but cannot retrieve it. Most people have experienced the phenomenon of not being able to immediately recall some piece of information (e.g., the name of their second grade teacher), and then having it suddenly "pop" into memory. This is viewed as a failure to retrieve the information that is eventually overcome.

The multiple stores model of memory discussed above is not the only model of memory. Another popular model of memory is the activation model of memory. In this model, memory is viewed as a single entity, but only certain parts of it can be activated at any one time. The processing of incoming information takes place in the activated portion. The amount of memory that is currently activated depends on the nature of the task being performed, with more difficult tasks requiring greater processing effort or capacity, which results in greater activation. This model is not inconsistent with the multiple stores model. In fact, if short-term memory is viewed as the activation of some part of long-term memory, then the multiple stores model can be thought of as an activation model of memory.

F. Summary of Information Processing

Information processing is the process by which an individual converts an incoming message into some sort of usable information. The next step in the consumer behavior sequence is to use the information to form an opinion about the topic of the message. In other words, the individual is now ready to form an attitude about some object or set of objects. These attitudes will be instrumental in deciding which good or service is most likely to satisfy his or her needs, and therefore which one she is most likely to purchase.

III. ATTITUDES

As stated earlier, attitudes have been a central focus of research in consumer behavior for a long time. One of the primary reasons for this is that attitudes tend to be very useful predictors of behavior, and predicting behavior is an important task in both theoretical and applied areas of consumer research. This section will discuss what an attitude is, how attitudes are formed and changed, and how attitudes relate to behavior.

A. Definition and Models of Attitudes

The most common definition of attitude is that it is "a learned predisposition to respond in a consistently favorable or unfavorable manner with respect to a given object." There are three important aspects of this definition that should be discussed in more detail. First, attitudes are learned. That is, a person is not born with an already existing set of attitudes. Second, attitudes have intensity. This means that a person's attitudes can vary from positive to negative. Third, attitudes have an object. In other words, an attitude has to be about something. Attitude research in consumer psychology is concerned with how a consumer learns his or her attitudes about goods or services and how these attitudes affect purchase behavior with respect to the good or service (i.e., the attitude object).

There are several models of attitudes. The classical model of attitudes assumes that an attitude has three components. In this model, attitudes are viewed as being composed of a cognitive component, an affective component, and a conative component. The cognitive component is based on what the person knows or believes about the attitude object. This knowledge can come either from direct experience with the object or from information obtained from other sources. For example, a consumer's cognitive component about a new car he is considering purchasing may include the following:

(1) it is a luxury car, (2) it is high priced, (3) it has lots of extra features, and (4) it is a prestigious brand.

The affective component of attitude consists of the consumer's feelings about the attitude object. These feelings tend to be evaluative. These evaluative feelings can be very specific with respect to the attitude object, or they can be general overall evaluations. Examples of specific evaluations about a new car might be: (1) I like luxury cars, (2) I do not like the high price, (3) having lots of extra features is good, and (4) the prestige of the brand does not matter. Note that for two attributes, luxury car and extra features, the evaluations are positive, for price the evaluation is negative, and for prestige the evaluation is relatively neutral. Thus, the evaluations do not have to be all positive or negative. The affective component can also be a general overall evaluation of the attitude object such as "I really like this car."

The conative component of attitudes reflects the likelihood of an individual to behave in a particular manner with respect to the attitude object. For this reason, it is often referred to as the behavioral component of attitudes. The conative component of a person's attitude about a particular brand of luxury automobile would be illustrated by the person visiting several dealers that sell that brand, taking one for a test drive, and talking to a salesperson about getting a good deal on the price.

While the tri-component model of attitude is often viewed as having all three components occurring simultaneously, a recent conceptualization views the three components as sequential. The three components are typically viewed as starting with cognition, which leads to affect, which in turn leads to conation. In other words, a person's knowledge and beliefs about the attitude object determine whether she likes the object, which in turn influences her behavior with respect to the object. In the new car purchase scenario, if the person believes the car is a luxury car and he likes luxury cars, then he is more likely to buy the car than is a person that likes luxury cars but does not believe the model is a luxury car, or a person that believes the model is a luxury car but does not like luxury cars. In this model, attitude tends to be more narrowly defined as simply the affective component.

B. Attitude Formation and Change

As stated earlier, an individual is not born with a set of attitudes. Attitudes must be learned. The two major theories of learning are classical and instru-mental conditioning. Attitudes can be learned through either mechanism, but the mechanisms are quite different.

Classical conditioning is based on the premise that repeated paring of an object that does not elicit the desired response with an object that does elicit the desired response will eventually lead to either object being able to elicit the response. In Pavlov's experiments, he was able to make dogs salivate at the sound of a bell by repeatedly ringing the bell each time the dogs were fed. The dogs eventually learned to associate the bell with being fed, and therefore began to salivate when the bell was rung even though no food was present. For consumers, the same thing can happen. For example, most people would associate the name Cadillac with a luxury automobile. This association came about through classical conditioning. Cadillac has repeatedly paired itself with the idea of being a luxury car through its advertising and marketing strategy to the point that when most people think of luxury cars, they think of Cadillac. The use of Joe DiMaggio in the Mr. Coffee ads is another example of attempting to create a positive attitude toward the product based on classical conditioning. By repeatedly pairing a well-known and respected celebrity with a product that people are unlikely to have an attitude about, marketers hope that some of the attitude toward the celebrity will be transferred to the product. [See CLASSICAL CONDITIONING.]

Instrumental conditioning causes attitudes to be formed on the basis of trial and error. In other words, a person performs a certain behavior with respect to an object, and then based on that incident or a series of similar incidents, forms an attitude toward that object. If the behavior results in a positive outcome, the attitude is likely to be favorable, and if the outcome is negative the attitude is likely to be unfavorable. Thus, unlike classical conditioning, in instrumental conditioning, behavior precedes attitude formation. For example, a consumer may try a new fast food restaurant, and, based on this or several visits, forms either a positive or negative attitude toward the restaurant. [See OPERANT LEARNING.]

Once attitudes are formed, the next question is how can they be changed. Attitudes are changed by persuasive messages, and these persuasive messages are processed using information-processing mechanisms discussed above. The manipulation of source characteristics (e.g., source credibility and attractiveness) and message characteristics (e.g., one-sided versus two-sided arguments) in order to change a person's attitude about a particular object is a major area of interest in both theoretical and applied areas of consumer research. Most of these strategies have already been discussed in the section on information processing and in the discussion of classical and instrumental conditioning, and will not be repeated here.

However, one model of attitude change that does deserve some mention is the Elaboration Likelihood Model (ELM). While this model is too complicated to discuss in detail, the basic assumptions can be described. The ELM assumes that persuasion occurs along one of two routes. The central route to persuasion results in relatively long-term attitude change. This attitude change is based on a careful analysis of the message content (e.g., strength of the arguments presented). The peripheral route results in relatively short-term attitude change, and tends to be based on message cues (e.g., number of arguments presented as opposed to the content of the arguments themselves). Which route is operative depends on numerous factors. For example, a person that is highly involved in a purchase decision may examine relevant information fairly critically, and thus be persuaded along the central route. A person that is not highly involved in the purchase decision may simply note the number of arguments presented in the information and use that as a cue to form his or her attitude. This would result in persuasion along the peripheral route.

C. Attitude–Behavior Relationships

One of the main reasons attitudes and attitude change are so important in consumer behavior research is that attitudes can be used to predict behavior. The prediction of behavior based on attitudes is not perfect, and there have been many attempts to understand exactly how attitudes and behavior are related and how prediction can be improved.

One of the most important improvements in using attitudes to predict behavior has been to change the focus of the attitude under study. So far, attitudes have been discussed as being about objects. However, attitudes about a particular object have been shown not to be very good predictors of behavior with respect to that object. For example, a consumer considering the purchase of a new car may have a very favorable attitude toward Cadillacs, but have very little likelihood of actually purchasing one because they are out of his or her feasible price range.

However, by examining a person's attitude toward the particular behavior instead of the object, prediction can be improved. Staying with the new car purchasing example, instead of measuring the consumer's attitude toward Cadillacs, the consumer's attitude toward the act of purchasing a Cadillac is measured. When this attitude is measured, it may reveal that the consumer thinks buying a Cadillac would be extravagant, unaffordable, and foolish. Given this attitude, the consumer is not likely to purchase a Cadillac even though she may hold a very favorable attitude about Cadillac automobiles.

Another improvement in using attitudes to predict behavior was the realization that many other factors affect the performance of a behavior besides attitudes. One of the main determinants of a person's behavior is their intention to perform that behavior. The relationship between a person's intention to perform a particular behavior and the actual performance of that behavior is not perfect because of the other factors that can influence behavior. For example, a consumer may have very strong intentions to buy a new car, but then discover that the particular car he desires has been sold, it may take a long time to order from the manufacturer, or he may lose his job and decide to wait until his financial situation improves. Therefore, since so many uncontrollable factors may affect behavior, attitudes are frequently used to predict intention to perform a particular behavior rather than the actual behavior itself. If a person has a positive attitude toward performing some behavior, her intentions to perform that behavior are likely to be quite high, whereas a person with a negative attitude toward performing some behavior is likely to have a very low, if any, intention to perform the behavior.

The prediction of intention to perform a behavior based on attitudes toward performing that behavior can be strengthened by observing some general guidelines for measuring attitudes. The first guideline concerns the timing of the measure. In general, the shorter the time interval between the measure of attitudes and the likely performance of the actual behavior, the better the prediction. This allows less time for intervening variables to occur that may degrade the prediction.

A second guideline useful in improving the prediction of behavior based on attitudes is to ensure that both are measured at the same level of specificity. For example, knowing that a consumer has a positive attitude toward purchasing a luxury automobile does not necessarily mean that the individual has a positive attitude toward purchasing a Cadillac. In this case, using the positive attitude toward purchasing a luxury car to predict the purchase of a particular brand of luxury car may be quite misleading. However, using the person's attitude toward purchasing a Cadillac is likely to produce a better prediction of intentions to purchase a Cadillac since both measures are at the same level of specificity.

D. Summary

This section has provided a brief introduction to the nature of attitudes and how attitudes can be used to predict consumer behavior. Now that the consumer has processed the information and formed an attitude, she is ready to make a decision about which good or service to purchase. How this decision gets made is the topic of the next and last section.

IV. CONSUMER DECISION MAKING

Once the consumer has obtained and processed enough relevant information, he is ready to make a decision as to which good or service to purchase in order to satisfy his needs or desires. In order to make a decision, some sort of strategy has to be selected. These strategies are commonly called decision rules. These decision rules can be grouped into two broad categories, compensatory and noncompensatory.

To arrive at a decision using a compensatory rule, the consumer evaluates each brand on all of the important attributes and arrives at a "weighted score" for each brand. This weighted score is arrived at based on the consumer's evaluation of the brand's performance on each attribute and the relative importance of each attribute. The consumer would then choose the brand with the highest score. In compensatory rules, a negative evaluation of a particular attribute, or feature, may be offset, or compensated for, by a positive evaluation on another attribute of the same brand. In contrast, noncompensatory rules do not allow for tradeoffs of positive and negative evaluations, and brands with negative evaluations would simply be removed from further consideration.

The implementation of these rules involves having the consumer assign numerical values to the importance of each attribute and to the evaluation of each brand's performance on that attribute. Then the consumer performs some mental algebra and arrives at a "score" for each brand. This does not mean, however, that consumers actually go through this process each time they make a purchase decision. Instead, these models serve as representations, or approximations, of the process consumers go through when making a decision. In fact, it is not clear which rules are used by consumers in particular purchase decisions. Nevertheless, the models described below do provide useful insight into understanding the consumer decision-making process.

A. Noncompensatory Rules

The noncompensatory decision rules tend to be the simplest to implement. When consumers are not motivated to process information about a product because they are not highly involved with the decision, or they are not familiar with a product class, and therefore are not sure how to evaluate it, they tend to use noncompensatory rules. There are several common noncompensatory rules.

The conjunctive rule requires the consumer to establish cutoff points for each relevant attribute in the product class. In order for a particular brand to be considered acceptable, it must surpass the cutoff point on each attribute. If a brand falls below a cutoff point on any attribute, it would be eliminated from further consideration. The major drawback to using this model is that it does not guarantee that a single brand will emerge as the choice. Since more than one brand may surpass the cutoff points, some other decision rule will have to be implemented to arrive at a unique choice.

The disjunctive decision rule is somewhat similar to the conjunctive rule in that minimum acceptable cutoff points are established for each attribute. However, unlike the conjunctive rule which required the brand to meet the cutoff point on all attributes, the disjunctive rule would consider a brand acceptable if it meets the cutoff on any attribute. In other words, as long as a brand meets the minimum cutoff on one attribute, it is considered acceptable regardless of whether it meets the cutoffs on the other attributes. Like the conjunctive rule, this rule also allows more than one brand to be considered acceptable, so another rule must be applied if a unique choice is desired.

The lexicographic rule is a little more complex, but it does have the advantage of providing a unique choice. To implement the lexicographic decision rule, the consumer must first rank all of the relevant attributes in terms of their importance. Then the consumer selects the brand that performs the best on the most important attribute. If two or more brands perform equally well on the most important attribute, the second most important attribute is considered. This process is repeated until one brand performs better than the rest.

A similar rule, called elimination by aspects, requires the consumer to rank each attribute in terms of importance, and to establish cutoff points on each attribute. Unlike the lexicographic rule which looks for the best brand on the most important attribute, elimination by aspects looks at all of the brands that meet the cutoff point on the most important attribute. This process is repeated until one brand remains.

B. Compensatory Rules

Compensatory decision rules allow the consumer to balance out some undesirable attributes with high scores on desirable attributes. Consumers that use this type of decision rule tend to be familiar with the product class or highly involved with the purchase decision. The compensatory rule is essentially the importance of a particular attribute multiplied by the evaluation of the brand on that attribute, summed across all of the relevant attributes. This sum of products represents the consumer's overall rating of that particular brand. In this type of decision rule, a negative evaluation on an attribute can be offset by a positive evaluation on a more important attribute, allowing the brand to have an overall positive evaluation.

C. Summary

The rules described above provide useful models of the consumer decision-making process. There is no guarantee that these rules are actually used in the exact manner described. In fact, there are many instances where such decision rules would not be expected to be used at all. For example, if the consumer is purchasing a brand from a product class that she has purchased many times before, such rules would not be necessary. Instead, the consumer would rely on information stored in long-term memory to simply retrieve the name of the desired brand. Nevertheless, the rules are useful in situations where a choice is being made among unfamiliar brands or in an unfamiliar product class.

V. OVERALL SUMMARY

This article provided a brief introduction into three areas of consumer psychology. The section on information processing described how consumers obtain and process information relevant to making a decision. The section on attitudes described how consumer's evaluations of products are related to their behavior with respect to those products. Finally, some basic models of consumer decision rules were discussed. While these three areas are vitally important to the study of consumer psychology, they are by no means all of the topics that are important in the area of consumer psychology. Indeed, there are numerous other areas that were not discussed in this article. Nevertheless, this brief overview should have piqued the reader's curiosity enough to cause him or her to pursue the fascinating discipline of consumer psychology in more detail.

Bibliography

Bettman, J. R. (1979). An Information Processing Theory of Consumer Behavior." Addison-Wesley, Reading, MA.

Fishbein, M., and Ajzen, I. (1975). "Belief, Attitude, Intention, and Behavior." Addison-Wesley, Reading, MA.

Hawkins, D., Best, R., and Coney, K. (1986). "Consumer Behavior." Business Publications, Inc., Plano, TX.

Holbrook, M. B. (1987). What is consumer research? *J. Consumer Res.* **14**(1), 128–132.

Kassarjian, H. H., and Robertson, T. S. (1991). "Perspectives in Consumer Behavior." Prentice-Hall, Englewood Cliffs, NJ.

Petty, R. E., and Cacioppo, J. T. (1986). "Communication and Persuasion: Central and Peripheral Routes to Persuasion." Springer-Verlag, New York.

Robertson, T., and Kassarjian, H. H. (1991). "Handbook of Consumer Behavior." Prentice-Hall, Englewood Cliffs, NJ.

CONTROL

Beth A. Morling and Susan T. Fiske
University of Massachusetts at Amherst

Glossary

Control The ability intentionally to influence environmental, psychological, or behavioral events.
Mental control Control over one's own thoughts and feelings.
Outcome control Control of exteral events motivationally relevant to the self.

CONTROL, the ability intentionally to influence environmental, psychological, or behavioral events, appears to be fundamental to people's well-being. People who feel they have control also perceive that they are competent, that they can influence events, and that they can predict what happens to them. People who temporarily feel out of control may be upset that they cannot alter events, and may engage in compensatory behaviors to restore a feeling of control. People who consistently feel out of control may give up, feel helpless, and cope less well with adversity. Psychological research in Western industrialized cultures indicates that people who feel in control live longer, suffer from fewer serious illnesses, and have better psychological health than people who do not feel in control. And regardless of culture, people everywhere strive to influence, learn about, and gain competence in culturally relevant areas of experience. Robert White's concept, "competence motivation" or "effectance," perhaps best captures this universal goal of control. From infancy, all animals exhibit a fundamental motivation to explore, act upon, and master their environment. People's motivation for effectance is reflected in their desire to control events and have an impact on the world.

I. INTRODUCTION TO CONTROL RESEARCH

Because of its fundamental importance to people, control plays an important role in theories of human behavior. Many psychologists view control as a motivation for human action; others cite it as an important individual difference. Psychologists study control from two perspectives: (a) individual differences in control, especially as it relates to the self-concept and psychological health, and (b) environmental effects on control, including contexts that make people feel out of control and people's reactions to control deprivation.

Control can be directed internally or externally (toward the self or toward others) in order to influence different environmental or psychological events (outcomes or mental processes). Most psychological research deals with perceived outcome control, that is, people's perceived control over external, self-relevant events (for example, a student's feeling that studying will produce a passing grade, or a patient's feeling that a change in diet will affect the course of a disease). Outcome control is the focus of the first two parts of this article. Other psychological research studies mental control, people's perceived control over their own internal thoughts and feelings (for example, a dieter's attempts to avoid thinking about food, or an anxious person's intrusive worries about physical danger). Mental control is covered in the third and last section of this article. Thus, the entire article covers attempts by individuals to control their *own* outcomes and mental processes. People can also control another person's thoughts, feelings, and behavior, which psychologists call social influence, or they can control another person's outcomes, which psychologists call social power.

In this article, we first describe personality psychological approaches to own-outcome control: individual differences and correlates of feelings of outcome control. There we describe how feelings of outcome control are related to a stable self-concept and to general coping ability. We also list some of the many theories that treat an individual's sense of outcome control as an important mediating or moderating variable. Second, we describe the social psychological approach to outcome control: ways that feelings of control can be manipulated, and what people do when they feel deprived of control. There we explain that people's strategies for control involve either acting on the environment or thinking about a situation differently. In addition, we explain that when people feel control-deprived, they search for information to regain control, or they may give up trying. In the last section of the article, we describe theory related to mental control, the control over one's own thoughts and feelings. In that section, we focus on the degree of control people have over their own cognition and affect.

II. PERSONALITY APPROACHES: INDIVIDUAL DIFFERENCES IN PERCEIVED OUTCOME CONTROL

Personality approaches to control have traditionally focused on differences between people who believe they can control their own outcomes and people who believe they cannot. One of the most well-known attempts to measure these differences is Rotter's Internal–External Locus of Control construct, based in learning theory. We will explore this construct and its limitations in some depth, because many of the same assumptions, predictions, and criticisms can apply to constructs to be described later.

A. Locus of Control Theory

According to Rotter, people with an internal locus of control (LOC) perceive contingencies between their behavior and subsequent events (such as reinforcements), whereas people with an external locus of control do not. Implied in the construct is that people's behavior will, to some extent, be determined by their control expectancies. Rotter's Internal–External Locus of Control scale contains 23 forced-choice items measuring the extent to which

people believe that the things that happen to them are caused by their own actions or are caused by external forces such as chance, luck, or powerful others. People who score low on the scale have an internal locus of control, meaning they believe their outcomes result from their own efforts. People who score high on the scale have an external locus of control, meaning they believe their outcomes result from environmental forces. Importantly, the scale, and the construct itself, concerns people's *beliefs* about outcome contingencies; it does not concern the *actual* correlation between people's actions and subsequent events.

Much research has explored social correlates of the LOC construct, and the studies suggest that people who have an internal LOC are more likely to resist persuasion, to try to act on their environments, and to place a high value on achievement. Studies show that people with an internal LOC conform less to external standards, have higher self-esteem, are more creative, are more optimistic, and persevere longer at difficult tasks. Internal LOC is related to political activism among students, to knowledge of prison regulations among inmates, and to knowledge of one's physical condition among hospital patients. Most researchers have concluded from these studies that an internal LOC is more psychologically healthy and adaptive than an external LOC.

Rotter's locus of control construct has been extremely widely used in personality, social, and health psychology, but it has also been criticized. Behavioral correlates (such as activism and achievement) of LOC often fail to replicate in different studies. And many writers have debated the construct, addressing its implication that an internal LOC is always preferable and an external LOC is always devalued. Furthermore, many studies show that lower social classes tend to score in the external direction, and thus more prone to an external LOC's achievement "deficits." One common critique separates locus of control beliefs into two separate constructs. One, perceived personal control, addresses individuals' beliefs about control in their own lives. The other, control ideology, is an individual's philosophy about how rewards are distributed in the larger world. Critics hold that the two kinds of control are independent. Therefore, for example, someone from a lower socio-economic status might hold an internal control ideology that individuals, in general, should be rewarded for their actions, but may also have an external sense of personal control reflecting that, in the past, his or her own actions have gone unrewarded.

Others have criticized the explicit bias toward an internal locus of control on the grounds that an accurate assessment of reward contingencies is more important than whether a person's LOC is internal or external. For some people, particularly those in lower social classes, an external locus of control may be an accurate picture of their worlds. Furthermore, an internal locus of control can be used by middle-or upper-class people to justify their position in life; thus, advantaged people hold a philosophy that one deserves one's superior position. The LOC construct (and also the related constructs of self-efficacy and learned helplessness, discussed below) may ignore or oversimplify the social contexts that surround individuals and influence their feelings of control. Control theories may be biased by an individualistic context, common to Western cultures, in which individuals are expected to stand out and make their own way instead of working together and fitting in with others.

B. Related Control Theories

Several personality constructs are related to the locus of control construct (Table I). To the extent that they are similar to locus of control, they are also subject to the same criticisms for being biased toward internality. Two of these theories (self-efficacy and learned helplessness) treat individual differ-

TABLE I
Summary of Major Personality Approaches to Individual Differences in Outcome Control

Major theorist	Construct	Variables affecting and affected by feelings of control
Rotter	Locus of control	Perceived contingency between one's actions and subsequent events leads to feelings of internal control
Seligman	Learned helplessness	Perceived lack of contingency between one's efforts and subsequent aversive events leads to feelings of no control
Bandura	Self-efficacy	Perceived ability to enact a behavioral outcome enhances feelings of personal control

ences in outcome control as a central variable, much like locus of control theory.

1. Self-Efficacy Theory

First, Bandura's self-efficacy theory addresses people's feelings of competence regarding an activity. Like locus of control theory, self-efficacy theory studies how people perceive their own abilities to act successfully in the world. If people feel they will be successful at an activity, they express agency, initiative, and achievement; i.e., they put more active, persistent, effort into that activity and are more likely to succeed. Self-efficacy is related to setting high goals for oneself, being optimistic about achieving those goals, and being motivated to try again if progress toward the goal is frustrated. Bandura explicity relates self-efficacy to the ability to control and predict one's outcomes. Bandura extends the self-efficacy construct to groups, with a parallel theory of collective efficacy, which refers to groups acting together to achieve some outcome, for example, social change. Like self-efficacy, collective efficacy involves agency, initiative, and achievement, and describes how groups can influence outcomes that are related to the welfare of the group or the larger world. [*See* SELF-EFFICACY.]

2. Learned Helplessness Theory

Learned helplessness, first studied in dogs who became passive in an experiment in which they received uncontrollable shocks, is also used to describe people who perceive their own outcomes to be uncontrollable. Because learned-helpless people do not feel they have control over outside events, they act passive and persist less in activities. Learned-helpless people resemble those with an external locus of control; they do not perceive a contingency between their efforts and their outcomes. The learned helplessness construct has been used as a model for depression. [*See* LEARNED HELPLESSNESS.]

3. Control as Moderator or Mediator

Scores of psychological theories include an individual's feelings of outcome control as a variable that moderates people's behavior (i.e., people who feel in control act one way and people who do not feel in control act another way) or mediates people's behavior (i.e., one variable influences people's feelings of control, which then influence a third variable). Still other theories view people's strivings for control as motivation for their behavior or beliefs about the world. There are simply too many theories that use control to catalog them all here; briefly mentioning the scope of the theories will suffice. For instance, research on stressful life events has studied how feelings of control can sometimes, but not always, help people cope. Other theories that focus on everyday life have used control to predict what people will do, such as when they will act on their attitudes, attend to their environments, feel good about things they have done, or try hard at an academic task. Still other theories have used the desire for prediction and control to explain why people tend to act in certain ways, such as why they choose particular romantic partners. The wide range of theories that have found control to be a useful predictive and explanatory variable attests to how important it is to people to influence environmental, psychological, and behavioral events.

III. SOCIAL PSYCHOLOGICAL APPROACHES: SITUATIONAL DETERMINANTS OF OUTCOME CONTROL

Whereas personality theories of control describe how people differ in their relatively stable, dispositional feelings of outcome control, social psychological theories of outcome control focus on more temporary, changeable feelings of control. In particular, they focus on the techniques people use to feel in control, the effects of control feelings in stressful situations, and the effects of control deprivation on people's behavior.

A. Ways of Feeling in Control: Techniques for Mastering the Situation

This section first addresses six major avenues to feeling in control, first identified by Suzanne Thompson. Each of these has been related to how people cope in stressful situations. Although there are six main control behaviors, they can all be summed up in two general techniques: acting to influence an aversive situation or thinking about the situation differently (Table II).

First, in *behavior control* people take steps to end an event, make it less likely, or change its timing or intensity. An example of behavioral control is people having the opportunity to press a button to control the intensity of an impending shock or loud noise,

or a cancer patient having control over when to administer his or her own pain medication. Behavior control can still be effective even if it is illusory (that is, even if a person never uses the response and does not know whether it would actually reduce the loudness of a noise). Perceptions of behavior control reduce people's distress before and after an aversive stimulus. People with behavioral control can also tolerate higher levels of the aversive stimulus. However, it is less clear whether people feel less distress during the event as a result of behavioral control.

In *cognitive control,* people think differently about an impending or ongoing noxious event through (a) avoidant strategies, for example, directing attention away from the stressful aspects of the event; or (b) nonavoidant strategies, for example, coping with the event by focusing on benefits of the event, conjuring images inconsistent with the stressful event, or talking calmly to the self. For example, a beginning graduate student might focus on the benefits, instead of the trials, of years of graduate training, or a person might mentally withdraw from a fight with a romantic partner. In general, cognitive control appears to help people cope with stressful events before, during, and after the event. However, specific kinds of cognitive control appear to help in particular ways: Mental withdrawal appears more effective in reducing pre-event distress, whereas reinterpretation (focusing on benefits) reduces postevent distress more effectively.

Decision control refers to the ability to make decisions about the type of aversive event, its onset, or its timing. For example, a patient might be given a choice between two kinds of surgery, or a student may be given a choice of several courses to take in fulfilling a requirement. In some cases, decision control can be illusory, when the choices are presented in such a way that people almost always choose one particular option. Decision control appears effective if the choice leads to positive outcomes (e.g., the surgery is successful) or to outcomes that can be reinterpreted with dissonance-reduction strategies (e.g., the chosen class is not really as boring as the other students say). But it is unclear whether decision control helps people cope when the outcome of the choice is decidedly unfavorable (e.g., when the surgery is unsuccessful).

When people gather information about an aversive event, they practice *information control*. The information can include details about how the event will feel, how long it will last, or what will cause it.

TABLE II
Summary of Types of Control and Their Effects on Adjustment to Stress

Type of control	Definition	Example	Effects
Behavior control	Acting in a concrete way to reduce aversiveness of a negative event	Pressing a button to reduce the intensity of a loud noise	Reduces pre-event anxiety, increases tolerance for the aversive event, reduces postevent distress
Cognitive control	Thinking about an aversive event differently or focusing on nonnoxious features of event	Focusing on benefits of a noxious medical procedure while it is occurring	Appears to improve coping with all phases of an aversive event
Decision control	Ability to make decisions regarding timing, onset, or type of aversive event	Choosing between two types of surgery	Is beneficial if the outcome of the event is favorable, but may not help if outcome is unfavorable
Information control	Obtaining or seeking information about details of an aversive event (e.g., sensations, duration, timing)	Learning the side effects of surgery	Sensation information and procedure information reduce the stress of an aversive event
Retrospective control	Beliefs that one can control an event that already occurred	Believing that one could have prevented an accident	Effects are yet unknown, may improve adjustment to some noxious events but not others
Control achieved through mastering the self. Techniques: predictive control, vicarious control, illusory control, and interpretive control	Bringing thoughts and behaviors in line with environmental forces	Carefully learning what might happen, aligning oneself with a powerful group, accepting what fate brings, or viewing events in beneficial terms	May help adjustment to events when situation mastery is not possible; may be a culturally proscribed control expectancy

Source: Fiske, S. T., and Taylor, S. E. (1991). "Social Cognition," 2nd ed. McGraw-Hill, New York.

Having a general understanding of what will happen, and why, appears to help people adjust to and cope with noxious events. Information control may be an easy way to implement control when more direct forms of control are less possible. In this particular way, it is related to predictive control, a form of mastering the self (described below).

In *retrospective control,* people construct control-related beliefs about an event that has already occurred. For example, a rape victim might blame herself for not locking her windows or for walking alone at night. Retrospective control beliefs might help victims feel more control over the event and over future recurrences of the event, perhaps restoring a positive sense of self. Another kind of retrospective control concerns beliefs about how replicable, rather than how controllable, a past event is. For example, cancer patients might not feel they had control over the onset of their disease, but may feel they can prevent a recurrence by changing their diet. Retro-spective control is still relatively unstudied in social psychology.

B. Ways of Feeling in Control: Techniques for Mastering the Self

Control attempts in which individuals attempt to master the self (traditionally called secondary control) differ from the previous five types of control. These five, behavior control, decision control, retrospective control, and, to a lesser extent, information control and cognitive control, are all examples of attempting control through mastering the situation (also called primary control). When people master the situation, they take action to bring the environment in line with their wishes. But when people attempt control by mastering the self, they do not attempt to influence the environment; instead, they attempt to bring themselves in line with it. Whereas the targets of mastering the situation are other people, objects, or environmental conditions, the targets of mastering the self are the *self's* expectations, goals, perceptions, or interpretations. Some theorists suggest that people from Western cultures are more likely to attempt situation mastery and that people from Eastern cultures are more likely to attempt self mastery; however, both kinds of control are prevalent in both cultures.

Mastering the self can take many forms. In *predictive control,* people attempt to avoid uncertainty by accurately predicting a future event. For example, they may learn their status in an impending social situation and the relevant rules of etiquette to avoid feeling unprepared or uncomfortable. (Note that predictive control is similar to information control, described earlier). In *vicarious control,* people align themselves closely with people or groups who have power, in order to participate indirectly in their control. For example, people may derive feelings of self-esteem by their close alignment with a successful work group. In *illusory control,* people align themselves with chance and accept their fate. People practice illusory control when they accept streaks of good and bad luck as they come. Finally, in *interpretive control,* people perceive events as purposeful and meaningful. An example of interpretive control is viewing a failure as an opportunity for growth, or interpreting a chronic anxiety problem in more positive terms (e.g., it makes one more vigilant and alert).

Theory on self-mastery control techniques is an important complement to the situation mastery research. It suggests that people can feel in control even when opportunities to alter the environment are unavailable. Control theories focusing on self mastery grew out of cross-cultural research in much the same way that critiques of the personality approaches to control (see Section II) reacted to findings of external control expectancies in lower social classes. In particular, some cultures appear to encourage self-mastery control expectancies by emphasizing a close relationship with one's social group. In such cultures, people may be encouraged to fit in and go along rather than stand out and make their own way without the group. Similarly, systems in society may reduce opportunities for situation mastery for people from lower social classes. Self-mastery implies that even when people's actual opportunities to alter the environment are low (as may be the case for lower social classes or in cultures where social behaviors are more strictly proscribed), people can still feel in control by altering the self or

identifying with a group. It therefore brings a broader and more universal perspective to control theory.

Although much of the social psychological work on control has focused on how feelings of control can help buffer stress, some research indicates that control is not always adaptive. In some situations, having control can actually cause higher distress. One such situation occurs when people have high levels of control but low levels of perceived self-efficacy. A person who is placed into a powerful position may have high control, but may feel incapable of fulfilling the responsibilities of the position, creating significant distress. Another situation occurs when people have too much control, so that the amount of control becomes overwhelming (for example, a medical procedure in which a patient is given too much information about the experience *and* given choices about treatment). Attempts at control can also be stressful when they require much more effort than not attempting control. Control is also aversive when efforts at control are unsuccessful. Some people may be able to identify situations when attempts at control are likely to be effective and situations when they are not, an ability that is part of a more general theory of coping called constructive thinking. Finally, some people prefer to cope with negative situations by repressing them. For these people, control options are aversive.

C. Effects of Control Deprivation

The previous discussion has focused on the effects of perceived control on people's coping with aversive life events. In social psychology, perceived control has also been tied to other psychological responses: increased information search, psychological reactance, and helplessness. These three responses are people's typical reactions to control deprivation. People can feel control-deprived when they experience a lack of contingency between their efforts and their outcomes or when they perceive a restriction of behavioral choice. Each of these three reactions and the specific type of control deprivation that typically causes them follows next.

One typical response to control deprivation is to look for more information. This *information search* likely responds to the kind of control deprivation caused by noncontingent or unpredictable outcomes. At times, control-deprived people become desperate for information, making them more susceptible to social influence and less able to process the information carefully. An indiscriminate information search can lead people to make inappropriate decisions or inaccurate predictions about their outcomes. But other times the search is more careful (and more adaptive), as when people vigilantly scan the environment.

Information search is significantly related to control motivation in impression formation. Heider, Kelley, and Jones, all original attribution theorists, unanimously proposed that people make attributions (i.e., casual judgments) about others to render the world more predictable and controllable. It follows that attributions should be especially important when control is threatened. Pittman and Heller proposed three kinds of situations in which people's feelings of control deprivation lead to more careful, information-driven impressions of others. The first occurs when people feel momentarily control-deprived, such as when they experience noncontingent feedback. Second, some interpersonal situations take control away from an individual. For example, people who are dependent on another person for an outcome (such as a reward) lose sole control over their own outcomes. Third, a situation that contains negative or surprising information threatens people's model of a predictable and benevolent world, so it also leads to increased information search. In these three situations, people respond to the lack of outcome control by paying more attention to interpersonal information and processing it more thoroughly and carefully. [See IMPRESSION FORMATION.]

Information search, then, is one typical reaction to control deprivation. Another common response is *reactance*. Reactance is most likely to occur when people's control is arbitrarily withdrawn or when people's previous freedoms are taken away. Reactance leads to anger and hostility, efforts to restore the lost freedoms, and a higher evaluation of the restricted option. For example, if a class originally had a choice between two paper topics and were then arbitrarily told to write on a particular one, the students might feel angry, might protest the action, and might also evaluate the unassigned topic as the better one. Reactance often causes physiological responses that can persist a long time and exacerbate health problems.

Another typical response to control deprivation is helplessness. In this response, people typically give in to the situation and act passively. People often act helpless when they feel that events are completely beyond their control: for example, an extremely stressful or shocking event (such as the death of a spouse) or alternatively, attempts at control that have been unsuccessful (such as repeated, vain attempts to escape an aversive situation). In addition to promoting passive behavior, helpless reactions are related to anxiety, depression, and depleted physiological reserves. Helplessness is directly related to learned helplessness theory. It also resembles the lack of persistence and low desire for achievement hypothesized in people with an external locus of control or low feelings of self-efficacy. In addition, it ties in with the theory of mindfulness, in that people who act mindlessly give up control over their environment by resorting to default levels of processing. A helpless reaction to control deprivation is therefore similar to people's more dispositional differences in low feelings of outcome control.

To summarize, social psychological approaches to outcome control have covered two domains. First, people can use a variety of strategies to feel in control, and often people's control attempts help them cope with stressful events. Second, people react to control deprivation by seeking information, reacting to restore lost freedoms, or by withdrawing effort when they perceive that they will have little impact.

Thus, the social psychological perspective on outcome control in many ways parallels the personality psychology approaches. Just as dispositional differences in control beliefs are related to perseverance, optimism, information-seeking, self-esteem, creativity, and other positive variables, social environments can create similar effects on a situationally specific (though not necessarily less potent) scale. Environments that provide choices for behavior and in which a person feels competent lead to greater personal interest, less tension, more trust, more creativity, improved mood, higher self-esteem, greater persistence, and better health. In large doses, such environments may well change people's dispositional differences in control beliefs.

Control beliefs in social environments also play a role in current theories of social cognition, the study of how people think about other people. Recently, social cognitive theorists viewed social perceivers as "cognitive misers," doing only as much mental work as they had to to get by. But currently, social perceivers are being viewed as "motivated tacticians." The current view emphasizes that people's social thinking is pragmatic: purposeful and affected by people's plans and goals. Therefore, sometimes it is in the interest of people's goals to make a careful, thoughtful impression, whereas other times, people may find a simple, "good-enough" impression suitable. Both the variations in the amount of control a situation affords and people's changing motivations for control can influence people's impression goals. In addition, social perceivers can use different degrees of controlled mental processing (discussed next) when they allocate their attention according to relevant goals. [*See* SOCIAL COGNITION.]

IV. APPROACHES TO MENTAL CONTROL

People's ability to control their thoughts and feelings varies tremendously. Some types of thinking are highly deliberate and controlled, whereas other types of thinking do not require as much effort or allow as much conscious intervention, so they qualify as less controlled processing. This section briefly describes the differences between controlled and uncontrolled (typically called automatic) mental processes. Psychological approaches to mental control appear to have little in common with the psychological approaches to outcome control mentioned in Sections I and II. Indeed, the domains of research do not overlap much, and very little research has explored the links, if any, between people's relative control over their thoughts and feelings and their control over their outcomes.

A continuum from automatic to controlled mental processes, outlined by John Bargh and James Uleman, provides a framework for a discussion of mental control. Starting at the most automatic end of the continuum, automatic processes include: preconscious automaticity, postconscious automaticity, and goal-directed automaticity. Moving toward the more controlled end of the continuum, controlled processes include: spontaneous thought, ruminations, and intentional thought. We discuss automatic and controlled thinking in separate sections; however, they are theoretically arranged on a single continuum. Criteria and forms of both automatic and controlled mental processes are presented in Table III.

A. Types of Automatic Processing

Automatic (uncontrolled) processes are so called because they are unintentional and occur without a person's awareness. They do not require cognitive capacity or mental effort to operate. Different types of automatic processes adhere to a greater or lesser extent of these criteria. *Preconscious* automaticity

TABLE III
Automatic and Controlled Mental Processes

Type of process	Criteria	Forms (corresponding to the criteria for each process)
Automatic	Process must be unintentional, involuntary, effortless, and outside awareness	Preconscious automaticity (most automatic) Postconscious automaticity Goal-dependent automaticity
Controlled	Process must be able to be started, monitored, and terminated at will	Spontaneous thought Ruminative thought Intentional thought (most controlled)

Source: Fiske, S. T., and Taylor, S. E. (1991). "Social Cognition," 2nd ed. McGraw-Hill.

is a name for the most automatic kind of mental processing, conforming to all of the criteria. When people process information preconsciously, they react immediately and spontaneously. People are not aware of a preconscious mental process. An example is subliminal encoding, where stimuli are presented at a rate too fast for conscious processing, but they are still processed and can still affect people's subsequent judgments.

A less pure form of automaticity on the continuum is called *postconscious* automaticity. This form occurs when people are aware of a stimulus in the environment, but are not aware of its effects on their mental processes. For example, people are often aware of their moods, but may not be aware that their moods affect the way they make judgments about stimuli. Similarly, sometimes activated schemas spur immediate, category-based affective responses. Such "schema-triggered affect" is postconscious in that people are aware of the stimulus, but not necessarily of their retrieval of the schema and its accompanying affective response.

An even less pure form of automaticity is *goal-dependent* automaticity. In this kind of processing, people need to initiate the processing, but once it is started, it does not require conscious effort to continue. For example, people may have a conscious goal of forming an accurate impression of another person, but their increased attention and individuating processes occur without intentional monitoring.

B. Types of Controlled Processing

Controlled processes are characterized by people's ability deliberately to stop and start them, and by people's ability consciously to monitor their progress. As with automatic processes, controlled processes adhere more or less to these criteria. The first form of controlled mental processes, which is the least controlled of the three, is *spontaneous* thought. Spontaneous thought begins without intent or awareness, but takes up cognitive capacity and can be terminated or inhibited at will. It overlaps to some extent with the least automatic of automatic mental processes, goal-dependent automaticity; indeed, the two are next to each other on the continuum from controlled to automatic processes. An example of spontaneous thought is people's rapid judgment of other people in terms of dispositional traits. People categorize others into traits relatively easily and with little cognitive effort; however, the trait judgments can be altered if people's goals or the situation changes. Therefore, spontaneous processes occur rapidly and unintentionally, but they can also be controlled.

A more controlled kind of thought is *ruminative* thought. Ruminations are controlled in that people are aware of the thoughts, but they are uncontrolled in that people are unable to end them at will. Ruminations are common when people's goals are interrupted. Ruminative thought can focus on searching for alternative means to achieve an interrupted goal, or, if alternative means are unavailable, ruminations focus on the feelings associated with the goal. It appears that as long as a goal remains unmet, ruminations continue unless people find a way to overcome the obstacle or abandon the goal altogether.

Related to rumination is a more general inability for people to prevent an unwanted thought from coming into consciousness. People have a difficult time purposefully suppressing thoughts (for example, it is difficult for a dieter to suppress thoughts of tempting foods). Furthermore, after a period of attempting to suppress a thought, people often experience a rebound, in which they think the unwanted thought more than people who had not been deliberately suppressing it. Focusing on an alternative thought during the suppression period can help prevent this rebound effect.

Thought suppression and ruminations appear prevalent in depression and coping with traumatic events. Depressed people ruminate about failures more and have more trouble suppressing negative thoughts than nondepressed people do. And people who experience negative life events often ruminate about them until they have worked them through. For these people, ruminations can be helped by intentionally focusing on the very thoughts they are trying to suppress. Talking or writing about the negative event appears to lower victims' distress, helps prevent ruminations from recurring, and attenuates medical complaints for weeks after the talking or writing. [*See* DEPRESSION.]

At the most controlled end of the continuum are *intentional* processes. When people perceive that they have choices or different interpretations of a situation, whatever choice they make can be said to be an intentional one. People's intent is especially obvious when they make a more difficult choice (one requiring more mental effort). People enact their mental intents by paying attention to the chosen alternative. For example, if a person intends to view a group of people in less stereotypical terms, he or she would consciously attend to stereotype-inconsistent information, instead of relying on the easier process of attending only to stereotype-consistent information. [*See* PREJUDICE AND STEREOTYPES.]

V. SUMMARY

In their efforts to feel in control of their worlds, people can attempt to control their outcomes or their own mental processes. People differ in the extent to which they feel their actions can alter their outcomes, a difference that personality psychologists have sometimes labeled locus of control, self-efficacy, or learned helplessness. Social psychologists have shown that people can feel in control by actually influencing an event or by changing the way they think about it. These attempts at control can help people adapt to stress and lead to improved physical health and longer life expectancy. When people's outcome control is threatened, they may seek information, protest to restore lost freedoms, or give up trying. And when people process information, they sometimes have considerable control over their thoughts and feelings, and other times they operate more automatically. People's desire for mastery and competence, reflected in their need to control events, is a primary motivating force. When this motivation is challenged, people react strongly: they fight or they give up. When it is promoted in culturally appropriate ways, people try, persist, learn, cope, and thrive.

Bibliography

Averill, J. R. (1973). Personal control over aversive stimuli and its relationship to stress. *Psychol. Bull.* **80**, 286–303.

Bandura, A. (1989). Human agency in social cognitive theory. *Am. Psychol.* **44**, 1175–1184.

Bargh, J. A. (1989). Conditional automaticity: Varieties of automatic influence on social perception and cognition. In "Unintended Thought." (J. S. Uleman and J. A. Bargh, Eds.), Guilford, New York.

Dépret, E., and Fiske, S. T. (in press). Social cognition and power: Some cognitive consequences of social structure as a source of control deprivation. In "Control Motivation and Social Cognition" G. Weary, F. Gleicher and K. Marsh, Eds.), Springer-Verlag, New York.

Fiske, S. T., and Taylor, S. E. (1984). "Social Cognition," Chapt. 5. Addison-Wesley, Reading, Ma.

Fiske, S. T., and Taylor, S. E. (1991). "Social Cognition," 2nd ed., Chapt. 6. McGraw-Hill, N. Y.

Lefcourt, H. M. (1973). The function of the illusions of control and freedom. *Am. Psychol.* **28**, 417–425.

Pittman, T. S., and Heller, J. F. (1987). Social motivation. *Annu. Rev. Psychol.* **38** 461–489.

Rotter, J. B. (1966). Generalized expectancies for internal versus external control of reinforcement. *Psychol. Monogr.* **80** (1), 609.

Strickland, B. R. (1989). Internal-external control expectancies: From contingency to creativity. *Am. Psychol.* **44**, 1–12.

Thompson, S. C. (1981). Will it hurt less if I can control it? A complex answer to a simple question. *Psychol. Bull.* **90**, 89–101.

Uleman, J. S. (1989). A framework for thinking intentionally about unintended thoughts. In "Unintended Thought " J. S. Uleman and J. A. Barge, Eds.), pp. 425–449, Guilford, New York.

Wegner, D. M., and Pennebaker, J. W. (Eds.) (1992) "Handbook of Mental Control." Prentice-Hall, Englewood Cliffs, N.J.

Weisz, J. R., Rothbaum, F. M. and Blackburn, T. C. (1984). Standing out and standing in: The psychology of control in America and Japan. *Am. Psychol.* **39**, 955–969.

ISBN 0-12-226921-7

90018
9 780122 269219